Shooter's Bible
114TH EDITION

SKYHORSE PUBLISHING

Skyhorse Publishing books may be purchased in bulk at special discounts for sales promotion, corporate gifts, fund-raising, or educational purposes. Special editions can also be created to specifications. For details, contact the Special Sales Department, Skyhorse Publishing, 307 West 36th Street, 11th Floor, New York, NY 10018 or info@skyhorsepublishing.com.

Skyhorse® and Skyhorse Publishing® are registered trademarks of Skyhorse Publishing, Inc.®, a Delaware corporation.

Visit our website at www.skyhorsepublishing.com.

10 9 8 7 6 5 4 3 2 1

Library of Congress Cataloging-in-Publication Data is available on file.

Cover design by Brian Peterson
Cover photos courtesy of Franchi Firearms, Kimber America, and AREX Defense

Print ISBN: 978-1-5107-7318-9
Ebook ISBN: 978-1-5107-7319-6
ISSN: 0080-0635

Printed in the United States of America

Note: Every effort has been made to record specifications and descriptions of guns, ammunition, and accessories accurately, but the Publisher can take no responsibility for errors or omissions. The prices shown for guns, ammunition, and accessories are manufacturers' suggested retail prices (unless otherwise noted) and are furnished for information only. These were in effect at press time and are subject to change without notice.

CONTENTS

INTRODUCTION

Last December, I flew from my home in New York to Jackson, Mississippi, where I met up with long-time hunting buddy Andy Dyess (we first met in a remote elk camp in Wyoming, twenty years ago, and have been friends ever since). Andy has a hunting camp on the Black River Delta, not too far from Jackson, and has been telling me for years that the trophy whitetail hunting there is out of this world. He insisted that I come for a visit and see it for myself.

Hunting in Mississippi is sure different from hunting in upstate New York. For starters, the temperatures were in the 80s, not 20s. And the hunting—at least, the hunting we did—was over food plots, not in hardwoods. The best time to hunt was from mid-afternoon until dark, so that's what we did, heading out after lunch, then hiking deep into the delta, where we climbed into our respective shooting houses and watched the food plots for any incoming bucks. I did see one nice buck right before dark on the third day—a 7-pointer I judged to weigh about 180 pounds—but I passed on him, electing to hold out for one of the monsters Andy said were in the area. Turns out that the hot temps did me in, as the big bucks were moving after dark. I flew home full of good memories of time spent with an old friend, but no buck to show for my efforts. There is always next year!

Andy with his 9-pointer, taken with the .257 Weatherby he carefully modified to make his own.

As it turns out, Andy shot a nice buck right before New Year's Eve—a 280-pound (!) 9-point that scored 146 B&C points and aged out at 7½ years old (a literal Methuselah). He came out to the food plot at dusk, and Andy took him with his Weatherby .257, a gun he had customized by dipping the stock in a synthetic camo that made it easy to grip and easier to look at, then adding a new Timney trigger and 4.5x14x56mm Kahles scope. He shot that monster with a 110-grain Weatherby Magnum cartridge.

Andy had shown me the gun in camp, proud of the work he had done on it, and proud of the half-inch groups it shot consistently. It was clearly a labor of love.

Isn't that why many of us own firearms? We don't just shoot them, we tinker with them, work to improve their accuracy, work to make them our own. If we take some nice game animals with them, so much the better.

People who buy the annual *Shooter's Bible* feel the same way. They like to see what's out there, what's available, what they might want to add to their collection of firearms. And when they get a gun they have been drooling over, they often fix it up a bit and make it their own special firearm.

I recently did that with my new Caesar Guerini 12-gauge over/under Summit. I bought it from a favorite firearms dealer, then had the stock worked on and the butt shortened so it fit me well. Tomorrow, I'm taking it shooting for the first time. It's my new favorite gun, and I can't wait to use it.

If you're looking for a new gun this year, then your first step should be to pore over the pages of this, the 114th edition of the *Shooter's Bible*. It's the most recent version of Skyhorse's annual firearms reference book, the source millions of people look to when they want information on new firearms, ammunition, optics, and accessories, as well as current prices and specs for thousands of in-production firearms. More than seven million copies of the *Shooter's Bible* have been sold since 1925, when it was first published. The book not only highlights all the new and in-production products, it also lets you see what the firearm industry has been producing and is planning to feature in the coming months.

This past year was, in fact, a solid one for the firearm industry. According to statistics compiled by the National Shooting Sports Foundation (NSSF), the trade association for the firearm industry, since 2020, more Americans than ever before have been exercising their Second Amendment right to purchase a firearm for the purposes of personal and home security, target shooting, and hunting. The following data points illustrate this increase in ownership and the diversification of gun owners in America.

- In October 2021, a Gallup poll found that 42 percent of American households had a firearm, an increase from recent years.
- Firearm purchases in 2020 and 2021 totaled more than 40 million, a record, with more than 13.8 million being first-time gun owners. In the first half of 2022, purchasing declined from those record levels but remained above pre-pandemic levels.
- According to NSSF firearm retailer surveys, more firearm purchases are being made by the African American, Asian, and Latina communities and women. This is not true. The organizations were in formation long before the pandemic sales increases.
- Of the 5.4 million first-time gun purchasers in 2021, 49.2 percent were under age 40, and 33.2 percent (1.8 million) were female. Nearly 48 percent were African American, 37 percent were Hispanic/Latino, and 27 percent were Asian. In short, gun purchasers and the shooting community are looking different than before; they are looking more like America.
- Due to excise taxes on the sale of firearms and ammunition, federal Pittman-Robertson funding made available to state wildlife agencies to support wildlife conservation, hunter education, and state shooting ranges reached a record high of more than $1.1 billion in 2021.

- The *Shooting Sports Participation in the U.S. 2020 Report* showed that participation in recreational shooting increased from 34.4 million in 2009 to 56.4 million in 2020. It seems likely that this upward trend of people enjoying the shooting sports will continue, given the increase in firearm sales in 2020 and 2021.
- New shooters are continuing to be attracted to shooting sports in nontraditional ways ("traditional" being a young male being introduced to shooting by his family, usually his father, in a rural setting).
- Compared to established shooters, new shooters are . . .
  - much less likely to go target shooting with a rifle.
  - much more likely than established shooters to go to an indoor range.
  - less likely to have grown up in a household with a firearm present; therefore, less likely to have been introduced to shooting in a family setting.
- Personal protection is a prime motivator for purchasing by new gun owners, with "home defense" and "self-defense" the two leading survey responses.
- 43 percent of first-time buyers signed up for training.
- Over the years, surveys by NSSF and others have continually shown that many Americans want to try target shooting and also hunting but are unsure how to get started and where to go. The importance of assisting those who have an interest by providing an invitation to go to the range, purchase an apprentice hunting license, or visit a firearm retailer cannot be overstated. NSSF's First Shots seminars, available at ranges around the country, provide a great introduction to target shooting, along with the safety and legal considerations of owning a firearm.
- Information on ownership, target shooting, and hunting—for newcomers as well as experienced gun owners—can be found at the NSSF's websites LetsGoShooting.org and LetsGoHunting.org.

Despite some production and inventory challenges created by the growing demand for firearms and ammunition, NSSF expects ongoing trends to continue through the year. To meet the continuing demand, manufacturers are coming out with a variety of new and exciting products. To summarize what Robert Sadowski details in depth in the New Products 2022 section (page 13).

The good news in lever-action rifles is that Marlin is back, with design modifications by Ruger. CZ has also introduced a new Model 600 centerfire rifle, a first for that company, while in the rimfire world, Savage has a number of new offerings. In shotguns, Benelli is now making a Super Black Eagle in 28 gauge. Mossberg's 590S pump can accommodate any size 12-gauge shell, from minis to 3-inch shells, while in handguns, FN has a new High Power pistol, as does Springfield Armory. And after almost one hundred years, Savage has reentered the handgun market.

The new Savage Stance, one of a number of new offerings from Savage.

Meanwhile, in ammunition, the big news is the .30 Super Carry, a cartridge designed for self-defense that's in-between the .380 Auto and the 9mm. And Remington is back, again cranking out quality rimfire, centerfire, and shotgun ammo.

As for Skyhorse, we continue to publish more useful firearms titles. One *Shooter's Bible* guidebook that came out in 2022 is Laurie Wiles's *Shooter's Bible Guide to Shotgun Sports for Women*, a comprehensive guide to the art and science of wing and clay shooting. This one is well worth reading—not only by women, but by men as well. It covers a huge array of topics, including (but not limited to) such things as gun safety and gun respect, the mental game of shooting, the basic groundwork of shooting, how to practice effectively, and much more. Also published in 2022 is the long-awaited *Shooter's Bible Guide to Sporting Shotguns*, by firearms expert Alex Brant. This one is sure to capture your interest, whether you currently own fine shotguns or are considering getting one (or more). This monster book not only tells you what's available from manufacturers in the U.S., Italy, the U.K., and other countries, it teaches you how to shoot correctly, where to shoot, and what type of ancillary gear you'll need to enjoy your sport to the fullest.

If you own or are looking to buy currently produced firearms, then check out the existing products section in the *Shooter's Bible*, starting on page 113. Here is where you'll find every firearm currently in production, with current prices and specs. If you have a gun that isn't in this section, it is probably out of production, in which case you need to pick up the *Gun Trader's Guide*. The 44th edition came off the presses at the same time this edition of the *Shooter's Bible* did.

The Skyhorse staff is quite proud of this newest edition of the *Shooter's Bible*, a book that has been continually updated and fact checked for the past twelve months. Now that this edition is off the presses, we're already starting to work on the 115th edition. It's an ongoing process, one we have to stay on top of and pay close attention to, given all the changes going on in the world of firearms.

—Jay Cassell
Editorial Director
Shooter's Bible

GUNS, OPTICS, AND AMMO 2023

By Robert A. Sadowski

The Marlin lever-action rifle is back with design tweaks from Ruger. Other rifle news includes CZ introducing the Model 600 centerfire rifle. And if rimfire shooting is your thing, check out the new rimfire rifles from Savage. Did you ever think Benelli would make the Super Black Eagle in 28 gauge? Well, guess what. It did. Mossberg's 590S will pump any size 12-gauge shell. Yes, you read that right—from mini shells to 3-inch shells. The news of the demise of the Hi-Power is greatly exaggerated. FN, the original manufacturer of the High-Power, has evolved the pistol. Springfield Armory has also introduced its versions of the High Power. Savage has reentered the handgun market after a hiatus since 1928. In optics, the shift is to more FFP (first focal plane) riflescopes. There are more new models of FFP scope models being offered by brands that traditionally only offered SFP (second focal plane) scopes. In ammo, the big news is the .30 Super Carry, a cartridge designed for self-defense that's in-between the .380 Auto and the 9mm. And Remington is again cranking out ammo—rimfire, centerfire, and shotshells. Here are the details.

Rifles

Benelli (benelliusa.com)

New to the Lupo bolt-action rifle series is the Lupo BE.S.T. series (MSRP: $2,199) with premium AA-grade walnut wood stock and BE.S.T. (Benelli Surface Treatment), a new glossy metal finish.

Benelli Lupo BES.T.

Bergara (bergara.online)

The new Canyon rifle (MSRP: $2,149) is designed for hunting the backcountry, a featherweight of 6.2 pounds. The MgLite (MSRP: $2,999) looks like a heavy chassis rifle, but weighs just 6.8 pounds. Available in four popular long-range calibers and either a 22- or 24-inch carbon-fiber wrapped barrel.

Bergara Canyon Rifle

Bergara MgLite

Browning (browning.com)

A new X-Bolt Pro McMillan (MSRP: $2,679.99-$2,699.99) rifle features a Cerakote Carbon Gray finish, fluted barrel with Recoil Hawg muzzle brake, and McMillan Game Scout carbon-fiber stock. The tactical-cool makeover in the Semi-Auto 22 Challenge (MSRP: $959.99) features a 16.25-inch matte blued bull barrel with compensator.

Browning 22 Challenge

Century Arms (centuryarms.com)

The all-new BFT47 AK rifle is all-American-made and designed to be a reliable and accurate AK at an affordable price.

Century Arms BFT47 AK

CZ-USA (cz-usa.com)

The CZ 600 series is an all-new bolt-action rifle design replacing all of CZ's existing centerfire bolt action rifles. The CZ 600 Alpha (MSRP: $749) has a threaded barrel and a black polymer stock, the CZ 600 Lux (MSRP: $849) features a wood Bavarian-style stock and open sights, the CZ 600 Range (MSRP: $1,199) is for long-range shooting and has a sub ¾-MOA guarantee, and the CZ 600 Trail (MSRP: $1,155) is a lightweight chassis rifle with a collapsable stock.

CZ-USA CZ 600 Alpha

Franchi (franchiusa.com)

The Momentum Elite line now has a model chambered in .350 Legend (MSRP $899), and the Momentum Elite Varmint is now available in .22-250 (MSRP $999).

Franchi Momentum Elite

Henry Repeating Arms (henryusa.com)

The new Long Ranger Express (MSRP: $1,235) carbine is chambered in .223 Rem/5.56 NATO and features a Picatinny rail, 16.5-inch threaded barrel, and laminate stock.

Henry Repeating Arms
Long Ranger Express

Legacy Sports (legacysports.com)

The Howa Super Light (MSRP: $1,399) has an unloaded weight of 4.4 pounds and has a sub-MOA guarantee, too. Need to scratch that 6mm ACR itch? The Howa Mini Action (MSRP: $559) and Mini EXCL Lite (MSRP: $579) are now chambered in 6mm ACR.

Legacy Sports
Howa Super Lite

Marlin (marlinfirearms.com)

Long live the lever gun! Marlin is back and being manufactured by Ruger. The first Ruger-produced Marlin is the popular 1895 SBL (MSRP: $1,399) chambered in .45-70 Government.

Marlin 1895 SBL

Savage (savagearms.com)

Savage is rolling out a truckload of new rimfire rifles that range from a single-shot plinker to a chassis precision rifle. The Rascal Minimalist (MSRP: $299) is a single-shot bolt-action chambered in .22 LR with a laminated stocks in pink/purple and teal/gray. The B22 Precision (MSRP: $659) in .22 LR features a custom one-piece MDT aluminum chassis.

Savage Rascal Minimalist

The minimalist laminated stock treatment has been applied to the model 93R17 Minimalist Brown (MSRP: $379) chambered in .17 HMR and the 93 Minimalist Brown (MSRP: $369) in .22 WMR. The A22 semi-auto line now has a model (MSRP: $529) featuring an ergonomic laminate stock coupled with a button-rifled barrel with a threaded muzzle and adjustable AccuTrigger. Want long-range precision without taking out a mortgage? The Axis II Precision (MSRP: $999)

features an MDT Chassis platform and a .22-inch, threaded, carbon-steel, button-rifled heavy barrel.

Savage Axis Precision II

Springfield Armory (springfield-armory.com)

The Hellion Bullpup rifle (MSRP: $1,999) is based on the proven VHS-2 bullpup and sports a 16-inch barrel, fully ambidextrous controls, and is chambered in 5.56mm NATO. The Saint Edge ATC AR-15 is built on an ATC chassis to deliver maximum precision in the AR platform. Models include the standard (MSRP: $1,549) and Elite (MSRP: $1,899).

Weatherby (weatherby.com)

Weatherby updated the lightweight Mark V Backcountry and Backcountry Ti rifles with 2.0 versions. The 2.0 Carbon (MSRP: $3,299-$3,399) features a BSF-tensioned carbon-fiber barrel. The Backcountry 2.0 Ti (MSRP: $3,449-$3,599) is built around a lightweight titanium receiver and fluted barrel and weighs a scant 4.7 pounds. All come with a sub-MOA accuracy guarantee.

Winchester (winchesterguns.com)

New to the iconic Model 70 line is the Extreme Hunter—Strata MB (MSRP: $1,679) with a Cerakote FDE finish on the barreled action and a tough Bell and Carlson synthetic stock with a sculpted cheekpiece and TrueTimber VSX finish. The XPR—TrueTimber Strata MB (MSRP: $749) features a composite stock with TrueTimber Strata camo finish and a barrel and action with Flat Dark Earth Perma-Cote finish. The Wildcat 22 TrueTimber Strata (MSRP: $309) has a molded polymer stock, Picatinny rail, and camouflage finish.

Shotguns

Benelli (benelliusa.com)

A Super Black Eagle 3 in 28 gauge? Yes, you read that right, the new Super Black Eagle 3 (MSRP: $1799-$1899) is chambered for 3-inch 28-gauge shotshells. The 828U Limited Edition (MSRP: $6,499) over/under features a nickel-plated steel frame and satin-finished AA-grade walnut furniture.

Browning (browning.com)

New to the Cynergy over/under series is the Wicked Wing—Vintage Tan (MSRP: $2,499.99), which features a camouflage composite stock and Burnt Bronze Cerakote metal.

Browning Cynergy Wicked Wing—Vintage Tan

Synergy also gets its turkey hunt on with Cynergy Ultimate Turkey, Mossy Oak Bottomland (MSRP: $2,549.99) outfitted with a short Picatinny rail and fiber-optic front sight. New to the Citori O/U line is the Hunter Grade II (MSRP: $2,269.99-$2,339.99) with silver-nitride finish and gold-enhanced receiver with gloss-blued barrels. The Citori 725 Sporting Medallion High Grade (MSRP: $7,069.99) is built for sporting clays and features a gloss oil-finish Grade IV Turkish walnut stock with cut checkering and right-hand palm swell. The semi-auto, recoil-operated A5 series now includes two new Sweet Sixteen models: The A5 Sweet Sixteen Upland (MSRP: $2,029.99) with an oil-finish walnut stock and brushed-nickel receiver, and the A5 Lightning Sweet Sixteen (MSRP: $1,819.99) with a gloss finish, walnut stock and a rounded, Lightning-style grip. New 12-gauge A5s include the A5—Vintage Tan (MSRP: $1,939.99) that sports a composite stock, plus full retro Vintage Tan camo finish. The A5 Wicked Wing—Vintage Tan (MSRP: $2,159.99) has a composite stock with retro camo and Cerakote Burnt Bronze finish. New to the 12-gauge, gas-operated Maxus II line are the Maxus II Wicked Wing—Vintage Tan (MSRP: $2,159.99), which features a Cerakote Burnt Bronze finish and composite stock with retro camouflage and the Maxus II (MSRP: $2,059.99) that features a Grade III walnut stock with oil finish and a nickel-plated receiver with scroll engraving. The Silver series now includes the Silver Rifled Deer, Mossy Oak Bottomland (MSRP: $1,389.99-$1,469.99) with a rifled barrel, cantilever scope mount, and full Mossy Oak Bottomland camouflage.

Henry Repeating Arms (henryusa.com)

The new Brass Axe .410 (MSRP: $1,132) features a polished hardened-brass receiver, a blued-steel 15.14-inch barrel threaded for choke tubes, and its namesake "axe handle" grip.

Mossberg (mossberg.com)

The new 590S will pump any size 12-gauge shell and is capable of cycling 1.75-, 2.75- and 3-inch shotshells interchangeably, in any combination. There are two full-length stock options (MSRP: $605-$708) and two versions of the bird's-head-gripped Shockwave (MSRP: $605). The 940 autoloading shotgun family now has the 940 Pro Field (MSRP: $868) equipped with a 28-inch vent rib barrel and synthetic black stock. If waterfowl are on the agenda, the 12-gauge workhorse 940 Pro Waterfowl (MSRP: $1,050) has a 28-inch, vent rib barrel and wears a Cerakote finish in Patriot Brown. The 940 Snow Goose (MSRP: $1,120)

features an extended 12-round magazine tube. If turkeys are more your game, then try the 940 Pro Turkey (MSRP: $1,120) with either an 18.5- or 24-inch optic-ready barrel in Mossy Oak Greenleaf camo.

Savage Arms (savagearms.com)

The Renegauge Security (MSRP: $1,499) 12-gauge autoloader is built on the Renegauge D.R.I.V. (Dual Regulating Inline Valve) gas system and features an 18.5-inch fluted barrel and adjustable ghost-ring sights. The Stevens 555 Single Barrel Trap shotgun (MSRP: $770) offers performance and value with a light aluminum receiver scaled to 12 or 20 gauge.

Winchester (winchesterguns.com)

Mossy Oak DNA camo finish is now available on the SX4 Universal Hunter—Mossy Oak DNA (MSRP: $1,149) autoloader and the SXP Universal Hunter—Mossy Oak DNA (MSRP: $509) pump gun.

Handguns

Browning (browning.com)

Browning tricked-out the Buck Mark Plus Vision Americana Suppressor Ready (MSRP $799.99) in red, white, and blue colors with an anodized blue receiver with white stars.

Colt's Manufacturing Co. (colt.com)

The Python line now has a 3-inch barrel variant (MSRP: $1,499), a semi-bright stainless finish, checkered walnut grips, and adjustable sights.

CZ-USA (cz-usa.com)

New to the P-10 series is the compact P-10 M (MSRP: $505), a 9mm with an internal slide stop. There are no controls nor levers on the outside of the gun other than the magazine-release button. The 9mm P-10 F Competition-Ready (MSRP: $1,009) is built on a full-size P-10 F frame and is equipped with competition features. An updated CZ TS 2 (MSRP: $1,695) is built for speed with a highly modified CZ-75 similar to the Shadow 2. The CZ TS 2 Racing Green (MSRP: $2,055) is the next rendition of the new TS2, with green anodized grips, magazine bases, and magazine release.

FN (fnamerica.com)

FN, the original manufacturer of the classic Hi-Power 9mm single-action pistol, has introduced a modern update, the new High-Power (MSRP: $1,269-$1,369), with improved ergonomics and easier takedown. Available in stainless steel, blued, or FDE. The 502 Tactical (MSRP: $519) is FN's first .22 LR pistol.

Heckler & Koch

New to the VP9 line is the VP9-SK (MSRP: $899-$999), which is optic-ready.

Heritage Mfg. (heritagemfg.com)

The new Rough Rider TC (MSRP: $212) blends the Old West with modern tactical enhancements like a Picatinny rail for mounting a red-dot and a threaded barrel. The Barkeep Boot (MSRP: $196-$205) six-shot rimfires have a birdshead grip and short 1.68-inch barrel, small enough to EDC in your boot.

Heritage Mfg. Barkeep Boot

Kimber (kimberamerica.com)

Kimber is giving the Rapide treatment to other 1911s like the Rapide (Dawn) (MSRP: $1,733) with a Kimpro Silver finish, brush-polished flats, and gold-finish barrel. The Rapide (Scorpius) (MSRP: $1,733) has a black finish with brush-polished flats. Two new Mako micro nines include the R7 Mako O.R. (MSRP: $599) with TruGlo night sights, and the R7 Mako O.I. (MSRP: $799) with a Crimson Trace CTS-1500 red-dot co-witnessed with TruGlo night sights.

Kel-Tec (keltecweapons.com)

The P15 (MSRP: $425) is KelTec's new 9mm striker-fire compact pistol with a 15+1 capacity.

Ruger (ruger.com)

New to the Wrangler rimfire six-shooter roundup is the Wrangler with a bird's-head grip (MSRP: $279) available in three Cerakote finishes: black, silver, and burnt bronze.

Savage Arms (savagearms.com)

The last time Savage produced a pistol was in 1928. The new micro-compact 9mm Stance (MSRP: $479) is designed for shooting comfort and concealed carry. The Stance uses a chassis system that is the serialized component of the pistol, giving shooters the ability to use a wide variety of grip frames.

SIG Sauer (sigsauer.com)

New to the P365 series is the P365XL Spectre Comp (MSRP: $1,299) with an integrated compensator. New to the

evolving P320 line are the P320 AXG Pro (MSRP: $1,199), P320 AXG Equinox (MSRP: $1,200), and P320 AXG Classic (MSRP: $1,299), all with alloy frames.

Smith and Wesson (smith-wesson.com)

The new CSX (MSRP: $609) is a hammer-fired subcompact 9mm built on an aluminum alloy frame. S&W is chambering the M&P Shield Plus (MSRP: $595) in the all-new .30 Super Carry cartridge. S&W is also introducing a new 10mm in the full-size M&P M2.0 (MSRP: $665).

Smith & Wesson CSX

Springfield Armory (springfield-armory.com)

SA introduced the SA-35 (MSRP: $699), which is not just another clone of the iconic Hi-Power pistol. The SA-35 features a forged frame and slide, larger thumb safety, and a big-dot front sight. The XD-M Elite Compact OSP (MSRP: $653) has a 3.8-inch match barrel and is chambered in .45 Auto and 10mm. New models based on the 1911 platform include the heirloom-quality Garrison series in either blue (MSRP: $849) or stainless steel (MSRP: $899), and the Emissary (MSRP: $1,349) with a tri-top cut slide, U-Dot sights, squared-off trigger guard, and flat trigger.

Springfield Armory SA-35

Stoeger (stoegerindustries.com)

There are three new models to the 9mm STR-9 striker-fire pistol series: the STR-9F full size (MSRP: $329) with a 4.6-inch barrel, the optic ready STR-9C compact (MSRP: $399) with a 3.8-inch barrel, and the optic ready STR-9SC sub-compact (MSRP: $329-$399) with a 3.5-inch barrel.

Taurus (taurususa.com)

The new GX4 T.O.R.O. (MSRP: $468) features the T.O.R.O. (Taurus Optic Ready Option) mounting system for adding a red-dot. New to the G3 series is the G3X (MSRP: $342), a compact 9mm with a full-size grip. The TX22 Competition SCR (MSRP: $589.00) rimfire features a compensator for added weight and custom bull barrel for enhanced accuracy. For new revolvers, check out the snubnose Taurus 327 (MSRP: $33) chambered in .327 Federal Magnum.

Black Powder

Traditions (traditionsfirearms.com)

Traditions is adding .45-caliber muzzleloader variants in both the popular Vortek StrikerFire series (MSRP: $428-$515) and the mid-level Pursuit XT series (MSRP: $362).

Optics

Axeon Optics (axeonoptics.com)

The Prism 3XRD 3X30mm Prism Dot Scope (MSRP: $129) features an illuminated, etched-glass ballistic reticle and fixed 3x magnification. The 4-16X50mm SF IGF rifle scope (MSRP $299) is both a solid performer and a solid value. This optic features an illuminated G126 tree reticle.

BSA Optics (bsaoptics.com)

The new Defiant4 scope series is packed with features that won't empty your bank account. Three models include 3-12x40mm (MSRP: $69.99), 3-16x40mm (MSRP: $69.99), and a 6-24x44mm (MSRP: $69.99).

Bushnell (bushnell.com)

Hunters will like the reintroduction of the Elite 4500 lineup of scopes, with a 1-4x24mm (MSRP: $230), 2.5-10x40mm (MSRP: $270), and 4-16x40mm (MSRP: $300). All have 4X magnification range, capped turrets, and are equipped with a Multi-X reticle. Two new rimfire rifle scopes include a 3-9x40mm with a DZ22 reticle (MSRP: $180) or an illuminated DZ22 retile (MSRP: $180). The DZ22 reticle was specifically designed for .22 LR rimfire ballistics, with drop points out to 125 yards. Two new Elite Tactical riflescopes—the DMR3 3.5-21x50mm FFP riflescope (MSRP: $1,199) and the XRS3 6-36x56 FFP (MSRP: $1,699)—are tailored to meet the demands of law-enforcement and military professionals, as well as long-range competition shooters.

Crimson Trace (crimsontrace.com)

CT has micro, sub-compact, compact, and full-size pistol sights covered with the CT RAD Micro Pro (Rapid Aiming Dot) Electronic Sight (MSRP: $275) and the CT RAD Pro

Electronic Sight (MSRP: $300). Both sights feature a red 3 MOA aiming dot, automatically adjusts the aiming dot's brightness to lighting condition, and automatically turns on when it detects movement.

EOTECH (eotechinc.com)

The new 1-10x28mm (MSRP: $1,799) first focal plane riflescope provides targeting from extremely close to long range.

HiLux Optics (hi-luxoptics.com)

The TD-3C (MSRP: $249) open reflex red-dot is tough. Built from aircraft-grade 7075-T6 aluminum alloy, the TD-3C is lightweight yet rugged.

Holosun (holosun.com)

The Holosun AEMS (Advanced Enclosed Micro Sight) Core (MSRP: $352.93/red reticle; $370.58/green reticle) rifle sight is 11-percent shorter in length than the standard micro-style optic yet offers twice the lens surface area for a wider field of view.

Konus (konuspro.com)

The Absolute 5-40x56mm (MSRP: $1,187) is designed for the competitive shooter, with a wide magnification range that goes from 5X to 40X. When you think of the two new Diablo riflescopes, think performance at a competitive price. Both models—the 4-16x50mm (MSRP: $510) and 6-24x50mm (MSRP: $530)—feature turrets that are lockable and resettable to zero.

Konus Diablo 4-16x50mm

Leapers/UTG (leapers.com)

The INTEGRIX 1-8x28mm riflescope features a first focal plane, T-Dot MOA reticle with 10 brightness levels. The UTG DSR Micro is a rugged and compact dot sight well suited for AR-style rifles.

Meopta (meoptasportsoptics.com)

The new Optika5 2-10x42 PA riflescope (MSRP: $349.99) features side parallax adjustment.

Primary Arms (primaryarms.com)

The PLx 1-8x24mm FFP Compact Rifle Scope features premium-grade Japanese ED lenses and AutoLive Motion-

Sensing illumination technology. The SLx RS10 Mini Reflex is a pistol-ready miniature reflex sight that offers a true daylight-bright 3-MOA reticle.

Sightmark (sightmark.com)

The lightweight and compact Wraith 4k Mini 2-16x32 Digital Riflescope (MSRP: $699) can detect objects up to 300 yards in the darkest of nights. Features include full-color, high-resolution imaging, video recording capabilities, 14 reticle options, and more.

Swarovski (swarovskioptik.com)

The new tM35 thermal imaging clip-on device (MSRP: $5554) offers impressive enhanced vision in twilight conditions or when hunting at night. The tM35 is compatible with the Z8i, Z6(i), Z5(i), and Z3 series riflescopes with an additional adapter (MSRP: $249).

Swarvoski tM35 Thermal Imaging Device

Ultradot (ultradotusa.com)

Ultradot is bringing back the Ultradot 4 (MSRP $269.95), the sight that helped launch red-dot optics on handguns.

Zeiss (zeiss.com)

The all-new LRP S5 first focal plane riflescopes are designed for precision long-range shooting. Two models include a 3-18x50mm (MSRP: $3299) and 5-25x56mm (MSRP: $3599). Both are equipped with the all-new Zeiss External Locking Windage Turret (ELWT) feature.

Ammunition

Browning (browningammo.com)

TSS Tungsten Turkey shells are loaded for dense shot patterns out to 70 yards. The new line of rimfire ammunition, the Browning PRO22 .22, features a 40-grain, round-nose lead bullet with a velocity of 1,085 fps.

Blazer (cci-ammunition.com)

New from Blazer is a .30 Super Carry cartridge load offered in a 115-grain FMJ with a muzzle velocity of 1,150 fps.

Federal Premium 30 Super Carry

Federal Premium (federalpremium.com)

New to the Personal Defense line is the .30 Super Carry loaded with a 100-grain HST bullet that travels at a muzzle velocity of 1,250 fps. Force X Shorty shotshells are 1¾ inches and hold a payload of six segmenting 00 buckshot pellets. New Upland Steel loads contain non-toxic shot plus biodegradable paper components. Leave a trail of shattered targets in your wake and more reloads per shell with High Over All shotshells.

Hornady (hornady.com)

The new CX (Controlled-alloy eXpanding) bullet is a mono-metal, lead-free bullet made from a single piece of copper. Ammo lines using the CX bullet include Outfitter, Custom, and Superformance.

Hornady CX (Controlled-alloy eXpanding) Bullet

Remington (remington.com)

Big Green is back in the ammo business and producing rifle, shotgun, handgun, and rimfire ammo. Premier Accutip-V ammo is now available in .224 Valkryie. New ultra-dense Tungsten Super Shot payload Premier TSS turkey shells deliver denser patterns and more knockdown power.

Winchester (winchester.com)

The USA Ready line of defense ammo also has new load in .40 S&W, .45 Auto, and 9mm; these use a Hex-Vent JHP bullet. The SilverTip line now includes a .22 LR load with a 37-grain segmenting hollowpoint bullet.

NEW PRODUCTS 2022–2023

ACCURACY INTERNATIONAL AT-X

ALLTERRA MOUNTAIN SHADOW STEEL

ALLTERRA CARBON

ALLTERRA STEEL

ALLTERRA MOUNTAIN SHADOW CARBON

AMERICAN TACTICAL ALPHA-15

ACCURACY INTERNATIONAL AT-X

Action: Bolt
Stock: Chassis
Barrel: 24 in.
Sights: None
Weight: 13 lb.
Caliber: 6.5 Creedmoor,
Magazine: 10 rounds
Features: This is a modular platform with a one-piece proofed steel action; AI's Quickloc quick-release barrel systeml; 20 MOA Stanag rail; six-lug bolt with a 60-degree throw; leaf-spring extractor; AI competition trigger; AI KeySlot fore-end mounting system; match-grade four-groove stainless steel barrel; dual quick-detach flush cups; adjustable friction-locking buttpad; height-adjustable cheekpiece
Price: $5250.00

ALLTERRA CARBON

Photo File Names: AllTerra Carbon
Action: Bolt
Stock: Carbon fiber
Barrel: 24, 26 in.
Sights: None
Weight: 7 lb. 8 oz.
Caliber: 6mm Creedmoor, .26 Nosler, 6.5 Creedmoor, 6.5 PRC, 6.5 SS, 6.5 SST, 6.5X284 Norma, 6.8 Westerner, .280 AI, 7mm Rem. Mag. 7 SS, 7mm SAUM, .28 Nosler, .308 Win., .300 PRC, .300 Win. Mag., .30 Nosler, .33 Nosler
Magazine: N/A
Features: A semi-custom build in the company's proprietary, ultralight Carbon Hunter stock that can be filled to customer-request weight; extended length magazine accommodates VLD bullets; match-grade, hand-lapped carbon fiber barrel; 2-lb. TriggerTech Diamond trigger; fluted bolt; dual ejectors; nickle-boron-coated mini M16 extractor; lengthened ejection

port; Cerakote finish on metal; lots of custom stock finishes, barrel configurations, stock weight, muzzle brakes, trigger, and other options
Price: . . . . Starting at $5825.00

ALLTERRA MOUNTAIN SHADOW CARBON

Action: Bolt
Stock: Carbon fiber
Barrel: 20, 22 in.
Sights: None
Weight: 6 lb.
Caliber: 6mm Creedmoor, 6.5 Creedmoor, 6.5 PRC, 6.5 SS, 6.5 SST, 7mm Rem. Mag., 7 SS, 7mm SAUM, .28 Nosler, .308 Win., .300 PRC, .33 Nosler
Magazine: N/A
Features: A compact and very lightweight rifle for the foot hunter with extended length magazine that accommodates VLD bullets; match-grade, hand-lapped carbon fiber barrel in a lightweight contour and threaded for suppressor; 2-lb. TriggerTech Diamond trigger; fluted, weight-reduced bolt; dual ejectors; nickle-boron-coated mini M16 extractor; skeletonized bolt shank; lengthened ejection port; Cerakote finish on metal; lots of custom stock finishes, barrel configurations, muzzle brakes, trigger, and other options
Price: . . . . Starting at $5995.00

ALLTERRA MOUNTAIN SHADOW STEEL

Action: Bolt
Stock: Carbon fiber
Barrel: 22 in.
Sights: None
Weight: 6 lb. 8 oz.
Caliber: 6mm Creedmoor, 6.5 Creedmoor, 6.5 PRC, 6.5 SS, 6.5 SST, .28o AI, 7mm Rem. Mag., 7 SS, 7mm

SAUM, .28 Nosler, .308 Win., .300 PRC, .33 Nosler
Magazine: N/A
Features: Similar to the Mountain Shadow Carbon, including the customizalbe feaures, but with a match-grade, hand-lapped, spiral-fluted stainless steel barrel
Price: . . . . Starting at $5495.00

ALLTERRA STEEL

Action: Bolt
Stock: Carbon fiber
Barrel: 24, 26 in.
Sights: None
Weight: 7 lb. 8 oz.
Caliber: 6mm Creedmoor, .26 Nosler, 6.5 Creedmoor, 6.5 PRC, 6.5 SS, 6.5 SST, 6.5X284 Norma, 6.8 Westerner, .280 AI, 7mm Rem. Mag. 7 SS, 7mm SAUM, .28 Nosler, .308 Win., .300 PRC, .300 Win. Mag., .30 Nosler, .33 Nosler
Magazine: N/A
Features: Very similar to the AllTerra Carbon, including customizable features, but with a match-grade, hand-lapped stainless steel barrel (choice of fluted or non-fluted), in a heavy sporter contour and threaded for suppressor use
Price: . . . . Starting at $5095.00

AMERICA TACTICAL ALPHA-15

Action: Semiautomatic
Stock: Synthetic
Barrel: 16 in.
Sights: Flip-up
Weight: 5 lb. 8 oz.
Caliber: 5.56 NATO
Magazine: 30 rounds
Features: A carbine-length AR-type rifle at a very light weight and with a Nano composite trigger kit; 1:8 twist pencil barrel; carbon-fiber infused buffer tube; 8-in. MLOK rail; flip-up sights
Price: $499.95

ANDERSON MFG RF85 AM-10

ANDERSON MFG RF85 AM-15

ANDERSON MFG RF85 AM-15 SNIPER

ANDRO CORP AR-10 .308 DIVERGENT

ANSCHÜTZ 1761 MPR MULTI-PURPOSE BEAVERTAIL

ANSCHÜTZ 1782 CLASSIC PRO

ANDERSON MFG RF85 AM-10 EXT

Action: Semiautomatic
Stock: Synthetic
Barrel: 18 in.
Sights: None
Weight: 10 lb.
Caliber: .308 Win.
Magazine: 20 rounds
Features: A powerhouse carbine for the hunter in .308 Win. Featuring a low-profile gas block assembly; top, bottom, and side Picatinny rails; Type-3 hard anodized forged aluminum uppers and lowers; Parkerized finish; forged aluminum AM-10 charging handle; Magpul MOE pistol grip; six-position buffer tube; Molding Solutions M17 buttstock; EXT handguard; billed as "the world's first no-lube rifles"
Price:.................$1504.99

ANDERSON MFG RF85 AM-15

Action: Semiautomatic
Stock: Synthetic
Barrel: 16 in.
Sights: None
Weight: 9 lb.
Caliber: .300 BLK, 5.56 NATO, 7.62X39
Magazine: 30 rounds
Features: A family of carbine-length AR-style rifles that Anderson bills as "the world's first no-lube rifle," with options that include 5.56 NATO and 7.62X39 models with traditional handguards, as well as 5.56 NATO and .300 BLK models with MLOK configurations; Type 3 hard anodized, forged 7075 T6 aluminum uppers and lowers; nitride-finished bolt, carrier, and barrel; high-rise carbine-length gas system; six-position buffer tube; six-position buttstock; M4 contour barrel of chrome moly vandium, threaded and with an A2 flash hider
Price:..........$772.89–$985.99

ANDERSON MFG RF85 AM-15 SNIPER

Action: Semiautomatic
Stock: Synthetic
Barrel: 24 in.
Sights: None
Weight: N/A
Caliber: 5.56 NATO
Magazine: 30 rounds
Features: A longer-barreled precision rifle in the "no-lube" family of RF85 rifles, this one features a low-profile rifle-length gas system; standard M16-profile bolt carrier group; straight fluting on the heavy-contour, unthreaded 416R stainless steel barrel with a target crown; 15-in. MLOK handguard; Ergo Tactical deluxe pistol grip with palm shelf; Magpul buttstock
Price:.................$1709.00

ANDRO CORP AR-10 .308 DIVERGENT

Action: Semiautomatic
Stock: Synthetic
Barrel: 16 in.
Sights: None
Weight: 8 lb.
Caliber: .308 Win.
Magazine: 20 rounds
Features: A carbine AR-10 platform with a Low Pro gas block; A2 flash hider; DPMS/SR25-style receiver; mid-length gas tube; 7075 billet aluminum upper and lower; charging handle; MLOK handguard; .308 carbine buffer and buffer spring; 4150 CMV melanite mid-gas barrel, threaded; finished in Armorers Black Cerakote
Price:.................$1781.00

ANSCHÜTZ 1761 MPR MULTI-PURPOSE BEAVERTAIL

Action: Bolt
Stock: Walnut
Barrel: 21 in.
Sights: None
Weight: 7 lb. 11 oz.
Caliber: .22 LR
Magazine: 5 rounds
Features: A precision rimfire, classicly styled, with an 11mm dovetail at the muzzle to accommodate a dipter front sight; two-stage trigger; MPR stock; detachable magazine; blued finish; cocked action has visible firing pin; 60-degree bolt throw; available left- or right-hand
Price:.................$2195.00

ANSCHÜTZ 1782 CLASSIC PRO

Action: Bolt
Stock: Walnut
Barrel: 18.5, 20.5, 22.8, 23.6, 25.9 in.
Sights: None
Weight: N/A
Caliber: .243 Win., 6.5 Creedmoor, 6.5X55 SE, .308 Win., .30-06 Spfd., 8X57 IS, 9.3X62, .300 Win. Mag.
Magazine: 3, 4 rounds
Features: A classicly designed centerfire rifle for the hunter but with an adjustable stock available in four grades of wood; recessed muzzle standard, threaded barrel optional; available right- and left-hand; travel MEGA lockable case included; steel action; non-slip checkering at pistol grip and forearm; ; detachable magazine; adjustable single-stage match trigger that can be changed to two-stage; top-side two-point Picatinny rail for scope mounting
Price:.....................N/A

ANSCHÜTZ 1827 F BIONIC

ARMALITE AR-10 A-SERIES SUPERSASS

ARMSCOR TM22

ARSENAL INC SAM7F-94E

AUTO ORDNANCE BOOTLEGGER THOMPSON

AWC SILENCERS ULTRA 13 MATCH

AWC SILENCERS ULTRA 13

ANSCHÜTZ 1827 F BIONIC

Action: Bolt
Stock: Synthetic
Barrel: 21.6 in.
Sights:
Weight: 7 lb. 9 oz.
Caliber: .22 LR
Magazine: 5 rounds
Features: A super-hip rifle for competitve biathletes, this snazzy model comes in a variety of bright-eye-catching stock colors and features the buyer's choice of standard or luxury biathlon sights; standard or extra-long hand stop; standard, Annett, Alexa, or individual palm rests; optional biathlon sight set; large, mediaum, small, or extra-small Bionic grip; MEGA transport case; tool set; damping ring; replacement firing pin; cheek piece with integral spare cartridge holder; biathlon hooked buttplate; magnetized fore-end magazine holders; adjustable two-stage match trigger
Price:. **$5495.00**

ARMALITE AR-10 A-SERIES SUPERSASS

Action: Semiautomatic
Stock: Synthetic
Barrel: 20 in.
Sights: None
Weight: 11 lb. 7 oz.
Caliber: 7.62 NATO
Magazine: 20 rounds
Features: The SASS stands for "Semi-Automatic Sniper System." Originally designed for the U.S. military, the civlian version sports an Armalite Gen II MLOK free-floating handguard; an adjustable gas systems to support suppressed and unsuppressed fire; Armalite tactical brake; nitride-finished heavy barrel; two-stage drop-in precision trigger; adjustable stock
Price:. **$3150.00**

ARMSCOR TM22

Action: Semiautomatic
Stock: Synthetic
Barrel: 18, 20 in.
Sights: None
Weight: 7 lb.
Caliber: .22 LR
Magazine: 10 rounds
Features: Highly maneuverable rimfire rifle with an AR-type grip; fixed minimal-profile buttstock; left-hand conversion kit; topside-rail; accessory-compatible MLOK fore-end; black anodized finish
Price:. **$278.00**

ARSENAL INC. SAM7F-94E

Action: Semiautomatic
Stock: Synthetic
Barrel: 16.33 in.
Sights: None
Weight: 8 lb. 8 oz.
Caliber: 7.62X39
Magazine: 30 rounds
Features: A limited edition rifle with a Bulgarian hot-die hammer-forged receiver, bolt, bolt group, and fire-control group; cold hammer-forged barrel built in Bulgaria on Steyr technology; removeable muzzle brake; right-hand folding tubular stock; side-mounted scope rail; ARM5F rail system
Price:. **$2499.99**

AUTO ORDNANCE BOOTLEGGER THOMPSON

Action: Semiautomatic
Stock: Walnut
Barrel: 16.5 in.
Sights: None
Weight: 12 lb. 8 oz.
Caliber: .45 ACP
Magazine: 20, 50 rounds
Features: A tribute to the Roaring '20s and the age of moonshine runners, this special Thompson features multiple era-specific scenes etched in the wood, "White Lightning" and "Bootlegger" engraved on the receiver," and "Speakeasy" emblazoned on the finned barrel; comes with a 20-round stick magazine and a 50-round drum; Bootlegger 1911 pistol was made to match for those wishing a set
Price:. **$2883.00**

AWC SILENCERS ULTRA 13 MATCH

Action: Semiautomatic
Stock: Synthetic
Barrel: 16.5 in.
Sights: None
Weight: 6 b. 1 oz.
Caliber: .22 LR
Magazine: 10 rounds
Features: An integrally suppressed rimfire, designed to be effective with both standard and high-velocity ammo, with a removeable core; match-grade barrel; Hogue stock in black, OD green, or flat dark earth
Price:. **$1799.00**

AWC SILENCERS ULTRA 13 SEMIAUTOMATIC

Action: Semiautomatic
Stock: Synthetic
Barrel: 16.5
Sights: None
Weight: 4 lb. 14 oz.
Caliber: .22 LR
Magazine: 10 rounds
Features: Featuring a removeable core, this integrally suppressed rifle is available in blue or stainless metal finish; stock in black, OD green, or flat dark earth
Price:. **$1395.00**

NEW Products: **Rifles**

B&T SPR300 PRO

BENELLI BE.S.T. LUPO

BERETTA BRX1

BEGARA BMR STEEL

BERGARA PREMIER CANYON

BERGARA PREMIER COMPETITION

BERGARA PREMIER DIVIDE

B&T SPR300 PRO

Action: Bolt
Stock: Synthetic
Barrel: 9.8 in.
Sights: None
Weight: N/A
Caliber: .300 Whisper, .300 BLK
Magazine: 5 rounds
Features: For sniper applications, this shorty-short barreled rifle includes a suppressor; adjustable folding stock; bipod; scope rings; soft and hard cases; Timney trigger; two-lug bolt; numerous rails
Price: $5200.00

BENELLI BE.S.T. LUPO

Action: Bolt
Stock: Synthetic
Barrel: 22, 24 in.
Sights: None
Weight: 6 lb. 15 oz.–7 lb. 1 oz.
Caliber: 6.5 Creedmoor, .308 Win., .300 Win. Mag.
Magazine: 5 rounds
Features: With a chassis-style configuration of a separate buttstock, receiver, and fore-end, this field rifle also features Benelli's Progressive Comfort recoil-taming system; Combtech cheek pad; adjustable trigger reach; Airtouch grip surfaces; threaded barrel. Three versions, all with B.E.S.T. surface treatment: AA-grade satin walnut stock with high-polished blue metal; Elevated II camo stock with matte Labrador Gray metal; Open Country camo stock with matte black metal
Price: $1899.00

BERETTA BRX1

Action: Bolt
Stock: Synthetic
Barrel: 20, 22.5, 24.5 in.
Sights: None
Weight: 7 lb. 3 oz.–7 lb. 5 oz.
Caliber: .308 Win., .30-06 Spfd., .300 Win. Mag.
Magazine: 5 rounds
Features: Beretta declares an entry into the hunting rifle market, chambered in just three calibers and featuring a flush-fit, removeable, five-round magazine; interchangeable barrels; three trigger weight options; ambidextrous bolt and extraction; locked trigger for safe unloading; threaded barrel with thread cover; adjustable length-of-pull stock; straight-pull 16-lug bolt head (8+8 inline); topside optics rail if equipped without sights (sights available as an option); anti-slip stock finish; integral sling swivels
Price: . . . . N/A

BERGARA BMR STEEL

Action: Bolt
Stock: Synthetic
Barrel: 18, 20 in.
Sights: None
Weight: 5 lb. 8 oz.–5 lb. 13 oz.
Caliber: .22 LR, .22 WMR, .17 HMR
Magazine: 5, 10 rounds
Features: Nice, lightweight rimfire with both five- and 10-round mags included; match chamber; Bergara Remington 700-style trigger; carbon-wrapped 4140 steel barrel threaded for supressor; stock in Tactical Gray with balck spots; 30 MOA rail
Price: $565.00

BERGARA PREMIER CANYON

Action: Bolt
Stock: Carbon fiber
Barrel: 20, 22 in.
Sights: None
Weight: 6 lb. 3 oz.–6 lb. 8 oz.
Caliber: 6.5 Creedmoor, 6.5 PRC, .308 Win., .375 H&H, .28 Nosler, .300 Win. Mag., .300 PRC
Magazine: 3, 5 rounds
Features: With a nice range of calibers to choose from (think varmints to targets to some bigger big-game), hunters get a lightweight carbon fiber composite stock; TriggerTech Frictionless Release Technology trigger; fluted No. 4 fully free-floated barrel, threaded and equipped with an Omni muzzle brake; AICS-style detachable magazine; Sniper Grey Cerakote metal finish;
Price: . . . . $2379.00–$2429.00

BERGARA PREMIER COMPETITION

Action: Bolt
Stock: Chassis
Barrel: 26 in.
Sights: None
Weight: 12 lb. 10 oz.
Caliber: 6.5 Creedmoor, 6mm Creedmoor
Magazine: 10 rounds
Features: Built for the PRS crowd, this long-range option features Graphite Black Cerakoting; MPA Comp Chassis Kit B foundation; AICS-style detachable magazine; threaded No. 7 taper barrel; TriggerTech Special trigger; integral QD flush cup mounts in fore-end and buttstock; Arca Swiss 3-in-1 rail;
Price: $2499.00

BERGARA PREMIER DIVIDE

Action: Bolt
Stock: Carbon fiber
Barrel: 22, 24 in.
Sights: None
Weight: 7 lb. 3 oz.–7 lb. 6 oz.
Caliber: 6.5 Creedmoor, 6.5 PRC, .308 Win., .300 Win. Mag.
Magazine: 3, 5 rounds
Features: For the hunter who's going to spend some time behind their gun before the perfect shot presents itself, they'll appreciate this rifle's carbon-fiber composite AG stock in Chalk Branch, with an adjustable cheekpiece and a steep pistol grip; free-floated CURE carbon barrel in a No. 6 taper and with an Omni muzzle brake; Patriot Brown Cerakoting; TriggerTech Frictionless Release Technology trigger; AICS-style detachable magazine
Price: . . . . $2749.00–$2799.00

BERGARA PREMIER LRP 2-0

BERGARA PREMIER MGLITE

BLASER R8 ULTIMATE X

BROWNING X-BOLT PRO

BROWNING X-BOLT SPEED–OVIX CAMO

BROWNING X-BOLT SPEED LONG-RANGE– OVIX CAMO

BROWNING X-BOLT WESTERN HUNTER LR– OVIX CAMO

BERGARA PREMIER LRP 2.0

Action: Bolt
Stock: Synthetic
Barrel: 24, 26 in.
Sights: None
Weight: 9 lb. 9 oz.–9 lb. 14 oz.
Caliber: 6.5 Creedmoor, 6.5 PRC, .300 Win. Mag., .300 PRC
Magazine: 5, 7 rounds
Features: A lighterweight offering for long-range practitioners, with an AICS-style detachable magazine; Bergara Premier Action with threaded-in bolt handle; XLR Element 3.0 stock; TriggerTech Frictionless Release Technology trigger; threaded muzzle with thread protector
Price: . . . . $2,000.00–$2100.00

BERGARA PREMIER MGLITE

Action: Bolt
Stock: Chassis
Barrel: 22, 24 in.
Sights: None
Weight: 6 lb. 13 oz.–6 lb. 24 oz.
Caliber: 6.5 Creedmoor, 6.5 PRC, .308 Win., .300 Win. Mag.
Magazine: 5 rounds
Features: Based on Bergara's XLR Element 4.0 magnesium folding chassis, this rifle has a No, 6 CURE carbon fiber barrel, free-floated, threaded, and with an Omni muzzle brake; AICS detachable magazine; metal finished in Graphite Black Cerakote; two-lug action system with a floating bolt head
Price: . . . . $3229.00–$3349.00

BLASER R8 ULTIMATE X

Action: Bolt
Stock: Synthetic
Barrel: Varies
Sights: None
Weight: N/A
Caliber: 6XC, .243 Win., 6.5X65 RWS, 6.5 Creedmoor, 6.5X55 SE, .270 Win., 7X64, .308 Win., .30-06 Spfd., 8X57 IS, 9.3X62, 6.5 PRC, .270 WSM, 7mm Rem. Mag., .300 Win. Mag., .300 Norma Mag., .338 Win. Mag., 8.5X55 Blaser, .338 Lapua Mag.
Magazine: 10 rounds

Features: This is apparently a very big deal for Blaser fans, with the favorite barrel-swapping, straight-pull bolt R8 reconfigured to house 10 round magazines, even for the magnum cartridges for which the rifle is chambered; .22 LR conversion kit available
Price: $5428.00

BROWNING X-BOLT PRO

Action: Bolt
Stock: Carbon Fiber
Barrel: 22, 24, 26 in.
Sights: None
Weight: 5 lb. 14 oz.–6 lb. 6 oz.
Caliber: 6.5 Creedmoor, 6.5 PRC, 6.8 Western, .280 AI, 7mm Rem. Mag., .28 Nosler, .300 Win. Mag., .300 PRC
Magazine: 3, 4 rounds
Features: Browning considers this X-Bolt Pro line of rifles to be "semi-custom" with highlights such as a ¼-pound weight reduction over previous models; sporter contour barrel threaded and skip-fluted; Recoil Hawg muzzle brake; removeable Picatinny rail; carbon fiber stock with a natural finish; Carbon Gray Elite finish on barrel, action, and spiral-fluted bolt
Price: $2229.99

BROWNING X-BOLT SPEED — OVIX CAMO

Action: Bolt
Stock: Composite
Barrel: 22, 23, 24, 26 in.
Sights: None
Weight: 6 lb. 5 oz.–6 lb. 13 iz,
Caliber: .243 Win., 6.5 Creedmoorm 6.5 PRC, 6.8 Western, 7mm-08 Rem., .308 Win., .270 WSM, .300 WSM, .270 Win., .30-06 Spfd., 7mm Rem. Mag., .280 AI, .28 Nosler, .300 Win, Mag., .300 PRC, .300 RUM
Magazine: 3, 4 rounds
Features: Wearing a new for 2022 OVIX camo designed by Browning, this rifle's metalwork is finished in Cerakote Smoked Bronze; sporter contour free-floating barrel is fluted and has a threaded radial muzzle

brake; sling swivels; detachable magazine
Price: . . . . $1339.99–$1399.99

BROWNING X-BOLT SPEED LONG-RANGE— OVIX CAMO

Action: Bolt
Stock: Composite
Barrel: 26 in.
Sights: None
Weight: 7 lb. 3 oz.–7 lb. 8 oz.
Caliber: 6.5 Creedmoor, 6.5 PRC, 6.8 Western, .270 WSM, .300 WSM, 7mm Rem. Mag., .280 AI, .28 Nosler, .300 Win. Mag., .300 PRC, .300 RUM
Magazine: 3, 4 rounds
Features: Similar to the X-Bolt Speed, but with a standardized 26-in. barrel across the calibers and a little bit more weight; adjustable Feather trigger; 60-degree short-throw bolt with extended handle; Inflex recoil pad; detachable rotary magazine with inline feed; sporter style stock with adjustable comb; free-floating barrel with target crown; stock in Browning's OVIX camo; metalwork in Smoked Bronze Cerakote
Price: . . . . $1359.99–$1439.99

BROWNING X-BOLT WESTERN HUNTER LR— OVIX CAMO

Action: Bolt
Stock: Composite
Barrel: 24, 26 in.
Sights: None
Weight: 6 lb. 6 oz.–7 lb. 8 oz.
Caliber: 6.5 Creedmoor, 6.5 PRC, 6.8 Western, .280 AI, 7mm Rem. Mag., .28 Nosler, .300 Win. Mag., .300 PRC
Magazine: 3, 4 rounds
Features: For western hunters taking long pokes in big country, this rifle has a sporter-style stock in Browning's OVIX camo; heavy sporter contour barrel, threaded and with a muzzle brake; adjustable comb; extended bolt handle; non-rflective matte blue metal finish
Price: . . . . $1149.99–$1259.99

NEW Products: Rifles

BUSHMASTER BA30

CAA AGADA

CADEX DEFENCE CDX-SS SEVEN S.T.A.R.S. PRO

CARACAL CAR814 A2 PATROL

CENTURY ARMS WASR-M

CHIAPPA M1-9 MBR

CHRISTENSEN ARMS MESA FFT

BUSHMASTER BA30

Action: Bolt
Stock: Synthetic
Barrel: 18, 24 in.
Sights: None
Weight: N/A
Caliber: 6.5 Creedmoor, .308 Win.
Magazine: 10 rounds
Features: Bushmaster makes a splash with a straight-pull bolt-action rifle that features interchangeable barrels, triggers, recoil pads; AR-style grips, and handguards; MLOK free-floating rail; XM-10 magazine; adjustable BFI stock; Snake Charmer muzzle brake; ambidextrous bolt handle; Type III hard-coat anodizing
Price: . . . .

CAA AGADA

Action: Semiautomatic
Stock: Synthetic
Barrel: 10, 16 in.
Sights: None
Weight: N/A
Caliber: 9mm
Magazine: 10, 15, 17 rounds
Features: An unusual pistol-caliber carbine—Agada is Hebrew for "legend"—that's suppressor ready and sports the pistol grip and fore-grip on opposite sides of the gun; ample rail top and bottom for optics and accessories; used with Glock or CAA-proprietary magazines; folding stock features an adjustable cheek riser; NFA regs apply to 10-in. barrel SBR, and a 10-in. non-NFA will also be available with a pinned and welded faux suppressor; available in left- and right-hand configurations
Price: **$899.00**

CADEX DEFENCE CDX-SS SEVEN S.T.A.R.S. PRO, COVERT

Action: Bolt
Stock: Chassis
Barrel: 11, 16.65, 26 in.
Sights: None
Weight: 11 lb. 14 oz.
Caliber: .223 Rem., 6.5 BR Norma, 6mm Dasher, 6mm Creedmoor, 6.5X47 Lapua, 6.5 Creedmoor, .308 Win., .300 BLK
Magazine: 10, 12 rounds
Features: An entry for the PRS crowd and LE sniper applications,, S.T.A.R.S. stands for Sport and Tactical Application Rifle System and features a STRIKE PRO chassis; Bartlein 5R barrel; 17-in. Acra Elite Systems rail; folding, tool-free adjustable stock; ambidextrous extended magazine latch; rubber vertical grip; 10 MLOK slots; barricade stop; Covert NFA 11-in. barrel available in .223 Rem. and .300 Blk.; all Pro models have 26-in. barrels
Price: . . . . **N/A**

CARACAL CAR814 A2 PATROL

Action: Semiautomatic
Stock: Synthetic
Barrel: 7.5, 11.5, 14.5, 16 in.
Sights: None
Weight: 5 lb. 8 oz.–6 lb. 7 oz.
Caliber: 5.56 NATO, .300 BLK
Magazine: 10, 30 rounds
Features: Designed primarily for law enforcement and military use, this MSR has a modified M4 barrel contour; 12-in. free-floating MLOK/QD handguard; Magpul CTR Carbine buttstock; EDT Sharp Shooter trigger; A2-style flash hider; gas operation, direct impingement; optional select fire for LE agency/military sales; 7.5-in. version is an SBR and different than the 7.5 Patrol pistol
Price: . . . . **$1399.99–$1489.99**

CENTURY ARMS WASR-M

Action: Semiautomatic
Stock: Wood
Barrel: 17.5 in.
Sights: Adjustable front, fixed rear
Weight: 7 lb. 11 oz.
Caliber: 9mm
Magazine: 33 rounds
Features: A fun, pistol-caliber carbine AK with direct blowback operation; AKM side optic mount; RAK-1 enhanced trigger group; original Romanian-made barrel; takes Glock 17/19 magazines
Price: **$919.99**

CHIAPPA M1-9 MODERN BLACK RIFLE (MBR)

Action: Semiautomatic
Stock: Wood
Barrel: 19 in.
Sights: Flip-up front and rear
Weight: 6 lb. 9 oz.
Caliber: 9mm
Magazine: 10 rounds
Features: Interesting PCC with a textured finish on the wood stock; straight blowback design; topside and under-fore-end rails; takes Beretta 92-style magazines, two included
Price: **$814.00**

CHRISTENSEN ARMS MESA FFT

Action: Bolt
Stock: Carbon fiber
Barrel: 20, 22 in.
Sights: None
Weight: 5 lb. 8 oz.
Caliber: .450 Bushmaster, .6.5 CRD, 6.5 PRC, 7mm-08 Rem., .308 Win., .300 Win. Mag., .300 PRC
Magazine: 3, 4 rounds
Features: A lightweight rifle—FFT stands for Flash Forge Technology and is applied in features like the FFT carbon fiber floot plate and bolt knob for weight reduction—with an ultra-light contour stainless barrel; seamless removeable radial muzzle brake; sporter-style stock; Tungsten Cerakote metal with black/gray stock or Burnt Bronze Cerakote metal with green/black/tan stock
Price: . . . . **Staring at $1599.99**

**CHRISTENSEN ARMS
RIDGELINE FFT**

**CHRISTENSEN ARMS
RIDGELINE SCOUT**

CVA CASCADE SB

CZ-USA 600 LUX

CZ-USA 600 RANGE

CZ-USA 600 ALPHA

CZ-USA 600 TRAIL

CHRISTENSEN ARMS RIDGELINE FFT

Action: Bolt
Stock: Carbon fiber
Barrel: 20, 22 in.
Sights: None
Weight: 5 lb. 4 oz.
Caliber: .450 Bushmaster, .22-250 Rem., .243 Win., 6.5 CRD, 6.5 PRC, 6.5-284 Norma, .26 Nosler, .270 Win., 7mm-08 Rem., .280 AI, .28 Nosler, 7mm Rem. Mag., .308 Win., .30-06 Spfd., .30 Nosler, .300 WSM, .300 Win. Mag., .300 PRC, .300 RUM
Magazine: 3, 4 rounds
Features: FFT stands for Flash Forge Technology and is applied in features like the FFT carbon fiber floot plate and bolt knob for weight reduction; carbon fiber-wrapped barrel, handlapped and with a match chamber, button rifling, and free-floating; removeable side-baffle stainless brake; TriggerTech trigger; Rem. 700 optics base compatible; metal in natural stainless or Burnt Bronze Cerakote; multiple stock finishes; some chamberings available left-hand; sub-MOA guarantee
Price: . . . . **Starting at $2399.99**

CHRISTENSEN ARMS RIDGELINE SCOUT

Action: Bolt
Stock: Carbon fiber composite
Barrel: 16 in.
Sights: None
Weight: 5 lb. 15 oz.
Caliber: .300 BLK, .223 Rem., 6.5 CRD, .308 Win,
Magazine: 10 rounds
Features: All the things you love about the full-size Ridgeline packaged into a nimble Scout configuration with an AICS-style detachable magazine; flat-shoe TriggerTech trigger; removeable three-prong flash hider; black nitride-coated action; barricade stop; topside and under-forearm rails
Price: **$2,199.99**

CVA CASCADE SB

Action: Bolt
Stock: Synthetic
Barrel: 16.5, 18 in.
Sights: None
Weight: 6 lb. 12 oz.
Caliber: 6.5 Creedmoor, .308 Win., .300 BLK
Magazine: 4 rounds
Features: SB stands for "short-barreled" but this one steers clear of NFA territory; threaded barrel; stock is in Veil Tec black and has SoftTouch finish and an adjustable length of pull; dual front swivel studs; 70-degree bolt throw; meatal finished in Graphite Black Cerakote; .300 BLK gets the shorter of the two barrel lengths
Price: $670.00

CZ-USA 600 ALPHA

Action: Bolt
Stock: Synthetic
Barrel: 24 in.
Sights: None
Weight: 7 lb.
Caliber: .223 Alpha, .224 Valkyrie, .300 Win. Mag., .308 Win., 6.5 Creedmoor, .30-06 Spfd., 6.5 PRC, 6mm Creedmoor, 7.62X39
Magazine: 5 rounds
Features: Promising sub-MOA performance, this rifle has an aluminum receiver; semi-heavy barrel profile; threaded muzzle for suppressor use; serrated grip points; ADJ single-stage trigger; detachable locking magazine
Price: $749.00

CZ-USA 600 LUX

Action: Bolt
Stock: Walnut

Barrel: 20, 24 in.
Sights: Adjustable rear; fiber-optic front
Weight: 8 lb. 3 oz.
Caliber: .308 Win., .300 Win. Mag., .30-06 Spfd., .223 Rem.
Magazine: 3, 5 rounds
Features: Wearing a distinctly old-world look with a Bavarian-style stock; steel receiver; modern iron sights; drilled and tapped for Remington 700-style bases; ADJ single-stage trigger; suppressor-ready barrel
Price: $849.00

CZ-USA 600 RANGE

Action: Bolt
Stock: Laminate
Barrel: 24 in.
Sights: None
Weight: 10 lb.
Caliber: 6mm Creedmoor, .308 Win.
Magazine: 5 rounds
Features: One for the bench, with a hefty 10 pounds of overall weight; detachable locking magazine; precision stock in laminate; heavy barrel contour; suppressor-ready; ADJ single-stage trigger
Price: **$1,199.00**

CZ-USA 600 TRAIL

Action: Semiautomatic
Stock: Synthetic
Barrel: 16.2 in.
Sights: None
Weight: 6 lb. 1 oz.
Caliber: .223 Rem., 7.62X39
Magazine: 10 rounds
Features: Great portability in a carbine-length package; four-position PDW ADJ stock; semi-heavy, suppressor-ready barrel; ADJ two-stage trigger; detachable magazine; ambidextrous mag release and safety; lots of topside rail
Price: **$1,155.00**

NEW Products: **Rifles**

DANIEL DEFENSE DD4 RIII

DANIEL DEFENSE DD4 RIII S

DANIEL DEFENSE DELTA 5 PRO HPALMA

DANIEL DEFENSE M4A1 RIII

DANIEL DEFENSE MK18 RIII

DANIEL DEFENSE DELTA 5 PRO VARMINT

DARK STORM INDUSTRIES DS-25 TYPHOON

DANIEL DEFENSE DD4 RIII

Action: Semiautomatic
Stock: Synthetic
Barrel: 16 in.
Sights: None
Weight: 6 lb. 8 oz.
Caliber: 5.56 NATO
Magazine: 10, 30 rounds
Features: Fully ambidextrous MSR with an MLOK 12.5-in. rail; heavy-phosphate-covered government-profile barrel; mid-length gas system;
Price: . . . . **N/A**

DANIEL DEFENSE DD4 RIII S

Action: Semiautomatic
Stock: Synthetic
Barrel: 11.5
Sights: None
Weight: 5 lb. 15 oz.
Caliber: 5.56 NATO
Magazine: 10, 30 rounds
Features: The SBR version of the full-size RIII; carbine-length gas system; 10.5-in. RIII rail; NFA regs apply
Price: . . . . **N/A**

DANIEL DEFENSE DELTA 5 PRO HPALMA

Action: Bolt
Stock: Chassis
Barrel: 20 in.
Sights: None
Weight: 10 lb. 14 oz.
Caliber: .308 Win.
Magazine: 10 rounds
Features: Competition ready for PRS Production Division with .5 sub-MOA accuracy; threaded, interchangeable cold hammer-forged barrel with Area 419 Hellfire muzzle brake; adjustable single-stage Timney Elite Hunter trigger; chassis base; multiple MLOK attachment points; 10, MLOK QD sling points; 20 MOA/5.8 MRAD rail; removeable bolt knob; mechanically bedded stainless steel action; left/right

adjustable thumb rest; buttstock adjustable for length of pull and cheek riser; Magpul PMAG magazine
Price: **$2499.00**

DANIEL DEFENSE DELTA 5 PRO VARMINT

Action: Bolt
Stock: Chassis
Barrel: 16, 18 in.
Sights: None
Weight: 11 lb. 13 oz.
Caliber: .308 Win., 6.5 Creedmoor
Magazine: 10 rounds
Features: Wearing most of the features to the Delta Pro 5 HPalma, this chassis rifle arrives in two calibers (18-in. barrel in 6.5 Creedmoor, 16-in. barrel in .308 Win.) and is intended for varmint work, including coyotes and hogs, thanks to the rifle's bridge that's compatible with an extended Picatinny rail for mounting nightvision and thermal optics
Price: **$2499.00**

DANIEL DEFENSE M4A1 RIII

Action: Semiautomatic
Stock: Synthetic
Barrel: 14.5 in.
Sights: None
Weight: 6 lb. 5 oz.
Caliber: 5.56 NATO
Magazine: 10, 30 rounds
Features: An adaptation of the proven M4A1 design, with a 12.5-in. RIII MLOK rail that replaces the Picatinny design and reduces weight; carbine-length gas system; flash suppressor pinned and welded to extend length to civilian-legal 16 in.
Price: . . . . **N/A**

DANIEL DEFENSE MK18 RIII

Action: Semiautomatic
Stock: Synthetic

Barrel: 10.5 in.
Sights: None
Weight: 5 lb. 12 oz.
Caliber: 5.56 NATO
Magazine: 10, 30 rounds
Features: Super-short, fully ambidextrous version for LE/military applications, with a carbine-length gas system; 9.5-in. RIII rail with MLOK slots; government profile barrel; NFA regs apply
Price: . . . . **N/A**

DARK STORM INDUSTRIES DS-25 TYPHOON

Action: Semiautomatic
Stock: Synthetic
Barrel: 12.5, 16 in.
Sights: None
Weight: 6 lb. 12 oz.
Caliber: .308 Win.
Magazine: 10, 20 rounds
Features: Dark Storm continues to innovate—especially on behalf of those citizens living in states with onerous firearm ownership restrictions—this time with an AR-15 chambered in .308. This novel rifle comes in several configurations to satisfy ownership requirements anywhere in the 50, including the Standard model with a 16-in. barrel, mid-length gas system, and 13-in. MLOK handguard; Non-NFA, which has no buttstock, a forward pistol grip, a 12.5-in. barrel, and is not classified as a rifle, pistol, or AOW; a 16-in. Fixed Magazine model; a Post-Ban 16-in. model; and a Featureless 16-in. model. Features across the board include a DSI Chinook ambidextrous charging handle; ambidextrous 90-degree safety selector; billet aluminum receiver; Type III hard-coat anodizing; some models available in flat dark earth and OD green
Price: . . . . $1495.00–$1595.00

DARK STORM INDUSTRIES DSI VARIANT 1

DAVIDE PEDERSOLI 86-71 BOARBUSTER EVOLUTION

DAVIDE PEDERSOLI 86-71 BOARBUSTER SHADOW

DERYA TM22

FIRECE FIREARMS CT RAGE

FIERCE FIREARMS TWISTED RIVAL

DARK STORM INDUSTRIES DSI VARIANT 1

Action: Semiautomatic
Stock: Synthetic
Barrel: 12.5, 16 in.
Sights: None
Weight: N/A
Caliber: 5.56 NATO, .300 BLK
Magazine: 10, 20 rounds
Features: A competition-ready MSR in several variations, including the Standard model with a 16-in. barrel, mid-length gas system, and 13-in. MLOK handguard; Non-NFA, which has no buttstock, a forward pistol grip, a 12.5-in. barrel, and is not classified as a rifle, pistol, or AOW; a 16-in. Fixed Magazine model; a Post-Ban 16-in. model; and a Featureless 16-in. model. Features across the board include a lightened aerospace-grade aluminum receiver; M4 feed ramp extensions; deburred edges; forward assist; Allen screw bolt catch and forward assist pins; winter trigger guard; ambidextrous charging handle; ultralight, narrow-profile MLOK handguard; competition compensator; Hogue adjustable stock (on buttstock models); available in Tungsten Cerakote or Type III hard-coat anodized black.
Price: . . . . **$1595.00–$1695.00**

DAVIDE PEDERSOLI 86/71 BOARBUSTER EVOLUTION

Action: Lever
Stock: Wood
Barrel: 19 in.
Sights: Fiber optic front, rear sight on Picatinny rail
Weight: 8 lb. 2 oz.
Caliber: .45-70 Gov't.
Magazine: 3 rounds
Features: A handsome lever made for hog hunters, with a wood stock; matte stainless receiver; polished blue barrel, lever, and magazine; drilled and tapped for optics mounts; Picatinny rail for forward-receiver mounting; side-gate loading
Price: . . . . **N/A**

DAVIDE PEDERSOLI 86/71 BOARBUSTER SHADOW

Action: Lever
Stock: Synthetic
Barrel: 19 in.
Sights: Fiber optic front, peep rear
Weight: 7 lb. 13 oz.
Caliber: .45-70 Gov't.
Magazine: 3 rounds
Features: For the all-weather hog hunter, this lever has a gray synthetic stock with grooved grip areas and an adjustable cheekpiece; matte black metalwork; drilled and tapped for optics mounting; side-gate loading
Price: **$1,791.04**

DERYA TM-22-A-18

Action: Semiautomatic
Stock: Aluminum
Barrel: 18 in.
Sights: None
Weight: 6 lb. 2 oz.
Caliber: .22 LR
Magazine: 10, 15, 25 rounds
Features: Made in Turkey, this rimfire auto-loader features a fixed aluminum stock; MLOK fore-end; blowback operation; aluminum receiver; left-side charging handle; alloy magazines; can accommodate most aftermarket AR-15 stocks; available in black, Sniper Gray, Arctic White, and flat dark earth
Price: . . . . **N/A**

FIERCE FIREARMS CT RAGE, CARBON RAGE, TWISTED RAGE

Action: Bolt
Stock: Carbon fiber
Barrel: 24, 26 in.
Sights: None
Weight: 6 lb. 1 oz.
Caliber: .22-250 Rem., 6.5 Creedmoor, 6.5 PRC, 7mm-08 Rem., .308 Win., 7mm Rem. Mag., .28 Nosler, .300 Win. Mag., .300 PRC, .300 RUM, .338 Lapua, .375 H&H Mag.
Magazine: 3, 4 rounds
Features: A super-lightweight hunter with a C3 carbon fiber barrel with radial muzzle brake; Firece titanium action (CT Rage) with a 70-degree bolt throw; adjustable Bix'n Andy trigger; carbon fiber stock with integral bipod rail and Monte Carlo cheekpiece; detachable speed-box magazine; numerous digital color patterns to choose from for the stock and choice of gray, black, bronze, or tungsten Cerakote; Carbon Rage has stainless steel action; Twisted Rage has stainless steel action and twisted stainless barrel
Price: . . . . **N/A**

FIERCE FIREARMS CT RIVAL, CARBON RIVAL, TWISTED RIVAL

Action: Bolt
Stock: Carbon fiber
Barrel: 24, 26 in.
Sights: None
Weight: 5 lb. 14 oz.–6 lb. 3 oz.
Caliber: 6mm Creedmoor, 6.5 Creedmoor, 6.5 PRC, .280 AI, .22 Creedmoor, .22-250 Rem., 7mm Rem. Mag., .28 Nosler, .300 Win. Mag., .300 PRC, .300 RUM
Magazine: 3, 4 rounds
Features: Lightweight and then some, this hunter's rifle has a titanium action (CT Rival) with a 70-degree bolt throw; C3 carbon fiber barrel; Limbsaver recoil pad; C3 carbon fiber stock with built-in bipod rail; minimum CNC tolerances overall; adjustable Bix'n Andy Dakota trigger; Fierc's Guard Cerakote finish in choice of gray, black, bronze, or tungsten to go with multiple digital color stock patterns; .50-MOA accuracy guarantee; Carbon Rival has C3 carbon barrel with stainless steel action; Twisted Rival has a vertical pistol grip, palm swell, high negative comb cheekpiece, spiral-fluted match-grade stainless steel barrel
CT Rival . . . . . . **starting at $3050.00**
Carbon Rival . . **starting at $2699.00**
Twisted Rival . . . **starting at $2299.00**

NEW Products: **Rifles**

FIERCE FIREARMS F-10 SIDEWINDER

FIERCE FIREARMS REAPER

FN AMERICA FN 15 TAC3

FN AMERICA FN PS90

H&K MP5 .22 LR

H&K SL8

HENRY REPEATING ARMS LONG RANGER EXPRESS

FIERCE FIREARMS FT SIDEWINDER

Action: Semiautomatic
Stock: Synthetic
Barrel: 16 in.
Sights: None
Weight: 5 lb. 14 oz.
Caliber: 6.5 Creedmoor, .308 Win.
Magazine: 20 rounds
Features: A very modern MSR with a unique and streamlined receiver design; carbon fiber MLOK handguard, grip; full-length aluminum rail; C3 carbon fiber match-grade barrel; side-charging without forward assist; TriggerTech Diamond trigger; .75-MOA accuracy guarantee
Price: $2,995.00

FIERCE FIREARMS REAPER

Action: Bolt
Stock: Chassis
Barrel: 20, 22, 24, 26 in.
Sights: None
Weight: 6 lb. 8 oz.–6 lb. 14 oz.
Caliber: 6mm Creedmoor, 6.5 Creedmoor, 6.5 PRC, 7mm Rem. Mag., .28 Nosler, .308 Win., .300 Win. Mag., .300 PRC, .300 RUM
Magazine: 5 rounds
Features: Aimed at both serious mountain hunters and PRS competitors, this chassis rifle features an adjustable carbon fiber stock in choice of fixed or folding; carbon fiber MLOK handguard; carbon fiber grip; C3 carbon fiber match-grade, hand-lapped, cryo-treated barrel with a stainless liner and suppressor ready; Bix'm Andy Dakota adjustable trigger; Fierc's Rival action (also available in a titanium upgrade that shaves five to six ounces off the overall rifle weight) with a 70-degre bolt throw; positve horizontal ejection via a dual plunger and mini claw extractor; Accurate Mag detachable magazine; available

in black, Bronze, or Tungsten Cerakote
Price: . . . . Starting at $2895.00

FN AMERICA FN 15 TAC3

Action: Semiautomatic
Stock: Synthetic
Barrel: 16 in.
Sights: None
Weight: 7 lb.
Caliber: 5.56 NATO
Magazine: 30 rounds
Features: A carbine MSR with a mil-spec foundation; M16 bolt carrier group; mid-length gas system with "H" buffer; fully free-floated barrel; Hodge Defense wedge lock handguard with continuous 12 o'clock rail space and multiple MLOK slots; ambidextrous charging handle and selector; six-position buttstock; government barrel profile; available in black, flat dark earth, or gray
Price: $1,799.00

FN AMERICA FN PS90

Action: Semiautomatic
Stock: Synthetic
Barrel: 16 in.
Sights: Backup iron sight
Weight: 6 lb. 4 oz.
Caliber: 5.7X28mm
Magazine: 10, 30 rounds
Features: A blowback operated, civilian-legal bullpup that fires from a closed bolt and has dual magazine latches; thumbhole stock with molded-in sling attachment points; fully ambidextrous operation; hammer-forged chrome-lined barrel with integral ported muzzle brake; enlarged trigger guard; mil-std 1913 accessory rail; backup iron sight
Price: $1,949.00

H&K MP5 .22 LR

Action: Semiautomatic

Stock: Synthetic
Barrel: 16.1 in.
Sights: Ghost ring front, adjustable aperture rear
Weight: 7 lb.
Caliber: .22 LR
Magazine: 10, 25 rounds
Features: Based on the famous submachine gun, this semi-auto .22 LR offers up lots of fun with blowback operation; single-stage trigger; retractable stock; adjustable bolt speed
Price: $489.00

H&K SL8

Action: Semiautomatic
Stock: Synthetic
Barrel: .223 Rem.
Sights: None
Weight: 8 lb. 10 oz.
Caliber: .223 Rem.
Magazine: 10 rounds
Features: The SL8 returns to the H&K stable in 2021 after a long absence and features the G36/SL8 short-stroke gas piston; match trigger; adjustable stock; free-floating bull barrel with recessed crown; ample top-side rail
Price: . . . . $1789.00–$1849.00

HENRY REPEATING ARMS LONG RANGER EXPRESS

Action: Lever-action
Stock: Laminate
Barrel: 16.5 in.
Sights: None
Weight: 7 lb.
Caliber: .223 Rem.
Magazine: 5 rounds
Features: A carbine-length lever-action with a birch laminate stock; hard-anodized black receiver; solid rubber buttpad; blued steel barrel, threaded; hammer extension; detachable box magazine; sling swivel studs; topside Picatinny rail
Price: $1,235.00

CITADEL HOWA CARBON ELEVATE

CITADEL HOWA CARBON STALKER

CITADEL SUPER LITE

IRON HORSE FIREARMS DMR CLASSIC

IRON HORSE FIREARMS SPR

IRON HORSE FIREARMS SPR 6MM ARC

ISTANBUL SILAH MONZA

LAZZERONI MODEL 2012 MOUNTAIN-LITE LONG-RANGE

HOWA CARBON ELEVATE
Action: Bolt
Stock: Carbon fiber
Barrel: 20, 24 in.
Sights: None
Weight: 4 lb. 10 oz.–6 lb. 7 oz.
Caliber: 6.5 Grendel, 6.5 Creedmoor, .308 Win., 6.5 PRC
Magazine: 3, 4 rounds
Features: Sporting both a carbon fiber stock and a carbon fiber-wrapped barrel; stock in Kryptek Altitude or all black; Limbsaver buttpad; suppressor-ready; detachable magazine in 6.5 Grendel mini-action only
Price:. $1,639.00

HOWA CARBON STALKER
Action: Bolt
Stock: Carbon fiber
Barrel: 16.25, 20, 22, 24 in.
Sights: None
Weight: 4 lb. 10 oz.–6 lb. 4 oz.
Caliber: .223 Rem., 6.5 Grendel, 7.62X39, 6mm ARC, .350 Legend, 7mm-08 Rem., .308 Win., .270 Win., 6.5 PRC, .300 Win. Mag., 7mm Rem. Mag.
Magazine: 3, 4 rounds
Features: Available in a mini short action, short action, and long action depending on caliber; this rifle has a super-lightweight custom carbon fiber stock (black or Kryptek Altitude); detachable magazine in the mini action; Accublock lug bed; Limbsaver buttpad;
Price:. $1,029.00

HOWA SUPER LITE
Action: Bolt
Stock: Synthetic
Barrel: 20 in.
Sights: None
Weight: 4 lb. 7 oz.
Caliber: 6.5 Creedmoor, .308 Win.
Magazine: 3 rounds
Features: This one really pushes the boundaries of lightweight at a smidge under 4.5 pounds; two-stage match trigger; one-piece topside rail; flush-fit detachable magazine; reduced short action build; tool-less firing pin removal; Kryptek Altitude and Obskura Transitional camo stock finishes; sub-MOA guarantee
Price:. $1,399.00

IRON HORSE FIREARMS DMR CLASSIC
Action: Semiautomatic
Stock: Aluminum billet
Barrel: 18 in.
Sights: None
Weight: 8 lb. 8 oz.
Caliber: .223 Rem.
Magazine: 30 rounds
Features: Features Iron Horse's lever-operated lower, said to cure trigger jerk and other shooting errors at the trigger; flared magazine well; aluminum billet stock; ambidextrous charging handle; QD handguard and stock; ambidextrous controls; window magazines
Price:. $2,099.00

IRON HORSE FIREARMS SPR
Action: Semiautomatic
Stock: Synthetic
Barrel: 18 in.
Sights: None
Weight: 8 lb. 8 oz.
Caliber: .223 Wylde
Magazine: 30 rounds
Features: Similar to the DMR, but chambered in the .223 Wylde and with a Fab Defense GL-Core S stock
Price:. $1,799.00

IRON HORSE FIREARMS SPR 6MM ARC
Action: Semiautomatic
Stock: Synthetic
Barrel: 18 in.
Sights: None
Weight: 6 lb. 15 oz.
Caliber: 6mm ARC
Magazine: 25 rounds
Features: Nearly identical to the original SPR, but chambered in the relatively new 6mm ARC (Advanced Rifle Cartridge), developed by Hornady; carbon fiber Helix6 barrel; metal magazines; rifle +1" gas system
Price:. $2999.00

ISTANBUL SILAH MONZA
Action: Bolt
Stock: Synthetic
Barrel: 20, 22, 24 in.
Sights: Fiber optic blade front, hidden adjustable rear
Weight: 7 lb.
Caliber: .308 Win.
Magazine: 4 rounds
Features: A Turkish-made rifle with an adjustable cheekpiece; button-rifled four-groove barrel with an 11-degree crown (optional threaded muzzle); detachable steel magazine; topside rail; fiber optic front sight paired with a hidden and adjustable rear sight; anodized finish; tool-less bolt disassembly; universal bipod rail
Price:. . . . . N/A

LAZZERONI MODEL 2012 MOUNTAIN-LITE LONG-RANGE
Action: Bolt
Stock: Graphite composite
Barrel: 26 in.
Sights: None
Weight: 7 lb. 5 oz.
Caliber: 6.53 Scramjet, 7.21 Firebird, 7.82 Warbird
Magazine: 3 rounds
Features: Some word argue that a rifle over seven pounds doesn't really qualify for "light weight," but there's no doubt about the quaility of a rifle like this from Lazzeroni, with a single-piece diamond-fluted bolt shaft; stainless-steel receiver; custom-molded and hand-bedded stock; Timney trigger; Vais muzzle brake; Limbsaver recoil pad; available right- and left-hand
Price:. $5,999.99

NEW Products: **Rifles**

LAZZERONI MODEL 2012 THUMBHOLE EXTRA LONG-RANGE RIFLE

MARLIN1895 SBL

MASTERPIECE ARMS MPA AR9 PCC

MASTERPIECE ARMS MPA BA PMR PRO RIFLE II

MASTERPIECE ARMS MPA PORK CHOP

MAUSER 18 FELDJAGD

LAZZERONI MODEL 2012 THUMBHOLE EXTRA LONG RANGE

Action: Bolt
Stock: Graphite composite
Barrel: 26 in.
Sights: None
Weight: 7 lb.15 oz.
Caliber: 7.21 Firebird, 7.82 Warbird, 9.53 Saturn
Magazine: 3 rounds
Features: For hunters taking long pokes at big game, this rifle offers a one-piece diamond-fluted bolt shaft; match-grade button-rifled barrel; Vais muzzle brake; Limbsaver recoil pad; High Mountain Desert Camo stock finish; 20 MOA Picatinny rail; choice of 30mm or 34mm ring sets; right-hand only
Price: **$6,999.99**

MARLIN 1895 SBL

Action: Lever-action
Stock: Laminate
Barrel: 19 in.
Sights: Fiber optic front, ghost ring rear
Weight: 7 lb. 4 oz.
Caliber: .45-70 Gov't.
Magazine: 6 rounds
Features: The first Marlin made by Ruger and released to the public at the tail end of 2021, this modernized lever-action includes a handsome gray laminate stock; polished stainless steel metal; cold hammer-forged stainless steel barrel with a match-polished thread cap; checkered grip panels; oversized leverl loop; nickel-plated spiral fluted bolt; lengthy topside PIcatinny rail
Price: **$1399.00**

MASTERPIECE ARMS MPA AR9 PCC

Action: Semiautomatic

Stock: Synthetic
Barrel: 16 in.
Sights: None
Weight: 6 lb. 4 oz.
Caliber: 9mm
Magazine: 17 rounds
Features: Up your pistol caliber carbine game with this offering from MPA that features an aluminum billet machined lower; Type-III hard coat anodized and Cerakoted finish in choice of black, blue, red, or green; machined aluminum S2 grip; anodized low-profile handguard; Cerakoted, multi-port compensator; adjustable buttstock; suppressor ready; takes Glock 17 magazines
Price: **$1499.00**

MASTERPIECE ARMS MPA BA PMR PRO RIFLE II

Action: Bolt
Stock: Chassis
Barrel: 26 in.
Sights: None
Weight: 12 lb. 8 oz.
Caliber: 6mm Creedmoor, 6GT, 6.5 Creedmoor, 6.5 PRC, 6 Dasher, 6BR, 6BRA, 6XC, 7=6X47 Lapua, .223 Rem., .308 Win.
Magazine: 10 rounds
Features: Designed to meet the specs of PRS Production Class, this rifle has MPA's BA Comp chassis with a built-in inclinometer, V-bedding system, thumb notch, EVG grip, Ultra Bag Rider, V4 spigot mount, and finished in black or Tungsten Cerakote; Lothar Walther hand-lapped, stress-relieved barrel; MPA/Curtis short action with a Remington 700 footprint; three-lug bolt with a 60-degree throw; choice of TriggerTech Diamond or Timney HIT triggers; comes with Plano rifle case
Price: **$2499.00**

MASTERPIECE ARMS MPA PORK CHOP

Action: Bolt

Stock: Chassis
Barrel: 18, 20, 22, 24, 26 in.
Sights: None
Weight: 8 lb. 7 oz.
Caliber: .22 Creedmoor, .223 Wylde, 6 GT, 6.5 Creedmoor, 6.5 PRC, 6mm Creedmoor
Magazine: 10 rounds
Features: MPA says this one is for ranch work and pest control, with a 6061 aluminum hybrid chassis in a special Pork Chop-themed Cerakote finish; stock adjustable for length of pull, cheek riser, and bag rider, is spigot-mount ready and incudes a V4 spigot mount, includes an incolmeter, thumb notch, and enhanced vertical pistol grip, and is V-bedded with additional clearance for glass bedding at the barrel; threaded carbon fiber barrel chambered by MPA, cut rifled, and stress relieved in choice of Sendero or Sendero Lite profiles; one-piece bolt with spiral fluting; TriggerTech Special Trigger; includes Plano rifle case
Price: . . . .**$3700.00–$3850.00**

MAUSER M18 FELDJAGD

Action: Bolt
Stock: Polymer
Barrel: 22, 24 in.
Sights: None
Weight: 6 lb. 15 oz.
Caliber: .223 Rem., .243 Win., .270 Win., .30-06 Spfd., 6.5X55 SE, 6.5 Creedmoor, 8X57 IS, 9.3X62, 6.5 PRC, 7mm Rem. Mag., .300 Win. Mag.
Magazine: 4, 5 rounds
Features: Feldjagd is German for "hunting in the fields," and this one fits the bill with a polymer stock that offers the convenience of an adjustable cheekpiece; soft-grip inlays at pistol grip and fore-end; fluted, threaded, cold hammer-forged barrel
Price: **$699.99**

MAUSER M18 LR
CHASSIS

MAUSER M18
WALDJAGD

MCMILLAN FIREARMS
TAC-65

MCMILLAN FIREARMS
TAC-50C

MOSSBERG PATRIOT
LR HUNTER

NOSLER MODEL 21

PATRIOT ORDNANCE
ROARING REBEL

MAUSER M18 LR CHASSIS

Action: Bolt
Stock: Chassis
Barrel: 24 in.
Sights: None
Weight: 9 lb. 15 oz.
Caliber: .308 Win., .243 Win., 6.5 Creedmoor, 6XC
Magazine: 10 rounds
Features: Mauser enters the long-range game with a rifle on an aluminum Oryx chassis that's adjustable for length of pull and cheekpiece height and features MLOK slots; free-floated, threaded, cold hammer-forged barrel; three-position safety; AR-15-compatible pistol grip; receiver Picatinny rail; barricade stop; two QD sling swivel sockets; double-stack detachable magazine
Price: . . . . **N/A**

MAUSER M18 WALDJAGD

Action: Bolt
Stock: Polymer
Barrel: 20 in.
Sights: Fiber optic front, adjustable leaf rear
Weight: 6 lb. 14 oz.
Caliber: .223 Rem., .243 Win., .270 Win., .308 Win., .30-06 Spfd., 6.5X55 SE, 6.5 Creedmoor, 8X57 IS, 9.3X62
Magazine: 5 rounds
Features: A shorter, more compact version of the Feldjagd, because Waldjagd means "hunting in the woods," thus the polymer stock in pine green and with grip inlays at the pistol grip and fore-end; high-contrast sights; fluted barrel is threaded
Price: **$699.99**

MCMILLAN FIREARMS TAC-6.5

Action: Bolt
Stock: Synthetic
Barrel: 24 in.
Sights: None
Weight: 11 lb. 8 oz.

Caliber: 6.5 Creedmoor
Magazine: 5 rounds
Features: A weighty sniper rifle in 6.5 Creedmoor with a five-round A1 detachable magazine; McMillan's own A3-5 stock; threaded and capped muzzle; match-grade stainless steel barrel in a medium-heavy contour; topside rail; flush-mount swivel cups; Cerakote meta finish
Price: **$5440.84**

MCMILLAN FIREARMS TAC-50C

Action: Bolt
Stock: Chassis
Barrel: 29 in.
Sights: None
Weight: 24 lb.
Caliber: .50 BMG
Magazine: 5 rounds
Features: This one's a beast at almost 25 pounds, but that weight will help suck up the recoil from the .50 BMG. Features include a folding Cadex Dual Strike chassis; slimmed pistol grip; three 193 Mil-Std rails; match-grade, fluted, Navy contour stainless steel barrel with an impressive muzzle brake; adjustable buttstock; Cerakote finish
Price: **$11,250.00**

MOSSBERG PATRIOT LR HUNTER

Action: Bolt
Stock: Synthetic
Barrel: 22, 24 in.
Sights: None
Weight: 6 lb. 8 oz.–7 lb. 8 oz.
Caliber: .308 Win., .300 Win. Mag., 6.5 Creedmoor, 6.5 PRC
Magazine: 3, 4, 5 rounds
Features: With a distinctive Monte Carlo-style stock, this rifle has a flat-bottomed tapered fore-end; adjustable trigger; fluted and threaded barrel; oversized bolt handle
Price: **$797.00**

NOSLER MODEL 21

Action: Bolt
Stock: Carbon fiber
Barrel: 22, 24 in.
Sights: None
Weight: 6 lb. 14 oz.–7 lb. 1 oz.
Caliber: .22 Nosler, 6.5 Creedmoor, 6.5 PRC, .26 Nosler, .27 Nosler, .280 AI, .28 Nosler, .308 Win., .300 Win. Mag., .30 Nosler, .33 Nosler, .375 H&H Mag.
Magazine: 3, 4 rounds
Features: A hunter's rifle with premium features like an EDM machined receiver; nitride-coated fluted bolt; TriggerTech Field trigger with Frictionless Release Technology; Shilen match-grade stainless steel barrel threaded and with a recessed crown McMillan stock; tool-less fire-control group takedown; threaded bolt handle for knob change-out;
Price: **$2795.00**

PATRIOT ORDNANCE ROARING REBEL

Action: Semiautomatic
Stock: Hardwood
Barrel: 16 in.
Sights: Post front, adjustable rear
Weight: N/A
Caliber: .22 LR
Magazine: 10, 30 rounds
Features: Commemorating POF's 20th anniversary in 2022, this nifty rimfire features retro styling that includes a 30-round drum and a Savior Equipment guitar case; 14-in. barrel with a pinned and welded Cutt's-type compensator to keep it off the NFA list; Boyd's hardwood stock and furniture; MLOK topside monolithic rail
Price: **$1663.00**

NEW Products: **Rifles**

PROOF RESEARCH MDT ACC CHASSIS RIFLE

PROOF RESEARCH TUNDRA

ROCK ISLAND ARMORY TM22

ROCK RIVER ARMS ASSURANCE CARBINE

ROSSI RIMFIRE RIFLE THREADED BARREL

RUGER 10-22 COMPETITION

SAVAGE ARMS 110 CARBON TACTICAL

PROOF RESEARCH MDT ACC CHASSIS RIFLE

Action: Bolt
Stock: Chassis
Barrel: 26 in.
Sights: None
Weight: 15 lb. 14 oz.
Caliber: .22 LR, .223 Rem., 6 ARC, 6 Dasher, 6 GT, 6mm Creedmoor, 6.5 Creedmoor, .308 Win.
Magazine: 12 rounds
Features: Built on a an MDT ACC chassis, this competition-ready rifle features a Zermatt Arms TL3 action; adjustable TriggerTech Pro Curved Diamond trigger; AICS detachable steel magazine; Proof's competition-contour steel barrel; Area 419 Hellfire muzzzle brake; 20 MOA rail
Price:................$5699.00

PROOF RESEARCH TUNDRA

Action: Bolt
Stock: Carbon fiber
Barrel: 20, 22, 24, 26 in.
Sights: None
Weight: 7 lb.–8 lb. 2 oz.
Caliber: 6mm Creedmoor, 6.5 Creedmoor, 6.5 PRC, 7mm Rem. Mag., .28 Nosler, .308 Win., .300 Win. Mag., .300 WSM , .300 PRC, .300 RUM, .338 Lapua
Magazine: 3, 4 rounds
Features: For hunters pushing distance, this rifle includes a threaded, match-grade, carbon fiber barrel, in a Sendero profile, and metalwork in choice of FDE, OD green, black, Tungsten, or Sniper Grey Cerakote; single-piece pinned rail; Defiance Ruckus action; extreme-accuracy bedding; TriggerTech trigger; choice of single or multiple-color stock options
Price:........ $7699.00–$7799.00

ROCK ISLAND ARMORY TM-22

Action: Semiautomatic

Stock: Synthetic
Barrel: 20 in.
Sights: None
Weight: N/A
Caliber: .22 LR
Magazine: 10 rounds
Features: A nimble rimfire with an fixed aluminum stock; AR-type grip; short-travel trigger pull; MLOK fore-end; ambidextrous design allows the user to switch from right- to left-handed controls easily; threaded barrel
Price:...................299.00

ROCK RIVER ARMS ASSURANCE CARBINE

Action: Semiautomatic
Stock: Synthetic
Barrel: 16 in.
Sights: None
Weight: N/A
Caliber: 5.56 NATO
Magazine: 30 rounds
Features: Originally designed for military and LE use and now offered for civilians, the Assurance has a RRA two-stage trigger; forged lower and upper; six-position operator's stock; gas block with receiver-height rail; A2 flash hider; chrome-moly barrel; free-floating quad rail handguard with Picatinny rails at 3, 9, and 12 o'clock and an MLOK slot on the 9 o'clock bottom; Hogue overmolded pistol grip; carbine-length gas system; hard case provided
Price:.................**$1000.00**

ROSSI RIMFIRE RIFLE WITH THREADED BARREL

Action: Semiautomatic
Stock: Synthetic
Barrel: 18 in.
Sights: Fiber optic front, adjustable rear
Weight: 4 lb. 8 oz.
Caliber: .22 LR
Magazine: 10 rounds
Features: Good for plinking and

small-varmint hunting, you can slap a suppressor on this rimfire thanks to its threaded barrel
Price:..................**$172.17**

RUGER 10/22 COMPETITION, COMPETITION LEFT-HAND

Action: Semiautomatic
Stock: Laminate
Barrel: 16.12 in.
Sights: None
Weight: 6 lb.
Caliber: .22 LR
Magazine: 10 rounds
Features: Yet another in the endless line of 10/22 iterrations, this one with a speckled gray/black laminate stock; hard-coat anodized receiver; 30 MOA Picatinny rail; fully adjustable cheekpiece; BX trigger; dual bedding system; rear cleaning port in the receiver; detachable rotary magazine; cold hammer-forged steel barrel in a bull profile and with a muzzle brake; match bolt release; compatible with Silent SR suppressor; includes hard case; left-hand variant available
Price:..................**$929.00**

SAVAGE ARMS 110 CARBON TACTICAL

Action: Bolt
Stock: Synthetic
Barrel: 22, 24 in.
Sights: None
Weight: 7 lb. 10 oz.–7 lb. 14 oz.
Caliber: .308 Win., 6.5 Creedmoor, 6mm Creedmoor
Magazine: 10 rounds
Features: You get a lightweight, threaded, Proof Research carbon fiber barrel on this rifle; AccuTrigger; carbon steel receiver in matte black; AccuStock with AccuFit technology; beavertail fore-end with three swivel studs; one-piece 20 MOA rail; stock in dark gray or flat dark earth
Price:..................**$1789.00**

SAVAGE ARMS 110 MAGPUL HUNTER

SAVAGE ARMS A22 PRECISION LITE

SAVAGE ARMS B17 PRECISION LITE

SEEKINS PRECISION HAVAK PH2

SEEKINS PRECISION HAVAK HIT

SAVAGE ARMS IMPULSE ELITE PRECISION

SIG SAUER MCX-SPEAR

SAVAGE ARMS 110 MAGPUL HUNTER

Action: Bolt
Stock: Synthetic
Barrel: 18 in.
Sights: None
Weight: 8 lb. 15 oz.
Caliber: .308 Win., 6.5 Creedmoor
Magazine: 5 rounds
Features: This short and stout rifle wears an adjustable Magpul Hunter stock with aluminum bedding block; AICS Magpul magazine; carbon steel barrel in a heavy profile and threaded; MLOK slots on fore-end sides and bottom; AccuTrigger; Tungsten Cerakote metalwork; available left-hand
Price:. **$1045.00**

SAVAGE ARMS A22 PRECISION LITE

Action: Semiautomatic
Stock: Chassis
Barrel: 18 in.
Sights: None
Weight: 6 lb. 11 oz.
Caliber: .22 LR
Magazine: 10 rounds
Features: A fast-handling rimfire with a carbon fiber-wrapped barrel; MDT aluminum chassis; oversized charging handle; rotary magazine; MDT pistol grip; MLOK fore-end
Price:. **$949.00**

SAVAGE ARMS B17 PRECISION LITE, B22 PRECISION LITE, B22 MAGNUM PRECISION LITE

Action: Bolt
Stock: Chassis
Barrel: 18 in.
Sights: None
Weight: 6 lb. 11 oz.
Caliber: .17 HMR, .22 LR, .22 WMR
Magazine: 10 rounds

Features: Similar to the A17 Precision Lite but in a bolt-action
Price:. **$949.00**

SAVAGE ARMS IMPULSE ELITE PRECISION

Action: Bolt
Stock: Chassis
Barrel: 26, 30 in.
Sights: None
Weight: 13 lb. 11 oz.
Caliber: .308 Win., 6.5 Creedmoor, 6mm Creedmoor, 6.5 PRC, .300 PRC, .300 Win. Mag., .338 Lapua
Magazine: 5 rounds
Features: An aluminum Adjustable Core chassis foundation from Modular Driven Technologies supports a straight-pull bolt action; ARCA MLOK fore-end; adjustable Accutrigger; ambidextrous bolt handle; button-rifled stainless steel Palma-contour barrel; 20 MOA rail
Price:. **$2619.00**

SEEKINS PRECISION HAVAK HIT

Action: Bolt
Stock: Chassis
Barrel: 24 in.
Sights: None
Weight: 11 lb. 8 oz.
Caliber: 6GT, 6mm Creedmoor, 6,5 Creedmoor, 6.5 PRC, .308 Win,
Magazine: 10 rounds
Features: A chassis for hunters or competitors, with a folding stock; changeable bolt head to go with the quick-change barrel system; 20mm Picatinny rail; tool-less cheekpiece, buttstock, and recoil pad adjustment; MLOK forearm; bag rider; AR-style vertical grip; LT Tactical barrel contour
Price:. **$2100.00**

SEEKINS PRECISION HAVAK PH2

Action: Bolt

Stock: Carbon composite
Barrel: 24 in.
Sights: None
Weight: 6 lb. 15 oz.–7 lb. 3 oz.
Caliber: 6mm Creedmoor, 6.5 Creedmoor, 6.5 PRC, .308 Win., .28 Nosler, .300 Win. Mag., .300 PRC, .338 Win, Mag., 7mm Rem. Mag.
Magazine: 3, 5 rounds
Features: A super choice for the foot hunter with a carbonfiber composite stock in choice of Mountain Shadow, Desert Shadow, or Urban Shadow finishes; hand-bedded barreled actions; carbon-fiber magazines; threaded 5R 416 stainless steel barrel; Timney Elite Hunter trigger; 4 lug bolt with 90-degree throw and removeable bolt head; 20 MOA Picatinny rail; bead-blasted charcoal gray metal finish
Price:. **$1895.00**

SIG SAUER MCX-SPEAR

Action: Semiautomatic
Stock: Synthetic
Barrel: 13 in.
Sights: None
Weight: 8 lb. 5 oz.
Caliber: .277 SIG Fury
Magazine: 20 rounds
Features: A commercial variant of the U.S. Army's Next Generation Squad Weapon (NGSW), this top-end MSR is a multi-caliber firearm (in addition to the .277 SIG Fury, it accepts 6.5 Creedmoor and 7.62 NATO with the appropriate barrel changes); rear and side non-reciprocating charging handle; six-position folding stock; adjustable two-position gas piston; free-floating MLOK handguard; full-length Picatinny rail; ambidextrous magazine release, bolt catch, and fire control; two-stage match trigger; ships with two 20-round magazines; Coyote finish; suppressor-ready; SBR, NFA regs apply
Price:. **$7,999.00**

NEW Products: **Rifles**

SIG SAUER SIGM400 TREAD PREDATOR

S&W M&P VOLUNTEER XV

S&W M&P VOLUNTEER XV DMR

S&W M&P VOLUNTEER XV VOLUNTEER OPTICS READY

S&W M&P VOLUNTEER XV PRO

S&W M&P VOLUNTEER XV VOLUNTEER RED DOT SIGHT

SPRINGFIELD ARMORY HELLION

SIG SAUER SIGM400 TREAD PREDATOR

Action: Semiautomatic
Stock: Synthetic
Barrel: 16 in.
Sights: None
Weight: 7 lb. 8 oz.
Caliber: 5.56 NATO
Magazine: 5 rounds
Features: Coyote and other varmint hunters will like the shorter barrel on this direct impingement MSR and its adjustable stock; adjustable comb height; TREAD handguard with a flat bottom surface; threaded stainless steel barrel with thread protector; QD sling mounts; Cerakote Elite Jungle finish
Price: **$1,099.00**

SMITH & WESSON M&P VOLUNTEER XV

Action: Semiautomatic
Stock: Synthetic
Barrel: 16 in.
Sights: None
Weight: 9 lb.
Caliber: 5.56 NATO
Magazine: 30 rounds
Features: The base model in the Volunteer lineup introduced for 2022, with choice of WGS Tactical folding sights, adjustable A2 post, Magpul BUS sights, or no sights; BCMGunfighter MLOK fore-end; dust cover; BS Systems Bravo buttstock and P-Grip; forward assist; Armonite metal finish; A2 flash suppressor; forged, integral trigger guard; flat-faced trigger
Price: . . . . **Starting at $1049.00**

SMITH & WESSON M&P VOLUNTEER XV DMR

Action: Semiautomatic

Stock: Synthetic
Barrel: 20 in.
Sights: Folding front and rear
Weight: 8 lb. 2 oz.
Caliber: 5.56 NATO
Magazine: 30 rounds
Features: Builds on the base Volunteer VX model with a longer barrel; rifle-length gas system; PWS 556 muzzle brake; BS Systems SOPMOD stock; WGS folding sights; ambidextrous Radian Rapto-LT charging handle; target crowned and threaded barrel
Price: . . . . **Starting at $1599.00**

SMITH & WESSON M&P VOLUNTEER XV OPTICS READY

Action: Semiautomatic
Stock: Synthetic
Barrel: 16 in.
Sights: None
Weight: 9 lb.
Caliber: 5.56 NATO
Magazine: 30 Rounds
Features: Adds to the base Volunteer VX model with a topside Picatinny rail for optics mounting
Price: . . . . **Starting at $1049.00**

SMITH & WESSON M&P VOLUNTEER XV PRO

Action: Semiautomatic
Stock: Synthetic
Barrel: 14.5, 16 in.
Sights: Folding front and rear
Weight: 6 lb. 12 oz.
Caliber: 5.56 NATO
Magazine: 30 rounds
Features: A step up from the base model Volunteer VX with the additions of a B5 Systems SOPMOD stock; folding Wiliams sights; B5 Systens P-Grip; target crowned and

threaded barrel; aluminum MLOK fore-end; assume 14.5-in.has welded PWS 556 muzzle brake
Price: . . . . **Starting at $1569.00**

SMITH & WESSON M&P VOLUNTEER XV RED DOT SIGHT

Action: Semiautomatic
Stock: Synthetic
Barrel: 16 in.
Sights: None
Weight: 9 lb. 5 oz.
Caliber: 5.56 NATO
Magazine: 30 rounds
Features: The base model Volunteer VX dressed up with a Crimson Trace red dot optic
Price: . . . . **Starting at $1099.00**

SPRINGFIELD ARMORY HELLION

Action: Semiautomatic
Stock: Synthetic
Barrel: 16 in.
Sights: Adjustable flip-up front and rear
Weight: 8 lb.
Caliber: 5.56 NATO
Magazine: 30 rounds
Features: Springfield colors outside the lines with a bullup having enough weight to appreciably suck up some recoil; two-position adjustable short-stroke gas piston; BCMGunfighter Mod 3 grip; Magpul PMAG magazine; ambidextrous non-reciprocating charging handle; five-position stock with cheek riser; four-prong flash hider; ambidextrous safety; dual-side QD mount points; reversible case ejection system;
Price: **$1,199.00**

SPRINGFIELD ARMORY MODEL 2020 WAYPOINT

SPRINGFIELD ARMORY SAINT EDGE ATC

SPRINGFIELD ARMORY SAINT EDGE ATC ELITE

STAG ARMS 15 3-GUN ELITE

STAG ARMS 15 COVENANT

STAG ARMS 15 LEO

STAG ARMS 15 M4

SPRINGFIELD ARMORY MODEL 2020 WAYPOINT

Action: Bolt
Stock: Carbon fiber
Barrel:
Sights: None
Weight: 6 lb. 15 oz.
Caliber: .308 Win., 6mm Creedmoor, 6.5 Creedmoor, 6.5 PRC
Magazine: 3 rounds
Features: One for hunters, with a carbon fiber stock in Evergreen or Ridgeline camo; carbon fiber barrel; nitride-treated fluted bolt; adjustable TriggerTech trigger; SA's radial muzzle brake; topside Picatinny rail; models in Ridgline camo stocks have metal in Desert Verde Cerakote, those in Evergreen have Mil-Spec Green Cerakote; some models have adjustable stocks
Price: . . . . $1923.00–$2527.00

SPRINGFIELD ARMORY SAINT EDGE ATC

Action: Semiautomatic
Stock: Synthetic
Barrel: 18 in.
Sights: None
Weight: 9 lb. 8 oz.
Caliber: .223 Wylde
Magazine: 20 rounds
Features: ATC stands for Accurized Tactical Chassis, and Springfield Armory adds to it with a monolithic lower/handguard system; free-floating barrel; B5 Systems adjustable Enhanced SOPMOD stock; Springfield Armory's flat-faced modular match trigger; in black with Type III hard-coat anodizing
Price: $1,549.00

SPRINGFIELD ARMORY SAINT EDGE ATC ELITE

Action: Semiautomatic
Stock: Synthetic
Barrel: 18 in.

Sights: None
Weight: 10 lb. 1 oz.
Caliber: .223 Wylde
Magazine: 20 rounds
Features: ATC stands for "Accurized Tactical Chassis, and Springfield Armory builds on that with a B5 Systems precision stock; LaRue Tactical MBT flat-faced, two-stage trigger; direct impingement mid-length gas system; GI-style charging handle; muzzle brake; Magpul PMAG magazine; carbine "H" heavy tungsten buffer assembly; integral MLOK handguard; in Coyote Brown with Coyote Brown Cerakote metal
Price: $1,899.00

STAG ARMS 15 3-GUN ELITE

Action: Semiautomatic
Stock: Synthetic
Barrel: 18 in.
Sights: None
Weight: N/A
Caliber: 5.56 NATO
Magazine: 10 rounds
Features: As the name implies, this one's intended for 3-Gun competition with features like a Geissele Super-Dynamic 3-Gun trigger; heavy profile fluted barrel; VG6 Gamma muzzle brake; Magpul SL-S stock; 16.5-in. MLOK handguard; MOE pistol grip; optional configurations include left-hand, New York-/California-/New Jersey-compliant left- and right-hand versions
Price: . . . . $1619.99–$1669.99

STAG ARMS 15 COVENANT

Action: Semiautomatic
Stock: Synthetic
Barrel: 16, 18, 20 in.
Sights: None
Weight: N/A
Caliber: 6 ARC, 6.5 Grendel
Magazine: 10 rounds
Features: A direct-impingement MSR in the 6 ARC round; choice of three

barrel lengths; oversized aluminum trigger guard; two-stage trigger; Magpul MOE pistol grip; Stag 15 MLOK handguard; Type III hard-anodized coating; VG6 Gamma muzzle brake; available left-hand
Price: . . . . $1399.99–$1599.99

STAG ARMS 15 LEO

Action: Semiautomatic
Stock: Synthetic
Barrel: 16 in.
Sights: A2 front
Weight: N/A
Caliber: 5.56 NATO
Magazine: 10 rounds
Features: Carbine-length MSR with a chrome-phosphate-finished government-profile barrel; carbine buffer spring and tube; mil-spec six-position stock; pinned front sight; Magpul PMAG magazine; Stag Arms flash hider; glass-filled nylon Stag Arms pistol grip; available left- and right-hand standard and left- and right-hand New York-/California-/Maryland-compliant
Price: . . . . $1149.99–$1219.99

STAG ARMS 15 M4

Action: Semiautomatic
Stock: Synthetic
Barrel: 16 in.
Sights: A2 front, adjustable rear
Weight: N/A
Caliber: 5.56 NATO
Magazine: 10 rounds
Features: A traditional take on the AR-15, with a chrome-phosphate-finished barrel; carbine-length handguard and gas system; single-stage trigger; rear sight Picatinny interface; glass-filled nylon A2 pistol grip; threaded-on Stag flash hider; Type 3 hard-coat anodizing; mil=spec six-position stock; available left- and right-hand standard and left- and right-hand New York-/California-/Maryland-compliant
Price: . . . . $1119.99–$1169.99

NEW Products: **Rifles**

STAG ARMS 15 RETRO

STAG ARMS 15 SPR

STAG ARMS SUPER VARMINTER

STAG ARMS 15 TACTICAL

STEYR MONOBLOC

SWORD INTL MK-15 IDC GARAND THUMB EDITION

STAG ARMS 15 RETRO

Action: Semiautomatic
Stock: Synthetic
Barrel: 20 in.
Sights: A2 front, adjustable rear
Weight: N/A
Caliber: 5.56 NATO
Magazine: 10 rounds
Features: Retro indeed, with a full 20 inches of chrome-phosphate-treated barrel; A2 mil-spec buttstock, pistol grip, and charging handle; rifle-length handguard and gas system; Type III hard-coat andozing; available left- and right-hand standard and left- and right-hand New York-/California-/New Jersey-compliant
Price: . . . . $1149.99–$1219.99

STAG ARMS 15 SPR

Action: Semiautomatic
Stock: Synthetic
Barrel: 18 in.
Sights: None
Weight: N/A
Caliber: 5.56 NATO
Magazine: 10 rounds
Features: A modern MSR with a nitride-finished barrel, bolt, and carrier group; slimline MLOK handguard; Magpul PMAG magazine; Stag Arms flash hider; Magpul MOE pistol grip; choice of Type III hard-coat anodizing in black or Cerakote Flat Dark Earth; available left- and right-hand and left- and right-hand Maryland-compliant
Price: . . . . $1199.99–$1319.99

STAG ARMS 15 SUPER VARMINTER

Action: Semiautomatic
Stock: Synthetic
Barrel: 20 in.
Sights: None

Weight: N/A
Caliber: 6.8 SPC
Magazine: 10 rounds
Features: With a longer, 416R, heavy profile stainless steel barrel that wears an 11-degree target crown, this rifle also zeros in on pesky varmints with a SAAMI Spec II chamber; Magpul MOE fixed stock; free-floating Picatinny rail; aluminum handguard, upper, and lower; Magpul PMAG magazine and MOE pistol grip; Stag Arms two-stage trigger; oversized aluminum trigger guard; Type III hard-coat anodizing; available left- and right-hand and left- and right-hand New York-/California-compliant
Price: . . . . $1349.99–$1419.99

STAG ARMS 15 TACTICAL

Action: Semiautomatic
Stock: Synthetic
Barrel: 16 in.
Sights: None
Weight: N/A
Caliber: 5.56 NATO, .300 BLK,
Magazine: 10 rounds
Features: A modern carbine-length MSR with acres of free-floating Picatinny rail on the topside; mid-lengthlow-profile gas block; government profile barrel in choice of nitride- or chrome-phosphate-treated; carbine buffer spring and tube; mil-spec Magpul MOE SL carbine stock; MLOK handguard; Magpul MOE pistol grip; Stag Arms flash hider; in Type III hard-coat anodizing in black or in Cerakote Flat Dark Earth; available left- and right-hand and left- and right-hand New York-/California-/New Jersey-/Maryland-compliant
Price: . . . . $899.99–$1199.99

STEYR MONOBLOC

Action: Bolt

Stock: Synthetic
Barrel: 22 in.
Sights: None
Weight: 8 lb. 3 oz.
Caliber: .308 Win., .30-06 Spfd.
Magazine: 4 rounds
Features: A thoroughly modern rifle wearing a synthetic stock with leather inlays; detachable, forward set trigger that can be stored in the stock; aluminum bedding; detachable steel magazine; hand-cocking system; barrel and housing made from one piece; multiple stock/inlay color combinations to choose from
Price: $5200.00

SWORD INTL MK-15 IDC GARAND THUMB EDITION

Action: Semiautomatic
Stock: Synthetic
Barrel: 16 in.
Sights: None
Weight: 6 lb. 11 oz.
Caliber: 5.56 NATO
Magazine: 30 rounds
Features: A collaborative effort between social media enterprise Garand Thumb and S.W.O.R.D., this distinctive MSR—IDC stands for "Individual Duty Carbine"—has a nitride-coated, cold hammer-forged barrel with a 1:7 twist that accommodates 5.56 NATO and .223 Rem. bullets from 55 to 75 grains; short-stroke gas system; mono piston-style bolt carrier; 15-in. free-floated modular rail; mil-spec trigger group, bolt, and flash suppressor; Radian Raptor ambidextrous charging handle; Tango Down pistol grip; B5 System stock; Splinter Camo Cerakote paired with flat dark earth hardware
Price: $3200.00

TACTICAL SOLUTIONS
X-RING VR GRS
HUNTER LITE STOCK

TAYLOR'S &
CO 1886 TC86
TAKEDOWN RIFLE

TRAILBLAZER
FIREARMS PIVOT

UINTAH
PRECISION UP-10

UINTAH
PRECISION UP-15

VOLQUARTSEN
VF-ORYX

WEATHERBY MARK V
ACCUMARK LIMITED

TACTICAL SOLUTIONS X-RING VR GRS HUNTER LITE STOCK

Action: Semiautomatic
Stock: Laminate
Barrel: 16.5 in.
Sights: None
Weight: 4 lb. 11 oz.
Caliber: .22 LR
Magazine: 10 rounds
Features: Tac Sol's upgrade to the Ruger 10/22 with a GRS Hunter Lite stock in choice of Nordic Wolf (Gun Metal Gray metal), black/green stock (matte black metal), Green Mountain Camo stock (matte black metal), or orange/black stock (matte black metal); milled aluminum receiver; aluminum fluted barrel with 11-degree target crown and threaded; machined stainless steel bolt with topside flutes; 15 MOA Picatinny rail; adjustable comb; adjustable length of pull; right- or left-hand charging; rear port cleaning access; extended magazine release
Price: **$1,500.00**

TAYLOR'S & CO 1886 TC86 TAKEDOWN RIFLE

Action: Lever-action
Stock: Walnut
Barrel: 16.5 in.
Sights: Fiber optic front, Skinner peep rear
Weight: 7 lb. 14 oz.
Caliber: .45-70 Gov't.
Magazine: 4 rounds
Features: A very handsome lever with a deeply colored case-hardened frame; semi-gloss stock; topside rail and modern firber optics with a traditional rear peep; topside Picatinny rail; threaded barrel for suppressor use; simple takedown—open the action, unscrew the mag tube; twist where the barrel meets the receiver, and you have two neat pieces for easy transport
Price: **$1,977.69**

TRAILBLAZER FIREARMS PIVOT

Action: Semiautomatic
Stock: Synthetic
Barrel: 16 in.
Sights: None
Weight: 5 lb.
Caliber: 9mm
Magazine: 10, 15, 17 rounds
Features: A very lightweight pistol-caliber carbine (non-NFA) with a corrosion-resistant finish; direct blowback action; threaded barrel; extendable folding stock with magazine storage; takes Glock magazines
Price: **$1,795.00**

UINTAH PRECISION UP-10

Action: Bolt
Stock: Synthetic
Barrel: 20, 22, 26 in.
Sights: None
Weight: N/A
Caliber: 6.5 Creedmoor, 6mm Creedmoor, .308 Win.
Magazine: 10 rounds
Features: A bolt-action "AR" with a three-lug bolt that has a 50-degree throw; Uintah Precision single-stage trigger; Ergo Deluxe Overmold Suregrip; Luth MBA-1 stock; Magpul magazine; choice of 416R stainless match barrel or carbon fiber-wrapped; comes with Pelican hard case
Price: . . . . **$1875.00–$2275.00**

UINTAH PRECISION UP-15

Action: Bolt
Stock: Synthetic
Barrel: 10.5, 16, 20, 22 in.
Sights: None
Weight: N/A
Caliber: 6mm ARC, .223 Wylde, .300 BLK, 6.5 Grendel, .224 Valkyrie
Magazine: 10 rounds
Features: Similar to the UP-10, but

with a wider caliber selection; .300 BLK available in 10.5-in. barrel (NFA regs apply)
Price: . . . . **$1675.00–$2075.00**

VOLQUARTSEN VF-ORYX .22 LR

Action: Semiautomatic
Stock: Chassis
Barrel: 18.5 in.
Sights: None
Weight: 9 lb. 3 oz.
Caliber: .22 LR
Magazine: 10 rounds
Features: This is an eye-catcher with Volquartsen's snake-fluted barrel; adjustable TG2000 trigger group; ambidextrous, aluminum MDT Oryx chassis; forward blow comp; stainless steel receiver; Picatinny rail; available with a 6–24X50mm Zeiss Conquest scope factory mounted in TPS scope rings
Price: . . . Rifle only **$2041.00**; With scope **$3432.00**

WEATHERBY MARK V ACCUMARK LIMITED

Action: Bolt
Stock: Fiberglass
Barrel: 24, 26 in.
Sights: None
Weight: 8 lb. 5 oz.
Caliber: .257 Wby. Mag., .300 Wby. Mag., 6.5 Creedmoor, 6.5-300 Wby. Mag., 6.5 Wby. RPM
Magazine: 3, 4 rounds
Features: Built on the six-lug Mark V receiver, this rifle sports a #3 contour spiral-fluted barrel; hand-laid fiberglass stock with a matte gel coat and brown/gray accents; barrel and receiver in Flat Dark earth Cerakote; bolt, bolt knob and safety in Graphite Black Cerakote
Price: **$2599.00**

NEW Products: **Rifles**

WEATHERBY MARK V BACKCOUNTRY 2.0

WEATHERBY MARK V BACKCOUNTRY 2.0 CARBON

WEATHERBY MARK V BACKCOUNTRY 2.0 TI

WEATHERBY MARK V BACKCOUNTRY 2.0 TI CARBON

WEATHERBY MARK V HUNTER

WEATHERBY MARK V MEATEATER EDITION

WEATHERBY MARK V TLR SIGNATURE SERIES

WEATHERBY MARK V BACKCOUNTRY 2.0

Action: Bolt
Stock: Carbon fiber
Barrel: 24, 26 in.
Sights: None
Weight: 5 lb. 7 oz.
Caliber: .240 Wby. Mag., .257 Wby. Mag., .270 Wby. Mag., .280 AI, .300 Wby. Mag., .308 Win., 6.5 Creedmoor, 6.5 Wby. Mag., 6.5 Wby. RPM, 6.5-300 Wby. Mag.
Magazine: 3, 4 rounds
Features: A very lightweight rifle on a Mar V action with a super-thin fluted barrel in a #1 or #2 contour depending on caliber; Peak 44 Blacktooth stock in dark green with brown sponge accents; Accubrake ST; barrel, triggerguard, and receiver in Patriot Brown Cerakote; bolt, bolt knob, and safety in Graphite Black Cerakote; spiral-fluted bolt body; skeletonized bolt knob; 2nd generation, 3D printed 3DHEX recoil pad
Price: $2699.00

WEATHERBY MARK V BACKCOUNTRY 2.0 CARBON

Action: Bolt
Stock: Carbon fiber
Barrel: 24, 26 in.
Sights: None
Weight: 6 lb. 9 oz.
Caliber: .257 Wby. Mag., .30-378 Wby. Mag., .300 Wby. Mag., 6.5 Creedmoor, 6.5 Wby. RPM, 6.5-300 Wby. Mag.
Magazine: 3, 4 rounds
Features: Similar to the Backcountry 2.0 but with a carbon fiber barrel in a #4 profile; 30-port Accubrake ST brake; threaded bolt handle; steel Mark V action
Price: $3399.00

WEATHERBY MARK V BACKCOUNTRY 2.0 TI

Action: Bolt
Stock: Carbon fiber
Barrel: 24, 26 in.
Sights: None
Weight: 4 lb. 15 oz.–5 lb. 9 oz.
Caliber: .240 Wby. Mag., .257 Wby. Mag., .270 Wby. Mag., .280 AI, .300 Wby. Mag., .308 Win., 6.5 Creedmoor, 6.5 Wby. Mag., 6.5 Wby. RPM, 6.5-300 Wby. Mag.
Magazine: 3, 4 rounds
Features: Similar to the Backcountry 2.0 but with its carbon fiber stock in grey with a white sponge pattern; titanium action left in the raw and, along with the bolt, barrel, bolt knob, triggerguard, and safety, sealed under Graphite Black Cerakote
Price: . . . . $3449.00–$3599.00

WEATHERBY MARK V BACKCOUNTRY 2.0 TI CARBON

Action: Bolt
Stock: Carbon fiber
Barrel: 24, 26 in.
Sights: None
Weight: 5 lb. 4 oz.–6 lb. 1 oz.
Caliber: .257 Wby. Mag., .300 Wby. Mag., 6.5 Creedmoor, 6.5 Wby. RPM, 6.5-300 Wby. Mag.
Magazine: 3, 4 rounds
Features: Similar to the Backcountry 2.0 Ti but carbon fiber barrel in a #4 profile
Price: . . . . $3849.00–$3949.00

WEATHERBY MARK V HUNTER

Action: Bolt
Stock: Polymer
Barrel: 22, 24, 26 in.
Sights: None
Weight: 6 lb. 1 oz.–7 lb. 5 oz.
Caliber: .240 Wby. Mag., .243 Win., .25-06 Rem., .257 Wby. Mag., .270 Wby. Mag., .270 Win., .280 AI, .30-06 Spfd., .300 Wby. Mag., .300 Win. Mag., .308 Win., 6.5 Creedmoor, 6.5 Wby. RPM, 6.5-300 Wby. Mag., 7mm Rem. Mag., 7mm Wby. Mag., 7mm-08 Rem.
Magazine: 3, 4 rounds

Features: With a more traditionally designed stock than other Weatherby rifles sport, this long gun also has a flat-bottomed fore-end; ambidextrous palm swell; aluminum pillars; fluted threaded barrel; barrel, receiver, and triggerguard in Cobalt Cerakote; bolt, bolt knob, and safety in Graphite Black Cerakote; stock in Urban and black speckle
Price: $1499.00

WEATHERBY MARK V MEATEATER EDITION

Action: Bolt
Stock: Fiberglass
Barrel: 26 in.
Sights: None
Weight: 7 lb. 1 oz.
Caliber: .257 Wby. Mag., .300 Wby. Mag., 6.5-300 Wby. Mag.
Magazine: 3 rounds
Features: A left-hand-only offering with a spiral fluted #2 contour barrel; hand-laid fiberglass stock with Monte Carlo cheekpiece; hinged floorplate engraved with MeatEater branding; barrel, brake, receiver, and triggerguard in Tungsten Cerakote; bolt, bolt knob, and safety in Graphite Cerakote; stock has a black base with gray/brown accents
Price: $2099.00

WEATHERBY MARK V TLR SIGNATURE SERIES

Action: Bolt
Stock: Polymer
Barrel: 26 in.
Sights: None
Weight: 8 lb. 4 oz.
Caliber: .257 Wby. Mag.
Magazine: 3 rounds
Features: A nine-lug Mark V action customized by Thompson Long Range to include a fluted bolt body with a 54-degree bolt lift; full-length bedding block; hand-lapped free-floating barrel in a #3 contour; Leupold fixed reticle 4.5–14X40mm scope
Price: $3,900.00

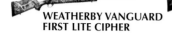

WEATHERBY VANGUARD FIRST LITE CIPHER

WEATHERGUARD VANGUARD MEATEATER

WEE 1 TACTICAL JR-15

WINCHESTER MODEL 70 EXTREME HUNTER STRATA MB

WINCHESTER MODEL 94 DELUXE SPORTING

WINCHESTER MODEL 1873 COMPETITION CARBINE HIGH GRADE

WINCHESTER MODEL 1873 DELUXE SPORTING

WINCHESTER 1886 SADDLE RING CARBINE

WEATHERBY VANGUARD FIRST LITE CIPHER

Action: Bolt
Stock: Polymer
Barrel: 24, 26 in.
Sights: None
Weight:
Caliber: .257 Wby. Mag., .300 Win. Mag., .300 Wby. Mag., 6.5-300 Wby. Mag., 6.5 Creedmoor, 6.5 PRC, .270 Win., .308 Win., 7mm Rem. Mag.
Magazine: 3, 4, 5 rounds
Features: A Davidson's distributor exclusive featuring a #2 spiral fluted barrel with Accubrake; Vanguard recoil pad; stock in First Lite Cipher camo; metalwork in Flat Dark Earth Cerakote
Price:. **$1,099.00**

WEATHERGUARD VANGUARD MEATEATER EDITION

Action: Bolt
Stock: Polymer
Barrel: 24, 26 in.
Sights: None
Weight: 7 lb.–7 lb. 2 oz.
Caliber: .300 Wby. Mag., .300 Win, Mag., .308 Win., 6.5 Creedmoor, 6.5-300 Wby. Mag., 7mm Rem. Mag.
Magazine: 3, 4 rounds
Features: Features a threaded, spiral-fluted #2 contour barrel; MeatEater branding on flooplate; Tungsten and black Cerakotingl; stock with a black base adnd gray/brown highlights
Price:. **$999.00**

WEE 1 TACTICAL JR-15

Action: Semiautomatic
Stock: Synthetic
Barrel: 16 in.
Sights: None
Weight: 2 lb.
Caliber: .22 LR
Magazine: 1, 5, 10 rounds
Features: Designed and sized specifically for youth shooters, this rifle is intended to make learning rifle handling easier for kids new to the shooting sports; tamper-resistant safety; mini mil-spec trigger; skimpy

two-pound weight; topside rail for scope mounting
Price:. . . . .

WINCHESTER MODEL 70 EXTREME HUNTER STRATA MB

Action: Bolt
Stock: Synthetic
Barrel: 22, 24, 26 in.
Sights: None
Weight: 6 lb. 12 oz.–7 lb. 4 oz.
Caliber: .243 Win., 6.5 Creedmoor, 7mm-08 Rem., .308 Win., 6.5 PRC, 6.8 Western, .270 WSM, .300 WSM, .25-06 Rem., .270 Win., .30-06 Spfd., .264 Win. Mag., 7mm Rem. Mag., .300 Win. Mag.
Magazine: 3, 5 rounds
Features: This rifle wears a Bell & Carlson stock with a sculpted cheekpiece and dressed in TrueTimber Strata; MOA trigger system; pre-'64 action; jeweled bolt body; knurled bolt knob; free-floating barrel with muzzle brake; hinged floorplate; combination of Flat Dark Earth and Tungsten Cerakoting
Price:. . . . . **$1679.99–$1719.99**

WINCHESTER MODEL 94 DELUXE SPORTING

Action: Lever
Stock: Walnut
Barrel: 24 in.
Sights: Gold bead front, semi-buckhorn rear
Weight: 7 lb. 8 oz.
Caliber: .30-30 Win., .38-55 Win.
Magazine: 8 rounds
Features: A striking Model 94 with a Grade IV/V checkered walnut stock; Marble Arms gold bead front sight; crescent buttplate; gloss-blue barre; color case-hardened receiver, lever, and forearm cap; drilled and tapped for scope mounting
Price:. **$2,169.99**

WINCHESTER MODEL 1873 COMPETITION CARBINE HIGH GRADE

Action: Lever

Stock: Walnut
Barrel: 20 in.
Sights: Gold bead front, semi-buckhorn rear
Weight: 7 lb. 4 oz.
Caliber: .38 Spec./.357 Mag., .45 Colt
Magazine: 10 rounds
Features: Show off a little at your next SASS match with Grade III/IV walnut stock; color case-hardened receiver, buttplate, and barrel bands; polished blue round barrel; rear tang drilled and tapped for peep sight
Price:. **$1,839.99**

WINCHESTER MODEL 1873 DELUXE SPORTING

Action: Lever
Stock: Walnut
Barrel: 24 in.
Sights: Gold bead front, semi-buckhorn rear
Weight: 8 lb.
Caliber: .38 Spec./.357 Mag., .45 Colt, .44-40 Win.
Magazine: 14 rounds
Features: Very pretty lever with a Grade V/VI walnut stock; shotgun buttplate, receiver, sideplates, lever, forearm cap are color case-hardened; gloss blue half-octagon barrel
Price:. **$2,119.99**

WINCHESTER MODEL 1886 SADDLE RING CARBINE

Photo File Names: Winchester 1886 Saddle Ring Carbine.jpg
Action: Lever
Stock: Walnut
Barrel: 22 in.
Sights: Blade front, ladder rear
Weight: 8 lb.
Caliber: .45-70 Gov't., .45-90 Win.
Magazine: 7 rounds
Features: Wearing a Grade I walnut stock with a straight grip; carbine fore-end; polished blue receiver with saddle ring; drilled and tapped for scope mounting; round barrel; full-length magazine tube
Price:. **$1,549.99**

NEW Products: Rifles

WINCHESTER MODEL 1895 HIGH GRADE

WINCHESTER MODEL-1892 DELUXE TAKEDOWN

WINCHESTER MODEL 1895 GRADE I

WINCHESTER WILDCAT STRATA

WINCHESTER XPERT-22

WINCHESTER XPR EXTREME HUNTER MIDNIGHT MB

WINCHESTER XPR HUNTER MOSSY OAK DNA

WINCHESTER MODEL 1892 DELUXE OCTAGON TAKEDOWN

Action: Lever
Stock: Walnut
Barrel: 24 in.
Sights: Gold bead front, semi-buckhorn rear
Weight: 7 lb.
Caliber: .38 Spec./.357 Mag., .45 Colt, .44 Mag., .44-40 Win.
Magazine: 11 rounds
Features: An upgraded 1892 with a Grade V/VI walnut stock with pistol grip; full octagon barrel in polished blue; receiver, lever, forearm cap, and buttplate are color cas-hardened; top tang drilled and tapped for peep sight
Price: **$2,199.99**

WINCHESTER MODEL 1895 GRADE I

Action: Lever
Stock: Walnut
Barrel: 24 in.
Sights: Gold bead front, semi-buckhorn rear
Weight: 8 lb.
Caliber: .30-06 Spfd., .405 Win.
Magazine: 4 rounds
Features: A powerhouse lever with a gloss blue metalwork; Grade I walnut stock with straight grip and schnable forearm; drilled and tapped for side-mounting optics; top tang safety
Price: **$1,369.99**

WINCHESTER MODEL 1895 HIGH GRADE

Action: Lever
Stock: Walnut
Barrel: 24 in.
Sights: Gold bead front, semi-buckhorn rear
Weight: 8 lb.
Caliber: .30-06 Spfd., .405 Win., .30-40 Krag

Magazine: 4 rounds
Features: Similar to the Grade I but with a Grade II/IV checkered walnut stock
Price: **$1,699.99**

WINCHESTER WILDCAT STRATA, STRATA SR

Action: Semiautomatic
Stock: Synthetic
Barrel: 18 in.
Sights: Ramped post front, ghost ring rear
Weight: 4 lb.
Caliber: .22 LR
Magazine: 10 rounds
Features: A fun rimfire with a skeletonized stock in TrueTimber Strata camo; button-rifled barrel; reversible safety; underside and topside Picatinny rails; last round bolt hold-open; ambidextrous magazine release; accepts aftermarket 10/22 magazines; lower receiver removes with the push of a button for easy takedown and transport; SR version has a recess crown and is threaded for a suppressor
Strata **$309.99**
Strata SR **$329.99**

WINCHESTER XPERT-22

Action: Bolt
Stock: Synthetic
Barrel: 18 in.
Sights: Ramped post front, ghost ring rear
Weight: 4 lb. 8 oz.
Caliber: .22 LR
Magazine: 10 rounds
Features: Very similar to the Wildcat, but in a bolt-action; three-lever rimfire MOA trigger; drilled and tapped for optics mounting; accepts aftermarket 10/22 magazines
Price: **$319.99**

WINCHESTER XPR EXTREME HUNTER MIDNIGHT MB

Action: Bolt
Stock: Composite
Barrel: 22, 24, 26 in.
Sights: None
Weight: 6 lb. 12 oz.–7 lb.
Caliber: .223 Rem., .243 Win., 6.5 Creedmoor, 7mm-08 Rem., .308 Win., .350 Legend, 6.5 PRC, 6.8 Western, .270 WSM, .300 WSM, .270 Win., .30-06 Spfd., 7mm Rem. Mag., .300 Win. Mag.
Magazine: 3, 5 rounds
Features: With a stock in TrueTimber Midnight camo, the rifle has Winchester's MOA trigger system; free-floating, button-rifled, and threaded barrel with a recessed target crown; Inflex recoil pad; metalwork in Tungsten Cerakote; detachable box magazine
Price: **$769.99**

WINCHESTER XPR HUNTER MOSSY OAK DNA

Action: Bolt
Stock: Composite
Barrel: 22, 24, 26 in.
Sights: None
Weight: 6 lb. 12 oz.–7 lb.
Caliber: .223 Rem., .243 Win., 6.5 Creedmoor, 7mm-08 Rem., .308 Win., .350 Legend, 6.5 PRC, 6.8 Western, .270 WSM, .300 WSM, .270 Win., .30-06 Spfd., 7mm Rem. Mag., .300 Win. Mag., .338 Win. Mag.
Magazine: 3, 5 rounds
Features: This rifle has a composite stock in Mossy Oak DNA camo; Inflex recoil pad; MOA trigger system; free-floating barrel with a recessed crown; metalwork in matte Perma-Cote finish
Price: **$649.99**

**WINCHESTER XPR
HUNTER STRATA MB**

**ZASTAVA ARMS
M07-AS**

ZASTAVA ARMS M91

**ZASTAVA ARMS
ZPAPM70**

**ZASTAVA ARMS
ZPAPM90PS**

**ZEV TECHNOLOGIES
CORE DUTY RIFLE**

**ZEV TECHNOLOGIES
LARGE-FRAME BILLET
.308**

WINCHESTER XPR HUNTER STRATA MB

Action: Bolt
Stock: Composite
Barrel: 22, 24, 26 in.
Sights: None
Weight: 6 lb. 12 oz.–7 lb.
Caliber: .223 Rem., .243 Win., 6.5 Creedmoor, 7mm-08 Rem., .308 Win., .350 Legend, 6.5 PRC, 6.8 Western, .270 WSM, .300 WSM, .270 Win., .30-06 Spfd., 7mm Rem. Mag., .300 Win. Mag.
Magazine: 3, 5 rounds
Features: The composite stock of this Model 70 is dressed in TrueTimber Strata; Inflex recoil pad; metalwork in Flat Dark Earth Perma-Cote; threaded, free-floating barrel with muzzle brake and recessed crown; MOA trigger system
Price:. $749.99

ZASTAVA ARMS M07-AS

Action: Semiautomatic
Stock: Bolt
Barrel: 26 in.
Sights: None
Weight: N/A
Caliber: .308 Win.
Magazine: 10 rounds
Features: A sniper rifle based on the Mauser 98 platform and featuring a threaded barrel; effective range of 1,000 meters; adjsutable trigger; adjustable stock; three-position mechanical safety; topside optics rail; ships with two magazines, sling, and cleaning kit
Price:. $3,139.00

ZASTAVA ARMS M91

Action: Semiautomatic
Stock: Synthetic
Barrel: 24 in.
Sights: None
Weight: N/A
Caliber: 7.62X54R
Magazine: 10 rounds

Features: Based on the Kalishnikov, this is a Serbian sniper rifle with a cold hammer-forged, chrome-lined, threaded barrel; adjustable stock; adjustable gas flow regulator; POSP 4X24 scope; ships with two magazines and a sling
Price:. $3,499.99

ZASTAVA ARMS ZPAPM70

Action: Semiautomatic
Stock: Polymer
Barrel: 16.3 in.
Sights: Adjustable front and rear
Weight: 7 lb. 15 oz.
Caliber: 7.62X39
Magazine: 30 rounds
Features: Based on the M70 automatic rifle, this semiauto has tough polymer furniture; four-position adjustable buttstock of carbon fiber glass-reinforced polymer; slip-on recoil pad; ergonomic pistol grip with storage compartment; three rail sections and a smooth top cover for modularity; rubber overmolded fiberglass handguard; double-stack bolt; cold hammer-forged chrome-lined barrel
Price:. $1,038.99

ZASTAVA ARMS ZPAPM90PS

Action: Semiautomatic
Stock: Polymer
Barrel: 18.25 in.
Sights: Adjustable front and rear
Weight: 8 lb. 8 oz.
Caliber: 5.56 NATO
Magazine: 30 rounds
Features: A sporting rifle in 5.56 NATO based on the M70 automatic and featuring a two-piece Hogue overmolded handguard; smooth top cover with three rail add-ons; Magpul MOE grip; folding adjustable Magpul Zhukov stock; adjustable gas block; double-stack bolt

Price:. $1,279.99

ZEV TECHNOLOGIES CORE DUTY RIFLE

Action: Semiautomatic
Stock: Synthetic
Barrel: 16 in.
Sights: None
Weight: 7 lb.
Caliber: 5.56 NATO
Magazine: 30 rounds
Features: A compact MSR with a low-profile gas block; mid-length gas system; forged mil-spec upper and lower; chrome-lined barrel with magnesium phosphate finish; Magpul SL adjustable buttstock and MOE pisotl grip; Radian Weapons Talon ambidextrous safety selector; boron-coated two-stage trigger; Zev muzzle device; Wedge Lock free-floating MLOK handguard
Price:. $1,574.00

ZEV TECHNOLOGIES LARGE-FRAME BILLET .308

Action: Semiautomatic
Stock: Synthetic
Barrel: 16 in.
Sights: None
Weight: 7 lb. 8 oz.
Caliber: .308 Win.
Magazine: 20 rounds
Features: A compact AR-10-type MSR with tons of Zev upgrades, including an ambidextrous slide lock charging handle, muzzle device, match-grade stainless steel barrel with bronze PVD coating, Wedge Lock MLOK handguard, and forged aluminum upper and lower in true black Type III class 2 hard anodizing; H3 carbine buffer; ATC flat-face gold AR trigger; ambidextrous operating controls; Magpul furniture and magazine
Price:. $2,649.00

AIR VENTURI AVENGER BULLPUP

AIR VENTURI AV-46M

AIR VENTURI SENECA DRAGONFLY MK2

BARRA AIRGUNS 1866

AIR VENTURI SPRINGFIELD ARMORY M1A UNDERLEVER

BARRA AIRGUNS 1911

BARRA AIRGUNS JUNIOR

AIR VENTURI AVENGER BULLPUP

Action: PCP
Stock: Synthetic
Barrel: 22.75 in.
Sights: None
Weight: 7 lb. 8 oz.
Caliber: .177, .22, .25
Magazine: 10, 8 rounds
Features: A precharged pneumatic with synthetic bullpup stock that has built-in magazine storage; two-stage adjustable trigger; externally adjustable regulator; fully shrouded barrel; 180cc air cylinder; three Picatinny rail sections; male quick-disconnect fill fitting; Picatinny optics rail; comes with two magazines (.25 cal. holds eight rounds) and a single-shot tray
Price:................$439.99

AIR VENTURI AV-46M MATCH

Action: Single-stroke pneumatic
Stock: Laminate
Barrel: 11 in.
Sights: Post front, adjustable rear
Weight: N/A
Caliber: .177
Magazine: 1 round
Features: Competition ready, with bolt-action operation; fixed power; rifled barrel; two-stage adjustable trigger; dry-fire capability; 18-lb. pumping effort
Price:................$699.99

AIR VENTURI SENECA DRAGONFLY MK2

Action: Pump
Stock: Wood
Barrel: 22.75 in.

Sights: Fiber optic front, adjustable rear
Weight: 6 lb. 8 oz.
Caliber: .177, .22
Magazine: 9, 7 rounds
Features: A multi-pump pneumatic with the patented Butterfly High Efficiency Pump System; hardwood stock; variable power across three to 15 pumps; bolt action; threaded muzzle adapter; 11mm dovetail optics rail; ships with one magazine and a single-shot tray
Price:................$229.99

AIR VENTURI SPRINGFIELD ARMORY M1A UNDERLEVER

Action: Spring piston
Stock: Wood
Barrel: 18.9 in.
Sights: Blade front, adjustable rear
Weight: 9 lb. 15 oz.
Caliber: .177
Magazine: 1 round
Features: A single-shot M1 Garand replica with underlever activation; 1,000 fps velocity; sliding breech cover exposes loading port; two-stage trigger; ambidextrous stock; anti-bear-trap safety mechanism; non-functional bolt handle
Price:................$245.99

BARRA AIRGUNS 1866

Action: Multi-pump pneumatic
Stock: Plastic
Barrel: 20 in.
Sights: Blade front, adjustable leaf rear

Weight: 5 lb. 14 oz.
Caliber: .177
Magazine: 50 rounds
Features: A multi-pump pneumatic fashioned off the 1866 of the Old West; thick-wall ABS plastic stock with wood-grain finish; 50-round capacity; 800 fps velocity
Price:................$75.00

BARRA AIRGUNS 1911

Action: CO2
Stock: Metal
Barrel: 4.25 in.
Sights: Three-dot front, rear
Weight: 1 lb. 11 oz.
Caliber: .177
Magazine: 12 rounds
Features: An all-meatl modern 1911 air pistol powered by CO2; non-rifled barrel; underside Picatinny rail; blowback action
Price:................$110.00

BARRA AIRGUNS JUNIOR

Action: Single-pump
Stock: Plastic
Barrel: 16.5 in.
Sights: Blade front, adjustable leaf rear
Weight: 4 lb. 1 oz.
Caliber: .177
Magazine: 50 rounds
Features: Similar to the 1866, this is a shorter, lighter model that younger shooters will find easier to handle; shrouded smooth barrel; metal frame; single-pump powerplant
Price:................$45.00

BARRA AIRGUNS ROSIE

BARRA AIRGUNS SCHOFIELD AGED

BEEMAN 1357

BROCOCK RANGER XR

BSA ULTRA CLX

CROSMAN 362

CROSMAN CHALLENGER

BARRA AIRGUNS ROSIE

Action: Single-pump
Stock: Plastic
Barrel: 16.5 in.
Sights: Blade front, adjustable leaf rear
Weight: 4 lb. 1 oz.
Caliber: .177
Magazine: 50 rounds
Features: Identical to the Junior but with a rose-gold-finished electroplated receiver
Price:..................$45.00

BARRA AIRGUNS SCHOFIELD AGED, GUN METAL

Action: CO2
Stock: Wood
Barrel: 5, 7 in.
Sights: Blade front, adjustable rear
Weight: 2 lb.
Caliber: BB
Magazine: 6 rounds
Features: Modeled on the vintage breaktop Schofield, this single-action, CO2-powered revolver comes in five- or seven-inch barrel lengths; choice of Aged or Gun Metal finishes; wood stocks
Price:.......... $110.00–$120.00

BEEMAN 1357

Action: PCP
Stock: Wood
Barrel: N/A
Sights: None
Weight: 7 lb. 4 oz.
Caliber: .177
Magazine: 12 rounds
Features: Utilizes a front underlever cocker; integral noise suppressor; scope and mounts included; wood thumbhole, skeletonized stock; springless design
Price:.................$399.99

BROCOCK RANGE XR

Action: PCP
Stock: Synthetic
Barrel: N/A
Sights: None
Weight: N/A
Caliber: .177, .22
Magazine: 10 shots
Features: Side-lever operation; Huma-Air regulator; topside and underside Picatinny rails; Silencer Adaptor; ambidextrous stock with adjustable, folding butt portion; single-shot tray and auto-indexing rotary magazine
Price:.................$1795.00

BSA ULTRA CLX

Action: PCP
Stock: Wood
Barrel: 12.5 in.
Sights: None
Weight: 5 lb. 11 oz.
Caliber: .177, .22
Magazine: 12 rounds
Features: A collaboration between Minelli and BSA, this PCP has a fully adjustable trigger; monoblock patform; anti-double load 12-shot magazine with shot countdown indicator; cold hammer-forged barrel; easy-grip magazine rotor
Price:.................... N/A

CROSMAN 362

Action: Pump
Stock: Synthetic
Barrel: N/A
Sights: Blade front, adjustable rear
Weight:
Caliber: .22
Magazine: 1 round
Features: A single-shot pump with a variable power plant; velocity up to 875 fps;
Price:.................$109.99

CROSMAN CHALLENGER PCP

Action: PCP
Stock: Synthetic
Barrel: N/A
Sights: None
Weight: 7 lb. 1 oz.
Caliber: .177
Magazine: 1 round
Features: One for competition, with an adjustable stock; two-stage, match-grade adjustable trigger; Lothar Walther barrel; operates on CO2 or compressed air; visible pressure gauge; patented linear bolt; approved for use in National Three-Position Air Rifle Sport Class
Price:...................$800.75

CROSMAN DRIFTER KIT

CROSMAN FULL-AUTO A4-P

CROSMAN FULL AUTO P1

CROSMAN MAG-FIRE EXTREME

CROSSMAN SEMI-AUTO R1

CROSMAN MAG-FIRE MISSION

CROSMAN DRIFTER KIT

Action: Pump
Stock: Synthetic
Barrel: N/A
Sights: Fiber optic front, peep rear
Weight: 2 lb. 12 oz.
Caliber: .22
Magazine: 1 round
Features: A super lightweight variable pump single-shot with an adjustable rear sight; rifled barrel; velocity up to 550 fps; crossbolt safety; kit comes with shoulder stock, stock pouch, pistol grips, 400 .22 pellets, and roll-out carry case
Price: **$169.99**

CROSMAN FULL-AUTO A4-P

Action: CO2
Stock: Synthetic
Barrel: N/A
Sights: None
Weight: 6 lb.
Caliber: BB
Magazine: 25 rounds
Features: A full-auto BB rifle with a firing rate of 1,400 rounds per minute; 400 fps velocity; uses two CO2 cartridges; realistic weight and blowback action; topside optics rail
Price: **$231.30**

CROSMAN FULL-AUTO P1

Action: CO2
Stock: Synthetic
Barrel: N/A
Sights: Front blade, notched rear
Weight: 2 lb. 7 oz.
Caliber: BB
Magazine: 19 rounds
Features: Modeled on the Beretta Model 92, this BB pistol has all-metal construction; 400 fps velocity; cycle rate up to 850 rounds per minute; removeable magazine houses the CO2 cartridge; accessory rail; removeable red laser
Price: **$206.51**

CROSMAN MAG-FIRE EXTREME

Action: Break barrel
Stock: Synthetic
Barrel: N/A
Sights: Fixed blade front, adjustable rear
Weight: 9 lb. 1 oz.
Caliber: .177, .22
Magazine: 10 rounds
Features: A mult-shot break-barrel capable of 975 fps velocities; all-weather chassis-style stock; rifled steel barrel; adjustable two-stage clean-break trigger; QuietFire suppression; powered by Nitron Piston Elite;

3–9X40mm adjustable objective scope included
Price: **$251.61**

CROSMAN MAG-FIRE MISSION

Action: Break barrel
Stock: Synthetic
Barrel: N/A
Sights: Blade front, adjustable rear
Weight: N/A
Caliber: .177, .22
Magazine: 12 rounds
Features: Multi-shot break-barrel with QuietFire suppression; 12-shot magazine; equipped with 4X32mm scope
Price: **$205.91**

CROSMAN SEMI-AUTO R1

Action: CO2
Stock: Synthetic
Barrel: N/A
Sights: Flip-up front and rear
Weight: 6 lb.
Caliber: BB
Magazine: 25 rounds
Features: Semi-auto BB AR pistol utilizing two CO2 cartridges; quad forearm rail; adjustable stock; red dot sight
Price: **$228.82**

EVANIX MAX AIR CARBON FIBER

EVANIX MAX ML BIG BORE PCP

EVANIX REX

EVANIX REX-IBEX

EVANIX REX P

EVANIX SNIPER

EVANIX MAX AIR CARBON FIBER

Action: PCP
Stock: Wood, Synthetic
Barrel: 21.6, 25.5 in.
Sights: None
Weight: 7 lb.
Caliber: .177, .22, .25, .30
Magazine: N/A
Features: A magazine-fed semiauto with a 290cc air reservoir; built in manometer; ambidextrous thumbhole stock in wood or synthetic; shrouded barrel; Weaver dovetail rail; adjustable power; two-stage adjustable trigger;
Wood. . . . . $1249.00–$1549.00
Synthetic . . . . . . $1149.00–$1449.00

EVANIX MAX ML PCP BULLPUP

Action: PCP
Stock: Wood
Barrel: 18.8, 21.6 in.
Sights: None
Weight: 7 lb. 3 oz.–7 lb. 13 oz.
Caliber: .177, .22, .25, .30, .35, .40, .50
Magazine: N/A
Features: For hunters, with calibers up to .50, this bullpup has a handsome hardwood stock in a thumbhole configuration; threaded barrel; side-lever action; Picatinny rail; 280cc carbon fiber cylinder
Price: . . . . $1050.00–$1350.00

EVANIX REX

Action: PCP
Stock: Synthetic
Barrel: 19.7 in.
Sights: None
Weight: 5 lb. 8 oz.
Caliber: .177, .22, .25, .30, .35, .40, .50
Magazine: 1 round
Features: A single-shot with under-lever cocking action; automatic safety; lightweight build; two-stage adjustable trigger; Picatinny rail; 200cc cylinder; adjustable power via cocking lever position
Price: . . . . $849.00–$1149.00

EVANIX REX-IBEX

Action: PCP
Stock: Synthetic
Barrel: 28.7 in.
Sights: None
Weight: 7 lb.
Caliber: .177, .22, .25, .30, .35, .40, .50
Magazine: 1 round
Features: A single-shot chassis-type air rifle with a rifled barrel; Picatinny rail; two-stage adjustable trigger;

adjustable cocking lever position, 480cc carbon fiber cylinder
Price: $1334.00

EVANIX REX P

Action: PCP
Stock: Synthetic
Barrel: 10.2 in.
Sights: None
Weight: 4 lb.
Caliber: .177, .22, .25, .30, .35, .40, .50
Magazine: 1 round
Features: A single-shot pistol with under-lever action; Picatinny rail; two-stage adjustable trigger; adjustable power via cocking lever position; 120cc cylinder
Price: . . . . $799.00–$1099.00

EVANIX SNIPER

Action: PCP
Stock: Synthetic
Barrel: 18.9, 21.6 in.
Sights: None
Weight: 8 lb. 2 oz.
Caliber: .177, .22, .25, .30, .35, .40, .50
Magazine: 5 rounds
Features: A magazine-fed air rifle with side-lever activation; Picatinny rail; 280cc carbon steel cylinder; adjustable stock is combination of metal and synthetic; two-stage adjustable trigger
Price: . . . .$1149.00–$1449.00

NEW Products: **Airguns**

GAMO ARROW

GAMO PR-776

GAMO PT-80 DARK
LIMITED EDITION

HATSAN FACTOR RC

SIG SAUER 1911
EMPEROR SCORPION
AIRGUN

SIG SAUER MCX
CANEBRAKE AIR RIFLE

GAMO ARROW

Action: PCP
Stock: Synthetic
Barrel: 20.8
Sights: None
Weight: 5 lb.
Caliber: .177, .22
Magazine: 10 rounds
Features: A PCP straight-loader with a two-stage adjustable CAT trigger; non-slip stock texturing; dovetail scope mount grooves; 10-shot Quick Shot technology; metal jacketed rifled steel barrel; Whisper Fusion noise dampening
Price:. $229.90

GAMO PR-776

Action: CO2
Stock: N/A
Barrel: 6 in.
Sights: Blade front, adjustable rear
Weight: 2 lb. 4 oz.
Caliber: .177
Magazine: 8 rounds
Features: A single-/double-action air revolver functioning via CO2; all-metal construction; rifled barrel; 400 fps velocity
Price:. $109.90

GAMO PT-80 DARK LIMITED EDITION

Action: CO2
Stock: N/A
Barrel: 3.75 in.
Sights: Blade front, notch rear
Weight: 1 lb.
Caliber: .177
Magazine: 8 rounds
Features: A single-/double-action limited edition air pistol utilzing CO2; non-blowback operation; 400 fps velocity; manual safety; comes with white camo grips and a padded hard case
Price:. $89.00

HATSAN FACTOR-RC

Action: PCP
Stock: Synthetic
Barrel: 23 in.
Sights: None
Weight: 7 lb. 15 oz.
Caliber: .177, .22, .25
Magazine: 24, 21, 19 rounds
Features: A magazine-fed PCP with topside and under rails; side-lever action; manual loading; pressure-adjustable regulator; carbon fiber air botle; externally adjustable hammer preload; built-in cylinder pressure gauge; reversible cocking handle; two-stage adjustable Quatro match-grade trigger; patented anti-knock system; manual safety; hard case
Price:. $1099.99

SIG SAUER 1911 EMPEROR SCORPION AIRGUN

Action: CO2
Stock: N/A
Barrel: 5 in.
Sights: Three-dot fixed front and rear
Weight: 41.6 oz.
Caliber: BB
Magazine: 17 rounds
Features: Sporting an M1913 accessory rail, this air pistol comes with one magazine; 300 fps velocity; similar wieght to the firearm; skeletonized hammer and trigger; Hogue-style grip and magwell; full blowback metal slide
Price:. $139.99

SIG SAUER MCX CANEBRAKE AIR RIFLE

Action: CO2
Stock: Synthetic
Barrel: N/A
Sights: Folding front and rear
Weight: 7 lb. 9 oz.
Caliber: .177
Magazine: 30 rounds
Features: Based on the MCX Canebrake firearm, this air rifle sports a 30-round magazine; velocity up to 600 fps; flat-blade trigger; MLOK handguard and shroud trainer; flip-up sights
Price:. $279.99

SIG SAUER MODEL 65

Action: Spring piston
Stock: Wood
Barrel: 14.5 in.
Sights: Fiber optic front, adjustable rear
Weight: 6 lb. 9 oz.
Caliber: .177, .22, .25
Magazine: 1 round
Features: A single-stho break barrel with a Turkish walnut stock that has an adjustable cheekpiece and checkering; fully shrouded barrel with intetrated sound moderator; two-stage adjustable match-grade Quatro trigger; manual and automatic cocking safeties; anti-bear-trap safety
Price:. . . . . N/A

STOEGER XM1
BULLSHARK

UMAREX EMERGE

UMAREX GLOCK 17
GEN 3 AIR PISTOL

UMAREX HECKLER &
KOCH HK416

UMAREX NOTOS

UMAREX NXG

UMAREX ORIGIN

UMAREX PRIMAL 20

STOEGER XM1 BULLSHARK

Action: PCP
Stock: Synthetic
Barrel: N/A
Sights: None
Weight: N/A
Caliber: .177, .22
Magazine: N/A
Features: This certainly marks a modern turn in air rifle design from Stoeger, with an innovative bullpup stock featuring Proadaptive checkering; manual cross-bolt safety; interchangeable Multi-Grip System; Stoeger claims Olympic-level accuracy with premium pellets; two-stage adjustable trigger
Price:. $479.00

UMAREX EMERGE

Action: Gas piston
Stock: Synthetic
Barrel: N/A
Sights: Fiber optic front, rear
Weight: N/A
Caliber: .177, .22
Magazine: 12 rounds
Features: A break-barrel gas piston-powered air rifle that comes with both upgradeds sights and a 4X32 scope; SilencAir Technology; two-stage adjustable trigger; automatic safety; 1,000 fps velocity; auto-advancing magazine
Price:. $189.99

UMAREX GLOCK GEN3

Action: CO2
Stock: Synthetic
Barrel: N/A
Sights: Blade front, notch rear
Weight: N/A
Caliber: .177, BB
Magazine: N/A
Features: A blowback repeater that fires both BBs and pellets; 365 fps velocity
Price:. $114.99

UMAREX HECKLER & KOCH HK416

Action: CO2
Stock: Synthetic
Barrel: N/A
Sights: Flip-up front and rear
Weight: N/A
Caliber: BB
Magazine: 36
Features: Modeled on the full-auto firearm, this air rifle has a 500 BB magazine reservoir with a 36-count feeding hold; fires in single shots or in a six-shot burst; Picatinny rail; quad rail; drop-free magazine; adjustable stock; utilizes two 12-gram CO2 cartridges
Price:. $159.99

UMAREX NOTOS

Action: PCP
Stock: Synthetic
Barrel: 11.75 in.
Sights: Fiber optic front, adjustabble rear
Weight: N/A
Caliber: .22
Magazine: N/A
Features: A high-performance air pistol with a fixed high-pressure air tank; removeable auto-indexing rotary magazine; three-baggle SilencAir muzzle device; side-lever cocking; topside Picatinny rail
Price:. $229.99

UMAREX NXG

Action: CO2
Stock: Synthetic
Barrel: N/A

Sights: Fiber optic front, notch rear
Weight: N/A
Caliber: BB
Magazine: 10 rounds
Features: A pump-action BB "shotgun" with the CO2 cartridge housed in the grip; drop-free rotary magazine; 490 fps velocity
Price:. $59.99

UMAREX ORIGIN

Action: PCP
Stock: Synthetic
Barrel: N/A
Sights: None
Weight: N/A
Caliber: .25
Magazine: 8 rounds
Features: Using an eight-shot auto-advancing magazine, this air rifle has side-lever charging; Picatinny rail; all-weather stock; 950 fps velocity; side-mounted pressure gauge; adjustable trigger; Ever-Pressure Tank System
Price:. $329.99

UMAREX PRIMAL 20

Action: PCP
Stock: Synthetic
Barrel: N/A
Sights: None
Weight: N/A
Caliber: 20-ga.
Magazine: 2 rounds
Features: A 20-gauge air "slug shotgun" in a bolt-action that utilizes a 395-grain slug; 24cc onboard aluminum air tank; drop and manual safeties; generates 700 fps velocity with 430 ft-lbs of pressure; topside rail; ergonomic thumbhole stock; cocked bolt indicator; fully ambidextrous design; laterally sliding magazine
Price:. $649.99

AMERICAN TACTICAL, INC. MILSPORT 410

ARMSCOR VRF14

BENELLI 828 U LIMITED EDITION

BENELLI ETHOS BE.S.T.

BERETTA A300 ULTIMA

BERETTA A400 XCEL SPORTING

BERETTA ULTRALEGGERO

AMERICAN TACTICAL MILSPORT .410

Action: Semiautomatic
Stock: Synthetic
Barrel: 18.5 in.
Chokes: 1
Sights: Flip-up front and rear
Weight: N/A
Gauge: .410
Magazine: 5, 15 shells
Features: An AR-platform shotgun with a custom 13-in. keymod rail; six-position Rogers Super Stoc; Cylinder choke; adjustable gas system; short-stroke piston system; can be converted ot 5.56 NATO or .300 BLK; chambered for 2.5-in. .410-bore shells
Price: $799.95

ARMSCOR VRF14

Action: Semiautomatic
Stock: Synthetic
Barrel: 14 in.
Chokes: Mobil Choke
Sights: Flip-up front and rear
Weight: 6 lb. 11 oz.
Gauge: 12
Magazine: 5, 9, 19 shells
Features: Armscor claims this is the first short-barrel 12-ga. of its kind with a pistol-style grip that enables shooting from the hip; gas operation; polymer fore-end; familiar AR-type controls; Mobil Choke choke tubes; topside Picatinny rail and plenty of room on the fore-end for accessories; black Cerakote finish; takes 2 ¾- and 3-in. shells, but does not qualify as a "shotgun" by ATF standards, instead falling under the non-Class 3/NFA "firearm" category according to various sources; comes with a five-round magazine but is compatible with larger-capacity VR-series mags
Price: $599.00

BENELLI 828 U LIMITED EDITION

Action: Over/under
Stock: Walnut
Barrel: 28 in.
Chokes: 5
Sights: Fiber optic front
Weight: 7 lb. 7 oz.
Gauge: 12
Magazine: 2 shells
Features: Just 250 in this limited edition; B.E.S.T. gloss treatment on barrels; AA-grade walnut stock in a satin finish; game scenes and floral engravings, some in gold, on the nickel-plated receiver; steel frame; right-hand stock
Price: $6499.00

BENELLI ETHOS BE.S.T.

Action: Semiautomatic
Stock: Synthetic
Barrel: 26, 28 in.
Chokes: 5
Sights: Fiber optic front
Weight: 6 lb. 9 oz.–6 lb. 11 oz.
Gauge: 12
Magazine: 4 shells
Features: With a black Comfort Tech 3 synthetic stock, this shotgun has a black anodized barrel with the BE.S.T. treatment; interchangeabble fiber optic front sight; comes with hard case; flush-fit Crio chokes
Price: $2199.00

BERETTA A300 ULTIMA

Action: Semiautomatic
Stock: Synthetic
Barrel: 28 in.
Chokes: 5
Sights: Fiber optic front
Weight: 7 lb. 11 oz.
Gauge: 12
Magazine: 4 shells
Features: A gas-operated semi-auto with an extended bolt handle; large bolt-release button; Kick-off recoil system; 3-in. chamber; available with the stock in black, Mossy Oak Bottomloand, or Realtree Max-5
Price: . . . .$800.00-$900.00

BERETTA A400 XCEL SPORTING

Action: Semiautomatic
Stock: Walnut
Barrel: 28, 30, 32 in.
Chokes: 5
Sights: Fiber optic front
Weight: 7 lb. 12 oz.
Gauge: 12
Magazine: 4 shells
Features: For 2022, this is an updated version of the first A400 Xcel so we're calling it new, with oversized controls; Blink gas operating system which increases follow-up shot speeds b 36%; Kick-Off recoil reduction system; Optima extended choke tube set; 10X10mm carbon fiber rib
Price: $1979.00

BERETTA ULTRALEGGERO

Action: Over/under
Stock: Walnut
Barrel: 24, 26, 28, 30 in.
Chokes: 5
Sights: Silver front bead
Weight: 6 lb. 2 oz.–6 lb. 9 oz.
Gauge: 12
Magazine: 2 shells
Features: Beretta says this marks a new point in lightweight craftsmanship with a "skeletonised" steel receiver; single selective trigger; techno-polymer receiver with floral motif that fades in and out as it shifts in the light; 3-in. chambers; aluminum 694 fore-end; enlarged stock cavity for weight reduction; Extralight recoil pad; steel shot-compatible Steelium Optima Bore HP barrels; anti-reflection 6X6 rib; flush-fit choke tubes
Price: . . . . .N/A

BROWNING A5 SWEET SIXTEEN UPLAND

BROWNING A5 SWEET SIXTEEN MOSSY OAK SHADOW GRASS HABITAT

BROWNING CITORI 725 SPORTING MEDALLION HIGH GRADE

BROWNING CYNERGY ULTIMATE TURKEY MOSSY OAK BOTTOMLAND

BROWNING MAXUS II ULTIMATE

BROWNING A5 SWEET SIXTEEN MOSSY OAK SHADOW GRASS HABITAT

Action: Semiautomatic
Stock: Synthetic
Barrel: 26, 28 in.
Chokes: 3
Sights: Fiber optic front
Weight: 7 lb. 3 oz.
Gauge: 16
Magazine: 4 shells
Features: In full coverage camo, this Sweet 16 comes with Full, Modified, and Improved Cylinder flush Invector-DS chokes; sling swivel studs; TurnKey magazine plug; Inflex recoil pad; Speed Load Plus feeding system; length of pull stock spacers
Price: $1999.99

BROWNING A5 SWEET SIXTEEN UPLAND

Action: Semiautomatic
Stock: Walnut
Barrel: 26, 28 in.
Chokes: 3
Sights: Fiber optic front
Weight: 5 lb. 12 oz.
Gauge: 16
Magazine: 4 shells
Features: Very lightweight at under 6 lb., this Sweet 16 has an oil-finished Turkis walnut stock with 18 lines-per-inch checkering; brushed nickel receiver; Inflex recoil pad; Speed Load Plus feeding system; stock shim

kit; Vector Pro forcing cones and back-boring; hard case included
Price: $2029.99

BROWNING CITORI 725 SPORTING MEDALLION HIGH GRADE

Action: Over/under
Stock: Walnut
Barrel: 30, 32 in.
Chokes: 5
Sights: Fiber optic front, ivory mid-rib
Weight: 7 lb. 8 oz.
Gauge: 12
Magazine: 2 shells
Features: Browning's flagship competition shotgun with Grade IV Turkish walnut with hand-cut checkering and right-hand palm swell; extended Invector-DS choke set; HiViz Pro Comp front fiber optic sight with ivory mid-rib bead; deep blue receiver with gold inlaid floral-type engraving; Inflex II recoil pad; Triple Trigger System; 50/50 point of impact; floating rib; chrome chambers; full-width hing pin; tapered locking bolt Negrini locking hard case with leather trim
Price: $7069.99

BROWNING CYNERGY ULTIMATE TURKEY MOSSY OAK BOTTOMLAND

Action: Over/under
Stock: Synthetic

Barrel: 24, 26 in.
Chokes: 5
Sights: Fiber optic front, adjustable rear
Weight: 7 lb. 4 oz.
Gauge: 12
Magazine: 2 shells
Features: An over/under for turkey hunters, featuring a fiber optic front sight paired with a Marble Arms Bullseye adjustable rear; a composite stock with an adjustable cheek riser, Inflex recoil pad, and shim spacers; topside Picatinny rail; 60/40 point of impact; full coverage Mossy Oak Bottomland camo
Price: $2549.99

BROWNING MAXUS II ULTIMATE

Action: Semiautomatic
Stock: Walnut
Barrel: 26, 28 in.
Chokes: 3
Sights: Fiber optic front, ivory mid-rib
Weight: 7 lb. 1 oz.
Gauge: 12
Magazine: 4 shells
Features: An upgraded semiauto with an oil-finished Grade III Turkish walnut stock shim adjustable for length of pull; 22 lines-per-inch checkering; close-radius pistol grip; nickel-Teflon-coated bolt; ramped trigger guard; flush-fit Invector Plus choke set; oversized bolt release and handle; satin-finished nickel-plated receiver with scroll engraving; gloss blue barrel
Price: $2059.99

BROWNING SILVER
RIFLED DEER MOSSY OAK
BOTTOMLAND

CAESAR GUERINI
REVENANT SPORTING

CHARLES DALY 101
12-GA. MOSSY OAK

CHARLES DALY 101
.410-BORE

CHARLES DALY 600 LEFT-
HAND MOSSY OAK
OBSESSION

CHARLES DALY 301
TRUE TIMBER PRAIRIE

BROWNING SILVER RIFLED DEER MOSSY OAK BOTTOMLAND

Action: Semiautomatic
Stock: Synthetic
Barrel: 22 in.
Chokes: None
Sights: None
Weight: 6 lb. 12 oz.–7 lb. 12 oz.
Gauge: 20, 12
Magazine: 4 shells
Features: Featuring a 3-inch chrome-lined chamber; thick-walled rifled barrel; topside cantilever scope mount; 12-ga. has full-coverage Mossy Oak Bottomland while the 20-ga. has a checkered walnut stock
Price:. 12-ga. $1389.99; 20-ga. $1469.99

CAESAR GUERINI REVENANT SPORTING

Action: Over/under
Stock: Walnut
Barrel: 30, 32 in.
Chokes: 6
Sights: White bead front, silver mid-rib bbead
Weight: 7 lb. 6 oz–7 lb. 8 oz.
Gauge: 20, 28
Magazine: 2 shells
Features: A gorgeous subgauge for the clays crowd with a hand-polished, coin-finished receiver with full-cover engraving in an organic floral design and with gold inlays and game birds; round-body action; 10mm vent rib; manual safety; 26 lines-per-inch checkering; supplied with hard case;

left-hand stock available for both gauges
**Price:. $15,785;
Left-hand add. $420.00**

CHARLES DALY 101 12-GA. MOSSY OAK

Action: Break-open
Stock: Synthetic
Barrel: 20 in.
Chokes: 1
Sights: Fiber optic front
Weight: 5 lb.
Gauge: 12
Magazine: 1 shell
Features: A single shot for turkey hunters as it comes with one extended ported XXFull choke tube; checkered synthetic stock in Mossy Oak Bottomland; topside Picatinny rail for optics; metal in Flat Dark Earth Cerakote
Price:. $206.00

CHARLES DALY 101 .410-BORE

Action: Break-open
Stock: Synthetic
Barrel: 20 in.
Chokes: 1
Sights: Fiber optic front
Weight: 5 lb.
Gauge: .410
Magazine: 1 shell
Features: The diminutive .410 in a black checkered synthetic stock; one XXFull extended and ported choke tube; topside rail for optics
Price:. $153.00

CHARLES DALY 301 TRUETIMBER PRAIRIE, MOSSY OAK BOTTOMLAND

Action: Pump
Stock: Synthetic
Barrel: 24, 28 in.
Chokes: 3
Sights: Fiber optic front
Weight: 7 lb.
Gauge: 12
Magazine: 4 shells
Features: A nice, sturdy pump for deer and turkey hunters, with a choice of stock in TrueTimber Prairie camo or Mossy Oak Bottomland; Flat Dark Earth Cerakote metal; Mossy Oak model has 24-in barrel and comes with flush-fit Modified and Full and extended ported XXFull chokes; TrueTimber has a 28-in. barrel and Improved, Modified, and Full flush-fit chokes
Price:. . TrueTimber Prairie $355.00; Mossy Oak Bottomland $384.00

CHARLES DALY 600 LEFT-HAND MOSSY OAK OBSESSION

Action: Semiautomatic
Stock: Synthetic
Barrel: 22, 26
Chokes: 3
Sights: Fiber optic front
Weight: 6 lb. 14 oz.
Gauge: 20
Magazine: 5 shells
Features: A pair of 20-ga. semi-autos dressed in Mossy Oak Obsession; gas operation; Improved, Modified, and Full chokes
Price:. $629.00

CHARLES DALY 601
DPS SPORTING CLAYS

CHARLES DALY 601
TRUE TIMBER PRAIRIE

CHARLES DALY 601 TURKEY
MOSSY OAK BOTTOMLAND

CHARLES DALY TRIPLE
MAGNUM TRUETIMBER
PRAIRIE

CITADEL/LEGACY
SPORTS BOSSHOG 1

CITADEL/LEGACY
SPORTS BOSS 25

CHARLES DALY 601 DPS SPORTING CLAYS

Action: Semiautomatic
Stock: Wood
Barrel: 30 in.
Chokes: 5
Sights: Fiber optic front
Weight: 7 lb. 15 oz.
Gauge: 12
Magazine: 4 shells
Features: A long, 30-in. barrel for long clay games; aluminum receiver; adjustable cheekpiece; gas operation; slim, checkered, ergonomic fore-end
Price: **$784.00**

CHARLES DALY 601 TRUETIMBER PRAIRIE

Action: Semiautomatic
Stock: Synthetic
Barrel: 28 in.
Chokes: 3
Sights: Fiber optic front
Weight: 7 lb. 3 oz.
Gauge: 12
Magazine: 4 shells
Features: Medium-weight field gun with a stock dressed in TrueTimber Prairie; Flat Dark Earth Cerakote metal; aluminum receiver; checkered synthetic stock; receiver grooved for scope mount; 3-in. chamber
Price: **$379.00**

CHARLES DALY 601 TURKEY MOSSY OAK BOTTOMLAND

Action: Semiautomatic
Stock: Synthetic
Barrel: 24 in.
Chokes: 3
Sights: Fiber optic front
Weight: 6 lb.
Gauge: 12
Magazine: 4 shells
Features: For deer or turkey, this shotgun has a stock in Mossy Oak Bottomland; Flat Dark Earth Cerakote metal; aluminum receiver, flush-ft Modified and Full chokes with an extended, ported XXFull choke; 3-in. chamber; topside Picatinny rail
Price: **$399.00**

CHARLES DALY TRIPLE MAGNUM TRUETIMBER PRAIRIE

Action: Drilling
Stock: Synthetic
Barrel: 28 in.
Chokes: 5
Sights: Fiber optic front
Weight: 8 lb. 10 oz.
Gauge: 12
Magazine: 3 shells
Features: Three barrels of 12-ga. all dressed up in TrueTimber Prairie; black receiver; single non-selective

trigger with mechanical reset; single barrel tops the double; five Rem-Choke threaded chokes provided; 3.5-in. chambers
Price: **$2073.00**

CITADEL/LEGACY SPORTS BOSS 25

Action: Semiautomatic
Stock: Synthetic
Barrel: 18.75 in.
Chokes: 5
Sights: Flip-up front and rear
Weight: N/A
Gauge: 12
Magazine: 5, 10 shells
Features: A detachable-magazine-fed shotgun on an AR-type platform; 3-in. chamber; muzzle brake; pistol grip; topside Picatinny rail; adjustable stock; available in black, flat dark earth, tactical gray, and a U.S.A. flag theme; California-compliant version available
Price: **$579.00**

CITADEL/LEGACY SPORTS BOSSHOG 1

Action: Semiautomatic
Stock: Synthetic
Barrel: 20 in.
Chokes: 3
Sights: Blade front sight
Weight: 6 lb. 14 oz.
Gauge: 12
Magazine: 4 shells
Features: A simple tactical shotgun with a dovetailed receiver; blad front sight; chrome-lined barrel; ventilated buttpad
Price: **$299.00**

NEW Products: **Shotguns**

CITADEL/LEGACY SPORTS
BOSSHOG 2

CITADEL/LEGACY
SPORTS PAT

CITADEL/LEGACY SPORTS
PAX

EAA AKKAR CHURCHILL
220 OPTICS READY

EAA AKKAR CHURCHILL
620 OPTICS READY

EAA GIRSAN MC312
SPORT WOOD

EAA GIRSAN MC312
GOOSE

CITADEL/LEGACY SPORTS BOSSHOG 2

Action: Semiautomatic
Stock: Synthetic
Barrel: 20
Chokes: 5
Sights: Fiber optic front, adjustable rear
Weight: 6 lb. 14 oz.
Gauge: 12
Magazine: 4 shells
Features: A more advanced tactical shotgun with a fiber optic front sight and adjustable rear; rubberized pistol grip; grooved fore-end; Picatinny rails topside and under the forearm
Price: **$299.00**

CITADEL/LEGACY SPORTS PAT

Action: Pump
Stock: Synthetic
Barrel: 20 in.
Chokes: 5
Sights: Fiber optic front
Weight: 7 lb. 5 oz.
Gauge: 12, 20
Magazine: 4 shells
Features: A tactical pump with a chrome-lined barrel; pistol grip; raised fiber optic front sight; topside and under-forearm Picatinny rails; metalwork in black or nickel
Price: **$219.00**

CITADEL/LEGACY SPORTS PAX

Action: Pump
Stock: Synthetic
Barrel: 20 in.
Chokes: 5
Sights: Fiber optic front
Weight: 7 lb. 5 oz.
Gauge: 12, 20
Magazine: 4 shells
Features: Wearing a skeletonized synthetic stock, this shotgun has a dovetailed receiver; chrome-lined barrel; pistol grip; 3-in. chamber; available with black or nickel metalwork
Price: **$199.00**

EAA AKKAR CHURCHILL 220 OPTICS READY

Action: Semiautomatic
Stock: Synthetic
Barrel: 18.5 in.
Chokes: 1
Sights: Fiber optic front, red-dot optic
Weight: 5 lb.
Gauge: 20
Magazine: 5 shells
Features: A 20-ga. self-defense shotgun that comes equipped with a red-dot reflex sight; breach/break choke tube; checkered pistol grip; enhanced loading port
Price: **$627.00**

EAA AKKAR CHURCHILL 620 OPTICS READY

Action: Pump
Stock: Synthetic
Barrel: 18.5
Chokes: 1
Sights: Fiber optic front, red-dot optic
Weight: 5 lb.
Gauge: 20
Magazine: 5 shells
Features: Identical to the 220 Optics Ready but in a pump-action
Price: **$467.00**

EAA GIRSAN MC312 GOOSE

Action: Semiautomatic
Stock: Synthetic
Barrel: 30 in.
Chokes: 3
Sights: Fiber optic front, red-dot optic
Weight: 6 lb. 15 oz.
Gauge: 12
Magazine: 5 shells
Features: A long barrel for long pokes on geese; included red-dot sight; inertia action; vent rib; extended choke tubesq
Price: **$627.00**

EAA GIRSAN MC312 SPORT WOOD

Action: Semiautomatic
Stock: Walnut
Barrel: 28 in.
Chokes: 4
Sights: Fiber optic front, red-dot optic
Weight: 6 lb. 15 oz.
Gauge: 12
Magazine: 5 shells
Features: A nice, budget-friendly field gun complete with an included red-dot sight; inertia action; checkered Turkish walnut stock in an oil-rubbed finish
Price: **$699.00**

FABARM ELOS ELITE 2

FABARM XLR CHESAPEAKE

FRANCHI AFFINITY 3 CERAKOTE

FRANCHI AFFINITY 3.5 TURKEY ELITE

FRANCHI INSTINCT SIDEPLATE

HATSANUSA ESCORT BTS

HATSANUSA ESCORT PS YOUTH

FABARM ELOS 2 ELITE FIELD

Action: Over/under
Stock: Walnut
Barrel: 28, 30 in.
Chokes: 5
Sights: Ivory front bead
Weight: 7 lb.
Gauge: 20, 12
Magazine: 2 shells
Features: Designed for the tasteful upland hunter, this model has a matte-finished, hand-oiled deluxe Turkish Walnut stock; steel case-colored receiver with gold game bird inlays; 6mm rib; Tribore HP barrels; 3-in. chambers; INTEGRALE case; left-hand available for both gauges
Price:.....**$3560.00; Left-hand add $175.00**

FABARM XLR CHESAPEAKE

Action: Semiautomatic
Stock: Synthetic
Barrel: 28, 30 in.
Chokes: 4
Sights: Fiber optic front
Weight: 6 lb. 14 oz.
Gauge: 12
Magazine: 4 shells
Features: Strong choice for tough field condigtions with an All-Terrain composite stock in TrueTimber Strata; metalwork in Midnight Bronze Cerakote; Pulse Piston gas operation; Tribore HP barrel; 3-in. chamber; three flush-fit chokes and one extended choke; left-hand available
Price:... **Right-hand $1995.00; Left-hand $2,200**

FRANCHI AFFINITY 3 CERAKOTE

Action: Semiautomatic
Stock: Synthetic
Barrel: 26, 28 in.
Chokes: 3
Sights: Fiber optic front
Weight: 6 lb., 6 lb. 15 oz.

Gauge: 20, 12
Magazine: 4 shells
Features: Available in 12- and 20-ga., this hunter has a 3-in. chamber; choice of Realtree Max-5 stock with Midnight Bronze Cerakote or Mossy Oak Bottomland stock with Patriot Brown Cerakot; Improved, Modified, and Full chokes;
Price:.................**$1099.00**

FRANCHI AFFINITY 3.5 TURKEY ELITE

Action: Semiautomatic
Stock: Synthetic
Barrel: 24 in.
Chokes: 2
Sights: Dual-color fiber optic front
Weight: 7 lb. 14 oz.
Gauge: 12
Magazine: 4 shells
Features: With a pistol-grip stock in Gore Optifade Subalpine, this turkey-specific gun has a hooded dual-color fiber-optic bar front sight; adjustable rear fiber optic sight; Picatinny top rail; shim kit; removeable trigger group; Rhino extended choke tubes in Turkey and Extra Full Turkey; metal in Midnight Bronze Cerakote; 3.5-in. chamber
Price:.................**$1449.00**

FRANCHI INSTINCT SIDEPLATE

Action: Over/under
Stock: Walnut
Barrel: 28 in.
Chokes: 3
Sights: Fiber optic front
Weight: 6 lb. 8 oz., 7 lb. 8 oz.
Gauge: 20, 12
Magazine: 2 shells
Features: Nicely configured upland gun with a Prince of Wales grip; side rib and vent rib; gloss blue barrels; engraved, color-case hardened receiver with a sideplate layout that includes a gold pheasant on the right

side and a gold quail on the left on the 12-ga. and quail on both sides of the 20-ga.; AA-grade walnut stock in a satin finish; 3-in. chambers; sculpted top-lever
Price:.................**$2229.00**

HATSANUSA ESCORT BTS

Action: Semiautomatic
Stock: Synthetic
Barrel: 20 in.
Chokes: N/A
Sights: Adjustable carry handle front and rear, adjustable flip-up front and rear
Weight: 6 lb. 13 oz.
Gauge: .410
Magazine: 5 shells
Features: A small-bore bullup with an aircraft alloy receiver; polymer lower; adjustable comb; 3-in. chamber; hard chrome-plated steel barrel; Picatinny rail; gas operation; detachable magazines; reversible cocking handle; ambidextrous magazine release;
Price:.................**$549.99**

HATSANUSA ESCORT PS YOUTH

Action: Semiautomatic
Stock: Synthetic
Barrel: 22 in.
Chokes: 5
Sights: Brass bead front
Weight: 6 lb.
Gauge: 20
Magazine: 4 shells
Features: Not another featureless shrunken "youth" gun, this 20-ga. has it all with a full five-choke set; 3-in. chamber; gas operation; manual cross-button safety; lightweight alloy receiver; oxidation-proof chrome-plated barrel; TioPad recoil-absorbing buttpad; stock shim kit; sling studs; in Realtree Timber
Price:.................**$449.97**

HATSANUSA ESCORT SDX12

 HATSANUSA ESCORT XTREMEMAX

HENRY LEVER-ACTION AXE .410

 **IRON HORSE FIREARMS SENTRY 12 ELITE**

 IRON HORSE FIREARMS SENTRY 12 PRO

 MOSSBERG 590S

MOSSBERG 590S SHOCKWAVE

MOSSBERG 940 PRO FIELD

HATSANUSA ESCORT SDX12

Action: Semiautomatic
Stock: Synthetic
Barrel: 18 in.
Chokes: 3
Sights: Adjustable carry handle front and rear, adjustable flip-up front and rear
Weight: 9 lb.
Gauge: 12
Magazine: 5 shells
Features: A detachable magazine-fed tactical 12-ga. with a black anodized aircraft alloy receiver; hard-chrome-plated steel barrel; pistol grip stock with adjustable comb; 3-in. chamber; gas operation; Full, Improved Cylinder, and breach/brake Cylinder chokes
Price: $499.99

HATSANUSA ESCORT XTREMEMAX

Action: Semiautomatic
Stock: Synthetic
Barrel: 28 in.
Chokes: 5
Sights: Fiber optic front
Weight: 7 lb. 8 oz.
Gauge: 12
Magazine: 4 shells
Features: Gas-operated semi-auto with a 3.5-in. chamber; full five-choke set; HiVIz Spark fiber optic front sight; chrome finished Ni-Cr-Mo steel barrel; checkered anti-glare vent rib; stock shim kit; sling studs; in full-coverage Realtree Max-5
Price: $899.99

HENRY LEVER-ACTION AXE .410

Action Axe .410
Action: Lever
Stock: Walnut
Barrel: 15.4 in.
Chokes: 1
Sights: Brass bead front
Weight: 5 lb. 12 oz.
Gauge: .410
Magazine: 5 shells

Features: Takings its name from the axe-style pistol grip, this handy lever has a five-round capacity with 2.5-in. shells; comes with Full choke and threaded for Invector-style chokes; drilled and tapped for scope mount; transfer-bar safety; choice of blued or brass receivers
Blued $1049.00
Brass $1132.00

IRON HORSE FIREARMS SENTRY 12 ELITE

Action: Pump
Stock: Synthetic
Barrel: 18.5 in.
Chokes: N/A
Sights: Flip-up sights
Weight: 6 lb. 2 oz.
Gauge: 12
Magazine: 5 shells
Features: A monolithic aluminum design; magazine-fed; Pro adds two more magazines, a stippled fore-end and pistol grip, Fab Defense flip-up sights, polished internals, and a single-point QD sling, custom Cerakote finish, to the base Sentry 12 model
Price: $1449.00

IRON HORSE FIREARMS SENTRY 12 PRO

Action: Pump
Stock: Synthetic
Barrel: 18.5 in.
Chokes: N/A
Sights: Flip-up sights
Weight: 6 lb. 2 oz.
Gauge: 12
Magazine: 5 shells
Features: A monolithic aluminum design; magazine-fed; Pro adds two more magazines, a stippled fore-end grip, Fab Defense flip-up sights, and a single-point QD sling to the base Sentry 12 model
Price: $1149.00

MOSSBERG 590S

Action: Pump
Stock: Synthetic
Barrel: 18.5, 20 in.

Chokes: 1
Sights: Ghost ring rear, blade front; bead front
Weight: 7 lb. 4 oz.
Gauge: 12
Magazine: 7, 8, 13 shells; 5, 6, 9 shells
Features: The 590S comes in two versions a 20-in. version with ghost ring sights ad an 18.5-in. version with no sights; chambers 3-in., 2.75-in., and the shorty 1.75-in. shells; MLOK-compatible fore-end; AccuChoke system, Cylinder choke included
Price: 20-in. $731.00; 18.5-in. $623.00

MOSSBERG 590S SHOCKWAVE

Action: Pump
Stock: Synthetic
Barrel: 14.375, 18.5 in.
Chokes: None
Sights: Bead front
Weight: 5 lb. 8 oz.
Gauge: 12
Magazine: 5, 6, 9 shells; 4, 5, 8 shells
Features: Like the full-size 590S, this model is designed to take 12-ga. shotshells 3-in., 2.75-in., and 1.75-in.; Cylinder bore; short-barreled model has heavy-wall barrel; Raptor grip; corncob fore-end with strap
Price: $623.00

MOSSBERG 940 PRO FIELD

Action: Semiautomatic
Stock: Synthetic
Barrel: 28 in.
Chokes: 3
Sights: Fiber optic front
Weight: 7 lb. 12 oz.
Gauge: 12
Magazine: 4 shells
Features: A utilitarian field gun with a black synthetic stock, adjustable for length of pull, cast, and drop; matte blue metalwork; supplied with full set of AccuChokes; vent rib; fiber optic front sight
Price: $903.00

MOSSBERG 940 PRO SNOW GOOSE

MOSSBERG 940 PRO TURKEY

MOSSBERG 940 PRO WATERFOWL

POINTER ACRIUS CERAKOTE

POINTER/LEGACY SPORTS FIELD TEK 3 CERAKOTE

POINTER/LEGACY SPORTS FIELD TEK 3 CERAKOTE YOUTH

POINTER/LEGACY SPORTS FIELD TEK 4

POINTER/LEGACY SPORTS FIELD TEK 5

MOSSBERG 940 PRO SNOW GOOSE

Action: Semiautomatic
Stock: Synthetic
Barrel: 28 in.
Chokes: 1
Sights: Fiber optic front
Weight: 8 lb. 4 oz.
Gauge: 12
Magazine: 12 shells
Features: Features an extended magazine, TrueTimber Viper Snow camo on the stock; Battleship Gray Cerakote metalwork; 3-in. chamber
Price:. $1165.00

MOSSBERG 940 PRO TURKEY

Action: Semiautomatic
Stock: Synthetic
Barrel: 18.5, 24 in.
Chokes: 1
Sights: Fiber optic front
Weight: 7 lb. 8 oz.
Gauge: 12
Magazine: 4 shells
Features: Equipped with a Compsight fiber optic front sight, the shotgun is optics ready; stock adjustable for length of pull, drop, and cast; vent rib; comes with one X-Factor XX Full turkey choke; full-coverage Mossy Oak Greenleaf
Price:. $1120.00

MOSSBERG 940 PRO WATERFOWL

Action: Semiautomatic
Stock: Synthetic
Barrel: 28 in.
Chokes: 1
Sights: Fiber optic front
Weight: 7 lb. 12 oz.
Gauge: 12
Magazine: 4 shells
Features: Full-coverage TrueTimber Prairie stock; Patriot Brown Cerakote metalwork; TriComp fiber optic front sight; supplied with one X-Factor

extended choke tube; stock is adjustable for length of pull, cast, and drop
Price:. $1092.00

POINTER/LEGACY SPORTS ACRISU CERAKOTE SERIES

Action: Over/under
Stock: Walnut
Barrel: 28 in.
Chokes: 5
Sights: Fiber optic front sight
Weight: 7 lb. 3 oz.
Gauge: 12
Magazine: 2 shells
Features: Budget-friendly upland hunter with a Turkish walnut stock; mechanical trigger; extractors; raised vent rib and side rib; choice of metalwork in Bronze, Gray, or OD Green Cerakote
Price:. $639.00

POINTER/LEGACY SPORTS FIELD TEK 3 CERAKOTE & WOOD SERIES

Action: Semiautomatic
Stock: Walnut
Barrel: 28 in.
Chokes: 5
Sights: Fiber optic front
Weight: 5 lb. 15 oz.–7 lb. 3 oz.
Gauge: 12, 20, .410
Magazine: 4 shells
Features: Gas-operated semiauto with Turkish walnut stock; chrome-lined barrels; vent rib; fiber optic front sight; ventilated recoil pad; choice of Bronze or Gray Cerakote receiver; barrel in polished blue
Price:. $479.00

POINTER/LEGACY SPORTS FIELD TEK 3 CERAKOTE & WOOD SERIES YOUTH

Action: Semiautomatic
Stock: Walnut
Barrel: 26

Chokes: 5
Sights: Fiber optic front
Weight: 5 lb. 13 oz.–6 lb. 3 oz.
Gauge: 20, .410
Magazine: 4 shells
Features: A smaller version of the Pointer Field Tek 3, with a 12.5-in. length of pull and shorter barrel
Price:. $479.00

POINTER/LEGACY SPORTS FIELD TEK 4, FIELD TEK 4 YOUTH

Action: Semiautomatic
Stock: Synthetic
Barrel: 28 in.
Chokes: 5
Sights: Fiber optic front
Weight: 5 lb. 15 oz.–7 lb. 3 oz.
Gauge: 12, 20, .410
Magazine: 4 shells
Features: Gas-operated semi-auto with chrome-lined barrel; vent rib; fiber optic front sight; stock in black, Realthree Max-5, or Mossy Oak Bottomland; cammo stocks have Midnight Bronze Cerakote metalwork; youth versions have shorter, 12.5-in. length of pull, 26-in. barrels, and are only available in Realtree Max-5
Price:. $469.00

POINTER/LEGACY SPORTS FIELD TEK 5 TURKEY, FIELD TEK 5 TURKEY YOUTH

Action: Semiautomatic
Stock: Synthetic
Barrel: 28 in.
Chokes: 5
Sights: Fiber optic front
Weight: 5 lb. 15 oz.–7 lb. 3 oz.
Gauge: 12, 20, .410
Magazine: 4 shells
Features: Similar to the Tek 4, but with a topside Picatinny rail; youth versions have same 12.5-in. length of pull and 26-in. barrel as other Pointer Youth models
Price:. $469.00

NEW Products: Shotguns

POINTER/LEGACY SPORTS SPORT TEK 5 SPORT CLAYS

POINTER/LEGACY SPORTS SPORT TEK 8

POINTER/LEGACY SPORTS SPORT TEK TRAP OVER/UNDER

POINTER/LEGACY SPORTS SPORT TEK TRAP SINGLE BARREL

REMINGTON 870 FIELDMASTER

ROCK ISLAND ARMORY VR80

ROCK ISLAND ARMORY VR80 REALTREE TIMBER

ROCK ISLAND ARMORY VR82

POINTER/LEGACY SPORTS SPORT TEK 5 SPORT CLAYS

Action: Over/under
Stock: Walnut
Barrel: 30 in.
Chokes: 5
Sights: Fiber optic front, mid-rib bead
Weight: N/A
Gauge: 12
Magazine: 2 shells
Features: A nicely priced over/under for sporting clays, with 30-in. chrome-lined barrels; wide vent rib; side ribs; extractors; Turkish walnut stock; blued barrels and receiver with red highlights; extended choke tube set
Price:..................**$669.00**

POINTER/LEGACY SPORTS SPORT TEK 8, SPORT TEK 8 YOUTH

Action: Semiautomatic
Stock: Walnut
Barrel: 28, 30 in.
Chokes: 5
Sights: Fiber optic front, mid-rib bead
Weight: N/A
Gauge: 12, 20
Magazine: 4 shells
Features: Handsome semiauto for the clay games with a 30-in. barrel; squared-back, low-profile receiver in blue with racy red highlights; checkered Turkish walnut stock; wide vent rib; set of 5 extended choke tubes; Youth model has 12.5-in. length of pull and 28-in. barrel
Price:..................**$519.00**

POINTER/LEGACY SPORTS SPORT TEK TRAP OVER/UNDER

Action: Over/under
Stock: Walnut
Barrel: 30 in.
Chokes: 5
Sights: Fiber optic front
Weight: N/A
Gauge: 12
Magazine: 2 shells
Features: Budget-friendly over/under for trap, with an adjustable comb on the Turkish walnut stock; wide vent rib; side ribs; extractors; set of five extended choke tubes
Price:..................**$669.00**

POINTER/LEGACY SPORTS SPORT TEK TRAP SINGLE BARREL

Action: Break-open
Stock: Walnut
Barrel: 30 In.
Chokes: 5
Sights: Fiber optic front
Weight: N/A
Gauge: 12
Magazine: 1 shell
Features: Identical to the over/under Sport Tek Trap but in a single-barrel configuration
Price:..................**$539.00**

REMINGTON 870 FIELDMASTER

Action: Pump
Stock: Walnut
Barrel: 26, 28 in.
Chokes: 3
Sights: Steel bead front
Weight: N/A
Gauge: 12
Magazine: 4 shells
Features: This seems to be the only "new" gun from Remington--under new owner RemArms--that seemed to debut at the 2022 SHOT Show. Word has it the new owners are dumping the 870 Express in favor of the FieldMaster; A-grade walnut stock; fleur-de-lis laser checkering; receiver drilled and tapped; 3-in. chamber
Price:..................**$600.00**

ROCK ISLAND ARMORY VR80

Action: Semiautomatic
Stock: Synthetic
Barrel: 20 in.
Chokes: 3
Sights: Flip-up front and rear
Weight: 7 lb. 7 oz.
Gauge: 12
Magazine: 5 shells
Features: A detachable-magazine-fed AR-type 12-ga. with familiar AR controls; 3-in. chamber; 7075 T6 aluminum upper and lower; fixed thumbhole stock; black anodized finish; left-hand model also available
Price:....**Right-hand $699.00; Left-hand $739.00**

ROCK ISLAND ARMORY VR80 REALTREE

Action: Semiautomatic
Stock: Synthetic
Barrel: 20 in.
Chokes: 3
Sights: None
Weight: 8 lb. 5 oz.
Gauge: 12
Magazine: 5 shells
Features: Dressed in Realtree Timber, this version of the VR80 comes with a Vortex Optics Strikerfire II red-dot optic
Price:..................**$949.00**

ROCK ISLAND ARMORY VR82

Action: Semiautomatic
Stock: Synthetic
Barrel: 18 in.
Chokes: 3
Sights: Flip-up front and rear
Weight: 7 lb. 8 oz.
Gauge: 20
Magazine: 5 shells
Features: A 20-ga. version of the V80 with a slightly shorter 18-in. barrel; black anodized finish; flip-up sights; detachable magazine; fixed thumbhole stock
Price:..................**$729.00**

ROCK ISLAND ARMORY
VRBP-100

ROCK ISLAND
ARMORY VRF14

ROCK ISLAND
ARMORY VRPA40

SAVAGE RENEGAUGE
SECURITY

STANDARD
MANUFACTURING DP-12
PROFESSIONAL

STANDARD
MANUFACTURING
SKO SHORTY WITH
DRUM MAGAZINE

STANDARD
MANUFACTURING SP-12
COMPACT

STANDARD
MANUFACTURING
SP-12 STANDARD

ROCK ISLAND ARMORY VRBP-100

Action: Semiautomatic
Stock: Synthetic
Barrel: 20 in.
Chokes: 3
Sights: Flip-up front and rear
Weight: 7 lb. 15 oz.
Gauge: 12
Magazine: 5 shells
Features: With a bull-pup design, this shotgun has weight to suck up recoil; three rubber buttpad spacers; black anodized and Parkerized finishes; flip-up sights; full-length top rail
Price: **$599.00**

ROCK ISLAND ARMORY VRF-14

Action: Semiautomatic
Stock: Synthetic
Barrel: 14 in.
Chokes: 3
Sights: Flip-up front and rear
Weight: 6 lb. 9 oz.
Gauge: 12
Magazine: 5 shells
Features: A non-NFA, "other" ATF firearm that's a 12-ga. shotgun; plenty of rail top and bottom; nine and 19-round VR mags from Rock Island are compatible
Price: **$599.00**

ROCK ISLAND ARMORY VRPA40

Action: Semiautomatic
Stock: Synthetic
Barrel: 20 in.
Chokes: 3
Sights: Fiber optic front, adjustable rear
Weight: 6 lb. 15 oz.
Gauge: 12
Magazine: 5 shells
Features: A more traditionally styled tactical 12-ga. with detachable magazine; topside Picatinny rail for optics mounting; aluminum heat shield; 3-in. chamber
Price: **$399.00**

SAVAGE ARMS RENEGAUGE SECURITY

Action: Semiautomatic
Stock: Synthetic
Barrel: 18.5 in.
Chokes: 3
Sights: Ghost ring front and rear
Weight: 7 lb.
Gauge: 12
Magazine: 6 shells
Features: Snazzy looking tactical semi-auto with a gray stock; aluminum receiver; ghost ring sights; extended magazine; fluted barrel; D.R.I.V. gas system; stock rod buffer to reduce recoil; easy-load magazine port; Beretta/Benelli-threaded flush-mount chokes in Improved, Modified, and Full
Price: **$1499.00**

STANDARD MANUFACTURING DP-12 PROFESSIONAL

Action: Pump
Stock: Synthetic
Barrel: 18.9 in.
Chokes: 2
Sights: None
Weight: 9 lb. 12 oz.
Gauge: 12
Magazine: 14 shells
Features: A double-barrel pump that fires two shots from a single trigger pull; each barrel has a spreader choke tube with Tru-Choke threads; aircraft-grade aluminum receiver; aluminum front grip with integral laser; full-length topside rail with reflex sight; hand-lapped barrels; heavy-duty magazine followers; hard-anodized finish in black or OD green; soft case and hard case included; handbuilt by master gunsmiths
Price: **$3250.00**

STANDARD MANUFACTURING SKO SHORTY WITH DRUM MAGAZINE

Action: Semiautomatic
Stock: Synthetic
Barrel: 18.9 in.
Chokes: N/A

Sights: None
Weight: 7 lb. 2 oz.
Gauge: 12
Magazine: 25 shells
Features: Machined from aircraft-grade aluminum, internal components are salt-bath nitride-coated; barrel threaed in a Tru-Choke pattern; 3-in. chamber; gas operation; ambidextrous controls; AR-style poymer grip; MOE-slotted composite fore-end with vertical grip; drum mag holds 25 shells, two-, five-, and 10-round magazines also available; last-round bolt hold-open
Price: **$979.00**

STANDARD MANUFACTURING SP-12 COMPACT

Action: Pump
Stock: Synthetic
Barrel: 14. 5 in.
Chokes: N/A
Sights: None
Weight: 5 lb. 12 oz.
Gauge: 12
Magazine: 7 shells
Features: A non-NFA "other" shotgun, this one sports a long topside rail; bird's-head grip; fully ambidextrous configuration; barrel threaded for choke tubes; full-length MLOK rail; handguard with strap
Price: **$799.00**

STANDARD MANUFACTURING SP-12 STANDARD

Action: Pump
Stock: Synthetic
Barrel: 18.5 in.
Chokes: N/A
Sights: None
Weight: 7 lb. 4 oz.
Gauge: 12
Magazine: 7 shells
Features: Similar to the compact, but with a more standardized 18.5-in. barrel; adjustable AR-type stock; 3-in. chamber; aggressively grooved fore-end grip; pistol grip
Price: **$799.00**

STANDARD MANUFACTURING TOROS COPPOLA T4

SYREN ELOS D2

TRISTAR ARMS BRISTOL SIVER

TRISTAR ARMS TT-15 SPORTING

TRISTAR ARMS VIPER G2 CAMO

TRISTAR ARMS VIPER G2 TURKEY

WEATHERBY 18I WATERFOWLER

STANDARD MANUFACTURING TORROS COPPOLA T4

Action: Semiautomatic
Stock: Synthetic
Barrel: 18 in.
Chokes: N/A
Sights: Ghost ring front and rear
Weight: 7 lb. 8 oz.
Gauge: 12
Magazine: 5 shells
Features: A tactical entry made in Turkey, with an M4 platform that has complete component interchangeability with the USMC M4; gas operation; standard M4 screw-in chokes; aluminum receiver; tactical anti-glare matte black metal finish; sling mounts
Price: $899.00

SYREN ELOS D2

Action: Over/under
Stock: Walnut
Barrel: 28 in.
Chokes: 5
Sights: Bead front
Weight: 6 lb. 7 oz.
Gauge: 20, 28
Magazine: 2 shells
Features: Wearing a beautifully figured Turkish walnut stock with a full pistol grip and slightly raised comb; Triwood finish; 6mm vent rib; single-selective trigger; Tribore HP barrels with 3-in. chambers; case-colored receiver with gold game birds; cupplied with INTEGRALE hard case; left-hand available in both gauges
Price: . . . . .$3150.00; Left-hand add $175.00

TRISTAR ARMS BRISTOL, BRISTOL SILVER

Action: Side-by-side
Stock: Walnut
Barrel: 28 in.
Chokes: 5
Sights: Bead front
Weight: 5 lb. 1 oz.–6 lb. 12 oz.
Gauge: 12, 16, 20, 28, .410
Magazine: 2 shells
Features: Side-by-side with choice of case-colored receiver or a nickel finish with 24K gold inlays; brass front bead; single selective trigger; straight-grip English stock of Turkish walnut with an oil finish; ejectors
Price: . Standard $1160.00–$1190.00; Silver $1100.00–$1130.00

TRISTAR ARMS VIPER G2 CAMO

Action: Semiautomatic
Stock: Synthetic
Barrel: 28, 30 in.
Chokes: 3
Sights: Fiber optic front
Weight: 5 lb. 14 oz.–6 lb. 14 oz.
Gauge: 12, 20, .410
Magazine: 5 shells
Features: Full-coverage camo in Realtree Edge or Realtree Max-5; 3-in. chamber; chrome-line barrel; soft-touch areas on grip and fore-arm; vent rib with matte sight plane; gas operation; last round bolt hold open
Price: . . . . $700.00–$740.00

TRISTAR ARMS VIPER G2 TURKEY

Action: Semiautomatic
Stock: Synthetic
Barrel: 24 in.
Chokes: 4
Sights: Fiber optic front
Weight: 6 lb.–6 lb. 14 oz.

Gauge: 12, 20, .410
Magazine: 5 shells
Features: Pistol-grip stock with full-coverage Mossy Oak Bottomland camo; Midnight Bronze Cerakote metal; topside Picatinny rail
Price: . . . . $730.00–$790.00

TRISTAR ARMS TT-15 SPORTING

Action: Over/under
Stock: Walnut
Barrel: 30 in.
Chokes: 5
Sights: Fiber optic front, mid-rib bead
Weight: 7 lb. 15 oz.
Gauge: 12
Magazine: 2 shells
Features: Good-looking over/under for clay sports, with fiber optic front sight and a mid-rib bead; chrome-lined barrels and chamber; ported barrels; Turkish walnut stock; wide target rib; single selective trigger; engraved nickel receiver; set of five extended choke tubes
Price: $1085.00

WEATHERBY 18I WATERFOWLER

Action: Semiautomatic
Stock: Synthetic
Barrel: 28 in.
Chokes: 5
Sights: Fiber optic front
Weight: 7 lb.
Gauge: 12
Magazine: 4 shells
Features: Choice of full-coverage camo in Mossy Oak Bottomland, Mossy Oak Shadow Grass Blades, Realtree Max-5, or Realtree Timber; elastomer stock helps reduce recoil; vent rib; chrome-line bore; 3.5-in. chamber; LPA fiber optic front sight
Price: . . . . $1239..00–$1249.00

AMERICAN TACTICAL
FXH

ANGSTADT ARMS
MDP-9

AREX DEFENSE DELTA
GEN2 TACTICAL

AREX DEFENSE
ZERO 2S

ARMSCOR/ROCK
ISLAND ARMORY
AL3.1

ARMSCOR/ROCK ISLAND
ARMORY AL9.0

ARMSCOR/ROCK ISLAND
ARMORY AL22M

AMERICAN TACTICAL FIREPOWER XTREME HYBRID 1911, HYBRID COMPACT 1911 (FXH SERIES)

Action: Semiautomatic
Grips: Synthetic
Barrel: 5, 4.25 in.
Sights: Fiber optic front, notch rear
Weight: 27.5 oz.
Caliber: .45 ACP
Capacity: 8 rounds
Features: A full-size and Commander-size pair of 1911s that have polymer frames with two metal inserts that add stability; built-in finger grooves; optics-ready steel slide accepts Glock sights, has aggressive serrations in the rear, and has lightning cuts; underside accessory rail; match-grade barrel; skeletonized trigger adjustable for over-travel; accpets standard 1911 magazines; offered in all black or with a two-tone flat dark earth frame/black slide
Price: $599.95

ANGSTADT ARMS MDP-9

Action: Semiautomatic
Grips: Synthetic
Barrel: 5.85 in.
Sights: None
Weight: 3 lb. 9 oz.
Caliber: 9mm
Capacity: 10, 15, 17 rounds
Features: A roller-delayed blowback on an AR-compatible foundation; utlizes all Glock double-stack 9mm magazines; can be comfortably carried concealed via a sling or in a backpack; non-reciprocating forward charging handle; plenty of topside rail; monolithic upper; SB side-folding, telescopic pistol brace option; available in black, flat dark earth and Tactical Gray
Price: $2,599.00

AREX DEFENSE DELTA GEN.2 TACTICAL

Action: Semiautomatic
Grips: Synthetic
Barrel: 4.6 in.
Sights: High-profile sights
Weight: 18.5 oz.
Caliber: 9mm
Capacity: 15, 17 rounds
Features: A very lightweight carry with a threaded, suppressor-ready barrel; high-profile sights; extremely aggressive slide serrations front and rear; extended magazine release button; accessory rail; optics-ready slide; modular frame design with front and rear inserts that can be customized; interchangeable backstraps
Price: . . . . N/A

AREX DEFENSE ZERO 2 S

Action: Semiautomatic
Grips: Synthetic
Barrel: 4.2 in.
Sights: Three-dot white sights
Weight: 32 oz.
Caliber: 9mm
Capacity: 18, 20 rounds
Features: Arex improves on 2021's model with redesigned, low-profile magazine release button; generous magazine capacity; aggressive slide serrations; underside accessory rail; extended magwell bevel; reengineered wraparound grip panel
Price: . . . . N/A

ARMSCOR/ROCK ISLAND ARMORY AL3.0, AL3.1

Action: Revolver
Grips: Rubber
Barrel: 2 in.
Sights: Low-profile ramp front, integral notch rear
Weight: 32 oz.
Caliber: .357 Mag.
Capacity: 6 rounds

Features: Nice choice for those who prefer a wheelgun for self-defense, with enough weight to handle a .357 round better than others; low-profile front ramp sight; traditional single-/double-action; textured rubber grips with finger groove; 3.1 is in stainless, 3.0 is blue
Blued $699.00
Stainless. $799.00

ARMSCOR/ROCK ISLAND ARMORY AL9.0

Action: Revolver
Grips: Rubber
Barrel: 3 in.
Sights: Ramp front, adjustable rear
Weight: 32 oz.
Caliber: 9mm
Capacity: 6 rounds
Features: Nicely balanced 9mm revolver for target shooting or home-/self-defense with a polished blue finish; textured rubber grip with finger grooves; full barrel shroud
Price: $699.00

ARMSCOR/ROCK ISLAND ARMORY AL22, AL22M

Action: Revolver
Grips: Rubber
Barrel: 4 in.
Sights: Fixed ramp front, adjustable rear
Weight: 38.4 oz.
Caliber: .22 LR, .22 Mag.
Capacity: 8, 9 rounds
Features: A generously sized rimfire revolver for a superb target-shooting experience; all-steel construction; soft rubber grips with finger grooves; ramp front sight with orange insert; in stainless or blue; M-designated models are in .22 Mag and have eight-round capacities
Price: $499.00

ARMSCOR/ROCK ISLAND ARMORY M206

ARMSCOR/ROCK ISLAND ARMORY ARMSCOR PRO ULTRA MATCH HC

ARMSCOR/ROCK ISLAND ARMORY ARMSCOR STK100

ARMSCOR/ROCK ISLAND ARMORY ARMSCOR TCM STANDARD FS HC

ARSENAL INC BS-1 BRIEFCASE

AUTO ORDNANCE OLD GLORY

ARSENAL INC KNIFE WITH INTERNAL SHOOTING MECHANISM

AUTO ORDNANCE BOOTLEGGER 1911

ARMSCOR/ROCK ISLAND ARMORY M206

Action: Revolver
Grips: Wood
Barrel: 2 in.
Sights: Low-profile ramp front, integral notch rear
Weight: 24 oz.
Caliber: .38 Spec.
Capacity: 6 rounds
Features: Pretty CCW revolver with a matte nickel finish; concealed hammer; bird's-head-type wood grips with checkering
Price:. $369.00

ARMSCOR/ROCK ISLAND ARMORY ARMSCOR PRO ULTRA MATCH HC

Action: Semiautomatic
Grips: G10
Barrel: 5 in.
Sights: Fiber optic front, adjustable rear
Weight: 48 oz.
Caliber: 9mm, .40 S&W
Capacity: 10, 16, 17 rounds
Features: A full-size 2011-style 9mm for speed games with a generous accessory rail and Picatinny rail underside; front and rear slide serrations; beveled mag well; adjustable rear sight; skeletonized trigger and hammer
Price:. $1,099.00

ARMSCOR/ROCK ISLAND ARMORY ARMSCOR STK100

Action: Semiautomatic
Grips: Aluminum
Barrel: 4.5 in.
Sights: Fixed front and rear
Weight: 28.8 oz.
Caliber: 9mm
Capacity: 10 rounds
Features: The first striker-fire from Armscor, with an aluminum grip frame that's highly textured on front, sides, and back; billet machined slide with lightning cuts and serrations; fixed rear sight on the included optics plate; Picatinny accessory rail; extended beavertail
Price:. $599.00

ARMSCOR/ROCK ISLAND ARMORY ARMSCOR TCM STANDARD FS HC

Action: Semiautomatic
Grips: Synthetic
Barrel: 5 in.
Sights: Fiber optic front, adjustable rear
Weight: 40 oz.
Caliber: .22 TCM
Capacity: 10, 17 rounds
Features: A 1911-style semiauto chambered for the .22 TCM; Parkerized finish; double-stack magwell; adjustable over-travel stop
Price:. $749.00

ARSENAL INC BS-1 BRIEFCASE

Action: Revolver
Grips: Synthetic
Barrel: N/A
Sights: None
Weight: 16 oz.
Caliber: .22 Short
Capacity: 6 rounds
Features: Introduced a few years ago, this isn't truly new for 2022, but too cool to leave out now that we've discovered it; aluminum briefcase is fully functional, with dual combination locks; .22 Short revolver concealed in the handle; NFA Any Other Weapon taxes and paperwork apply
Price:. $7,499.00

ARSENAL INC KNIFE WITH INTERNAL SHOOTING MECHANISM

Action: Revolver
Grips: Synthetic
Barrel: N/A
Sights: None
Weight: 16 oz.
Caliber: .22 Short
Capacity: 6 rounds
Features: This also isn't new for 2022, having been introduced a few years ago but, like the briefcase, we though it was cool enough to add in; barrel and cylinder concealed in the knife handle; a rotating trigger release mechanism aligns the trigger for proper index finger manipulation; NFA Any Other Weapon paperwork and taxes apply
Price:. $7,499.00

AUTO ORDNANCE BOOTLEGGER 1911

Action: Semiautomatic
Grips: Walnut
Barrel: 5 in.
Sights: Blade front, adjustable rear
Weight: 36.8 oz.
Caliber: .45 ACP
Capacity: 7 rounds
Features: This is part of a pair of Bootlegger's offered by Auto-Ordnance, the other half a Thompson model; Distressed Bronze Cerakote metalwork; slide is marked with "Bootlegger Prohibiiton Edition" and "Proof Tennessee Moonshine;" walnut grips and some metal have scrollwork
Price:. $1,215.00

AUTO ORDNANCE OLD GLORY 1911

Action: Semiautomatic
Grips: Aluminum
Barrel: 5 in.
Sights: Truglo night sights
Weight: 36.8 oz.
Caliber: .45 ACP
Capacity: 7 rounds
Features: Paying tribute to the original American flag, "Old Glory" is emlazoned in vintage script across the slide and upper frame on the left side; "I'm Mighty Proud of that Ragged Old Flag" appears on the right side of the slide and upper frame; finished in Distressed Burnt Bronze Cerkote; aluminum grip panels with "76," "USA," and stars and stripes; match-grade barrel; adjustable trigger; skeletonized hammer; night sights; flared ejection port; checkered front strap and mainspring housing
Price:. $1,785.00

AUTO ORDNANCE RALLY CRY

AUTO ORDNANCE UNITED WE STAND

BERETTA 92X PERFORMANCE DEFENSIVE

BERETTA 92X RDO COMPACT

BERETTA M9A4 CENTURION

BERETTA M9A4 FULL SIZE

BOND ARMS CUB

BOND ARMS GRIZZLY

AUTO ORDNANCE RALLY CRY 1911

Action: Semiautomatic
Grips: Aluminum
Barrel: 5 in.
Sights: Truglo night sights
Weight: 36.8 oz.
Caliber: .45 ACP
Capacity: 7 rounds
Features: No one would ever doubt Auto-Ordnance/Kahr Group's devotion to Donald Trump, with yet another model commemorating his administration (and no doubt hoping for a second); engraved by Outlaw Ordnance artists with depictions of MAGA rallies, American flag imageru, and Trump's portrait; finished in black Cerakote with a clear gold-flake Cerakote overlay; extended magazine release; adjustable trigger; match-grade barrel; checkered front strap and mainspring housing
Price:. $1,535.00

AUTO ORDNANCE UNITED WE STAND 1911

Action: Semiautomatic
Grips: Aluminum
Barrel: 5 in.
Sights: Truglo night sights
Weight: 36.8 oz.
Caliber: .45 ACP
Capacity: 7 rounds
Features: Calling on America to stand together, this 1911 sports a Bible verse from the book of Mathew engraved on the slide along with "United We Stand; Statue of Liberty image and "In God We Trust" appear on the aluminum grip panels; unique slide serrations; checkered front strap and mainspring housing; adjustable trigger; match-grade barrel; Black Armor Cerakote; flared ejection port
Price:. $1,849.00

BERETTA 92X PERFORMANCE DEFENSIVE

Action: Semiautomatic

Grips: Polymer
Barrel: 4.9 in.
Sights: Fiber optic front, adjustable rear
Weight: 42.7 oz.
Caliber: 9mm
Capacity: 10, 15 rounds
Features: Designed for IDPA competition, this sleek 92X is optics ready and sports a non-decocking frame-mounted safety; slimline grips; lightened steel slide and frame; front strap and backstrap checkering; sawtooth front and rear slide serrations; skeletonized hammer; adjustable trigger; Nistan finish
Price:. $1,649.00

BERETTA 92X RDO COMPACT

Action: Semiautomatic
Grips: Polymer
Barrel: 4.25 in.
Sights: Orange dot front, notch rear
Weight: 27.2 oz.
Caliber: 9mm
Capacity: 10 rounds
Features: A compact, optics-ready carry gun with front and rear slide serrations; high-visibility orange dot front sight; decocker safety convertible to decock-only; slimline and wraparound grips; Picatinny accessory rail
Price:. $729.00

BERETTA M9A4 CENTURION

Action: Semiautomatic
Grips: Polymer
Barrel: 5.1 in.
Sights: Three-dot night sights
Weight: 33.4 oz.
Caliber: 9mm
Capacity: 10, 15, 18 rounds
Features: A very updated 92 in a Centurion configuration with a unique vertical backstrap; wear-resistant flat dark earth finish; slimline, stippled grips; decoker-only slide; undeside Picatinny rail; optics plate and

removeable front sight; oversized magazine release button
Price:. $1,099.00

BERETTA M9A4 FULL-SIZE

Action: Semiautomatic
Grips: Polymer
Barrel: 5.1 in.
Sights: Three-dot night sights
Weight: 33.4 oz.
Caliber: 9mm
Capacity: 10, 15, 18 rounds
Features: A very updated 92 with a unique vertical backstrap; wear-resistant flat dark earth finish; slimline, stippled grips; decoker-only slide; undeside Picatinny rail; optics plate and removeable front sight; oversized magazine release button
Price:. $1,099.00

BOND ARMS CUB

Action: Derringer
Grips: Rubber
Barrel: 2.5 in.
Sights: Blade front, integral rear
Weight: 19 oz.
Caliber: .38 Spec./.357 Mag.
Capacity: 2 rounds
Features: A tiny flip-barrel two-shot with rubber grips; stainless steel barrels and frame; automatic extractor; cross-bolt safety
Price:. $541.00

BOND ARMS GRIZZLY

Action: Derringer
Grips: Rosewood
Barrel: 3 in.
Sights: Blade front, integral rear
Weight: 20 oz.
Caliber: .45 LC/.410-bore
Capacity: 2 rounds
Features: With a three-inch barrel that accommodates both .45 LC and .410 shotshells, this flip-barrel has checkered rosewood grips with a pinkie extension and an relief of a grizzly bear
Price:. $377.00

NEW Products: **Handguns**

BROWNING BUCK MARK HUNTER 5.9

BROWNING BUCK MARK MEDALLION ROSEWOOD VORTEX RED DOT

BROWNING BUCK MARK VISION BLACK/GOLD SUPPRESSOR READY VORTEX RED DOT

BRÜGGER & THOMET SPC9-PDW

CABOT GUNS NERO

CABOT GUNS SERENITY

CANIK USA METE SFT

BROWNING BUCK MARK HUNTER 5.9

Action: Semiautomatic
Grips: Laminate
Barrel: 5.9 in.
Sights: Fiber optic front sight, adjustable rear
Weight: 40.96 oz.
Caliber: .22 LR
Capacity: 10 rounds
Features: A longer-barreled rimfire for hunters with a matte blue bull barrel; lamimated target grips; includes Vortex Crossfire red-dot optic with co-witnessed sights; threaded on ported muzzle accessory
Price:..................$839.99

BROWNING BUCK MARK MEDALLION ROSEWOOD VORTEX RED DOT

Action: Semiautomatic
Grips: Laminate
Barrel: 5.5 in.
Sights: Fiber optic front sight, adjustable rear
Weight: 39 oz.
Caliber: .22 LR
Capacity: 10 rounds
Features: Wearing laminate grip that are checkered and have a rosewood color this rimfire comes with a Vortex Crossfire red-dot sight with co-witnessed irons; slab-sided barrel with polished flats
Price:..................$869.99

BROWNING BUCK MARK VISION BLACK/GOLD SUPPRESSOR READY VORTEX RED DOT

Action: Semiautomatic
Grips: Composite
Barrel: 5.87 in.
Sights: Fiber optic front sight, adjustable rear
Weight: 31 oz.
Caliber: .22 LR
Capacity: 10 rounds

Features: A snazzy rimfire with a steel-sleeved barrel in a Gold Cerakoted aluminum sleeve; aluminum frame; UFX grips with rubber overmolding; threaded barrel with muzzle brake; Vortex Crossfire red-dot sight with co-witnessing iron sights
Price:..................$979.99

BRÜGGER & THOMET SPC9-PDW

Action: Semiautomatic
Grips: Synthetic
Barrel: 4.5 in.
Sights: None
Weight: 88 oz.
Caliber: 9mm
Capacity: 10, 30, 30 rounds
Features: A personal defense weapon with a non-reciprocating charging handle; ambidextrous AR-type controls; topside Picatinny rail; three-lug muzzle adaptor; telescipic shoulder brace; flip-up sights; takes Glock magazines
Price:...............$2,523.00

CABOT GUNS NERO

Action: Semiautomatic
Grips: G10
Barrel: 4.25, 5 in.
Sights: Fiber optic front, ledge rear
Weight: N/A
Caliber: 9mm, .45 ACP
Capacity: 8, 9 rounds
Features: Top-notch defensive pistol in choice of two calibers and two hand-fit, crown-cut, match-fit barrel lengths; 13-degree front and rear slid serrations as well as top of slide serrations; rhombus-cut front strap and mainspring housing checkering; "idiot-scratch-proof" slide stop; integral frame rail; reverse dovetail fiber optic front sight in red; ledge rear sight designed by master gunsmith Rob Schauland; machined in place "perfect fit" ejector; Plasma Black Diamond Like carbon finish with proprietary hardening
Price:........ **Starting at $5295.00**

CABOT GUNS SERENITY

Action: Semiautomatic
Grips: Steel
Barrel: 4.25, 5 in.
Sights: Blade front, ledge rear
Weight: N/A
Caliber: 9mm, .45 ACP
Capacity: 8, 9 rounds
Features: Super-sleek 1911 in choice of Commander or full-size configurations; slide of Damascus steel, deep-etched and polished; unusual, completely smooth stainless grips; Big Bang cocking serrations; hand-fit, crown-cut, match-grade barrel; integral frame rail; rhombus-cut, 24 lines-per-inch checkering on front strap and backstrap; one-piece extended mag well and mainspring housing; lowered and flared ejection port
Price:........ **Starting at $8495.00**

CANIK USA METE SFT

Action: Semiautomatic
Grips: Synthetic
Barrel: 4.5 in.
Sights: Three-dot white sights
Weight: 27.8 oz.
Caliber: 9mm
Capacity: 18, 20 rounds
Features: A gun for gamers and serious self-defense practitioners, with an angled rear sight edge to aid with weak- and one-handed operation; optics- and co-witness sights-ready slide in Tungsten Grey Cerakote; short reset trigger; underside Picatinny rail; match-grade barrel; loaded chamber indicator; interchangeable backstraps; front and rear slide serrations; reversible magazine release; textured side, rear, and front grip panels; comes with 18- and 20-round magazines, hard case, EZ loader, reversible IWB/OWB holster; two optics bases, cleaning kit
Price:..................$519.99

CANIK USA METE SFX

CANIK USA TP9DA

CANIK USA SFX RIVAL

CANIK USA SIGNATURE SERIES TP9SFX WHITEOUT

CANIK USA TP9SA MOD.2

CANIK USA TP9 ELITE COMBAT EXECUTIVE

CANIK USA TP9SF

CANIK USA METE SFX

Action: Semiautomatic
Grips: Synthetic
Barrel: 5.2
Sights: Three-dot white sights
Weight: 30 oz.
Caliber: 9mm
Capacity: 18, 20 rounds
Features: Similar to the SFT, but with a longer barrel and lightning cuts on the top of the slide to aid with cooling and reduce weight
Price: $574.99

CANIK USA SFX RIVAL

Action: Semiautomatic
Grips: Synthetic
Barrel: 5 in.
Sights: Fiber optic front, adjustable rear
Weight: 29.5 oz.
Caliber: 9mm
Capacity: 18 rounds
Features: Striker-fire, optics-read pistol designed for competition, with a lightened, 90-degree diamond-cut, aluminum flat trigger; ambidextrous slide release; reversible magazine release; double undercut trigger guard; texturing on front, back, and sides of grip; slide has both front and rear serrations and lightning cuts; in Canik Rival Grey with gold Cerakote accents or allover Canik Rival Dark Side; comes with a custom holster, two magazines with aluminum base plates; magazine loader, three interchangeable backstraps; three magazine release extensions; additional front sight fiber optics; four optics plats on the Rival, five for the Rival Dark Side
Price: $679.99

CANIK USA SIGNATURE SERIES TP9SFX WHITEOUT

Action: Semiautomatic
Grips: Synthetic
Barrel: 5.2 in.
Sights: Fiber optic front, black-out rear

Weight: 30.7 oz.
Caliber: 9mm
Capacity: 18, 21 rounds
Features: Neato-keen, optics-ready striker-fire in Whiteout Cerakote, with interchangeable backstraps; IWB/OWB holster; Warren tactical sights; red striker set indicator; extended tactical slide release; extended reversible magazine release; limited run of 7,500; comes with Signature Series storage and transportation box
Price: $769.99

CANIK USA TP9 ELITE COMBAT EXECUTIVE

Action: Semiautomatic
Grips: Synthetic
Barrel: 4.73 in.
Sights: Fiber optic front, black-out rear
Weight: 28.5 oz.
Caliber: 9mm
Capacity: 15, 18
Features: Sharp-looking carry or games gun with a gold barrel by Salient that is fluted, match-grade, suppressor-ready, and has a PVD-over-nitride coating; nitride-coated jet black slide is optics ready; aluminum Speed Funnel mag well; plus-3 magazine extensions; flat-faced aluminum Canik Enhanced Trigger set to 4.8-lb.; underside Picatinny rail; comes with a retention holster
Price: $779.99

CANIK USA TP9DA

Action: Semiautomatic
Grips: Synthetic
Barrel: 4 in.
Sights: White dot front, blackout U-notch rear
Weight: 27.8 oz.
Caliber: 9mm
Capacity: 18 rounds
Features: A striker-fire with true double-action/single-action performance, including a external de-cocker topside that also serves as

the disassembly button; interchangeable backstraps; match-grade barrel; Warren tactical sights; underside accessory rail; in black nitride on a black frame or Burnt Bronze Cerakote over nitride with a bronze frame
Price: $404.99

CANIK USA TP9SA MOD.2

Action: Semiautomatic
Grips: Synthetic
Barrel: 4.5 in.
Sights: White dot front, blackout U-notch rear
Weight: 28.5 oz.
Caliber: 9mm
Capacity: 18 rounds
Features: Canik claims this model has a very smooth single-action trigger; top-side decocker is also the disassembly button; interchangeable backstraps; Warren tactical sights; match-grade barrel; underside accessory rail; in black or flat dark earth; comes with patented holster and two magazines
Price: $379.99

CANIK USA TP9SF

Action: Semiautomatic
Grips: Synthetic
Barrel: 4.5 in.
Sights: White dot front, blackout U-notch rear
Weight: 28.5 oz.
Caliber: 9mm
Capacity: 18, 20 rounds
Features: In nitride black or Cerakote Flat Dark Earth with black highlight points, this good-looking and durable carry gun comes with two 18-round magazines; 20-round magazines from Canik also fit; interchangeable backstraps; Warren tactical sights; match-grade barrel; underside accesssory rail; reversible magazine release; premium Canik trigger; includes Canik holster
Price: $399.99

NEW Products: **Handguns**

CANIK USA TP9SF ELITE

CHARLES DALY 1911 EMPIRE GRADE

CHARLES DALY SUPERIOR 1911 SUPERIOR GRADE

CHARTER ARMS BOXER

CHIAPPA 30DS NEBULA

CHRISTENSEN ARMS MPP

CIMARRON FIREARMS ANGEL EYES

CANIK USA TP9SF ELITE

Action: Semiautomatic
Grips: Synthetic
Barrel: 4.2 in.
Sights: Fiber optic front, black-out rear
Weight: 28.3 oz.
Caliber: 9mm
Capacity: 15 rounds
Features: A medium-sized gunin the TP9 family with an ambidexterous slide release; reversible magazine catch; Warrant tactical sights with a fiber optic front; match-grade barrel; interchangeable backstraps; comes with carrying case, holster, speed-loader, and two MecGar magazines
Price:.................$429.99

CHARLES DALY 1911 EMPIRE GRADE

Action: Semiautomatic
Grips: G10
Barrel: 5 in.
Sights: Blade front, adjustable rear
Weight: 41.1 oz.
Caliber: .45 ACP
Capacity: 8 rounds
Features: Classy Gov't.-sized 1911 with adjustable target sights; steel frame; chrome finish; G10 grip panels; narrow front and rear slide serrations; skeletonized hammer and trigger; flat mainspring housing
Price:.................$999.00

CHARLES DALY 1911 SUPERIOR GRADE

Action: Semiautomatic
Grips: Rubber
Barrel: 5 in.
Sights: Fiber optic front, two-dot rear
Weight: 41.1 oz.
Caliber: .45 ACP
Capacity: 8 rounds
Features: Full-size Gov't. 1911 similar to the Empire but with wider slide serrations; checkered black rubber grip panels; low-profile three-dot Novak sights; includes two magazines and cleaning kit
Price:.................$769.00

CHARTER ARMS BOXER

Action: Revolver
Grips: Rubber
Barrel: 2.2 in.
Sights: Fiber optic front, notch rear
Weight: 16 oz.
Caliber: .38 Spec.
Capacity: 6 rounds
Features: This is a reconfiguration of the five-shot .44 Special Bulldog model, now in a six-shot .38 Special revolver on an aluminum frame
Price:.................$357.00

CHIAPPA RHINO 30DS NEBULA, 30 SAR NEBULA

Action: Revolver
Grips: Laminate
Barrel: 3 in.
Sights: Fiber optic front, adjustable rear
Weight: 27.2 oz.
Caliber: .357 Mag.
Capacity: 6 rounds
Features: With very cool blue laminate grips and the unique rainbow finish of the Nebula line, this revolver has a red fiber optic front sight paired with an adjustable green fiber optic rear for superior contrast; machined 7075-T6 alloy frame; steel barrel and cylinder; includes three moon clips, gun lock, and holster; SAR is California-compliant
Price:............... $1,912.00

CHRISTENSEN ARMS MPP

Action: Bolt
Grips: Aluminum
Barrel: 7.5, 10.5, 12.5 in.
Sights: None
Weight: 4 lb. 7 oz.
Caliber: .300 BLK, .223 Rem., 6.5 Creedmoor, .308 Win.
Capacity: 10 rounds
Features: MPP stands for Modern Precision Pistol; Chirstensen Arms' own 7075 billet aluminum pistol chassis; twin-lug spiral-fluted bolt with oversized bolt knob and skeletonized bolt handle; M16-style extractor; TriggerTech flat trigger; enlarged ejection port; forward-mount Picatinny rail with barricade stop; MLOK fore-end; QD flushcup mounts; button-rifled, hand-lapped, free-floating carbon fiber-wrapped barrel with a target profile, threaded and with a match chamber; stabilizing brace; .300 BLK has 7.5-in. barrel, .223 Rem. has 10.5-in. barrel, and 6.5 Creedmoor and .308 Win. have 12.5-in. barrel
Price:............... $2,399.99

CIMARRON FIREARMS ANGEL EYES

Action: Revolver
Grips: Walnut
Barrel: 8 in.
Sights: Post front
Weight: N/A
Caliber: .45 LC/.44 Percussion
Capacity: 6 rounds
Features: A replica of the 1858 Remington firearm from the movie The Good, The Bad, and The Ugly, this conversion revolver has fixed sights; two-piece walnut grips; case-hardened frame and hammer with laser engraved borders
Price:.................$662.84

CIMARRON FIREARMS DOC HOLLIDAY

CIMARRON FIREARMS MAN WITH NO NAME CONVERSION

CIMARRON FIREARMS ROOSTER SHOOTER

COLT PYTHON 3-IN.

CZ-USA P10-F COMPETITION READY

CZ-USA P-10 M

CZ-USA P-10 M

EAA GIRSEN MCP35

EAA GIRSAN REGARD MC BX

CIMARRON FIREARMS DOC HOLLIDAY THUNDERER

Action: Revolver
Grips: True Ivory
Barrel: 3.5 in.
Sights: Blade front, integral notch rear
Weight: 39.8 oz.
Caliber: .45 LC
Capacity: 6 rounds
Features: Short-barreled single action with Tru Ivory grips in a bird's head configuration; polished stainless steel metalwok; "Doc Holliday" engraved on backstrap
Price: **$1,155.20**

CIMARRON FIREARMS MAN WITH NO NAME CONVERSION

Action: Revolver
Grips: Walnut
Barrel: 7.5 in.
Sights: Brass bead front, notch rear
Weight: 48.8 oz.
Caliber: .38 Spec.
Capacity: 6 rounds
Features: Replica of the 1851 Navy Conversion that often appeared in Spaghetti Westerns; steel case-hardened frame; walnut grips with silver coiled snake inlay and brass backstrap; unadorned wood grip version also available; brass triggerguard; takes modern smokeless powder .38 Spec. or .38 S&W Spec. ammo;
Plain grips **$630.12**
Snake inlay grips **$882.74**

CIMARRON FIREARMS ROOSTER SHOOTER

Action: Revolver
Grips: Synthetic
Barrel: 4.75 in.
Sights: Blade front, integral notch rear
Weight: 39.7 oz.
Caliber: .45 LC
Capacity: 6 rounds

Features: Cimarron claims the material for the orange grips hadn't been made in 50 years and had to have it remade; grips have finger grooves; replica of the revolver carried by John Wayne in movies such as True Grit and Rooster Cogburn; no-blue original finish
Price: **$1,010.72**

COLT PYTHON 3-IN.

Action: Revolver
Grips: Wood
Barrel: 3 in.
Sights: Ramp front, adjustable rear
Weight: 40 oz.
Caliber: .357 Mag.
Capacity: 6 rounds
Features: With Colt's the only thing ever new is the old, and for 2022 the company brings back the Python with a 3-in. barrel; orange insert front ramp sight with adjustable rear; recessed target crown; checkered walnut grips; stainless steel frame with 30-percent more steel below the rear sight improves this revolver's strength
Price: **$1,499.00**

CZ-USA P-10 F COMPETITION READY

Action: Semiautomatic
Grips: Synthetic
Barrel: 5 in.
Sights: Fiber optic front, notch rear
Weight: 30 oz.
Caliber: 9mm
Capacity: 19 rounds
Features: CZ's full-size P-10 F frame provides the foundation for generous capacity; longer barrel than other P-10 Fs provides a longer sight radius; extended magazine release and slide release; HB Industries trigger; optics-ready slide; gold accents; three included magazines have Henning Group aluminum bases
Price: **$1,009.00**

CZ-USA P-10 M

Action: Semiautomatic
Grips: Synthetic
Barrel: 3.19 in.
Sights: Three dot white front and rear
Weight: 20.1 oz.
Caliber: 9mm
Capacity: 7 rounds
Features: A compact carry gun with a fiber-reinforced polymer frame; internal slide release prevents snagging on clothing when drawing from a holster; single takedown pin for easy disassembly; underside rail for small accessories
Price: **$505.00**

EAA GIRSAN MCP35

Action: Semiautomatic
Grips: Synthetic
Barrel: 4.8 in.
Sights: Three-dot white front and rear
Weight: 28.8 oz.
Caliber: 9mm
Capacity: 15 rouds
Features: If you think this looks an awful lot like a Browning Hi-Power, you wouldn't be wrong; 15-round capacity; steel frame and slide; short trigger reset; ambidextrous safety; available in black, flat dark earth, or two-tone
Price: **$528.00**

EAA GIRSAN REGARD MC BX

Action: Semiautomatic
Grips: G10
Barrel: 5 in.
Sights: Three-dot white front and rear
Weight: 33.6 oz.
Caliber: 9mm
Capacity: 18 rounds
Features: Modeled on the legendary Beretta Model 92, this Girsan tak features G10 grips; threaded barrel; slide-mounted ambidextrous decocker; underside accessory rail blued/black finish or flat dark earth
Price: **$588.00**

NEW Products: **Handguns**

EAA GIRSAN REGARD MC DELUXE

EAA GIRSAN REGARD MC SPORT GEN 4

EAA GIRSAN MC1911 GOLD LUX

EAA GIRSAN MC1911 LUX

EAA GIRSAN MC1911 NOEL

EAA GIRSAN MC1911 SC ULTIMATE

EAA GIRSAN MC28 SA

EAA GIRSAN MC28 SA-TV

EAA GIRSAN REGARD MC DELUXE

Action: Semiautomatic
Grips: G10
Barrel: 5 in.
Sights: Blade front, notch rear
Weight: 33.6 oz.
Caliber: 9mm
Capacity: 18 rounds
Features: With a polished gold finish and hand engraving over the slide and forged aluminum frame, this 92-type pistol also has finger grips; underside accessory rail; slide-mounted safety/decocker
Price: $745.00

EAA GIRSAN REGARD MC SPORT GEN 3, GEN 4

Action: Semiautomatic
Grips: G10
Barrel: 4.9 in.
Sights: Blade front, notch rear
Weight: 34.4 oz.
Caliber: 9mm
Capacity: 18 rounds
Features: Featuring both windowed G10 grips (choice of blue or gray) and windowed magazines, you'll never lose count of your on-board rounds; Gen 3 has frame-mounted thumb safety; Gen 4 has slide-mounted decocker/safety; both generations have slide serrations, oversized magazine releases, and underside accessory rail; Gen 3 also available optics-ready and equipped with Far Dot reflex red-dot sight
Gen 4 . . . .$594.00
Gen 3 . . . . $$631.00–$653.00

EAA GIRSAN MC1911 GOLD LUX

Action: Semiautomatic
Grips: G10
Barrel: 5 in.
Sights: Blade front, adjustable rear

Weight: 40.8 oz.
Caliber: .45 ACP
Capacity: 8 rounds
Features: Gov't-sized 1911-type pistol with a flashy gold and hand engraved finish; black G10 grips with swirl design; skeletonized hammer and trigger; flat mainspring housing
Price: $1,297.00

EAA GIRSAN MC1911 LUX

Action: Semiautomatic
Grips: Synthetic
Barrel: 5 in.
Sights: Blade front, adjustable rear
Weight: 40.8 oz.
Caliber: .45 ACP
Capacity: 8 rounds
Features: Similar to the MC1911 Gold Lux but in a polished blue finish; engravings on slide and frame; Ivory Lite grips; custom carry case included
Price: $1,133.00

EAA GIRSAN MC1911 NOEL

Action: Semiautomatic
Grips: G10
Barrel: 5 in.
Sights: Fiber optic front, adjustable rear
Weight: 40.8 oz.
Caliber: .45 ACP
Capacity: 8 rounds
Features: Finished in what EAA calls Wonder, which appears to be a matte medium gray, this pistol has complimentary gray-striped G10 grips; thumb-shield safety; skeletonized competition trigger
Price: $952.00

EAA GIRSAN MC1911 SC ULTIMATE

Action: Semiautomatic
Grips: G10
Barrel: 3.4 in.
Sights: Blade front, adjustable rear

Weight: 25.6 oz.
Caliber: 9mm, .45 ACP
Capacity: 6, 7 rounds
Features: Officer-sized 1911 with windowed G10 grips and magazine; in black or flat dark earth finish; optional optics-ready slide equipped with Far Dot red-dot sight; frame-mounted thumb shield safety
Price: . . . . $732.00–$855.00

EAA GIRSAN MC28 SA

Action: Semiautomatic
Grips: Synthetic
Barrel: 4.25 in.
Sights: Blade front, notch rear
Weight: 28.8 oz.
Caliber: 9mm
Capacity: 17 rounds
Features: A double-stack striker fire with a forward-angled grip frame; Novak-style rear sight; underside accessory rail; rear slide serrations; interchangeable backstrap set
Price: $376.00

EAA GIRSAN MC28 SA-TV, SA-TV-BX

Action: Semiautomatic
Grips: Synthetic
Barrel: 4.25 in.
Sights: Three dot front and rear, adjustable rear
Weight: 28.8 oz.
Caliber: 9mm
Capacity: 17 rounds
Features: An upgraded version of the MC28 SA, with lightning cuts in the slide; optics-ready and red-dot sight-equipped option; interchangeable backstraps; accessory rail, avaiable in all black, flat dark earth, or two-tone; SA-TV-BX version adds a threaded barrel and is available only in black or flat dark earth
SA-TV . . . . $477.00–$499.00
SA-TV-BX . . . . $517.00–$541.00

FLIGHTLITE INDUSTRIES MXR PRO

FLIGHTLITE INDUSTRIES MXR PRO

FK BRNO US PSD MULTI-CALIBER PISTOL

FN AMERICA FN-502 TACTICAL

FN AMERICA FN 509 MIDSIZE MRD

FN AMERICA FN HIGH POWER

FLIGHTLITE INDUSTRIES MXR PRO

Action: Semiautomatic
Grips: Synthetic
Barrel: 5 in.
Sights: None
Weight: 52 oz.
Caliber: 9mm
Capacity: 10, 15, 17 rounds
Features: Functions off of Glock magazines, with a tool-less quick-change barrel system–.22 LR, 9mm, .40 S&W, 10mm, .45 ACP, 5.7X28mm; threaded barrel of chrome-moly steel; mil-std 1913 rail at 12 o'clock and MLOK slots at 3 and 9 o'clcok; ambidextrous charging knob and magazine release; closed-bolt blowback operation; last-round hold-open with optional overide
Price:. **$799.99**

FLIGHTLITE INDUSTRIES MXR PRO

Action: Semiautomatic
Grips: Synthetic
Barrel: 5, 7 in.
Sights: None
Weight: 68 oz.
Caliber: 9mm
Capacity: 10, 15, 17 rounds
Features: Taking Glock magazines, this PDW pistol has a closed bolt blowback operation; mil-std 1913 optics interface; A2-style flash hider; SB Tactical SBA3 or KAK Industry 2M pistol brace; Magpul MOE or K-grip pistol grip; ambidextrous magazine release and safety; adjustable cycle rate through buffer exchange; MLOK interfaces; tool-less quick-change barrel system–.22 LR, 9mm, .40 S&W, 10mm, .45 ACP, 5.7X28mm–with threaded barrel; ambidextrous charging knob;
Price:. . . . . **$969.99–$999.99**

FK BRNO US PSD MULTI-CALIBER PISTOL

Action: Semiautomatic
Grips: Synthetic
Barrel: 5.3 in.
Sights: Diamond or pin-point front, ring sight or two-dot rear
Weight: 38.8 oz.
Caliber: 7.5 FK, 9mm, 10mm/.40 S&W
Capacity: 16, 17, 10 rounds
Features: A single-action pistol with caliber interchangeability; comes standard with the 7.5 FK chamber/barrel, 9mm and 10mm/.40 S&W barrels available as add-ons; textured grip frame; accessory rail; external thumb safety; patented recoil attenuating system with a positive-lock tilting barrel; optics-ready slide; various sights available
Price:. **$1,750.00**

FN AMERICA FN-502 TACTICAL

Action: Semiautomatic
Grips: Synthetic
Barrel: 4.6 in.
Sights: Suppressor-height fixed front and rear
Weight: 23.7 oz.
Caliber: .22 LR
Capacity: 10, 15 rounds
Features: FN claims this is the firarm industry's first optics-ready .22 LR; target-crowned muzzle is suppressor-ready and comes with thread protector; anodized aluminum/steel slide with front and rear serrations; loaded chamber indicator; single-action hammer; ambidextrous controls; manual no-decock safety; in black or flat dark earth
Price:. **$519.00**

FN AMERICA FN 509 MIDSIZE MRD

Action: Semiautomatic
Grips: Synthetic
Barrel: 4 in.
Sights: Combat-style drift-adjustable front, rear
Weight: 26.5 oz.
Caliber: 9mm
Capacity: 10, 15 rounds
Features: Double-action striker-fire in a concealed-carry package; raised combat-style sights for easier slide racking and co-witnessing; fully ambidextrous controls; front and rear slide serrations; optics-ready slide; cold hammer-forged barrel with recessed target crown; interchangeable backstraps; grip texturing; flatter trigger; underside accessory rail; in black or flat dark earth; ships with soft case and locking device
Price:. **$799.00**

FN AMERICA FN HIGH POWER

Action: Semiautomatic
Grips: G10, wood
Barrel: 4.7 in.
Sights: Blade front, notch rear
Weight: 40 oz.
Caliber: 9mm
Capacity: 17 rounds
Features: The High Power returns to American buyers, albeit without the Browning name stamped on it and with High instead of Hi; ambidextrous safety and slide stop; reversible magazine release; target-crowned hammer forged barrel; larger than original magazine capacity; finished in black, stainless, or flat dark earth, each with multiple G10 and wood grip panel choices
Price:. . . . .**$1269.00–$1369.00**

GLOCK G22 GEN5

GLOCK G23 GEN5

GLOCK G27 GEN5

H&K HK416 PISTOL

H&K MP5 PISTOL

H&K SP5K PDW

H&K SP5L

H&K VP9 MATCH

GLOCK G22 GEN5, GEN5 MOS

Action: Semiautomatic
Grips: Synthetic
Barrel: 4.5 in.
Sights: Three-dot white front and rear
Weight: 37.32 oz.
Caliber: .40 S&W
Capacity: 15, 16, 22 rounds
Features: Full-size .40 S&W with Gen5 attributes such as the Glock Marksman Barrel; nDLC finish; flared mag well; ambidextrous slide-stop lever; MOS version has optics-ready slide
Price: $657.99

GLOCK G23 GEN5, GEN5 MOS

Action: Semiautomatic
Grips: Synthetic
Barrel: 4 in.
Sights: Three-dot white front and rear
Weight: 34.36 oz.
Caliber: .40 S&W
Capacity: 13, 14, 15, 16, 22 rounds
Features: Compact .40 S&W with Gen5 attributes such as the Glock Marksman Barrel; nDLC finish; flared mag well; ambidextrous slide-stop lever; MOS version has optics-ready slide
Price: $622.99

GLOCK G27 GEN5

Action: Semiautomatic
Grips: Synthetic
Barrel: 3.4 in.
Sights: Three-dot white front and rear
Weight: 29.17 oz
Caliber: .40 S&W
Capacity: 9, 10, 13, 14, 15, 16, 22 rounds
Features: Subcompact .40 S&W with Gen5 attributes such as the Glock

Marksman Barrel; nDLC finish; flared mag well; ambidextrous slide-stop lever
Price: $578.99

H&K HK416 PISTOL

Action: Semiautomatic
Grips: Synthetic
Barrel: 8.5 in.
Sights: Flip-up front, rear
Weight: 72 oz.
Caliber: .22 LR
Capacity: 10, 20, 30 rounds
Features: Class-act rimfire with a pistol grip that has a storage compartment; MLOK/mil-sted 1913 rail; functional dust cover; aluminum receiver; compatible with most AR-style arm braces; last-round bolt hold-open; threaded barrel; adjustable flip-up sights
Price: $529.00

H&K MP5 PISTOL

Action: Semiautomatic
Grips: Synthetic
Barrel: 8.5 in.
Sights: Front post in hooded ring, rotating aperture rear
Weight: 94.4 oz.
Caliber: .22 LR
Capacity: 10, 25 rounds
Features: H&K says this is a sub-gun "trainer" with blowback operation; single-stage trigger; developed with Umarex; threaded barrel for suppressor use
Price: $529.00

H&K SP5K PDW

Action: Semiautomatic
Grips: Synthetic
Barrel: 5.83
Sights: Front post in hooded ring, rotating aperture rear

Weight: 67.2 oz.
Caliber: 9mm
Capacity: 10, 30 rounds
Features: Semiauto personal defense pistol in 9mm in a roller-delayed blowback operating system; Navy style threaded tri-lug adaptor barrel; fluted chamber; paddle magazine release; comes with sling and sight tool
Price: $3,279.00

H&K SP5L

Action: Semiautomatic
Grips: Synthetic
Barrel: 16.57 in.
Sights: Front post in hooded ring, rotating aperture rear
Weight: 94.4 oz.
Caliber: 9mm
Capacity: 10, 15, 30 rounds
Features: Semiauto civilian version of the MP5 sub gun, with a carbine rifle-length Navy barrel that's threaded and features a tri-lug adaptor; paddle magazine release; fluted chamber; supplied with "bungie" sling
Price: $3,279.00

H&K VP9 MATCH

Action: Semiautomatic
Grips: Synthetic
Barrel: 5.5 in.
Sights: Fixed front and rear
Weight: 14.16 oz.
Caliber: 9mm
Capacity: 10, 20 rounds
Features: A full-size handgun for competition, with a longer than usual barrel; optics-ready slide with lightnight cuts in the front and deep serrations at the rear; underside accessory rail; comes with five optics mounting plates, three backstraps, and three sets of lateral grip plates
Price: $1,159.00

H&K VP9 TACTICAL OR

H&K VP9L OR

HERITAGE MANUFACTURING BARKEEP BOOT

HERITAGE MANUFACTURING ROUGH RIDER TC

HI-POINT FIREARMS YEET CANNON G1

IDEAL CONCEAL IC9MM

IWI JERICHO ENHANCED

KARH ARMS P9-2

H&K VP9 TACTICAL OR

Action: Semiautomatic
Grips: Synthetic
Barrel: 4.7 in.
Sights: Raised, drift-adjustable night sights
Weight: 26.87 oz.
Caliber: 9mm
Capacity: 10, 17 rounds
Features: Suppressor- and optics ready, this more compact tactical offering has raised sights that can make weak-handed and one-handed slide racking easier; sights are also 1/3 co-witness with a red-dot sight; underside accessory rail; supplied with three sets of backstraps, three sets of side plates, slide cover plate, and three magazines
Price:. **$1,059.00**

H&K VP9L OR

Action: Semiautomatic
Grips: Synthetic
Barrel: 5. in.
Sights: Raised, drift-adjustable night sights
Weight: 27.16 oz.
Caliber: 9mm
Capacity: 10, 20 rounds
Features: The optics-ready slide accommodates numerous red-dot reflex sights; three sets of backstraps and sideplates provide up to 27 grip options; extended slide has lightning cuts and rear serrations; underside accessory rail; also available without night sights
Price:. . . . . **$999.00–$1119.00**

HERITAGE MANUFACTURING BARKEEP BOOT

Action: Revolver
Grips: Wood
Barrel: 1.68 in.
Sights: Notch rear
Weight: 25.5 oz.
Caliber: .22 LR

Capacity: 6 rounds
Features: This one takes "snubnose" to a new level with a barrel just 1.68-in. long; manual external thumb safety; with choice of black wood, gray "pearl," or black wood with a burned-in image of a rattlesnake

Black	$196.80
Gray Pearl	$205.38
Wood Burnt Snake	$205.38

HERITAGE MANUFACTURING ROUGH RIDER TC

Rider TC
Action: Revolver
Grips: Carbon fiber
Barrel: 6.5 in.
Sights: Fiber optic front
Weight: 32.1 oz.
Caliber: .22 LR
Capacity: 6 rounds
Features: A tactical single-action .22? Yup, that's what this is with a fiber optic front sight; topside optics rail; threaded barrel; carbon fiber grips; compatible with .22 WMR cylinders
Price:. **$212.88**

HI-POINT FIREARMS YEET CANNON G1, G1 TB

Action: Semiautomatic
Grips: Synthetic
Barrel: 3.5, 3.93 in.
Sights: Yellow ramp front, red-dot rear
Weight: 29 oz.
Caliber: 9mm
Capacity: 8, 10 rounds
Features: Compact 9mm carry gun with a high-impact polymer frame and grips; magazine disconnect safety; +P rated; TB is threaded for suppressor and has the slightly longer barrel

Standard	$210.00
TB	$249.99

IDEAL CONCEAL IC9MM

Action: Two-shot

Grips: Synthetic
Barrel: N/A
Sights: None
Weight: 18 oz.
Caliber: 9mm
Capacity: 2 rounds
Features: Like its predecessor the IC380, this 9mm is designed to appear as a foldable cell phone; one-piece frame; available black, Blue Line edition, or Flag graphic

Black	$649.00
Blue Line	$724.00
Flag	$825.00

IWI JERICHO ENHANCED

Action: Semiautomatic
Grips: Synthetic
Barrel: 4.4 in.
Sights: Novak sights
Weight: 26.8 oz.
Caliber: 9mm
Capacity: 10, 17 rounds
Features: Well-built gun for carry, home-defense, or target shooting, this model is based on CZ's short recoil system; short-spur hammmer with serrations; front and rear slide serrations; interchangeable backstraps; underside accessory rail; improved external thumb safety; improved trigger profile; finger groove-less grip profile
Price:. **$559.00**

KARH ARMS P9-2

Action: Semiautomatic
Grips: Synthetic
Barrel: 3.6 in.
Sights: Truglo night sights
Weight: 15.8 oz.
Caliber: 9mm
Capacity: 7 rounds
Features: A very lightweight carry gun with a CNC-machined stainless steels slide; non-slip grip texturing; accessory rail; match-grade barrel with polyganol rifling; front and rear slide serrations
Price:. **$679.00**

KAHR ARMS TP9-2

KEL-TEC P15

KIMBER MICRO 9 BLACK OI

KIMBER MICRO 9 ESV TWO-TONE (MS) (TP)

KIMBER MICRO 9 RAPIDE (BLACK ICE)

KIMBER MICRO 9 RAPIDE (DAWN)

KIMBER MICRO 9 RAPIDE (SCROPIUS)

KIMBER MICRO 9 STAINLESS (MC) (TP)

KARH ARMS TP9-2

Action: Semiautomatic
Grips: Synthetic
Barrel: 4 in.
Sights: Truglo night sights
Weight: 18.5 oz.
Caliber: 9mm
Capacity: 8 rounds
Features: A slightly larger version of the P9-2
Price:...............$679.00

KEL-TEC P15

Action: Semiautomatic
Grips: Synthetic
Barrel: 4 in.
Sights: HiViz fiber optic front, adjustable tritium two-dot rear
Weight: 14 oz.
Caliber: 9mm
Capacity: 15 rounds
Features: Sporting a uniquely textured grip, this striker-fire carry gun is a skimpy 14 oz.; includes extended and flush-fit magazines; accessory rail; grip safety; 5-lb. trigger pull
Price:...............$425.00

KIMBER MICRO 9 BLACK OI, STAINLESS OI

Action: Semiautomatic
Grips: Rubber
Barrel: 3.15 in.
Sights: White dot front, integral rear groove
Weight: 18.4 oz.
Caliber: 9mm
Capacity: 7 rounds
Features: One of Kimbers most popular carry 9mms, this one complete with a Swamp Fox Sentinal red-dot optic; aluminum frame; match-grade stainless steel barrel; 7-lb. trigger; finish in Kimpro II Black or satin Kimpro II Silver
Price:...............$905.00

KIMBER MICRO 9 ESV TWO-TONE (MS) (TP)

Action: Semiautomatic
Grips: Rubber
Barrel: 3.45 in.
Sights: Truglo Pro night sights
Weight: 19.2 oz.
Caliber: 9mm
Capacity: 7 rounds
Features: Wearing a special mini compensator, this Micro 9 has Hogue wraparound rubber grips; Truglo Pro night sights with an orange front sight ring and a U-notch rear with green sight rings and a cocking ledge; Kimpro II Black frame finish, glass bead stainless slide finish; slide has muzzle end lightning cuts, rear serrations
Price:...............$976.00

KIMBER MICRO 9 RAPIDE (BLACK ICE)

Action: Semiautomatic
Grips: G10
Barrel: 3.15 in.
Sights: Truglo TFX Pro day/night sights
Weight: 15.6 oz.
Caliber: 9mm
Capacity: 7 rounds
Features: With uniquely textured gray G10 grips, this Micro 9 has stepped cocking serrations at the slide rear and lightning ports at the slide front; Stiplex front strap texturing; flush-fitting magwell; frame finished in Kimpro II Silver; frame finished in Silver and Kimpro II Grey
Price:...............$986.00

KIMBER MICRO 9 RAPIDE (DAWN)

Action: Semiautomatic
Grips: G10
Barrel: 3.15 in.
Sights: Truglo TFX Pro day/night sights
Weight: 15.6 oz.

Caliber: 9mm
Capacity: 7 rounds
Features: Similar to the Dawn iteration, but with a gold TiN-coated barrel; grey/black G10 grips; frame in Kimpro II Silver finish; slide has brushed stainless steel sides and Silver Kimpro II finish
Price:...............$986.00

KIMBER MICRO 9 RAPIDE (SCROPIUS)

Action: Semiautomatic
Grips: G10
Barrel: 3.15 in.
Sights: Truglo TFX Pro day/night sights
Weight: 15.6 oz.
Caliber: 9mm
Capacity: 7 rounds
Features: Similar to the Black Ice and Dawn Micro 9 models, but with a uniquely patterned, all-black G10 grip; frame finished in Kimpro II Black; slide has brushed stainless sides and Black Kimpro II finish; DLC-coated barrel for a striking color contrast with the slide sides
Price:...............$986.00

KIMBER MICRO 9 STAINLESS (MC) (TP)

Action: Semiautomatic
Grips: Rubber
Barrel: 3.45 in.
Sights: Truglo Pro night sights
Weight: 19.2 oz.
Caliber: 9mm
Capacity: 7 rounds
Features: Equipped with a mini-compensator; rear slide serrations; Hogue wraparound rubber grips with finger grooves; frame finished in Kimpro II Silver; slide in glass bead finished stainless
Price:...............$890.00

KIMBER R7 MAKO OI

LES BAER CUSTOM CARRY COMMANCHE

KIMBER R7 MAKO OR

LES BAER STINGER MONOLITH COMMANCHE

KIMBER RAPIDE (DAWN)

KIMBER RAPIDE (SCORPIUS)

LWRCI ICD PISTOL AND BRACE

KIMBER R7 MAKO OI

Action: Semiautomatic
Grips: Glass-filled nylong
Barrel: 3.37 in.
Sights: Truglo Pro night sights
Weight: 19.5 oz.
Caliber: 9mm
Capacity: 11, 13 rounds
Features: A tiny double-stack striker-fire with orange front ring and white rear dot sights in the TruGlo Tritium Pro line; glass-filled nylon grip with all-around texturing; grip is just 1-in. wide; 11-round flush-fit mag and extended 13-round mag; optics-ready slide; Performance Carry trigger; FNC hard-coated barrel; undercut triggerguard; ambidextrous controls; includes a factory-mounted Crimson Trace CTS-1500 red-dot sight; Performance Carry trigger; undercut triggerguard; nearly full-coverage grip texturing; FNC-hard-coated barrel with deep-cut crown
Price:. $799.00

KIMBER R7 MAKO OR

Action: Semiautomatic
Grips: Glass-filled nylong
Barrel: 3.37 in.
Sights: Truglo Pro night sights
Weight: 19.5 oz.
Caliber: 9mm
Capacity: 11, 13 rounds
Features: Identiacl to th OI version, but this model is optics-ready--OR-- with a cutout for any sight that fits the Shield-pattern RMSc footprint
Price:. $599.00

KIMBER RAPIDE (DAWN)

Action: Semiautomatic
Grips: G10
Barrel: 5.25 in.
Sights: Truglo TFX Pro day/night sights
Weight: 40 oz.
Caliber: 9mm
Capacity: 9 rounds
Features: A full-size 1911-type in

9mm with Kimber's gray/black RAPIDE G10 grips; V-cut aluminum trigger; front strap has Stiplex treatment; stepped cocking serrations; lightning ports; slide and frame are in Silver Kimpro II with brushed polished flats; barrel finished in gold TiN for smart contrast point
Price:. $1,733.00

KIMBER RAPIDE (SCORPIUS)

Action: Semiautomatic
Grips: G10
Barrel: 5.25
Sights: Truglo TFX Pro day/night sights
Weight: 40 oz.
Caliber: 9mm
Capacity: 9 rounds
Features: Identiacl in featues to the Rapide (Dawn), the (Scorpius) is finished all over in Black Kimpro II with polished flats; barrel has black DLC finish
Price:. $1,733.00

LES BAER CUSTOM CARRY COMMANCHE

Action: Semiautomatic
Grips: Walnut
Barrel: 4.25 in.
Sights: Rolo/Les Baer Custom adjustable night sights
Weight: N/A
Caliber: 10mm
Capacity: 7 rounds
Features: A carry gun in the powerful 10mm, with dehorned frame and slide; lowered and flared ejection port; tight 30 lines-per-inch front strap checkering; checkered slide stop; extended ejector; flat serrated mainspring housing; 4-lb Baer Speed trigger; Baer tactical ambidextrous safety; choice of Rolo night sights or Les Baer Custom low-mount adjustable night sights
Rolo night sights $3390.00
Les Baer night sights $3490.00

LES BAER STINGER MONOLITH COMMANCHE

Action: Semiautomatic
Grips: Synthetic
Barrel: 4.25 in.
Sights: Rolo adjustable night sights
Weight: N/A
Caliber: 10mm
Capacity: 6 rounds
Features: An Officer's-sized frame with a beefy Commanche (Commander) slide that adds muzzle weight to help soak up the 10mm recoil; extra-long dust cover; black Recon grips; adjustable Rolo night sights; tight rear cocking serrations; Les Baer Speed trigger
Price:. $3,584.00

LWRCI ICD PISTOL AND BRACE, SBM4 BRACE

Action: Semiautomatic
Grips: Synthetic
Barrel: 10. 5 in.
Sights: None
Weight: 105.6 oz.
Caliber: 5.56 NATO
Capacity: 20 rounds
Features: A direct impingement AR pistol with a modular one-piece free-floating rail; ambidextrous lower controls and charging handle; Magpul MOE+ grip; LWRCI's own rail panels and hand stop; keyless bolt carrier design; converts to a DI-version piston-driven system by swapping out the upper; standrad Brace model has an SBA3 tactical pistol brace or you can opt for the model with SMB4 brace from SB Tactical; in black or in flat dark earth, olive drab, patriot brown, or tungsten gray
Standard Brace. $1802.83
SBM4 Brace $1733.49
Colors add $156.06

NEW Products: Handguns

LWRCI IC-PSC PISTOL

MAGNUM RESEARCH 20TH ANNIVERSARY BFR

MASTERPIECE ARMS MPA DS9 HYBRID BLACK BUTLER CUT

MASTERPIECE ARMS MPA DS9 COMMANDER

MASTERPIECE ARMS MPA DS40 TT COMP

MAXIM DEFENSE MD-15 PISTOL

MAXIM DEFENSE MD-1505SPB PISTOL

LWRCI IC-PSD PISTOL

Action: Semiautomatic
Grips: Synthetic
Barrel: 8.5 in.
Sights: Flip-up front and rear
Weight: 94.4 oz.
Caliber: 5.56 NATO
Capacity: 20 rounds
Features: PSD is for "Personal Security Detail" and equips this pistol with an 8.5-in. barrel; fully ambidextrous lower controls; LWRCI Enhance Fire Control Group; NiCorr-treated cold hammer-forged barrel; Magpul MOE+ grip; LWRCI Skirmish iron sights; ambidextrous charging handle; pistol buffer tube recoil system; oversized LWRCI Advanced Trigger Guard; plenty of top-side rail; in black, flat dark earth, olive drab, patriot brown, or tungsten gray
Black **$2319.48**
Color add **$156.06**

MAGNUM RESEARCH 20TH ANNIVERSARY BFR

Action: Revolver
Grips: Polymer
Barrel: 7.5 in.
Sights: Ramp front, adjustable rear
Weight: 68.8 oz.
Caliber: .45-70 Gov't.
Capacity: 5 rounds
Features: Almost hard to believe the BFR has been around 20 years now. This limited edition celebratory run of just 20 revolvers features white, plow-style grip panels; full octagon barrel; brushed stainless steel finish with engraving from Tyler Gun Works; wood presentation case and letter of authenticity
Price: **$7,200.00**

MASTERPIECE ARMS MPA DS9 HYBRID BLACK BUTLER CUT

Action: Semiautomatic
Grips: Aluminum
Barrel: 5 in.
Sights: Fiber optic front, adjustable rear

Weight: N/A
Caliber: 9mm
Capacity: 17, 20 rounds
Features: A limited run competition gun with handlapped frame-to-slide fit; Accuracy X Multi-Sight optics ready slide; wide body double-stack frame; Koenig hammer, sear, and disconnector; aluminum trigger shoe; Wolff springs; MPA magwell; TriTop slide machining; 416R stainless bull barrel; 2.5-lb. trigger will relax to 2-lb. after break-in; butler cut frame; FGW slide serrations and lightning cuts; accessory rail
Price: **$2,999.99**

MASTERPIECE ARMS MPA DS9 COMMANDER

Action: Semiautomatic
Grips: Aluminum
Barrel: 4.25 in.
Sights: Fiber optic front, adjustable rear
Weight: N/A
Caliber: 9mm
Capacity: 17 rounds
Features: Commander-length slide; handlapped frame-to-slide fit; Accuracy X Multi-Sight optics ready slide; wide body double-stack frame; Koenig hammer, sear, and disconnector; aluminum trigger shoe; Wolff springs; MPA magwell; TriTop slide machining; 416R stainless bull barrel; 3.5-lb. trigger pull will drop in weight after break-in
Price: **$2,999.99**

MASTERPIECE ARMS MPA DS40 TT COMP

Action: Semiautomatic
Grips: Aluminum
Barrel: 5 in.
Sights: Fiber optic front, adjustable rear
Weight: N/A
Caliber: .40 S&W
Capacity: 20 rounds
Features: Jamming 20 rounds of .40 S&W into the MBX magazine, this wide-body competition gun was

designed with input from MPA Team Shooter and world champion Travis Tomasie; handlapped frame-to-slide fit; Koenig hammer, sear, and disconnector; aluminum trigger shoe; Wolff springs; MPA competition magwell; TriTop slide machining; 416R stainless bull barrel; 2.5-lb. trigger will relax to 2-lb. after break-in; rear slide serrations and fore lightning cuts; accessory rail
Price: **$2,999.99**

MAXIM DEFENSE MD:15 PISTOL

MD-15 Pistol
Action: Semiautomatic
Grips: Synthetic
Barrel: 8.5, 10.3 in.
Sights: None
Weight: N/A
Caliber: .300 BLK, 5.56 NATO, 7.62X39 NATO
Capacity: 20 rounds
Features: Designed to be used only as a fore-arm brace, this pistol has ample topside rail; Maxim's Hatebrake muzzle brake; monolithic-like upper platform with five-sided MLOK compatibility; available with SCW or CQB series fore-arm braces
Price: . . . . **$1595.00–$1695.00**

MAXIM DEFENSE MD:1505SPB PISTOL

Action: Semiautomatic
Grips: Synthetic
Barrel: 5.5 in.
Sights: None
Weight: 88 oz.
Caliber: .300 BLK, 5.56 NATO, 7.62X39 NATO
Capacity: 20 rounds
Features: Equipped with a Maxim Hatebrake muzzle brake; free-floating Slimline handguard with five-sided MLOK compatibility; ambidextrous mag release and selector; SCW forearm brace; ALG Combat trigger
Price: **$1,895.00**

MAXIM DEFENSE MD-1505SPS PISTOL

MAXIM DEFENSE MDX-508CPB PISTOL

MAXIM DEFENSE MDX-508SPB PISTOL

MAXIM DEFENSE MDX-510CPB

MAXIM DEFENSE MDX-510SPB

MAXIM DEFENSE PDX

MAXIM DEFENSE PDX SPS

MAXIM DEFENSE URBAN GRAY PDX

MAXIM DEFENSE MD:1505SPS PISTOL

Action: Semiautomatic
Grips: Synthetic
Barrel: 5.5 in.
Sights: None
Weight: 88 oz.
Caliber: .300 BLK, 5.56 NATO, 7.62X39 NATO
Capacity: 20 rounds
Features: Similar to the MD:1505SPB, but this model is equiped with Maxim's SCW pistol configuration that lacks a forearm brace
Price: **$1,895.00**

MAXIM DEFENSE MDX:508CPB PISTOL

Action: Semiautomatic
Grips: Synthetic
Barrel: 8.5 in.
Sights: None
Weight: N/A
Caliber: .300 BLK, 5.56 NATO, 7.62X39 NATO
Capacity: 20 rounds
Features: Configured as a CQB pistol with a CQB forearm brace, this compact AR-platform firearm includes the Hatebrake muzzle brake; available in black, Arid, or Urban Gray
Price: **$2,495.00**

MAXIM DEFENSE MDX:508SPB PISTOL

Action: Semiautomatic
Grips: Synthetic
Barrel: 8.5 in.
Sights: None
Weight: N/A
Caliber: .300 BLK, 5.56 NATO, 7.62X39 NATO
Capacity: 20 rounds
Features: Similar to the MDX:508CPB, but this version is equipped with the SCW pistol forearm brace; available in black, Urban Gray, or Arid
Price: **$2,495.00**

MAXIM DEFENSE MDX: 510CPB

Action: Semiautomatic
Grips: Synthetic
Barrel: 10.3 in.
Sights: None
Weight: N/A
Caliber: .300 BLK, 5.56 NATO, 7.62X39 NATO
Capacity: 20 rounds
Features: The 510 series builds on the shorter barreled MDX pistols with a longer 10.3-in. barrel; Radian Rapto chargin handle; ambidextrous QD sling points; adjustable gas block; ambidextrous Radian Talon selector; BBCM Gunfighter grip; ALG Defense Combat trigger; M-RAX/MLOK-compatible handguard; Hatebrake muzzle brake; in a CQB pistol configuration; available in black, Arid, or Urban Grey
Price: **$2,495.00**

MAXIM DEFENSE MDX:510SPB

Action: Semiautomatic
Grips: Synthetic
Barrel: 10.3 in.
Sights: None
Weight: N/A
Caliber: .300 BLK, 5.56 NATO, 7.62X39 NATO
Capacity: 20 rounds
Features: Similar to the MD:510CPB, but this version is vailable with SCW or CQB pistol forearm braces; in black or Arid
Price: **$2,495.00**

MAXIM DEFENSE PDX

Action: Semiautomatic
Grips: Synthetic
Barrel: 5.5 in.
Sights: None
Weight: 91 oz.
Caliber: 5.56 NATO, 7.62X39 NATO
Capacity: 20 rounds
Features: Maxim's premier PDW line with a short 5.5-in. barrel; Maxim SCW stock system that cust the stock length to just four inches; Hatebrake muzzle brake; ALG Combat trigger; direct impingement system
Price: **$2,295.00**

MAXIM DEFENSE PDX SPS

Action: Semiautomatic
Grips: Synthetic
Barrel: 5.5 in.
Sights: None
Weight: 94.4 oz.
Caliber: .300 BLK, 5.56 NATO, 7.62X39 NATO
Capacity: 20 rounds
Features: This PDX features Maxims SCW pistol system instead of wearing a forearm brace; HK-height rail provides rigidity to the upper; M-slot-compatible handguard; Hatebrake muzzle brake; in black, Urban Grey, or Arid
Price: **$2,295.00**

MAXIM DEFENSE URBAN GRAY PDX

Action: Semiautomatic
Grips: Synthetic
Barrel: 5.5 in.
Sights: None
Weight: 94.4 oz.
Caliber: .300 BLK, 5.56 NATO, 7.62X39 NATO
Capacity: 20 rounds
Features: Slightly different than the original PDX, this one in hard-coat anodized Urban Grey has an ALG Combat trigger; SCW pistol configuration forearm brace; Hatebrake muzzle brake
Price: **$2,295.00**

NEW Products: Handguns

MOSSBERG MC2SC,
CROSS-BOLT SAFETY,
TRU-GLO SIGHTS

NIGHTHAWK
COUNSELOR

NIGHTHAWK
DELEGATE

NIGHTHAWK
FALCON

NIGHTHAWK
PREDATOR

NIGHTHAWK SAND
HAWK

NIGHTHAWK
SHADOW HAWK

MOSSBERG MC2SC

Action: Semiautomatic
Grips: Synthetic
Barrel: 3.4 in.
Sights: Three-dot white front and rear
Weight: 19.5 oz.
Caliber: 9mm
Capacity: 10, 11, 14 rounds
Features: A micro-compact with tremendous capacity; optics-ready slide; DLC-finished slide and barrel; front and rear slide serrations; striker-fire; alternate version available with TruGlo Pro night sights; alternate version with standard sights available with cross-bolt safety

Standard **$556.00**
Cross-bolt safety **$556**
Night sights **$662.00**

NIGHTHAWK COUNSELOR

Action: Semiautomatic
Grips: G10
Barrel: 3.5 in.
Sights: Tritium front, Heinie Straight Eight Slant Pro rear
Weight: 27.9 oz.
Caliber: 9mm
Capacity: 8 rounds
Features: Sleek carry 9mm with positive slide serrations in which the serrations are raised on top of the slide metal rather than having metal removed to make them; thin-profile grip panels; Officer-sized frame; flush-fit magwell; ultra-high undercut triggerguard

Price: **$4,299.00**

NIGHTHAWK DELEGATE

Action: Semiautomatic
Grips: G10
Barrel: 4.25
Sights: Tritium front, Heinie black ledge rear
Weight: 38.2 oz.
Caliber: 9mm,. 45 ACP
Capacity: 7, 9 rounds
Features: A forged Commander frame

supports a Commander slide; Ambassador front and rear "positive" cocking serrations; Railscales G10 grips; crowned, flush-cut barrel; flush-fit magwell; black nitride finish; ultra high-cut front strap; match-grade bull barrel

Price: **$4,299.00**

NIGHTHAWK FALCON

Action: Semiautomatic
Grips: G10
Barrel: 5 in.
Sights: Tritium front, Heinie Straight Eight Ledge rear
Weight: 38.8 oz.
Caliber: .45 ACP
Capacity: 8 rounds
Features: Forged Government-sized frame with a match-grade barrel; ball-cut rear cocking serrations; G10 Golf Ball grip panels; front strap checkered at 25 lines per inch; lightweight tri-cavity trigger; complete frame dehorning; ultra high-cut front strap; shortened slide stop; top of slide has three ball-cut grooves

Price: **$3,999.00**

NIGHTHAWK PREDATOR, PREDATOR II, PREDATOR III

Action: Semiautomatic
Grips: Cocobolo
Barrel: 5, 4.25 in.
Sights: Tritium front, Heinie Straight Eight Slant Pro rear
Weight: 40.3 oz.
Caliber: 9mm, .45 ACP
Capacity: 6, 7, 9 rounds
Features: The original Predator is a Government-sized gun, Predator II is Commander-sized, and Predator III ihas an Officer-sized frame with a Commander-length slide; Nighthawk two-piece magwell; serrated slide top; match-grade barrel; complete dehorning; ultra high-cut front strap; 25 lines-per-inch checkered front strap; rear of sline at 40 lines-per-inch

serration to match the rear sight; black nitride finish; speial coned/wafered barrel reduce recoil

Price: **$4,299.00**

NIGHTHAWK SAND HAWK

Action: Semiautomatic
Grips: Aluminum
Barrel: 5 in.
Sights: Gold bead front, Heinie Ledge Black rear
Weight: 39.6 oz.
Caliber: 9mm
Capacity: 17 rounds
Features: A double-stack Government-sized 9mm in Tan Cerakote; monolithic slide with wide cocking serrations; complete dehorning; integral compensator; accessory rail; flat-face, serrated trigger

Price: **$5,399.00**

NIGHTHAWK SHADOW HAWK GOVERNMENT, COMMANDER

Action: Semiautomatic
Grips: G10
Barrel: 5, 4.25 in.
Sights: Tritium front, Heinie Straight Eight Ledge rear
Weight: 41.3 oz.
Caliber: 9mm, .45 ACP
Capacity: 7, 8, ,9, 10 rounds
Features: Wearing a black nitride finish, these two guns were designed in cooperation with Steve "Yeti" Fisher; flat-faced trigger; match-grade barrel; 25 lines-per-inch checkered front strap; 40 lines-per-inch serrated slide rear to match the rear sight; crowned barrel is situated flush with the bushing; shortened slide stop; beveled frame; front and rear cocking serrations; complete dehorning

Price: **$3,999.00**

NIGHTHAWK SHADOW HAWK LONG SLIDE

NIGHTHAWK TREASURER

NORTH AMERICAN ARMS ANTI-VENOM

NORTH AMERICAN ARMS GATOR GUN

NORTH AMERICAN ARMS PUG SHADOW

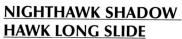

NORTH AMERICAN ARMS PUG TURQUOISE

PATRIOT ORDNANCE PHOENIX

POLYMER80 PF320

NIGHTHAWK SHADOW HAWK LONG SLIDE

Action: Semiautomatic
Grips: G10
Barrel: 6 in.
Sights: Tritium front, adjustable two-dot tritium rear
Weight: 42 oz.
Caliber: 10mm
Capacity: 9 rounds
Features: A Government frame supports a long 6-inch slide/barrel; Nighthawk rear sight; ball radius slide cuts; front and rear cocking serrations; match-grade barrel; one-piece magwell; shortened slide stop; 25 lines-per-inch front strap checkering; 40 lines-per-inch rear of slide checkering; flat-faced solid aluminum trigger; complete dehorning
Price: **$4,299.00**

NIGHTHAWK TREASURER

Action: Semiautomatic
Grips: G10
Barrel: 3.85 in.
Sights: Gold bead front, Heinie Ledge Black rear
Weight: 34.7 oz.
Caliber: 9mm
Capacity: 8 rounds
Features: An Officer-sized frame with a one-piece magwell; Railscale Ascend G10 grip panels; match-grade barrel; 25 lines-per-inch checkering on front strap and mainspring housing; 14K gold front bead; barrel finished in gold tatanium nitride; checkered recoil spring plug; ultra high-cut front strap; complete dehorning; one lightning cut on either side of lide at the muzzle
Price: **$4,599.00**

NORTH AMERICAN ARMS ANTI-VENOM MAGNUM, MAGNUM SNUB

Action: Revolver

Grips: Synthetic
Barrel: 1.9, 1.2 in.
Sights: Blade front, integral rear
Weight: 5.9 oz.
Caliber: .22 Mag.
Capacity: 5 rounds
Features: Jazzed up Magnum with a boot grip and a Magnum Snub with a bird's-head grip, both have grips covered in a snakeskin pattern and have a ready-to-bite-you snake head engraved on the frame by Black Ice Coatings of Spanish Fork, Utah
Price: . . . . **$240.00–$250.00**

NORTH AMERICAN ARMS GATOR GUN

Action: Revolver
Grips: Synthetic
Barrel: 1.2 in.
Sights: Blade front, integral rear
Weight: 5.9 oz.
Caliber: .22 Mag.
Capacity: 5 rounds
Features: Very cool to see NAA jazzing up its mini revolver line, this one with camo-covered grip panels on this .22 Mag.
Price: **$289.99**

NORTH AMERICAN ARMS PUG SHADOW

Action: Revolver
Grips: Rubber
Barrel: 1 in.
Sights: White dot front, notch rear
Weight: 6.4 oz.
Caliber: .22 LR, .22 Magnum
Capacity: 5 rounds
Features: The tiny and favorite Pug mini-revolver with a comfortable rubber bird's head grip and all-over black PVD coating
Price: **$449.99**

NORTH AMERICAN ARMS PUG TURQUOISE

Action: Revolver
Grips: Synthetic

Barrel: 1 in.
Sights: White dot front, notch rear
Weight: 6.4 oz.
Caliber: .22 LR, .22 Magnum
Capacity: 5 rounds
Features: The pug gets a shiny upgrade with frame and barrel in Turquoise Crerakote matched with simulated pearl grip panels
Price: **$399.00**

PATRIOT ORDNANCE PHOENIX

Action: Semiautomatic
Grips: Synthetic
Barrel: 8.5 in.
Sights: None
Weight: 73.6 oz.
Caliber: 9mm
Capacity: 35 rounds
Features: A 9mm PDW with huge capacity; mil-spec AR-style trigger; blowback action; threaded barrel; Mission First Tactical grip; ambidextrous fire-control group; black anodized finishl rear and top-side Picatinny rails; monolithi upper with MLOK compatibility
Price: **$1,699.00**

POLYMER80 PF320

Action: Semiautomatic
Grips: Synthetic
Barrel: 4.49 in.
Sights: Fiber optic front, notch rear
Weight: N/A
Caliber: 9mm
Capacity: 10, 15 rounds
Features: Some are calling this a "kit" but Polymer80 is selling this as a complete gun with a Sig P320 fire-control unit as its foundation; 1911-angled grip; Polymer80's P80 PTEX grip texture; proprietary ambidextrous magazine release; roomy underside rail; optics-ready slide; double undercut triggerguard; flared aluminum magazine well
Price: **$799.00**

NEW PRODUCTS

RUGER LCP MAX

RUGER MAX-9

RUGER-57

RUGER WRANGLER BIRDS HEAD

SAR USA BY SARSILMAZ ST9-SS

SAR USA BY SARSILMAZ ST45

SAR USA BY SARSILMAZ 109T

RUGER LCP MAX

Action: Semiautomatic
Grips: Glass-filled nylon
Barrel: 2.8 in.
Sights: Tritium fiber optic front, notch rear
Weight: 10.6 oz.
Caliber: .380 ACP
Capacity: 10, 12 rounds
Features: Talk about tiny, at just 10.6 oz., this micro carry gun is under an inch wide and fits in the included pocket holster; green tritium sight with white outline; reversible magazine release; comes with a 10-round flush-fit magazine and a finger rest extension; 12-round extended magazine available; black oxide finish on a steel alloy slide; front and rear cocking serrations
Price: $469.00

RUGER MAX-9, MAX-9 WITH CRIMSON TRACE COMPACT REFLEX SIGHT, MAX-9 WITH HOGUE GRIP SLEEVE

Action: Semiautomatic
Grips: Glass-filled nylon
Barrel: 3.2 in.
Sights: Tritium front, notch rear
Weight: 18.4 oz.
Caliber: 9mm
Capacity: 10, 12 rounds
Features: Compact, striker-fired 9mm carry with an external thumb safety; comes with both 10- and 12-round E-Nickel Teflon-coated magazines and a finger grip extension; optic ready steel alloy slide with cuts that take JPoint and Shield micro red-dots; available without external thumb safety; available with a factory-mounted, co-witnessed Crimson Trace Compact red-dot sight and external safety; available with a Hogue slip on grip sleeve and external safety
Price: . . . . $579.00–$709.00

RUGER-57 PRO

Action: Semiautomatic
Grips: Glass-filled nylon
Barrel: 4.94 in.
Sights: Fiber optic front, adjustable rear
Weight: 24.5 oz.
Caliber: 9mm
Capacity: 20 rounds
Features: A 9mm for target practice or competition with a generous 20-round magazine capacity; drop-free mags (two included); black nitride-treated alloy steel barrel; fully adjustable rear sight; Ruger's Secure Action striker-fire design; front and rear slide serrations; slide drilled and tapped for use with available optic adaptor plate; no-triggger-pull, no-tool takedown; reversible magazine release
Price: $869.00

RUGER WRANGLER WITH BIRD'S-HEAD GRIP

Action: Revolver
Grips: Synthetic
Barrel: 3.75 in.
Sights: Blade front, integral notch rear
Weight: 28 oz.
Caliber: .22 LR
Capacity: 6 rounds
Features: Interesting take on a single-action, with synthetic bird's-head-style grips; non-fluted cylinder; aluminum alloy frame in choice of Black, Silver, or Burnt Bronze Cerakote
Price: $279.00

SAR USA BY SARSILMAZ ST9, ST9-SS

Action: Semiautomatic
Grips: Synthetic
Barrel: 4.4 in.
Sights: Low-profile front, adjustable rear
Weight: 27.1 oz.

Caliber: 9mm
Capacity: 15, 17 rounds
Features: Striker-fired 9mm wihtout the annoying middle-trigger safety; external thumb safety; paddle magazine release; striker-status indicator; interchangeable backstraps; standard model available in blue or matte stainless; SS model has a slide with lightning cuts and a ported barrel; both models have underside accessory rail
Price: $367.97

SAR USA BY SARSILMAZ ST45

Action: Semiautomatic
Grips: Synthetic
Barrel: 4.5 in.
Sights: Low-profile front, adjustable rear
Weight: 32 oz.
Caliber: .45 ACP
Capacity: 12 rounds
Features: A striker-fire similar to the ST-9 but chambered in .45 ACP; no middle-trigger safety; external thumb safety and striker ready indicator; interchangeable backstraps
Price: $398.68

SAR USA BY SARSILMAZ 109T

Action: Semiautomatic
Grips: Synthetic
Barrel: 8.7 in.
Sights: Flip-up front and rear
Weight: 78.4 oz.
Caliber: 9mm
Capacity: 10, 20, 30 rounds
Features: A 9mm AR-type pistol with blowback operating system; free-floating handguard with rails at 3, 6, 9, and 12 o'clock; H1 buffer spring; non-reciprocating charging handle; two-part aluminum alloy receiver; overall length of just 27.8 inches
Price: $1,799.00

SAVAGE ARMS STANCE

SCCY CPX-4RD

SHADOW SYSTEMS XR920 ELITE

SIG SAUER M400 SWITCHBLADE PISTOL

SIG SAUER P210 CARRY

SIG SAUER P220 EQUINOX ELITE FULL-SIZE

SIG SAUER P226 EQUINOX ELITE FULL-SIZE

SAVAGE ARMS STANCE

Action: Semiautomatic
Grips: Synthetic
Barrel: 3.2 in.
Sights: Orange dot front, two-do white U-notch rear
Weight: 22 oz.
Caliber: 9mm
Capacity: 7, 8 rounds
Features: Savage goes handgun with a micro-compact striker-fire that features a short reset trigger; two interchangeable 18-degree backstraps; ambidextrous slide release and magazine release; 360-degree grip stippling; removeable chassis; snag-free high-visibility sights; stainless steel slide with black nitride finish and lightning cuts; glass-filled nylon grip; frame in black, gray, or flat dark earth
Price:................$479.00

SCCY CPX-4, CPX4RD

Action: Semiautomatic
Grips: Synthetic
Barrel: 2.96 in.
Sights: Low-profile front, fixed notch rear
Weight: 15 oz.
Caliber: .380 ACP
Capacity: 10 rounds
Features: Super compact carry gun with a hammer-fired double-action; SCCY's Roebuck Quadlock technology that virtually eliminates barrel wiggle; textured grip panels, external safety; RD model comes with Crimson Trace red-dot sight; with choice of blued or stainless slide finishes
Standard $329.99
Red-dot $429.99

SHADOW SYSTEMS XR920 COMBAT, ELITE

Action: Semiautomatic
Grips: Synthetic
Barrel: 4, 4.5 in.
Sights: Tritium front, serrated rear
Weight: 19.2, 20 oz.
Caliber: 9mm
Capacity: 10, 17 rounds
Features: A full-frame 9mm with a compact slide, these semiautos come standard with an optics-ready slide; choice of threaded or non-threaded barrel; front and rear slide serrations; choice of black or gold barrel finish with choice of black or flat dark earth frames/slides; extended upswept beavertail; interchangeable backstraps; recoil control ledge; aggressive grip texturing; Elite model adds top-side serrations and window slide cuts
Combat $889.00
Elite $989.00

SIG SAUER M400 SWITCHBLADE

Action: Semiautomatic
Grips: Synthetic
Barrel: 11.5 in.
Sights: None
Weight: N/A
Caliber: 5.56 NATO
Capacity: 30 rounds
Features: AR-platform rifle-caliber pistol with a two-stage Matchlite Duo trigger; direct impingement operating system; flash hider; polymer pistol grip; Magpul BSL brace; receiver finished in Cerakote Elite; MLOK accessory rail
Price:................ $1,549.99

SIG SAUER P210 CARRY

Action: Semiautomatic
Grips: G10

Barrel: 4.1 in.
Sights: Siglite night sights
Weight: 29 oz.
Caliber: 9mm
Capacity: 8 rounds
Features: A full-size carry gun based off SIG's P210 target pistol profile; curved trigger; single-action-only operation; carbon steel barrel' stainless steel slide in a black Nitron finish; alloy frame with G10 grip panels; large levers on slide release and thumb safety
Price:............... $1,699.00

SIG SAUER P220 EQUINOX ELITE FULL-SIZE

Action: Semiautomatic
Grips: G10
Barrel: 4.4 in.
Sights: X-Ray3 day/night sights
Weight: 30.4 oz.
Caliber: .45 ACP
Capacity: 8 rounds
Features: Full-size .45 with a curved trigger; hard coat-anoddized ally frame; carbon steel barrel; M1913 accessory rail; two-tone Equinox slide finish; steel slide with cocking serrations; frame-mounted decocker
Price:............... $1,429.99

SIG SAUER P226 EQUINOX ELITE FULL-SIZE

Action: Semiautomatic
Grips: G10
Barrel: 4.4 in.
Sights: X-Ray3 day/night sights
Weight: 34 oz.
Caliber: 9mm
Capacity: 15 rounds
Features: Double-stack 9mm on the traditional P226 profile; M193 accessory rail; two-tone Equinox slide finish; frame-mounted decocker
Price:................ $1,429.99

SIG SAUER P229 EQUINOX ELITE COMPACT

SIG SAUER P320 AXG EQUINOX

SIG SAUER P320 AXG PRO

SIG SAUER P320 AXG SCORPION

SIG SAUER P320 XCOMPACT

SIG SAUER P365-380

SIG SAUER P365XL SPECTRE COMP

SMITH & WESSON CSX

SIG SAUER P229 EQUINOX ELITE COMPACT

Action: Semiautomatic
Grips: G10
Barrel: 3.9 in.
Sights: X-Ray3 day/night sights
Weight: 34 oz.
Caliber: 9mm
Capacity: 15 rounds
Features: With a shorter barrel than the P226, the compact P229 has a slide with the two-tone Equinox finish; SIG rail; hard coat-anodized alloy frame; curved trigger; frame decocker
Price: **$1,429.99**

SIG SAUER P320 AXG EQUINOX

Action: Semiautomatic
Grips: G10
Barrel: 3.9 in.
Sights: X-Ray3 day/night sights
Weight: 31.3 oz.
Caliber: 9mm
Capacity: 10, 17 rounds
Features: Part of the AXG Alloy Grip Series, this P320 get the Equinox aesthetics; skeletonized flat trigger; hard coat-anodized frame; optics-ready slide; Negrini Custom Works case; challenge coin
Price: **$1,329.99**

SIG SAUER P320 AXG PRO

Action: Semiautomatic
Grips: G10
Barrel: 4.7 in.
Sights: X-Ray3 day/night sights
Weight: 35.4 oz.
Caliber: 9mm
Capacity: 17 rounds
Features: A street-tough-looking, full-size, striker-fire 9mm with big window cuts in the Nitron-finished stainless steel, optics-ready slide; Carry AXG grip module; Xseries

stright trigger; hard coat-anodized stainless steel frame; M1913 accessory rail; detachable magwell
Price: **$1,199.99**

SIG SAUER P320 AXG SCORPION

Action: Semiautomatic
Grips: G10
Barrel: 4.7 in.
Sights: X-Ray3 day/night sights
Weight: 35.4 oz.
Caliber: 9mm
Capacity: 10, 17 rounds
Features: Similar to the other P320 AXG Pro, but with the frame and slide in Flat Dark Earth Cerakote; snake-skin-like G10 grip panel design; skeletonized flat trigger
Price: **$1,299.99**

SIG SAUER P320 XCOMPACT

Action: Semiautomatic
Grips: Polymer
Barrel: 3.6 in.
Sights: X-Ray3 day/night sights
Weight: 25.3 oz.
Caliber: 9mm
Capacity: 10, 15 rounds
Features: Compact, lighterweight version of this model with an Xseries straight trigger; Xcompact medium polymer grip module; stainless steel frame; optics ready rear plate; accessory rail; raised cocking serrations
Price: **$679.99**

SIG SAUER P365-380

Action: Semiautomatic
Grips: Polymer
Barrel: 3.1 in.
Sights: Siglite night sights
Weight: 15.7 oz.
Caliber: .380 ACP
Capacity: 10 rounds
Features: Big .380 capacity in a little

gun weighing under 16 oz.; striker-fire action; curved trigger; optics-ready slide in a black Nitride finish
Price: **$579.99**

SIG SAUER P365XL SPECTRE, SPECTRE COMP

Action: Semiautomatic
Grips: Polymer
Barrel: 3.7 in.
Sights: X-Ray3 day/night sights
Weight: 20.7 oz.
Caliber: 9mm
Capacity: 10, 12 rounds
Features: Double-stack 9mm micro-compact with laser-engraved LXG grip texturing; striker-fire action; SIG rail; Xseries straight trigger; stainless steel slide with a distressed or nDLC finish; generous topside slide windows; TiN gold barrel and trigger for contrast on nDLC models; optics ready; Spectra Comp adds two-port muzzle compensator and comes standard with TiN gold barrel and trigger
Price: **$1,299.99**

SMITH & WESSON CSX

Action: Semiautomatic
Grips: Synthetic
Barrel: 3.1 in.
Sights: Three-dot white front and rear
Weight: 19.5 oz.
Caliber: 9mm
Capacity: 10, 12 rounds
Features: Built on a lightweight aluminum frame, this small carry gun has interchangeable backstraps; textured front strap; ambidextrous thumb safety and slide release; interchangeable left-/right-hand magazine release buttons; flat-faced trigger; slide with EZ-tabs for easier racking; Armonite metalwork finish
Price: **$609.00**

SMITH & WESSON M&P M2.0

SMITH & WESSON M&P SHIELD PLUS

SPRINGFIELD ARMORY 1911 EMISSARY

SPRINGFIELD ARMORY 1911 RONIN EMP

SPRINGFIELD AMORY 1911 GARRISON

SPRINGFIELD ARMORY 1911 OPERATOR

SPRINGFIELD ARMORY 1911 VICKERS TACTICAL MASTER CLASS

SMITH & WESSON M&P M2.0

Action: Semiautomatic
Grips: Synthetic
Barrel: 4, 4.25, 4.6, 5 in.
Sights: Varies
Weight: 29.3 oz.
Caliber: 9mm, .40S&W, 10mm, .45 ACP
Capacity: 10, 15, 17 rounds
Features: Lots of flexiblity with this model with four calibers to the platform, all with at least two barrel lengths to choose from; depending on barrel/caliber choice, choice of optic-height white dot, tall white dot, suppressor-height night sights, TFX white dot, and both standard and tall steel white dot sights; available with or without optics-ready and with included red-dot sight; some models available with a threaded barrel; choice of black, or flat dark earth; four interchangeable palmswell grips; 18-degree grip angle; aggressive grip texturing; a kit option, which comes as a dual-tone flat dark earth/black, has a threaded muzzle; suppressor height sights night sights, includes a red-dot sight, and comes with an M&P full-tang fixed blade boot knife, M&P Spec Series challenge coin, and a custom plastic case
Price:. . . . . **$629.00–$969.00**

SMITH & WESSON M&P SHIELD PLUS

Action: Semiautomatic
Grips: Synthetic
Barrel: 3.1 in.
Sights: Three-dot white front and rear; orange ring night sight front, black night sight rear
Weight: 19.3 oz.
Caliber: 9mm, .30 Super Carry
Capacity: 10, 12, 13, 15 rounds
Features: A micro that comes optics ready and has a flat-face trigger; enhanced grip texturing; extended and flush-fit magazines; 18-degree grip angle; Armonite metal finish; optional thumb safety
Price:. . . . . **$553.00–$595.00**

SPRINGFIELD ARMORY 1911 EMISSARY

Action: Semiautomatic
Grips: G10
Barrel: 4.25, 5 in.
Sights: Tritium front, U-notch rear
Weight: 38.5–40 oz.
Caliber: 9mm, .45 ACP
Capacity: 8, 9 rounds
Features: This two-toned 1911 wears a unique tri-top cut slide with 40 lines per inch flat-top serrations that reduce glare; oversized square triggerguard; VZ Grips Thin-Line G10 panels; match-grade bull barrel; rear slide serrations; flat-faced serrated solid trigger; textured front strap and front mainspring housing; .45 ACP available in both barrel lengths
Price:. **$1,349.00**

SPRINGFIELD ARMORY 1911 GARRISON

Action: Semiautomatic
Grips: Wood
Barrel: 5 in.
Sights: Low-profile combat 3-dot
Weight: 37 oz.
Caliber: .45 ACP
Capacity: 7 rounds
Features: A classy and very traditionally styled 1911 with thin, checkered wood grips; GI recoil system; match-grade barrel; forged steel construction; in blue or stainless
Blue **$849.00**
Stainless. **$899.00**

SPRINGFIELD ARMORY 1911 OPERATOR

Action: Semiautomatic
Grips: G10
Barrel: 5 in.
Sights: Tritium front, tactical rack white dot rear
Weight: 42 oz.
Caliber: .45 ACP
Capacity: 8 rounds
Features: This 1911 is dressed up with VZ Grips scalloped G10 panels; Black Cerakote finish; front and rear slide serrations; underside accessory rail; skeletonized trigger; two included magazines have bumper pads
Price:. **$1,159.00**

SPRINGFIELD ARMORY 1911 RONIN EMP

Action: Semiautomatic
Grips: Wood
Barrel: 3, 4 in.
Sights: Fiber optic front, tactical rack white dot rear
Weight: 24–27.5 oz.
Caliber: 9mm
Capacity: 9, 10 rounds
Features: This Enhanced Micro Pistol (EMP) is the smallest 1911 built (in the 3-in. barrel) and designed specifically around the 9mm roundA slim and compact carry 9mm with a dual captive recoil spring on 3-in., flat wire on 4-in.; full-length guide rod; forged aluminum alloy grame in Satin Aluminum Cerakote; match-grade bull barrel with fully supported ramp; blued slide; skeletonized trigger
Price:. **$899.00**

SPRINGFIELD ARMORY 1911 VICKERS TACTICAL MASTER CLASS

Action: Semiautomatic
Grips: G10
Barrel: 5 in.
Sights: Tritium front, Vickers Elite Battle U-notch rear
Weight: 41.5 oz.
Caliber: .45 ACP
Capacity: 8 rounds
Features: Built with guidance from Larry Vickers, a retired U.S. Army 1st SFOD-Delta combat veteran, this upgraded 1911 sports highly unique woven slide serrations at the rear with the same pattern repeated on the front strap; Wilson Combat hammer and safety; custom match-grade barrel; Cerakoted metalwork; G10 grips with Vickers logo
Price:. **$1,495.00**

SPRINGFIELD ARMOY
HELLCAT RDP

SPRINGFIELD
ARMORY
SA-35

SPRINGFIELD ARMORY
SAINT VICTOR PISTOL

SPRINGFIELD ARMORY
XD-M ELITE 3.8-IN.
DRAGONFLY

SPRINGFIELD ARMORY
XD-M ELITE 4.5 OSP
THREADED

SPRINGFIELD
ARMORY XD-M ELITE
5.25-IN. PRECISION

SPRINGFIELD ARMORY HELLCAT RDP

Action: Semiautomatic
Grips: Synthetic
Barrel: 3.8 in.
Sights: Tritium front, tactical rack U-notch rear
Weight: 19.3 oz.
Caliber: 9mm
Capacity: 11, 13 rounds
Features: A compact, lightweight, striker-fire carry 9mm with a billet-machined slide, optics-ready and with a Melonite finish; dual captive recoil spring; full-length guide rod; Adaptive Grip Texture; threaded and compensated forged steel barrel; flush-fit and extended mags included; comes with factory-mounted Springfield Armory HEX Wasp red-dot reflex sight; avialble with or without manual thumb safety
Price: $962.00

SPRINGFIELD ARMORY SA-35

Action: Semiautomatic
Grips: Wood
Barrel: 4.7 in.
Sights: White dot front, serrated tactical black rear
Weight: 31.5 oz.
Caliber: 9mm
Capacity: 15 rounds
Features: John Browning's iconic Hi-Power continues to make a resurgence in 2022, this time guised as SA's model SA-35, with a traditional round hammer; checkered walnut grips; forged carbons teel slide and frame in matte blue
Price: $699.00

SPRINGFIELD ARMORY SAINT VICTOR AR-15 PISTOL

Action: Semiautomatic
Grips: Synthetic
Barrel: 7.5 in.
Sights: None
Weight: 85 oz.
Caliber: 5.56 NATO
Capacity: 30 rounds
Features: This rifle-caliber pistol sports a direct impingement, pistol-length gas sytstem; low-profile pinned gas block; carbine "H" heavy tungsten buffer assembly; forged T6 aluminum upper and lower hard coat Type III anodized; ambidextrous safety; Springfield Armory forward blast diverter muzzle accessory; Magpul BTR pistol brace; B5 Systems triggerguard and Type 23 P-Grip
Price: $1,249.00

SPRINGFIELD ARMORY XD-M ELITE 3.8-IN. OSP, 3.8-IN. OSP HEX DRAGONFLY

Action: Semiautomatic
Grips: Synthetic
Barrel: 3.8 in.
Sights: Fiber optic front, tactical rack U-notch rear
Weight: 27–29 oz.
Caliber: 9mm
Capacity: 14 rounds
Features: Two barrel length/frame sizes offer lots of variety for concealed carry, target practice, and home-defense. Elite 3.8 is designed for deep concealment with a fiber optic front sight and U-notch rear and comes optics-ready or with SA's HEX Dragonfly red-dot optic factory installed

3.8 . . . . $653.00–$837.00
4.5-in. $733.00

SPRINGFIELD ARMORY XDM 4.5-IN. OSP THREADED

Action: Semiautomatic
Grips: Synthetic
Barrel: 4.5 in.
Sights:
Weight: 30 oz.
Caliber: 9mm
Capacity: 22 rounds
Features: The XD-M Elite 4.5 covers a lot of practice and carry ground and is available in black or flat dark earth; optics-ready; threaded muzzle
Price: $733.00

SPRINGFIELD ARMORY XD-M ELITE 5.25-IN. PRECISION

Action: Semiautomatic
Grips: Synthetic
Barrel: 5.25 in.
Sights: Fiber optic front, adjustable target rear
Weight: 30 oz.
Caliber: 9mm
Capacity: 22 rounds
Features: Designed for competition, this 9mm offers great capacity; Melonite-finished barrel and slide; lightning cut slide; "standard" flared and extended magwell; META Match Enhanced Trigger Assembly
Price: $674.00

STANDARD MANUFACTURING 1911 CASE-COLORED

STANDARD MANUFACTURING 1911 BLUED ENGRAVED #1

STANDARD MANUFACTURING 1911 DAMASCUS

STANDARD MANUFACTURING SG9

STANDARD MANUFACTURING SG22 CASE-COLORED ENGRAVED

STANDARD MANUFACTURING SG33 LTD ED RED

STANDARD MANUFACTURING SWITCH-GUN1 AND STANDARD SWITCH-GUN2

STANDARD MANUFACTURING 1911 BLUED, NICKEL-PLATED, CASE-COLORED

Action: Semiautomatic
Grips: Wood
Barrel: 5 in.
Sights: Low-mount tactical front and rear
Weight: N/A
Caliber: .45 ACP
Capacity: 8 rounds
Features: Classic 1911 with a lowered and flared ejection port; checkered front strap; extended tactical thumb safety, slide release, and magazine release; solid match-grade trigger; match-grade stainless steel barrel and bushing; nickel-plated has poished flats and bead-blasted contours; blue and case-colored models are high-polished all over
Blued $1295.00
Nickel-plated $1899.00
Case-colored $1599.00

STANDARD MANUFACTURING 1911 BLUED ENGRAVED #1, CASE-COLORED ENGRAVED #1

Action: Semiautomatic
Grips: Wood
Barrel: 5 in.
Sights: Low-mount tactical front and rear
Weight: N/A
Caliber: .45 ACP
Capacity: 8 rounds
Features: Identical to the base models of these finishes, but these have Deluxe #1 scroll engraving on the slides and frames
Blued $1579.00
Case-colored $1899.00

STANDARD MANUFACTURING 1911 DAMASCUS

Action: Semiautomatic
Grips: Wood
Barrel: 5 in.
Sights: Low-mount tactical front and rear
Weight: N/A
Caliber: .45 ACP
Capacity: 8 rounds
Features: A full Damascus steel rendition of the 1911; chain pattern; extra fancy American walnut grip panels
Price: $5,999.00

STANDARD MANUFACTURING SG9

Action: Semiautomatic
Grips: Glass-reinforced polymer
Barrel: 4 in.
Sights: Tritium front and rear
Weight: 26 oz.
Caliber: 9mm
Capacity: 18 rounds
Features: Standard's first striker-fired pistol with generous double-stack capacity; removeable machined 4140 steel chassis (much like the Sig P320; ambidextrous slide-stop and external safety; reversible magazine release; interchangeable backstraps; button-rifled six-groove barrel; cocking indicator; three-slot underside accessory rail; available as an optics-ready variant
Price: . . . . Standrd $649.00; Optics-ready $749.00

STANDARD MANUFACTURING SG22 ROYAL BLUE, CASE-COLORED

Action: Semiautomatic
Grips: Walnut

STANDARD MANUFACTURING SWITCH-GUN1 AND STANDARD SWITCH-GUN2

Barrel: 6.63 in.
Sights: Fixed flade front, adjustable rear
Weight: N/A
Caliber: .22 LR
Capacity: 10 rounds
Features: Reminiscent of the Hi Standards of yesteryear, this pretty target .22 has a button magazine release; partially checkered, two-piece target grips; rear slide cocking serrations; adjustable rear sight; in polished Royal Blue or with a blued barrel paired with a case-colored and engraved frame and slide
Price: .N/A

STANDARD MANUFACTURING SG333 THUNDERSTRUCK LIMITED EDITION RED

Action: Revolver
Grips: Polymer
Barrel: 1.5 in.
Sights: Three-dot white front and rear
Weight: 18 oz.
Caliber: .22 Mag.
Capacity: 8 rounds
Features: Unique double-action revolver that fires two rounds with each trigger pull; special limited edition with anodized red aluminum frame
Price: $479.99

STANDARD MANUFACTURING SWITCH-GUN

Action: Revolver
Grips: Polymer
Barrel: .88 in.
Sights: None
Weight: 8 oz.
Caliber: .22 Mag.
Capacity: 5 rounds
Features: This folding revolver is designed to fit in your pocket; trigger is completely covered in the folded position; single-action; frame and barrel are CNC-machined steel
Price: $449.00

STOEGER INDUSTRIES STR-9F FULL-SIZE

STOEGER INDUSTRIES STR-9SC OPTIC READY

TAURUS 327

TAURUS DEFENDER 605

TAURUS G3X

TAURUS G3XL

TAYLOR'S & CO. FIREARMS DEVIL ANSE

STOEGER INDUSTRIES STR9-F FULL-SIZE

Action: Semiautomatic
Grips: Synthetic
Barrel: 4.68 In.
Sights: Three-dot white front and rear
Weight: 26.4 oz.
Caliber: 9mm
Capacity: 10, 17 rounds
Features: Expanding the STR-9 line to include a full-size variant, this pistol has an integral rail; reversible magazine release; slide serrations; comes with one magazine and medium backstrap
Price: **$329.00**

STOEGER INDUSTRIES STR-9SC SUB-COMPACT, SUB-COMPACT OPTIC READY

Action: Semiautomatic
Grips: Synthetic
Barrel: 3.54 in.
Sights: Three-dot white front and rear
Weight: 22.4 oz.
Caliber: 9mm
Capacity: 10 rounds
Features: The smallest offering in the STR-9 lineup, this subcompact comes in both standard and optics-ready variants; comes with one backstrap and cable lock; optics-ready version has four mounting plates to accommodate most reflex sight models
Standard **$329.00**
Optic ready **$399.00**

TAURUS 327

Action: Revolver
Grips: Rubber
Barrel: 2 in.
Sights: Fixed front, integral rear
Weight: 22 oz.
Caliber: .327 Fed. Mag.
Capacity: 6 rounds
Features: A six-shot snubbie in .327 Fed. Mag.; removeable serrated blade front sight; soft rubber grips; stainless steel construction with matte stainless finish
Price: **$388.32**

TAURUS DEFENDER 605

Action: Revolver
Grips: Wood
Barrel: 3 in.
Sights: Tritium front, integral rear
Weight: 24 oz.
Caliber: .38 Spec.
Capacity: 5 rounds
Features: Handsome and functinal five-shot for home- or self-defense, with a orange-outline tritium front sight; Tungsten Cerakote metal finish; extended wood grips from Altamont; +P rated
Price: **$517.33**

TAURUS G3X

Action: Semiautomatic
Grips: Polymer
Barrel: 3.2 in.
Sights: Fixed front, drift-adjustable rear
Weight: 22.6 oz.
Caliber: 9mm
Capacity: 15 rounds

Features: Expanding on the G3 line, this version has a full-size grip with a barrel of concealable length; generous magazine capacity; Picatinny rail; unique restrike-capable single-action striker-fire trigger with a short reset; loaded chamber indicator
Price: **$342.98**

TAURUS G3XL

Action: Semiautomatic
Grips: Polymer
Barrel: 4 in.
Sights: Fixed front, drift-adjustable rear
Weight: 24.4 oz.
Caliber: 9mm
Capacity: 12 rounds
Features: The middle ground in the G3 family, with a slightly shorter grip than the G3X but a longer barrel
Price: **$342.98**

TAYLOR'S & CO. FIREARMS DEVIL ANSE

Action: Revolver
Grips: Wood
Barrel: 4.75 in.
Sights: Blade front, integral rear
Weight: N.A
Caliber: .357 Mag., .45 LC
Capacity: 6 rounds
Features: Inspired by a famous family feud in long-ago Kentucky and West Virginia, this sleek revolver has a blued forged steel frame; black-finished Navy-sized wood grips; round barrel; available as a Taylor Tuned option
Standard . . . . **$631.43–$637.74**
Taylor Tuned . . . . . **$777.68–$783.99**

TAYLOR'S & CO. FIREARMS DRIFTER

TAYLOR'S & CO. FIREARMS HICKOK OPEN TOP

TRISTAR ARMS AMERICAN CLASSIC COMMANDER

TRISTAR ARMS AMERICAN CLASSIC GOV'T

TRISTAR ARMS AMERICAN CLASSIC II GOV'T

TRISTAR ARMS AMERICAN CLASSIC TROPHY

TRISTAR ARMS SPS PANTERA

TAYLOR'S & CO. FIREARMS DRIFTER

Action: Revolver
Grips: Wood
Barrel: 4.75, 5.5, 7.5 in.
Sights: Blade front, integral rear
Weight: N.A
Caliber: .357 Mag., .45 LC
Capacity: 6 rounds
Features: Based on the Cattleman frame; full octagon barrel; forged steel case-hardened frame; Navy-size walnut grip; availabe as a Taylor Tuned upgrade
Standard . . . . $625.12–$631.43
Taylor Tuned . . . . . $771.37–$777.68

TAYLOR'S & CO. FIREARMS HICKOK OPEN TOP

Action: Revolver
Grips: Wood
Barrel: 3.5 in.
Sights: Blade front, integral rear
Weight: 35.2 oz.
Caliber: .38 Spec., .45 LC
Capacity: 6 rounds
Features: A replica of the first revolver from Colt's designed around a centerfire cartridge; case-hardened forged steel frame; round barrel; no ejector rod; Army-sized walnut grip
Price:. $635.64

TRISTAR ARMS AMERICAN CLASSIC COMMANDER

Action: Semiautomatic
Grips: Wood
Barrel: 4.25 in.
Sights: Blade front, Novak rear
Weight: 36.9 oz.
Caliber: 9mm, .45 ACP
Capacity: 8, 9 rounds

Features: Developed in partnership with Metro Arms, this traditional 1911 Commander has checkered wood grips; rear slide serrations; Novak rear sight; skeletonized trigger and combat hammer; flat mainspring housing; in blue or chrome; comes with one magazine, hard case, and gun lock
Blued $730.00
Chrome $840.00

TRISTAR ARMS AMERICAN CLASSIC GOV'T 1911

Action: Semiautomatic
Grips: Wood
Barrel: 5 in.
Sights: Blade front, notch rear
Weight: 39.5 oz.
Caliber: 9mm, .38 Super, .45 ACP
Capacity: 8, 9 rounds
Features: Similar to the American Classic Commander, but with in a full-size Gov't. configuration and with mil-spec front and rear sights; in blue or chrome
Blued $670.00
Chrome $760.00

TRISTAR ARMS AMERICAN CLASSIC II GOV'T 1911

Action: Semiautomatic
Grips: Wood
Barrel: 5 in.
Sights: Blade front, Novak rear
Weight: 39.5 oz.
Caliber: 9mm, .45 ACP, 10mm
Capacity: 8, 9 rounds
Features: Builds on the original American Classic Gov't. by adding front slide serrations; Novak rear sight; in blue or chrome

Blued $715.00
Chrome $810.00

TRISTAR ARMS AMERICAN CLASSIC TROPHY 1911

Action: Semiautomatic
Grips: Wood
Barrel: 5 in.
Sights: Fiber optic front, adjustable Novak rear
Weight: 39.5 oz.
Caliber: .45 ACP
Capacity: 8 rounds
Features: In .45 ACP only and intended for more serious target shooting, this model builds on TriStar/Metro Arms other 1911s by adding an adjustable rear Novak sight and a fiber optic front sight; in chrome only
Price:. $945.00

TRISTAR ARMS SPS PANTERA 1911

Action: Semiautomatic
Grips: Polymer
Barrel: 5 in.
Sights: Fiber optic front, adjustable Bomar rear
Weight: 43.36 oz.
Caliber: 9mm
Capacity: 18 rounds
Features: A single-action 9mm for the competition range, with generous double-stack capacity; over-wide magwell; ambidextrous thumb safety; polymer trigger; skeletonized combat hammer; extended beavertail; steel frame and slide; in blue, chrome, or black chrome
Blue $1985.00
Chrome $2060.00
Black chrome $2135.00

NEW Products: **Handguns**

TRISTAR ARMS SPS VISTA LONG

UBERTI CODY

UBERTI FRISCO

UBERTI HARDIN

UBERTI TEDDY

VOLQUARTSEN ENV PISTOL

WALTHER PDP PRO SD

TRISTAR ARMS SPS VISTA LONG 1911

Action: Semiautomatic
Grips: Polymer
Barrel: 5.5 in.
Sights: None
Weight: 43.36 oz.
Caliber: .38 Super
Capacity: 21 rounds
Features: Ready to win in Open Class right out of the box, this all-steel double-stack 1911 has a match-grade barrel with a threaded-on muzzle break; rear scope mount (just add a sight and you're ready to go); over-wide magwell; ambidextrous thumb safety; wide rear slide serrations; polymer trigger; skeletonized combat hammer
Price: **$2,825.00**

UBERTI CODY

Action: Revolver
Grips: Synthetic
Barrel: 4.75 in.
Sights: Blade front, integral rear
Weight: 36.8 oz.
Caliber: .45 LC
Capacity: 6 rounds
Features: Handsome polished nickel single-action with smooth ivory-like synthetic grips, based on the New Model 1863 Cattleman
Price: **$1,029.00**

UBERTI FRISCO

Action: Revolver
Grips: Synthetic
Barrel: 4.75 in.
Sights: Blade front, integral rear
Weight: 36.8 oz.

Caliber: .45 LC
Capacity: 6 rounds
Features: Striking single-action with charcoal blue round barrel, cylinder and grip; case-colored frame; pearl-like synthetic grips
Price: **$1,029.00**

UBERTI HARDIN

Action: Revolver
Grips: Synthetic
Barrel: 7 in.
Sights: Blade front, integral rear
Weight: 41.6 oz.
Caliber: .45 LC
Capacity: 6 rounds
Features: Gorgeous break-top inspired by the outlaw and gunfighter John Wesley Hardin; polished deep-blue barrel and fluted cylinder; case-colored frame; simulated buffalo horn grips
Price: **$1,699.00**

UBERTI TEDDY

Action: Revolver
Grips: Synthetic
Barrel: 5.5 in.
Sights: Blade front, integral rear
Weight: 36.8 oz.
Caliber: .45 LC
Capacity: 6 rounds
Features: Inspired by President Theodore "Teddy" Roosevelt, this 1873 Cattleman appears in full nickle-plated steel with western scroll engraving very similar to the engraving on Teddy's own gun and with simulated ivory grips
Price: **$1,399.00**

VOLQUARTSEN ENV-6, ENV-9

Action: Semiautomatic
Grips: Synthetic
Barrel: 6, 9 in.
Sights: None
Weight: 59 oz.
Caliber: .22 LR
Capacity: 10 rounds
Features: There's a 10/22 foundation under the Enoch Industries ODIN chassis system; ENV aluminum receiver; TG2000 trigger group; universal red-dot optics mount; threaded lightweight barrel; SB Tactical arm brace; Magpul MOE-K grip; Slat Stop hand stop; built to order
Price: **$1,554.00**

WALTHER PDP PRO SD FULL-SIZE, COMPACT

Action: Semiautomatic
Grips: Synthetic
Barrel: 4, 5.1 in.
Sights: Blade front, adjustable rear
Weight: 23.7 oz.
Caliber: 9mm
Capacity: 10, 15, 18 rounds
Features: The Pro SD builds out the original PDP models with a Performance Duty trigger; threaded barrel; aluminum magwell; magazines with aluminum base pads (three included); SuperTerrain slide serrations front and rear; underside accessory rail; optics-ready slide
Price: **$829.00**

WILSON COMBAT ACP FULL SIZE

WILSON COMBAT ACP COMPACT

WILSON COMBAT ACP COMMANDER

WILSON COMBAT CQB ELITE COMMANDER

WILSON COMBAT CQB ELITE COMPACT

WILSON COMBAT CQB PROFESSIONAI

WILSON COMBAT EDC X9

WILSON COMBAT ACP FULL SIZE

Action: Semiautomatic
Grips: G10
Barrel: 5 in.
Sights: Fiber optic front, adjustable rear
Weight: 41.6 oz.
Caliber: 9mm, .45 ACP
Capacity: 8, 10 rounds
Features: The ACP--Advanced Combat Pistol—is a full-size Govt. model with a carbon steel frame and slide; Eagle Claw cocking serrations; Bullet Proof high-grip beavertail safety, magazine release, and tactical thumb safety; contoured magazine well; flush-cut match-grade barrel and bushing; Eagle Claw G10 grips
Price:........ **$2595.00–$2695.00**

WILSON COMBAT ACP COMPACT

Action: Semiautomatic
Grips: G10
Barrel: 4
Sights: Fiber optic front, adjustable rear
Weight: 36.9 oz.
Caliber: 9mm, .45 ACP
Capacity: 7, 8 rounds
Features: The shorter barreled, shorter gripped version of the ACP Full-Size; match-grade cone barrel and bushing
Price:........ **$2595.00–$2695.00**

WILSON COMBAT ACP COMMANDER

Action: Semiautomatic
Grips: G10
Barrel: 4.25
Sights: Fiber optic front, adjustable rear
Weight: 37.8 oz.
Caliber: 9mm, .45 ACP
Capacity: 8, 10 rounds
Features: A Commander-length barrel on WC's Professional 1911 frame with all the features of the other ACP pistols; standard flush-cut match-grade barrel and bushing; 30 lines per inch slide top serrations; 40 lines per inch rear of slide serrations; cocking serrations fore and aft
Price:........ **$2595.00–$2695.00**

WILSON COMBAT CQB ELITE COMMANDER

Action: Semiautomatic
Grips: G10
Barrel: 4.25
Sights: Fiber optic front, adjustable rear
Weight: 38.3 oz.
Caliber: 9mm, .38 Super, .45 ACP
Capacity: 8, 10 rounds diagonally cut G10 grips; flush-cut match-grade bushing and barrel with reverse crown; 30 lines per inch top-of-slide serrations; 40 lines per inch rear-of-slide serrations
Features: A Commander-sized 1911 with Bullet Proof mag well, tactical thumb safety, magazine release, and high-rise beavertail; G10 diagonally lined grips; reverse-crown, match-grade, flush-cut barrel and bushing; standard flush-cut match-grade barrel and bushing; 30 lines per inch slide top serrations; 40 lines per inch rear of slide serrations; cocking serrations fore and aft
Price:........ **$3565.00–$3665.00**

WILSON COMBAT CQB ELITE COMPACT

Action: Semiautomatic
Grips: G10
Barrel: 4 in.
Sights: Fiber optic front, adjustable rear
Weight: 36.8 oz.

Caliber: 9mm, .38 Super, .45 ACP
Capacity: 7 rounds
Features: The smallest of the CQB Elite line with all the features of the others plus G10 Starburst grips; Bullet Proof round-butt magazine well; flush-cut, reverse crown, match-grade cone barrel and bushing
Price:........ **$3565.00–$3665.00**

WILSON COMBAT CQB PROFESSIONAL

Action: Semiautomatic
Grips: G10
Barrel: 4 in.
Sights: Fiber optic front, adjustable rear
Weight: 38.6 oz.
Caliber: 9mm, .38 Super, .45 ACP
Capacity: 8, 10 rounds
Features: A short barrel on WC's tall frame, this one sports all the other featuers of the CQB Elites in addition to G10 diagonally carved grips; flush-cut, match-grade, reverse-crown cone barrel and bushing; high-cut checkered front strap
Price:........ **$3565.00–$3665.00**

WILSON COMBAT EDC X9

Action: Semiautomatic
Grips: G10
Barrel: 4 in.
Sights: Fiber optic front, adjustable rear
Weight: 29.09 oz.
Caliber: 9mm
Capacity: 15, 18 rounds
Features: A sharp-looking 9mm for everyday carry (EDC), with aggressively textured Starburst G10 grips; X-Tac front strap, mainspring housing, and cocking serration treatment; Bullet Proof concealment hammer, thumb safety, and magazine release; heavy machine chamber on slide bottom; aluminum X-Frame; flush-cut, reverse-crown, fluted cone barrel; fluted chamber; 30 lines per inch slide top serrations; 40 lines per inch rear of slide serrations; carry cuts and ball endmills cuts througout; black DLC slide finish
Price:................ **$2,995.00**

NEW Products: **Handguns**

WILSON COMBAT EDC X9L

WILSON COMBAT SFX9

WILSON COMBAT TACTICAL CARRY COMMANDER

WILSON COMBAT VICKERS ELITE COMMANDER

WILSON COMBAT X-TAC COMMANDER

WILSON COMBAT X-TAC ELITE COMMANDER

WILSON COMBAT EDC X9L

Action: Semiautomatic
Grips: G10
Barrel: 5 in.
Sights: Fiber optic front, adjustable rear
Weight: 32.4 oz.
Caliber: 9mm
Capacity: 15, 18 rounds
Features: Similar to the X9, but with a longer flush-cut reverse crown stainless barrel; underside accessory rail; trip-top slide with external extractor; black DLC slide finish
Price: **$3,095.00**

WILSON COMBAT SFX9

Action: Semiautomatic
Grips: Polymer
Barrel: 3.25, 4 in.
Sights: Fiber optic front, adjustable rear
Weight: 25.2, 36 oz.
Caliber: 9mm
Capacity: 10, 15 rounds
Features: A double-stack carry sub-compact with single-stack ergonomics; aluminum X-Frame; Bullet Proof concealment hammer, concealment thumb safety, concealment magazine release, and concealment slide stop; stainless steel tri-top slide with external extractor, black DLC finish, and X-Tac rear cocking serrations; flush-cut, reverse crown, fluted cone barrel with a fluted chamber; 30 lines per inch top-side slide serrationc; carry cuts; accessory rail
Price: . . . . **$2795.00–$2895.00**

WILSON COMBAT TACTICAL CARRY COMMANDER

Action: Semiautomatic
Grips: G10
Barrel: 4.25 in.
Sights: Fiber optic front, adjustable rear
Weight: 37.8 oz.
Caliber: 9mm, .38 Super, .45 ACP
Capacity: 8, 10 rounds
Features: Commander barrel length on a Professional-size carbon steel frame; Bullet Proof round-butt magazine well, concealment beavertail grip safety and hammer, and tactical thumb safety; counter-sunk slide stop; rear slide cocking serrations; Starburst G10 grip panels; flush-cut reverse crown match-grade barrel and bushing; 30 lines per inch top-side slide serrations; 40 lines per inch rear of slide serrations; carry cuts and ball endmills cuts throughout
Price: . . . . **$3890.00–$3990.00**

WILSON COMBAT VICKERS ELITE COMMANDER

Action: Semiautomatic
Grips: G10
Barrel: 4.25 in.
Sights: Gold bead front sight, adjustable rear
Weight: 39.6 oz.
Caliber: 9mm, .45 ACP
Capacity: 8, 10 rounds
Features: Special pistol developed in coordination with Larry Vickers, this pistol sports G10 grips with the Vickers logo; Bullet Proof round-butt magazine well, magazine release, tactical thumb safety, and bobbed high-ride beavertail safety; countersunk slide stop; flush-cut, reverse crown match-grade barrel with thick flange; fluted chamber; wide rear cocking serrations; 30 lines per inch top-side slide serrations; 40 lines per inch rear of slide serrations; ball endmill cuts throughout
Price: . . . .**$3990.00–$4090.00**

WILSON COMBAT X-TAC COMMANDER

Action: Semiautomatic
Grips: G10
Barrel: 4.25 in.
Sights: Fiber optic front, adjustable rear
Weight: 38 oz.
Caliber: 9mm, .38 Super, .45 ACP
Capacity: 8, 10 rouonds
Features: Commander-length barrel on Professional-size frame with X-Tac front strap and mainspring housing treatment; Bullet Proof high-ride beavertail safety, magazine release, and tactical thumb safety; X-Tac pattern G10 grips; X-Tac cocking serrations; flush-cut reverse crown match-grade barrel; contoured magazine well; black Parkerized finish
Price: . . . .**$2860.00–$2960.00**

WILSON COMBAT X-TAC ELITE COMMANDER

Action: Semiautomatic
Grips: G10
Barrel: 4.25 in.
Sights: Fiber optic front, adjustable rear
Weight: 38.4 oz.
Caliber: 9mm, .38 Super, .45 ACP
Capacity: 8, 10 rounds
Features: All the features of the base X-Tac Elite, then adds 30 lines per inch top-side slide serrations; 40 lines per inch rear of slide serrations; carry cuts and ball endmill cuts throughout; countersunk slide stop
Price: . . . .**$3790.00–$3890.00**

ARMAMENT TECHNOLOGY SAI OPTICS SAI 6

ARMAMENT TECHNOLOGY TANGENT THETA 3–15X50MM PROFESSIONAL

ARMAMENT TECHNOLOGY TANGENT THETA 3–15X50MM LONG RANGE HUNTER

AMAMENT TECHNOLOGY TANGENT THETA 5–25X56MM PROFESSIONAL

ATN CORP. X-SIGHT LTV 5-15X

BLASER B1

SCOPES

ARMAMENT TECHNOLOGY SAI OPTICS SAI 6

Available in: 1–6X24mm
Weight: 18 oz.
Length: 10.07 in.
Main Dia.: 30mm
Exit Pupil: 9.5–4mm
Field of View: 39.8–6.5m@100m
Eye Relief: 3.54 in.
Features: Boasting an illuminated first focal plane Rapid Aiming Feature reticle; 10 illumination brightness settings; exteriror in Type II anodized matte flat dark earth; 120 MOA windage/elevation adjustment; finger-adjustable re-zero mechanism; supplied with Tennebrex Tactical Tough lens covers and killFlash Anti-Reflection Device; throw-lever available as an add-on
Price:. $1290.00

ARMAMENT TECHNOLOGY TANGENT THETA 3–15X50MM PROFESSIONAL

Available in: 3–15X50mm
Weight: 36.15 oz.
Length: 14.01 in.
Main Dia.: 34mm
Exit Pupil: 11.5–3.5mm
Field of View: 12.8–2.8m@100m
Eye Relief: 3.54 in.
Features: Designed for professional marksmen, the ultra-durable construction houses 11 illumination settings; Tool-Less Re-Zero; side parallax adjustment; lockable, rapid-adjusting diopter; elevation zero-stop; parallax adjustment range 50m to infinity; working elevation adjustmet 96 MOA; working windage adjustment 20.5 MOA; waterproof for four hours at a depth of 10m; available reticles include Gen2XR, MOA-calibrated reticle; Gen2 Mil-dot with .1 MRAD adjustment resolution, and Gen3XR
Price:. $4550.00

ARMAMENT TECHNOLOGY TANGENT THETA 3–15X50MM LONG RANGE HUNTER

Available in: 3–15X50mm
Weight: 36.15 oz.
Length: 14.01 in.
Main Dia.: 34mm
Exit Pupil: 11.5–3.5mm
Field of View: 12.8–2.8m@100m
Eye Relief: 3.54 in.
Features: For hunters, this iterration sports a single-piece main tube; reticle illumination and parallax controlled by the left-side dial; 32mm eyepiece; elevation revolutions indicator; rapid-access windage and elevation; working elevation 39 MOA; working windage 9.5 MOA; crosshair and stadia line reticles in MOA or MRAD
Price:. $3974.00

ARMAMENT TECHNOLOGY TANGENT THETA 5–25X56MM PROFESSIONAL

Available in: 5–25X56mm
Weight: 52.91 oz.
Length: 16.73 in.
Main Dia.: 34mm
Exit Pupil: 11–2.3mm
Field of View: 7.6–1.6m@100m
Eye Relief: 3.54 in.
Features: Designed for professional marksmen working at extreme ranges, this scope has a big 56mm objective; 11 reticle illumination settings; side parallax adjustment with parallax from 50mm to infinity; 906 MOA working elevation; 20 MOA working windage; double-turn elevation and revoultion indicators; Tool-Less Re-Zero; elevation zero-stop; lockable rapid-adjusting diopter; available reticles include Gen2 XR, MOA ER, Gen3 XR, Horus H59, Horus Tremor3, JTAC, and Gen3 XR Fine; external finish in Type II anodized matte black or coyote brown; supplied with Tennebrex lens covers and Anti-Reflective Device
Price:. . . . . $5092.00–$6180.00

ATN CORP. X-SIGHT LTV

Available in: 3–9X, 5–15X
Weight: 26.27, 27.5 oz.
Length: 12.2, 13 in.
Main Dia.: 30mm
Exit Pupil: N/A
Field of View: N/A
Eye Relief: 3.54
Features: This is a day/night optic complete with IR illuminator; 3D gyroscope and accelerometer; ATN Obsidian LT core; ATN QHD+ M584 sensor; 1280X720 video resolution and HD display; USB charging port; multiple reticle patterns; ultra-low power consumption for longevity in the field; One Shot Zero feature; 30mm rings included
Price:. .3–9X $599.00; 5–15X $679.00

BLASER B1

Available in: 1–7X28mm, 2.8–20X50mm, 4–20X58mm
Weight: 22.75, 27.6, 31.2 oz.
Length: 12.5, 13.5, 14.37 in.
Main Dia.: N/A
Exit Pupil: 4mm, 10–2.5mm, 12.3–2.9mm
Field of View: 44.6–6.6 yd@100 yd., 14.4–6.5 yd.@100 yd., 10–2 yd.@100 yd.
Eye Relief: 3.5 in.
Features: You'll note in the specifications that no tube diameters are listed and that's because Blaser's never-ending quest for the sleekest guns on the planet has expanded to include scopes that don't require a traditional ring and base mount and instead mount directly to the Blaser Saddle Mount via a notch design; all reticles are in the first focal plane; IC illumination built in and activated via the IC cocking slide on a Blaser R8 bolt rifle; Intelligent Variable Dot changes in size with magnification changes; Quick Distance Control allows for instant reticle changes to longer-distance targets without actually having to aim higher; lockable turrets and parallax setting
Price:. . . . . $3267.00–$4111.00

BLASER B2

BURRIS ELIMINATOR 5

BURRIS XTR III ILLUMINATED

BURRIS XTR PRO

BUSHNELL AR OPTICS 1–6X24MM ILLUMINATED

BUSHNELL ELITE 4500 1–4X24MM

BUSHNELL ELITE TACTICAL DMR3

BLASER B2

Available in: 1–6X24mm, 2–12X50mm, 2.5–15X56mm
Weight: 20.8, 25.9, 28.12 oz.
Length: 10.7, 13, 12.87 in.
Main Dia.: N/A,
Exit Pupil: 9.8–4mm, 9.8–4.2mm, 9.8–3.7mm
Field of View: 40–6.7m@100m, 20–3.3m@100m, 16–2.6m@100m
Eye Relief: 3.54 in.
Features: A more compact lineup than the B1 optics, this line features the same unique mounting and IC illumination activation; 1–6X designed for driven hunting, 2–12X works well for stalking or treestand work, and the 2.5–15X also works well for treestand work and longer shots; fiber optic 4A reticle in the second focal plane
Price: ....N/A

BURRIS ELIMINATOR 5

Available in: 5–25X50mm
Weight: 28.8 oz.
Length: 15.5 in.
Main Dia.: N/A
Exit Pupil: 10–2.5mm
Field of View: 22–5.8 ft.@100 yd.
Eye Relief: 3.5–4 in.
Features: Burris calls this a "plug and play"—all you have to do is feed the scope your ballistic information and it calculates holdover to the targer; Bluetooth technology; X96 reticle with 10mph wind values; mounts to any Weaver or Picatinny base without requiring rings
Price: ....N/A

BURRIS XTR III ILLUMINATED

Available in: 3.3–18X50mm, 5.5–30X56mm
Weight: 29.8 oz.
Length: 13.3 in.
Main Dia.: 34mm
Exit Pupil: 8.6–2.7mm
Field of View: 37.7–6.8 ft.@100 yd.
Eye Relief: 3.5–4 in.
Features: Burris builds on its popular XTR III line with illuminated reticles; choice of SCR MOA or SCR2 reticle in the first focal plane; red or green illumination; large eye box
Price: $1439.00

BURRIS XTR PRO

Available in: 5.5–30X56mm
Weight: 33.6 oz.
Length: 15.4 in.
Main Dia.: 34mm
Exit Pupil: 8.6–1.8mm
Field of View: 23–4.2 ft.@100 yd.
Eye Relief: 3.2–4 in.
Features: Developed for PRS and NRL competitors, this powerhouse scope features a quick-detach race dial with "whiteboard"-style coating that allows for use with a dry erase marker; tool-less zero stop; magnification throw lever; changeable reticle illumination colors with 11 brightness settings; waterproof, shockproof, and fogproof; spiffy red part highlights; available reticles include SCR 2, Horus THERMOR5, and SCR 2 ¼ Mil
Price: $2639.00

BUSHNELL AR OPTICS 1–6X24MM ILLUMINATED

Available in: 1–6X24mm
Weight: 16.5 oz.
Length: 10.2 in.
Main Dia.: 30mm
Exit Pupil: N/A
Field of View: 100–16 ft. @100 yd.
Eye Relief: 3.6 in.
Features: A second focal plane illuminated, etched glass BDC reticle in a compact package; reticle designe for use with .223 Rem/5.56 NATO;

capped turrets; throw-down power-change lever; IPX7 waterproof construction; fully multi-coated optics
Price: $279.99

BUSHNELL ELITE 4500

Available in: 1–4X24mm, 2.5–10X40mm, 4–16X50mm
Weight: 15.5, 19.7, 20 oz.
Length: 9.37, 13, 14.1 in.
Main Dia.: 30mm
Exit Pupil: N/A
Field of View: 88–26 ft@100 yd., 38–10 ft. @100 yd., 25–6 ft, @100 yd.
Eye Relief: 4.4, 4.3, 4.3 in.
Features: Generous eye relief backs toplow-light performance; EXO Barrier lens protection; fast-focus eyepiece; IPX7 waterproof construction; Multi-X reticle; 120 MOA windage/elevation adjustment
Price: ....$229.99–$299.99

BUSHNELL ELITE TACTICAL DMR3

Available in: 3.5–21X50mm
Weight: 35.5 oz.
Length: 13.2 in.
Main Dia.: 34mm
Exit Pupil: N/A
Field of View: 25.5–5.1 ft@100 yd.
Eye Relief: 4 in.
Features: Feature-rich scope for less money than the competition, with a RevLimiter zero-stop; ED Prime glass; IP67 water- and dust-proof rated; EXO Barrier protection; specially coated G4P reticle elements; two-position throw hammer; parallax adjustable to 25 yards; oversized turret markings; leveler; sunshade; fast-focus diopter; fully multi-coated lenses; locking windage turret; 32 MIL windage adjustment, 20 MIL elevation adjustmen; argon-gas purged fogproof
Price: $1499.99

**BUSHNELL ELITE
TACTICAL XRS3**

**BUSHNELL RIMFIRE
3–9X40MM**

CABELA'S
COVENANT 7

**CABLEA'S
COVENANT 5**

**CABELA'S
COVENANT AR**

**CABELA'S COVENANT
TACTICAL FFP**

**CABELA'S COVENANT
TACTICAL SFP**

CABELA'S CX
PRO HD FFP

BUSHNELL ELITE TACTICAL XRS3

Available in: 6–36X56mm
Weight: 38.9 oz.
Length: 14.8 in.
Main Dia.: 34mm
Exit Pupil: N/A
Field of View: 18–3 ft.@100 yd.
Eye Relief: 4 in.
Features: Big magnification backed by a glass-eteched G4P reticle with element coating in the first focal plane; multi-position throw hammer; oversized turret markings; RevLimiter zero stop; locking diopter; ED Prime glass; improved eyebox; side-focus parallax adjustment 50 yards to infinity; IP67 water- and dust-proof rated; locking windage turret; 29 MIL elevation adjustment, 15 MIL windage adjustment; sunshade included
Price:. **$1699.99**

BUSHNELL RIMFIRE 3–9X40MM, 3–9X40MM ILLUMINATED

Available in: 3–9X40mm
Weight: 15.4 oz.
Length: 12.2 in.
Main Dia.: 1 in.
Exit Pupil: N/A
Field of View: 39–13 ft.@100 yd.
Eye Relief: 3.6 in.
Features: Dedicated rimfire scope with a second focal plane, etched glass DZ22 BDC reticle available both illuminated and nonilluminated and calibrated for the .40-grain .22 LR with drop points to 125 yards; IPX7 waterproof; nitrogen-gas purged; fast-focus diopter; fully multi-coated lenses; EXO Barrier protection; 60 MOA windage/elevation adjustment
Price: . . . . **Non-illuminated $99.99;
Illuminated $119.99**

CABELA'S COVENANT 7

Available in: 3–21X50mm, 5–35X50mm, 5–35X56mm,
Weight: N/A
Length: 13.8, 15.4 in.
Main Dia.: 34mm
Exit Pupil: N/A
Field of View: N/A
Eye Relief: 3.5 in.
Features: A pair of 7Xs with enhanced power lever; exposed turrets; zero-stop elevation; side parallax adjustment; fully-multicoated lenses; water- and fog-proof; choice of TAC-36 MOA FFP, TAC-10 MIL FFP, or TAC-8 MIL SFP reticles
Price:. . . . . $349.99–$399.99

CABELA'S COVENANT 5 TACTICAL

Available in: 3–15X50mm, 5–25X50mm
Weight: 24, 26 oz.
Length: 14.1, 16.4 in.
Main Dia.: 30mm
Exit Pupil: N/A
Field of View: 36–7.5 ft.@100 yd.
Eye Relief: 3.5–4 in.
Features: Similar to the Covenant 7 line, but in a 5X zoom range; choice of TAC-10 MIL FFP, TAC-36 FFP, TAC-10S MIL SFP, or TAC-6 MIL SFP reticles
Price:. . . . . $299.99–$349.99

CABELA'S COVENANT AR

Available in: 1–8X24mm
Weight: 17.5 oz.
Length: 10.75 in.
Main Dia.: 30mm
Exit Pupil: N/A
Field of View: 124.2–15.6 ft.@100 yd.
Eye Relief: 4.75 in.
Features: Compact unit for MSR platforms, with big eye relief; quick-change maganification throw lever; fully multi-coated lenses; waterproof and fog-proof
Price:. **$249.99**

CABELA'S COVENANT TACTICAL FFP

Available in: 4–16X44mm, 6–24X50mm
Weight: 24, 26 oz.
Length: 14.1 in.
Main Dia.: 30mm
Exit Pupil: N/A
Field of View: 24.6–6.3 ft.@100 yds., 17.7–4.45 ft.@100 yds.
Eye Relief: 4 in.
Features: With a first focal plane TAC-36 ballistic reticle, this scope has a 4X power range; side-focus parallax; water- and fog-proof; low-profile turrets with ¼-MOA clicks
Price:. . . . .**$249.99–$299.99**

CABELA'S COVENANT TACTICAL SFP

Available in: 4–16X44mm
Weight: 24 oz.
Length: 14.1 in.
Main Dia.: 30mm
Exit Pupil: N/A
Field of View: 24.6–6.3 ft.@100 yds.
Eye Relief: 3.7–4 in.
Features: Similar to the FFP version, but with a TAC 32 reticle in the second focal plane
Price:. **$199.99**

CABELA'S CX PRO HD FFP

Available in: 5–25X56mm
Weight: 41 oz.
Length: 15.67 in.
Main Dia.: 34mm
Exit Pupil: N/A
Field of View: 22.1–4.7 ft.@100 yd.
Eye Relief: 3.74 in.
Features: A big 5X-range scope with a Cabela's proprietary glass-etched, illuminated CX-MOA or CX-MIL reticle in the first focal plane; exposed locking turrets; side-focus parallax adjustment; zero-stop elevation turret; fully multi-coated lenses; magnifcation change power lever; IPX7 waterproof; ED glass with index-matched and advanced ultra-wide-band coatings; includes soft stretch case, flip-up lens covers, removeable zoom lever, battery, and sunshade
Price:. **$799.99**

NEW Products: Optics

CABELA'S INTENSITY LR

CABELA'S INTENSITY RIMFIRE

CABELA'S LR

CARL ZEISS LRP S5

CRIMSON TRACE BRUSHLINE

CRIMSON TRACE BRUSHLINE PRO 2–7X32

CABELA'S INTENSITY LR

Available in: 4–16X44mm
Weight: 25 oz.
Length: 14 in.
Main Dia.: 30mm
Exit Pupil: N/A
Field of View: 28.3–7 ft@100 yd.
Eye Relief: 3.6 in.
Features: A lightweight option for hunters needing some range, with a 4X scope wearing an INT LR MOA reticle in the second focal plane; fast-focus eyepiece; generous eye relief; zero-stop elevation turret; side parallax adjustment; fully multi-coated lenses; rubber eye guard; easy-grip power selector; waterproof, shockproof, and fog-proof
Price:.................$299.99

CABELA'S INTENSITY RIMFIRE

Available in: 3–9X40mm, 4–12X40mm
Weight: N/A
Length: 15, 16.5 in.
Main Dia.: 1 in.
Exit Pupil: N/A
Field of View: 34.7–11.35 ft.@100 yd., 34.7–11.35 ft.@100 yd.
Eye Relief: 4 in.
Features: Dedicated rimfire scope with big eye relief; Intensity RF BDC reticle; ¼-MOA clicks; fast-focus eyepiece; parallax free at 50 yards; waterproof, shockproof, and fog-proof
Price:.......... **$119.99–$129.99**

CABELA'S LR

Available in: 4–16X44mm
Weight: 24 oz.
Length: 14.1 in.
Main Dia.: 30mm
Exit Pupil: N/A
Field of View: N/A
Eye Relief: N/A
Features: With a TAC 32 ballistic reticle in the seconf focal plane, this scope also features low-profile ¼-MOA turrets; side-focus parallax adjustment; shockproof, waterproof, and fog-proof via nitrogen-filled tube
Price:.................$199.99

CARL ZEISS LRP S5

Available in: 3.6–18X50mm, 5–25X56mm
Weight: 32.8, 36.3 oz.
Length: 13, 15.6 in.
Main Dia.: 34mm
Exit Pupil: 9.3–2.8mm, 9.2–2.4mm
Field of View: 30–6 ft.@100 yd., 23–5 ft.@100 yd.
Eye Relief: 3.54 in.
Features: A first focal plane rifle scope with a 34mm main tube designed for PRS or NRL competiton, with features like 140 MOA of elevation (optional 40.7 MRAD); daylight-visible illuminated reticle; lockable repeatable tactical turrets; fluoride lens elements; SCHOTT glass; Zeiss T* coatings; LutoTec protective exterior lens coating repels moisture, dust, and fingerprints; parallax setting from 27 yards to infinity
Price:........ **$3299.99–$3599.99**

CRIMSON TRACE BRUSHLINE

Available in: 3–9X40mm, 3–9X50mm, 4–12X40mm,
Weight: 14.1, 20.46, 16.2 oz.
Length: 12.3, 12.4, 14 in.
Main Dia.: 1 in.
Exit Pupil: N/A
Field of View: 33.9–11.3 ft.@100 yd., 23.6–7.9 ft.@100 yd.
Eye Relief: 3.5 in.
Features: Designed to function perfectly in extreme weather, this scope series features aerospace-grade aluminum bodies; nitorgen-purged, waterproof and shockproof; MOC-coated ELD glass; aggressive knurling on turret knobs and magnification ring; 95 MOA windage/elevation adjustment on 3–9x, 65 MOA on 4–12s; 3–9X40 and 4–12X40 have Crimson Trace Custom BDC Rimfire reticle or Crimson Trace Custom BDC reticle; 3–9X50 has Crimson Trace Custom BDC reticle;
Price:.......... **$159.99–$204.99**

CRIMSON TRACE BRUSHLINE PRO

Available in: 2–7X32mm, 2.5–8X28mm, 2.5–10X42mm, 3–9X40mm, 3–9X50mm, 3–12X42mm, 4–12X40mm 4–16X42mm, 4–16X50mm, 6–24X50mm
Weight: 16.08, 11.46, 16.48, 14.99, 17.64, 15.52, 18.87, 22.93, 20.46 oz.
Length: 11.5, 9.7, 12.6, 12.4, 12.5, 14.1, 13.5, 14.7, 15.5 in.
Main Dia.: 1 in., 30mm
Exit Pupil: N/A
Field of View: 44.5–12.8 ft.@100 yd., 13.1–4.1 ft.@100 yd., 40.2–10.1 ft.@100 yd., 33.9–11.3 ft.@100 yd., 33.9–11.3 ft.@100 yd., 23.6–7.9 ft.@100 yd., 25.2–6.3 ft.@100 yd., 28.5–7.2 ft.@100 yd., 16.8–4.2 ft.@100 yd.
Eye Relief: 3.5 in.
Features: For dedicated hunters, this line of second focal plane scopes has something for rifle, pistol, shotgun, and muzzleloader hunters, with fully multi-coated lenses; aerospace-grade aluminum bodies; capped turrets; 2–7X32 available with BDC or BDC rimfire reticle and 90 MOA windage/ elevation; 2.5–8X28 is a pistol scope with a BDC Pistol reticle, 9.3-in. eye relief; and 15 MOA windage/ elevation; 2.5–10X42 has Plex or BDC reticle, 100-yd. parallax, and 90 MOA windage/elevation; 3–9X40 has choice of BDC, BDC Predator, BDC Muzzleloader, BDC Legend (for .350 Legend rifles), BDC Slugger (for slug shotguns), or Plex reticle, 95 MOA windage/elevation, 100-yd. parallax on rifle scopes, 65 MOA windage/ elevation on Slugger and Muzzleloader, 90 MOA windage/ elevation on Legend; 3–50X only available with BDC reticle, has 95 MOA windage/elevation and 100-yd. parallax; 4–12X40 available in Plex, BDC, or BDC Predator reticles, 65 MOA windage/elevation, 100-yd. parallax; 4–16X42 in BDC reticle only, adjustable side parallax; 4–16X50 in either a 1-in. or 30mm tube, both with BDC reticle, 90 MOA windage/ elevation, and adjustable side parallax; 6–24X50 has BDC reticle; 36 MOA windage/elevation, adjustable parallax
Price:.......... **$224.99–$779.99**

CRIMSON TRACE
HARDLINE 4–12X40

EOTECH VUDU
1–10X28 FFP

GPO SPECTRA 7.5X50I

HAWKE SPORT OPTICS
FRONTIER 34 FFP

HAWKE SPORT OPTICS
OPTICS SIDEWINDER
30 FFP IR

HAWKE SPORT OPTICS SIDEWINDER 30
SF IR

CRIMSON TRACE HARDLINE

Available in: 2–7x32mm, 3–9X40mm, 3–12X42mm, 4–12X40mm, 4–16X42,
Weight: 16.08, 17.07, 20.5, 17.5, 20.6 oz.
Length: 11.5, 12.5, 13.1, 14.1, 13.6 in.
Main Dia.: 1 in., 30mm
Exit Pupil: N/A
Field of View: 44.5–12.8 ft.@100 yd., 33.9–11.3 ft.@100 yd., 37.3–9.5 ft.@100 yd., 23.6–7.9 ft.@100 yd., 28.5–7.2 ft.@100 yd.
Eye Relief: 3.5 in.
Features: Tactical operators and target shooters will appreciate the generous eye relief of this line, as well as its fully multi-coated optics and nitrogen-purged body for waterproofness; 2–7X32 has a BDC Blackout (.300 Blackout) reticle, 90 MOA windage/elevation adjustments, and 100-yd. side parallax; 3–9X40 available with MR1-MOA or BDC Carbine reticles, 75 MOA windage/elevation adjustment, 100-yd. side parallax; 3–12X42 has 30mm main tube, choice of MR1-MIL or MR1-MOA reticles, adjustable side parallax, 65 MOA/15 MIL windage/elevation adjustment; 4–12X40 has choice of BDC Carbine, Mildot, or BDC Long Range reticles, 65 MOA windage/elevation, 100-yd. side parallax; 4–16X42 gas cgiuce if BDC Carbine, MR1-MOA, or BDC Long Range reticles, 75 MOA windage/elevation, and side parallax adjustment; all reticles are second focal plane
Price: . . . . $259.99–$584.99

EOTECH VUDU 1–10X28 FFP

Available in: 1–10X28mm
Weight: 21.3 oz.
Length: 10.63 in.
Main Dia.: 34mm
Exit Pupil: N/A
Field of View: 116.6–11.7 ft.@100 yd.
Eye Relief: 3.27–3.9 in.
Features: With a big 34mm body and a robust 10X magnification range, this scope has an illuminated glass-etched reticle (choice of SR-4, SR-5, or LE-5) in the first focal plane; nitrogen gas purged for fog and shock resistance; water-resistent; XC high-density, low-dispersion glass with anti-reflective coatings; power throw lever; low-profile tactical turrets
Price: $1799.00

GPO SPECTRA 7.5X50I

Available in: 7X50mm
Weight: 21.7 oz.
Length: N/A
Main Dia.: 30mm
Exit Pupil: N/A
Field of View: N/A
Eye Relief: N/A
Features: GPO's first fixed-power scope, this one in a unique 7X with a big 50mm objective; illuminated G4i reticle; double HD glass system with GPOBright high-transmission lens coating
Price: $599.99

HAWKE SPORT OPTICS FRONTIER 34 FFP IR

Available in: 3–18X50mm, 5–30X56mm
Weight: 27.9, 29.3 oz.
Length: 13.3, 15.4 in.
Main Dia.: 34mm
Exit Pupil: 16.7–2.8mm, 11.2–1.9mm
Field of View: 37.5–6.3 ft.@100 yd., 22.5–3.8 ft.@100 yd.
Eye Relief: 4 in.
Features: A generous 34mm aluminum monotube body supports features such as a patented Lock-N-Stop exposed zero elevation turret; side focus knob; oversized eyebox; fast-focus eyepiece with locking ring; fully multi-coated, 21-layer lenses; wide-angle field of view; removeable magnification throw lever; multi-LED high-intensity illuminated Mil Pro Ext. or MOA Pro Ext. reticle
3–18X $1299.00
5–30X $1399.00

HAWKE SPORT OPTICS SIDEWINDER 30 FFP IR

Available in: 4–16X50mm, 6–24X56mm
Weight: 25.6, 27.3 oz.
Length: 13.3, 14.3 in.
Main Dia.: 30mm
Exit Pupil: 12.5–3.1mm, 9.2–2.3mm
Field of View: 31.8–8.1 ft.@100 yd., 21.3–5.4 ft.@100 yd.
Eye Relief: 4 in.
Features: Parallax free from 9m to infinity, this scope has a generous eyebox; removeable, index-matched sidewheel; side focus; ultra-wide 24-degree field of view; removeable magnification throw lever; 18-layer multi-coated lenses; fast-focus locking eye ring; low-dispersion crown glass; resettable locking turrets with witness window; glass-etched red illuminated Half Mil reticle in the first focal plane with six brightness levels
Price: . 4–16X $899.00; 6–24X $929.00

HAWKE SPORT OPTICS SIDEWINDER 30 SFP IR

Available in: 4–16X50, 4.5–14X44mm, 6–24X56mm, 6.5–20X44mm, 8–32X56mm
Weight: 25.6, 24, 27.3, 24, 27.3 oz.
Length: 13.3, 13.3, 14.3, 13.3 in., 15.5 in.
Main Dia.: 30mm
Exit Pupil: 12.5–3.1mm, 9.8–3.1mm, 9.3–2.3mm, 6.5–2.1mm, 1–1.8mm
Field of View: 31.8–8.1 ft.@100 yd., 28.2–9 ft.@100 yd., 21.3–5.4 ft.@100 yd., 19.5–6.3 ft.@100 yd., 15.9–3.9 ft.@100 yd.
Eye Relief: 4 in.
Features: Similar to the FFP models, but with the following etched-glass illuminated reticle configurations: 4–16X 10X Half Mil or SR Pro II; 4.5–14X 10X Half Mil; 6–24X 20X Half Mil or SR Pro II; 6.5–20X 20X Half Mil; 8X32 20X Half Mil or SR Pro II
Price: . . . . $679.00–$749.00

NEW Products: Optics

HAWKE SPORT OPTICS OPTICS VANTAGE 30 WA FFP IR

HI-LUX ACROSS THE COURSE XTC1–4X34 SERVICE RIFLE COMPETITON SCOPE 1–4X34MM 22 OZ.

HI LUX WM. MALCOLM 3X SHORT TELESCOPIC SIGHT

HI-LUX WM. MALCOLM 6X TWO TONE SHORT RIFLE SCOPE

KAHLES K525I DLR

KONUS ABSOLUTE 5X-40×56 ZOOM

KONUS DIABLO

HAWKE SPORT OPTICS OPTICS VANTAGE 30 WA FFP IR

Available in: 4–16X50mm, 6–24X50mm
Weight: 26.3, 26.6 oz.
Length: 13.7, 14.9 in.
Main Dia.: 30mm
Exit Pupil: 12.5–3.1mm, 8.3–2.1mm
Field of View: 32.5–8.1 ft.@100 yd., 21–5.2 ft.@100 yd.
Eye Relief: 3.5 in.
Features: With an illuminated red/green Half Mil Dot reticle in the first focal plane, this scope also has exposed locking turrets; fast-focus eyepiece; knurled posi-grip power selector; 11-layer multi-coated lenses; wide-angle objective; high-torque zoom ring
Price: . . .4–16X $519.00; 6–24X $549.00

HI-LUX ACROSS THE COURSE XTC1–4X34 SERVICE RIFLE COMPETITON SCOPE

Available in: 1–4X34mm
Weight: 22 oz.
Length: 10.2 in.
Main Dia.: 30mm
Exit Pupil: N/A
Field of View: 95–26.2 ft.@100 yd.
Eye Relief: 3.5 in.
Features: With a huge field of view, this scope was designed specifically for CMP and NRA "Across the Course" High Power competiton; ¼-MOA clicks; adjustable parallax; fully multi-coated air surfaces; high-density extra low-dispersion lenses; green center illuminated MOA Cross reticle
Price: $475.00

HI-LUX WM. MALCOLM 3X SHORT TELESCOPIC SIGHT

Available in: 3X
Weight: 17.5 oz.
Length: 17 in.
Main Dia.: .75-in.
Exit Pupil: N/A
Field of View: 15 ft.@100 yd.
Eye Relief: 4 in.
Features: Similar to the original Winchester A5 scopes from the late 1880s and '90s, this scope has a "caged" rear and front mount; elevation and windage adjusted via rear mount; fine crosshair reticle
Price: $360.00

HI-LUX WM. MALCOLM 6X TWO TONE SHORT RIFLE SCOPE

Available in: 6X
Weight: 18 oz.
Length: 18 in.
Main Dia.: .75-in.
Exit Pupil: N/A
Field of View: 12 ft.@100 yd.
Eye Relief: 4 in.
Features: Handsome polished blue scope with brass eyepiece and objective housings; clickless micrometer adjustment rear mount; fine crosshair reticle
Price: $475.00

KAHLES K525I DLR

Available in: 5X25–56mm
Weight: 35 oz.
Length: 14.8 in.
Main Dia.: 34mm
Exit Pupil: 9.5–2.3mm
Field of View: 25.2–5.2 ft.@100 yd.
Eye Relief: 3.74 in.
Features: DLR stands for Dynamic Long Range and means this scope was designed primarily for long-range competition; parallax adjustment from 20 yd. to infinity; first focal plane reticle in illuminated SKMR or newere SKMR4 Christmas tree configuration; twist-guard left/right elevation turret; zero-stop; oversized turret lettering; 100 clicks per turret rotation; extra-long throw lever and parallax spiner;
Price: $3549.00

KONUS ABSOLUTE

Available in: 5–40X56mm
Weight: 28.2 oz.
Length: 15.8 in.
Main Dia.: 30mm
Exit Pupil: 8–1.4mm
Field of View: 24–3 ft.@100 yd.
Eye Relief: 3.5–3.6 in.
Features: Excellent choice for long-range rifle shooters with a constant long eye relief across the magnification range; side parallax wheel; superb light transmission thanks to ED glass, ultra-wideband fully multi-coated lenses and hydrophobic lens coatings for all-weather use; locking tactical turrets; 1/10 mil clicks; magnification zoom throw lever; Modified Mil Dot reticle; sunshade included
Price: $869.99

KONUS DIABLO

Available in: 4–16X50mm
Weight: 23.9 oz.
Length: 13.5 in.
Main Dia.: 30mm
Exit Pupil: 9.8–3mm
Field of View: 19.4–5.2 ft.@100 yd.
Eye Relief: 3.2 in.
Features: Sporting a big exit pupil, this more compact scope has ¼-MOA clicks; an engraved, dual illumination 550 ballistic reticle; side parallax wheel; improved erector tube system designed to withstand heavy recoil; ultra-wideband fully multi-coated and hydrophobic lens coatings; sunshade included
Price: $393.99

KONUS KONUSPRO-275

KONUS KONUSPRO AS-34

KONUS KONUSPRO LZ-30

LEUPOLD MARK 3HD

LEUPOLD PATROL 6HD

MARCH OPTICS/DEON OPTICAL DESIGN CORP. 1.5–15X42 SFP

KONUS KONUSPRO-275

Available in: 3–9X40, 3–10X44
Weight: 14.1, 17.6 oz.
Length: 12.4, 13.2 in.
Main Dia.: 1 in.
Exit Pupil: 13.3–4.4mm, 14.7–4.4mm
Field of View: 38–12.5 ft.@100 yd., 35.1–10.8 ft.@100 yd.
Eye Relief: 3 in.
Features: These scopes were designed for use with muzzleloaders, with heavy recoil-proof reticles; dry nitrogen-filled for waterproof, shoockproof, and fog-proof performance; multi-coated optics; engraved Ballistic 275 reticle in the second focal plane on the 3–9X, while the 3–10 has the same reticle but with dual illumination; also approved for airgun use with 7.5 joule or less of energy
Price:. . . . . **$136.99–$206.99**

KONUS KONUSPRO AS-34

Available in: 2–6X28mm
Weight: 19.75 oz.
Length: 8.35 in.
Main Dia.: 34mm
Exit Pupil: 14–4.7m
Field of View: 54–7.3 ft.@100 yd.
Eye Relief: 4.8–4.09 in.
Features: A compact tactical scope with generous eye relief; engraved Mil Dot reticle in the second focal plane with dual red/green illumination and five brightness settings; illuminated level bubble; ¼-MOA clicks; locking tactical turrets; fully multi-coated optics; fast-focus ocular lens; wide angle objective; dry nitrogen filled for shockproof, waterproof, fog-proof performance
Price:. **$259.99**

KONUS KONUSPRO LZ-30

Available in: 2.5–10X50mm, 3–12X56mm
Weight: 22.58, 25.4 oz.
Length: 12.9, 13.4 in.
Main Dia.: 30mm
Exit Pupil: 20–5mm, 18.6–4.6mm
Field of View: 50.8–12.7 ft.@100 yd., 42.8–10.7 ft.@100 yd.
Eye Relief: 3.3 in.
Features: Great for deer hunters, these scopes are waterproof, shockproof, and fog-proof and have multi-coated optics; dual locking turrets with zero reset bezel; 30/30 dual red/blue illuminated floating cross reticle; fast-focus ocular lens
Price:. . . . . **$245.99–$379.99**

LEUPOLD MARK 3HD

Available in: 1.5–4X20mm, 3–9X40mm, 4–12X40mm, 6–18X50mm, 8–24X50mm
Weight: 13.1, 15, 16.2, 20.5, 21 oz.
Length: 9.4, 12.7, 12.6, 14.6, 14.6 in.
Main Dia.: 30mm
Exit Pupil: N/A
Field of View: 74.2–29.4 ft.@100 yd., 33.7–13.6 ft.@100 yd., 21.5–10.1 ft.@100 yd., 12.6–6.3 ft.@100 yd., 9.4–4.7 ft.@100 yd.
Eye Relief: 4.2–3.7mm, 4.2–3.7mm, 4.9–3.7mm, 5.1–3.7mm, 5.4–3.8mm
Features: A family of 3:1 zoom ratio riflescopes with Leupold's Elite Optical System; high-definition lenses; removeable throw levers; second focal plane reticles. Power-specific features: 1.5–4X illuminated FireDot BDC, illuminated FireDot TMR, illuminated FireDot SPR, or non-illuminated AR-Ballistic reticle, finger-click elevation; 3–9X Mil-Dot reticle or illuminated FIreDot TMR reticle, P5 elevation adjustment; 4–12X TMR illuminated FireDot or non-illuminated reticle, zero-stop, P5 elevation adjustment; 6–18X TMR reticle, zero-stop, side-focus adjustment, and P5 elevation adjustment; 8–24X TMR reticle, zero-stop, side-focus adjustment, and P5 elevation adjustment
Price:. . . . . **$599.99–$699.99**

LEUPOLD PATROL 6HD

Available in: 1–6X24mm
Weight: 16.2 oz.
Length: 10.8 in.
Main Dia.: 30mm
Exit Pupil: N/A
Field of View: 120.9–19.2 ft.@100 yd.
Eye Relief: 3.8–3.7 in.
Features: With a lightweight, low-profile design, this close-quarters scope features a choice of illuminated CMR-2 or FireDot Duplex second focal plane reticles; Guard-Ion hydrophobic lens coating; high-definition calcium-flouride lenses; CDS-ZL2 (Zerolock 2) elevation dial on the CM-R2 reticle; motion-sensor technology that turns off the reticle illumination after five minutes of inactivity to conserve battery life; electronic reticle level indicator; reversible throw lever
CM-R2 . . . .**$1499.99**
FireDot. **$1399.99**

MARCH OPTICS/DEON OPTICAL DESIGN CORP. 1.5–15X42 SFP—HUNTING

Available in: 1.5–15X42mm
Weight: 21.16 oz.
Length: 10.4 in.
Main Dia.: 30mm
Exit Pupil: 8.7–2.8mm
Field of View: 70.2–6.9 ft.@100 yd.
Eye Relief: 2.7–4.4 in.
Features: This second-focal-plane scope is intended for hunters; superb low-light performance; day-bright illuminated dot; 40 mil elevation/windage adjustment; FD-2 or FD-1 reticle; fast-focus eyepiece; waterproof to 4m; includes sunshade, fast-lever, hex wrench, and flip caps
Price:. **$2729.99**

NEW Products: Optics

MARCH OPTICS/DEON OPTICAL DESIGN CORP. MARCH OPTICS MARCH 1.5–15X42 SFP—TACTICAL

MARCH OPTICS/DEON OPTICAL DESIGN CORP. MARCH OPTICS MARCH-F 1–10X24MM SHORTY FFP

MAVEN OUTDOOR EQUIPMENT COMPANY RS.1

MAVEN OUTDOOR EQUIPMENT COMPANY RS.2

MAVEN OUTDOOR EQUIPMENT COMPANY RS.5

MAVEN OUTDOOR EQUIPMENT COMPANY RS.3

MAVEN OUTDOOR EQUIPMENT COMPANY RS.4

MARCH OPTICS/DEON OPTICAL DESIGN CORP. 1.5–15X42 SFP—TACTICAL

Available in: 1.5–15X42mm
Weight: 22.01 oz.
Length: 10.6 in.
Main Dia.: 30mm
Exit Pupil: 8.7–2.8mm
Field of View: 70.2–6.9 ft.@100 yd.
Eye Relief: 2.7–4.4 in.
Features: This second-focal-plane scope is different from the hunting scope with the same magnification range, being slightly longer and a smidge heavier; ¼-MOA clicks; MTR-3, MTR-4, and MTR-5 red illuminated reticles; tactical turrets; fast-focus eyepiece; designed for NRA mid-range tactical competition; comes with sunshade, flip-up caps, hex wrench, and fast-lever
Price:. $2779.00

MARCH OPTICS/DEON OPTICAL DESIGN CORP. MARCH-F 1–10X24MM SHORTY FFP

Available in: 1–10X24mm
Weight: 17.8 oz.
Length: 8.4 in.
Main Dia.: 30mm
Exit Pupil: 8.6–2.4mm
Field of View: 101.5–10.5 ft.@100 yd.
Eye Relief: 2.8–4 in.
Features: The DR-1 "Dual Reticle" in the first focal plane is said to serve the best of both FFP and SFP worlds; dot sight in the second focal plane at low magnifications as this is a true 1X; six illumination levels; .1-Mil clicks; side focus 10 yards to infinity;
Price:. $2750.00

MAVEN OUTDOOR EQUIPMENT COMPANY RS.1

Available in: 2.5–15X44mm
Weight: 24.5 oz.
Length: 14 in.
Main Dia.: 30mm
Exit Pupil: 28.5–2.93mm
Field of View: 41.7–7 ft.@100 yd.
Eye Relief:
Features: A First focal plane scope for hunters with side parallax adjustment; ED glass with 89% light transmission; waterproof to 3m; etched glass reticle in choice of SHR (MOA) or SHR-W (MOA-2); nitrogen gas purged body; available in black or gray/black combo
Price:. $1200.00

MAVEN OUTDOOR EQUIPMENT COMPANY RS.2

Available in: 2–10X38mm
Weight: 12.4 oz.
Length: 12.44 in.
Main Dia.: 1 in.
Exit Pupil: 12.2–3.8mm
Field of View: 41.2–10.5 ft.@100 yd.
Eye Relief: 3.1 in.
Features: A second focal plane scope in what Maven call its "Ultralight" design; ED glass; parallax at 150 yd.; 50 MOA elevation/windage adjustment; adjustable diopter; wire reticle in choice of Duplex or SHR
Price:. $550.00

MAVEN OUTDOOR EQUIPMENT COMPANY RS.3

Available in: 5–30X50mm
Weight: 26.9 oz.
Length: 13 in.
Main Dia.: 30mm
Exit Pupil: 8.9–1.7mm
Field of View: 22.2–3.7 ft.@100 yd.
Eye Relief: 2.9–3.7 in.
Features: This long-range scope for hunters has a first focal plane etched glass reticle in choice of SHR-W (MOA), MOA-2 (MOA), or SHR-MIL (MIL); exposed turrets; tool-less zero; lockable zero-stop; ED glass; ¼-MOA clicks; 80 MOA elevation/50 MOA windage adjustment; parallax adjustment 20 yd. to infinity
Price:. $1600.00

MAVEN OUTDOOR EQUIPMENT COMPANY RS.4

Available in: 5–30X56mm
Weight: 35.4 oz.
Length: 12.79 in.
Main Dia.: 34mm
Exit Pupil: 8.9–1.9mm
Field of View: 23.3–3.9 ft.@100 yd.
Eye Relief: 3–3.6 in.
Features: A contender for PRS matches and the like, with a dual red/green illuminated, etched glass first focal plane reticle available in SHR-W (MOA), MOA-2 (MOA), CFR-MIL (MIL), or SHR-MIL (MIL) designs; four brightness levels of illumination; mechanical zero stop; side parallax adjustment from 15 yd. to infinity; ED glass with 91.84% light transmission
Price:. $1800.00

MAVEN OUTDOOR EQUIPMENT COMPANY RS.5

Available in: 4–24X50mm
Weight: 26.9 oz.
Length: 14.4 in.
Main Dia.: 30mm
Exit Pupil: 8.5–2.1mm
Field of View: 27.8–4.6 ft.@100 yd.
Eye Relief: 3–3.8 in.
Features: A nice choice for hunters shooting at longer ranges, with a second focal plane etched glass reticle in choice of SHR-W (MOA) or SHR-MIL (MIL) configurations; reticle is illuminated with 10 available brightness levels; mechanical zero-stop; ED glass with 90.1% light transmission; side parallax adjustment from 10 yd. to infinity
Price:. $1400.00

MAVEN OUTDOOR EQUIPMENT COMPANY CRS.1

MAVEN OUTDOOR EQUIPMENT COMPANY CRS.2

MEOPTA MEOSPORT R

MEOPTA OPTIKA5

MINOX ALLAROUNDER 1–5X24

MINOX PRO ZP5

PRIMARY ARMS PLX

MAVEN OUTDOOR EQUIPMENT COMPANY CRS.1

Available in: 3–12X40mm
Weight: 14.2 oz.
Length: 12.44 in.
Main Dia.: 1 in.
Exit Pupil: 13.2–3.4mm
Field of View: 34–8.5 ft.@100 yd.
Eye Relief: 2–3.22 in.
Features: Classic magnification and objective size for hunters with 50 MOA elevation/windage adjustment; C Series glass with 88% light transmission; second focal plane wire CSHR (C-series Simplified Holdover Reticle)
Price:.................$450.00

MAVEN OUTDOOR EQUIPMENT COMPANY CRS.2

Available in: 4–16X44mm
Weight: 16.9 oz.
Length: 11.61 in.
Main Dia.: 1 in.
Exit Pupil: 9.3–2.8mm
Field of View: 25.6–6.4 ft.@100 yd.
Eye Relief: 2.4–3.4 in.
Features: With all the features of the CRS.1, including the second focal plane wire CSHR reticle, this model provides more magnificaton than its slightly smaller brother while maintaining a lightweight, compact design
Price:.................$550.00

MEOPTA MEOSPORT R

Available in: 3–15X50
Weight: 23.1 oz.
Length: 13.29 in.
Main Dia.: 30mm
Exit Pupil: N/A
Field of View: N/A
Eye Relief: 3.94 in.
Features: Built around a 30mm tube, this scope features an illuminated 4C

(duplex floating dot) reticle in the seconf focal plane; locking .1-MRAD turrets with zero reset; side focus from 10 yd. to infinity; ring mounts included; MeoDrop and MeoBright lens coatings
Price:.................$449.99

MEOPTA OPTIKA5

Available in: 2–10X42mm, 3–15X44mm, 4–20X44mm, 4–20X50mm
Weight: 20.8, 21.7, 21.5, 23.3 oz.
Length: 12.1, 13.6, 13.5, 13.6 in.
Main Dia.: 1 in.
Exit Pupil: N/A
Field of View: 55.7–11.5 ft.@100 yd., 37.2–7.9 ft.@100 yd., 27.8–5.8 ft.@100 yd., 27.8–5.8 ft.@100 yd.
Eye Relief: 3.6 in.
Features: A family of 1-in. tube, second focal plane scopes with MeoBright and MeoDrop (hydrophobic) lens coatings. Model specifics as follows: 2–10X available with side parallax (10 yd. to infinity) or without (parallax free at 100 yd.), Z-Plex or Z-Plus reticles, ¼-MOA clicks; 3–15X and 4–20X44 have power throw lever, Z-Plex or Z-Plus reticles, ¼-MOA clicks, parallax correction 10-yd. to infinity;4–20X50 has power throw lever, Z-Plex, Z-Plus, illuminated Z-Plus, and illuminated BDC-3 reticles,
Price:...........$500.00–$600.00

MINOX ALLAROUNDER

Available in: 1–5X24mm, 2–10X50mm, 3–15X56mm
Weight: 16, 22.9, 26.8 oz.
Length: 11.2, 13.1, 14.6 in.
Main Dia.: 30mm
Exit Pupil: 11.4–4.9mm, 11.4–5.2mm, 11.4–3.8mm
Field of View: 37.1–8.2m@100m, 18.9–4.0m@100m, 11.9–2.3m@100m
Eye Relief: 3.9 in.
Features: A second focal plane family of all-purpose scopes that Minox says

has 94% light transmission thanks to improved optical coatings; dimable fiber optic #4 crosshair reticle; nitrogen gas purged; IPX7 water/fog-proof; Fast Target Acquisition design for increased exit pupil; lens caps included
Price:......... $1125.88–$1432.94

MINOX PRO ZP5

Available in: 3–15X50mm, 5–25X56mm
Weight: 32.4, 34.2 oz.
Length: 13.6, 16.7 in.
Main Dia.: 34mm
Exit Pupil: 11.5–3.3mm, 12.0–4.4mm
Field of View: 12.8–2.8m@100m, 7.6–1.6m@100m
Eye Relief: 3.54 in.
Features: A pair of first focal plane scopes for hardcore hunters, with aircraft aluminum construction; M* multi-coatings; locking diopter adjustment ring; IPX7 waterproofing/ fog-proofing; illuminated MRAD MR2 or MR5 reticle for the 3–15X, MR2, MR4, MR5, or THLR for the 5–25X; battery and lens caps included
Price:.................$2825.21

PRIMARY ARMS PLX FFP

Available in: 1–8X24mm
Weight: 16.95 oz.
Length: 9.28 in.
Main Dia.: 30mm
Exit Pupil: 8–3mm
Field of View: 121–14.6 ft.@100 yd.
Eye Relief: 3.7–3.2 in.
Features: A first-focal plane compact scope with premium Japanese-made ED glass; power throw lever; user-configurable turrets; 100 MOA elevation/windage adjustment; night vision compatible; choice of illuminated ACSS Griffin-Mil-M8, ACSS Raptor-M8-Yards, or ACSS Raptor-M8-Meters reticles
Price:.................$1499.99

NEW Products: Optics

PRIMARY ARMS SLX SFP

PULSAR DIGEX C50

PULSAR THERMION 2
XP50

PULSAR DIGEX N455

PRIMARY ARMS SLX

Available in: 1–10X28mm, 3–9X40mm, 3–9X50mm, 4–12X40mm, 4–12X50mm
Weight: 19.1, 15.3, 18.17, 16.23, 18,52 oz.
Length: 10.5, 12.36, 12.64, 14.13, 14.25 in.
Main Dia.: 34mm, 1 in.
Exit Pupil: 9–2.8mm, 13.3–4.4mm, 16.67–5.6mm, 10–3.5mm, 12.5–4.1mm
Field of View: 110–10 ft.@100 yd., 33.8–11.2 ft.@100 yd., 23.57–7.9 ft.@100 yd.
Eye Relief: 3.5–2.1 in., 3.5
Features: A family of second focal plane reticle scopes with the hunter in mind. Model specifics include: 1–10X has 34mm tube, illuminated daylight bright ACSS-Griffin-M10S or ACSS Raptor-5.56-M10S reticles with 11 brightness settings including two night-vision compatible, 40 MOA elevation/windage adjustment; 3–9Xs have 1-in. tubes, two objective lens size choices, non-illuminated Duplex reticle, 80 MOA windage/elevation adjustment; 4–12Xs have choice of two objective lens sizes, 1-in. tubes, 80 MOA elevation/windage adjustment, and non-illuminated Duplex reticles
Price: .N/A

PULSAR DIGEX C50

Available in: 3.5–14X50mm
Weight: 52.9 oz.
Length: 16 in.
Main Dia.: 30mm
Exit Pupil: N/A
Field of View: N/A
Eye Relief: 1.96 in.
Features: This is a 24/7 day/night vision riflescope with a three-second startup time; 29.5-degree wide-angle eyepiece; zoom in 2X or gradual magnification change; 1024X76 HD AMOLED display; SumLight enhanced sensor sensitivity software; ability to load five shooting profiles and 50 zeroing distances; picture-in-picture mode; Stream Vision 2 Wifi integration with both Android and iOS devices; 10 hours of battery life on a single charge; 500m night viewing range; Colour Twilight mode for full color at sunrise/sunset; optional black and white viewing; 10 preloaded reticles; 16 GB video/photo memory; IPX7 waterproof; available with optional Digex 850S IR or Digex 940S IR illuminators
Price: $1539.99

PULSAR DIGEX N450/N455

Available in: 4–16X40mm
Weight: 33.5 oz.
Length: 13.3 in.
Main Dia.: 30mm
Exit Pupil: N/A
Field of View: N/A
Eye Relief: 1.96 in.
Features: A fully IPX7-waterproof night vision riflescope that can take shotgun recoil to 12-ga. and rifle caliber recoil to .375 H&H; 10 reticle shapes and ballistic scalable reticles; eight color modes; zoom zeroing with a stable aiming point across the magnification range; video recording; picture-in-picture; remote firmware updates; built-in Wifi compatible with Android and iOS; side incline indication; customizable shutdown; stadiametric rangefinder; removeable, magnet-fixed eye-cup; dual lithium-ion battery pack system, one internal and one external; N450 comes equipped with an 850nm long-range IR illuminator; N455 comes equipped with a 940nm invisibla IR illuminator
Price: $1439.99

PULSAR THERMION 2 XP50, XQ50, XQ38

Available in: 2–16X50mm, 3.5–14X50mm, 2.5–10X50mm
Weight: 31.7 oz.
Length: 16.37 in.
Main Dia.: 30mm
Exit Pupil: N/A
Field of View: N/A
Eye Relief: 1.96 in.
Features: This is a thermal-imaging riflescope with a sensor having NETD <35mK* that provides superior detail recognition in the harshest weather and environments; fast-aperture Germanium optics; IPX7 waterproof; rated for 12 ga/.375 H&H; all-metal housing; variable digitial zoom; five zeroing profiles; numerous, customizable reticle configurations available in black, white, red, and green; picture-in-picture capable; Image Boost technology for additonal detail; full-color HD AMOLED display with customizable color palettes; Stream Vision 2 WiFi capable with the mobile app on Android/iOs; video and still-picture recording; dual battery system, one internal and one external; 16 GB of storage; XP50 is 2–16X and has 640x480 @ 17 µm (NETD <25 mK) sensor and detection range to 1,800m/2,000 yd.; XQ50 is 3.5–14X and has 384x288 pix. @ 17 µm (NETD <40 mK) and detection range to 1,800m/2,000 yd.; XQ38 is 2.5–10X and 384x288 pix. @ 17 µm (NETD <40 mK) and detection range to 1,350m/1,476 yd.
Price: . . . .$3929.99–$5499.99

REDFIELD REBEL 1–6X

REVIC PMR 428

SCHMIDT & BENDER
PM II

SIGHTMARK CORE TX

SIGHTMARK PRESIDIO
5–30X

REDFIELD REBEL

Available in: 1–6X24mm, 3–9X40mm, 3–9X50mm, 4–12X40mm
Weight: N/A
Length: N/A
Main Dia.: 1 in.
Exit Pupil: N/A
Field of View: N/A
Eye Relief: N/A
Features: In April 2021, Leupold sold the Redfield brand, with which it had done virtually nothing for years, to the Academy Sports & Outdoors retail chain. Academy lists one model of riflescopes--the Rebel--with four magnification choices but couldn't be bothered to provide its customers any specs on its website. Still, the brand apparently lives on, if in name only, with the scopes apparently made in China and with 1-in. tubes, 100-yd. parallax setting, nitrogen purged and sealed, fully multi-coated low-dispersion glass, aluminum housings, duplex reticles, and cut checkering and a grip bump on the magnification ring
Price: . . . . $119.99–$179.99

REVIC PMR 428 SMART RIFLE SCOPE

Available in: 4.5–28X56mm
Weight: 47 oz.
Length: 14 in.
Main Dia.: 34mm
Exit Pupil: 8.4–2mm
Field of View: N/A
Eye Relief: 3.34 in.
Features: The company Revic declares this to be a "smart" riflescope, one that features real-time bullet trajectory after the user turns the turret, thanks to a built-in compass and inclination, cant, temperature, and pressure sensors; illuminated RX1 Mil reticle can be adjusted for both color (36

colors in all) and intensity; other sensors and algorithms sort latitude, nominal wind speed, wind vector, verical drop, directional wind, spin drift, Coriolis, aerodynamic jump, and a host of other ballistic inputs such as sight heigh, barret twist/direction, BC, bullet weight/length, and more
Price: $3250.00

SCHMIDT & BENDER PM II

Available in: 6–36X56mm
Weight: 33.15 oz.
Length: 15.3 in.
Main Dia.: 34mm
Exit Pupil: 8.3–1.6mm
Field of View: 7.3–1.25m@100m
Eye Relief: 3.54 in.
Features: Big 6X ratio with a big 34mm tube but in an overall more compact size compared to comparably powered scopes; waterproof to 3m and waterproof to 10m, 20m, and 25m upon request; available with illuminated GR2ID in the first focal plane or the new for 2022, uncluttered first focal plane P5FL reticle with a free-floating illuminated center dot; .1-MRAD clicks with 39.5 MRAD of elevation adjustment; parallax adjustment 20m to infinity
Price: . . . . N/A

SIGHTMARK CORE TX

Available in: 4X32mm, 1–4X24mm, 2.5–10X32mm, 3–12X44mm
Weight: 13.4, 16.2, 20, 20oz.
Length: 9.1, 9.64, 12.2, 13 in.
Main Dia.: 30mm
Exit Pupil: 8, 11–6mm, 12–3mm, 14.7–3.7mm
Field of View: 8.4m@100m, 32–8m@100m, 14.7–3.7m@100m, 12.25–3.1m@100m
Eye Relief: 4 in., 4–3.47 in.

Features: Budget priced line of second focal plane 4:1 scopes with single-piece 30mm tubes; hard-coat anodized finishes; throw levers; flip-up lens covers; pop-up locking turrets IP67 water- and dust-proof rating; fully multi-coated lenses. Model specifics include: fixed 4X and 1–4X with choice of 55-gr. .223 Rem.-calibrated BDC reticle with red/green illumination or dual-caliber red/green illuminated reticle for both .223 and .308; 2.5–10X and 3–12X both have the dual-caliber illuminated red/green reticle
Price: . . . . $107.96–$299.99

SIGHTMARK PRESIDIO

Available in: 1–6X24mm, 3–18X50mm, 5–30X56mm
Weight: 18, 30.8, 33 oz.
Length: 10.48, 13, 15.7 in.
Main Dia.: 30mm
Exit Pupil: 29.14, 35.5, 36.6mm
Field of View: 33.89–5.59m@100m, 11.9–1.86m@100m, 6.71–1.13m@100m
Eye Relief: 2.8–3.3 in., 3.8 in., 3.7 in.
Features: Mid-priced line of 6:1 scopes that feature aircraft-grade aluminum tubes; IP67 dust- and waterproof; throw lever; flip-up lens caps; 1–6X has 55-gr. .223 Rem.-calibrated illuminated BDC etched glass reticle in the second focal plane; 3–18X has illuminated etched-glass LR2 reticle in the first focal plane; 5–30X has more features with fully multi-coated optics, hard anodized finish, exposed locking turrets, zero-stop, scratch-resistant lens coating, AR riser fixed mount, and an etched glass LR2 illuminated reticle in the first focal plane
Price: . . . . $359.99–$539.99

NEW Products: Optics

SIGHTRON S1 G2

SIG SAUER BUCKMASTERS

SIG SAUER TANGO MSR LPVO

STEINER M8XI

STEINER PREDATOR 4

SWAROVSKI OPTIK DS GEN II

SIGHTRON S1 G2

Available in: 1.75–5X32mm, 3–9X40mm, 3.5–10X50mm, 4–12X40mm
Weight: 12.7, 13.9, 15.9, 14.5 oz.
Length: 10.3, 11.7, 12.6, 12.3 in.
Main Dia.: 1 in.
Exit Pupil: N/A
Field of View: N/A
Eye Relief: 3.4–3.3 in., 4.1–3.3 in.
Features: Sightron's second generation of 1-in. tube scopes; second focal plane reticle; ¼-MOA clicks; fully multi-coated all-glass optics; waterproof, shockproof, fog-proof. Model specifics: 1.75–5X duplex reticle and 120 MOA windage/ elevation adjustment; 3–9X available with Duplex, HHR2, or Mil-Dot reticle, 70 MOA windage/elevation adjustment; 3.5–10X has Duplex reticle and 60 MOA windage/ elevation adjustment; 4–12X available with Duple, HHR2, or Mil-Dot reticle and 60 MOA elevation/windage adjustment, standard, and also with an adjustable objective in either a Duplex or MOA-20 reticle
Price: . . . . **Starting at $204.99**

SIG SAUER BUCKMASTERS

Available in: 3–9X40mm, 3–9X50mm, 3–12X44mm
Weight: 14.1 oz.
Length: N/A
Main Dia.: 1 in.
Exit Pupil: 13.3–4.4mm, 16–4.17mm, 13.3–3.3mm
Field of View: 34.1–11.4 ft.@100 yd.
Eye Relief: 3.85mm
Features: An entry-level line of hunting scopes with 1-inch tubes; second focal plane Buckmasters BDC reticle; IPX7 waterproof; 60 MOA windage/elevation adjustment
Price: . . . . **$109.99–$143.99**

SIG SAUER TANGO MSR LPVO

Available in: 1–6X24mm
Weight: 18.5 oz.
Length: N/A
Main Dia.: 30mm
Exit Pupil: 10.5–4.5mm
Field of View: 124.8–19.6 ft.@100 yd.
Eye Relief: 10.5–4.5mm
Features: A second focal plane scope designed specifically for use with today's MSR platforms; illuminated MSR-BDC reticle; removeable throw lever; 100 MOA elevation/windage adjustment; IPX7 waterproof; adjustable diopter; hard-coat anodized finish; lay-flat flip-up lens covers; ALPHA-MSR one-piece cantilever mount included;
Price: **$337.99**

STEINER M8XI

Available in: 1–8X24mm
Weight: 26.5 oz.
Length: 10.8 in.
Main Dia.: 34mm
Exit Pupil: 10.4–3.3mm
Field of View: 34.2–4.8m@100m
Eye Relief: 3.54 in.
Features: Compact, lightweight tactical scope with a generous 8X magnification that provides improved resolution in close quarters; low-profile turrets; one-piece 34mm tube; submersible to 20m; DMR81 (Designated Marksman Riflescope) reticle, illuminated and in the second focal plane; fixed parallax at 100m; side focus; in black or coyote brown
Price: . . . . **$4073.99–$4341.99**

STEINER PREDATOR 4

Available in: 2.5–10X42mm, 4–16X50mm, 6–24X50mm
Weight: 22.7, 23.7, 23.5 oz.
Length: 13.3, 14.7, 14.7 in.

Main Dia.: 30mm
Exit Pupil: 8.7–4.2mm, 9.2–3mm, 8.2–2mm
Field of View: 48–12 ft.@100 yd., 30–7.5 ft.@100 yd., 20.1–5.1 ft.@100 yd.
Eye Relief: 3.5 in.
Features: A lineup of second focal plane scopes designed for predator hunting, with plenty of magnification range; generous eye relief; illuminated E3 reticle with five day and six night brightness settings; adjustable diopter; nitrogen-filled and fog-proof; waterproof to 3 ft.
Price: . . . .**$1039.99–$1149.99**

SWAROVSKI OPTIK DS GEN. II

Available in: 5–25X52mm
Weight: 38.4 oz.
Length: 15.87 in.
Main Dia.: 40mm
Exit Pupil: 9.6–2.1mm
Field of View: 21.9–4.5 ft.@100 yd.
Eye Relief: 3.7 in.
Features: This is a big scope in all the imagineable ways--magnification, eye relief, main tube diameter,field of view, and price; scope automatically corrects the user's aiming point, via the Configurator app and Bluetooth (OS and Android compatible), in real time, taking into account the shooting angle, distance to the target, magnification selected, temperature, and ballistic data; parallax correction from 55 yd. to infinity; illuminated 4A-1 reticle in the second focal plane is simple and uncluttered and has 64--sixty-four!--brightness settings; maximum aiming point correction is a stellar 1,120 yd.; available in ring or rail mount setups
Price: **$5221.00**

TRIJICON IR-HUNTER

TRIJICON REAP-IR

VORTEX OPTICS RAZOR HD GEN III 6–36X56MM

VORTEX RAZOR HD LHT

VORTEX OPTICS SONORA

VORTEX VENOM

TRIJICON IR-HUNTER

Available in: 1.2 base/9.6 combination, 1.75X base/14X combination, 3X base/24X combination
Weight: 28.4, 29.1, 40.7 oz.
Length: 9.6, 9.8, 11 in.
Main Dia.: N/A
Exit Pupil: N/A
Field of View: N/A
Eye Relief: 1.063 in.
Features: A collection of thermal imaging scopes for hunters with an advanced 640X480 12 micron imaging sensor that works in any lighting condition; digital turret controls;USB-C cable; mini Picatinny rail mount and Trijicon's Q-Loc quick-release technology provide mounting flexibility; top-loading battery compartment
1.2X $6499.00
1.75X $7499.00
3X. $8999.00

TRIJICON REAP-IR

Available in: 1.2 base/9.6 combination, 1.75X base/14X combination, 3X base/24X combination
Weight: 24.7, 26.5, 37.8 oz.
Length: 8.4, 8.6, 9.7 in.
Main Dia.: N/A
Exit Pupil: N/A
Field of View: N/A
Eye Relief: 1.063 in.
Features: Very similar to the IR-Hunter models but ina smaller, more compact presentation; thumbstick controller; numerous reticle options
Price: **1.2X $6999.00; 1.75X $7999.00; 3X $9499.00**

VORTEX OPTICS RAZOR HD GEN III 6–36X56MM

Available in: 6–36X56mm
Weight: 45.1 oz.
Length: 15.3 in.
Main Dia.: 34mm
Exit Pupil: N/A
Field of View: 20.5–3.5 ft.@100 yd.
Eye Relief: 3.5 in.
Features: Nice long-range optic for competition with parallax setting from 10 yd. to infinity; ¼-MOA clicks; 120 MOA elevation and 52.5 MOA windage adjustment; exposed locking turrets; locking side illumination control; throw lever; illuminated first focal plane glass-etched EBR-70 reticle that remains in proportion regardless the magnification level; L-Tec+ Zero system and micro-adjustable zero setting; Plasma Tech lens coatings; HD glass with XR Plus full multi-coatings; scratch-resistant ArmorTek lens coating; hard-anodized Stealth Shadow exterior finish; waterproof, shockproof, and fog-proof
Price: $3999.99

VORTEX OPTICS RAZOR HD LHT

Available in: 3–15X42mm, 3–15X50mm, 4.5–22X50mm
Weight: 19.1, 20.5, 21.7 oz.
Length: 13.3 in.
Main Dia.: 30mm
Exit Pupil: N/A
Field of View: 35.3–7 ft.@100 yd., 23.5–4.7 ft.@100 yd.
Eye Relief: 3.8 in., 4 in.
Features: High definition glass meets a trio of super lightweight full-size scopes with features like XR Plus full multi-coatings; APO System index-matched lenses for true-life color; RevStop Zero System; ArmoTek scratch-resistant lens coating; locking elevation turret; oversized and capped windage turret; 3–15X42mm has second focal plane HSR-5i reticle in choice of MOA or MRAD; 3–15X50mm has second focal plane G4i BDC MRAD reticle; 4.5–22X50mm has a first focal plane illuminated XLR-2 reticle in choice of MOA or MRAD
Price: . . . . $1799.99–$1999.99

VORTEX OPTICS SONORA

Available in: 4–12X44
Weight: 15.8 oz.
Length: 13.5 in.
Main Dia.: 1 in.
Exit Pupil: N/A
Field of View: 24.7–8.4 ft.@100 yd.
Eye Relief: 4 in.
Features: Great eye relief, ample field of view, and a budget-friendly price combine with features such as a locking diopter; hard anodized single-piece aluminum body; parallax setting from 100 yd.; ¼-MOA clicks; 60 MOA elevation/windage adjustment; capped turrets; fully multi-coated lenses; second focal plane Dead-Hold BDC reticle
Price: $209.99

VORTEX OPTICS VENOM

Available in: 5–25X56
Weight: 35 oz.
Length: 15.3 in.
Main Dia.: 34mm
Exit Pupil: N/A
Field of View: 21.2–4.7 ft.@100 yd.
Eye Relief: 3.6 in.
Features: Super magnification and eye relief in a 34mm tube for long-range work in tough conditions; XD extra low-dispersion glass, fully multi-coated; first focal plane glass-etched EBR-7C reticle in choice of MOA or MRAD; RevStop Zero System; power throw lever; fast-focus eyepiece; ArmoTek scratch-resistant lens coating; tactical turrets
Price: $699.99

NEW Products: Optics

NEW PRODUCTS

AIMPOINT ACRO P-2

AIMPOINT DUTY RDS

AIMPOINT MICRO H-2 6 MOA

AIMPOINT MICRO H-2 ORANGE CERAKOTE

AIMPOINT MICRO T-2

ATHLON MIDAS LE GEN2

BURRIS FASTFIRE4

RED-DOTS/REFLEX RED-DOTS

AIMPOINT ACRO P-2

Weight: 2.1 oz.
Length: 1.3 in.
Power: 1X
Obj. Dia.: N/A
Field of View: N/A
Eye Relief: Unlimited
Features: Now using a CR2032 battery and improved diode technology, this reflex red-dot is night vision device-compatible; battery change takes place without removing optic from the firearm; anodized high-strength aluminum housing; 3.5 MOA dot; no optical signature; submersible to 35m/115 ft.; 50,000 battery life; four night and six daytime brightness settings; multiple mounting options available
Price: $599.00

AIMPOINT DUTY RDS

Weight: 3.8 oz.
Length: 2.7 in.
Power: 1X
Obj. Dia.: N/A
Field of View: N/A
Eye Relief: Unlimited
Features: With a 2 MOA dot and 30,000 hours of battery life, this reflex collimator sight has a one-piece torsion nut mount; flip-up lens colors; advanced optical lenses; flush-mounted and waterproof windage/elevation adjustments with audible clicks; four night vision and six daytime brightness settings; submersible to 25m/80 ft.; no visible optical signature
Price: $499.00

AIMPOINT MICRO H-2 6 MOA

Weight: 3.3 oz.

Length: 2.7 in.
Power: 1X
Obj. Dia.: N/A
Field of View: N/A
Eye Relief: Unlimited
Features: Finally, a sight with a much biggerr dot, 6 MOA to be exact; integral Picatinny/Weaver-mount; 50,000 hours of battery life; see-through flip-up lens covers; 12 daylight and low-light settings
Price: $745.00

AIMPOINT MICRO H-2 ORANGE CERAKOTE

Weight: 3.3 oz.
Length: 2.7 in.
Power: 1X
Obj. Dia.: N/A
Field of View: N/A
Eye Relief: Unlimited
Features: In the deer woods, every bit of safety helps, so top your rifle or slug gun with this 2 MOA red dot dressed up in Cerakote Orange; 12 brightness settings; submersible to 5m/15 feet; 50,000 hours of battery life; includes Micro Standard mount and flip-up lens covers
Price: $765.00

AIMPOINT MICRO T-2

Weight: 3 oz.
Length: N/A
Power: 1X
Obj. Dia.: N/A
Field of View: N/A
Eye Relief: Unlimited
Features: Housing a 2MOA red dot, this optic was built to withstand abuse and features compatibility with Aimpoint 3XMag-1 and 6XMag-1 magnifiers and night vision devices;

recessed lenses with flip-up lens caps; hard-anodized aluminum housing; Spuhr mount; lower 1/3 co-witness for use with iron sights; submersible to 25m/80 ft.
Price: $922.00

ATHLON MIDAS LE GEN2

Weight: 6.9 oz.
Length: 3.4 in.
Power: N/A
Obj. Dia.: N/A
Field of View: N/A
Eye Relief: Unlimited
Features: This reflex is a few ounces heavier and a little longer than common these days in the world of micro red dots, but this one has three interchangeable reticles--dot, circle and dot/circle—available at the press of a button; motion wakeup; fully multi-coated optics; .5-MOA clicks; throw-lever for mount tightening; six brightness settings; 50,000 hours of battery life; side-access battery compartment
Price: $312.49

BURRIS FASTFIRE 4

Weight: 1.6 oz.
Length: 1.9 in.
Power: 1.07X
Obj. Dia.: N/A
Field of View: N/A
Eye Relief: Unlimited
Features: Users can toggle between reticles, which include a 3 MOA dot, 11 MOA dot, and both dot sizes within red circles; 26,000 hours of battery life; optional screw-on weather shield; auto brightness; auto-shutoff after eight hours
Price: $419.00

BURRIS RT-1

BURRIS RT-3 PRISM

BURRIS SPEEDBEAD SHOTGUN SIGHT SYSTEM

BURRIS T.M.P.R. PRISM SYSTEM 5X32

BURRIS TRS-125

EOTECH EFLX

HEX BY SPRINGFIELD ARMORYHEX DRAGONFLY

HEX BY SPRINGFIELD ARMORY HEX WASP

BURRIS RT-1

Weight: 4.8 oz.
Length: 2.75 in.
Power: 1X
Obj. Dia.: 25mm
Field of View: Unlimited
Eye Relief: Unlimited
Features: With a 2 MOA red dot, this optic allows for easy both eyes open shooting; equipped with both high and low mounts; .5-MOA clicks
Price:.................$359.00

BURRIS RT-3 PRISM

Weight: 8.8 oz.
Length: 3.5 in.
Power: 3X
Obj. Dia.: 33.8mm
Field of View: 38.2 ft.@100 yd.
Eye Relief: 2.6 in.
Features: A red-dot with actual magnification, this one in 3X; 50 MOA elevation/windage adjustment; red Ballistic 3X reticle; cantilever-style Picatinny mount
Price:.................$455.00

BURRIS SPEEDBEAD SHOTGUN SIGHT SYSTEM

Weight: 1.9 oz.
Length: 1.9 in.
Power: 1X
Obj. Dia.: 21X15mm
Field of View: N/A
Eye Relief: Unlimited
Features: This is actually a mount, meant to be placed between the stock and receiver of a variety of popular shotguns. Once installed, you can mount a Burris FastFire3 8 MOA red-dot optic on it, encouraging both eyes open shooting; parallax free; five-year battery life; will fit Benelli Super Black Eagle II, 12 ga. Benelli M2 Montefeltro or Ultralight; Beretta Xtrema/2, 391, and Urika/2,

Remington 870, 1100, and 11-87, and Beretta A400 Xplor
Price:.................$323.00

BURRIS T.M.P.R. PRISM SYSTEM 3X32, 5X32

Weight: 18.2, 19.1 oz.
Length: 5.6, 6 inn.
Power: 3X, 5X
Obj. Dia.: 32mm
Field of View: 40 ft., 24 ft.
Eye Relief: 2.2 in.
Features: Burris has created a modular system in which the user can employ the prism sight by itself or in combination with a Burris laser sight or FastFire M3 8 MOA red-dot (or all three together); each component has its own CR123 battery but used in combination utilize the prism sight battery; QD mount; ½-MOA clicks; ; fixed parallax at 100 yd.; 3X prism has Ballistic 3X red-dot reticle, 80 MOA windage/elevation adjustment, 10 ft. close focus; 5X has Ballistic 5X reticle, 50 MOA windage/elevation adjustment, 25 ft. close focus
3X32 .... $839.00–$1259.00
5X32 .... $899.00–$1319.00

BURRIS TRS-125

Weight: 5.4 oz.
Length: 2.9 in.
Power: 1X
Obj. Dia.: 22mm
Field of View: N/A
Eye Relief: Unlimited
Features: With an IPX7 waterproof rating, this closed reflex sight has a 3 MOA red dot with 10 brightness settings; 100 MOA windage/elevation adjustment; fully multi-coated lenses with EXO Barrier protection; includes high-rise and low-profile Weaver rail mounts; up to 15,000 hours of battery life
Price:.................$119.99

EOTECH EFLX

Weight: 1.4 oz.
Length: 1.9 in.
Power: 1X
Obj. Dia.: N/A
Field of View: N/A
Eye Relief: Unlimited
Features: A mini reflex sight from EoTech with a Leupold Delta Point Pro footprint; choice of 3MOA or 6 MOA red dot; seven daytime brightness settings, one ultra-bright setting, and one night vision setting for Gen1–GenIII+
Price:.................$389.00

HEX BY SPRINGFIELD ARMORY HEX DRAGONFLY

Weight: 1.2 oz.
Length: 1.9 in.
Power: 1X
Obj. Dia.: N/A
Field of View: N/A
Eye Relief: Unlimited
Features: Boasting a 3.5 MOA red dot, this sight has eight manual brightness adjustment; scratch-resistant, anti-glare glass lens; aluminum housing; manual on/off; IPX7 waterproof; 160 MOA windage/elevation adjustment in 1 MOA clicks; hard coat anodized finish
Price:.................$249.00

HEX BY SPRINGFIELD ARMORY HEX WASP

Weight: .7-oz.
Length: 1.6 in.
Power: 1X
Obj. Dia.: N/A
Field of View: N/A
Eye Relief: Unlimited
Features: Designed for direct, low-profile mounting on Springfield's Helcatt OSP and XD-S Mod.2 OSP handguns; always-on and auto-dimming technologies; 3.5 MOA red dot; IPX7 waterproof;
Price:.................$299.00

NEW Products: **Optics**

HOLOSUN AEMS

HOLOSUN EPS CARRY

HOLOSUN SCS

LEAPERS UTG OP3 MINI MICRO

NEWCON OPTIK HDS 3AA

PRIMARY ARMS MD-RBGII CLASSIC SERIES GEN II

PRIMARY ARMS SLX ADVANCED 30MM RED DOT

HOLOSUN AEMS, AEMS CORE

Weight: 3.9 oz.
Length: 2.2 in.
Power: 1X
Obj. Dia.: N/A
Field of View: N/A
Eye Relief: Unlimited
Features: A forged pressed aluminum housing in the CORE models has a boxy shape housing a 2 MOA red or green dot; shake-awake technology; super LED; motion on last setting recall; multi-layer reflective glass; 50,000 battery life; rear of sight controls; 50 MOA windage/elevation adjustment; IP67 waterproofing; parallax free; lower 1/3 co-witness mount; non-CORE models sport a multi-reticle system--2 MOA dot, 65 MOA circle, circle/dot--solar fail-safe and shake-awake technologies, and flip-down lens covers
CORE . . . . $352.93–$370.58
non-CORE . . . . . . $470.58–$505.87

HOLOSUN EPS, EPS CARRY

Weight: 1.4, 1.23 oz.
Length: 1.62 in.
Power: 1X
Obj. Dia.: N/A
Field of View: N/A
Eye Relief: Unlimited
Features: EPS stands for Enclosed Pistol Sight. A reflex red-dot sight in two sizes, the CARRY option the smaller of the two for CCW practitioners; choice of red or green dot; solar failsafe and shake-awake technologies;7075 T6 aluminum housing; IPX8 waterproofing; aspherical, zero-distortion, multi-layer reflective lens; Holosun K footprint; 6 MOA dot;
Price: . . . . $435.28–$458.81

HOLOSUN SCS

Weight: 1.3 oz.
Length: 1.93 in.
Power: 1X
Obj. Dia.: N/A
Field of View: N/A
Eye Relief: Unlimited
Features: SCS stands for Solar Charging Sight. This is reflex sight designed to work with the Glock MOS system; low-profile deck allows use of sights; titanium housing; super LED; solar failsafe technology; multi-reticle system offers up a 2 MOA dot, 32 MOA circle or a combo circle/dot; self-adjusting brightness control; in red or green
Price: . . . . $399.99–$435.28

LEAPERS UTG OP3 MINI MICRO

Weight: .7-oz.
Length: 1.6 in.
Power: 1X
Obj. Dia.: N/A
Field of View: N/A
Eye Relief: Unlimited
Features: A red-dot reflex sight under an ounce? That's just what Leapers offered in 2022 as part of its 30th annivesary new offerings; 3 MOA constant-on dot with automatic brightness; backup sight milled into the sight body; 30,000 hours battery life;
Price: $229.97

NEWCON OPTIK HDS 3AA

Weight: 11.71 oz.
Length: 4.51 in.
Power: 1
Obj. Dia.: 30mm
Field of View: N/A
Eye Relief: Unlimited
Features: This is a holographic red dot sight with a 4 MOA dot; compatible with Newcon's 3X and 5X magnifier; runs off a single AA battery for up to 800 hours; tool-free Picatinny mount; 11 settings include night-vision compatibles;
Price: $628.00

PRIMARY ARMS MD-RBGII CLASSIC SERIES GEN II

Weight: 4.2 oz.
Length: N/A
Power: 1X
Obj. Dia.: N/A
Field of View: N/A
Eye Relief: Unlimited
Features: A microdot with a daylight-bright 2 MOA red dot; 11 brightness settings; fully multi-coated anti-reflective lenses; night-vision compatible; parallax free past 33 yards; removeable Picatinny mount; hard anodized black finish; 1,000 hours of batttery life using one CR2032 battery; bikini lens cover included
Price: $89.99

PRIMARY ARMS SLX ADVANCED 30MM RED DOT

Weight: 7.1 oz.
Length: N/A
Power: 1X
Obj. Dia.: N/A
Field of View: N/A
Eye Relief: Unlimited
Features: A full-size, 30mm tube red-dot with up to 14,000 hours of batttery life; aluminum housing; ½-MOA click values; 10 brightness settings; in black or flat dark earth anodized finishes
Price: $129.99

PRIMARY ARMS SLX ROTARY KNOB 25MM MICRODOT

RITON OPTICS 3 TACTIC PRD 2

SHIELDS SIGHTS AMS

SHIELD SIGHTS RMSX

SIGHTMARK MTS 1X30

SIGHTMARK MINI SHOT A-SPEC M3

SIGHTMARK MTS MINI SOLAR

PRIMARY ARMS SLX ROTARY KNOB 25MM MICRODOT

Weight: 2 oz.
Length: N/A
Power: 1X
Obj. Dia.: N/A
Field of View: N/A
Eye Relief: Unlimited
Features: This one made a splash, awarded a Silver Tier rating by the National Tactical Officer's Association and winning the 2021 Industry Choice Red Dot Optic of the Year; aluminum housing; 12 brightness settings; night vision compatible; big-dot view on a micro-mount keeps things lightweight; ACS CQB reticle; hard coat anodized finish in black or flat dark earth
Price: $199.99

RITON OPTICS 3 TACTIC PRD 2

Weight: .9-oz.
Length: 1.77 in.
Power: 1X
Obj. Dia.: N/A
Field of View: N/A
Eye Relief: Unlimited
Features: A parallax-free 3 MOA red-dot sight with 1 MOA clicks at 100 yd.; 140 MOA windage/elevation adjustment; fully multi-coated, full wide-band, waterproof-coated lens with low-light enhancement; shake-awake technology; auto-brightness; auto-off after 3 minutes of no actitivy; 40,000 hours of battery life
Price: $349.99

SHIELDS SIGHTS AMS

Weight: N/A
Length: N/A
Power: 1X
Obj. Dia.: N/A
Field of View: N/A
Eye Relief: Unlimited
Features: An enclosed, co-witness-capable red-dot with a built-in rear peep sight; no-click zeroing adjustments for ultra-fine-tuning; aluminum housing; intelligent on/off returns to on at previous setting; 12 brightness settings include three that are night-vision compatible; three stages--high, medium, and low--of auto-brightness; LED interface permits four reticle choices; side-access battery compartment; 13,000 hours of battery life;
Price: . . . . **N/A**

SHIELDS SIGHTS RMSX

Weight: .8-oz.
Length: N/A
Power: 1X
Obj. Dia.: N/A
Field of View: N/A
Eye Relief: Unlimited
Features: Shields puts a huge, 34mm-wide lens on this uber-lightweight red-dot; HDC polymer lens with a 5H hardness rating; parallax free; fast refresh rate; lens position allows for co-witnessing; available with 4 MOA or 8 MOA dot
Price: $450.00

SIGHTMARK MINI SHOT A-SPEC M3

Weight: .7-oz.
Length: N/A
Power: 1X
Obj. Dia.: N/A
Field of View: N/A
Eye Relief: Unlimited
Features: This micro-dot sports a red 3 MOA dot; 80/130 MOA elevation/windage adjustment; parallax from 25 yd. to infinity; aluminum housing; IP55 water resistant; AR red lens coating; low-profile fixed mount; Weaver/Picatinny rail mount; up to 100,000 hours of battery life; auto-brightness for day/night use
Price: $186.99

SIGHTMARK MTS 1X30

Weight: 9.8 oz.
Length: 4.4 in.
Power: 1X
Obj. Dia.: 30mm
Field of View: N/A
Eye Relief: Unlimited
Features: Wearing an AR red lens coating, this tubular sight has a 2 MOA red dot; aluminum housing; takes recoil up to .338 Win. Mag.; 1 MOA clicks; 110 MOA elevation/windage adjustment; fog-proof and IP67 waterproof; nitrogen-filled; up to 15,000 hours of battery life; nine daylight and two night vision brightness settings; windage and elevation caps serve as adjustment tools; semi-cantilever clamp mount; compatible with magnifiers; includes flip-up lens covers and CR2032 battery
Price: $129.97

SIGHTMARK MTS MINI SOLAR

Weight: 5.5 oz.
Length: 2.96 in.
Power: 1X
Obj. Dia.: 22mm
Field of View: N/A
Eye Relief: Unlimited
Features: A 3 MOA red dot is accompanied by a combination aluminum and plastic housing; both solar and CR2032 battery power; up to 200,000 hours of battery life on the low setting; 1 MOA clicks; 120/160 MOA elevation/windage adjustment; 10 brightness settings; Eclipse Light Management System adjusts the brightness level automatically depending on the ambient light; hinged battery door; turret caps serve as adjustment tools; includes flip-up lens caps, low Picatinny mount, and co-witness mount
Price: $239.99

NEW Products: **Optics**

SIGHTMARK VOLTA SOLAR

SIG SAUER ROMEO5 TREAD

SIG SAUER ROMEO2

SIG SAUER ROMEO5X

SIG SAUER ROMEO5XDR

SIG SAUER ROMEO7S

SIG SAUER ROMEOZERO ELITE

SIGHTMARK VOLTA SOLAR

Weight: 7.3 oz.
Length: 3.23 in.
Power: 1X
Obj. Dia.: 28mm
Field of View: N/A
Eye Relief: Unlimited
Features: With a 2 MOA red dot, this enclosed red-dot is powered by both solar and AAA batteries (2); lenses are scratch-resistant and have anti-reflective coating; adjustable height mount; digital switch brightness controls; same-side windage (160 MOA) and elevation (120 MOA) with ½-MOA clicks; takes recoil up to .338 Win. Mag.; up to 400,000 hours of battery life on the low setting; supplied with rubber optic cover, low-profile Picatinny mount, and co-witness mount
Price:. **$359.99**

SIG SAUER ROMEO 1X20 TREAD

Weight: 5.1 oz.
Length: 2.5 in.
Power: 1X
Obj. Dia.: 20mm
Field of View: N/A
Eye Relief: Unlimited
Features: Sporting a 2 MOA red dot, this enclosed sight has eight daytime and two night vision brightness settings; 100 MOA elevation/windage adjustment; 40,000 hours of run time;

side-loading battery access; sight optimized for use on SIG's Tread rifle
Price:. **$168.99**

SIG SAUER ROMEO2

Weight: N/A
Length: 1.84 in.
Power: 1X
Obj. Dia.: 30mm
Field of View: N/A
Eye Relief: Unlimited
Features: Four models offer a choice of reticles--circle/dot, 3 MOA, 6 MOA, and 10 MOA; 12 daylight and three night vision settings; 1 MOA clicks; 25,000 hours of battery life at the medium setting
Price:. . . . . **$659.99–$768.99**

SIG SAUER ROMEO5X

Weight: 5.6 oz.
Length: N/A
Power: 1X
Obj. Dia.: 20mm
Field of View: N/A
Eye Relief: Unlimited
Features: An all-purpose tubular red dot with a 2 MOA dot; 50,000 hours of run time on one AAA battery; 100 MOA windage/elevation adjustment; eight daytime and two night vision brightness settings; IPX7 waterproof; modular Picatinny riser mount
Price:. **$219.99**

SIG SAUER ROMEO5XDR

Weight: 5.6 oz.
Length: N/A

Power: 1X
Obj. Dia.: 20mm
Field of View: N/A
Eye Relief: Unlimited
Features: Similar to the Romeo5X, but with reticles available in a circle/dot or as a dual predator/dot, either with 2 MOA center dot size
Price:. . . . . **$270.99–$295.99**

SIG SAUER ROMEO7S

Weight: 7.7 oz.
Length: 3.2 in.
Power: 1X
Obj. Dia.: 22mm
Field of View: N/A
Eye Relief: Unlimited
Features: Running off a single AAA battery, this sight comes with either a red or green 2 MOA dot; IPX7 waterproof; M1913 Picatinny mount; nine daytime and two night vision brightness settings; .5-MOA clicks;
Price:. **$177.99**

SIG SAUER ROMEOZERO ELITE

Weight: .5-oz.
Length: 1.6 in.
Power: 1X
Obj. Dia.: 24mm
Field of View: N/A
Eye Relief: Unlimited
Features: This is about as lightweight as a reflex optic gets; choice of 2MOA dot with a 32 MOA circle or the singular 3 MOA red dot; eight daytime settings; 20,000 hours of run time on the CR1632 battery
Price:. . . . . **$229.99–$259.99**

VORTEX OPTICS AMG UH-1 GEN II

VORTEX OPTICS SPITFIRE HD GEN II PRISM

ATHLON TALOS 800Y

BUSHNELL PRIME 1800

VORTEX OPTICS RAZOR

ATHLON MIDAS 1 MILE

ATN CORP. ABL 1500

HALO OPTICS CL300

VORTEX OPTICS AMG UH-1 GEN II

Weight: 11.6 oz.
Length: 3.9 in.
Power: 1X
Obj. Dia.: N/A
Field of View: N/A
Eye Relief: Unlimited
Features: A holographic 1 MOA red dot with 100 MOA elevation/windage adjustment; parallax free; standard Weaver/Picatinny mount; includes four night vision settings with a dediated night vision button
Price:.................$899.99

VORTEX OPTICS RAZOR

Weight: 1.3 oz.
Length: 1.83 in.
Power: 1X
Obj. Dia.: N/A
Field of View: N/A
Eye Relief: Unlimited
Features: Available with a choice of 3 or 6 MOA red dot; 114/170 MOA windage/elevation adjustment; parallax free; side-loading battery tray
Price:.................$499.99

VORTEX OPTICS SPITFIRE HD GEN II PRISM

Weight: 9, 10.3 oz.
Length: 3, 3.6 in.
Power: 3X, 5X
Obj. Dia.: 21, 25mm,
Field of View: 37.9 ft.@100 yd., 23.3 ft. @100 yd.
Eye Relief: 2.6, 2.7 in.
Features: A prism optic in a choice of 3X or 5X magnification; 100-yd. parallax setting; 250 MOA windage/ elevation adjustment for the 3X; 200 MOA windage/elevation adjustment for the 5X; 1 MOA clicks; multi-height mounting system; AR-BDC4 red-illuminated reticle subtends for

5.56 NATO; 10 daytime and two night vision brightness settings
Price:.......... **$549.99–$649.99**

RANGEFINDERS

ATHLON MIDAS 1 MILE

Weight: 4.75 oz.
Length: 3.8 in.
Power: 6X
Obj. Dia.: 21mm
Field of View: 7 degrees
Eye Relief: .55-in.
Features: Fast-scanning rangefinder shows distances from 5 yd. to 1 mile in horizontal, vertical, and angle-compensated modes; rain-proof; rubber grip panels; fully multi-coated lenses; diopter adjustment; yard/meter readouts
Price:.................$369.99

ATHLON TALOS 800Y

Weight: 4.75 oz.
Length: 3.8in.
Power: 6X
Obj. Dia.: 21mm
Field of View: 7 degrees
Eye Relief: .55-in.
Features: A lightweight tool for the hunter with a full reflective range of 800 and a "deer" range of 300 yd.; waterproof; adjustable diopter; fully multi-coated lenses; yard/meter readout; scan mode; angle compensation
Price:.................$199.99

ATN CORP. ABL 1000, 1500

Weight: 14 oz.
Length: 4.3 in.
Power: N/A
Obj. Dia.: N/A
Field of View: N/A
Eye Relief: N/A
Features: Designed to work in tandem

with ATN's Smart HD day, night, and thermal scopes (this rangefinder screws directly onto the front of the scope), the Applied Ballistic Laser (ABL) rangefinder reads to a maximum distance of 1,000 or 1,500 yd.; waterproof; sends distances to the scope ballistic calculator; avilable in black, or the Break-Up Country, Elements Terra, or Bottomland camo patterns from Mossy Oak
Price:.......... **$299.00–$379.00**

BUSHNELL PRIME 1800

Weight: 6 oz.
Length: 4.23 in.
Power: 6X
Obj. Dia.: 24mm
Field of View: N/A
Eye Relief: N/A
Features: This rangefinders feature's Bushnell's ActivSync technology, which changes the display readout from red to black with shading in between according to the ambient light so that the readout isn't lost against a too bright or too dark background; maximum range 1,800 yd.; deer range 900 yd.; IPX4 water resistant; EXO Barrier lens treatment; ARC, scan, bow, bull's-eye, brush, and rifle modes
Price:.................$249.99

HALO OPTICS CL300

Weight: 8 oz.
Length: 5 in.
Power: 5X
Obj. Dia.: N/A
Field of View: N/A
Eye Relief: N/A
Features: Economically priced rangefinder does the job on reflective targets to 500 yd., non-reflective to 300 yd.; scan mode; uses AAA battery; water-resistant housing
Price:.................$99.99

NEW Products: Optics

HALO OPTICS XL450

HALO OPTICS Z1000

REVIC BR4

SIG SAUER KILO5K

SIG SAUER KILO 8K-ABS

HALO OPTICS XLR1600

MUDDY/GSM OUTODOORS 650 W HD

SIG SAUER BUCKMASTERS 1500

HALO OPTICS XL450, XL600, XL700

Weight: 5.2 oz.
Length: 4.3 in.
Power: 6X
Obj. Dia.: 24mm
Field of View: N/A
Eye Relief: N/A
Features: Budget-minded line of rangefinders; water-resistant; ergonomic design; roof prism; anti-fog lens coatings; display in yards only; built-in inclometer; auto-off feature; maximum yardage reading indicated in the model number
Price:. . . . . **$119.99–$149.99**

HALO OPTICS XLR1600

Weight: 11 oz.
Length: 5 in.
Power: 6X
Obj. Dia.: 24mm
Field of View: N/A
Eye Relief: N/A
Features: It turns out you can get a big-distance rangefinder without spending a ton; auto-acquisiton target read feature; maxium 1,600-yd. reflective target reading; glass lenses; scan mode; angle intelligence; water resistant
Price:. **$249.99**

HALO OPTICS Z1000

Weight: 9 oz.
Length: 5 in.
Power: 6X
Obj. Dia.: 24mm
Field of View: N/A
Eye Relief: N/A
Features: Reads to a full 1,000 yd. on reflective targets, 600 to non-reflective; auto acquisiton technology; scan mode; water-resistant; non-slip ergonomic housing design
Price:. **$149.99**

MUDDY/GSM OUTODOORS 650 W HD, 850 W HD, 1300 W HD

Weight: 15 oz.
Length: N/A
Power: 6X
Obj. Dia.: 26mm
Field of View: N/A
Eye Relief: N/A
Features: A line of budget-friendly rangefinders that feature an ABS housing with rubber trim; IP54 waterproofing; scan mode; yard/meter radout; angle compensation; glass lenses; battery level indicator; carrying case and lanyard included; number in the model indicates maximum yardage readout
Price:. . . . . **$179.99–$229.99**

REVIC BR4

Weight: 10 oz.
Length: 4.85 in.
Power: 10X
Obj. Dia.: N/A
Field of View: N/A
Eye Relief: N/A
Features: This sleek-looking unit goes big, with a whopping 10X magnification; 4,000-yd. reflective target reading; on-board ballistic profiles; temperature, pressure, compass, and inclometer sensors; firing solutions in MRAD, MIL or Revic's own BDC "Shoot to Range" technology; Bluetooth connectivity with the Revic mobile app (iOS and Android) for instant ballistic calculations and syncing; metal housing; IP67 waterproofing
Price:. **$1350.00**

SIG SAUER BUCKMASTERS 1500

Weight: 5.2 oz.
Length: 3.9 in.
Power: 6X

Obj. Dia.: 22mm
Field of View: N/A
Eye Relief: .7-in.
Features: SIG goes economical both in rangefinder weight and in price; 600-yd. readings to deer, 800-yd. to trees, 1,500-yd. maximum reflective target; IPX-4 waterproofing; black circle reticle with a red LED readout
Price:. **$152.99**

SIG SAUER KILO5K

Weight: 7.5 oz.
Length: 4.4 in.
Power: 7X
Obj. Dia.: 25mm
Field of View: N/A
Eye Relief: .59-in.
Features: With a nice 7X magnification, this unit ranges up to 2,000 yd. on deer, 2,500 on trees, and a stellar 5,000 yd. for a maximum reflective target reading; diopter adjustment; IPX4 waterproofing; circle and milling grid reticle in an OLED display; extended range, fog, first, best, and last target modes; Gen II Lightwave DSP Ranging Engine; onboard enviornmental sensors; connects with BaseMap app via Bluetooth for waypoint dropping, custom bullet profiles, and onboard ballistic groups
Price:. **$718.99**

SIG SAUER KILO8K-ABS

Weight: 7.5 oz.
Length: 4.4 in.
Power: 7X
Obj. Dia.: 25mm
Field of View: N/A
Eye Relief: .6-in.
Features: Loaded with all the features of the Kilo5K, this one extends the refeflective target range to 8,000 yd.; ships with MOLLE bag, multicam carry pouch, lanyard, tripod adaptor, and WeatherFlow Bluetooth WindMETER
Price:. **$1791.99**

TACTICON
ARMAMENT
PREDATOR
V1

TACTICON
ARMAMENT
PREDATOR
V2

TACTICON
ARMAMENT
PREDATOR
V3

TRIJICON
VENTUS

VORTEX
OPTICS
IMPACT 1000

VORTEX
OPTICS
COPPERHEAD
1500

VORTEX
OPTICS
RANGER 1800

TACTICON ARMAMENT PREDATOR V1

Weight: 9.58 oz.
Length: 5 in.
Power: 1X
Obj. Dia.: 28mm
Field of View: N/A
Eye Relief: N/A
Features: This is a dual user-selectable red/green 3 MOA tubular sight; five brightness settings; glare-resistant lenses; includes elevated cantilever Picatinny mount and rubber lens caps
Price:..................$59.95

TACTICON ARMAMENT PREDATOR V2

Weight: 5.15 oz.
Length: 3.5 in.
Power: 1X
Obj. Dia.: N/A
Field of View: N/A
Eye Relief: Unlimited
Features: An economical reflex sight with user-selectable red or green reticles in four reticle choices; nine brightness settings; waterproof and fogproof; works with a 45-degree offset mount
Price:..................$69.95

TACTICON ARMAMENT PREDATOR V3

Weight: 4.87 oz.
Length: 2.5 in.
Power: 1X
Obj. Dia.: 22mm
Field of View: N/A
Eye Relief: N/A
Features: A micro redot that can serve the user well on a 45-degree offset mount; 2MOA red dot with 11 brightness settings; anti-reflective lens coatings; aluminum body is nitrogen injected to be fog proof and submersible to 10m; includes a

45-degree offset mount and a .83-in. riser mount
Price:..................$69.95

TRIJICON VENTUS

Weight: N/A
Length: N/A
Power: 9X
Obj. Dia.: N/A
Field of View: N/A
Eye Relief: N/A
Features: There was much anticipation about this device but very little detail when announced early in 2022, but suffice it to say that this is more than your usual rangefinder--much more. While the Ventus does indeed measure range, its soul belongs to reading the wind--at the device, 100 yards from the device, 200, 300, 400, 500 yards and beyond, measuring three-dimensional wind velocities via the Dopplerr shift of returning laser energy returned to the tool after. eing reflected by air particles; collimated fiber optic laser capable of reading target range up to an almost unimaginable 5,000 yd. even when it's snowing, raining, or you're socked in with fog; oversized control buttons for easy access; wealth of sensors collect all sorts of atmospheric data; Ventus communicates seamlessly with the mobile app (iOS and Android), providing ballistic solutions to Trijicon reticles, providing a wind overlay map of its readings, and the user can even "fire" the Ventus via the app. Bottom line, and though specs and pricing won't be available until later in 2022 after this volume has gone to print, if you're dead-serious about perfecting your long-range game, the Ventus looks to be an absolute game-changer
Price:.................. **N/A**

VORTEX OPTICS COPPERHEAD 1500

Weight: 7.7 oz.
Length: 3.9 in.
Power: 6X
Obj. Dia.: 22mm
Field of View: N/A
Eye Relief: .66-in.
Features: With distance readings to 1,500 yd., this rangefinder also has fully multi-coated lenses; yard/meter readout; Horizontal Component Distance (HCD) angle compensation; reversible side clip; waterproof; non-slip rubber armor; adjustable diopter; tripod mount recess
Price:..................$519.99

VORTEX OPTICS IMPACT 1000

Weight: 5.5 oz.
Length: 3.8 in.
Power: 6X
Obj. Dia.: 20mm
Field of View: 341 ft.@1000 yd.
Eye Relief: .66-in.
Features: Easy on the wallet, this rangefinder offers reflective target readings to 1,000 yd.; compact and lightweight package; waterproof design; adjustable diopter; angle-compensated "shoot to range" technology
Price:..................$269.99

VORTEX OPTICS RANGER 1800

Weight: 7.7 oz.
Length: 3.9 in.
Power: 6X
Obj. Dia.: 22mm
Field of View: 315 ft.@1000 yd.
Eye Relief: .66 in.
Features: Great for distance--out to 1,800 yd. on a reflective target--this rangefinder has built-in angle compensation; fully multi-coated lenses; waterproof construction; non-slip rubber armor housing; line of sight and scan modes; yard/meter readout; reversible belt clip
Price:..................$499.99

CRIMSON TRACE LG-RUGER MAX 9, LG HELLCAT

HOLOSUN LE117 LASER

HOLOSUN LS117 LASER

HOLOSUN LE221

HOLOSUN LS221 LASER

HOLOSUN LE321 LASER

HOLOSUN LS321 LASER

HOLOSUN RML

MAGPUL MBUS 3 FRONT AND MAGPUL MBUS 3 REAR

SIGHTS/LASERS

CRIMSON TRACE LG-RUGER MAX 9, LG HELLCAT

Weight: N/A
Length: N/A
Descriiption: Mounts forward of the triggerguard with activation at the grip; easy access battery compartment; windage and elevation adjustable; in red or green
Ruger . . . . **$269.99–$359.99**
Hellcat . . . . **$$359.99–$315.99**

HOLOSUN LE117, LE117IR

Weight: 6.7 oz.
Length: 3.43 in.
Descriiption: A collimated laser, available in red or green and also as an infrared laser; titanium body; quick-release Picatinny mount; remote cable switch; high and low brightness settings; IP67 waterproof
MSRP: $411.75–$470.58

HOLOSUN LS117, LS117IR

Weight: 4.9 oz.
Length: 3.43 in.
Descriiption: Similar-class laser to the LE117s, but this laser has a 7075 aluminum housing
MSRP: $317.64–$363.52

HOLOSUN LE221

Weight: 6.88 oz.
Length: 3.43 in.
Descriiption: This is a coaxial laser, with either a red or green laser paired with an infrared laser; titanium housing; remote cable switch; quick-release mount; high and low brightness settings; IP67 waterproof
MSRP: . . . . **$788.21–$858.81**

HOLOSUN LS221

Weight: 6.7 oz.
Length: 3.43 in.
Descriiption: Similar to the LE221 coaxial laser, but this model has a 7075 aluminum housing
MSRP: . . . . **$611.75–$670.58**

HOLOSUN LE321

Weight: 9.52 oz.
Length: 3.43 in.
Descriiption: There's a lot packed into this 9.52-oz. package, with an infrared laser and infrared illuminator paired with either a red or green laser, all coaxially mounted; titanium housing; IR illuminator focus adjustment; quick-release Picatinny mount; remote pressure switch; IPX8 water resistant
MSRP: . . . . **$1176.46–$1235.28**

HOLOSUN LS321

Weight: 8.64 oz.
Length: 3.43 in.
Descriiption: Simlilar to the LE321, but with a 7075 aluminum housing that shaves off almost an ounce
MSRP: . . . . **$905.87–$970.58**

HOLOSUN RML

Weight: 1.3 oz.
Length: 1.97 in.
Descriiption: RML stands for Rail Mounted Laser; available in red or green; universal rail mount; tactile windage and elevation adjustments; polymer housing; compatible with most weapon-light holsters
MSRP: . . . . **$111.75–$117.64**

MAGPUL MBUS 3 FRONT, REAR

Weight: N/A
Length: N/A
Descriiption: This is a backup sight system; front and rear sights available seperately; ambidextrous push-button depolyment via spring-loaded design; tool-less elevation adjustment; front sight is dual-width enhanced; standard AR height when in the upright position; polymer construction for reduced weight; available in black, flat dark earth, Stealth Gray, and OD green
MSRP: . . . .**N/A**

STEINER OPTICS TOR MINI IR

TACTICON FLIP-UP IRON SIGHTS

TACTICON 45-DEGREE BUIS

ULTRADYNE C4 FRONT/REAR SIGHT COMBO

XS SIGHTS R3D NIGHT SIGHTS

ULTRADYNE C2 45-DEGREE OFFSET COMBO

ULTRADYNE C4 DYNAMOUNT

XS SIGHTS XT12 45 DEGREE OFFSET BUIS NON-TRITIUM

STEINER OPTICS TOR MINI IR

Weight: 2.2 oz.
Length: 2.1 in.
Descriiption: A very small infrared laser from Steiner; auto-on function when drawn; Type III hard-anodized machined aluminum housing and rail mount; left or right pressure pad activation; adjustable power output, including as a pulse; constant laser output throughout life of battery; adjustable brightness; adjustable windage/elevation; water-resistant and dust-proof
MSRP: $286.99

TACTICON FLIP-UP IRON SIGHTS

Weight: 1.6 oz.
Length: N/A
Descriiption: Made of high-strength aluminum alloy, front and rear sight units are spring-loaded and activated via push button; fits standard 20mm Picatinny rails; fully adjustable for windage/elevation; front sight post adjustment tool included
MSRP: $44.95

TACTICON 45-DEGREE BUIS

Weight: 1.7 oz.
Length: N/A
Descriiption: Backup iron sights designed to be mounted at a 45-degree offset; spring-loaded and activated via push button; aircraft-grade aluminum; fully adjustable for windage and elevation; includes sight adjustment tool
MSRP: $44.95

ULTRADYNE C2 FRONT, REAR, COMBO

Weight: 2.2, 1.7 oz.
Length: N/A
Descriiption: Made from 416 stainless steel and aircraft-grade aluminum, this is a dual aperture sight pair; front sight features 12 MOA aperture or blade-style post, 40 MOA of windage adjustment in ½-MOA clicks, elevation adjustable in .36-clicks; rear sight has purely concentric sight picture, interchangeable apertures-- .07-in, .05-in, and ghost ring--with the spares stored in the windage knob, 40 MOA of windage adjustment in ½-MOA clicks; 100-percent target picture; standard mil-std 1913 mounting; front and rear sights also available individually; front sight and combo pair also available as a 45-degree offset

Front	$79.00
Rear	$79.00
Combo	$149.00
45-degree front	$89.00
45-degree combo	$159.00

ULTRADYNE C4 FRONT, REAR, COMBO

Weight: 1.3, 1.7 oz.
Length: N/A
Descriiption: Employing the unique Dynalign Technology sighting system of four concentric circles, inner and outer on each of the sights in this combo; front sight features tool-less elevation adjustment and windage adjustment for zeroing, includes 12 MOA Dynalign and front post, with 8, 10, and 14 MOA Dinaligns available; rear sight has purely concentric sight picture, interchangeable apertures-- .07-in, .05-in, and ghost ring--with the spares stored in the windage knob; both front and rear mount to standard mil-std 1913 rails; front and rear sights also available individually; front, rear, and combo also available as 45-degree offset

Front	$131.00
Rear	$131.00
Combo	$288.00
45-degree front	$136.00
45-degree rear	$178.00
45-degree combo	$299.00

ULTRADYNE C4 DYNAMOUNT

Weight: 2.2 oz.
Length: N/A
Descriiption: This sight solves the problem of sight movement on a free-floating handguard by being a barrel-mounted sight; windage adjustable for zeroing; tool-less elevation adjustment; 12 MOA Dynalign aperture standard with 8, 10, and 14 MOA available as well as a standard front post; indexable to standard upright or 45-degree offset mounting; choice of ½X28 thread for .223/5.56 or 5/8X24 thread for .308/7.62

.223	$141.00
.308	$152.00

XS SIGHTS R3D NIGHT SIGHTS

Weight: N/A
Length: N/A
Descriiption: This is a traditonal notch/post three-dot pistol sight arrangement with a choice of orange or green front sight, both colors with Ember Glow Technology; rear sight is blacked out; available for CZ, Canik, FN, Mossberg, H&K, Sig, S&W, Springfield Armory, Taurus, Walther, and Glock handguns
MSRP: $116.00

XS SIGHTS XT12 45 DEGREE OFFSET BUIS NON-TRITIUM

Weight: N/A
Length: N/A
Descriiption: Fully ambidextrous 45-degree offset backup irons for AR platforms; non-tritium high-visibility orange front with Ember Glow for use in low-light conditions;
MSRP: $129.99

NEW Products: Ammunition

ARMSCORPRECISION/ ADVANCED TACTICAL HANDGUN AMMUNITION

ARMSCORPRECISION/ ADVANCED TACTICAL RIFLE AMMO

ARMSCORPRECISION/ ADVANCED TACTICAL RIMFIRE AMMO

ARMSCOR SHOTSHELL AMMO

BERGER BULLETS ELITE HUNTER

BERGER BULLETS MATCH GRADE .223

BLACK HILLS AMMUNITION MK 262 MOD 1-C

BRENNEKE USA ORANGE LIGHTNING

BROWNING PRO22

BROWNING WICKED WING XD

BROWNING WICKED WING

ARMSCORPRECISION/ ADVANCED TACTICAL HANDGUN

Features: Full metal jacket, semi-wadcutter, and jacketed hollowpoint handgun ammunition
Available in: .32 ACP 71/72 gr.; .380 ACP 95-gr.; 38 Spec. 125/158 gr.; .357 Mag. 125/158 gr.; .38 Super 125 gr.; 9mm 115/124 gr.; .40 S&W 180 gr.; 10mm 180 gr.; .44 Mag. 240-gr.; .45 ACP 230-gr.; .45 LC 255 gr.; .50 AE 300 gr.; .500 S&W 300 gr.
Box of:. 20, 50
MSRP:. . . . . $11.84–$313.55

ARMSCORPRECISION/ ADVANCED TACTICAL RIFLE

Features: Full metal jacket line of rifle ammunition
Available in: .223 Rem., .308 Win., .270 Win., .300 BLK, .300 Win. Mag., .30-06 Spfd., .30-30 Win., .30 Carbine, .375 H&H, .45-70 Gov't., 5.56 NATO, 6.5 Creedmoor; 7mm Rem. Mag., 7.62X39mm
Box of:. 20, 50
MSRP:. . . . . $10.20–$59.88

ARMSCORPRECISION/ ADVANCED TACTICAL RIMFIRE

Features: Hollowpoint and solid point rimfire ammunition
Available in: .22 LR, .22 Short, .22 Magnum

BLACK HILLS AMMUNITION MK 262 MOD 1-C

Features: 5.56 in bulk! Exact military
Box of:. 50
MSRP: . . . .$5.50–$8.71

ARMSCORPRECISION/ ADVANCED TACTICAL SHOTGUN

Features: Slug, buckshot, and birdshot loads
Available in: 12 ga., 20 ga., .410-bore
Box of:. 10, 25
MSRP: . . . .$5.00–$18.25

BERGER BULLETS ELITE HUNTER

Features: Features a high BC, hybrid ogive Elite Hunter bullet with a J4 Hunting Jacket that allows the bullet to penetrate two to three inches before delivering hydrostatic shock to vitals
Available in: New for 2022 are 6.5 PRC in a 156-gr. Extreme Outer Limits and .300 PRC 205-gr. cartridges. They join the 6.5 PRC and .338 Lapua already in this line
Box of:. . . . .
MSRP: . . . .

BERGER BULLETS MATCH GRADE .223 REM.

Features: Two loads, a 73-gr. Berger Boat-Tail Target bullet traveling with a muzzle velocity of 2820 fps and muzzle energy of 1289 ft-lb., and a 77-gr. OTM Tactical bullet traveling with a muzzle velocity of 1293 and muzzle energy of 2750 ft-lb.
Available in: .223 Rem.
Box of:. .20
MSRP: $33.99

specification construction; sold in bulk military ammo cans; no lot ships unless it tests out at a sub 2-in. group
Available in: 5.56 NATO 77 gr.
Box of:. 450
MSRP: $649.95

BRENNEKE USA ORANGE LIGHTNING

Features: A 440-gr. 12-ga. slug with a Brenneke B.E.T. (Better Energy Transfer) wad;
Available in: 12-ga. 2¾-in.
Box of:. 5
MSRP: $19.99

BROWNING PRO22

Features: Target grade rimfire ammuniton with a precise target crimp to minimize jump; subsonic velocity at 1085 fps
Available in: .22 LR 40-gr.
Box of:. 100
MSRP: . . . . .N/A

BROWNING WICKED WING

Features: Steel shot waterfowl load; 1¼-oz. payload; 1,450 fps; No. 2, No. 4 shot
Available in: 12-ga. 3-in.
Box of:. 250
MSRP: $179.99

BROWNING WICKED WING XD

Features: Plated steel shot to reduce cost; 1-oz. payload in 20-ga. (No. 2 or No. 3), 1¼-oz. 12-ga. 3-in, 1½-oz. 3.5 12-ga. (BB or No. 2)
Available in: 20-ga 3-in., 12 ga. 3-in., 3½-in.
Box of:. 250
MSRP: . . . . $239.00–$329.00

**CCI BLAZER BRASS
LEAD-FREE**

**CCI BLAZER BRASS .30
SUPER CARRY FMJ**

**CCI CLEAN-22
REALTREE**

**D DUPLEKS USA BROADHEAD
DEVASTATOR**

**D DUPLEKS USA
ROSSA 32**

**D DUPLEKS USA STEELHEAD
PEN-TRACK**

**ELEY MINOR9
COMPETITION**

**ELEY SEMI-AUTO
BENCHREST OUTLAW**

**ELEY SEMI-AUTO
BENCHREST
PRECISION**

**FEDERAL .30 SUPER
CARRY HST**

CCI BLAZER BRASS LEAD-FREE

Features: Lead-free Clean Fire primers; lead-free flat-nosed projectiles
Available in: 9mm 100-gr.
Box of:. 50
MSRP: $27.99

CCI BLAZER BRASS .30 SUPER CARRY FMJ

Features: Devleoped by Federal, the .30 Super Carry has a .312-in.-diameter projectile but with the same muzzle energy as a traditional 9mm; reloadable brass
Available in: 115-gr.
Box of:. 50
MSRP: $30.99

CCI CLEAN-22 REALTREE

Features: Polymer-coated led bullet cuts lead build-up in barrel and suppressors; high-velocity; bullet coating colors in tan, grean, and black
Available in: .22 LR 40-gr.
Box of:. 400
MSRP: $43.99

D DUPLEKS USA BROADHEAD DEVASTATOR

Features: A lead-free, expanding steel slug that fragments; for thin-skinned mediaum-sized North American big game such as deer, wild boar, big cats, etc.; 11/16-oz. slug; muzzle

velocity 1475 fps; muzzle energy 1455 ft-lb.; safe for smoothbore and rifled barrels; safe for all chokes; non-fouling construction
Available in: 20-ga. 11/16-oz. slug
Box of:. 5
MSRP: $10.99

D DUPLEKS USA ROSSA 32

Features: An expanding steel slug for big-game hunters; hollowpoint ogive has six petals for controlled expansion; wasited body provides stable aerodynamics; can be used in smoothbore and rifled barrels and the company says it's safe for all chokes; fouling-free design; muzzle velocity 1330 fps; muzzle energy 1930 ft-lb.
Available in: 12 ga. 1/8-oz. slug
Box of:. 5
MSRP: . . . . N/A

D DUPLEKS USA STEELHEAD PEN-TRACK

Features: A 2/4-in. 20-ga. solid steel 11/16-oz. slug; waited slug body for stabilization; foul-less construction; flat ogive; muzzle velocity 1475 fps; muzzle energy 1455 ft-lb.
Available in: 20-ga. 11/16-oz. slug
Box of:. 5
MSRP: $7.50

ELEY MINOR 9 COMPETITION

Features: Designed for pistol-caliber carbines and action pistol limited divisions; PCC available in 115- and

124-gr.; action pistol available in 115-, 124-, and 147-gr.; round-nose full metal jacket
Available in: 9mm
Box of:. 50
MSRP: $20.00

ELEY SEMI-AUTO BENCHREST OUTLAW

Features: A higher-velocity .22 LR round developed for competitive rimfire shooters using semi-auto rifles; round-nose; paraffin-was lubricant; muzzle velocity 1090 fps
Available in: .22 LR 42-gr.
Box of:. 50
MSRP: $6.50

ELEY SEMI-AUTO BENCHREST PRECISION

Features: Developed with a 40-gr. round-nose bullet to function reliably in semi-automatic rifles; mizzle velocity 1040–1080 fps
Available in: .22 LR 40-gr.
Box of:. 50
MSRP: $9.99

FEDERAL .30 SUPER CARRY HST

Features: A new cartridge introduction for 2022, developed by Federal, with a an HST bullet smaller in diameter than a standard 9mm, but with the same muzzle energy; nickel-plated cases; HST hollowpoint expands reliably through many common barriers
Available in: .30 Super Carry 100-gr.
Box of:. 20
MSRP: $36.99

NEW Products: Ammunition

FEDERAL AMERICAN EAGLE .30 SUPER CARRY

FEDERAL HIGH OVER ALL

FEDERAL SHORTY FORCE X2

FEDERAL TOP GUN GAME LOADS

FEDERAL TOP GUN PAPER WAD

FEDERAL UPLAND STEEL PAPER WAD

FIOCCHI USA 3-GUN LEGACY SERIES

FIOCCHI USA BLUE GUARDIAN

FIOCCHI USA DEFENSE DYNAMICS HANDGUN

FIOCCHI USA DEFENSE DYNAMICS RIFLE

FEDERAL AMERICAN EAGLE .30 SUPER CARRY

Features: The more affordable answer for practice with the new Federal .30 Super Carry round; 100-gr. FMJ; reloadable brass; feel/point of impact mimics the Federal HST load in this caliber
Available in: .30 Super Carry 100-gr.
Box of: 50
MSRP: $31.99

FEDERAL HIGH OVER ALL

Features: Designed for clay target competitors; solid brass head; Podium wad represetnts a new wad design for 2022; reloadable single-piece plastic hull; high-antimony pellets
Available in: 12-ga. 2¾-in. all as follows: 24-g. 3¼ DE No. 7.5, 1-oz. 9; 2¾ DE No, 7.5, 8; 1-oz. 3 DE No. 7.5, 8; 1-oz. 3¼ DE No. 7.5, 8, 8.5; 1⅛-oz. 2¾ DE No. 7.5, 8, 9; 1⅛-oz. 3 DE No. 7.5, 8; 1⅛-oz. HDCP DE, No. 7.5,8
Box of: 25
MSRP: $14.99

FEDERAL SHORTY FORCE X2

Features: This is the shortened 12-ga. round that stands at 1¾-in.; payload consists of six 00 buckshot pellets that segment in half upon impact; copper-plated shot
Available in: 12-ga. 1¾-in.
Box of: 10
MSRP: $28.99

FEDERAL TOP GUN GAME LOADS

Features: A fresh 20-ga. offering for both bird and predator hunters; high brass-plated steel head; one-piece wad
Available in: 20-ga. 1¼-oz. No. 5, 6
Box of: 25
MSRP: $26.99

FEDERAL TOP GUN PAPER WAD

Features: For clay bird shooters, these loads have a proprietary paper gas-sealing over-powder wad; choice of lead or steel shot;
Available in: 12-ga. 2¾-in. all as follows: 1⅛-oz. 3 DE No. 7,5, 8 lead; 1-oz. 3 DE No. 7 steel at either 1,250 or 1,300 fps
Box of: 25
MSRP: . . . Lead $17.99; Steel $19.99

FEDERAL UPLAND STEEL PAPER WAD

Features: Like the Top Gun Paper Wad loads, this load for upland bird huntes has a proprietary paper gas-sealing over-powder wad; high-velocity 1,330 fps
Available in: 12-ga. 2¾-in. 1-oz. No, 7,5
Box of: 25
MSRP: $19.99

FIOCCHI USA 3-GUN LEGACY SERIES (JERRY MICULEK SERIES)

Features: A pair of slug loads, a buckshot load, and a slug round to gkeep 3-Gun competitors at the top of their game; developed in conjunction with renowned competitor Jerry Miculek
Available in: 12-ga. 2¾-in. 9-pellet 00 Buck (1,250 fps); 1⅛-oz. No 7.5

(1,200 fps); 1-oz. No. 7.5 (1,170 fps); 7/8-oz. slug (1,300 fps)
Box of: 25
MSRP: . . . . $10.99–$21.49

FIOCCHI USA BLUE GUARDIAN

Features: This line of handgun defense ammunition features a Reduced Recoil Hollow Point (RRHP) bullet; EnviroShield lead-free bullets and primers; online reviews claim this is frangible but the Fiocchi USA website doesn't mention that at all
Available in: .380 ACP 75-gr., 9mm 100-gr., .40 S&W 125-gr., .45 ACP 155-gr.
Box of: 20
MSRP: $29.99

FIOCCHI USA DEFENSE DYNAMICS HANDGUN

Features: A collection of semi-jacketed and jacketed hollowpoints for self-defense use; most calibers have more than one bullet-weight choice
Available in: .32 ACP, .380 ACP, 9mm, .38 Spec., .357 Mag., .40 S&W, 10mm, .44 Spec., .44 Mag., .45 ACP
Box of: 50
MSRP: . . . . $36.99–$50.99

FIOCCHI USA DEFENSE DYNAMICS RIFLE

Features: An odd, single choice for a self-defense rifle line, this one a round developed for the H&K MP7 PDW back in 1999
Available in: 4.6X30mm HK
Box of: 50
MSRP: $37.01

FIOCCHI USA DEFENSE DYNAMICS SHOTGUN

FIOCCHI USA EXACTA CRUSHER

FIOCCHI USA EXACTA INTERCEPTOR SPREADER

FIOCCHI USA LITTLE RINO

FIOCCHI USA EXACTA EXTRA LOW RECOIL

FIOCCHI USA EXACTA PAPER CRUSHER

FIOCCHI USA EXACTA PAPER LITTLE RINO

FIOCCHI USA EXACTA POWER SPREADER

FIOCCHI USA EXACTA STEEL TARGET

FIOCCHI USA EXACTA SUPER CRUSHER

FIOCCHI USA EXACTA VIP

FIOCCHI USA DEFENSE DYNAMICS SHOTGUN

Features: Fiocchi gets creative with both lethal and non-lethal options in this 12-ga. line of self-defense ammo; 2¾-in. shells
Available in: All 12-ga. 2¾-in. as follows: 1-oz. lead slug at 1,560 or 1,150 fps; lead nine-pellet 00 Buck at 1,250 fps; lead eight-pellet 00 Buck at 1,325 fps; rubber 15-pellet non-lethal load at 790 fps; 1-oz. frangible slug at 1,045 fps; 1-oz. rubber slug at 740 fps
Box of: **10, 25**
MSRP: . . . . **$9.99–$23.99**

FIOCCHI USA EXACTA CRUSHER

Features: For skeet, trap, sporting clays, and other clay sports
Available in: 12-ga. 2¾-in. 1-oz. No. 7.5, 8, at 1,300 fps
Box of: **25**
MSRP: **$10.99**

FIOCCHI USA EXACTA INTERCEPTOR SPREADER

Features: Fiocchi says this offers the same performance as a 1 1/8-oz. load but with less recoil
Available in: 12-ga. 2¾-in. 1-oz. No. 8 at 1,300 fps
Box of: **25**
MSRP: **$17.99**

FIOCCHI USA EXACTA LITTLE RINO

Features: A premium handicap-level load
Available in: 12-ga. 2¾-in. 1-oz. No. 7.5, 8, at 1,250 fps

Box of: **25**
MSRP: **$14.99**

FIOCCHI USA EXACTA EXTRA LOW RECOIL

Features: High-performaing, low-payload, low-recoil practice round
Available in: 12-ga. 2¾-in. 7/8-oz. No. 7.5, 8 at 1,200 fps; 20-ga. 2¾-in. ¾-oz. No. 7.5 at 1,075 fps
Box of: **25**
MSRP: **$12.99**

FIOCCHI USA EXACTA PAPER CRUSHER

Features: Water-resistant, wax-impregnated paper hull for clay competititon
Available in: 12-ga. 2¾-in. 1-oz. No. 7.5, 8, at 1,300 fps
Box of: **25**
MSRP: **$15.99**

FIOCCHI USA EXACTA PAPER LITTLE RINO

Features: Similar to the Paper Crusher, but with a bit less velocity
Available in: 12-ga. 2¾-in. 1-oz. No. 7.5, 8, at 1,250 fps; 12-ga. 2¾-in. 1 1/8-oz. No. 7.6, 8 at 1,250 fps
Box of: **25**
MSRP: **$11.29**

FIOCCHI USA EXACTA POWER SPREADER

Features: Features a fast-opening shot column with a heavy payload for peformance on rabbits, close-quarter

incoming targets and other close-up presentations
Available in: 12-ga. 2¾-in. 1 1/8-oz. No. 8, 8.5 at 1,250 fps
Box of: **25**
MSRP: **$16.29**

FIOCCHI USA EXACTA STEEL TARGET

Features: Payloads of steel pellets plated with zinc for anti-corrosion purposes and optimized flight performance
Available in: 12-ga. 2¾-in. No. 7 in 1⅛-oz (1,375 fps) and 1-oz. (1,200 fps) 20-ga. in 7/8-oz. No. 7 (1,225 fps)
Box of: **25**
MSRP: **$9.49**

FIOCCHI USA EXACTA SUPER CRUSHER

Features: High-speed loads with one-piece cushioned wads
Available in: 12-ga. 2¾-in. No. 7.5 at 1,400 fps
Box of: **25**
MSRP: **$9.49**

FIOCCHI USA EXACTA VIP

Features: A family of sub-gauge loads designed for competition use, built to meet Olympic- and world-class performance expectations
Available in: 20-ga. 2¾-in. 7/8-oz. No. 7.5, 8, 9 at 1,200 fps; 28-ga. 2¾-in. ¾-oz. No. 7.5, 8, 9 at 1,200 fps; .410-bore 2½-in. ½-oz. No. 7.5, 8, 9 at 1,250 fps
Box of: **25**
MSRP: **$13.99**

NEW Products: Ammunition

FIOCCHI USA EXACTA VIP HEAVY

FIOCCHI USA EXACTA WHITE RINO

FIOCCHI USA EXACTA WHITE RINO CRUSHER

FIOCCHI USA FIELD DYNAMICS AERO SLUG

FIOCCHI USA FIELD DYNAMICS DOVE LOADS

FIOCCHI USA FIELD DYNAMICS HIGH VELOCITY

FIOCCHI USA FLYWAY SERIES

FIOCCHI USA GOLDEN GOOSE

FIOCCHI USA EXACTA VIP HEAVY

Features: Similar to the VIP, but only for 20- and 28-ga. and with higher velocities
Available in: 20-ga. 2¾-in. 7/8-oz. No. 7.5, 8 at 1,250 fps; 28-ga. 2¾-in. ¾-oz. No. 7.5, 8, 9 at 1,300 fps
Box of:......................25
MSRP:...................$13.99

FIOCCHI USA EXACTA WHITE RINO

Features: Dense patterns, capable velocity and softer recoil for long days on the range
Available in: 12-ga. 2¾-in. 1 1/8-oz. No. 7.5, 8 at 1,250 fps
Box of:......................25
MSRP:...................$10.44

FIOCCHI USA EXACTA WHITE RINO CRUSHER

Features: Similar to the standard White Rino but with higher velocities
Available in: 12-ga. 2¾-in. 1 1/8-oz. No. 7.5, 8 at 1,300 fps
Box of:......................25
MSRP:...................$12.39

FIOCCHI EXACTA WHITE RINO LITE

Features: Similar to the standard White Rino but with less velocity for a high-volume shooting days
Available in: 12-ga. 2¾-in. 1 1/8-oz. No. 7.5, 8, 9 at 1,200 fps
Box of:......................25
MSRP:...................N/A

FIOCCHI USA EXACTA WHITE RINO SUPER LITE

Features: Similar to the White Rino Lite, but with even less velocity for a much softer shooting experience; ideal for new shooters and training
Available in: 12-ga. 2¾-in. 1 1/8-oz. No. 7.5, 8 at 1,150 fps
Box of:......................25
MSRP:...................$14.99

FIOCCHI USA FIELD DYNAMICS SHOTGUN—BUCK & SLUG

Features: Ample energy for the whitetail hunter with Fiocchi's lead Aero Slug, or nickel-plated 00 Buck or #4 Buck
Available in: 12-ga. 2¾-in. 7/8-oz. slug (1,300 fps); 9-pellet 00 Buck (1,325 fps); 27-pellet #4 Buck (1,325 fps)
Box of:......................10
MSRP:...........$10.00–$15.99

FIOCCHI USA FIELD DYNAMICS SHOTGUN—DOVE LOADS

Features: Full complement of dove and quail loads for every gauge, all in 2¾-in with the exception of the .410-bore which is in the field-appropriate 2½-inch shell
Available in: 12-ga. 1 1/8-oz. No. 7.5, 8 (1,250 fps); 12-ga. 1-oz. No. 7.5, 8 (1,250 fps); 16-ga. 1-oz. No. 7.5, 8 (1,165 fps); 20-ga. 7/8-oz. No. 7 (1,225 fps) and No. 7.5, 8 (1,210 fps); 28-ga. ¾-oz. No. 8 (1,200 fps); .410-bore ½-oz. No. 9 (1,200 fps)
Box of:......................25
MSRP:...................$12.99

FIOCCHI USA FIELD DYNAMICS SHOTGUNS—HIGH FIOCCHI VELOCITY

Features: A robust lineup of upland loads for all gauges, with velocities and shot sizes to take everything from quail and woodcock to grouse and pheasants
Available in: 12-ga. 3-in. 1¾-oz. No. 4, 5, 6 (1,330 fps); 12-ga. 2¾-in. 1¼-oz. No. 4, 5, 6, 7.5, 8, 9 (1,330 fps); 16-ga. 2¾-in. 1 1/8-oz. No. 5, 6, 7.5 (1,330 fps); 20-ga. 3-in. 1¼-oz. No. 4, 5, 6, 7.5, 8 (1,200 fps); 20-ga. 2¾-in. 1-oz. No. 5, 6, 7.5, 8, 9 (1,220 fps); 28-ga. 3-in. 1-oz. No. 5, 6, 7.5, 8 (1,300 fps); 28-ga. 2¾-in. ¾-oz. No. 6, 7.5, 8, 9 (1,300 fps); .410-bore 3-in. 11/16-oz. No. 6, 7.5, 8, 9 (1,140 fps)
Box of:......................25
MSRP:...................$13.49

FIOCCHI USA FLYWAY SERIES

Features: A complete line of magnum 12- and 20-ga. loads for waterfowlers; plated steel shot
Available in: 12-ga. 3½-in. 1 3/8-oz. No. 1, 2, 4, BB, BBB, T (1,470 fps); 12-ga. 3-in. 1 1/5-oz. No. 1, 2, 4, 6, BB (1,500 fps), and 1/18-oz. No. 1, 2, 3, 4, BB (1,550 fps); 20-ga. 3-in. 7/8-oz. No. 2, 3, 4 (1,500 fps)
Box of:......................25
MSRP:...........$16.99–$18.99

FIOCCHI USA GOLDEN GOOSE

Features: If geese are your game, then this is your load; plated steel high-velocity shot
Available in: 12-ga. 3½-in. 1 5/8-oz. No. 1, 2, BB, BBB, T
Box of:......................25
MSRP:...................$24.00

FIOCCHI USA GOLDEN PHEASANT

FIOCCHI USA GOLDEN PHEASANT BISMUTH

FIOCCHI USA GOLDEN TURKEY

FIOCCHI USA GOLDEN TURKEY TSS

FIOCCHI USA GOLDEN WATERFOWL

FIOCCHI USA GOLDEN WATERFOWL BISMUTH

FIOCCHI USA HERITAGE

FIOCCHI USA HYPERFORMANCE DEFENSE HANDGUN

FIOCCHI USA HYPERFORMANCE HUNT RIFLE

FIOCCHI USA GOLDEN PHEASANT

Features: Big lineup of shells for pheasant hunters; nickel-plated lead shot
Available in: 12-ga. 3-in. 1¾-oz. No. 4, 5, 6 (1,200 fps); 12-ga. 2¾-in. 1⅛-oz. No. 4, 5, 6 (1,250 fps and 1,485 fps); 16-ga. 2¾-in. 1⅛-oz. No. 5, 6 (1,310 fps); 20-ga. 3-in. 1¼-oz. No. 4, 5, 6, 7.5 (1,200 fps); 20-ga. 2¾-in. 1-oz. No. 5, 6, 7.5 (1,245 fps); 28-ga. 3-in. 1 11/16-oz. No. 5, 6, 7.5 (1,200 fps); 28-ga. 2¾-in. ⅞-oz. No. 5, 6, 7.5 (1,300 fps)
Box of: 25
MSRP: . . . . $20.99–$21.99

FIOCCHI USA GOLDEN PHEASANT BISMUTH

Features: High-density, premium bismuth shot for pheasant hunters
Available in: 12-ga. 3-in. No. 4, 6 (1,400 fps)
Box of: 10
MSRP: . . . . $22.99–$23.84

FIOCCHI USA GOLDEN TURKEY

Features: A definite upgrade in 2022 over previous turkey loads from this brand, with nickel-plated shot, clean-buring powder, and an improved wad design
Available in: 12-ga. 3-in. 1¾-oz. No. 4, 5, 6 (1,200 fps); 20-ga. 3-in. 1¼-oz. No. 5, 6 (1,200 fps)
Box of: 10
MSRP: $18.00

FIOCCHI USA GOLDEN TURKEY TSS

Features: Super-dense patterns, even in the .410-bore, thanks to the tungsten shot payloads
Available in: 12-ga. 3-in. 1 5/8-oz. No. 7, 9 (1,200 fps); 20-ga. 3-in. 1 3/8-oz. No. 9 (1,225 fps); .410-bore 3-in. 13/16-oz. No. 9 (1,100 fps)
Box of: 5
MSRP: . . . . N/A

FIOCCHI USA GOLDEN WATERFOWL

Features: Excellent choice for sea ducks, geese, and late-season, decoy-shy birds; plated steel shot
Available in: 12-ga. 3-in. 1¼-oz. No. 1, 2, 3, 4, BB, BBB, T at 1,350 fps
Box of: 25
MSRP: $19.99

FIOCCHI USA GOLDEN WATERFOWL BISMUTH

Features: Duck hunters will get their limits with these fast, hard-hitting loads of bismuth shot
Available in: 12-ga. 3-in. 1 3/8-oz. No. 2, 4, 6 (1,450 fps); 20-ga. 3-in. 1 1/16-oz No. 4 (1,250 fps) or 15/16-oz. No. 4 (1,350 fps)
Box of: 10
MSRP: . . . . N/A

FIOCCHI USA HERITAGE

Features: Rounds for collectors with hard to find chamberings; most have full metal jackets, some with truncated cones; one semi-jacketed softpoint (.30 Luger) and one lead roundnose (.455 Webley)
Available in: .30 Luger. 7.62 Nagant, 7.62 Tokarev, 7.63 Mauser, 8mm Gasser, 8mm Lebel, 8mm Steyr, 9mm Makarov, 9mm Steyr, 9X18mm Ultra, 9X21mm IMI, .455 Webley

Box of: 50
MSRP: . . . . $34.99–$75.00

FIOCCHI USA HYPERFORMANCE DEFENSE HANDGUN

Features: Full line of self-defense handgun cartridges wearing a copper-jacketed XTP hollowpoint; brass cases; lead-free primers
Available in: .25 ACP (35-, 60-gr.); .380 ACP (90-gr.); 9mm (115-, 124-, 147-gr.); .38 Spec. +P (110-, 125-gr.); .357 Mag. (158-gr.); .40 S&W (155-, 180gr.); .44 Mag. (200-, 240-gr.); .45 ACP (200-, 230-gr.)
Box of: 20
MSRP: . . . . N/A

FIOCCHI USA HYPERFOMANCE HUNT RIFLE

Features: Premium hunting loads with high-BC bullets that provide flat trajectories, controlled expansion, and top-end weight retention
Available in: .243 Win. (90-gr. Scirocco, 95-gr. Hornady SST); .260 Rem. (129-gr. SST); 6.5 Creedmoor (129-gr. SST, 130-Gr. Scirocco); .270 Win. (130-gr. Scirocco, 150-gr. SST); 7mm-08 Rem. (129-gr. SST); 7mm Rem. Mag. (150-gr. Scirocco, 154-gr. SST); .300 BLK (125-gr. SST); .308 Win. (150-gr. SST or Scirocco, 180-gr. SST); .30-06 SPfd. (165-gr. Scirocco or Sierra HPBT GameKing, 180-gr. SST); .300 Win. Mag. (180-gr. SST or Scirocco)
Box of: 20
MSRP: . . . . $32.99–$60.99

NEW Products: **Ammunition**

FIOCCHI USA HYPERFORMANCE MATCH RIFLE

FIOCCHI USA INTERNATIONAL TRAP & SKEET

FIOCCHI USA INTERNATIONAL SHOOTING DYNAMICS

FIOCCHI USA PAPER INTERNATIONAL TRAP & SKEET

GECO TARGET HP

GECO ACTION EXTREME FRAGMENTATION

HEVI-SHOT HEVI-XII

INCEPTOR PREFERRED HUNTING

NORMA .22 WMR

FIOCCHI USA HYPER-FORMANCE MATCH RIFLE

Features: For competitors, this premium lineup wears Sierra MatchKing hollowpoint boattail projectiles
Available in: .223 Rem. (69-, 77-gr.), 6.5 Creedmoor (142-gr.), .300 BLK (220-gr.); .308 Win. (168-, 175-gr.); .300 Win. Mag. (190-gr.)
Box of: 20
MSRP: . . . . $29.99–$35.99

FIOCCHI USA INTERNATIONAL TRAP & SKEET

Features: Traditional plastic hull holds a high-velocity 24-g. payload of premium shot for exacting internation
Available in: 12-ga. 2¾-in. No. 7.5 or 9 at 1,350 fps
Box of: 25
MSRP: $13.58

FIOCCHI USA INTERNATIONAL SHOOTING DYNAMICS

Features: Traditional plastic hull holds a high-velocity 24-g. payload of chilled shot for exacting internation; note that thisis not the same load as found in the general Shooting Dynamics line of target shotshell ammunition
Available in: 12-ga. 2¾-in. No. 7.5 or 9 at 1,350 fps
Box of: 25
MSRP: $7.21

FIOCCHI USA PAPER INTERNATIONAL TRAP & SKEET

Features: Paper hull holds a high-velocity 24-g. payload for exacting international-grade competition
Available in: 12-ga. 2¾-in. No. 7.5 or 9 at 1,350 fps
Box of: 25
MSRP: $12.54

FIOCCHI USA SHOOTING DYNAMICS SHOTGUN

Features: A full lineup of everyday target loads for trap, skeet, sporting clays and other clay games
Available in: 12-ga. 2¾-in. 1 1/8-oz. No. 7.5, 8 (1,200 or 1,280 fps), No. 7.5, 8, 9 (1,165 fps), and No. 7.5, 8 (1,250 fps); 1-oz. No. 7.5, 8, 9 (1,200, 1,170 fps) or No. 7.5, 8 (1,250 fps); ⅞-oz. No. 7.5, 8 (1,350 fps); 20-ga. 2¾-in. 7/8-oz. No. 7.5, 8, 9 (1,210 fps)
Box of: 25
MSRP: $9.49

GECO TARGET HP

Features: Offered in three of the most popular cartridges for general target shooting and long-range precision; boattail hollowpoint projectiles; softened recoil
Available in: 6.5X55 SE 130-gr.; 6.5 Creedmoor 130-gr.; .308 Win. 168-gr.
Box of: 50
MSRP: . . . . N/A

GECO ACTION EXTREME FRAGMENTATION

Features: Features a hollowpoint that breaks into five pieces, four "wings" and a center body core for deep penetration
Available in: 9mm Browning Short (.380 ACP) 85-gr.; 9mm 108-gr.; .40 S&W 155-gr.; .45 ACP 175-gr.
Box of: 20
MSRP: . . . . N/A

HEVI-SHOT HEVI-XII

Features: This isn't so much new as a repackaging and bigger quantity offering of the original Hevi-Shot load, now in a 25-count box
Available in: 12-ga. 3-in. 1⅛-oz. No. 2, 4, 6; 12-ga. 3-in. 1¼-oz. No. 4, 6; 20-ga. 3-in. ⅞-oz. No. 4, 6; 20-ga. 3-in. 1¼-oz. No. 6; 28-ga. 3-in. 1-oz. No 4, 6
Box of: 25
MSRP: . . . . $62.99–$69.99

INCEPTOR PREFERRED HUNTING

Features: Features the ARX non-expanding projectile, an injection-molded design of a polymer/copper matrix; penetrates soft tissue but breaks apart on encountering hard barriers like bone; flat trajectories; low recoil
Available in: .45 LC (lever-actions) 157-gr.; .450 Bushmaster 158-gr.; .458 SOCOM 200-gr.; .50 Beowulf 200-gr.
Box of: 20
MSRP: . . . . $48.99–$59.99

NORMA.22 WMR

Features: A new entry in the rimfire varmint hunters arsenal; jacketed hollowpoint
Available in: .22 WMR 40-gr. at 1,877 fps
Box of: 50
MSRP: $17.99

NEW Products: Ammunition

NORMA ECO-POWER 22 FRAGMENTATION **NORMA ECOSTRIKE** **NORMA NXD** **NORMA TAC-22** NOSLER ASSURED STOPPING POWER

NOVX PENTAGON RIFLE **NOVX PENTAGON HANDGUN** REMINGTON CORE-LOKT TIPPED REMINGTON PETERS PAPER REMINGTON PREMIER ACCUTIP-V REMINGTON PREMIER MAGNUM TURKEY HIGH VELOCITY

NORMA ECO-SPEED .22, .22 FRAGMENTATION

Features: Copper-plated bullets have a lead-free zinc core; lead-free primer; super-high muzzle velocity; also offered as in a fragmenting hollowpoint option
Available in: .22 LR
Box of: 50
MSRP: $8.42

NORMA ECO-STRIKE

Features: Non-lead, green polymer-tipped hunting rounds; core comprised of copper and nickel and is lighter overall than traditional lead bullets; boattail profile
Available in: 8X57 JRS, 8X57 IS, 9.3X62, 9.3X74R, 7mm Rem. Mag., 7X64, 7X65R, ,300 WSM, .300 Win. Mag., .308 Win., .30-06 Spfd., .375 H&H Mag., .338 Win. Mag.
Box of: 20
MSRP: ....N/A

NORMA NXD

Features: NXD is Non-Expanding Defensive ammunition; injection-molded copper projectile in a fluted design that promotes terminal performance and hydraulic displacement; brass case
Available in: 9mm 65-gr.
Box of: 20
MSRP: $19.99

NORMA TAC-22

Features: A lead roundnose training .22 in bulk pack; consistent velocities and grouping;
Available in: .22 LR
Box of: 500
MSRP: $52.60

NOSLER ASSURED STOPING POWER

Features: Match-grade accuracy with hollowpoint bullets; bullets have a skived jacket for reliable expansion and a jacketed mouth for reliable feeding
Available in: 9mm, 40 S&W, 10mm Auto, .45 ACP,
Box of: 20, 50
MSRP: ....$18.49–$58.49

NOVX PENTAGON RIFLE

Features: Monolithic copper hollowpoint designed for controlled expansion; lead-free; petal expansion to twice the bullet diameter; reduced muzzle rise;
Available in: .300 BLK 125-gr. at 2,080 fps; 5.56 NATO 55-gr. at 3,340 fps
Box of: 20
MSRP: ....$49.99–$54.99

NOVX PENTAGON HANDGUN

Features: Monolithic copper hollowpoint designed for controlled expansion; lead-free; petal expansion to twice the bullet diameter; reduced muzzle rise;
Available in: 9mm 115-gr. at 1,300 fps; .380 ACP at 1,150 fps
Box of: 20
MSRP: ....$34.99–$36.99

REMINGTON CORE-LOKT TIPPED

Features: Wears a distinctive Big Green polymer tip; traditional Core-Lokt jacket; match-grade accuracy
Available in: .243 Rem., 6.5

Creedmoor, .270 Win., .280 Win., .308 Win., .30-06 Spfd., .300 Win. Mag., .300 WSM, 7mm Rem. Mag.
Box of: 20
MSRP: ....$44.99–$65.99

REMINGTON PETERS PREMIER BLUE PAPER

Features: Premium lead shot; Peters paper hull; soft recoil; all-brass head; competition wad
Available in: 12-ga. No. 7.5, 8, at 1,145, 1,200, or 1,245 fps
Box of: 25
MSRP: $19.99

REMINGTON PREMIER ACCUTIP -V

Features: Designed for varmint hunting; gold polymer tip; soft lead core fragments dramatically
Available in: .17 Rem., .17 Rem. Fireball, .22 Hornet, .221 Fireball, .204 Ruger, .22-25 Rem., .222 Rem. .223 Rem., .243 Win.
Box of: 20
MSRP: ....$26.99–$80.99

REMINGTON PREMIER MAGNUM TURKEY HIGH VELOCITY

Features: Provides tight patterns over longer distances; Power-Piston one-piece wad; hardened copper-plated lead shot
Available in: 12-ga. No. 4, 5, 1¾-oz. or 2-oz., 1,300 fps; 20-ga. No. 5 1 1/8-oz., 1,300 fps
Box of: 5
MSRP: ....$8.99–$12.99

NEW Products: **Ammunition**

REMINGTON PREMIER TSS

REMINGTON UMC HANDGUN

REMINGTON UMC RIFLE

SIERRA MATCHKING COMPETITION

SPEER LAWNMAN CLEANFIRE

SPEER LAWMAN RHT TRAINING

WINCHESTER AA DIAMOND GRADE ELITE TRAP

BERGER LONG-RANGE HYBRID TARGET 30-CAL BULLETS

HORNADY CX BULLETS

REMINGTON PREMIER TSS

Features: Payloads of ultra-dense Tungsten Super Shot that allows for smaller shot sizes and denser patterns over longer ranges
Available in: 12-ga. No. 7, 9, 1¾-oz., 1,200 fps; 20-ga. No. 7, 9, 1½-oz., 1,100 fps; .410-bore No. 9, 7/8-oz., 1,100 fps
Box of: 5
MSRP: . . . . $45.99–$68.99

REMINGTON UMC HANDGUN

Features: Value-based, no-nonsense rifle ammunition with full metal jackets, softpoints, or jacketed hollowpoints; Kleanbore primers
Available in: .25 ACP, .32 ACP, .380 ACP, 9mm, .38 Super +P, .357 SIG, .38 Spec., .38 Spec. +P, .357 Mag., .40 S&W, 10mm Auto, .44 Mag., .45 ACP
Box of: . . .50, 100, 250, 300, 500, 600
MSRP: . . . . $24.99–$417.99

REMINGTON UMC RIFLE

Features: Value-based, no-nonsense rifle ammunition with full metal jackets or jacketed hollowpoints
Available in: .22-250 Rem., .223 Rem., .300 BLK, 6.8 Rem. SPC, .30 Carbine, .303 British, .308 Win., .30-06 Spfd., .450 Bushmaster
Box of: 20, 50, 200, 300
MSRP: . . . . $17.99–$270.99

SELLIER & BELLOT BLUE EXERGY

Features: Lead-free, all-copper polymer-tipped boattail projectiles
Available in: 6.5X55 SE, 6.5X57, 6.5 Creedmoor, .270 Win., 7X57, 7X57R,

7X64, 7X65R, 7mm Rem. Mag., .300 BLK, .308 Win., .30-06 SPfd., .300 Win. Mag., 8X57 JRS, 8X57 JS, 9.3X62, 9.3X74R
Box of: 20
MSRP: . . . . N/A

SIERRA MATCHKING COMPETITION

Features: High-quality brass, powder, primers, and bullets designed for match-grade competition performance
Available in: .223 Rem. .308 Win., 6mm Creedmoor, 6.5 Creedmoor
Box of: 20
MSRP: . . . . $39.99–$54.99

SPEER LAWMAN, LAWMAN CLEANFIRE

Features: Reloadable cases; full metal jacket projectiles with lead cores; CleanFire options have CCI CleanFire primer
Available in: .280 ACP, 9mm, .38 Spec. +P, .357 SIG, .40 S&W, .45 ACP, .45 G.A.P.
Box of: 50
MSRP: . . . . $30.99–$67.99

SPEER LAWMAN RHT

Features: A frangible round; lead-free; CCI CleanFire primers; bullet tip distinctly marked to differentiate from traditional ammo
Available in: .45 G.A.P.
Box of: 50
MSRP: $28.99

WINCHESTER AA DIAMOND GRADE ELITE TRAP

Features: Super-high-antimony lead

shot precision sorted for consistency; AA wads; nickel-plated head
Available in: 12-ga. 2¾-in. 1 1/8-oz., 1,250 fps
Box of: 25
MSRP: $15.99

COMPONENTS

BERGER LONG-RANGE HYBRID TARGET

Description: .30-caliber 245-gr.
Boxes of: 100
MSRP: . . . . .N/A

HORNADY CX

Description: CX stands for Copper alloy eXpanding; advanced monolithic hunting projectile; deep penetration and high weight retention; heat shield tip. Available in: 6mm/.243 80-, 90=-gr.; .25/.257 90-gr.; 6.5mm/.264 120-, 130-gr.; 6.8mm/.270/277 100-gr.; .270/.277 130-gr.; 7mm/.284 139-, 150-gr., .30/.308 110-, 165-, 180-, 190-gr.; .338 185-, 225-gr.; .375 250-gr.
Boxes of: 100
MSRP: . . . . $52.39–$60.91

HORNADY ECX

Description: ECX stands for Extreme Copper alloy eXpanding intended for international big-game hunting; monolithc; flat polymer tip; 95% weight retention. Available in: .22/.224 50-gr.; 6mm/.264 140-gr.; 7mm/.284 150-gr.; .30/.308 125-, 165-gr.; 8mm/.323 180-gr.; 9.3/.366 250-gr.
Boxes of: 100
MSRP: . . . . .N/A

Accuracy International

ACCURACY INTERNATIONAL AT308

ACCURACY INTERNATIONAL AX308

ACCURACY INTERNATIONAL AXMC

AT308
Action: Bolt
Stock: Synthetic
Barrel: 24 in.
Sights: None
Weight: 12 lb. 13 oz.
Caliber: .308 Win.
Magazine: 10 rounds
Features: "AT" stands for Accuracy Tactical and this short-action .308 features an adjustable cheekpiece; fixed buttplate with spacers; pistol grip; 20 MOA STANAG 4695/Mil Std 1913 rail; double-chamber standard muzzle brake; double-stack magazine; folding stock; barrels finished in choice of Cerakote black, green, or pale brown
MSRP **$4984.00**

AX308
Action: Bolt
Stock: Synthetic
Barrel: 24 in.
Sights: None
Weight: 13 lb. 11 oz.
Caliber: .308 Win.
Magazine: 10 rounds
Features: A short-action sniper design; two 80mm flush cup accessory rails; 13-in. forend tube and rail; flush cup sling attachment points; adjustable cheekpiece; adjustable buttstock with spacers; right-side folding stock over bolt; double-stack magazine; tactical muzzle brake; High-Performance H series in Cerakote dark earth, green and pale brown options, Elite series in Elite Sand or Elite Midnight
MSRP **$7535.00**

AXMC
Action: Semiautomatic
Stock: Synthetic
Barrel: 27 in.
Sights: None
Weight: 15 lb.
Caliber: .300 Win. Mag., .308 Win., .338 Lapua
Magazine: 10 rounds
Features: Multi-caliber, allowing users to switch calibers with a change of barrel, bolt, and magazine; AI's patent-pending Quicklok quick-release barrel; detachable magazine has a left-side cutout that eases insertion into the rifle; Cerakote finishes in Elite Sand, Elite Midnight, AI Dark Earth, AI Green, AI Pale Brown; other barrel lengths available on request; custom options available
MSRP . . . . **starting at $8687.00**

Adcor Defense

ADCOR DEFENSE ELITE

ADCOR DEFENSE ELITE GI

ELITE
Action: Semiautomatic
Stock: Synthetic
Barrel: 16 in.
Sights: None
Weight: 10 lb.
Caliber: 7.62x39, .300 BLK
Magazine: 30 rounds
Features: Gas piston action, billet upper and lower, free-floating chrome-lined barrel and forward charging handle are standard. Choice

of Quad or Key Mod rails; black, Flat Dark Earth, Olive Drab Green, or Patriot Brown
MSRP . . . . **$2295.00–$2545.00**

ELITE GI
Action: Semiautomatic
Stock: Synthetic
Barrel: 16 in., 18 in.
Sights: None
Weight: 6 lb. 13 oz.–6 lb. 15 oz.
Caliber: .223

Magazine: 31 rounds
Features: A gas impingement version of Adcor's popular gas pistol Elite; billet upper and lower; two barrel lengths to choose from, either length available with or without a forward-charging handle; choice of quad or Key-Mod rail; finishes in black, Flat Dark Earth, Olive Drab Green, and Patriot Brown
Black: **$1995.00**
Colors: **$2245.00**

AllTerra Arms, LLC

ALLTERRA ARMS ARID 1760

ARID 1760
Action: Bolt
Stock: Synthetic
Barrel: 24 in.
Sights: None
Weight: 10 lb. 10 oz.
Caliber: 6.5 SST
Magazine: 4 rounds
Features: A dedicated one-miler; Axial

Precision Convergence Series receiver; TriggerTech Diamond trigger; match-grade fluted steel barrel; Race bolt; Heavy Hitter 3-port muzzle brake; adjustable cheekpiece; Manners MCS-EH1A stock in green and tan camo; detachable box magazine; topside and underside Picatinny rails
MSRP . . . . **Starting at $6295.00**

American Tactical

AMERICAN TACTICAL GALEO

AMERICAN TACTICAL OMNI HYBRID MAXX

GALEO
Action: Semiautomatic
Stock: Synthetic
Barrel: 18.5 in.
Sights: Flip-up front, rear
Weight: N/A
Caliber: 5.56 NATO
Magazine: 30 rounds
Features: Completely assembled in Summerville, SC, with a combination of US-made parts and Israeli military Galil parts; available with wood or polymer handguard; side-folding stock
MSRP $1489.95

OMNI HYBRID MAXX
Action: Semiautomatic
Stock: Synthetic
Barrel: 16 in.
Sights: None
Weight: 6 lb. 4 oz., 6 lb. 8 oz.
Caliber: .223 Rem./5.56 NATO, .22 LR, .300 BLK
Magazine: Detachable box, 30 round
Features: Retractable stock; metal-reinforced polymer lower and upper receiver; Picatinny rail
.22 LR: $429.95
.223 Rem./5.56 NATO: . . .$449.95–$669.95
.300 BLK: . . . . $449.95–$579.95

Anderson Manufacturing

ANDERSON MANUFACTURING AM-9

ANDERSON MANUFACTURING AM-10

ANDERSON MANUFACTURING AM-10 SNIPER

AM-9
Action: Semiautomatic
Stock: Synthetic
Barrel: 16 in.
Sights: None
Weight: 7 lb.
Caliber: 9mm
Magazine: 10, 17, 19 rounds
Features: Super fun PCC rifle that takes Glock magazines and features a forged aluminum upper and lower receiver; blowback operating system; M4 contour barrel with a parkerized finish; open trigger guard; six-position buffer tube; six-position carbine stock
MSRP $793.89

AM-10
Action: Semiautomatic
Stock: Synthetic
Barrel: 18 in.
Sights: None
Weight: 10 lb.
Caliber: .308 Win.
Magazine: 10 rounds
Features: Manageable barrel length while still having enough weight to tamp recoil; collapsible stock; M-LOK handguard; muzzle brake; lots of accessory rail
MSRP $1218.29

AM-10 SNIPER
Action: Semiautomatic
Stock: Synthetic
Barrel: 24 in.
Sights: None
Weight: 12 lb.
Caliber: .308 Win.
Magazine: 10 rounds
Features: A solid contender for those looking for a long-range gun, one that features acres of rail; adjustable stock; stabilizing pistol grip; M-LOK handguard; bipod
MSRP $2006.59

Anschütz (J.G. Anschütz)

ANSCHÜTZ 1416 AMERICAN VARMINTER

ANSCHÜTZ 1416 D HB CLASSIC

1416 AMERICAN VARMINTER
Action: Bolt
Stock: Thumbhole walnut
Barrel: 18 in.
Sights: None
Weight: 5 lb. 10 oz.
Caliber: .22 LR
Magazine: 5 rounds
Features: 64 bolt-action repeater; 5098 two-stage trigger; blued finish; hex-key bolts; medium-weight barrel threaded ½ in. x 28 tpi; no iron sight provision; counter-bored crown
MSRP $1749.00

1416 D HB CLASSIC
Action: Bolt
Stock: Walnut
Barrel: 23 in.
Sights: None
Weight: 6 lb. 7 oz.
Caliber: .22 LR
Magazine: Detachable box, 5 rounds
Features: Heavy barrel; lacquered walnut wood stock (optional beavertail); pistol grip; black buttplate; studs for sling swivel; lateral sliding safety
MSRP $1099.00

Anschütz (J.G. Anschütz)

J.G. ANSCHÜTZ 1761, 1761 AV THREADED

J.G. ANSCHÜTZ 1782D

ANSCHÜTZ 1907 IN 1914 STOCK

ANSCHÜTZ 2013/690 WITH 2018 PRECISE STOCK

ANSCHÜTZ 1771 D

ANSCHÜTZ 1827 FORTNER SPRINT

J.G. ANSCHÜTZ 1927 CISM WALNUT

ANSCHÜTZ 1771 D GRS

ANSCHÜTZ 1903 TARGET

1761 D HB, HB, AV THREADED

Action: Bolt
Stock: Walnut
Barrel: 18 in., 20 in.
Sights: None
Weight: 6 lb. 6 oz.
Caliber: .22 LR, .17 HMR
Magazine: 5 rounds
Features: Simple target .22 LR with a Classic Anschütz stock; single-stage trigger; large bolt knob; AV model has an 18-in. heavy barrel with a threaded muzzle
D HB, HB: . . . . . **$1775.00–$2095.00**
AV Threaded: **$1850.00**

1771 D

Action: Bolt
Stock: Germany-styled walnut
Barrel: 21.5 in.
Sights: None
Weight: 7 lb. 7 oz.
Caliber: .22 Hornet, .222 Rem., .223 Rem., .204 Ruger
Magazine: 4 rounds
Features: 1771 bolt action repeater; six front locking lugs; blued finish; heavy barrel; no iron sight provision
MSRP **$2495.00**

1771 D GRS

Action: Bolt
Stock: Laminated birch
Barrel: 22 in.
Sights: None
Weight: 8 lb. 6 oz.
Caliber: .204 Ruger, .222 Rem., .223 Rem., .300 BLK
Magazine: Detachable box, 4 rounds
Features: Butt plate speed lock adjustment; GRS-rubber butt plate; cheek piece speed lock adjustment; ergo-

nomical and gripping forend; precision barrel
MSRP **$3300.00**

1782 D

Action: Bolt
Stock: Walnut
Barrel: 20.5 in., 22.8 in.
Sights: None
Weight:
Caliber: .243 Win., 6.5 Creedmoor, .308 Win., .30-06 Spfd., 8x57 IS, 9.3x62
Magazine: 3 rounds
Features: Classic or German-style walnut stocks in an oil finish; single-stage match-grade trigger with adjustable blade and ability to be changed to a two-stage; silent safety catch operation; 60-degree bolt throw; integrated recoil lug; V bedding; double Picatinny rails; Fast Release magazine; choice of threaded barrel or barrel with recessed crown
MSRP . . . . **$2795.00–$2995.00**

1827 FORTNER SPRINT

Action: Bolt
Stock: Biathlon, walnut
Barrel: 22 in.
Sights: None
Weight: 8 lb. 2 oz.
Caliber: .22 LR
Magazine: Detachable box, 5 rounds
Features: Combination of an extra light 1827 Fortner barreled action with the stock of the 1827 model; lacquered walnut stock with stippled checkering; heavy, cylindrical match barrel; match stage two or single trigger
MSRP **$3950.00**

1903 TARGET

Action: Bolt
Stock: Hardwood
Barrel: 26 in., heavy
Sights: None
Weight: 9 lb. 11 oz.

Caliber: .22 LR
Magazine: None
Features: A match rifle for small bore shooters; anatomically perfect walnut stock with vertically adjustable cheek piece; optional aluminum, hook, or rubber buttplate; aluminum accessories rail
MSRP **$1695.00**

1907 IN 1914 STOCK

Action: Bolt
Stock: Walnut
Barrel: 32.28 in.
Sights: None
Weight: 10 lb. 12 oz.
Caliber: .22 LR
Magazine: None
Features: Match 54 action; heavy, cylindrical barrel; match two-stage or single-stage trigger; safety signal pin
MSRP **$4095.00**

1927 CISM WALNUT

Action: Bolt
Stock: Walnut
Barrel: 26 in.
Sights: None
Weight: 10 lb. 1 oz.
Caliber: .22 LR
Magazine: 10 rounds
Features: Top-end fast-fire (CISM) rimfire competition rifle; hefty walnut stock, lacquered finish and stippled checkering; sliding safety catch; 1927 action (similar to biathlon 1827 F) with a Match 54 Fortner straight-pull bolt; heavy-weight tapered barrel
MSRP **$4995.00**

2013/690 WITH 2018 PRECISE STOCK

Action: Bolt
Stock: Aluminum
Barrel: 27.17 in.
Sights: None
Weight: 13 lb.
Caliber: .22 LR
Magazine: None
Features: Single loader; two-stage trigger; optional buttplate; new backend offers large range of adjustment for small shooters
MSRP **$5695.95**

RIFLES

Anschütz (J.G. Anschütz)

ANSCHÜTZ MATCH 54.30

MATCH 54.30

Action: Barreled
Stock: Aluminum or walnut
Barrel: 26 in.
Sights: None
Weight: 11 lb. 3 oz.
Caliber: .22 LR
Magazine: 8 rounds

Features: Improved ergonomics; reduced weight of firing pin for increase in velocity and shorter lock time; newly designed target chamber for better accuracy; threaded receiver and barrel connection; available in aluminum or walnut stock
MSRP **$5895.00**

ArmaLite

ARMALITE AR-10 COMPETITION RIFLE

ARMALITE AR-10 DEF 10

ARMALITE AR-50 .50 BMG PRECISION BOLT-ACTION RIFLE

ARMALITE SUPER SASS GEN II

AR-10 COMPETITION RIFLE

Action: Semiautomatic
Stock: Synthetic
Barrel: 13 in., 18 in.
Sights: None
Weight: 8 lb. 3 oz.–8 lb. 14 oz.
Caliber: .308 Win./7.62 NATO
Magazine: Detachable box, 25 rounds
Features: Picatinny rail; Armalite tunable brake pinned and welded; 12-in. free-floating handguard; stock adjustable for length-of-pull and comb height; ambidextrous safety and charging handle
MSRP **$2231.00**

AR-10 DEF 10

Action: Semiautomatic
Stock: Synthetic
Barrel: 16 in.
Sights: Front
Weight: 7 lb. 14 oz.
Caliber: 7.62 NATO, .308 Win.
Magazine: 10, 20 rounds
Features: No-frills rifle built for sporting or defensive use; mid-length gas system, six-position collapsible stock, forged flat top with Mil-Std 1913 rail, 7075 forged aluminum lower and receiver, standard charging handle, single-stage trigger are standard; supplied with one 20-round Magpul Pmag; Colorado-compliant version comes with 10-round Magpul Pmag
MSRP **$1126.00**

AR-50 .50 BMG BOLT-ACTION RIFLE

Action: Bolt
Stock: Synthetic

Barrel: 33 in.
Sights: None
Weight: 33 lb. 3 oz.
Caliber: .50 BMG
Magazine: None
Features: Chromoly barrel; muzzle-brake; 15 minute rail; single-stage trigger
MSRP **$3985.00**

SUPER SASS GEN II

Action: Semiautomatic
Stock: Synthetic
Barrel: 20 in., 22 in.
Sights: None
Weight: 11 lb. 14 oz.
Caliber: 7.62 NATO, 6.5 Creedmoor
Magazine: 20 rounds
Features: Magpul mag; Armalite-designed upper, lower, 15-in. free-floating Gen II handguard; POF two-stage trigger; Armalite Tac Brake on a stainless steel match grade barrel
MSRP **$3150.00**

Armscor/Rock Island Armory

ARMSCOR/ROCK ISLAND ARMORY M22 TCM TACTICAL

M22 TCM TACTICAL

Action: Bolt
Stock: Synthetic
Barrel: 20 in.
Sights: None
Weight: 7 lb.
Caliber: .22 TCM

Magazine: 5 rounds
Features: Adjustable comb and length of pull; metal top rail; compatible with 17-round magazines from Armscor/RRI's .22 TCM 1911
MSRP **$449.00**

Arsenal, Inc.

ARSENAL, INC. SAS M-7 CLASSIC

ARSENAL, INC. SAM7R

ARSENAL, INC. SLR-107R

SAS M-7 CLASSIC
Action: Semiautomatic
Stock: Metal
Barrel: 16.25 in.
Sights: A-4-type front, 800m adjustable rear
Weight: 7 lb. 8 oz.
Caliber: 7.62X39mm
Magazine: 30 rounds
Features: Built in Nevada, a classic AK-47 design with under-folding stock; chrome-lined heavy barrel; left-hand threaded muzzle
MSRP $1999.00

SAM7R
Action: Semiautomatic
Stock: Polymer
Barrel: 16.25 in.
Sights: Scope rail
Weight: 8 lb.
Caliber: 7.62x39 Warsaw
Magazine: Detachable box, 10 rounds
Features: Milled receiver; chrome-lined, hammer-forged barrel; removeable muzzle brake; cleaning rod; intermediate-length, U.S.-made buttstock with cleaning kit compartment; FIME Group Enhanced Fire Control Group; also available with an AR-M5F rail system and a serial-numbered 30-round M-47W Circle 10 magazine
Standard $1929.99
AR-M5F rail $2449.99

SLR-107R
Action: Semiautomatic
Stock: Polymer
Barrel: 16.25 in.
Sights: Front sight, 800m rear
Weight: 7 lb. 5 oz.
Caliber: 7.62x39mm
Magazine: 5 rounds
Features: Manufactured in Las Vegas with a Bulgarian-made stamped receiver; anti-slap double-stage trigger; Warsaw-length buttstock with a cleaning kit compartment; stainless steel heat shield, side rail, and slings; available in black, Plum, Desert Sand, or OD Green
MSRP $1519.99

Auto-Ordnance

AUTO-ORDNANCE AOM150

AUTO-ORDNANCE IWO JIMA THOMPSON

AUTO-ORDNANCE TANKER THOMPSON

AUTO-ORDNANCE THOMPSON 1927 A-1 "COMMANDO" CARBINE

AOM150
Action: Semiautomatic
Stock: Walnut; handguard
Barrel: 18 in.
Sights: Blade front; flip style rear
Weight: 5 lb. 6 oz.
Caliber: .30
Magazine: Detachable stick, 15 rounds
Features: Folding stock; Parkerized finish
MSRP $1342.00

IWO JIMA THOMPSON
Action: Semiautomatic
Stock: Wood
Barrel: 16.5 in.
Sights: Pinned front blade, open adjustable rear
Weight: 11 lb. 8 oz.
Caliber: .45 ACP
Magazine: 20, 30 rounds
Features: Honors the 75th anniversary of the Battle of Iwo Jima with grips emblazoned with "Among the men who fought on Iwo Jima, uncommon valor was a common virtue" (engraving by Outlaw Ordnance); finished in Cerakote OD green and Distressed Copper
MSRP $1886.00

TANKER THOMPSON
Action: Semiautomatic
Stock: Walnut
Barrel: 16.5 in.
Sights: Blade front, fixed battle rear
Weight: 11 lb. 8 oz.
Caliber: .45 ACP
Magazine: 20, 30 rounds
Features: Commemorative firearm dedicated to soldiers who fought in M4 Sherman tanks; Cerakoted in Army O.D. green; Sherman tank white star engraved in front of the mag well; U.S. logo on buttstock; stick magazines
MSRP $1501.00

THOMPSON 1927 A-1 "COMMANDO" CARBINE .45-CALIBER
Action: Semiautomatic
Stock: Black finish stock and forend
Barrel: 16.5 in.
Sights: Blade front, open rear adjustable
Weight: 13 lb.
Caliber: .45 ACP
Magazine: Detachable stick, 30 rounds
Features: Frame and receiver made from solid steel; compensator; black nylon sling
MSRP $1618.00

RIFLES

Auto-Ordnance

AUTO-ORDNANCE THOMPSON 1927 A-1 DELUXE CARBINE

AUTO-ORDNANCE THOMPSON 1927 A-1 DELUXE CARBINE HARD CHROME PLATED

AUTO-ORDNANCE THOMPSON 1927 A-1C LIGHTWEIGHT DELUXE SEMI-AUTO

AUTO-ORDNANCE THOMPSON M1 CARBINE "TOMMY GUN"

AUTO-ORDNANCE THOMPSON M1SB

THOMPSON 1927 A-1 DELUXE CARBINE .45-CALIBER

Action: Semiautomatic
Stock: Walnut, vertical foregrip
Barrel: 10.5 in., 16.5 in.
Sights: Blade front, open rear adjustable
Weight: 13 lb.
Caliber: .45 ACP
Magazine: 20 rounds
Features: Finned barrel with compensator; blued steel or color case-hardened; magazine options range from 10- and 20-round sticks to 50- and 100-round drums; horizontal fore-grip option; detachable stock option; SBR 10.5-in. barrel option
Standard . . . . . . $1697.00–$2393.00
Detachable
   buttstock . . . . $2218.00–$2913.00
Case-hardened. $2003.00
10.5-in. SBR $2900.00

THOMPSON 1927 A-1 DELUXE CARBINE .45-CALIBER HARD CHROME PLATED, GOLD PLATED

Action: Semiautomatic
Stock: Walnut

Barrel: 16.5 in.
Sights: Blade front, open rear adjustable
Weight: 13 lb.
Caliber: .45 ACP
Magazine: One each round 50 drum and 20 stick magazines
Features: Finned barrel; fixed stock with vertical foregrip; tiger strip detailing option available on both chrome and gold models
Gold/Chrome. $3671.00
Tiger Stripe $4465.00

THOMPSON 1927A-1C LIGHTWEIGHT DELUXE SEMI-AUTO 9MM

Action: Semiautomatic
Stock: Walnut
Barrel: 16.5 in.
Sights: Blade front, adjustable open rear
Weight: 13 lb.
Caliber: 9mm
Magazine: 20 rounds
Features: The famous 1927 in a pistol caliber; aluminum frame; finned barrel with compensator; comes with one 20-round magazine
MSRP. $1364.00

THOMPSON M1 CARBINE "TOMMY GUN" .45-CALIBER

Action: Semiautomatic
Stock: Walnut, vertical foregrip
Barrel: 10.5 in., 16.5 in.
Sights: Blade front, fixed battle rear
Weight: 11 lb. 8 oz.
Caliber: .45 ACP
Magazine: 10, 30 rounds
Features: Choice of steel or aluminum receiver; 10- or 30-round stick magazines; no vertical fore-grip
MSRP. . . . . $1441.00–$1594.00

THOMPSON M1 SBR

Action: Semiautomatic
Stock: Walnut, vertical foregrip
Barrel: 10.5 in.
Sights: Blade front, fixed battle rear
Weight: 10 lb. 8 oz.
Caliber: .45 ACP
Magazine: Detachable stick, 30 rounds
Features: Will not accept drum magazines; frame and receiver made from solid steel
MSRP. $2234.00

RIFLES

Barrett

BARRETT M107A1

BARRETT 82A1

M107A1

Action: Semiautomatic
Stock: Synthetic
Barrel: 20 in., 29 in.
Sights: Flip-up iron sights
Weight: 30 lb. 14 oz.
Caliber: .50 BMG
Magazine: Detachable box, 10 rounds
Features: Chrome-lined barrel, Flat Dark Earth stock finish; suppressor-ready muzzlebrake; pelican case;

M1913 optics rail; detachable adjustable lightweight bipod legs; lightweight monopod; black, Flat Dark Earth, OD Green, or Tungsten Grey Cerakote receiver finishes
MSRP. $13,999.99

MODEL 82A1

Action: Semiautomatic
Stock: Synthetic
Barrel: 20 in., 29 in.

Sights: Flip-up iron sights or Leupold scope
Weight: 30 lb. 14 oz.
Caliber: .416 Barrett, .50 BMG
Magazine: Detachable box, 10 rounds
Features: Pelican case; detachable adjustable bipod legs; cleaning kit; carry handle; muzzlebrake; Picatinny rail; chrome-lined barrel; manganese phosphate finish or Cerakote receiver finishes in Flat Dark Earth, Burnt Bronze, Tungsten Grey, or OD Green
MSRP. . . . . $7873.00–$9499.99

Barrett

BARRETT 95

BARRETT MRAD

BARRETT 99

BARRETT REC7 D1

BARRETT REC10

MODEL 95

Action: Semiautomatic
Stock: Synthetic
Barrel: 29 in.
Sights: Flip-up iron sights
Weight: 25 lb.
Caliber: .50 BMG
Magazine: Detachable box, 5 rounds
Features: Pelican case; detachable adjustable bipod legs; cleaning kit; Picatinny rail
MSRP **$6472.00**

MODEL 99

Action: Bolt
Stock: Synthetic
Barrel: 29 in., 32 in.
Sights: None
Weight: 25 lb.
Caliber: .416 Barrett, .50 BMG
Magazine: None
Features: Picatinny rail; pelican case; detachable adjustable bipod; cleaning kit; available in black anodized or Cerakote Flat Dark Earth receiver
MSRP . . . . **$4745.00–$5030.00**

MRAD

Action: Bolt action repeater
Stock: Synthetic
Barrel: 17 in., 20 in., 22 in., 24 in., 26 in.
Sights: None
Weight: 12 lb. 15 oz.–14 lb. 8 oz.
Caliber: .338 Lapua Magnum, .338 Norma Magnum, .300 Norma Magnum, .300 PRC, .300 Win. Mag., .309 Win., 6.5 Creedmoor
Magazine: Detachable box, 10 rounds
Features: Fluted, carbon fiber, or heavy barrel; multi-role brown finish stock; folding stock; adjustable cheekpiece and buttplate; includes two 10-round magazines, two sling loops, and three adjustable accessory rails; receivers in black anodized or in Cerakote Tungsten Grey, Flat Dark Earth, OD Green, or Burnt Bronze
MSRP . . . . **$5060.00–$6970.00**

REC7 D1

Action: Semiautomatic
Stock: Synthetic
Barrel: 10.25 in., 16 in., 18 in.
Sights: None
Weight: 5 lb. 8 oz.–6 lb. 3 oz.
Caliber: 5.56 NATO
Magazine: 10, 20, 30 rounds
Features: Hand-built, lightweight, direct impingement; Magpul MOE six-position stock, Barrett designed 15-in. KeyMod handguard, Bravo Company Gunfighter charging handle, and ALG Defense ACT trigger; bolt carrier group plated in nickel boron finish; Black, Flat Dark Earth, OD Green, Tungsten Grey, or Burnt Bronze Cerakote.
MSRP **$2599.00**

REC10

Action: Semiautomatic
Stock: Synthetic
Barrel: 16 in.
Sights: Flip-up front and rear
Weight: 8 lb.
Caliber: .308 Win.
Magazine: 20 rounds
Features: This one might find favor with the 3-gun crowd with its direct impingement gas system; anti-tilt bolt carrier; Barrett gas block and barrel; Barrett three-prong flash hider or muzzle brake; Barrett M-LOK rail handguard; ALG QMS trigger; Radian charging handle; Magpul stock, pistol grip, magazine and flip-up sights; available in black, flat dark earth, or tungsten grey
MSRP **$2995.00**

Benelli USA

BENELLI R1 BIG GAME

BENELLI LUPO

LUPO

Action: Bolt
Stock: Synthetic
Barrel: 22 in., 24 in.
Sights: None
Weight: 7 lb.–7 lb. 2 oz.
Caliber: .30-06 Spfd., .300 Win. Mag., .270 Win., 6.5 Creedmoor, .308 Win., .243 Win., 6.5 PRC, 7mm Rem. Mag., 6mm Creedmoor
Magazine: 3 rounds
Features: Benelli's first bolt-action rifle with a streamlined synthetic stock; Crio-treated free-floating barrel; alloy receiver; built-in Progressive Comfort combined with Combtech cheek pad reduce felt recoil
MSRP **$1699.00**

R1 BIG GAME

Action: Semiautomatic
Stock: AA-grade satin walnut, synthetic or Realtree APG
Barrel: 22 in., 24 in.
Sights: None
Weight: 7 lb. 2 oz.–7 lb. 5 oz.
Caliber: .30-06 Spfd., .300 Win. Mag., .338 Win. Mag.
Magazine: Detachable box, 3+1 or 4+1 rounds
Features: Picatinny rail; synthetic and APG finish come with GripTight coating; raised comb; auto-regulating gas-operated system
Walnut **$1249.00**
Synthetic **$1449.00**

Benelli USA

BENELLI R1 PRO BIG GAME

R1 PRO BIG GAME
Action: Semiautomatic
Stock: Walnut
Barrel: 22 in.
Sights: Fiber optic front, adjustable rear
Weight: 7 lb. 3.2 oz.
Caliber: .30-06 Spfd.
Magazine: 4 rounds
Features: Includes Benelli's Progressive Comfort technology; AA walnut satin finish stock; receiver drilled and tapped for scope mount, Picatinny rail and shim kit included; CRIO treated barrel
MSRP $1499.00

Beretta USA

BERETTA USA ARX100

BERETTA CX4 STORM

ARX100
Action: Semiautomatic
Stock: Telescopic folding
Barrel: 16 in.
Sights: Removable back-up sights
Weight: 6 lb. 13 oz.
Caliber: 5.56 NATO (other barrels available)
Magazine: 30 rounds
Features: Cold hammer forged barrel

can be replaced with barrels in different lengths and calibers; case ejection switches from right to left at a button push; completely ambidextrous; technopolymer receiver; contains no pins and can be disassembled without the use of tools; optional .300 Black Out kit available
MSRP $1950.00

CX4 STORM
Action: Single-action
Stock: Synthetic
Barrel: 16.6 in.
Sights: Front sight post
Weight: 5 lb. 12 oz.
Caliber: 9mm
Magazine: 10, 15 rounds
Features: Picatinny rail; allows for reverse ejection and extraction; ideal for left-handed shooters; adjustable length-of-pull; easy to accessorize; takes Beretta series 92 pistol magazines
MSRP $899.00

Bergara

BERGARA B-14 HMR

BERGARA B-14 HUNTER

BERGARA B-14 RIDGE

B-14 HMR
Action: Bolt
Stock: Bergara BMP HMR molded with mini-chassis
Barrel: 20 in. (.308 Win.), 22 in. (6.5 Creedmoor)
Sights: None
Weight: 9 lb. 2.4 oz.–9 lb. 4 oz.
Caliber: 6.5 Creedmoor, 6.5 PRC, .308 Win., .22-250 Rem., .450 Bushmaster, .300 Win. Mag., .300 PRC
Magazine: 5 rounds
Features: Field or competition use; buttstock has adjustable cheekpiece, and LOP spacers, integrated mini-chassis; one-piece Bergara B-14 action, Bergara Performance trigger, AICS detachable magazine, threaded muzzle and thread protector; left-hand available in 6.5 Creedmoor,

.308 Win., .22-250 Rem., and .300 Win. Mag.
MSRP $1249.00

B-14 HUNTER
Action: Bolt
Stock: Glass fiber-reinforced polymer
Barrel: 22 in. (short actions), 24 in. (long actions)
Sights: None
Weight: 7 lb.–7 lb. 2 oz.
Caliber: .30-06 Spfd., .300 Win. Mag., .270 Win., .308 Win., 6.5 Creedmoor, 7mm Rem. Mag., .243 Win., .22-250 Rem., 7mm-08 Rem.
Magazine: 3, 4 rounds
Features: Stock has Soft Touch coating for better purchase; drilled and tapped for Remington 700-style bases; barrel is matte blue
MSRP $899.00

B-14 RIDGE
Action: Bolt
Stock: Glass fiber-reinforced polymer
Barrel: 18, 22, 24 in.
Sights: None
Weight: 7 lb. 3 oz.–7 lb. 15 oz.
Caliber: 6.5 Creedmoor, 6.5 PRC, .308 Win., .243 Win., .22-250 Rem., 7mm-08 Rem., .450 Bushmaster, .270 Win., .30-06 Spfd., 7mm Rem. Mag., .300 Win. Mag., .300 PRC
Magazine: 3, 4 rounds
Features: Stock has Soft Touch coating for better purchase; drilled and tapped for Remington 700-style bases; barrel is a #5 profile of 4140 CrMo steel in matte blue and threaded for suppressor or muzzle brake use; choice of hinged floor plate or detachable magazine; .308 and 6.5 Creedmoor available in an 18-inch Special Purpose Short Barrel
MSRP $949.00

Bergara

BERGARA B-14 TIMBER

BERGARA B-14 WILDERNESS HMR

BERGARA B-14 WILDERNESS HUNTER

BERGARA B-14 WILDERNESS RIDGE

BERGARA B-14 WILDERNESS TERRAIN

BERGARA B-14R TRAINER CARBON

BERGARA B-14R TRAINER STEEL

BERGARA BMR CARBON

B-14 TIMBER

Action: Bolt
Stock: Walnut
Barrel: 22 in. (short actions), 24 in. (long actions)
Sights: None
Weight: 7 lb. 5 oz.–7 lb. 9 oz.
Caliber: 6.5 Creedmoor, .308 Win., .30-06 Spfd., .270 Win., .300 Win. Mag., .243 Win.
Features: Monte Carlo cheekpiece; drilled and tapped for Remington 700-style bases; barrel is a #3 profile of 4140 CrMo steel in matte blue; integral epoxy resin pillars surround the action screws in the stock
MSRP $1149.00

B-14 WILDERNESS HMR

Action: Bolt
Stock: Molded mini-chassis
Barrel: 20 in., 24 in., 26 in.
Sights: None
Weight: 9 lb. 8 oz.–9 lb. 15 oz.
Caliber: 6.5 Creedmoor, 6.5 PRC, .308 Win., 7mm Rem. Mag., .28 Nosler, .300 Win. Mag., .300 PRC
Magazine: 3, 5 rounds
Features: HMR is Hunting-Match Rifle; two-lug B-14 action; AICS detachable magazine; mini-chassis stock in hand-painted camo; multi-port muzzle brake; free-floated #6 barrel; metalwork in Cerakote Sniper Grey
MSRP . . . . $1149.00–$1249.00

B-14 WILDERNESS HUNTER

Action: Bolt
Stock: Synthetic
Barrel: 22 in., 24 in., 26 in.
Sights: None
Weight: 7 lb. 2 oz.–7 lb. 8 oz.
Caliber: 6.5 Creedmoor, .308 Win., .28 Nosler, 7mm Rem. Mag., .300 Win. Mag.
Magazine: 2, 3, 4 rounds
Features: Two-lug B-14 action in a traditionally styled stock having soft-touch features; hinged floorplate magazine; free-floated #3 barrel; metalwork in Cerakote Sniper Grey
MSRP . . . . $899.00–$965.00

B-14 WILDERNESS RIDGE

Action: Bolt
Stock: Synthetic
Barrel: 18 in., 20 in., 22 in., 24 in., 26 in.
Sights: None
Weight: 7 lb. 3 oz.–7 lb. 15 oz.
Caliber: 6.5 Creedmoor, 6.5 PRC, .308 Win., 7mm Rem. Mag., .28 Nosler, .300 Win. Mag., .300 PRC
Magazine: 2, 3, 4 rounds
Features: Two-lug B-14 action in a traditionally styled stock having soft-touch features; hinged floorplate magazine; free-floated #5 barrel with Omni muzzle brake; Bergara Performance Trigger; metalwork in Cerakote Sniper Grey
MSRP . . . . $975.00–$1055.00

B-14 WILDERNESS TERRAIN

Action: Bolt
Stock: Molded mini-chassis
Barrel: 20 in., 24 in., 26 in.
Sights: None
Weight: 8 lb. 15 oz.–10 lb. 2 oz.
Caliber: 6.5 Creedmoor, 6.5 PRC, .308 Win., 7mm Rem. Mag., .28 Nosler, .300 Win. Mag., .300 PRC
Magazine: 3, 5 rounds
Features: Two-lug B-14 action in a Bergara Terrain molded mini-chassis stock with adjustable cheekpiece; free-floated #5.5 barrel with Omni muzzle brake; Bergara Performance Trigger; metalwork in Cerakote Sniper Grey
MSRP . . . . $1199.00–$1279.00

B-14R TRAINER CARBON

Action: Bolt
Stock: Molded mini-chassis
Barrel: 18 in.
Sights: None
Weight: 8 lb. 2 oz.
Caliber: .22 LR
Magazine: 10 rounds
Features: A training rifle with some heft and a threaded #6 carbon-fiber barrel; AICS-style detachable magazine; Bergara Performance Trigger; Bergara HMR molded mini-chassis stock with adjustable cheekpiece and adjustable length of pull; QD flush cup sling mounts and swivels
MSRP $1245.00

B-14R TRAINER STEEL

Action: Bolt
Stock: Molded mini-chassis
Barrel: 18 in.
Sights: None
Weight: 9 lb. 3 oz.
Caliber: .22 LR
Magazine: 10 rounds
Features: Similar to the Trainer Carbon, but with a threaded steel barrel in #6 taper
MSRP $1150.00

BMR CARBON

Action: Bolt
Stock: Synthetic
Barrel: 18 in., 20 in.
Sights: None
Weight: 5 lb.–5 lb. 7 oz.
Caliber: .22 LR, .22 WMR, .17 HMR
Magazine: 5, 10 rounds
Features: A delightful rimfire, the BMR (Bergara Micro Rimfire) comes with a carbon fiber Bergara barrel in a No. 6 profile; 30 MOA rail; Bergara Performance trigger; synthetic stock in black with gray speckling; steel barrel is optional
MSRP $659.00

BERGARA BXR CARBON

BERGARA PREMIER HIGHLANDER

BERGARA PREMIER RIDGEBACK

BERGARA BXR STEEL

BERGARA PREMIER HMR PRO

BERGARA PREMIER APPROACH

BERGARA MOUNTAIN 2.0

BXR CARBON

Action: Bolt
Stock: Synthetic
Barrel: 16.5 in.
Sights: None
Weight: 4 lb. 12 oz.
Caliber: .22 LR
Magazine: 10 rounds
Features: Similar to the BXR base model, but with a carbon-fiber barrel for reduced weight; gray-flecked black stock
MSRP. **$659.00**

BXR STEEL

Action: Bolt
Stock: Synthetic
Barrel: 16.5 in.
Sights: None
Weight: 6 lb. 2 oz.
Caliber: .22 LR
Magazine: 10 rounds
Features: Feature-rich rimfire for competitors with a black-flecked green stock adjustable for length of pull; threaded fluted steel barrel; 30 MOA Picatinny rail; Cerakote ceramic coating on metalwork; rotary magazine (Ruger 10/22 mag compatible)
MSRP. **$565.00**

PREMIER APPROACH

Action: Bolt
Stock: Synthetic
Barrel: 20, 22, 24, 26 in.
Sights: None
Weight: 8 lb. 3 oz.–8 lb. 10 oz.
Caliber: 6.5 Creedmoor, .308 Win., .22-250 Rem., 6.5 PRC, 7mm Rem. Mag., .300 PRC, .300 Win. Mag., .28

Nosler
Features: Hand-laid fiberglass stock in a mottled gray and tan; barrel is threaded; a #5 taper profile; bronze Cerakote finish; TriggerTech Frictionless Release Technology; integral QD cup sling; swivel mounts
MSRP. . . . . **$1960.00–$2060.00**

PREMIER HIGHLANDER

Action: Bolt
Stock: Fiberglass
Barrel: 20 in., 24 in.
Sights: None
Weight: 7 lb. 3 oz.–7 lb. 11 oz.
Caliber: 6.5 Creedmoor, 6.5 PRC, .28 Nosler, .308 Win., 7mm Rem. Mag., .300 Win. Mag., .300 PRC
Magazine: 3, 4 rounds
Features: For the hunter looking for reach, a rifle featuring Graphite Black Cerakote-finished metalwork; No. 5.5 tapered barrel with threads; TriggerTech Friction Release Technology trigger
MSRP. . . . . **$1885.00–$1985.00**

PREMIER HMR PRO

Action: Bolt
Stock: Synthetic
Barrel: 20, 22, 24, 26 in.
Sights: None
Weight: 9 lb. 5 oz.–9 lb. 13 oz.
Caliber: 6.5 Creedmoor, .308 Win., .22-250 Rem., 6mm Creedmoor, 6.5 PRC, .28 Nosler, 7mm Rem. Mag., .300 Win. Mag., .300 PRC
Magazine: 5, 7 rounds
Features: Stainless one-piece bolt with a cone-shaped nose and a spring-loaded sliding plate extractor; bolt shroud is fully nitrided and self-lubricating; free-floating #5 taper barrel in gray Cerakote; full-length mini

chassis; stock adjustable for comb height and length of pull; threaded barrel; detachable AICS-style magazine
MSRP. . . . . **$1715.00–$1815.00**

PREMIER MOUNTAIN 2.0

Action: Bolt
Stock: Carbon fiber composite
Barrel: 22 in., 24 in.
Sights: None
Weight: 6 lb. 3 oz.–6 lb. 6 oz.
Caliber: 6.5 Creedmoor, 6.5 PRC, .308 Win., .300 Win. Mag., .300 PRC, .28 Nosler
Magazine: 2, 3, 4 rounds
Features: Part of Bergara's Premier Series with a 100-percent carbon-fiber stock; TriggerTech trigger; No. 3 taper barrel; hinged floor-plate magazine
MSRP. . . . . **$2150.00–$2250.00**

PREMIER RIDGEBACK

Action: Bolt
Stock: Fiberglass
Barrel: 20 in., 24 in., 26 in.
Sights: None
Weight: 10 lb.–10 lb. 9 oz.
Caliber: 6mm Creedmoor, 6.5 Creedmoor, 6.5 PRC, .308 Win., .300 Win. Mag., .300 PRC, .28 Nosler
Magazine: 5, 7 rounds
Features: Dedicated long-range games rifle in all the latest cartridges. Features include: Cerakote black metalwork; medium Palma barrel profile; adjustable cheekpiece with M-LOK compatibility; AICS-type detachable magazine; TriggerTech Frictionless Release Technology trigger
MSRP. . . . . **$2000.00–$2100.00**

Big Horn Armory

BIG HORN ARMORY AR500

AR500

Action: Semiautomatic
Stock: Synthetic
Barrel: 18 in.
Sights: None
Weight: 9 lb. 8 oz.

Caliber: .500 Auto Max
Magazine: 10 rounds
Features: Adjustable gas block; Picatinny rail; flash suppressor; adjustable buttstock; includes a hard case
MSRP. **$1999.00**

RIFLES

Blaser USA

BLASER K95 STUTZEN

BLASER K95 ULTIMATE CARBON

BLASER R8 INTUITION

BLASER R8 JAEGER

BLASER R8 PROFESSIONAL AMBI SYNTHETIC

BLASER R8 PROFESSIONAL SUCCESS

BLASER R8 ULTIMATE

K95 STUTZEN

Action: Single shot
Stock: Walnut
Barrel: 19.75 in.
Sights: None
Weight: 5 lb. 11 oz.
Caliber: .243 Win., 6.5x57R, 6.5x55 SE, .270 Win., 7x65R, 7x57 R, .308 Win., .30-06 Spfd., 8x57 IRS
Magazine: None
Features: Octagonal barrel standard, barrels are interchangeable; split forearm for continuous precision even in extreme weather; black forearm tip; range of ornamentation and game engravings
Luxus $11,416.00
Baronesse $26,775.00

K95 ULTIMATE CARBON

Action: Break-action
Stock: Carbon fiber
Barrel: 19.5 in., 23.6 in., 25.5 in., 27.5 in.
Sights: None
Weight: N/A
Caliber: More than 25 cartridges ranging from .22 Hornet to .338 Blaser Mag., plus 10.3X60R
Magazine: 1 round
Features: Featuring a unique, two-piece thumbhole stock with an adjustable comb option; special recoil absorption system or optional adjustable recoil pad; Blaser's cocking slide automatically illuminates the dot in Blaser illuminated riflescopes
MSRP $15,824.00

R8 INTUITION

Action: Bolt
Stock: Wood (various grades)
Barrel: Varies
Sights: Varies
Weight: N/A
Caliber: All common short-action, long-action, and magnum centerfire calibers from .204 Ruger to .338 Lapua.
Magazine: 1, 2, 3, 4, 5 rounds by caliber

Features: Designed specifically for women with a shorter length of pull and a buttstock designed to fit a woman's unique anatomy, including a higher comb, slimmer pistol grip, and a reduction of distance between the trigger and the grip; available in all R8 wood stock configurations
MSRP $6556.00

R8 JAEGER

Action: Straight-pull bolt-action
Stock: Walnut, pistol grip
Barrel: 20.5 in., 23 in., 25.75 in.
Sights: None
Weight: 6 lb. 6 oz.
Caliber: .222 Rem. to .338 Win. Mag.
Magazine: Detachable box, 3 rounds with lock
Features: Cold-hammer-forged barrels and chambers; black forearm tip; synthetic stock in dark green or walnut, straight comb; manual cocking system; integrated trigger/magazine unit; original Blaser saddle mount
MSRP $7511.00

R8 PROFESSIONAL AMBI SYNTHETIC

Action: Straight-pull bolt-action
Stock: Matte dark green synthetic stock, pistol grip
Barrel: 20.5 in., 23 in., 25.75 in.
Sights: None
Weight: 6 lb. 6 oz.
Caliber: .222 Rem. to .338 Win. Mag.
Magazine: Detachable box, 3 rounds with lock
Features: Shatter-proof synthetic stock in dark green brown/black, Savannah or camo with elastomere inlay; detachable magazine/trigger unit; single-stage trigger; quick-release scope mount; ergonomically optimized pistol grip; kickstop optional; precision trigger; black forearm tip; integrated receiver
Single color $4692.00
Camo $5679.00

R8 PROFESSIONAL SUCCESS

Action: Bolt
Stock: Synthetic
Barrel: 22.8 in., 25.6 in.

Sights: Open
Weight: 7 lb.
Caliber: .222 Rem., .204 Ruger, .223 Rem., .22–250 Rem., .243 Win., 6XC, 6.5x55 Swedish, 6.5x57, 6.5x65 RWS, .270 Win., 7x64 Brenneke, .308 Win., .30-06 Spfd., 8x57 IS, 8.5x63, 9.3x57, 9.3x62 Mauser, 6.5x68, 7.5x55 Suisse, 8x68 S, .257 Wby. Mag., .270 Wby. Mag., .270 WSM, 7mm Blaser Mag., 7mm Rem. Mag., .300 Blaser Mag., .300 Win. Mag., .300 Wby. Mag., .300 WSM, .338 Blaser Mag., .338 Win. Mag., .375 Blaser Mag., .375 H&H
Magazine: 3+1, 4+1, 5+1 rounds
Features: Blaser precision trigger; radial locking system; ergonomically optimized stock in dark green or dark brown and elastomer grips; double loading option; leather model available
Elastomere inlays $5329.00
Leather inlays $6719.00
Monza $7544.00
Left-hand . . . . add $715.00

R8 ULTIMATE

Action: Bolt
Stock: Carbon fiber
Barrel: 19.5 in., 22 in., 25.5 in., 23.6 in., 27.5 in.
Sights: None
Weight: N/A
Caliber: More than 40 cartridges ranging from .204 Ruger to .500 Jeffery, plus 10.3X60R
Magazine: 2, 3, 4 rounds
Features: Similar to the K95 break-action Ultimate Carbon, but in the renowned switch-barrel, box magazine R8 configuration; optional leather or elastomer stock inserts
Standard/elastomere inlays . . $5329.00
Adjustable comb/elastomere inlays $5921.00
Standard/eather inlays $6719.00
Adjustable comb/leather inlays $7414.00
Ultimate Carbon/elastomere inlays $10540.00
Ultimate Carbon/leather inlays $11,890.00
Left-hand . . . . add $715.00

Browning

BROWNING AB3 COMPOSITE STALKER

BROWNING AB3 HUNTER

BROWNING AB3 MICRO STALKER

BROWNING BAR MARK III

BROWNING BAR MARK III DBM

BROWNING BAR MARK III DBM, WOOD

BROWNING BAR MARK III STALKER

BROWNING BLR LIGHTWEIGHT '81

AB3 COMPOSITE STALKER

Action: Bolt
Stock: Synthetic
Barrel: 22 in., 26 in.
Sights: None
Weight: 6 lb. 9 oz.–7 lb. 3 oz.
Caliber: .243 Win., .270 Win., .270 WSM, .30-06 Spfd., .300 Win. Mag., .300 WSM, .308 Win., 6.5 Creedmoor, 7mm Rem. Mag., 7mm-08 Rem.
Magazine: Detachable box, 4 rounds
Features: Inflex Technology recoil pad; top tang safety; blued barrel and action
MSRP $659.99

AB3 HUNTER

Action: Bolt
Stock: Satin
Barrel: 22 in.
Sights: Drilled and tapped for sights
Weight: 6 lb. 11 oz.–7 lb. 6 oz.
Caliber: .243 Win., .270 Win., .270 WSM, .30-06 Spfd., .300 Win. Mag., .300 WSM, .308 Win., 6.5 Creedmoor, 7mm Rem. Mag., 7mm-08 Rem.
Magazine: Detachable box
Features: 5-round mag capacity; steel barrel; polished finish
MSRP $749.99

AB3 MICRO STALKER

Action: Bolt
Stock: Composite
Barrel: 20 in.
Sights: None
Weight: 6 lb. 6 oz.–6 lb. 8 oz.
Caliber: .243 Win., 6.5 Creedmoor, 7mm-08 Rem., .308 Win.
Magazine: 5 rounds
Features: Intended for smaller-statured hunters; 13 in. length of pull; Pachmayr Decelerator recoil pad; drilled and tapped for scope mounts
MSRP $659.99

BAR MARK III

Action: Semiautomatic
Stock: Walnut
Barrel: 22 in., 23 in., 24 in.
Sights: None
Weight: 7 lb. 2 oz.–7 lb. 11 oz.
Caliber: .243 Win., .270 Win., .270 WSM, .30-06 Spfd., .300 Win. Mag., .300 WSM, .308 Win., 7mm Rem. Mag., 7mm-08 Rem.
Magazine: Detachable rotary, 3 or 4 rounds
Features: Oil-finished walnut; precision alloy receiver; hammer-forged barrel; drilled and tapped for scope; left-hand version available
MSRP . . . . $1399.99–$1499.99

BAR MARK III DBM

Action: Semiautomatic
Stock: Composite
Barrel: 18 in.
Sights: None
Weight: 6 lb. 10 oz.
Caliber: .308 Win.
Magazine: 10 rounds
Features: Detachable box magazine with a magwell instead of the standard hinged floor plate design; QD swivel cups (QD sling swivels included); 1913 Picatinny rail scope bases; hammer-forged barrel
MSRP $1629.99

BAR MARK III DBM, WOOD

Action: Semiautomatic
Stock: Wood
Barrel: 18 in.
Sights: None
Weight: 6 lb. 10 oz.
Caliber: .308 Win.
Magazine: 10 rounds
Features: With a hybrid military/European hunting look, this lightweight and fast-handling .308 has detachable box magazine; two top-side scope mount rails; sling swivel studs; matte-finish metal; composite

trigger guard; multi-lug rotary bolt; gas-piston functionality
MSRP $1659.99

BAR MARK III STALKER

Action: Semiautomatic
Stock: Composite
Barrel: 22 in., 23 in., 24 in.
Sights: None
Weight: 6 lb. 10 oz.–7 lb. 8 oz.
Caliber: .243 Win., 7mm-08 Rem., .308 Win., .270 Win., .30-06 Spfd., 7mm Rem. Mag., .300 Win. Mag., .300 WSM, .270 WSM
Magazine: 3, 4 rounds
Features: Composite stock with contemporary design; shim-adjustable for cast and drop at comb; gas-piston operation; lightweight aluminum alloy receiver drilled and tapped for scope mounts; hinged floor plate with detachable box magazine; Browning's own Ovix camo, paired with smoked bronze metalwork, added in 2022
Standard . . . . . . $1389.99–$1499.99
Mossy Oak Break-Up
Country . . . . . $1519.99–$1659.99
Ovix . . . . $1719.99–$1829.99

BLR LIGHTWEIGHT '81

Action: Lever
Stock: Walnut, straight grip
Barrel: 20 in., 22 in., 24 in.
Sights: None
Weight: 6 lb. 8 oz.–7 lb. 12 oz.
Caliber: .22-250 Rem., .223 Rem., .243 Win., .270 Win., .270 WSM, .30-06 Spfd., .300 Win. Mag., .300 WSM, .308 Win., .325 WSM, .358 Win., .450 Marlin, 7mm Rem. Mag., 7mm WSM, 7mm-08 Rem., .222 Rem., 6.5 Creedmoor
Magazine: Detachable box
Features: Aircraft-grade alloy receiver; drilled and tapped for scope mounts; crowned muzzle; adjustable sights; gloss finish walnut stock; recoil pad
MSRP . . . . $959.99–$1019.99

Browning

BROWNING BLR LIGHTWEIGHT '81 STAINLESS TAKEDOWN

BROWNING BLR LIGHTWEIGHT STAINLESS WITH PISTOL GRIP

BROWNING SEMI-AUTO 22 CHALLENGE

BROWNING SEMI-AUTO GRADE II OCTAGON

BROWNING T-BOLT GRAY LAMINATED TARGET/VARMINT STAINLESS, SUPPRESSOR READY

BROWNING T-BOLT TARGET WITH MUZZLE BRAKE

BROWNING X-BOLT HUNTER

BLR LIGHTWEIGHT '81 STAINLESS TAKEDOWN

Action: Lever-action
Stock: Laminate, straight grip
Barrel: 20 in., 22 in., 24 in.
Sights: Open
Weight: 6 lb. 8 oz.–7 lb. 12 oz.
Caliber: .243 Win., 6.5 Creedmoor, 7mm-08 Rem., .308 Win., .300 WSM, .30-06 Spfd., .300 Win. Mag.
Magazine: Detachable box
Features: Aircraft-grade alloy receiver; drilled and tapped for scope mounts; stainless steel barrel with matte finish; gray laminate wood stock in satin finish; recoil pad; separates for storage or transportation; optional Scout-style scope mount; TRUGLO/Marble's fiber optic front sight
MSRP . . . . $1229.99–$1419.99

BLR LIGHTWEIGHT STAINLESS WITH PISTOL GRIP

Action: Lever-action
Stock: Walnut, pistol grip
Barrel: 20 in., 22 in., 24 in.
Sights: None
Weight: 6 lb. 8 oz.–7 lb. 12 oz.
Caliber: .450 Marlin, .22-250 Rem., .223 Rem., .243 Win., 6.5 Creedmoor, .270 Win., .270 WSM, .30-06 Spfd., .300 Win. Mag., .300 WSM, .308 Win., .325 WSM, .358 Win., 7mm Rem. Mag., 7mm-08 Rem., 7mm WSM
Magazine: Detachable box
Features: Aircraft-grade alloy receiver; drilled and tapped for scope mounts; steel barrel with matte finish; crowned muzzle; adjustable sights; gloss finish walnut stock with pistol grip; sling swivel studs installed; recoil pad
MSRP . . . . $1159.99–$1239.99

SEMI-AUTO 22 CHALLENGE

Action: Semiautomatic
Stock: Walnut
Barrel: 16.25 in.
Sights: None
Weight: 6 lb. 10 oz.
Caliber: .22 LR
Magazine: 10 rounds
Features: Certainly one for rimfire competition, with metal buttplate; satin-finished Grade 1 walnut stock; fixed bull barrel with threaded-on muzzle brake; matte blued metalwork; topside Picatinny rail
MSRP $959.99

SEMI-AUTO GRADE II OCTAGON

Action: Semiautomatic
Stock: Grade II/III black walnut
Barrel: 19.4 in.
Sights: Blade front, notch rear
Weight: 5 lb. 3 oz.
Caliber: .22 LR
Magazine: 10 rounds
Features: A John Browning original gets a gloss-finish black walnut stock; takedown design; octagon barrel; metal buttplate; satin nickel receiver with scroll engraving; steel trigger guard; drilled and tapped for optic mounting
MSRP $1079.99

T-BOLT GRAY LAMINATED TARGET/VARMINT STAINLESS, SUPPRESSOR READY

Action: T-bolt
Stock: Laminate
Barrel: 22 in.
Sights: None
Weight: 5 lb. 10 oz.
Caliber: .22 LR, .22 WMR, .17 HMR
Magazine: 10 rounds
Features: Gray laminate stock with a Monte Carlo comb; a free-floating barrel with a medium target profile and recessed crown; semi-match grade chamber; adjustable trigger; installed sling swivels; threaded for suppressor use; thread protector included
MSRP . . . . $999.99–$1099.99

T-BOLT TARGET WITH MUZZLE BRAKE

Action: Bolt
Stock: Black walnut
Barrel: 16.5 in.
Sights: None
Weight: 6 lb. 2 oz.
Caliber: .22 LR, .22 WMR, .17 HMR
Magazine: 10 rounds
Features: Handy rimfire for ranch work, casual target practice, or rimfire competition with a Grade 1 black walnut stock in a satin finish; Monte Carlo cheekpiece; free-floating heavy bull target barrel with a semi-match chamber and a threaded-on in-profile muzzle brake; steel receiver; sling swivel studs; straight-pull action; top-tang safety; Double Helix magazine
MSRP . . . . $719.99–$759.99

X-BOLT HUNTER

Action: Bolt
Stock: Satin finish walnut stock
Barrel: 22 in., 23 in., 24 in., 26 in.
Sights: None
Weight: 6 lb. 13 oz.–7 lb.
Caliber: 6.5 Creedmoor, .223 Rem., .22-250 Rem., .243 Win., 7mm-08 Rem., .308 Win., .270 WSM, .300 WSM, .25-06 Rem., .270 Win., .280 Rem., .30-06 Spfd., 7mm Rem. Mag., .375 H&H Mag., 338 Win. Mag., .300 Win. Mag.
Magazine: Detachable rotary box
Features: Adjustable feather trigger; top-tang safety with bolt unlock button; sling swivel studs installed; Inflex technology recoil pad
Standard . . . . $939.99–$1049.99
Left-hand . . . . . . $1069.99–$1099.99

BROWNING X-BOLT MAX FLAT DARK EARTH LONG RANGE

BROWNING X-BOLT MAX LONG RANGE

BROWNING X-BOLT MEDALLION

BROWNING X-BOLT MICRO COMPOSITE

BROWNING X-BOLT MICRO MIDAS

BROWNING X-BOLT MOUNTAIN PRO BURNT BRONZE, MOUNTAIN PRO TUNGSTEN

BROWNING X-BOLT MOUNTAIN PRO LONG RANGE BURNT BRONZE, MOUNTAIN PRO LONG-RANGE TUNGSTEN

X-BOLT MAX FLAT DARK EARTH LONG RANGE

Action: Bolt
Stock: Composite
Barrel: 26 in.
Sights: None
Weight: 8 lb. 3 oz.–8 lb. 7 oz.
Caliber: 6.5 Creedmoor, 6.5 PRC, 6.8 Western, .280 Ackley Improved, .300 Win. Mag., .300 PRC
Magazine: 3, 4 rounds
Features: Long-range target option with an adjustable cheekpiece and length of pull stock spacers; fluted heavy sporter barrel with threaded on Recoil Hawg muzzle brake; extended bolt handle with a 60-degree lift; detachable rotary magazine; X-Lock scope mounts; bolt unlock button; Feather trigger
MSRP . . . . $1279.99–$1319.99

X-BOLT MAX LONG RANGE

Action: Bolt
Stock: Composite
Barrel: 26 in.
Sights: None
Weight: 8 lb. 3 oz.–8 lb. 7 oz.
Caliber: 6mm Creedmoor, 6.5 Creedmoor, .308 Win., .300 WSM, 7mm Rem. Mag., .28 Nosler, .300 Win. Mag., .300 RUM, 6.5 PRC, .30 Nosler, .300 PRC, 6.8 Western
Magazine: 3, 4 rounds
Features: Viable entry for those looking to get into the long-range game, featuring Composite Max stock with adjustable comb and a black-and-gray textured finish; fluted, stainless steel, heavy contour barrel; TPI threaded muzzle brake and thread protector; length of pull spacers; three swivel studs
MSRP . . . . $1379.99–$1459.99

X-BOLT MEDALLION

Action: Bolt

Stock: Walnut
Barrel: 22 in., 23 in., 24 in., 26 in.
Sights: Open
Weight: 6 lb. 6 oz.–7 lb.
Caliber: .223 Rem., .243 Win., .270 Win., .308 Win., .25-06 Rem., .280 Rem., .30-06 Spfd., 7mm Rem. Mag., .300 Win. Mag., .300 WSM, .270 WSM, .375 H&H Mag., 6.5 Creedmoor
Magazine: Detachable rotary box
Features: Gloss finish walnut stock, rosewood forend grip and pistol cap; Inflex technology recoil pad; adjustable feather trigger; drilled and tapped for scope mounts; left-hand option
MSRP . . . . $1039.99–$1219.99

X-BOLT MICRO COMPOSITE

Action: Bolt
Stock: Composite
Barrel: 20 in.
Sights: None
Weight: 6 lb. 5 oz.
Caliber: .243 Win., 6.5 Creedmoor, 7mm-08 Rem., .308 Rem.
Magazine: 4 rounds
Features: Shorter length of pull at 13 in.; stock is a non-glare composite in black and with textured gripping surfaces and a palm swell; free-floating barrel features a threaded muzzle brake, thread protector, target crown, and light sporter contour; sling swivel studs; Pachmayr Decelerator recoil pad
MSRP . . . . $999.99–$1069.99

X-BOLT MICRO MIDAS

Action: Bolt
Stock: Walnut
Barrel: 20 in.
Sights: None
Weight: 6 lb. 1 oz–6 lb. 6 oz.
Caliber: .243 Win., 7mm-08 Rem., .308 Win., 6.5 Creedmoor

Magazine: Detachable rotary magazine
Features: Drilled and tapped for scope mounts, low-luster blued finish, free-floating barrel; adjustable feather trigger; top-tang safety; left-hand option
MSRP . . . . $859.99–$959.99

X-BOLT MOUNTAIN PRO BURNT BRONZE, TUNGSTEN

Action: Bolt
Stock: Carbon fiber
Barrel: 22 in., 23 in., 24 in., 26 in.
Sights: None
Weight: 5 lb. 14 oz.–6 lb. 6 oz.
Caliber: 6.5 Creedmoor, 6.5 PRC, 6.8 Western, .300 WSM, .30-06 Spfd., 7mm Rem. Mag., .28 Nosler, .300 Win. Mag., .30 Nosler, .300 PRC, .300 RUM
Magazine: 3, 4 rounds
Features: Browning says that this is a limited production gun and one that gives the company entry into the semi-custom production category, with features like a carbon fiber stock; Cerakote burnt bronze finish on metalwork; spiral-fluted, lapped sporter contour barrel; removable Picatinny rail; Feather trigger; X-Lock scope mounts; bolt unlock button; detachable rotary magazine
MSRP . . . . $2479.99–$2539.99

X-BOLT MOUNTAIN PRO LONG RANGE BURNT BRONZE, TUNGSTEN

Action: Bolt
Stock: Carbon fiber
Barrel: 26 in.
Sights: None
Weight: 6 lb. 12 oz.–7 lb. 1 oz.
Caliber: 6.5 Creedmoor, 6.5 PRC, 6.8 Western, .300 WSM, .30-06 Spfd., 7mm Rem. Mag., .28 Nosler, .300 Win. Mag., .30 Nosler, .300 PRC, .300 RUM
Magazine: 3, 4 rounds
Features: Similar to the Mountain Pro, but with the barrel standardized at 26 inches across all calibers; fast-twist rifling in some calibers
MSRP . . . . $2519.99–$2579.99

RIFLES

Browning

BROWNING X-BOLT PRO LONG RANGE

BROWNING X-BOLT PRO MCMILLAN LONG RANGE

BROWNING X-BOLT STAINLESS STALKER

BROWNING X-BOLT PRO MCMILLAN

BROWNING X-BOLT RMEF WHITE GOLD MEDALLION

BROWNING X-BOLT STALKER LONG RANGE

X-BOLT PRO LONG RANGE

Action: Bolt
Stock: Composite
Barrel: 26 in.
Sights: None
Weight: 6 lb. 12 oz.–7 lb. 1 oz.
Caliber: 6.5 Creedmoor, 6.5 PRC, 6.8 Western, .280 Ackley Improved, 7mm Rem. Mag., .28 Nosler, .300 Win. Mag., .300 PRC, .300 RUM
Magazine: 4, 5 rounds
Features: With a standardized 26-inch barrel across the caliber choices, this rifle features a skip-fluted heavy sporter contour barrel threaded and equipped with the Recoil Hawg muzzle brake; removable Picatinny rail on forend underside; spiral-fluted bolt; natural finish on stock; Carbon Gray Elite Cerakote on metalwork; gun is quarter-pound lighter than previous iterations
MSRP . . . .$2239.99–$2269.99

X-BOLT PRO MCMILLAN

Action: Bolt
Stock: Carbon fiber
Barrel: 22 in., 23 in., 24 in., 26 in.
Sights: None
Weight: 6 lb. 5 oz.–6 lb. 12 oz.
Caliber: 6.5 Creedmoor, 6.5 PRC, 6.8 Western, .280 Ackley Improved, .300 WSM, .30-06 Spfd., 7mm Rem. Mag., .28 Nosler, .300 Win. Mag., .300 PRC, .300 RUM
Magazine: 3, 4 rounds
Features: This X-bolt wears a McMillan Game Scout stock in Sonoran Carbon Ambush finish; metalwork in Cerakote carbon gray; a skip-fluted sporter contour barrel

wearing a threaded-on Recoil Hawg muzzle brake; spiral fluted bolt and fluted bolt knob; 20 MOA Picatinny rail topside plus more under the forend; quick-detach sling attachments
MSRP . . . . $2679.99–$2699.99

X-BOLT PRO MCMILLAN LONG RANGE

Action: Bolt
Stock: Carbon fiber
Barrel: 26 in.
Sights: None
Weight: 7 lb.–7 lb. 7 oz.
Caliber: 6.5 Creedmoor, 6.5 PRC, 6.8 Western, .280 Ackley Improved, 7mm Rem. Mag., .28 Nosler, .300 Win. Mag., .300 PRC, .300 RUM
Magazine: 3, 4 rounds
Features: Similar to the X-Bolt Pro McMillan, but with the barrel standardized to 26 inches across all available calibers
MSRP . . . . $2659.99–$2779.99

X-BOLT RMEF WHITE GOLD MEDALLION

Action: Bolt
Stock: Walnut
Barrel: 26 in.
Sights: None
Weight: 7 lb.
Caliber: .300 Win. Mag.
Magazine: Detachable rotary box
Features: Monte Carlo stock; stainless steel barrel and receiver, receiver etched in gold; raised cheekpiece; Inflex technology recoil pad; adjustable feather trigger; top-tang safety
MSRP $1799.99

X-BOLT STAINLESS STALKER

Action: Bolt
Stock: Composite
Barrel: 22 in., 23 in., 24 in., 26 in.
Sights: None
Weight: 6 lb. 3 oz.–6 lb. 13 oz.
Caliber: .243 Win., 6.5 Creedmoor, 7mm-08 Rem., .308 Win., .270 WSM, .300 WSM, .25-06 Rem., .270 Win., .30-06 Spfd., 7mm Rem. Mag., .300 Win. Mag., .338 Win. Mag., .375 H&H Mag.
Magazine: Detachable rotary box
Features: Composite stock in matte black with textured gripping surfaces; Dura-Touch armor coating; adjustable feather trigger; top-tang safety; bolt unlock button; palm swell
MSRP . . . . $1899.99–$1299.99

X-BOLT STALKER LONG RANGE

Action: Bolt
Stock: Composite
Barrel: 26 in.
Sights: None
Weight: 7 lb. 8 oz.–7 lb. 13 oz.
Caliber: 6.5 Creedmoor, 6.5 PRC, .270 Win., 7mm Rem. Mag., .28 Nosler, .30 Nosler, .300 Win. Mag., .300 RUM, .300 PRC
Magazine: 3, 4 rounds
Features: A no-frills rifle for those getting started in the long-range game; heavy sporter barrel with a threaded on Recoil Hawg muzzle brake; adjustable comb; matte blued metal on a matte blue composite stock; extended bolt handle; Feather trigger; X-Lock scope mounts; also available in flat dark earth
MSRP . . . . $1069.99–$1119.99

Cadex Defence

CADEX DEFENCE CDX-40 SHADOW

CADEX DEFENCE CDX-MC KRAKEN

CADEX DEFENCE CDX-50 TREMOR

CADEX DEFENCE CDX-R7 CRBN

CADEX DEFENCE CDX-LITE SERIES

CADEX DEFENCE CDX-R7 FCP SERIES

CDX-40 SHADOW

Action: Bolt
Stock: Synthetic
Barrel: 29 in., 32 in.
Sights: None
Weight: 18 lb. 8 oz.
Caliber: .375 CT, .375 EnABLER, .408 CT
Magazine: 5 rounds
Features: Designed for anti-materiel shooting and other targets out to 4,000 yards; tool-less adjustable at cheek, length of pull, and buttplate; V-shaped bedding system that eliminates action movement in the chassis; mirage control tube; three-lug bolt with 60-degree throw; DX2 Evo single-/double-stage selectable trigger; Bartlein heavy straight-taper fluted barrel with a threaded muzzle, and 5R mil-spec match-grade single-point cut rifling; Ergo rubberized finger-groove grip; reverse folding stock; oversized trigger guard; detachable base for easy trigger care; full-length dual top rail in 20, 40, or 60 MOA
MSRP . . . . $8576.95–$8591.95

CDX-50 TREMOR

Action: Bolt
Stock: Synthetic
Barrel: 29 in.
Sights: None
Weight: 22 lb. 7 oz.
Caliber: .50 BMG
Magazine: 5 rounds
Features: Tool-less adjustable cheek, length of pull, and buttplate; V-shaped bedding system that eliminates action movement in the chassis; mirage control tube; four-lug bolt with 50-degree throw; DX2 Evo single-/double-stage selectable trigger; Bartlein straight-taper fluted barrel with a threaded muzzle, and 5R mil-spec match-grade single-point cut rifling; Ergo rubberized finger-groove grip; full-length dual top rail in 20 or 40 MOA
MSRP . . . . $9452.95–$9529.95

CDX-LITE SERIES

Action: Bolt
Stock: Synthetic
Barrel: 24 in., 26 in., 27 in.
Sights: None
Weight: 13 lb. 7 oz.–14 lb. 8 oz.
Caliber: 6mm Creedmoor, .260 Rem., 6.5 Creedmoor, 6.5x47 Lapua, 6.5 PRC, .308 Win., .300 Win. Mag., .300 PRC, .300 Norma Mag., .338 Lapua Mag., .338 Norma Mag.
Magazine: 10 rounds
Features: Designed for long-range sniper work; V-shaped bedding eliminates action movement in the chassis; mirage-control tube; Bartlein straight-taper fluted barrel with threaded muzzle, 5R mil-spec match-grade single-point cut rifling; built-in recoil lug; DX2 Evo single-/double-stage selectable trigger; Ergo rubberized finger-grooved grip; full-length lite top rail; Cerakote finishing
MSRP . . . . $5599.95–$5719.95

CDX-MC KRAKEN

Action: Bolt
Stock: Synthetic
Barrel: 24 in., 26 in., 27 in.
Sights: None
Weight: 15 lb. 3 oz.
Caliber: 6mm Creedmoor, .260 Rem., 6.5 Creedmoor, 6.5x47 Lapua, .308 Win., .300 Win. Mag., .300 PRC, .300 Norma Mag., .338 Lapua Mag., .338 Norma Mag.
Magazine: 10 rounds
Features: V-shaped bedding that eliminates action movement in the chassis; mirage-control tube; three-lug bolt with 50-degree throw and choice of round bulb or cross-hatched pattern knob; Bartlein straight-taper heavy barrel with barrel band, threaded muzzle, 5R mil-spec single-point cut rifling; built-in recoil lug; DX2 Evo single-/double-stage selectable trigger; Ergo rubberized finger-grooved grip; full-length top rail; Cerakote finishing
MSRP . . . . $7174.95–$7195.95

CDX-R7 CRBN

Action: Bolt
Stock: Synthetic
Barrel: 24 in., 26 in.
Sights: None
Weight: 8 lb. 3 oz.–8 lb. 4 oz.
Caliber: 6.5 Creedmoor, 6.5 PRC, .308 Win., .300 WSM, 7mm Rem. Mag., .28 Nosler, .300 Win. Mag., .300 PRC, .338 Lapua Mag.
Magazine: 3, 4 rounds
Features: Hunting-style in-profile muzzle brake; aluminum bedding blocks; choice of 20 or 30 MOA top action rails; four-lug spiral-fluted bolt with 50-degree throw and slim round knob; Proof Research carbon fiber match-grade barrel with a stainless core; CX2 Evo single-/two-stage selectable trigger; neoprene cheek-piece; rubberized grip insert; oversized trigger guard; numerous stock colors
MSRP . . . . $3359.95–$4169.95

CDX-R7 FCP SERIES

Action: Bolt
Stock: Synthetic
Barrel: 24 in., 26 in., 27 in.
Sights: None
Weight: 12 lb. 15 oz.–13 lb. 2 oz.
Caliber: 6mm Creedmoor, .260 Rem., 6.5 Creedmoor, 6.5x47 Lapua, 6.5 PRC, .308 Win., .300 Win. Mag., .300 PRC, .300 Norma Mag., .338 Lapua Mag., .338 Norma Mag.
Magazine: 10 rounds
Features: Fixed skeleton stock; tool-less adjustable at cheek, length of pull, and buttplate; DX2 Evo single-/double-stage selectable trigger; Bartlein heavy straight-taper barrel with barrel band, threaded muzzle and 5R mil-spec single-point cut rifling; Ergo rubberized finger-groove grip; oversized trigger guard; detachable base for easy trigger care; multiple stock color options
MSRP . . . . $4459.95–$4649.95

Cadex Defence

CADEX DEFENCE
CDX-R7 SHP SERIES

CADEX DEFENCE
CDX-R7 SPTR

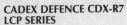

CADEX DEFENCE CDX-R7
LCP SERIES

CADEX DEFENCE
CDX-TAC SERIES

CDX-R7 LCP SERIES

Action: Bolt
Stock: Synthetic
Barrel: 24 in., 26 in., 27 in.
Sights: None
Weight: 12 lb. 15 oz.–13 lb. 2 oz.
Caliber: 6mm Creedmoor, .260 Rem., 6.5 Creedmoor, 6.5x47 Lapua, 6.5 PRC, .308 Win., .300 Win. Mag., .300 PRC, .300 Norma Mag., .338 Lapua Mag., .338 Norma Mag.
Magazine: 10 rounds
Features: Designed for Precision Rifle Series competition; four-lug bolt with a 50-degree throw and oversized knob in choice of round bulb or crosshatch design; Cerakote finish; Bartlein straight-taper heavy barrel with a barrel band, threaded muzzle, and 5R mil-spec single point cut rifling; Ergo finger-grooved and rubberized pistol grip; reverse folding buttstock; DX2 Evo single-/double-stage selectable trigger; choice of 0, 20, or 30 MOA rail; numerous stock colors
MSRP . . . . **$4899.95–$5069.95**

CDX-R7 SHP SERIES

Action: Bolt
Stock: Synthetic
Barrel: 20 in., 24 in., 26 in., 27 in.
Sights: None
Weight: 13 lb.–13 lb. 8 oz.
Caliber: 6mm Creedmoor, .260 Rem., 6.5 Creedmoor, 6.5x47 Lapua, 6.5 PRC, .308 Win., .300 Win. Mag., .300 PRC, .300 Norma Mag., .338 Lapua Mag., .338 Norma Mag.
Magazine: 10 rounds
Features: Cerakoting; MX2 Tactical muzzle brake; aluminum micro-chassis; choice of 0, 20, or 30 MOA action rails; spiral-fluted bolt with a 50-degree throw; oversized bolt knob in choice of round bulb or cross-hatch body; straight taper fluted match-grade barrel; DX2 Evo single-/two-stage selectable trigger; tool-less adjustable spring-loaded cheekpiece; dual-sided built-in quick-detach sling attachment flush cups; ambidextrous palm swell grip; oversized trigger guard; numerous stock colors available
MSRP . . . . **$3269.95–$3369.95**

CDX-R7 SPTR

Action: Bolt
Stock: Synthetic
Barrel: 24 in., 26 in.
Sights: None
Weight: 8 lb. 8 oz.
Caliber: 6.5 Creedmoor, 6.5 PRC, .308 Win., .300 WSM, 7mm Rem. Mag., .28 Nosler, .300 Win. Mag., .300 PRC, .338 Lapua Mag.
Magazine: 3, 4 rounds
Features: Hunting-style in-profile muzzle brake; aluminum bedding blocks; choice of 20 or 30 MOA top action rails; four-lug spiral-fluted bolt with 50-degree throw and slim round knob; Cadex sporter-profile stainless steel barrel; CX2 Evo single-/two-stage selectable trigger; neoprene cheekpiece; rubberized grip insert; oversized trigger guard; numerous stock colors
MSRP . . . . **$2769.95–$3079.95**

CDX-TAC SERIES

Action: Bolt
Stock: Synthetic
Barrel: 24 in., 26 in., 27 in.
Sights: None
Weight: 12 lb. 3 oz.–13 lb. 5 oz.
Caliber: 6.5 Creedmoor, 6.5 PRC, .300 Win., .300 WSM, .28 Nosler, .300 Win. Mag., .300 PRC, .300 Lapua Mag.
Magazine: 10 rounds
Features: Fixed skeleton stock; tool-less adjustable at cheek, length of pull, and buttplate; V-shaped bedding system that eliminates action movement in the chassis; mirage control tube to reduce visual mirage from barrel heat; DX2 Evo single-/double-stage selectable trigger; Bartlein heavy straight-taper barrel with barrel band, threaded muzzle, and 5R mil-spec single-point cut rifling; Ergo rubberized finger-groove grip; oversized trigger guard; detachable base; full-length lite top rail in 20, 30, or 40 MOA; multiple stock colors
MSRP . . . . **$4989.95–$5139.95**

Caracal USA

CARACAL USA
CAR814 A2 MOE

CARACAL USA
CAR816 A2

CAR814 A2 MOE

Action: Semiautomatic
Stock: Synthetic
Barrel: 11.5, 14.5, 15 in.
Sights: A2 front sight, flip-up rear
Weight: 7 lb.
Caliber: 5.56 NATO
Magazine: 30 rounds
Features: Direct impingement gas-operated system; Magpul MOE M-LOK handguard; Magpul CTR mil-spec carbine stock; Caracal grip
MSRP . . . . **$739.00–$1199.00**

CAR816 A2

Action: Semiautomatic
Stock: Synthetic
Barrel: 11.5, 14.5, 16 in.
Sights: Flip-up front and rear
Weight: 7 lb. 6.4 oz.
Caliber: 5.56 NATO
Magazine: 30 rounds
Features: Short-stroke push rod gas piston system; three-position adjustable gas valve; Caracal handguard; full-length 1913 Picatinny rail; Modified M4 barrel contour; Magpul STR Carbine stock or SBA3 Pistol Brace stock; A2-style flash hider; select-fire option available; EDT Sharp Shooter trigger
MSRP . . . . **$1254.00–$1929.00**

RIFLES

Caracal USA

VERSUS COMPETITION

Action: Semiautomatic
Stock: Synthetic
Barrel: 18 in.
Sights: None
Weight: 6 lb. 3 oz.
Caliber: .223 Wylde
Magazine: 10, 30 rounds
Features: A lightweight nimble gun for the 3-Gun crowd in an outside-the-box caliber. Features include carbon fiber-wrapped 416R stainless barrel; two-port, self-timing muzzle brake; 15-inch Caracal free-floating handguard with MLOK and QD attachment points; Caracal grip; direct impingement gas system
MSRP $2199.00

CARACAL USA VERSUS COMPETITION

Century Arms

CENTURY ARMS VSKA

VSKA

Action: Semiautomatic
Stock: American maple
Barrel: 16.3 in.
Sights: A2-style front, ladder-type adjustable rear
Weight: N/A
Caliber: 7.62X39
Magazine: 30 rounds
Features: An upscale, heavy-duty AK-47-style rifle with American maple stock; heat-treated S7 tool steel bolt carrier, front trunnion, and feed ramp; chrome moly 4150 barrel; RAK-1 Enhanced Trigger Group; manganese-phosphate finish; available in synthetic stock and California-compliant versions
MSRP . . . . $799.99–$899.99

Chiappa Firearms

CHIAPPA FIREARMS 1886 LEVER ACTION DELUXE

CHIAPPA FIREARMS DOUBLE BADGER

CHIAPPA FIREARMS 1892 WILDLANDS

CHIAPPA FIREARMS LA322 KODIAK CUB TAKEDOWN

1886 LEVER ACTION DELUXE

Action: Lever
Stock: Walnut
Barrel: 26 in.
Sights: Dovetail front, buckhorn rear
Weight: 9 lb.
Caliber: .45-70 Govt.
Magazine: 8 rounds
Features: High-grade current production of Browning's classic 1886 rifle; color case finished receiver; select walnut; checkering at wrist and forend; octagonal barrel
MSRP $1880.00

DOUBLE BADGER

Action: Break-open
Stock: Beech
Barrel: 19 in., 20 in.
Sights: Fixed red fiber optic front, Williams green fiber optic rear
Weight: 5 lb. 13 oz.
Caliber: .22 LR/.410-bore, .243 Win./.410-bore, .22 LR/20-gauge, .22 WMR/.410-bore
Magazine: 2 rounds
Features: A folding combo gun with double triggers; firearm folds by lowering the trigger guard; all shotgun bores are 3-inch chambers; blued finish metalwork; beech stocks
MSRP . . . . $441.00–$647.00

LA322 KODIAK CUB TAKEDOWN

Action: Lever action
Stock: English-style black soft touch
Barrel: 18.5 in.
Sights: Hooded front, adjustable rear
Weight: 5 lb. 8 oz.
Caliber: .22 LR
Magazine: 15 rounds
Features: Stainless Cerakote receiver with a blued barrel; black soft touch coating makes the stock easier to grip and protects from the elements; easy take down
MSRP $680.00

LA322 TAKEDOWN DELUXE

Action: Lever action
Stock: Walnut
Barrel: 18.5 in.
Sights: Hooded front, adjustable rear
Weight: 5 lb. 8 oz.
Caliber: .22 LR
Magazine: 15 rounds
Features: A takedown lever-action rimfire with a dovetail groove for scope mounting; pistol grip wood stock; Tactical Grey Cerakote receiver; blued barrel
MSRP $592.00

Chiappa Firearms

CHIAPPA FIREARMS LA322 TAKEDOWN STANDARD CARBINE

CHIAPPA FIREARMS M1-9 CARBINE

CHIAPPA FIREARMS MFOUR-22 GEN II PRO CARBINE, RIFLE

CHIAPPA FIREARMS LITTLE BADGER

CHIAPPA FIREARMS M1-22 CARBINE

CHIAPPA FIREARMS RAK-9

CHIAPPA FIREARMS LITTLE BADGER OD GREEN WITH SCOPE

CHIAPPA FIREARMS M6

CHIAPPA FIREARMS RAK-22

LA322 TAKEDOWN STANDARD CARBINE

Action: Lever action
Stock: English-style wood
Barrel: 18.5 in.
Sights: Hooded front, adjustable rear
Weight: 5 lb. 8 oz.
Caliber: .22 LR
Magazine: 15 rounds
Features: 3/8-inch dovetail on top of receiver for scope mounting; take-down design; straight wood stock; blued or matte black metalwork
MSRP . . . . $389.00–$399.00

LITTLE BADGER

Action: Single shot
Stock: Metal foldable
Barrel: 16.5 in.
Sights: Adjustable rear
Weight: 3 lb. 8 oz.
Caliber: .22 LR, .22WMR, .17 HMR
Magazine: None
Features: Single barrel; foldable rifle; extremely light for comfortable carry; folds to 16.5 in. total length; nylon carry bag and special cartridge holder available; in Desert Sand Cerakote or all-over blue
MSRP . . . . $228.00–$264.00

LITTLE BADGER OD GREEN WITH SCOPE

Action: Break-open single-shot
Stock: Wire steel
Barrel: 16.5 in.
Sights: None
Weight: 3 lb. 10 oz.
Caliber: .22 LR
Magazine: 1 round
Features: Chiappa's handy folding survival rifle gets a makeover in all-over OD Green; four-sided Picatinny rail for optics and accessories
MSRP $233.00

M1-9 CARBINE

Action: Semiautomatic
Stock: Polymer, wood
Barrel: 18 in.
Sights: Winged front, sliding rear
Weight: 5 lb. 14.4 oz.–6 lb. 4.8 oz.
Caliber: 9mm
Magazine: 10 rounds
Features: Classic M1 carbine taking Beretta 9mm magazines; metals matte blue; two magazines included
Polymer: $597.32
Wood: $676.12

M1-22 CARBINE

Action: Semiautomatic
Stock: Polymer
Barrel: 18 in.
Sights: Adjustable rear
Weight: 5 lb. 8 oz.
Caliber: .22 LR
Magazine: Detachable box, 10 rounds
Features: The M1 carbine is a light-weight, easy-to-use semiautomatic carbine that became a standard firearm for the U.S. military during World War II, the Korean War, and the Vietnam War, and was produced in several variants
Polymer: $332.93
Wood: $460.37

M6

Action: Lever
Stock: Polypropylene closed cell foam
Barrel: 18.5 in.
Sights: Fiber optic front, military adjustable rear
Weight: 5 lb. 12.8 oz.–6 lb.
Caliber: 12 ga./.22 LR, 20 ga./.22 LR, 12 ga./.22 WMR, 20 ga./.22 WMR
Magazine: 2 rounds
Features: Combo gun, shotgun barrel top, .22 rimfire barrel bottom; folding stock, interchangeable choke tubes, and dedicated triggers for each barrel;

cleaning kit and 4–8 additional rounds stored in the stock
MSRP . . . . $729.00–$999.00

MFOUR-22 GEN II PRO CARBINE, RIFLE

Action: Semiautomatic
Stock: Synthetic
Barrel: 16 in.
Sights: None
Weight: 5 lb. 11.2 oz.
Caliber: .22 LR
Magazine: 28 rounds
Features: Fully equipped MSR in .22 LR; eight-position Picatinny rail; six-position adjustable buttstock; heavy barrel profile; two magazines
MSRP . . . . $473.00–$569.00

RAK-9

Action: Semiautomatic
Stock: Synthetic
Barrel: 17.25 in.
Sights: Adjustable military-style
Weight: 6 lb. 10 oz.
Caliber: 9mm
Magazine: 10 rounds
Features: A pistol-caliber take on the AK-47 with a skeletonized synthetic stock; steel frame; adjustable sights
MSRP $719.00

RAK-22

Action: Semiautomatic
Stock: Wood
Barrel: 17.25 in.
Sights: Adjustable
Weight: 6 lb.
Caliber: .22 LR
Magazine: Detachable box, 10 rounds
Features: Steel blued receiver and barrel
MSRP $665.00

Chipmunk Rifles (Keystone Sporting Arms, LLC)

CHIPMUNK RIFLES CHIPMUNK

CHIPMUNK

Action: Bolt
Stock: Walnut, laminated
Barrel: 16.125 in.
Sights: Target
Weight: 2 lb. 8 oz.

Caliber: .22 LR
Magazine: None
Features: Designed with younger shooters in mind; single-shot; manual-cocking action; receiver-mounted rear sights; metal with blued finish or stainless steel; post sight on ramp front, fully adjustable peep rear; adjustable trigger; extendable buttplate and front rail; available in black, walnut, deluxe walnut, camo laminate, and brown laminate
Standard . . . . $275.00–$405.00
Standard left-hand $275.00
Barracuda. . . . . $315.00–$335.00

Christensen Arms

CHRISTENSEN ARMS BA TACTICAL

CHRISTENSEN ARMS CA-10 G2

CHRISTENSEN ARMS CA5FIVE6

CHRISTENSEN ARMS CA-10 DMR

CHRISTENSEN ARMS CA-15 G2

BA TACTICAL

Action: Bolt
Stock: Hand-laid fiberglass
Barrel: 16 in., 20 in., 22 in., 24 in., 26 in., 27 in.
Sights: None
Weight: 7 lb. 11 oz.–8 lb. 2 oz.
Caliber: .223 Rem., 6mm Creedmoor, 6.5 Creedmoor, 6.5 PRC, .308 Win., .300 Win. Mag., .338 Lapua Mag., .300 PRC
Magazine: Detachable box, 5 rounds
Features: Integral full-length rail incorporates a 20 MOA taper; front stud with five flush cups; adjustable cheek piece via inserts; stainless steel side-port muzzle brake
MSRP. $2899.99

CA-10 DMR

Action: Semiautomatic
Stock: Synthetic
Barrel: 18 in., 20 in., 22 in., 24 in.
Sights: None
Weight: 7 lb. 13 oz.–8 lb. 3 oz.
Caliber: 6.5 Creedmoor, .308 Win.
Magazine: Detachable box
Features: Picatinny rail; OSS suppressor; ambidextrous magazine release; Magpul stock; various finishes available
MSRP. $3399.99

CA-10 G2

Action: Semiautomatic
Stock: Synthetic
Barrel: 18 in., 20 in.
Sights: None
Weight: 7 lb. 12.8 oz.–8 lb. 3.2 oz.
Caliber: 6.5 Creedmoor, .308 Win.
Magazine: N/A
Features: Upper and lower of billet 7075 aluminum; integrated undercut trigger guard on lower, aerograde carbon fiber handguard on an upper with KeyMod or M-Lok configurations; match chamber and trigger; direct impingement system; Magpul adjustable STR stock; 416R stainless barrel wrapped in steel aerograde carbon fiber; Titanium side baffle brake; carbon-fiber-wrapped stainless steel barrel
MSRP. $3199.99

CA-15 G2

Action: Semiautomatic
Stock: Synthetic
Barrel: 16 in.
Sights: None
Weight: 5 lb. 12.8 oz.
Caliber: .223 Wylde
Magazine: N/A

Features: Custom-built AR optimized for weight and accuracy; newly designed matched receiver with a contour-matching carbon fiber handguard; single-stage match trigger; match chamber; flared magwell; button rifled, threaded, and carbon fiber-wrapped barrel; BCM Gunfighter adjustable stock; stainless steel flash hider; in stainless steel or carbon fiber
Stainless steel $1799.99
Carbon fiber $2399.99

CA5FIVE6

Action: Semiautomatic
Stock: Synthetic
Barrel: 16 in.
Sights: None
Weight: 6 lb. 5 oz.
Caliber: .223 Wylde
Magazine: 10 rounds
Features: Maneuverable carbine; Trigger Tech single-stage trigger; match chamber; ½X28 threaded muzzle with a stainless 3-prong flash hider; carbon fiber-wrapped stainless barrel; forged aluminum upper and lower; 15-in. aluminum hybrid carbon fiber M-LOK handguard; direct impingement system; adjustable MFT minimalist buttstock
Black anodized. 1699.99
Cerakote $1749.99

Christensen Arms

CHRISTENSEN ARMS ELR

CHRISTENSEN ARMS MESA

CHRISTENSEN ARMS MESA LONG RANGE

CHRISTENSEN ARMS MESA TITANIUM

CHRISTENSEN ARMS MODERN PRECISION RIFLE

CHRISTENSEN ARMS RANGER 22

ELR

Action: Bolt
Stock: Hand-laid carbon fiber
Barrel: 26 in.–27 in.
Sights: None
Weight: 7 lb. 8 oz.
Caliber: 6.5 Creedmoor, 6.5 PRC, .28 Nosler, 7mm Rem. Mag., .300 Win. Mag., .300 PRC, .338 Lapua Mag.
Magazine: 4 rounds
Features: Machined aluminum hinged floorplate; dual front studs with flush cups; adjustable cheek piece via inserts; titanium side-port muzzle brake
MSRP **$2899.00**

MESA

Action: Bolt
Stock: Carbon fiber composite
Barrel: 20 in., 22 in., 24 in., 26 in.
Sights: None
Weight: 6 lb. 8 oz.–6 lb. 11.2 oz.
Caliber: .450 Bushmaster, 6.5 Creedmoor, 6.5 PRC, 7mm-08 Rem., 7mm Rem. Mag., .308 Win., .28 Nosler, .300 Win. Mag., .300 PRC
Magazine: 3 (magnum), 4 rounds
Features: Featherweight contour barrel with removable stainless radial muzzle brake and tungsten Cerakote finish; skeletonized bolt handle; Limbsaver recoil pad; Invar pillars and spot bedding; match chamber and trigger; and button rifled, free-floating barrel
MSRP . . . . **Starting at $1349.00**

MESA LONG RANGE

Action: Bolt
Stock: Carbon fiber
Barrel: 24 in., 26 in., 27 in.
Sights: None
Weight: 8 lb. 14 oz.

Caliber: 6.5 Creedmoor, 6.5 PRC, .308 Win., .28 Nosler, 7mm Rem. Mag., .300 Win. Mag., .300 PRC, .338 Lapua Mag.
Magazine: 3, 4 rounds
Features: Stainless steel, medium Palma contour barrel that's hand lapped and button rifled; threaded-on seamless side-baffle brake in stainless steel; CA's own carbon-fiber composite long-range stock with spacer-adjustable comb; match chamber; spot bedding and Invar pillars; internal magazine with hinged floorplate; Trigger Tech trigger; twin-lug spiral fluted bolt and fluted bolt knob; dual ejectors in magnum calibers; M16-style extractor
MSRP **$1649.99**

MESA TITANIUM

Action: Bolt
Stock: Carbon fiber composite
Barrel: 22 in., 24 in.
Sights: None
Weight: 6 lb. 2 oz.
Caliber: 6.5 Creedmoor, 6.5 PRC, .308 Win., .300 Win. Mag., .28 Nosler, .300 PRC, 7mm Rem. Mag.
Magazine: 3, 4 rounds
Features: An upgraded Mesa with a titanium receiver; hand-lapped, free-floating, button-rifled, and threaded barrel with a featherweight contour, bead-blasted finish, and radial brake; match chamber; match-grade trigger; stock in gray metallic with black webbing
MSRP **$1949.00**

MODERN PRECISION RIFLE

Action: Bolt

Stock: Billet aluminum
Barrel: 16 in., 20 in., 22 in., 24 in., 26 in., 27 in.
Sights: None
Weight: 6 lb. 14 oz.–8 lb. 2 oz.
Caliber: .223 Rem., 6mm Creedmoor, 6.5 PRC, 6.5 Creedmoor, .308 Win., .300 Win. Mag., .300 PRC, .338 Lapua Mag.
Magazine: N/A
Features: 416 stainless steel barrel is carbon fiber wrapped; removable stainless side-baffle brake in a black nitride finish; barrel is hand lapped, button rifled and free floating; chassis is 7075 billet aluminum with an adjustable carbon fiber cheek riser and adjustable length of pull; six Q/D flush cup mounts; carbon fiber handguard with M-LOK; V-Block bedding; monopod mount ready via Picatinny rail; match chamber; skeletonized bolt handle; twin lug spiral fluted bolt; flat match-grade trigger; 20 MOA of rail
MSRP . . . . **Starting at $2499.00**

RANGER 22

Action: Bolt
Stock: Carbon fiber composite
Barrel: 18 in.
Sights: None
Weight: 5 lb. 2 oz.
Caliber: .22 LR
Magazine: 10 rounds
Features: An above-average rimfire with upgraded features such as Christensen Arms's own hand-lapped, threaded, carbon fiber tension barrel; Bentz match chamber; dual ejectors; stock in choice of black with gray webbing or tan with black webbing
MSRP **$849.99**

Christensen Arms

CHRISTENSEN ARMS RIDGELINE

CHRISTENSEN ARMS RIDGELINE TITANIUM

CHRISTENSEN ARMS SUMMIT TI

CHRISTENSEN ARMS TFM

CHRISTENSEN ARMS TRAVERSE

RIDGELINE

Action: Bolt
Stock: Hand-laid fiberglass with carbon fiber reinforced stock
Barrel: 20 in., 24 in., 26 in.
Sights: None
Weight: 6 lb. 5 oz.–6 lb. 11 oz.
Caliber: .22-250 Rem., 6.5 Creedmoor, 6.5 PRC, 6.5-284 Norma, .26 Nosler, .270 Win., .270 WSM, 7mm-08 Rem, .28 Nosler, .280 Ackley Improved, 7mm Rem. Mag., .308 Win., .30 Nosler, .30-06 Spfd., .300 RUM, .300 Win. Mag., .300 WSM, .300 PRC, .450 Bushmaster
Magazine: 4 rounds
Features: Carbon fiber–wrapped barrel; a spiral fluted bolt; scalloped bolt knob; dual front studs; SUB MOA accuracy; bedded recoil lug and invar pillar inserts; machined aluminum hinged floorplate
MSRP . . . . **Starting at $2099.99**

RIDGELINE TITANIUM

Action: Bolt
Stock: Carbon fiber composite
Barrel: 22 in., 24 in.
Sights: None
Weight: 5 lb. 13 oz.
Caliber: 6.5 Creedmoor, 6.5 PRC, .308 Win., .300 Win. Mag., .28 Nosler, .300 PRC, 7mm Rem. Mag.
Magazine: 3, 4 rounds
Features: The hot feature on this premium rifle is its aerograde carbon fiber–wrapped, button-rifled barrel with a titanium radial brake; stock in metallic gray with black webbing
MSRP $2599.99

SUMMIT TI

Action: Bolt
Stock: Aerograde carbon fiber
Barrel: 24 in.–27 in.
Sights: None
Weight: 5 lb. 8 oz.–6 lb.
Caliber: .25-06 Rem., 6.5 Creedmoor, 6.5 PRC, 6.5-284 Norma, .26 Nosler, .270 Win., .270 WSM, .28 Nosler, .280 Ackley Improved, 7mm Rem. Mag., .30-06 Spfd., .308 Win., .30 Nosler, .300 Win. Mag.
Magazine: 3 rounds
Features: 416R stainless steel, aerograde carbon fiber-wrapped barrel is hand lapped and button rifled and sports a removable radial titanium muzzle brake; trued receiver has integrated Picatinny rail; fully adjustable match trigger, Nitride-treated bolt with fluted knob, enlarged ejection port, full-length bedding with carbon fiber pillars are standard; sporter or thumbhole stock
MSRP $5999.99

TFM

Action: Bolt
Stock: Carbon fiber
Barrel: 16 in., 24 in., 26 in., 27 in.
Sights: None
Weight: 7 lb. 4 oz.
Caliber: 6mm Creedmoor, 6.5 Creedmoor, 6.5 PRC, .300 Win. Mag., .338 Lapua Mag., .300 PRC
Magazine: 3, 4 rounds
Features: Carbon fiber-wrapped barrel in a target profile; removable and adjustable titanium side-baffle brake; integrated 20 MOA Picatinny rail; fully adjustable match trigger; over-sized and fluted bolt knob; tactical mag release; AICS-compatible magazines; CA's carbon fiber long-range tactical stock with thumb-wheel adjustable comb and length of pull; modified beavertail forend, tactical grip with palm swell and thumb shelf; tactical hook; full-length bedding with carbon fiber pillars; nitride-treated, twin-lug, spiral-fluted bolt; dual ejector in magnum calibers; M16-style extractor; barrel is hand lapped, button rifled, free-floating, has a match chamber and a 5/8x24 threaded muzzle
MSRP $4999.99

TRAVERSE

Action: Bolt
Stock: Carbon fiber composite
Barrel: 24 in., 26 in.
Sights: None
Weight: 7 lb. 5 oz.–7 lb. 11 oz.
Caliber: .22–250 Rem., .243 Win., 6.5 Creedmoor, 6.5 PRC, 6.5–284, .26 Nosler, .270 Win., .270 WSM, 7mm-08 Rem., .280 Ackley Improved, .28 Nosler, 7mm Rem. Mag., .308 Win., .30-06 Spfd., .30 Nosler, .300 WSM, .300 Win. Mag., .300 RUM, .30 PRC, .338 Lapua Mag.
Magazine: 3 rounds
Features: Classically styled and thoroughly modern backcountry rifle with a carbon fiber composite stock with Monte Carlo profile; full palm swell; light target contour, hand-lapped, carbon fiber-wrapped, free-floating threaded barrel with match chamber and 4-inch bottom rail; skeletonized bolt with fluted bolt knob; 0 MOA top rail; Invar pillars; spot bedding; Limbsaver recoil pad; black/gray or green/black spiderweb finish on stock
MSRP $2549.99

Cimarron Firearms Co.

CIMARRON 1860 HENRY CIVILIAN

CIMARRON 1860 IRON FRAME HENRY

CIMARRON 1873 SADDLE RIFLE

CIMARRON FIREARMS COMPANY 1873 TRAPPER

CIMARRON 1876 CENTENNIAL

CIMARRON FIREARMS COMPANY 1876 CENTENNIAL TOM HORN

CIMARRON 1876 CROSSFIRE CARBINE

1860 HENRY CIVILIAN

Action: Lever
Stock: Walnut
Barrel: 24 in.
Sights: Open
Weight: 9 lb. 2 oz.
Caliber: .44 WCF, .45 LC
Magazine: Under-barrel tube, 12 rounds
Features: Reproduction of 1860 Civil War Henry rifle; includes military sling swivels; frame comes in charcoal blue or original finish
MSRP **$1676.21**

1860 IRON FRAME HENRY

Action: Lever
Stock: Walnut
Barrel: 24 in.
Sights: Ivory front blade, adjustable rear
Weight: 9 lb. 3 oz.
Caliber: .44 WCF, .45 LC
Magazine: 12 rounds
Features: An authentic reproduction any collector would be proud of, featuring case hardened frame; walnut stock; octagon barrel
MSRP **$1768.17**

1873 SADDLE RIFLE

Action: Lever
Stock: Wood
Barrel: 18 in.
Sights: Open
Weight: 8 lb.
Caliber: .357 Mag., .45 Colt, .44 WCF
Magazine: Fixed tube
Features: Full octagon barrel; straight stock with checkered forearm and stock
MSRP **$1575.21**

1873 TRAPPER

Action: Lever
Stock: Walnut
Barrel: 16 in.
Sights: Blade front, leaf rear
Weight: 7 lb. 2 oz.
Caliber: .44-40 (.44 WCF), .32-20 (.32 WCF), .45 LC
Magazine: 9 rounds
Features: Handy short-barreled lever with a straight stock in a polished finish; blued round barrel and magazine; choice of blued or case-colored receiver with blued barrel and magazine tube
Blued **$1529.85**
Case-colored **$1465.89**

1876 CENTENNIAL

Action: Lever
Stock: Walnut
Barrel: 28 in.
Sights: Open
Weight: 9 lb. 15 oz.–10 lb. 2 oz.
Caliber: .45-60, .50-95
Magazine: Under-barrel tube, 12 rounds
Features: Originally dubbed the "Centennial Model" because of its introduction during America's 100th anniversary of the Declaration of Independence from British rule, and featured at Philadelphia's Centennial Exposition, this enlarged version of the famed 1873 Winchester was designed to handle stronger loads than its predecessor; finished in a standard blue octagonal barrel, tubular magazine, barrel band and foreend, with a color case hardened receiver, lever, trigger, hammer and butt plate
MSRP . . . . **$1895.97–$1940.95**

1876 CENTENNIAL TOM HORN

Action: Lever single-shot
Stock: Walnut
Barrel: 28 in.
Sights: Blade front, aperture rear
Weight: 10 lb.
Caliber: .45-60
Magazine: 1 round
Features: Inspired by the movie Tom Horn starring Steve McQueen, this single-shot wears a polished blue finish; Tom Horn "signature" engraved on the receiver sideplate; storage in the stock accessed through the crescent buttplate; folding leaf rear for use when the user does not wish to employ the wrist-mounted aperture rear
MSRP **$2083.27**

1876 CROSSFIRE CARBINE

Action: Lever
Stock: Walnut
Barrel: 22 in.
Sights: None
Weight: 8 lb. 15 oz.
Caliber: .45-60, .45-75
Magazine: Under-barrel tube, 8 rounds
Features: Gun was glorified in the movie Crossfire Trail; case-hardened stock with standard blued finish
MSRP **$2133.37**

Cimarron Firearms Co.

CIMARRON 1885 HIGH WALL SPORTING RIFLE

CIMARRON 1886 RIFLE

CIMARRON 1894 CARBINE

CIMARRON 1894 RIFLE

CIMARRON MODEL 71 CLASSIC

1885 HIGH WALL SPORTING RIFLE

Action: Dropping block
Stock: Walnut, pistol grip
Barrel: 30 in.
Sights: Open
Weight: 9 lb. 4 oz.–10 lb. 6 oz.
Caliber: .38-55, .45-70
Magazine: None
Features: Reproduction of the Winchester single-shot hunting rifle popular in 1880s; standard blued finish on octagonal barrel; single- or double-set triggers
Standard $1405.45
Deluxe $1433.98

1886 RIFLE

Action: Lever
Stock: Walnut
Barrel: 26 in.
Sights: None
Weight: 8 lb.–9 lb.
Caliber: .45-70 Govt.

Magazine: Under-barrel tube, 7+1, 8+1 rounds
Features: Made by Armi Sport in Italy; color case-hardened receiver and buttplate; octagonal barrel; standard blued finish
Standard $1708.63
Deluxe . . . . $2114.97–$2252.87

1894 CARBINE

Action: Lever
Stock: Walnut
Barrel: 20 in.
Sights: Blade front, adjustable rear
Weight: N/A
Caliber: .30-30 Win., .38-55 Win.
Magazine: N/A
Features: Faithful to John Browning's original, with both calibers available in case-colored frame
MSRP $1324.70

1894 RIFLE

Action: Lever

Stock: Walnut
Barrel: 24.25 in., 26 in.
Sights: Blade front, adjustable rear
Weight: N/A
Caliber: .30-30 Win., .38-55 Win.
Magazine: N/A
Features: Identical to Cimarron's 1894 Carbine, though with a more pronounced crescent shape to the buttstock and with an appropriately longer barrel; .30-30 also available in all blue instead of case-hardened
MSRP . . . . $1393.00–$1506.44

MODEL 71 CLASSIC

Action: Lever
Stock: Walnut
Barrel: 24 in.
Sights: Open
Weight: 8 lb. 11 oz.
Caliber: .45-70 Gov't., .348 Win.
Magazine: Fixed tube
Features: Blued receiver; pistol grip stock
.45-70 Gov't. $1751.10
.348 Win. $1846.48
Premium .45-70 Gov't. $2199.83
Premium .348 Win. $2160.05

Citadel by Legacy Sports

CITADEL BY LEGACY SPORTS LEVTAC-92

CITADEL BY LEGACY SPORTS TRAKR .22 LR

LEVTAC-92

Action: Lever
Stock: Synthetic
Barrel: 18 in.
Sights: Blade front, peep rear
Weight: N/A
Caliber: .357 Mag., .44 Mag., .454 Casull
Magazine: 3, 4 rounds

Features: Super-handy and tough lever-action with an M-LOK handguard; topside Picatinny rail; oversized lever for gloved hands
MSRP $899.00

TRAKR .22 LR

Action: Semiautomatic
Stock: Synthetic
Barrel: 18 in.

Sights: Fiber optic front
Weight: N/A
Caliber: .22 LR
Magazine: 10 rounds
Features: Economical choice for plinking, fun competition, and even small game, this rifle gets a lightweight MSR-style stock and pistol grip
MSRP $369.00

Colt's Manufacturing Company

COLT M4 MONOLITHIC

COLT M4 TROOPER

M4 MONOLITHIC
Action: Semiautomatic
Stock: Combat-style, synthetic
Barrel: 16.1 in.
Sights: Flip-up front flip-up rear
Weight: 6 lb. 11 oz.
Caliber: 5.56 NATO
Magazine: Detachable box, 20, 30 rounds

Features: Incorporates a continuous Picatinny rail from the rear of the upper receiver to the front sight, free-floating chrome-line barrel, folding locking front sight, Magpul MBUS rear sight, integrated quad-rail; single-stage trigger, direct gas impingement system are standard
MSRP $1399.00

M4 TROOPER
Action: Semiautomatic
Stock: Synthetic
Barrel: 16.1 in.
Sights: None
Weight: 6 lb. 7 oz.
Caliber: 5.56 NATO
Magazine: 30 rounds
Features: Centurion free-floating fore-end M-Lok capable; 12 o'clock Picatinny rail; black M4 buttstock; black A2 pistol grip; Magpul P-Mag 30-round magazine
MSRP $1049.00

Connecticut Valley Arms (CVA)

CVA CASCADE

CVA SCOUT

CASCADE
Action: Bolt
Stock: Synthetic
Barrel: 18 in., 22 in.
Sights: None
Weight: N/A
Caliber: .243 Win., 6.5 Creedmoor, 7mm-08 Rem., .308 Win., .450 Bushmaster, .350 Legend, .22-250 Rem., 6.5 PRC, 7mm Rem. Mag., .300 Win. Mag., .300 BLK
Magazine: 3 roumds
Features: CVA's first centerfire bolt-action featuring a fiberglass-reinforced CVA stock in Veil Camo with Cascade Cerakote metalwork, in Veil Tac Black with Graphite Black Cerakote (short-barrel) or in charcoal gray with blued metalwork; 70-degree bolt throw; 4140 carbon steel barrel; flush-fit detachable box magazine; spacers for adjustable length of pull; dual front swivel studs; short-barrel model available in 6.5 Creedmoor, .308 Win., .300 BLK only
MSRP . . . . $566.95–$670.00

SCOUT, SCOUT COMPACT
Action: Break-open single-shot
Stock: Synthetic
Barrel: 20 in., 25 in.
Sights: None
Weight: 5 lb. 13 oz.
Caliber: .444 Marlin, .44 Mag., .45-70 Gov't., .450 Bushmaster, .35 Whelen, .243 Win., .300 BLK, 7mm-09 Rem., 6.5 Creedmoor, .350 Legend
Magazine: N/A
Features: Fluted stainless steel barrel; ambidextrous stock; reversible hammer spur; CrushZone recoil pad; black stock with stainless steel barrel; some models available with factory-mounted Konus 3–9x40mm scope; DF muzzlebrake on unscoped model, scoped model available with or without muzzlebrake
MSRP . . . . $348.95–$418.95

Cooper Firearms of Montana

COOPER FIREARMS MODEL 21 VARMINT EXTREME

MODEL 21 CLASSIC
Action: Bolt
Stock: AA Claro Walnut
Barrel: 24 in.
Sights: None
Weight: 6 lb.–7 lb. 12 oz.

Caliber: .17 Fireball, .17 Rem., .20 VarTag, .20 Tactical, .204 Ruger, .221 Fireball, .22 Rem., .222 Rem. Mag., .222 Rem., .223 Rem. AI,.300 BLK
Features: Hand-rubbed oil-finished stock with four-panel hand checker-ing, Pachmayer recoil pad, chrome-moly premium match grade Wilson Arms barrel, steel grip cap are standard
Right-hand $3325.00
Left-hand $3575.00

Cooper Firearms of Montana

COOPER FIREARMS MODEL 21
VARMINTER (LAMINATE STOCK)

COOPER FIREARMS MODEL 51

COOPER FIREARMS MODEL 52 WESTERN CLASSIC

COOPER FIREARMS MODEL 57-M CLASSIC

COOPER FIREARMS MODEL 52
TIMBERLINE

MODEL 22 CLASSIC

Action: Bolt
Stock: AA Claro Walnut
Barrel: N/A
Sights: None
Weight: N/A
Caliber: .More than 30 calibers available, from .22 BR to .338 Federal
Magazine: None
Features: Hand-rubbed oil-finished stock with four-panel hand checkering, Pachmayer recoil pad, chrome-moly premium match grade Wilson Arms barrel, steel grip cap are standard
Right-hand: **$3325.00**
Left-hand: **$3575.00**

MODEL 51

Action: Bolt
Stock: AA Claro Walnut
Barrel: 24 in.
Sights: None
Weight: 6 lb. –7 lb. 12 oz.
Caliber: .17 Rem., .20 Tactical, .204 Ruger, .222 Rem., .223 Rem., .223 Rem. AI
Magazine: None
Features: Longer barrel standard on all varmint models; fully adjustable single-stage trigger; Sako style extraction machined from solid bar stock
Right-hand **$3325.00**
Left-hand **$3575.00**

MODEL 52 TIMBERLINE

Action: Bolt
Stock: Composite
Barrel: N/A
Sights: None
Weight: 7 lb.
Caliber: Thirty-five calibrs available

ranging from .240 Wby. Mag. to .340 Wby. Mag.
Magazine: N/A
Features: Cooper's own carbon-fiber and Kevlar reinforced composite stock in black with tan webbing; semi-vertical grip; palm swell; raised comb; adjustable single-stage trigger; spiral-fluted three-lug bolt; muzzle brake
Right-hand **$3295.00**
Left-hand **$3545.00**

MODEL 52 WESTERN CLASSIC

Action: Bolt
Stock: AAA+ Claro Walnut
Barrel: 24 in.
Sights: None
Weight: 6 lb. 12 oz.–8 lb.
Caliber: More than 30 calibers available from .257 Wtby. Mag. to .375 H&H
Magazine: 3 rounds
Features: Stock has shadowline beaded cheekpiece, African ebony tip, and western fleur wraparound checkering. Steel grip cap, sling swivels, and case coloring on selected metal work are standard
Right-hand **$5495.00**
Left-hand **$5745.00**

MODEL 54 CLASSIC

Action: Bolt
Stock: AA Claro Walnut
Barrel: 24 in.

Sights: None
Weight: 6 lb.–7 lb. 12 oz.
Caliber: .22-250 Rem., .22-250 AI, .220 Swift, .243 Win., .243 Win. AI, 6mm Rem., 6mm Creedmoor, .250 Savage, .250 Savage AI, .257 Roberts, .257 Roberts AI, 6.5 Creedmoor, 6.5x47 Lapua, .260 Rem., 7mm-08, .308 Win., .338 Federal, .358 Win.
Magazine: 3 rounds
Features: Three-rear locking lug bolt action magazine fed repeater; centerfire action, also available in stainless steel; Sako style extraction machined from solid bar stock; plunger style ejector machined form solid bar; fully adjustable single-stage trigger
Right-hand **$3325.00**
Left-hand **$3575.00**

MODEL 57-M CLASSIC

Action: Bolt
Stock: AA Claro walnut
Barrel: 24 in,
Sights: None
Weight: 6 lb.–7 lb. 12 oz.
Caliber: .17 HMR, .22 LR, .22 WMR
Magazine: 4, 5 rounds
Features: Hand-rubbed oil-finished stock with four-panel hand checkering, Pachmayer recoil pad, chrome-moly premium match grade Wilson Arms barrel, steel grip cap are standard
Right-hand **$3475.00**
Left-hand **$3725.00**

Cooper Firearms of Montana

COOPER FIREARMS EXCALIBUR

COOPER FIREARMS MODEL 92 BACKCOUNTRY

MODEL 92 BACKCOUNTRY
Action: Bolt
Stock: Composite
Barrel: 24 in.
Sights: None
Weight: 5 lb. 12 oz.
Caliber: All standard long-action calibers and magnums up to .340 Wby. Mag.
Magazine: 3 rounds
Features: Lightweight Cooper Model 92 all-stainless steel action (Chromoly available on request); detachable magazine; Jewell trigger; Wilson Arms fluted barrel with muzzle brake; guaranteed ½-MOA accuracy
Right-hand $3955.00
Left-hand $4205.00

MODEL TRP-3
Action: Bolt
Stock: Wood; synthetic
Barrel: 26 in.
Sights: None
Weight: 8 lb.
Magazine: N/A
Caliber: A wide variety of calibers across three Cooper platforms
Features: Available in the Model 21, Model 22, and Model 57-M platforms; choice of wood or synthetic stock; adjustable single-stage trigger; matte stainless steel barrel with straight taper
Model 21 . . . .$4045.00
Model 22 . . . .$4045.00
Model 57-M $3355.00

"VARIATIONS"

1. Classic
AA Claro walnut; steel grip; four-panel hand checkering; oil finish; matte metal finish; no options; available in all Cooper models

2. Custom Classic
AAA Claro walnut stock, shadowline beaded cheekpiece, African ebony tip, and western fleur wraparound checkering; sling swivel studs and chorome-moly premium match-grade Wilson Arms barrel are standard; all metal work has high gloss finish; available in all models

3. Excalibur
Hand-laid synthetics with Kevlar reinforcing material surrounding an aircraft-grade aluminum bedding block. Spiral fluted bolt, chrome-moly premium match grade Wilson Arms fluted barrel are standard; all metal work is matte finish; available for models 51, 52, and 54

4. Jackson Game
AA+ Claro walnut stock, rollover cheekpiece, semi-beavertail forearm. VE hand checkered grip in crossover multi-point pattern; stainless steel premium match grade Wilson Arms barrel; laminate version available; available for Models 51, 52, and 54

5. Jackson Hunter
Hand-laid synthetics with Kevlar reinforcing material surrounding an aircraft-grade aluminum bedding block; stainless steel premium match grade Wilson Arms barrel is standard; all metal work is matte finish; available for models 51, 52, 54, and 57-M

6. Jackson Squirrel
AA+ Claro walnut stock with rollover cheekpiece and semi-beavertail forearm. Grip has VE hand checkering in a crossover multi-point pattern; stainless steel premium match Wilson Arms barrel; also available in laminate; all metal work is matte finish; available in Model 57-M only

7. Mannlicher
AAA+ Claro walnut, shadowline beaded cheekpiece, African ebony tip, western fleur wraparound hand checking, chrome-moly premium match grade Wilson Arms octagonal barrel; all metal work is high gloss finish; available in all models

8. Montana Varminter
AA+ Claro walnut stock, hand-check-

ered grip, stainless steel straight taper premium match grade Wilson Arms barrel; all metal work is matte finish; available in models 21, 22, 38, 51, 52, 54, and 57-M

9. Phoenix
Hand-laid synthetics with Kevlar reinforcing material surrounding an aircraft-grade aluminum bedding block; spiral fluted bolt, chrome-moly premium match grade Wilson Arms fluted barrel are standard; all metal work is matte finish; available for models 21, 22, 38, 51, 54; left-hand options only in models 21 and 38

10. Schnabel
Available in models 52, 54, 56, and 57; AA+ Claro walnut; raised comb; slim taper forearm; multi-point two panel hand checkering; oil finish; standard grade sling swivel studs; Pachmayr pad; steel grip cap; chromoly premium match grade barrel; metal work is matte finished; available in Models 51, 52, 54, 57-M, 58, and muzzleloader

11. Varminter
AA Claro walnut stock, hand checkered grip, stainless steel straight taper premium match grade Wilson Arms barrel; all metal work is matte finish; available in Models 21, 22, 38, 51, 52, 54, and 57-M

12. Varmint Extreme
AAA Claro walnut stock, hand checkered grip in a crossover western fleur pattern; stainless steel straight taper matte finish premium match grade Wilson Arms barrel; all blued steel is high gloss finish; available in models 21, 22, 38, 51, 52, 54, and 57-M

13. Western Classic
AAA+ Claro walnut, shadowline beaded cheekpiece, African ebony tip, western fleur wraparound hand checking, chrome-moly premium match grade Wilson Arms octagonal barrel; all metal work is high gloss finish, selected metal work is highlighted with case coloring

RIFLES

CZ-USA (Ceska Zbrojovka)

CZ-USA 457 AMERICAN

CZ-USA 457 AMERICAN COMBO

CZ-USA 457 JAGUAR

CZ-USA 457 LUX

CZ-USA 457 PREMIUM

CZ-USA 457 PRO VARMINT SUPPRESSOR-READY

CZ-USA 457 ROYAL

CZ-USA 457 SCOUT

CZ-USA 457 VARMINT

457 AMERICAN
Action: Bolt
Stock: Turkish walnut
Barrel: 24.8 in.
Sights: None
Weight: 6 lb. 3 oz.
Caliber: .22 LR, .17 HMR, .22 WMR
Magazine: 5 rounds
Features: Classically styled, walnut-stocked rimfire with a cold hammer-forged barrel; integral 11mm dovetail scope mount cutouts; detachable magazine
MSRP $569.00

457 AMERICAN COMBO
Action: Bolt
Stock: Turkish walnut
Barrel: 24.8 in.
Sights: None
Weight: 6 lb. 2 oz.
Caliber: .22 LR/.17 HMR
Magazine: 5 rounds
Features: A nimble, pretty rimfire in two-caliber combo featuring a Turkish walnut stock; detachable magazine; cold hammer forged barrel; adjustable trigger; 60-degree bolt rotation
MSRP $725.00

457 JAGUAR
Action: Bolt
Stock: Beechwood
Barrel: 28.6 in.
Sights: Adjustable iron
Weight: 6 lb. 6 oz.
Caliber: .22 LR
Magazine: 10 rounds
Features: Wearing a stock in the European style, this rimfire features a fully adjustable trigger
MSRP $645.00

457 LUX
Action: Bolt
Stock: Turkish walnut

Barrel: 24.8 in.
Sights: Hooded front, tangent adjustable rear
Weight: 6 lb. 3 oz.
Caliber: .22 LR, .17 HMR, .22 WMR
Magazine: 5 rounds
Features: A rimfire with a European flair; detachable box magazine; fully adjustable trigger; 60-degree bolt rotation for easier scope use; swappable barrel system
MSRP $605.00

457 PREMIUM
Action: Bolt
Stock: Turkish walnut
Barrel: 24.8 in.
Sights: Adjustable tangent
Weight: 6 lb. 6 oz.
Caliber: .22 LR
Magazine: 5 rounds
Features: With a European-styled stock in Turkish walnut, this rimfire features adjustable tangent sights; adjustable trigger; detachable magazine; 60-degree bolt rotation; threaded muzzle
MSRP $879.00

457 PRO VARMINT SUPPRESSOR-READY
Action: Bolt
Stock: Laminate
Barrel: 16.5 in.
Sights: None
Weight: 7 lb. 4 oz.
Caliber: .22 LR
Magazine: 5 rounds
Features: A short-barreled, suppressor-ready rifle for small varmints: detachable box magazine; laminate stock with black paint; fully adjustable trigger; barrel threaded ½X28
MSRP $679.00

457 ROYAL
Action: Bolt
Stock: Turkish walnut
Barrel: 16.5 in., 20.5 in.
Sights: None
Weight: 5 lb. 15 oz.–6 lb. 2 oz.
Caliber: .22 LR
Magazine: 5 rounds
Features: Specifically designed for scope use, this rimfire has an adjustable trigger
MSRP $849.00

457 SCOUT
Action: Bolt
Stock: Beechwood
Barrel: 16.5 in.
Sights: Skeletonized hooded blade front, leaf rear
Weight: 5 lb.
Caliber: .22 LR
Magazine: 1 round
Features: A youth rifle with a 12-inch length of pull; ½X28 threaded muzzle for suppressor use; modular 457 platform; single-shot adaptor, but accepts all 457/455 magazines; American style beechwood stock; adjustable trigger
MSRP $525.00

457 VARMINT
Action: Bolt
Stock: Turkish walnut
Barrel: 20.5 in.
Sights: None
Weight: 7 lb. 1 oz.
Caliber: .22 LR, .17 HMR, .22 WMR
Magazine: 5 rounds
Features: A maneuverable varmint rifle with: heavy barrel profile; detachable box magazine; swappable barrel system; 60-degree bolt rotation for easier use with optics; laser-cut stippling
MSRP $625.00

CZ-USA (Ceska Zbrojovka)

CZ-USA 457 VARMINT AT-ONE

CZ-USA 457 VARMINT MTR

CZ-USA 457 VARMINT PRECISION CHASSIS

CZ-USA 457 VARMINT PRECISION TRAINER CAMO

CZ-USA 512 SEMI-AUTOMATIC

CZ-USA BREN 2 MS CARBINE

CZ-USA SCORPION BULLPUP CARBINE KIT

CZ–USA SCORPION EVO 3 S1 CARBINE

457 VARMINT AT-ONE

Action: Bolt
Stock: Laminate
Barrel: 16.5 in., 24 in.
Sights: None
Weight: 7 lb. 12 oz.
Caliber: .22 LR
Magazine: 5 rounds
Features: A varmint-getter made to fit with a Boyd's AT-ONE laminate stock adjustable at cheekpiece and for length of pull; swappable barrel system; fully adjustable trigger
MSRP $759.00

457 VARMINT MTR

Action: Bolt
Stock: Turkish walnut
Barrel: 20.5 in.
Sights: None
Weight: 7 lb. 1 oz.
Caliber: .22 LR
Magazine: 5 rounds
Features: A rock-steady small-varmint or paper-puncher gun- (MTR = Match Target Rifle) with a handsome target-style stock of Turkish walnut; fully adjustable trigger; detachable box magazine; match chamber; heavy barrel profile; flat fore-end; dual QD studs front, single rear
MSRP $865.00

457 VARMINT PRECISION CHASSIS

Action: Bolt
Stock: Aluminum chassis
Barrel: 16.5 in., 24 in.
Sights: None
Weight: 7 lb.
Caliber: .22 LR
Magazine: 5 rounds
Features: A suppressor-ready rimfire with a chassis foundation for serious competition; fully adjustable trigger;

heavy cold hammer forged barrel; adjustable Luth-AR stock; AR-style grip; multiple M-LOK slots; QD sling pockets
MSRP $1149.00

457 VARMINT PRECISION TRAINER CAMO

Action: Bolt
Stock: Composite
Barrel: 16.5, 20.5 in., 24 in.
Sights: None
Weight: 7 lb. 2 oz.–7 lb. 9 oz.
Caliber: .22 LR
Magazine: 5 rounda
Features: A dedicated rimfire training rifle or small-game getter with a Manners carbon-fiber/fiberglass composite stock in a three-color camo; ½X28 threaded barrel; swappable barrel system
MSRP $1315.00

512 SEMI-AUTOMATIC

Action: Semiautomatic
Stock: Lacquered beech wood
Barrel: 20.7 in.
Sights: Adjustable
Weight: 5 lb. 14 oz.
Caliber: .22 WMR
Magazine: Detachable box, 5 rounds
Features: Aluminum alloy upper receiver and fiberglass reinforced polymer lower half; dual guide rods; hammer-forged CZ barrel; integral 11mm dovetail for mounting optics
MSRP $549.00

BREN 2 MS CARBINE

Action: Semiautomatic
Stock: Synthetic
Barrel: 26.5 in.
Sights: None
Weight: 7 lb. 5 oz.
Caliber: .223 Rem.
Magazine: 30 rounds

Features: Based off the original select-fire Bren 2, this semiautomatic has a manual safety; folding adjustable stock; aluminum upper; carbon-fiber composite lower; Ms designation stands for modular forearm
MSRP $2259.00

SCORPION BULLPUP CARBINE KIT

Action: Semiautomatic
Stock: Synthetic
Barrel: Less than 16 in.
Sights: None
Weight: N/A
Caliber: 9mm
Magazine: N/A
Features: Fun bullpup in you-build-it kit form; short-barreled firearm requires appropriate tax stamps and Class III paperwork
MSRP $399.00

SCORPION EVO 3 S1 CARBINE

Action: Semiautomatic
Stock: Synthetic
Barrel: 16.2 in.
Sights: Low-profile fully adjustable aperture and post, 4 rear aperture sizes
Weight: 7 lb.
Caliber: 9mm
Magazine: 10 or 30 rounds
Features: 16.2 in. barrel fitted with either a compensating muzzle brake or a faux suppressor built specifically for CZ-USA by SilencerCo; newly designed forend covered in M-LOK attachment points to keep the profile slim while still being big enough to swallow most pistol-caliber suppressors; top Picatinny rail; low-profile aluminum adjustable sights; ambidextrous controls; swappable non-reciprocating charging handle; adjustable trigger
MSRP . . . . $1429.00–$1499.00

DAMKO MARTINI RIFLE PEEP SIGHT

DAMKO MARTINI RIFLE STANDARD

DAMKO MARTINI RIFLE SCOPE VERSION

MARTINI RIFLE PEEP SIGHT

Action: Single-shot Martini falling block
Stock: Walnut
Barrel: 20 in., 24 in.
Sights: Hooded bead front, threaded rear peep
Weight: N/A
Caliber: .25–35 Win., .30–30 Win., .30–40 Krag, .44 Rem. Mag.
Magazine: 1 round
Features: All the features of the standard Martini, with the addition of DAMKO's own peep sight with a 12–40 thread
MSRP $1956.99

MARTINI RIFLE SCOPE VERSION

Action: Single-shot Martini falling block
Stock: Walnut
Barrel: 20 in., 26 in.
Sights: None
Weight: N/A
Caliber: .25–35 Win., .30–30 Win., .30–40 Krag, .44 Rem. Mag.
Magazine: 1 round
Features: An original take on the Martini rifle with a flat-top PAC-NOR barrel mounted with DAMKO's own cantilever scope mount base
MSRP $2059.99

MARTINI RIFLE STANDARD

Action: Single-shot Martini falling block
Stock: Walnut
Barrel: 20 in., 24 in.
Sights: Hooded bead front, tangent-adjustable flat-top rear
Weight: N/A
Caliber: .25–35 Win., .30–30 Win., .30–40 Krag, .44 Rem. Mag.
Magazine: 1 round
Features: An updated take on a classic Martini falling block action in four popular calibers; .44 Rem. Mag with 20-inch barrel, all others 24 inches; steel butt plate; Chromoly Pac-Nor barrel
MSRP $1853.99

Daniel Defense

DANIEL DEFENSE DDM4ISR

DANIEL DEFENSE DDM4 PDW SBR

DANIEL DEFENSE DD5 V3

DDM4ISR

Action: Semiautomatic
Stock: Synthetic
Barrel: 9 in.
Sights: None
Weight: 7 lb. 9 oz.
Caliber: .300 BLK
Magazine: DD magazine
Features: Integrally suppressed weapon system optimized for the .300 BLK cartridge; cold-hammer-forged barrel is fluted, has a target crown; standard pistol length gas system; direct impingement; MFR XL 15.0 rail with KeyMod attachments on sides and bottom; Mil-Spec with enhanced flared magwell; rear receiver QD swivel attachment point;

available in black, Deep Woods, or Mil Spec+
MSRP $3390.00

DDM4 PDW SBR

Action: Semiautomatic
Stock: Synthetic
Barrel: 7 in.
Sights: None
Weight: 5 lb. 11 oz.
Caliber: .300 BLK
Magazine: 30 rounds
Features: Super-compact SBR—short-barreled rifle—featuring a Maxim Defense CQB Gen 7 stock; 6-in. MFR flat front rail; carbine-length gas system
MSRP $2092.00

DD5 V3

Action: Semiautomatic
Stock: Synthetic
Barrel: 16 in.
Sights: None
Weight: 8 lb. 5 oz.
Caliber: .308 Win.
Magazine: 20 rounds
Features: Ample .308 power in a nimble configuration that includes dual ejectors; super-finished DLC-coated bolt carrier group; proprietary chrome-lined barrel; four-bolt connection system; GRIP-N-RIP independent and ambidextrous charging handle; adjustable gas block in an intermediate-length gas system
MSRP $2599.00

Daniel Defense

DANIEL DEFENSE DD5 V4

DANIEL DEFENSE DD5 V5

DANIEL DEFENSE DDM4 HUNTER

DANIEL DEFENSE DDM4V4S

DANIEL DEFENSE DDM4V7

DANIEL DEFENSE DDM4V7 PRO

DANIEL DEFENSE DDM4V7 S

DANIEL DEFENSE DDM4V9

DD5 V4

Action: Semiautomatic
Stock: Synthetic
Barrel: 18 in.
Sights: None
Weight: 8 lb. 10 oz.
Caliber: 6.5 Creedmoor, .308 Win.
Magazine: 20 rounds
Features: Similar to the DD5 V3, but with a slightly longer barrel, a couple more ounces, and a rifle-length gas system; in black or Mil Spec+ choice of finishes
MSRP . . . .$2599.00–$2779.00

DD5 V5

Action: Semiautomatic
Stock: Synthetic
Barrel: 18 in.
Sights: None
Weight: 8 lb. 10 oz.
Caliber: 6.5 Creedmoor, .260 Rem.
Magazine: 20 rounds
Features: Super-finished DLC-coated bolt carrier group; dual ejectors; proprietary chrome-lined barrel; four-bolt connection system; GRIP-N-RIP independent and ambidextrous charging handle; threaded muzzle; both calibers available in black, 6.5 Creedmoor also available in Mil Spec+ finish
MSRP . . . .$2599.00–$2779.00

DDM4 HUNTER

Action: Semiautomatic
Stock: Glass-filled polymer
Barrel: 16 in.
Sights: None
Weight: 6 lb. 8 oz.
Caliber: 5.56 NATO, .300 BLK, 6.8 SPC
Magazine: 5 rounds
Features: Lightweight and nimble, this rifle clad in Kryptek Highlander camo gets a mil-spec upper and lower; flared magwell; mid-length direct impingement gas system; pinned low-profile gas block; H buffer; staked gas key; Grip-N-Rip charging handle; soft-touch overmolding on stock and pistol grip; DD MFR 15-in rail with M-LOK points; takes PRI magazines
MSRP . . . . $1946.00–$2024.00

DDM4V4S

Action: Semiautomatic
Stock: Synthetic
Barrel: 11.5 in.
Sights: None
Weight: 5 lb. 14 oz.
Caliber: 5.56 NATO
Magazine: Detachable box, 30 rounds
Features: Lightweight, ergonomic rail system affords ample room for multiple accessories and offers the longest possible sight radius with iron sights; three removable high-temperature-resistant Daniel Defense Rail Panels; compatibility with a wide variety of muzzle devices and sound suppressors; free-floating, cold hammer-forged barrel
MSRP $1975.00

DDM4V7

Action: Semiautomatic
Stock: Synthetic
Barrel: 16 in.
Sights: None
Weight: 6 lb. 3 oz.
Caliber: 5.56 NATO
Magazine: Detachable box, 30 rounds
Features: M-LOK attachment technology with Daniel Defense MFR XS 15.0 rail; DD improved flash suppressor; mid-length gas system; uninterrupted 1913 Picatinny rail; black, Deep Woods, Daniel Defense Tornado or Mil Spec+ choice of finishes
MSRP . . . . $1870.00–$2057.00

DDM4V7 PRO

Action: Semiautomatic
Stock: Synthetic
Barrel: 18 in.
Sights: None
Weight: 7 lb. 6.4 oz.

DDM4V4S

Caliber: 5.56 NATO
Magazine: DD magazine
Features: Designed for multi-gun competitors; 18-in. Strength-to-Weight (S2W), cold-hammer-forged barrel; rifle-length direct impingement gas system; Muzzle Climb Mitigator; Geissele Automatics Super Dynamic 3 Gun trigger; MFR XS 15.0 rail with M-LOK attachment system; Grip-N-Rip charging handle; glass-filled polymer stock with soft-touch overmolding; in black or Rattlecan finish
MSRP . . . . $2162.00–$2259.00

DDM4V7 S

Action: Semiautomatic
Stock: Synthetic
Barrel: 11.5 in.
Sights: None
Weight: 5 lb. 9.6 oz.
Caliber: 5.56 NATO
Magazine: DD magazine
Features: Short-barreled rifle featuring M-LOK attachment technology; free-floating, cold-hammer-forged barrel; carbine-length gas system; free-floating MFR XS 10.0 rail; M-LOK attachment points that run along seven positions; uninterrupted 1913 Picatinny rail on top
MSRP $1870.00

DDM4V9

Action: Semiautomatic
Stock: Synthetic
Barrel: 16 in.
Sights: None
Weight: 6 lb. 10 oz.
Caliber: 5.56 NATO
Magazine: Detachable box, 30 rounds
Features: Daniel Defense glass-filled polymer stock, pistol and vertical grips; rail panels of Santoprene heat-resistant to 300-degrees; flash suppressor; H buffer; mid-length direct impingement system; M4 rail; Grip-N-Rip charging handle; adjustable six-position buttstock; upper and lower Type III hard-coat anodized
MSRP $1979.00

RIFLES

Daniel Defense

DANIEL DEFENSE DELTA 5

DANIEL DEFENSE DELTA 5 ACCURACY PACKAGE

DANIEL DEFENSE DELTA 5 PRO HPALMA

DANIEL DEFENSE DELTA 5 PRO VARMINT

DELTA 5

Action: Bolt
Stock: Synthetic
Barrel: 20 in., 24 in.
Sights: None
Weight: 8 lb. 15 oz.–9 lb. 8 oz.
Caliber: .308 Win., 6.5 Creedmoor
Magazine: 5 rounds
Features: DD's first bolt-action featuring a user-interchangeable stainless steel barrel; bedded stainless steel action with integral recoil lug; removeable bolt knob; carbon fiber-reinforced stock adjustable for length of pull and height; 11 M-LOK points on the fore-end, one on the buttstock, and three M-LOK sling points; AICS single-feed mag compatible; adjustable Timney Elite Hunter trigger, single-stage with two-position safety
MSRP **$1871.00**

DELTA 5 ACCURACY PACKAGE

Action: Bolt
Stock: Synthetic

Barrel: 24 in.
Sights: None
Weight: 11 lb. 13 oz.
Caliber: 6.5 Creedmoor
Magazine: 5 rounds
Features: Daniel Defense builds on the success of the Delta 5 with an upgraded package that includes a Nightforce SHV 4-14X50 scope; Atlas bipod; heavy Palma barrel profile
MSRP **$3744.00**

DELTA 5 PRO HPALMA

Action: Bolt
Stock: Chassis
Barrel: 24 in.
Sights: None
Weight: 11 lb. 6 oz.
Caliber: 6.5 Creedmoor
Magazine: 10 rounds
Features: Interchangeable barrel in a heavy Palma profile and with a Cerakote finish; Area 419 Hellfire muzzle brake; Timney Elite Hunter adjustable single-stage trigger; chassis base; interchangeable AR-15 grip attachment; adjustable left/right thumb rest; three-lug bolt with removable bolt knob; 10 quick-detach sling points; six M-LOK attachment points

on forend, one on buttstock bottom; adjustable buttstock and cheekpiece; 20 MOA Picatinny rail
Black: **$2499.00**
Cerakote color: **$2673.00**

DELTA 5 PRO VARMINT

Action: Bolt
Stock: Chassis
Barrel: 26 in.
Sights: None
Weight: 13.3 lb.
Caliber: 6.5 Creedmoor, 6mm Creedmoor
Magazine: 10 rounds
Features: A varmint gun with a chassis foundation; interchangeable barrels; Area 419 Hellfire muzzle brake; three-lug bolt with removable bolt knob; 20 MOA Picatinny scope base; 10 M-LOK quick-detach sling points; integral ARCA lock along entire lower rail; interchangeable AR-15 grip attachment; left/right adjustable thumb rest; tool-less adjustable cheekpiece ad buttstock; single-stage adjustable Timney Elite Hunter trigger; in black or Cerakote olive drab or coyote tan
Black: **$2499.00**
Cerakote color: **$2673.00**

Dark Storm Industries

DARK STORM INDUSTRIES DS1 VARIANT 1 FEATURELESS

DARK STORM INDUSTRIES DS1 VARIANT 1 FIXED MAGAZINE RIFLE

DS1 VARIANT 1 FEATURELESS

Action: Semiautomatic
Stock: Synthetic
Barrel: 16 in.
Sights: None
Weight: N/A
Caliber: 5.56 NATO
Magazine: 10 rounds
Features: Featureless version fits the bill with a weird but workable stock; 7075 aluminum billet receiver set;

deburred edges; M4 feed ramp extensions; winter trigger guard; 90-degree ambidextrous safety selector; 9-in. narrow-profile M-LOK forearm; in black or tungsten finishes
Black: **$1595.00**
Tungsten: **$1695.00**

DS1 VARIANT 1 FIXED MAGAZINE RIFLE

Action: Semiautomatic
Stock: Synthetic
Barrel: 16 in.

Sights: None
Weight: N/A
Caliber: 5.56 NATO
Magazine: 10 rounds
Features: Similar to the Featureless model, but with a Magpul CTR adjustable stock and a fixed magazine; Dark Storm says this rifle is legal to own in all 50 states; in a tungsten or black finish
Black: **$1595.00**
Tungsten: **$1695.00**

Dark Storm Industries

DARK STORM INDUSTRIES DS1 VARIANT 1 NON-NFA FIREARM

DARK STORM INDUSTRIES DS1 VARIANT 1 POST-BAN

DARK STORM INDUSTRIES DS1 VARIANT 1 RIFLE

DS1 VARIANT 1 NON-NFA FIREARM
Action: Semiautomatic
Stock: Synthetic
Barrel: 12.5 in.
Sights: None
Weight: N/A
Caliber: 5.56 NATO
Magazine: 10, 30 rounds
Features: Dark Storm says this is not a rifle, not a pistol, and not an AOW—any other weapon. It also says it fails to qualify as an "assault weapon" under CT and NJ law, but it is not currently legal to own this firearm in MA, NY, CA, or MD.; in black or tungsten finishes
Black:.................**$1595.00**
Tungsten:..............**$1695.00**

DS1 VARIANT 1 POST-BAN
Action: Semiautomatic
Stock: Synthetic
Barrel: 16 in.
Sights: None
Weight: N/A
Caliber: 5.56 NATO
Magazine: 10 rounds
Features: Similar to the Featureless model, but with a Magpul fixed carbine stock; DSI Competition Compensator; carbine gas system; steel micro gas block; optics ready; in black or tungsten finishes
Black:.................**$1595.00**
Tungsten:..............**$1695.00**

DS1 VARIANT 1 RIFLE
Action: Semiautomatic
Stock: Synthetic
Barrel: 16 in.
Sights: None
Weight: N/A
Caliber: 5.56 NATO
Magazine: 30 rounds
Features: No AR restrictions to worry about? Then this is the Dark Storm rifle for you with a carbine gas system; threaded barrel; DSI competition compensator; Magpul CTR adjustable stock; optic ready design; ambidextrous sling; ambidextrous 90-degree safety selector; ambidextrous charging handle; winter trigger guar; in black or tungsten finishes; HBAR variant available
Black:.................**$1595.00**
Tungsten:..............**$1695.00**

Davide Pedersoli & C.

DAVIDE PEDERSOLI 1874 SHARPS OLD WEST

DAVIDE PEDERSOLI 1886 HUNTER LIGHT

DAVIDE PEDERSOLI 1886 SPORTING CLASSIC

1874 SHARPS OLD WEST MAPLE
Action: Dropping block
Stock: Maple
Barrel: 30 in.
Sights: None
Weight: 11 lb. 7 oz.
Caliber: .45-70 Govt.
Magazine: None
Features: Optional Creedmoor and tunnel sights; brass plate on right side of butt stock can be personalized; forend has wedge plates; pistol grip cap is made of hardened steel
MSRP.................**$2560.00**

1886 HUNTER LIGHT
Action: Lever
Stock: Walnut
Barrel: 22 in.
Sights: Ramped front, buckhorn rear
Weight: 7 lb. 2 oz.
Caliber: .45-70 Govt., .444 Marlin
Magazine: 3 rounds
Features: Lighter, shorter version of standard 1886 lever-action; designed to accommodate a left side-mounted Creedmoor sight; barrel is broach rifled; sling swivels included
.45-70: **$1885.00**
.444 Marlin: **$1935.00**

1886 SPORTING CLASSIC
Action: Lever
Stock: American walnut
Barrel: 26 in.
Sights: Blade front sight, semi-buckhorn rear
Weight: 9 lb. 4 oz.
Caliber: .45-70 Gov't.
Magazine: 8 rounds
Features: Straight English stock of American walnut; case hardened receiver; blued round barrel; crescent buttplate; receiver can accept a peep sight
MSRP.................**$2110.00**

Davide Pedersoli & C.

DAVIDE PEDERSOLI
KODIAK MARK IV

DAVIDE PEDERSOLI MODEL 86/71
LEVER ACTION BOARBUSTER CAMO

DAVIDE PEDERSOLI MODEL
86/71 BOARBUSTER MARK II

DAVIDE PEDERSOLI MODEL
86/71 LEVER ACTION CLASSIC

DAVIDE PEDERSOLI MODEL 86/71
LEVER ACTION STAINLESS STEEL

DAVIDE PEDERSOLI MODEL 86/71
LEVER ACTION WILDBUSTER

KODIAK MARK IV
Action: Breech loading
Stock: Walnut
Barrel: 22 in., 24 in.
Sights: Open
Weight: 9 lb. 11 oz.–10 lb. 5 oz.
Caliber: .450 NE, .45-70 Govt.
8x57JRS, 9.3x74R
Magazine: None
Features: Double-leave rear sight in a dovetail; tapered round barrels made of blued steel; select walnut stock with checkering and oil finish; available with an interchangeable 20-gauge barrel in all calibers except the .450 NE
Rifle calibers
   only: . . . . **$6665.00–$8935.00**
With 20-gauge
   barrel: . . . . . . **$9050.00–$9115.00**

MODEL 86/71 LEVER ACTION BOARBUSTER
Action: Lever
Stock: Walnut
Barrel: 19 in.
Sights: Drilled and tapped for scopes
Weight: 7 lb. 4 oz.
Caliber: .444 Marlin, .45-70 Govt.
Magazine: 5 rounds
Features: Barrel equipped with European Picatinny style base with integral rear sight; half cock safety on hammer; safety slide catch at the rear of the frame; checkered pistol grip stock and forend are made from walnut; also available in soft touch

orange camo color; metal parts are blued; drilled and tapped for sights
MSRP . . . . **$2085.00–$2125.00**

MODEL 86/71 LEVER ACTION BOARBUSTER MARK II
Action: Lever
Stock: Synthetic
Barrel: 19 in.
Sights: Superluminova front and rear
Weight: 7 lb. 4 oz.
Caliber: .444 Marlin, .45-70
Magazine: 5 rounds
Features: Adjustable comb synthetic stock Cerakoted metalwork in bronze; ample rail for optics
MSRP **$2645.00**

MODEL 86/71 LEVER ACTION CLASSIC
Action: Lever
Stock: Walnut
Barrel: 24 in.
Sights: Drilled and tapped for scopes
Weight: 8 lb. 3 oz.
Caliber: .348 Win., .45-70 Govt.
Magazine: 5 rounds
Features: Last "big frame" rifle for Winchester; drilled and tapped for scopes; broach rifled barrel and magazine are blued finished; checkered walnut pistol grip; frame is forged and CNC-machined, with a blued finish on the standard version and case-hardened frame and buttcap on the

Premium model with select walnut stock and forend
Standard: . . . . . . **$1945.00–$1980.00**
Premium: **$2100.00**

MODEL 86/71 LEVER ACTION STAINLESS STEEL
Action: Lever
Stock: Synthetic
Barrel: 19 in.
Sights: Adjustable rear, fixed front
Weight: 7 lb. 15 oz.
Caliber: .45-70 Govt.
Magazine: N/A
Features: PMG barrel, broach rifled; fiber optic front sight and Weaver/Picatinny base with integrated rear sight; stock is made of American walnut covered with a camouflage film; microcell thick butt plate and swivel stud
MSRP **$2640.00**

MODEL 86/71 LEVER ACTION WILDBUSTER
Action: Lever
Stock: Walnut
Barrel: 24 in.
Sights: Drilled and tapped for scopes
Weight: 8 lb. 3 oz.
Caliber: .45-70 Govt.
Magazine: 5 rounds
Features: Ramp rear sight; walnut forend and pistol grip stock with checkered buttplate; blued finish on metal parts; drilled and tapped for scopes
MSRP **$1900.00**

Davide Pedersoli & C.

DAVIDE PEDERSOLI ROLLING BLOCK MISSISSIPPI CLASSIC

DAVIDE PEDERSOLI ROLLING BLOCK TARGET

DAVIDE PEDERSOLI SHARPS 1877 OVERBAUGH LONG RANGE

DAVIDE PEDERSOLI SHARPS LITTLE BESTY

RIFLES

ROLLING BLOCK MISSISSIPPI CLASSIC

Action: N/A
Stock: Wood
Barrel: 26 in.
Sights: Adjustable rear, fixed front
Weight: 7 lb. 8 oz.
Caliber: .357 Mag, .38-55, .45 Colt
Magazine: N/A
Features: High carbon steel barrel is broach rifled; alloy frame is embellished with a engraving; old silver colour finishing; equipped with a blade front sight and an adjustable rear sight, drilled to assemble the Creedmoor sight; stock and forend are made of American walnut with brass fittings
MSRP **$1243.00**

ROLLING BLOCK TARGET

Action: Dropping block
Stock: Walnut
Barrel: 30 in.
Sights: Open
Weight: 10 lb. 9 oz.
Caliber: .357 Mag., .45–70 Govt.
Magazine: None

Features: Octagonal, conical blued barrel; case-hardened color frame is equipped with ramp rear sight adjustable in elevation; steel buttplate and trigger guard; straight stock and forend made of walnut with oil finish; Deluxe grade also available
Standard **$1459.00**
Deluxe **$2898.00**

SHARPS 1877 OVERBOUGH LONG RANGE

Action: Sharps
Stock: Walnut
Barrel: 30 in.
Sights: Blade front, military-style rear
Weight: 8 lb. 4.8 oz.
Caliber: .45-70 Govt.
Magazine: N/A
Features: Designed to meet the 10-lb. weight limitations in NRA competition; forged frame and parts; oil-finished American walnut stock with

checkering; double set triggers are standard; rifle is drilled and tapped for Creedmoor sights
MSRP **$2464.00**

SHARPS LITTLE BETSY

Action: N/A
Stock: Wood
Barrel: 24 in.
Sights: Creedmoor
Weight: 7 lb. 10 oz.
Caliber: .17 HRM, .22LR, .22 Hornet, .357 Mag, .30-30 Win.
Magazine: N/A
Features: Forged and CNC machined frame features a floral engraving; stock is made of American walnut; barrel PMG quality features a matt blue finish; sights includes a tunnel front sight and the folding Creedmoor sight; with double set trigger
MSRP **$2211.00**

Del-Ton

DEL-TON DT SCOUT

DT SCOUT

Action: Semiautomatic
Stock: Synthetic
Barrel: 16 in.

Sights: A2 front sight, flip-up rear
Weight: 5 lb. 14 oz.
Caliber: 5.56 NATO
Magazine: 30 rounds
Features: Lightweight MSR in A3 flat-top configuration; forged aluminum upper and lower; chrome-lined carrier

and carrier key; lightweight barrel profile with a threaded-on A2 flash hider; mid-length gas system with staked and sealed gas key; mid-length aluminum Delta Ring handguard with heat shield; ejection port cover; round forward assist; A2 grip; carbine buffer
MSRP **$680.00**

Del-Ton

DEL-TON DTI EXTREME DUTY 316–CALIFORNIA-COMPLIANT

DEL-TON DTI SXT

DEL-TON ECHO 316H OR

DEL-TON ECHO 7.62X39

DEL-TON SIERRA 316L

DTI EXTREME DUTY– CALIFORNIA-COMPLIANT

Action: Semiautomatic
Stock: M4 reinforced fiber
Barrel: 16 in.
Sights: Samson quick flip dual aperture rear sight
Weight: 6 lb. 6.4 oz.
Caliber: 5.56 NATO
Magazine: Detachable box
Features: Hammer forged CMV chrome-lined barrel; H-buffer
MSRP **$1133.33**

DTI SXT

Action: Semiautomatic
Stock: Synthetic
Barrel: 16 in.
Sights: None
Weight: 6 lb. 3 oz.

Caliber: 5.56 NATO
Magazine: 30 rounds
Features: Forged aluminum upper and lower in Cerakote flat dark earth; 15-in Samson free-floating handguard with M-LOK attachment points; lightweight profile barrel of chrome moly vanadium; M4 feed ramp; DTI low-profile gas block; M4 five-position buttstock with a mil-spec buffer tube; round forward assist; ejection port cover
MSRP **$750.00**

ECHO 7.62X39

Action: Semiautomatic
Stock: Synthetic
Barrel: 16 in.
Sights: Adjustable front sight
Weight: 6 lb. 10 oz.
Caliber: 7.62x39
Magazine: Detachable box, 30 rounds
Features: Carbine gas system; phosphated under F-marked front sight base; chrome-lined carrier interior; carbine-length hand guards; aluminum delta ring; single heat shield
MSRP **$753.42**

ECHO 316H OR

Action: Semiautomatic
Stock: M4 five-position
Barrel: 16 in.
Sights: None
Weight: 6 lb. 10 oz.
Caliber: 5.56 NATO
Magazine: Detachable box, 30 rounds
Features: Single rail gas block; CAR handguards with single heat shields; A2 flash hider; forged 7075 T6 aluminum upper and lower receivers
MSRP **$675.00**

SIERRA 316L OPTICS READY/MLOK

Action: Semiautomatic
Stock: Synthetic
Barrel: 16 in.
Sights: None
Weight: 6 lb. 3 oz.
Caliber: 5.56 NATO
Magazine: 30 rounds
Features: Optics-ready MSR with a mid-length lightweight barrel; A2 flash hider; DTI low-profile gas block; threaded muzzle; M4 feed ramp; forged aluminum upper and lower receiver hard anodized and mil-spec; M4 five-position buttstock with mil-spec buffer tube; 15-in M-LOK free-floating handguard
MSRP **$675.00**

Desert Tech

DESERT TECH MDRX

DESERT TECH SRS A2 STANDARD

MDRX

Action: Semiautomatic
Stock: Synthetic
Barrel: 16 in., 20 in.

Sights: None
Weight: 8 lb. 8 oz.–8 lb. 14 oz.
Caliber: .223 Wylde, .300 BLK, .308 Win.
Magazine: 10, 20, 30 rounds
Features: This is a convertible bullpup available in either forward-eject or side-eject configurations, both options in state-compliant models as well; trigger pull weight set at 4.7 lb.; ambidextrous controls; barrel threaded ½X28 or 5/8x28 depending on caliber
MSRP . . . . **Starting at $2245.00**

SRS A2

Action: Bolt
Stock: Synthetic
Barrel: 22 in., 26 in.

Sights: None
Weight: 8 lb. 15 oz.–9 lb. 8 oz.
Caliber: .308 Win., 6.5 Creedmoor, .300 Win. Mag., .300 Norma Mag., .338 Lapua Mag., .338 Norma Mag.
Magazine: 5, 6, 8, 10 rounds
Features: Similar to the Covert model, but with more caliber choices, including several in the very long-range game; 6-second reload time; adjustable trigger; monopod-ready stock; integral tripod mount; barrel threaded 5/8x24; handguard with M-LOK attachment points; integral Picatinny rails top and bottom
MSRP . . . . **Starting at $5749.00**

Desert Tech

DESERT TECH SRS A2 COVERT

DESERT TECH SRS A2 ULTRA-LIGHT

SRS A2 COVERT
Action: Bolt
Stock: Synthetic
Barrel: 16 in., 18 in.
Sights: None
Weight: 8 lb.–8 lb. 4 oz.
Caliber: .308 Win., 6.5 Creedmoor, .300 Win.
Magazine: 5, 6, 8, 10 rounds
Features: Buffered bolt carrier; cold hammer-forged, steel chrome-lined barrel in a 2SW (strength-to-weight) profile; direct impingement gas system with a pinned user adjustable gas block; Daniel Defense Superior Suppression Device; two-stage Geissele Super Semiautomatic trigger; 15-in. DD5 rail with M-LOK attachment; soft-touch overmolding on stock and pistol grip; takes all SR-25 magazines
MSRP . . . . Starting at $5749.00

SRS A2 ULTRA-LIGHT
Action: Bolt
Stock: Synthetic
Barrel: 24 in., 26 in.
Sights: None
Weight: 8 lb. 4 oz.–9 lb.
Caliber: 6.5 Creedmoor, .300 Win. Mag. .300 RUM, 7mm Rem. Mag.
Magazine: 5, 6, 8, 10 rounds
Features: Rifle weight is marginally less than the standard; 6-second reload time; adjustable trigger; mono-pod-ready stock; integral tripod mount; barrel threaded 5/8x24; handguard with M-LOK attachment points; integral Picatinny rails top and bottom
MSRP . . . . Starting at $5549.00

DoubleStar Corp.

DOUBLESTAR 3GR 2.0 GO-FAST RED

DOUBLESTAR STAR10-B

DOUBLESTAR STAR10-BX

DOUBLESTAR ZERO CARBINE RIFLE

3GR 2.0 GO-FAST RED
Action: Semiautomatic
Stock: Synthetic
Barrel: 16 in.
Sights: None
Weight: N/A
Caliber: 5.56 NATO
Magazine: 30 rounds
Features: The Go-Fast title and bright red cosmetics tell you this is one for the 3-Gun game; direct impingement gas system; ACE ARFX stock; low-profile steel gas block; billet backbone charging handle; billet winter trigger guard; forged aircraft 7075 upper and lower
MSRP $1629.99

STAR10-B
Action: Semiautomatic
Stock: Synthetic
Barrel: 18 in.
Sights: None
Weight: 9 lb. 13 oz.
Caliber: .308 cal
Magazine: 20 rounds
Features: Hogue pistol grip; Wilson air gauged stainless steel barrel (fluted); Samson Evolution handguard; brass deflector and dust cover; integrated trigger guard
MSRP $2728.99

STAR10-BX
Action: Semiautomatic
Stock: Synthetic
Barrel: 22 in.
Sights: None
Weight: 10 lb.
Caliber: .260 Rem.
Magazine: 20 rounds
Features: Direct impingement; stainless steel free-floating barrel; Bullseye muzzle brake; 15-in. Samson .309 Evolution handguard; brass deflector; dust cover; enhanced magazine well; CMC flat trigger group set to 3.5 pounds; ACE Hammer stock
MSRP $2728.99

ZERO CARBINE RIFLE
Action: Semiautomatic
Stock: Synthetic
Barrel: 16 in.
Sights: None
Weight: N/A
Caliber: 5.56 NATO
Magazine: 30 rounds
Features: A premium accuracy rifle with a 1:8 twist Wilson Air Gauge heavy barrel; low-profile gas block; Cloak 15 ½-inch M-LOK handguard; Alpha AR Comp compensator; flattop receiver; billet winter triggerguard and backbone charging handle; forward assist; ACE SOCOM stock; Ergo Ambi Sure Grip; direct gas impingement action
MSRP $1629.99

RIFLES

DRD Tactical

DRD TACTICAL KIVAARI

DRD TACTICAL
PARATUS P762 GEN-2

KIVAARI

Action: Semiautomatic
Stock: Synthetic
Barrel: 24 in.
Sights: None
Weight: 13 lb. 9 oz.
Caliber: .338 Lapua, .300 Norma Mag.
Magazine: 10 rounds
Features: Billet aircraft aluminum receiver; direct gas operated action; fully adjustable Magpul PRS stock is mated with 17-in. QD Magpul M-LOK rail; SilencerCo QD muzzle brake; ambidextrous safety; Wilson Combat two-stage match trigger; choice of hard case or Tactical-Tailor Trekker backpack; available in anodized black, Cerakote Flat Dark Earth, or NiB Battle Worn finishes
MSRP......... **$5500.00–$6250.00**

PARATUS P762 GEN-2

Action: Semiautomatic
Stock: Synthetic
Barrel: 16 in.
Sights: None
Weight: 9 lb. 3 oz.
Caliber: 7.62x51 NATO, 6.5 Creedmoor
Magazine: 20 rounds
Features: Compact enough when disassembled to be stowed in a briefcase or backpack; adjustable Magpul folding stock; Mil-Std 1913 rail; direct gas operated; rifle may be fired with the stock in the folded position; in black or NiB Battle Worn finishes.
MSRP......... **$3700.00–$4300.00**

Excel Arms

EXCEL ARMS ACCELERATOR RIFLE

EXCEL ARMS X-5.7R

ACCELERATOR RIFLE
MR-22, MR-5.7

Action: Semiautomatic
Stock: Polymer composite, pistol grip
Barrel: 18 in.
Sights: Standard includes Red/Green dot optic
Weight: 8 lb.
Caliber: .22 WMR, 5.7X28mm
Magaine: 9 rounds
Features: Corrosion-resistant 17-4 stainless steel, including its fluted barrel; manual and firing pin safeties; last-round-fired hold-open bolt; flat-top accessory rail; choice of black or silver shroud. Basic model is supplied with one magazine; Package P-2 comes with a sling, two magazines, and a 3–9X40mm scope; Package P-5 is available only in .22 WMR and comes with a red dot optic, tactical rails, flashlight, bipod, detachable iron sights, and two magazines

MR-22...................	$648.00
MR-5.7.................	$809.00
Package P2 MR-22........	$844.00
Package P2 MR-5.7......	$1009.00
Package P5 MR-22.......	$1187.00

X-5.7R

Action: Semiautomatic
Stock: Synthetic
Barrel: 18 in.
Sights: None
Weight: 6 lb. 4 oz.
Caliber: 5.7X28mm, 9mm
Magazine: 10, 17, 20 rounds
Features: CNC-machined aluminum; Picatinny rail; tactical AR styling; collapsible stock; tapped holes in the handguard for mounting accessory rails; 5.7x28mm takes FN Five-SeveN magazines; 9mm takes Glock magazines; 10-round models are California-compliant featureless rifles
MSRP........... **$897.00–$912.00**

FN America

FN AMERICA FN M249S PARA

FN AMERICA FN SCAR 17S CARBINE

FN AMERICA FN SCAR 20S

FN M249S PARA

Action: Semiautomatic
Stock: Metal
Barrel: 16.1 in.
Sights: Graduated 1000-meter front and rear combo
Weight: 17 lb.
Caliber: 5.56 NATO
Magazine: 30, 200 rounds
Features: Semiauto version of the full-auto M249 Para light machine gun; originally developed by FN Herstal as the FN MINIMI and adopted by the U.S. military in 1988; features signature 16-in. FN cold-hammer-forged, chrome-lined barrel in a quick-change configuration; formed steel frame receiver with claw extractor and fixed, pivoting ejector that ejects to the side; rotating, telescoping stock

assembly with a hydraulic recoil buffer system; operates from a closed bolt and will accept both magazine and linked ammunition belts; Picatinny top rail and integral Mil-Std bipod
MSRP..............$10,499.00

FN SCAR 16S, 17S

Action: Gas-operated semiautomatic
Stock: Polymer
Barrel: 16.25 in.
Sights: Adjustable, folding, removable
Weight: 8 lb.
Caliber: .308 Win., 7.62 NATO
Magazine: Detachable box, 10, 20 rounds
Features: Fully adjustable stock; Picatinny rail plus three accessory rails for attaching a variety of sights and lasers; free-floating, cold-hammer-forged barrel; available in black or Flat

Dark Earth tactical, telescoping, side-folding polymer stock
16S...................$3609.00
17S...................$3644.00

FN SCAR 20S

Action: Semiautomatic
Stock: Synthetic
Barrel: 20 in.
Sights: None
Weight: 11 lb. 3 oz.
Caliber: 7.62x51mm, 6.5 Creedmoor
Magazine: 10 rounds
Features: Slick, short-stroke gas piston semiauto with miles of rail; two-stage match Geissele "Super SCAR" trigger; stock adjustable for length of pull and comb height; Hogue finger-groove pistol grip; monolithic aluminum receiver; left- or right-hand charging handle mounting; polymer trigger module; adjustable cheekpiece
MSRP..................$4699.00

Franchi

FRANCHI MOMENTUM

FRANCHI MOMENTUM ELITE

FRANCHI MOMENTUM ELITE VARMINT

MOMENTUM

Action: Bolt
Stock: Synthetic
Barrel: 22 in., 24 in.
Sights: None
Weight: 6 lb. 11 oz.–7 lb. 13 oz.
Caliber: 6.5 Creedmoor, .308 Win., .300 Win. Mag., .350 Legend
Magazine: 3, 4 rounds
Features: Franchi's first ever rifle; synthetic stocks in flat dark earth or hunter gray; free-floating barrels; 60-degree bolt throws; adjustable triggers; barrels are available plain or threaded for suppressor use
MSRP...................$609.00

MOMENTUM ELITE

Action: Bolt
Stock: Synthetic
Barrel: 22 in., 24 in.
Sights: None
Weight: 7 lb. 2 oz.–7 lb. 8 oz.
Caliber: 6.5 Creedmoor, .308 Win., 6.5 PRC, .300 Win. Mag., .350 Legend, .223 Rem., 22-250 Rem., .224 Valkyrie
Magazine: 3, 4 rounds
Features: Trim, ergonomic stock; muzzle brake; topside Picatinny scope rail; TrueTimber Strata/Midnight Bronze Cerakote and Realtree Excape/Burnt Bronze Cerakote available in 6.5 Creedmoor, .308 Win., 6.5 PRC, and .300 Win. Mag.; Optifade Elevated II/Cobalt Cerakote available

for 6.5 Creedmoor, .308 Win., and .350 Legend; Optifade Subalpine/Midnight Bronze Cerakote available in .223 Rem., .22-250 Rem., .224 Valkyrie; Gore Optifade Elevated II/Cobalt Cerakote in 6.5 PRC
MSRP..................$899.00

MOMENTUM ELITE VARMINT

Action: Bolt
Stock: Synthetic
Barrel: 24 in.
Sights: None
Weight: 9 lb.–9 lb. 7 oz.
Caliber: 6.5 Creedmoor, .308 Win., .223 Rem., .22-250 Rem., .224 Valkyrie
Magazine: 3, 4 rounds
Features: Synthetic stock in Optifade camo; free-floating, heavy profile fluted barrel with muzzle brake in Midnight Bronze Cerakote; flush-fit magazine (¾ rounds) and one extended magazine (8 rounds); soft-touch overmolds on grip and cheekpiece; topside Picatinny rail
MSRP..................$999.00

FRANKLIN ARMORY
BSFIII M4

FRANKLIN ARMORY
XO-26 R3

FRANKLIN ARMORY M4-HTF
R3 XTD

FRANKLIN ARMORY
REFORMATION RS7, RS11

BSFIII M4

Action: Semiautomatic
Stock: Synthetic
Barrel: 16 in.
Sights: None
Weight: N/A
Caliber: 5.56 NATO
Magazine: 20 rounds
Features: Franklin's Binary Firing System Gen III, a 3-position trigger: Position 1 is safe, position 2 is one shot per pull, and position 3 fires one round on pull and one on release; LTW contour barrel; 15-in. FST handguard; standard charging handle; mid-length gas system; low-profile gas block; A2 flash hider and grip; M4 stock
MSRP $1109.99

M4-HTF R3 XTD

Action: Semiautomatic
Stock: Synthetic
Barrel: 16 in.

Sights: None
Weight: N/A
Caliber: 5.56 NATO, .350 Legend
Magazine: 20 rounds
Features: Binary Firing System Gen III, a 3-position trigger: position 1 is safe, position 2 is one shot per pull, and position 3 fires one round on pull and one on release; LTW contour barrel; 15-in. FSR M-LOK handguard; mil-spec charging handle; mid-length gas system; low-profile gas block; Aura XTD muzzle device; B5 grip; B5 Bravo stock
MSRP . . . . $1259.99–$1369.99

REFORMATION RS7, RS11

Action: Semiautomatic
Stock: Synthetic
Barrel: 7.5 in., 11.5 in.
Sights: MBUS
Weight: N/A
Caliber: 5.56 NATO, .300 BLK
Magazine: 20 rounds
Features: The Reformation barrel does not impart spin on the projectile, so it does not meet the definition of 'rifling.' Franklin Armory has safely

tested off-the-shelf ammunition in a Reformation barrel and routinely achieved 3.5 in. @100 yards with white box ammunition. .300 BLK has 11.5-in. barrel and choice of black or OD green receiver; 5.56 NATO has 7.5-in. barrel and is available in black; both calibers can option Franklin Armory's Binary Firing System Gen III trigger
RS7: . . . . $1254.99–$1429.99
RS-11: . . . . $1594.99–$1757.99

XO-26 R3

Action: Semiautomatic
Stock: Synthetic
Barrel: 12 in.
Sights: None
Weight: N/A
Caliber: 5.56 NATO, .350 Legend
Magazine: 10, 30 rounds
Features: Barrel has an LTW contour; 11.5-in. FST handguard; standard charging handle; pistol lower; BFSIII or custom-tuned trigger; carbine-length gas system; low-profile gas block; Triumvir muzzle device; Magpul SL grip; Magpul M-LOK MVG
MSRP . . . . $1369.99–$1519.99

Heckler & Koch

HECKLER & KOCH
MR556A1

HECKLER &
KOCH MR762A1

HECKLER & KOCH MR762A1
LONG RIFLE PACKAGE II

MR556A1

Action: Semiautomatic
Stock: Synthetic
Barrel: 14 in., 16.5 in.
Sights: Troy microsights
Weight: 8 lb. 10 oz.
Caliber: 5.56 NATO
Magazine: Detachable box, 30 rounds
Features: Free-floating Picatinny rail; gas operated piston system
MSRP $3499.00

MR762A1

Action: Semiautomatic
Stock: Synthetic
Barrel: 16.5 in.
Sights: None
Weight: 9 lb. 15 oz.
Caliber: 7.62 NATO

Magazine: Detachable box, 10, 20 rounds
Features: Match rifle features; direct descendant of HK416/417 series, but made for civilians; uses a piston and a solid operating "pusher" rod in place of the common gas tube normally used in AR-style rifles; cold-hammer-forged barrel; adjustable stock
MSRP $3999.00

MR762A1 LONG RIFLE PACKAGE II

Action: Semiautomatic
Stock: Synthetic
Barrel: 16.5 in.
Sights: 3–9x40mm scope
Weight: 10 lb. 7 oz.

Caliber: 7.62 NATO
Magazine: Detachable box, 10, 20 rounds
Features: Semi-auto descendent of the full-auto HK416/417; short-stroke gas piston; cold hammer-forged barrel; adjustable cheekpiece; Long Rifle Package adds an a buttstock with an adjustable cheekpiece, LaRue Tactical BRM-S bipod, a second magazine, MLOK handguard, hard case, and Vortex Viper PSTII 3–15X44mm first focal plane MRAD scope
Standard $4129.00
Package $7249.00

Henry Repeating Arms

HENRY REPEATING ARMS .30-30 LEVER ACTION–BRASS

HENRY REPEATING ARMS .45-70 LEVER ACTION

HENRY REPEATING ARMS ALL-WEATHER LEVER ACTION SIDE GATE

HENRY REPEATING ARMS AMERICAN EAGLE

HENRY REPEATING ARMS BIG BOY ALL WEATHER SIDE GATE

HENRY REPEATING ARMS BIG BOY, BIG BOY CARBINE COLOR CASE HARDENED SIDE GATE

HENRY REPEATING ARMS BIG BOY, BIG BOY CARBINE STEEL SIDE GATE

.30-30 LEVER ACTION–BRASS

Action: Lever
Stock: Walnut
Barrel: 20 in.
Sights: Open
Weight: 7 lb.
Caliber: .30-30 Win.
Magazine: Under-barrel tube, 5 rounds
Features: Octagon barrel: straight-grip American walnut with buttplate; marble fully adjustable semi-buckhorn rear sight, with diamond insert, beaded front sight; brass receiver, drilled and tapped for easy scope mounting
Brass: **$1087.00**

.45-70 LEVER ACTION OCTAGON

Action: Lever
Stock: Wood
Barrel: 22 in.
Sights: Adjustable
Weight: 8 lb. 2 oz.
Caliber: .45-70 Govt.
Magazine: 4 rounds
Features: Straight-grip American Walnut stock with brass buttplate; fully adjustable semi-buckhorn rear, and brass beaded front sight; brass drilled and tapped for a Weaver 63B mount
MSRP **$1087.00**

ALL-WEATHER LEVER ACTION SIDE GATE

Action: Lever
Stock: Hardwood
Barrel: 20 in.
Sights: Brass bead front, fully adjustable semi-buckhorn rear
Weight: 7 lb.

Caliber: .30-30 Win., .45-70 Gov't.
Magazine: 4, 5 rounds
Features: A side-loader for deer hunters, with a darkly stained hardwood stock; metalwork in an industrial hard chrome satin finish; drilled and tapped; swivel studs
MSRP **$1198.00**

AMERICAN EAGLE

Action: Lever
Stock: Walnut
Barrel: 20 in.
Sights: Brass bead front, adjustable buckhorn rear with diamond insert
Weight: 6 lb. 12 oz.
Caliber: .22 LR
Magazine: 16 rounds
Features: A unique salute to America with a ivory-washed walnut stock engraved with border patterns, an American eagle head, and aggressive, distinctive checkering; blued octagon barrel
MSRP **$1071.00**

BIG BOY ALL WEATHER SIDE GATE

Action: Lever
Stock: Hardwood
Barrel: 20 in.
Sights: Brass bead front, fully adjustable semi-buckhorn rear
Weight: 7 lb.
Caliber: .38 Spl./.357 Mag., .44 Spl./.44 Mag., .45 LC
Magazine: 10 rounds
Features: Convenient side-gate loading; metalwork is hard-chrome plated and sealed to be moisture resistant; darkly stained hardwood stock; drilled

and tapped; swivel studs included
MSRP **$1198.00**

BIG BOY, BIG BOY CARBINE COLOR CASE HARDENED SIDE GATE

Action: Lever
Stock: American walnut
Barrel: 16.5 in. (carbine), 20 in. (standard)
Sights: Brass bead front, fully adjustable semi-buckhorn rear
Weight: 7 lb. 7 oz.–7 lb. 14 oz.
Caliber: .38 Spl./.357 Mag., .44 Spl./.44 Mag., .45 LC
Magazine: 7 rounds (carbine), 10 rounds (standard)
Features: A side-loading gate; case-hardened frame finish; octagon barrel in blue; carbines have large loop lever; drilled and tapped
MSRP **$1198.00**

BIG BOY, BIG BOY CARBINE STEEL SIDE GATE

Action: Lever
Stock: American walnut
Barrel: 16.5 in., 20 in.
Sights: Brass bead front, fully adjustable semi-buckhorn rear
Weight: 6 lb. 9 oz.–7 lb.
Caliber: .38 Spl./.357 Mag., .44 Spl./.44 Mag., .45 LC
Magazine: 7 rounds (carbine), 10 rounds (standard)
Features: This variant wears a steel frame instead of brass; full-length version also available with a large loop lever; drilled and tapped; swivel studs
Standard lever **$1017.00**
Large loop lever **$1035.00**

Henry Repeating Arms

HENRY REPEATING ARMS
BIG BOY CLASSIC

HENRY REPEATING ARMS BIG
BOY SILVER

HENRY REPEATING
ARMS BIG BOY STEEL
CARBINE

HENRY REPEATING ARMS
BIG BOY X-MODEL

HENRY REPEATING
ARMS COLOR CASE
HARDENED LEVER
ACTION SIDE GATE

HENRY REPEATING ARMS
FREEMASONS TRIBUTE
EDITION

HENRY REPEATING ARMS FRONTIER
MODEL LONG BARREL 24"

BIG BOY CLASSIC

Action: Lever
Stock: Walnut
Barrel: 20 in.
Sights: Open
Weight: 8.68 lb.
Caliber: .41 Mag., .327 Fed. Mag., .44 Mag., .45 Colt, .357 Mag.
Magazine: Under-barrel tube, 10 rounds
Features: Adjustable marble semi-buckhorn rear with white diamond insert and brass beaded front sight; solid top brass receiver, brass buttplate and brass barrel band; straight-grip American walnut stock; octagonal barrel
MSRP $1051.00

BIG BOY SILVER

Action: Lever
Stock: Walnut
Barrel: 20 in.
Sights: Semi-buckhorn rear, brass bead front
Weight: 8 lb. 11 oz.
Caliber: .44 Magnum, .45 Colt, .357 Mag/.38 Spl.
Magazine: Under-barrel tube, 10 rounds
Features: Nickel plating; octagon barrel; buckhorn/bead sights; drilled and tapped scope option; straight stock wrist; carbine-style buttplate; okay for left-handed shooters
MSRP $1161.00

BIG BOY STEEL CARBINE

Action: Lever

Stock: Checkered walnut
Barrel: 16.5 in.
Sights: Adjustable semi-buckhorn rear with adjustable white diamond insert, brass bead front
Weight: 6 lb. 9 oz.
Caliber: .44 Magnum, .45 Colt, .357 Mag/.38 Spl., .327 Fed., .41 Mag.
Magazine: Under-barrel tube, 7 rounds
Features: Sliding transfer bar safety system in its hammer; lighter steel frame; ventilated rubber recoil pad; sling swivel studs; rifle-style fore-end cap; glove-friendly oversized lever
MSRP $998.00

BIG BOY X-MODEL

Action: Lever
Stock: Synthetic
Barrel: 17.4 in.
Sights: Fiber optic front, adjustable fiber optic rear
Weight: 7 lb. 5 oz.
Caliber: .45 Colt, .357 Mag., .44 Mag.
Magazine: 7 rounds
Features: Who knew you could modernize a lever-action to this extent? Henry did, adding features like a tough synthetic stock and forend with an ergonomic design
MSRP $1049.00

COLOR CASE HARDENED LEVER ACTION SIDE GATE

Action: Lever
Stock: American walnut
Barrel: 20 in., 22 in.

Sights: Brass bead front, fully adjustable semi-buckhorn rear
Weight: 8 lb. 2 oz.–8 lb. 8 oz.
Caliber: .30-30 Win., .45-70 Gov't.
Magazine: 4, 5 rounds
Features: Workhorse levers with sidegate loading wearing octagon barrels and rich color case-hardened steel receivers; .30-30 gets a straight grip and standard lever, .45-70 gets a pistol grip stock and large loop lever
MSRP $1198.00

FREEMASONS TRIBUTE EDITION

Action: Lever
Stock: Walnut
Barrel: 20 in.
Sights: Adjustable semi-buckhorn rear with adjustable white diamond insert, brass bead front
Weight: 6 lb. 12 oz.
Caliber: .22 S/L/LR
Magazine: 16 rounds (long range), 21 rounds (short)
Features: Receiver engraving with 24K gold plating; engraved/painted stock; depicts our first president in full Masonic regalia
MSRP $1178.00

FRONTIER MODEL LONG BARREL 24"

Action: Lever
Stock: Walnut
Barrel: 24 in.
Sights: Brass bead front, fully adjustable semi-buckhorn rear with adjustable white diamond insert
Weight: 7 lb.
Caliber: .22 LR, .22 Mag.
Magazine: 12, 16, 21 rounds by caliber
Features: Merge of Henry's Lever Octagon and Frontier models; octagonal barrel adds weight, rigidity, and stability; grooved receiver for scope mounting
.22 LR $553.00
.22 Mag. $660.00

Henry Repeating Arms

HENRY REPEATING ARMS FRONTIER MODEL THREADED BARREL 24"

HENRY REPEATING ARMS GARDEN GUN SMOOTHBORE .22 LR SHOTSHELL

HENRY REPEATING ARMS GOD BLESS AMERICA EDITION GOLDEN BOY

HENRY REPEATING ARMS GOLDEN BOY DELUXE ENGRAVED 3RD EDITION

HENRY REPEATING ARMS GOLDEN BOY SILVER AMERICAN RODEO TRIBUTE

HENRY REPEATING ARMS GOLDEN BOY SILVER YOUTH

HENRY REPEATING ARMS LEVER ACTION .22 CARBINE RIFLE

FRONTIER MODEL THREADED BARREL 24"

Action: Lever
Stock: Walnut
Barrel: 24 in.
Sights: Brass bead front, fully adjustable semi-buckhorn rear with adjustable white diamond insert
Weight: 7 lb.
Caliber: .22 LR, .22 Mag.
Magazine: 12, 16, 21 rounds by caliber
Features: Similar to the standard Frontier Long Barrel 24-in. model but with a ½x28 threads for suppressor use
.22 LR **$580.00**
.22 Mag. **$688.00**

GARDEN GUN SMOOTHBORE .22 LR SHOTSHELL

Action: Lever
Stock: Black ash
Barrel: 18.5 in.
Sights: Hooded blade front, adjustable rear
Weight: 5 lb. 4 oz.
Caliber: .22 LR shotshell
Magazine: 15 rounds
Features: Designed to rid your vegetable garden of undesirable four-legged critters
MSRP **$468.00**

GOD BLESS AMERICA EDITION GOLDEN BOY

Action: Lever
Stock: American walnut
Barrel: 20 in.
Sights: Brass bead front, fully adjustable semi-buckhorn rear with diamond insert
Weight: 6 lb. 12 oz.
Caliber: .22 LR

Magazine: 16 rounds
Features: Nickel receiver is engraved on both sides with floral scrollwork; right side features 24k gold banner reading "Home of the Free Because of the Brave" and gold American flag; left side features the Liberty Bell and a bald eagle in gold; the right side of the stock has a painted rendition of the Statue of Liberty's raised arm and torch; the forend has painted engraving that reads "God Bless America"
MSRP **$1361.00**

GOLDEN BOY DELUXE ENGRAVED 3RD EDITION

Action: Lever
Stock: Walnut
Barrel: 20 in.
Sights: Fully adjustable rear, brass-beaded front
Weight: 6 lb. 12 oz.
Caliber: .22 LR, .22 WMR, .17 HMR
Magazine: Under-barrel tube, 16 rounds (LR), 12 rounds (Short)
Features: American walnut stock; adjustable buckhorn rear sight, beaded front sight; brasslite receiver, brass buttplate, and blued barrel
.22 LR **$1724.00**
.22 Mag. **$1778.00**
.17 HMR **$1795.00**

GOLDEN BOY SILVER AMERICAN RODEO TRIBUTE

Action: Lever
Stock: Walnut
Barrel: 20 in.
Sights: Brass bead front, adjustable rear
Weight: 6 lb. 12 oz.
Caliber: .22 LR
Magazine: 16 rounds

Features: A tribute to the sport and cowboys of American rodeo, featuring a blued octagon barrel; engraved stock with 24K gold highlights; bucking bull rider engraved in color on stock
MSRP **$1361.00**

GOLDEN BOY SILVER YOUTH

Action: Lever
Stock: Walnut
Barrel: 17 in.
Sights: Brass bead front, adjustable semi-buckhorn rear
Weight: 6 lb.
Caliber: .22 LR
Magazine: 12 rounds
Features: An easy shooting lever .22 (short, long, and long rifle) with a high-shine nickel-plated receiver and butt plate; quarter-cock safety; blued octagon barrel; drilled and tapped for scope mounting; 13-in. length of pull
MSRP **$696.00**

LEVER ACTION .22 CARBINE RIFLE

Action: Lever
Stock: Walnut
Barrel: 16.13 in.
Sights: Open
Weight: 4 lb. 8 oz.
Caliber: .22 LR
Magazine: 15 rounds (.22 LR), 17 rounds (.22 L), 18 rounds (.22 S), 21 rounds (.22)
Features: Straight-grip American walnut stock; adjustable rear, hooded front sight; blued round barrel; large loop lever
MSRP **$436.00**

Henry Repeating Arms

HENRY REPEATING ARMS LEVER ACTION OCTAGON FRONTIER

HENRY REPEATING ARMS LEVER-ACTION X-MODEL .45-70

HENRY REPEATING ARMS PUMP-ACTION OCTAGON

HENRY REPEATING ARMS MINI BOLT YOUTH

HENRY REPEATING ARMS NEW ORIGINAL HENRY

HENRY REPEATING ARMS SIDE GATE LEVER-ACTION

HENRY REPEATING ARMS SINGLE-SHOT RIFLE STEEL

RIFLES

LEVER-ACTION OCTAGON FRONTIER

Action: Lever
Stock: Walnut
Barrel: 20 in.
Sights: Open
Weight: 6 lb. 4 oz.
Caliber: .22 LR, .22 WMR, .17 HMR
Magazine: Under-barrel tube, 21 rounds (.22 S), 16 rounds (.22 LR); 12 rounds (.22 Mag.); 11 rounds (.17 HMR)
Features: American walnut; marble fully adjustable semi-buckhorn rear with reversible white diamond insert and brass beaded front sight; blued barrel and lever
.22 LR $525.00
.22 Mag. $636.00
.17 HMR $636.00

LEVER-ACTION X-MODEL .45-70

Action: Lever
Stock: Synthetic
Barrel: 19.8 in.
Sights: Fiber optic front, adjustable fiber optic rear
Weight: 7 lb. 6 oz.
Caliber: .45-70 Govt.
Magazine: 4 rounds
Features: Similar to the Big Boy X-Model, but in a longer barrel to accommodate the fat .45-70 round
MSRP $1049.00

MINI BOLT YOUTH

Action: Bolt
Stock: Synthetic
Barrel: 16.25 in.
Sights: Open

Weight: 3 lb. 4 oz.
Caliber: .22 LR
Magazine: None
Features: Single-shot; one-piece fiberglass synthetic stock; Williams fire sights; stainless steel receiver and barrel; black, Muddy Girl Camo, or Instant Orange stock finishes; right-hand only
MSRP $319.00

NEW ORIGINAL HENRY

Action: Lever
Stock: Walnut
Barrel: 24.5
Sights: Folding ladder rear
Weight: 9 lb.
Caliber: .44-40, .45 Colt
Magazine: Under-barrel tube, 13+1 rounds
Features: True to original 1860 specifications; fancy American walnut stock; blade front sight with a folding ladder rear; half-cock safety hammer notch
MSRP $2720.00

PUMP-ACTION OCTAGON

Action: Pump
Stock: Walnut
Barrel: 19.75 in.
Sights: Open
Weight: 6 lb.
Caliber: .22 LR, .22 WMR
Magazine: Under-barrel tube, 15 rounds (.22 LR), 12 rounds (.22 WMR)
Features: American walnut stock; adjustable rear, beaded front sight; blued octagonal barrel
.22 LR $636.00
.22 Mag. $680.00

SIDE GATE LEVER-ACTION

Action: Lever
Stock: American walnut
Barrel: 20 in.
Sights: Ramp front, adjustable semi-buckhorn rear
Weight: 7 lb. 8 oz.
Caliber: .38-55, .30-30 Win., .45-70 Govt., .35 Rem.
Magazine: 4, 5 rounds
Features: Henry says this is SASS-approved, with a brass receiver; deep checkering; ramp front sight with ivory bead; round barrel
MSRP $1166.00

SINGLE-SHOT RIFLE IN STEEL & BRASS

Action: Break-open single-shot
Stock: Walnut
Barrel: 22 in.
Sights: Brass bead front, fully adjustable folding leaf rear
Weight: 6 lb. 15 oz.
Caliber: .223 Rem., .350 Legend, .450 Bushmaster, .243 win., .308 Win., .44 Spec./.44 Mag., .45-70 Gov't., .30-30 Win., .38 Spec./.357 Mag.
Magazine: N/A
Features: Centerfire top-lever rifle; matte finish on steel frame or a high-polished finish on hardened brass frame; steel models get curved pistol grip and rubber recoil pad; brass version have straight English grip and and brass buttplate; top lever is ambidextrous
Brass $679.00
Steel $552.00

Henry Repeating Arms

HENRY REPEATING ARMS SINGLE-SHOT YOUTH RIFLE

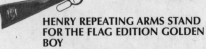

HENRY REPEATING ARMS STAND FOR THE FLAG EDITION GOLDEN BOY

HENRY REPEATING ARMS STEEL LEVER ACTION SIDE GATE

HENRY REPEATING ARMS TEXAS TRIBUTE EDITION

HENRY REPEATING ARMS THE LONG RANGER DELUXE ENGRAVED

HENRY REPEATING ARMS THE LONG RANGER WITH SIGHTS

SINGLE-SHOT YOUTH RIFLE

Action: Break-open
Stock: Walnut
Barrel: 22 in.
Sights: Folding fully adjustable leaf rear, brass bead front
Weight: 6 lb. 15 oz.
Caliber: .243 Win.
Magazine: 1 round
Features: The first time Henry's single-shot youth rifle offered in a caliber other than .22. Features include solid rubber recoil pad; blued steel receiver; round blued steel barrel
MSRP. **$552.00**

STAND FOR THE FLAG EDITION GOLDEN BOY

Action: Lever
Stock: American walnut
Barrel: 20 in.
Sights: Brass bead front, fully adjustable semi-buckhorn rear with diamond insert
Weight: 6 lb. 12 oz.
Caliber: .22 LR
Magazine: 16 rounds
Features: Bright nickel receiver 90 percent covered with a Cerakote American flag; on the stock's right side, a man pays homage to the flag with his hand over his heart, surrounded by a circle bearing the opening line from the National Anthem
MSRP. **$1361.00**

STEEL LEVER ACTION SIDE GATE

Action: Lever
Stock: American walnut
Barrel: 18.43 in.
Sights: Brass bead front, fully adjustable semi-buckhorn rear

Weight: 7 lb. 1 oz.
Caliber: .30-30 Win., .45-70 Gov't.
Magazine: 4 rounds
Features: A traditional lever with side-gate loading; pistol grip stock with checkering; ventilated rubber recoil pad; drilled and tapped; swivel studs; .30-30 gets a straight grip and choice of standard or large loop lever, .45-70 gets a pistol grip stock and large loop lever
MSRP. **$1017.00**

STEEL WILDLIFE EDITION SIDE GATE

Action: Lever
Stock: American walnut
Barrel: 18.43 in., 20 in.
Sights: Brass bead front, fully adjustable semi-buckhorn rear
Weight: 7 lb.–7 lb. 1 oz.
Caliber: .30-30 Win., .45-70 Gov't.
Magazine: 4, 5 rounds
Features: .30-30 has 20-in. barrel, whitetail deer in gold with gold highlights on engraved receiver, straight stock, and standard loop; the .45-70 has an 18.43-in. barrel, moose engraved in gold with gold highlights on the receiver, pistol grip stock, and large loop lever
MSRP. **$1699.00**

TEXAS TRIBUTE EDITION

Action: Lever
Stock: American walnut
Barrel: 20 in.
Sights: Brass bead front, adjustable semi-buckhorn rear
Weight: 6 lb. 12 oz.
Caliber: .22 LR
Magazine: 16 rounds
Features: This one certainly screams Texas—literally—with the state's name and shape in 24K, plus a number of

brass stars, highlighting the dark walnut stock, an ode to Texas's "black gold" history
MSRP. **$1071.00**

THE LONG RANGER

Action: Lever
Stock: Walnut
Barrel: 20 in.
Sights: Ramp ivory bead front, fully adjustable folding rear
Weight: 7 lb.
Caliber: .223 Rem.. .243 Win., .308 Win. 6.5 Creedmoor
Magazine: 4 rounds
Features: Henry's first long-range hunting rifle; exposed hammer and forged steel lever; geared action that drives a machined and chromed steel bolt with a six-lug rotary head into a rear extension of the barrel; side-ejection from alloy receiver; drilled and tapped for scope mounts; laser-cut checkering
MSRP. **$1195.00**

THE LONG RANGER DELUXE ENGRAVED

Action: Lever
Stock: Walnut
Barrel: 20 in.
Sights: Folding fully adjustable rear, ramp front with ivory bead
Weight: 7 lb.
Caliber: .223 Rem./5.56 NATO, .243 Win., .308 Win.
Magazine: 5, 4 rounds
Features: Freshly updated versions of Henry's popular hunting rifle. All have checkered American walnut straight-wrist stocks; solid rubber recoil pads; sling swivels; detachable steel magazines; high-polished nickel receivers with gold-inlay enhanced scroll engraving
MSRP. **$2072.00**

Henry Repeating Arms

HENRY REPEATING ARMS THE LONG RANGER WILDLIFE EDITION

HENRY REPEATING ARMS U.S. SURVIVAL AR-7

HENRY REPEATING ARMS VARMINT EXPRESS

THE LONG RANGER WILDLIFE EDITION

Action: Lever
Stock: Walnut
Barrel: 20 in.
Sights: Folding fully adjustable rear, ramp front with ivory bead
Weight: 7 lb.
Caliber: .223 Rem./5.56 NATO, .243 Win., .308 Win.
Magazine: 5, 4 rounds
Features: Similar to the Long Ranger Deluxe Engraved, but each caliber is dedicated to a specific game animal with appropriate portrait engravings highlighted in 24K gold: the Coyote in .223/5.56 NATO; the Antelope in .243; and the Elk in .308
MSRP $1973.00

US SURVIVAL AR-7

Action: Semiautomatic
Stock: ABS Plastic
Barrel: 16 in.
Sights: Adjustable rear, blade front
Weight: 3 lb. 8 oz.
Caliber: .22 LR

Magazine: Detachable box, 8 rounds
Features: ABS plastic in black; Teflon coated receiver and coated steel barrel; in black or choice of True Timber-Kanati or Viper Western full-coverage camo
Black: $319.00
Camo: $388.00

VARMINT EXPRESS

Action: Lever
Stock: Walnut
Barrel: 20 in.
Sights: Open
Weight: 5 lb. 12 oz.
Caliber: .17 HMR
Magazine: Under-barrel tube, 11 rounds
Features: Checkered American walnut stock; Williams fire sights; blued round barrel and lever
MSRP $605.00

Heritage Manufacturing, Inc.

HERITAGE MANUFACTURING ROUGH RIDER RANCHER CARBINE

ROUGH RIDER RANCHER CARBINE

Action: Revolver
Stock: Wood
Barrel: 16 in.
Sights: Blade front, adjustable buck-horn rear
Weight: 4 lb. 2 oz.
Caliber: .22 LR

Magazine: 6 rounds
Features: A different take on the PCC, with a straight wood shoulder stock; six-round cylinder; black oxide finish; single-action only; leather sling included
MSRP $333.80

Hi-Point Firearms

HI-POINT FIREARMS MODEL 995

HI-POINT FIREARMS 1095

HI-POINT FIREARMS 4095

995

Action: Blow-back semiautomatic
Stock: Black, skeleton-style, all-weather molded polymer
Barrel: 16.5 in.
Sights: Adjustable
Weight: 7 lb.
Caliber: 9mm
Magazine: Detachable box, 10 rounds
Features: Sling, swivels, and base mount included; last round lock-open latch; multiple Picatinny rails; internal recoil buffer; also available in digital tan, pink, and woodland camos
MSRP . . . . $339.00–$471.00

1095

Action: Semiautomatic
Stock: Synthetic
Barrel: 17.5 in.
Sights: Fully adjustable front, rear
Weight: 7 lb.
Caliber: 10mm
Magazine: 10 rounds
Features: Skeletonized stock; fully adjustable front and rear sights; a raised soft-rubber cheekpiece; sling swivels; scope base; accessory rails; threaded barrel; available in black, flat dark earth, and Realtree Edge, Kryptek Yeti, and Mothwing Winter Mimicry camo patterns
Black $427.98
Realtree Edge $501.00
Flat dark earth $445.00

Kryptek Yeti $490.00
Mothwing Winter Mimicry . . . $490.00

4095

Action: Semiautomatic
Stock: Polymer
Barrel: 17.5 in.
Sights: Adjustable
Weight: 7 lb.
Caliber: .40 S&W
Magazine: 9 rounds
Features: All-weather; black polymer skeletonized stock sling; swivels and scope base internal recoil buffer in stock weaver style rails; fully adjustable sights ("ghost ring" rear peep and post front); quick on/off thumb safety; grip-mounted clip release; also available in digital tan, pink, and woodland camos
MSRP . . . . $349.00–$480.00

Howa by Legacy Sports

HOWA BY LEGACY SPORTS
APC FLAG CHASSIS

HOWA BY LEGACY SPORTS
HOGUE GAMEPRO 2

HOWA BY LEGACY
SPORTS HOGUE RIFLE

HOWA BY LEGACY
SPORTS HS PRECISION
RIFLE

HOWA BY LEGACY
SPORTS KUIU RIFLE

HOWA BY LEGACY SPORTS
MINI ACTION

APC FLAG CHASSIS

Action: Bolt
Stock: Aluminum
Barrel: 16.25 in., 24 in.
Sights: Nikko Sterling Diamond 4–16X50 Long Range scope
Weight: 11 lb. 8 oz.–12 lb. 5 oz.
Caliber: .223 Rem., 6mm Creedmoor, 6.5mm Creedmoor, .308 Win.
Magazine: 10 rounds
Features: Chassis rifle Cerakoted in red-white-and-blue or a gray-scale American flag graphics; Nikko Sterling Diamond 4–16X50 Long Range scope; heavy barrel with muzzle three-chamber Midwest Industries muzzle brake (semi-heavy barrel option does not include brake); Hogue finger groove pistol grip; adjustable bipod
MSRP **$1229.00**

HOGUE GAMEPRO 2

Action: Bolt
Stock: Synthetic
Barrel: 22 in., 24 in.
Sights: Nikko Stirling Gamepro scope
Weight: 7 lb. 13 oz.–8 lb.
Caliber: .22-250 Rem., .243 Win., 6.5 Creedmoor, 7mm-08 Rem., .308 Win., .270 Win., .30-06 Spfd., 7mm Rem. Mag., .300 Win. Mag., .300 PRC, 6.5 PRC
Magazine: N/A
Features: Users of this rifle get a Hogue pillar-bedded stock; suppres-sor-ready threaded barrel
MSRP **$719.00**

HOGUE RIFLE

Action: Bolt
Stock: Synthetic
Barrel: 22 in., 24 in.
Sights: None
Weight: 7 lb. 12 oz.–8 lb.
Caliber: .22-250 Rem., .243 Win., 6.5 Creedmoor, 7mm-08 Rem., .308 Win., .270 Win., .30-06 Spfd., 7mm Rem. Mag., .300 Win. Mag., .300 PRC, 6.5 PRC
Magazine: Internal box
Features: Blue metalwork; Hogue overmolded stock with pillar bedding; hinged floor plate; sling; swivel studs; threaded barrel
MSRP **$579.00**

HS PRECISION RIFLE

Action: Bolt
Stock: HS precision
Barrel: 22 in., 24 in.
Sights: None
Weight: 7 lb. 9 oz.–7 lb. 12 oz.
Caliber: .22-250 Rem., .243 Win., 6.5 Creedmoor, .308 Win., .270 Win., .30-06 Spfd., 7mm Rem. Mag., .300 Win. Mag., .300 PRC, 6.5 PRC
Magazine: 3, 4 rounds
Features: HOWA 1500 barreled action set in an aluminum bedding block with hand-laminated stock of Kevlar, fiberglass, carbon fiber molded around it; two-stage HACT trigger;

stocks in gray, tan, or OD green with black webbing
MSRP **$1059.00**

KUIU RIFLE

Action: Bolt
Stock: Synthetic
Barrel: 22 in., 24 in.
Sights: None
Weight: 7 lb. 12 oz.–8 lb.
Caliber: .22-250 Rem., .243 Win., 6.5 Creedmoor, 7mm-08 Rem., .308 Win., .270 Win., .30-06 Spfd., 7mm Rem. Mag., .300 Win. Mag.
Magazine: 5 rounds
Features: KUIU camo on Hogue pillar-bedded stock and recoil pad; Cerakote Gun Metal finish on barrel and action; KUIU Vias or Verde camo finishes
MSRP **$739.00**

MINI ACTION

Action: Bolt
Stock: Synthetic
Barrel: 16.25 in., 20 in., 22 in.
Sights: None
Weight: 5 lb. 11 oz.–6 lb. 10 oz.
Caliber: .223 Rem., 7.62X39, 6.5 Grendel, .350 Legend , 6mm ARC
Magazine: Detachable box, 10 rounds
Features: HOWA's Mini Action is only 6 in. long and weighs just 10.2 oz., 3 oz. and almost a full inch less than a standard short action and two ounces nearly 1.5 in. less than a long-action; barrels in lightweight (#1), standard (#2), and heavy (#6) options, as well as stocks in black, OD Green, Kryptek Highlander, Multicam and Yote camo finishes; package includes Nikko Stirling 3-9x40mm scope and one-piece base and rings
MSRP **$559.00**

Howa by Legacy Sports

**HOWA BY LEGACY SPORTS
MINI EXCL LITE CHASSIS**

**HOWA BY LEGACY
SPORTS ORYX**

**HOWA BY LEGACY SPORTS
RIMFIRE GAMEPRO
PACKAGE**

**HOWA BY LEGACY SPORTS
ORYX MINI-ACTION**

**HOWA BY LEGACY
SPORTS TSP X FOLDING
CHASSIS**

MINI EXCL LITE CHASSIS
Action: Bolt
Stock: Synthetic
Barrel: 16.25 in., 20 in.
Sights: None
Weight: N/A
Caliber: .223 Rem., 7.62X39, 6.5
Grendel, .350 Legend, 6mm ARC
Magazine: 5, 10 rounds
Features: An ultra-compact light-
weight chassis rifle with threaded bar-
rel; detachable box magazine;
adjustable length of pull from 12.75
to 15.75 in.
MSRP $579.00

ORYX
Action: Bolt
Stock: Aluminum
Barrel: 20 in., 24 in., 26 in.
Sights: None
Weight: 10 lb. 13 oz.–11 lb. 4 oz
Caliber: 6.5 PRC, .300 PRC, 6.5
Creedmoor, .308 Win.
Magazine: N/A

Features: A full monolithic aluminum
chassis with a back end adjustable for
length of pull and comb height; heavy
barrel; available in grey, green, or flat
dark earth; barrel threaded 5/8X24
MSRP . . . . $1099.00–$1119.00

ORYX MINI-ACTION
Action: Bolt
Stock: Aluminum
Barrel: 16 in..25 in., 20 in.
Sights: None
Weight: 8 lb. 3 oz.–8 lb. 23 oz.
Caliber: .223 Rem., 7.62X39, 6.5
Grendel, 6mm ARC
Magazine: N/A
Features: The compact chassis foot-
print of the full-size Oryx and with a
different set of caliber offerings
MSRP $1059.00

RIMFIRE GAMEPRO
PACKAGE
Action: Bolt

Stock: Synthetic
Barrel: 18 in.
Sights: Nikko Stirling Gamepro scope
Weight: 6 lb. 5 oz.
Caliber: .22 LR, .22 WMR, .17 HMR
Magazine: N/A
Features: Great rifle for the aspiring
rimfire competitor; comes with 3.5–
10x44mm Nikko Stirling Gamepro
scope; available in green, black, or
Kryptek Obskura Transitional camo
stocks
MSRP $459.00

TSP X FOLDING CHASSIS
Action: Bolt
Stock: Aluminum
Barrel: 24 in.
Sights: N/A
Weight: 13 lb. 8 oz.
Caliber: 6.5 Creedmoor, .300 PRC,
6.5 PRC, .308 Win.
Magazine: N/A
Features: A dedicated rifle for the
long-range game made more portable
with a folding stock design; available
in black or in a Cerakoted American
flag graphic overlay; muzzle brake;
top-side optics rail
MSRP $1159.00

H-S Precision

PHR (PROFESSIONAL
HUNTER RIFLE)
Action: Bolt
Stock: Synthetic
Barrel: 20 in., 22 in., 24 in., 26 in.,
28 in.
Sights: None
Weight: 7 lb. 12 oz.–8 lb. 4 oz.
Caliber: All popular magnum calibers
up to .458 Lott
Magazine: Detachable box, 3,
4 rounds
Features: Pro-Series 2000; cheekpiece
and built-in recoil reduction system;
steel barrel; optional muzzlebrake;
synthetic stock comes in sand, black,
olive, gray, and spruce green
MSRP $4599.00

H-S PRECISION HTR

H-S PRECISION PHR

HTR (HEAVY TACTICAL
RIFLE)
Action: Bolt
Stock: Synthetic
Barrel: 20 in., 22 in., 24 in., 26 in.,
28 in.
Sights: None

Weight: 10 lb. 12 oz.–11 lb. 4 oz.
Caliber: Any standard SAAMI, LR calibers
Magazine: Detachable box, 3, 10
rounds
Features: Pro-Series 2000; fully
adjustable synthetic stock comes in
sand, black, olive, gray, and spruce
green; heavy fluted barrel
MSRP $4779.00

H-S Precision

H-S PRECISION PLC (PROFESSIONAL LONG-RANGE CARBON FIBER)

H-S PRECISION TTD

PLC (PROFESSIONAL LONG-RANGE CARBON FIBER)

Action: Bolt
Stock: Synthetic
Barrel: Varies with caliber
Sights: None
Weight: Varies
Caliber: More than 50 calibers from .17 Rem. to .338 Win.
Magazine: 3, 4, 5 rounds
Features: A rifle of nearly unending customization, from barrel length, caliber, and left- or right-hand setups to length of pull, trigger, and dozens of accessories and scopes; features a carbon fiber barrel; completely redesigned stock
MSRP . . . . . . Starting at $5,550.00

TTD (TACTICAL TAKE-DOWN RIFLE)

Action: Bolt
Stock: Composite
Barrel: 22 in., 24 in.

Sights: None
Weight: 11 lb. 4 oz.–11 lb. 12 oz.
Caliber: Available in all standard SA SAAMI and LR calibers
Magazine: Detachable box, 3, rounds
Features: Stainless steel barrel and floor plate; synthetic stock with full length bedding block chassis system; metal parts are finished in matte black Teflon; stock colors include sand, black, olive, gray, and spruce green
MSRP $6499.00

Iron Horse Firearms

BLACKWATER FIREARMS/ IRON HORSE FIREARMS DMR

DMR

Action: Semiautomatic
Stock: Synthetic
Barrel: 18 in.

Sights: None
Weight: 8 lb. 7 oz.
Caliber: .223 Wylde
Magazine: 30 rounds
Features: Designated Marksman Rifle; 4150 steel button-rifled barrel in nitride coating; billet 7075 aluminum upper and lower; rifle-length gas system; A2 buffer, spring, and tube; adjustable length of pull and cheekpiece; ambidextrous charging handle and safety selector; 15.25-in. aluminum handlock with 3, 6, and 9 o'clock M-LOK points; oversized magazine release; supplied with 2 MFT magazines
MSRP $2099.00

Israel Weapons Industry (IWI)

ISRAEL WEAPON INDUSTRIES X95 FLATTOP

X95 FLATTOP

Action: Semiautomatic
Stock: Polymer
Barrel: 13, 16.5 in.
Sights: Folding front and rear
Weight: 7 lb. 15 oz.
Caliber: .300 BLK, .5.56 NATO, 5.45X39mm, 9mm
Magazine: 30 rounds
Features: Bullpup with a long-stroke gas-piston action and a closed rotating bolt; ambidextrous mag release; Picatinny rail; pistol grip or X95 customized trigger guard; in black or Flat Dark Earth; conversion kits for 9mm and 5.56 NATO available; submachine gun option available for law enforcement; NFA paperwork, taxes, etc. for SBR 13-in. barrel
MSRP . . . . .Starting at $2,000.00

Iver Johnson

IVER JOHNSON 1911A1 CARBINE

1911A1 CARBINE

Action: Semiautomatic
Stock: Walnut
Barrel: 16.125 in.
Sights: Blade front, notch rear
Weight: 4 lb.
Caliber: .45 ACP
Magazine: 8, 28 rounds

Features: Detachable walnut stock; barrel has a black oxide finish; walnut pistol grips with checkering and the Iver Johnson logo; 28-round drum magazine is available; includes one eight-round magazine
MSRP $881.00

Jarrett Rifles

JARRETT BEANFIELD

JARRETT PROFESSIONAL HUNTER

JARRETT SHIKAR SERIES

JARRETT WIND WALKER

BEANFIELD

Action: Bolt
Stock: Synthetic
Barrel: Various lengths available
Sights: None
Weight: Varies depending on options
Caliber: Any popular standard or magnum chambering
Magazine: Comes with 20 rounds
Features: Can build rifle on any receiver provided; optional caliber, stock style, color, muzzlebrake, barrel size, and taper; includes load data and 20 rounds of custom ammo
MSRP . . . . **starting at $6050.00**

PROFESSIONAL HUNTER

Action: Bolt
Stock: Synthetic or walnut
Barrel: Various lengths available
Sights: None
Weight: Varies depending on options
Caliber: .375 H&H, .416 Rem., .416 Rigby, .450 Rigby
Magazine: Comes with 40 rounds
Features: Includes 40 rounds of soft pointed bullets and solids created custom for each gun; ballistics printout and last three targets the gun shot also provided; optional scopes; .416 Rem. comes with Jarrett Tri-Lock receiver
MSRP . . . . **starting at $11,700.00**

SHIKAR SERIES

Action: Bolt
Stock: Wood
Barrel: N/A
Sights: None
Weight: 8 lb.
Caliber: Any long action, standard or magnum caliber
Magazine: N/A

Features: Muzzle brake; decelerator pad; hand checkering; trap door plate; Shilen or Jewell trigger; aged American black walnut stock; Jarrett Tri-Lock left or right hand receiver
MSRP . . . . **starting at $10,320.00**

WIND WALKER

Action: Bolt
Stock: Synthetic
Barrel: Up to 24 in.
Sights: None
Weight: 7 lb. 8 oz.
Caliber: Any popular short-action
Magazine: Comes with 20 rounds
Features: Jarrett Tri-Lock action; muzzlebrake; Tally scope mounting system; phenolic resin metal finish with choice of stock colors; ballistic print out included
MSRP . . . . **starting at $8320.00**

RIFLES

J.P. Sauer & Sohn

J.P. SAUER & SOHN
SAUER S100 CERATECH

J.P. SAUER & SOHN SAUER S100
CHEROKEE

S100 CERATECH

Action: Bolt
Stock: Synthetic
Barrel: 22 in., 24 in.
Sights: None
Weight: N/A
Caliber: .223 Rem., .243 Win. .270 Win., 7mm-08 Rem., 6.5x55 SE, 6.5 Creedmoor, 6.5 PRC, .308 Win., .30-06 Spfd., 8x57 IS, 9.3x62, 7mm Rem. Mag., .300 Win Mag.
Magazine: N/A

Features: Adjustable trigger; detachable magazine; ERGO MAX Stock; cold hammer forged barrel; receiver and barrel are in Cerakote Grey Ice
MSRP **$899.99**

S100 CHEROKEE

Action: Bolt
Stock: Synthetic
Barrel: 22 in., 24 in.
Sights: None
Weight: N/A

Caliber: .270 Win., .300 Win. Mag., .308 Win., 6.5 Creedmoor, 7mm Rem. Mag., 7mm-08 Rem., 6.5 PRC
Magazine: N/A
Features: Schnabel forend in soft-touch green/gold Digi-Camo; bolt, steel receiver, and barrel are in Cerakote Tundra Green; adjustable trigger; optional threaded muzzle
MSRP **$1000.00**

J.P. Sauer & Sohn

J.P. SAUER & SOHN SAUER S100 FIELDSHOOT

J.P. SAUER & SOHN SAUER S100 PANTERA

J.P. SAUER & SOHN S101 HIGHLAND XTC

J. P. SAUER & SOHN SAUER S404 CLASSIC

J.P. SAUER & SOHN S404 SYNCHRO XTC

RIFLES

S100 FIELDSHOOT

Action: Bolt
Stock: Wood
Barrel: 24 in.
Sights: None
Weight: N/A
Caliber: .223 Rem., .243 Win., .308 Win., 6.5x55 SE, 6.5 Creedmoor, 6.5 PRC
Magazine: N/A
Features: Oiled wood stock is adjustable for vertical height and length of pull; adjustable cheekpiece; vented forend is trim and has a bipod adaptor; barrel has a varmint match profile; bolt knob is an oversized cone design; threaded muzzle
MSRP $1575.00

S100 PANTERA

Action: Bolt
Stock: Laminated wood
Barrel: 20 in., 22 in.
Sights: None
Weight: N/A
Caliber: .223 Rem., .243 Win., .300 Win. Mag., .30-06 Spfd., .308 Win., 6.5 Creedmoor, 6.5 PRC
Magazine: N/A
Features: Threaded fluted barrel treated in Cerakote Black Recon; adjustable cheek piece; vented forend is trim and has a bipod adaptor; threaded muzzle
MSRP $1575.00

S101 HIGHLAND XTC

Action: Bolt
Stock: Carbon fiber
Barrel: 20 in., 22 in.

Sights: None
Weight: 5 lb. 8 oz.–5 lb. 10 oz.
Caliber: .243 Win., .270 Win., 6.5x55 SE, 7x64, .308 Win., .30-06 Spfd., 8x57 IS, 9.3x62, .300 Win. Mag., 7mm Rem. Mag.
Magazine: 4, 5 rounds
Features: Super lightweight, this rifle has a hand-laid carbon-fiber stock; fluted and threaded barrel; fluted bolt; Diamond-like Carbon surface treatment on metalwork; DURA SAFE firing pin safety; EVER REST bedding system; cold hammer-forged barrel; match rifle-shaped single-stage trigger
MSRP $3000.00

S404 CLASSIC

Action: Bolt
Stock: Wood
Barrel: 20–24.4 in.
Sights: Adjustable
Weight: 7 lb.–7 lb. 3 oz.
Caliber: .243 Win., 6.5x55 Swedish, .270 Win., 7x64 Brenneke, .308 Win., .30-06 Spfd., 8x57IS, 9.3x62 Mauser, 7mm Rem. Mag., .300 Win. Mag., 8x68 S, .338 Win. Mag., .375 H&H Mag.
Magazine: 2–3 rounds
Features: ERGO LUX stock in grade-5 figured walnut; aviation-grade high-alloy aluminum receiver; perfectly placed ergonomic manual cocking slide on the bolt shroud; easily replaceable bolt head makes switching from standard to magnum calibers a snap; twin ejectors for a precisely perpendicular ejection pattern; 6-lug bolt locks directly into the barrel; jeweled bolt body; SAUER Quattro

trigger with choice of four trigger pull weights: 550 g (1.2 lbs), 750 g (1.7 lbs), 1000 g (2.2 lbs) and 1250 g (2.7 lbs); infinitely adjustable trigger blade with 8 mm (0.3 in) adjustment range for length of pull and a left-to-right swivel range of 5 degrees; SAUER Universal Mount (SUM) integral to with receiver for an extremely low build height; SAUER universal key (SUS) integrated into the front sling swivel for forend and buttstock removal, barrel removal or replacement, and selection of trigger pull weight; MagLock magazine safety
MSRP . . . . $4685.00–$5301.00

S404 SYNCHRO XTC

Action: Bolt
Stock: Carbon fiber
Barrel: 22 in.
Sights: None
Weight: 6 lb. 2 oz.–6 lb. 5 oz.
Caliber: .223 Rem., .243 Win., 6.5x55 Swedish, 6.5 Creedmoor, .270 Win., 7x64, .308 Win., .30-06 Spfd., 8x57 IS, 9.3x62, 7mm Rem. Mag., .300 Win. Mag., 8x68 S, 10.3x60R
Magazine: 2, 3, 4 rounds
Features: Hand-laid carbon-fiber thumbhole stock of unique and trim design that's also modular, allowing the user to change stocks and barrel speedily with a Sauer SUS universal key integrated into the detachable forend swivel; adjustable cheekpiece; two-step bolt head from bolt body separation to render the gun instantly inoperable as needed; push-button manual cocking system; adjustable trigger pull weight and trigger blade position; cold hammer-forged threaded barrel
MSRP $8199.00

Kel-Tec

KEL-TEC RDB

KEL-TEC RFB

KEL-TEC SUB CQB

KEL-TEC SUB-2000

RDB

Action: Semiautomatic
Stock: Synthetic
Barrel: 17.3 in.
Sights: None
Weight: 7 lb.
Caliber: 5.56 NATO
Magazine: 20, 30 rounds
Features: A bullpup that features downward ejection; high impact-resistant Zytel forend; completely ambidextrous; top and bottom Picatinny rails
MSRP . . . .$1000.00–$1300.00

RFB, RFB HUNTER

Action: Semiautomatic
Stock: Synthetic
Barrel: 18 in., 24 in.
Sights: None
Weight: 8 lb.–8 lb. 11 oz.
Caliber: .308 Win.
Magazine: Detachable box, 10 or 20 rounds
Features: Picatinny rail; short-stroke gas piston operation; A2-style flash hider
MSRP . . . . $1800.00–$2000.00

SUB-2000

Action: Semiautomatic
Stock: Polymer
Barrel: 16.1 in.
Sights: Target
Weight: 4 lb.
Caliber: 9mm, .40 S&W
Magazine: 10+1 rounds
Features: Accepts Smith & Wesson M&P an SIG P226 magazines in 9mm or .40 S&W, Beretta 92 and 96 magazines, and Glock 17, 19, 22, and 23 magazines; folds away for storage and transportation
MSRP . . . . $578.00–$621.00

SUB CQB

Action: Semiautomatic
Stock: Synthetic
Barrel: 16.2 in.
Sights: None
Weight: 9 lb. 8 oz.
Caliber: 9mm
Magazine: 10, 15, 17, 30 rounds
Features: Super interesting entry in the self-defense genre, an integrally suppressed 9mm (one NFA stamp—this is not an SBR) that folds in half and tales Glock magazines; lots of rail for lights and lasers; only 4.25 inches of rifling in a 16-in. baffled barrel
MSRP $995.00

Kimber

KIMBER ADVANCED TACTICAL
SOC II FDE, SG

KIMBER ADVANCED
TACTICAL SRC II

ADVANCED TACTICAL SOC II FDE, SG

Action: Bolt
Stock: Aluminum
Barrel: 22 in.
Sights: None
Weight: 11 lb.
Caliber: 6.5 Creedmoor, .308 Win.
Magazine: 5 rounds
Features: Sub .5-MOA accuracy guarantee; match grade chamber; threaded barrel; side-folding stock adjustable for length and comb height; night vision mount; M-LOK rail; 1913 Mil-Spec tripod mount; Mauser claw extractor; in Flat Dark Earth (FDE) or anodized black (SG) stocks; barrels and action are finished in matte black Kim Pro II; SOC stands for Special Operations Capable
MSRP $2661.00

ADVANCED TACTICAL SRC II

Action: Bolt
Stock: Aluminum
Barrel: 16 in.
Sights: None
Weight: 10 lb.
Caliber: .308 Win.
Magazine: 5 rounds
Features: Similar to the SOC II, but with a shorter, suppressor-ready barrel; SRC stands for Suppressor Ready Compact
MSRP $2661.00

Kimber

KIMBER ADIRONDACK

KIMBER HUNTER

KIMBER MONTANA

KIMBER MOUNTAIN ASCENT

KIMBER MOUNTAIN ASCENT (SUBALPINE)

KIMBER OPEN RANGE PRO CARBON GRANITE

ADIRONDACK
Action: Bolt
Stock: Synthetic
Barrel: 18 in.
Sights: None
Weight: 4 lb. 13 oz.
Caliber: .308 Win., 7mm-08 Rem., 6.5 Creedmoor
Magazine: Internal, 4 rounds
Features: Kevlar/carbon fiber stock with Optifade Forrest finish; recoil pad; fluted barrel threaded for muzzle break/suppressor
MSRP.................**$1955.00**

HUNTER
Action: Bolt
Stock: FDE composite
Barrel: 22 in., 24 in.
Sights: None
Weight: 5 lb. 10 oz.
Caliber: .243 Win., .257 Roberts, 6.5 Creedmoor, .270 Win., .280 Ackley Imp., 7mm-08 Rem., .308 Win., .30-06 Spfd.
Magazine: 3 rounds
Features: Lightweight stock; match-grade adjustable trigger; match-grade chamber; sporter contour stainless barrel; removable box magazine; available in Flat Dark Earth stocks with either blue or stainless hardware
MSRP.................**$1026.00**

MONTANA
Action: Bolt
Stock: Reinforced carbon fiber
Barrel: 22 in., 24 in., 26 in.

Sights: None
Weight: 5 lb. 2 oz.–6 lb. 13 oz.
Caliber: .300 Win. Mag., .300 WSM, .30-06 Spfd., .280 Ackley Improved, .308 Win., 7mm-08 Rem., 6.5 Creedmoor
Magazine: 4, 5 rounds
Features: A Montana rifle with Kimber enhancements; match-grade chamber; threaded barrel; sling swivel studs; pillar bedding; sporter contour stainless barrel with satin finish; adjustable trigger; green stock; stainless hardware
MSRP.................**$1522.00**

MOUNTAIN ASCENT
Action: Bolt
Stock: Reinforced carbon fiber
Barrel: 22 in., 24 in., 26 in.
Sights: None
Weight: 4 lb. 13 oz.–6 lb. 7 oz.
Caliber: .280 Ackley Improved, .270 Win., .30-06 Spfd., .308 Win., .300 WSM, .270 WSM, .300 Win. Mag., 7mm Rem. Mag., 7mm-08 Rem., 6.5 Creedmoor
Magazine: 4 rounds
Features: Stainless fluted barrel with muzzle brake and thread protector; adjustable trigger; 1-inch Pachmayr Decelerator pad; three-position M70-type safety; Mauser claw extractor; match-grade chamber; 84M action; Moss Green stock
MSRP.................**$2302.00**

MOUNTAIN ASCENT (SUBALPINE)
Action: Bolt

Stock: Carbon fiber
Barrel: 22 in., 24 in.
Sights: None
Weight: 5 lb. 6 oz.
Caliber: .308 Win., .280 Ackley Improved, .30–06 Spfd., .300 WSM, .300 Win. Mag.
Magazine: 4 rounds
Features: A very lightweight offering for back-country wilderness hunters featuring reinforced carbon fiber stock wrapped in Gore Optifade SubAlpine camo; four-groove, fluted, sporter-contour barrel; muzzle brake and thread protector; stainless steel 84M action; Mauser claw extractor; spiral-fluted bolt
MSRP.................**$2302.00**

OPEN RANGE PRO CARBON GRANITE
Action: Bolt
Stock: Carbon fiber
Barrel: 24 in.
Sights: None
Weight: 6 lb. 3 oz.
Caliber: 6.5 Creedmoor
Magazine: 4 rounds
Features: With both a carbon fiber stock and barrel, this lightweight rifle also features a threaded muzzle with muzzle brake; metalwork finish in black KimPro II; medium-heavy barrel contour; stainless steel action; pillar-bedded stock in textured granite
MSRP.................**$3301.00**

RIFLES

KIMBER OPEN RANGE PRO CARBON OPEN COUNTRY

OPEN RANGE PRO CARBON OPEN COUNTRY

Action: Bolt
Stock: Carbon fiber
Barrel: 24 in.
Sights: None
Weight: 6 lb. 3 oz.
Caliber: 6.5 Creedmoor
Magazine: 4 rounds
Features: With both a carbon fiber stock and barrel, this lightweight rifle also features a threaded muzzle with muzzle brake; metalwork finish in black KimPro II; medium heavy barrel contour; stainless steel action finished in KimPro II gray; pillar-bedded stock in Tru Timber O2 Octane camo
MSRP. $3301.00

Knight's Armament Company

KNIGHT'S ARMAMENT SR-15 E3 CARBINE MOD 2 M-LOK

KNIGHT'S ARMAMENT SR-15 E3 LPR MOD 2 M-LOK

KNIGHT'S ARMAMENT SR-15 E3 MOD 2 M-LOK

KNIGHT'S ARMAMENT SR-30 M-LOK

SR-15 E3 CARBINE MOD 2 M-LOK

Action: Semiautomatic
Stock: Synthetic
Barrel: 14.5 in.
Sights: Adjustable
Weight: 6 lb. 6.4 oz.
Caliber: 5.56mm NATO
Magazine: 30 rounds
Features: Free-floated barrel inside a URX4 M-LOK handguard; improved E3 round-lug bolt design; ambidextrous bolt release, selector lever, and magazine release; drop-in two-stage trigger; 3-prong flash eliminator
MSRP. $2855.00

SR-15 E3 LPR MOD 2 M-LOK

Action: Semiautomatic
Stock: Synthetic
Barrel: 18 in.
Sights: Adjustable
Weight: 7 lb. 6.4 oz.
Caliber: 5.56mm NATO
Magazine: 30 rounds
Features: Free-floated barrel inside a URX4 M-LOK handguard; improved E3 round-lug bolt design; ambidextrous bolt release, selector lever, and magazine release; drop-in two-stage trigger; 3-prong flash eliminator
MSRP. $2883.99

SR-15 E3 MOD 2 M-LOK

Action: Semiautomatic
Stock: Synthetic
Barrel: 16 in.
Sights: Adjustable
Weight: 6 lb. 9 oz.
Caliber: 5.56mm NATO
Magazine: 30 rounds
Features: Free-floated barrel inside a URX4 M-LOK handguard; improved E3 round-lug bolt design; ambidextrous bolt release, selector lever, and magazine release; drop-in two-stage trigger; 3-prong flash eliminator
MSRP. $2699.99

SR-30 M-LOK

Action: Semiautomatic
Stock: Synthetic
Barrel: 9.5 in.
Sights: Adjustable
Weight: 6 lb. 3 oz.
Caliber: .300 BLK (7.62x35mm)
Magazine: 30 rounds
Features: QDC-compatible flash hider will mount any of the KAC 7.62mm QDC suppressors; ambidextrous controls; two-stage match trigger; M-Lok accessory mounting system
MSRP. $2653.00

Krieghoff

KRIEGHOFF "BIG FIVE" DOUBLE RIFLE

"BIG FIVE" DOUBLE RIFLE
Action: Hinged breech
Stock: Walnut
Barrel: 23.5 in.
Sights: Open

Weight: 9 lb. 8 oz.–10 lb. 8 oz.
Caliber: .375 H&H Mag., .375 Flanged Magnum N.E., .450/.400 NE, .500/.416 N.E., .470 N.E., .500 N.E.
Magazine: None

Features: Double triggers; V-shaped rear sight with a white, vertical middle line and a pearl front sight; optional Super-Express sight; Monte Carlo style cheekpiece; European walnut stock with small game scene engraving; steel trigger and floor plate; straight comb and large recoil pad
MSRP . . . . starting at $15,995.00

Kriss USA

KRISS USA DMK22C

KRISS USA DMK22C LVOA

KRISS USA VECTOR 22-CRB

KRISS USA VECTOR CRB

KRISS USA VECTOR SBR ENHANCED

DMK22C
Action: Semiautomatic
Stock: Synthetic
Barrel: 16 in.
Sights: Adjustable
Weight: N/A
Caliber: .22 LR
Magazine: 10 or 15 rounds
Features: Full metal construction; mil-spec buffer tube; free-floating modular handguard; bolt stays open when magazine is pulled; compatible with most AR-15 parts; six-position adjustable stock; black nitride finish on barrel; direct blowback action; in black, flat dark earth, Alpine, camo black, camo Alpine
MSRP . . . . $725.00–$985.00

DMK22C LVOA
Action: Semiautomatic
Stock: Synthetic
Barrel: 16 in.
Sights: None
Weight: 7 lb. 1 oz.
Caliber: .22 LR
Magazine: 15 rounds
Features: Licensed reproduction of War Sport Manufacturing's Low Visibility Operations Application rifle, this rimfire has an adaptor that allows for the installation of aftermarket Ruger 10/22 barrels; patented bolt lock keeps action open when magazine is removed; compatible with most AR-15 furniture and accessories; LVOA free-floating rail; low-profile flip-up sights; mil-spec buffer tube; six-position adjustable stock; direct blowback action; single-stage trigger; in black, flat dark earth, or alpine white
MSRP . . . . $825.00–$925.00

VECTOR 22-CRB, 22-CRB ENHANCED
Action: Semiautomatic
Stock: Synthetic
Barrel: 16 in.
Sights: Flip-up front, rear
Weight: 7 lb. 6 oz.
Caliber: .22 LR
Magazine: 10 rounds
Features: A very sophisticated rimfire in the Kriss bull-pup style with an ambidextrous safety; six-position adjustable stock; direct blowback action with last round bolt hold-open; aluminum M-LOK handguard; enhanced gets a free-floating M-LOK handguard; standard model in black, Alpine, or flat dark earth Nitride finish; Enhanced model in camo black or camo white
22-CRB: . . . . $675.00–$695.00
Enhanced: $895.00

VECTOR CRB
Action: Semiautomatic
Barrel: 16 in.
Sights: Low-profile folding front and rear
Weight: 8 lb.
Caliber: 9mm, .45 ACP, 10mm, .40 S&W
Magazine: Glock magazines
Features: Patented Kriss Super V recoil mitigation system; closed bolt/delayed blowback action; six-position adjustable stock; full-length top rail; low-profile flip-up sights; compatible with Glock magazines; in black, flat dark earth or Alpine white; California, Maryland, Massachusetts, New Jersey and Canada compliant variants available
MSRP . . . . $1575.00–$1615.00

VECTOR SBR, SBR ENHANCED
Action: Semiautomatic
Stock: Synthetic
Barrel: 5.5 in., 6.5 in.
Sights: Custom flip-up iron
Weight: 7 lb.–7 lb. 4 oz.
Caliber: .45 ACP, 9mm, 10mm, .40 S&W
Magazine: Glock magazines
Features: Kriss's Super V recoil management system; topside and under muzzle rails; Glock magazine compatibility; threaded barrel; Enhanced has slightly longer barrel and additional rail space; both versions available in black, flat dark earth, or Alpine white
SBR . . . .$1625.00–$1665.00
Enhanced . . . .$1825.00–$1865.00

Lazzeroni Arms, Inc.

LAZZERONI M2012 MOUNTAIN-LITE LONG-RANGE

LAZZERONI M2012 SHORT-MAG HEAVY BARREL DANGEROUS GAME

LAZZERONI M2012 THUMBHOLE EXTRA LONG-RANGE

M2012 MOUNTAIN-LITE LONG-RANGE

Action: Bolt
Stock: Graphite/composite
Barrel: 26 in.
Sights: None
Weight: 7 lb. 5 oz.
Caliber: 6.53 Scramjet, 7.21 Firebird, 7.82 Firebird
Magazine: 4 rounds
Features: All new precision CNC-machined chromoly receiver; one-piece diamond-fluted bolt shaft; stainless steel match-grade button-barrel; custom molded hand-bedded graphite/composite stock designs; precision-machined aluminum alloy floor plate/trigger guard assembly; jewel competition trigger; Vais muzzlebrake; Limbsaver recoil pad
MSRP $5999.99

M2012 SHORT-MAG HEAVY BARREL DANGEROUS GAME

Action: Bolt
Stock: Composite
Barrel: 22 in.
Sights: None
Weight: 7 lb. 3 oz.
Caliber: 9.53 Hellcat, 10.57 Maverick, 12.04 Lilmufu
Magazine: 3 rounds
Features: Designed around Lazzeroni's short magnums, but for the larger calibers in this group; stainless steel match-grade button-rifled barrel; Timney trigger; High-tech Vais muzzle brake; barrel band with sling eye
MSRP $7499.99

M2012 THUMBHOLE EXTRA LONG-RANGE

Action: Bolt
Stock: Graphite/composite
Barrel: 25 in.
Sights: None
Weight: 7 lb. 11 oz.
Caliber: 7.21 Warbird, 7.82 Warbird, 8.59 Titan, 9.53 Saturn
Magazine: 4 rounds
Features: 20 MOA Picatinny style rail; 34mm or 30mm ring sets; right hand only
MSRP $6999.99

Lithgow Arms

LITHGOW ARMS LA101 CROSSOVER RIMFIRE

LITHGOW ARMS LA105 WOOMERA

LA101 CROSSOVER RIMFIRE

Action: Bolt
Stock: Synthetic, laminate
Barrel: 20.9 in.
Sights: None
Weight: 6 lb. 9.6 oz.–7 lb. 3.2 oz.
Caliber: .22 LR, .22 WMR, .17 HMR
Magazine: N/A
Features: Free-floating barrel; integral molded trigger guard; length of pull adjustment spacers; Cerakote-finished barrel; receiver, bolt handle, and integral scope bases; black synthetic and laminate stock options
MSRP . . . . $1249.00–$1383.00

LA105 WOOMERA

Action: Bolt
Stock: Polymer
Barrel: 24 in.
Sights: None
Weight: 11 lb.
Caliber: 6.5 Creedmoor, .308 Win.
Magazine: 10 rounds
Features: Adjustable KRG tactical rifle stock; muzzle brake; Cerakote finish; threaded muzzle; 20 MOA Picatinny rail; in black or Flat Dark Earth finishes
MSRP $3299.00

Live Q or Die Q, LLC

LIVE Q OR DIE HONEY BADGER SBR

HONEY BADGER SBR

Action: Semiautomatic
Stock: Synthetic
Barrel: 7 in.
Sights: None
Weight: 4 lb. 8 oz.
Caliber: .300 BLK
Magazine: 20 rounds
Features: This is an NFA short-barreled rifle (no suppressor), so paperwork/tax stamps apply; adjustable low-profile gas block; two-position collapsible PDW stock; free-floating 6-inch M-LOK handguard; Cherry Bomb muzzle brake threaded at 5/8x24
MSRP $2999.00

Live Q or Die Q, LLC

LIVE Q OR DIE HONEY BADGER SD

LIVE Q OR DIE THE FIX

HONEY BADGER SD

Action: Semiautomatic
Stock: Synthetic
Barrel: 7 in.
Sights: None
Weight: 5 lb. 6 oz.
Caliber: .300 BLK
Magazine: 20 rounds
Features: This an NFA short-barrel rifle with silencer, so all paperwork/tax stamps apply; free-floating 6061 aluminum M-LOK handguard; tapered muzzle threaded 5/8x24; AR-type controls; two-stage trigger; finished in clear hard coat anodized over tan; company's own Honey Badger silencer
MSRP **$3499.00**

THE FIX

Action: Bolt
Stock: Synthetic
Barrel: 16 in.
Sights: None
Weight: 6 lb. 4 oz.–6 lb. 6 oz.
Caliber: 6.5 Creedmoor, .308 Win.
Magazine: 20 rounds
Features: 45-degree short-throw bolt; fully adjustable folding stock; free-floating Q-sert handguard; 5/8X24 threaded tapered muzzle with Cherry Bomb muzzle brake; two-stage match trigger; one-piece receiver; SR-25 magazine compatible; AR-type controls
MSRP **$3299.00**

LWRC International

LWRCI IC A5

LWRCI IC DI COMPETITION

LWRCI IC DI STANDARD 5.56

LWRCI IC DI STANDARD .300 BLK

IC A5

Action: Semiautomatic
Stock: Composite
Barrel: 10.5 in., 14.7 in., 16.1 in.
Sights: Skirmish back up iron sights
Weight: 6 lb. 8 oz.–7 lb. 5 oz.
Caliber: .5.56 NATO
Magazine: 10 or 30 rounds
Features: Enhanced Fire Control Group; dual-control fully ambidextrous lower receiver; Magpul MOE grip; NiCorr treated cold hammer-forged barrel; ambidextrous charging handle; Monoforge upper receiver with modular rail system; adjustable two-position gas block; A2 birdcage flash hider
MSRP **$2704.02**

IC DI COMPETITION

Action: Semiautomatic
Stock: Polymer
Barrel: 16.1 in.
Sights: None
Weight: 7 lb.
Caliber: 5.56 NATO
Magazine: 10, 30 rounds
Features: A shorter-barreled direct impingement AR platform; fully ambidextrous controls; sling mount; charging handle; LWRCI's new four-port Ultra Brake and M-LOK free-float handguard; Timney 6675 straight competition trigger; short-throw selector; in black, Flat Dark Earth, OD Green, Patriot Brown, or Tungsten Grey
MSRP **$2267.19**

IC DI STANDARD 5.56

Action: Semiautomatic
Stock: Synthetic
Barrel: 16.1 in., 18.1 in.
Sights: None
Weight: 6 lb. 10 oz.
Caliber: 5.56 NATO, .300 Blackout
Magazine: Detachable box
Features: Direct impingement system; modular, one-piece free-float rail; angled ergonomic fore grip with QD sling point; fully ambidextrous lower controls; A2 birdcage flash hider
MSRP **$1649.44**

IC DI STANDARD .300 BLK

Action: Semiautomatic
Stock: Polymer
Barrel: 16.1 in.
Sights: None
Weight: 6 lb. 10 oz.
Caliber: .300 Blackout
Magazine: 30 rounds
Features: Direct impingement AR platform; A2 flash hider; ambidextrous controls; six-position Mil-Spec buffer tube; NiCorr-treated barrel; gas block; gas tube; in black, Patriot Brown, or Gun Metal Gray
MSRP **$1715.41**

LWRC International

LWRCI IC SPR

LWRCI VALKYRIE 224 DI

LWRCI REPR MK II

IC SPR

Action: Semiautomatic
Stock: Composite
Barrel: 14.7 in., 16.1 in.
Sights: Skirmish back up iron sights
Weight: 7 lb.–7 lb. 5 oz.
Caliber: 5.56 NATO
Magazine: 10 or 30 rounds
Features: Monoforge upper receiver with user-configurable 12-inch rail system; cold hammer-forged spiral fluted barrel that is 20 percent lighter; Enhanced Fire Control Group; advanced trigger guard; adjustable compact stock; compact high-efficiency flash hider; patented short-stroke gas piston system; Magpul MOE grip
MSRP $2443.92

R.E.P.R. MK II, MK II ELITE

Action: Semiautomatic
Stock: Synthetic
Barrel: 12.7 in., 16.1 in., 20 in.
Sights: None
Weight: 9 lb. 4.8 oz.
Caliber: 6.5 Creedmoor, 7.62x39
Magazine: N/A
Features: Rapid Engagement Precision Rifle utilizes patented Short Stroke Gas Piston System; billet 7075 aluminum upper and lower; 12.5-in. modular rail system; gas system normal and suppressed settings; side-mounted non-reciprocating charging handle; NiCorr-treated cold-hammer-forged heavy barrel; Patriot Brown, OD Green, Flat Dark Earth, and black anodized finishes available, plus many custom options
Standard: $4233.00
Elite: $4763.40

VALKYRIE 224 DI

Action: Semiautomatic
Stock: Polymer
Barrel: 20.1 in.
Sights: None
Weight: 8 lb. 2 oz.
Caliber: .224 Valkyrie
Magazine: N/A
Features: Direct impingement, Rifle+1-length system with LWRCI fire control group; LWRCI's news four-port Ultra Brake; NiCorr-treated gas block; cold hammer-forged non-fluted NiCorr-treated barrel; Magpul MOE stock; LWRCI's all-new SnakeSkin Pistol grip provides for sight tool and battery storage; in black, Flat Dark Earth, Olive Drab, Patriot Brown, and Tungsten Grey
MSRP $2179.78

RIFLES

Magnum Research

MAGNUM RESEARCH SWITCHBOLT

SWITCHBOLT

Action: Semiautomatic
Stock: Laminate, synthetic
Barrel: 17 in.
Sights: None
Weight: 4 lb. 8 oz.
Caliber: .22 LR
Magazine: 10 rounds
Features: Designed for rimfire speed competitions; operating bolt handle on the left side of the right-handed bolt, so that right-handed shooters never have to release their trigger hand grip to charge after a gone-dry reload or otherwise manipulate the bolt; skeletonized hardwood laminate (red, blue, black pepper, or forest camo) or black synthetic thumbhole stock; carbon barrel; gas-assisted blowback operation; Ruger 10/22 magazines
MSRP . . . . $638.00–$849.00

MasterPiece Arms

MASTERPIECE ARMS MPA AR9 PCC

MPA AR9 PCC

Action: Semiautomatic
Stock: Aluminum
Barrel: 16 in.
Sights: None
Weight: 6 lb. 4 oz.
Caliber: 9mm
Magazine: 10, 15, 17, 30 rounds
Features: Closed-bolt blowback operating system; aluminum receiver that takes standard AR accessories and furniture; proprietary bolt carrier group; heavy duty claw extractor; suppressor compatibility; Glock magazine compatibility; multi-port steel Cerakoted compensator; adjustable buttstock; cool colors
MSRP $1499.00

MasterPiece Arms

MASTERPIECE ARMS MPA BA PRECISION MATCH RIFLE (PMR) COMPETITION

MASTERPIECE ARMS MPA BA ULTRA LITE HUNTER CF

MASTERPIECE ARMS MPA BA ULTRA LITE HUNTER RIFLE SS

MASTERPIECE ARMS MPA PORK CHOP RIFLE

MPA BA PRECISION MATCH RIFLE (PMR) COMPETITION

Action: Bolt
Stock: Aluminum
Barrel: 26 in.
Sights: None
Weight: 11 lb. 8 oz.
Caliber: 6mm Creedmoor, 6.5 Creedmor, .308 Win.
Magazine: 10 rounds
Features: Developed specifically for the Production Class in formal Precision Rifle Series competition, this rifle sport's MPA's BA Hybrid Chassis in Cerakote with v-bedding, built-in inclinometer, thumb notch, and lower rail; MPA/Curtis short action; X-Caliber hand-lapped barrel with a #7 profile threaded 5/8X24; TriggerTech Special trigger; Magpul AICS-type magazine
MSRP . . . . $2200.00–$2350.00

MPA BA ULTRA LITE HUNTER CF (CARBON FIBER)

Action: Bolt
Stock: Aluminum
Barrel: customer determined

Sights: None
Weight: 7 lb. 8 oz.
Caliber: 6.5 Creedmoor, 6.5 PRC, .300 PRC, .28 Nosler
Magazine: 3 rounds
Features: Nearly 2 pounds lighter than the Hybrid Hunter, this chassis rifle features a Proof carbon fiber barrel in a Sendero light contour and threaded 5/8X25; Curtis Axiom action; MPA's Ultra-Light Chassis with V-bedding system; vertical grip; built-in inclinometer; TriggerTech trigger; Cerakote finish
MSRP . . . . $3575.00–$3700.00

MPA BA ULTRA LITE HUNTER RIFLE SS

Action: Bolt
Stock: Aluminum
Barrel: Customer choice
Sights: N/A
Weight: 7 lb. 8 oz.
Caliber: .300 Win. Mag., .300 WSM, 7mm SAUM, .243 Win., .28 Nosler, 6.5 PRC, .300 PRC, .308 Win., 6.5 Creedmoor, 6mm Creedmoor
Magazine: 3 rounds
Features: Curtis Custom Axiom bolt action in a Remington 700 configuration; stainless hand-lapped, pull-button-rifled barrel in a sendero pro-

file and threaded 5/8-24
MSRP . . . . $3200.00–$3325.00

MPA PORK CHOP

Action: Bolt
Stock: Chassis
Barrel: 18 in., 20 in., 22 in., 24 in., 26 in.
Sights: None
Weight: 8 lb. 6 oz.
Caliber: .22 Creedmoor, .223 Wylde, 6 GT, 6mm Creedmoor, 6.5 Creedmoor, 6.5 PRC
Magazine: N/A
Features: Customer choice of barrel length, left-/right-hand setup, and stock type; MPA RAT rail (Arca Swiss Rail); adjustable cheekpiece and length of pull; EVG—enhanced vertical grip; inclinometer level; V4 spigot mount; length of pull ranging from 11.75 to 13.25 in.; one-piece spiral-fluted bolt; carbon fiber barrel hand-lapped, stress relieved, and threaded in choice of Sendero or Sendero Lite profiles; V bedding system with clearance glass bedding; thumb notch; bag rider; Trigger Tech Special trigger; choice of Cerakote finish
MSRP . . . . $3700.00–$3850.00

Mauser

MAUSER M18

M18

Action: Bolt
Stock: Polymer
Barrel: 22 in., 24 in.

Sights: None
Weight: 6 lb. 6 oz.–6 lb. 10 oz.
Caliber: .243 Win., .270 Win., .300 Win. Mag., .30-06 Spfd., .308 Win.,

6.5 Creedmoor, 6.5 PRC, 7mm Rem. Mag.
Magazine: 5 rounds
Features: All-steel receiver; an all-weather polymer stock with soft-grip inserts; three-position safety; cold-hammer-forged barrel; adjustable trigger; buttstock has a removable cap for small-tool or compact cleaning kit storage
MSRP $699.99

M98 MAGNUM

Action: Bolt
Stock: Wood
Barrel: 24.4 in.
Sights: Windage and elevation adjustable two-leaf express sights.
Weight: 9 lb. 7 oz.–10 lb. 1.6 oz.
Caliber: .375 H&H Mag., .416 Rigby, .450 Rigby
Magazine: 4, 5 rounds
Features: Premium steel construction with plasma nitriding; long extractor; controlled round feed; double recoil

MAUSER M98 MAGNUM

lugs; pillar bedding; newly designed horizontal safety; double square bridge system designed for swing-off scope mounts; heavy barrel contour option for .416 and .450 Rigby calibers. Two variants: Expert has noble walnut root WG5 grade, while Diplomat has upgraded WG7 grade;

both have M98 Classic Sporter stock profile, ebony fore-end caps; hinged floorplate steel magazine, M98 express open sights
Expert: $15,081.00
Diplomat: $16,146.00

McMillan Firearms

MCMILLAN TAC-338

TAC-338

Action: Bolt
Stock: Composite
Barrel: 27 in.
Sights: None
Weight: 11 lb.

Caliber: .338 Alpha Mag.
Magazine: Detachable box, 1 to 5 rounds
Features: Featuring McMillan's own TAC-338 action designed for the .338 Lapua; the 27-in. barrel has a medi-

um-heavy contour, is match grade and stainless steel, and has a muzzle brake with ¾-24 threads; McMIllan's Tactical stock with adjustable cheekpiece, length-of-pull spacers, one stud, and six flush-mount cups with ¼-in. sling loops; 20 MOA 1913 Mil-Std rail is standard; metalwork finished to match the stock, available in black, OD Green, and Flat Dark Earth
MSRP . . . . **starting at $6063.75**

Mossberg (O. F. Mossberg & Sons)

MOSSBERG 702 PLINKSTER

MOSSBERG 702 YOUTH BANTAM PLINKSTER

MOSSBERG 715T FLAT TOP

702 PLINKSTER

Action: Semiautomatic
Stock: Synthetic
Barrel: 18 in.
Sights: Hooded fiber optic front, adjustable rear
Weight: 4 lb.
Caliber: .22 LR
Magazine: 10, 25 rounds
Features: A handy, economical youth rimfire; black synthetic stock; rounded fore-end; vented rubber recoil pad
MSRP . . . . **$153.00–$227.00**

702 YOUTH BANTAM PLINKSTER

Action: Semiautomatic
Stock: Synthetic

Barrel: 18 in.
Sights: Hooded fiber optic front, adjustable rear
Weight: 4 lb.
Caliber: .22 LR
Magazine: 10 rounds
Features: Black synthetic stock; adjustable rifle sights with a fiber optic front; rounded fore-end; Bantam is two inches shorter overall than standard Plinkster
MSRP $217.00

715T FLAT TOP

Action: Semiautomatic
Stock: Synthetic
Barrel: 16.25 in.
Sights: Mounted front, adjustable rear;

rail mount and adjustable front and rear; 30mm red-dot
Weight: 5 lb. 8 oz.
Caliber: .22 LR
Magazine: Detachable box, 11 or 26 rounds
Features: Adjustable stock; 10-round magazine or 25-round magazine/loader; FLEX Pad; standard model has rail mount adjustable sights and is available with choice of black or Muddy Girl Serenity synthetic stock; red-dot combo has black synthetic stock; green-dot combo has flat dark earth stock
Sights only $381.00
Red-/green-dot sight $434.00

Mossberg (O. F. Mossberg & Sons)

MOSSBERG 802 PLINKSTER

MOSSBERG 802 PLINKSTER SCOPED COMBO

MOSSBERG 817

MOSSBERG MVP LR

MOSSBERG MVP PATROL

MOSSBERG MVP PRECISION RIFLE

MOSSBERG MVP SCOUT

RIFLES

802 PLINKSTER

Action: Bolt
Stock: Synthetic
Barrel: 18 in.
Sights: Hooded fiber optic front, adjustable rear
Weight: 4 lb.
Caliber: .22 LR
Magazine: 10 rounds
Features: Black synthetic stock; adjustable rifle sights with a fiber optic front; rounded fore-end; vented rubber recoil pad
MSRP $217.00

802 PLINKSTER SCOPED COMBO

Action: Bolt
Stock: Synthetic
Barrel: 18 in.
Sights: Hooded fiber optic front, adjustable rear/4X scope
Weight: 4 lb. 8 oz.
Caliber: .22 LR
Magazine: 10 rounds
Features: Black synthetic stock; adjustable rifle sights with a fiber optic front; factory mounted 4X scope; rounded fore-end; vented rubber recoil pad
MSRP $230.00

817

Action: Bolt
Stock: Synthetic or wood
Barrel: 21 in.
Sights: None
Weight: 4 lb. 8 oz.–5 lb.
Caliber: .17 HMR
Magazine: Detachable box, 6 rounds
Features: Factory-mounted Weaver-style scope bases; cross-bolt safety

and magazine release buttons; free gun lock included
MSRP $252.00

MVP LR

Action: Bolt
Stock: Synthetic
Barrel: 20 in.
Sights: None
Weight: 8 lb.
Caliber: 7.62 NATO, 6.5 Creedmoor
Magazine: 10 rounds
Features: Features include a textured OD green stock with adjustable cheekpiece; detachable box magazine; fluted and threaded barrel; topside optics rail; dual swivels front, single rear
MSRP $976.00

MVP PATROL

Action: Bolt
Stock: Synthetic
Barrel: 16.25 in.
Sights: Adjustable
Weight: 7 lb.–7 lb. 8 oz.
Caliber: 5.56 NATO, 7.62 NATO, .300 BLK
Magazine: Detachable box, 10+1 rounds
Features: Picatinny rail; threaded barrel for flash suppressor; Lightning Bolt action adjustable trigger system; Standard Patrol rifles have 16.25-in. barrels and come in black
MSRP $638.00

MVP PRECISION RIFLE

Action: Bolt
Stock: Aluminum
Barrel: 20 in., 24 in.

Sights: None
Weight: 9 lb. 4 oz. (7.62 NATO), 10 lb. (6.5 Creedmoor)
Caliber: 7.62 NATO, 6.5 Creedmoor
Magazine: 11 rounds
Features: Mossberg chassis; UTH-AR MBA-3 adjustable stock; Magpul MOE grip; accepts both M1A/M14 and AR10-SR25 magazines; Magpul M-LOK modular mounting system; medium bull barrel is free-floating and threaded; the Mossberg Lightning Trigger System adjusts from three to seven pounds; oversized bolt and trigger guard; 20 MOA Picatinny rail
MSRP $1509.00

MVP SCOUT

Action: Bolt
Stock: Synthetic
Barrel: 16.25 in.
Sights: Fiber optic front ghost ring
Weight: 6 lb. 12 oz.
Caliber: 7.62 NATO
Magazine: Detachable box, 11 rounds
Features: Has an 11-inch receiver/barrel-mounted Picatinny rail; an integrated, rail-mounted, Ghost Ring rear sight is paired with a barrel-mounted, fiber optic front sight; two Picatinny side rails, located near the front of the forend; a compact 16 ¼-inch medium bull, carbon steel button-rifled, threaded barrel with an A2-style suppressor, with a 1:10 twist rate; a protective thread cap is provided; an adjustable rifle sling; scoped package includes Vortex 2-7x32 rifle scope
Sights only $669.00
With scope. $836.00

Mossberg (O. F. Mossberg & Sons)

MOSSBERG PATRIOT
NIGHT TRAIN

MOSSBERG PATRIOT
PREDATOR

MOSSBERG PATRIOT PREDATOR
CERAKOTE/STRATA CAMO

MOSSBERG PATRIOT
SYNTHETIC

MOSSBERG PATRIOT
SYNTHETIC CERAKOTE

MOSSBERG PATRIOT SYNTHETIC
VORTEX SCOPED COMBO

MOSSBERG PATRIOT
WALNUT

PATRIOT NIGHT TRAIN

Action: Bolt
Stock: Synthetic
Barrel: 24 in.
Sights: 6–24X50mm scope
Weight: N/A
Caliber: .308 Win., 6.5 Creedmoor, .300 Win. Mag.
Magazine: 5 rounds
Features: A long-range rifle, complete with factory-mounted scope, that won't break the bank; matte finished fluted barrel; OD green in .308, flat dark earth stock in 6.5 Creedmoor, O.D. green stock in .300 Win. Mag.
MSRP. $906.00

PATRIOT PREDATOR

Action: Bolt
Stock: Synthetic
Barrel: 16.25 in.
Sights: None
Weight: 6 lb. 4 oz.
Caliber: .243 Win., .308 Win., 6.5 Creedmoor, .450 Bushmaster, 6.5 PRC
Magazine: 4, 5 rounds
Features: Threaded fluted barrel and Picatinny rail on all calibers, and the .450 Bushmaster also gets adjustable sights; flat dark earth stock with matte blued metalwork
MSRP. . . . . $504.00–$535.00

PATRIOT PREDATOR
CERAKOTE/STRATA CAMO

Action: Bolt
Stock: Synthetic
Barrel: 22 in.
Sights: None
Weight: 6 lb. 8 oz.
Caliber: .22-250 Rem., .243 Win., .3008 Win. 6.5 Creedmoor, 6.5 PRC
Magazine: 4, 5 rounds
Features: Synthetic stock in Strata camo; metalwork in Cerakote Patriot Brown; fluted threaded barrel
MSRP. $598.00

PATRIOT SYNTHETIC

Action: Bolt
Stock: Synthetic
Barrel: 20 in.
Sights: None
Weight: 6 lb. 8 oz.
Caliber: .243 Win., .22-250 Rem., 7mm-08 Rem., .308 Win., .25-06 Rem., .270 Win., .30-06 Spfd., 6.5 Creedmoor, .450 Bushmaster, .350 Legend, .300 Win. Mag., 7mm Rem. Mag.
Magazine: 3, 4, 5 rounds
Features: Utilitarian hunting rifle in the straight-wall .450 Bushmaster round; threaded barrel; Weaver-type bases
MSRP. . . . . $440.00–$455.00

PATRIOT SYNTHETIC
CERAKOTE

Action: Bolt
Stock: Synthetic
Barrel: 22 in.
Sights: None; adjustable
Weight: 6 lb. 8 oz.
Caliber: 6.5 Creedmoor, .243 Win., .308 Win., 7mm-08 Rem., .270 Win., .30-06 Spfd., .22-250 Rem., .25-06 Rem., 7mm Rem. Mag., .300 Win. Mag., .338 Win. Mag., .375 Ruger
Magazine: 3, 5 rounds
Features: Cerakote Stainless with black synthetic stocks; button-rifled, carbon steel, free-floating fluted barrel; Weaver-style optics bases; spiral-fluted bolts; the Lightning Bolt Action Trigger System
MSRP. . . . . $503.00–$540.00

PATRIOT SYNTHETIC
VORTEX SCOPED COMBO

Action: Bolt
Stock: Synthetic
Barrel: 22 in.
Sights: Vortex Crossfire II 3–9X40mm scope
Weight: 7 lb. 8 oz.
Caliber: .243 Win., .308 Win., .270 Win., .30-06 Spfd., 6.5 Creedmoor, .22-250 Rem., 7mm-08 Rem., .25-06 Rem., .300 Win. Mag., 7mm Rem. Mag.
Magazine: 3, 5 rounds
Features: Utilitarian hunting rifle featuring a fluted barrel; Vortex scope; matte blue metalwork
MSRP. . . . . $594.00–$609.00

PATRIOT WALNUT

Action: Bolt
Stock: Walnut
Barrel: 20 in.
Sights: None
Weight: 7 lb.
Caliber: .243 Win., .308 Win., .270 Win., .30-06 Spfd., 6.5 Creedmoor, .22-250 Rem., 7mm-08 Rem., .25-06 Rem., .300 Win. Mag., 7mm Rem. Mag., .350 Legend, .450 Bushmaster
Magazine: 4 rounds
Features: A traditionally styled rifle for the straight-wall .450 Bushmaster with walnut stock; matte blue metalwork; vented rubber recoil pad; threaded barrel; Weaver-style bases
MSRP. . . . . $617.00–$634.00

Mossberg (O. F. Mossberg & Sons)

MOSSBERG PATRIOT WALNUT VORTEX SCOPED COMBO

MOSSBERG PATRIOT YOUTH SUPER BANTAM SCOPED COMBO

PATRIOT WALNUT VORTEX SCOPED COMBO

Action: Bolt
Stock: Walnut
Barrel: 22 in.
Sights: Vortex Crossfire II 3–9X40mm scope
Weight: 8 lb.
Caliber: .243 Win., .308 Win., .270 Win., .30-06 Spfd., 6.5 Creedmoor, .22-250 Rem., 7mm-08 Rem., .25-06 Rem., .300 Win. Mag., 7mm Rem. Mag.
Magazine: 3, 5 rounds
Features: The walnut-stocked Patriot in a variety of common calibers; factory-mounted Vortex scope; fluted barrel; vented recoil pad
MSRP . . . . $783.00–$797.00

PATRIOT YOUTH SUPER BANTAM SCOPED COMBO

Action: Bolt
Stock: Synthetic
Barrel: 20 in.
Sights: 3-9x40mm scope
Weight: 7 lb. 8 oz.
Caliber: .243 Win., 6.5 Creedmoor, 7mm-08 Rem., .308 Win., .243 Win., .350 Legend
Magazine: 5 rounds
Features: Adjustable stock; fluted matte blue barrel; stock in black or choice of Muddy Girl Wild or Strata camo
MSRP . . . . $483.00–$540.00

New Ultra Light Arms

NEW ULTRA LIGHT ARMS MODEL 20 ULTIMATE MOUNTAIN RIFLE

MODEL 20 ULTIMATE MOUNTAIN RIFLE

Action: Bolt
Stock: Kevlar/graphite composite
Barrel: 22 in.
Sights: None
Weight: 5 lb.
Caliber: .308 Win., .243 Win., 6mm Rem., .257 Roberts, 7mm-08, .284 Win.
Magazine: Detachable box
Features: Available in left-hand; choice of stock colors; 20-oz. action; two-position safety
MSRP $4200.00

Nosler

NOSLER M48 LONG-RANGE CARBON

NOSLER M48 MOUNTAIN CARBON

M48 LONG-RANGE CARBON

Action: Bolt
Stock: Carbon Fiber
Barrel: 26 in.
Sights: None
Weight: 7 lb.
Caliber: 6.5 Creedmoor, .26 Nosler, .27 Nosler, .300 Win. Mag., .30 Nosler, .33 Nosler
Magazine: 3, 4 rounds
Features: Proof Research carbon-fiber-wrapped match-grade barrel; Manners MCS carbon-fiber stock in Elite Midnight Camo; action and bottom metal in Cerakote Sniper Grey; glass and aluminum pillar bedding; threaded muzzle; muzzle brake is available
MSRP $3285.00

M48 MOUNTAIN CARBON

Action: Bolt
Stock: Carbon fiber
Barrel: 24 in.
Sights: None
Weight: 6 lb.
Caliber: 6mm Creedmoor, 6.5 Creedmoor, 6.5 PRC, .26 Nosler, .27 Nosler, .280 Ackley Improved, .28 Nosler, .300 Win. Mag., .30 Nosler, .33 Nosler
Magazine: 3, 4 rounds
Features: Super-light hunter with a carbon-wrapped, Tungsten Grey Cerakote, free-floating barrel with Sendero profile; textured carbon fiber Aramid-reinforced, pillar-bedded Mountain Hunter stock; aluminum floorplate
MSRP $3235.00

Noveske

NOVESKE GEN III HEAVY INFIDEL N6

NOVESKE GEN IV SERIES

Barrel: 8.5 in., 10.5 in., 13.7 in., 16 in.
Sights: Open, none
Weight: N/A
Caliber: 5.56 NATO, .300 BLK, 9mm
Magazine: 30 rounds
Features: Gen I series of Noveske modern sporting rifles include cold hammer-forged barrels with extended feed ramps; Geissele Super Badass charging handle, Q-bolt, and carrier group; free-floating M-LOK or Keymod handguards; hard coat Type III anodizing with Cerakote; ALG Defense ACT trigger; Magpul stocks and grips; Magpul MBUS folding sights on some model. Current production includes Infidel, Space Invader SBR, Noveske9, and Shorty models
MSRP. . . . . $2900.00–$3425.00

GEN III SERIES

Action: Semiautomatic
Stock: Synthetic
Barrel: 18, 20 in.
Sights: Adjustable
Weight: N/A
Caliber: .5.56 NATO, 6.5 Grendl
Magazine: Detachable box, 30 rounds
Features: Noveske's Gen III rifles come in a wide variety of barrel lengths, handguard and stock config-urations, rails, and sight options. Current Gen III models includes OMW (One More Wave); Light Recce; Diplomat; Switchblock; 6.5 Grendel; Varmageddon; N6; Afghan; Infidel; Leonidas Switchblock N6; Leonidas Switchblock
MSRP. $3150.00–

GEN IV SERIES

Action: Semiautomatic
Stock: Synthetic

Patriot Ordnance Factory

PATRIOT ORDNANCE FACTORY MINUTEMAN

PATRIOT ORDNANCE FACTORY RENEGADE PLUS

PATRIOT ORDNANCE FACTORY P415 EDGE

PATRIOT ORDNANCE FACTORY PRESCOTT

MINUTEMAN

Action: Semiautomatic
Stock: Synthetic
Barrel: 16.5 in.
Sights: None
Weight: 6 lb. 3 oz.
Caliber: 5.56 NATO, .350 Legend
Magazine: N/A
Features: Direct impingement carbine with a straight, drop-in match-grade trigger; ambidextrous rear QD sling swivel plate; mid-length gas system; POF three-prong flash-hider; Renegade rail; in black or tungsten finishes; California-compliant versions offered in 5.56 NATO
MSRP. . . . . $1518.00–$1716.00

P415 EDGE

Action: Semiautomatic
Stock: Synthetic
Barrel: 16.5 in.
Sights: None
Weight: 7 lb.
Caliber: 5.56 NATO, .300 Blackout
Magazine: N/A
Features: Short-stroke gas piston action; nitride heat-treated barrel; 14½-in. M-LOK rail; triple port muzzle break; six-position anti-tilt buffer tube; chrome-plated bolt; Mission First Tactical furniture; E2 Dual Extraction Technology chamber; POF drop-in trigger group; black, NP3, Burnt Bronze, and Tungsten finishes
MSRP. . . . . $2059.00–$2218.00

PRESCOTT

Action: Semiautomatic
Stock: Synthetic
Barrel: 20 in.
Sights: None
Weight: 7 lb.
Caliber: 6.5 Creedmoor
Magazine: 10 rounds
Features: Nitride heat-treated single port muzzle brake; rifle-length gas block; match-grade stainless steel barrel; E2 dual extraction; Renegade handguard and heat sink barrel nut; multiple quick-detach points; direct impingement operation; match-grade straight drop-in trigger with anti-walk pins; ambidextrous safety and quick-detach end plate; anti-tilt extension tube with Luth-AR MBA-4 stock; in black or burnt bronze
MSRP. . . . . $1952.00–$2084.00

RENEGADE PLUS

Action: Semiautomatic
Stock: Synthetic
Barrel: 16.5 in. (5.56 NATO), 18.5 in. (.223 Wylde)
Sights: None
Weight: 6 lb. 6 oz. (5.56 NATO), 7 lb. 11 oz. (.223 Wylde)
Caliber: 5.56 NATO, .300 Blackout
Magazine: Detachable box
Features: M-LOK compatible Renegade rail; heat sink barrel nut; Dictator 9-position adjustable gas block with straight gas tube; nitride heat-treated barrel; Gen 4 POF-USA ambidextrous billet lower receiver and POF-USA Ultimate Bolt Carrier Group; flat 3.5 lb match-grade trigger with KNS Precision anti-walk pins; NP3 coated for maximum protection and reliability; integrated gas key (no screws required)
MSRP. . . . . $1927.00–$2086.00

Patriot Ordnance Factory

PATRIOT ORDNANCE FACTORY REVOLUTION

PATRIOT ORDNANCE FACTORY ROGUE

PATRIOT ORDNANCE FACTORY WONDER

REVOLUTION

Action: Semiautomatic
Stock: Synthetic
Barrel: 14.5, 16.5. 20 in.
Sights: None
Weight: 7 lb. 4 oz.–9 lb. 4 oz.
Caliber: .308 Win., 6.5 Creedmoor
Magazine: N/A
Features: A .308/6.5 Creedmoor that handles like a 5.56; Edge handguard with four built-in QD mounts; five-position gas operating system; single stage match grade trigger; 6.5 Creedmoor available in 20-inch barrel only; both calibers available in black or burnt bronze finishes; gas piston and direct impingement operating systems available

Gas piston: . . . . $2792.00–$2924.00
Direct
impingement:. . $2699.00–$2831.00

ROGUE

Action: Semiautomatic
Stock: Synthetic
Barrel: 16.5 in.
Sights: None
Weight: 5 lb. 14 oz.
Caliber: .308 Win.
Magazine: N/A
Features: A direct impingement carbine .308 under six pounds and featuring an anti-tilt buffer tube; 11-in. Renegade forearm; key-lock DI bolt carrier group; multiple QD sling attachment points; Micro B muzzle

brake
MSRP . . . . $1889.00–$2031.00

WONDER

Action: Semiautomatic
Stock: Synthetic
Barrel: 16.5 in.
Sights: None
Weight: 6 lb. 3 oz.
Caliber: 5.56 NATO
Magazine: 30 rounds
Features: A lightened up and eye-catching AR platform featuring an eye-catching titanium blue Cerakote receiver and 14.5-inch M-LOK Renegade handguard; match-grade Puritan barrel heat-treated and threaded ½X28; single-port Micro-B muzzle brake; carbine length low-profile gas block; direct impingement system
MSRP . . . . $1703.00–$1769.00

Primary Weapons Systems

PRIMARY WEAPONS SYSTEMS MK216 MOD-1 M

MK216 MOD-1 M

Action: Semiautomatic
Stock: Synthetic
Barrel: 16 in.
Sights: Adjustable
Weight: 8 lb. 10 oz.
Caliber: .308 Win., 7.62 NATO

Magazine: Detachable box, 10 or 20 rounds
Features: FSC muzzle brake and suppressor; Picatinny rail; adjustable stock
MSRP $2199.95

Proof Research

PROOF RESEARCH CONVICTION

PROOF RESEARCH ELEVATION

CONVICTION

Action: Bolt
Stock: Synthetic
Barrel: 20 in., 22 in., 24 in., 26 in., 28 in.
Sights: None
Weight: 6 lb. 13 oz.–8 lb. 8 oz.
Caliber: 6 Creedmoor, 6.5 Creedmoor, 6.5 PRC, .28 Nosler, .308 Win., 7mm Rem. Mag.,.300 Win. Mag., .300 WSM, .300 PRC, .300 RUM, .338 Lapua
Magazine: 3, 4 rounds

Features: A competition-ready long-range rifle built with PR's Conviction carbon-fiber stock; PR carbon-fiber wrapped match-grade barrel; tactical action; modified ball or tactical bolt knob; Triggertech trigger; Sendero contour barrel
MSRP . . . . $8399.00–$8499.00

ELEVATION

Action: Bolt
Stock: Synthetic
Barrel: 20 in., 22 in., 24 in.

Sights: None
Weight: 5 lb. 14 oz.–6 lb. 8 oz.
Caliber: 6mm Creedmoor, 6.5 Creedmoor, .308 Win., 7mm Rem. Mag., .300 Win. Mag.
Magazine: 3, 4 rounds
Features: A light rifle for backcountry hunters with PR's carbon fiber-wrapped match-grade barrel; PR's carbon fiber stock; TriggerTech trigger; Zermatt Arms Origin action
MSRP . . . . $3099.00–$3199.00

PROOF RESEARCH ELEVATION MTR

PROOF RESEARCH GLACIER TI

PROOF RESEARCH MPA CHASSIS RIFLE

ELEVATION MTR
Action: Bolt
Stock: Synthetic
Barrel: 20 in., 22 in., 24 in.
Sights: None
Weight: 6 lb. 5 oz.–7 lb. 2 oz.
Caliber: .223 Rem., 6 ARC, 6mm Creedmoor, 6.5 Creedoor, 6.5 PRC, .308 Win., 7mm Rem. Mag., .300 Win. Mag.
Magazine: 3, 4 rounds
Features: MTR is for Mountain Tactical Rifle; it features PR's carbon fiber-wrapped match-grade barrel; PR's carbon fiber stock; TriggerTech trigger; Zermatt Arms Origin action; detachable box magazine or hinged floorplate; Sendero Light contour barrel; black metalwork finish; topside scope rail
MSRP . . . .$3399.00–$3499.00

GLACIER, GLACIER TI
Action: Bolt

Stock: Synthetic
Barrel: 20 in., 22 in., 24 in., 26 in.
Sights: None
Weight: 5 lb. 5 oz.–7 lb. 2 oz.
Caliber: 6 Creedmoor, 6.5 Creedmoor, 6.5 PRC, .308 Win., 7mm Rem. Mag., .28 Nosler, .300 WSM, .300 Win. Mag., .300 PRC
Magazine: 3, 4 rounds
Features: Superbly accurate rifle for the mountain hunter, featuring PR's carbon fiber-wrapped match-grade barrel; PR's carbon fiber stock; TriggerTech trigger; Lone Peak Arms Razor action; detachable BDL-type magazine; threaded Sendero or Sendero Light contour barrel; Cerakote metalwork in flat dark earth, olive drab, black, tungsten or Sniper Gray; topside scope rail; stock in several single colors and a wide range of multi-color and patterns; stock and barrel can be ordered in custom lengths; TI variant has titanium action

Glacier: . . . .$6299.00–$6399.00
Glacier TI: . . . . . .$7099.00–$7199.00

MDT ACC CHASSIS RIFLE
Action: Bolt
Stock: Synthetic
Barrel: 26 in.
Sights: None
Weight: 15 lb. 4 oz.
Caliber: .22 LR, .223 Rem., 6mm ARC, 6 Dasher, 6 GT, 6mm Creedmoor, 6.5 Creedmoor, .308 Win.
Magazine: 12 rounds
Features: A competition-ready (and flashy!) rifle built on a MDT ACC chassis; Triggertech Pro Curved Diamond adjustable trigger; Area 419 Hellfire muzzle brake; Zermatt Arms TL3 action; 20 MOA rail; steel Competition contour barrel; AICS steel magazine
MSRP $5699.00

PTR Industries

Features: H&K Navy-type polymer trigger group housing, HK 91-length handguards, cocking tube, welded scope mount, paddle magazine release, delayed blowback roller lock system are standard; now with 5/8-24 barrel threading.
MSRP . . . .$1336.00–$1418.00

PTR INDUSTRIES 32 KFR PTR 200

32 KFR PTR 200
Action: Semiautomatic
Stock: Synthetic
Barrel: 16 in.
Sights: Fixed
Weight: 9 lb. 5 oz.
Caliber: 7.62X39
Magazine: 10, 30 rounds

Red Arrow Weapons

RED ARROW WEAPONS RAW10

RED ARROW WEAPONS RAW15

RAW10
Action: Semiautomatic
Stock: Synthetic
Barrel: 18 in.
Sights: None
Weight: 8 lb. 7.5 oz.
Caliber: .308 Win., 6.5 Creedmoor
Magazine: 20 rounds
Features: A heavier AR-10–type for

action shooting, with stainless fluted barrel; rifle-length gas system; high-pressure firing pin; 15-in. M-LOK S rail; Magpul ACS-L carbine stock; DB10 threaded on muzzle brake; Magpul K grip; CMC 2.5-lb. single-stage trigger; dressed in midnight bronze
MSRP . . . .$1550.00–$1650.00

RAW15
Action: Semiautomatic
Stock: Synthetic
Barrel: 16 in.
Sights: None
Weight: 6 lb. 9 oz.

Caliber: .223 Rem/5.56 NATO, .300 BLK
Magazine: 30 rounds
Features: Melonite-coated 4150 chromoly barrel; mid-length gas system on .223, pistol-length system on .300 BLK; CMC 3.5-lb. single-stage trigger; A3 flattop upper and lower of 7075 T-6 forged aluminum; 15-in. M-LOK handguard; Magpul K2+ grip; Magpul P-Mag magazine; DB15 556 threaded-on muzzle brake; Magpul CTR stock; in black with red highlights or in midnight bronze
MSRP . . . . $815.00–$1287.00

RIFLES

Rifles Inc.

RIFLES INC. CANYON

RIFLES INC. MASTER'S SERIES

RIFLES INC. CLASSIC

RIFLES INC. SAFARI

RIFLES INC. LIGHTWEIGHT STRATA

CANYON

Action: Bolt
Stock: McMillan HTG
Barrel: 24 in.
Sights: None
Weight: 10 lb.
Caliber: Most popular calibers
Magazine: Internal
Features: Blind or hinged floor plate; customer-supplied Rem. 700 action; match grade stainless steel Lilja number 6 barrel; optional muzzle-brake; matte stainless metal finish, optional black Teflon; adjustable cheekpiece; custom buttpad
MSRP $3500.00

CLASSIC

Action: Bolt
Stock: Laminated fiberglass
Barrel: 24 in.–26 in.
Sights: None
Weight: 6 lb. 8 oz.
Caliber: All popular chamberings up to .375 H&H
Magazine: Internal
Features: Customer-supplied Rem. 700 action; match grade stainless steel Lilja barrel; blind or hinged floor plate; matte stainless metal finish, optional Black Teflon finish; black

laminated fiberglass, pillar glass bedded stock
MSRP $3500.00

LIGHTWEIGHT STRATA, LIGHTWEIGHT 70

Action: Bolt
Stock: Laminate
Barrel: 22 in.–26 in.
Sights: None
Weight: 4 lb. 8 oz.–5 lb. 12 oz.
Caliber: All popular chamberings up to .375 H&H
Magazine: Internal
Features: Customer-supplied Rem. 700 action; match grade stainless steel Lilja barrel; fluted bolt and hollowed-handle; blind or hinged floor plate; matte stainless metal finish, optional black Teflon finish; hand-laminated blend of Kevlar/graphite and boron, pillar glass bedded stock; Titanium Strata has hand-laminated graphite stock with pillar glass bedded; custom buttpad; Quiet Slimbrake II muzzle-brake
Lightweight Strata $3600.00
Lightweight 70 . . . . $3500.00

MASTER'S SERIES

Action: Bolt
Stock: Laminated fiberglass

Barrel: 24 in.–27 in.
Sights: None
Weight: 7 lb. 12 oz.
Caliber: All popular chamberings up to .375 H&H
Magazine: Internal
Features: Customer-supplied Rem. 700 action; match grade stainless steel Lilja number 5 barrel; hinged floor plate; matte stainless metal finish, optional black Teflon finish; black laminated fiberglass, pillar glass bedded stock; optional muzzlebrake
MSRP $3600.00

SAFARI

Action: Bolt
Stock: Laminated fiberglass
Barrel: 23 in.–25 in.
Sights: Optional Express Sights
Weight: 8 lb. 8 oz.
Caliber: .375 H&H, .416 Rem. Mag., and other large game cartridges
Magazine: 4 rounds
Features: Customer-supplied Winchester Model 70 Classic action; lapped and face trued bolt; match grade stainless steel Lilja barrel; Quiet Slimbrake II muzzlebrake; hinged floor plate or optional drop box; matte stainless finish, optional black Teflon; double laminated fiberglass, pillar glass bedded stock; Pachmayr decelerator; optional barrel band
MSRP $3500.00

Rock River Arms

ROCK RIVER ARMS LAR-8 PREDATOR HP

ROCK RIVER ARMS LAR-8 PREDATOR HP MID-LENGTH

LAR-8 PREDATOR HP

Action: Semiautomatic
Stock: Synthetic
Barrel: 20 in.
Sights: None
Weight: 8 lb. 10 oz.
Caliber: .243 Win., 6.5 Creedmoor
Magazine: Detachable box
Features: Forged A4 receiver with forward assist and port door; stainless

steel barrel; gas block sight Base; two-stage trigger; Hogue rubber grip; RRA aluminum free-float tube; A2 buttstock or operator stock
MSRP $1650.00

LAR-8 PREDATOR HP MID-LENGTH

Action: Semiautomatic
Stock: Synthetic
Barrel: 16 in.

Sights: None
Weight: 8 lb. 14.4 oz.–9 lb. 3.2 oz.
Caliber: .308 Win.
Magazine: N/A
Features: Forged LAR-8 lower and A4 upper; stainless steel barrel has 1:10 twist, is fluted, bead-blasted, and cryogenically treated; available with or without muzzle brake; two-stage match trigger with winter trigger guard; RRA Operator CAR or A2 buttstock; RRA LAR-8 DLX rifle-length free-floating handguard with three short accessory rails; Hogue pistol grip
MSRP $1690.00

ROCK RIVER ARMS LAR-8 X-1

ROCK RIVER ARMS LAR-8M .243 PREDATOR HP

ROCK RIVER ARMS LAR-8M 6.5 CREEDMOOR PREDATOR HP

ROCK RIVER ARMS LAR-15 FES LIGHT PREDATOR2L

ROCK RIVER ARMS LAR-15 FES PREDATOR2 GHOST CAMO

ROCK RIVER ARMS LAR-15LH LEF-T COYOTE RIFLE

ROCK RIVER ARMS LAR-15M .350 LEGEND CAR A4, CAR A4 STAINLESS

LAR-8 X-1

Action: Semiautomatic
Stock: Synthetic
Barrel: 18 in.
Sights: None
Weight: 9 lb. 8 oz.
Caliber: .308 Win., 7.62 NATO
Magazine: Detachable box, 20 rounds
Features: RRA Beast of Hunter muzzle brake; available in black or tan; available with A2 or CAR stocks
MSRP . . . . $1770.00–$1805.00

LAR-8M .243 PREDATOR HP

Action: Semiautomatic
Stock: Synthetic
Barrel: 20 in.
Sights: None
Weight: 9 lb. 3.2 oz.–9 lb. 8 oz.
Caliber: .243 Win.
Magazine: N/A
Features: Rifle features a forged, multi-caliber marked LAR-8M lower and a forged A4 upper; stainless steel barrel has 1:10 twist, is fluted, and cryogenically treated; Rock River's Operator muzzle brake available; low-profile gas block; two-stage match trigger with a winter trigger guard; RRA Operator A2 or CAR stock; RRA LAR-8 DLX free-floating rifle-length handrail with three short accessory rails; Hogue pistol grip
MSRP $1655.00

LAR-8M 6.5 CREEDMOOR PREDATOR HP

Action: Semiautomatic
Stock: Synthetic
Barrel: 20 in.
Sights: None
Weight: 9 lb. 3.2 oz.–9 lb. 6.4 oz.
Caliber: 6.5 Creedmoor
Magazine: N/A
Features: Rifle features a forged,

multi-caliber marked LAR-8M lower and a forged A4 upper; barrel has 1:8 twist, is bead blasted, and cryogenically treated; Rock River's Operator muzzle break available; low-profile gas block; two-stage match trigger with a winter trigger guard; RRA Operator A2 stock; RRA LAR-8 DLX free-float handrail with three short accessory rails; Hogue pistol grip
MSRP $1650.00

LAR-15 FES LIGHT PREDATOR2L

Action: Semiautomatic
Stock: Synthetic
Barrel: 16 in.
Sights: None
Weight: 6 lb. 14 oz.
Caliber: .223 Wylde
Magazine: 20 rounds
Features: Free-floating, extended length, top rail handguard; FES muzzle brake; lightweight fluted steel barrel; mid-length gas system with low-profile gas block; Rock River's Operator stock; two-stage trigger; Winter trigger guard; BCM GUNFIGHTER charging handle; furniture is black; receiver and lower can be upgraded to Rock River's ROCKote Gunmetal Gray
MSRP $2045.00
ROCKote Gunmetal Gray receiver: $2115.00

LAR-15 FES PREDATOR2 GHOST CAMO

Action: Semiautomatic
Stock: Synthetic
Barrel: 16 in.
Sights: None
Weight: 7 lb. 10 oz.
Caliber: .223 Wylde
Magazine: 20 rounds
Features: FES stands for Fred Eichler Series; Ghost Camo stock; handguard

emblazoned with paw prints; Rock River's FES muzzle brake; Operator CAR stock; chrome two-stage trigger; FES extended free-floating handguard with full-length rail; Cryo-treated fluted barrel; Hogue rubber pistol grip; Rock River's Winter trigger guard; BCM GUNFIGHTER charging handle
MSRP $2205.00

LAR-15LH LEF-T COYOTE RIFLE & CARBINE

Action: Semiautomatic
Stock: Synthetic A2
Barrel: 16 in., 20 in.
Sights: None
Weight: 7 lb.-8 lb. 6.4 oz.
Caliber: 5.56 NATO, .223 Rem., .223 Wylde
Magazine: Detachable box, 20 rounds
Features: Smith Vortex Flash Hider; Hogue free float tube; Hogue grip; two stage trigger
MSRP $1355.00

LAR-15M .350 LEGEND CAR A4, CAR A4 STAINLESS

Action: Semiautomatic
Stock: Synthetic
Barrel: 16 in.
Sights: None
Weight: 6 lb. 13 oz.
Caliber: .350 Legend
Magazine: 10 rounds
Features: Operator CAR stock, over-molded A2 grip, two-stage trigger, and winter trigger guard; low-profile gas block; carbine-length gas system; chrome-moly barrel; forged upper and lower; 13-inch free-floating M-LOK compatible rail
Standard $1220.00
Stainless $1275.00

Rock River Arms

ROCK RIVER ARMS LAR-15M .450 BUSHMASTER

ROCK RIVER ARMS LAR-6.8 COYOTE CARBINE

ROCK RIVER ARMS LAR-6.8 X-1

ROCK RIVER ARMS LAR-15 RRAGE CARBINE

ROCK RIVER LAR-15 R3 COMPETITION RIFLE

ROCK RIVER ARMS LAR-15 RRAGE 3G

ROCK RIVER ARMS LAR-15M VARMINT A4

ROCK RIVER ARMS LAR-22 MID A4

ROCK RIVER ARMS LAR-22 NM A4 RIFLE

LAR-15M .450 BUSHMASTER

Action: Semiautomatic
Stock: Synthetic
Barrel: 16 in.
Sights: None
Weight: 6 lb. 13 oz.
Caliber: .450 Bushmaster
Magazine: N/A
Features: One for the new straight-wall cartridge, featuring cryo-treated 1:14 twist barrel; RRA's Operator muzzle brake with 5/8X24 threads; mid-length gas system; 13-inch free-floating M-LOK rail; two-stage trigger; winter trigger guard
Standard $1170.00
Stainless $1220.00 LAR-15M 6.8
Coyote Carbine
Action: Semiautomatic
Stock: Synthetic
Barrel: 16 in.
Sights: None
Weight: 7 lb.
Caliber: 6.8 SPC II
Magazine: 1 round
Features: Smith Vortex flash hider; chromoly barrel; RRA two-stage match trigger
MSRP $1355.00

LAR-15M 6.8 X-1

Action: Semiautomatic
Stock: Synthetic
Barrel: 18 in.
Sights: None
Weight: 7 lb. 13 oz.
Caliber: 6.8 SPC II
Magazine: Detachable box, 25 rounds
Features: RRA Beast of Hunter muzzle brake; available in black or tan; available with A2 or CAR stocks
MSRP . . . . $1565.00–$1600.00

LAR-15M R3 COMPETITION RIFLE

Action: Semiautomatic
Stock: Synthetic A2 or CAR
Barrel: 18 in.
Sights: None
Weight: 7 lb. 9.6 oz.
Caliber: .223 Wylde
Magazine: Detachable box, 30 rounds
Features: RRA tuned and ported muzzle brake; low profile gas block; two stage trigger; Hogue Rubber grip
MSRP $1385.00

LAR-15M RRAGE CARBINE, VEIL TAC-BLACK CARBINE, PINK CARBINE

Action: Semiautomatic
Stock: Synthetic
Barrel: 16 in.
Sights: None
Weight: 5 lb. 11 oz.
Caliber: 5.56mm NATO/.223 Rem.
Magazine: 30 rounds
Features: Feature-rich AR carbine with an extruded aluminum A4 upper with port door; A2 flash hider; single-stage trigger; six-position tactical CAR stock; CAR-length free-floating aluminum handguard with M1913 top rail and M-LOK compatible;
Standard $840.00
Veil Tac-Black $975.00
Pink $820.00

LAR-15M RRAGE 3G

Action: Semiautomatic
Stock: Synthetic
Barrel: 16 in.
Sights: None
Weight: 6 lb. 3 oz.
Caliber: 5.56mm NATO/.223 Rem.
Magazine: 30 rounds
Features: For the 3-Gun crowd, a carbine featuring a low-profile carbine-length gas block; single-stage trigger; forged lower; 15-inch RRA 3G hand-guard; A2 grip; adjustable stock; no forward assist
MSRP $905.00

LAR-15M VARMINT A4

Action: Semiautomatic
Stock: Synthetic
Barrel: 16, 18, 20, 24 in.
Sights: None
Weight: 9 lb. 1.6 oz.
Caliber: .204 Ruger
Magazine: N/A
Features: Forged, multi-caliber marked LAR-15M lower and A4 upper; stainless steel bull barrel has 1:12 twist, is fluted, air gauged, and cryogenically treated; low-profile gas block; two-stage match trigger with a winter trigger guard; A2 buttstock; RRA TRO-STD free-floating handrail with octagonal top rail providing one STD and two short accessory rails; Hogue pistol grip
MSRP . . . . $1275.00–$1385.00

LAR-22 MID A4

Action: Semiautomatic
Stock: Synthetic
Barrel: 16 in.
Sights: None
Weight: 5 lb. 6 oz.
Caliber: .22 LR
Magazine: N/A
Features: A classic look in a .22 LR featuring single-stage trigger; six-position tactical CAR stock; mid-length handguard with heat shield; choice of poly or forged aluminum A4 upper
Aluminum $590.00
Poly $490.00

LAR-22 NM A4

Action: Semiautomatic
Stock: Synthetic
Barrel: 20 in.
Sights: None
Weight: 8 lb. 14 oz.
Caliber: .22 LR
Magazine: 30 rounds
Features: A vintage look with modern features like a free-floating, high-temp thermo-molded handguard with NM barrel sleeve; stainless steel HBAR barrel; two-stage match chrome trigger group
MSRP $920.00

ROCK RIVER ARMS LAR-22 NM CMP TRAINER

ROCK RIVER ARMS LAR-22 TACTICAL CARBINE

ROCK RIVER ARMS LAR-47 CAR A4

ROCK RIVER ARMS LAR-BT9G

ROCK RIVER ARMS LAR-9 R9 COMPETITION

ROCK RIVER ARMS LAR-PDS CARBINE

ROCK RIVER ARMS RBG BOLT GUN

ROCK RIVER ARMS BT-3 .308 18-INCH PRECISION RIFLE

LAR-22 NM A4 20-INCH CMP TRAINER

Action: Semiautomatic
Stock: Synthetic
Barrel: 20 in.
Sights: None
Weight: 8 lb. 13 oz.
Caliber: .22 LR
Magazine: N/A
Features: One for serious small-bore competition with added weight; two-stage chrome match trigger group; stainless steel HBAR barrel with 1:16 twist; NM CMP TRO free-floating rifle-length handguard with rail and swivel; A2 pistol grip; forged aluminum upper and lower
MSRP $980.00

LAR-22 TACTICAL CARBINE

Action: Semiautomatic
Stock: Synthetic
Barrel: 16 in.
Sights: None
Weight: N/A
Caliber: .22 LR
Magazine: 30 rounds
Features: AR plinking fun or serious rimfire competition thanks to features such as a two-stage trigger; winter trigger guard; six-position stock; A2 flash hider; Hogue rubber grip; 11-inch free-floating M-LOK handguard; choice of aluminum or poly receiver construction
Aluminum $700.00
Poly $610.00

LAR-47 CAR A4

Action: Semiautomatic
Stock: Synthetic
Barrel: 16 in.
Sights: None
Weight: 6 lb. 6 oz.
Caliber: 7.62x39
Magazine: Detachable box, 30

rounds, standard AK-47 mag
Features: RRA 6-postion tactical CAR stock; A2 pistol grip; CAR handguards; RRA two-stage trigger; A2 flash hider; ambidextrous mag release
MSRP $1135.00

LAR-BT9G CAR A4, MID-LENGTH A4

Action: Semiautomatic
Stock: Synthetic
Barrel: 16 in.
Sights: None
Weight: 6 lb. 14 oz.–7 lb. 1 oz.
Caliber: 9mm
Magazine: 10, 15, 17 rounds
Features: Two configurations that take Glock 9mm magazines and have six-position CAR stock: CAR A4 carbine with a 16-in. barrel, gas block with receiver-height sight base, single-stage trigger, R-4 handguard, winter trigger guard, and Hogue rubber grip; R9 Competition with a 16-in. chromoly barrel, threaded-on mini brake, two-stage trigger, 15-in. free-floating M-LOK-compatible rail
CAR A4. . . . .$1050.00
Mid-Length A4 . . . .$1030.00

LAR-BT9G R9 COMPETITION

Action: Semiautomatic
Stock: Synthetic
Barrel: 16 in.
Sights: None
Weight: 7 lb. 6.4 oz.
Caliber: 9mm
Magazine: N/A
Features: Forged LAR-9 lower with integral Magwell and a forged A4 upper; barrel has 1:10 twist, is chain-link fluted, and cryogenically treated; wears a 9mm Mini-Break; two-stage match trigger; RRA Operator CAR

stock; RRA Lightweight Extended Mid-Length handguard; Hogue pistol grip
MSRP $1300.00

LAR PDS CARBINE RIBBED, TRI-RAIL

Action: Semiautomatic
Stock: Synthetic
Barrel: 16 in.
Sights: None
Weight: 7 lb. 6 oz.
Caliber: .223 Rem.
Magazine: Detachable box
Features: Ambidextrous non-reciprocating charging handle; A2 flash hider; RRA two-stage trigger; Hogue rubber grip; tri-rail handguard available
Ribbed $1495.00
Tri-Rail $1575.00

RBG BOLT GUN

Action: Bolt
Stock: Synthetic
Barrel: 20 in.
Sights: None
Weight: 10 lb. 3 oz.
Caliber: .308 Win., 6.5 Creedmoor
Magazine: 10 rounds
Features: Serious competitors will appreciate the KRG chassis foundation; air-gauged, cryogenically-treated fluted stainless barrel; Triggertech trigger
MSRP $4450.00

LAR-BT3 .308 18-INCH PRECISION RIFLE

Action: Semiautomatic
Stock: Synthetic
Barrel: 18 in.
Sights: None
Weight: 8 lb. 3 oz.
Caliber: .308 Win.
Magazine: 10 rounds
Features: Features a six-position adjustable stock; cryogenically treated fluted stainless barrel; Rock River's BT-3 billet lower and billet A4 upper; two-stage trigger; low-profile gas block; mid-length gas block
MSRP $1720.00

RIFLES

Rock River Arms

ROCK RIVER ARMS BT-3 .308 20-INCH SELECT TARGET RIFLE

ROCK RIVER ARMS BT-3 .308 20-INCH VARMINT RIFLE

ROCK RIVER ARMS BT-3 ENHANCED MID-LENGTH A4

ROCK RIVER ARMS BT-6 .338 LAPUA

LAR-BT3 .308 20-INCH SELECT TARGET RIFLE

Action: Semiautomatic
Stock: Synthetic
Barrel: 20 in.
Sights: None
Weight: 8 lb. 10 oz.
Caliber: .308 Win.
Magazine: 10 rounds
Features: Features a Gen3 Precision Rifle stock; cryogenically treated fluted stainless barrel with heavy profile; Rock River's BT-3 billet lower and billet A4 upper; two-stage trigger
MSRP $1990.00

LAR-BT3 .308 20-INCH VARMINT RIFLE

Action: Semiautomatic
Stock: Synthetic
Barrel: 20 in.
Sights: None

Weight: 9 lb. 13 oz.
Caliber: .308 Win.
Magazine: 10 rounds
Features: More than a pound over the other BT-3 models for steadiness on long-distance critters; six-position NSP-2 CAR stock; Rock River's BT-3 billet lower and billet A4 upper; two-stage trigger; low-profile gas block; rifle-length gas block; 17-in. M-LOK compatible free-floating handrail; Hogue rubber grip
MSRP $1655.00

LAR-BT3 ENHANCED MID-LENGTH A4

Action: Semiautomatic
Stock: Synthetic
Barrel: 16 in.
Sights: None
Weight: 8 lb. 3 oz.
Caliber: .308 Win.
Magazine: 10 rounds

Features: Features a six-position Operator CAR stock; cryogenically treated fluted stainless barrel with heavy profile; Rock River's BT-3 billet lower and billet A4 upper; two-stage trigger; low-profile gas block
MSRP $1656.00

LAR-BT6 .338 LAPUA

Action: Semiautomatic
Stock: Synthetic
Barrel: 24 in.
Sights: None
Weight: 13 lb. 8 oz.
Caliber: .338 Lapua
Magazine: 10 rounds
Features: Two-stage Ultra Match trigger; Magpul Gen Precision Rifle stock; Rock River overmolded A2 pistol grip; black nitride stainless steel barrel; adjustable low-profile gas block; four-port muzzle brake; quick takedown design
MSRP $5580.00

Rossi

ROSSI RB22LR

ROSSI RS22LR

RB22LR, RB22WMR, RB17HMR

Action: Semiautomatic
Stock: Bolt
Barrel: 18 in., 21 in.
Sights: Fiber optic
Weight: 5 lb. 4 oz.–5 lb. 7 oz.
Caliber: .22 LR, .22 WMR, .17 HMR
Magazine: 5, 10 rounds
Features: Super-economical choice in a bolt-action rimfire for new shooters

with; fiber optic sights on the .22 LR with dovetail scope bases; .22 WMR and .17 HMR have scope bases and five-round magazines; cross-bolt safety
MSRP . . . . $171.83–$201.05

RS22LR, RS22WMR

Action: Semiautomatic
Stock: Synthetic
Barrel: 18 in., 21 in.
Sights: Fiber optic

Weight: 5 lb. 4 oz.–5 lb. 7 oz.
Caliber: .22 LR, .22 WMR
Magazine: 10 rounds
Features: A wallet-friendly rimfire to start new shooters with; fiber optic sights on the .22 LR, topside rail on .22 WMR, dovetail scope bases on both; cross-bolt safety on both, .22 WMR also gets a trigger safety
.22 LR: $171.83
.22 WMR: $312.18

Ruger (Sturm, Ruger & Co.)

RUGER 10/22 CARBINE

RUGER 10/22 COMPACT WITH MODULAR STOCK SYSTEM

RUGER 10/22 TAKEDOWN

RUGER 10/22 TAKEDOWN WITH MAGPUL BACKPACKER STOCK

RUGER 10/22 TARGET

RUGER 77/17

RIFLES

10/22 CARBINE

Action: Semiautomatic
Stock: Synthetic or hardwood
Barrel: 18.5 in.
Sights: Gold bead front sight, adjustable rear
Weight: 5 lb.
Caliber: .22 LR
Magazine: Detachable rotary, 10 rounds
Features: Available versions come in wood, black, gray or Go Wild Rock Star camo synthetic stocks with blue metalwork or a black synthetic stock with stainless steel hardware; extended magazine release; hammer-forged barrel; polymer trigger housing; aluminum receiver; contoured buttpad; barrel band; modular stock version has topside Picatinny rail
Wood, black synthetic: **$379.00**
Gray synthetic **$369.00**
Black synthetic/
  stainless: **$419.00**
Wood, black synthetic
  with scope: **$439.00**
Go Wild Rock Star camo: . .**$429.00**

10/22 COMPACT WITH MODULAR STOCK SYSTEM

Action: Semiautomatic
Stock: Synthetic
Barrel: 16.12 in.
Sights: Adjustable fiber optic rear, fiber optic front
Weight: 4 lb. 9 oz.
Caliber: .22 LR
Magazine: 10 rounds
Features: The rugged, reliable 10/22 now with a Modular Stock System;

low comb and short length of pull
MSRP **$369.00**

10/22 TAKEDOWN

Action: Semiautomatic
Stock: Black synthetic
Barrel: 16.12 in.–18.5 in.
Sights: Gold bead front, adjustable rear
Weight: 4 lb. 9.6 oz.–5 lb. 5 oz.
Caliber: .22 LR
Magazine: Detachable rotary, 10 rounds
Features: Built of alloy steel with satin black finish; easy takedown and reassembly; detachable rotary magazine; extended magazine release; available in three configurations: black synthetic stock with 18.5-in. stainless barrel; black synthetic stock with 16.4-in. threaded barrel with flash suppressor in blue; black synthetic Ruger modular stock with 16.12-in. satin black threaded, fluted target barrel
Stainless: **$539.00**
Blued with flash
  suppressor: **$559.00**
Blued threaded/fluted: **$769.00**

10/22 TAKEDOWN WITH MAGPUL BACKPACKER STOCK

Action: Semiautomatic
Stock: Synthetic
Barrel: 16.4 in.
Sights: Fiber optic front and rear
Weight: 4 lb. 3 oz.
Caliber: .22 LR
Magazine: 10 rounds
Features: A new configuration in the

10/22 breakdown family that wears a Magpul X-22 Backpacker stock in Stealth Gray; threaded stainless barrel
MSRP **$529.00**

10/22 TARGET

Action: Semiautomatic
Stock: Laminate
Barrel: 16.13 in.
Sights: None
Weight: 5 lb.
Caliber: .22 LR
Magazine: 10 rounds
Features: Laminated thumbhole stock adjustable for length of pull; vented forearm; cold hammer-forge barrel; scope base adapter that works with Weaver-style and .22 tip-off mounts; metal has a satin blue finish
MSRP **$769.00**

77/17

Action: Bolt
Stock: Walnut
Barrel: 20 in.
Sights: None
Weight: 5 lb. 11 oz.
Caliber: .17 WSM, .17 Hornet
Magazine: 6 rounds
Features: Traditionally styled smallbore for varmint or target work with: detachable rotary magazine; sling swivel studs; integral scope mounts; three-position safety; both calibers available in Green Mountain laminate stock, .17 WSM also available in American walnut
MSRP . . . . **$1209.00–$1309.00**

Ruger (Sturm, Ruger & Co.)

RUGER AMERICAN RIFLE

RUGER AMERICAN RIFLE HUNTER

RUGER AMERICAN RIFLE PREDATOR

RUGER AMERICAN RIFLE RANCH

RUGER AMERICAN RIFLE WITH GO WILD CAMO

RUGER AMERICAN RIFLE WITH VORTEX RIFLESCOPE

AMERICAN RIFLE

Action: Bolt
Stock: Synthetic
Barrel: 22 in.
Sights: Drilled and tapped for scopes
Weight: 6 lb. 2 oz.–6 lb. 4 oz.
Caliber: .22-250 Rem., .223 Rem., 6.5 Creedmoor, 7mm-08 Rem., .243 Win., .270 Win., .30-06 Spfd., .308 Win.
Magazine: Detachable rotary, 4 rounds
Features: Ruger Marksman adjustable trigger; ergonomic, lightweight stock; soft rubber recoil pad; three-lug 70 degree bolt; Power Bedding positively locates the receiver and free-floats the barrel; hammer-forged barrel; tang safety; round rotary magazine
MSRP **$579.00**

AMERICAN RIFLE HUNTER

Action: Bolt
Stock: Synthetic
Barrel: 20 in.
Sights: None
Weight: 9 lb. 3 oz.
Caliber: 6.5 Creedmoor, .308 Win.
Magazine: 5 rounds
Features: This long-range-game rifle gets a Magpul Hunter American short-action adjustable stock; Ruger Marksman Adjustable trigger
MSRP **$989.00**

AMERICAN RIFLE PREDATOR

Action: Bolt
Stock: Synthetic
Barrel: 22 in.
Sights: None
Weight: 6 lb. 9 oz.
Caliber: .22-250 Rem., 6.5 Creedmoor, .308 Win., .243 Win., 7mm-08 Rem., 6.5 Grendel, .223 Rem., 6mm Creedmoor, .204 Ruger
Magazine: 10 rounds
Features: Moss Green synthetic stock; Ruger Marksman Adjustable Trigger and Power Bedding; threaded barrel; unscoped model has installed Picatinny rail; scoped model comes with a Vortex Crossfire II 4-12x44mm scope factory mounted and the Dead-Hold BDC reticle; left-hand version available
Rifle only: . . . . **$599.00–$679.00**

AMERICAN RIFLE RANCH

Action: Bolt
Stock: Synthetic
Barrel: 16.1 in.
Sights: None
Weight: 6 lb.–6 lb. 8 oz.
Caliber: 5.56 NATO, .300 BLK, .450 Bushmaster, 7.62x39, .350 Legend, 6.5 Grendel
Magazine: Detachable rotary, 3–5 rounds
Features: Ruger Marksman Adjustable trigger offers a pull weight that is adjustable between 3 and 5 pounds; ergonomic, lightweight flat dark earth composite stock with modern forend contouring and grip serrations and swivel studs; soft rubber recoil pad; Power Bedding positively locates the receiver and free-floats the barrel for outstanding accuracy; threaded barrel is cold hammer-forged; tang safety; rotary magazine; factory installed one-piece aluminum scope rail
MSRP **$659.00**

AMERICAN RIFLE WITH GO WILD CAMO

Action: Bolt
Stock: Synthetic
Barrel: 22 in.
Sights: None
Weight: 6 lb. 9 oz.
Caliber: 7mm-08 Rem., .243 Win., 6.5 Creedmoor, .308 Win., .30-06 Spfd., .450 Bushmaster, .300 Win. Mag., .350 Legend, .25-06 Rem., 6.5 PRC
Magazine: 3 rounds
Features: Go Wild I-M Brush camo; action and barrel in Bronze Cerakote; Picatinny rail; muzzle brake; Ruger's Marksman Adjustable Trigger and Power Bedding
MSRP **$769.00**

AMERICAN RIFLE WITH VORTEX SCOPE

Action: Bolt
Stock: Synthetic
Barrel: 22 in.
Sights: None
Weight: 7 lb. 3 oz.
Caliber: .223 Rem., .243 Win., .270 Win., .30-06 Spfd., 6.5 Creedmoor, .204 Ruger
Magazine: 5 rounds
Features: Vortex 3–9x40mm or 4–12x44mm Crossfire II scope (Dead-Head BDC reticle) already mounted; Ruger Marksman Adjustable Trigger and Power Bedding; a cold hammer forged barrel
MSRP **$769.00–899.00**

Ruger (Sturm, Ruger & Co.)

RUGER AMERICAN RIMFIRE TARGET

RUGER AMERICAN RIMFIRE TARGET STAINLESS

RUGER AMERICAN RIMFIRE WITH WOOD STOCK

RUGER AR-556

RUGER AR-556 MPR

RUGER AR-556 MPR FLAG SERIES

AMERICAN RIMFIRE TARGET

Action: Bolt
Stock: Laminate
Barrel: 18 in.
Sights: None
Weight: 6 lb. 8 oz.–6 lb. 11 oz.
Caliber: .17 HMR, .22 LR, .22 WMR
Magazine: 9, 10 rounds
Features: Ruger Marksman Adjustable trigger; aluminum Picatinny rail; cold hamme-forged threaded bull barrel; Power Bedding; flush-fit BX-1 magazines. Variants include GO Wild Camo I-M stocks with burnt bronze Cerakote or black synthetic stocks, some with adjustable stock modules, and blue or stainless metalwork
MSRP . . . . $449.00–$559.00

AMERICAN RIMFIRE TARGET STAINLESS

Action: Bolt
Stock: Laminate
Barrel: 18 in.
Sights: None
Weight: 6 lb. 11 oz.
Caliber: .22 LR, .22 WMR, .17 HMR
Magazine: 9, 10 rounds
Features: The durability and rust-resistance of a stainless receiver and barrel meet the Ruger American rimfire; flush-mount BX-1 magazine; Ruger Marksman Adjustable trigger; Power Bedding bedding block system
MSRP . . . . $659.00–$689.00

AMERICAN RIMFIRE WOOD STOCK

Action: Bolt
Stock: Wood
Barrel: 22 in.

Sights: Fiber optic front, adjustable rear
Weight: 6 lb. 2 oz.
Caliber: .22 LR
Magazine: 10 rounds
Features: Extended magazine release; patent-pending Power Bedding integral bedding block system; Ruger Marksman Adjustable trigger offers a crisp release with a pull weight that is user adjustable between 3 and 5 lb.; wood stock with checkering on the grip and forend and a rubber buttpad for a comfortable length of pull; cold hammer-forged barrel
MSRP $569.00

AR-556

Action: Semiautomatic
Stock: Synthetic
Barrel: 16.1 in.
Sights: Adjustable
Weight: 6 lb. 8 oz.
Caliber: .223 Rem./5.56 NATO
Magazine: Detachable box, 30 rounds
Features: The milled gas block is located at a carbine length (M4) position; multiple attachment points include a QD socket and bayonet lug; front sight post is elevation adjustable, and a front sight tool is included; A-2 Style F-Height allows co-witness with many optics; Ruger Rapid Deploy folding rear sight provides windage adjustability; six-position telescoping M4-style buttstock and Mil-Spec buffer tube; barrel is cold hammer-forged; Ruger flash suppressor; matte black oxide finish on the exterior of the bolt carrier

Standard $989.00
Magpul MOE furniture. . . . $1039.00

AR-556 MPR

Action: Semiautomatic
Stock: Synthetic
Barrel: 18 in.
Sights: Adjustable post front, adjustable Ruger rapid deploy rear
Weight: 6 lb. 8 oz.
Caliber: 5.56 NATO, .450 Bushmaster, .350 Legend
Magazine: 5, 10, 30 rounds
Features: M-LOK accessory-compatible 15-in. free-floating handguard; Ruger's Elite 452 AR trigger; rifle-length gas system; contoured barrel that reduces overall weight; low-profile gas block; stock is adjustable; long topside Picatinny rail; variants include a model with Magpul furniture, and state-compliant models that have either a non-threaded barrel or a fixed magazine
MSRP . . . . $1089.00–$1269.00

AR-556 MPR FLAG SERIES

Action: Semiautomatic
Stock: Synthetic
Barrel: 18 in.
Sights: None
Weight: 6 lb. 13 oz.
Caliber: 5.56 NATO
Magazine: 30 rounds
Features: A subtle if somewhat battle-worn American flag graphic is overlaid on the upper, lower, and handguard of this MSR; rifle-length gas system; Magpul MOE grip; Magpul MOE SL collapsible stock
MSRP $1139.00

Ruger (Sturm, Ruger & Co.)

RUGER CUSTOM SHOP 10/22 COMPETITION

RUGER CUSTOM SHOP 10/22 COMPETITION WITH SKELETONIZED GREEN MOUNTAIN STOCK

RUGER HAWKEYE ALASKAN

RUGER HAWKEYE LONG-RANGE TARGET

RUGER CUSTOM SHOP PRECISION RIFLE

RUGER HAWKEYE HUNTER

RUGER HAWKEYE PREDATOR

CUSTOM SHOP 10/22 COMPETITION

Action: Semiautomatic
Stock: Laminate
Barrel: 16.12 in.
Sights: None
Weight: 6 lb.
Caliber: .22 LR
Magazine: 10 rounds
Features: A next-level .22 for the serious rimfire competitor with features that include: heat-treated and stress-relieved aluminum receiver; 30mm Picatinny rail for optics mounting; adjustable cheekpiece; free-floating barrel with rear cleaning port; extended ambidextrous magazine release; match-grade bolt release; BX Trigger; choice of traditional speckled black/gray laminate stock with satin black metalwork, natural brown laminate traditional stock with stainless steel hardware, or a Green Mountain skeletonized laminate thumbhole stock with angled forend, hard-coat anodized black receiver, and satin stainless barrel with black Cerakote accents
Speckled black/gray laminate stock..............**$899.00**
Natural brown laminate stock..............**$1029.00**

CUSTOM SHOP 10/22 COMPETITION WITH SKELETONIZED GREEN MOUNTAIN STOCK

Action: Semiautomatic
Stock: Laminate
Barrel: 16.12 in.
Sights: None
Weight: 5 lb. 8 oz.
Caliber: .22 LR
Magazine: 10 rounds
Features: Skeletonized laminate stock from Green Mountain; free-floating stainless steel barrel with black Cerakote highlights; 30 MOA topside

Picatinny rail; black hard-coat anodized receiver with rear cleaning port; dual bedding system; BX-Trigger; match bolt release; includes Ruger hard case, Custom Shop letter of authenticity, and challenge coin
MSRP................**$1019.00**

HAWKEYE ALASKAN

Action: Bolt
Stock: Hogue synthetic
Barrel: 20 in.
Sights: Bead front, adjustable rear
Weight: 8 lb. 2 oz.
Caliber: .375 Ruger, .338 Win. Mag., .300 Win. Mag.
Magazine: 3 rounds
Features: Ruger brings back the Alaskan in three bear/moose/wolf-stopping cartridges and with enough weight to sop up some of the recoil; Hogue overmolded stock; Hawkeye Matte durable metal finish; non-rotating, Mauser-type controlled round feed extractor; LC6 trigger
MSRP................**$1569.00**

CUSTOM SHOP PRECISION RIFLE

Action: Bolt
Stock: Synthetic
Barrel: 26 in.
Sights: None
Weight: 12 lb. 14 oz.
Caliber: 6mm Creedmoor
Magazine: 10 rounds
Features: Custom heavy-contour barrel that's free-floating, cold hammer-forged, and has R5 rifling; threaded muzzle with an APA muzzle brake; free-floating M-LOK handguard with slots on four sides and is flat-bottomed and compatible with RRS S.O.A.R. and other quick-detach systems; Magpul MOE K2 grip; Sorbothane cheek pad; Trigger Tech trigger; folding stock adjustable at cheekpiece and for length of pull; gray Cerakote finish
MSRP................**$2419.00**

HAWKEYE HUNTER

Action: Bolt
Stock: American walnut
Barrel: 20 in., 22 in., 24 in.
Sights: None
Weight: 7 lb.–8 lb. 2 oz.
Caliber: 6.5 Creedmoor, 6.5 PRC, .308 Win., .30-06 Spfd., .300 Win. Mag., 7mm Rem. Mag., .204 Ruger
Magazine: 3, 4 rounds
Features: American walnut stock; satin stainless hardware; non-rotating, Mauser-type controlled round feed extractor; 20 MOA topside Picatinny rail; free-floating cold hammer-forged barrel with 5R rifling
MSRP................**$1359.00**

HAWKEYE LONG-RANGE TARGET

Action: Bolt
Stock: Laminate
Barrel: 24 in.
Sights: None
Weight: 10 lb. 11 oz.
Caliber: .300 Win. Mag., 6.5 Creedmoor, 6.5 PRC, .204 Ruger, .308 Win.
Magazine: 5 rounds
Features: Heavy contour barrel; Ruger's Precision Rifle Muzzle Brake; two-stage target trigger; controlled round feed; fixed-blade ejecto;, a 20 MOA rail that screws down on top of Ruger's own integral mounts; adjustable laminate stock
MSRP................**$1569.00**

HAWKEYE PREDATOR

Action: Bolt
Stock: Laminate
Barrel: 22 in., 24 in.
Sights: None
Weight: 7 lb. 11 oz.–8 lb. 2 oz.
Caliber: .22-250 Rem., .223 Rem., .204 Ruger, .6.5 Creedmor
Magazine: 4 rounds
Features: Non-rotating, Mauser-type controlled round feed extractor; hinged solid-steel floorplate; cold hammer-forged barrel; patented integral scope mounts
MSRP........**$1399.00–$1429.00**

Ruger (Sturm, Ruger & Co.)

RUGER MINI-14 RANCH RIFLE

RUGER MINI-14 TACTICAL

RUGER MINI-14 TACTICAL WOOD STOCK

RUGER NO. 1

RUGER PC CARBINE

RUGER PC CARBINE CHASSIS

RUGER PC CARBINE FLAG SERIES

MINI-14 RANCH

Action: Semiautomatic
Stock: Hardwood, synthetic
Barrel: 18.5 in.
Sights: Blade front sight, adjustable rear
Weight: 6 lb. 12 oz.–7 lb.
Caliber: 5.56 NATO, .223 Rem.
Magazine: 5 rounds, or detachable box, 20 rounds
Features: Stock comes in hardwood or black synthetic; Garand style action; hammer-forged barrel; sighting system; integral scope mounts; flat buttpad; integral sling swivels on hardwood or black synthetic stocks
MSRP . . . . $1229.00–$1409.00

MINI-14 TACTICAL

Action: Semiautomatic
Stock: Synthetic
Barrel: 16.1 in.
Sights: Adjustable
Weight: 6 lb. 12 oz.–7 lb. 4 oz.
Caliber: 5.56 NATO, .223 Rem., .300 BLK
Magazine: Detachable box, 5, 20 rounds
Features: Standard features include Garand-style action; flash suppressor; adjustable ghost ring rear sight, non-glare protected-post front sight; drilled and tapped receiver; Picatinny rail; scope rings; two magazines. Variants include black synthetic stock with stainless or blued hardware; ATI six-position collapsible/folding stock with blued hardware; speckled black/brown hardwood stock with blued hardware
MSRP . . . . $1339.00–$1439.00

MINI-14 TACTICAL WOOD STOCK

Action: Semiautomatic
Stock: Hardwood

Barrel: 16.12 in.
Sights: Blade front, adjustable rear
Weight: 7 lb. 3 oz.
Caliber: 5.56 NATO
Magazine: 20 rounds
Features: The Mini-14 gets a new look and improved gripping surface with a speckled black-and-brown hardwood stock while retaining standard features such as its Garand-style, breech-bolt locking action
MSRP $1299.00

NO. 1

Action: Single-shot
Stock: American walnut
Barrel: 20 in.
Sights: Blade front and rear
Weight: 7 lb. 1 oz.
Caliber: .450 Marlin, .308 Win., .450 Bushmaster
Magazine: 1 round
Features: Falling-block breech mechanism rifle includes a sliding tang safety; Ruger's patented scope mounting system; ejector that can be adjusted to perform as an extractor only; caliber changes from year to year and rifle is available in limited quantities; for 2022, this model is available through Lipsey's Distributors in: American walnut/satin blue in .257 Wby., .275 Rigby, and 6.5 Creedmoor
MSRP . . . . N/A

PC CARBINE

Action: Semiautomatic
Stock: Synthetic
Barrel: 16.12 in.
Sights: Protected blade front, adjustable ghost ring rear
Weight: 6 lb. 12 oz.
Caliber: 9mm
Magazine: 10, 17 rounds
Features: Interchangeable magwell that lets the operator use a variety of

Ruger or Glock magazines; buttstock is adjustable for length of pull via included spacers; magazine release and charging handle are both reversible; dead blow action with a tungsten weight both shortens the overall bolt trave, reduces felt recoil and muzzle rise
MSRP $759.00

PC CARBINE CHASSIS

Action: Semiautomatic
Stock: Glass-filled polymer
Barrel: 16.12 in.
Sights: None
Weight: 7 lb. 5 oz.
Caliber: 9mm
Magazine: 10, 17 rounds
Features: A favorite carbine gets a technology upgrade; glass-filled polymer chassis foundation; aluminum free-floating handguard; threaded and fluted heavy-contour barrel; telescopic, six-position Magpul MOE buttstock; SR series magazine
MSRP $979.00

PC CARBINE FLAG SERIES

Action: Semiautomatic
Stock: Glass-filled nylon
Barrel: 16.12 in.
Sights: Blade front, adjustable ghost ring rear
Weight: 7 lb.
Caliber: 9mm
Magazine: 17 rounds
Features: Quick-handling and visibly startling, you'll have loads of fun in PCC competitions thanks to the rifle's free-floating aluminum handguard; reversible magazine release and charging handle; heavy contour barrel; Type III hard coat anodizing
MSRP $899.00

Ruger (Sturm, Ruger & Co.)

RUGER PRECISION RIFLE

RUGER PRECISION RIMFIRE

RUGER PRECISION RIMFIRE FLAG SERIES

RUGER SCOUT RIFLE

PRECISION RIFLE

Action: Bolt
Stock: Synthetic
Barrel: 20 in., 24 in.
Sights: None
Weight: 9 lb. 12 oz.–10 lb. 12 oz.
Caliber: .308 Win., 6.5 Creedmoor, 6mm Creedmoor, ,338 Lapua, .300 Win. Mag., 6.5 PRC, .300 PRC, 6mm Creedmoor
Magazine: 10 rounds
Features: Cold hammer-forged chrome-moly steel barrel with 5R rifling at minimum bore and groove dimensions, minimum, headspace and centralized chamber; Samson Evolution KeyMod handguard; 20 MOA Picatinny rail; in-line recoil path manages recoil directly from the rear of the receiver to the buttstock; patent-pending multi-magazine interface functions interchangeably with M110, SR25, DPMS, and Magpul-style magazines and AICS magazines (works with some M14 magazines); Ruger Marksman Adjustable trigger
MSRP . . . . $1879.00–$2459.00

PRECISION RIMFIRE

Action: Bolt
Stock: Synthetic
Barrel: 18 in.
Sights: None
Weight: 6 lb. 12 oz.
Caliber: .22 LR, .22 WMR, .17HMR
Magazine: 10, 15 rounds
Features: One-piece molded chassis is mated with an oversized bolt; adjustable bolt throw to prevent short stroking; Ruger's Marksman Adjustable trigger; reversible safety; glass-filled nylon buttstock is fully adjustable; Picatinny rail bag rider for monopod use; a molded in window allows squeeze bag attachment
MSRP $599.00

PRECISION RIMFIRE FLAG SERIES

Action: Bolt
Stock: Glass-filled nylon chassis
Barrel: 18 in.
Sights: None
Weight: 6 lb. 13 oz.
Caliber: .22 LR
Magazine: 15 rounds
Features: Competition-ready rimfire features a one-piece chassis and

Quick-Fit adjustable buttstock, both of glass-filled nylon; Ruger Marksman Adjustable trigger
MSRP $649.00

SCOUT RIFLE

Action: Bolt
Stock: Laminate; synthetic; wood
Barrel: 16.50 in.
Sights: Post front sight, adjustable rear
Weight: 7 lb.
Caliber: .308 Win., .350 Legend,.450 Bushmaster
Magazine: Detachable box, 10 rounds
Features: Flash suppressor, Picatinny rail; recoil pad; integral scope mounts; Mauser-type extractor; detachable magazine; stainless finish bolt. Variants include black laminate stock with matte blue barrel/receiver and 10-round magazine; black laminate stock with stainless barrel/receiver and 10-round magazine; black synthetic stock with matte black barrel/receiver and five-round magazine; black synthetic stock with stainless barrel/receiver and 10-round magazine; wood stock in .450 Bushmaster only with Ruger Precision Rifle Hybrid Muzzle Brake, blued barrel/receiver, four-round magazine
MSRP . . . .$1409.00–$1479.00

Sako

SAKO 85 BAVARIAN CARBINE

SAKO 85 CARBONLIGHT

85 BAVARIAN CARBINE

Action: Bolt
Stock: Walnut
Barrel: 22.5, 24.3 in.
Sights: Rifled sights
Weight: N/A
Caliber: .308 Win., .270 Win., .30-06 Spfd., .300 Win. Mag., 6.5 Creedmoor
Features: Featuring a full Mannlicher

stock with Schnabel fore-tip and Bavarian cheekpiece/comb; iron sights; sling swivel studs; single set trigger
MSRP: $2225.00

85 CARBONLIGHT

Action:Bolt
Stock: Carbon fiber
Barrel: 20 in.

Sights: None
Weight: 5 lb. 5 oz.
Caliber: .308 Win., .260 Rem., 7mm-08 Rem.
Magazine: Detachable box, 5 rounds
Features: Fluted barrel; stainless steel action; stainless steel barrel; single stage trigger; single set trigger available
MSRP $3175.00

Sako

SAKO 85 CARBON WOLF

SAKO 85 CLASSIC

SAKO 85 FINNLIGHT

SAKO 85 FINNLIGHT II

SAKO 85 GREY WOLF (AKA 85 HUNTER LAMINATED STAINLESS)

SAKO 85 KODIAK

SAKO 85 LONG RANGE

85 CARBON WOLF

Action: Bolt
Stock: Carbon fiber
Barrel: 24 in.
Sights: None
Weight: 7 lb. 4 oz.–7 lb. 11 oz.
Caliber: .308 Win., .30-06 Spfd., .300 Win. Mag., 7mm Rem. Mag., 6.5 Creedmoor
Magazine: 5, 6
Features: Carbon fiber stock with a RTM technology and a soft-touch coating; stock is adjustable for length of pull and cheek-piece height
MSRP $3600.00

85 CLASSIC

Action: Bolt
Stock: Walnut
Barrel: 22.4 in., 24.4 in.
Sights: Open
Weight: 7 lb.–7 lb. 12 oz.
Caliber: .308 Win., .25-06 Rem., .270 Win., .30-06 Spfd., .300 Win. Mag., .338 Win. Mag., .375 H&H, .270 WSM, .300 WSM, 7mm Rem. Mag.
Magazine: Detachable box, S/M 6 rounds, SM/L 5 rounds
Features: Comes in short actions Extra Short (XS), Short (S) and Short Magnum (SM), medium action (M), and long action (L); straight, classic walnut stock with rosewood forend tip and pistol grip cap; integral rails for scope mounts; free-floating barrel is cold-hammer-forged; adjustable single-stage trigger
MSRP . . . . $2275.00–$2325.00

85 FINNLIGHT

Action: Bolt
Stock: Synthetic
Barrel: 20.25, 22.4, 24.3 in.
Sights: None
Weight: 6 lb. 3 oz.–6 lb. 13 oz.

Caliber: (Short): .22-250 Rem., .243 Win., .260 Rem., .7mm-08 Rem., .308 Win.; (SM) .270 Win. Short Mag., .300 Win. Short Mag.; (Medium): .25-06 Rem., 6.5x55 Swedish, .270 Win., .30-06 Spfd.; (Long) 7mm Rem. Mag., .300 Win. Mag.
Magazine: Detachable box, S/M 6 rounds, SM/L 5 rounds
Features: Comes in short actions Short (S) and Short magnum (SM), Medium action (M), and Long action (L); single-stage trigger; two-way Sako safety locks both trigger and bolt handle; black synthetic stock with soft gray grip areas; pistol grip stock; integral rails for scope mounts; free-floating barrel is cold-hammer-forged of stainless steel
MSRP . . . . $1800.00–$1850.00

85 FINNLIGHT II

Action: Bolt
Stock: Fiberglass
Barrel: 20 in., 23 in., 24 in.
Sights: None
Weight: 6 lb. 3 oz.–6 lb. 13 oz.
Caliber: .22-250 Rem., .243 Win., .308 Win., .25-96 Rem., .270 Win., .30-06 Spfd., .260 Rem., .300 Win. Mag., .270 WSM, .300 WSM, 6.5x55 Swedish Mauser, 7mm-08 Rem., 7mm Rem. Mag., 6.5 Creedmoor
Magazine: 4, 5 rounds
Features: Fiberglass stock with RTM technology; fully adjustable cheek-piece; improved gripping surfaces; barrel finished in Cerakote
MSRP $2475.00

85 GREY WOLF

Action: Bolt
Stock: Laminated
Barrel: 23 in., 24 in.

Sights: None
Weight: 6 lb. 6 oz.–7 lb. 8 oz.
Caliber: .270 Win., .30-06 Spfd., .300 Win. Mag., .270 WSM, .300 WSM, 7mm Rem. Mag.
Magazine: 4, 5 rounds
Features: Gray matte-lacquered laminate stock; stainless hardware throughout; single stage trigger is standard, single set trigger optional; detachable magazine
MSRP . . . . $1725.00–$1775.00

85 KODIAK

Action: Bolt
Stock: Laminated hardwood
Barrel: 12.25 in.
Sights: Open
Weight: 7 lb. 15 oz.
Caliber: .375 H&H
Magazine: Detachable box, 5 rounds
Features: Adjustable single-stage trigger; barrel band for front swivel; integral dovetail rails for secure scope mounting; straight stock made of gray matte-lacquered laminated hardwood and reinforced with two cross-bolts; free-floating "bull" barrel
MSRP $1950.00

85 LONG RANGE

Action: Bolt
Stock: Wood
Barrel: 26 in.
Sights: None
Weight: 9 lb. 12 oz.
Caliber: .300 Win. Mag., .338 Lapua Mag.
Magazine: Detachable box, 4+1 rounds
Features: Flush design muzzle brake; designed for long range hunting
MSRP $2875.00

Sako

SAKO S20

SAKO TRG 22

SAKO TRG 22/42 A1

SAKO TRG M10

S20

Action: Bolt
Stock: Synthetic
Barrel: 20 in., 24 in.
Sights: None
Weight: N/A
Caliber: 6.5 Creedmoor, .308 Win., .243 Win., .30-06 Spfd., .270 Win., 6.5 PRC, 7mm Rem. Mag., .300 Win. Mag.
Magazine: 3, 4 rounds
Features: A modular configuration offers a semi-custom fit, with buyers able to choose from interchangeable stocks, barrel lengths and styles, and numerous accessories; full aluminum chassis; adjustable stock; cold hammer-forged barrels; adjustable trigger; double-stack magazines designed to prevent bullet damage; interchangeable bolt handle face; three-lug stainless steel bolt; receiver with integrated Picatinny rails; full aluminum bedding
MSRP . . . . **$1599.00–$1699.00**

TRG 22

Action: Bolt
Stock: Synthetic
Barrel: 20 in., 26 in., 27.1 in.
Sights: None
Weight: 10 lb. 4 oz.–10 lb. 12 oz.
Caliber: .308 Win., 6.5 Creedmoor
Magazine: Detachable box, 5, 7, 10 rounds
Features: Double-stage trigger; two-way Sako safety locks both trigger and bolt handle; base of stock is made of polyurethane with aluminum skeleton; adjustable cheekpiece and buttplate; Ambidextrous stock in green or desert tan color; includes integral dovetail on receiver and is drilled and tapped for Picatinny rail mounting
MSRP **$3500.00**

TRG 22/42 A1

Action: Bolt
Stock: Aluminum
Barrel: 26 in., 27 in.
Sights: None
Weight: 11 lb. 11 oz.–13 lb. 3 oz.
Caliber: .308 Win., .260 Rem., 6.5 Creedmoor, .300 Win. Mag., .338 Lapua
Magazine: 5, 7, 10 rounds
Features: Adjustable folding stock with two hinge points that eliminate wobble; M-LOK forend for accessory attachments; threaded muzzles; phosphatized steel parts; detachable magazine; muzzle brake and Picatinny or Weaver rail is standard on some models, optional on others
MSRP . . . . **$6400.00–$7400.00**

TRG M10

Action: Bolt
Stock: Synthetic
Barrel: 20–27 in.
Sights: None
Weight: 13 lb. 4 oz.–14 lb. 5 oz.
Caliber: .308 Win., .300 Win. Mag., .338 Lapua
Magazine: Detachable box, 8 or 11 rounds
Features: Threaded muzzle; muzzle break available; phosphatized steel parts; stainless steel barrel; double stage trigger; Picatinny or Weaver rail; fully adjustable rear stock; ambidextrous controls
MSRP **$11,275.00**

Savage Arms

SAVAGE ARMS 12BTCSS

SAVAGE ARMS 110 APEX HUNTER XP

SAVAGE ARMS 110 APEX PREDATOR XP

SAVAGE ARMS 110 APEX STORM XP

SAVAGE ARMS 110 BEAR HUNTER

SAVAGE ARMS 110 CLASSIC

12BTCSS

Action: Bolt
Stock: Laminate
Barrel: 26 in.
Sights: None
Weight: 10 lb.
Caliber: .204 Ruger, .223 Rem., .22-250 Rem.
Magazine: Detachable box, 4 rounds
Features: Drilled and tapped for scope mounts; stainless steel barrel with high luster finish; AccuTrigger; wood laminate with thumbhole and satin finish
MSRP **$1459.00**

110 APEX HUNTER XP

Action: Bolt
Stock: Synthetic
Barrel: 20 in., 22 in., 24 in.
Sights: Vortex Crossfire II 3–9X40mm scope
Weight: 7 lb. 11 oz.–8 lb. 2 oz.
Caliber: .223 Rem., .204 Ruger, .22–250 Rem., .243 Win., 6.5 Creedmoor, .260 Rem., .308 Win., .270 WSM, .300 WSM, .25–06 Rem., 6.5x284 Norma, .270 Win., .270 WSM, .30–06 Spfd., 7mm Rem. Mag., .300 Win. Mag., .338 Win. Mag., 7mm-08 Rem., .350 Legend, .450 Bushmaster, 6.5 PRC
Magazine: 3, 4 rounds
Features: With a caliber for every hunting pursuit except the most dangerous; adjustable AccuTrigger; detachable box magazine; matte black metalwork; stock with adjustable length of pull; left and right-hand configurations in black synthetic stock; right-hand stock in Muddy Girl camo in limited calibers
MSRP. **$709.00**

110 APEX PREDATOR XP

Action: Bolt
Stock: Synthetic
Barrel: 20 in., 24 in.
Sights: Vortex Crossfire II 4–12X44mm scope
Weight: 8 lb. 7 oz.
Caliber: .223 Rem., .22–250 Rem., .204 Ruger, .243 Win., 6.5 Creedmoor, .308 Win.
Magazine: 3, 4 rounds
Features: A package rifle with a factory-mounted and bore-sighted Vortex scope; AccuTrigger; button-rifled heavy barrel; adjustable length of pull; matte blue metalwork; Mossy Oak camo coverage on stock; detachable box magazine
MSRP. **$829.00**

110 APEX STORM XP

Action: Bolt
Stock: Synthetic
Barrel: 20 in., 22 in., 24 in.
Sights: Vortex Crossfire II 3–9X40mm scope
Weight: 7 lb. 11 oz.–8 lb. 2 oz.
Caliber: .223 Rem., .204 Ruger, .22–250 Rem., .243 Win., 6.5 Creedmoor, .260 Rem., .308 Win., .270 WSM, .25–06 Rem., 6.5x284 Norma, .270 Win., .270 WSM, .30–06 Spfd., 7mm Rem. Mag., .300 Win. Mag., .338 Win. Mag., 7mm-08 Rem., .350 Legend, 6.5 PRC
Magazine: 3, 4 rounds
Features: Similar to the 110 Apex Hunter XP, but with matte stainless metalwork
MSRP. **$819.00**

110 BEAR HUNTER

Action: Bolt
Stock: Synthetic
Barrel: 23 in.
Sights: None
Weight: 8 lb. 6 oz.
Caliber: .300 Win. Mag., .300 WSM, .338 Federal, .338 Win. Mag., .375 Ruger
Magazine: 2 rounds
Features: AccuFit System Accustock; four ¼-in. length-of-pull spacers and five 1/8-in. comb risers, all easily swappable; stainless steel finish; hinged floorplate magazine; straight fluted barrel; stock in Mossy Oak Breakup Country.
MSRP. **$1119.00**

110 CLASSIC

Action: Bolt
Stock: Walnut
Barrel: 22 in.
Sights: None
Weight: 8 lb.
Caliber: .243 Win., .270 Win., .30-06 Spfd., .300 Win. Mag., .308 Win., 6.5 Creedmoor, 7mm Rem. Mag., 7mm-08 Rem.
Magazine: 3, 4 rounds
Features: Classic indeed! Totally retro look from the grain and color of the hardwood stock to the funky slashed checkering, but you also get modern upgrades like an adjustable AccuTrigger
MSRP. **$1099.00**

Savage Arms

SAVAGE ARMS 110 ENGAGE HUNTER XP

SAVAGE ARMS 110 HIGH COUNTRY

SAVAGE ARMS 110 HOG HUNTER

SAVAGE ARMS 110 HUNTER

SAVAGE ARMS 110 LIGHTWEIGHT STORM WITH ADJUSTABLE LENGTH OF PULL

SAVAGE ARMS 110 LONG RANGE HUNTER

110 ENGAGE HUNTER XP

Action: Bolt
Stock: Synthetic
Barrel: 22 in.
Sights: None
Weight: 7 lb. 4 oz.
Caliber: .243 Win., 6.5 Creedmoor, 7mm-08 Rem., .308 Win., .260 Rem., .270 WSM, .300 WSM, .338 Win. Mag., .25-06 Rem., .270 Win., 6.5x284 Norma, .30-06 Spfd., 7mm Rem. Mag., .300 Win. Mag., .280 Ackley Improved, .350 Legend, .450 Bushmaster, 6.5 PRC
Magazine: 4 rounds
Features: Adjustable stock for length of pull; user-adjustable AccuTrigger; detachable box magazine; Weaver Grand Slam bases and rings; Bushnell Engage 3–9x40mm drop-compensating reticle scope mounted and bore sighted
MSRP **$669.00**

110 HIGH COUNTRY

Action: Bolt
Stock: Synthetic
Barrel: 22 in., 24 in.
Sights: None
Weight: 8 lb. 1 oz.
Caliber: .243 Win., 6.5 Creedmoor, 6.5 PRC, .270 Win., .280 Ackley Improved, 7mm-08 Rem., 7mm Rem. Mag., .308 Win., .30–06 Spfd., .300 Win. Mag., .300 WSM
Magazine: 3, 4, 5 rounds
Features: One for the backcountry hunters featuring Accufit stock with overmold gripping surfaces and full-coverage TrueTimber Strata camo; PVD-coated stainless action; spiral-0fluted bolt and barrel in bronze;

threaded barrel (magnum barrels include taplock-interface muzzle brake); detachable box magazine; AccuTrigger; Accufit adjustable stock
MSRP **$1239.00**

110 HOG HUNTER

Action: Bolt
Stock: Synthetic
Barrel: 20 in.
Sights: Adjustable iron
Weight: 7 lb. 4 oz.
Caliber: .223 Rem., .308 Win., .350 Legend
Magazine: 4 rounds
Features: A responsive gun for today's growing legions of wild boar hunters with a medium contour, threaded, carbon steel barrel; oversize bolt handle; olive drab stock; detachable box magazine; adjustable length of pull; AccuTrigger
MSRP **$669.00**

110 HUNTER

Action: Bolt
Stock: Synthetic
Barrel: 22 in., 24 in.
Sights: None
Weight: 7 lb. 2 oz.–7 lb. 5 oz.
Caliber: .204 Ruger, .22-250 Rem., .223 Rem., .243 Win., .25-06 Rem., .270 Win., .280 Ackley Imp., .30-06 Spfd., .300 Win Mag., .308 Win., 7mm Rem. Mag., 7mm-08 Rem., 6.5 Creedmoor
Magazine: 3, 4 rounds
Features: AccuFit System Accustock; four ¼-inch length-of-pull spacers and five 1/8-inch comb risers, all easily swappable; black matte finish; detachable box magazine
MSRP **$795.00**

110 LIGHTWEIGHT STORM WITH ADJUSTABLE LENGTH OF PULL

Action: Bolt
Stock: Synthetic
Barrel: 20 in.
Sights: None
Weight: 5 lb. 9 oz.–5 lb. 13 oz.
Caliber: .270 Win., .223 Win., 7mm-08 Rem., .308 Win., .243 Win., 6.5 Creedmoor
Magazine: 4 rounds
Features: Savage takes its popular Storm model and shaves off more than a pound with a light-contour barrel that gets spiral fluting. Other features include: detachable box magazine; AccuTrigger; adjustable length of pull; skeletonized receiver
MSRP **$849.00**

110 LONG RANGE HUNTER

Action: Bolt
Stock: Synthetic
Barrel: 26 in.
Sights: None
Weight: 8 lb.
Caliber: .280 Ackley Imp., .300 Win. Mag., .300 WSM, .308 Win., 6.5 Creedmoor, 6.5x284 Norma, 7mm Rem. Mag., .28 Nosler
Magazine: 3, 4 rounds
Features: AccuFit System Accustock; four ¼-inch length-of-pull spacers and five ⅛-inch comb risers, all easily swappable; black matte finish barrel; hinged floorplate magazine; muzzle brake
MSRP **$1239.00**

SAVAGE ARMS 110
LONG RANGE HUNTER
.338 LAPUA

SAVAGE ARMS 110
SCOUT

SAVAGE ARMS 110
PREDATOR

SAVAGE ARMS 110
STORM

SAVAGE ARMS 110
RIDGE WARRIOR

SAVAGE ARMS 110 TACTICAL

SAVAGE ARMS 110
TACTICAL DESERT

SAVAGE ARMS 110
TACTICAL LEFT-HAND

110 LONG RANGE HUNTER .338 LAPUA

Action: Bolt
Stock: Synthetic
Barrel: 26 in.
Sights: None
Weight: 8 lb. 14 oz.
Caliber: .338 Lapua
Magazine: 5 rounds
Features: AccuFit System Accustock; four ¼-inch length-of-pull spacers and five ⅛-inch comb risers, all easily swappable; black matte finish barrel; detachable box magazine; muzzle brake
MSRP $1469.00

110 PREDATOR

Action: Bolt
Stock: Synthetic
Barrel: 22 in., 24 in.
Sights: None
Weight: 8 lb. 4 oz.–8 lb. 11 oz.
Caliber: .204 Ruger, .22-250 Rem., .223 Rem., .243 Win., .260 Rem., 6.5 Creedmoor, .308 Win.
Magazine: 4 rounds
Features: AccuFit System Accustock; four ¼-inch length-of-pull spacers and five ⅛-inch comb risers, all easily swappable; black matte finish barrel; detachable box magazine; stock in Realtree Max-1 camo stock; two-piece Weaver-style bases
MSRP $1009.00

110 RIDGE WARRIOR

Action: Bolt
Stock: Synthetic
Barrel: 24 in.
Sights: None
Weight: 8 lb. 13 oz.
Caliber: 6.5 Creedmoor, .308 Win.
Magazine: 10 rounds
Features: AccuFit AccuStock and an adjustable AccuTrigger; Mossy Oak Overwatch camo on the stock; Gunsmoke gray receiver with PVD coating; fluted, threaded heavy barrel

MSRP $1049.00

110 SCOUT

Action: Bolt
Stock: Synthetic
Barrel: 16.5 in.
Sights: Adjustable iron
Weight: 7 lb. 11 oz.
Caliber: .223 Rem., .308 Win., .450 Bushmaster
Magazine: 10 rounds
Features: AccuFit System Accustock; four ¼-inch length-of-pull spacers and five ⅛-inch comb risers, all easily swappable; black matte finish barrel; detachable Magpul AICS box magazine; Flat Dark Earth stock; adjustable iron sights; forward-mounted accessory/optic rail
MSRP $919.00

110 STORM

Action: Bolt
Stock: Synthetic
Barrel: 22 in., 24 in.
Sights: None
Weight: 7 lb. 2 oz.–7 lb. 5 oz.
Caliber: .22-250 Rem., .223 Rem., .243 Rem., .25-06 Rem., .270 Win., .270 WSM, .280 Ackley Imp., .30-06 Spfd., 300 Win. Mag., .300 WSM, .308 Win., 6.5 Creedmoor, 6.5x284 Norma, 7mm Rem., Mag., 7mm-08 Rem., .338 Win. Mag.
Magazine: 3, 4 rounds
Features: AccuFit System Accustock; four ¼-inch length-of-pull spacers and five 1/8-inch comb risers, all easily swappable; matte stainless steel barrel finish; detachable box magazine; left-hand versions available
MSRP $959.00

110 TACTICAL

Action: Bolt
Stock: Synthetic
Barrel: 20 in., 24 in.

Sights: None
Weight: 8 lb. 11 oz.–8 lb. 14 oz.
Caliber: .308 Win., .300 Win. Mag., 6.5 Creedmoor, 6.5 PRC, 6mm ARC
Magazine: 10 rounds
Features: AccuFit System Accustock; four ¼-inch length-of-pull spacers and five 1/8-inch comb risers, all easily swappable; matte black barrel finish; detachable box magazine; threaded heavy barrel with end cap; an oversized bolt; a 20 MOA EGW accessory/optic rail; left-hand available in .308 Win. and 6.5 Creedmoor
MSRP $889.00

110 TACTICAL DESERT

Action: Bolt
Stock: Synthetic
Barrel: 24 in., 26 in.
Sights: None
Weight: 8 lb. 14 oz.–9 lb.
Caliber: 6.5 Creedmoor, .300 Win. Mag., 6.5 PRC, 6mm Creedmoor
Magazine: 10 rounds
Features: AccuFit System Accustock; four-inch length-of-pull spacers and five 1/8-inch comb risers, all easily swappable; a matte black barrel finish; detachable box magazine; Flat Dark Earth stock; threaded heavy barrel with end cap; oversized bolt; 20 MOA EGW accessory/optic rail; left-hand available in 6.5 Creedmoor
MSRP $869.00

110 TACTICAL LEFT-HAND, 110 TACTICAL DESERT LEFT-HAND

Action: Bolt
Stock: Synthetic
Barrel: 24 in.
Sights: None
Weight: 8 lb. 13 oz.
Caliber: 6.5 Creedmoor
Magazine: 10 rounds
Features: A true tactical for lefties in a matte gray or a spiffy desert tan stock with detachable Magpul AICS magazine; adjustable AccuTrigger; oversize bolt knob; soft-grip surfaces; AccuFit stock; threaded heavy barrel
MSRP . . . . $869.00–$889.00

Savage Arms

SAVAGE ARMS 110 VARMINT

SAVAGE ARMS A SERIES A17 OVERWATCH

SAVAGE ARMS A SERIES A22

SAVAGE ARMS A SERIES A17

SAVAGE ARMS A SERIES A17 TARGET SPORTER LAMINATE

SAVAGE ARMS A SERIES A22 FV-SR, FV-SR OVERWATCH

SAVAGE ARMS A17 HM2

SAVAGE ARMS A17 TARGET THUMBHOLE

SAVAGE ARMS A SERIES A22 MAGNUM

110 VARMINT
Action: Bolt
Stock: Synthetic
Barrel: 26 in.
Sights: None
Weight: N/A
Caliber: .204 Ruger, .22-250 Rem., .223 Rem.,
Magazine: 4 rounds
Features: AccuFit System Accustock; four ¼-inch length-of-pull spacers and five 1/8-inch comb risers, all easily swappable; matte black barrel finish; detachable box magazine
MSRP $849.00

A SERIES A17
Action: Semiautomatic
Stock: Synthetic
Barrel: 22 in.
Sights: Drilled and tapped for scope mounts
Weight: 5 lb. 7 oz.
Caliber: .17 HMR
Magazine: Detachable rotary
Features: Carbon steel barrel; high luster barrel finish; Delayed Blowback Action, Hard Chromed Bolt with Dual Controlled Round Feed, Case Hardened Receiver, Button-Rifled Barrel
MSRP $539.00

A SERIES A17 HM2
Action: Semiautomatic
Stock: Synthetic
Barrel: 20 in.
Sights: None
Weight: 5 lb. 8 oz.
Caliber: .17 HMR
Magazine: 10 rounds
Features: This varmint-getter is easy on the wallet and has a sporter-profile carbon steel barrel, free-floating and with button rifling
MSRP $409.00

A SERIES A17 OVERWATCH
Action: Semiautomatic
Stock: Synthetic
Barrel: 22 in.
Sights: None
Weight: 5 lb. 13 oz.
Caliber: .17 HMR
Magazine: 10 rounds
Features: Neat-looking .17 HMR rimfire semiautomatic dressed in Mossy Oak Overwatch camo; rotary magazine; adjustable AccuTrigger; carbon steel barrel in heavy profile
MSRP $599.00

A SERIES A17 TARGET SPORTER LAMINATE
Action: Semiautomatic
Stock: Wood laminate
Barrel: 22 in.
Sights: None
Weight: 6 lb. 15 oz.
Caliber: .17 HMR
Magazine: Detachable rotary, 10 rounds
Features: Delayed blowback action; hard chromed bolt with dual controlled round feed; case hardened receiver; button-rifled barrel
MSRP $649.00

A SERIES A17 TARGET THUMBHOLE
Action: Semiautomatic
Stock: Wood laminate
Barrel: 22 in.
Sights: None
Weight: 7 lb. 1 oz.
Caliber: .17 HMR
Magazine: Detachable rotary, 10 rounds
Features: Grey laminate thumbhole stock; delayed blowback action; hard chromed bolt with dual controlled round feed; case hardened receiver; button-rifled barrel
MSRP $709.00

A SERIES A22
Action: Semiautomatic
Stock: Synthetic
Barrel: 21 in.
Sights: Adjustable
Weight: 5 lb. 10 oz.
Caliber: .22 LR
Magazine: 10 rounds
Features: Modeled after the A17, but chambered for .22 LR; straight blowback action; steel billet receiver; user-adjustable AccuTrigger
MSRP $309.00

A SERIES A22 FV-SR, FV-SR OVERWATCH
Action: Semiautomatic
Stock: Synthetic
Barrel: 16.5 in.
Sights: None
Weight: 5 lb. 4 oz.
Caliber: .22 LR
Magazine: 10 rounds
Features: This rimfire wears a shorter, medium-contour button-rifled barrel of carbon steel; carbon steel receiver; rotary magazine; one-piece Picatinny rail topside; adjustable AccuTrigger
Black stock: $389.00
Camo stock: $429.00

A SERIES A22 MAGNUM
Action: Semiautomatic
Stock: Synthetic
Barrel: 21 in.
Sights: None
Weight: 5 lb. 9 oz.
Caliber: .22 WMR
Magazine: Detachable rotary, 10 rounds
Features: Delayed blowback action; hard chromed bolt with dual controlled round feed; case hardened receiver; button-rifled barrel
MSRP $539.00

Savage Arms

SAVAGE ARMS AXIS (LEFT-HAND)

SAVAGE ARMS AXIS COMPACT

SAVAGE ARMS AXIS XP, XP STAINLESS

SAVAGE ARMS AXIS XP CAMO

SAVAGE ARMS AXIS XP COMPACT MUDDY GIRL CAMO

SAVAGE ARMS AXIS II

SAVAGE ARMS AXIS II OVERWATCH

SAVAGE ARMS AXIS II .300 BLACKOUT

SAVAGE ARMS AXIS II LEFT-HAND

AXIS

Action: Bolt
Stock: Synthetic
Barrel: 18 in., 22 in.
Sights: None
Weight: 6 lb. 5 oz.
Caliber: .223 Rem., .22-250 Rem., .243 Win., .25-06 Rem., .270 Win., .308 Win., .30-06 Spfd., .350 Legend, 6.5 Creedmoor, 7mm-08 Rem.
Magazine: 4 rounds
Features: Budget-friendly, lightweight hunting rifle great for treestand use and featuring a detachable magazine; button-rifled carbon steel barrel
MSRP..................$419.00

AXIS COMPACT

Action: Bolt
Stock: Synthetic
Barrel: 20 in.
Sights: None
Weight: 6 lb. 4 oz.
Caliber: .223 Rem., .243 Win., 6.5 Creedmoor, 7mm-08 Rem.
Magazine: 4 rounds
Features: Identical to the Axis, but with a shorter 12.75-in. length of pull and shorter barrel; left-hand available in .243 Win. and 7mm -08 Rem. only
MSRP..................$419.00

AXIS XP, XP STAINLESS

Action: Bolt
Stock: Synthetic
Barrel: 22 in.
Sights: Weaver 3–9X40mm scope
Weight: 7 lb. 5 oz.
Caliber: .223 Rem., .22–250 Rem., .243 Win., .25–06 Rem., 6.5 Creedmoor, .270 Win., 7mm-08 Rem., .308 Win., .30–06 Spfd., .350 Legend
Magazine: 5 rounds
Features: A package rifles with a factory-mounted and boresighted Weaver scope; detachable box magazine; sporter-contour barrel
XP $459.00
Stainless..............$569.00

AXIS XP CAMO

Action: Bolt

Stock: Synthetic
Barrel: 22 in.
Sights: Weaver 3–9X40mm scope
Weight: 7 lb. 5 oz.
Caliber: .223 Rem., .22–250 Rem., .243 Win., .25–06 Rem., 6.5, .350 Legend
Magazine: 5 rounds
Features: The popular, no-frills, scope-packaged rifle available in Muddy Girl or Mossy Oak Break-Up Country full-coverage stocks; sporter barrel contour; carbon steel barreled action
MSRP..................$509.00

AXIS XP COMPACT

Action: Bolt
Stock: Synthetic
Barrel: 20 in.
Sights: None
Weight: 7 lb. 5 oz.
Caliber: 6.5 Creedmoor
Magazine: 4 rounds
Features: The popular 6.5 Creedmoor in an ergonomic stock with a 12.75-in. length of pull; factory mounted 3–9x40mm Weaver scope; carbon-steel barrel; detachable box magazine; stock available in black, camo, and Muddy Girl camo
Black stock..............$459.00
Camo stock $509.00

AXIS II

Action: Bolt
Stock: Synthetic
Barrel: 22 in.
Sights: None
Weight: 6 lb. 4 oz.
Caliber: .223 Rem., .22–250 Rem., .243 Win., .25–06 Rem., 6.5 Creedmoor, .270 Win., 7mm-08 Rem., .280 Ackley Improved, .308 Win., .30–06 Spfd., .350 Legend
Magazine: 5 rounds
Features: Improved ergonomics with a redesigned stock; adjustable AccuTrigger; four-round detachable box magazine; button-rifled sporter barrel
MSRP..................$479.00

AXIS II .300 BLACKOUT

Action: Bolt
Stock: Synthetic
Barrel: 16.125 in.
Sights: None
Weight: 6 lb. 10 oz.
Caliber: .300 BLK
Magazine: 4 rounds
Features: This shorty rifle has a threaded carbon-steel barrel with a heavy profile; adjustable AccuTrigger; detachable box magazine; topside optics rail; ergonomic stock with textured grip areas
MSRP..................$469.00

AXIS II LEFT-HAND

Action: Bolt
Stock: Synthetic
Barrel: 22 in.
Sights: None
Weight: 6 lb. 5 oz.
Caliber: .223 Rem., .22-250 Rem., .243 Win., .25-06 Rem., .270 Win., .308 Win., .30-06 Spfd., 6.5 Creedmoor, 7mm-08 Rem.
Magazine: 4 rounds
Features: A great, budget-friendly choice for southpaws; adjustable AccuTrigger; detachable box magazine; button-rifled carbon steel barrel in a sporter contour; thread-in barrel headspacing
MSRP..................$479.00

AXIS II OVERWATCH

Action: Bolt
Stock: Synthetic
Barrel: 20 in.
Sights: None
Weight: 6 lb. 8 oz.
Caliber: .223 Rem., .22-250 Rem., .243 Win., .25-06 Rem., .270 Win., .280 Ackley Improved, .20-06 Spfd., .308 Win., 6.5 Creedmoor, 7mm-08 Rem.
Magazine: 4 rounds
Features: Stainless steel receiver and sporter-profile barrel in PVD-coated Gunsmoke gray; detachable box magazine; EGW one-piece optics rail; adjustable AccuTrigger; stock in Mossy Oak Overwatch camo
MSRP..................$549.00

Savage Arms

SAVAGE ARMS AXIS II XP

SAVAGE ARMS AXIS II XP COMPACT

SAVAGE ARMS AXIS II XP STAINLESS STEEL

SAVAGE ARMS B SERIES (B17 F, B22 F, B22 MAGNUM F)

SAVAGE ARMS B SERIES B17 FV-SR OVERWATCH

SAVAGE ARMS B SERIES B22 FV-SR OVERWATCH

SAVAGE ARMS IMPULSE PREDATOR

SAVAGE ARMS MAGNUM SERIES 93 BRJ

AXIS II XP

Action: Bolt
Stock: Synthetic
Barrel: 22 in.
Sights: None
Weight: 6 lb. 8 oz.
Caliber: .22-250 Rem., .223 Rem., .243 Win., .25-06 Rem., .270 Win., .280 Ackley Improved, .30-06 Spfd., .308 Win., 6.5 Creedmoor, 7mm-08 Rem., .350 Legend
Magazine: 4 rounds
Features: Carbon steel, button-rifled barrel; user-adjustable AccuTrigger; detachable box magazine; factory-mounted and bore-sighted 3–9x40mm Bushnell Banner scope; also available in a FDE stock
MSRP **$529.00**

AXIS II XP COMPACT

Action: Bolt
Stock: Synthetic
Barrel: 20 in.
Sights: None
Weight: 6 lb. 3 oz.
Caliber: .243 Win., .350 Legend, 6.5 Creedmoor
Magazine: 4 rounds
Features: Shorter length of pull; carbon steel, button-rifled barrel; user-adjustable AccuTrigger; detachable box magazine; factory-mounted and bore-sighted 3–9x40mm Bushnell Banner scope
MSRP **$529.00**

AXIS II XP STAINLESS

Action: Bolt
Stock: Synthetic
Barrel: 22 in.
Sights: None
Weight: 6 lb. 8 oz.
Caliber: .223 Rem., .22-250 Rem., 6.5 Creedmoor, .243 Win., .25-06 Rem., .280 Ackley Improved, 7mm-08 Rem., .308 Win., .30-06 Spfd., .270 Win., .350 Legend

Magazine: 4 rounds
Features: Carbon steel, button-rifled barrel; user-adjustable AccuTrigger; detachable box magazine; factory-mounted and bore-sighted 3–9x40mm Bushnell Banner scope; stainless-finish barrel, receiver, and bolt
MSRP **$629.00**

B SERIES

Action: Bolt
Stock: Synthetic
Barrel: 16.25 in., 21 in.
Sights: None
Weight: 5 lb. 8 oz.–6 lb.
Caliber: .17 HMR, .22 LR, .22 WMR
Magazine: 10 rounds
Features: In 2021, In 2022, this series boasts more than 30 models; three available calibers; wood and synthetic stocks; some left-hand models; G models get a raised cheekpiece and vertical pistol grip on a hardwood stock and a fore-end with grooves; compact models has 12.5-inch length of pull
MSRP . . . . **$369.00–$949.00**

B SERIES B17 FV-SR OVERWATCH

Action: Bolt
Stock: Synthetic
Barrel: 16.5 in.
Sights: None
Weight: 5 lb. 10 oz.
Caliber: .17 HMR
Magazine: 10 rounds
Features: Handy .17 HMR rimfire with a carbine-length threaded barrel of carbon steel in a heavy profile and with a target crown; rotary magazine; adjustable AccuTrigger; stock with raised comb and vertical target grip in Mossy Oak Overwatch camo; topside optics rail; sling swivel studs
MSRP **$379.00**

B SERIES B22 FV-SR OVERWATCH

Action: Bolt
Stock: Synthetic

Barrel: 16.5 in.
Sights: None
Weight: 5 lb. 10 oz.
Caliber: .22 LR
Magazine: 10 rounds
Features: A .22 LR with a carbine-length threaded barrel of carbon steel in a heavy profile and with a target crown; rotary magazine; adjustable AccuTrigger; stock with raised comb and vertical target grip in Mossy Oak Overwatch camo; topside optics rail; sling swivel studs
MSRP **$439.00**

IMPULSE PREDATOR

Action: Bolt
Stock: Synthetic
Barrel: 20 in.
Sights: None
Weight: 8 lb. 12 oz.
Caliber: .22-250 Rem., .243 Win., .308 Win., 6.5 Creedmoor
Magazine: 10 rounds
Features: Straight-pull bolt design; matte black aluminum receiver; matte black carbon steel barrel, threaded, in a medium contour; detachable AICS magazine with ambidextrous release; 20 MOA rail machined into receiver; user-adjustable AccuTrigger; adjustable AccuFit stock in Mossy Oak Terra Gila camo
MSRP **$1379.00**

MAGNUM SERIES 93 BRJ

Action: Bolt
Stock: Wood laminate
Barrel: 21 in.
Sights: None
Weight: 7 lb.
Caliber: .22 WMR
Magazine: Detachable box, 5 rounds
Features: Carbon steel barrel in blued satin finish; wood laminate stock; AccuTrigger
MSRP **$609.00**

RIFLES

Savage Arms

SAVAGE ARMS MARK II MINIMALIST

SAVAGE ARMS MODEL 64 TAKEDOWN

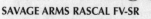

SAVAGE ARMS MSR15 RECON 2.0

SAVAGE ARMS RASCAL FV-SR

SAVAGE ARMS MARK II SERIES MARK II BTV

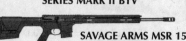

SAVAGE ARMS MSR 15 LONG RANGE

SAVAGE ARMS MSR 15 RECON LRP

SAVAGE ARMS MSR 10 HUNTER

SAVAGE ARMS MSR 10 LONG RANGE

MARK II MINIMALIST
Action: Bolt
Stock: Laminate
Barrel: 18 in.
Sights: None
Weight: 5 lb. 9 oz.
Caliber: .22 LR
Magazine: 10 rounds
Features: A futuristic looking rimfire with a Boyd's laminate hardwood stock in choice of green or brown tones; carbon steel barrel in matte finish and threaded ½x28; adjustable AccuTrigger; detachable magazine; two-piece Weaver bases
MSRP.................$379.00

MARK II SERIES MARK II BTV
Action: Bolt
Stock: Wood laminate
Barrel: 21 in.
Sights: None
Weight: 6 lb. 8 oz.
Caliber: .22 LR
Magazine: Detachable box, 5 rounds
Features: Carbon steel barrel with blued satin finish; wood laminate stock with thumbhole; AccuTrigger
MSRP.................$439.00

MODEL 64 TAKEDOWN
Action: Semiautomatic
Stock: Synthetic
Barrel: 16.5 in.
Sights: Front post, ladder-type leaf rear
Weight: 5 lb.
Caliber: .22 LR
Magazine: 10 rounds
Features: A portable, tear-apart rimfire that comes with an Uncle Mike's Bug-Out Bag; detachable box magazine; available left or right hand; drilled

and tapped for scope mount; sling swivel studs
MSRP.................$269.00

MSR 10 HUNTER
Action: Semiautomatic
Stock: Synthetic
Barrel: 16.125 in.
Sights: None
Weight: 7 lb. 13 oz.–8 lb.
Caliber: .308 Win., 6.5 Creedmoor
Magazine: 20 rounds
Features: Light, compact sporting platform with 5R rifled upgraded barrel; target chamber; BLACKHAWK! AR Blaze trigger; Melonite QPQ finish
MSRP.................$1719.00

MSR 10 LONG RANGE
Action: Semiautomatic
Stock: Synthetic
Barrel: 20 in.
Sights: None
Weight: 9 lb. 12 oz.
Caliber: .308 Win., 6.5 Creedmoor, 6mm Creedmoor
Magazine: 10 rounds
Features: Long distance capabilities built on a compact frame; non-reciprocating side-charging handle; fluted heavy barrel; BLACKHAWK! two-stage target trigger; Magpul PRS adjustable stock; target chamber
MSRP.................$2659.00

MSR 15 LONG RANGE
Action: Semiautomatic
Stock: Synthetic
Barrel: 22 in.
Sights: None
Weight: 10 lb. 8 oz.
Caliber: .224 Valkyrie
Magazine: 11 rounds
Features: Savage adds weight and stability for the long range crowd. Features include two-port muzzle brake; Hogue pistol grip; free-floating MLOK-capable handguard; low-

profile adjustable gas block; Magpul Gen 3 PRS adjustable stock; custom-forged upper and lower; custom length gas system; non-reciprocating side charging handle
MSRP.................$1979.00

MSR 15 RECON 2.0
Action: Semiautomatic
Stock: Synthetic
Barrel: 16.125 in.
Sights: None
Weight: 7 lb. 5 oz.
Caliber: .223 Rem.
Magazine: 30 rounds
Features: Compact MSR with a nickel-boron-coated trigger; custom-forged lower; Melonite QPQ finish; Magpul buttstock and pistol grip; lots of rail for optics and accessories
MSRP.................$1159.00

MSR 15 RECON LRP
Action: Semiautomatic
Stock: Synthetic
Barrel: 18 in.
Sights: None
Weight: 7 lb. 14 oz.
Caliber: .22 Nosler, .224 Valkyrie, 6.8 SPC
Magazine: 25 rounds
Features: Fast-handling MSR with an adjustable gas block; two-stage trigger; Melonite QPQ finish; Magpul CTR stock; tunable muzzle brake
MSRP.................$1439.00

RASCAL FV-SR
Action: Bolt
Stock: Synthetic
Barrel: 16.125 in.
Sights: None
Weight: 2 lb. 11 oz.
Caliber: .22 LR
Magazine: 1 round
Features: A bolt-cocking single-shot for youths, but one with "big gun" features like a heavy barrel with threaded muzzle and AccuTrigger; pink or black synthetic stock; left- or right-handed
MSRP.................$249.00

Savage Arms

SAVAGE ARMS MARK II MINIMALIST

SAVAGE ARMS RASCAL MINIMALIST

SAVAGE ARMS RASCAL SYNTHETIC LEFT-HAND

SAVAGE ARMS RASCAL TARGET

SAVAGE ARMS RASCAL TARGET XP

SAVAGE ARMS SPECIALTY SERIES MODEL 42 TAKEDOWN, COMPACT

SAVAGE ARMS TARGET SERIES 12 BENCHREST

SAVAGE ARMS TARGET SERIES 112 MAGNUM TARGET

SAVAGE ARMS VARMINT SERIES 25 WALKING VARMINTER

SAVAGE ARMS VARMINT SERIES 25 LIGHTWEIGHT VARMINTER

RASCAL MINIMALIST

Action: Bolt
Stock: Laminate
Barrel: 16.125 in.
Sights: Blade front, peep rear
Weight: 3 lb. 8 oz.
Caliber: .22 LR
Magazine: 1 round
Features: Single-shot; Boyd's Minimalist stock of laminated hardwood in gray/teal or pink/purple; 11.25-in. length of pull; barrel has target crown and is threaded ½x28; can be unloaded without pulling the trigger; adjustable AccuTrigger; comes with firearm lock and eye and ear plugs
MSRP **$299.00**

RASCAL RED, WHITE, & BLUE

Action: Bolt
Stock: Synthetic
Barrel: 16.125 in.
Sights: Blade front, peep rear
Weight: 2 lb. 13 oz.
Caliber: .22 LR
Magazine: 1 round
Features: A Rascal with a classic stock swathed in American flag graphics; 11.25-in. length of pull; adjustable AccuTrigger; carbon steel sporter barrel
MSRP **$249.00**

RASCAL SYNTHETIC LEFT-HAND

Action: Bolt
Stock: Synthetic
Barrel: 16.125 in.
Sights: Peep sights
Weight: 2 lb. 11 oz.
Caliber: .22 LR
Magazine: 1 round
Features: The popular youth rifle in a lightweight synthetic stock for left-handers; available in black or pink
MSRP **$209.00**

RASCAL TARGET

Action: Bolt
Stock: Hardwood

Barrel: 16.125 in.
Sights: None
Weight: 4 lb. 8 oz.
Caliber: .22 LR
Magazine: 1 round
Features: A wood-stocked Rascal for the youth shooter ready to improve on the basics, with a rifle two pounds heavier than its synthetic-stocked cousins; a threaded barrel; and topside Picatinny rail for optics mounting.
MSRP **$349.00**

RASCAL TARGET XP

Action: Bolt
Stock: Hardwood
Barrel: 16.125 in.
Sights: 4X32mm scope
Weight: 5 lb. 14 oz.
Caliber: .22 LR
Magazine: 1 round
Features: For the youth shooter getting serious about improving skills and target acquisition with a single-shot .22 LR that includes a factory-installed and sighted 4X32mm scope; heavy barrel; threaded muzzle; AccuTrigger; bipod; swivel mounts; left-hand available
MSRP **$449.00**

SPECIALTY SERIES MODEL 42 TAKEDOWN, COMPACT

Action: Over/under
Stock: Synthetic
Barrel: 20 in.
Sights: Adjustable
Weight: 6 lb.
Caliber: .22 LR/.410-bore, .22 WMR/.410-bore
Magazine: 2 rounds
Features: Carbon steel barrel; matte barrel finish; break-open combination gun, .22 LR over .410
MSRP **$559.00**

TARGET SERIES 12 BENCHREST

Action: Bolt, single shot
Stock: Wood laminate
Barrel: 29 in.

Sights: None
Weight: 12 lb. 12 oz.
Caliber: .308 Win., 6 Norma BR
Magazine: None
Features: Drilled and tapped for scope mounts; stainless steel barrel with high luster finish; wood laminate stock with satin finish; AccuTrigger
MSRP **$1889.00**

TARGET SERIES 112 MAGNUM TARGET

Action: Bolt
Stock: Wood laminate
Barrel: 26 in.
Sights: None
Weight: 12 lb.
Caliber: .338 Lapua Mag.
Magazine: Single shot
Features: Carbon steel barrel; matte barrel finish
MSRP **$1109.00**

VARMINT SERIES 25 LIGHTWEIGHT VARMINTER

Action: Bolt
Stock: Wood laminate
Barrel: 24 in.
Sights: None
Weight: 8 lb. 4 oz.
Caliber: .17 Hornet, .204 Ruger, .22 Hornet, .223 Rem.
Magazine: Detachable box, 4 rounds
Features: Drilled and tapped for scope mounts; carbon steel barrel with blued satin finish; wood laminate stock with satin finish
MSRP **$869.00**

VARMINT SERIES 25 WALKING VARMINTER

Action: Bolt
Stock: Synthetic
Barrel: 22 in.
Sights: None
Weight: 6 lb. 14 oz.
Caliber: .17 Hornet, .204 Ruger, .22 Hornet, .222 Rem., .223 Rem.
Magazine: Detachable box, 4 rounds
Features: Matte black synthetic stock; matte black carbon steel barrel; AccuTrigger; camo version has stock in Realtree Max-1
Black stock **$699.00**
Camo stock **$759.00**

Seekins Precision

SEEKINS PRECISION HAVAK ELEMENT

HAVAK ELEMENT

Action: Bolt
Stock: Carbon composite
Barrel: 21 in., 22 in.
Sights: None
Weight: 5 lb. 8 oz.–6 lb.
Caliber: 6mm Creedmoor, 6.5 Creedmoor, 6.5 PRC, .308 Win., .28 Nosler, .300 Win. Mag., .300 PRC
Magazine: 3, 5 rounds

Features: Seekins calls this a "hybrid" hunting rifle; Mountain Hunter contoured fluted barrel in stainless steel; integrated recoil lug; 20 MOA rail; bubble level; M16-style extractor; 90-degree bolt throw; removable bolt head; 2.5-lb. Timney Elite Hunter trigger; muzzle threaded 5/8X24; stock finished in Element camo; short-actions have 21-in. barrel and five-round Magpul PMag magazines (except 6.5 PRC), long-actions have 22-in. barrel and three-round detachable carbon fiber magazine (6.5 PRC also has the carbon fiber three-round mag)
MSRP. **$2795.00**

Sero International

SERO INTERNATIONAL GM6 LYNX

GM6 LYNX

Action: Semiautomatic
Stock: N/A
Barrel: 28.7 in.
Sights: None
Weight: 25 lb. 6 oz.
Caliber: .50 BMG
Magazine: 5 rounds

Features: Hungarian-made .50 BMG bullpup; "unique barrel recoil technology" knocks the punch down to half of any other comparable rifle; a match-grade Lothar Walther barrel; long-recoil action; an effective range of 1500 meters
MSRP. **$14,750.00**

Shaw Barrels & Rifles

SHAW CUSTOM RIFLES ERS10

SHAW BARRELS & RIFLES MK. VII GEN II

SHAW CUSTOM RIFLES MARK X

ERS10

Action: Semiautomatic
Stock: Synthetic
Barrel: 16 in., 18 in., 20 in. (ERS15), 20 in. (ERS10)
Sights: None
Weight: Varies
Caliber: 5.56 NATO, .308, .300 Blackout (ERS15).308, 6.5 Creedmoor (ERS10)
Magazine: N/A
Features: Barrels have continuous twist fluted profiles and can be matte or polished finish; the handguard is either a Magpul MOE or a T-Mod rail heat shield; 7075-T6 forged aluminum upper/lowers; uppers with an M4 feed ramp and finished in black anodized, dry film lube, or Cerakote; lowers in anodized black or Cerakote; button-rifled barrel with an H-bar profile, one-piece hard anodized T-Mod heat shield
MSRP. . . . . **starting at $1200.00**

MK. VII GEN II

Action: Bolt
Stock: Laminate, walnut
Barrel: Customer choice
Sights: None
Weight: 7 lb. 8 oz.–8 lb. 8 oz.
Caliber: Customer choice
Magazine: 2, 3, 4, 5 rounds
Features: Choice of #2.5 heavy sporter or #3 light varmint barrel contour with button rifling, choice of helical fluting, straight fluting, or no fluting, and 11-degree target crown; Shaw-tuned AccuTrigger; teardrop bolt handle; walnut stock or laminate stock in nutmeg or pepper, glass bedded and steel pillar bedded; drilled and tapped for Savage round-action scope bases; Pachmayr recoil pad
MSRP. . . . . . **Contact manufacturer**

MARK X

Action: Bolt
Stock: Walnut
Barrel: Varies
Sights: None
Weight: Varies
Caliber: Customer choice
Magazine: Varies
Features: Customizable in thousands of combinations; choice of two barrel profiles; more than 80 caliber choices; Grade 5 walnut stocks; integral scope mount bases machined into the receiver; hybrid push/controlled-round feeding; Savage's AccuTrigger; numerous upgrades offered
MSRP. . . . . **starting at $1400.00**

Shiloh Sharps

SHILOH SHARPS 1874 MILITARY CARBINE

1874 MILITARY CARBINE

Action: Hammer
Stock: Wood
Barrel: 22 in., 24 in.
Sights: Blade front, Lawrence ladder buckhorn rear
Weight: 7 lb. 8 oz.
Caliber: .30-40 Krag, .38-55, .40-65, .45-70, .40-50 Sharps Straight
Magazine: 1 round
Features: We're slotting this in center-fire rifles based solely on the fact that .30-40 Krag was never a blackpowder cartridge, and all the other cartridges can be loaded with modern smokeless powders; tons of features and upgrades include color case-hardened finish as standard or pack harden and various levels of antique metal finish upgrades, patchbox, ebony pistol grip, barrel finish, saddle bar and ring, upgraded wood and finishes, brass escutcheons, custom bedding, various sling swivels, forearm designs, rear barrel sights, vernier tang sights, drilling and tapping, and checkering upgrades
MSRP . . . . Starting at $2057.00

SIG Sauer

SIG SAUER SIG716I TREAD

SIG SAUER CROSS RIFLE

SIG SAUER MCX RATTLER SBR

SIG SAUER MCX VIRTUS PATROL

SIG SAUER MPX PCC

SIG SAUER SIGM400 TREAD 16-INCH

716I TREAD

Action: Semiautomatic
Stock: Synthetic
Barrel: 16 in.
Sights: None
Weight: 8 lb. 8 oz.
Caliber: 7.62 NATO
Magazine: 20 rounds
Features: A direct impingement MSR with a telescoping stock; two-stage Matchlite Duo trigger; hard-coat anodized receiver; alloy forend; polymer grip; barrel threaded 5/8x24; M-LOK accessory rail
MSRP $1616.99

CROSS RIFLE

Action: Bolt
Stock: Synthetic
Barrel: 16 in., 18 in.
Sights: None
Weight: 6 lb. 8 oz.–6 lb. 13 oz.
Caliber: .277 Fury, .308 Win., 6.5 Creedmoor
Magazine: 5 rounds
Features: SIG's own fully adjustable folding Precision Stock; a one-piece receiver of aluminum ; M-LOK rail; AICS mags; alloy forend; threaded stainless steel barrel
MSRP . . . . $1599.99–$1799.99

MCX RATTLER SBR

Action: Semiautomatic
Stock: Aluminum
Barrel: 5.5 in.
Sights: None
Weight: 5 lb. 11 oz.
Caliber: .300 Blackout
Magazine: 30 rounds
Features: Takes AR mags; PDW upper and Ultra Thin Folding Aluminum Stock; M-LOK handguard is free-floating; action is gas piston
MSRP . . . . $2499.99–$2699.99

MCX VIRTUS PATROL

Action: Semiautomatic
Stock: Synthetic
Barrel: 16 in.
Sights: None
Weight: 7 lb. 15 oz.
Caliber: 5.56 NATO, .300 BLK
Magazine: 30 rounds
Features: An AR platform designed for patrol use and featuring user-changeable barrels; free-floating M-LOK handguard in four lengths; ambidextrous controls; adjustable folding stock; available in Stealth Grey or Flat Dark Earth
MSRP $2399.99

MPX PCC

Action: Semiautomatic
Stock: Synthetic
Barrel: 16 in.
Sights: None
Weight: 6 lb. 9 oz.
Caliber: 9mm
Magazine: 30 rounds
Features: Jumping into the trendy pistol-caliber carbine game with an AR platform featuring a gas piston operating system; free-floating M-LOK handguard; folding, telescoping stock; three-chamber compensator; MPX magazine; 1:10 twist barrel; Timney single-stage MPX trigger
MSRP $2099.99

SIG M400 TREAD 16-INCH

Action: Semiautomatic
Stock: Synthetic
Barrel: 16 in.
Sights: None
Weight: 7 lb.
Caliber: 5.56 NATO
Magazine: 30 rounds
Features: An AR for on-the-go, featuring: reduced weigh MLOK handguard; direct impingement mid-length gas system functionality; aluminum frame; ambidextrous controls; single-stage trigger; Magpul SL-K6 telescoping buttstock
MSRP $951.00

RIFLES

SIG SAUER SIGM400
TREAD COIL

SIG SAUER SIG MCX RATTLER
CANEBRAKE

SIG SAUER SIG MCX VIRTUS SBR

SIG M400 TREAD COIL

Action: Semiautomatic
Stock: Synthetic
Barrel: 16 in.
Sights: Flip-up rear
Weight: 7 lb.
Caliber: 5.56 NATO
Magazine: 30 rounds
Features: A direct impingement MSR with a telescoping stock; two-stage Matchlite Duo trigger; hard-coat anodized receiver; alloy forend; polymer grip; barrel threaded ½x28; M-LOK accessory rail with lightning cuts, choice of 13- or 15-inch lengths; ambidextrous charging handle of aircraft-grade aluminum; M-LOK front sight adapter with co-witness height; upgraded flat-blade single-stage trigger; three-chamber compensa-tor; ROMEO5 electro optic with 2 MOA dot
MSRP.................$1211.99

SIG MCX RATTLER CANEBRAKE

Action: Semiautomatic
Stock: Synthetic
Barrel: 5.5 in.
Sights: None
Weight: 6 lb. 8 oz.
Caliber: .300 BLK
Magazine: 30 rounds
Features: Gas-piston SBR (NFA regs apply) with a receiver in Cerakote E190 (aka bronze); two-stage flat-blade trigger; folding PCB brace; Magpul magazine; inert training device factory installed so buyer can train while waiting for NFA paper-work to clear
MSRP.................$2897.00

SIG MCX VIRTUS SBR

Action: Semiautomatic
Stock: Synthetic
Barrel: 5 in., 9 in., 11.5 in.
Sights: None
Weight: 7 lb.–5 lb. 11 oz.
Caliber: 5.56 NATO, .300 BLK
Magazine: 30 rounds
Features: Gas-piston SBR (NFA regs apply) with a Matchlite Duo trigger; M-LOK handguard; cold hammer-forged barrel; 5.56 NATO available in 11-in. barrel, five-position telescop-ing/folding stock, and choice of gray or hard-coat anodized receiver finish; .300 BLK available in a 9-in. barrel with a five-position folding/telescop-ing stock, and flat dark earth receiver or in a 5.5-in. barrel with a folding Minimalist stock and hard-coat anod-ized receiver
MSRP.................$2893.99

Silver Shadow Advanced Security Systems, Inc.

SILVER SHADOW
GILBOA DBR SNAKE

SILVER SHADOW
GILBOA M43
CARBINE

GILBOA DBR SNAKE

Action: Semiautomatic
Stock: Synthetic
Barrel: 11.5 in.
Sights: Flip-up
Weight: 10 lb. 13 oz.
Caliber: 5.56 NATO
Magazine: 40 rounds
Features: Double the fun with a two-barrel, two-magazine, two-trigger gas impingement semiauto that fires two shots at the same time; made in Israel
MSRP.................$2574.99

GILBOA M43 CARBINE

Action: Semiautomatic
Stock: Synthetic
Barrel: 16 in.
Sights: Flip-up
Weight: 6 lb. 7 oz.
Caliber: 7.62X39mm NATO
Magazine: 30 rounds
Features: Lightweight, Israeli-made; gas impingement system; hard anod-ized billet aircraft aluminum alloy upper and lower; ample rail; accepts standard AK-47 magazines; free-floating key-mod handguard; Gilboa compensator
MSRP.................$1599.00

Smith & Wesson

SMITH & WESSON M&P10 6.5 CREEDMOOR

SMITH & WESSON M&P10 SPORT OPTICS READY

SMITH & WESSON M&P15

SMITH & WESSON M&P15 COMPETITION

SMITH & WESSON M&P15 SPORT II

SMITH & WESSON M&P15-22 SPORT, SPORT M-LOK

SMITH & WESSON M&P15-22 SPORT ROBIN'S EGG BLUE PLATINUM FINISH

M&P10 6.5 CREEDMOOR

Action: Semiautomatic
Stock: Synthetic
Barrel: 20 in.
Sights: None
Weight: 9 lb.
Caliber: 6.5 Creedmoor
Magazine: 10 rounds
Features: MSR flattop platform; threaded muzzle with thread protector; two-stage match trigger; 15-in. free-floating Troy Alpha M-LOK handguard; 2-in. aluminum M-LOK accessory rail; Magpul MOE stock; gas-operated
MSRP $2095.00

M&P10 SPORT OPTICS READY

Action: Semiautomatic
Stock: Synthetic
Barrel: 16. in.
Sights: None
Weight: 8 lb.
Caliber: .308 Win.
Magazine: 20 rounds
Features: Mid-length gas system; ambidextrous safety; bolt and magazine releases; mid-length handguard; A2 suppressor; chromed firing pin; six-position telescoping stock; gas block with Picatinny rail; barrel is finished inside and out with Armornite
MSRP . . . . $1129.00–$1679.00

M&P15

Action: Semiautomatic
Stock: Synthetic
Barrel: 16 in.
Sights: Troy adjustable front post, folding rear battle sight
Weight: 6 lb. 12 oz.
Caliber: 5.56 NATO, .223 Rem.
Magazine: Detachable box, 30 rounds

Features: Six-position telescopic black stock; chrome-lined gas key and bolt carrier; flash suppressor compensator; two-position safety lever; available options include optics ready, optics-ready with red-dot sight included, California-legal grip, threaded barrel, adjustable A2 front sight post, WGS folding sights, Magpul MBUS sights, and custom engraving
MSRP . . . . $1079.00–$1599.00

M&P15 COMPETITION

Action: Semiautomatic
Stock: Synthetic
Barrel: 18 in.
Sights: None
Weight: 7 lb. 6 oz.
Caliber: 5.56 NATO
Magazine: 30 rounds
Features: Performance Center muzzle brake; two-stage match trigger; 15-in. free-floating Troy Alpha M-LOK handguard; 2-in. aluminum M-Lok rail; VLTOR I-Mod stock; Hogue pistol grip; aluminum frame; gas-operated
MSRP $1639.00

M&P15 SPORT II

Action: Semiautomatic
Stock: Synthetic
Barrel: 16 in.
Sights: Adjustable front, Magpul MBUS rear
Weight: 6 lb. 7 oz.
Caliber: 5.56 NATO
Magazine: 10, 30 rounds
Features: Forged, integral trigger guard; Armornite finish (durable corrosion-resistant finish); chromed firing pin; forward assist; dust cover; available in Colorado- and California-compliant versions, MOE M-LOK,

and as Optics Ready variant with or without M-LOK handguard
MSRP . . . . $796.00–$840.00

M&P15-22 SPORT

Action: Semiautomatic
Stock: Synthetic
Barrel: 16.5 in.
Sights: Folding Magpul MBUS front and rear
Weight: 4 lb. 12 oz.
Caliber: .22 LR
Capacity: 10, 25 rounds
Features: Updated version of the original M&P 15-22, with a slightly shorter barrel; six-position collapsible stock, 10-in. slim handguard, M-LOK compatible, functioning charging handle, shell deflector, two-position receiver-mounted safety, and Armonite barrel finish are standard; available in black, Kryptek, and Muddy Girl finishes; California-compliant version available in black only
MSRP . . . . $489.00–$552.00

M&P15-22 SPORT ROBIN'S EGG BLUE PLATINUM FINISH

Action: Semiautomatic
Stock: Synthetic
Barrel: 16.5 in.
Sights: MBUS folding front and rear
Weight: 5 lb.
Caliber: .22 LR
Magazine: 25 rounds
Features: carbon steel barrel; folding sights; six-position CAR stock; 2-in. M-LOK rail panel; M&P handguard with Magpul's M-LOKTM
MSRP $552.00

Springfield Armory

SPRINGFIELD ARMORY M1A LOADED

SPRINGFIELD ARMORY M1A SCOUT SQUAD

SPRINGFIELD ARMORY M1A SOCOM 16

SPRINGFIELD ARMORY M1A SOCOM 16 CQB

SPRINGFIELD ARMORY M1A STANDARD ISSUE

SPRINGFIELD ARMORY M1A TANKER

SPRINGFIELD ARMORY MODEL 2020 WAYPOINT

M1A LOADED
Action: Semiautomatic
Stock: Synthetic
Barrel: 22 in.
Sights: Adjustable
Weight: 11 lb. 4 oz.
Caliber: 7.62 NATO, 6.5 Creedmoor
Magazine: 10 rounds
Features: 1:11 inch barrel twist; match grade aperture with ½ MOA adjustment for windage and 1 MOA for elevation; FDE precision adjustable stock
MSRP . . . . $1880.00–$2083.00

M1A SCOUT SQUAD
Action: Semiautomatic
Stock: Walnut, composite
Barrel: 18 in.
Sights: National Match front military post sight; rear military aperture
Weight: 9 lb. 5 oz.
Caliber: 7.62 NATO, .308 Win.
Magazine: Detachable box, 10 rounds
Features: Mounted optical sight base; muzzle stabilizers; black or green fiberglass composite, American walnut stock or Mossy Oak camo stock; two-stage military trigger
MSRP . . . . $1883.00–$2023.00

M1A SOCOM 16
Action: Semiautomatic
Stock: Composite
Barrel: 16.25 in.
Sights: Tritium front sight
Weight: 8 lb. 13 oz.

Caliber: 7.62 NATO, .308 Win
Magazine: Detachable box, 10 rounds
Features: Muzzlebrake; forward mounted scope base; two-stage military trigger; composite black or green stock
MSRP $2026.00

M1A SOCOM 16 CQB
Action: Semiautomatic
Stock: Synthetic
Barrel: 16.25 in.
Sights: XS Post with tritium insert front, adjustable rear
Weight: 9 lb. 3 oz.
Caliber: .308 Win., 7.62x51mm NATO
Magazine: 10 or 20 rounds
Features: Adjustable buttstock; five-position length and two-position adjustable cheek piece; standard AR-type commercial buffer tube; AK-style pistol grip; accepts any standard AK-style replacement; M-Lok compatible system; fixed top rail
Standard: $2183.00
With Vortex Venom
   Red-Dot: $2464.00

M1A STANDARD ISSUE
Action: Semiautomatic
Stock: Composite or walnut
Barrel: 22 in.
Sights: National Match military front post, adjustable rear aperture sight
Weight: 9 lb. 5 oz.
Caliber: 7.62 NATO, .308 Win.
Magazine: Detachable box, 10 rounds
Features: Stocks available in

Highlander camo, solid Flat Dark Earth, walnut, or black composite; parkerized carbon steel barrels; two-stage military trigger
MSRP . . . . $1717.00–$1819.00

M1A TANKER
Action: Semiautomatic
Stock: Walnut
Barrel: 16.25 in.
Sights: XS post with tritium insert front, ghost ring rear
Weight: 8 lb. 12 oz.
Caliber: .308 Win.
Magazine: 10 rounds
Features: A throwback to WWII's Tanker Garands, with a carbine-length barrel; Parkerized metalwork; detachable magazine; carbon steel barrel
MSRP $2023.00

MODEL 2020 WAYPOINT
Action: Bolt
Stock: Carbon fiber
Barrel: 20 in., 22 in., 24 in.
Sights: None
Weight: 6 lb. 15 oz.–7 lb. 5 oz.
Caliber: .308 Win., 6mm Creedmoor, 6.5 Creedmoor, 6.5 PRC
Magazine: 3 rounds
Features: Fluted bolt with dual locking lugs and removable bolt knob; enlarged ejection port; hybrid dual-plane feed ramp; AG Composites carbon-fiber stock in choice of fixed or adjustable cheekpiece configurations and in Evergreen or Ridgeline camo; TriggerTech adjustable trigger; five quick-detach mount inserts; removable Springfield Armory radial muzzle brake; AICS pattern magazine; Pachmayr Decelerator recoil pad; BSF barrel in a carbon-fiber sleeve or fluted stainless steel and free-floated
MSRP . . . . $1797.00–$1923.00

Springfield Armory

SPRINGFIELD ARMORY SAINT EDGE

SPRINGFIELD ARMORY SAINT M-LOK

SPRINGFIELD ARMORY SAINT VICTOR

SPRINGFIELD ARMORY SAINT VICTOR SBR

SAINT EDGE

Action: Semiautomatic
Stock: Synthetic
Barrel: 16 in.
Sights: Flip-up front and rear
Weight: 6 lb. 3 oz.
Caliber: 5.56 NATO
Magazine: 30 rounds
Features: Mid-length multi-mode adjustable gas block; Bravo Company M3 pistol grip; Mod 0 SOPMOD buttstock; Springfield mid-size charging handle; free-floating full-length aluminum handguard; Tungsten Carbine H heavy buffer; flip-up sights are Springfield Armory's low-profile, dual-aperture rear; Springfield multiport muzzle brake
MSRP. **$1379.00**

SAINT M-LOK

Action: Semiautomatic
Stock: Synthetic
Barrel: 16 in.
Sights: Standard post front, Springfield

Armory low profile flip-up dual aperture rear
Weight: 6 lb. 11 oz.
Caliber: 5.56 NATO
Magazine: 30 rounds
Features: Type III aircraft-grade 7075 T6 aluminum upper and lower receivers are joined using the Accu-Tite system; 16-inch chrome moly vanadium barrel treated with Melonite; 1:8-inch twist; mid-length gas system paired with a heavier carbine "H" heavy tungsten buffer; Bravo Company Mod 0 pistol grip and Bravo Company buttstock; QD and fixed sling swivels; Bravo PKMT two-piece handguard; aluminum heat shields; black or Flat Dark Earth; California-compliant in black only
MSRP **$1023.00**

SAINT VICTOR

Action: Semiautomatic
Stock: Synthetic
Barrel: 16 in.
Sights: Flip-up
Weight: 6 lb. 9 oz.
Caliber: 5.56 NATO, .308 Win., .350 Legend
Magazine: 30 rounds
Features: Game-ready AR-platform with direct impingement mid-length

gas system; Bravo Company six-position buttstock and Mod.3 grip; carbine H heavy tungsten buffer; forged Type III aluminum upper, Accu-Tite lower, both hard anodized; GI-type charging handle; 15-inch M-LOK handguard; spring-loaded flip-up sights; soft rifle case
MSRP. . . . . **$1150.00–$2497.00**

SAINT VICTOR SBR

Action: Semiautomatic
Stock: Synthetic
Barrel: 11.5 in.
Sights: None
Weight: 5 lb. 9 oz.
Caliber: 5.56 NATO
Magazine: 30 rounds
Features: A loaded SBR with features that include a forged lower with Accu-Tite tension system; ambidextrous safety; Type III hard coat anodized upper and lower; low-profile, adjustable carbine-length gas block; forward assist; Bravo Company Gunfighter buttstock; Carbine "H" heavy tungsten buffer; Melonite finish on barrel and bolt-carrier group; nickel-boron coated GI-style trigger; Magpul PMAG; full-length, free-floating handguard M-LOK compatible
MSRP. **$1150.00**

Stag Arms

STAG ARMS MODEL 3GUN ELITE

MODEL 3GUN ELITE

Action: Semiautomatic
Stock: Synthetic
Barrel: 18 in.
Sights: None
Weight: N/A
Caliber: 5.56 NATO, .223 Rem.
Features: A2 flash hider; Picatinny rail; Magpul ACS buttstock; aluminum

enhanced trigger guard; manganese phosphate-coated chrome-lined bolt carrier group; Stag 3G compensator; Geissele Super 3-Gun trigger; New York-, New Jersey-, California, and 10-round-compliant models available in left and right hand
MSRP. . . . . **$1599.99–$1669.99**

Standard Manufacturing Co., LLC

STANDARD MANUFACTURING MODEL 16721

MODEL 16721

Action: Semiautomatic
Stock: Synthetic

Barrel: 16 in.
Sights: None
Weight: 6 lb. 7 oz.
Caliber: 5.56 NATO
Magazine: 30 rounds
Features: Direct impingement carbine-length gas system; A2 flash hider;

A3 upper and lower of aluminum with mil-spec hard-anodized finish; standard charging handle; Rogers Super Stock; 13-in. M-LOK handguard; heavy-profile barrel with M4 feed ramp; two magazines
MSRP. **$999.00**

STEYR ARMS AUG A3 M1

STEYR ARMS SCOUT

STEYR ARMS SSG 08

STEYR ARMS ZEPHYR II

AUG A3 M1

Action: Semiautomatic
Stock: Synthetic
Barrel: 16 in.
Sights: None
Weight: 7 lb. 11 oz.–8 lb. 13. oz.
Caliber: 5.56 NATO, .223 Rem.
Magazine: Detachable box, 30 rounds
Features: Bullpup rifle has adjustable short-stroke gas piston, hard Eloxalcoated aircraft aluminum receiver, chrome-lined CHF barrel with muzzle brake, two-position trigger-blocking safety; short rail, high rail, and optics configurations; available in white/ black, OD Green, or MUD; choice of short, long, or extended rails; choice of 1.5X or 3X optic
MSRP $2199.00

SCOUT

Action: Bolt
Stock: Synthetic
Barrel: 19, 22 in.
Sights: None
Weight: 6 lb. 10 oz.
Caliber: .308 Win., 7mm-08 Rem.
Magazine: Detachable box, 5 rounds (optional 10 round magazine)
Features: Weaver scope mounting rail; set trigger or direct trigger; synthetic stock in black, white, mud, green, Mossy Oak Bottomland, or Mossy Oak Break-Up Country; fluted or unfluted barrel depending on chosen barrel length and stock choice
MSRP . . . .$1749.00–$1889.00

SSG 08

Action: Bolt
Stock: Synthetic
Barrel: 20, 23.6, 25.6 in.
Sights: None
Weight: 5 lb. 8 oz.–5 lb. 11 oz.
Caliber: .300 Win. Mag., .308 Win., .338 Lapua
Magazine: Detachable box, 10 rounds
Features: Direct trigger; Mannox TM system; high grade aluminum folding stock; adjustable cheekpiece and buttplate with height marking; ergonomic exchangeable pistol grip; UIT rail and Picatinny rail; muzzlebrake; Versa-Pod
MSRP . . . .$3549.00–$9827.00

ZEPHYR II

Action: Bolt
Stock: Walnut
Barrel: 19.7 in.
Sights: None
Weight: 5 lb. 13 oz.
Caliber: .17 HMR, .22 LR, .22 WMR
Magazine: 5 rounds
Features: Trim, European walnut stock; fish scale checkering; tang safety; detachable magazine; available with threaded barrel
MSRP . . . .$1099.00–$1129.00

RIFLES

S.W.O.R.D. International

S.W.O.R.D. INTERNATIONAL MK-17 MOD 1 GUNGNIR

MK-17 MOD 1 GUNGNIR

Action: Semiautomatic
Stock: Synthetic
Barrel: 20 in.
Sights: None
Weight: 8 lb. 15 oz.
Caliber: 6.5 Creedmoor
Magazine: 10, 20 rounds
Features: Gungnir is the name of the mighty spear that belongs to Odin, the leader of the Norse Gods, and is said to have had the most accurate and deadly aim; tuned compensator on a single-point-cut rifled barrel with a black nitride coating; self-regulating gas system; free-floating M-LOK rail system; ambidextrous bolt catch, bolt release pad, and magazine release; tungsten-filled heavy buffer; retractable stock; piston-rated heavy-duty action spring; in coyote brown Cerakote or mil-spec type 3 hardcoat anodized black
MSRP $4800.00

S.W.O.R.D. International

S.W.O.R.D. INTERNATIONAL MK-18 MOD 1 MJÖLNIR

MK-18 MOD 1 MJÖLNIR

Action: Semiautomatic
Stock: Synthetic
Barrel: 20 in., 24 in.
Sights: None
Weight: 12 lb. 4 oz.

Caliber: .338 Lapua, .338 Norma, .300 Norma
Magazine: 10 rounds
Features: It's all long-distance business with the MK-18, featuring a proprietary self-regulating short-stroke gas piston system; mil-spec Type 3 hard anodized coating in Coyote Brown; single-point cut-rifled barrel with nitride coating; free-floating M-LOK rail; ambidextrous mag release; tungsten-filled heavy buffer; tuned compensator to reduce muzzle rise
MSRP................$8425.00

Tactical Solutions

TACTICAL SOLUTIONS OWYHEE TAKEDOWN RIFLE

TACTICAL SOLUTIONS X-RING TD VR

TACTICAL SOLUTIONS X-RING TSS INTEGRALLY SUPPRESSED RIFLE

TACTICAL SOLUTIONS X-RING VR HOGUE STOCK OPEN SIGHTS

TACTICAL SOLUTIONS X-RING VR VANTAGE RS STOCK

OWYHEE TAKEDOWN RIFLE

Action: Bolt
Stock: Synthetic
Barrel: 16.5 in.
Sights: Fiber optic front, adjustable rear
Weight: 3 lb. 14 oz.
Caliber: .22 LR
Magazine: N/A
Features: For hikers, new shooters, ranchers, and home-defense; aluminum receiver; extended mag release; fluted, threaded barrel with chromoly bore; modified Magpul X-22 Backpacker stock
MSRP................$1155.00

X-RING TD VR

Action: Semiautomatic
Stock: Synthetic
Barrel: 16.5 in.
Sights: Adjustable rear, fiber-optic front
Weight: 3 lb. 11 oz.–4 lb. 10 oz.
Caliber: .22 LR
Magazine: 1 round, 10 rounds
Features: With a Ruger 10/22 as its backbone, hikers, ranch workers and survivalists get an ultralightweight, packable, takedown (TD) rifle in choice of a variety of metal and stock colors
MSRP.........$1255.00–$1333.00

X-RING TSS INTEGRALLY SUPPRESSED RIFLE

Action: Bolt
Stock: Synthetic
Barrel: 16.75 in.
Sights: None
Weight: 4 lb. 14 oz.
Caliber: .22 LR
Magazine: N/A
Features: Integrally suppressed for the .22 LR with a lightweight aluminum barrel, interlocking titanium baffles, and a stainless steel split tube; Magpul X-22 Hunter stock; topside 15 MOA Picatinny rail; Ruger BX trigger; receiver adjustable for right- or left-hand charging; black, flat dark earth, OD green and Stealth Gray stock options
MSRP................$1533.00

X-RING VR HOGUE STOCK

Action: Semiautomatic
Stock: Synthetic
Barrel: 16.5 in.
Sights: None
Weight: 4 lb. 5 oz.
Caliber: .22 LR
Magazine: 10 rounds
Features: Features an ambidextrous bolt; 15 MOA rail; Ruger BX-Trigger; variety of stock color; threaded barrel options; various metal/stock finish options
MSRP................$1055.00

X-RING VR MAGPUL HUNTER X-22 STOCK

Action: Semiautomatic
Stock: Synthetic
Barrel: 16.5 in.
Sights: None, open
Weight: 5 lb. 2 oz.
Caliber: .22 LR
Magazine: 10 rounds
Features: Similar in features to the other VRs, but with Magpul's Hunter X-22 chassis stock designed specifically for Ruger 10/22 actions and with M-LOK slots and adjustable length of pull; variety of stock/metal finishes
MSRP.........$1188.00–$1277.00

RIFLES

Taylor's & Co. Firearms

TAYLOR'S & CO. 1860 HENRY
LEVER ACTION RIFLE

TAYLOR'S & CO. 1886 RIDGE
RUNNER

TAYLOR'S & CO.
FIREARMS ALASKAN
THREADED

TAYLOR'S & CO. 1873 RIFLE -
CHECKERED STRAIGHT STOCK

TAYLOR'S & CO. LIGHTNING
SLIDE ACTION RIFLE

1860 HENRY LEVER ACTION RIFLE

Action: Lever
Stock: Walnut
Barrel: 24.25 in.
Sights: Open
Weight: 9 lb. 3 oz.
Caliber: .44-40 Win., .45 LC
Magazine: Under-barrel tube, 9–13 rounds
Features: Brass frame; octagonal barrel with blued finish; includes sling swivels
MSRP . . . . **$1463.00–$1845.59**

1873 RIFLE - CHECKERED STRAIGHT STOCK

Action: Lever
Stock: Walnut
Barrel: 20 in.
Sights: Open
Weight: 8 lb. 8 oz.
Caliber: .357 Mag., .45 LC
Magazine: Under-barrel tube, 10+1

rounds
Features: Case-hardened frame; straight stock with checkering; available with full octagon barrel
MSRP **$1383.00**

1886 RIDGE RUNNER

Action: Lever
Stock: Wood or synthetic
Barrel: 18.5 in.
Sights: Skinner rear peep sight, fiber optic front
Weight: 7 lb. 13 oz.
Caliber: .45-70 Govt.
Magazine: 4, 8 rounds
Features: Available in matte blue or matte chrome metalwork. Stock is wood with soft-touch rubber over-mold; Integrated Skinner rear peep sight, Weaver rail, front fiber optic sight, D-shaped lever, muzzle brake, and half-octagonal barrel are standard
MSRP . . . . **$1956.69–$2061.68**

1892 ALASKAN TAKEDOWN

Action: Lever
Stock: Wood
Barrel: 16, 20 in.
Sights: Fiber optic front, peep rear
Weight: 5 lb. 15 oz.
Caliber: .357 Mag., .44 Mag.
Magazine: 5 rounds
Features: Handy takedown rifle with a wood stock wearing a coverage of soft-touch finish in black; matte chrome finish metalwork; rear peep sight sits at back of topside Picatinny rail
MSRP . . . . **$1603.90–$1704.69**

LIGHTNING SLIDE ACTION RIFLE

Action: Slide
Stock: Walnut
Barrel: 20 in., 24 in.
Sights: Open
Weight: 6 lb. 6 oz.–6 lb. 14 oz.
Caliber: .357 Mag., .45 LC
Magazine: 10 rounds
Features: Case-hardened steel receiver; fancy walnut stock; octagonal barrel; made by Pedersoli
MSRP **$1836.00**

Thompson/Center Arms

THOMPSON/CENTER
ARMS T/C COMPASS II

THOMPSON/CENTER
ARMS T/C COMPASS
UTILITY

T/C COMPASS II

Action: Bolt
Stock: Synthetic
Barrel: 16.5 in., 21.6 in., 24 in.
Sights: None
Weight: 6 lb. 8 oz.–7 lb.
Caliber: .243 Win., .270 Win., .308 Win., .223 Rem., .30-06 Spfd., 6.5 Creedmoor, .300 Win. Mag., 7mm Rem. Mag.
Magazine: 4, 5 rounds
Features: A step up from the Compass Utility with a Gen 2 trigger; threaded

muzzle; available with no sights or with Crimson Trace scope (7mm Rem. Mag. unscoped only); Compact version available in .243 Win., 6.5 Creedmoor, and .308 Win. only, 16.5-in barrel only, and has a 12.5-in. length of pull
Standard: **$417.00**
Scoped: **$595.00**

T/C COMPASS UTILITY

Action: Bolt
Stock: Synthetic
Barrel: 21.6 in.

Sights: None
Weight: 7 lb.
Caliber: .243 Win., .270 Win., .308 Win., .223 Rem., .30-06 Spfd., 6.5 Creedmoor
Magazine: 5 rounds
Features: Great entry-level rifle in several common cartridges; flush-fit rotary magazine; 60-degree bolt throw; 5R rifling; three-position safety; available as a scoped package
Standard: **$370.00**
Scoped: **$459.00**

Thompson/Center Arms

THOMPSON/CENTER ARMS T/CR22

THOMPSON/CENTER ARMS T/C VENTURE II

T/CR22

Action: Semiautomatic
Stock: Synthetic
Barrel: 17 in.
Sights: Fiber optic front, adjustable rear
Weight: 4 lb. 6 oz.
Caliber: .22 LR
Magazine: 10 rounds
Features: Handy small-game, varmint, or target rimfire with both sights and a topside rail; detachable magazine; blued metalwork with stock in choice of green, Realtree Edge, or Mossy Oak Break-Up Country
Green: $399.00
Camo: $419.00

T/C VENTURE II

Action: Bolt
Stock: Synthetic
Barrel: 22 in., 24 in.
Sights: None
Weight: 7 lb. 8 oz.
Caliber: .243 Win., .270 Win., .308 Win., .223 Rem., .30-06 Spfd., 6.5 Creedmoor, .300 Win. Mag., 7mm Rem. Mag., .350 Legend
Magazine: 3 rounds
Features: With a Generation II trigger, this rifle also features a corrosion-resistant Weather Shield coating; 5R rifling; composite stock with Hogue panels at grip areas
MSRP. $540.00

Tikka

TIKKA T1X MTR

TIKKA T3X COMPACT TACTICAL

TIKKA T3X FOREST

TIKKA T3X HUNTER, HUNTER STAINLESS

T1X MTR

Action: Bolt
Stock: Synthetic
Barrel: 20 in.
Sights: None
Weight: 5 lb. 5 oz.
Caliber: .22 LR, .17 HMR
Magazine: 10 rounds
Features: Detachable magazine; threaded muzzle; modular stock with grip adjustable for angle
MSRP. . . . . $569.99–$619.99

T3X COMPACT TACTICAL

Action: Bolt
Stock: Synthetic
Barrel: 20 in.
Sights: None
Weight: 5 lb. 14.4 oz.
Caliber: .308 Win., .260 Rem., 6.5 Creedmoor
Magazine: 3, 4 rounds
Features: Designed specifically for low-recoiling centerfire rifle rounds; 30mm spacer and larger recoil pad to further improve fit and reduce felt recoil; black synthetic stock; stainless steel barrel; single-stage adjustable trigger; integral 17mm rail; drilled and tapped for scope mounts; blue or stainless metal finishes
MSRP. $1079.99

T3X FOREST

Action: Bolt
Stock: Synthetic
Barrel: 20 in., 22.4 in., 24.4 in.
Sights: Optional open
Weight: 6 lb. 9.8 oz.–7 lb.
Caliber: .270 Win., .300 Win. Mag., .308 Win., .30-06 Spfd., 7mm Rem. Mag.
Magazine: 3, 4 rounds
Features: Designed for hunters using scopes with large variable optics that require higher mounting; modular synthetic stock has interchangeable pistol grip and optional attachment point that allows the user to change the width of the forend; asymmetrical grip pattern provides solid grip in adverse conditions; stocks without cheekpieces have foam insert that lowers stock-generated noise; widened ejection port improves cycling; extra top-side receiver screw permits Picatinny rail mounting; set and standard triggers available
MSRP. $1049.00

T3X HUNTER, HUNTER STAINLESS

Action: Bolt
Stock: Walnut
Barrel: 22.4 in.
Sights: None
Weight: 6 lb. 12.8 oz.
Caliber: .243 Win., 6.5x55mm, .270 Win., .308 Win., .30-06 Spfd., 7mm-08 Rem., 7mm Rem. Mag. 6.5 Creedmoor
Magazine: 3 rounds
Features: Classic walnut stock has improved checkering and enhanced recoil pad; stainless finish barrel is fluted and has hand-cut target crown; receiver has widened ejection port; integral 17mm rail drilled and tapped to accept standard scope mounts or Picatinny rail
Blue $899.00
Blue left-hand $949.00
Stainless. $1099.00

TIKKA T3X LAMINATED STAINLESS

TIKKA T3X LITE

TIKKA T3X LITE COMPACT

TIKKA T3X LITE ROUGHTECH

TIKKA T3X LITE VEIL ALPINE, VEIL WIDELAND

TIKKA T3X SUPERLITE

TIKKA T3X TAC A1

T3X LAMINATED STAINLESS

Action: Bolt
Stock: Laminate
Barrel: 22.4 in., 24.3 in.
Sights: None
Weight: 6 lb. 9.6 oz.–7 lb.
Caliber: .243 Win., .260 Rem., .270 Rem., .270 WSM, .308 Win., .30-06 Spfd., 7mm Rem. Mag, .300 WSM, 6.5 Creedmoor
Magazine: N/A
Features: Weather-resistant gray laminate stock; cold-hammer-forged stainless steel free-floating barrel with hand-cut target crown; receiver has widened ejection port; integral 17mm rail drilled and tapped to accept standard scope mounts or Picatinny rail
MSRP **$1099.00**

T3X LITE

Action: Bolt
Stock: Synthetic
Barrel: 22 in., 24 in.
Sights: None
Weight: 7 lb. 3 oz.
Caliber: .223 Rem., .22-250 Rem., .243 Win., .25-06 Rem., .270 Win., .270 WSM, .300 Win. Mag., .300 WSM, .30-06 Spfd., .308 Win., 7mm-08 Rem., 7mm Rem. Mag., 6.5 Creedmoor
Magazine: 3, 4 rounds
Features: Weather-resistant rifle; modular stock that allows for grip angle adjustment; new recoil pad; improved textured gripping surfaces; stock's foam insert reduces noise; left-hand models available
Right-hand . . . . **$749.00–$849.00**
Left-hand **$899.00**

T3X LITE COMPACT

Action: Bolt
Stock: Synthetic
Barrel: 20 in.

Sights: None
Weight: 6 lb. 10 oz.
Caliber: .204 Ruger, .22-250 Rem., .223 Rem., .243 Win., .308 Win., 7mm-08 Rem., 6.5 Creedmoor
Magazine: 3, 4 rounds
Features: Stock comes with a 1-in. spacer and a thick recoil pad; length of pull is 12.5 in.; detachable magazine; textured grip panels; blued hardware
MSRP **$749.00**

T3X LITE ROUGHTECH

Action: Bolt
Stock: Synthetic
Barrel: 20 in., 22.4 in., 24.3 in.
Sights: None
Weight: 6 lb. 6 oz.
Caliber: 6.5 Creedmoor, .270 Win., .270 WSM, .300 Win. Mag., .300 WSM, .7mm Rem. Mag.
Magazine: 3 rounds
Features: Great for hunting in wet, inclement conditions thanks to the textured Roughtech stock; blued metalwork; fluted bolt with oversized bolt knob; integral rail; single-stage trigger; fluted barrel with threaded-on muzzle brake; modular stock in black or tan with black webbing
MSRP **$1079.00**

T3X LITE VEIL ALPINE, VEIL WIDELAND

Action: Bolt
Stock: Synthetic
Barrel: 20 in., 22.4 in., 24.3 in.
Sights: None
Weight: 6 lb. 6 oz.
Caliber: .22-250 Rem., .223 Rem., .243 Win., .25-06 Rem., .270 Win., .270 WSM, .30-06 Spfd., .300 Win. Mag., .300 WSM, .308 Win., 6.5 Creedmoor, 7mm Rem. Mag., 7mm-08 Rem.
Magazine: 3 rounds
Features: A lightweight hunter with a fluted bolt and barrel; modular stock with interchangeable pistol grip; improved grip and recoil pad; stock

designed for reduced noise; widened ejection port; barrel is Cerakoted; muzzle brake included; in Alpine or Wideland camo patterns from Veil Camo
MSRP **$1279.00**

T3X SUPERLITE

Action: Bolt
Stock: Synthetic
Barrel: 22.4 in.
Sights: None
Weight: 6 lb.
Caliber: .243 Win., .308 Win., .270 Win., .30-06 Spfd., 7mm Rem. Mag., 6.5 Creedmoor, .300 Win. Mag., 7mm-08 Rem.
Magazine: 3 rounds
Features: Enhanced gripping areas; new recoil pad; stock's foam insert reduces noise; black stock model is exclusive to Sportsmen's Warehouse; Camo model is available only through Cabela's; both models have a single-stage adjustable trigger, fluted barrels
MSRP . . . . **$899.99–$949.99**

T3X TAC A1

Action: Bolt
Stock: Aluminum rear stock and middle chassis
Barrel: 16 in., 20 in., 24 in.
Sights: None
Weight: 10 lb. 5.7 oz.–11 lb. 4 oz.
Caliber: .260 Rem., 6.5 Creedmoor, .308 Win.
Magazine: 10 rounds
Features: Long-range chassis rifle; aluminum rear stock with height- and angle-adjustable cheekpiece; adjustable-height recoil pad; Picatinny rail for monopod attachment; aluminum middle chassis with modular, removable forend connector; AR-15 buffer tube-compatible interface; AR-15 pistol grip compatible slot; barrel is threaded and mid-contour; trigger is two-stage and adjustable; detachable magazine; two-way safety with bolt release lever; topside Picatinny rail
MSRP . . . . **$1899.00–$2088.00**

RIFLES

Tikka

TIKKA T3X UPR

TIKKA T3X VARMINT

T3X UPR
Action: Bolt
Stock: Synthetic
Barrel: 20 in., 24.3 in.
Sights: None
Weight: 8 lb. oz.
Caliber: .260 Rem., .308 Win., 6.5 Creedmoor
Magazine: 10 rounds

Features: A long-range entry with an adjustable cheekpiece; choice of flat rail or 20 MOA inclined rail; modular stock with interchangeable pistol grip; improved grip and recoil pad; stock designed for reduced noise; Tikka website says the stock is an olive drab green, but the picture shows a light beige with black flecking
MSRP . . . . **$1399.00–$1498.00**

T3X VARMINT
Action: Bolt
Stock: Synthetic
Barrel: 23.7 in.
Sights: None
Weight: 7 lb. 8 oz.
Caliber: .223 Rem., .22-250 Rem. 6.5 Creedmoor
Magazine: 5, 6 rounds
Features: Raised Varmint cheekpiece aids in alignment with larger scopes; free-floating barrel; wide forend perfect for sandbag use
MSRP **$898.00**

TNW Firearms

TNW FIREARMS AERO SURVIVAL RIFLE LTE

TNW FIREARMS AERO SURVIVAL RIFLE

AERO SURVIVAL RIFLE
Action: Semiautomatic
Stock: Synthetic
Barrel: 16.25 in.
Sights: None
Weight: 5 lb.
Caliber: 9mm, 10mm, .45 ACP, .460 Rowland, .40 S&W, .357 SIG
Magazine: 10, 15, 24, 29, 31 rounds by caliber
Features: Specialty survival/home-defense rifle; removable barrel and collapsible AR stock; calibers can easily be converted; TNW offers barrel threading services for suppressor use; black, Tiger Green, Pink Attitude, Dark Earth, and OD Green finishes
MSRP **$799.00**

AERO SURVIVAL RIFLE LTE
Action: Semiautomatic
Stock: Synthetic
Barrel: 16.25 in.

Sights: None
Weight: 3 lb. 15 oz.
Caliber: 9mm
Magazine: 10, 15, 17 rounds
Features: Perhaps the lightest pistol-caliber carbine on the modern market; takes Glock magazines; hard anodized coating; direct blowback action; integrated child safety lock; rapid takedown design; in gray, black, dark earth, or OD green
MSRP **$799.00**

Troy Industries

TROY INDUSTRIES M4A4

TROY INDUSTRIES PUMP-ACTION RIFLE WITH FOLDING STOCK

M4A4
Action: Semiautomatic
Stock: Synthetic
Barrel: 12 in., 16 in., 20 in.
Sights: Troy folding battle sights front, rear
Weight: N/A
Caliber: .308 Win., 6.5 Creedmoor
Magazine: 10 rounds
Features: A conventionally styled MSR with acres of top rail; CMC trigger; Magpul stock; Troy Control Grip;

M-LOK forend; hard-coat anodized finish; 6.5 Creedmoor available only in 20-in. barrel
.308 Win. **$1500.00**
6.5 Creedmoor **$1900.00**

PUMP-ACTION RIFLE WITH FOLDING STOCK
Action: Pump
Stock: Synthetic
Barrel: 16 in.
Sights: None

Weight: 6 lb.
Caliber: .223 Rem., .300 BLK
Magazine: 10 rounds
Features: An AR platform in a pump-action configuration; optic ready; TRX2-style handguard; full-length top rail; Troy SAR folding stock; uses brass-cased ammo only
MSRP . . . . **$1230.00–$1250.00**

UBERTI 1860 HENRY RIFLE

UBERTI 1866 YELLOWBOY

UBERTI 1873 COMPETITION

UBERTI 1873 CARBINE

UBERTI 1874 SHARPS RIFLE

UBERTI 1876 CENTENNIAL

UBERTI 1885 COURTNEY STALKING RIFLE

UBERTI 1885 HIGH WALL SPORTING RIFLE STRAIGHT STOCK

UBERTI SPRINGFIELD TRAPDOOR ARMY

1860 HENRY RIFLE

Action: Lever
Stock: Walnut
Barrel: 18.5 in., 24.5 in.
Sights: Adjustable
Weight: 9 lb.
Caliber: .45 Colt, .44-40 Win.
Magazine: Under-barrel tube, 8+1 or 13+1 rounds
Features: Several versions: Trapper has 18.5-in barrel, brass frame/buttplate, and case-hardened lever, Rifle has 24.5-in. barrel, brass frame/buttplate, and case-hardened receiver; Steel Rifle has 24.5-in. barrel, case-hardened frame/lever, blue buttplate
MSRP . . . . **$1549.00–$1599.00**

1866 YELLOWBOY

Action: Lever
Stock: Walnut
Barrel: 19 in., 20 in., 24.25 in.
Sights: Adjustable
Weight: 8 lb. 3 oz.
Caliber: .45 Colt, .44-40 Win., .38 Spl.
Magazine: Under barrel tube, 10+1 or 13+1 rounds
Features: Three versions, all calibers available in all three: Carbine, 19-in. barrel; Short Rifle, 20-in. barrel; Sporting Rifle, 24.25-in. barrel. All have brass frames and buttplates, case-hardened levers
MSRP **$1299.00**

1873 COMPETITION

Action: Lever
Stock: Wood
Barrel: 20 in.
Sights: Adjustable
Weight: 8 lb.
Caliber: .357 Mag., .45 Colt
Magazine: Under-barrel tube, 10+1 rounds
Features: Octagonal barrel; A-grade walnut; lever lock; side loading gate for ease of loading
MSRP **$1479.00**

1873 RIFLE & CARBINE

Action: Lever
Stock: Walnut
Barrel: 16.1 in., 18 in., 19 in., 20 in., 24.5 in.
Sights: Adjustable
Weight: 7 lb. 3 oz.–8 lb. 3 oz.
Caliber: .45 Colt, .357 Mag., .44-44
Magazine: Under-barrel tube, 9+1, 10+1 or 13+1 rounds
Features: Octagonal barrel on rifle; round barrel on trapper; A-grade walnut with checkered pistol grip and forend
Half Octagon Rifle **$1399.00**
Short Rifle **$1349.00**
Special Sporting **$1479.00**
Special Sporting Short **$1479**
Sporting **$1349.00**
Trapper **$1399.00**

1874 SHARPS RIFLE

Action: Falling block
Stock: Walnut
Barrel: 32 in., 34 in.
Sights: Creedmoor Sight
Weight: 10 lb. 4 oz.–11 lb.
Caliber: .45-70 Govt.
Magazine: None
Features: Blued octagonal barrel; checkered walnut stock; case-hardened; double-set trigger; pewter forend cap
Special **$2479.00**
Down Under **$3229.00**
Buffalo Hunter **$3229.00**

1876 CENTENNIAL

Action: Lever
Stock: Walnut
Barrel: 28 in.
Sights: Adjustable
Weight: 10 lb.
Caliber: .50-95
Magazine: Under-barrel tube, 11+1 rounds
Features: Case-hardened frame and lever; blued buttplate; octagonal barrel; straight stock
MSRP **$1749.00**

1885 COURTNEY STALKING RIFLE

Action: Single-shot
Stock: Walnut
Barrel: 24 in.
Sights: Blade front, adjustable rear
Weight: 7 lb. 2 oz.
Caliber: .303 British, .45-70 Gov't.
Magazine: 1 round
Features: A lovely rifle in a nearly forgotten cartridge, featuring a Grade A walnut stock with a Prince of Wales grip; color case receiver; round barrel in polished blue
MSRP **$1749.00**

1885 HIGH WALL SPORTING RIFLE STRAIGHT STOCK

Action: Falling block
Stock: Walnut
Barrel: 28 in., 30 in., 32 in.
Sights: Adjustable
Weight: 9 lb. 5 oz. (carbine), 10 lb.
Caliber: .45-70
Magazine: None
Features: Case-hardened frame and lever; blued buttplate; octagonal barrel; straight stock
MSRP **$1199.00**

SPRINGFIELD TRAPDOOR ARMY

Action: Hinged breech
Stock: Walnut
Barrel: 32.5 in.
Sights: Adjustable
Weight: 8 lb. 13 oz.
Caliber: .45-70 Govt.
Magazine: None
Features: Blued steel, case-hardened breechblock and buttplate
MSRP **$2449.00**

RIFLES

Uberti

UBERTI SPRINGFIELD TRAPDOOR CARBINE

SPRINGFIELD TRAPDOOR CARBINE

Action: Hinged breech
Stock: Walnut
Barrel: 22 in.
Sights: Adjustable
Weight: 7 lb. 5 oz.

Caliber: .45-70 Govt.
Magazine: None
Features: Blued steel, case-hardened breechblock and buttplate; fitted with sliding ring and bar for cavalryman to carry it clipped to carbine sling
MSRP $2199.00

Ultimate Arms

ULTIMATE ARMS MOUNTAIN LITE RIFLE

ULTIMATE ARMS WARRIOR LITE TACTICAL LONG RANGE RIFLE

MOUNTAIN LITE RIFLE

Action: Bolt
Stock: Synthetic
Barrel: 26 in.
Sights: None
Weight: N/A
Caliber: .308 Warbird (7.82 Lazzeroni)
Magazine: 3 rounds
Features: Housing a most powerful round, this custom-built rifle has a six-groove fluted medium-contour barrel with button rifling; removeable muzzle brake; proprietary Warrior Mountain Lite action; center feed
MSRP $5899.95

WARRIOR LITE TACTICAL LONG RANGE RIFLE

Action: Bolt
Stock: Carbon Kevlar
Barrel: 26 in.
Sights: None
Weight: 10 lb. 8 oz.
Caliber: 7.82 Lazzeroni Warbird
Magazine: 5 rounds
Features: 416 stainless steel fluted barrel and action dressed in a ceramic coat finish; one-piece helical cut bolt; button rifling; removable muzzle brake; carbon Kevlar stock
MSRP $6999.95

Volquartsen Firearms

VOLQUARTSEN FIREARMS .22 LR WITH OPEN SIGHTS

VOLQUARTSEN FIREARMS SUMMIT

.22 LR WITH OPEN SIGHTS

Action: Semiautomatic
Stock: Synthetic
Barrel: 16.5 in.
Sights: HiViz fiber optic front, TL tritium rear
Weight: 6 lb.
Caliber: .22 LR
Magazine: 10 rounds
Features: CNC-machined stainless steel receiver; carbon fiber THM tension barrel; TG2000 trigger guard; Magpul X-22 Hunter stock; black, OD Green, or Flat Dark Earth stock colors
MSRP $1668.00

SUMMIT

Action: Bolt
Stock: Synthetic
Barrel: N/A
Sights: None
Weight: 5 lb. 13 oz.
Caliber: .22 LR, .17 Mach 2
Magazine: N/A
Features: Lightweight Magpul stock adjustable for length of pull; carbon fiber barrel; 1.75-pound trigger; ample rail on the top for optics; threaded barrel accommodates suppressor use; a variety of colored stocks from Magpul, a laminate thumbhole configuration, plus a Hogue stock option in .17 Mach; .22 LR available with Magpul stocks, lightweight thumbhole, or ambidextrous stocks/tapered barrel
Magpul stock: $1331.00
Thumbhole laminate: $1575.00

WEATHERBY MARK V
ACCUMARK

WEATHERBY MARK V
ACCUMARK ELITE

WEATHERBY MARK V
ACCUMARK PRO

WEATHERBY MARK V CAMILLA
ULTRA LIGHTWEIGHT

WEATHERBY MARK V
CARBONMARK

WEATHERBY MARK V
CARBONMARK ELITE

MARK V ACCUMARK

Action: Bolt
Stock: Composite
Barrel: 24 in., 26 in., 28 in. by caliber
Sights: None
Weight: 7 lb. 4 oz.–8 lb. 8 oz.
Caliber: .240 Wby. Mag., .257 Wby. Mag., .270 Wby. Mag., .30-378 Wby. Mag., .300 Wby. Mag., .300 Win. Mag., .338 Lapua, .338-378 Wby. Mag., .340 Wby Mag., 6.5 Creedmoor, 6.5-300 Wby. Mag. 6.5 Wby. RPM, 7mm Wby. Mag.
Magazine: 2, 3, 4, 5 rounds by caliber
Features: Overhauled Mark V line; enhanced ergonomic stock; reduced grip diameter with added palm swell; overall weight reduction; LXX Trigger; fluted #3 contour barrel; Accubrake available
MSRP . . . .$2199.00–$2399.00

MARK V ACCUMARK ELITE

Action: Bolt
Stock: Carbon fiber
Barrel: 24 in., 26 in.
Sights: None
Weight: 7 lb. 10 oz.–8 lb. 6 oz.
Caliber: .240 Wby. Mag., .257 Wby. Mag., 6.5 Creedmoor, 6.5 Wby. RPM, 6.5-300 Wby. Mag., .270 Wby. Mag., 7mm Wby. Mag., .300 Win. Mag., .300 Wby. Mag., .30-378 Wby. Mag., .340 Wby. Mag., .338 Lapua Mag., .338-378 Wby. Mag.
Magazine: 2, 3, 4 rounds
Features: Similar to the Accumark Pro, but with the fluted barrel, muzzle brake, trigger guard, and receiver in Elite Cerakote Coyote Tan; fluted bolt, bolt knob, and safety in Cerakote Graphite Black; adjustable stock is dark brown with tan splotching
MSRP . . . .$3149.00–$3249.00

MARK V ACCUMARK PRO

Action: Bolt
Stock: Carbon fiber
Barrel: 24 in., 26 in.
Sights: None
Weight: 7 lb. 2 oz.–7 lb. 14 oz.
Caliber: .240 Wby. Mag., .257 Wby. Mag., 6.5 Creedmoor, 6.5 Wby. RPM, 6.5-300 Wby. Mag., .270 Wby. Mag., 7mm Wby. Mag., .300 Win. Mag., .300 Wby. Mag., .30-378 Wby. Mag., .340 Wby. Mag., .338 Lapua Mag., .338-378 Wby. Mag.
Magazine: 2, 3, 4 rounds
Features: The carbon fiber stock appears in dark gray with lighter gray splotches; fluted barrel, muzzle brake, trigger guard, and receiver are in Tungsten Cerakote
MSRP . . . .$2699.00–$2899.00

MARK V CAMILLA ULTRA LIGHTWEIGHT

Action: Bolt
Stock: Composite
Barrel: 22 in., 24 in.
Sights: None
Weight: 5 lb. 12 oz.
Caliber: .240 Wby. Mag., .243 Win., 6.5 Creedmoor, .280 Ackley Improved, 6.5 Wby. RPM
Magazine: 4, 5 rounds
Features: One for the hiker with a stock made to better fit a woman's physique; hand-laid composite stock with full-length aluminum bedding block and wearing a Forest Green/black web gel coating; fluted stainless barrel with #1 contour; fluted bolt body; LXX trigger with grooves
MSRP $2049.00

MARK V CARBONMARK

Action: Bolt
Stock: Composite
Barrel: 26 in.
Sights: None
Weight: 7 lb. 12 oz.
Caliber: .257 Wby. Mag., .300 Wby. Mag., 6.5 Creedmoor, 6.5 Wby. RPM, 6.5-300 Wby.
Magazine: 3 rounds
Features: A collaboration with Proof Research featuring a stock with a reduced grip diameter, right-hand palm swell, aluminum bedding block, and a dark gray/black matte gel finish; Proof Research carbon fiber barrel with a stainless steel core, #4 contour, cut-rifled, hand-lapped, and threaded 5/8X24; Tactical Grey Cerakote metalwork; magnum 9-lug action; fluted bolt body; LXX trigger
MSRP . . . . $2649.00–$2749.00

MARK V CARBONMARK ELITE

Action: Bolt
Stock: Carbon fiber
Barrel: 22 in., 24 in., 26 in.
Sights: None
Weight: 7 lb. 3 oz.–8 lb. 6 oz.
Caliber: 6.5 Creedmoor, 6.5 Wby. RPM, .257 Wby. Mag., 6.5-300 Wby. Mag., .300 Wby. Mag.
Magazine: 3, 4 rounds
Features: Similar to the Carbonmark Pro, but with an adjustable stock in dark gray with a tan sponge pattern; bolt, bolt knob, and safety in Graphite Black Cerakote; receiver, muzzle brake, and trigger guard in Elite Cerakote Coyote Tan
MSRP . . . .$3549.00–$3649.00

RIFLES

Weatherby

WEATHERBY MARK V CARBONMARK PRO

WEATHERBY MARK V COWPOKE EDITION

WEATHERBY MARK V DELUXE

WEATHERBY MARK V WEATHERMARK

WEATHERBY MARK V WEATHERMARK LIMITED

WEATHERBY MARK V WEATHERMARK LT

MARK V CARBONMARK PRO

Action: Bolt
Stock: Carbon fiber
Barrel: 22 in., 24 in., 26 in.
Sights: None
Weight: 6 lb. 11 oz.–7 lb. 8 oz.
Caliber: 6.5 Creedmoor, 6.5 Wby. RPM, .257 Wby. Mag., 6.5-300 Wby. Mag., .300 Wby. Mag.
Magazine: 3, 4 rounds
Features: Carbon fiber sleeve with a 416 stainless steel barrel; receiver, muzzle brake, and trigger guard in Tungsten Cerakote; fluted bolt, bolt knob, and safety in Cerakote Graphite Gray; charcoal stock
MSRP . . . . **$3199.00–$3299.00**

MARK V COWPOKE EDITION

Action: Bolt
Stock: Fiberglass
Barrel: 24 in., 26 in.
Sights: None
Weight: 8 lb. 6 oz.
Caliber: .257 Wby. Mag., .30-378 Wby. Mag., .300 Wby. Mag., 6.5 Wby. RPM, 6.5-300 Wby. Mag.
Magazine: 3, 4 rounds
Features: This is a pretty fancy rifle to be dubbed the "Cowpoke," but surely the folks at Weatherby had a vision (okay, really, it's a Wyoming thing); receiver and #3 contour barrel in Cerakote brown but with its flutes in Cerakote gold; handlaid fiberglass stock mimics the color mix; TriggerTech trigger; Accubrake ST; 54-degree bolt
MSRP **$2499.00**

MARK V DELUXE, CAMILLA DELUXE

Action: Bolt
Stock: Walnut
Barrel: 24 in., 26 in., 28 in.
Sights: None
Weight: 6 lb. 12 oz.–10 lb.
Caliber: 240 Wby. Mag., .243 Win., .257 Wby. Mag., .270 Wby., .30-378 Wby. Mag., .300 Wby. Mag., .338-378 Wby. Mag., .340 Wby. Mag., .378 Wby. Mag., .416 Wby. Mag., .460 Wby. Mag., 6.5 Creedmoor, 6.5 Wby. RPM, 6.5-300 Wby. Mag., 7mm Wby. Mag.
Magazine: 2+1, 3+1, 5+1 rounds
Features: Weatherby overhauled the Mark V in 2018 with ergonomically enhanced stocks that include reduced grip diameter and lighter overall weight, an improved LXX trigger with a wider face, and the company's sub-MOA accuracy gurantee; also new to the Deluxe line is the addition of the Camilla Deluxe, the upgraded sister to the previous Vanguard Camilla, with a six-lug action and a stock designed to better fit the female form
Deluxe . . . . **$2599.00–$2999.00**
Camilla Deluxe **$2499.00**

MARK V WEATHERMARK, WEATHERMARK BRONZE

Action: Bolt
Stock: Composite
Barrel: 24 in., 26 in., 28 in. by caliber
Sights: None
Weight: 6 lb. 4 oz.–8 lb. 4 oz.
Caliber: .240 Wby. Mag., .243 Win., .257 Wby. Mag.,, .270 Wby. Mag., .300 Wby. Mag., .30-378 Wby. Mag., .340 Wby. Mag., .338-378 Wby. Mag., 6.5 Creedmoor, 6.5 Wby. RPM, 6.5-300 Wby. Mag., 7mm Wby. Mag.
Magazine: 2, 3, 5 rounds by caliber
Features: First Mark V to feature a Cerakote finish; #2 contour threaded barrels; hand-laid fiberglass stock with Monte Carlo cheekpiece; aluminum bedding block; spiral-fluted bolt body; standard Weathermark has barrel and receiver in Tac Gray Cerakote, Bronze model in Burnt Bronze Cerakote
MSRP . . . . **$1699.00–$1899.00**

MARK V WEATHERMARK LIMITED

Action: Bolt
Stock: Composite
Barrel: 22 in., 24 in., 26 in.
Sights: None
Weight: 7 lb. 3 oz.
Caliber: .257 Wby. Mag., .300 Wby. Mag., 6.5 Creedmoor, 6.5 Wby. RPM, 6.5-300 Wby. Mag.
Magazine: 3, 4 rounds
Features: Weatherby's first spiral-fluted barrel on a Mark V rifle; fluted bolt knob; flat-faced TriggerTech trigger; combination of black and burnt bronze Cerakote on the metal; black based composite stock with grey and brown accents; Accubrake ST
MSRP **$2299.00**

MARK V WEATHERMARK LT

Action: Bolt
Stock: Fiberglass
Barrel: 22 in., 24 in., 26 in.
Sights: None
Weight: 5 lb. 14 oz.–7 lb. 3 oz.
Caliber: .240 Wby. Mag., .257 Wby. Mag., .270 Wby. Mag., 6.5 Creedmoor, 6.5 Wby. RPM, 6.5-300 Wby. Mag., 7mm Wby. Mag., .300 Wby. Mag.
Magazine: 3, 4 rounds
Features: Handlaid fiberglass stock in traditional Weatherby styling; raised comb, with a green base and flat dark earth flecking; fluted barrel, muzzle brake, receiver, and trigger guard in flat dark earth Cerakote; fluted bolt, bolt knob, and safety in Graphite Black Cerakote; 6mm Creedmoor, 6.5 Creedmoor, 6.5 Wby. RPM, and .240 Wby Mag. have six-lug actions and are the lightest of the lineup at 5 lb. 14 oz.; left-hand available in .257, 6.5-300, and .300 Wby. Mags.
MSRP . . . . **$2099.00–$2199.00**

WEATHERBY VANGUARD BADLANDS

WEATHERBY VANGUARD FIRST LITE

WEATHERBY VANGUARD LAMINATE SPORTER

WEATHERBY VANGUARD CAMILLA

WEATHERBY VANGUARD HIGH COUNTRY

WEATHERBY VANGUARD CAMILLA WILDERNESS

WEATHERBY VANGUARD HUSH EDITION

VANGUARD BADLANDS

Action: Bolt
Stock: Composite
Barrel: 25 in., 28 in.
Sights: None
Weight: 7 lb. 8 oz.
Caliber: .25-06 Rem., .257 Wby. Mag., .270 Win., .30-06 Spfd., .300 Wby. Mag., .300 Win. Mag., .308 Win., 6.5 Creedmoor, 6.5 PRC, 6.5-300 Wby. Mag., 7mm Rem. Mag., 7mm-08 Rem.
Magazine: 3, 4, 5 rounds
Features: Standard Vanguard features; #2 contour barrel; metalwork in Burnt Bronze Cerakote; polymer stock with textured gripping surfaces, all dressed in Badlands Approach camo; adjustable match-grade two-stage trigger; fluted, one-piece machined bolt body with fully enclosed bolt sleeve
MSRP $899.00

VANGUARD CAMILLA

Action: Bolt
Stock: Turkish walnut
Barrel: 20 in.
Sights: None
Weight: 6 lb. 4 oz.
Caliber: .22-250 Rem., .243 Win., .308 Win., 6.5 Creedmoor, 7mm-08 Rem.
Magazine: 4, 5 rounds
Features: SUB-MOA accuracy guarantee; "creep-free," match-quality, two-stage trigger; three-position safety; slimmer grip angle; shorter, slimmer forearm and grip with right side palm swell for better balance and fit; fleur de lis checkering pattern; recoil pad has been given a negative angle, reduced in size, and the toe canted away from the body to better fit a woman's shoulder
MSRP $899.00

VANGUARD CAMILLA WILDERNESS

Action: Bolt
Stock: Fiberglass
Barrel: 20 in.
Sights: None
Weight: 7 lb.
Caliber: .243 Win., 6.5 Creedmoor, 7mm-08 Rem., .308 Win.
Magazine: 4, 5 rounds
Features: The Wilderness sports a green handlaid fiberglass stock with black webbing; #2 contour barrel; fluted bolt body; skeletonized aluminum bedding block
MSRP $999.00

VANGUARD FIRST LITE

Action: Bolt
Stock: Composite
Barrel: 26 in., 28 in.
Sights: None
Weight: 7 lb. 8 oz.
Caliber: .240 Wby. Mag., .25-06 Rem., .257 Wby. Mag., 6.5-3000 Wby. Mag., .270 Win., .308 Win., .30-06 Spfd., .300 Win. Mag. .300 Wby. Mag., 6.5 Creedmoor, 6.5 PRC
Magazine: 3, 5 rounds
Features: Stock finished in First Lite Fusion camo; stock has texturing at the grip and forearm; Flat Dark Earth Cerakote finish on the barrel and action; one-piece machined fluted bolt body; #2 contour fluted barrel with Accubrake; adjustable match-grade two-stage trigger
MSRP $1099.00

VANGUARD HIGH

Action: Bolt
Stock: Composite
Barrel: 24 in., 26 in.
Sights: None
Weight: 7 lb. 4 oz.
Caliber: .257 Wby. Mag., .270 Win., .30-06 Spfd., .300 Wby. Mag., .300 Win. Mag., .308 Win., 6.5 Creedmoor, 6.5 PRC, 6.5-300 Wby. Mag.
Magazine: 3, 4, 5 rounds

Features: Monte Carlo stock with a right-hand palm swell; black base with green and tan accents; textured forearm and grip; adjustable two-stage trigger; fluted bolt body; Accubrake ST; metalwork in flat dark earth Cerakote
MSRP $1049.00

VANGUARD HUSH EDITION

Action: Bolt
Stock: Composite
Barrel: 24 in., 26 in.
Sights: None
Weight: 7 lb. 4 oz.
Caliber: .257 Wby. Mag., .300 Wby. Mag., 6.5 Creedmoor, 6.5-300 Wby. Mag.
Magazine: 3, 4 rounds
Features: A collaborative effort between Weatherby and HUSH, this rifle's receiver is in full graphite black Cerakote with a fluted bolt to match; straight-flute #2 contour barrel; stock in cement gray with black webbing, textured grip areas, and right-hand palm swell; threaded barrel with Accubrake ST
MSRP $1049.00

VANGUARD LAMINATE SPORTER

Action: Bolt
Stock: Laminate
Barrel: 24 in., 26 in.
Sights: None
Weight: 7 lb. 4 oz.–7 lb. 8 oz.
Caliber: .223 Rem., .22-250 Rem., .243 Win., .240 Wby. Mag., .25-06 Rem., .257 Wby. Mag., 6.5 Creedmoor, .270 Win., 7mm-08 Rem., 7mm Rem. Mag., .308 Win., .30-06 Spfd., .300 Win. Mag., .300 Wby. Mag.
Magazine: 3, 4, 5 rounds
Features: Handsome laminate stock in Nutmeg from Boyds; fluted bolt body; cold hammer-forged barrel in a #2 contour; matte blue metalwork
MSRP . . . . $849.00–$949.00

RIFLES

Weatherby

WEATHERBY VANGUARD MEATEATER EDITION

WEATHERBY VANGUARD MULTICAM

WEATHERBY VANGUARD SPORTER

WEATHERBY VANGUARD SYNTHETIC

WEATHERBY VANGUARD SYNTHETIC COMPACT BLUE

WEATHERBY VANGUARD WEATHERGUARD

VANGUARD MEATEATER EDITION

Action: Bolt
Stock: Composite
Barrel: 24 in., 26 in.
Sights: None
Weight: 7 lb. 2 oz.
Caliber: .300 Wby. Mag., .300 Win. Mag., .308 Win., 6.5 Creedmoor, 6.5-300 Wby. Mag., 7mm Rem. Mag.
Magazine: 3, 4 rounds
Features: A collaborative effort with the MeatEater brand, this rifle's receiver and #2 contour spiral-fluted barrel are in tungsten Cerakote; fluted bolt is in black Cerakote; black-based stock has gray and brown accents, right palmswell, and textured grip areas; barrel is threaded but does not come with Accubrake
MSRP $999.00

VANGUARD MULTICAM

Action: Bolt
Stock: Polymer
Barrel: 24 in., 26 in.
Sights: None
Weight: 7 lb. 4 oz.–7 lb. 8 oz.
Caliber: .243 Win., .240 Wby. Mag., .25-06 Rem., .257 Wby. Mag., 6.5 Creedmoor, 6.5-300 Wby. Mag., .270 Win., 7mm-08 Rem., 7mm Rem. Mag., .308 Win., .30-06 Spfd., .300 Win. Mag., .300 Wby. Mag., 6.5 PRC
Magazine: 3, 4, 5 rounds
Features: The MultiCam finish on the stock lends a lot of versatility to this rifle, which also features metalwork with Cerakote flat dark earth finish; fluted bolt body; #2 contour barrel
MSRP $999.00

VANGUARD SPORTER

Action: Bolt
Stock: Walnut
Barrel: 24 in.
Sights: None

Weight: 7 lb. 4 oz.–7 lb. 8 oz.
Caliber: .223 Rem., .22-250 Rem., .243 Win., .25-06 Rem., .270 Win., 7mm-08 Rem., .308 Win., .30-06 Spfd., .257 Wby. Mag., 7mm Rem. Mag., .300 Win. Mag., .300 Wby. Mag., 6.5 Creedmoor, 6.5-300 Wby. Mag.
Magazine: 3+1, 5+1 rounds
Features: Two-stage trigger; raised comb, Monte Carlo stock with satin urethane finish; hand-selected A fancy grade Turkish walnut; rosewood forend; low luster, matte blued metalwork; fine line diamond point checkering; low density recoil pad
MSRP $929.00

VANGUARD SYNTHETIC

Action: Bolt
Stock: Synthetic
Barrel: 24 in.
Sights: None
Weight: 7 lb. 4 oz.
Caliber: .22-250 Rem., .223 Rem., .240 Wby. Mag., .243 Win., .25-06 Rem., .257 Wby. Mag., .270 Win., .30-06 Spfd., .300 Wby. Mag., .300 Win. Mag., .308 Win., 6.5 Creedmoor, 6.5 PRC, 6.5-300 Wby. Mag., 7mm Rem. Mag., 7mm-08 Rem.
Magazine: Internal, 6+1 rounds
Features: Matte bead blasted blued metalwork; low density recoil pad; two-stage trigger; fluted bolt body; Monte Carlo Griptonite stock available in grey or green with black grip inserts
MSRP $699.00

VANGUARD SYNTHETIC COMPACT

Action: Bolt
Stock: Composite
Barrel: 20 in.

Sights: None
Weight: 6 lb. 8 oz.
Caliber: .243 Win., .308 Win., 6.5 Creedmoor, 7mm-08 Rem.
Magazine: 4, 5 rounds
Features: Handy rifle for backcountry hunters or ranch work; injection-molded composite stock that includes a spacer for length-of-pull adjustment; #1 contour barrel in matte, bead-blasted blued finish; base model has the stock in black, while the blue model has splashes of gray and neon blue
Standard: $629.00
Blue: $699.00

VANGUARD WEATHERGUARD, WEATHERGUARD BRONZE

Action: Bolt
Stock: Monte Carlo Griptonite
Barrel: 24 in.
Sights: None
Weight: 7 lb. 12 oz.
Caliber: .22-250 Rem., .223 Rem., .240 Wby. Mag., .243 Win., .25-06 Rem., .257 Wby. Mag., .270 Win., .30-06 Spfd., .300 Wby. Mag., .300 Win. Mag., .308 Win., 6.5 Creedmoor, 6.5 PRC, 7mm Rem. Mag., 7mm-08 Rem.
Magazine: 3+1 or 5+1 rounds
Features: Guaranteed SUB-MOA accuracy; Monte Carlo Griptonite stock features pistol grip, forend inserts, and right-side palm swell (aids shooter's comfort and control); Tactical Gray or Burnt Bronze Cerakoting on receiver and barrel for exceptional weather and corrosion resistance; fluted bolt body; three-position safety; hinged floorplate; cold hammer-forged barrel; match quality two-stage trigger
Standard $799.00
Bronze $829.00

RIFLES

Wilson Combat

WILSON COMBAT PAUL HOWE TACTICAL CARBINE

WILSON COMBAT PROTECTOR SERIES AR CARBINE

WILSON COMBAT RANGER

WILSON COMBAT RECON TACTICAL

WILSON COMBAT SBR TACTICAL

WILSON COMBAT SUPER SNIPER

WILSON COMBAT TACTICAL HUNTER

PAUL HOWE TACTICAL CARBINE

Action: Semiautomatic
Stock: Synthetic
Barrel: 14.7 in.
Sights: Detachable fixed front, flip-up BUS rear, Leupold scope
Weight: 6 lb. 4 oz.
Caliber: .223 Rem.
Magazine: N/A
Features: Super-compact MSR; two-stage TTU trigger with heavy mil-spec springs; fluted Recon barrel with a permanent flash hider; M-LOK rail; Daniel Defense detachable fixed front sight; flip-up BUS rear sight with CSAT aperture; Leupold VX-6HD scope; Streamlight TLR-1 HL light; Wilson Combat/BCM Starburst Gunfighter grip; Vickers sling; Armor-Tuff camo finish; California magazine options available; multiple barrel options; kit version available
MSRP . . . . starting at **$2800.00**

PROTECTOR SERIES AR CARBINE

Action: Semiautomatic
Stock: Synthetic
Barrel: 16.25 in.
Sights: None
Weight: 6 lb. 1 oz.
Caliber: .300 HAM'R, .223 Rem., .300 BLK
Magazine: 30 rounds
Features: Wilson Combat match-grade barrel; low-profile gas block; QComp muzzle brake; M-LOK handguard with 4-in. rail; direct impingement mid-length operation in 5.56 and .300 HAM'R, pistol length on .300 BLK; TTU M2 two-stage trigger; Rogers/Wilson Super Stoc stock; Wilson

Combat/BCM Starburst Gunfighter pistol grip; oversized tactical trigger guard; in black or Coyote Tan Armor-Tuff finish; left-hand options available; no forward assist available
MSRP . . . . starting at **$1995.95**

RANGER

Action: Semiautomatic
Stock: Synthetic
Barrel: 16 in., 16.2 in.
Sights: None
Weight: 8 lb.
Caliber: .300 BLK, 5.56 NATO, 6.8 SPC II, 7.62X40 WT, .350 Legend, .300 Ham'r
Magazine: N/A
Features: Match-grade WC Ranger barrel; Rogers/Wilson Super-Stoc stock; Wilson Combat/BCM Starburst Gunfighter grip; threaded muzzle with QComp brake; 1-in. M-LOK rail with three Falcon/Ergo rail covers
MSRP . . . . starting at **$2500.00**

RECON TACTICAL

Action: Semiautomatic
Stock: Synthetic tactical
Barrel: 16 in.
Sights: Optional rail
Weight: 7 lb.
Caliber: .204 Ruger, .224 Valkyrie, .300 BLK, .458 SOCOM, 5.56 NATO, 6.5 Grendel, 6.8 SPC, 7.62X40 WT, .300 Ham'R, .350 Legend, .375 SOCOM, .450 Bushmaster
Magazine: Detachable box, 30 rounds
Features: Match grade medium weight stainnless steel barrel; forged 7075 upper (flat top) and lower receiver; mid-length gas system with low-profile gas block; Wilson Combat T.R.I.M. rail; ergo pistol grip
MSRP . . . . starting at **$2450.00**

SBR TACTICAL

Action: Semiautomatic
Stock: Synthetic
Barrel: 11.3 in.
Sights: Flip-up front, rear

Weight: 6 lb. 5 oz.
Caliber: .300 BLK, .300 HAM'R, 6.8 SPC II, .223 Rem.
Magazine: N/A
Features: SBR (short-barreled rifle) with BILLet upper and lower; match-grade SBR Tactical barrel with a threaded muzzle; choice of Accu-Tac or QComp flash hider; carbine-length gas system with low-profile gas block
MSRP . . . . starting at **$2425.00**

SUPER SNIPER

Action: Semiautomatic
Stock: Synthetic, telescoping
Barrel: 20 in.
Sights: None
Weight: 10 lb. 11 oz.
Caliber: .260 Rem., 6mm Creedmoor, 6.5 Creedmoor, .308 Win.
Magazine: 10 rounds, 20 rounds
Features: Barrel is precision button rifled from 416-R stainless steel; 1:10 twist; Picatinny rail; BILLet-AR machined aluminum upper and lower receivers; 12 inch or 14 inch free-floating TRIM rail; available with a fluted or non-fluted barrel
MSRP . . . . starting at **$3235.00**

TACTICAL HUNTER

Action: Semiautomatic
Stock: Synthetic
Barrel: 18 in., 20 in.
Sights: None
Weight: 7 lb. 11 oz.
Caliber: 7mm-08 Rem., .308 Win., .338 Fed., 6mm Creedmoor, 6.5 Creedmoor, .260 Rem.
Magazine: N/A
Features: Ready for the predator and game fields; threaded match-grade Tactical Hunter barrel; rifle-length gas system; SLR Rifleworks adjustable gas block; Rogers/Wilson Super Stoc stock; 14.6-in. M-LOK rail with three three-section Magpul Type 1 rail covers; nickel-boron low-mass bolt carrier; small-latch BCM charging handle
MSRP . . . . starting at **$3335.00**

Wilson Combat

WILSON COMBAT ULTRALIGHT RANGER

WILSON COMBAT URBAN SUPER SNIPER

ULTRALIGHT RANGER

Action: Semiautomatic
Stock: Carbon fiber
Barrel: 16, 18 in.
Sights: None
Weight: 7 lb. 6 oz.
Caliber: .300 BLK, .223 Rem., 6.8 SPC, 7.62x40 WT, .300 HAM'R, .350 Legend
Magazine: N/A
Features: Composite carbon fiber stock in smoke and with a closed shoulder buttstock; match-grade Ranger barrel; SLR Rifleworks adjust-able gas block; 10-in. M-LOK rail with three Falcon/Ergo rail covers; TTU M2 #4 trigger; Mission First tacti-cal pistol grip; fluted barrel in .350 Legend (16-in.) and .30 HAM'R (18 in.); Armor-Tuff finish over hard anod-ize finish, standard in green/black with other color choices and camo available
MSRP . . . . starting at $2615.00

URBAN SUPER SNIPER

Action: Semiautomatic, mid-length gas system with low-profile gas block

Stock: Synthetic, telescoping
Barrel: 18 in.
Sights: None
Weight: 7 lb. 5 oz.
Caliber: .223 Wylde
Magazine: 10, 20, or 30 rounds
Features: Medium heavy-weight, flut-ed, stainless steel premium match-grade barrel; 1:8 twist; Picatinny rail; 10.4 inch free-floating TRIM rail
MSRP . . . . starting at $2400.00

Winchester Repeating Arms

WINCHESTER MODEL 70 ALASKAN

WINCHESTER REPEATING ARMS MODEL 70 EXTREME TRUETIMBER VSX MB

WINCHESTER MODEL 70 EXTREME TUNGSTEN

MODEL 70 ALASKAN

Action: Bolt
Stock: Walnut
Barrel: 25 in.
Sights: Open
Weight: 8 lb. 8 oz.
Caliber: .30-06 Spfd., .300 Win. Mag. .338 Win. Mag., .375 HH Mag.
Magazine: None
Features: Satin finish Monte Carlo walnut stock with cut checkering; folding adjustable rear sight with hooded gold bead front sight; recessed target crown
MSRP . . . . $1489.99–$1549.99

MODEL 70 EXTREME TRUETIMBER VSX MB

Action: Bolt
Stock: Composite
Barrel: 22 in., 24 in., 26 in.
Sights: None
Weight: 6 lb. 12 oz.–7 lb. 4 oz.
Caliber: .243 Win., 6.5 Creedmoor, 7mm-08 Rem., .308 Win., 6.5 PRC, 6.8 Western, .270 WSM, .300 WSM, .25-06 Rem., .270 Win., .30-06 Spfd., .264 Win. Mag., 7mm Rem. Mag., .300 Win. Mag.
Magazine: 3, 4, 5 rounds
Features: Receiver and barrel finished in tungsten Cerakote; Bell & Carlson stock has sculpted cheekpiece and TrueTimber VSX camo; jeweled bolt body; MOA trigger system
MSRP . . . . $1679.99–$1719.99

MODEL 70 EXTREME TUNGSTEN MB

Action: Bolt
Stock: Synthetic
Barrel: 22 in., 24 in., 26 in.
Sights: None
Weight: 6 lb. 12 oz.–7 lb. 4 oz.
Caliber: .243 Win., 6.5 Creedmoor, 7mm-08 Rem., .308 Win., .270 WSM, .300 WSM, .25-06 Rem., 270 Win., .30-06 Spfd., .264 Win. Mag., 7mm Rem. Mag., .300 Win. Mag., 6.8 Western
Magazine: 3, 5 rounds
Features: Wearing a charcoal gray Bell & Carlson synthetic stock, this rifle has a free-floating barrel with a muzzle brake in Tungsten Cerakote; receiver in Tungsten Cerakote; Pachmayr Decelerator recoil pad MOA trigger system; pre-'64 action
MSRP . . . . $1609.99–$1649.99

Winchester Repeating Arms

WINCHESTER REPEATING ARMS MODEL 70 EXTREME WEATHER MB

WINCHESTER MODEL 70 FEATHERWEIGHT COMPACT

WINCHESTER MODEL 70 SAFARI EXPRESS

WINCHESTER REPEATING ARMS MODEL 70 LONG RANGE MB

WINCHESTER MODEL 70 SUPER GRADE FRENCH WALNUT

MODEL 70 EXTREME WEATHER MB

Action: Bolt
Stock: Composite
Barrel: 22 in., 24 in., 26 in.
Sights: None
Weight: 6 lb. 12 oz.–7 lb. 4 oz.
Caliber: .243 Win., 6.5 Creedmoor, 7mm-08 Rem., .308 Win., 6.5 PRC, 6.8 Western, .270 WSM, .300 WSM, .25-06 Rem., .270 Win., .30-06 Spfd., .264 Win. Mag., 7mm Rem. Mag., .300 Win. Mag.
Magazine: 3, 4, 5 rounds
Features: Receiver and sporter contour barrel are finished in matte stainless finish; Bell & Carlson lay-up composite stock has sculpted cheekpiece and is in TrueTimber VSX camo; aluminum bedding block; MOA trigger system
MSRP . . . .$1679.99–$1719.99

MODEL 70 FEATHERWEIGHT COMPACT

Action: Bolt
Stock: Walnut
Barrel: 20 in.
Sights: None
Weight: 6 lb. 8 oz.

Caliber: 6.5 Creedmoor 7mm-08 Rem., .308 Win., 6.8 Western, 6.5 PRC
Magazine: 5 rounds
Features: Pachmayr decelerator recoil pad; action is drilled and tapped for optics
MSRP . . . . $1089.99–$1129.99

MODEL 70 SAFARI EXPRESS

Action: Bolt
Stock: Satin-finished checkered walnut with deluxe cheekpiece
Barrel: 24 in.
Sights: Hooded-blade front and express-style rear
Weight: 9 lb.
Caliber: .375 H&H Mag., .416 Rem. Mag., .458 Win. Mag.
Magazine: 3 rounds
Features: Pre-'64 type claw extractor; Pachmayr decelerator recoil pad; barrel band front swivel base; dual recoil lugs and three-position safety; MOA trigger system; matte blued finish; two steel cross-bolts and one-piece steel trigger guard and hinged floor plate
MSRP $1679.99

MODEL 70 LONG RANGE MB

Action: Bolt
Stock: Composite
Barrel: 24 in.
Sights: None
Weight: 7 lb. 8 oz.
Caliber: .22-250 Rem., .243 Win., 6.5 Creedmoor, .308 Win., 6.5 PRC, .270 WSM, .300 WSM, 6.8 Western
Magazine: 3, 4 rounds
Features: Hand-laid Bell & Carlson stock is in tan with black spider webbing and a flat forend; aluminum bedding blocks; fluted barrel in a light varmint contour has muzzle brake; MOA trigger system; Pachmayr Decelerator pad
MSRP . . . .$1609.99–$1649.99

MODEL 70 SUPER GRADE FRENCH WALNUT

Action: Bolt
Stock: French walnut
Barrel: 22 in., 24 in., 26 in.
Sights: None
Weight: 7 lb. 12 oz.–8 lb. 8 oz.
Caliber: .243 Win., 6.5 Creedmoor, .308 Win., .270 Win., .30-06 Spfd., .264 Win. Mag., 7mm Rem. Mag., .300 Win. Mag., 6.8 Western
Magazine: 3, 5 rounds
Features: Grade AAA French walnut stock that features an ebony forearm tip, Shadowline cheekpiece, and polished steel pistol grip cap; free-floating barrel with target crown is in a high-polished blue; M.O.A. trigger assembly; pre-'64 action
MSRP . . . .$2109.99–$2149.99

RIFLES

Winchester Repeating Arms

WINCHESTER MODEL 70 SUPER GRADE MAPLE

WINCHESTER MODEL 94 CARBINE

WINCHESTER REPEATING ARMS MODEL 94 DELUXE SPORTING

WINCHESTER MODEL 94 SHORT RIFLE

WINCHESTER MODEL 94 SPORTER

WINCHESTER REPEATING ARMS MODEL 94 TRAILS END TAKEDOWN

WINCHESTER MODEL 1873 CARBINE

WINCHESTER REPEATING ARMS MODEL 1873 COMPETITION CARBINE HIGH GRADE

MODEL 70 SUPER GRADE MAPLE

Action: Bolt
Stock: Maple
Barrel: 24 in., 26 in.
Sights: None
Weight: 7 lb. 12 oz.–8 lb. 6 oz.
Caliber: .243 Win., .308 Win., .270 Win., .30-06 Spfd., .264 Win. Mag., 7mm Rem. Mag., .300 Win. Mag., 6.5 Creedmoor, 6.8 Western
Magazine: 3, 5 rounds
Features: Gloss-finished AAA maple stock with ebony forend tip; Shadowline cheekpiece; Super Grade engraved hinged floorplate; jeweled bolt body; knurled bolt handle; pre-64 action with MOA Trigger System; hammer-forged, free-floating steel barrel with target crown
MSRP . . . . $1789.99–$1829.99

MODEL 94 CARBINE

Action: Lever
Stock: Walnut
Barrel: 20 in.
Sights: Adjustable semi-buckhorn rear, Marble Arms front
Weight: 6 lb. 8 oz.
Caliber: .30-30 Win., .38-55 Win.
Magazine: 7 rounds
Features: Triple-checked button rifled barrel; round locking bolt trunnions; top-tang safety; rebounding hammer; bolt relief cut; steel loading gate; articulated cartridge stop; available knurled hammer spur extension
MSRP $1279.99

MODEL 94 DELUXE SPORTING

Action: Lever
Stock: Walnut
Barrel: 24 in.

Sights: Gold bead front, semi-buckhorn rear
Weight: 7 lb. 8 oz.
Caliber: .30-30 Win., .38-55 Win.
Magazine: 8 rounds
Features: Very attractive upgrade on a classic, with a steel receiver in a color case-hardened finish; button-rifled semi-gloss blue barrel; Grade V/VI walnut stock with crescent buttplate; hammer spur extension; Marble Arms sights
MSRP $2169.99

MODEL 94 SHORT RIFLE

Action: Lever
Stock: Walnut
Barrel: 20 in.
Sights: Front, adjustable rear
Weight: 6 lb. 12 oz.
Caliber: .30-30 Win., .450 Marlin, .38-55 Win.
Magazine: 7 rounds
Features: Straight grip; rifle-style forearm and black grip cap; semi-buckhorn rear sights, Marble Arms gold-bead front sight; drilled and tapped for optics
MSRP $1309.99

MODEL 94 SPORTER

Action: Lever
Stock: Walnut
Barrel: 24 in.
Sights: Marble Arms front, adjustable rear
Weight: 7 lb. 8 oz.
Caliber: .30-30 Win., .38-55 Win.
Magazine: 8 rounds
Features: Half-round, half-octagon blued barrel; straight grip stock with a crescent butt and finely checkered blued-steel buttplate with double-line bordering; drilled and tapped for optics
MSRP $1479.99

MODEL 94 TRAILS END TAKEDOWN

Action: Lever
Stock: Walnut
Barrel: 20 in.
Sights: Adjustable
Weight: 6 lb. 12 oz.
Caliber: .30-30 Win., .38-55 Win., .450 Marlin
Magazine: 6 rounds
Features: Walnut stock and forearm with satin finish and straight-grip styling; blued steel receiver and barrel; Marble Arms front sight with semi-buckhorn rear sight; Pachmayr Decelerator recoil pad (450 model)
MSRP $1549.99

MODEL 1873 CARBINE

Action: Lever-action
Stock: Black walnut
Barrel: 20 in.
Sights: Marble Arms gold bead front, semi-buckhorn rear
Weight: 7 lb. 4 oz.
Caliber: .357-38, .44-40 Win., .45 Colt
Magazine: 10 rounds
Features: Blued carbine strap buttplate; round barrel; full-length magazine; receiver is drilled and tapped for a tang-mounted rear sight; saddle ring is also in blue
MSRP $1389.99

MODEL 1873 COMPETITION CARBINE HIGH GRADE

Action: Lever
Stock: Walnut
Barrel: 20 in.
Sights: Blade front, carbine ladder-style rear
Weight: 7 lb. 4 oz.
Caliber: .357 Mag., .45 Colt
Magazine: 10 rounds
Features: SASS ready and has a polished blue round barrel with barrel band; Grade III/IV walnut stock; color case-hardened carbine buttplate and steel receiver; top tang drilled for peep sight; saddle ring
MSRP $1839.99

RIFLES

Winchester Repeating Arms

WINCHESTER MODEL 1873 DELUXE SPORTING

WINCHESTER MODEL 1873 SHORT RIFLE

WINCHESTER MODEL 1873 SHORT RIFLE COLOR CASE HARDENED

WINCHESTER MODEL 1873 SPORTER OCTAGON COLOR CASE HARDENED

WINCHESTER REPEATING ARMS MODEL 1885 LOW WALL HUNTER HIGH GRADE

WINCHESTER MODEL 1886 DELUXE RIFLE CASE HARDENED

WINCHESTER REPEATING ARMS MODEL 1886 SADDLE RING CARBINE

MODEL 1873 DELUXE SPORTING

Action: Lever
Stock: Black walnut
Barrel: 24 in.
Sights: Hooded front, semi-buckhorn rear
Weight: 8 lb.
Caliber: .357-38, .44-40 Win., .45 Colt
Magazine: 14 rounds
Features: Grade V/VI black walnut stock with a metal "shotgun" butt-plate; color case-hardened receiver, lever, forearm cap and buttplate; drilled and tapped for peep sights; barrel is half round/half octagon, button rifled, and has a gloss blue finish
MSRP **$2119.99**

MODEL 1873 SHORT RIFLE

Action: Lever
Stock: Wood
Barrel: 20 in.
Sights: Adjustable
Weight: 7 lb. 4 oz.
Caliber: .357 Mag., .45 Colt, .44-40 Win.
Magazine: Under-barrel tube, 10 rounds
Features: Walnut straight grip stock with satin oil finish; classic rifle style forearm with blued steel cap; semi-buckhorn rear sight with Marble Arms gold bead front sights; steel loading gate; receiver rear tang drilled and tapped for optional tang-mounted rear sight
MSRP **$1389.99**

MODEL 1873 SHORT RIFLE COLOR CASE HARDENED

Action: Lever
Stock: Wood
Barrel: 20 in.
Sights: Adjustable

Weight: 7 lb. 4 oz.
Caliber: .357 Mag., .38 Spl., .44-40 Win., .45 Colt
Magazine: 10–11 rounds
Features: Steel receiver, color case hardened; steel loading gate; rear tang is drilled and tapped for scope mount; steel barrel, polished blued finish; full-length magazine tube; grade II/III walnut stock; straight grip; classic rifle-style forearm; steel forend cap; semi-buckhorn rear sight; Marble's gold bead front sight; color case hardened crescent buttplate, lever, forend cap, and loading gate
MSRP **$1679.99**

MODEL 1873 SPORTER OCTAGON COLOR CASE HARDENED

Action: Lever
Stock: Walnut
Barrel: 24 in.
Sights: Marble Arms gold bead front, semi-buckhorn rear
Weight: 8 lb.
Caliber: .357 Mag., .44-40 Win., .45 Colt
Magazine: 14 rounds
Features: Classic lever has octagon barrel; pistol grip Grade II/III walnut stock; top tang drilled and tapped for tang-mounted rear sight; crescent buttplate; deep-polished blue finish
MSRP **$1839.99**

MODEL 1885 LOW WALL HUNTER HIGH GRADE

Action: Lever
Stock: Walnut
Barrel: 24 in.
Sights: None
Weight: 7 lb. 8 oz.
Caliber: .22 Hornet, .222 Rem., .223

Rem., .243 Win., 6.5 Creedmoor,
Magazine: 1 rounds
Features: One of the prettiest single-shots around; full octagon barrel; Pachmayr Decelerator recoil pad; 22 lpi checkering; upgraded black walnut stock; drilled and tapped
MSRP **$1789.99**

MODEL 1886 DELUXE RIFLE CASE HARDENED

Action: Lever
Stock: Black walnut
Barrel: 24 in.
Sights: Hooded front, semi-buckhorn rear
Weight: 9 lb. 12 oz.
Caliber: .45-90 Win., .45-70 Gov't.
Magazine: 8 rounds
Features: Grade III/IV black walnut stock; color case-hardened receiver, crescent buttplate, forearm cap, lever, and lower tang; full octagon barrel in polished blue
MSRP **$1839.99**

MODEL 1886 SADDLE RING CARBINE

Action: Lever
Stock: Walnut
Barrel: 22 in.
Sights: Blade front, carbine ladder-style rear
Weight: 8 lb.
Caliber: .45-70 Gov't., .45-90 Win.
Magazine: 7 rounds
Features: A lever with some heft to soak up recoil; Grade I walnut stock; straight grip stock; carbine-style forend; round barrel in polished blue with barrel band; full-length magazine tube; saddle ring; drilled and tapped
MSRP **$1549.99**

Winchester Repeating Arms

WINCHESTER MODEL 1886 SHORT RIFLE

WINCHESTER MODEL 1892 CARBINE

WINCHESTER REPEATING ARMS MODEL 1892 DELUXE OCTAGON TAKEDOWN

WINCHESTER MODEL 1892 DELUXE TRAPPER TAKEDOWN CASE-HARDENED

WINCHESTER MODEL 1892 LARGE LOOP CARBINE

WINCHESTER REPEATING ARMS MODEL 1895 HIGH GRADE

WINCHESTER WILDCAT 22

WINCHESTER REPEATING ARMS WILDCAT 22 COMBO

MODEL 1886 SHORT RIFLE

Action: Lever
Stock: Walnut
Barrel: 20 in., 24 in.
Sights: Front with brass bead, adjustable rear
Weight: 8 lb. 6 oz.
Caliber: .45-70 Govt., .45-90 Win.
Magazine: Under-barrel tube, 8 rounds
Features: Deeply blued receiver and lever; end cap and steel crescent buttplate; straight grip
MSRP $1409.99

MODEL 1892 CARBINE

Action: Lever-action
Stock: Black walnut
Barrel: 20 in.
Sights: Marble Arms gold bead front, semi-buckhorn rear
Weight: 6 lb.
Caliber: .357 Mag., .44 Rem. Mag., .44-40 Win., .45 Colt
Magazine: 10 rounds
Features: Blued carbine strap buttplate; barrel band; saddle ring; straight-grip stock; top tang is drilled and tapped to add a peep sight
MSRP $1129.99

MODEL 1892 DELUXE OCTAGON TAKEDOWN

Action: Lever
Stock: Walnut
Barrel: 24 in.
Sights: Gold bead front, semi-buckhorn rear
Weight: 7 lb.
Caliber: .357 Mag., .44 Rem. Mag., .44-40 Win., .45 Colt
Magazine: 11 rounds
Features: Color case-hardened steel receiver; full octagon barrel in a polished blue finish; Grade V/VI walnut stock with steel shotgun buttplate; Marble Arms sights; top tang drilled for peep sight
MSRP $2199.99

MODEL 1892 DELUXE TRAPPER TAKEDOWN CASE-HARDENED

Action: Lever
Stock: Black walnut
Barrel: 16 in.
Sights: Hooded front, semi-buckhorn rear
Weight: 5 lb. 14 oz.
Caliber: .357 Mag., .44 Rem. Mag., .45 Colt
Magazine: 7 rounds
Features: Grade III/IV black walnut stock in an oil finish; full-octagon button-rifled barrel in polished blue; metal crescent buttplate, receiver, lever, and forearm cap in color case-hardened; drilled and tapped for peep sights
MSRP $1859.99

MODEL 1892 LARGE LOOP CARBINE

Action: Lever
Stock: Walnut
Barrel: 20 in.
Sights: Marble Arms brass bead front, adjustable rear
Weight: 6 lb.
Caliber: .357 Mag., .44 Rem. Mag., .44–40 Win., .45 Colt
Magazine: 10 rounds
Features: Classic saddle rifle with Grade I walnut; large loop with radiused edges; rebounding hammer, metal carbon buttplate; saddle ring; button rifled barrel with recessed crown
MSRP $1349.99

MODEL 1895 HIGH GRADE

Action: Lever
Stock: Walnut
Barrel: 24 in.
Sights: Gold bead front, buckhorn rear
Weight: 8 lb.

Caliber: .30-06 Spfd., .30-40 Krag, .405 Win.
Magazine: 4 rounds
Features: A classic lever with a box magazine; Grade III/IV in an oil finish with a straight grip and metal buttplate; Marble Arms sights; polished blue metalwork; schnabel forend; drilled and tapped for side-mount sight; traditional checkering
MSRP $1699.99

WILDCAT 22

Action: Semiautomatic
Stock: Polymer
Barrel: 18 in.
Sights: Ramped post front, adjustable ghost ring rear
Weight: 4 lb.
Caliber: .22 LR
Magazine: 10 rounds
Features: Super-fun plinker is super portable at just 4 pounds and has a number of innovative features such as a lower receiver that drops out at the push of a button; removeable rotary magazine; adjustable rear ghost sight; striker-fired mechanism; slide lock; top-side Picatinny rail and a second rail at fore-end tip; ambidextrous skeletonized stock in black or True Timber Strata camo
Black $269.99
Camo $309.99

WILDCAT 22 COMBO

Action: Semiautomatic
Stock: Composite
Barrel: 18 in.
Sights: Ramped post front, adjustable ghost ring rear
Weight: 4 lb.
Caliber: .22 LR
Magazine: 10 rounds
Features: Budget-friendly rimfire; reflex-style red-dot sight factory mounted on it composite receiver, stock, and integrated sling swivels; sporter contour barrel in matte blue; detachable magazine with dual ambidextrous releases and spring-assisted ejection; reversible manual safety; integral Picatinny rail
MSRP $309.99

RIFLES

Winchester Repeating Arms

WINCHESTER REPEATING ARMS WILDCAT SR

WINCHESTER REPEATING ARMS XPR COMPACT SCOPE COMBO

WINCHESTER XPR HUNTER MOSSY OAK ELEMENTS TERRA BAYOU

WINCHESTER XPR

WINCHESTER REPEATING ARMS XPR EXTREME HUNTER TRUETIMBER MIDNIGHT MB

WINCHESTER XPR COMPACT

WINCHESTER REPEATING ARMS XPR HUNTER MOSSY OAK DNA

RIFLES

WILDCAT SR

Action: Semiautomatic
Stock: Composite
Barrel: 16.5 in.
Sights: Ramped post front, adjustable ghost ring rear
Weight: 4 lb.
Caliber: .22 LR
Magazine: 10 rounds
Features: The "SR" stands for suppressor ready; composite receiver, stock, and integrated sling swivels; sporter contour barrel in matte blue; detachable magazine with dual ambidextrous releases and spring-assisted ejection; reversible manual safety; integral Picatinny rail
MSRP $299.99

XPR

Action: Bolt
Stock: Composite polymer
Barrel: 24 in., 26 in.
Sights: None
Weight: 7 lb.
Caliber: .243 Win., 7mm-08, .308 Win., .270 WSM, .300 WSM, .325 WSM, .270 Win., .30-06 Spfd., 7mm Rem. Mag., .300 Win. Mag., .338 Win. Mag., 6.5 Creedmoor, .350 Legend, .223 Rem., 6.5 PRC, 6.8 Western
Magazine: Detachable box, 3 rounds
Features: Chromoly steel barrel; matte blue finish; hardened steel components; recessed target-style crown; Inflex recoil pad
MSRP $569.99

XPR COMPACT

Action: Bolt
Stock: Composite
Barrel: 20 in., 22 in., 24 in.
Sights: None
Weight: 6 lb. 12 oz.–7 lb.

Caliber: .243 Win., 6.5 Creedmoor, 7mm-08 Rem., .308 Win., .270 WSM, .300 WSM, .325 WSM, .350 Legend, 6.5 PRC
Magazine: 3 rounds
Features: Shorter 13-in. length of pull; advanced polymer stock in black, matte blue metal finish; detachable box magazine
MSRP $569.00

XPR COMPACT SCOPE COMBO

Action: Bolt
Stock: Composite
Barrel: 20 in.
Sights: None
Weight: 6 lb. 12 oz.–7 lb.
Caliber: .243 Win., 6.5 Creedmoor, 7mm-08 Rem., .308 Win., .300 WSM, .270 WSM, .350 Legend, 6.5 PRC, 6.8 Western
Magazine: 3 rounds
Features: Package includes a rifle with a steel receiver in black Perma-Cote; free-floating barrel with a recessed crown in black Perma-Cote; 13-in. length of pull; Vortex Crossfire II 3–9x40 scope with BDC reticle; sling swivels; MOA trigger system; matte black stock
MSRP $759.99

XPR EXTREME HUNTER TRUETIMBER MIDNIGHT MB

Action: Bolt
Stock: Composite
Barrel: 22 in., 24 in., 26 in.
Sights: None
Weight: 6 lb. 12 oz.–7 lb.
Caliber: .223 Rem., .243 Win., 6.5 Creedmoor, 7mm-08 Rem., .308 Win., .350 Legend, 6.5 PRC, 6.8 Western, .270 WSM, .300 WSM, .270 Win., .30-06 Spfd., 7mm Rem. Mag., .300 Win. Mag.
Magazine: 3, 4, 5 rounds
Features: Steel receiver is drilled and tapped and appears in tungsten Cerakote; barrel is in tungsten

Cerakote, free-floating, has a recessed crown, is threaded 9/16x24, and has a muzzle brake; MOA trigger system; Inflex Technology recoil pad; detachable box magazine; stock is dressed in TrueTimber Midnight camo
MSRP $769.99

XPR HUNTER MOSSY OAK DNA

Action: Bolt
Stock: Composite
Barrel: 22 in., 24 in., 26 in.
Sights: None
Weight: 6 lb. 12 oz.–7 lb. 4 oz.
Caliber: .223 Rem., .243 Win., 6.5 Creedmoor, 7mm-08 Rem., .308 Win., .350 Legend, 6.5 PRC, 6.8 Western, .270 WSM, .300 WSM, .270 Win., .30-06 Spfd., 7mm Rem. Mag., .300 Win. Mag., .338 Win. Mag.
Magazine: 3, 4, 5 rounds
Features: Steel receiver is drilled and tapped and appears in matte black Perma-Cote; barrel is in matte black Perma-Cote, free-floating, and has a recessed crown; MOA trigger system; Inflex Technology recoil pad; detachable box magazine; stock is dressed in Mossy Oak DNA camo
MSRP $649.99

XPR HUNTER MOSSY OAK ELEMENTS TERRA BAYOU

Action: Bolt
Stock: Composite
Barrel: 22 in., 24 in., 26 in.
Sights: None
Weight: 6 lb. 12 oz.–7 lb. 4 oz.
Caliber: .243 Win., 7mm-08 Rem., .308 Win., .350 Legend, 6.5 PRC, .270 WSM, .300 WSM, .270 Win., .30-06 Spfd., 7mm Rem. Mag., .300 Win. Mag., .338 Win. Mag.
Magazine: 3, 4, 5 rounds
Features: Receiver, barrel, and bolt in flat dark earth Perma-Cote; M.O.A. trigger system; stock in full-coverage Mossy Oak Elements Terra Bayou camo pattern and with textured grip panels; Inflex Technology recoil pad
MSRP $649.00

Winchester Repeating Arms

WINCHESTER REPEATING ARMS XPR HUNTER SCOPE COMBO TRUE TIMBER STRATA

WINCHESTER XPR SCOPED COMBO

WINCHESTER XPR SR

WINCHESTER XPR HUNTER TRUE TIMBER STRATA

WINCHESTER XPR SPORTER

WINCHESTER XPR STEALTH SR

WINCHESTER XPR RENEGADE LONG-RANGE SR

XPR HUNTER SCOPE COMBO TRUE TIMBER STRATA

Action: Bolt
Stock: Composite
Barrel: 20 in., 22 in.
Sights: None
Weight: 6 lb. 12 oz.–7 lb.
Caliber: .270 WSM. .243 Win., 6.5 Creedmoor, 7mm-08 Rem., .300 WSM, .308 Win.
Magazine: 3 rounds
Features: Steel receiver is drilled and tapped and appears in flat dark earth Perma-Cote; barrel is in flat dark earth Perma-Cote, free-floating, has a recessed crown and muzzle brake; MOA trigger system; Inflex Technology recoil pad; 13-in length of pull stock is dressed in TrueTimber Strata camo; comes mounted with a Vortex Crossfire II 3–9x40 scope with BDC reticle; sling swivel studs
MSRP **$829.99**

XPR HUNTER TRUE TIMBER STRATA

Action: Bolt
Stock: Composite
Barrel: 22 in., 24 in., 26 in.
Sights: None
Weight: 6 lb. 12 oz.–7 lb. 4 oz.
Caliber: ..223 Rem., 243 Win, 6.5 Creedmoor, 7mm-08 Rem., .308 Win., .270 Win., .30-06 Spfd., 7mm Rem. Mag., .300 Win. Mag., .338 Win. Mag., .300 WSM, .270 WSM, .325 WSM, .350 Legend, 6.5 PRC, 6.8 Western
Magazine: 3 rounds
Features: The popular XPR bolt rifle with a stock dressed in True Timber Strata camo; Permacoat Flat Dark Earth metalwork finish; MOA trigger system
MSRP **$649.00**

XPR RENEGADE LONG-RANGE SR

Action: Bolt
Stock: Composite
Barrel: 22 in., 24 in.
Sights: None
Weight: 8 lb. 8 oz.
Caliber: .243 Win., 6.5 Creedmoor, 7mm-08 Rem., .308 Win., .270 WSM, .300 WSM, 6.5 PRC, 6.8 Western
Magazine: 3 rounds
Features: Advance Grayboe Renegade Long-Range stock with an upright grip profile, flattened forend, and undercut butt for bench use, as well as length-of-pull spacers; a button-rifled, fluted, free-floating barrel threaded and with a recessed target crown
MSRP **$1149.99**

XPR SCOPED COMBO

Action: Bolt
Stock: Composite
Barrel: 22 in., 24 in., 26 in.
Sights: None
Weight: 6 lb. 12 oz.–8 lb. 8 oz.
Caliber: .243 Win., 7mm-08 Rem., .308 Win., .350 Legend, 6.5 PRC, .270 WSM, .300 WSM, .325 WSM, .270 Win., .30-06 Spfd., 7mm Rem. Mag., .300 Win. Mag., .338 Win. Mag., 6.5 Creedmoor, 6.8 Western
Magazine: 3, 4 rounds
Features: Vortex Crossfire II 3–9x4mm scope with BDC reticle; Weaver-style rings and bases; Inflex Technology recoil pad; MOA trigger assembly; matte blue metalwork; free-floating button-rifled barrel with target crown
MSRP **$759.99**

XPR SPORTER

Action: Bolt
Stock: Walnut
Barrel: 22 in., 24 in., 26 in.
Sights: None
Weight: 6 lb. 12 oz.–7 lb. 4 oz.
Caliber: .243 Win., 6.5 Creedmoor, 7mm-08 Rem., .308 Win., .270 Win., .30-06 Spfd., 7mm Rem. Mag., .300 Win. Mag., .338 Win. Mag., .300 WSM, .270 WSM, .325 WSM, .350 Legend 6.5 PRC, 6.8 Western
Magazine: 3 rounds
Features: Button-rifled free-floating barrel; M.O.A. Trigger System; detachable box magazine; Inflex Technology recoil pad; metal is finished in matte black Perma-Cote
MSRP **$649.99**

XPR SR

Action: Bolt
Stock: Composite
Barrel: 20 in.
Sights: None
Weight: 6 lb. 12 oz.
Caliber: 6.5 Creedmoor, .243 Win., .308 Win., .30-06 Spfd., .300 Win. Mag., .350 Legend, .223 Rem., 6.5 PRC, 6.8 Western
Magazine: 3, 4, 5 rounds
Features: A suppressor-ready rifle for hunters with a sporter-contour, button-rifled, free-floating barrel threaded and with a recessed target crown; M.O.A. trigger assembly; Inflex Technology recoil pad; matte blue metalwork
MSRP **$699.99**

XPR STEALTH SR

Action: Bolt
Stock: Composite
Barrel: 16.5 in.
Sights: None
Weight: 6 lb. 8 oz.
Caliber: .223 Rem., .243 Win., 6.5 Creedmoor, 7mm-08 Rem., .308 Win., .250 Legend, 6.5 PRC, .270 WSM, .300 WSM, 6.8 Western
Magazine: 3, 4, 5 rounds
Features: A suppressor-ready rifle in a handy barrel length with a button-rifled, free-floating, threaded barrel in a black Perma-Cote finish and with a recessed target crown; dark-green composite stock; swivel studs
MSRP **$689.99**

Winchester Repeating Arms

WINCHESTER XPR THUMBHOLE VARMINT SUPPRESSOR READY

WINCHESTER REPEATING ARMS XPR TRUE TIMBER STRATA MB

XPR THUMBHOLE VARMINT SUPPRESSOR READY

Action: Bolt
Stock: Laminate
Barrel: 24 in.
Sights: None
Weight: 6 lb. 12 oz.
Caliber: .243 Win., 6.5 Creedmoor, .308 Win., .270 Win., .30-06 Spfd., .350 Legend, .223 Rem., 6.5 PRC, 6.8 Western
Magazine: 3 rounds
Features: Laminate thumbhole stock; raised cheekpiece; vented forearm

aids cooling; two front sling swivels accommodate sling and bipod simultaneously; metal is matte blue finished; barrel is threaded
MSRP $859.99

XPR TRUE TIMBER STRATA MB

Action: Bolt
Stock: Composite
Barrel: 22 in., 24 in., 26 in.
Sights: None
Weight: 6 lb. 12 oz.–7 lb.
Caliber: .223 Rem., .243 Win., 6.5 Creedmoor, 7mm-08 Rem., .308

Win., .350 Legend, 6.5 PRC, 6.8 Western, .270 WSM, .300 WSM, .270 Win., .30-06 Spfd., 7mm Rem. Mag., .300 Win. Mag.
Magazine: 3, 4, 5 rounds
Features: Steel receiver is drilled and tapped and appears in flat dark earth Perma-Cote; barrel is in flat dark earth Perma-Cote, threaded 9/16x24, free-floating, has a recessed crown and muzzle brake; MOA trigger system; Inflex Technology recoil pad; stock is dressed in TrueTimber Strata camo
MSRP $749.00

Windham Weaponry

WINDHAM WEAPONRY 6.5 CREEDMOOR

WINDHAM WEAPONRY 20-INCH WOOD GRAIN VEX

WINDHAM WEAPONRY .223 SUPERLIGHT

WINDHAM WEAPONRY .224 VALKYRIE

WINDHAM WEAPONRY .450 THUMPER

6.5 CREEDMOOR

Action: Semiautomatic
Stock: Synthetic
Barrel: 20 in.
Sights: None
Weight: 9 lb. 2 oz.
Caliber: 6.5 Creedmoor
Magazine: 5 rounds
Features: Fluted barrel with threaded muzzle; Luth-AR adjustable buttstock; Windham Weaponry free-floating handguard; Hogue overmolded beavertail grip; acres of optics/accessory rail; Hiperfire EDT3 Trigger; gas impingement system
MSRP $2056.00

20-INCH WOOD GRAIN VEX

Action: Semiautomatic
Stock: Synthetic
Barrel: 20 in.
Sights: None
Weight: 8 lb. 5 oz.
Caliber: .223 Rem.
Magazine: 5 rounds
Features: Standard A4 stock gets a

dipped wood grain finish, while the receiver gets a hardcoat anodized Coyote finish. Other features include a flattop upper with optic riser blocks; 15-in. M-LOK free-float handguard
MSRP $1544.00

.223 SUPERLIGHT

Action: Semiautomatic
Stock: Synthetic
Barrel: 16 in.
Sights: Flip-up front and rear
Weight: 6 lb.
Caliber: .223 Rem.
Magazine: 30 rounds
Features: Ultralight .223 MSR with a superlight barrel profile wearing a Melonite QPQ finish and A2 flash suppressor; Mission First Tactical Minimalist buttstock; mil-spec buffer tube; Mission First Tactical Engage pistol grip; Kriss flip-up sights
MSRP $1368.00

.224 VALKYRIE

Action: Semiautomatic
Stock: Synthetic
Barrel: 22 in.

Sights: None
Weight: 8 lb. 13 oz.
Caliber: .224 Valkyrie
Magazine: 5 rounds
Features: A gas impingement MSR designed specifically for the .224 Valkyrie round, with a fluted barrel threaded ½X28 and 1:7 right-hand twist; flat-top upper hard coat anodized; Luth-AR adjustable buttstock; 15-inch free-floating fore-end; Hogue overmolded beavertail pistol grip
MSRP $1800.00

.450 THUMPER

Action: Semiautomatic
Stock: Synthetic
Barrel: 16 in.
Sights: None
Weight: 7 lb. 3 oz.
Caliber: .450 Bushmaster
Magazine: 5 rounds
Features: Designed specifically for the straight-wall .450 Bushmaster, with Luth-AR adjustable buttstock; free-floating handguard with rail; Hogue overmolded beavertail pistol grip; chrome-lined barrel with A2 flash hider
MSRP $1608.00

Windham Weaponry

WINDHAM WEAPONRY R20FFTM-308

WINDHAM WEAPONRY RMCS-2 (MULTI-CALIBER SYSTEM) RIFLE KIT

WINDHAM WEAPONRY RMCS-3 (MULTI-CALIBER SYSTEM) RIFLE KIT

WINDHAM WEAPONRY RMCS-4 (MULTI-CALIBER SYSTEM) RIFLE KIT

R20FFTM-308

Action: Semiautomatic
Stock: Synthetic
Barrel: 20 in.
Sights: None
Weight: 9 lb. 0.8 oz.
Caliber: .308 Win.
Magazine: 5+1 rounds
Features: Magpul fixed length buttstock with multiple sling attachments; comfortable rubber recoil pad under which is a handy storage compartment; multiple attachment options for M-Lok accessory rails; internal heat shielding; Hogue overmolded rubber pistol grip; Mil Std 1913 Picatinny rails on both receiver and gas block
MSRP $1888.00

RMCS-2 (MULTI-CALIBER SYSTEM) RIFLE KIT

Action: Semiautomatic
Stock: Synthetic
Barrel: 16 in.
Sights: None
Weight: N/A
Caliber: .223 Rem./5.56 NATO–300 BLK
Magazine: 30 rounds
Features: Two calibers in the same AR platform by simply switching out the barrel; chrome-lined barrels; Mil Std 1913 railed gas block; receivers are CNC machined from forged 7075 T6 aircraft aluminum and finished in hardcoat black anodize; twist rates differ depending on barrel
MSRP $1738.00

RMCS-3 (MULTI-CALIBER SYSTEM) RIFLE KIT

Action: Semiautomatic
Stock: Synthetic
Barrel: 16 in.
Sights: None
Weight: N/A
Caliber: .223 Rem./5.56 NATO–300 BLK–7.62x36mm
Magazine: Standard 30 rd. for .223 Rem./5.56 NATO; standard Magpul for 7.62x39mm; standard Colt type Mag for 9mm
Features: Two calibers in the same AR platform by simply switching out the barrels and magazine wells; chrome-lined barrels; Mil Std 1913 railed gas block; receivers are CNC machined from forged 7075 T6 aircraft aluminum and finished in hardcoat black anodize; twist rates differ depending on barrel
MSRP $2391.00

RMCS-4 (MULTI-CALIBER SYSTEM) RIFLE KIT

Action: Semiautomatic
Stock: Synthetic
Barrel: 16 in.
Sights: None
Weight: N/A
Caliber: .223 Rem./5.56 NATO–300 BLK–7.62x36mm–9mm
Magazine: Standard 30 rd. for .223 Rem./5.56 NATO; standard Magpul for 7.62x39mm; standard Colt type Mag for 9mm
Features: Two calibers in the same AR platform by simply switching out the barrels and magazine wells; chrome-lined barrels; Mil Std 1913 railed gas block; receivers are CNC machined from forged 7075 T6 aircraft aluminum and finished in hardcoat black anodize; twist rates differ depending on barrel
MSRP $2971.00

RIFLES

AirForce Airguns

AIRFORCE AIRGUNS CONDOR

AIRFORCE AIRGUNS CONDOR SS

AIRFORCE AIRGUNS EDGE

AIRFORCE AIRGUNS ESCAPE

AIRFORCE AIRGUNS ESCAPE SS

AIRFORCE AIRGUNS ESCAPE UL

AIRFORCE AIRGUNS TALON P

AIRFORCE AIRGUNS TALON

AIRFORCE AIRGUNS TALON P CARBINE

CONDOR

Power: Pre-charged pneumatic, user adjustable
Stock: Composite
Overall Length: 38.7 in.
Sights: None
Weight: 6 lb. 8 oz.
Caliber: .25, .22, .20, .177
Features: Black, red, or blue composite stock; integral extended scope rail; detachable air tank; Lothar Walther barrel; pressure relief device; adjustable power; scopes optional
Spin-Loc: $879.95

CONDOR SS

Power: Compressed air
Stock: Composite
Overall Length: 38.125 in.
Sights: Open or optical may be installed
Weight: 6 lb. 2 oz.
Caliber: .177, .20, .22, .25
Features: CondorSS combines the major attributes of the TalonSS's quiet operation and the Condor's high power levels; new sound reduction technology; 18-inch barrel blue, red, or original black; 600–1300 fps; two-stage trigger; single shot
MSRP. $914.95

EDGE

Power: Pre-charged pneumatic
Stock: Composite
Overall Length: 35–40 in.
Sights: TS1 peep sight system
Weight: 6 lb. 2 oz.
Caliber: .177
Features: Ambidextrous cocking knob; regulated air system; adjustable length of pull; adjustable forend; hooded front sight only or front and rear sight available; two-stage adjust-

able trigger; composite stock in red or blue finish; scopes optional
Front sight only: $639.95
Front and rear sights:. $799.95

ESCAPE

Power: Compressed air
Stock: Synthetic
Overall Length: 34.5 in.–39 in.
Sights: Open or optical
Weight: 5 lb. 4.8 oz
Caliber: .22, .25
Features: Lothar Walther Barrels; Quick-Detach or Spin-Loc air tanks; lightweight and compact; geared for survival situations; user adjustable length
MSRP. $819.95

ESCAPE SS

Power: Compressed air
Stock: Synthetic
Overall Length: 27.75 in.–32.25 in.
Sights: Open or optical
Weight: 4 lb. 4.8 oz
Caliber: .22, .25
Features: Lothar Walther Barrels; Quick-Detach or Spin-Loc air tanks; lightweight and compact; geared for survival situations; user adjustable length; Sound-Loc sound reduction technology installed
MSRP. $809.95

ESCAPE UL

Power: Compressed air
Stock: Synthetic
Overall Length: 28.5 in.–33 in.
Sights: Open or optical
Weight: 4 lb. 4 oz
Caliber: .22, .25
Features: Lothar Walther Barrels; Quick-Detach or Spin-Loc air tanks; lightweight and compact; geared for survival situations; user adjustable length

MSRP. $754.95

TALON

Power: Compressed air
Stock: Composite
Overall Length: 32.6 in.
Sights: None
Weight: 5 lb. 8 oz.
Caliber: .25, .22, .20, .177
Features: Lothar Walther barrel; pressure relief device; adjustable power; detachable air tank; black composite stock; scopes optional
MSRP. $714.95

TALON P

Power: Compressed air
Stock: Composite
Overall Length: 24 in.
Sights: None
Weight: 3 lb. 8 oz.
Caliber: .25
Features: Designed to deliver over 50 ft.-lbs. of energy with a .25-caliber hunting pellet; integral extended scope rail; Lothar Walther barrels; variant with buttstock and moderator
MSRP. $569.95

TALON P CARBINE

Power: PCP
Stock: Synthetic
Barrel: 12 in.
Sights: None
Weight: 4 lb. 5 oz.
Caliber: .25
Magazine: 1 shot
Features: A single-shot PCP with adjustable power; pressure relief valve; two-stage adjustable trigger; moderator similar to the one on Airforce's LSS air rifles, which helps mitigate sound
MSRP. $839.95

AIRGUNS

AIRFORCE AIRGUNS TALON SS

AIRFORCE AIRGUNS TEXAN

AIRFORCE AIRGUNS TEXAN CF

AIRFORCE AIRGUNS TEXAN LSS

AIRFORCE AIRGUNS TEXAN LSS-CF

TALON SS

Power: Compressed air
Stock: Composite
Overall Length: 32.7 in.
Sights: None
Weight: 5 lb. 4 oz.
Caliber: .25, .22, .20, .177
Features: Improved sound reduction; Lothar Walther barrel; pressure relief device; adjustable power; detachable air tank; black, red, or blue composite stock; multiple mounting rails; two-stage trigger; innovative muzzle cap that strips away air turbulence and reduces discharge sound levels; scopes optional
MSRP $765.95

TEXAN

Power: Compressed air
Stock: Synthetic
Overall Length: 48 in.
Sights: Open or optical
Weight: 8 lb.
Caliber: .257, .308, .357, .457, .50
Features: With the ability to launch

.45 caliber projectiles at over 1000 feet per second and generating energy levels of over 500 foot pounds, the Texan takes its place as the world's most powerful production air rifle. Easy to load and simple to use, this Big Bore air rifle will let you focus on hunting with the knowledge you have enough power to get the job done.
MSRP $1214.95

TEXAN CF

Power: PCP
Stock: Synthetic
Barrel: 34 in.
Sights: None
Weight: 8 lb.
Caliber: .457, .50
Magazine: 1 shot
Features: Luthar Walther barrel; carbon fiber tank with pressure relief valve can be filled with compressed air or dried nitrogen to a max fill pressure of 3,625 psi; auto-safe upon cocking with side-lever
MSRP . . . . $1379.95–$1549.95

TEXAN LSS

Power: PCP
Stock: Synthetic
Barrel: 34 in.
Sights: None
Weight: 8 lb.
Caliber: .257, .308, .357, .457, .510
Magazine: N/A
Features: Capable of taking medium-sized game animals, this suppresses big-bore rifle features adjustable power; pressure relief device; side-cocking lever; two-stage position-adjustable trigger; automatic safety on cocking
MSRP . . . . $1254.95–$1399.95

TEXAN LSS-CF

Power: PCP
Stock: Synthetic
Barrel: 34 in.
Sights: None
Weight: 9 lb. 5 oz.
Caliber: .457, .50
Magazine: 1 shot
Features: A big-bore air rifle with a carbon fiber tank; Lothar Walther barrel; side-lever cocking; auto-safe upon cocking; two-stage adjustable trigger; adjustable power; pressure relief valve; TX2 valve
MSRP $1569.95

Air Venturi

AIR VENTURI AVENGER

AIR VENTURI M1A UNDERLEVER

AIR VENTURI V10 TARGET AIR PISTOL

AVENGER

Power: PCP
Stock: Synthetic
Barrel: 22.75 in.
Sights: None
Weight: 6 lb.
Caliber: .177, .22, .25
Magazine: 10 shots
Features: Features a regulator that can be adjusted externally; adjustable two-stage trigger; regulated and fill pressure gauges; fully shrouded barrel; scope rail tp, accessory rail at underside of forearm; pre-drilled holes for stud installation
MSRP $399.99

M1A UNDERLEVER

Power: Spring piston
Stock: Wood
Barrel: N/A
Sights: M1A iron sights
Weight: N/A
Caliber: .177, .22
Magazine: 1 shot
Features: With nearly the heft and balance of the real thing, this single-shot spring-piston air rifle has a forward-cocking underlever
MSRP $245.99

V10 TARGET AIR PISTOL

Power: Single-stroke pneumatic
Stock: Wood
Barrel: 8.26 in.
Sights: Blade ramp front, adjustable rear
Weight: 1 lb. 17 oz.
Caliber: .177
Magazine: 1 shot
Features: Competition-ready air pistol with a two-stage adjustable trigger; single-stroke pneumatic power plant; recoil and vibration free
MSRP $299.99

AIRGUNS

Anschütz (J.G. Anschütz)

ANSCHÜTZ 8001 CLUB

ANSCHÜTZ 9003
PREMIUM S2 PRECISE

ANSCHÜTZ 8001 JUNIOR

ANSCHÜTZ 9015
ONE

ANSCHÜTZ 8002 S2

8001 CLUB
Power: Compressed air
Stock: Walnut
Overall Length: 42.1 in.
Sights: Open, includes sight set 6834
Weight: 8 lb. 6 oz.
Caliber: .177
Features: Walnut stock with stippled checkering and non-stained aluminum or rubber buttplate; adjustable trigger; match grade barrel
MSRP $1999.99

8001 JUNIOR
Power: Compressed air
Stock: Laminate
Overall Length: 37.4 in.
Sights: Open, includes sight set 6834
Weight: 8 lb. 2 oz.
Caliber: .177
Features: Laminated wood in blue and orange with aluminum buttplate

stock; cylindrical match grade barrel; comes with accessory box
MSRP $1999.99

8002 S2
Power: Compressed air
Stock: Aluminum and synthetic pistol grip or laminated wood pistol grip
Overall Length: 42.1 in.
Sights: Open, includes sight set 6834
Weight: 10 lb. 2 oz.
Caliber: .177
Features: Aluminum stock in silver and blue with laminated wood or synthetic pistol grip; blue air cylinder; ProGrip cheekpiece and forend; includes accessory box; aluminum accessory rail
Wood: $2619.99

9003 PREMIUM S2 PRECISE
Power: Compressed air
Stock: Aluminum
Overall Length: 43.7 in.

Sights: Open, includes sight set 6834
Weight: 9 lb. 15 oz.
Caliber: .177
Features: Silver/black aluminum stock pistol grip; Soft Link shock absorber pads; adjustable forend stock, cheekpiece, and buttplate; includes plastic rifle case; steel match barrel; aluminum accessory rail on stock
MSRP $3183.29

9015 ONE
Power: Barreled action
Stock: Aluminum; stainless steel; carbon
Overall Length: 39 in.–47.2 in.
Sights: Adjustable
Weight: 10.1 lb.
Caliber: .177
Features: New patented 5065 4K trigger with ball bearings and versatile adjustable trigger blade; a stainless steel barrel unit; thin, special coated barrel extension; maintenance free stabilizer; air filter against pollutions; cocking lever mountable left and right; adjustable cheekpiece; scalloped grip
MSRP $5349.99

Beeman Precision Airguns

BEEMAN PRECISION
AIRGUNS 2027

BEEMAN PRECISION
AIRGUNS 10616,
10616GP

BEEMAN PRECISION
AIRGUNS CHIEF II

2027
Power: PCP
Stock: Wood
Barrel: N/A
Sights: Fiber optic front and rear
Weight: 3 lb. 12 oz.
Caliber: .177
Magazine: 12 shots
Features: Adjustable velocity target pistol with ergonomic wood stock; adjustable trigger; capable of 60 shots at 600 fps
MSRP $189.99

10616, 10616GP
Power: Spring piston
Stock: Synthetic
Barrel: N/A
Sights: Fiber optic front and rear
Weight: 8 lb. 8 oz.
Caliber: .177
Magazine: 1 shot
Features: A break-barrel air rifle that includes a 4x32 scope; automatic gas safety; available in gas ram; velocity of 1,200 fps with lead pellets; single cocking stroke
MSRP . . . . $159.99–$207.35

CHIEF II
Power: PCP
Stock: Wood
Barrel: 21.5 in.
Sights: Fiber optic front and rear
Weight: 6 lb. 14 oz.
Caliber: .177, .22
Magazine: 10 shots
Features: Similar to the Chief, but as a 10-shot repeating model; max velocity 1,000 fps; 50 shots per fill
MSRP . . . . $239.99–$259.99

AIRGUNS

Beeman Precision Airguns

BEEMAN PRECISION AIRGUNS COMMANDER

BEEMAN PRECISION AIRGUNS COMPETITION 1380

BEEMAN PRECISION AIRGUNS GRIZZLY X2 DUAL CALIBER

BEEMAN PRECISION AIRGUNS MARKSMAN 1018

BEEMAN PRECISION AIRGUNS MARKSMAN 2066

BEEMAN PRECISION AIRGUNS PCP UNDER-LEVER 1378

BEEMAN PRECISION AIRGUNS SILVER KODIAK X2 DC

BEEMAN PRECISION AIRGUNS TETON

BEEMAN PRECISION AIRGUNS WOLVERINE CARBINE

COMMANDER
Power: PCP
Stock: Wood
Barrel: 24.5 in.
Sights: Fiber optic front and rear
Weight: 10 lb. 1 oz.
Caliber: .177, .22
Magazine: 10 shots
Features: A more serious target rifle; bolt-action; rubber buttpad; 100 shots per fill max; max velocity 1,100 fps; integrated sound suppressor; ambidextrous hardwood thumbhole stock; include Beeman 5013 4x32mm scope and mounts
MSRP. $269.99

COMPETITION 1380
Power: PCP
Stock: Wood
Barrel: N/A
Sights: None
Weight: 9 lb.
Caliber: .177
Magazine: 1 shot
Features: Designed for regulation competition; fully adjustable two-stage trigger with dry-fire option; adjustable cheekpiece, buttstock, forearm, and grip; 200 shots per fill; side lever; integral manometer; meets ISSF requirements
MSRP. $1059.99

GRIZZLY X2 DUAL CALIBER
Power: Spring piston
Stock: Wood
Overall Length: 45.5 in.
Sights: Fixed and scope
Weight: 8 lb. 8 oz.

Caliber: .177, .22
Features: 4x32 scope and fiber optics sights; break barrel action; interchangeable barrels; available with case
MSRP. $179.99

MARKSMAN 1018
Power: Spring piston
Stock: Synthetic
Barrel: N/A
Sights: Fiber optic front and rear
Weight: 1 lb. 5 oz.
Caliber: .177, BB
Magazine: 18 shots
Features: Slide-cocking plinking air pistol with a smooth bore; 18-shot BB reservoir; fiber optic sights; a single shot with .177 pellets and bolts
MSRP. $34.99

MARKSMAN 2066
Power: Spring piston
Stock: Wood
Barrel: 18.5 in.
Sights: Fiber optic front and rear
Weight: 6 lb. 4 oz.
Caliber: .177, .22
Magazine: 1 shot
Features: A break-barrel single-shot that includes a noise suppressor; 4x32 scope with mounts; automatic safety
MSRP. $109.00

PCP UNDERLEVER 1378
Power: PCP
Stock: Wood
Barrel: N/A
Sights: Fiber optic front and rear
Weight: 7 lb. 4.5 oz.
Caliber: .177, .22
Magazine: 1 shot

Features: A unique underlever cocking design makes for faster shot-to-shot transition; supplied with scope
MSRP. $449.99

SILVER KODIAK X2 DC
Power: Break action, spring piston
Stock: All-weather synthetic
Overall Length: 47.5 in.
Sights: 3–9x32 or 4x32 scope
Weight: 8 lb. 12 oz.
Caliber: .177, .22
Features: Two airguns in one; satin nickel plated barrel and receiver; ported muzzle brake; 1000 fps max velocity
MSRP. $179.99

TETON
Power: Spring piston
Stock: Wood
Overall Length: 44.5 in.
Sights: Fixed and scope
Weight: 9 lb.
Caliber: .177, .22
Features: 4x32 scope and fiber optic sights; break barrel action; rifled barrel
MSRP. $169.99

WOLVERINE CARBINE
Power: Spring piston
Stock: Synthetic
Overall Length: 45.5 in.
Sights: Fixed and scope
Weight: 8 lb. 8 oz.
Caliber: .177, .22
Features: 4x32 scope and fiber optic sights; break barrel action; rifled barrel; rubber recoil pad
MSRP. $129.95

Bo Manufacture/Black Ops Soul

**BO MANUFACTURE/
THE BLACK OPS SOUL
LANGLEY**

**BO MANUFACTURE/
THE BLACK OPS SOUL
PENDLETON**

**BO MANUFACTURE
BLACK OPS
QUANTICO**

LANGLEY
Power: Spring piston
Stock: Synthetic
Barrel: 14.5 in.
Sights: Fiber optic front and rear
Weight: 3 lb. 15 oz.
Caliber: .177, .22
Magazine: 1 shot
Features: A lightweight break-barrel with fiber optic sights (adjustable rear); 21mm Picatinny rail; shrouded barrel; detachable polymer stock

transforms the air rifle to an air pistol
MSRP **$132.00**

PENDLETON
Power: Break barrel
Stock: Synthetic
Barrel: 18.8 in.
Sights: Fiber optic front and rear
Weight: 6 lb. 14 oz.
Caliber: .177
Magazine: 1 shot
Features: A break-barrel with an adjustable high-density polymer stock; acres of topside, side, and

bottom rails for optics and accessories; three sets of grip replacement modules
MSRP **$139.00**

QUANTICO
Power: Spring piston
Stock: Synthetic
Barrel: 18.8 in.
Sights: Fiber optic front, rear
Weight: 7 lb. 3 oz.
Caliber: .17, .22
Magazine: 1 shot
Features: Features a super-adjustable buttstock; top-side Picatinny rail
MSRP **$109.99**

BSA Guns

BSA DEFIANT

BSA R-10 TH

DEFIANT
Power: PCP
Stock: Walnut, laminate
Barrel: 18.5 in.
Sights: N/A
Weight: 9 lb.
Caliber: .177, .22

Magazine: 10 shots
Features: Ambidextrous stock that is adjustable, soft-touch cheekpiece, and magazine housing; pressure gauge with quick-fill design; barrel with shroud and integrated silencer
MSRP **$1599.00**

R-10 TH
Power: PCP

Stock: Walnut, laminate
Barrel: 15 in.
Sights: N/A
Weight: 8 lb.
Caliber: .177, .22
Magazine: 10 shots
Features: Ambidextrous thumbhole stock in maple or black pepper laminate; adjustable cheekpiece and adjustable buttstock; rotary numbered magazine with last shot indicator; fully regulated
MSRP **$1299.99**

Chiappa Firearms

CHIAPPA AG92

AG92
Power: CO2
Stock: Polymer
Barrel: 4.8 in.
Sights: Fixed front, windage adjustable rear
Weight: 1 lb. 4 oz.
Caliber: .177
Magazine: 14 shots
Features: A true double-/single-action air pistol replica of Beretta's iconic Model 92; automatic feed; pellets fed via seven-round cylinders
MSRP **$139.00**

AIRGUNS

Chiappa Firearms

CHIAPPA CHARGING RHINO DS AIRSOFT

CHIAPPA FAS 6004

CHIAPPA RHINO 50DS

CHARGING RHINO DS AIRSOFT
Power: CO2
Stock: Imitation wood
Barrel: 5 in.
Sights: Fixed fiber optic front, adjustable rear
Weight: 2 lb. 5 oz.
Caliber: 6mm
Magazine: 6 shots
Features: An airsoft revolver that arms via an active pedal; metal barrel and body; double-/single-action; active safety flag; active barrel lock pedal; in a black frame/white grip as a standard selection, or a white frame/black grip as a limited edition
MSRP . . . . Black/white: $229.00
White/black: $239.00

FAS 6004
Power: Break barrel
Stock: Wood
Barrel: 7.5 in.
Sights: Fixed front, adjustable rear
Weight: 2 lb.
Caliber: .177
Magazine: 1 shot
Features: A single-shot pneumatic air pistol for target shooters, with an ambidextrous walnut grip in non-target design or right-hand adjustable target grip; adjustable trigger; aluminum receiver; steel barrel in anodized black
Adjustable grip:. $443.00
Target grip: $569.00

RHINO 50DS
Power: CO2
Stock: Synthetic
Barrel: 5 in.
Sights: Fixed front, adjustable rear
Weight: 38.4 oz.
Caliber: 6mm, 4.5BB
Magazine: 6 shots
Features: A 6mm airsoft or 4.5 BB revolver with underlug accessory rail; double-/single-action; metalwork available in black, nickel, black/white, white/black
MSRP. . . . . $149.00–$239.00

Cometa (Carabinas Cometa, S.A.)

AIRFORCE AIRGUNS COMETA LYNX V10

AIRFORCE AIRGUNS COMETA ORION

LYNX V10
Power: PCP
Stock: Wood
Barrel: 18.5 in.
Sights: None
Weight: 7 lb. 14 oz.
Caliber: .177
Magazine: 1 shot
Features: Single-shot loading tray; 11mm dovetail grooves; adjustable power; two-stage adjustable trigger; ambidextrous stock with dual-raised cheekpieces; checkered grip and forearm; built-in manometer; manual safety
MSRP. $699.99

ORION
Power: PCP
Stock: Wood
Barrel: 18.5 in.
Sights: None
Weight: 7 lb. 4 oz.
Caliber: .177, .22, .25
Magazine: 17, 13, 11 shots
Features: A bolt-action PCP with a checkered hardwood stock; adjustable trigger; hammer-forged barrel; high-efficiency barrel shroud; integrated gauge; quick-fill port; adjustable cheekpiece
MSRP. $499.99

Crosman

CROSMAN 760 PUMPMASTER KIT

CROSMAN 1911

760 PUMPMASTER, PUMPMASTER KIT
Power: Pump
Stock: Synthetic
Barrel: N/A
Sights: Ramp blade front, adjustable rear
Weight: N/A
Caliber: BB, .177
Magazine: 18 shots
Features: In 2019, a total revamp of this tried and true airgun, with all new stock, trigger design, 1,000-shot BB reservoir, and easier to access loading port; stocks in turquoise blue, pink and, both available with optional scope; earth brown stock available for Canadian market; kits include 4X scope, Copperhead BBs, Crosman pellets, safety glasses, and targets
Air rifle only. $64.99
With scope. $64.99
Kit . . . . $64.99–$77.44

1911
Power: CO2
Stock: Polymer
Overall Length: 8 in.
Sights: Fixed
Weight: 1 lb. 14 oz.
Caliber: .177
Magazine: 6 rounds
Features: In traditional Colt 1911 style; polymer frame; metal slide; accessory rail; removable metal magazine with two six-round rotary clips; available in blue or stainless finishes
MSRP. $60.11

Crosman

CROSMAN AIRMASTER

CROSMAN BENJAMIN 392S

CROSMAN BENJAMIN 397S

CROSMAN BENJAMIN AKELA

CROSMAN BENJAMIN CAYDEN

CROSMAN BENJAMIN ARMADA

CROSMAN BENJAMIN BULLDOG .357

CROSMAN BENJAMIN DISCOVERY

CROSMAN BENJAMIN FORTITUDE GEN 2

AIRMASTER
Power: Variable pump
Stock: Synthetic
Overall length: 39.75 in.
Sights: Fiber optic front, adjustable rear
Weight: 4 lb. 12 oz.
Caliber: BB, .177
Features: Variable pump; rifled steel barrel; single-stage trigger; crossbolt safety; 4x15mm scope; optional kit includes metal swinging target, 500 pellets, 1,500 BBs, and safety glasses
MSRP...................$110.44

BENJAMIN 392S
Power: Variable pump
Stock: Synthetic
Barrel: 19.25 in.
Sights: Fixed front, adjustable rear
Weight: 5 lb. 8 oz.
Caliber: .22
Magazine: 1 shot
Features: Good for plinking or small game, this favorite in the Benjamin lineup gets a new all-weather synthetic stock; fully rifled brass barrel; easier-to-pump forearm
MSRP...................$236.77

BENJAMIN 397S
Power: Variable pump
Stock: Synthetic
Barrel: 19.25 in.
Sights: Fixed front, adjustable rear
Weight: 5 lb. 8 oz.
Caliber: .177
Magazine: 1 shot
Features: An old favorite gets a new look with an all-weather synthetic stock; fully rifled brass barrel; easier-to-pump forearm
MSRP...................$236.77

BENJAMIN AKELA
Power: PCP
Stock: Turkish walnut
Barrel: N/A
Sights: None
Weight: 7 lb. 11 oz.
Caliber: .22
Magazine: 12 shots
Features: Similar to the Cayden model, but with a slightly lighter and more compact bullpup stock with texturing at the grip area
MSRP................. $632.00

BENJAMIN ARMADA
Power: Multi-shot pneumatic, bolt
Stock: Synthetic
Overall Length: 42 in.
Sights: None
Weight: 7 lb. 5 oz.
Caliber: .177, .22, .25
Features: Modular, versatile design; backwards compatible with Mil-Spec AR-15 grips and stocks; machined receiver featuring 5 inches of Picatinny rail space; delivers over 30 consistent shots per fill (up to 16 in .25 cal); bolt action is reversible; integrated resonance dampener; 10-round magazine delivers fast follow up shots (8-rd magazine in .25 cal); rifled barrel, choked and shrouded; optics and bipod not included
MSRP................. $959.03

BENJAMIN BULLDOG .357
Power: Multi-shot pneumatic, bolt
Stock: Synthetic
Overall Length: 36 in.
Sights: None
Weight: 7 lb. 11 oz.
Caliber: .357
Features: Bullpup configuration; 26

inches of picatinny rail; Baffle-less SoundTrap shroud for big bore sound suppression; sidelever bolt reversible for left hand shooters; intuitive, easy to load 5-shot magazine; reversible bolt; 10 shots per fill
Airgun only: $949.99
Value pack: $1349.99

BENJAMIN CAYDEN
Power: PCP
Stock: Turkish walnut
Barrel: N/A
Sights: None
Weight: 7 lb. 15 oz.
Caliber: .22
Magazine: 12 shots
Features: Bolt-action operation with a two-stage trigger; rotary magazine; rifled steel barrel; sling swivel studs; side cocking lever; adjustable trigger shoe; adjustable cheekpiece
MSRP...................$632.00

BENJAMIN DISCOVERY
Power: Dual fuel compressed air
Stock: Walnut
Overall Length: 39 in.
Sights: Fiber optic front, adjustable rear
Weight: 5 lb. 2 oz.–5 lb. 3 oz.
Caliber: .22, .177
Features: Rifled steel barrel; velocity up to 900 fps; cross-bolt safety; built-in pressure gauge; high pressure pump included
MSRP................. $279.95

BENJAMIN FORTITUDE GEN 2
Power: PCP
Stock: Synthetic
Barrel: N/A
Sights: None
Weight: N/A
Caliber: .177, .22
Magazine: 10 shots
Features: Cocking force is light; rotary magazine; 3,000 psi regulated pressure gauge; shrouded barrel; suppressor; rifled barrel
MSRP................. $455.70

CROSMAN BENJAMIN IRONHIDE

CROSMAN BENJAMIN KRATOS

CROSMAN BENJAMIN MARAUDER

CROSMAN BENJAMIN MARAUDER LOTHAR BARREL

CROSMAN BENJAMIN MARAUDER SEMI-AUTOMATIC

CROSMAN CHALLENGER PCP

CROSMAN BENJAMIN TRAIL NP2

CROSMAN BENJAMIN VAPORIZER

CROSMAN BENJAMIN MPW

BENJAMIN IRONHIDE

Power: Gas piston
Stock: Synthetic
Overall Length: N/A
Sights: Fixed front, adjustable open rear
Weight: 10 lb.
Caliber: .177, .22
Magazine: 1 round
Features: Thumbhole-stocked break-barre; two-stage adjustable trigger; SBD Gold Sound Suppression; CenterPoint 3–9x40mm scope
MSRP.................$191.83

BENJAMIN KRATOS

Power: PCP
Stock: Turkish walnut
Barrel: N/A
Sights: None
Weight: 8 lb. 3 oz.
Caliber: .22, .25
Magazine: 10, 12 shots
Features: Similar to the Cayden model with a different powerplant arrangement and availability in .25
MSRP.................$664.00

BENJAMIN MARAUDER

Power: Compressed air
Stock: Wood
Overall Length: 42.8 in.
Sights: None
Weight: 8 lb. 3 oz.
Caliber: .177, .22, .25
Features: Bolt action; ten round magazine; reversable bolt; dovetail mounting rail; available in wood, black synthetic, and Realtree Max1, Realtree Xtra, and Muddy Girl camo stocks
MSRP..........$695.16–$769.99

BENJAMIN MARAUDER LOTHAR BARREL

Power: PCP
Stock: Wood
Barrel: N/A
Sights: None
Weight: N/A
Caliber: .177, .22
Magazine: 10 shots
Features: Adjustable cheekpiece; rifled barrel; reversible bolt handle; Picatinny breech; Lothar Walther barrel; multi-shot bolt-action
MSRP.................$609.99

BENJAMIN MARAUDER SEMI-AUTOMATIC

Power: PCP
Stock: Hardwood
Barrel: N/A
Sights: None
Weight: 8 lb. 3 oz.
Caliber: .22
Magazine: 10 shots
Features: Semiautomatic air rifle; ambidextrous charging handle; shrouded rifled barrel with resonance damper; regulated for 60 shots per fill; adjustable cheekpiece on hardwood stock; auto-indexing magazine is backwards compatible
MSRP.................$736.00

BENJAMIN TRAIL NP2

Power: NP2 nitro piston
Stock: Synthetic or wood
Overall Length: 46.25 in.
Sights: CenterPoint 3–9x32mm scope
Weight: 8 lb. 5 oz.
Caliber: .177
Features: Break barrel; first to feature new NP2 power system; enhanced Clean Break Trigger; integrated sound

suppression system; shoots up to 1200 fps alloy, 900 fps pellet
MSRP.................$339.99

BENJAMIN VAPORIZER

Power: Gas piston
Stock: Synthetic
Overall Length: N/A
Sights: Fixed front sight, adjustable rear
Weight: 10 lb.
Caliber: .177, .22
Magazine: 1 round
Features: Crosman's SBD Gold Sound Suppression; synthetic stock with soft-touch inserts; Picatinny rail; CenterPoint 3–9x40mm scope
MSRP.................$240.65–

BUSHMASTER MPW

Power: CO2
Stock: Synthetic
Barrel: N/A
Sights: Red dot
Weight: N/A
Caliber: BB
Magazine: 25 shots
Features: An AR-style CO2 BB gun with adjustable buttstock; quad rail forearm; red dot sight; full-auto and semiauto modes; 25-round drop magazine; can be customized with AR-compatible buffer tubes and grips; speedloader included
MSRP.................$245.93

CHALLENGER PCP

Power: Pneumatic pump and CO2
Stock: Synthetic
Overall Length: 41.5 in.
Sights: Open
Weight: 7 lb. 2 oz.
Caliber: .177
Features: Two-stage match grade adjustable trigger; Lothar Walther barrel; adjustable cheekpiece and buttpiece; black synthetic stock; 11mm scope mount rails; ambidextrous
Without sights...........$800.75
Sights.................$915.16

Crosman

CROSMAN CLASSIC 1911 PISTOL KIT

CROSMAN CLASSIC 2100

CROSMAN DIAMONDBACK

CROSMAN COWBOY

CROSMAN FULL AUTO R1

CROSMAN DPMS CLASSIC M4 NITRO PISTON

CROSMAN M4-177

CROSMAN FURY NP

CLASSIC 1911 PISTOL KIT

Power: CO2
Stock: Synthetic
Barrel: 5 in.
Sights: Low-profile blade front, notch rear
Weight: N/A
Caliber: BB
Magazine: N/A
Features: A full-size 1911-type BB pistol with textured grip; skeletonized trigger; under rail; tan frame with black slide and grips; comes with targets and 250 BBs
MSRP **$36.96**

CLASSIC 2100

Power: Pneumatic pump
Stock: Synthetic
Overall Length: 39.75 in.
Sights: Visible impact front, adjustable rear
Weight: 4 lb. 13 oz.
Caliber: .177
Features: Cross-bolt safety; BB up to 755 fps, pellet up to 725 fps
Airgun only **$89.99**
With scope **$83.44**

COWBOY

Power: Lever
Stock: Wood
Barrel: N/A
Sights: Ramp blade front, adjustable rear
Weight: N/A
Caliber: BB
Magazine: 1 shot
Features: Have your kid watch a couple John Wayne movies, then buy

them this fun lever BB gun with a ratcheted lever that locks to prevent pinched fingers during cocking; all-metal receiver; hardwood stock
MSRP **$39.99**

DIAMONDBACK

Power: Gas piston
Stock: Synthetic
Overall Length: N/A
Sights: Fixed front sight, adjustable rear
Weight: N/A
Caliber: .177, .22
Magazine: 1 round
Features: Sturdy pistol grip stock; rifled barrel; SBD Gold Sound Suppression; CenterPoint 4x32mm scope
MSRP . . . . **$161.28–$177.31**

DPMS CLASSIC M4 NITRO PISTON

Power: Nitro Piston 2
Stock: Synthetic
Overall length: 40 in.
Sights: None
Weight: 5 lb. 12.8 oz.
Caliber: .177
Features: Break-barrel action modeled after DPMS A4 platform; two-stage adjustable trigger; Picatinny rail; CenterPoint 4x32mm scope included
MSRP **$265.48**

FULL AUTO R1

Power: C02
Stock: Nylon fiber
Barrel: N/A
Sights: Reflex red-dot
Weight: 6 lb.
Caliber: .177
Magazine: 25 shots

Features: This "MSR" utilizes two 12-gram CO2 cartridges to empty the 25-round magazine of its BBs in no time at all—1,400 rounds per minute, in fact; six-position adjustable buttstock; rails for light and laser add-ons; smooth bore
MSRP **$189.99**

FURY NP

Power: Break action Nitro Piston
Stock: Synthetic all-weather
Overall Length: 45 in.
Sights: 4X32mm scope; rifled sights
Weight: 6 lb. 6 oz.
Caliber: .177
Features: Velocities up to 1200 fps; rifled steel barrel; adjustable two-stage trigger; Nitro Piston technology delivers smooth cocking, reduced vibration and shoots with 70 percent less noise
Scope: **$139.99**

M4-177

Power: Multi-pump pneumatic
Stock: Synthetic
Length: 34 in.
Sights: Adjustable front and rear
Weight: 3 lb. 9 oz.
Caliber: .177
Features: Rifled steel barrel; shoots both pellets and BBs; variable pump action easy to use for right- or lefthanded shooters; Picatinny rails; front and rear sights and stock are removable for upgrades; adjustable stock; velocities up to 660 fps with BBs and 625 fps with 7.9gr, .177 caliber pellets
MSRP . . . . **$72.30–$83.00**

AIRGUNS

Crosman

CROSMAN MAG-FIRE ULTRA

CROSMAN MAKO

CROSMAN MAXIMUS

CROSMAN MK45

CROSMAN NIGHT STALKER

CROSMAN OPTIMUS

CROSMAN P10KT

CROSMAN REMINGTON 1875

CROSMAN REMINGTON R1100 PUMP RIFLE

CROSMAN REPEATAIR 1077

MAG-FIRE ULTRA

Power: Break barrel
Stock: Synthetic
Barrel: N/A
Sights: Blade front, adjustable rear
Weight: 9 lb. 14 oz.
Caliber: .177, .22
Magazine: 12 shots
Features: Rifled/overmolded barrel; Quietfire sound suppression technology; 3–9x40 adjustable objective scope; Picatinny rail
MSRP $228.82

MAKO

Power: CO2
Stock: Synthetic
Overall Length: 8.56 in.
Sights: Fiber optic front and rear
Weight: 1 lb. 11 oz.
Caliber: BB
Magazine: 20 rounds
Features: Designed based on the Beretta Model 92; tri-color look; finger grips on the front strap; removable backstraps; accessory rail
MSRP $71.63

MAXIMUS

Power: Bolt
Stock: Synthetic
Overall Length: N/A
Sights: Fiber optic front and rear
Weight: N/A
Caliber: .22, .177
Features: Easy filling 2000 PSI reservoir; rifled barrel; up to 30 effective shots per fill
Airgun only $219.99
With scope $263.87

MK45

Power: CO2
Stock: Synthetic
Overall Length: 7.5 in.
Sights: Fixed blade front, notch rear

Weight: N/A
Caliber: BB
Magazine: 20 rounds
Features: Removable grip makes CO2 cartridge loading easy; tan with a black grip; accessory rail
MSRP $42.83

NIGHT STALKER

Power: CO2
Stock: Synthetic
Barrel: N/A
Sights: Low-profile blade front, notch rear, laser
Weight: N/A
Caliber: BB
Magazine: 18 shots
Features: A Walther lookalike with a built-in red laser; 18-shot BB magazine; blowback action
MSRP $120.22

OPTIMUS

Power: Break action
Stock: Hardwood
Overall Length: 43 in.
Sights: 4x32mm CenterPoint scope
Weight: 6 lb. 8 oz.
Caliber: .177, .22
Features: Ambidextrous hardwood stock; relatively light cocking force and a two-stage adjustable trigger; barrel incorporates a micro-adjustable rear sight and fiber optic front sight; .177 also available without scope
MSRP $164.73

P10KT

Power: CO2
Stock: Synthetic
Overall Length: 6.9 in.
Sights: Fixed blade front, notch rear
Weight: 1 lb. 1.6 oz.
Caliber: BB
Magazine: 20 rounds
Features: Steel barrel; grip removes

for CO2 cartridge replacement; accessory rail
MSRP $49.99

REMINGTON 1875

Power: CO2
Stock: Faux ivory
Overall length: 13.125 in.
Sights: Fixed blade front, fixed notch rear
Weight: 2 lb. 4.8 oz.
Caliber: BB, .177
Features: Replica of Remington 1875 revolver; single-action; functional hammer, load gate, and extractor; nickel finish
MSRP $144.95

REMINGTON R1100 PUMP RIFLE

Power: Pump
Stock: Synthetic
Barrel: N/A
Sights: Blade front, adjustable rear
Weight: N/A
Caliber: BB, .177
Magazine: 1 shot
Features: A variable speed pump (more pumps equal more velocity) in a shotgun-style stock of youth proportions
MSRP $61.76

REPEATAIR 1077

Power: CO2
Stock: All-weather, synthetic, wood
Overall Length: 36.88 in.
Sight: Fiber optic front, adjustable rear
Weight: 3 lb. 11 oz.
Caliber: .177
Features: Exclusive 12-shot rotary pellet clip lets you shoot longer; maximum velocity 625 fps; cross-bolt safety
Synthetic $78.92
Wood $136.13

Crosman

CROSMAN SILVER FOX NITRO PISTON

CROSMAN THRASHER

CROSMAN TRAIL MARK II NP PISTOL

CROSMAN TRIPLE THREAT

CROSMAN TYRO

CROSMAN VALIANT

CROSMAN VANTAGE NP

SILVER FOX NITRO PISTON
Power: Nitro Piston
Stock: Synthetic
Overall length: 43.5 in.
Sights: None
Weight: 6 lb.
Caliber: .177, .22
Features: Break-barrel action; dovetail mounting rail; two-stage trigger; CenterPoint 4x32mm scope
MSRP **$199.99**

THRASHER
Power: Gas piston
Stock: Synthetic
Overall Length: 45.5 in.
Sights: Fixed front, adjustable rear
Weight: 8 lb. 5 oz.
Caliber: .22
Magazine: 1 round
Features: Skeleton stock; rifled barrel; two-stage adjustable trigger; CenterPoint 4x32mm scope
MSRP **$184.99**

TRAIL MARK II NP PISTOL
Power: Nitro Piston
Stock: Synthetic
Overall length: N/A
Sights: Fiber optic front, adjustable notch rear
Weight: 3 lb. 7 oz.
Caliber: .177

Features: Break-barrel action; rifled steel barrel; tactical frame; removable cocking aid
MSRP **$123.99**

TRIPLE THREAT
Power: CO2
Stock: Polymer
Barrel: 3 in., 6 in., 8 in.
Sights: Ramp front, adjustable rear
Weight: N/A
Caliber: BB, .177
Magazine: 6, 10 shots
Features: A fun CO2 revolver with three barrels, all with vent ribs and rifled; grips remove to replace CO2 cartridge; 10-shot pellet clip; 6-shot BB clip
MSRP **$120.22**

TYRO
Power: Spring
Stock: Synthetic
Overall Length: 30.5 in.–32.75 in.
Sights: Fiber optic front, adjustable rear
Weight: 5 lb.
Caliber: .177
Magazine: 1 round
Features: Designed for younger shooters; soft shooting; ambidextrous stock with a number of spacers to adjust for length of pull
MSRP **$83.44**

VALIANT
Power: Gas piston
Stock: Wood
Overall Length: N/A
Sights: Fixed front sight, adjustable rear
Weight: 6 lb. 4 oz.
Caliber: .177, .22
Magazine: 1 round
Features: Ambidextrous thumbhole stock of hardwood; two-stage adjustable trigger; CenterPoint 4x32mm scope
MSRP . . . . **$177.31–$188.71**

VANTAGE NP
Power: Break action
Stock: Hardwood
Length: 45 in.
Sights: Fiber optic front, adjustable rear 4x32mm scope included
Weight: 7 lb. 2 oz.
Caliber: .177, .22
Features: Crosman's own version of the Bantage NP; hardwood stock; fiber optic front sight and fully adjustable rear sight; .177-caliber comes with scope; .22-caliber only with fiber optic sights and 11mm dovetail groove for optics mounting
.177 . . . .**$188.71**
.22 . . . .**$124.62**

Daisy

DAISY MODEL 599 COMPETITION

MODEL 599 COMPETITION
Power: PCP
Stock: Beechwood

Barrel: N/A
Sights: Hooded front, diopter rear
Weight: N/A
Caliber: .177
Magazine: 1 shot
Features: Competition ready air rifle with integral dovetail scope rail; sling

rail; pressure gauge; adjustable stock; position and weight adjustable trigger; cold hammer forged BSA barrel; straight-pull T handle
MSRP **$595.00**

DAISY POWERLINE MODEL 880

DAISY POWERLINE MODEL 901

POWERLINE MODEL 880

Power: Multi-pump pneumatic
Stock: Molded wood grain
Overall Length: 37.6 in.
Sights: TruGlo fiber optic front, adjustable rear
Weight: 3 lb. 11 oz.
Caliber: .177
Features: Wood-grained, Monte Carlo stock and forearm; rifled steel barrel; cross-bolt trigger block; velocity up to 750 fps; engineering resin with dovetail mount for scope

Airgun only $54.90
With scope. $60.50
Shadow Plus kit $65.90
Powerline scope kit $87.90

POWERLINE MODEL 901

Power: Multi-pump pneumatic
Stock: Composite
Overall Length: 37.5 in.
Sights: Fiber optic front, adjustable rear
Weight: 3 lb. 11 oz.
Caliber: .177
Features: Rifled steel barrel; black advanced composite stock; dovetail mounts for optics

Airgun only $71.40
Kit $82.50

DIANA Mayer & Grammelspacher

AIR VENTURI DIANA STORMRIDER

STORMRIDER

Power: PCP
Stock: Wood
Barrel: 19 in.
Sights: Blade front, adjustable leaf rear
Weight: 5 lb.
Caliber: .177, .22

Magazine: 7, 9 shots
Features: Bolt-action repeater with a checkered beech stock; two-stage adjustable trigger; integrated pressure gauge; 11mm dovetail; rotary magazine and single-shot tray; Air Venturi G9 pump; barrel shroud
MSRP. $449.98

FX Airguns

FX AIRGUNS CROWN MKII

FX AIRGUNS DREAMLINE CLASSIC

CROWN MKII

Power: PCP
Stock: Wood, laminate, synthetic
Barrel: 14.96 in., 19.69 in., 23.62 in., 27.56 in.
Sights: None
Weight: 6 lb. 3 oz.–9 lb. 9 oz.
Caliber: .177, .22, .25, .30
Magazine: 22, 18, 16, 13 shots
Features: Ambidextrous thumbhole stock paired with a fully-shrouded barrel; interchangeable calibers via barrel liners; rigid breech block; externally adjustable AMP; adjustable hammer spring; three-step transfer port adjustment; 480cc carbon fiber air cylinder; dual pressure gauges; STX fully barrel with built-in shroud; switch-style safety; Picatinny optics rail with 20 MOA angle; two-stage adjustable match trigger; adjustable buttpad; multiple stock/barrel/caliber choices
MSRP. . . . . $1799.99–$1849.99

DREAMLINE CLASSIC

Power: PCP
Stock: Walnut
Barrel: 19.69 in., 23.62 in.
Sights: None
Weight: 6 lb. 4 oz.
Caliber: .177, .22, .25, .30
Magazine: 22, 18, 16, 13 shots
Features: Removable rotary magazine; ambidextrous stock; match-grade free-floating Twist X barrel; 11mm dovetail optics mount; interchangeable caliber barrel liner system; externally adjustable AMP regulator; fixed DonnyFL moderator; adjustable hammer weight; two-stage adjustable trigger
MSRP. $1249.99

AIRGUNS

FX Airguns

FX AIRGUNS DREAMLINE LITE

FX AIRGUNS DREAMLINE TACTICAL

FX AIRGUNS DREAMLINE LITE COMPACT

FX AIRGUNS DREAMLINE TACTICAL COMPACT

FX AIRGUNS IMPACT X MKII

FX AIRGUNS MAVERICK SNIPER

FX AIRGUNS ROYALE 400

DREAMLINE LITE
Power: PCP
Stock: Synthetic
Barrel: 19.69 in., 23.62 in.
Sights: None
Weight: 5 lb. 8 oz.
Caliber: .177, .22, .25, .30
Magazine: 22, 18, 16, 13 shots
Features: Skeletonized buttstock; lightweight trigger guard with integrated rail; threaded FX Smooth Twist X match-grade, free-floating barrel; interchangeable barrel liner system; externally adjustable AMP regulator; adjustable match trigger; side-lever cocking system; 11mm dovetail scope mount; Hogue AR grip; DonnyFL and Huggett moderators, hard case, and bottle upgrades available
MSRP **$1299.99**

DREAMLINE LITE COMPACT
Power: PCP
Stock: Synthetic
Barrel: 15.75 in., 19.29 in.
Sights: None
Weight: 5 lb. 1 oz.
Caliber: .177, .22, .25
Magazine: 22, 18, 16 shots
Features: Similar to the standard lite, but without the .30-caliber option and with shorter barrel options; side-lever cocking action; DonnyFL moderator and bottle options available
MSRP . . . . **$1149.99–$1349.99**

DREAMLINE TACTICAL
Power: PCP
Stock: Synthetic
Barrel: 19.69 in., 23.62 in.
Sights: None
Weight: 6 lb.–7 lb. 15 oz.

Caliber: .177, .22, .25, .30
Magazine: 22, 18, 16, 13 shots
Features: Similar to the Dreamline Lite, but with a Hogue mil-spec buttstock, Hogue grip; bottle, stock color, six-position buffer tube, DonnyFL moderator and hard case upgrades available
MSRP . . . . **$1149.99–$1784.95**

DREAMLINE TACTICAL COMPACT
Power: PCP
Stock: Synthetic
Barrel: 15.75 in., 19.29 in.
Sights: None
Weight: 6 lb.–7 lb. 7 oz.
Caliber: .177, .22, .25
Magazine: 22, 18, 16 shots
Features: Similar to the standard Tactical, but without the .30-caliber option and with shorter barrel options; DonnyFL moderator, buffer tube/stock, and bottle options available
MSRP . . . . **$1249.99–$1704.95**

IMPACT X MKII
Power: PCP
Stock: Synthetic
Barrel: 19.69 in., 23.62 in., 31.50 in.
Sights: None
Weight: 6 lb. 9 oz.
Caliber: .177, .22, .25, .30, .35
Magazine: 38, 28, 28, 23, 18 shots
Features: Completely adjustable including hammer spring tension and air valve control; FX Smooth Twist X barrel with interchangeable liner system; side-cocking lever; power upgrade with FX Power Plenum; in a 9mm (.35) with 500cc bottle and 800mm barrel; Sniper with 700mm

barrel; Compact with a 300cc bottle and shorter barrel; choice of black or bronze receiver
MSRP **$2199.99**

MAVERICK SNIPER
Power: PCP
Stock: Synthetic
Barrel: 27.56 in.
Sights: None
Weight: 7 lb. 3 oz.
Caliber: .22, .25, .30
Magazine: 18, 16, 13 shots
Features: A side-lever repeater that utilizes side-shot magazines; ½-in. UNF threaded Superior STX barrel; adjustable match trigger; Picatinny optics; textured AR-style grip; dual pressure gauges; 580cc carbon fiber air cylinder; dual AMP regulators
MSRP . . . . **$1799.99–$1914.97**

ROYALE 400
Power: PCP
Stock: Synthetic, walnut, laminate
Barrel: 19.69 in.
Sights: None
Weight: 7 lb.–7 lb. 7 oz.
Caliber: .177, .22
Magazine: 16, 14 shots
Features: Side-lever repeater; thumbhole stock in choice of synthetic (adjustable recoil pad), laminate, or walnut (adjustable recoil pad and ambidextrous); adjustable match trigger; 11mm dovetail scope mount; shrouded muzzle; match-grade free-floating FX Smooth Twist barrel; manual safety
MSRP . . . . **$1599.99–$1799.99**

AIRGUNS

FX Airguns

FX AIRGUNS ROYALE 500

FX AIRGUNS WILDCAT MKIII COMPACT

FX AIRGUNS WILDCAT MKIII SNIPER

ROYALE 500

Power: PCP
Stock: Synthetic, walnut, laminate
Barrel: 23.62 in.
Sights: None
Weight: 7 lb.–7 lb. 7 oz.
Caliber: .25
Magazine: 11 shots
Features: Similar to the 400, but in .25 caliber and with a longer barrel
MSRP . . . . **$1599.99–$1799.99**

WILDCAT MKIII COMPACT

Power: PCP
Stock: Synthetic
Barrel: 19.69 in.

Sights: None
Weight: 6 lb.
Caliber: .177, .22, .25, .30
Magazine: 22, 18, 16, 13 shots
Features: A compact side-lever bullpup with a 230cc aluminum air cylinder; manual safety; Picatinny scope rail; moderator-ready ½-in. UNF threaded muzzle; Twist X barrel; externally adjustable AMP regulator; dual manometers; seven-position macro hammer spring tension adjustment
MSRP . . . . **$1399.00–$1664.97**

WILDCAT MKIII SNIPER

Power: PCP
Stock: Synthetic
Barrel: 27.56 in.
Sights: None
Weight: 6 lb. 11 oz.
Caliber: .22, .25, .30
Magazine: 18, 16, 13 shots
Features: A sweet bullpup side-lever with a seven-position macro hammer spring tension adjustment; Twist X barrel; 300cc aluminum air cylinder; manual safety; Picatinny optics rail; dual manometers; externally adjustable AMP regulator
MSRP . . . . **$1499.99–$1764.97**

Gamo USA

GAMO USA COYOTE WHISPER FUSION

GAMO USA P-430

GAMO SWARM FUSION 10X GEN2

GAMO USA SWARM MAGNUM 10X GEN2

COYOTE WHISPER FUSION

Power: PCP
Stock: Beechwood
Overall length: 42.9 in.
Sights: None
Weight: 7 lb. 13.6 oz.
Caliber: .177, .22
Features: An entry-level PCP-power plant bolt-action air rifle that boasts a 10-pellet rotary clip, hammer forged rifled barrel, selve-regulating valve, Custom Action Trigger, Shock Wave Absorber, double-sided molded cheekpiece, and Whisper Fusion technology
MSRP **$797.90**

P-430

Power: CO2
Stock: Polymer
Barrel: N/A

Sights: Fixed front and rear
Weight: 15.5 oz.
Caliber: .177
Magazine: 16 shots
Features: Non-blowback air pistol with single-/double-action; smoothbore barrel; tactical accessory rail; aggressive slide, grip and trigger guard serrations
MSRP **$47.40**

SWARM FUSION 10X GEN2

Power: Gas piston
Stock: Synthetic
Barrel: 20.5 in.
Sights: None
Weight: 5 lb. 13 oz.
Caliber: .22
Magazine: 10 shots
Features: Already upgraded after just a year, with a new horizontal magazine design and fiber optic sights front and (adjustable) rear; two-stage adjustable trigger; recoil reducing rail; Inert Gas Technology piston; Gamo 3–9x40mm scope; fluted, rifled barrel with a polymer jacket, and Whisper Fusion noise suppression
MSRP **$293.90**

SWARM MAGNUM 10X GEN2

Power: Inert gas
Stock: Glass-filled nylon
Barrel: N/A
Sights: Fiber optic front and rear
Weight: 6 lb. 14 oz.
Caliber: .177, .22
Magazine: 10 shots
Features: Break-action air rifle with a two-stage adjustable trigger; automatic cocking safety system; RRR-recoil reducing rail; inertia-fed technology; thumbhole stock of glass-filled nylon; Gamo 3–9x40 scope; jacketed rifled steel barrel; Whisper Fusion noise dampening
MSRP **$319.90**

Gamo USA

GAMO USA SWARM
MAXXIM 10X GEN2

GAMO USA WHISPER
FUSION MACH 1

GAMO USA URBAN PCP

SWARM MAXXIM 10X GEN2

Power: Inert gas
Stock: Glass-filled nylon
Barrel: N/A
Sights: Fiber optic front and rear
Weight: 5 lb. 10 oz.
Caliber: .177, .22
Magazine: 10 shots
Features: Similar to the Swarm Magnum 10X Gen2, but with a lighter weight; inertia-fed technology; fluted polymer jacketed rifled steel barrel with Whisper Maxxim noise reduction technology; stock with magazine compartment; Gamo 3–9x40 scope
MSRP $209.90

URBAN PCP

Power: PCP
Stock: Synthetic
Overall length: 42.9 in.
Sights: None
Weight: 6 lb. 11.2 oz.
Caliber: .22
Features: Bolt-action air rifle features Whisper Fusion technology multi-shot mechanism, Custom Action Trigger,

hammer forged barrel, and thumbhole stock with double-sided molded cheekpiece
MSRP $419.99

WHISPER FUSION MACH 1

Power: IGT Mach 1
Stock: Synthetic
Overall length: 46.5 in.
Sights: Fiber optic front, adjustable rear
Weight: 8 lb.
Caliber: .177, .22
Features: Break-barrel, single-cocking action; single-shot; fluted polymer jacketed steel barrel; Custom Action Trigger; Recoil Reducing Rail; 3-9x40 air rifle scope
MSRP $289.90

Gletcher

GLETCHER M712

GLETCHER M1891

GLETCHER M1944

GLETCHER PM 1951

GLETCHER NGT F

M712

Power: CO2
Stock: Wood
Overall length: 23 in.
Sights: Post front, tangent rear
Weight: 3 lb.
Caliber: .177
Features: Reproduction of WWII 1932 broomhandle Mauser; breech mechanism moves when firing; full-auto functionality and blowback system
MSRP $189.99

M1891

Power: CO2
Stock: Imitation wood
Overall length: 22.43 in.
Sights: Hooded front post, tangent rear
Weight: 5 lb. 9.6 oz.
Caliber: .177
Features: Reproduction of Russian Civil War "Obrez" model, a sawed-off Mosin-Nagant; mechanism works as in the original; built-in hex key for CO2 cartridge installation
MSRP $199.99

M1944

Power: CO2
Stock: Imitation wood
Overall length: 52.75 in.
Sights: Post front, tangent rear
Weight: 8 lb. 3 oz.
Caliber: .177
Features: Reproduction of M44 Russian Mosin-Nagant carbine; barrel, bolt mechanism, and magazine are metal; action operates like the original firearm; integral folding bayonet; built-in hex wrench for CO2 cartridge installation
MSRP $329.99

NGT F

Power: CO2
Stock: Plastic
Overall length: 9 in.

Sights: Front post, cutout rear
Weight: 1 lb. 8 oz.
Caliber: .177
Features: Reproduction of the Belgian Nagant revolver; steel BBs fired through decorative snap cap "cartridges"; seven-shot true revolving action; blue or silver finishes
MSRP $159.99

PM 1951

Power: CO2
Stock: Plastic
Overall length: 6.3 in.
Sights: Low-profile integral front and rear
Weight: 1 lb. 10 oz.
Caliber: .177
Features: Reproduction of Russian Makarov sidearm; metal body and slide; safety lever; magazine pinky finger extension
MSRP $124.99

AIRGUNS

Gletcher

GLETCHER STECHKIN

STECHKIN
Power: CO2
Stock: Plastic
Overall length: 8.8 in.
Sights: Low-profile integral front, adjustable rear
Weight: 2 lb. 4.8 oz.

Caliber: .177
Features: Reproduction of Soviet Stretchkin pistol; weight is identical to the firearm version; double-action, with gold finish, engraving on slide and frame; comes in a presentation box
MSRP $259.99

HatsanUSA, Inc.

HATSAN USA AIRMAX BULLPUP

HATSAN USA AIRTACT

HATSAN USA ALPHA YOUTH QE

HATSAN USA AT44PA-10 PUMP QES, PUMP LONG QES

HATSAN USA BARRAGE

HATSAN USA BLITZ

AIRMAX
Power: PCP
Stock: Turkish walnut
Barrel: 23 in.
Sights: None
Weight: 10 lb. 14 oz.
Caliber: .177, .22, .25
Magazine: 9, 10 shots
Features: A bullpup design featuring the QuietEnergy fully shrouded barrel; ambidextrous thumbhole stock with adjustable cheekpiece; detachable magazine; Anti-Double Pellet Feed technology; under rail; sling swivels; Quattro adjustable two-stage match trigger
MSRP $629.99

AIRTACT
Power: Break-barrel
Stock: Synthetic
Barrel: 14.5 in.
Sights: Fiber optic front, adjustable rear, 4X32mm Optima scope
Weight: 5 lb. 11 oz.
Caliber: .177, .22, .25
Magazine: 1 shot
Features: Beginner's single-shot with a slim, skeletonized thumbhole stock; large muzzle break for easy cocking; steel rifled barrel with molded shroud; manual firing safety; automatic cocking safety; adjustable trigger; scope and sights provided
MSRP $109.99

ALPHA YOUTH QE
Power: Spring piston
Stock: Synthetic
Barrel: 15.4 in.
Sights: Red fiber optic front, green fiber optic rear
Weight: 5 lb. 4 oz.
Caliber: .177
Magazine: 1 shot
Features: Perhaps the perfect starter air rifle for your kids, with an ambidextrous stock; easy break-action cocking mechanism
MSRP $109.99

AT44PA-10 PUMP QES, PUMP LONG QES
Power: PCP
Stock: Synthetic
Barrel: 19.4 in., 23 in.
Sights: None
Weight: 9 lb. 10 oz.–9 lb. 15 oz.
Caliber: .177, .22, .25
Magazine: 10, 9 shots
Features: This repeater features a two-stage adjustable trigger; pump action; 11mm/22mm combo scope rail; TruGlo sights; Quiet Energy fully shrouded barrel with integrated sound moderator; Monte Carlo thumbhole stock with adjustable buttpad; long version sports the 23-in. barrel for added velocity
Standard: $449.99
Long: $499.99

BARRAGE
Power: PCP
Stock: Synthetic
Overall length: 19.7 in.
Sights: Fiber optic front and rear
Weight: 10 lb. 1.6 oz.
Caliber: .177, .22
Features: Semiautomatic; fitted with a 500cc air bottle mounted to the forearm; barrel is precision rifled, choked, and fully shrouded; ambidextrous thumbhole stock; Picatinny rail on the forearm; includes magazines for both calibers (.177 mag holds 14 shots, .22 holds 12 shots); TruGlo sights; HatSan's patented anti-knock system that prevents gas discharge and waste if the rifle is knocked or bounced
MSRP $799.99

BLITZ
Power: PCP
Stock: Synthetic
Barrel: 23 in.
Sights: None
Weight: 8 lb. 13 oz.
Caliber: .22, .25, .30
Magazine: 16, 19, 21 shots
Features: A select-fire—semiauto or full-auto—air rifle with a rotary magazine; buttstock adjustable at buttpad and comb; three forearm accessory rails; quick-fill nozzle; anti-knock safety system prevents firing when the air rifle is knocked or bounced; fully shrouded barrel
MSRP $999.99

AIRGUNS

HatsanUSA, Inc.

HATSAN USA
BULLMASTER

HATSAN USA
FLASHPUP QE, SYN QE

HATSAN USA
HYDRA QE

HATSAN USA INVADER
AUTO

HATSAN USA MOD
130S QE

HATSAN USA
NEUTRONSTAR

HATSAN USA
PILEDRIVER

HATSAN
USA SORTIE,
SORTIE TACT

BULLMASTER

Power: PCP
Stock: Synthetic
Overall length: 19.7 in.
Sights: None
Weight: 10 lb. 4.8 oz.
Caliber: .177, .22
Features: Semiautomatic bullpup design; 500cc air bottle mounted to the forearm; barrel is precision rifled, choked, and fully shrouded; includes magazines for both calibers (.177 mag holds 14 shots, .22 holds 12 shots); topside and and under forearm Picatinny rails; elevation adjustable cheekpiece; HatSan's patented anti-knock system that prevents gas discharge and waste if the rifle is knocked or bounced
MSRP $799.99

FLASHPUP SYN QE

Power: PCP
Stock: Wood, synthetic
Barrel: 19.4 in.
Sights: None
Weight: 6 lb. 1 oz.
Caliber: .177, .22, .25
Magazine: 14, 12, 10 shots
Features: A bolt-action repeater in a synthetic bullpup-style stock; Quattro trigger; QuietEnergy fully shrouded barrel; two indexing magazines and a single-shot tray included; combo 11mm/22mm rail; adjustable cheekpiece on via adjustment wheel; anti-knock system prevents gas waste
MSRP $359.99

HYDRA QE

Power: PCP
Stock: Turkish walnut
Barrel: 17.7 in.
Sights: None

Weight: 6 lb. 13 oz.
Caliber: .177, .22, .25
Magazine: 10, 12, 14 shots
Features: Features interchangeable barrel system; detachable magazine; aluminum receiver; built-in pressure gauge; ambidextrous, ergonomic stock with an adjustable cheekpiece and checkering at grip locations
MSRP $399.99

INVADER AUTO

Power: PCP
Stock: Synthetic
Barrel: 19.7 in.
Sights: Adjustable fiber optic
Weight: 8 lb. 2 oz.
Caliber: .177, .22, .25
Magazine: 10, 12, 14 shots
Features: Bolt-action; QuietEnergy shrouded rifled barrel; three Picatinny rails; detachable magazine; built-in pressure gauge; rotating dust cover; anti-knock system to prevent accidental discharges
Auto: $609.99

MOD 130S QE

Power: Gas piston
Stock: Synthetic
Barrel: 10.6 in.
Sights: Fiber optic front and rear
Weight: 9 lb. 9 oz.
Caliber: .30
Magazine: 1 shot
Features: A single-shot break-action with a two-stage adjustable trigger; Vortex gas piston; anti-bear trap safety; TruGlo sights; SaS Shock Absorber System; QuietEnergy integrated suppressor; automatic safety; sling swivels
Airgun only $239.99
With scope $329.99

NEUTRONSTAR

Power: PCP
Stock: Wood
Barrel: 23 in.
Sights: None
Weight: 8 lb. 7 oz.
Caliber: .177, .22, .25
Magazine: 14, 12, 10 shots
Features: A repeater with a shrouded barrel and threaded muzzle cap; Turkish walnut thumbhole stock with adjustable comb; two-stage adjustable Quattro trigger; Picatinny rail; combo optics rail; spare magazine storage in stock; comes with two magazines and single-shot tray; anti-knock system prevents wasted gas
MSRP . . . . $799.99–$889.99

PILEDRIVER

Power: PCP
Stock: Synthetic
Barrel: 33 in.
Sights: Adjustable fiber optic
Weight: 10 lb.
Caliber: .45, .50
Magazine: 1 shot
Features: A big-bore air rifle in a compact bullpup package; gas piston hammer spring; rifled barrel; long optics rail; adjustable cheekrest
MSRP . . . . $1173.99–$1179.99

SORTIE, SORTIE TACT

Power: PCP
Stock: Synthetic
Barrel: 7.9 in.
Sights: Fiber optic front and rear
Weight: 4 lb. 7 oz.
Caliber: .177, .22, .25
Magazine: 14, 12, 10 shots
Features: Hatsan's first PCP air pistol with a 62cc cylinder; detachable sights; ergonomic all-weather grip; Tact version has a removable folding rear stock; includes three magazines and hard case
MSRP $599.99

AIRGUNS

HATSAN USA SPEEDFIRE

HATSAN USA VECTIS

SPEEDFIRE

Power: Break-barrel
Stock: Synthetic
Barrel: 14.5 in.
Sights: Green fiber optic front, red fiber optic rear, Optima 3–9x32mm scope
Weight: 6 lb. 9 oz.
Caliber: .177, .22
Magazine: 10, 12 shots
Features: Modern-looing ergonomically designed stock with raised cheekpiece; removeable Rapid

Performance Mag; front sight folds down for use with optics on the top-side rail; rifled steel barrel with QuickEnergy synthetic shroud; Quattro two-stage adjustable trigger; manual, automatic cocking, and anti-beartrap safeties; SAS shock absorber system
MSRP. **$189.99**

VECTIS

Power: PCP
Stock: Synthetic

Barrel: 17.7 in.
Sights: Flip-up green fiber optic front, red fiber optic rear
Weight: 7 lb. 2 oz.
Caliber: .177, .22, .25
Magazine: 10, 12, 14 shots
Features: A lever-activated thoroughly modern PCP air rifle featuring the QuietEnergy barrel shroud; S/Roto magazines and single-shot tray; Quattro adjustable two-stage trigger; all-weather thumbhole stock with Monte Carlo cheekpiece; removeable fiber optic flip-up sights; acres of rail top and bottom; rifled and choked barrel
MSRP. **$369.99**

Sig Air

SIG AIR 1911 SPARTAN CO2 BB GUN

SIG AIR 1911 WE THE PEOPLE BB PISTOL

SIG AIR MCX AIR RIFLE

SIG AIR MCX AIR RIFLE SCOPED

SIG AIR MCX VIRTUS PCP

1911 SPARTAN CO2 BB GUN

Power: CO2
Stock: Custom Spartan
Overall length: 8.7 in.
Sights: White dot front and rear
Weight: 2 lb. 9.6 oz.
Caliber: BB (4.5mm)
Features: CO2-operated BB gun replication of SIG Spartan 1911 pistol; MOLON LABE engraved slide; custom Spartan grips; skeletonized trigger; cam-lever CO2 loading port; functional grip safety; full blowback metal slide; 16-round magazine; oil-rubbed bronze finish
MSRP. **$129.99**

1911 WE THE PEOPLE BB PISTOL

Power: CO2
Stock: Aluminum
Overall Length: 8.5 in.
Sights: Fixed
Weight: 2 lb. 3 oz.

Caliber: BB
Magazine: 17 rounds
Features: Custom aluminum 50-star grips (25 each side); distressed finish slide and frame
MSRP. **$139.99**

MCX AIR RIFLE

Power: CO2
Stock: Synthetic
Barrel: 18 in.
Sights: Flip-up front and rear
Weight: 7 lb. 4 oz.
Caliber: .177
Magazine: 39 shots
Features: An MSR-style air rifle; synthetic handguard; Picatinny rail; tactical front grip; in black or flat dark earth
MSRP. **$249.99**

MCX AIR RIFLE SCOPED

Power: CO2
Stock: Synthetic
Barrel: 18 in.

Sights: Flip-up front and rear
Weight: 7 lb. 14 oz.
Caliber: .177
Magazine: 30 shots
Features: An MSR-style air rifle with rifled steel barrel; synthetic handguard; Picatinny rail; tactical front grip; 1–4x24mm scope; in black or flat dark earth
MSRP. **$309.99**

MCX VIRTUS PCP

Power: PCP
Stock: Synthetic
Barrel: 17.5 in.
Sights: Folding front and rear
Weight: 7 lb. 8 oz.
Caliber: .22
Magazine: 30 shots
Features: SIG's premium PCP pellet rifle sends .22-caliber pellets at velocities up to 700 fps; SIG Rapid Pellet Magazine
MSRP. **$409.99**

AIRGUNS

Sig Air

SIG AIR MPX AIR RIFLE

SIG AIR P226 AIR PISTOL

SIG AIR P320 AIR PISTOL

SIG AIR P320 M17 AIR PISTOL

SIG AIR P365 AIR PISTOL

SIG AIR PROFORCE M17 AIRSOFT

SIG AIR PROFORCE MCX VIRTUS AIRSOFT AEG

SIG AIR PROFORCE P229

MPX AIR RIFLE
Power: CO2
Stock: Synthetic
Barrel: 8 in.
Sights: Flip-up front and rear
Weight: 6 lb. 3 oz.
Caliber: .177
Magazine: 30 shots
Features: Compact and light, this SBR air rifle has a metal housing; integral Picatinny rail; side rails; flip-up adjustable front and rear sights; muzzle velocity up to 498 fps; available in black
MSRP **$229.99**

P226 AIR PISTOL
Power: CO2
Stock: Metal
Barrel: 4.75 in.
Sights: Fixed front and rear
Weight: 2 lb. 5 oz.
Caliber: .177
Magazine: 16 shots
Features: Metal frame; 8x2 rotary magazine; rifled steel barrel; Picatinny rail mount; can also use BBs; white dot fixed sights
MSRP **$129.99**

P320 AIR PISTOL, AIR PISTOL COYOTE TAN
Power: CO2
Stock: Polymer
Overall length: 7.9 in.
Sights: White dot front and rear
Weight: 1 lb. 11 oz.
Caliber: .177
Features: CO2-operated airgun model of SIG's P320 carry gun; rotary maga-

zine holds 30 rounds; rifled steel barrel; manual safety; all-metal slide; black or Coyote Tan finishes
MSRP **$139.99**

P320 M17 AIR PISTOL
Power: CO2
Stock: Polymer
Barrel: N/A
Sights: Fixed
Weight: 34 oz.
Caliber: .177
Magazine: 20 shots
Features: Copy of the U.S. Army's M17 semiautomatic. Features full blowback action for realistic shooting
MSRP **$159.99**

P365 AIR PISTOL
Power: CO2
Stock: Polymer
Barrel: 3.2 in.
Sights: Fixed front and rear
Weight: 13 oz.
Caliber: .177 BB
Magazine: 12 shots
Features: High visibility green dot fixed sights; similar in weight, feel, and action to its 9mm counterpart; full blowback metal slide that locks back on last shot fired; manual safety
MSRP **$129,99**

PROFORCE M17 AIRSOFT, M18 AIRSOFT
Power: CO2; green gas
Stock: Synthetic
Barrel: N/A
Sights: Fixed front, optics-ready rear
Weight: 48 oz.

Caliber: 6mm BB
Magazine: 21 shots
Features: An airsoft pistol nearly identical to the US Army's M17 sidearm that can use both CO2 or green gas power supply (M18 is green gas only); metal slide with full blowback action
MSRP **$209.99**

PROFORCE MCX VIRTUS AIRSOFT AEG
Power: AEG
Stock: Synthetic
Barrel: 11.5 in.
Sights: None
Weight: 7 lb.
Caliber: 6mm BB
Magazine: 120 shots
Features: AEG (Auto Electric Gun) powered by an 11.1-volt LIPO battery and featuring a three-position telescoping stock; M-LOK accessory rail; muzzle velocity up to 370 fps
MSRP **$209.99**

PROFORCE P229
Power: Green gas
Stock: Metal
Barrel: 7 in.
Sights: Fixed front and rear
Weight: 29.6 oz.
Caliber: 6mm BB
Magazine: 25 shots
Features: A full-size metal-frame airsoft pistol with a generous 25-round capacity powered by green gas and featuring a full-metal slide with realistic blowback action
MSRP **$199.99**

AIRGUNS

Sig Air

SIG AIR X-FIVE

X-FIVE
Power: CO2
Stock: Metal
Overall Length: 8.7 in.
Sights: Adjustable
Weight: 2 lb. 11.2 oz.
Caliber: .177
Magazine: 20 rounds
Features: Advanced Sport Pellet; full blowback, metal-framed CO2 air pistol; cam-lever CO2 housing; ambidextrous safety
MSRP $159.99

Stoeger Airguns

STOEGER S3000-C COMPACT COMBO

STOEGER S4000-E SUPPRESSED COMBO

STOEGER S6000-E UNDERLEVER COMBO

STOEGER S8000-E TAC SUPPRESSED

STOEGER XM1 SUPPRESSED PCP

S3000-C COMPACT, COMPACT COMBO
Power: Spring piston
Stock: Synthetic, hardwood
Barrel: N/A
Sights: Fiber optic front, rear, scope
Weight: N/A
Caliber: .177
Magazine: N/A
Features: One for the younger or shorter-statured air rifle aficionado, with an ergonomic stock featuring ProAdaptive checkering; fully adjustable rear sight with a fiber optic front; 4x32mm scope
Synthetic sights only $99.00
Synthetic combo: $119.00
Hardwood combo: $149.00

S4000-E SUPPRESSED
Power: Break-barrel
Stock: Synthetic
Barrel: N/A
Sights: Interchangeable fiber optic front, adjustable fiber optic rear; 4X32 scope
Weight: N/A
Caliber: .177, .22
Magazine: 1 shot

Features: Employing the Gas Ram System break-action design; ProAdaptive stock texturing; adjustable two-stage trigger; integral S3 suppressor; MultiGrip system; comes with both the fiber optic sights and a 4x32 scope; sights-only variant; stock options include black synthetic, hardwood, synthetic OD green, and synthetic in Realtree Edge camo
MSRP . . . . $149.00–$199.00

S6000-E UNDERLEVER COMBO
Power: Spring piston
Stock: Synthetic, hardwood
Barrel: N/A
Sights: Fiber optic front, rear, scope
Weight: N/A
Caliber: .177, .22
Magazine: N/A
Features: A well-balanced air rifle with the cocking lever placed under the barrel for better handling while aiming; hooded front sight with red fiber optic pipe; 4x32mm scope; black synthetic or hardwood stock
Synthetic: $199.00
Hardwood: $229.00

S8000-E TAC SUPPRESSED
Power: Gas ram
Stock: Synthetic
Overall Length: 42.5 in.
Sights: 3–9x40mm scope
Weight: 8 lb. 14 oz.
Caliber: .177, .22
Features: Airflow control technology and dual-stage noise reduction system; automatic ambidextrous safety; black tactical stock; up to 1200 fps with alloy pellets (.177); adjustable length of pull; integral Picatinny rails
MSRP $249.00

XM1 SUPPRESSED PCP
Power: PCP
Stock: Synthetic
Barrel: N/A
Sights: Fiber optic front, rear, scope
Weight: 5 lb. 11 oz.
Caliber: .177, .22
Magazine: 7, 9 shots
Features: Interchangeable pistol grip inserts; cross-bolt safety; integral suppression; on-board air reservoir; two-stage adjustable trigger; also available in choice of black or Realtree Edge stock as a combo air rifle with a 4x32 scope
MSRP . . . . $199.00–$249.00

Umarex USA

UMAREX 850 M2

850 M2
Power: CO2
Stock: Synthetic
Barrel: N/A
Sights: Fiber optic front, rear
Weight: 6 lb. 12 oz.
Caliber: .177, .22
Magazine: 8 shots
Features: A sweet little repeater with a threaded muzzle; three Picatinny rails; removeable additional cheekpiece for scope use; no energy loss shot to shot
MSRP $349.99

Umarex USA

UMAREX BERETTA APX

UMAREX A-REX

UMAREX DX17

UMAREX EMBARK

UMAREX FORGE

UMAREX FUSION 2

UMAREX GAUNTLET

UMAREX GLOCK 19X

UMAREX HAMMER

A-REX
Power: TNT gas system
Stock: Synthetic
Barrel: 14.7 in.
Sights: Fiber optic front and rear
Weight: 7 lb. 14 oz.
Caliber: .177
Magazine: 1 shot
Features: A break-barrel single-shot with velocity up to 1,000 fps; SilencAir muzzle device; 3–9x32 adjustable objective scope included
MSRP..................$179.99

BERETTA APX
Power: CO2
Stock: N/A
Overall length: 7.25 in.
Sights: Fixed front and rear
Weight: 1 lb. 12 oz.
Caliber: BB
Features: Semiautomatic; 20-shot; double-action repeater has realistic recoil action; CO2 cartridge housed in grip; drop-free steel BB magazine; integrated Picatinny rail
MSRP..................$74.99

DX17
Power: Spring-powered
Stock: Synthetic
Overall length: 9.5 in.
Sights: Fixed fiber optic front, fixed rear
Weight: 1 lb.
Caliber: BB
Features: Single-action air pistol shoots steel BBs; built-in BB reservoir; integrated accessory rail; 15-shot capacity; includes 200 steel BBs
MSRP..................$21.99

EMBARK
Power: Break-barrel spring piston

Stock: Synthetic
Overall Length: 40 in.
Sights: Fixed open blade front, micrometer adjustable rear
Weight: 4 lb. 7 oz.
Caliber: .177
Magazine: 1 round
Features: An electric-green, ambidextrous thumbhole stock; official air rifle of the Student Air Rifle Program; cocking poundage is 16.25 lbs
MSRP..................$99.99

FORGE
Power: T.N.T. Turbo Nitrogen Technology gas piston
Stock: Wood
Overall length: 44.8 in.
Sights: 4x32mm scope
Weight: 7 lb. 13 oz.
Caliber: .177
Features: T.N.T. fast piston system; spring piston break barrel with a single-shot cocking mechanism and automatic safety; adjustable trigger; integrated rail platform; 4x32 airgun scope; rifled barrel; enhanced SilencAir noise dampener
MSRP..................$199.99

FUSION 2
Power: CO2
Stock: Synthetic
Barrel: N/A
Sights: None
Weight: N/A
Caliber: .177
Magazine: 9 shots
Features: Topside optics rail; SilencAir noise suppression
MSRP..................$159.99

GAUNTLET
Power: Pre-charged pneumatic

Stock: Synthetic
Overall length: 46.75 in.
Sights: N/A
Weight: 8 lb. 8 oz.
Caliber: .177, .22, .25
Features: Bolt-action repeater; removable 3000 psi 13 cubic in. tank; 1100 psi regulator; adjustable stock comb; pressure key release; rotary magazine; single-shot tray; stock in black or in "multi-purpose" camo pattern
MSRP..................$369.99

GLOCK 19X
Power: CO2, green gas
Stock: Polymer
Barrel: 3.36 in.
Sights: Fixed front, rear
Weight: 1 lb. 10 oz.
Caliber: .177
Magazine: 18 shots
Features: Glock replica; realistic blowback action; double-action trigger; metal slide
MSRP..................$144.99

HAMMER
Power: PCP
Stock: Synthetic
Barrel: 29.5 in.
Sights: None
Weight: 8 lb. 8 oz.
Caliber: .510
Magazine: 2 shots
Features: Intended for big-game hunting with a straight-pull speed bolt action; shrouded rifled barrel; manual safety; two-round magazine; built in manometer; Picatinny optics rail; PolyOne stock; three M-LOK forend slots
MSRP..................$899.99

AIRGUNS

UMAREX HECKLER & KOCH USP BLOWBACK

UMAREX LEGENDS ACE IN THE HOLE

UMAREX LEGENDS M3 GREASE GUN

UMAREX LEGENDS MP

UMAREX M1A1

UMAREX MCP KIT

UMAREX RUGER 10/22

UMAREX OCTANE ELITE

HECKLER & KOCH USP BLOWBACK

Power: CO2
Stock: Synthetic
Overall Length: 7.75 in.
Sights: Fixed front blade, fixed rear
Weight: 2 lb. 2 oz.
Caliber: BB
Magazine: 16 rounds
Features: Replica of H&K's semiautomatic pistol; magazine houses both BBs and the CO2 capsule; blowback action
MSRP **$114.99**

LEGENDS ACE IN THE HOLE

Power: CO2
Stock: Synthetic
Overall Length: 9 in.
Sights: Blade front, groove rear
Weight: 1 lb. 15 oz.
Caliber: .177
Magazine: 6 rounds
Features: Single-action CO2 revolver; weathered finish; black grips with an embossed spade; speed-draw thumb spur; by Umarex
MSRP **$120.95**

LEGENDS M3 GREASE GUN

Power: CO2
Stock: Metal
Barrel: N/A
Sights: Blade front, peep rear
Weight: 7 lb. 10 oz.
Caliber: .177
Magazine: 30 shots
Features: A full-auto replica of the

iconic WWII gun with open-bolt action; drop-free magazine; collapsible wire stock
MSRP **$249.99**

LEGENDS MP

Power: CO2
Stock: Metal
Overall length: 33 in.
Sights: Fixed front, elevation adjustable rear
Weight: N/A
Caliber: .177
Features: Distinctive German replication; 10-in. barrel; folding stock; full-auto blowback action; 60-shot drop-free steel BB magazine; two CO2 cartridges housed in the magazine
MSRP . . . . **$239.99–$267.50**

M1A1

Power: CO2
Stock: Wood
Barrel: 12 in.
Sights: Fixed front and rear
Weight: 7 lb. 13 oz.
Caliber: .177 BB
Magazine: 30 shots
Features: A full-auto replica of the Thompson M1A1, including its open-bolt functionality; sling mounts; drop-free magazine that also houses the CO2 cartridge; full metal frame
MSRP **$279,99**

MCP KIT

Power: CO2
Stock: Synthetic
Overall Length: 7.75 in.

Sights: Fixed blade front, fixed rear
Weight: 14.4 oz.
Caliber: BB
Magazine: 19 rounds
Features: Safety glasses; packet of 250 BBs; pair of CO2 cartridges; CO2 is housed in the grip; accessory rail
MSRP **$42.99**

OCTANE ELITE

Power: ReAxis gas-powered piston
Stock: Synthetic
Overall length: 48.6 in.
Sights: 3-9x40mm scope
Weight: 9 lb. 8 oz.
Caliber: .177, .22
Features: Lockdown rail mounting system; 3-9x40mm airgun scope with adjustable objective; Stopshox anti-recoil system; SilencAir 5 chamber noise dampener; all-weather stock; rifled barrel; single-shot cocking mechanism
.22: **$279.99**
.177: **$249.99**

RUGER 10/22

Power: CO2
Stock: Synthetic
Barrel: 18 in.
Sights: Blade front, adjustable rear
Weight: 4 lb. 8 oz.
Caliber: .177
Magazine: 10 shots
Features: Faithful replica of Rugers rimfire autoloader; semiautomatic functionality; rifled barrel; rubber buttpad
MSRP **$149.99**

AIRGUNS

Umarex USA

UMAREX RUGER TARGIS HUNTER MAX

UMAREX RUGER TARGIS MAX

UMAREX RUGER YUKON MAGNUM

UMAREX RWS MODEL 34

UMAREX RWS MODEL 48 WITH SCOPE

UMAREX RWS MODEL 54

UMAREX RWS MODEL 350 MAGNUM

UMAREX SA10

UMAREX SMITH & WESSON M29

RUGER TARGIS HUNTER MAX

Power: Gas piston
Stock: Synthetic
Barrel: 14 in.
Sights: Fiber optic front and rear
Weight: 8 lb. 8 oz.
Caliber: .22
Magazine: 1 shot
Features: A single-shot break-barrel with adjustable rear sight; all-weather stock; automatic safety; SilencAir muzzle device; 3–9x42 adjustable objective scope; sling and swivels
MSRP. **$229.99**

RUGER TARGIS MAX

Power: Spring piston
Stock: Synthetic
Barrel: 18.7 in.
Sights: Fiber optic front and rear
Weight: N/A
Caliber: .177
Magazine: 1 shot
Features: A single-shot break-barrel with fiber optics sights (adjustable rear); all-weather stock; automatic safety; SilencAir muzzle device; 3–9x42 adjustable objective scope
MSRP. **$179.99**

RUGER YUKON MAGNUM

Power: Break-barrel gas piston
Stock: Wood
Overall Length: 48.25 in.
Sights: Fiber optic front, adjustable rear
Weight: 9 lb. 3 oz.
Caliber: .22
Magazine: 1 round
Features: ReAxis piston for improved velocities; equipped with a 3–9x42mm scoped premounted on the air rifle's Picatinny rail; two-stage

adjustable trigger; SilencAir suppressor; cocking effort is 47 pounds
MSRP. **$197.97**

RWS MODEL 34

Power: Break action/spring piston
Stock: Hardwood, synthetic
Overall Length: 45 in.
Sights: 4x32mm scope
Weight: 7 lb. 8 oz.–8 lb.
Caliber: .177, .22
Features: Polished with blued metalwork; full-sized hardwood stock; two-stage adjustable trigger; automatic safety; finely rifled barrel; 34 Pro large muzzlebrake
.22 airgun only. **$399.99**
.22 with scope **$419.99**
.177 airgun only **$332.00**
.177 with scope **$385.99**

RWS MODEL 48

Power: Side lever/spring piston
Stock: Hardwood
Overall Length: 42.5 in.
Sights: Adjustable rear
Weight: 8 lb. 8 oz.
Caliber: .177
Features: Extended breech stock to reduce recoil; fixed barrel system; adjustable trigger; automatic safety; optional RWS 4x32mm scope and mounts
.22 airgun only: **$589.99**
.177 with scope:. **$599.99**
.22 with scope: **$599.99**

RWS MODEL 54

Power: Side lever/spring piston
Stock: Hardwood
Overall Length: 43.75 in.
Sights: Adjustable rear
Weight: 9 lb.
Caliber: .177, .22

Features: Adjustable trigger; scope rail; Monte Carlo hardwood stock with cheekpiece and checkering; automatic safety; 1100 fps maximum velocity
.22 airgun only: **$809.99**
.22 with scope: **$869.99**
.177 with scope:. **$695.45**

RWS MODEL 350 MAGNUM

Power: Break action/spring piston
Stock: Hardwood
Overall Length: 48.3 in.
Sights: 4x32mm scope
Weight: 8 lb. 3 oz.
Caliber: .177, .22
Features: Two-stage trigger; mounted scope rail
Sight Airgun only: **$549.99**
With scope:. **$569.99**

SA10

Power: CO2
Stock: Synthetic
Overall length: 9.25 in.
Sights: None
Weight: 2 lb. 1 oz.
Caliber: BB, .177
Features: Dual-ammo air pistol accommodating both BBs and .177-caliber pellets; uses one CO2 cartridge; blowback action; DA/SA trigger; eight-round rotary magazine; integrated accessory rail; gold-colored barrel
MSRP. **$94.99**

SMITH & WESSON M29

Power: CO2
Stock: Wood
Barrel: 8.375 in.
Sights: Ramp blade front, adjustable rear
Weight: N/A
Caliber: .177 BB
Magazine: 6 shots
Features: True to the firearm, this is a CO2 six-shot revolver; single-/double-action
MSRP. **$149.99**

Umarex USA

UMAREX STEEL FORCE

UMAREX STEEL STRIKE

UMAREX STRIKE POINT

UMAREX SURGEMAX ELITE

UMAREX SYNERGIS

UMAREX TREVOX

UMAREX WALTHER PPQ

UMAREX WALTHER PPS M2

UMAREX WALTHER REIGN UXT

STEEL FORCE
Power: CO2
Stock: Synthetic
Barrel: 7.5 in.
Sights: Flip-up front and rear
Weight: 3 lb. 5 oz.
Caliber: .177 BB
Magazine: 30 shots
Features: Full-auto with a 300 BB reservoir above the handguard; fires in six-shot bursts; collapsible stock; dual C02 compartment in false vertical magazine; can also be fired in semiauto
MSRP $128.35

STEEL STRIKE
Power: CO2
Stock: Synthetic
Barrel: 9 in.
Sights: Flip-up front and rear
Weight: N/A
Caliber: .177 BB
Magazine: 30 shots
Features: Full-auto with a 900 BB reservoir above the handguard; fires in six-shot bursts; CO2 housed in collapsible stock; integrated railing; can also be fired in semiauto
MSRP $124.99

STRIKE POINT
Power: Multi-pump pneumatic
Stock: Synthetic
Overall length: 14 in.
Sights: Fiber optic
Weight: 2 lb. 10 oz.
Caliber: .177, .22
Features: Variable pump power; easy grip pump-action; easy load bolt-action; SilencAir 3 chamber noise dampener
MSRP $56.99

SURGEMAX ELITE
Power: Gas piston
Stock: Synthetic
Barrel: N/A
Sights: Fiber optic front and rear
Weight: N/A
Caliber: .177
Magazine: 1 shot
Features: A single-shot break-barrel with an all-weather stock featuring an ambidextrous cheekpiece; adjustable rear sight; two-stage adjustable trigger; integrated Nucleus rail system that absorbs and minimizes noise and vibration; automatic safety; muzzle brake; 4x32 adjustable objective scope; Turbo Nitrogen Technology (TNT) gas piston action
MSRP $159.99

SYNERGIS
Power: Gas piston
Stock: Synthetic
Barrel: 18.5 in.
Sights: None
Weight: 8 lb.
Caliber: .177, .22
Magazine: 12 shots
Features: A gas-piston underlever repeater with a two-stage adjustable trigger; Picatinny top rail; Airflow Boost Technology auto-indexing pellet probe; RapidMag cartridge system; 3–9x40 scope included
MSRP $199.99

TREVOX
Power: T.N.T. Turbo Nitrogen Technology gas piston
Stock: Synthetic
Overall length: 18.11 in.
Sights: Fiber optic
Weight: 3 lb. 2 oz.
Caliber: .177
Features: Rifled barrel accuracy with an easy-grip; single-stroke cocking mechanism; SilencAir 3 chamber noise dampener; 11mm dovetail cuts for optics mounting; blued finish
MSRP $89.99

WALTHER PPQ
Power: CO2
Stock: Synthetic
Barrel: N/A
Sights: Fixed front, adjustable rear
Weight: N/A
Caliber: .177
Magazine: 8 shots
Features: Fun BB pistol powered by a 12-gram CO2 cartridge; under-muzzle accessory rail
MSRP $72.00

WALTHER PPS M2
Power: CO2
Stock: Synthetic
Overall Length: 6.3 in.
Sights: Fixed blade front, fixed rear
Weight: 1 lb. 2 oz.
Caliber: BB
Magazine: 18 rounds
Features: Blowback design; metal parts for added weight; CO2 housing is hidden in the backstrap; from Umarex
MSRP $84.99

WALTHER REIGN UXT
Power: PCP
Stock: Synthetic
Barrel: N/A
Sights: None
Weight: 5 lb. 8 oz.
Caliber: .22, .25
Magazine: 9 shots
Features: A bullpup stock houses high-grade aluminum components; cocking lever can be operated without coming off the stock; topside optics rail
.22 . . . .$599.99
.25 . . . .$569.99

AIRGUNS

SHOTGUNS

American Tactical

AMERICAN TACTICAL CAVALRY

AMERICAN TACTICAL CAVALRY SV YOUTH

AMERICAN TACTICAL NOMAD WITH SURVIVOR PACK

CAVALRY, CAVALRY SPORT

Action: Over/under
Stock: Walnut
Barrel: 26 in., 28 in.
Chokes: 5
Sights: Brass bead front
Weight: 4 lb. 1 oz.–5 lb. 15 oz.
Bore/Gauge: 12, 20, 28, .410
Capacity: 2 shells
Features: An economically priced group of lightweight shotguns with Turkish walnut stocks; 3-in. chambers (2¾-in. 28-ga.); all but the .410 threaded for Benelli choke tubes; extractors; single selective trigger; long length of pull at 14.23 in. on the 12-ga.; Sport model has engraved receiver, between barrel venting
MSRP . . . . $535.96–$659.95

CAVALRY SV YOUTH

Action: Over/under
Stock: Walnut
Barrel: 26 in.
Chokes: 5
Sights: Brass bead front
Weight: N/A
Bore/Gauge: 20
Capacity: 2 shells
Features: Similar to the standard Cavalry, but with a much shorter length of pull at 12.47 in.; extractors only
MSRP $659.99

NOMAD WITH SURVIVOR PACK

Action: Single-shot
Stock: Synthetic
Barrel: 18.5 in.
Chokes: None
Sights: Bead front
Weight: N/A
Bore/Gauge: .410, 20, 12
Capacity: 1 shell
Features: Break-action folder with a hardy, checkered, synthetic stock and schnabel forend; 3-in. chamber; combo pack comes with a water-resistant Rukx Gear Survivor backpack made for this shotgun and with a hidden handgun pocket, among other features
MSRP $209.95

Armscor/Rock Island Armory

ARMSCOR/ROCK ISLAND ARMORY ALL GENERATIONS

ARMSCOR/ROCK ISLAND ARMORY LION TACTICAL SA (X4)

ARMSCOR/ROCK ISLAND ARMORY MERIVA

ARMSCOR/ROCK ISLAND ARMORY PA 3-IN-1 CHROME SHOTGUN

ALL GENERATIONS

Action: Pump
Stock: Synthetic
Barrel: 18.5 in., 26 in., 28 in.
Chokes: F, M
Sights: Bead front
Weight: 7 lb. 1 oz.–8 lb. 14 oz.
Bore/Gauge: 12, 20, .410
Capacity: 5 shells
Features: Modernized, affordable pump with an ergonomic synthetic stock and forend; 3-in. chamber; aluminum receiver; unique adjustable cheekpiece; stock spacers; 12-ga. available in a 28-in. barrel and in a self-defense 18.5-in. length, 20-ga. and .410-bore in 26-in. barrels
MSRP $299.00

LION TACTICAL SA (X4)

Action: Semiautomatic
Stock: Polymer
Barrel: 18.5 in.
Chokes: F, M, IC
Weight: 7 lb.
Bore/Gauge: 12
Magazine: 4 shells
Features: Economical shotgun for home-defense or 3-Gun competition; flash hider at the muzzle; fiber optic front sight, rear sight; Picatinny rail; aluminum receiver in black chrome finish; polymer stock with pistol grip
MSRP $299.00

MERIVA

Action: Pump
Stock: Synthetic
Barrel: 18.5 in.
Chokes: None
Sights: Fixed blade/ramp front
Weight: 5 lb. 15 oz.
Bore/Gauge: 12
Capacity: 5 shells
Features: A no-frills pump for self-defense
MSRP $199.00

MERIVA 3-1 CHROME SHOTGUN

Action: Pump
Stock: Polymer
Barrel: 18.5 in., 28 in.
Chokes: S, F, M, IC
Weight: 6 lb. 2.7 oz.
Bore/Gauge: 12
Magazine: 4 shells
Features: 28-in. vent rib barrel with removable chokes; 18.5-in. cylinder bored barrel with front post sight; full polymer stock; add-on pistol grip; aluminum receiver; metalwork finished in Marine Chrome
MSRP $349.00

Armscor/Rock Island Armory

ARMSCOR/ROCK ISLAND ARMORY VR60 SHOTGUN STANDARD

ARMSCOR/ROCK ISLAND ARMORY VR80

ARMSCOR/ROCK ISLAND ARMORY VR82

ARMSCOR/ROCK ISLAND ARMORY VRBP100

ARMSCOR/ROCK ISLAND ARMORY VRPA40

VR60 SHOTGUN STANDARD

Action: Semiautomatic
Stock: Polymer
Barrel: 20 in.
Chokes: F, M, IC
Weight: 7 lb. 6.2 oz.
Bore/Gauge: 12
Magazine: 5 shells
Features: AR-platform semiautomatic; conventional gas-operated action; removable carry handle; full-length Picatinny rail
MSRP **$499.00**

VR80

Action: Semiautomatic
Stock: Synthetic
Barrel: 20 in.
Chokes: Mobil Choke
Sights: Flip-up front and rear
Weight: 8 lb. 4 oz.

Bore/Gauge: 12
Capacity: 5 shells
Features: A gas-operated tactical shotgun with aluminum upper, lower, and forend; THS buffer tube stock; fluted barrel shroud
MSRP **$699.00**

VR82

Action: Semiautomatic
Stock: Synthetic
Barrel: 18 in.
Chokes: 3
Sights: Flip-up front, rear
Weight: 7 lb. 8 oz.
Bore/Gauge: 20
Capacity: 5 shells
Features: Contoured barrel with lightning cuts; thumbhole stock; black anodized finish; barrel shroud and forend compatible with aftermarket accessories; ambidextrous controls; aluminum frame
MSRP **$729.00**

VRBP100

Action: Semiautomatic
Stock: Synthetic

Barrel: 20 in.
Chokes: Mobil Choke
Sights: Flip-up front and rear
Weight: 7 lb. 15 oz.
Bore/Gauge: 12
Capacity: 5 shells
Features: A tactical shotgun in bullpup configuration featuring a spacer-adjustable buttstock with adjustable cheekpiece; detachable VR series magazine; side and top Picatinny rails; aluminum receiver
MSRP **$699.99**

VRPA40

Action: Pump
Stock: Synthetic
Barrel: 20 in.
Chokes: Mobil Choke
Sights: Fiber optic front, adjustable rear
Weight: 6 lb. 15 oz.
Bore/Gauge: 12
Capacity: 5 shells
Features: A versatile pump with a detachable VR series magazine; heat shield; topside optic rail; 3-in. chamber
MSRP **$399.00**

AYA (Aguirre y Aranzabal)

AYA CENTENARY

AYA IMPERIAL

CENTENARY

Action: Side-by-side
Stock: Wood
Barrel: 28 in.
Chokes: N/A
Weight: 6 lb. 12 oz.
Bore/Gauge: 12, 16, 20, 28, .410
Magazine: 2 shells
Features: Forged steel action with double locking mechanism and gas vents; hardened steel intercepting safety sears; gold lined cocking indicators; double trigger with hinged front trigger; optional selective or

non-selective single trigger; chopper lump steel barrels; concave rib; straight hand, finely chequered oil finished walnut stock; exhibition wood; custom Centenary engraving, gold inlays; initial oval; automatic safety
MSRP . . . . . . **Contact manufacturer**

IMPERIAL

Action: Side-by-side hammerless sidelock
Stock: Walnut
Barrel: 28 in., with other lengths to order

Chokes: Screw-in tubes
Weight: 6 lb. 12 oz.
Bore/Gauge: 12, 16, 20, 28, .410
Magazine: None
Features: Forged steel action with double locking mechanism and gas vents; gold washed internal lock parts; gold lined cocking indicators; optional selective or non-selective single trigger; concave rib; straight hand, finely checkered walnut stock; gold initial oval
MSRP . . . . . . **Contact manufacturer**

SHOTGUNS

AYA (Aguirre y Aranzabal)

AYA MODEL NO. 4/53

MODEL NO. 4/53

Action: Side-by-side hammerless boxlock ejector
Stock: Walnut
Barrel: 28 in., with other lengths to order
Chokes: Screw-in tubes
Weight: 6 lb. 10 oz.
Bore/Gauge: 12, 16, 20, 28, .410
Magazine: None
Features: Double locking mechanism with replaceable hinge pin; disk set firing pins; double trigger; chopper

AYA MODEL NO. 37

lump barrels with concave rib; light scroll engraving; metal finish available in hardened, old silver, or white finish; automatic safety
MSRP . . . . . . Contact manufacturer

MODEL NO. 37

Action: Over/under sidelock
Stock: Walnut
Barrel: 28 in.
Chokes: Screw-in tubes
Weight: 7 lb. 8 oz.

Bore/Gauge: 12
Magazine: None
Features: Double underlocking lugs and double crossbolt; chopper lump chrome nickel steel barrels; hardened steel intercepting safety sears; gold line cocking indicators; gold washed internal lock parts; double trigger with hinged front trigger; fine rose and scroll, game scene, or bold relief engraving on action plates; full pistol grip walnut stock
MSRP . . . . . . Contact manufacturer

Benelli USA

BENELLI 828U

BENELLI 828U SPORT

BENELLI ETHOS BE.S.T.

BENELLI 828U LEFT-HAND ENGRAVED RECEIVER

BENELLI ETHOS

828U

Action: Over/under
Stock: Wood
Barrel: 26 in., 28 in.
Chokes: C, IC, M, IM, F, wrench
Weight: 6 lb. 8 oz.
Bore/Gauge: 12, 20
Magazine: 2 shells
Features: Patented steel locking system and plate; easily removable trigger group receiver; adjustable drop and cast; ergonomic opening lever; impulse activated ejectors; available with the receiver in either black anodized finish or engraved nickel finish
MSRP . . . . $2799.00–$3299.00

828U LEFT-HAND ENGRAVED RECEIVER

Action: Over/under
Stock: Walnut
Barrel: 26 in., 28 in.
Chokes: Crio (C, IC, M, IM, F)
Weight: 6 lb. 8 oz.–6 lb. 9.6 oz.
Bore/Gauge: 12

Magazine: 2 shells
Features: Left-hand stock orientation with engraved nickel-plated receiver
MSRP $3299.00

828U SPORT

Action: Over/under
Stock: Walnut
Barrel: 30 in., 32 in.
Chokes: 5 (C, IC, M, IM, F)
Sights: White bead front
Weight: 8 lb.
Bore/Gauge: 12
Capacity: 2 shells
Features: For the sporting clays crowd, the 828U gets an adjustable trigger; automatic ejectors; AA-grade walnut stock; Crio barrel; shim plates for drop and cast adjustments; wide carbon fiber rib with sight channel; balancing weight system; custom hardshell case
MSRP $4399.00

ETHOS

Action: Inertia-operated semiautomatic
Stock: Walnut
Barrel: 26 in., 28 in.
Chokes: C, IC, M, IM, F

Weight: 5 lb.–6 lb. 5 oz.
Bore/Gauge: 12, 20, 28
Magazine: 4+1 shells
Features: Progressive Comfort recoil reduction system; two-part carrier latch for easy reloading; interchangeable fiber optic sights; available with engraved nickel-plated receiver
MSRP . . . . $1999.00–$2149.00

ETHOS BE.S.T.

Action: Semiautomatic
Stock: Synthetic
Barrel: 26 in., 28 in.
Chokes: 5 (C, IC, M, IM, F)
Sights: Interchangeable fiber optic front
Weight: 6 lb. 10 oz.–6 lb. 11 oz.
Bore/Gauge: 12
Capacity: 4 shells
Features: BE.S.T. stands for Benelli Surface Treatment, a metal surface treatment that Benelli says is impenetrable and actually stops rust and corrosion with a twenty-five-year warranty.
MSRP $2199.00

Benelli USA

BENELLI ETHOS CORDOBA BE.S.T.

BENELLI ETHOS SPORT

BENELLI ETHOS SUPERSPORT

BENELLI M2 FIELD 12 GA.

BENELLI M2 FIELD 20 GA.

BENELLI M4 TACTICAL

BENELLI MONTEFELTRO

ETHOS CORDOBA BE.S.T.

Action: Semiautomatic
Stock: Synthetic
Barrel: 28 in., 30 in.
Chokes: 5
Sights: Fiber optic front
Weight: 5 lb. 7 oz.–7 lb.
Bore/Gauge: 12, 20, 28
Capacity: 2, 4 shells
Features: Semiauto with a ported barrel; ComforTech recoil system; inertia-driven operating system; Benelli Surface Treatment (BE.S.T.) aids in rust/corrosion resistance; Broadway rib; Shell View magazine; Crio choke set; right-hand only; recommended minimum load is 3-dram 1 1/8-oz.; 28-ga. magazine holds only two shells
MSRP $2349.00

ETHOS SPORT

Action: Semiautomatic
Stock: Walnut
Barrel: 28 in., 30 in.
Chokes: Five Extended Crio (C, IC, M, IM, F)
Sights: Interchangeable fiber optic front, mid-rib bead
Weight: 5 lb. 6 oz.–6 lb. 11 oz.
Bore/Gauge: 12, 20, 28
Magazine: 4 shells
Features: Cycles loads from featherweight to heavy without interruption; stocks are AA walnut satin finished; receivers are nickel-plated and anodized with light engraving; red, green, and yellow fiber optic sight inserts; stock shim kit; hard case
MSRP $2269.00

ETHOS SUPERSPORT

Action: Semiautomatic
Stock: Carbon fiber
Barrel: 28 in., 30 in.
Chokes: 5
Sights: Fiber optic front
Weight: 5 lb. 7 oz.–7 lb.
Bore/Gauge: 12, 20, 28
Capacity: 2, 4 shells
Features: Semiauto with a ported barrel; ComforTech 3 stock system; Shell View magazine; flush Crio choke set; right-hand only.; 28-ga. magazine holds only two shells
MSRP $2299.00

M2 FIELD 12 GA.

Action: Inertia operated semiautomatic
Stock: Synthetic, Realtree APG
Barrel: 21 in., 24 in., 26 in., 28 in.
Chokes: Crio Chokes (IC, M, F)
Weight: 6 lb. 14 oz.–7 lb. 3 oz.
Bore/Gauge: 12
Magazine: 3+1 shells
Features: ComforTech gel recoil pad and comb insert; ComforTech shim kit; red bar front sight; stock comes in black synthetic, Realtree MAX-5, Mossy Oak Shadow Grass Blades, or Gore Optifade Timber full-coverage camo; left-hand available in full-size model in black or Max-5; Compact and Rifled Slug versions; all 12-gauge models chamber 3-inch shells
Black: $1449.00
Realtree Max-5, Mossy Oak Shadow Grass Blades, Gore Optifade Timber: $1559.00
Compact: $1449.00
Rifled slug: . . . . $1449.00–$1559.00

M2 FIELD 20 GA.

Action: Inertia operated semiautomatic
Stock: Synthetic
Barrel: 24 in., 26 in.
Chokes: Crio Chokes (IC, M, F)
Weight: 5 lb. 13 oz.–6 lb. 8 oz.
Bore/Gauge: 20
Magazine: 3+1 shells
Features: ComforTech gel recoil pad and comb insert; ComforTech shim kit; red bar front sight; stock comes in black synthetic, Realtree MAX-5, Mossy Oak Shadow Grass Blades, or Gore Optifade Timber full-coverage camo; left-hand available in full-size model in black; Compact and Rifled Slug versions; all 12-gauge models chamber 3-inch shells
MSRP: . . . . $1449.00–$1559.00

M4 TACTICAL

Action: Pump
Stock: Synthetic
Barrel: 18.5 in.
Chokes: M
Weight: 7 lb. 12.8 oz.
Bore/Gauge: 12
Magazine: 5 shells
Features: Titanium Cerakote or anodized black phosphate finish on barrel, receiver, and magazine tube; black Cerakote on bolt; internal components receive corrosion-resistant coatings; ghost ring sights; Picatinny rail; standard or pistol grip stocks
Black phosphate $2099.00
Cerakote $2269.00

MONTEFELTRO

Action: Semiautomatic
Stock: Synthetic, walnut
Barrel: 24 in., 26 in., 28 in., 30 in.
Chokes: IC, M, F
Weight: 5 lb. 5 oz.–5 lb. 10 oz. (20 ga.); 6 lb. 15 oz.–7 lb. 3 oz. (12 ga.)
Bore/ Gauge: 12, 20
Magazine: 4 +1 shells
Features: A traditionally styled semiauto field gun with a low-profile rib, slim fore-end, and a lightweight anodized receiver; Sporting 12-ga. has a 30-inch barrel and walnut stock; field 12-ga. has choice of 26- or 28-inch barrel with either walnut stock or black synthetic stock (non-Comfort Tech); left-hand 12-ga. choice of 26- or 28-inch barrel in walnut stock only; 20-ga. and Compact 20-ga. in walnut stock only with 24- or 26-inch barrel; all walnut stocks are satin-finished
MSRP: $1299.00

BENELLI MONTEFELTRO SILVER FEATHERWEIGHT

BENELLI NOVA PUMP

BENELLI NOVA TACTICAL

BENELLI PERFORMANCE SHOP 828U UPLAND

BENELLI PERFORMANCE SHOP ETHOS UPLAND

BENELLI PERFORMANCE SHOP M2 TURKEY 20-GAUGE

MONTEFELTRO SILVER FEATHERWEIGHT

Action: Semiautomatic
Stock: Walnut
Barrel: 26 in.
Chokes: Five
Sights: Red bar front
Weight: 6 lb. 3 oz.
Bore/Gauge: 12, 20
Capacity: 3 shells
Features: A lightweight field gun with a 26-inch barrel; AA-grade walnut stock; slim fore-end; low-profile vent rib; engraved nickel-plated alloy receiver; Inertia Driven system; full set of extended Crio chokes
MSRP $1999.00

NOVA PUMP

Action: Pump
Stock: Synthetic
Barrel: 28 in., 26 in.
Chokes: Three
Sights: Red bar front, mid bead
Weight: 8 lb. (12 ga.); 6 lb. 9 oz. (20 ga.)
Bore/Gauge: 12, 20
Capacity: 3 shells
Features: The Nova Pump now available in Mossy Oak Bottomland, Realtree Max-5 or black; 12-gauge chambered for 3 ½-inch and with 28- or 26-inch barrel; 20-gauge chambered for 3-inch, 26-inch barrel only
MSRP . . . .$449.00–$559.00

NOVA TACTICAL

Action: Pump
Stock: Synthetic
Barrel: 18.5 in.
Chokes: Fixed cylinder choke
Weight: 7 lb. 3 oz.
Bore/Gauge: 12
Magazine: 4+1 shells
Features: Available with ghost-ring or open rifle sights; push-button shell stop; grooved grip surface stocks in black synthetic stock; available with H2O technology, including a matte nickel-plated metal work
Standard rifled sights: $439.00
Standard ghost ring sights: . .$449.00
H2O: $669.00

PERFORMANCE SHOP 828U UPLAND

Action: Over/under
Stock: Walnut
Barrel: 24 in.
Chokes: Eight
Sights: Red fiber optic front
Weight: 6 lb. 6 oz.
Bore/Gauge: 12
Capacity: 2 shells
Features: A short-barreled upland gun with upgraded AA walnut stock in a satin finish; five flush-mount chokes plus three Rob Roberts Triple Threat chokes; carbon fiber stepped rib; drop and cast adjustment shims; no automatic ejectors; lengthened forcing cones; reduced 14.25-inch length of pull; 3-inch chambers; Dark Bronze anodized metalwork
MSRP $3499.00

PERFORMANCE SHOP ETHOS UPLAND

Action: Semiautomatic
Stock: Walnut
Barrel: 26 in.
Chokes: 8 (C, IC, M, IM, F, T1, T2, T3)
Sights: Interchangeable fiber optic front
Weight: 5 lb. 10 oz.–6 lb. 10 oz.
Bore/Gauge: 20, 12
Capacity: 4 shells
Features: Performance gun for the bird fields with lengthened forcing cone; ported barrel; enlarged bolt release and bolt handle; 3-in. chamber; Progressive Comfort stock in AA-grade satin-finished walnut; nickel-plated receiver (20-ga. has alloy receiver); barrel in gloss blue
MSRP $2999.00

PERFORMANCE SHOP M2 TURKEY 20-GAUGE

Action: Semiautomatic
Stock: Synthetic
Barrel: 24 in.
Chokes: Six
Sights: Burris Fast-Fire II red dot
Weight: 5 lb. 11 oz.
Bore/Gauge: 20
Capacity: 4 shells
Features: With custom enhancements from patterning expert Rob Roberts; five flush-fit Crio tubes in normal constrictions, plus one extended custom XFT choke; Burris Fast-Fire red dot factory installed; Mossy Oak Bottomland coverage on stock; Burnt Bronze metalwork; ComforTech stock
MSRP $2999.00

SHOTGUNS

Benelli USA

BENELLI PERFORMANCE SHOP M2 WATERFOWL 20-GAUGE

BENELLI SUPER BLACK EAGLE 3

BENELLI SUPER BLACK EAGLE 3 RIFLED SLUG

BENELLI PERFORMANCE SHOP SUPER BLACK EAGLE 3 TURKEY 12-GAUGE

BENELLI SUPER BLACK EAGLE 3 BE.S.T.

BENELLI SUPER BLACK EAGLE 3 WITH STEADY GRIP

PERFORMANCE SHOP M2 WATERFOWL 20-GAUGE

Action: Semiautomatic
Stock: Synthetic
Barrel: 28 in.
Chokes: Three
Sights: Hi-Viz Comp front, metal mid-rib
Weight: 5 lb. 15 oz.
Bore/Gauge: 20
Capacity: 4 shells
Features: Honed and polished action; custom-tuned trigger group; oversized bolt handle; paracord survival sling; three Rob Roberts Triple Threat chokes; chambers 3-inch shells; Gore Optifade Marsh camo on stock; Burnt Bronze metalwork
MSRP $2699.00

PERFORMANCE SHOP SUPER BLACK EAGLE 3 TURKEY 12-GAUGE

Action: Semiautomatic
Stock: Synthetic
Barrel: 24 in.
Chokes: Six
Sights: Burris Fast-Fire II red dot
Weight: 6 lb. 13 oz.
Bore/Gauge: 12
Capacity: 4 shells
Features: With custom enhancements from patterning expert Rob Roberts; five flush-fit Crio tubes in normal constrictions, plus one extended custom XFT choke; Burris Fast-Fire red dot factory installed; full-coverage Mossy Oak Bottomland camo; ComforTech stock
MSRP $3399.00

SUPER BLACK EAGLE 3

Action: Semiautomatic

Stock: Synthetic
Barrel: 26 in., 28 in.
Chokes: Crio (C, IM, F), Extended Crio (IC, M)
Weight: 7 lb.–7 lb. 3 oz.
Bore/Gauge: 12, 20
Magazine: 2 shells
Features: Inertia-driven action with 3.5-in. chamber; Easy Locking System; oversized safety, bolt handle, and bolt release button; enlarged loading port; Easy Fitting System shim kit; ComforTech stock; Combtech cheek pad; Crio-treated barrel; stocks in black synthetic, A-Grade satin walnut, Realtree Max-5, GORE OPTIFADE Timber, GORE OPTIFADE Marsh, or Mossy Oak Bottomlands; red bar front sight, midbead; drilled and tapped for 93A Weaver scope mounts
MSRP . . . . $1799.00–$2099.00

SUPER BLACK EAGLE 3 BE.S.T.

Action: Semiautomatic
Stock: Synthetic
Barrel: 26 in., 28 in.
Chokes: 3
Sights: Red bar front
Weight: 5 lb. 15 oz.–7 lb.
Bore/Gauge: 12, 20
Capacity: 3 shells
Features: BE.S.T. stands for Benelli Surface Treatment, a metal surface treatment that Benelli says is impenetrable and stops rust and corrosion with a 25-year warranty. Other features include a 3.5-in. chamber in the 12-ga., 3-in. chamber in the 20-ga,; six Crio chokes (extended chokes get BE.S.T. treatment); drilled and tapped for scope mounts; minimum

recommended 12-ga. load is 3 DE/1 1/8-oz. payload, 2 ½ DE 7/8-oz. payload for the 20-ga.; shim kit; black stock and black anodized receiver
MSRP $2199.00

SUPER BLACK EAGLE 3 RIFLED SLUG

Action: Semiautomatic
Stock: Synthetic
Barrel: 24 in.
Chokes: None
Sights: Adjustable rifle sights
Weight: 7 lb. 2 oz.
Bore/Gauge: 12
Capacity: 4 shells
Features: Dedicated rifled bore in an easy to manage 24-inch length; adjustable rifled sights; 3-inch chamber
MSRP $1999.00

SUPER BLACK EAGLE 3 WITH STEADY GRIP

Action: Semiautomatic
Stock: Synthetic
Barrel: 24 in.
Chokes: Five
Sights: Red bar front
Weight: 6 lb. 13 oz.
Bore/Gauge: 12
Capacity: 4 shells
Features: The SBE3 now with a Steady Grip and short barrel for turkey hunters; three flush and two extended Crio chokes; stock adjustment shim kit; ComforTech3 and Combtech pads; Crio barrel; custom fitted hard case; full-coverage Mossy Oak Bottomlands
MSRP $2099.00

SUPERNOVA PUMP SHOTGUN

Action: Pump
Stock: Synthetic
Barrel: 24 in., 26 in., 28 in.
Chokes: Standard choke (IC, M, F)
Weight: 7 lb. 13 oz.–8 lb.
Bore/Gauge: 12
Magazine: 4+1 shells
Features: Stock comes in black synthetic or Realtree Max-5 camo; receiver drilled and tapped for scope mounting; standard chokes; vented recoil pad; standard model chambers up to 3 ½-inch shells
MSRP:. . . . . $559.00–$669.00

SUPERSPORT

Action: Semiautomatic
Stock: Synthetic
Barrel: 28 in., 30 in.
Chokes: Extended Crio Chokes(C, IC, M, IM, F)
Weight: 6 lb. 5 oz.–7 lb. 5 oz.
Bore/Gauge: 12, 20
Magazine: 4+1 shells
Features: Stock comes in black SuperSport carbon fiber finish; red bar front sight and metal bead mid sight; Crio ported barrels; ComforTech gel recoil pad and comb insert
MSRP. $2299.00

SUPER VINCI

Action: Semiautomatic
Stock: Synthetic, Realtree APG
Barrel: 26 in., 28 in., 30 in.
Chokes: Crio Chokes (C, IC, M, IM, F)
Weight: 6 lb. 14 oz.–7 lb. 2 oz.
Bore/Gauge: 12
Magazine: 3+1 shells
Features: In-line inertia driven system; enlarged trigger and trigger guard for use with gloves; ComforTech Plus recoil pad; QuadraFit shim kit; drilled and tapped for scopes; available in black, Realtree Max-5. or Mossy Oak Shadow Grass Blades or Gore Optifade Concealment Marsh; all models chamber up to 3 ½-inch shells
MSRP. . . . . $1599.00–$1699.00

ULTRA LIGHT

Action: Semiautomatic
Stock: Walnut
Barrel: 24 in., 26 in.
Chokes: Crio Chokes (IC, M, F)
Weight: 5 lb. 3 oz.–6 lb. 2 oz.
Bore/Gauge: 12, 20, 28
Magazine: 2+1 shells
Features: Weather-coated walnut stock; red bar front sight and metal bead mid sight; gel recoil pad; option of checkered Montefeltro forend or ultra light forend
MSRP. . . . . $1669.00–$1799.00

VINCI

Action: Semiautomatic
Stock: Synthetic
Barrel: 26 in., 28 in.
Chokes: Crio Chokes (C, IC, M, IM, F)
Weight: 6 lb. 13 oz.–6 lb. 14 oz.
Bore/Gauge: 12
Magazine: 3+1 shells
Features: Stock in black, or Realtree MAX-5 camo; red bar front sight and metal bead mid sight; drilled and tapped for scope mounting; ComforTech Plus recoil pads
MSRP: . . . . $1349.00–$1449.00

BENELLI SUPERNOVA PUMP SHOTGUN

BENELLI SUPERSPORT

BENELLI SUPER VINCI

BENELLI ULTRA LIGHT

BENELLI VINCI

Beretta USA

BERETTA 486 PARALLELO

BERETTA 686 SILVER PIGEON I

486 PARALLELO

Action: Side-by-side
Stock: Wood
Barrel: 28 in., 30 in.
Chokes: Fixed, Optima-Choke
Weight: 7 lb.
Bore/Gauge: 12
Magazine: 2 shells
Features: Round action with lavish scroll engraving; new leaf springs, trigger group, barrel technology
MSRP. $5799.00

686 SILVER PIGEON I

Action: Over/under
Stock: Walnut
Barrel: 26 in., 28 in., 30 in.
Chokes: MC
Weight: 6 lb. 13 oz.
Bore/Gauge: 12, 20, 28, .410
Magazine: 2 shells
Features: Extensive but refined floral and scroll decoration on the frame; dual-conical locking mechanism; automatic safety; oil finish on checkered walnut stock and forend; metal bead sight
MSRP. $2350.00

SHOTGUNS

Beretta USA

BERETTA 686 SILVER PIGEON 1 SPORTING

BERETTA 687 SILVER PIGEON III

BERETTA 692 SPORTING BLACK

BERETTA 694

BERETTA 1301 COMP

BERETTA 1301 TACTICAL

BERETTA A300 OUTLANDER

BERETTA A300 OUTLANDER SPORTING

686 SILVER PIGEON 1 SPORTING

Action: Over/under
Stock: Walnut
Barrel: 28, 30, 32 in.
Chokes: 3
Sights: Steel bead front
Weight: N/A
Bore/Gauge: 12, 20, 29, .410-bore
Capacity: 2 shells
Features: Longer barrels across all gauges, including 30-in. barrels available in all four bore sizes; 12-ga. available with 28- and 32-in. barrels as well; Opti-Bore HP barrels; two mid-action conical locking lugs allow for a lower-profile receiver; 2 ¾-in. and 3-in. chambers available in all but the 28-ga.; 12-ga. has 10X8 rib, all others have 8X8; Optima Chokes; oil-finished stock; scroll-engraved receiver
MSRP $2399.00

687 SILVER PIGEON III

Action: Over/under
Stock: Wood
Barrel: 26 in., 26.5 in., 28 in., 30 in.
Chokes: 3
Sights: White front bead
Weight: N/A
Bore/Gauge: 12, 20, 28, .410
Capacity: 2 shells
Features: Several improvements over earlier models, including 5-axis laser engraving on the receiver with game scenes and floral motifs; class 2.5 walnut with a high-gloss finish; Steelium Optima Bore HP tri-alloy barrels; 20mm MicroCore buttpad; 6x6 windowed top rib with anti-reflective checkering
MSRP $2699.00

692 SPORTING BLACK

Action: Over/under
Stock: Walnut

Barrel: 30 in., 32 in.
Chokes: 5 OCHP
Weight: 7 lb. 11 oz.
Bore/ Gauge: 12
Magazine: 2 shells
Features: Steelium Plus barrels; longer forcing cone; Beretta Fast Adjustment System Technology; Adjustable Balance System; adjustable trigger
MSRP . . . . $5250.00–$5750.00

694

Action: Over/under
Stock: Walnut
Barrel: 30 in., 32 in.
Chokes: 5
Sights: Steel bead front
Weight: 7 lb. 13 oz.
Bore/Gauge: 12
Capacity: 2 shells
Features: A slick offering for clay games with new action shape and stock configuration including grip designed to increase the shooter's field of vision; Steelium Plus barrels; MicroCore recoil pad; expanded pitch checkering at handhold points; steel action in Nistan gray finish; three-position adjustable trigger; new ejector design
MSRP $4549.00

1301 COMP

Action: Gas-operated semiautomatic
Stock: Synthetic
Barrel: 21 in., 24 in.
Chokes: IC
Weight: 7 lb. 2 oz.
Bore/Gauge: 12
Magazine: 5+1 shells
Features: Fiber optic sights; oversized bolt release and handle; Optima Bore HP interchangable choke system
MSRP $1349.00

1301 TACTICAL

Action: Gas-operated semiautomatic

Stock: Synthetic
Barrel: 18.5 in.
Chokes: F
Weight: 7 lb. 2 oz.
Bore/Gauge: 12
Magazine: 5+1 shells
Features: Ghost ring sight; front blade sight; Picatinny rail; oversized bolt release and handle; fixed cylinder choke
Standard $1429.00
Tactical pistol grip $1449.00
Standard Flat Dark Earth . . $1359.00

A300 OUTLANDER

Action: Gas-operated semiautomatic
Stock: Synthetic, camo, walnut
Barrel: 28 in.
Chokes: MC3
Weight: 7 lb. 10 oz.
Bore/Gauge: 12
Magazine: 3+1 shells
Features: Gas operation with compensating exhaust valve and self-cleaning piston; adjustable shim system on stock; aluminum alloy receiver; crossbolt safety with ergonomics; front metal bead sight; oiled wood stock finish
MSRP $899.00

A300 OUTLANDER SPORTING

Action: Semiautomatic
Stock: Wood
Barrel: 30 in.
Chokes: Three MobilChoke Victory (IC, M, F)
Sights: Front and mid-rib beads
Weight: N/A
Bore/Gauge: 12
Magazine: 3 shells
Features: High-grade wood with checkering pattern; gas-operated; valve with a self-cleaning cylinder and piston combination
MSRP $1100.00

BERETTA A300 OUTLANDER TURKEY

BERETTA A350 EXTREMA MAX-5

BERETTA A400 LITE SYNTHETIC

BERETTA A400 XPLOR ACTION

BERETTA A400 XTREME PLUS CAMO

BERETTA A400 XTREME PLUS SYNTHETIC

BERETTA A400 XTREME UNICO

A300 OUTLANDER TURKEY

Action: Semiautomatic
Stock: Synthetic
Barrel: 24 in.
Chokes: 3 chokes (F, M, IC)
Weight: 7 lb. 9 oz.
Bore/Gauge: 12
Magazine: 3+1 shells
Features: TRUGLO fiber optic sights; Realtree Xtra or Xtra Green camo choices; adjustable drop cast; reliable/clean gas operating system; sling attachment
MSRP $900.00

A350 EXTREMA MAX-5

Action: Semiautomatic
Stock: Synthetic
Barrel: 28 in.
Chokes: Optima HP
Weight: 7 lb. 2 oz.
Bore/Gauge: 12
Magazine: N/A
Features: Adjustable shim system for drop and right-hand or left-hand configuration; 3.5 in. chamber; steelium barrel; fiber optic bead front sight; sling points; Micro Core recoil pad; Max-5 camo finish
MSRP $1150.00

A400 LITE SYNTHETIC

Action: Semiautomatic
Stock: Walnut and polymer
Barrel: 24 in., 26 in., 28 in., 30 in.
Chokes: OptimaChoke screw-in tube
Weight: 6 lb. 3 oz.–6 lb. 10 oz.
Bore/Gauge: 12, 20
Magazine: 3+1 or 2+1 shells
Features: Steelium barrel design, walnut stock with polymer forend insert, trigger guard and kick-off interface; 3-in. chamber; blink operating system; Micro-Core recoil pad; available with Kick-Off damper system; available in a standard-length 20-ga. and a Compact 20-ga., both with 3-inch chambers; Compact does not include the Kick-Off system
12-ga.: $1600.00
20-ga.: $1600.00
Compact 20-ga.: $1500.00

A400 XPLOR ACTION

Action: Gas-operated semiautomatic
Stock: Walnut
Barrel: 26 in., 28 in.
Chokes: F
Weight: 5 lb. 8 oz.
Bore/Gauge: 12, 20, 28
Magazine: 3+1 shells
Features: Fiber optic sights; Gun Pod shell counter, cartridge tester, and temperature display; Kick-Off recoil reduction system; Optima Bore interchangable bore system; left-hand available in 12-ga. 3-inch chamber with 28-inch barrel only
MSRP . . . . $1679.00–$1829.00

A400 XTREME PLUS CAMO

Action: Semiautomatic
Stock: Synthetic
Barrel: 26 in., 28 in.
Chokes: Five
Sights: Red bar front, integral mid bead
Weight: N/A
Bore/Gauge: 12
Capacity: 4 shells
Features: Improved stock features a soft-touch comb; barrels are Steelium Plus and reduce felt recoil; stepped rib with integral mid-rib bead; 3 ½-inch chamber; full-coverage Realtree Max-5, Kryptek Wraith, True Timber DTR, Realtree Timber, or MO Bottomland camo; five extended Black Edition choke tubes
MSRP . . . . $1899.00–$1949.00

A400 XTREME PLUS SYNTHETIC

Action: Semiautomatic
Stock: Synthetic
Barrel: 26, 28, 30 in.
Chokes: Five
Sights: Red bar front, integral mid bead
Weight: N/A
Bore/Gauge: 12
Capacity: 4 shells
Features: Kick-Off Mega/Kick-Off3 stock features a soft-touch comb; barrels are Steelium Plus and reduce felt recoil; stepped rib with integral mid-rib bead; 3 ½-inch chamber; black synthetic stock with complementary dark-gray receiver finish; five extended Black Edition choke tubes
MSRP . . . . $1899.00–$1949.00

A400 XTREME UNICO SYNTHETIC

Action: Semiautomatic
Stock: Synthetic or camo
Barrel: 26 in., 28 in., 30 in.
Chokes: Optima Bore HP (C, Mod, Full)
Weight: 7 lb. 10 oz.
Bore/Gauge: 12
Magazine: 4+1 or 3+1 shells
Features: Adjustable buttstock shim kits, anti-corosion coatings on the barrel, Beretta's fast-cycling Blink technology, fast-assembly B-Lock fore-end cap, Kick-Off 3/Kick-Off Mega recoil reduction system, and Steelium Optma Bore HP barrels; chamber 3 ½-in. shells; left-hand available
MSRP: . . . . $1750.00–$1800.00

Beretta USA

BERETTA DT11 SPORTING BLACK

BERETTA SL3

DT11 SPORTING BLACK

Action: Over/under
Stock: Walnut
Barrel: 30 in., 32 in.
Chokes: OCHPe
Weight: 9 lb.
Bore/ Gauge: 12
Magazine: 2 shells
Features: Steelium Pro barrel; top rib with hollowed bridges; ergonomic top lever; safety selector switch; increased receiver side wall thickness; select high-quality walnut wood finished in oil; stock and forend can be fitted to customer's measurement; pistol grip and forend are hand-checkered; B-Fast adjustable stock available; left-hand model available in both barrel lengths, but without B-Fast stock option
MSRP . . . . . . $12,550.00–$12,950.00

SL3

Action: Over/under
Stock: Walnut
Barrel: 28 in., 30 in.
Chokes: N/A
Sights: Bead front
Weight: Fixed
Bore/Gauge: 12, 20
Capacity: 2 shells
Features: A handmade boxlock with superior walnut stock; double triggers; Optima Bore HP barrels; rounded body design; light scroll, deep scroll, or game scene engravings, as well as a striking unengraved high-polish receiver option available
MSRP . . . . . . $21,100.00–$21,500.00

Blaser USA

BLASER F16 GAME

BLASER F16 GAME INTUITION

BLASER F16 SPORTING

BLASER F16 SPORTING INTUITION

F16 GAME

Action: Over/under
Stock: Walnut
Barrel: 28 in., 30 in.
Chokes: Blaser chokes flush to muzzle
Weight: 6 lb. 13 oz.
Bore/Gauge: 12
Magazine: 2 shells
Features: Sleak English-style forearm design; crisp trigger pull; Triplex bore design; tapered rib; proven Blaser ejection system; Inertial Block System (IBS) prevents an involuntary second shot or the unintentional triggering of a second shot while maintaining a superb trigger pull; many options available within three grades: Standard, Grande Luxe, and Heritage
Standard/wood grade 4 . . . $5213.00
Grande Luxe/wood grade 6. . . $9268.00
Heritage/wood grade 8. . .$12,744.00

F16 GAME INTUITION

Action: Over/under
Stock: Wood grade II
Barrel: 28 in., 30 in.
Chokes: Three flush chokes (¼, ½, ¾)
Weight: 6 lb. 10 oz.
Bore/Gauge: 12
Magazine: 2 shells
Features: Designed specifically for women, with a specially designed buttstock tailored to the female anatomy, including a more slender pistol grip, higher comb, and reduced pitch; non-adjustable trigger; 13.8-in. length of pull; sling swivel (not mounted); silver F16 logo and silver front bead; many options available, including upgraded wood and weight balancer
Standard/wood grade 4: . . $5792.00
Grande Luxe/wood grade 6: . . . $9731.00
Heritage/wood grade 8: . .$13,091.00

F16 SPORTING

Action: Over/under
Stock: Walnut
Barrel: 30 in., 32 in.
Chokes: Blaser chokes flush to muzzle
Weight: 7 lb. 8 oz.–8 lb. 6 oz.
Bore/Gauge: 12
Magazine: 2 shells
Features: Balancer system allows the adjustment of the weight distribution to shooter's personal needs; sleak English-style forearm design; crisp trigger pull; Triplex bore design; tapered rib; proven Blaser ejection system; Inertial Block System (IBS) prevents an involuntary second shot or the unintentional triggering of a second shot while maintaining a superb trigger pull; many options available within three grades: Standard, Grande Luxe, and Heritage
Standard/wood grade 4 . . $5,792.00
Grande Luxe/wood grade 6. . . $9731.00
Heritage/wood grade 8. . .$13,091.00

F16 SPORTING INTUITION

Action: Over/under
Stock: Wood grade II
Barrel: 30 in., 32 in.
Chokes: Three flush chokes (¼, ½, ¾)
Weight: 7 lb. 5 oz.–8 lb. 3 oz.
Bore/Gauge: 12
Magazine: 2 shells
Features: Designed specifically for women, with a specially designed buttstock tailored to the female anatomy, including a more slender pistol grip, higher comb, and reduced pitch; non-adjustable trigger; 13.8-in. length of pull; Blaser Comfort recoil pad; adjustable trigger length; prep for barrel balancer and stock balancer; red F16 logo and red fiber optic front bead; many options available, including upgraded wood and barrel balancer weights
Standard/wood grade 4: . . . $5299.00
Grande Luxe/wood grade 6:. . . $8903.00
Heritage/wood grade 8: . . .$11,977.00

BROWNING A5 CAMO

BROWNING A5 CAMO VINTAGE TAN

BROWNING A5 HUNTER

BROWNING A5 HUNTER HIGH GRADE

BROWNING A5 LIGHTNING SWEET 16

A5 MOSSY OAK BREAK-UP COUNTRY

BROWNING A5 STALKER

A5 CAMO, REALTREE TIMBER, MO BREAKUP COUNTRY, MO SHADOW GRASS HABITAT, REALTREE MAX-7

Action: Semiautomatic
Stock: Synthetic
Barrel: 26 in., 28 in., 30 in.
Chokes: 3
Sights: Fiber optic front sight
Weight: 7 lb. 3 oz.–7 lb. 7 oz.
Bore/Gauge: 12
Capacity: 4 shells
Features: The A5 goes all things camo with three coverages to choose from; 3½-in. chamber; textured grip panels; aluminum alloy receiver; back-bored; VectorPro lengthened forcing cones; Invector DS chokes; nickel-Teflon coating on operating controls; stock shims; Speed Load Plus design; TurnKey magazine plug; Kinematic Drive action; Ergo Balanced design
MSRP . . . .$1799.99–$1939.99

A5 CAMO VINTAGE TAN

Action: Semiautomatic
Stock: Synthetic
Barrel: 26 in., 28 in.
Chokes: 3
Sights: Fiber optic front sight
Weight: 7 lb. 3 oz.–7 lb. 5 oz.
Bore/Gauge: 12
Capacity: 4 shells
Features: Vintage is in with an old duck hunter's type of camo; 3½-in. chamber; textured grip panels; aluminum alloy receiver; back-bored; VectorPro lengthened forcing cones; Invector DS chokes; nickel-Teflon coating on operating controls; stock shims; Speed Load Plus design; TurnKey magazine plug; Kinematic Drive action; Ergo Balanced design
MSRP **$1939.99**

A5 HUNTER

Action: Semiautomatic
Stock: Walnut

Barrel: 26 in., 28 in.
Chokes: Invector-DS
Weight: 6 lb. 15 oz.
Bore/Gauge: 12
Magazine: None
Features: Strong, lightweight aluminum alloy; black anodized bi-tone finish; flat, ventilated rib; recoil operated Kinematic Drive cycles a wide range of loads; gloss finish walnut with close radius pistol grip; shim adjustable for length of pull, cast and drop; Vector Pro lengthened forcing cone; three invector-DS choke tubes; brass front bead sight; ivory mid-bead sight; included ABS case
3-inch: **$1799.99**
3½-inch: **$1939.99**

A5 HUNTER HIGH GRADE

Action: Semiautomatic
Stock: Walnut
Barrel: 26 in., 28 in.
Chokes: Invector-DS (F, M, IC)
Weight: 6 lb. 11 oz.–6 lb. 13 oz.
Bore/Gauge: 12
Magazine: 4 shells
Features: 3-in. chambered gun; gloss finished barrel; receiver with intricate scrollwork, pheasant and mallard engraving; grade 2.5 gloss varnish finish walnut stock with 22 lines-per-inch checkering; lightweight profile barrel; aluminum alloy receiver; recoil-operated Kinematic drive; Vector Pro lengthened forcing cones
MSRP **$2039.99**

A5 LIGHTNING SWEET 16

Action: Semiautomatic
Stock: Walnut
Barrel: 26 in., 28 in.
Chokes: 3
Sights: Fiber optic front sight, ivory mid-bead
Weight: 5 lb. 12 oz.–5 lb. 13 oz.
Bore/Gauge: 16
Capacity: 4 shells
Features: Turkish walnut stock in gloss finish; Prince of Wales grip; high-gloss

blued barrel; 2¾-in. chamber; aluminum alloy receiver in a gloss black anodized finish; back-bored; VectorPro lengthened forcing cones; Invector DS chokes; nickel-Teflon coating on operating controls; stock shims; Kinematic Drive action; SpeedLoad Plus design; TurnKey magazine plug; Ergo Balanced design; ABS case included
MSRP **$1819.99**

A5 MOSSY OAK BREAK-UP COUNTRY

Action: Semiautomatic
Stock: Composite
Barrel: 26 in., 28 in.
Chokes: 3 (F, M, IC)
Sights: Fiber optic front
Weight: 7 lb. 3 oz.–7 lb. 7 oz.
Bore/Gauge: 12, 20
Capacity: 4 shells
Features: The "new" A5 with Kinetic Drive System; aluminum alloy receiver; Vector Pro lengthened forcing cones; Inflex recoil pad; stock spacers; length of pull/drop/cast shims; Invector DS chokes; 3.5-in. chamber; ABS case
3-inch: **$1799.99**
3½-inch: **$1939.99**

A5 STALKER

Action: Semiautomatic
Stock: Composite
Barrel: 26 in., 28 in.
Chokes: Invector-DS
Weight: 7 lb. 3 oz.–7 lb. 7 oz.
Bore/Gauge: 12
Magazine: None
Features: Strong, lightweight aluminum alloy; flat, ventilated rib; recoil operated Kinematic Drive cycles a wide range of loads; composite with close radius pistol grip; textured gripping surfaces; shim adjustable for cast and drop; matte black finish; Dura-Touch armor coating; Vector Pro lengthened forcing cone; fiber-optic front sight; included ABS case
3-inch: **$1659.99**
3½-inch: **$1799.99**

Browning

BROWNING A5 SWEET SIXTEEN

BROWNING A5 WICKED WING

BROWNING A5 WICKED WING VINTAGE TAN

BROWNING B15 BEAUCHAMP

BROWNING BPS FIELD

BROWNING BPS FIELD COMPOSITE REALTREE MAX-5

BROWNING BT-99 MAX HIGH-GRADE

BROWNING BT-99

A5 SWEET SIXTEEN

Action: Semiautomatic
Stock: Turkish walnut
Barrel: 28 in.
Chokes: Invector-DS flush
Weight: 5 lb. 13 oz.
Bore/Gauge: 16
Magazine: 4 shells
Features: Gloss walnut stock; brass bead front sight; humpback receiver; short recoil-operated Kinematic Drive System; Invector-DS choke tubes; built on a smaller, lighter receiver for reduced weight
MSRP $1869.99

A5 WICKED WING

Action: Semiautomatic
Stock: Composite
Barrel: 26 in., 28 in.
Chokes: Extended Invector-DS Banded (F,M,IC)
Weight: 7 lb. 3 oz.–7 lb. 5 oz.
Bore/Gauge: 12
Magazine: 4 shells
Features: Chambered for 3.5-in. shells; Cerakote Burnt Bronze camo receiver and Burnt Bronze barrel with Mossy Oak Shadow Grass Habitat, Mossy Oak Bottomland, or Realtree Max-7; Briley extended bolt handle and oversize bolt release; fully chromed bore; recoil operated Kinematic Drive; Vector Pro lengthened forcing cone; fiber-optic front sight and ivory mid-bead
MSRP $2229.99

A5 WICKED WING VINTAGE TAN

Action: Semiautomatic
Stock: Synthetic
Barrel: 26 in., 28 in.
Chokes: 3
Sights: Fiber optic front sight
Weight: 7 lb. 3 oz.–7 lb. 5 oz.
Bore/Gauge: 12

Capacity: 4 shells
Features: Wearing full-coverage old duck hunter's type of camo; 3½-in. chamber; textured grip panels; aluminum alloy receiver; back-bored; VectorPro lengthened forcing cones; Invector DS chokes; nickel-Teflon coating on operating controls; stock shims; Speed Load Plus design; TurnKey magazine plug; Kinematic Drive action; Ergo Balanced design
MSRP $2159.99

B15 BEAUCHAMP

Action: Over/under
Stock: Walnut
Barrel: 26 in., 28 in., 30 in.
Chokes: Five Invector DS
Sights: Front bead
Weight: 6 lb. 6 oz.
Bore/Gauge: 12
Magazine: 2 shells
Features: Part of Belgium-produced John M. Browning Collection; offered in four wood grades and three barrel lengths, with various forearms, buttplates and engraving levels; mechanical triggers; back-bored Vector Pro barrels; full flush-mounted choke set; leather case
MSRP . . . . . . $19,299.95–$28,999.99

BPS FIELD

Action: Pump
Stock: Walnut
Barrel: 26 in., 28 in.
Chokes: 3 (F, M, IC)
Sights: Silver bead front
Weight: 7 lb.–7 lb. 10 oz.
Bore/Gauge: 12, 20, 28, .410
Capacity: 4 shells
Features: This long-standing pump was overhauled in 2020, with an upgraded stock and forend design in a satin-finish walnut; Inflex recoil pad; improved checkering at grip points; floating rib; classic bottom feed/ ejection; flush Invector Plus chokes
MSRP: . . . . $759.99–$829.99

BPS FIELD COMPOSITE

Action: Pump
Stock: Composite
Barrel: 26 in., 28 in.
Chokes: 3 (F, M, IC)
Sights: Silver bead front
Weight: 7 lb.–8 lb. 1 oz.
Bore/Gauge: 10, 12, 20
Capacity: 4 shells
Features: A redesigned stock and forend for a faster feel, and other changes in 2020 include an Inflex recoil pad; textured grip points; floating rib; classic bottom feed/ ejection; flush Invector Plus chokes
MSRP . . . . $719.99–$749.99

BT-99

Action: Pump
Stock: Walnut
Barrel: 32 in., 34 in.
Chokes: Screw-in tubes
Weight: 8 lb. 3 oz.–8 lb. 5 oz.
Bore/Gauge: 12
Magazine: None
Features: Satin finish walnut stock with beavertail forearm; steel receiver with blued finish; high-post ventilated rib
MSRP $1619.99

BT-99 MAX HIGH-GRADE

Action: Break-open
Stock: Grade V/VI walnut
Barrel: 32 in., 34 in.
Chokes: Three extended
Sights: Hi-Viz Pro Comp fiber optic front, mid-rib bead
Weight: 9 lb. 5 oz.
Bore/Gauge: 12
Capacity: 1 shell
Features: Top-of-the-line single-shot trap model with three extended Midas grade choke tubes; Pachmayr Decelerator XLT recoil pad; adjustable Graco buttpad, comb, and recoil reduction system; point of impact adjustable high rib; gloss oil stock finish; fitted Universal BT Trap case
MSRP $5799.99

Browning

BROWNING BT-99 TRAP, TRAP MICRO WITH ADJUSTABLE BUTTPLATE AND COMB

BROWNING BT-99 MICRO WITH ADJUSTABLE LOP

BROWNING CITORI 725 FEATHER

BROWNING CITORI 725 FEATHER SUPERLIGHT

BROWNING CITORI 725 FIELD

BROWNING CITORI 725 PRO SPORTING WITH PRO FIT ADJUSTABLE COMB

BROWNING CITORI 725 PRO TRAP WITH PRO FIT ADJUSTABLE COMB

BT-99, BT-99 MICRO WITH ADJUSTABLE BUTTPLATE AND COMB

Action: Single-shot
Stock: Black walnut
Barrel: 30 in., 32 in., 34 in.
Chokes: One Invector-Plus flush
Sights: Ivory bead
Weight: 7 lb. 12 oz.–8 lb. 5 oz.
Bore/Gauge: 12
Magazine: 1 shell
Features: Graco Pro Fit adjustable buttpad plate and comb; barrels and receiver are satin blue; stock is in a satin finish; standard model (32-in., 34-in. barrel); Micro version (30-in., 32-i.n barrel) has shorter length of pull and is 12 ga., 2.75-in. chamber
MSRP. $2019.99

BT-99 MICRO WITH ADJUSTABLE LOP

Action: Single-shot
Stock: Black walnut
Barrel: 30 in.
Chokes: Invector Plus flush (F)
Sights: Ivory front sight, mid-bead
Weight: 7 lb. 12 oz.
Bore/Gauge: 12
Capacity: 1 shell
Features: A dedicated trap gun for smaller-statured shooters with an adjustable length of pull; Graco trap recoil pad; satin-finish stock; 2¾-in. chamber
MSRP. $1779.99

CITORI 725 FEATHER

Action: Over/under
Stock: Walnut
Barrel: 26 in., 28 in.
Chokes: 3 Invector-DS
Weight: 5 lb. 14 oz.–6 lb. 9 oz.
Bore/ Gauge: 12, 20
Magazine: 2 shells
Features: Lightweight alloy receiver; low-profile; silver nitride finish; ventilated top rib barrel; Fire Lite Mechanical Trigger system; hammer ejectors; ivory front and mid-bead sights
MSRP. $2919.99

CITORI 725 FEATHER SUPERLIGHT

Action: Over/under
Stock: Grade II/III walnut
Barrel: 26 in.
Chokes: Three (F, M, IC)
Sights: Ivory bead front
Weight: 6 lb. 2 oz. (12-ga.); 5 lb. 7 oz. (20-ga.)
Bore/Gauge: 12, 20
Capacity: 2 shells
Features: Super lightweight swinger for the upland hunter who goes all day, featuring: flush-mounted Invector DS chokes; aluminum alloy receiver with silver nitride receiver; gloss-finish straight-grip stock; 2¾-inch chrome-plated chambers
MSRP. $2839.00

CITORI 725 FIELD

Action: Over/under
Stock: Walnut
Barrel: 26 in., 28 in.
Chokes: Invector-DS
Weight: 6 lb. 7 oz.–7 lb. 8 oz.
Bore/Gauge: 12, 20, 28, .410
Magazine: 2 shells
Features: Steel receiver with silver nitride finish; accented, high-relief engraving; ventilated top rib action; mechanical trigger system; hammer ejectors; top-tang barrel selector/safety; gloss oil finish Grade II/III walnut with close radius pistol grip; Vector Pro lengthened forcing cones; ivory front and mid-bead sights
MSRP. . . . . $2759.99–$2839.99

CITORI 725 PRO SPORTING WITH PRO FIT ADJUSTABLE COMB

Action: Over/under
Stock: Wood
Barrel: 30 in., 32 in.
Chokes: F, IM, M, IC, S
Weight: 7 lb. 5 oz.–7 lb. 13 oz.
Bore/Gauge: 12, 20
Magazine: 2 shells
Features: Polished blue barrel finish; grade III/IV black walnut stock with gloss oil finish; HiViz ProComp sights; vented ribs; drilled and tapped for scopes
MSRP. $4349.99

CITORI 725 PRO TRAP WITH PRO FIT ADJUSTABLE COMB

Action: Over/under
Stock: Wood
Barrel: 30 in., 32 in.
Chokes: F, LF, M, 2IM
Weight: 8 lb. 8 oz., 8 lb. 11 oz.
Bore/Gauge: 12
Magazine: 2 shells
Features: Polished blue barrel finish; grade III/IV black walnut stock with gloss oil finish; HiViz ProComp sights; vented ribs; drilled and tapped for scopes
MSRP. $4349.99

SHOTGUNS

Browning

BROWNING CITORI 725 SPORTING

BROWNING CITORI 725 SPORTING MAPLE

BROWNING CITORI 725 TRAP LEFT-HAND, LEFT-HAND ADJUSTABLE COMB

BROWNING CITORI 725 SPORTING ADJUSTABLE COMB

BROWNING CITORI 725 SPORTING PARALLEL COMB, PARALLEL COMB ADJUSTABLE COMB

BROWNING CITORI 725 SPORTING LEFT-HAND, LEFT-HAND ADJUSTABLE COMB

BROWNING CITORI 725 SPORTING GOLDEN CLAYS

CITORI 725 SPORTING

Action: Over/under
Stock: Walnut
Barrel: 30, 32 in.
Chokes: Invector-DS
Weight: 6 lb. 4 oz.–7 lb. 10 oz.
Bore/Gauge: 12, 20, 28, .410
Magazine: 2 shells
Features: Steel receiver with silver nitride finish; gold accented engraving; ventilated top and side rib action; mechanical trigger system; hammer ejectors; top-tang barrel selector/safety; gloss oil finish Grade III/IV walnut with close radius pistol grip; Vector Pro lengthened forcing cones; five Invector-DS choke tubes; HiViz Pro-Comp sight and ivory mid-bead
MSRP . . . . $3419.99–$3479.99

CITORI 725 SPORTING ADJUSTABLE COMB

Action: Over/under
Stock: Wood
Barrel: 30 in., 32 in.
Chokes: F, IM, M, IC, S
Weight: 7 lb. 13 oz.
Bore/Gauge: 12
Magazine: 2 shells
Features: Steel low-profile receiver with silver nitride finish and gold accented engraving; ventilated barrel with top and side ribs; Fire Lite mechanical trigger system; top-tang barrel selector/safety; gloss oil finish Grade III/IV walnut stock with close radius pistol grip and adjustable comb; HiViz Pro-Comp sight and ivory mid-bead
MSRP $3829.99

CITORI 725 SPORTING LEFT-HAND, LEFT-HAND ADJUSTABLE COMB

Action: Over/under
Stock: Walnut
Barrel: 30 in., 32 in.
Chokes: 5

Sights: HiViz Pro Comp fiber optic front
Weight: 7 lb. 8 oz.–7 lb. 13 oz.
Bore/Gauge: 12
Capacity: 2 shells
Features: Browning's Fire Lite mechanical trigger with three shoes; Invector-DS chokes; Ergo balance design; Inflex II recoil pad; gloss oil-finished Grade III/IV walnut stock; true left-hand top lever; wide floating rib and between barrel venting; ported barrels; optional adjustable comb model
Standard:. $3419.99
Adjustable Comb: $3829.99

CITORI 725 SPORTING MAPLE

Action: Over/under
Stock: Maple
Barrel: 30 in., 32 in.
Chokes: 5
Sights: HiViz Pro Comp fiber optic front
Weight: 7 lb. 6 oz.–7 lb. 8 oz.
Bore/Gauge: 12
Capacity: 2 shells
Features: AAAA-grade maple stock; Fire Lite mechanical trigger with three shoes; Invector-DS chokes; Ergo balance design; Inflex II recoil pad; low post floating rib and between barrel venting; ported barrels; gold-enhanced engraving
MSRP $3549.99

CITORI 725 SPORTING PARALLEL COMB, PARALLEL COMB ADJUSTABLE COMB

Action: Over/under
Stock: Walnut
Barrel: 30 in., 32 in.
Chokes: 5
Sights: HiViz Pro Comp fiber optic front
Weight: 7 lb. 6 oz.–7 lb. 8 oz.
Bore/Gauge: 12
Capacity: 2 shells
Features: Fire Lite mechanical trigger with three shoes; Invector-DS chokes; Ergo balance design; Inflex II recoil pad; gloss oil-finished Grade III/IV

walnut stock; low-post floating rib and between barrel venting; ported barrels; parallel comb stock; optional adjustable comb model; silver nitride receiver with gold-enhanced engraving; point of aim 50/50
Standard $3399.99
Adjustable comb $3829.00

CITORI 725 SPORTING GOLDEN CLAYS

Action: Over/under
Stock: Walnut
Barrel: 30 in., 32 in.
Chokes: Extended Invector-DS (F, IM, M, IC, Skeet)
Weight: 7 lb. 13 oz.
Bore/Gauge: 12
Magazine: 2 shells
Features: Unique "Golden Clays" accented gold engraving; Pro Fit adjustable comb; ported barrels with vented top and side ribs; HiViz Pro-Comp fiber optic front side and ivory mid-bead; grade V/VI walnut stock; low-profile silver nitride finish steel receiver; FireLite mechanical trigger
MSRP. $5799.99

CITORI 725 TRAP LEFT-HAND, LEFT-HAND ADJUSTABLE COMB

Action: Over/under
Stock: Walnut
Barrel: 30 in., 32 in.
Chokes: 3
Sights: HiViz Pro Comp fiber optic front, ivory mid bead
Weight: 8 lb. 10 oz.–9 lb. 1 oz.
Bore/Gauge: 12
Capacity: 2 shells
Features: Fire Lite mechanical trigger with three shoes; Invector-DS chokes; Ergo balance design; gloss oil-finished Grade III/IV walnut stock; true left-hand top lever; high post floating rib and between barrel venting; ported barrels; steel receiver in silver nitride finish with gold-enhanced engraving; supplied with three extended Invector-DS chokes; 2¾-chamber; optional adjustable comb model
Standard $3619.99
Adjustable comb $4059.99

BROWNING CITORI 725 TRAP MAPLE

BROWNING CITORI 725 TRAP MAX

BROWNING CITORI 725 TRAP ADJUSTABLE COMB

BROWNING CITORI CX

BROWNING CITORI CXS 20-/28-GAUGE COMBO

BROWNING CITORI 725 TRAP GOLDEN CLAYS

BROWNING CITORI CX WHITE ADJUSTABLE COMB

CITORI 725 TRAP MAPLE

Action: Over/under
Stock: Maple
Barrel: 30 in., 32 in.
Chokes: 3
Sights: HiViz Pro Comp fiber optic front
Weight: 8 lb. 2 oz.–8 lb. 4 oz.
Bore/Gauge: 12
Capacity: 2 shells
Features: AAAA-grade maple; Fire Lite mechanical trigger with three shoes; Invector-DS extended chokes; Ergo balance design; ventilated trap-style recoil pad; Monte Carlo comb; semi-beavertail forend; high post floating rib and between barrel venting; ported barrels; gold-enhanced engraving; point of impact 70/30
MSRP **$3619.00**

CITORI 725 TRAP ADJUSTABLE COMB

Action: Over/under
Stock: Wood
Barrel: 30 in., 32 in.
Chokes: F, IM, M
Weight: 8 lb. 8 oz.–8 lb. 11 oz.
Bore/Gauge: 12
Magazine: 2 shells
Features: Steel low-profile receiver with silver nitride finish and gold accented engraving; ventilated barrel with top and side ribs; Fire Lite mechanical trigger system; top-tang barrel selector/safety; gloss oil finish Grade III/IV walnut stock with close radius pistol grip and Monte Carlo or adjustable straight comb; HiViz Pro-Comp sight and ivory mid-bead
MSRP **$4059.99**

CITORI 725 TRAP GOLDEN CLAYS

Action: Over/under
Stock: Walnut
Barrel: 30 in., 32 in.
Chokes: Extended Invector-DS (F, LF, IM, IM, M)
Weight: 8 lb. 8 oz.–8 lb. 11 oz.

Bore/Gauge: 12
Magazine: 2 shells
Features: 2¾ in. chamber; hammer ejectors and top-tang barrel selector/safety; gloss grade V/VI walnut stock with close radius pistol grip and right-hand palm swell; receiver has a silver nitride finish and gold-accented engraving; adjustable Monte Carlo comb; Pachmayr Decelerator XLT Trap recoil pad; ventilated top and side ribs; Vector Pro lengthened forcing cones; GraCoil recoil reduction system; HiViz Pro-Comp front sight and ivory mid-bead
MSRP **$6229.99**

CITORI 725 TRAP MAX

Action: Over/under
Stock: Black walnut
Barrel: 30 in., 32 in.
Chokes: 5 (F, LF, M, IM x2)
Sights: Hi-Viz Pro Comp front, ivory mid bead
Weight: 9 lb.–9 lb. 2 oz.
Bore/Gauge: 12
Capacity: 2 shells
Features: You'll be aiming for gold with this trap gun featuring a Graco buttpad plate for cant/toe-in/toe-out adjusting; adjustable GraCoil Recoil Reduction System; Grade V/VI gloss-finished walnut stock; Triple Trigger System with three shoes; Pachmayr Decelerator XLT recoil pad; adjustable high trap rib changes POI from 50/50 up to 90/10; ported barrels
MSRP **$6229.99**

CITORI CX

Action: Over/under
Stock: Grade II American walnut
Barrel: 28 in., 30 in., 32 in.
Chokes: Three extended (F, M, IC)
Sights: Ivory bead front
Weight: 8 lb. 1 oz.–8 lb. 5 oz.
Bore/Gauge: 12
Capacity: 2 shells
Features: Browning calls this a "crossover" gun with a 60/40 point of

impact to address targets or game and featuring: high-polished blued finish with CX logo in gold on the receiver; 3-inch chrome chambers; Vector Pro lengthened forcing cones; Inflex recoil pad; gloss-finish stock; Midas-grade extended chokes; ventilated high-post rib and vented barrel joint; Triple Trigger System with one trigger included
MSRP **$2339.00**

CITORI CX WHITE

Action: Over/under
Stock: Black walnut
Barrel: 28 in., 30 in., 32 in.
Chokes: Invector Plus Midas
Sights: Ivory front, mid-bead
Weight: 8 lb. 1 oz.–8 lb. 9 oz.
Bore/Gauge: 12
Capacity: 2 shells
Features: Similar to the standard CX, but with a receiver in a silver nitride finish
Standard stock: **$2519.99**
Adjustable comb: **$2949.99**

CITORI CXS 20-/28-GAUGE COMBO

Action: Over/under
Stock: Black walnut
Barrel: 30 in., 32 in.
Chokes: 6 (F, M, IC)
Sights: Ivory front, mid-bead
Weight: 7 lb. 2 oz.–7 lb. 15 oz.
Bore/Gauge: 20/28
Capacity: 2 shells
Features: A two-barrel set for sub-gauge competitors with a Grade II walnut stock with 18 lines-per-inch checkering and in a gloss finish; polished blue receiver and barrels; wide floating rib with 50/50 point of impact; Inflex 2 recoil pad; six extended Invector Plus Midas-grade chokes, three for each gauge
MSRP **$4379,99**

SHOTGUNS

Browning

BROWNING CITORI CXS

BROWNING CITORI CXS MICRO

BROWNING CITORI CXT

BROWNING CITORI CXT
MICRO ADJUSTABLE LOP

BROWNING CITORI CXS
WHITE ADJUSTABLE COMB

BROWNING CITORI
FEATHER LIGHTNING

BROWNING CITORI FEATHER
SUPERLIGHT 16-GAUGE

CITORI CXS, CXS WITH ADJUSTABLE COMB

Action: Over/under
Stock: Black walnut
Barrel: 28 in., 30 in., 32 in.
Chokes: Three Invector-Plus Midas (F, M, IC)
Sights: Ivory bead
Weight: 6 lb. 3 oz.–6 lb. 7 oz. (20-gauge); 7 lb. 10 oz.–7 lb. 14 oz. (12-gauge); 7 lb. 14 oz.–8 lb. 2 oz. (12-gauge with adjustable comb)
Bore/Gauge: 12, 20
Magazine: 2 shells
Features: Barrels with a lightweight profile, vented top and side; shoots 50/50 point of impact; Grade II American walnut with a gloss finish; Vector Pro lengthened forcing cones; Triple Trigger system (one trigger included); ivory mid-bead
Standard **$2399.99**
Adjustable comb. . .**$2749.99–$2839.99**

CITORI CXS MICRO

Action: Over/under
Stock: Grade II/III American walnut
Barrel: 24 in., 26 in.
Chokes: Three extended (F, M, IC)
Sights: Ivory bead front and mid-rib
Weight: 6 lb. 7 oz.–7 lb. 8 oz.
Bore/Gauge: 12, 20
Capacity: 2 shells
Features: In Browning's "crossover" category of over/unders, this one with shorter barrels for nimble handling on the skeet field or in the grouse woods. Features include: 50/50 point of impact; Inflex recoil pad; shorter 13-inch length of pull; extended Midas-grade chokes; front and mid-rib beads; 3-inch chambers both gauges
MSRP. **$2419.99**

CITORI CXT, CXT WITH ADJUSTABLE COMB

Action: Over/under
Stock: Black walnut
Barrel: 30 in., 32 in.
Chokes: Three Invector-Plus Midas Extended (F, M, IC)
Sights: Ivory bead
Weight: 8 lb. 6 oz.–8 lb. 8 oz. (CXT); 8 lb. 10 oz.–8 lb. 12 oz. (CXT with adjustable comb)
Bore/Gauge: 12
Magazine: 2 shells
Features: Raised comb (in the non-adjustable model); high-post floating rib; point of impact is 70/30; 3-in. chamber
Standard **$2469.99**
Adjustable comb **$2919.99**

CITORI CXT MICRO ADJUSTABLE LOP

Action: Over/under
Stock: Black walnut
Barrel: 28 in., 30 in.
Chokes: 3 (F, M, IC)
Sights: Ivory front sight, mid-bead
Weight: 8 lb. 9 oz.–8 lb. 11 oz.
Bore/Gauge: 12
Capacity: 2 shells
Features: Stock adjustable for length of pull and with a Graco butt pad and Inflex recoil pad; Grade II American walnut stock with gloss finish; 70/30 point of impact; three-position trigger; 3-inch chambers; ported barrels; vented mid-rib
MSRP. **$2699.99**

CITORI CXT WHITE

Action: Over/under
Stock: Black walnut
Barrel: 30 in., 32 in.
Chokes: 3 (F, IM, M)
Sights: Ivory front, mid-bead
Weight: 8 lb. 2 oz.–8 lb. 4 oz.
Bore/Gauge: 12
Capacity: 2 shells
Features: This member of the crossover CXT family is intended for Trap, with a Monte Carlo-type stock and a wide, floating higher-shooting rib designed for a 70/30 point of impact; silver nitride barrel; side venting; ported barrels; supplied with extended Invector-Plus Midas-grade chokes; adjustable comb model has Graco comb
Standard **$2669.99**
Adjustable comb **$3119.99**

CITORI FEATHER LIGHTNING

Action: Over/under
Stock: Grade III/IV walnut
Barrel: 26 in., 28 in.
Chokes: Three extended (F, M, IC)
Sights: Ivory bead front and mid-rib
Weight: 7 lb.–7 lb. 2 oz.
Bore/Gauge: 12, 20
Capacity: 2 shells
Features: A super-lightweight hunter's favorite returns to the Browning family with: three extended Invector Plus chokes; 3-inch chambers; upgraded wood; updated receiver engraving in a pronounced leaf pattern; rounded pistol grip
MSRP. **$3059.99**

CITORI FEATHER SUPERLIGHT 16-GAUGE

Action: Over/under
Stock: Black walnut
Barrel: 26 in., 28 in.
Chokes: 3 (F, M, IC)
Sights: Ivory bead front
Weight: 6 lb. 2 oz.–6 lb. 4 oz.
Bore/Gauge: 16
Capacity: 2 shells
Features: Another entry in the 16-ga. revival field, and one with a British flare thanks to its Grade II/III straight-grip stock and hard, snag-free buttplate; 18 lines-per-inch checkering; low-profile vent rib; flush-fit Invector chokes; 2 ¾-in. chamber
MSRP. **$2469.99**

BROWNING CITORI WHITE LIGHTNING

BROWNING CITORI GRAN LIGHTNING

BROWNING CITORI GRAN LIGHTNING 16-GA.

BROWNING CITORI HUNTER GRADE I, GRADE II

BROWNING CITORI WHITE LIGHTNING 16-GA.

BROWNING CYNERGY CLASSIC TRAP UNSINGLE COMBO WITH ADJUSTABLE COMB

BROWNING CYNERGY CX, CX COMPOSITE

BROWNING CYNERGY CX FEATHER

CITORI GRAN LIGHTNING

Action: Over/under
Stock: Grade V/VI walnut
Barrel: 26 in., 28 in.
Chokes: Three extended (F, M, IC)
Sights: Ivory bead front and mid-rib
Weight: 6 lb. 13 oz.–8 lb. 2 oz.
Bore/Gauge: 12, 20, 28, .410
Capacity: 2 shells
Features: Top-grade wood; rounded pistol grip; all-new leaf-pattern engraving in polished blue with gold accents; Midas-grade extended choke tubes; 3-inch chambers on 12- and 20-gauge and .410 bore, 28-gauge has 2¾-inch chambers
MSRP . . . . $3549.99–$3619.99

CITORI GRAN LIGHTNING 16-GA.

Action: Over/under
Stock: Walnut
Barrel: 26 in., 28 in.
Chokes: 3
Sights: Ivory bead front, mid bead
Weight: 6 lb. 14 oz.–7 lb.
Bore/Gauge: 16
Capacity: 2 shells
Features: A very pretty 16-ga. with a gloss oil-finished Lightning-style stock; Prince of Wales grip; Grade V/VI walnut; Inflex 2 recoil pad; blued receiver with unique broad-coverage engraving and gold accents; three-set of extended Invector Plus Midas chokes
MSRP $3619.99

CITORI HUNTER GRADE I, GRADE II

Action: Over/under
Stock: Walnut
Barrel: 26 in., 28 in.
Chokes: 3
Sights: Silver bead
Weight: 6 lb. 15 oz.–7 lb. 11 oz.
Bore/Gauge: 12, 16, 20, 28, .410
Capacity: 2 shells
Features: One for the hunters in every gauge available; Invector-Plus flush chokes; Grade I black walnut stock; Inflex 2 recoil pad; polished blue barrels and receiver with gold

enhancements; 50/50 point of impact; Grade II has Grade II/III American walnut stock
Grade I . . . . $2069.99–$2139.99
Grade II . . . . $2269.99–$2339.99

CITORI WHITE LIGHTNING

Action: Over/under
Stock: Grade IIiI/IV walnut
Barrel: 26 in., 28 in.
Chokes: Three extended (F, M, IC)
Sights: Ivory bead front and mid-rib
Weight: 6 lb. 12 oz.–8 lb. 2 oz.
Bore/Gauge: 12, 20, 28, .410
Capacity: 2 shells
Features: Mid-grade wood paired with a silver nitride receiver left naturally "in the white" and polished blue barrels; chrome-plated 3-inch chambers; extended Invector Plus chokes; new engraving in a bold leaf pattern
MSRP . . . . $2839.99–$2919.99

CITORI WHITE LIGHTNING 16-GA.

Action: Over/under
Stock: Walnut
Barrel: 26 in., 28 in.
Chokes: 3
Sights: Ivory bead front, mid bead
Weight: 6 lb. 14 oz.–7 lb.
Bore/Gauge: 16
Capacity: 2 shells
Features: Similar to the Gran Lightning 16-ga.; Grade III/IV walnut stock; silver nitride receiver with engraving and gold accents; extended black Invector Plus Midas chokes
MSRP $2899.99

CYNERGY CLASSIC TRAP UNSINGLE COMBO WITH ADJUSTABLE COMB

Action: Single shot and over/under
Stock: Walnut
Barrel: 32/34 in.
Chokes: Four Invector-Plus Midas Grade choke tubes
Weight: 8 lb. 13 oz.–8 lb. 15 oz.
Bore/Gauge: 12
Magazine: 1 or 2 shells

Features: Steel receiver with MonoLock hinge; double- and single-barrel sets included; reverse striker ignition system; impact ejectors; top-tang barrel selector/safety; gloss finish Monte Carlo grade III/IV walnut stock with right-hand palm swell
MSRP $4499.99

CYNERGY CX, CX COMPOSITE

Action: Over/under
Stock: Black walnut, composite
Barrel: 30 in., 32 in.
Chokes: Invector-Plus Midas Grade (F, M, IC)
Weight: 7 lb. 14 oz.–8.0 lb. (CX); 7 lb. 11 oz.–7 lb. 13 oz. (CX Composite)
Bore/Gauge: 12
Magazine: 2 shells
Features: Crossover barrel design with a 60/40 POI; ventilated top and side ribs; ivory front and mid-bead sights; steel ultra-low profile receiver with MonoLock Hinge engraved with a silver nitride finish; reverse striker ignition system; mechanical trigger design; Impact Ejectors; top-tang barrel selector/safety; 3-in. chamber; composite version features black rubber overmolding at grip points and adjustable comb
Wood $1959.99
Composite $1869.99

CYNERGY CX FEATHER

Action: Over/under
Stock: Walnut
Barrel: 28 in., 30 in.
Chokes: 3
Sights: Ivory bead front, mid bead
Weight: 6 lb. 13 oz.–6 lb. 15 oz.
Bore/Gauge: 12
Capacity: 2 shells
Features: Grade I walnut stock; stock spacer; three-position trigger with one shoe; Invector Plus Midas extended choke tubes; Inflex recoil pad; 3-in. chamber; silver nitride receiver; 60/40 point of impact
MSRP $2269.99

SHOTGUNS

Browning

BROWNING CYNERGY FIELD

BROWNING CYNERGY MICRO MIDAS

BROWNING CYNERGY WICKED WING CAMO

BROWNING CYNERGY WICKED WING VINTAGE TAN

BROWNING CYNERGY CX WITH ADJUSTABLE COMB

BROWNING MAXUS II CAMO REALTREE MAX-5

BROWNING MAXUS II CAMO VINTAGE TAN

CYNERGY FIELD

Action: Over/under
Stock: Walnut
Barrel: 26 in., 28 in.
Chokes: Three Invector-Plus
Weight: 6 lb. 2 oz.–7 lb. 11 oz.
Bore/Gauge: 12, 20
Magazine: 2 shells
Features: Steel receiver with MonoLock hinge; reverse striker ignition system; impact ejectors; oil finish walnut stock; ivory front and mid-bead sights
MSRP . . . . **$2099.99–$2179.99**

CYNERGY MICRO MIDAS

Action: Over/under
Stock: Wood
Barrel: 24 in., 26 in.
Chokes: F, M, IC
Weight: 6 lb.–6 lb. 2 oz.
Bore/Gauge: 20
Magazine: 2 shells
Features: Matte blued barrel finish; grade I/II black walnut stock with satin finish; ivory bead front sight; Cynergy Inflex recoil pad
MSRP **$2179.99**

CYNERGY WICKED WING CAMO

Action: Over/under
Stock: Composite
Barrel: 26 in., 28 in., 30 in.
Chokes: 3 (F, M, IC)
Sights: Ivory bead front
Weight: 7 lb. 6 oz.–7 lb. 10 oz.
Bore/Gauge: 12
Capacity: 2 shells
Features: A big one for geese or far away toms with 3.5-in. chamber; stock with adjustable comb, length-of-pull spacers, and in choice of Realtree Max-7, Mossy Oak Bottomland, or Mossy Oak Shadowgrass Habitat; full chrome bore; receiver and barrels in burnt bronze Cerakote; with extended, banded Invector-Plus chokes
MSRP **$2499.99**

CYNERGY WICKED WING CAMO VINTAGE TAN

Action: Over/under
Stock: Synthetic
Barrel: 26 in., 28 in., 30 in.
Chokes: 3
Sights: Ivory bead front
Weight: 7 lb. 6 oz.–7 lb. 10 oz.
Bore/Gauge: 12
Capacity: 2 shells
Features: Retro meets modern with a vintage tan camo pattern; burnt bronze Cerakote barrels and receiver; hard-chromed chambers and bores; Invector Plus Goose Band extended chokes; adjustable comb and stock spacer; textured grip surfaces
MSRP **$2499.99**

CYNERGY CX WITH ADJUSTABLE COMB

Action: Over/under
Stock: Black walnut
Barrel: 30 in., 32 in.
Chokes: Three Invector-Plus Midas Extended (F, M, IC)
Sights: Ivory bead
Weight: 8 lb. 2 oz.–8 lb. 6 oz.
Bore/Gauge: 12
Magazine: 2 shells
Features: Shoots 60/40 point of impact; adjustable comb; trigger adjustable for length of pull; 0.25-in. stock spacer; reverse striker ignition system; mechanical trigger; impact ejectors; Grade 1 walnut in a satin finish; Vector Pro lengthened forcing cones
MSRP **$2399.99**

MAXUS II CAMO

Action: Semiautomatic
Stock: Synthetic
Barrel: 26 in., 28 in.
Chokes: 3
Sights: Fiber optic front, ivory mid bead
Weight: 7 lb.–7 lb. 2 oz.
Bore/Gauge: 12
Capacity: 4 shells
Features: Full-coverage camo in choice of Realtree Timber, Mossy Oak Original Bottomland and newer Bottomland, Realtree Max-7, or Mossy Oak Shadow Grass Habitat make this Power Drive gas-operated semiauto the tool for every hunter; SoftFlex cheekpiece; oversized bolt and bolt handle; shims for cast, drop, and length of pull adjustment; ramped trigger guard for improved loading; reduced weight magazine tube; chrome chamber and bore; back-bored barrels; Lightning trigger; Speed Load Plus design; magazine cut-off and TurnKey magazine plug; extended Invector Plus choke tubes; hard case
MSRP . . . . **$1869.99–$1979.99**

MAXUS II CAMO VINTAGE TAN

Action: Semiautomatic
Stock: Synthetic
Barrel: 26 in., 28 in.
Chokes: 3
Sights: Fiber optic front, ivory mid bead
Weight: 7 lb.–7 lb. 2 oz.
Bore/Gauge: 12
Capacity: 4 shells
Features: Power Drive gas-operated repeater; stock can be trimmed, dressed in a vintage "old duck hunters" tan splotch camo; over-molded grip panels; SoftFlex cheekpiece; oversized bolt and bolt handle; shims for cast, drop, and length of pull adjustment; ramped trigger guard for improved loading; reduced weight magazine tube; chrome chamber and bore; Lightning trigger; Speed Load Plus design; magazine cut-off and TurnKey magazine plug; extended Invector Plus choke tubes; hard case
MSRP **$1979.99**

SHOTGUNS

BROWNING MAXUS II HUNTER

BROWNING MAXUS II RIFLED DEER

BROWNING MAXUS II SPORTING CARBON FIBER

BROWNING MAXUS II STALKER

BROWNING MAXUS II WICKED WING

BROWNING SILVER BLACK LIGHTNING AND SILVER HUNTER MATTE

BROWNING SILVER FIELD

MAXUS II HUNTER

Action: Semiautomatic
Stock: Walnut
Barrel: 26 in., 28 in.
Chokes: 3
Sights: Fiber optic front, ivory mid bead
Weight: 7 lb.–7 lb. 2 oz.
Bore/Gauge: 12
Capacity: 4 shells
Features: Turkish walnut stock in a satin finish; oversized bolt and bolt handle; shims for cast, drop, and length of pull adjustment; matte black anodized receiver; ramped trigger guard for improved loading; reduced weight magazine tube; chrome chamber and bore; Lightning trigger; Speed Load Plus design; magazine cut-off and TurnKey magazine plug; Invector Plus choke tubes; hard case
MSRP. **$1669.99**

MAXUS II RIFLED DEER

Action: Semiautomatic
Stock: Synthetic
Barrel: 22 in.
Chokes: None
Sights: None
Weight: 7 lb. 3 oz.
Bore/Gauge: 12
Capacity: 4 shells
Features: With a 3-in. chamber, this gun for deer hunters has a topside Picatinny rail cantilever scope mount; full-coverage Mossy Oak Bottomland; Lightning trigger; Speed Load Plus design; TurnKey magazine plug; rubber overmolding on grip areas; Power Drive gas operating system; SoftFlex cheekpad; oversized controls
MSRP. **$1869.99**

MAXUS II SPORTING CARBON FIBER

Action: Semiautomatic
Stock: Synthetic
Barrel: 28 in., 30 in.
Chokes: 5
Sights: HiViz TriComp front, ivory mid bead

Weight: 7 lb. 2 oz.
Bore/Gauge: 12
Capacity: 4 shells
Features: Stock, receiver, and barrel are carbon fiber-dipped; receiver has satin-finished flats; oversized controls; reduced weight magazine tube; Invector Plus Midas extended choke tubes; ramped trigger guard for easier loading; SoftFlex cheekpiece; rubber overmolding on grip areas; Lightning trigger; Speed Load Plus; chrome chamber and bore; ABS hard case
MSRP. **$1939.99**

MAXUS II STALKER

Action: Semiautomatic
Stock: Synthetic
Barrel: 26 in., 28 in.
Chokes: 3
Sights: HiViz TriComp front, ivory mid bead
Weight: 6 lb. 14 oz.–6 lb. 15 oz.
Bore/Gauge: 12
Capacity: 4 shells
Features: A deer or turkey hunter's friend, with a durable, all-black finish on stock and metal; oversized controls; reduced weight magazine tube; Invector Plus flush choke tubes; ramped trigger guard for easier loading; SoftFlex cheekpiece; rubber overmolding on grip areas; Lightning trigger; Speed Load Plus; chrome chamber and bore; ABS hard case included; 3½- or 3-in. chamber
MSRP. . . . . **$1659.99–$1859.99**

MAXUS II WICKED WING CAMO

Action: Semiautomatic
Stock: Synthetic
Barrel: 26 in., 28 in.
Chokes: 3
Sights: Fiber optic front, ivory mid bead
Weight: 7 lb.–7 lb. 2 oz.
Bore/Gauge: 12
Capacity: 4 shells
Features: Realtree Max-7, Realtree Timber, Mossy Oak Original

Bottomland and newer Bottomland, Mossy Oak Shadow Grass Habitat; and Browning's own Vintage Tan camo; oversized controls; reduced weight magazine tube; Invector Plus Midas extended choke tubes; ramped trigger guard for easier loading; SoftFlex cheekpiece; rubber overmolding on grip areas; Lightning trigger; Speed Load Plus; chrome chamber and bore; ABS hard case included; 3½-in. chambers on all
MSRP. . . . . **$2019.99–$2159.99**

SILVER BLACK LIGHTNING

Action: Semiautomatic
Stock: Turkish walnut
Barrel: 26 in., 28 in.
Chokes: Invector-Plus (F, M, IC)
Weight: 7 lb. 4 oz.–7 lb. 6 oz.
Bore/Gauge: 12
Magazine: 4 shells
Features: Gloss black and deep blued metal with gloss finish walnut Lightweight aluminum alloy receiver; Active Valve System regulates light and heavy loads; semi-humpback receiver styling; brass front bead; back-bored barrel; matte version features satin finish stock and bi-tone matte black and silver finish on the receiver
MSRP. **$1229.99**

SILVER FIELD

Action: Semiautomatic
Stock: Turkish walnut
Barrel: 26 in., 28 in.
Chokes: Three Invector-Plus flush (F, M, IC)
Sights: Brass bead
Weight: 7 lb. 4 oz.–7 lb. 5 oz. (12-gauge); 6 lb. 5 oz.–6 lb. 6 oz. (20-gauge)
Bore/Gauge: 12, 20
Magazine: 4 shells
Features: Aluminum receiver; matte blue barrel; satin-finished bi-tone receiver; 3-in. chamber; square pistol grip
MSRP. . . . . **$1199.99–$1259.99**

Browning

BROWNING SILVER FIELD CAMO FDE VINTAGE TAN

BROWNING SILVER FIELD CAMO VINTAGE TAN

BROWNING SILVER FIELD COMPOSITE

BROWNING SILVER FIELD MICRO MIDAS

BROWNING SILVER FIELD MO BOTTOMLAND/FDE

BROWNING SILVER FIELD REALTREE MAX-5

BROWNING SILVER RIFLED DEER MATTE

SILVER FIELD CAMO

Action: Semiautomatic
Stock: Composite
Barrel: 26 in., 28 in.
Chokes: 3 (F, M, IC)
Sights: Brass front bead
Weight: 7 lb. 8 oz.–7 lb. 9 oz.
Bore/Gauge: 12
Capacity: 4 shells
Features: One of Browning's more budget-friendly semiauto field guns with the company's Active Valve gas system; lightweight profile barrel; alloy receiver with semi-humpback design; flush Invector Plus chokes; 3.5-in. chamber, metalwork in two-tone gray/black; stocks in Mossy Oak Shadow Grass Habitat stock, Vintage Tan, Mossy Oak Bottomland or Realtree Max-7
MSRP **$1269.99**

SILVER FIELD CAMO/ CERAKOTE

Action: Semiautomatic
Stock: Composite
Barrel: 26 in., 28 in.
Chokes: 3 (F, M, IC)
Sights: Brass front bead
Weight: 7 lb. 8 oz.–7 lb. 9 oz.
Bore/Gauge: 12
Capacity: 4 shells
Features: One of Browning's more budget-friendly semiauto field guns with the company's Active Valve gas system; lightweight profile barrel; alloy receiver with semi-humpback design; flush Invector Plus chokes; 3.5-in. chamber, metalwork in flat dark earth Cerakote; stocks in Mossy Oak Shadow Grass Habitat stock, Vintage Tan, Mossy Oak Bottomland or Realtree Max-7
MSRP **$1319.99**

SILVER FIELD CAMO FDE VINTAGE TAN

Action: Semiautomatic
Stock: Synthetic
Barrel: 26 in., 28 in.
Chokes: 3
Sights: Brass bead front
Weight: 7 lb. 8 oz.–7 lb. 10 oz.
Bore/Gauge: 12
Capacity: 4 shells
Features: Identical to the other Silver Field Cerakote/camo shotguns, but with a stock in the duck hunter's camo of yesteryear for an almost-Vintage look
MSRP **$1319.99**

SILVER FIELD CAMO VINTAGE TAN

Action: Semiautomatic
Stock: Synthetic
Barrel: 26 in., 28 in.
Chokes: 3
Sights: Brass bead front
Weight: 7 lb. 8 oz.–7 lb. 10 oz.
Bore/Gauge: 12
Capacity: 4 shells
Features: Identical to the other Silver Field non-Cerakote camo shotguns, but with a stock in the duck hunter's camo of yesteryear for an almost-Vintage look; aluminum alloy receiver in a combo black/charcoal finish
MSRP **$1269.99**

SILVER FIELD COMPOSITE

Action: Semiautomatic
Stock: Composite
Barrel: 26 in., 28 in.
Chokes: Three Invector-Plus flush (F, M, IC)
Sights: Brass bead
Weight: 7 lb. 8 oz.–7 lb. 9 oz.
Bore/Gauge: 12

Magazine: 4 shells
Features: Active Valve system for reliable cycling across a variety of loads; stock in a matte black finish; two-tone gray/black receiver emblazoned with Buckmark logo; choice of 3-in. or 3.5-in. chamber
MSRP . . . . **$1119.99–$1199.99**

SILVER FIELD MICRO MIDAS

Action: Semiautomatic
Stock: Turkish walnut
Barrel: 24 in., 26 in.
Chokes: Three Invector-Plus flush (F, M, IC)
Sights: Brass bead
Weight: 6 lb. 2 oz.
Bore/Gauge: 20
Magazine: 4 shells
Features: A reduced stock version (13 in.) for young and shorter-statured hunters; two-tone silver and black receiver; Inflex 1 small buttpad with a hard heel insert; 3-in. chamber
MSRP **$1259.99**

SILVER RIFLED DEER MATTE

Action: Semiautomatic
Stock: Turkish walnut
Barrel: 22 in.
Chokes: N/A
Weight: 6 lb. 12 oz.
Bore/Gauge: 20
Magazine: 4 shells
Features: Fully rifled barrel for sabot slugs; top cantilever scope mount; gas operation; 3-in. chamber; satin finish stock
MSRP **$1299.99**

SHOTGUNS

Caesar Guerini

CAESAR GUERINI ELLIPSE EVO

CAESAR GUERINI INVICTUS I SPORTING

CAESAR GUERINI INVICTUS III SPORTING

CAESAR GUERINI INVICTUS III TRAP COMBO

CAESAR GUERINI INVICTUS V SPORTING

CAESAR GUERINI INVICTUS VII SPORTING

CAESAR GUERINI MAGNUS SPORTING

ELLIPSE CURVE, EVO
Action: Round body
Stock: Hand-rubbed oil on walnut
Barrel: 28 in.
Chokes: 5 nickel plated, flush fitting
Weight: 6 lb. 1 oz.–7 lb. 4 oz.
Bore/ Gauge: 12, 20, 28
Magazine: 2 shells
Features: Engraving pattern coated with Invisalloy; brass front bead sight; single (selective optional) trigger; manual safety; tapered, solid top rib; three variants available: the Curve (rose scroll engraving with nude goddess on receiver bottom), Evo (tight scroll engraving with large oak leaf carvings, and Evo Light (a lighter Evo); left-hand and English stocks available
Curve . . . . $8445.00–$8715.00
Evo . . . . $7735.00–$8005.00

INVICTUS I SPORTING
Action: Over/under
Stock: Wood
Barrel: 30 in., 32 in.
Chokes: 6 MAXIS competition chokes
Weight: 8 lb. 1 oz.–8 lb. 3 oz.
Bore/Gauge: 12
Magazine: 2 shells
Features: White Bradley style front silver center bead; manual safety (automatic optional); DTS-2 trigger system with two trigger pull weight options, take up, over travel and length of pull adjustments
Standard $8320.00
Left-hand . . . . add $270.00
Adjustable comb . . . . . add $425.00

INVICTUS III SPORTING
Action: Over/under
Stock: Walnut
Barrel: 30 in., 32 in.
Chokes: Six
Sights: White Bradley-style front, silver mid-bead
Weight: 8 lb. 1 oz.–8 lb. 3 oz.

Bore/Gauge: 12
Capacity: 2 shells
Features: This one's a head-turner on the sporting clays course, with features like the receiver's hand-polished coin finish gold highlights; ventilated barrel joint; tapered 10mm–8mm top rib; chrome-line barrels; 5-inch DuoCon forcing cones; MAXIS competition chokes; available in left-hand option and with adjustable comb
Standard $9545.00
Left-hand . . . . add $270.00
Adjustable comb . . . . . add $425.00

INVICTUS III TRAP COMBO
Action: Unsingle, over/under
Stock: Walnut
Barrel: 32 in., 34 in.
Chokes: 3 unsingle (M, IM, Fl), 5 O/U (LM, M, IM, LF, F)
Sights: White bead front, silver mid-bead
Weight: 8 lb. 15 oz.–9 lb. 5 oz.
Bore/Gauge: 12
Capacity: 1, 2 shells
Features: Available as a 32-in. over/under with a 34-in Unsingle barrel, this high-grade trap-specific combo shotgun features a stock with a hand-rubbed oil finish and four-way adjustable DTS Monte Carlo comb; 5-in. DuoCon forcing cones; semi-beavertail forearm with finger grooves; 12mm tapered vent rib 25mm high, DTS adjustable 60/40–100 for over/under, 60/40–120 for Unsingle; ventilated center rib on over/under; manual safety (can option automatic); adjustable DPS trigger
Standard $15,765.00
Left-hand . . . . add $270.00

INVICTUS V SPORTING
Action: Over/under
Stock: Wood
Barrel: 30 in., 32 in.

Chokes: 6 MAXIS competition chokes
Weight: 8 lb. 1 oz.–8 lb. 3 oz.
Bore/Gauge: 12
Magazine: 2 shells
Features: DPS2 trigger system; factory selective release triggers available in single and double release; contemporary Italian Ornato-style engraving with deep relief game scenes; white Bradley-style front silver center bead
Standard $10,585.00
Left-hand . . . . add $270.00
Adjustable comb . . . . . add $425.00

INVICTUS VII SPORTING
Action: Over/under
Stock: Walnut
Barrel: 30 in., 32 in.
Chokes: Six
Sights: White Bradley-style front, silver mid-bead
Weight: 8 lb. 1 oz.–8 lb. 3 oz.
Bore/Gauge: 12
Capacity: 2 shells
Features: Similar to the Invictus III Sporting, but with additional gold engravings of five flushing quail on the right side panels, three quail on the rise on the left side, a pheasant and quail on the receiver's underside
Standard $10,875.00
Left-hand . . . . add $270.00
Adjustable comb . . . . . add $425.00

MAGNUS SPORTING
Action: Over/under
Stock: Hand-rubbed oil on walnut
Barrel: 30 in., 32 in., 34 in.
Chokes: 6 CCP competition chokes (6 MAXIS for 12 Ga. models)
Weight: 7 lb. 6 oz.–8 lb. 2 oz.
Bore/Gauge: 12, 20, 28, .410
Magazine: 2 shells
Features: Single selective trigger; manual safety; ventilated center rib; available 20/28 gauge combo and 20/28/.410 gauge combo
Standard right-hand $5765.00
20-/28-ga. combo $8370.00
20-/28-/.410 combo $11,180.00
Left-hand . . . . add $270.00
English stock . . . . add $270.00

Caesar Guerini

CAESAR GUERINI REVENANT

CAESAR GUERINI TEMPIO

CAESAR GUERINI WOODLANDER

REVENANT

Action: Over/under
Stock: Walnut
Barrel: 28 in., 30 in.
Chokes: 5
Sights: Silver bead front
Weight: 6 lb. 6 oz.–6 lb. 11 oz.
Bore/Gauge: 20, 28
Capacity: 2 shells
Features: A beautiful round-body sub-gauge with an Ellipse rounded forend; radiused sideplates gorgeously engraved by master engravers Bottega C. Giovanelli and Dario Cortini and featuring an organic motif of maple leaves and branches in a hand-polished coin finish and gold game birds; solid 8–6mm tapered rib
Standard **$14,995.00**
Left-hand . . . . **add $420.00**

TEMPIO

Action: Over/under

Stock: Turkish walnut
Barrel: 26 in., 28 in., 30 in.
Chokes: 5 nickel plated, flush fitting chokes
Weight: 6 lb.–7 lb.
Bore/Gauge: 12, 20, 28, .410
Magazine: 2 shells
Features: Designed to be a sleek and fast pointing shotgun in the field; perfect companion for upland game hunters; low-profile receiver matched with a trim stock, classic Prince-of-Wales grip and schnabel forend make the gun a perfect match for fast game birds; contemporary style of "ornato" style scroll with tasteful gold accents; Invisalloy protective coating
Standard 12-, 20-, 28-ga.: . . **$4845.00**
Standard .410-bore: **$5050.00**
20/28-ga.combo: **$7400.00**
20/28/.410 combo: **$10,155.00**
Left-hand or English
  stock: . . . . **add $270.00**

WOODLANDER

Action: Over/under
Stock: English walnut
Barrel: 26 in., 28 in., 30 in.
Chokes: Five precision patterned flush chokes (CYL, IC, M, IM, F)
Weight: 6 lb.–7 lb.
Bore/Gauge: 12, 20, 28, .410
Magazine: 2 shells
Features: Gun reflects passion for fall coverts, autumn foliage, wet gun dogs, and the smell of wood; understated elegance of color case hardening and nicely figured, oil-finished English walnut that speaks of quality from a bygone era; a superior-handling upland game gun that's perfect for tight cover and fast-flushing birds
Standard 12-, 20-, 28-ga.: . . **$4275.00**
20/28-ga.combo: **$6825.00**
20/28/.410 combo: **$89585.00**
Left-hand or English
  stock: . . . . **add $270.00**

Charles Daly/Chiappa Firearms

CHARLES DALY/CHIAPPA FIREARMS 204X

CHARLES DALY 520

CHARLES DALY 512

CHARLES DALY 512 T

204X

Action: Over/under
Stock: Synthetic
Barrel: 24 in.
Chokes: Skeet, IC, MOD, IM, F
Weight: 6 lb. 6 oz.–6 lb. 13 oz.
Bore/Gauge: 20, 12
Magazine: 2 shells
Features: Fiber optic sights; black receiver with full-coverage camo in Realtree APG or Mossy Oak Obsession; 3 ½-in. chamber; topside Picatinny rail for optics; Improved, Modified, Full, 2X and XF Rem Choke threaded chokes included
MSRP **$899.00**

512

Action: Side-by-side

Stock: Walnut
Barrel: 28 in.
Chokes: Five (F, IM, M, IC, Skeet)
Sights: Bead front
Weight: 5 lb. 10 oz.
Bore/Gauge: 12
Capacity: 2 shells
Features: A lightweight side-by-side with single selective trigger; extractors; Rem Choke threads; gloss blue barrels; receiver left in the white; one sling swivel stud only under barrel joint
MSRP **$945.00**

512 T

Action: Side-by-side
Stock: Walnut
Barrel: 20 in.
Chokes: Five
Sights: Bead front
Weight: 5 lb. 8 oz.
Bore/Gauge: 12

Capacity: 2 shells
Features: The coach gun version of the 512, with matte blue barrels; sling swivel studs under barrel joint and buttstock
MSRP **$945.00**

520

Action: Side-by-side
Stock: Walnut
Barrel: 26 in.
Chokes: Five (F, IM, M, IC, Skeet)
Sights: Bead front
Weight: 5 lb. 10 oz.
Bore/Gauge: 20
Capacity: 2 shells
Features: Single selective trigger; extractors; Rem Choke threads; gloss blue barrels; receiver left in the white; one sling swivel stud only under barrel joint
MSRP **$945.00**

Charles Daly/Chiappa Firearms

CHARLES DALY 520 T

CHARLES DALY 528

CHARLES DALY 536

CHARLES DALY 601, 601 COMPACT

CHARLES DALY 601 DPS

CHARLES DALY AR-12A, 12T

CHARLES DALY AR-12S

CHARLES DALY CA612 TACTICAL

520 T
Action: Side-by-side
Stock: Walnut
Barrel: 20 in.
Chokes: Five
Sights: Bead front
Weight: 5 lb. 4 oz.
Bore/Gauge: 20
Capacity: 2 shells
Features: The coach gun version of the 520, with matte blue barrels; sling swivel studs under barrel joint and buttstock
MSRP **$946.00**

528
Action: Side-by-side
Stock: Walnut
Barrel: 26 in.
Chokes: Five
Sights: Bead front
Weight: 5 lb. 8 oz.
Bore/Gauge: 28
Capacity: 2 shells
Features: Nice little grouse or quail gun with polished blue barrels; single trigger; receiver left in the white; extractors; one sling swivel stud only under barrel joint
MSRP **$945.00**

536
Action: Side-by-side
Stock: Walnut
Barrel: 26 in.
Chokes: Five
Sights: Bead front
Weight: 5 lb. 6 oz.
Bore/Gauge: .410
Capacity: 2 shells
Features: Properly scaled .410 with polished blue barrels with Rem Choke threads; receiver left in the white; single trigger; extractors; extended chokes; no sling swivel studs
MSRP **$946.00**

601, 601 COMPACT
Action: Semiautomatic
Stock: Synthetic
Barrel: 22 in., 28 in.
Chokes: 3
Sights: Fiber optic front
Weight: 7 lb.–7 lb. 3 oz.
Bore/Gauge: 12, 20
Capacity: 4 shells
Features: An affordable shotgun for the hunter with a black synthetic stock, wood stock, or synthetic stock in Realtree Edge or Mossy Oak Bottomland; cammo available with either flat dark earth metal or full-coverage camo; Beretta/Benelli Mobil chokes (thread MC-3); Compact model is the 20-ga. with the 22-in. barrel
MSRP . . . . **$332.00–$432.00**

601 DPS
Action: Semiautomatic
Stock: Synthetic
Barrel: 18.5 in.
Chokes: 1
Sights: Hooded front, ghost-ring rear
Weight: 8 lb. 1 oz.
Bore/Gauge: 12
Capacity: 5 shells
Features: The short barrel makes this a smart choice for home defense; topside rail for optics; pistol grip has finger grooves; Modified Beretta/Benelli Mobil choke
MSRP **$678.00**

AR-12A, 12T
Action: Semiautomatic
Stock: Synthetic
Barrel: 18.5 in.
Chokes: 1
Sights: Flip-up front, rear
Weight: 8 lb. 3 oz.
Bore/Gauge: 12
Capacity: 5 shells

Features: Scattergun AR with bells and whistles; stock with an adjustable cheekpiece; lots of top-side rail; handguard with M-LOK slots; 12T version has additional rail sections at 3, 6, and 9 o'clock
AR-12A **$531.00**
AR-12T **$615.00**

AR-12S
Action: Semiautomatic
Stock: Synthetic
Barrel: 20 in.
Chokes: One (M)
Sights: A4-style front, adjustable carry handle rear
Weight: 7 lb. 8 oz.
Bore/Gauge: 12
Capacity: 5 shells
Features: Proving the AR really is a do-it-all firearm, this one chambered for the 3-inch 12-gauge and featuring choke with Beretta/Benelli Mobil Choke threads; adjustable buttstock;
MSRP **$432.00**

CA612 TACTICAL
Action: Semiautomatic
Stock: Synthetic
Barrel: 22 in.
Chokes: 5
Sights: Hooded front, ghost-ring rear
Weight: 6 lb. 11 oz.
Bore/Gauge: 12
Capacity: 4 shells
Features: Nice choice for home defense or 3-gun games; Beretta/Benelli Mobil chokes that include two breaching chokes; 3-in. chamber; aluminum receiver; topside Picatinny rail
MSRP **$439.00**

Charles Daly/Chiappa Firearms

CHARLES DALY HONCHO TACTICAL TRIPLE

CHARLES DALY/CHIAPPA FIREARMS TRIPLE THREAT

CHARLES DALY N4S BULLPUP

CHARLES DALY/CHIAPPA FIREARMS TRIPLE CROWN

Weight: 8 lb. 11 oz.
Bore/Gauge: 12, 20, 28, .410
Magazine: 3 shells
Features: Side-by-side and middle arrangement sporting model with three shotgun barrels; chokes in all three barrels; sling swivel studs
Standard $1983.00
Two-barrel set $2823.00
Compact $1983.00

HONCHO TACTICAL TRIPLE

Action: Over/under
Stock: Rubber-coated walnut
Barrel: 18.5 in.
Chokes: None
Sights: Bead front
Weight: 6 lb.
Bore/Gauge: 12
Capacity: 3 shells
Features: A single over double three-shot self-defense shotgun with rubber-coated walnut fore-end and pistol grip for added weight and improved grip; overall length 27 inches; top-tang safety; single trigger; sling swivels
MSRP $1480.00

N4S BULLPUP

Action: Semiautomatic
Stock: Synthetic
Barrel: 18.5 in.
Chokes: One
Sights: Flip-up
Weight: 8 lb. 8 oz.
Bore/Gauge: 12
Capacity: 5 shells
Features: A bullpup with a little weight for better handling; fixed Modified choke with Beretta/Benelli Mobil Choke thread; adjustable flip-up sights front and rear; detachable magazine
MSRP $408.00

TRIPLE CROWN

Action: Break-action
Stock: Wood
Barrel: 26 in., 28 in.
Chokes: Rem-choke in all barrels

TRIPLE THREAT

Action: Break-action
Stock: Wood, synthetic
Barrel: 18.5 in.
Chokes: Rem-choke in all barrels
Weight: 8 lb.
Bore/Gauge: 12, 20, .410
Magazine: 3 shells
Features: Side-by-side and middle arrangement defense model with three shotgun barrels; chokes in all three barrels; sling swivel studs; wooden stock can be partly disassembled
Wood $2014.00
Synthetic $1968.00

Cimarron Firearms Co.

CIMARRON 1878 COACH GUN

1878 COACH GUN

Action: Side-by-Side
Stock: Wood
Barrel: 20 in., 26 in.
Chokes: Open
Weight: 8 lb.–8 lb. 15 oz.

Bore/Gauge: 12
Magazine: 2 shells
Features: 3 in. blue steel real working hammers; available in standard blue
MSRP . . . . $661.67–$648.41

Connecticut Shotgun Mfg. Co.

CONNECTICUT SHOTGUN MFG. CO. A-10

A-10

Action: Sidelock over/under
Stock: Checkered American black walnut
Barrel: 26 in.–32 in.
Chokes: 5 TruLock tubes
Weight: 6 lb. 8 oz.–7 lb. 8 oz.

Bore/Gauge: 12, 20, 28
Magazine: 2 shells
Features: Finely engraved, cut checkering; ventilated rib; pistol grip or straight grip; auto ejectors, single selective trigger; Galazan pad
MSRP . . . .$13,000.00–$39,999.00

Connecticut Valley Arms (CVA)

CVA SCOUT .410 SHOTGUN COMPACT

SCOUT .410 SHOTGUN COMPACT

Action: Break-open single-shot
Stock: Synthetic
Barrel: 20 in.
Chokes: 1 Full turkey
Sights: None
Weight: 6 lb. 5 oz.

Bore/Gauge: .410
Capacity: 1 shell
Features: An affordable single-shot .410 for home-defense or close-range turkey hunting with a stock in Realtree Timber camo; optic rail
MSRP $450.00

SHOTGUNS

CZ-USA (Ceska Zbrojovka)

CZ-USA 612 FIELD

CZ-USA CZ 612 TARGET

CZ-USA CZ 620/628 FIELD SELECT

CZ-USA 712 G2

CZ-USA 712 TARGET G2

CZ-USA 712 UTILITY G2

CZ-USA 1012 ALL-TERRAIN

CZ-USA 1012

CZ-USA 1012 SYNTHETIC BOTTOMLAND

612 FIELD
Action: Pump
Stock: Walnut
Barrel: 28 in.
Chokes: 3 chokes
Weight: 6 lb. 3 oz.
Bore/Gauge: 12
Magazine: 4+1 shells
Features: Satin chrome finish; capable of shooting 2 ¾-in. and 3-in. shells; supplied with three chokes
MSRP $415.00

612 TARGET
Action: Pump
Stock: Turkish walnut
Barrel: 32 in.
Chokes: Extended knurled
Weight: 7 lb. 5 oz.
Bore/Gauge: 12
Magazine: 4 shells
Features: Select grade wood with a glossy oil finish; metal is a deep polished blue; tuned trigger system; raised rib; comfortable Monte Carlo stock; pair of Bradley-style white beads
MSRP $615.00

620/628 FIELD SELECT
Action: Pump
Stock: Turkish walnut
Barrel: 28 in.
Chokes: F, M, C
Weight: 5 lb. 6 oz.
Bore/Gauge: 28 (628); 20 (620)
Magazine: 4 shells
Features: Gauge-specific 7075 aluminum action; deep glossy blue finish; select grade Turkish Walnut; full forend
MSRP $469.00

712 G2
Action: Semiautomatic
Stock: Turkish walnut
Barrel: 26 in., 28 in.

Chokes: 5 included
Weight: 7 lb. 5 oz.–7 lb. 6 oz.
Bore/Gauge: 12
Magazine: 4+1 shells
Features: Accepting 2¾ and 3-inch shells, it is an all-arounder, a great choice for upland game, waterfowl, or clays; barrel is chrome-lined and has a matte black hard chrome exterior that will resist corrosion for many seasons in the field; G2 stock adds new laser-engraved checkering, right-hand palm swell as well as a barrel lock-ring to make assembly easier
MSRP $565.00

712 TARGET G2
Action: Semiautomatic
Stock: Walnut
Barrel: 30 in.
Chokes: Interchangeable chokes (F, M, IC)
Weight: 7 lb. 10 oz.
Bore/Gauge: 12
Magazine: 4+1 shells
Features: Gas operated aluminum alloy action with target-grade enhancements; chrome-lined barrel; fiber optic front sight on a 10mm stepped rib; Schnabel forend; smooth rounded heel; Monte Carlo buttstock
MSRP $759.00

712 UTILITY G2
Action: Semiautomatic
Stock: Synthetic
Barrel: 20 in.
Chokes: Screw-in chokes (F, IM, M, IC, C)
Weight: 6 lb. 10 oz.
Bore/Gauge: 12
Magazine: 4+1 shells
Features: 3-in. chamber cross-bolt safety; black synthetic stock; matte chrome black barrel
MSRP $565.00

1012
Action: Semiautomatic
Stock: Turkish walnut
Barrel: 26, 28 in.
Chokes: Five (F, MIM, M, IC, C)
Sights: Bead front
Weight: 6 lb. 8 oz.
Bore/Gauge: 12
Capacity: 5 shells
Features: A unique gas-less inertia operating system that features the softest shooting 2 ¾ shells to the hottest 3-inch shells. Features include: 8mm flat vent rib; 14 ½-inch length of pull; choice of Bronze, Grey, or gloss black receiver finishes
MSRP . . . . $645.00–$679.00

1012 ALL-TERRAIN
Action: Semiautomatic
Stock: Turkish walnut
Barrel: 28 in.
Chokes: Extended black
Sights: Front bead
Weight: 6 lb. 8 oz.
Bore/Gauge: 12
Capacity: 4 shells
Features: A favorite semiauto gets a Turkish walnut stock paired with metalwork in Cerakote OD Green; flat 8mm vent rib; extended choke tubes provided; crossbolt safety
MSRP $749.00

1012 SYNTHETIC
Action: Semiautomatic
Stock: Synthetic
Barrel: 28 in.
Chokes: Five
Sights: Bead front
Weight: 6 lb. 8 oz.
Bore/Gauge: 12
Capacity: 5 shells
Features: Similar to the standard 1012, but in Mossy Oak Shadow Grass Blades or Bottomland
MSRP $749.00

SHOTGUNS

CZ-USA (Ceska Zbrojovka)

CZ-USA CZ ALL-AMERICAN

CZ–USA ALL AMERICAN TRAP COMBO

CZ-USA CZ BOBWHITE G2

CZ-USA BOBWHITE G2 ALL-TERRAIN

CZ–USA DRAKE

CZ-USA DRAKE ALL-TERRAIN

CZ-USA REAPER MAGNUM

CZ–USA REDHEAD PREMIER

CZ-USA REDHEAD PREMIER ALL-TERRAIN

ALL-AMERICAN

Action: Over/under
Stock: Turkish walnut
Barrel: 30 in., 32 in.
Chokes: Extended black
Weight: 8 lb. 8 oz.
Bore/Gauge: 12
Magazine: 2 shells
Features: CNCed throughout; drop-in replacement parts (including locking blocks for those who shoot tens of thousands of rounds a year); four-way comb; adjustable buttplate hardware; barrels have lengthened forcing cones and are ported; 3-in. chambers
MSRP . . . . **$2649.00–$2789.00**

ALL-AMERICAN TRAP COMBO

Action: Over/under
Stock: Turkish walnut
Barrel: 32 in.
Chokes: 1 Skeet, 1 IC, 2 M, 1 IM, 2 F
Weight: 8 lb. 8 oz.
Bore/Gauge: 12
Magazine: 2 shells
Features: Comes with a single-shot un-single with a dial-adjustable aluminum rib (adjustable from 50/50 up to 90/10 point of impact) and a standard set of barrels with stepped rib (50/50 point of impact); replaceable locking blocks; adjustable parallel comb; competition trigger; auto ejectors
MSRP **$3765.00**

BOBWHITE G2

Action: Side-by-side
Stock: Wood
Barrel: 28 in.
Chokes: Five (F, M, IM, IC, C)
Sights: Bead front
Weight: 5 lb 8 oz.–7 lb. 4 oz.
Bore/Gauge: 12, 20, 28
Capacity: 2 shells
Features: Features a straight, English-style stock; flush-mount choke tubes;

double triggers; black chrome finish; gauge-specific frames
MSRP . . . . **$709.00–$765.00**

BOBWHITE G2 ALL-TERRAIN

Action: Side-by-side
Stock: Turkish walnut
Barrel: 28 in.
Chokes: 5 (F, IM, M, IC, C)
Sights: Front bead
Weight: 6 lb.–7 lb. 5 oz.
Bore/Gauge: 20, 12
Capacity: 2 shells
Features: Wearing a straight English-style stock of walnut, the All-Terrain has barrels and receiver in Cerakote OD Green; dual triggers
MSRP **$899.00**

DRAKE

Action: Over/under
Stock: Turkish walnut
Barrel: 28 in.
Chokes: 5 chokes
Weight: 6 lb.–7 lb. 6 oz.
Bore/Gauge: 12, 20, 28, .410
Magazine: 2 shells
Features: CNC action; extractor operation; single selectable trigger; .410-bore has fixed Improved Cylinder/Modified chokes; left-hand Southpaw model available in 12- and 20-gauge.
MSRP . . . . **$709.00–$765.00**

DRAKE ALL-TERRAIN

Action: Over/under
Stock: Turkish walnut
Barrel: 28 in.
Chokes: Extended black
Sights: Front bead
Weight: 6 lb. 8 oz.–7 lb.
Bore/Gauge: 20, 12
Capacity: 2 shells
Features: A balanced over under with a pretty walnut stock paired with

metalwork in Cerakote OD Green; single selectable trigger
MSRP **$859.00**

REAPER MAGNUM

Action: Over/under
Stock: Polymer
Barrel: 26 in.
Chokes: Five extended
Sights: Front bead
Weight: 7 lb.
Bore/Gauge: 12
Magazine: 2 shells
Features: Dressed in Realtree Xtra Green with a black receiver; topside Picatinny rail for optics mounting; mechanical trigger
MSRP **$1079.00**

REDHEAD PREMIER

Action: Over/under
Stock: Turkish walnut
Barrel: 26 in., 28 in.
Chokes: 5 flush-mount
Weight: 6 lb. 14 oz.
Bore/Gauge: 12, 20
Magazine: 2 shells
Features: The tried-and-true Redhead also gets CZ's new 1-piece CNCed receiver; laser-cut checkering, solid mid-ribs, pistol grip, and a classy white bead; silver receiver and ejectors that kick out the spent shells automatically, hard plastic case included
MSRP **$1075.00**

REDHEAD PREMIER ALL-TERRAIN

Action: Over/under
Stock: Turkish walnut
Barrel: 28 in., 30 in.
Chokes: Extended black
Sights: Front bead
Weight: 6 lb. 14 oz.–8 lb.
Bore/Gauge: 20, 12
Capacity: 2 shells
Features: Nice field gun with extended choke tubes; single selectable trigger; Turkish walnut stock; metalwork in Cerakote OD Green; 3-in. chamber; extended choke tubes provided; both gauges available in both barrel lengths
MSRP **$1219.00**

CZ-USA (Ceska Zbrojovka)

CZ-USA SCTP STERLING   CZ–USA SHARP-TAIL   CZ-USA SHARP-TAIL COACH

CZ-USA SUPREME FIELD

CZ-USA CZ SWAMP MAGNUM CAMO

CZ–USA WINGSHOOTER ELITE

CZ-USA UPLAND ULTRALIGHT

CZ-USA UPLAND ULTRALIGHT ALL-TERRAIN

SCTP STERLING

Action: Over/under
Stock: Turkish walnut
Barrel: 28 in.
Chokes: Five flush chokes (C, IC, M, IM, F)
Sights: None
Weight: 7 lb. 8 oz.
Bore/Gauge: 12
Magazine: 2 shells
Features: Stock designed to fit female and young shooters; silver receiver is finished in two-tone satin and gloss chrome; the barrels are gloss black chrome; stock features laser stippling; 3-in. chambers; left-hand Southpaw model available
MSRP $1519.00

SHARP-TAIL

Action: Side-by-side
Stock: Wood
Barrel: 28 in.
Chokes: 5 flush interchangeable
Weight: 6 lb.– 7 lb. 5 oz.
Bore/Gauge: 12, 20, 28, .410
Magazine: 2 shells
Features: Black hard chrome barrel finish; color case hardened receiver finish; semi-beavertail forend; extractor; manual safety
MSRP . . . . $1165.00–$1399.00

SHARP-TAIL COACH

Action: Side-by-side
Stock: Turkish walnut
Barrel: 20 in.
Chokes: Fixed chokes (C/C)
Sights: Front bead
Weight: 6 lb. 11 oz.
Bore/Gauge: 12, 20
Magazine: 2 shells
Features: Semi-beavertail forearm for a solid grip; single selectable trigger; extractors
MSRP $1095.00

SUPREME FIELD

Action: Over/under
Stock: Grade III Turkish walnut
Barrel: 28 in.
Chokes: Five extended
Sights: Front bead
Weight: 6 lb.–7 lb. 14 oz.
Bore/Gauge: 12, 20, 28
Magazine: 2 shells
Features: Grade III walnut; polished nickel chrome receiver with border engraving; ejectors; solid mid-rib; sharp checkering
MSRP $1935.00

SWAMP MAGNUM CAMO

Action: Over/under
Stock: Polymer
Barrel: 30 in.
Chokes: Extended black
Weight: 7 lb. 2 oz.
Bore/Gauge: 12
Magazine: 2 shells
Features: Only over/under in CZ's line with an automatic safety, which engages every time the action is opened; polymer stocks in camo; all metal work blacked out; chambered for 3 ½ in.
MSRP $1169.00

UPLAND ULTRALIGHT

Action: Over/under
Stock: Turkish walnut
Barrel: 26 in., 28 in.
Chokes: 5 (F, IM, M, IC, C)
Sights: Front bead
Weight: 5 lb. 3 oz.–6 lb.
Bore/Gauge: 12
Capacity: 2 shells
Features: Super upland choice with a mechanical trigger selectable for barrel; aluminum alloy frame with black anodized finish; matte black finish on barrels; flat 6mm vent rib;

separated barrels; 3-in. chamber; extractors
MSRP $855.00

UPLAND ULTRALIGHT ALL-TERRAIN

Action: Over/under
Stock: Turkish walnut
Barrel: 28 in.
Chokes: Extended black
Sights: Front bead
Weight: 5 lb. 14 oz.–6 lb. 5 oz.
Bore/Gauge: 20, 12
Capacity: 2 shells
Features: Upland hunters putting in the miles will appreciate this lightweight over/under with its Turkish walnut stock; metalwork in Cerakote OD Green; separated barrels for reduced ounces
MSRP $965.00

WINGSHOOTER ELITE

Action: Over/under
Stock: Turkish walnut
Barrel: 28 in.
Chokes: 5 flush-mount
Weight: 7 lb. 6 oz.
Bore/Gauge: 12, 20
Magazine: 2 shells
Features: Replaces the Wingshooter; new CNCed 1-piece receiver; fully hand-engraved side-plates, reminiscent of custom-grade Super Scroll; single selectable trigger, solid mid-ribs, ejectors, and two-tone chromed finish; laser-cut checkering, solid mid-ribs, pistol grip stock, white bead; hard plastic case
MSRP $1195.00

European American Armory

EUROPEAN AMERICAN ARMORY AKKAR CHURCHILL 212 FIELD LEFT-HAND

EUROPEAN AMERICAN ARMORY CHURCHILL 220

EUROPEAN AMERICAN ARMORY CHURCHILL 220 FIELD

EUROPEAN AMERICAN ARMORY CHURCHILL 220 GOBBLER

EUROPEAN AMERICAN ARMORY CHURCHILL 228 FIELD

EUROPEAN AMERICAN ARMORY CHURCHILL 612, 612 PISTOL GRIP, 612 TACTICAL

EUROPEAN AMERICAN ARMORY CHURCHILL 612 HUNTER

EUROPEAN AMERICAN ARMORY CHURCHILL 812 FIELD

AKKAR CHURCHILL 212 FIELD LEFT-HAND

Action: Semiautomatic
Stock: Synthetic
Barrel: 28 in.
Chokes: 1
Sights: Fiber optic front
Weight: 6 lb. 4 oz.
Bore/Gauge: 12
Capacity: 3 shells
Features: A no-nonsense, lightweight, easy swinging autoloader for left-hand shooters; left-side bolt, ejection, and controls; vent rib barrel; blued metalwork; aluminum receiver
MSRP $502.00

AKKAR CHURCHILL 220

Action: Semiautomatic
Stock: Synthetic
Barrel: 18.5 in.
Chokes: 1
Sights: Bead front
Weight: 5 lb.
Bore/Gauge: 20
Capacity: 5 shells
Features: Intended for home defense, with a lightweight 18.5-in. barrel
MSRP $433.00

AKKAR CHURCHILL 220 FIELD

Action: Semiautomatic
Stock: Synthetic
Barrel: 24 in., 26 in., 28 in.
Chokes: 1
Sights: Bead front
Weight: 5 lb. 14 oz.
Bore/Gauge: 20
Capacity: 3 shells
Features: Similar to the home-defense

220, but with a longer barrel and reduced magazine capacity
MSRP $449.00

AKKAR CHURCHILL 220 GOBBLER

Action: Semiautomatic
Stock: Synthetic
Barrel: 24 in.
Chokes: 1
Sights: Fiber optic front
Weight: 5 lb. 14 oz.
Bore/Gauge: 20
Capacity: 3 shells
Features: Burnt bronze Cerakote receiver and vent rib barrel; camo stock; receiver is optics ready and includes red-dot sight; length of pull stock spacers
MSRP $661.00

AKKAR CHURCHILL 228 FIELD

Action: Semiautomatic
Stock: Synthetic
Barrel: 24 in., 26 in., 28 in.
Chokes: 1
Sights: Bead front
Weight: 5 lb. 14 oz.
Bore/Gauge: 28
Capacity: 3 shells
Features: A lightweight 28-gauge for the field with vent rib barrel
MSRP $467.00

AKKAR CHURCHILL 612 HOME DEFENSE

Action: Pump
Stock: Synthetic
Barrel: 18.5 in.
Chokes: 1
Sights: Blade front

Weight: 5 lb. 8 oz.
Bore/Gauge: 12
Capacity: 5 shells
Features: A home-defense pump; Tactical pistol grip stock option; Picatinny optics rail; breaching-type choke tube
Standard $285.00
Pistol Grip $296.00
Tactical $353.00
Combo $467.00

AKKAR CHURCHILL 612 HUNTER

Action: Pump
Stock: Synthetic
Barrel: 28 in.
Chokes: 3
Sights: Bead front
Weight: 5 lb. 8 oz.
Bore/Gauge: 12
Capacity: 5 shells
Features: You can carry this one all day at under six pounds; full vent rib
MSRP $331.00

AKKAR CHURCHILL 812 FIELD

Action: Over/under
Stock: Walnut
Barrel: 26 in., 28 in.
Chokes: 3
Sights: Fiber optic front
Weight: N/A
Bore/Gauge: .410, 28, 20, 12
Capacity: 2 shells
Features: A no-frills, well-made over/under by Turkish manufacturer Akkar Firearms; automatic safety; extractors; standard grip profile; checkering; fiber optic front sight; blued barrels with stainless receiver
MSRP $870.00

SHOTGUNS

EUROPEAN AMERICAN ARMORY AKKAR CHURCHILL 815 SPORTING

EUROPEAN AMERICAN ARMORY GIRSAN MC312 GOBBLER

EUROPEAN AMERICAN ARMORY GIRSAN MC312 SPORT

EUROPEAN AMERICAN ARMORY GIRSAN MC312 TACTICAL

AKKAR CHURCHILL 812 SPORTING

Action: Over/under
Stock: Walnut
Barrel: 28 in., 30 in.
Chokes: 5
Sights: Fiber optic front, mid-bead
Weight: N/A
Bore/Gauge: 12
Capacity: 2 shells
Features: Similar to the Sporting 812 ORCAP, this clays gun has its receiver in stainless with light engraving
MSRP $1751.00

GIRSAN MC312 GOBBLER

Action: Semiautomatic
Stock: Synthetic
Barrel: 24 in.
Chokes: 1
Sights: Fiber optic front, red-dot optic

Weight: 6 lb. 12 oz.
Bore/Gauge: 12
Capacity: 5 shells
Features: Totally ready for the turkey woods with a barrel and receiver in burnt bronze Cerakote; camo stock; red-dot optic included; enhanced loading port and controls
MSRP $641.00

GIRSAN MC312 SPORT

Action: Semiautomatic
Stock: Synthetic
Barrel: 24 in.
Chokes: 5
Sights: Fiber optic front, red-dot optic
Weight: 6 lb. 12 oz.
Bore/Gauge: 12
Capacity: 5 shells
Features: Ready for 3-gun or other target games; low-profile accessory

rail; stock in black; fully machined receiver in choice of blue, black, or red; pistol grip stock optional; red-dot optic included
MSRP $653.00

GIRSAN MC312 TACTICAL

Action: Semiautomatic
Stock: Synthetic
Barrel: 18.5 in.
Chokes: 1
Sights: Fiber optic front
Weight: 6 lb. 12 oz.
Bore/Gauge: 12
Capacity: 5 shells
Features: A home-defense 12-ga. with a breaching-type choke tube; black synthetic pistol grip stock; red-dot optic included
MSRP $578.00

Fabarm

FABARM AUTUMN

FABARM AXIS ALLSPORT QUICK RELEASE RIB (QRR)

FABARM ELOS D2

AUTUMN

Action: Side-by-side
Stock: Wood
Barrel: 28 in., 30 in.
Chokes: 5
Sights: White bead front
Weight: 5 lb. 9 oz.–6 lb. 2 oz.
Bore/Gauge: 20
Capacity: 2 shells
Features: A beautiful first side-by-side; stock of deluxe Turkish walnut; color case-hardened receiver with full-coverage engraving; four-lug locking system; "swamped" rib textured to reduce glare; Tribore HP barrels; choice of straight English stock with splinter forend or pistol-grip stock with semi-beavertail forend; add $160 for left-hand stock
MSRP $4425.00

Left-hand . . . . add $175.00
Double triggers . . . . . . add $469.00

AXIS ALLSPORT QUICK RELEASE RIB (QRR)

Action: Over/under
Stock: Wood
Barrel: 30–32 in.
Chokes: 5 Exis HP
Weight: 8 lb. 6 oz.
Bore/Gauge: 12
Magazine: 2 shells
Features: Quick Release Rib design allows configuration for varying shooting styles and disciplines; standard offering includes two 10mm high ramp style ribs—one with a 50/50 percent point-of-impact and a second for a higher 65/35 percent; includes Tribore free floating barrels for improved balance and

performance; 97mm Exis HP hyperbolic choke tubes; integrated recoil reducer; adjustable trigger; Triwood enhanced stock finish; Micro Metric adjustable stock comb
MSRP $4675.00
Left-hand: . . . . add $160.00

ELOS D2

Action: Over/under
Stock: Wood
Barrel: 28 in.
Chokes: Five INNER HP chokes
Sights: Front bead
Weight: 5 lb. 8 oz.–6 lb. 8 oz.
Bore/Gauge: 12, 20, 28
Magazine: 2 shells
Features: A lightweight upland bird gun; stainless receiver with scroll and game birds engravings
MSRP $2995.00
Left-hand . . . . add $175.00

SHOTGUNS

Fabarm

FABARM ELOS N2 ALLSPORT

FABARM L4S INITIAL HUNTER

FABARM XLR5 VELOCITY AR

FABARM ELOS N2 SPORTING

FABARM L4S SPORTING, GREY SPORTING, DELUXE SPORTING

FABARM L4S SERIES

FABARM L4S SPORTING COMPACT

ELOS N2 ALLSPORT

Action: Over/under
Stock: Turkish walnut
Barrel: 30 in., 32 in.
Chokes: 5
Sights: White front bead, silver mid-bead
Weight: 7 lb. 11 oz.
Bore/Gauge: 12
Capacity: 2 shells
Features: Truly meant to cover all the clay sports with an interchangeable rib system that includes one QRR (Quick Release Rib) at 50/50 and another at 65/35, as well as a Micro Metric adjustable stock; stock has Triwood finish; barrels are Tribore
MSRP **$3425.00**
Left-hand . . . . **add $175.00**

ELOS N2 SPORTING

Action: Over/under
Stock: Wood
Barrel: 30 in., 32 in.
Chokes: Five EXIS HP Competition tubes
Sights: Front bead
Weight: 7 lb. 7 oz.
Bore/Gauge: 12
Magazine: 2 shells
Features: Micro-meter adjustable comb; vented barrel separation; adjustable competition trigger
MSRP **$3150.00**
Left-hand . . . . **add $175.00**

L4S DELUXE HUNTER, GREY HUNTER

Action: Semiautomatic
Stock: Wood
Barrel: 26 in., 28 in.
Chokes: 3 Inner HP
Weight: 6 lb. 5 oz.–6 lb. 13 oz.
Bore/Gauge: 12
Magazine: 4 shells
Features: Stock shim system for adjusting fit; Tribore HP tapered barrels; available in three grades: Initial Hunter (black action), Grey Hunter (silver action with game

scene), and Deluxe Hunter (silver action with detailed game scene with gold inlays and upgraded wood); Initial Hunter available in left-hand
Deluxe **$2525.00**
Grey **$2060.00**

L4S INITIAL HUNTER

Action: Semiautomatic
Stock: Turkish walnut
Barrel: 26 in., 28 in.
Chokes: 3 inner HP
Weight: 6 lb. 5 oz.–6 lb. 13 oz
Bore/Gauge: 12
Magazine: 4 shells
Features: Pulse Piston system; TRIBORE HP tapered barrels; innovative new design that allows the fore-end to be removed without disassembling the shotgun; gas-operating system that significantly reduces recoil; stock shim system for adjusting fit; left-hand versions available in both barrel lengths; model chambers 3-in. shells
Right-hand **$1475.00**
Left-hand **$1680.00**

L4S SPORTING, GREY SPORTING, DELUXE SPORTING

Action: Semiautomatic
Stock: Walnut
Barrel: 28 in., 30 in., 32 in.
Chokes: Five EXIS HP Competition tubes
Sights: White bead
Weight: 7 lb. 3 oz.
Bore/Gauge: 12
Magazine: 4 shells
Features: Designed around the 2.75-in.,12 ga. shell; Fabarm's tapered Tribore that improves patterns and velocities; oversized bolt handle and bolt release; highlights in bright red; stock can accept Kinetik recoil reducer; available left-handed; Grey and Deluxe include engraving and gold inlays of game birds
Sporting . . . . **$2170.00–$2375.00**
Grey **$2675.00**
Deluxe **$3150.00**

L4S SPORTING COMPACT

Action: Semiautomatic

Stock: Walnut
Barrel: 28 in.
Chokes: 5
Sights: White bead front
Weight: 6 lb. 12 oz.
Bore/Gauge: 12
Capacity: 4 shells
Features: With a lively swing at under 7 lbs. and a 13.75-in. length of pull, youth and small-statured shooters will appreciate this gun's Tribore HP barrel; stainless steel piston gas operation
Right-hand **$2170.00**
Left-hand **$2375.00**

XLR5 GRYPHON

Action: Semiautomatic
Stock: Synthetic
Barrel: 30 in., 32 in.
Chokes: 5
Sights: White bead front
Weight: 7 lb. 5 oz.
Bore/Gauge: 12
Capacity: 4 shells
Features: A limited edition shotgun dressed in the flashy True Timber blue Viper camo with soft-touch finish; stainless steel piston gas operation; black hard anodized receiver; five Exis HP competition choke tubes; calibrated for use with only 2 3/4-in. target loads
MSRP **$2475.00**

XLR5 VELOCITY AR

Action: Semiautomatic
Stock: Walnut
Barrel: 30 in., 32 in.
Chokes: 5
Sights: White bead front
Weight: 7 lb. 9 oz.–7 lb. 12 oz.
Bore/Gauge: 12
Capacity: 4 shells
Features: Semiauto users get what over/under users have benefitted from for years: perfect weight and balance thanks to a magazine cap with adjustable weight; integrated recoil reducer; adjustable rib; Pulse Piston gas operation; receiver in black anodized or titanium silver finishes; matte-finish hand-oiled stock with adjustable cheekpiece; Tribore HP barrel
Right-hand **$3775.00**
Left-hand **$3980.00**

Fabarm

FABARM XLR5 WATERFOWLER

XLR5 WATERFOWLER
Action: Semiautomatic
Stock: Synthetic
Barrel: 28 in., 30 in.
Chokes: 3 inner HP, 1 EXIS DK
Weight: 7 lb.

Bore/Gauge: 12
Magazine: 5 shells
Features: Pulse Piston system; TRIBORE HP barrel design for reduced recoil and improved pattern performance; special competition choke tube, the EXIS DK, tuned for non-toxic ammo in the most popular pellet sizes; a top rib increases the sighting plain by 4 in. and allows the shooter to see down the rib with a more comfortable head-up posture; chrome plated barrel extension and bores; left-hand versions available in both barrel lengths; model chambers 3-in. shells; in True Timber Viper camo stock with OD green receiver or a left-hand-only version in full-coverage Kryptec Banshee camo
Right-hand **$2025.00**
Left-hand **$2230.00**

Fausti USA

FAUSTI USA CALEDON L4   **FAUSTI USA CLASS**

FAUSTI USA ITALYCO

FAUSTI USA MAGNIFICENT

CALEDON
Action: Over/under
Stock: Walnut
Barrel: 26 in., 28 in., 30 in.
Chokes: Fixed or interchangeable choke tubes
Weight: 5 lb. 12 oz.–7 lb. 4 oz.
Bore/Gauge: 12, 16, 20, 28, .410
Magazine: 2 shells
Features: Single selectable trigger; A+ Turkish walnut stock with oil finish; laser-engraved lower receiver; automatic ejectors; metallic bead sight
MSRP . . . . **$1999.00–$2600.00**

CLASS
Action: Over/under
Stock: Walnut
Barrel: 26 in., 28 in., 30 in.
Chokes: Fixed or interchangeable choke tubes
Weight: 5 lb. 12 oz.–7 lb. 5 oz.

Bore/Gauge: 12, 16, 20, 28, .410
Magazine: 2 shells
Features: Features automatic ejectors; metallic bead; single-selectable trigger; 14–3/8-in. length of pull; timeless AA walnut oil-polished stock; Prince of Wales style stock; receiver laser-engraved with flushing quail
MSRP . . . . **$2799.00–$3840.00**

ITALYCO
Action: Over/under
Stock: Wood
Barrel: 23–32 in.
Chokes: Fixed
Weight: N/A
Bore/Gauge: 12 (2 ¾ in., 3 in.), 16 (2 ¾ in.), 20 (2 ¾ in., 3 in.), 28 (2 ¾ in.), .410 (3 in.)
Magazine: 2 shells
Features: Single selective trigger (double trigger available); automatic ejector (manual ejector available); box lock round body; pistol grip with steel grip cap or Prince of Wales or English
MSRP . . . . . . **Contact manufacturer**

MAGNIFICENT
Action: Over/under
Stock: Walnut
Barrel: 26 in., 28 in., 30 in.
Chokes: Fixed or interchangeable choke tubes
Weight: 5 lb. 12 oz.–7 lb. 6 oz.
Bore/Gauge: 12, 16, 20, 28, .410
Magazine: 2 shells
Features: AAA+ walnut stock with oil finish; precision scroll engraving accompanies Aphrodite, the Greek goddess of love and beauty, on the receiver; the Crest of the city of Brescia, Italy, where all Fausti shotguns are produced, is on the underside of the receiver; single selectable trigger; automatic ejectors; metallic bead sight
MSRP: . . . . **$4999.00–$5559.00**

Fox by Savage Arms

FOX (BY SAVAGE ARMS) A GRADE

A GRADE
Action: Side-by-side
Stock: American black walnut
Barrel: 26 in., 28 in.
Chokes: IM, M, F
Sights: Front brass bead

Weight: N/A
Bore/Gauge: 12, 20
Magazine: 2 shells
Features: Splinter forend; checkered stock; straight grip; case-colored receiver; three interchangeable chokes; double triggers; made by Connecticut Shotgun Manufacturing Company
MSRP **$4250.00**

Franchi

FRANCHI AFFINITY 3

FRANCHI AFFINITY CATALYST

FRANCHI AFFINITY 3 COMPACT

FRANCHI AFFINITY 3 ELITE UPLAND

FRANCHI AFFINITY LEFT-HAND

FRANCHI AFFINITY 3 SPORTING

FRANCHI AFFINITY 3 TURKEY 20-GA.

FRANCHI AFFINITY 3 ELITE TURKEY

FRANCHI AFFINITY 3.5

AFFINITY 3

Action: Semiautomatic
Stock: Synthetic, walnut
Barrel: 26 in., 28 in.
Chokes: Three chokes (F, IC, M)
Sights: Fiber optic bar front sight
Weight: 5 lb. 15 oz.–6 lb. 15 oz.
Bore/Gauge: 12, 20
Magazine: 4 shells
Features: Drop at heel is adjustable; in black, Realtree Max-5, or Mossy Oak Bottomland synthetic stocks or A-grade satin-finished walnut; chambers 3-inch shells
MSRP. . . . . **$899.00–$999.00**

AFFINITY 3 CATALYST

Action: Semiautomatic
Stock: Walnut
Barrel: 28 in.
Chokes: IC, M, F
Weight: 6 lb. 10 oz.
Bore/Gauge: 12
Magazine: 4+1 shells
Features: Drop, cast, pitch, and length-of-pull are all tailored to a woman's build; fiber optic red-bar front sight
MSRP. **$969.00**

AFFINITY 3 COMPACT

Action: Semiautomatic
Stock: Synthetic
Barrel: 24 in., 26 in.
Chokes: Three chokes (F, IC, M)
Sights: Fiber optic bar front sight
Weight: 5 lb. 15 oz.–6 lb. 11 oz.
Bore/Gauge: 12, 20
Magazine: 4 shells
Features: A hunting semiautomatic for youth, women, and shorter-statured shooters; length of pull and drop at heel are adjustable; chambers 3-inch shells; both gauges available in full-coverage Realtree Max-5; 20 ga. available in all-black
MSRP. . . . . **$949.00–$1049.00**

AFFINITY 3 ELITE UPLAND

Action: Semiautomatic
Stock: Walnut
Barrel: 26 in., 28 in.
Chokes: 3 (CR, MR, LR)
Sights: TruGlo dual-color front
Weight: 6 lb.–6 lb. 15 oz.
Bore/Gauge: 20, 12
Capacity: 4 shells
Features: Satin-finished Grade A walnut stock; gun metal-gray Cerakote metal finish; stock adjustable for drop at heel
MSRP. **$1279.00**

AFFINITY 3 LEFT-HAND

Action: Semiautomatic
Stock: Synthetic
Barrel: 26, 28 in.
Chokes: Three chokes (F, IC, M)
Sights: Fiber optic bar front sight
Weight: 6 lb.–6 lb. 15 oz.
Bore/Gauge: 12, 20
Magazine: 4 shells
Features: Drop at heel is adjustable; in black, Realtree Max-5, or Mossy Oak Bottomland synthetic stocks or A-grade satin-finished walnut; chambers 3-inch shells
MSRP. **$899.00**

AFFINITY 3 SPORTING

Action: Semiautomatic
Stock: Walnut
Barrel: 28 in., 30 in.
Chokes: 3 (IC, M, F)
Sights: Red fiber optic front
Weight: 6 lb. 3 oz.–7 lb. 2 oz.
Bore/Gauge: 20, 12
Capacity: 4 shells
Features: Neatly priced semiautomatic for the sporting clays crowd, with a red fiber optic front sight; A-grade satin-finished walnut stock adjustable for drop at heel; TSA recoil pad; extended chokes
MSRP. . . . . **$1049.00–$1179.00**

AFFINITY 3 TURKEY

Action: Semiautomatic

Stock: Synthetic
Barrel: 24 in.
Chokes: 2
Sights: Hooded dual-color fiber optic front
Weight: 6 lb. 12 oz.–7 lb. 7 oz.
Bore/Gauge: 12, 20
Capacity: 4 shells
Features: Not everyone feels the need to throw a super-magnum 12-ga. load at a turkey; dual-color front sight; Extended Turkey and Extended Turkey XF chokes; Steadygrip pistol-grip stock and metalwork in full-coverage MO Bottomland
MSRP. **$999.00**

AFFINITY 3 TURKEY ELITE

Action: Semiautomatic
Stock: Synthetic
Barrel: 24 in.
Chokes: 2
Sights: Hooded dual-color fiber optic front
Weight: 6 lb. 14 oz.–7 lb. 10 oz.
Bore/Gauge: 12, 20
Capacity: 4 shells
Features: The Affinity 3 line gains a turkey gun; pistol grip stock in Optifade Subalpine; metalwork in midnight bronze Cerakote; Exteded Turkey and Exteneded Turkey XF chokes included
MSRP. **$1279.00**

AFFINITY 3.5

Action: Semiautomatic
Stock: Synthetic
Barrel: 26 in., 28 in.
Chokes: Three chokes (F, IC, M)
Sights: Fiber optic bar front sight
Weight: 6 lb. 15 oz.–7 lb.
Bore/Gauge: 12
Magazine: 4 shells
Features: Chambers 3.5-in. shells; adjustable drop at heel; 26-in. barrel model available in black synthetic or Realtree Max-5; 28-in. barrel model available in Realtree Max-5 or Mossy Oak Bottomland
Black:. **$999.00**
Camo: **$1129.00**

SHOTGUNS

Franchi

FRANCHI AFFINITY 3.5 CERAKOTE

FRANCHI INSTINCT L

FRANCHI INSTINCT SLX

FRANCHI INSTINCT L CATALYST, SL CATALYST

FRANCHI INSTINCT LX

FRANCHI INSTINCT SPORTING II

FRANCHI INSTINCT L CATALYST, SL CATALYST

FRANCHI INSTINCT SL

AFFINITY 3.5 CERAKOTE
Action: Semiautomatic
Stock: Synthetic
Barrel: 26 in., 28 in.
Chokes: 3
Sights: Fiber optic red bar front
Weight: 6 lb. 15 oz.–7 lb.
Bore/Gauge: 12
Capacity: 4 shells
Features: Lots of power with a 3½-in. chamber; receiver drilled and tapped; stock is adjustable for drop; stepped ventilated rib; 28-in. model has stock in Realtree Max-5 and metalwork in Midnight Bronze Cerakote; 26-in. model has stock in MO Bottomland and metalwork in Patriot Bronze Cerakote
MSRP. $1279.00

AFFINITY 3.5 TURKEY
Action: Semiautomatic
Stock: Synthetic
Barrel: 24 in.
Chokes: 2
Sights: Hooded dual-color fiber optic front
Weight: 7 lb. 8 oz.
Bore/Gauge: 12
Capacity: 4 shells
Features: Powerhouse turkey gun; Extended Turkey and Extended Turkey XF chokes; receiver drilled and tapped; Steadygrip pistol grip stock and metalwork in full-coverage MO Bottomland
MSRP. $1179.00

INSTINCT CATALYST
Action: Over/under
Stock: Wood
Barrel: 26 in.
Chokes: 3
Sights: Fiber optic front
Weight: 5 lb. 7 oz.–6 lb. 14 oz.
Bore/Gauge: 20
Capacity: 2 shells
Features: These field-grade 20-gauges have walnut stocks in a satin finish

designed to better fit women shooters; auto ejectors; L wears a red fiber optic front bead, while the SL has a red fiber optic front bar; automatic safety; two versions include a color case-hardened receiver and matte blue barrels with flush-fit choke tubes or a brushed aluminum receiver and gloss blue barrels with extended choke tubes
Case-colored **$1549.00**
Aluminum alloy **$1779.00**

INSTINCT L
Action: Over/under
Stock: Walnut
Barrel: 26 in., 28 in.
Chokes: Interchangeable (IC, M, F)
Weight: 6 lb. 2 oz.–6 lb. 6 oz.
Bore/Gauge: 12, 20
Magazine: 2 shells
Features: Ventilated raised rib; red fiber optic front sight; blued and color-case-hardened finish on the receiver, with gold inlay; A-grade walnut stock in Prince-of-Wales style with cut checkering on the forend and pistol grip; satin oil finish; single gold-plated trigger; chrome-lined barrels proofed for steel shot; hard-shell custom-fitted gun case included
MSRP. $1449.00

INSTINCT LX
Action: Over/under
Stock: Walnut
Barrel: 28 in.
Chokes: 3 (IC, M, F)
Sights: Red fiber optic front
Weight: 6 lb. 10 oz.–7 lb.
Bore/Gauge: 12, 20, 28
Capacity: 2 shells
Features: A much fancier Instinct with AA-grade walnut in a satin finish and with fine line checkering, Prince of Wales grip, and schnabel forearm; deep color case-hardened receiver with gold inlays; barrel selector; extended chokes
MSRP. $1779.00

INSTINCT SL
Action: Over/under
Stock: Walnut
Barrel: 26 in., 28 in.
Chokes: Interchangeable (IC, M, F)
Weight: 5 lb. 2 oz.–6 lb. 2 oz.
Bore/Gauge: 12, 20, 16, 28, .410
Magazine: 2 shells
Features: Vent rib; red fiber optic front bead; aluminum alloy receiver; blued barrels; AA-grade satin walnut stock in Prince-of-Wales style with cut checkering and oil finish; tang-mounted automatic safety; custom-fitted, hard-shell gun case included
MSRP. . . . . $1679.00–$1779.00

INSTINCT SLX
Action: Over/under
Stock: Walnut
Barrel: 28 in.
Chokes: 5 (C, IC, M, IM, F)
Sights: Red fiber optic front
Weight: 5 lb. 10 oz.–6 lb. 5 oz.
Bore/Gauge: 12, 16, 20, 28
Capacity: 2 shells
Features: AA-grade walnut stock in a satin finish and with a Prince of Wales grip and schnabel forearm; a satin stainless receiver with floral engraving; between barrel venting; auto ejectors; barrel select switch; extended chokes
MSRP. . . . . $2099.00–$2299.00

INSTINCT SPORTING II
Action: Over/under
Stock: Walnut
Barrel: 30 in.
Chokes: 3 (IC, M, F)
Sights: Red fiber optic front
Weight: 7 lb. 7 oz.–7 lb. 13 oz.
Bore/Gauge: 20, 12
Capacity: 2 shells
Features: A-Grade walnut stock in a satin finish; between-barrel venting; matte stainless receiver; adjustable comb
MSRP. $2099.00

SHOTGUNS

HatsanUSA, Inc.

HATSAN USA
ESCORT DF12

HATSAN USA ESCORT
DYNAMAX

HATSAN USA ESCORT
SLUGGER, SLUGGER TACTICAL

ESCORT DF12

Action: Semiautomatic
Stock: Synthetic
Barrel: 18 in.
Chokes: Five (F, M, IM, IC, C)
Sights: A4-style front, adjustable rear, flip-up front and rear
Weight: 8 lb. 15 oz.
Bore/Gauge: 12
Capacity: 6 shells
Features: An AR-platform shotgun for the 3-Gun crowd; 3-inch chambers; oxidation-proof chrome-plated barrel; reversible cocking handle; ample rail acreage; elevation-adjustable comb
MSRP **$699.99**

ESCORT DYNAMAX

Action: Semiautomatic
Stock: Synthetic
Barrel: 28 in.
Chokes: Five (F, M, IM, IC, C)
Sights: Fiber optic front
Weight: 7 lb.
Bore/Gauge: 12
Capacity: 5 shells
Features: A fast-handling semiauto with three-inch chamber; DaSoft soft-touch stock finish; checkered anti-glare vent rib; Hi-Viz fiber optic front bead; detachable sling swivels; 11mm grooved receiver for optics mounting; steel-shot acceptable chokes
MSRP **$699.99**

ESCORT SLUGGER, SLUGGER TACTICAL

Action: Pump-action
Stock: Synthetic
Barrel: 18 in.
Chokes: None
Sights: Fixed blade front
Weight: 6 lb. 6 oz.–6 lb. 8 oz.
Bore/Gauge: 12
Capacity: 5 shells
Features: Sling swivel studs; aggressively textured forearms; Tactical version gets a pistol grip and a five-shot shellholder built into the skeletal buttstock, as well as a Picatinny rail in front of the forend or light mounting
Slugger **$209.99**
Slugger Tactical **$219.99**

Henry Repeating Arms Co.

HENRY REPEATING ARMS
LEVER-ACTION X-MODEL .410

HENRY REPEATING
ARMS SIDE GATE LEVER-
ACTION .410

HENRY REPEATING ARMS SINGLE SHOT
SHOTGUN IN STEEL & BRASS

LEVER-ACTION X-MODEL .410

Action: Lever
Stock: Synthetic
Barrel: 19.8 in.
Chokes: Invector-style Full
Sights: Fiber optic front
Weight: 7 lb. 8 oz.
Bore/Gauge: .410
Capacity: 5 shells
Features: A very modernized lever-action with an ergonomically designed lever loop and tough synthetic stock; Picatinny rail and M-LOK slots; 2.5-in shells only
MSRP **$1049.00**

SIDE GATE LEVER-ACTION .410

Action: Lever
Stock: American walnut
Barrel: 19.75 in., 24 in.
Chokes: None
Sights: Ramp ivory bead, adjustable semi-buckhorn rear
Weight: 7 lb. 1 oz.
Bore/Gauge: .410
Capacity: 5 shells
Features: A handsome .410-bore with deep engraving at wrist and forend; Cylinder bore (no chokes); swivel studs; polished brass receiver and butt plate; 2.5-in. shells only
Blue . . . . **$1017.00–$1063.00**
Brass **$1166.00**

SINGLE SHOT SHOTGUN IN STEEL & BRASS

Action: Break-open single-shot
Stock: Walnut
Barrel: 26 in., 28 in.
Chokes: 1 (varies with gauge)
Weight: 6 lb. 10 oz.–6 lb. 12 oz.
Bore/Gauge: 12, 20, .410
Magazine: 1 shell
Features: Sharing the same action as the single-shot rifle; front brass bead; steel models have pistol grip, brass models sport a straight grip; Rem-Choke style threaded chokes
Steel **$552.00**
Brass **$679.00**

SHOTGUNS

Henry Repeating Arms Co.

HENRY REPEATING ARMS SINGLE-SHOT SLUG BARREL

HENRY REPEATING ARMS SINGLE-SHOT TURKEY CAMO

SINGLE-SHOT SLUG BARREL

Action: Single-shot
Stock: Walnut
Barrel: 24 in.
Chokes: None
Sights: Fiber optic front, rear
Weight: 6 lb. 14 oz.
Bore/Gauge: 12
Capacity: 1 shell
Features: American walnut stock topped with a round blued-steel rifled barrel with a 1:35 twist; rebounding hammer; dual-direction pivoting locking lever mechanism; 3-in. chamber
MSRP $587.00

SINGLE-SHOT TURKEY CAMO

Action: Single-shot
Stock: Walnut
Barrel: 24 in.
Chokes: 1
Sights: Fiber optic front, rear
Weight: 6 lb. 11 oz.
Bore/Gauge: 12
Capacity: 1 shell
Features: Sporting a 3½-inch chamber, this single-shot break-action has metalwork dressed in full-coverage MO Obsession; Turkey choke; threaded for Remington-style chokes; solid rubber buttpad
MSRP $721.00

Iron Horse Firearms

IRON HORSE FIREARMS SENTRY 12

SENTRY 12

Action: Pump
Stock: Synthetic
Barrel: N/A
Chokes: N/A
Sights: None
Weight: N/A
Bore/Gauge: 12
Capacity: 5 shells
Features: An easy to take apart modular pump shotgun with plenty of rail on top for optics mounting; detachable box magazine; ambidextrous controls
MSRP $899.99

Israel Weapon Industries (IWI)

ISRAEL WEAPON INDUSTRIES (IWI) TAVOR TS 12

TAVOR TS 12

Action: Semiautomatic
Stock: Synthetic
Barrel: 18.5 in.
Chokes: One
Sights: None
Weight: 8 lb.
Bore/Gauge: 12
Magazine: 15 shells
Features: Triple-magazine bullpup semiauto shotgun; each magazine can hold a maximum of four 3-in. or five 2.75-in. 12-ga. shells and can be both fed and unloaded from either side; available in black, Flat Dark Earth, and OD Green
MSRP $1499.99

Ithaca Gun Company

ITHACA DEERSLAYER II

ITHACA DEERSLAYER III

DEERSLAYER II

Action: Pump
Stock: Walnut
Barrel: 24 in.
Chokes: None
Weight: 6.8 lb.–8 lb. 6 oz.
Bore/Gauge: 12, 20
Magazine: 4+1 shells
Features: Solderless barrel system; thumbhole or standard black walnut Monte Carlo stock; fat deluxe checkered forend; sling swivel studs; Pachmayr 750 Decelerator recoil pad; matte blued finish on barrel; gold-plated trigger; Marble Arms rifle sights; drilled and tapped for Weaver #62 scope rail
MSRP . . . . $1199.00–$1749.00

DEERSLAYER III

Action: Pump
Stock: Walnut
Barrel: 20 in., 26 in., 28 in.
Chokes: None
Weight: 8.1 lb.–9 lb. 8 oz.
Bore/Gauge: 12, 20
Magazine: 4+1 shells
Features: Heavy-walled, fluted, fixed barrel in blue matted finish; walnut Monte Carlo stock with optional thumbhole; Pachmayr 750 Decelerator recoil pad; sling swivel studs; gold-plated trigger; Weaver #62 rail pre-installed on receiver
MSRP . . . . $1399.00–$1949.00

Ithaca Gun Company

ITHACA MODEL 37
DEFENSE SYNTHETIC

ITHACA GUN CO. MODEL
37 28-GAUGE

ITHACA MODEL 37
FEATHERLIGHT

ITHACA MODEL 37
WATERFOWL

MODEL 37 28-GAUGE

Action: Pump
Stock: Walnut
Barrel: 24 in., 26 in., 28 in.
Chokes: N/A
Sights: Bead
Weight: N/A
Bore/Gauge: 28
Magazine: 4 shells
Features: Choice of A, AA, or AAA walnut; chrome finish with light engraving at the edges of the receiver; available in blue
MSRP . . . . $1399.00–$2549.00

MODEL 37 DEFENSE

Action: Pump
Stock: Walnut
Barrel: 18.5 in., 20 in.
Chokes: None
Weight: 6.5 lb.–7 lb. 2 oz.
Bore/Gauge: 12, 20
Magazine: 4+1 or 7+1 shells
Features: Choice of walnut or black synthetic stock; 3 in. chamber; matte blued finish barrel; Pachmayr decelerator recoil pad
MSRP . . . . $1099.00–$1199.00

MODEL 37 FEATHERLIGHT

Action: Pump
Stock: Walnut
Barrel: 26 in., 28 in., 20 in.
Chokes: 3 Briley Choke tubes (F, M, IC, and wrench)

Weight: 6.1 lb.–7 lb. 10 oz.
Bore/Gauge: 12, 16, 20, 28
Magazine: 4+1 rounds
Features: Solderless shells system; classic game scene engraving; black walnut stock with semi-pistol butt stock; TruGlo red front sight; Pachmayr 752 Decelerator recoil pad
MSRP . . . . $1199.00–$2154.00

MODEL 37 WATERFOWL

Action: Pump
Stock: Camo, synthetic black
Barrel: 28 in., 30 in.
Chokes: Briley choke tubes
Weight: 7 lb. 3 oz.–7 lb. 6 oz.
Bore/ Gauge: 12, 20
Magazine: 4+1 shells
Features: 3 in. chamber; gold plated trigger; gamescene engraving; perma-guard protection
MSRP . . . . $1099.00–$1369.00

Iver Johnson Arms

IVER JOHNSON HP 18

IVER JOHNSON IJ500

IVER JOHNSON IJ700

IVER JOHNSON IJ600

HP 18

Action: Semiautomatic
Stock: Synthetic
Barrel: 18.5 in.
Chokes: N/A
Weight: 6 lb. 6 oz.
Bore/Gauge: 12, 20
Magazine: 5+1 shells
Features: High grade alloy receiver for reduced weight; two-piece detachable pistol grip stock; rubber buttpad on the stock to help reduce felt recoil; Picatinny rail on top of the receiver, with a fully adjustable white dot rear sight; fiber optic front sight; finger grooves on the forend to ensure a solid grip while firing; muzzle break externally threaded onto the barrel; 12-ga. available in black or Digital Tan, 20-ga. in black only
Black: $379.00
Digital Tan 12-ga.: $486.00

IJ500

Action: Semiautomatic
Stock: Walnut
Barrel: 28 in.
Chokes: 3 internally threaded choke tubes (F, IM, M)
Weight: 7 lb. 2 oz.
Bore/Gauge: 12
Magazine: 5+1 shells
Features: Front brass bead sight; checkered stock and forend; chambered for 2 ¾" and 3" shotshells. —12-ga. now available in synthetic stock in Max-4 camo.
Wood stock: $385.00
Max-4 camo: $486.00

IJ600

Action: Over/under
Stock: Walnut
Barrel: 28 in.
Chokes: 5 internal (F, IM, M, IC, C)
Weight: 6 lb. 1 oz.–7 lb. 5 oz.

Bore/Gauge: 12, 20, .410
Magazine: N/A
Features: Vent rib on top and bottom barrel; extractors on both barrels; engraved receiver with birds accented in gold colored coating; selector switch located on the safety for choosing which barrel fires first; checkered stock and forend; sling swivel on barrel and stock; 20 gauge has a scaled down receiver, stock, and forend
MSRP $527.00

IJ700

Action: Break-open single-shot
Stock: Walnut
Barrel: 18 in., 26 in.
Chokes: None
Weight: 4 lb. 8 oz.–4 lb. 14 oz.
Bore/Gauge: .410
Magazine: 1 shell
Features: Silver receiver; blued barrel; single extractor; sling swivels
MSRP $180.00

Iver Johnson Arms

IVER JOHNSON PAS12, PAS12-PG

PAS12, PAS12-PG
Action: Pump
Stock: Synthetic
Barrel: 18 in.
Chokes: N/A
Sights: Blade front

Weight: 6 lb.
Bore/Gauge: 12
Magazine: 4 shells
Features: Lightweight alloy frame; chambers 3-in. shells; forend is grooved and belled on the back end

to ensure proper stroking of the action; PAS12 is available with or without a muzzle brake; PAS12 PG is equipped with a pistol grip; PAS12 standard barrel is available in all-over satin nickel

PAS12: .... **$257.00–$297.00**
PAS12-PG: .... **$257.00–$338.00**

Kalashnikov USA

KALASHNIKOV USA KS-12, KS-12T

KS-12, KS-12T
Action: Semiautomatic
Stock: Polymer
Barrel: 18.25 in.
Chokes: None

Sights: Fixed
Weight: 8 lb. 8 oz.
Bore/Gauge: 12
Magazine: 5 shells
Features: Based on historical Kalashnikov rifle platform goes

shotgun; threaded barrel; T–Tactical–version has a skeletonized collapsible stock, a 10-round magazine, and side accessory rails on the handguard; available in black or flat dark earth

KS-12 .... **$856.80**
KS-12T **$933.69**

Kel-Tec

KEL-TEC KS7

KEL-TEC KSG

KEL-TEC KSG-25

KS7
Action: Pump
Stock: Synthetic
Barrel: 18.5 in.
Chokes: None
Sights: None
Weight: 5 lb. 15 oz.
Bore/Gauge: 12
Capacity: 8 shells
Features: A shotgun in compact bullpup design with a 13-inch length of pull; carry handle; ambidextrous adjustable stock
MSRP **$580.00**

KSG
Action: Pump
Stock: Glass reinforced nylon
Barrel: 18.5 in.
Chokes: Cylinder bore
Weight: 6 lb. 14.4 oz.-8 lb. 8 oz.
Bore/Gauge: 12 gauge (3 in.)
Magazine: 6+6+1
Features: KSG receiver is made from hardened steel and includes the magazine tubes which have been welded in place; pump action feeds from either the left or right tube
MSRP **$900.00**

KSG-25
Action: Pump
Stock: Synthetic
Barrel: 30 in.
Chokes: None
Weight: 9 lb. 4 oz.
Bore/Gauge: 12
Magazine: 21, 25 shells
Features: Magpul MBUS and an RVG vertical grip on the pump; 3-in. chambers; holds a full box of 2¾-in. or 3-in. shells
MSRP **$1150.00**

SHOTGUNS

Krieghoff

KRIEGHOFF K-20 SPORTING

KRIEGHOFF K-80 SPORTER

KRIEGHOFF K-80 ACS

KRIEGHOFF K-80 PARCOURS-X

KRIEGHOFF KX-6

K-20 SPORTING

Action: Over/under
Stock: Walnut
Barrel: 30 in., 32 in.
Chokes: 5 choke tubes (C, S, IC, LM, M, LIM, IM, F)
Weight: 7 lb. 8 oz.
Bore/Gauge: 20, 28, .410
Magazine: 2 shells
Features: Top-tang push safety button; classic scroll engraving; white pearl front bead and metal center bead; single-selective mechanical trigger; hand-checkered select European walnut stock with satin epoxy finish
Single gauge $12,895.00
Two-gauge set $18,495.00
Three-gauge set $23,995.00

K-80

Action: Over/under
Stock: Walnut

Barrel: 30 in., 32 in., 34 in.
Chokes: Steel or Titanium choke tubes (C, S, IC, LM, M, LIM, IM, F, SF)
Weight: 8 lb. 4 oz.
Bore/Gauge: 12
Magazine: 2 shells
Features: White pearl front sight and metal center bead; nickel-plated steel receiver with satin grey finish; single select trigger; top-tang push button safety; fine-checkered Turkish walnut
From: . . . . . . $12,395.00–$19,495.00

K-80 ACS COMBO

Action: Single barrel
Stock: Walnut
Barrel: 30 in., 32 in., 34 in.
Chokes: 8 factory steel choke tubes
Weight: 8 lb. 12 oz.
Bore/Gauge: 12
Magazine: 2 shells
Features: White pearl front bead and

metal center bead sight; case-hardened action, nickel-plated steel receiver with nitride silver finish; single selective trigger; Combo is a an over/under and Unsingle.
From: $19,495.00

K-80 PARCOURS-X

Action: Over/under
Stock: Walnut
Barrel: 32 in.
Chokes: 2
Sights: White pearl front, metal mid-bead
Weight: 8 lb. 8 oz.
Bore/Gauge: 12
Capacity: 2 shells
Features: A new gun specifically for sporting clays and FITASC competitors; Turkish walnut stock, checkered and with a satin epoxy finish; top-tang safety can be locked in "off" position; soldered 10mm-8mm tapered Parcours-X rib; M and IM Krieghoff Thin Wall chokes; nickel-plated steel receiver in a satin grey finish; right- or left-hand stock with adjustable comb and palm swell; 3-in. chambers
MSRP $13,695.00

KX-6

Action: Single-shot trap
Stock: Walnut
Barrel: 34 in.
Chokes: IM, LIM, F
Weight: 8 lb. 12 oz.
Bore/ Gauge: 12
Magazine: 1 shell
Features: White pearl front sight and metal center bead; case hardened, long lasting black nitro carbonized finish; semiautomatic ejector; adjustable tapered rib; readily available add-ons include adjustable butt-plate, installed release trigger, and upgraded titanium choke tubes
MSRP . . . . starting at $6695.00

K-Var

K-VAR VEPR 12

VEPR 12

Action: Semiautomatic
Stock: Synthetic
Barrel: 19 in.

Chokes: Cylinder
Weight: 6 lb. 14 oz.
Bore/Gauge: 12
Magazine: 5+1 shells
Features: AK safety selector with levers on both sides for easy

operation; ability to insert magazines straight into the magazine well without canting; RPK-style windage adjustable rear sights; windage and elevation adjustable front sights integrated to the gas block; Picatinny rail incorporated into the hinged dust cover; left-side folding tubular buttstock with cheek rest and sling loop
MSRP . . . . $2399.99–$3999.99

LJUTIC ADJUSTABLE RIB MONO GUN

LJUTIC MONO GUN

LJUTIC PRO 3

ADJUSTABLE RIB MONO GUN

Action: Single barrel
Stock: Walnut
Barrel: 34 in.
Chokes: Fixed or Ljutic SIC
Weight: 10 lb.
Bore/Gauge: .740, 12
Magazine: 1 shell
Features: "One Touch" adjustable rib allows you to change your point-of-impact; adjustable comb stock
MSRP: . . . .**POR**

MONO GUN

Action: Single barrel
Stock: Walnut
Barrel: 32 in.–34 in.
Chokes: Optional screw in chokes (Fixed, Ljutic SIC, Briley SIC)
Weight: 10 lb.
Bore/Gauge: .740, 12
Magazine: 1 shell
Features: Comes with American walnut wood; optional roll over combs and cheek pieces; various upgrades available
MSRP . . . .**POR**

PRO 3

Action: Single barrel
Stock: Walnut
Barrel: 34 in.
Chokes: 4 Briley Series 12 chokes
Weight: 9 lb.
Bore/Gauge: .740, 12
Magazine: 1 shell
Features: Aluminum baseplate; interchangeable two-pad system; adjustable comb; English or American walnut stock; screw in hinge pin; stainless or blued barrel
MSRP . . . .**POR**

Merkel

MERKEL 147EL

147EL

Action: Side-by-side
Stock: Wood
Barrel: 27 in., 28 in.

Chokes: Steel-shot proofed chokes
Weight: 6 lb. 3 oz.
Bore/Gauge: 12
Magazine: None
Features: English stock finished with fine hand-cut checkering at buttplate; silver monogram plate; steel action is

gray nitrated; Anson & Deeley locks; Greener-style cross bolt and double bottom bite; double trigger; automatic safety
MSRP **$8885.00**

Mossberg (O. F. Mossberg & Sons)

MOSSBERG 500 ATI TACTICAL

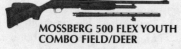

MOSSBERG 500 FLEX YOUTH COMBO FIELD/DEER

MOSSBERG 500 FLEX ALL-PURPOSE

MOSSBERG 500 FLEX SUPER BANTAM ALL-PURPOSE

500 ATI TACTICAL

Action: Pump
Stock: Synthetic
Barrel: 18.5 in.
Chokes: Cylinder
Weight: 6 lb. 12 oz.
Bore/Gauge: 12
Magazine: 5 shells
Features: ATI TacLite six-position adjustable buttstock; Scorpion Recoil ATI Akita fore-end; heat shield; topside and muzzle-end rails; three-shell side-saddle; in Flat Dark Earth or Destroyer Gray
MSRP: **$685.00**

500 FLEX ALL-PURPOSE

Action: Pump
Stock: Synthetic
Barrel: 28 in.

Chokes: Accu-Set
Weight: 7 lb. 8 oz.
Bore/Gauge: 12
Magazine: 5 shells
Features: Matte metal finishes; stock with medium recoil pad; stock and forend constructed of synthetic with black matte finish; twin bead sights
MSRP **$553.00**

500 FLEX SUPER BANTAM ALL-PURPOSE

Action: Pump
Stock: Synthetic
Barrel: 22 in.
Chokes: Accu-Set
Sights: Front and mid-rib beads
Weight: 6 lb. 8 oz.
Bore/Gauge: 20
Capacity: 6 shells
Features: A gun to grow with thanks to the FLEX stock system; vent rib;

chokes; mid-rib and front beads; 12 ½-inch length of pull
MSRP **$514.00**

500 FLEX YOUTH COMBO FIELD/DEER

Action: Pump
Stock: Synthetic
Barrel: 22 in., 24 in.
Chokes: Accu-Set
Sights: Front and mid-rib beads/adjustable rifle sights
Weight: 6 lb. 8 oz.–6 lb. 12 oz.
Bore/Gauge: 20
Capacity: 6 shells
Features: A combo youth gun with a 24-inch vent rib barrel with Accu-Set chokes and dual beads; 22-inch fully rifled slug barrel with adjustable sights; FLEX four-position adjustable stock; three-inch chamber
MSRP **$601.00**

Mossberg (O. F. Mossberg & Sons)

MOSSBERG 500 RETROGRADE

MOSSBERG 500 TURKEY

MOSSBERG 500 SUPER
BANTAM TURKEY

MOSSBERG 510 YOUTH MINI
SUPER BANTAM ALL-PURPOSE

MOSSBERG 500
TACTICAL JIC

MOSSBERG 500
TACTICAL JIC FLEX

MOSSBERG 500 YOUTH SUPER
BANTAM ALL-PURPOSE

MOSSBERG 590
7-SHOT

MOSSBERG 590 9-SHOT

500 RETROGRADE

Action: Pump
Stock: Walnut
Barrel: 18.5 in.
Chokes: None
Sights: Bead front
Weight: 6 lb. 4 oz.
Bore/Gauge: 12
Capacity: 6 shells
Features: Designed to celebrate Mossberg's 100th anniversary, buyers get a pump shotgun they revere for its technology with the retro look of yesteryear. Features include Cylinder-bore barrel; full-length buttstock; corncob fore-end; single brass bead; blued finish
MSRP $570.00

500 SUPER BANTAM TURKEY

Action: Pump
Stock: Synthetic
Barrel: 22 in.
Chokes: Interchangeable Accu-Choke (X-full and wrench)
Weight: 5 lb. 4 oz.
Bore/Gauge: 20
Magazine: 6 shells
Features: Adjustable synthetic stock in Mossy Oak Obsession; adjustable fiber optic sights; drilled and tapped for scopes; gun lock
MSRP $550.00

500 TACTICAL JIC

Action: Pump
Stock: Synthetic
Barrel: 18.5 in.
Chokes: Cylinder bore chokes
Weight: 5 lb. 8 oz.
Bore/Gauge: 12
Magazine: 6 shells
Features: Bead sight; Marinecote metal finish; comes with multi-tool, survival knife and cordura carrying case; gun lock; swivel studs; black synthetic stock; only pump-action shotguns to pass all U.S. Military Mil-Spec 3443 standards; available with matte blued metalwork

Blue $566.00
Marinecoat $731.00

500 TACTICAL JIC FLEX

Action: Pump
Stock: Synthetic
Barrel: 18.5 in.
Chokes: C
Weight: 5 lb. 8 oz.
Bore/Gauge: 12
Magazine: 6 shells
Features: Bead sights; FLEX pistol grip; 3-in. barrel with matte black finish
MSRP $573.00

500 TURKEY

Action: Pump
Stock: Synthetic
Barrel: 20 in., 22 in., 26 in.
Chokes: X-Factor; none
Weight: 6 lb. 8 oz.–7 lb.
Bore/Gauge: 12, 20, .410
Magazine: 5, 6 shells
Features: 12-gauge has X-Factor ported choke tube, adjustable fiber optic sights, full-coverage Mossy Oak Obsession; 20-gauge has X-Factor choke, adjustable fiber optic sights, full-coverage Mossy Oak Obsession; .410-bore has fixed Full choke, front fiber optic sight, full-coverage Mossy Oak Bottomland
MSRP: $549.00

500 YOUTH SUPER BANTAM ALL-PURPOSE

Action: Pump
Stock: Synthetic
Barrel: 22 in.
Chokes: Accu-Set
Sights: Bead
Weight: 5 lb. 4 oz.
Bore/Gauge: 20
Magazine: 6 shells
Features: Designed for youth and people with a shorter length of pull; black or Muddy Girl Wild camo adjustable stock; Accu-Set chokes; vent rib
MSRP . . . . $473.00–$532.00

510 YOUTH MINI SUPER BANTAM ALL-PURPOSE

Action: Pump
Stock: Synthetic
Barrel: 18.5 in.
Chokes: None
Sights: Bead
Weight: 5 lb.
Bore/Gauge: 20, .410
Magazine: 4 shells
Features: Designed for youth and people with a shorter length of pull; stock in black, Muddy Girl Wild, or Mossy Oak Break-Up Country; adjustable stock; vent rib on the fixed-choke Modified barrel
MSRP . . . . $473.00–$533.00

590 7-SHOT

Action: Pump
Stock: Synthetic
Barrel: 18.5 in.
Chokes: None
Sights: Bead front
Weight: 5 lb. 12 oz.–7 lb.
Bore/Gauge: 20, 12, .410
Capacity: 6 shells
Features: Handy pump for self-defense and even 3-Gun games, with a FLEX stock adjustable for length of pull; FLEX pistol grip; Cylinder bore; matte blue finish
MSRP . . . . $515.00–$680.00

590 9-SHOT

Action: Pump
Stock: Synthetic
Barrel: 20 in.
Chokes: None
Sights: None; ghost ring
Weight: 5 lb. 12 oz.–7 lb. 12 oz.
Bore/Gauge: 20, 12
Capacity: 8 shells
Features: Three 12-ga. configurations include 1) ghost ring sights and a heat shield 2) no sights, with heat shield, with adjustable stock and pistol grip kit, and 3) ghost ring sights, no heat shield, and with the six-position Flex buttstock and Flex pistol grip; all models are fixed Cylinder bore
MSRP . . . . $536.00–$680.00

Mossberg (O. F. Mossberg & Sons)

MOSSBERG 590 CHAINSAW

MOSSBERG 590 CRUISER

MOSSBERG 590 M-LOK

MOSSBERG 590 NIGHTSTICK

MOSSBERG 590 RETROGRADE

MOSSBERG 590 SHOCKWAVE

MOSSBERG 590 SHOCKWAVE 7-SHOT

MOSSBERG 590 SHOCKWAVE 20-GAUGE (NON-NFA)

MOSSBERG 590 SHOCKWAVE FLAT DARK EARTH CERAKOTE (NON-NFA)

MOSSBERG 590 JIC SHOCKWAVE

590 CHAINSAW

Action: Pump
Stock: Synthetic
Barrel: 18.5 in.
Chokes: None
Sights: White dot front
Weight: 6 lb.
Bore/Gauge: 12
Capacity: 5 shells
Features: A pistol-grip-only model with a removeable top handle for more secure hip-shooting technique; accessory rails on forend at 3, 6, and 9 o'clock; breaching "stand-off" barrel; matte blue finish
MSRP $619.00

590 CRUISER

Action: Pump
Stock: Synthetic
Barrel: 18.5 in.
Chokes: None
Sights: White dot front
Weight: 5 lb. 12 oz.
Bore/Gauge: 12
Capacity: 6 shells
Features: The reliable Cruiser in a pistol-grip configuration gets a breaching "stand-off" barrel; matte blue finish; forend hand strap
MSRP $515.00

590 M-LOK

Action: Pump
Stock: Synthetic
Barrel: 20 in.
Chokes: Accu Choke Cylinder
Sights: Ghost ring
Weight: 7 lb. 4 oz.
Bore/Gauge: 12
Capacity: 8 shells
Features: A great pump for ranch work or 3-Gun with a longer barrel; ghost ring sights; M-LOK forend
MSRP $622.00

590 NIGHTSTICK

Action: Pump
Stock: Hardwood
Barrel: 14 in.

Chokes: None
Sights: Bead front
Weight: 5 lb. 3 oz.
Bore/Gauge: 12, 20
Capacity: 6 shells
Features: Five-round magazine; non-NFA (no ATF tax stamp required) fixed Cylinder choke barrel; hardwood bird's-head grip and corncob fore-end; matte blue finish; chambers 3-inch shells
MSRP $609.00

590 RETROGRADE

Action: Pump
Stock: Walnut
Barrel: 18.5 in., 20 in.
Chokes: None
Sights: Bead front
Weight: 7 lb.–7 lb. 4 oz.
Bore/Gauge: 12
Capacity: 6, 8 shells
Features: A 3-Gun or ranch work pump with a good-looking walnut stock in traditional styling; heat shield; fixed Cylinder bore; matte blue metalwork
MSRP . . . . $612.00–$629.00

590 SHOCKWAVE

Action: Pump
Stock: Synthetic
Barrel: 14 in.
Chokes: None
Weight: 5 lb. 4.8 oz.
Bore/Gauge: 12
Magazine: 6 shells
Features: Features unique Raptor pistol grip
MSRP $515.00

590 SHOCKWAVE 7-SHOT

Action: Pump
Stock: Synthetic
Barrel: 18.5 in.
Chokes: None
Sights: Bead front
Weight: N/A
Bore/Gauge: 12
Capacity: 7 shells
Features: The Shockwave with a

higher-capacity magazine tube; Raptor grip; sling; corncob fore-end
MSRP $515.00

590 SHOCKWAVE 20-GAUGE

Action: Pump
Stock: Synthetic
Barrel: 14.375 in.
Chokes: None
Sights: Front bead
Weight: 4 lb. 14 oz.
Bore/Gauge: 20
Magazine: 6 shells
Features: Bird's head Raptor pistol grip; strapped forend for additional stability; no NFA paperwork needed
MSRP $515.00

590 SHOCKWAVE FLAT DARK EARTH CERAKOTE

Action: Pump
Stock: Synthetic
Barrel: 14.375 in.
Chokes: None
Sights: Bead
Weight: 5 lb. 5 oz.
Bore/Gauge: 12
Magazine: 6 shells
Features: Flat Dark Earth Cerakote treatment; Raptor pistol grip; corn-cob forend; forend hand strap; barrel is Cylinder bore; no NFA paperwork needed
MSRP $570.00

590 SHOCKWAVE JIC

Action: Pump
Stock: Synthetic
Barrel: 14.375 in.
Chokes: None
Sights: Bead
Weight: 5 lb. 5 oz.
Bore/Gauge: 12
Magazine: 6 shells
Features: Mossberg's Shockwave in the Just in Case package; water-resistant carry tube; non-reflective Cerakote Stainless finish on the metal
MSRP $731.00

Mossberg (O. F. Mossberg & Sons)

MOSSBERG 590 SHOCKWAVE LASER SADDLE

MOSSBERG 590 SHOCKWAVE SHOCK 'N' SAW

MOSSBERG 590 SHOCKWAVE SPX

MOSSBERG 590 SPX

MOSSBERG 590 THUNDER RANCH

MOSSBERG 5901A1 CLASS III PUMP-ACTION 6-SHOT

MOSSBERG 590A1 RETROGRADE

590 SHOCKWAVE LASER SADDLE

Action: Pump
Stock: Synthetic
Barrel: 14 in.
Chokes: None
Sights: Front bead
Weight: N/A
Bore/Gauge: 12, 20
Capacity: 6 shells
Features: The Shockwave with the addition of a Crimson Trace Laser Saddle; Raptor grip, sling; corncob fore-end
MSRP $672.00

590 SHOCKWAVE SHOCK 'N' SAW

Action: Pump
Stock: Synthetic
Barrel: 14 in.
Chokes: None
Sights: Bead front
Weight: 6 lb.
Bore/Gauge: 12
Capacity: 6 shells
Features: This non-NFA (no ATF tax stamp required) shotgun features: fixed Cylinder choke barrel; Shockwave's polymer Raptor grip; aluminum MLOK fore-end with Mossberg's own Chainsaw grip; breacher muzzle; matte blue finish; chambers 3-inch shells
MSRP $633.00

590 SHOCKWAVE SPX

Action: Pump
Stock: Synthetic
Barrel: 14 in.

Chokes: None
Sights: Bead front
Weight: 5 lb. 12 oz.
Bore/Gauge: 12
Capacity: 6 shells
Features: This non-NFA (no ATF tax stamp required) shotgun features: fixed Cylinder choke barrel; Shockwave's polymer Raptor grip; corncob fore-end with strap; polymer seven-round side-saddle shell holder; heat shield; top-side Picatinny rail; matte blue finish; chambers 3-inch shells
MSRP $633.00

590 SPX

Action: Pump
Stock: Synthetic
Barrel: 18.5 in.
Chokes: None
Sights: Fiber optic front, ghost ring
Weight: 5 lb. 12 oz.–7 lb.
Bore/Gauge: 12
Capacity: 6 shells
Features: Lots of options with this scattergun thanks to its six-position Flex buttstock and Flex pistol grip; ghost ring rear sight paired with fiber optic front; topside Picatinny rail; forend hand strap
MSRP $802.00

590 THUNDER RANCH

Action: Pump
Stock: Synthetic
Barrel: 18.5 in.
Chokes: None
Sights: Fiber optic front
Weight: 6 lb. 12 oz.
Bore/Gauge: 12

Capacity: 6 shells
Features: Dressed in Kuiu camo; muzzle sports a door breaching add-on; matte blue metalwork
MSRP $624.00

5901A1 CLASS III PUMP-ACTION 6-SHOT

Action: Pump
Stock: Synthetic
Barrel: 14 in.
Chokes: None
Sights: Bead, ghost ring
Weight: 6 lb. 12 oz.
Bore/Gauge: 12
Magazine: 6 shells
Features: fore-end with hand strap; Parkerized finish, 3-inch chamber; heavy-walled Cylinder barrel; Compact Synthetic has 13-in. length of pull and ghost ring sights; Parkerized finish; ghost ring sights; Plus-4 shell-holder stock
MSRP $806.00

590A1 RETROGRADE

Action: Pump
Stock: Walnut
Barrel: 20 in.
Chokes: None
Sights: Ghost ring
Weight: 7 lb 4 oz.
Bore/Gauge: 12
Capacity: 9 shells
Features: The sister companion to the 500 Persuader Retrograde, features on this MIL-SPEC pump include: Parkerized finish; metal trigger and safety button; heat shield; bayonet lug; full-length stock; corncob fore-end; heavy-wall barrel with Cylinder fixed choke
MSRP $1018.00

Mossberg (O. F. Mossberg & Sons)

MOSSBERG 590M MAG-FED

MOSSBERG 590M SHOCKWAVE

MOSSBERG 835 ULTI-MAG

MOSSBERG 930 HUNTING ALL PURPOSE FIELD

MOSSBERG 930 PRO SPORTING

MOSSBERG 930 TACTICAL 8 SHOT

MOSSBERG 930 THUNDER RANCH

590M MAGFED

Action: Pump
Stock: Synthetic
Barrel: 18.5 in.
Chokes: none; Accu-Choke
Sights: Bead; ghost ring
Weight: 7 lb. 12 oz.–8 lb.
Bore/Gauge: 12
Magazine: 10 shells
Features: Detachable double-stack magazine; magazine tube is inactive and serves as support for the pumping action of the fore-end and rails; basic version gets a fixed Cylinder bore with a front bead; heat-shield option gets heat shield, ghost ring sights, a Cylinder Accu-Choke only
Standard **$617.00**
Heat shield. **$703.00**

590M SHOCKWAVE

Action: Pump
Stock: Synthetic
Barrel: 15 in.
Chokes: None
Sights: Bead front
Weight: 6 lb. 8 oz.
Bore/Gauge: 12
Capacity: 11 shells
Features: This non-NFA (no ATF tax stamp required) shotgun features: fixed Cylinder choke barrel; Shockwave's polymer Raptor grip; corncob fore-end with strap; increased 11-round overall capacity with a 10-round double-stack removeable magazine; drilled and tapped for optics; chambers 3-inch shells
MSRP **$617.00**

835 ULTI-MAG

Action: Pump
Stock: Synthetic
Barrel: 20 in., 24 in., 28 in.
Chokes: Ulti-full tube chokes, Accu-Mag Set, or Modified Tube

Weight: 7 lb. 8 oz.–7 lb. 12 oz.
Bore/Gauge: 12
Magazine: 5 shells
Features: Features 3 ½-inch chambers; dual extractors; over-bored and ported barrels. Variations include Turkey/Waterfowl combo in MO Break-Up Country, fiber optic front sight; Turkey/Deer combo with dual combs, Ulti- Full barrel/fully rifled barrel with cantilever scope base in MO Break-Up Country; Field/Deer combo with wood stock, 28-inch vent rib/24-in. rifled barrel adjustable rifle sights; Turkey with Marble Arms Bullseye fiber optic sights, Ulti-Full choke, MO Obsession; Waterfowl with Accu-Set chokes, fiber optic front sight, MO Shadow Grass Blades; Tactical Turkey with six-position adjustable stock, fiber optic front sight, and full-coverage MO Obsession; All-Purpose Field with Accu-Mag chokes, X-Factor ported turkey choke, MO New Bottomland
All-Purpose Field Camo **$587.00**
Combo Field/Deer **$557.00**
Combo Turkey/Deer **$644.00**
Combo Turkey/Waterfowl . . **$644.00**
Tactical Turkey **$736.00**
Waterfowl **$587.00**
Turkey w/Marble Arms
 Sight **$612.00**

930 HUNTING ALL PURPOSE FIELD

Action: Semiautomatic
Stock: Walnut
Barrel: 28 in.
Chokes: Accu-Set (F, M, IC)
Sights: Fiber optic
Weight: 7 lb. 12 oz.
Bore/Gauge: 12
Magazine: 5 shells
Features: A wood stock and blued metal make for a classic field semi-

auto shotgun; dual beads; vent rib; Accu-Set chokes included
MSRP **$797.00**

930 PRO SPORTING

Action: Semiautomatic
Stock: Walnut
Barrel: 28 in.
Chokes: 3 chokes (F, M, IC)
Weight: 7 lb. 12 oz.
Bore/Gauge: 12
Magazine: 5 shells
Features: Chambered in 2 ¾ in. and 3 in.; engraved Cerakote receiver; beveled loading gate; Briley extended chokes; vented rib ported barrel; boron nitride-coated gas piston, piston rings, magazine tube, hammer, and sear prevents corrosion and facilitates cleaning
MSRP **$1162.00**

930 TACTICAL 8-SHOT

Action: Semiautomatic
Stock: Synthetic
Barrel: 18.5 in.
Chokes: None
Weight: 6 lb. 12 oz.
Bore/Gauge: 12
Magazine: 8 shells
Features: The popular 930 tactical autoloader gets an extended eight-shot magazine
MSRP **$699.00**

930 THUNDER RANCH

Action: Semiautomatic
Stock: Synthetic
Barrel: 18.5 in.
Chokes: None
Sights: Fiber optic front
Weight: 6 lb. 12 oz.
Bore/Gauge: 12
Capacity: 5 shells
Features: Self-defense gun with a door-breeching muzzle accessory; Kuiu camo stock; matte blue metalwork; Cylinder bore
MSRP **$797.00**

Mossberg (O. F. Mossberg & Sons)

MOSSBERG 935 PRO WATERFOWL

MOSSBERG 935 MAGNUM TURKEY

MOSSBERG 940 JM PRO

MOSSBERG 940 JM PRO 5-SHOT

MOSSBERG INTERNATIONAL GOLD RESERVE SUPER SPORT

MOSSBERG INTERNATIONAL GOLD RESERVE

MOSSBERG INTERNATIONAL GOLD RESERVE BLACK LABEL

MOSSBERG MAVERICK 88 ALL-PURPOSE

935 MAGNUM PRO WATERFOWL

Action: Semiautomatic
Stock: Synthetic
Barrel: 28 in.
Chokes: 3 chokes (F, M, IC)
Weight: 7 lb. 12 oz.
Bore/Gauge: 12
Magazine: 5 shells
Features: Synthetic stock covered in Mossy Oak Shadowgrass Blades; overbored vent rib barrel; Stock Drop System; 3.5-in chamber
MSRP $997.00

935 MAGNUM TURKEY

Action: Semiautomatic
Stock: Synthetic
Barrel: 22 in.
Chokes: Vent rib. overbored
Weight: 7 lb. 8 oz.
Bore/Gauge: 12
Magazine: 5 shells
Features: Chambers 3 ½-inch shells; over-bored barrels; dual vent system; Quick Empty magazine release button; stock spacer system; drilled and tapped receivers; X-Factor choke; adjustable fiber optic sights; standard stock option in MO Bottomland or pistol grip stock in MO Obsession
Standard stock $862.00
Pistol-grip stock $1053.00

940 JM PRO

Action: Semiautomatic
Stock: Synthetic
Barrel: 24 in.
Chokes: 3 (C, IC, M)
Sights: HiViz TriComp
Weight: 7 lb. 12 oz.
Bore/Gauge: 12
Capacity: 10 shells
Features: One for the 3-Gun crowd, developed by Jerry and Lena Miculek; newly designed gas system that cycles a wide variety of 2¾- and 3-in. shells reliably; loading port designed to quad-load the magazine tube;

adjustable stock; interchangeable light tube HiViz sights; Briley extended chokes; base model in black stock, matte blue barrel, tungsten gray anodized receiver, and gold-highlighted parts accents
MSRP $1122.00

940 JM PRO 5-SHOT

Action: Semiautomatic
Stock: Synthetic
Barrel: 24 in.
Chokes: 3
Sights: Fiber optic front
Weight: 7 lb. 12 oz.
Bore/Gauge: 12
Capacity: 4 shells
Features: With champion shooter Jerry Miculek's name on it, this one is surely meant for 3-gun games; stock adjustable for length of pull, drop, and cast; Briley extended choke set; oversized gold controls; extended magazine tube holds four with the crimped plug; 3-in. chamber
MSRP $1122.00

GOLD RESERVE

Action: Over/under
Stock: Walnut
Barrel: 28 in., 30 in.
Chokes: 5
Sights: Fiber optic front
Weight: 6 lb. 8 oz.–7 lb. 8 oz.
Bore/Gauge: 12, 20, .410 bore
Capacity: 2 shells
Features: Grade-A black walnut stocks; ejectors; silver-finish receiver with scroll engraving and gold inlays; 24K gold inlay "M" in a circle on bottom of receiver; extended sport chokes; 10mm rib; between barrel ventilation
MSRP $1043.00

GOLD RESERVE BLACK LABEL

Action: Over/under

Stock: Walnut
Barrel: 30 in.
Chokes: 5
Sights: Fiber optic front
Weight: 7 lb. 8 oz.
Bore/Gauge: 12
Capacity: 2 shells
Features: Same as the International Gold Reserve standard model but with the receiver finished in polished black
MSRP $1043.00

GOLD RESERVE SUPER SPORT

Action: Over/under
Stock: Walnut
Barrel: 30 in.
Chokes: 5
Sights: Fiber optic front
Weight: 7 lb. 8 oz.
Bore/Gauge: 12
Capacity: 2 shells
Features: Based on the standard International Gold Reserve, this model upgrades with an adjustable cheekpiece, fully adjustable buttstock, and a higher-profile rib
MSRP $1295.00

MAVERICK 88 ALL-PURPOSE

Action: Pump
Stock: Synthetic
Barrel: 26 in., 28 in.
Chokes: Modified
Sights: Bead front
Weight: 7 lb.
Bore/Gauge: 20, 12
Capacity: 5 shells
Features: Simple pump has vent rib; stock in Mossy Oak Treestand; 3-inch chamber; 28-in. barrel on 12 ga., 26-in. barrel on 20 ga.
MSRP . . . . $245.00–$274.00

SHOTGUNS

Mossberg (O. F. Mossberg & Sons)

MOSSBERG MAVERICK 88-SECURITY WITH TOP FOLDING STOCK

MOSSBERG MAVERICK 88 YOUTH ALL-PURPOSE

MOSSBERG SA-20 YOUTH BANTAM WALNUT, SYNTHETIC

MOSSBERG SA-28 YOUTH BANTAM WALNUT, SYNTHETIC

MOSSBERG MAVERICK 88 CRUISER 6-SHOT, 8-SHOT

MOSSBERG SA-20 ALL-PURPOSE FIELD

MOSSBERG INTERNATIONAL SA-28 ALL-PURPOSE FIELD

MOSSBERG SA-410 FIELD

MAVERICK 88 CRUISER 6-SHOT, 8-SHOT

Action: Pump
Stock: Synthetic
Barrel: 18.5 in.
Chokes: None
Sights: Bead front
Weight: 5 lb. 8 oz.–5 lb. 12 oz.
Bore/Gauge: 20, 12
Capacity: 5, 7 shells
Features: Pistol grip pump with a 5+1 or 7+1 capacity; fixed Cylinder bore
MSRP................$245.00

MAVERICK 88-SECURITY WITH TOP FOLDING STOCK

Action: Pump
Stock: Glass-reinforced polymer
Barrel: 18.5 in.
Chokes: None
Sights: Bead
Weight: 6 lb.
Bore/Gauge: 12
Magazine: 6 shells
Features: Top-folding stock by Advanced Technology International; chambers 3-in. rounds
MSRP................$274.00

MAVERICK 88 YOUTH ALL-PURPOSE

Action: Pump
Stock: Synthetic
Barrel: 22 in.
Chokes: Modified
Sights: Bead front
Weight: 5 lb. 4 oz.
Bore/Gauge: 20
Capacity: 5 shells
Features: A great pump for new youth shooters with a shorter length of pull

and barrel; stock in black synthetic or camo
MSRP..........$245.00–$272.00

SA-20 ALL-PURPOSE FIELD

Action: Semiautomatic
Stock: Walnut, synthetic
Barrel: 26 in.
Chokes: 5 chokes (C, IC, M, IM, F)
Weight: 5 lb. 12 oz.
Bore/Gauge: 20
Magazine: 5 shells
Features: Smooth cycling gas-operated system; bead sight; blue finish on barrel; available in walnut or synthetic stocked All-Purpose Field, pink Muddy Girl synthetic stock, a Turkey version in Mossy Oak Obsession, railed versions with and without pistol grips in black synthetic stock, and in a 13-in. length of pull Youth Bantam version with a black synthetic stock
Walnut................$760.00
Synthetic..............$662.00

SA-20 YOUTH BANTAM

Action: Semiautomatic
Stock: Walnut, synthetic
Barrel: 24 in.
Chokes: Five tubes (F, IM, M, IC, C)
Sights: Bead
Weight: 5 lb. 8 oz. (synthetic), 6 lb. 4 oz. (walnut)
Bore/Gauge: 20
Magazine: 5 shells
Features: Easy recoiling, semiautomatic youth shotgun with shortened stock and barrel; chambers 3-in. shells; synthetic stock has metal with a matte blue finish; high-gloss walnut stock has polished blue metalwork
Walnut................$760.00
Synthetic..............$662.00

SA-28 ALL-PURPOSE FIELD

Action: Semiautomatic
Stock: Walnut
Barrel: 26 in.
Chokes: Sport Set
Weight: 6 lb. 8 oz.
Bore/Gauge: 28
Magazine: 5 shells
Features: Lightweight field gun in 2¾-in.; front bead; high-polish blue metal; high-gloss walnut stock
MSRP................$760.00

SA-28 YOUTH BANTAM ALL-PURPOSE FIELD

Action: Semiautomatic
Stock: Synthetic
Barrel: 24 in.
Chokes: Five tubes (F, IM, M, IC, C)
Sights: Bead
Weight: 5 lb. 8 oz.
Bore/Gauge: 28
Magazine: 5 shells
Features: Easy recoiling, semiautomatic youth shotgun with shortened stock and barrel; chambers 2¾-inch shells
MSRP:................$662.00

SA-410 FIELD

Action: Semiautomatic
Stock: Synthetic
Barrel: 26 in.
Chokes: Sport set
Sights: Bead front
Weight: 6 lb. 8 oz.
Bore/Gauge: .410
Capacity: 4 shells
Features: A reliably functioning semiauto in .410-bore with a 3-in. chamber; gas-operation
MSRP................$696.00

Mossberg (O. F. Mossberg & Sons)

MOSSBERG SA-410 TURKEY

MOSSBERG INTERNATIONAL SILVER RESERVE

MOSSBERG INTERNATIONAL SILVER RESERVE EVENTIDE

MOSSBERG INTERNATIONAL SILVER RESERVE YOUTH BANTAM

SA-410 TURKEY

Action: Semiautomatic
Stock: Synthetic
Barrel: 26 in.
Chokes: XX-Full turkey
Sights: FO ghost ring
Weight: 6 lb. 8 oz.
Bore/Gauge: .410
Capacity: 4 shells
Features: Same as the Field SA-410, but in full-coverage Mossy Oak Bottomland camo; FO ghost ring sights
MSRP $829.00

SILVER RESERVE

Action: Over/under
Stock: Walnut
Barrel: 26 in., 28 in.
Chokes: 5

Sights: Bead front
Weight: 6 lb. 8 oz.–7 lb. 8 oz.
Bore/Gauge: 12, 20, 28, .410
Capacity: 2 shells
Features: If you can live without ejectors, then this shotgun will serve you well for field or range; extractors only; field chokes; select black walnut stocks; satin finished receiver unadorned except for the laser-engraved Mossberg name; matte blue barrels; vet rib and between barrel venting
MSRP $734.00

SILVER RESERVE EVENTIDE

Action: Over/under
Stock: Synthetic
Barrel: 28 in.
Chokes: 5
Sights: Fiber optic front
Weight: 7 lb.
Bore/Gauge: 12
Capacity: 2 shells

Features: A great choice for hunting (or shooting skeet or trap in the pouring rain), with a synthetic stock; matte blue metalwork; field chokes
MSRP $675.00

SILVER RESERVE YOUTH BANTAM

Action: Over/under
Stock: Walnut
Barrel: 26 in.
Chokes: 5
Sights: Bead front
Weight: 7 lb.
Bore/Gauge: 20
Capacity: 2 shells
Features: Nice choice for a youth or smaller-statured person getting serious about competing or hunting; 13.25-in. length of pull; satin silver receiver; matte blue barrels
MSRP $734.00

Nighthawk Custom

NIGHTHAWK OVERSEER MODEL 3

OVERSEER

Action: Pump
Stock: Synthetic
Barrel: 18 in.
Chokes: None
Sights: Fiber optic front
Weight: N/A
Bore/Gauge: 12
Capacity: 6 shells

Features: Based on a Remington 870 action, the standard-package Model 1 includes hand-honed action and rails, Nighthawk tactical ghost ring rear sight with a fiber optic rear, Picatinny receiver mount, six-round side saddle; Hogue overmolded stock and fore-end, and a black Cerakote finish on the metalwork; Model 2 adds an SGA Magpul fore-end and stock with adapter plates; Model 2.5 builds on Model 2 by adding a Vang Comp System barrel porting; Model 3 builds on Model 2 with a custom Shadow

Tan finish on stock and fore-end; Model 4 builds on Model 2 with a custom Shadow Urban camo stock and fore-end, a Surefire Z2X combat light, a barrel clamp with swivel, and a Picatinny rail; Model 5 builds on Model 2 with a custom Battle-Worn Silver Patriot overall finish; Model 6 builds on Model 1 with a collapsible stock, Hogue pistol grip, SureFire DSF870 fore-end, ambidextrous and selectable light switch, three-shot mag extension, and breeching device
MSRP . . . . $1499.00–$2199.00

Perazzi

PERAZZI HIGH TECH

HIGH TECH

Action: Over/under
Stock: Wood
Barrel: 27–31 in.
Chokes: Can be specified or made interchangeable
Weight: N/A
Bore/Gauge: 12

Magazine: 2 shells
Features: High Tech has a sporty and futuristic look; a large logo engraved in black smoke color on both sides of the receiver, under clear varnish, in contrast to the rest of the receiver; hinge pins are engraved with a checkered design; action is two-tone and varnished "in the white" only in the areas where the logo appears; frame has a greater weight than other

Perazzi models and it is distributed within the median line between the grip of the hands, which both improves the fluidity of handling and further reduces recoil; divergent rib that goes from 7mm wide at the action to 10mm at the front end of the barrels allows you to greatly speed up your perception of the target and also expands your field of vision.
MSRP . . . **Contact retailers for pricing**

SHOTGUNS

Perazzi

PERAZZI MX8

MX8
Action: Over/under
Stock: Walnut
Barrel: 29 in., 30 in., 31 in.
Chokes: Interchangeable chokes
Weight: 7 lb. 5 oz.
Bore/Gauge: 12, 20
Magazine: 2 shells

Features: Custom walnut stock with beavertail forend; half-ventilated side ribs on barrel; removable trigger with flat or coil springs; blue or nickel plating; Sporting, Skeet and Trap models; 28 Ga. and .410 models also available
MSRP . . . . Contact retailers for pricing

Pointer By Legacy Sports

POINTER BY LEGACY SPORTS ACRIUS

ACRIUS
Action: Over/under
Stock: Walnut
Barrel: 28 in.
Chokes: 5
Sights: Fiber optic front
Weight: 6 lb. 10 oz.
Bore/Gauge: 12

Capacity: 2 shells
Features: Turkish walnut stock; coin-finished receiver with light floral laser-etching; vent rib and between barrel venting; chrome-lined barrels; supplied with extended chokes
MSRP $519.00

Retay USA

RETAY USA GORDION SYNTHETIC

RETAY USA GORDION TURKEY

RETAY USA GORDION WALNUT

RETAY USA GPS DEFENSE

GORDION SYNTHETIC
Action: Semiautomatic
Stock: Synthetic
Barrel: 26 in., 28 in.
Chokes: 5 (F, IM, M, IC, C), 6
Sights: TruGlo red front
Weight: N/A
Bore/Gauge: 12
Capacity: 4 shells
Features: Feature-loaded shotgun for the field, with a stock in black synthetic or choice of full-coverage camo in Realtree Max-5 or Mossy Oak New Bottomland; TruGlo fiber-optic front sight; flat 8mm vent rib; adjustable stock shim kit; five-set of MaraPro chokes; single piece aluminum receiver; inertia piston system; 3-in. chamber
Black $799.00
Camo $899.00

GORDION TURKEY
Action: Semiautomatic
Stock: Synthetic
Barrel: 24 in.
Chokes: 5 (IC, SK, M, IM, F)
Sights: Fibe optic front
Weight: 6 lb. 8 oz.
Bore/Gauge: 12
Capacity: 4 shells
Features: Similar to the Gordion Synthetic, but with the addition of a receiver-mounted Picatinny rail for optics mounting; available in full-coverage Realtree Timber, NWTF Mossy Oak Obsession or Mossy Oak New Bottomland
MSRP $949.00

GORDION WALNUT
Action: Semiautomatic
Stock: Turkish walnut
Barrel: 26 in., 28 in.
Chokes: 5 (IC, SK, M, IM, F)
Sights: TruGlo red front
Weight: N/A
Bore/Gauge: 12
Capacity: 4 shells
Features: Reasonably priced semiauto for upland bird work or clay games; Inertia-Plus bolt system; Mara bolt; hard case included
MSRP $899.00

GPS
Action: Pump
Stock: Synthetic
Barrel: 18.5 in.
Chokes: 3
Sights: Blade front
Weight: N/A
Bore/Gauge: 12
Capacity: 5 shells
Features: Geometric Pump Shotgun (GPS)—what that really means is Retay used computer-enhanced geometry to produce a gun that required shorter pump strokes and made loading easier; 3-in. chamber; matte anodized receiver; matte black chrome-lined barrel; MaraPro chokes in C, M, and F included
MSRP $349.00

Retay USA

RETAY USA MASAI MARA
CERAKOTE

RETAY USA MASAI MARA
WALNUT

MASAI MARA CERAKOTE

Action: Semiautomatic
Stock: Synthetic
Barrel: 26 in., 28 in.
Chokes: 5 (IC, SK, M, IM, F)
Sights: TruGlo red front
Weight: N/A
Bore/Gauge: 12, 20
Capacity: 4 shells
Features: Designed for the tough conditions found in waterfowling, this 12-ga. has a 3.5-in. chamber; MaraPro five-choke set; removeable trigger group; aluminum lower receiver with a milled Bohler steel upper receiver; chrome-lined barrel; lengthened forcing cones. Color/gauge combos include: 12- or 20-ga. (3.5- and 3-in. chambers, respectively) in Realtree Timber stock with Flat Dark Earth Cerakote; 12-ga. (3.5-in. chamber) Realtree Max- with OD Green Cerakote; 12- or 20-ga. (3.5- and 3-in. chambers, respectively) in Mossy Oak New Bottomland with Burnt Bronze Cerakote
MSRP . . . . $1499.00–$1600.00

MASAI MARA WALNUT

Action: Semiautomatic
Stock: Turkish walnut
Barrel: 24 in., 26 in., 28 in., 30 in.
Chokes: 5 (IC, SK, M, IM, F)
Sights: TruGlo red front
Weight: N/A
Bore/Gauge: 20, 12
Capacity: 4 shells
Features: Features: Pretty line of streamlined upland or sporting semiautomatics; Turish walnut stocks; 3-in. chambers; intertia piston system with rotating bolt; flat 8mm vent rib; removeable trigger group; red TruGlo fiber optic front sight; shim kit with adjustable butt plate; lengthened forcing cones; chrome-line barrel. Available in: Comfort–12- or 20-ga., upgraded Grade 2 or 4 walnut stocks in an oil finish in the 12-ga. only, matte stainless receiver finish; Satin ST–20-ga. only with a satin-finishe stainless receiver; Jet Black–20-ga. only with a polished black receiver; Dark Black–20-ga. only with a matte black receiver; Bronze Pure–20-ga. only with a Bronze Cerakote receiver
MSRP . . . . $1355.00–$2149.00

Savage Arms

SAVAGE ARMS 220 SLUG GUN

SAVAGE RENEGAUGE
COMPETITION

SAVAGE ARMS 220
TURKEY

220 SLUG GUN

Action: Bolt
Stock: Synthetic
Barrel: 22 in.
Sights: None
Weight: 7 lb. 8 oz.
Caliber: 20
Magazine: 2 shells
Features: Detachable box magazine; AccuTrigger; button-rifled barrels; left-hand in black synthetic stock and matte black metalwork; right-hand version in Mossy Oak Break-Up stock and matte stainless metalwork or Mossy Oak Break-Up Infinity with matte black metalwork
Black $699.00
Black left-hand. $699.00
Camo/black $769.00
Camo/stainless. $889.00

220 TURKEY

Action: Bolt
Stock: Synthetic
Barrel: 22 in.
Chokes: Extra-full turkey
Sights: None
Weight: 7 lb.
Bore/Gauge: 20
Capacity: 3 shells
Features: A dedicated turkey gun on a bolt-action platform; Winchester-thread for chokes; adjustable AccuFit stock in Mossy Oak Obsession; matte black metal; topside optics rail; detachable two-round box magazine
MSRP $769.00

RENEGAUGE COMPETITION

Action: Semiautomatic
Stock: Synthetic
Barrel: 24 in.
Chokes: 3
Sights: Fiber optic front
Weight: 8 lb. 3 oz.
Bore/Gauge: 12
Capacity: 9 shells
Features: Ready for 3-gun out of the box; competition-ready easy-load magazine port; extended Skeet 2/Light Mod Beretta/Benelli Mobil-type choke; aluminum receiver, magazine tube, and choke extension in red Cerakote; carbon-steel vent rib; Hi-Viz Tri-Comp fiber optic sight; stock rod buffer to reduce recoil; stock adjustable for length of pull, cast, and drop; D.R.I.V. dual-regulating inline valve gas system
MSRP $2089.00

Savage Arms

SAVAGE RENEGAUGE FIELD

SAVAGE RENEGAUGE PRAIRIE

SAVAGE RENEGAUGE TURKEY

SAVAGE RENEGAUGE WATERFOWL

SAVAGE ARMS STEVENS 301 SINGLE-SHOT

SAVAGE ARMS STEVENS 301 SINGLE-SHOT COMPACT

SAVAGE ARMS STEVENS 301 TURKEY

SAVAGE STEVENS 301 TURKEY THUMBHOLE

RENEGAUGE FIELD

Action: Semiautomatic
Stock: Synthetic
Barrel: 26 in., 28 in.
Chokes: 3 (IC, M, F)
Sights: Front fiber optic
Weight: 7 lb. 13.6 oz.–7 lb. 14.4 oz.
Bore/Gauge: 12
Capacity: 4 shells
Features: The first semiautomatic shotgun produced by Savage and featuring the new DRIV (Dual Regulating Inline Valve) system that speeds cycling while minimizing recoil across a spectrum of payloads; fluted vent-rib barrel with red fiber optic front sight; easy-load ejection port; oversized bolt handle and safety
MSRP $1592.00

RENEGAUGE PRAIRIE

Action: Semiautomatic
Stock: Synthetic
Barrel: 28 in.
Chokes: 3
Sights: Fiber optic front
Weight: 7 lb. 15 oz.
Bore/Gauge: 12
Capacity: 4 shells
Features: Stock in TrueTimber Prairie camo; receiver and barrel in Brown Sand Cerakote; D.R.I.V. gas system; aluminum receiver; carbon steel barrel; vent rib; stock rod buffer to reduce recoil; oversized controls; easy-load magazine port; I, M, and F flush-mount Beretta/Benelli Mobil-type chokes and hard case included
MSRP $1707.00

RENEGAUGE TURKEY

Action: Semiautomatic
Stock: Synthetic

Barrel: 24 in.
Chokes: 4 (XF, IC, M, F)
Sights: Front fiber optic
Weight: 7 lb. 12 oz.
Bore/Gauge: 12
Capacity: 4 shells
Features: Similar to the Field but with a shorter barrel for tom hunting; Beretta/Benelli chokes; choice of Mossy Oak Bottomland or Obsession full-coverage camo
MSRP $1707.00

RENEGAUGE WATERFOWL

Action: Semiautomatic
Stock: Synthetic
Barrel: 26 in., 28 in.
Chokes: 3 (IC, M, F)
Sights: Front fiber optic
Weight: 7 lb. 13.6 oz.–7 lb. 14 oz.
Bore/Gauge: 12
Capacity: 4 shells
Features: Similar to the Field but in full-coverage Mossy Oak Shadow Grass Blades camo; melonite finish on barrel; Beretta/Benelli chokes
MSRP $1707.00

STEVENS 301 SINGLE-SHOT

Action: Single-shot
Stock: Synthetic
Barrel: 26 in. (12-ga.); 22, 24 in. (20-ga.); 22, 26 in. (.410-bore)
Chokes: None
Sights: Front bead
Weight: N/A
Bore/Gauge: 12, 20, .410
Magazine: 1 shell
Features: Break-action single-shot with a receiver-side safety; synthetic stock; carbon steel barrel
MSRP $206.00

STEVENS 301 SINGLE-SHOT COMPACT

Action: Single-shot
Stock: Synthetic
Barrel: 22 in. (Compact); 26 in. (Standard)
Chokes: Interchangeable
Sights: Bead

Weight: 5 lb. 4 oz. (Compact); 5 lb. 8 oz. (Standard)
Bore/Gauge: 20, .410
Magazine: 1 shell
Features: Interchangeable chokes; two-position safety; 3-in. chambers; compact available only in the 20 ga. and .410-bore
MSRP $206.00

STEVENS 301 TURKEY

Action: Single-shot
Stock: Synthetic
Barrel: 26 in.
Chokes: Extra-full
Sights: Bead front, rear rail
Weight: 5 lb.
Bore/Gauge: 12, 20, .410
Capacity: 1 shell
Features: Designed to be optimized in barrel length for Federal's HEAVYWEIGHT TSS turkey loads; available in Mossy Oak Bottomland or Obsession; sling swivel studs; removeable front sight can be replaced with TruGlo fiber optics; 3-inch chamber
MSRP $227.00

STEVENS 301 TURKEY THUMBHOLE

Action: Single-shot
Stock: Synthetic
Barrel: 26 in.
Chokes: 1
Sights: Bead front
Weight: 5 lb. 1 oz.
Bore/Gauge: .410
Capacity: 1 shell
Features: Handy thumbhole stock in an olive drab green keeps a turkey hunter steady; carbon steel receiver and chrome alloy steel barrel in matte black; ambidextrous cheek riser; removable topside rail; Extra Full choke Winchester-type ½x32UN threads; barrel optimized for use with Federal Premium Heavyweight TSS Turkey ammunition; swivel studs on forend and stock
MSRP $248.00

Savage Arms

SAVAGE STEVENS 301 TURKEY OBSESSION, 301 TURKEY XP OBSESSION

SAVAGE ARMS STEVENS 320 FIELD GRADE

SAVAGE ARMS STEVENS 320 FIELD GRADE COMPACT

SAVAGE ARMS STEVENS 320 SECURITY

SAVAGE ARMS STEVENS 555

SAVAGE STEVENS 320 SECURITY THUMBHOLE

SAVAGE ARMS STEVENS 555 E

SAVAGE STEVENS 555 TRAP, TRAP COMPACT

STEVENS 301 TURKEY XP

Action: Single-shot
Stock: Synthetic
Barrel: 26 in.
Chokes: 1
Sights: Bead front, 1x3 red-dot optic
Weight: 5 lb. 1 oz.
Bore/Gauge: 20, .410
Capacity: 1 shell
Features: Beware the turkey hunter who trusts in a single-shot; barrel optimized for Federal Premium Heavyweight TSS Turkey loads; removable rail; stock and forend in Mossy Oak Bottomland or Obsession; matte black barrel and receiver; chambered for 3½-in.; includes Extra-Full choke tube in a Winchester ½x32UN thread pattern
MSRP $268.00

STEVENS 320 FIELD GRADE

Action: Pump
Stock: Synthetic
Barrel: 26 in., 28 in.
Chokes: M
Weight: 6 lb. 15.2 oz.–7 lb. 7.2 oz.
Bore/Gauge: 12, 20
Magazine: 5 shells
Features: Base model has black synthetic stock; camo options in MO Shadow Grass or Obsession and matte blue metalwork, mid-length fore-end and fiber-optic front sight;
Black $280.00
Camo (12-ga. only) $331.00

STEVENS 320 FIELD GRADE COMPACT

Action: Pump
Stock: Synthetic
Barrel: 22 in.
Chokes: N/A
Weight: 7 lb.
Bore/Gauge: 20
Magazine: 2 shells

Features: Carbon steel barrel; compact size and light recoil make it the ideal shotgun for introducing young people to the shooting sports; in all-black, MO Shadow Grass Blades, or Muddy Girl camo
Black $280.00
Camo $319.00

STEVENS 320 SECURITY

Action: Pump
Stock: Synthetic
Barrel: 18.5 in.
Chokes: M
Weight: 6 lb. 13.6 oz.–7lb.
Bore/Gauge: 12, 20
Magazine: 5 shells
Features: Intended for home and personal defense, five versions available: heat shield with top-side optics rail; ghost ring with pistol grip stock; ergonomic stock with bead sight; ergonomic stock with ghost ring sights; bead sight and pistol grip
MSRP: . . . . $278.00–$330.00

STEVENS 320 SECURITY THUMBHOLE

Action: Pump
Stock: Synthetic
Barrel: 18.5 in.
Chokes: None
Sights: Bead front, ghost ring
Weight: 7 lb.–7 lb. 3 oz.
Bore/Gauge: 12, 20
Capacity: 5 shells
Features: This is a smart choice for home defense with its shorter than average 13.75-in. length of pull; thumbhole stock has ambidextrous cheek riser; textured grip areas; 3-in. chamber; bottom-loading magazine tube; all-over matte black appearance; choice of front bead or front/rear ghost ring sights
Bead $298.00
Ghost ring $330.00

STEVENS 555

Action: Over/under
Stock: Wood
Barrel: 28 in.
Chokes: 5 interchangeable chokes
Weight: 6 lb.
Bore/Gauge: 12, 20, 16, 28, .410
Magazine: 2 shells
Features: Lightweight alloy receiver, Turkish walnut stock & forearm, single selective trigger, mechanical triggers, extractors, manual safetys
MSRP $709.00

STEVENS 555 E

Action: Over/under
Stock: Walnut
Barrel: 28 in. (12-ga.); 26 in. (20- and 28-ga, .410)
Chokes: SK, IC, M, IM, F
Weight: 5 lb. 8 oz.–6 lb.
Bore/Gauge: 12, 20, 16, 28, .410
Magazine: 2 shells
Features: Lightweight aluminum receiver is scaled to gauge; imperial walnut stock; automatic shell ejectors; laser-engraved filigree decoration on the receiver
MSRP $937.00

STEVENS 555 TRAP, TRAP COMPACT

Action: Single-shot
Stock: Walnut
Barrel: 30 in.
Chokes: 3
Sights: Bead front
Weight: 6 lb. 9 oz.–7 lb. 8 oz.
Bore/Gauge: 12, 20
Capacity: 1 shell
Features: Oil-finished Turkish walnut stock with adjustable cheekpiece; raised vent rib; aluminum alloy receiver in a semi-gloss finish; carbon steel barrel in a semi-gloss finish; 3-in. chamber; F, M, and I chokes; standard model has 14.75-in. length of pull, Compact is 13.75 in.
MSRP $770.00

SRM Arms

SRM ARMS MODEL 1216

MODEL 1216

Action: Semiautomatic
Stock: Synthetic
Barrel: 18 in.
Chokes: N/A
Weight: 7 lb. 4 oz.
Bore/Gauge: 12
Magazine: 16 shells

Features: Picatinny rail combined with a three face handguard rail; ambidextrous receiver and controls; quad-tube, revolving detachable magazine
MSRP $1799.00

Standard Manufacturing Co.

STANDARD MANUFACTURING CO. SKO MINI

STANDARD MANUFACTURING CO. SKO MINI WORKS PACKAGE

SKO MINI

Action: Semiautomatic
Stock: Polymer, composite
Barrel: 14.75 in.
Chokes: N/A
Sights: None
Weight: 7 lb. 2 oz.
Bore/Gauge: 12
Capacity: 2, 5, 10 shells
Features: Overall length 27 inches; internal parts salt bath nitride coated; gas-operation; ready for user to add optics, accessories, and chokes, including specialty chokes such as breaking types; accepts most AR-type grips; 3-inch chamber
MSRP $750.00

SKO MINI WORKS PACKAGE

Action: Semiautomatic
Stock: Polymer, composite
Barrel: 14.75 in.
Chokes: One
Sights: Flip-up AR-style, reflex red dot
Weight: 7 lb. 2 oz.
Bore/Gauge: 12
Capacity: 2, 5, 10 shells
Features: An NFA "other" firearm featuring a 3-inch chamber; gas operation; aluminum receiver; composite fore-end with MOE slots; vertical forward grip; Tru-Choke threading; aluminum tactical grip
MSRP $1200.00

Stoeger Industries

STOEGER COACH GUN

STOEGER CONDOR

STOEGER CONDOR COMPETITION

STOEGER CONDOR OUTBACK

COACH GUN

Action: Side-by-side
Stock: Walnut, hardwood
Barrel: 20 in.
Chokes: Fixed chokes (IC, M)
Weight: 6 lb. 5 oz.–7 lb.
Bore/Gauge: 12, 20, .410
Magazine: 2 shells
Features: A-grade satin or black finished hardwood stock; brass bead sights; nickel or blued metal finish
MSRP . . . . $479.00–$549.00

CONDOR

Action: Over/under
Stock: Walnut
Barrel: 22 in., 24 in., 26 in., 28 in.
Chokes: Screw-in and fixed chokes on

12 Ga., 20 Ga., 28 Ga. (IC, M), 16 Ga. (M, F), .410 (F&F)
Weight: 5 lb. 8 oz.–7 lb. 6 oz.
Bore/Gauge: 12, 16, 20, 28, .410
Magazine: 2 shells
Features: Walnut stock; brass bead sight; single trigger; auto-ejectors
Field . . . . $349.00–$479.00
Youth $479.00
Skeet $479.00
Supreme $619.00
Longfowler $479.00

CONDOR COMPETITION

Action: Over/under
Stock: Walnut
Barrel: 30 in.
Chokes: Screw-in (IC, M, F)
Weight: 7 lb. 5 oz.–7 lb. 13 oz.
Bore/Gauge: 12, 20

Magazine: 2 shells
Features: Walnut stock; brass bead with silver mid-bead sight; single selective trigger; automatic ejector; ported barrel
MSRP $669.00

CONDOR OUTBACK

Action: Over/under
Stock: Walnut, hardwood
Barrel: 20 in.
Chokes: Screw-in (IC, M)
Weight: 6 lb. 8 oz.–7 lb.
Bore/Gauge: 12, 20
Magazine: 2 shells
Features: Notched rear sight and fixed blade front sight; shell extractor; single trigger; A-grade satin walnut or black finished hardwood
Outback . . . . $479.00–$499.00

Stoeger Industries

STOEGER DOUBLE DEFENSE OVER/UNDER

STOEGER M3K 3-GUN

STOEGER M3000 DEFENSE

STOEGER M3000 SPORTING

STOEGER DOUBLE DEFENSE

STOEGER M3000

STOEGER INDUSTRIES M3000 FREEDOM SERIES DEFENSE SHOTGUN

STOEGER M3000 WALNUT/BURNT BRONZE

DOUBLE DEFENSE OVER/UNDER

Action: Over/under
Stock: Hardwood
Barrel: 20 in.
Chokes: Screw-in chokes (IC/IC fixed)
Weight: 6 lb. 3 oz.–6 lb. 8 oz.
Bore/Gauge: 12, 20
Magazine: 2 shells
Features: Black hardwood stock; green fiber optic front sight; ported barrels; two Picatinny rails; single trigger design; tang-mounted automatic safety
MSRP **$479.00**

DOUBLE DEFENSE SIDE-BY-SIDE

Action: Side-by-side
Stock: Hardwood
Barrel: 20 in.
Chokes: Screw-in chokes (IC/IC fixed)
Weight: 6 lb. 8 oz.
Bore/Gauge: 12, 20
Magazine: 2 shells
Features: Black hardwood stock; fiber optic front sight; ported barrels; two Picatinny rails; single trigger design; tang-mounted automatic safety
MSRP **$489.00**

M3K 3-GUN, FREEDOM SERIES 3-GUN

Action: Semiautomatic, inertia-driven
Stock: Synthetic
Barrel: 24 in.
Chokes: XC, IC, M
Weight: 7 lb. 5 oz.
Bore/Gauge: 12
Magazine: 4+1
Features: Fiber optic sights; based on the M3000 line of shotguns; 3-gun ready; oversized anodized aluminum bolt release, oversized safety, and

extended tactical-style anodized aluminum bolt handle; elongated carrier and enlarged, beveled loading port for quicker and easier reloading
MSRP . . . . **$669.00–$699.00**

M3000

Action: Semiautomatic
Stock: Black synthetic, Realtree APG, Realtree APG SteadyGrip, Realtree Max-5
Barrel: 24 in.
Chokes: IC, M, XFT, wrench
Weight: 7 lb. 5 oz.
Bore/ Gauge: 12
Magazine: 4+1 shells
Features: Inertia driven; red-bar front sight; drilled and tapped; shim kit; 3-in. loads; available with stocks in A-grade satin walnut, black synthetic, Mossy Oak Bottomland or Realtree Max-5, all with blue metalwork
MSRP . . . . **$559.00–$669.00**

M3000 DEFENSE

Action: Semiautomatic
Stock: Synthetic
Barrel: 18.5 in.
Chokes: Cylinder fixed
Weight: 7 lb.
Bore/Gauge: 12
Magazine: 4 shells
Features: 3-in. chamber; blade front sight; field or pistol grip stock
Pistol grip: **$619.00**
Standard: **$559.00**

M3000 FREEDOM SERIES DEFENSE

Action: Semiautomatic
Stock: Synthetic
Barrel: 18.5 in.
Chokes: None
Sights: Blade front sight

Weight: 6 lb. 10 oz.–7 lb.
Bore/Gauge: 12
Magazine: 7 shells
Features: A super self-defense shotgun with a seven-round magazine, blade front sight, fixed Cylinder choke. Includes a stock shim kit included. Available with a pistol grip stock.
MSRP **$619.00**
Pistol grip: **$669.00**

M3000 SPORTING

Action: Semiautomatic
Stock: Synthetic
Barrel: 30 in.
Chokes: SK1, SK2, IC
Weight: 7 lb. 8 oz.
Bore/Gauge: 12
Magazine: 4 shells
Features: Built for clay game competition; 3-in. chamber; fiber optic front sight; extended choke tubes
MSRP **$669.00**

M3000 WALNUT/BURNT BRONZE

Action: Semiautomatic
Stock: Walnut
Barrel: 28 in.
Chokes: Three
Sights: Red bar front
Weight: 7 lb. 6 oz.
Bore/Gauge: 12
Capacity: 4 shells
Features: Inertia Driven semiauto in a 3-inch 12-gauge; satin-finished walnut stock paired with Burnt Bronze Cerakote metalwork; also available with a Realtree Max-5 stock; stepped vent rib; drilled and tapped
MSRP **$669.00**

SHOTGUNS

Stoeger Industries

STOEGER M3020 WALNUT/BURNT BRONZE

STOEGER INDUSTRIES M3020 DEFENSE SHOTGUN 20-GAUGE

STOEGER INDUSTRIES M3020 UPLAND SPECIAL

STOEGER MODEL 3500

STOEGER M3500 WATERFOWL

STOEGER INDUSTRIES M3500 PREDATOR/TURKEY

STOEGER INDUSTRIES M3500 SNOW GOOSE

STOEGER INDUSTRIES P3000

M3020 DEFENSE SHOTGUN 20-GAUGE

Action: Semiautomatic
Stock: Synthetic
Barrel: 18.5 in.
Chokes: None
Sights: Ghost ring sights
Weight: 5 lb. 8 oz.
Bore/Gauge: 20
Magazine: 4 shells
Features: Self-defense shotgun; fixed Cylinder choke; ghost ring sights; chambers 3-in. shells
MSRP $619.00

M3020 UPLAND SPECIAL

Action: Semiautomatic
Stock: Walnut
Barrel: 26 in.
Chokes: 3 (M, F, C)
Sights: Red bar front
Weight: 5 lb. 7 oz.
Bore/Gauge: 20
Capacity: 4 shells
Features: Nice upland semiauto with an anodized silver receiver; gloss-finished walnut stock; extended chokes; 3-in. chamber; Inertia-Driven system
MSRP $649.00

M3020 WALNUT/BURNT BRONZE

Action: Semiautomatic
Stock: Walnut
Barrel: 28 in.
Chokes: Three
Sights: Red bar front
Weight: 5 lb. 12 oz.
Bore/Gauge: 20
Capacity: 4 shells
Features: Who says you have to pay big bucks for today's upgraded finishes? Stoeger adds Burnt Bronze Cerakote metalwork to a satin-finished walnut stock, all within a working man's budget
MSRP $649.00

M3500

Action: Semiautomatic
Stock: Synthetic
Barrel: 24 in., 26 in., 28 in.
Chokes: Screw-in choke tubes (C, IC, M, F, XFT) and wrench
Weight: 7 lb. 7 oz.–7 lb. 10 oz.
Bore/Gauge: 12
Magazine: 4+1 shells
Features: Synthetic stock comes in black or camo finish in Realtree Max-5 or Mossy Oak Bottomland; one Mossy Oak Bottomland version offered with Burnt Bronze Cerakote metalwork; satin walnut stock version available; inertia drive system; recoil reducer; red-bar front sight; Weaver scope base; includes shim kit
Black synthetic: $669.00
Camo or walnut stock: $769.00
Camo with Cerakote: $799.00

M3500 PREDATOR/TURKEY

Action: Semiautomatic
Stock: Synthetic
Barrel: 24 in.
Chokes: 5 (Predator, Turkey, M, IC, C)
Sights: Red bar front
Weight: 7 lb. 8 oz.
Bore/Gauge: 12
Capacity: 4 shells
Features: Drilled and tapped for optics mounting; full-coverage Mossy Oak Overwatch camo; pistol grip stock
MSRP $929.00

M3500 SNOW GOOSE

Action: Semiautomatic
Stock: Synthetic
Barrel: 28 in.
Chokes: 5

Sights: Red fiber optic front
Weight: 8 lb. 3 oz.
Bore/Gauge: 12
Capacity: 10 shells
Features: Designed for high-volume, extreme weather shooting with oversized controls; full-coverage distressed white Cerakote; huge magazine capacity; Close-Range, Mid-Range, Modified, Improved, and XFT extended choke tubes; drilled and tapped receiver; paracord sling
MSRP $929.00

M3500 WATERFOWL

Action: Semiautomatic
Stock: Synthetic
Barrel: 28 in.
Chokes: Five
Sights: Red bar front
Weight: 7 lb. 13 oz.
Bore/Gauge: 12
Capacity: 4 shells
Features: Dressed in Realtree Max-5 on the stock and Flat Dark Earth metalwork, this one handles all waterfowl with a 3½-inch chamber; extended chokes in Close-Range, Mid-Range, Modified, Improved Cylinder, and XFT; paracord sling; drilled and tapped
MSRP $849.00

P3000

Action: Pump
Stock: Synthetic
Barrel: 18.5 in., 26 in., 28 in.
Chokes: M inner choke
Weight: 6 lb. 6 oz.–6 lb. 14 oz.
Bore/Gauge: 12
Magazine: 4+1 shells
Features: Chambered for 2¾- and 3-in. shells; in black or Realtree Max-5 camo in long barrel options; 18.5-in. barrel option only in black synthetic but with choice of pistol grip or standard buttstock
MSRP . . . . $289.00–$339.00

Stoeger Industries

STOEGER P3000 DEFENSE

STOEGER THE GRAND

STOEGER INDUSTRIES P3000 FREEDOM SERIES DEFENSE

STOEGER UPLANDER

STOEGER P3500

P3000 DEFENSE

Action: Pump
Stock: Synthetic, wood
Barrel: 18.5 in.
Chokes: Cylinder fixed
Weight: 6 lb. 8 oz.
Bore/Gauge: 12
Magazine: 4 shells
Features: Blade front sight; 3-in. chamber; field or pistol grip stock
MSRP . . . . $289.00–$339.00

P3000 FREEDOM SERIES DEFENSE

Action: Pump
Stock: Synthetic
Barrel: 18.5 in.
Chokes: None
Sights: Blade front sight
Weight: 6 lb. 4 oz.
Bore/Gauge: 12
Magazine: 7 shells
Features: A pump self-defense

shotgun with added capacity; fixed Cylinder choke
MSRP $339.00

P3500

Action: Pump
Stock: Synthetic
Barrel: 26 in., 28 in.
Chokes: M
Weight: 6 lb. 14 oz.–7 lb.
Bore/Gauge: 12
Magazine: 4 shells
Features: Chambered for 2 ¾-, 3-, and 3 ½-in.; mechanical rotating bolt; dual action rails; red fiber optic front sight; chrome-lined steel barrel; black or Realtree Max-5
Black: $339.00
Camo: $389.00

THE GRAND

Action: Break-action
Stock: Wood
Barrel: 30 in.
Chokes: M, IM, F

Weight: 9 lb.
Bore/Gauge: 12
Magazine: 1 shell
Features: Single-barrel target gun designed for shooting trap; stepped ventilated rib and fiber optic front sight; automatic safety that engages when the lever is activated to open the action
MSRP $629.00

UPLANDER

Action: Side-by-side
Stock: Walnut
Barrel: 22 in. (youth), 26 in., 28 in., 28 in.
Chokes: Screw-in and fixed tubes
Weight: 6 lb. 8 oz.–7 lb. 8 oz.
Bore/Gauge: 12, 16, 20, 28, .410
Magazine: 2 shels
Features: Brass bead sights; A-grade satin walnut stock; tang-mounted safety; single or double triggers; extractors included
Uplander Field: $479.00
Uplander Supreme: $549.00
Uplander Youth: $479.00
Uplander Longfowler: $479.00

Syren USA

SYREN USA ELOS N2 ELEVATE

SYREN ELOS N2 SPORTING

ELOS N2 ELEVATE

Action: Over/under
Stock: Walnut
Barrel: 30 in.
Chokes: 5
Sights: White bead front, brass mid-bead
Weight: 7 lb. 10 oz.
Bore/Gauge: 12
Capacity: 2 shells
Features: Turkish walnut stock having a TRIWOOD finish and an adjustable stock; 10mm-8mm tapered vet rib and set of two quick-detach ribs, one pointing 50/50, the other 65/35;

ventilated center rib; black satin finish receiver; microcell 22mm soft black rubber buttpad; TRIBORE HP bores; schnabel forend; trigger adjustable for length of pull; EXIS HP extended competition choke tubes; overall geometry designed for a more upright shooting stance; add $160 for left-hand configuration
MSRP $3425.00
Left-hand . . . . add $175.00

ELOS N2 SPORTING

Action: Semiautomatic
Stock: Turkish walnut

Barrel: 30 in.
Chokes: 5 EXIS HP
Weight: 7 lb. 14 oz.
Bore/Gauge: 12
Magazine: 4+1 shells
Features: Turkish walnut stock enhanced by a proprietary TRIWOOD finish, which adds grain and water resistance; TRIBORE HP barrels for the ultimate in ballistic performance; adjustable trigger; lefthand option; 32-in. barrels can be optioned for additional charge
Standard $3150.00
Left-hand . . . . add $175.00

SYREN USA JULIA SPORTING

SYREN L4S SPORTING

SYREN TEMPIO TRAP UNSINGLE AND TEMPIO TRAP OVER/UNDER

JULIA SPORTING

Action: Over/under
Stock: Walnut
Barrel: 28, 30 in.
Chokes: 6
Sights: White bead front, silver mid-bead
Weight: 7 lb. 15 oz.
Bore/Gauge: 12, 20
Capacity: 2 shells
Features: Beautiful hand-rubbed oil stock with a rounded forend; tapered 10mm-8mm rib; MAXIS competition chokes; ventilated center rib; receiver is case colored and bears a fantasy engraving of syren Julia, Caesar's daughter, that portrait emerging from floral engraving that begins as her flowing hair; 20-ga. available in both 28- and 30-in. barrels, while the 12-ga. is available only with 30-in. tubes

MSRP **$6495.00**
Left-hand . . . . **add $270**
Adjustable stock
(right-hand only) . . . . . **add $425.00**

L4S SPORTING

Action: Semiautomatic
Stock: Walnut
Barrel: 28 in., 30 in.
Chokes: N/A
Sights: Bead
Weight: N/A
Bore/Gauge: 12
Magazine: 4 shells
Features: Syren's firearms are designed for women shooters; Monte Carlo comb; slimmed pistol grip; drop and cast dimensions that are better suited to the female form; lefthand model available

Right-hand **$2170.00**

Left-hand **$2375.00**

TEPIO TRAP UNSINGLE & OVER/UNDER COMBO

Action: Over/under
Stock: Turkish walnut
Barrel: 30 in., 32 in.
Chokes: 3 MAXIS (unsingle); 5 MAXIS (over/under)
Weight: 8 lb. 5 oz.–8 lb. 6 oz.
Bore/Gauge: 12
Magazine: 2 shells
Features: Stock designed to fit the female shooter with specialized dimensions, including length of pull, smaller grip, and increased pitch; calibrated barrel and stock weight; DTS trigger system with two trigger pull weight options, take up, over travel, and length of pull adjustments; hand-polished coin finish with Invisalloy protective finish; 30-in. barreled over/under, 32-in. barrel Unsingle, and combo with both barrel sets

MSRP **$10,755.00**
Left-hand . . . . **add $270.00**

Taylor's & Co. Firearms

TAYLOR'S & CO. 1887 T-MODEL LEVER-ACTION SHOTGUN

TAYLOR'S & CO. WYATT EARP SHOTGUN

1887 T-MODEL LEVER-ACTION SHOTGUN

Action: Lever
Stock: Synthetic
Barrel: 18.5 in.
Chokes: None
Weight: 7 lb.
Bore/Gauge: 12
Magazine: 5+1 shells
Features: Black soft touch stock, matte blued finish; Bootleg Model
MSRP **$1702.97**

WYATT EARP SHOTGUN

Action: Side-by-side
Stock: Walnut checkered pistol grip
Barrel: 20.06 in.
Chokes: N/A
Weight: 7 lb. 1 oz.
Bore/ Gauge: 12
Magazine: 2 shells
Features: Easily opened with one hand for fast shell loading; case-hardened frame stamped with 'Wyatt Earp'; chromed barrel bores with blued finish
MSRP **$1908.17**

SHOTGUNS

Thompson/Center Arms

ENCORE PRO HUNTER TURKEY
Action: Hinged-breech single-shot

THOMPSON/CENTER ENCORE PRO HUNTER TURKEY

Stock: AP camo with Flextech
Barrel: 24 in. or 26 in.
Chokes: T/C extra full
Weight: 6 lb. 4 oz.–6 lb. 12 oz.
Bore/Gauge: 12, 20
Magazine: 1 shell
Features: Fiber optic sights; 14 in. length pull
MSRP $892.00

TriStar Arms

TRISTAR ARMS BRISTOL

TRISTAR ARMS BRISTOL SILVER

TRISTAR ARMS COBRA III FIELD PUMP CAMO

TRISTAR ARMS COBRA III FORCE

TRISTAR ARMS COBRA III FIELD PUMP YOUTH

TRISTAR ARMS COBRA III MARINE

TRISTAR ARMS COBRA III TACTICAL

BRISTOL
Action: Side-by-side
Stock: Walnut
Barrel: 28 in.
Chokes: 5
Sights: Bead front
Weight: 5 lb. 1 oz.–6 lb. 11 oz.
Bore/Gauge: 12, 20, 28, .410
Capacity: 2 shells
Features: Straight English stock of select Turkish walnut; splinter forend; checkering; case-colored, single-selective trigger; ejectors; Beretta Mobil flush-fit choke tubes
12-, 20-ga.. . . . . $1160.00
28-, 16-ga., .410-bore $1190.00

BRISTOL SILVER
Action: Side-by-side
Stock: Walnut
Barrel: 28 in.
Chokes: 5
Sights: Bead front
Weight: 5 lb. 1 oz.–6 lb. 11 oz.
Bore/Gauge: 12, 20, 28, .410
Capacity: 2 shells
Features: An upgrade from the standard Bristol, with improved wood; nickel-finished receiver with scroll engraving and gold inlays
12-, 20-ga.. . . . . $1100.00
28-, 16-ga., .410-bore $1130.00

COBRA III FIELD PUMP
Action: Pump
Stock: Synthetic
Barrel: 24 in., 26 in., 28 in.
Chokes: 3 (IC, M, F)
Sights: Fiber optic front
Weight: 5 lb.–7 lb.
Bore/Gauge: 20, 12

Capacity: 5 shells
Features: 3-in. pump-action that allows you to shoot light target to heavy waterfowl loads; removable choke system uses Beretta/Benelli Mobil Threads; injection molded stock and forearm; camo available in Advantage Timber Turkey or Max-5
Black synthetic. $345.00
Realtree Max-5, Advantage
   Timber . . . . $410.00–$450.00
Walnut . . . . $395.00–$410.00

COBRA III FIELD PUMP YOUTH
Action: Pump
Stock: Walnut, synthetic
Barrel: 24 in.
Chokes: 3 (IC, M, F)
Sights: Fiber optic front
Weight: 5 lb. 6 oz.–6 lb. 8 oz.
Bore/Gauge: 20
Capacity: 5 shells
Features: Extended forearm for superior fit and feel; vent rib with matted sight plane; fiber optic sight; five-round magazine, shot plug included; Quick Shot Plug Removal; chrome-lined chamber and barrel; youth stock LOP 13 in.
Black synthetic. $345.00
Realtree Max-5 . . . .$410.00
Walnut . . . . $395.00–$410.00

COBRA III FORCE
Action: Pump
Stock: Synthetic
Barrel: 18.5 in.
Chokes: 2

Sights: Fiber optic bridge front, ghost ring rear
Weight: 6 lb. 8 oz.
Bore/Gauge: 12
Capacity: 5 shells
Features: Spring-loaded forearm; Picatinny under rail and top rail; pistol grip stock has soft rubber grip; Cylinder Beretta/Benelli Mobil choke plus a muzzle brake
MSRP $365.00

COBRA III MARINE
Action: Pump
Stock: Synthetic
Barrel: 18.5 in.
Chokes: 1
Sights: Blade front
Weight: 6 lb. 3 oz.
Bore/Gauge: 12
Capacity: 5 shells
Features: Spring-loaded forearm speeds cycling; underside forearm rail; matte stainless metalwork with black synthetic stock
MSRP $335.00

COBRA III TACTICAL
Action: Pump
Stock: Synthetic
Barrel: 18.5 in.
Chokes: 1
Sights: Blade front
Weight: 6 lb. 3 oz.
Bore/Gauge: 12
Capacity: 5 shells
Features: Similar to the Cobra III Marine, but all metalwork is in matte black
MSRP $320.00

SHOTGUNS

TriStar Arms

TRISTAR ARMS COMPACT TACTICAL

TRISTAR ARMS HUNTER MAG II

TRISTAR ARMS KRX TACTICAL

TRISTAR ARMS RAPTOR A-TAC

TRISTAR ARMS SETTER S/T

TRISTAR ARMS TRINITY

TRISTAR ARMS TRINITY LT

TRISTAR ARMS TT-15 FIELD

COMPACT TACTICAL

Action: Semiautomatic
Stock: Synthetic
Barrel: 20 in.
Chokes: One
Sights: Flip-up front, rear
Weight: 8 lb.
Bore/Gauge: 12
Capacity: 5 shells
Features: A gas-operated bullpup design for action shooting games or home defense featuring a detachable magazine; forward grip; carry handle; 30-inch overall length
MSRP $795.00

HUNTER MAG II

Action: Over/under
Stock: Synthetic
Barrel: 26 in., 28 in., 30 in.
Chokes: 5 (SK, IC, M, IM, F)
Sights: Fiber optic front
Weight: 7 lb. 5 oz.–7 lb. 14 oz.
Bore/Gauge: 12
Capacity: 2 shells
Features: 3.5-in. chamber; sealed actions to keep dirt out; self-adjusting locking lugs; top tang barrel selector and safety; steel mono-block barrel construction; injection-molded stock and forearm; Beretta/Benelli Mobil style choke tubes with choke box and choke wrench; rubber recoil pad; swivel studs; four camo options
MSRP . . . . $810.00–$825.00

KRX TACTICAL

Action: Semiautomatic
Stock: Synthetic
Barrel: 20 in.
Chokes: Extended tactical choke
Weight: 7 lb. 6.4 oz.
Bore/Gauge: 12
Magazine: 5 shells
Features: AR-platform with a 3-in. chamber; controls similar to those of an actual AR; gas-operated; full-length Picatinny rail; removable carry handle; bridge front sight; injection-molded stock and forearm; two detachable magazines
Black $565.00
Flat dark earth $595.00

RAPTOR A-TAC

Action: Semiautomatic
Stock: Synthetic
Barrel: 20 in.
Chokes: N/A
Weight: 7 lb.
Bore/Gauge: 12
Magazine: 5 shells
Features: Gas-operated; bridge-front sight with fiber optic bead; Picatinny rail mounted on of the receiver with a ghost ring sight installed; fixed pistol grip stock, swivel studs, and a tactical style operating handle; comes with an Extended Tactical Beretta/Benelli style choke; available in Kryptec Typhon and digital camo finishes
MSRP $470.00

SETTER S/T

Action: Over/under
Stock: Walnut
Barrel: 26 in., 28 in.
Chokes: 3-Beretta style tubes (IC, M, F)
Weight: 6 lb. 3 oz.–7 lb. 3 oz.
Bore/Gauge: 12, 20, 28, .410
Magazine: 2 shells
Features: Fiber optic front sight; high-gloss wood; single selective trigger; extractors; ventilated rib
12-, 20-gauge: $635.00
28-gauge, .410-bore: $665.00

TRINITY

Action: Over/under
Stock: Turkish walnut
Barrel: 26 in., 28 in.
Chokes: 5 (SK, IC, M, IM, F)
Sights: Fiber optic front
Weight: 6 lb. 5 oz.–6 lb. 14 oz.
Bore/Gauge: 20, 16, 12
Capacity: 2 shells
Features: Sealed actions to keep dirt out; self-adjusting locking lugs; top tang barrel selector and safety; steel mono-block barrel construction; Turkish walnut with semi-gloss finish; rubber recoil pad; 24k inlay on the receiver
MSRP $745.00

TRINITY LT

Action: Over/under
Stock: Turkish walnut
Barrel: 26 in., 28 in.
Chokes: 5 (SK, IC, M, IM, F)
Sights: Fiber optic front
Weight: 5 lb. 5 oz.–6 lb. 5 oz.
Bore/Gauge: .410, 28, 20, 12
Capacity: 2 shells
Features: 3-in. chamber; lightweight aluminum alloy frame with steel inserts at contact points for added strength; sealed actions to keep dirt out; self-adjusting locking lugs; top tang barrel selector and safety; steel mono-block barrel construction; Turkish Walnut with semi-gloss finish
12-, 20-gauge: $745.00
28-gauge, .410-bore: $765.00

TT-15 FIELD

Action: Over/under, top-single, top-unsingle, or combo
Stock: Turkish walnut
Barrel: 30 in., 32 in., 34 in.
Chokes: 3 or 5 extended Benelli/Beretta chokes
Weight: 7 lb. 13 oz.–8 lb. 14 oz.
Bore/Gauge: 12, 20, 28, .410
Magazine: 1 shell, 2 shells
Features: Monte Carlo stock; fully adjustable comb; elegant hand-engraved receiver with nickel finish; fitted with high-standing 3-point adjustable rib, auto-ejectors, and fiber optic front sight
12-, 20-gauge: $945.00
28-gauge, .410-bore: $975.00

TriStar Arms

TRISTAR ARMS VIPER G2 LH

TRISTAR ARMS VIPER G2 BRONZE, G2 SILVER

TRISTAR ARMS VIPER G2 SPORTING

TRISTAR ARMS VIPER G2 YOUTH

TRISTAR ARMS VIPER MAX

VIPER G2 BRONZE
Action: Semiautomatic
Stock: Turkish walnut
Barrel: 26, 28 in.
Chokes: Three Beretta-style chokes
Sights: Fiber optic front sight
Weight: 5 lb. 3 oz.–6 lb. 13 oz.
Bore/Gauge: 12, 20, 28, .410
Magazine: 5 shells
Features: High-grade Turkish walnut stock and Cerakote Bronze receiver; tight checkering; shim kits; vent rib with a matte sighting plane; 20-ga. has a 26-in. barrel and chambers 2.75-in; other models have 28-in. barrels and 3-in. chambers.
12-, 20-gauge: **$860.00**
16-gauge, 28-gauge,
.410-bore:. **$915.00**

VIPER G2 LH
Action: Semiautomatic
Stock: Synthetic
Barrel: 28 in.
Chokes: IC, M, F
Weight: 6 lb. 14.4 oz.
Bore/ Gauge: 12
Magazine: N/A
Features: Chrome-lined chambers; barrels threaded for Beretta/Benelli style choke tubes; 3 in. chambers
Black synthetic: **$655.00**
Realtree Max-5: **$745.00**

VIPER G2 SILVER
Action: Semiautomatic
Stock: Turkish walnut
Barrel: 26 in., 28 in.

Chokes: 3 (IC, M, F)
Sights: Fiber optic
Weight: 5 lb. 3 oz.–6 lb. 3 oz.
Bore/Gauge: .410, 28, 20, 12
Capacity: 5 shells
Features: A gas-operated semiauto vent rib that has a matte sight plane; stock shim kit; chrome-lined chamber and barrel; Quick Shot Plug removal; receiver in bronze or silver Cerakote
12-, 20-ga.. . . . . **$740.00**
28-ga., .410-bore **$785.00**

VIPER G2 SPORTING
Action: Semiautomatic
Stock: Synthetic, walnut
Barrel: 30 in.
Chokes: 4 (SK, IC, M, F)
Sights: Middle bead, fiber optic
Weight: 7 lb. 3 oz.–7 lb. 6 oz.
Bore/Gauge: 12
Capacity: 5 shells
Features: Gas-operated semiauto; tubular magazine; manual E-Z Load magazine cutoff; wood stock has "TriStar Select" Turkish walnut stock and forearm with cut checkering and semi-gloss finish; synthetic stock comes with blue or red accents; adjustable comb; raised target rib
Synthetic **$700.00**
Walnut **$900.00**

VIPER G2 YOUTH
Action: Semiautomatic, gas-operated
Stock: Synthetic
Barrel: 26 in.
Chokes: SK, IC, M, F

Weight: 5 lb. 11 oz.–6 lb. 3 oz.
Bore/Gauge: 12, 20
Magazine: 5 shells
Features: Manual E-Z Load magazine cut-off; raised target rib w/ matted sight plane; middle bead and fiber pptic sight; quick shot plug removal; chrome-lined chamber and barrel; adjustable comb; available in wood stock, black synthetic, Advantage Timber, black synthetic two-stock combo, and a black synthetic stock Sport model with red or blue metallic finish on receiver and magazine cap
MSRP. . . . . **$625.00–$755/00**

VIPER MAX
Action: Semiautomatic
Stock: Synthetic
Barrel: 28 in., 30 in.
Chokes: Beretta Mobil (SK, IC, M, F)
Weight: 7 lb. 6.4 oz.
Bore/Gauge: 12
Magazine: 4 shells
Features: Gas-operated; 3 ó -in. chamber; heavy and light load pistons; extra piston can be stored in the forearm for instant in-the-field change-out; fiber optic front sight; sling swivel studs; magazine cut-off; Quick Shot plug removal; chrome-lined barrel and chamber; black synthetic stock with black metalwork, Mossy Oak Max-5 full-coverage camo, or Mossy Oak Shadow Grass Blades stock with bronze metalwork
Black:. **$715.00**
Realtree Max-5: **$810.00**
Bronze Cerakote/MO
Shadow Grass Blades:. . . . **$825.00**

Weatherby

WEATHERBY 18I DELUXE

18I DELUXE
Action: Semiautomatic
Stock: Walnut
Barrel: 26 in., 28 in.

Chokes: 5 (IC, IM, M, I, F)
Sights: LPA fiber optic
Weight: 6 lb.–7 lb.
Bore/Gauge: 20, 12
Capacity: 4 shells

Features: An inertia-operated shotgun with a matte-finished walnut stock; 3-in. chamber; four-round magazine tube; custom Lasertech engraving on the single-piece billet aluminum receiver in a matte silver; vent rib; includes choke tube wrench
MSRP. **$1899.00**

Weatherby

WEATHERBY 18I SYNTHETIC

WEATHERBY ELEMENT SYNTHETIC

WEATHERBY ELEMENT TUNGSTEN SYNTHETIC

WEATHERBY ELEMENT UPLAND

WEATHERBY ELEMENT WATERFOWLER MAX-5

WEATHERBY ORION I

WEATHERBY ORION SPORTING

WEATHERBY SA-08 SYNTHETIC, SYNTHETIC COMPACT

18I SYNTHETIC

Action: Semiautomatic
Stock: Synthetic
Barrel: 28 in.
Chokes: 5 (IC, IM, M, I, F)
Sights: LPA fiber optic
Weight: 7 lb.
Bore/Gauge: 12
Capacity: 4 shells
Features: An inertia-operated semiautomatic for turkeys or big geese with a 3.5-in. chamber; elastomer stock for reduced recoil despite the firearm's relatively light weight; matte finish all over
MSRP $1149.00

ELEMENT SYNTHETIC

Action: Semiautomatic
Stock: Synthetic
Barrel: 26 in., 28 in.
Chokes: 4 application specific chokes (IC, Mod, Full, Long Range Steel)
Weight: 6 lb. 4 oz.–6 lb. 12 oz.
Bore/Gauge: 12, 20
Magazine: 4+1 shells
Features: Griptonite stock features pistol grip and forend inserts gray/black design color; matte, bead blasted finish
MSRP $649.00

ELEMENT TUNGSTEN SYNTHETIC

Action: Semiautomatic
Stock: Synthetic
Barrel: 26 in., 28 in.
Chokes: 3, 4
Sights: Fiber optic front
Weight: 6 lb. 4 oz.–6 lb. 12 oz.
Bore/Gauge: 12, 20
Capacity: 4 shells
Features: Black synthetic stock; all metalwork in tungsten Cerakote; inertia action; chrome-lined bore; Griptonite stock has textured grip

inserts; 3-in. chamber; F, M, and I chokes; 12-ga. also comes with a Long Range Steel choke; stock shims
MSRP $699.00

ELEMENT UPLAND

Action: Semiautomatic
Stock: Walnut
Barrel: 26 in., 28 in.
Chokes: Three (F, M, IM)
Sights: Fiber optic front
Weight: 6 lb. 9 oz.–6 lb. 12 oz.
Bore/Gauge: 12, 20
Capacity: 5 shells
Features: Inertia-operated semiauto made for the grouse woods and pheasant fields, featuring a chrome-line vent rib barrel; both gauges chamber 3-inch shells
MSRP $799.00

ELEMENT WATERFOWLER MAX-5

Action: Semiautomatic
Stock: Synthetic
Barrel: 26 in., 28 in.
Chokes: 3, 4
Sights: Fiber optic front
Weight: 6 lb. 4 oz.–6 lb. 12 oz.
Bore/Gauge: 12, 20
Capacity: 4 shells
Features: Full-coverage Realtree Max-5 camo; dual-purpose bolt release; inertia action; chrome-lined bore; Griptonite stock has textured grip inserts; 3-in. chamber; F, M, and I chokes; 12-ga. also comes with a Long Range Steel choke; stock shims
MSRP $799.00

ORION I

Action: Over/under
Stock: Walnut
Barrel: 30 in.
Chokes: IC, M, F
Weight: 7 lb.

Bore/Gauge: 12
Magazine: 2 shells
Features: Brass front sights; ambidextrous top tang safety; automatic ejectors; low profile receiver; chrome-lined bores; matte ventilated top rib with brass bead; traditional boxlock action; integral multi choke system
MSRP $1049.00

ORION SPORTING

Action: Over/under
Stock: Walnut
Barrel: 30 in.
Chokes: Five (F, M, IM, IC, S)
Sights: Fiber optic front
Weight: 7 lb. 8 oz.
Bore/Gauge: 12
Capacity: 2 shells
Features: A dedicated sporting clays gun featuring an "A"-grade stock with diamond point checkering and adjustable comb; tapered vent rib; ported barrels; automatic ejectors; chrome-lined bores; 3-inch chamber; knurled extended chokes
MSRP $1149.00

SA-08 SYNTHETIC COMPACT

Action: Semiautomatic
Stock: Synthetic
Barrel: 24 in.
Chokes: 3 (F, M, IC)
Sights: Brass bead
Weight: 5 lb. 12 oz.
Bore/Gauge: 20
Capacity: 5 shells
Features: An economical do-everything shotgun with a 3-in. chamber; low-profile vent rib; swivel studs front and rear; aircraft-grade alloy receiver; chrome-lined bore
MSRP $679.00

Wilkinson Tactical

WILKINSON TATICAL CR12

CR12

Action: Semiautomatic
Stock: Synthetic
Barrel: 18 in.
Chokes: N/A
Sights: None
Weight: N/A

Bore/Gauge: 12
Capacity: 5, 10, 12 shells
Features: MAWS stands for Modular Advanced Weapons System; .308 AR lower pairs with an upper chambered for 12-ga.; upper can be exchanged for one in .308/7.62X39 NATO or the 6mm and 6.5 Creedmoors in seconds; direct impingement gas operation; smooth barrel threaded for Winchester chokes; FAILZERO EXO nickel boron-plated bolt carrier group; M4-type adjustable stock; black anodized finish; standard buffer on Basic model; Performance model gets Kynshot hydraulic buffer, Carlson breaching muzzle device, PDQ boly catch, and custom color upgrade
MSRP **$1995.00**

Winchester Repeating Arms

WINCHESTER REPEATING ARMS MODEL 101 FIELD

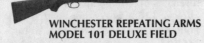

WINCHESTER REPEATING ARMS MODEL 101 DELUXE FIELD

WINCHESTER REPEATING ARMS SX4 COMPACT

WINCHESTER REPEATING ARMS SX4 HYBRID

WINCHESTER REPEATING ARMS SX4 HYBRID HUNTER

WINCHESTER REPEATING ARMS SX4 NWTF CANTILEVER TURKEY HUNTER

MODEL 101

Action: Over/under
Stock: Walnut
Barrel: 26 in., 28 in., 30 in., 32 in.
Chokes: Invector-Plus choke system, 3 tubes
Weight: 6 lb. 12 oz.–7 lb. 6 oz.
Bore/Gauge: 12
Magazine: 2 shells
Features: Solid brass bead front sight on Field; Truglo front sight on Sporting; deep relief receiver engraving; high-gloss grade II/III walnut stock; vented Pachmayr Decelerator pad with classic white line spacer
Field **$2039.99**
Sporting **$2549.99**

MODEL 101 DELUXE FIELD

Action: Over/under
Stock: Walnut
Barrel: 26 in., 28 in.
Chokes: Invector-Plus (F, M, IC)
Weight: 6 lb. 12 oz.
Bore/Gauge: 12
Magazine: 2 shells
Features: Grade III European walnut stock; detailed engraving on steel receiver; back-bored, hard-chromed barrels; front bead; 3-in. chambers
MSRP **$2149.99**

SX4 COMPACT

Action: Semiautomatic
Stock: Composite

Barrel: 24 in., 26 in., 28 in.
Chokes: Three (F, M, IC)
Sights: Fiber optic front
Weight: 6 lb. 8 oz.–6 lb. 12 oz.
Bore/Gauge: 12, 20
Capacity: 5 shells
Features: For youth or shorter-statured shooters with a 13-inch length of pull; all over matte black finish; aluminum alloy receiver; flush Invector-Plus chokes; 3-inch chamber
MSRP . . . . **$849.99–$999.99**

SX4 HYBRID

Action: Semiautomatic
Stock: Composite
Barrel: 26 in., 28 in.
Chokes: 3 (F, M, IC)
Sights: Fiber optic
Weight: 6 lb. 10 oz.–7 lb. 2 oz.
Bore/Gauge: 20, 12
Capacity: 4 shells
Features: An upgraded SX4 Hunter with a barrel and alloy receiver in gray Cerakote finish; Active Valve operating system; enlarged trigger guard for gloved hand use; Invector Plus choke tubes; Inflex Technology recoil pad; TruGlo fiber optic sight; vent rib; enlarged bolt handle; black synthetic stock with length of pull spacers
MSRP . . . . **$919.99–$1069.99**

SX4 HYBRID HUNTER

Action: Semiautomatic
Stock: Composite

Barrel: 26 in., 28 in.
Chokes: 3 (F, M, IC)
Sights: Fiber optic
Weight: 6 lb. 10 oz.–7 lb. 2 oz.
Bore/Gauge: 20, 12
Capacity: 4 shells
Features: An upgraded SX4 Hunter with a barrel and alloy receiver in FDE Cerakote finish; Active Valve operating system; enlarged trigger guard for gloved hand use; Invector Plus choke tubes; Inflex Technology recoil pad; TruGlo fiber optic sight; vent rib; six camo stock options
MSRP . . . . **$849.99–$1119.99**

SX4 NWTF CANTILEVER TURKEY HUNTER

Action: Semiautomatic
Stock: Composite
Barrel: 24 in.
Chokes: One Invector-Plus Extended
Sights: TruGlo fiber optic front, adjustable rear
Weight: 7 lb. 8 oz.
Bore/Gauge: 12
Magazine: 4 shells
Features: Created with input from the National Wild Turkey Federation; 3.5-in. chamber; back-bored barrels; reengineered stock with gripping surfaces; Quadra-Vent ports; cantilever optics mount; drop-out trigger group; stock spacers and one Extra-Full turkey choke are included; full-coverage Mossy Oak Obsession
MSRP **$1149.99**

Winchester Repeating Arms

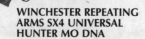

WINCHESTER REPEATING ARMS SX4 UNIVERSAL HUNTER MO DNA

WINCHESTER REPEATING ARMS SX4 WATERFOWL HUNTER COMPACT

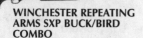

WINCHESTER REPEATING ARMS SXP BUCK/BIRD COMBO

WINCHESTER REPEATING ARMS SX4 UPLAND FIELD

WINCHESTER REPEATING ARMS SXP BLACK SHADOW

WINCHESTER REPEATING ARMS SXP DARK EARTH DEFENDER

WINCHESTER REPEATING ARMS SX4 WATERFOWL HUNTER

WINCHESTER REPEATING ARMS SXP BLACK SHADOW DEER 20-GAUGE

SX4 UNIVERSAL HUNTER MO DNA

Action: Semiautomatic
Stock: Synthetic
Barrel: 24 in., 26 in., 28 in.
Chokes: 3
Sights: Fiber optic front
Weight: 6 lb. 8 oz.–7 lb.
Bore/Gauge: 12, 20
Capacity: 4 shells
Features: Drop-out trigger group; Quadra-Vent ported and back-bored barrel; stock with new ergonomics, spacers, and dressed in MO DNA pattern; drilled and tapped receiver; ambidextrous safety; oversized bolt handle and release; Inflex recoil pad; Invector Plush flush choke tubes
MSRP $1149.99

SX4 UPLAND FIELD

Action: Semiautomatic
Stock: Walnut
Barrel: 26 in., 28 in.
Chokes: Three (F, M, IC)
Sights: Fiber optic front
Weight: 6 lb. 10 oz.
Bore/Gauge: 12, 20
Capacity: 5 shells
Features: Grade II/III walnut stock with a satin finish, 20 lines per inch checkering; aluminum alloy receiver with a matte nickel finish and engraved game bird scenes; length of pull spacers; 3-inch chamber; flush Invector-Plus chokes
MSRP . . . . $1189.99–$1329.99

SX4 WATERFOWL HUNTER

Action: Semiautomatic
Stock: Synthetic
Barrel: 26 in., 28 in.
Chokes: Invector-Plus (F, M, IC)
Weight: 6 lb. 10 oz.–7 lb. 2 oz.
Bore/Gauge: 12, 20
Magazine: 4 shells
Features: Improved stock ergonomics with smaller pistol grip and textured

gripping surfaces; back-bored barrels; vent rib; Active Valve gas system; Quadra-Vent ports; drop-out trigger group; oversized bolt handle; stock spacers; ambidextrous crossbolt safety; True Timber Prairie, Mossy Oak Shadowgrass Habitat, Reeltree Timber, Mossy Oak Shadowgrass Blades, Mossy Oak Bottomlands, and Realtree Max-5 camo finishes; 3- and 3 ½-inch chambers in 12-gauge; 3-inch chamber 20-gauge
MSRP . . . . $999.99–$1149.99

SX4 WATERFOWL HUNTER COMPACT

Action: Semiautomatic
Stock: Composite
Barrel: 24 in., 26 in., 28 in.
Chokes: Three (F, M, IC)
Sights: Fiber optic front
Weight: 6 lb. 8 oz.–6 lb. 12 oz.
Bore/Gauge: 12, 20
Capacity: 5 shells
Features: For youth or shorter-statured hunters with a 13-inch length of pull; full-coverage Mossy Oak Shadow Grass Habitat camo; Inflex-1 recoil pad with hard heel; flush Invector-Plus chokes; vent rib; 3-inch chamber
MSRP . . . . $999.99–$1149.99

SXP BLACK SHADOW

Action: Pump
Stock: Synthetic
Barrel: 26 in., 28 in.
Chokes: Invector Plus
Weight: 6 lb. 12 oz.–7 lb.
Bore/Gauge: 12, 20
Magazine: 4 shells
Features: Hard chrome chamber and bores; drop-out trigger group for easy cleaning; synthetic stock with non-glare black matte finish on barrel and receiver
MSRP . . . . $389.99–$409.99

SXP BLACK SHADOW DEER

Action: Pump
Stock: Synthetic
Barrel: 22 in.
Chokes: None
Weight: 6 lb. 10 oz.
Bore/Gauge: 12, 20
Magazine: 4 shells
Features: Rotary-bolt pump; fully rifled barrel; alloy receiver; TruGlo fiber optic front sight; adjustable rear sight; three-shot Speed Plug adaptor; drop-out trigger; ambidextrous crossbolt safety; drilled and tapped for scope mounts
MSRP . . . . $529.99–$559.99

SXP BUCK/BIRD COMBO

Action: Pump
Stock: Composite
Barrel: 26 in., 28 in.
Chokes: 3 (F, M, IC)
Sights: Fiber optic, brass bead
Weight: 6 lb. 12 oz.–6 lb. 14 oz.
Bore/Gauge: 20, 12
Capacity: 4 shells
Features: A two-for-one pump with a vent rib barrel at 26 or 28 inches, as well as a shorter rifled deer barrel; Invector-Plus flush chokes; Inflex recoil pad; deer barrel has TruGlo fiber optic, field barrel has brass bead
20-ga.: $679.00
12-ga.: $649.99

SXP DARK EARTH DEFENDER

Action: Pump
Stock: Synthetic
Barrel: 18 in.
Chokes: Fixed cylinder
Weight: 6 lb. 4 oz.
Bore/Gauge: 12, 20
Magazine: 5 shells
Features: Aluminum alloy receiver; 3-in. chamber; front brass bead with removable TruGlo fiber optic sight; finished in Dark Earth
MSRP . . . . $389.99–$409.99

Winchester Repeating Arms

WINCHESTER REPEATING ARMS SXP DEFENDER

WINCHESTER REPEATING ARMS SXP FIELD COMPACT

WINCHESTER REPEATING ARMS SXP NWTF TURKEY HUNTER

WINCHESTER REPEATING ARMS SXP EXTREME DEER HUNTER

WINCHESTER REPEATING ARMS SXP HYBRID HUNTER

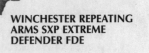

WINCHESTER REPEATING ARMS SXP EXTREME DEFENDER FDE

WINCHESTER REPEATING ARMS SXP LONG BEARD

SXP DEFENDER
Action: Pump
Stock: Composite
Barrel: 18 in.
Chokes: Fixed cylinder choked barrel
Weight: 6 lb.–6 lb. 5 oz.
Bore/Gauge: 12, 20
Magazine: 5+1 shells
Features: Uses Foster-type slugs; non-glare metal surfaces with a tough black composite stock; deeply grooved forearm for control and stability
MSRP . . . . $359.99–$389.99

SXP EXTREME DEER
Action: Pump
Stock: Synthetic
Barrel: 22 in.
Chokes: None
Weight: 7 lb.
Bore/Gauge: 12
Magazine: 4 shells
Features: Rotary-bolt pump with fully rifled barrel; alloy receiver; TruGlo fiber optic front sight; adjustable rear sight; three-shot Speed Plug adaptor; drop-out trigger; ambidextrous crossbolt safety; drilled and tapped for scope mounts; 3-in. chamber; synthetic pistol grip stock has textured grip surfaces, two interchangeable cheek pieces, and two length-of-pull spacers
MSRP $569.99

SXP EXTREME DEFENDER FDE
Action: Pump
Stock: Composite
Barrel: 18 in.
Chokes: 2
Sights: Steel blade front
Weight: 7 lb.
Bore/Gauge: 12
Capacity: 5 shells

Features: Nice choice for 3-Gun games or law enforcement with a stock that has two interchangeable comb pieces and two length of pull spacers; 3-in.chamber; aluminum alloy receiver with a topside Picatinny rail; finger-groove pistol grip; flat dark earth finish on barrel and most of stock; supplied with a flush Invector-Plus Cylinder choice and a door-breeching choke
MSRP $549.99

SXP FIELD COMPACT
Action: Pump
Stock: Satin finish
Barrel: 24 in., 26 in., 28 in.
Chokes: Three Invector-Plus chokes
Weight: 6 lb. 4 oz.–6 lb. 10 oz.
Bore/ Gauge: 12, 20
Magazine: None
Features: Aluminum alloy receiver; matte black finish; hard chrome chamber and bore; Speed plug system; brass bead front sight; Inflex technology recoil pad
MSRP . . . . $409.99–$439.99

SXP HYBRID HUNTER
Action: Pump
Stock: Composite
Barrel: 26 in., 28 in.
Chokes: 3 (F, M, IC)
Sights: Fiber optic
Weight: 6 lb. 8 oz.–7 lb.
Bore/Gauge: 20, 12
Capacity: 4 shells
Features: Barrel and receiver in FDE Perma-Cote; back-bored chrome-plated barrel; alloy receiver; Invector Plus choke tubes; Inflex Technology recoil pad; TruGlo fiber optic sight; vent rib; sling swivel studs; six dipped camo stock options

20-ga.: $449.99
3-inch 12-ga.: $429.99
3.5-inch 12-ga.: $449.99

SXP LONG BEARD
Action: Pump
Stock: Composite
Barrel: 24 in.
Chokes: Invector-Plus flush, extra full
Weight: 6 lb. 14 oz.–7 lb.
Bore/Gauge: 12, 20
Magazine: 4 shells
Features: TRUGLO fiber optic sights; two user-interchangeable combs and height adjust spacers; hard chromeplated chamber and bore; easily operated crossbolt safety; inflex technology recoil pad; in full-coverage Mossy Oak Obsession or Mossy Oak Break-Up Country; 12-gauge available in both 3- and 3½-inch chamber versions; 20-gauge chambers 3-inch shells
MSRP . . . . $549.99–$589.99

SXP NWTF TURKEY HUNTER
Action: Pump
Stock: Synthetic
Barrel: 24 in.
Chokes: Invector Plus
Weight: 6 lb. 4 oz.–6 lb. 10 oz.
Bore/Gauge: 12, 20
Magazine: 4 shells
Features: Hard chrome chamber and bores; drop-out trigger group for easy cleaning; Invector Plus Extra-Full Turkey Choke Tube; crossbolt safety; Inflex technology recoil pad; synthetic stock with textured gripping surfaces in Mossy Oak Break-Up Country or Mossy Oak Obsession; 12-gauge with 3 ½-inch chamber, 20-gauge with 3-inch chamber
MSRP $529.99

Winchester Repeating Arms

WINCHESTER REPEATING ARMS SXP SHADOW DEFENDER

WINCHESTER REPEATING ARMS SXP SHADOW MARINE DEFENDER

WINCHESTER REPEATING ARMS REPEATING ARMS SXP TURKEY

WINCHESTER REPEATING ARMS SXP UPLAND FIELD

WINCHESTER REPEATING ARMS SXP WATERFOWL HUNTER

WINCHESTER REPEATING ARMS SXP YOUTH FIELD

SXP SHADOW DEFENDER

Action: Pump
Stock: Synthetic
Barrel: 18 in.
Chokes: One Invector-Plus flush
Sights: TruGlo fiber optic
Weight: 7 lb. 8 oz.
Bore/Gauge: 12, 20
Magazine: 5 shells
Features: Pistol grip stock with textured gripping surfaces; two interchangeable comb modules; two length-of-pull spacers; ribbed forend; TruGlo fiber optic front sight; accessory rail; 3-in. chamber; one Cylinder choke tube
MSRP . . . . $449.99–$479.99

SXP SHADOW MARINE DEFENDER

Action: Pump
Stock: Synthetic
Barrel: 18 in.
Chokes: Invector-Plus (C)
Weight: 7 lb. 8 oz.
Bore/Gauge: 12, 20
Magazine: 5 shells
Features: Hard chrome plating on most exterior metal surfaces and bore; alloy receiver is drilled and tapped for scope mounts; 3-in. chamber; synthetic pistol grip stock has textured grip surfaces; two interchangeable cheek pieces; two length-of-pull spacers
MSRP . . . . $499.99–$519.99

SXP TURKEY

Action: Pump
Stock: Synthetic
Barrel: 24 in.
Chokes: Invector-Plus Extra Full Turkey
Weight: 6 lb. 4 oz. (20-ga.), 6 lb. 10 oz. (12-ga.)
Bore/Gauge: 12, 20
Magazine: 4 shells
Features: Hard chrome plated chamber and bore; back-bore technology; TruGlo fiber optic adjustable sights; 12-ga. has 3½-in. chamber; 20-ga. has 3-in. chamber
MSRP $449.99

SXP UPLAND FIELD

Action: Pump
Stock: Turkish walnut
Barrel: 26 in., 28 in.
Chokes: 3 (F, M, IC)
Sights: Fiber optic
Weight: 6 lb. 12 oz.–7 lb. 2 oz.
Bore/Gauge: 20, 12
Capacity: 4 shells
Features: A very pretty pump with Grade II/III Turkish walnut stock; matte nickel receiver with game bird engravings on both sides; chrome-lined barrel in a matte finish; flush Invector-Plus chokes; Infex 1 recoil pad; 3-in chamber in both gauges
20-ga.: $529.99
12-ga.: $509.99

SXP WATERFOWL HUNTER

Action: Pump
Stock: Synthetic
Barrel: 26 in., 28 in.
Chokes: Invector Plus
Weight: 6 lb. 8 oz.–7 lb.
Bore/Gauge: 12, 20
Magazine: 4 shells
Features: Hard chrome chamber and bores; drop-out trigger group; synthetic stock with textured gripping surfaces; in full-coverage True Timber Prairie, Mossy Oak Shadow Grass Habitat, Mossy Oak Shadow Grass Blades, Mossy Oak Bottomlands, Realtree Max-5, Realtree Timber
MSRP . . . . $469.99–$499.99

SXP YOUTH FIELD

Action: Semiautomatic
Stock: Walnut
Barrel: 18 in., 20 in., 22 in., 24 in.
Chokes: Three (F, M, IC)
Sights: Brass bead front
Weight: 5 lb. 14 oz.–6 lb. 6 oz.
Bore/Gauge: 12, 20
Capacity: 5 shells
Features: A youth field shotgun in either 12- or 20-gauge, both with 3-inch chambers; flush Invector-Plus chokes; Grade I walnut stock with satin finish, laser-cut 18 lines per inch checkering; 12-inch length of pull
MSRP . . . . $409.99–$439.99

Accu-Tek

ACCU-TEK AT-380 II

ACCU-TEK HC-380

ACCU-TEK LT-380

AT-380 II

Action: Semiautomatic
Grips: Composite
Barrel: 2.8 in.
Sights: Target
Weight: 23.5 oz.
Caliber: .380 ACP
Capacity: 6+1 rounds
Features: Stainless steel construction; adjustable rear sight; one hand manual safety blocks; stainless steel magazine
MSRP $329.00

HC-380

Action: Semiautomatic
Grips: Composite
Barrel: 2.8 in.
Sights: Target
Weight: 26 oz.
Caliber: .380 ACP
Capacity: 13 rounds
Features: Adjustable rear sight; black checkered grip; one-hand manual safety block; includes two magazines and cable lock
MSRP $330.00

LT-380

Action: SA semiautomatic
Grips: Composite
Barrel: 2.8 in.
Sights: Adjustable rear sight
Weight: 15 oz.
Caliber: .380 ACP
Capacity: 6 rounds
Features: Aluminum frame; stainless steel slide; exposed hammer; manual safety; European type magazine release
MSRP $324.00

Altor Corp.

ALTOR CORP. SINGLE-SHOT

ALTOR SINGLE-SHOT

Action: Single-shot
Grips: Nylon
Barrel: 3 in.
Sights: Low-profile
Weight: 10 .5 oz.
Caliber: .380 ACP, 9mm
Capacity: 1 round

Features: There are just six parts—SIX!—to this detachable barrel, breech-loading single-shot pistol; all metal parts are stainless steel
.380 ACP $109.00
9mm $119.00

American Derringer

AMERICAN DERRINGER LM4 SIMMERLING

AMERICAN DERRINGER LM5

AMERICAN DERRINGER MODEL 1

LM4 SIMMERLING

Action: Hinged breech
Grips: Mesquite, Rosewood, custom
Barrel: 2 in.
Sights: Open, fixed
Weight: 24 oz.
Caliber: .45 ACP
Capacity: 5 rounds
Features: Vest pocket pistol; first round carried in the chamber; only 1in. thick; stainless steel
MSRP . . . . . . **Contact manufacturer**

LM5

Action: Hinged breech
Grips: Rosewood
Barrel: 2 in.
Sights: Open, fixed
Weight: 15 oz.
Caliber: .25 ACP
Capacity: 5
Features: Stainless steel; cam lock safety
MSRP . . . . . . **Contact manufacturer**

MODEL 1

Action: Hinged breech
Grips: Rosewood or stag
Barrel: 3 in.
Sights: Fixed, open
Weight: 15 oz.
Caliber: .45 Colt, .410, .45-70, .45 ACP, .45 Win. Mag., .44-40 Win., .44 Mag., .44 Spl., .41 Mag., .40 S&W, .380 ACP, .38 Spl., .38 Super, .357 Mag., .32-20, .32 Mag. S&W Long, .30-30 Win., .30 Carbine, .22 LR, .22 WMR, 10mm, 9mm, .223
Capacity: 2 rounds
Features: Single-action; automatic barrel selection; manually operated hammer-block safety
MSRP . . . . . . **Contact manufacturer**

American Derringer

AMERICAN DERRINGER MODEL 4

AMERICAN DERRINGER MODEL 6

AMERICAN DERRINGER MODEL 7

AMERICAN DERRINGER MODEL 8

MODEL 4
Action: Hinged breech
Grips: Rosewood
Barrel: 4.1 in
Sights: Fixed open
Weight: 16.5 oz.
Caliber: .375 Mag., 357 Max., .45-70 Govt.,
.45 Colt/.410, .44 Mag.
Capacity: 2 rounds
Features: Satin or high polish stainless steel finish; single-action; automatic barrel selection; manually operated hammer-block type safety
MSRP . . . . . . Contact manufacturer

MODEL 6
Action: Hinged breech
Grips: Rosewood, walnut, black
Barrel: 6 in.
Sights: Fixed open
Weight: 21 oz.
Caliber: .22 WMR, .357 Mag., .45 ACP, .45 Colt/.410
Capacity: 2 rounds
Features: Satin or high polish stainless steel finish; single-action; automatic barrel selection; manually operated hammer-block type safety
MSRP . . . . . . Contact manufacturer

MODEL 7 LIGHTWEIGHT & ULTRA LIGHTWEIGHT
Action: Hinged breech
Grips: Blackwood
Barrel: 3 in.
Sights: Fixed open
Weight: 7.5 oz.
Caliber: .44 Spl., .380 ACP, .38 Spl., .32 Mag./.32 S&W Long, .22 LR, .22 Mag.

Capacity: 2 rounds
Features: Grey matte finish; single-action; automatic barrel selection; manually operated hammer-block type safety
MSRP . . . . . . Contact manufacturer

MODEL 8
Action: Hinged breech
Grips: Rosewood, walnut, black
Barrel: 6 in.
Sights: Optional Adco red dot scope
Weight: 24 oz.
Caliber: .45 Colt/.410
Capacity: 2 rounds
Features: Satin or high polish stainless steel finish; single-action; automatic barrel selection; manually operated hammer-block type safety
MSRP . . . . . . Contact manufacturer

American Tactical Imports

AMERICAN TACTICAL IMPORTS FIREPOWER XTREME 45ACP G1 1911 (FX SERIES)

AMERICAN TACTICAL IMPORTS FX FIREPOWER XTREME 45ACP MILITARY 1911 (FX SERIES)

FIREPOWER XTREME 45ACP G1 1911 (FX SERIES)
Action: Semiautomatic
Grips: Mahogany
Barrel: 4.25 in.
Sights: Fixed
Weight: 33.5 oz.
Caliber: .45 ACP
Capacity: 7+1 rounds
Features: Steel parts; black matte military-style fixed front and rear sights; military-style slide stop and thumb safety, solid mahogany grip panels
MSRP $479.95

FIREPOWER XTREME 45ACP MILITARY 1911 (FX SERIES)
Action: Semiautomatic
Grips: Mahogany
Barrel: 5 in.
Sights: Fixed
Weight: 37 oz.
Caliber: .45 ACP
Capacity: 7+1 rounds
Features: Steel parts; black matte military-style fixed front and rear sights; military-style slide stop and thumb safety, solid mahogany grip panels
MSRP $479.95

American Tactical Imports

AMERICAN TACTICAL IMPORTS FIREPOWER XTREME HYBRID 45ACP FXH-45 1911

FIREPOWER XTREME HYBRID 45ACP FXH-45 1911 (FX SERIES)

Action: SA semiautomatic
Grips: Polymer
Barrel: 5 in.
Sights: Fixed
Weight: 27.5 oz.
Caliber: .45 ACP
Capacity: 8 rounds
Features: Polymer frame with 2 metal inserts for added stability and durability; steel match grade barrel and a custom designed steel slide; ergonomic frame with built-in finger grooves; accepts Glock front and rear sights, including aftermarket night sights
MSRP $599.95

Anderson Manufacturing

AM-15 EXT 5.56 7.5-INCH PISTOL

Action: Semiautomatic
Grips: Synthetic
Barrel: 7.5 in. extended barrel
Sights: None
Weight: 4 lb. 14 oz.
Caliber: 5.56 NATO, .300 BLK
Capacity: Detachable box, 30 rounds
Features: Picatinny rail; Anderson Knight Stalker flash hider; Magpul grip; available treated with proprietary no lube RF85 treatment
MSRP $599.99

ANDERSON MANUFACTURING AM-15 EXT 5.56 7.5-INCH PISTOL

Angstadt Arms

ANGSTADT ARMS MDP-9

ANGSTADT ARMS UDP-9 WITH MAXIM CQB BRACE

ANGSTADT ARMS UDP-9 WITH SBA3 BRACE

MDP-9

Action: Semiautomatic
Grips: Synthetic
Barrel: 5.3 in.
Sights: None
Weight: 57.6 oz.
Caliber: 9mm
Capacity: 10, 15, 17 rounds
Features: Patent-pending roller-delayed action that the maker says "significantly reduces" both recoil and the overall weight of the gun; 15 inches long; rear 1913 rail with SB tactical braces in choice of telescoping or side-folding options; non-reciprocating left- or right-side charging handle; extended mag release; last round bolt hold-open
MSRP $2599.00

UDP-9 WITH MAXIM CQB BRACE

Action: Semiautomatic
Grips: Synthetic
Barrel: 4.5 in.
Sights: None
Weight: 5 lb.
Caliber: 9mm
Capacity: 10, 15, 17, 30 rounds
Features: Takes all Glock aftermarket mags; threaded barrel ½x28; billet aluminum lower and slick-side upper in black hardcoat anodized ; assembly uses standard AR-15 hammer; Maxim Defense CQB pistol stabilizing brace with PCC pistol buffer; Magpul K2 pistol grip; Angstadt Arms 4-in. free-floating M-LOK handguard; topside mil-spec Picatinny rail
MSRP $1849.00

ARMS UDP-9 WITH SBA3 BRACE

Action: Semiautomatic
Grips: Synthetic
Barrel: 6, 10.5 in.
Sights: None
Weight: < 5 lb.
Caliber: 9mm
Capacity: 10, 15, 17, 30 rounds
Features: Oversized trigger guard; flared magwell; SBTactical SBA3 five-position adjustable stabilizing brace; Magpul K2 or B5 Systems pistol grip; bolt assembly uses standard AR-15 hammer; billet aluminum lower and slick-side upper in hard-coat anodized matte black or Cerakote Tactical Grey or flat dark earth; barrel threaded ½x28; mil-spec topside Picatinny rail; Angstadt Arms 5.5-in. free-floating M-LOK handguard with seven-side design
Black 6-in. $1499.00
Black 10.5-in. $1699.00
Cerakote 6-in. $1599.00

AREX defense (Fime Group)

AREX ALPHA

AREX DELTA GEN2

AREX (FIME GROUP) REX ZERO 1CP

AREX (FIME GROUP) REX ZERO 1S

AREX (FIME GROUP) REX ZERO 1 TACTICAL

ALPHA
Action: Semiautomatic
Grips: Polymer
Barrel: 5 in.
Sights: Fiber optic front, adjustable rear
Weight: 39 oz.
Caliber: 9mm
Capacity: 17 rounds
Features: A hammer-fired competition handgun based on the Zero platform with ambidextrous controls; SA/DA; steel frame; competition-grade trigger; front and rear slide serrations; highly textured grip; under rail; grip panels available in choice of black, white, red, or blue
MSRP **$999.00**

DELTA
Action: Semiautomatic
Grips: Polymer
Barrel: 4 in.
Sights: Steel
Weight: 22.2 oz.

Caliber: 9mm
Capacity: N/A
Features: Arex's first striker-fired pistol featuring a two-stage trigger; angled edges for improved carry; double-stack magazine; front and rear slide serrations
MSRP **$479.99**

ZERO 1CP
Action: Semiautomatic
Grips: Polymer
Barrel: 3.85 in.
Sights: White dot
Weight: 25.2 oz.
Caliber: 9mm, 9x21
Capacity: 17 rounds
Features: Produced in Slovenia, this is the company's first entry into the U.S. market; DA/SA semiauto with a short-recoil, modified Browning linkless locking design; combo slide stop/decocker; hard anodized T7075 aluminum frame; nitrocarburized steel slide and cold-hammer-forged barrel; ambidextrous safety and magazine release; loaded chamber indicator; Picatinny rail; oversized trigger guard for use with gloves
MSRP **$589.99**

ZERO 1S
Action: Semiautomatic
Grips: Polymer

Barrel: 4.3 in.
Sights: White dot
Weight: 29 oz.
Caliber: 9mm, 9x21
Capacity: 17 rounds
Features: Produced in Slovenia, this is the company's first entry into the U.S. market; DA/SA semiauto with short-recoil, modified Browning linkless locking design; combo slide stop/decocker; hard anodized T7075 aluminum frame; nitrocarburized steel slide and cold-hammer-forged barrel; ambidextrous safety and magazine release; loaded chamber indicator; Picatinny rail; oversized trigger guard for use with gloves
MSRP **$589.99**

ZERO 1 TACTICAL, TACTICAL COMPACT
Action: Semiautomatic
Grips: Synthetic
Barrel: 4.9 in., 4.5 In.
Sights: Blade front, drift-adjustable rear
Weight: 30 oz., 28 oz.
Caliber: 9mm
Capacity: 20, 17 rounds
Features: This aluminum-framed pistol has generous capacity; DA/SA with an exposed hammer; frame in black, flat dark earth, or grey
MSRP **$699.99**

Armscor/Rock Island Armory

ARMSCOR/ROCK ISLAND ARMORY AL3.0, AL3.1

ARMSCOR/ROCK ISLAND ARMORY AL9.0

AL3.0, AL3.1
Action: Revolver
Grips: Rubber
Barrel: 2 in.
Sights: Ramp front, notch rear
Weight: 24 oz.
Caliber: .357 Mag.
Capacity: 6 rounds
Features: There's a lot of power in a snubby in .357; exposed hammer for DA/SA; blued finish on 3.0, stainless on 3.1; drop safety
Blued: **$699.00**
Stainless: **$799.00**

AL9.0
Action: Revolver
Grips: Rubber
Barrel: 4 in.
Sights: Ramp front, adjustable rear
Weight: 24 oz.
Caliber: 9mm
Capacity: 6 rounds
Features: Fun to have a revolver in 9mm and keeps ammo simple when you have a semiautomatic of the same caliber; exposed hammer; DA/SA; blued finish; no moon clips needed
MSRP **$699.00**

Armscor/Rock Island Armory

ARMSCOR/ROCK ISLAND ARMORY AL22

ARMSCOR/ROCK ISLAND ARMORY AL22M

ARMSCOR/ROCK ISLAND ARMORY BABY ROCK

ARMSCOR/ROCK ISLAND ARMORY BBR 3.10

ARMSCOR/ROCK ISLAND ARMORY GI STANDARD FS HC-45ACP

ARMSCOR/ROCK ISLAND ARMORY GI STANDARD MS-45ACP

ARMSCOR/ROCK ISLAND ARMORY PRO MATCH ULTRA 6-IN-10MM

ARMSCOR/ROCK ISLAND ARMORY PRO MATCH ULTRA HC

ARMSCOR/ROCK ISLAND ARMORY ROCK ULTRA CS

AL22
Action: Revolver
Grips: Rubber
Barrel: 4 in.
Sights: Ramp front, adjustable rear
Weight: 39 oz.
Caliber: .22 LR
Capacity: 9 rounds
Features: Fully shrouded barrel; in all blue or a blue frame with stainless cylinder, barrel and shroud
Blued: **$659.00**
Stainless: **$784.00**

AL22M
Action: Revolver
Grips: Rubber
Barrel: 4 in.
Sights: Ramp front, adjustable rear
Weight: 39 oz.
Caliber: .22 WMR
Capacity: 8 rounds
Features: Same as the AL22, but chambered in the .22 WMR round
Blued: **$669.00**
Stainless: **$794.00**

BABY ROCK
Action: Semiautomatic
Grips: Rubber
Barrel: 4 in.
Sights: Fixed
Weight: 1 lb. 8 oz.
Caliber: .380 ACP
Capacity: 7 rounds
Features: Parkerized frame; front post, Novak-style rear sight
MSRP. **$399.00**

BBR 3.10
Action: Semiautomatic
Grips: G10

Barrel: 3.1 in.
Sights: Fiber optic front, adjustable rear
Weight: 32 oz.
Caliber: .45 ACP
Capacity: 10 rounds
Features: G10 grips; parkerized finish; snag-free sights; beavertail grip safety
MSRP. **$699.00**

GI STANDARD FS HC-45ACP
Action: Semiautomatic
Grips: Rubber
Barrel: 5 in.
Sights: Fixed
Weight: 2 lb. 9 oz.
Caliber: .45 ACP
Capacity: 10 rounds
Features: Parkerized frame; 1:16 in. twist; 4–6 lb. trigger pull
MSRP. **$599.00**

GI STANDARD MS-45ACP
Action: Semiautomatic
Grips: Wood
Barrel: 4.25 in.
Sights: Fixed
Weight: 2 lb. 6 oz.
Caliber: .45 ACP
Capacity: 8 rounds
Features: Parkerized frame; 1:16 in. twist; 4–6 lb. trigger pull
MSRP. **$549.00**

PRO MATCH ULTRA 6-IN. 10MM
Action: Semiautomatic
Grips: Rubber
Barrel: 6 in.
Sights: Dovetail mounted fiber optic front, LPA TRT1 adjustable rear
Weight: 2 lb. 8 oz.

Caliber: 10mm
Capacity: 8 rounds
Features: Parkerized frame; orange fiber-optic front sight, tactical adjustable rear sight; comes with 9mm conversion kit; 1:16 twist; 4–6 lb. trigger pull; ambidextrous safety; combat hammer; extended beavertail
MSRP. **$1169.00**

PRO MATCH ULTRA HC-40S&W
Action: Semiautomatic
Grips: G10
Barrel: 5 in., 6 in.
Sights: Dovetail mounted fiber-optic front, LPA TRT-type rear
Weight: 2 lb. 14 oz.
Caliber: .40 S&W,
Capacity: 16 rounds
Features: Parkerized frame; orange fiber-optic front sight, tactical adjustable rear sight; comes with 9mm conversion kit; 1:16 twist; 4–6 lb. trigger pull; ambidextrous safety; combat hammer; extended beavertail
MSRP. **$1099.00**

ROCK ULTRA CCO
Action: Semiautomatic
Grips: G10
Barrel: 4.25 in.
Sights: Dovetail fiber optic front, LPA MPS1-type adjustable rear
Weight: N/A
Caliber: .45 ACP
Capacity: 8 rounds
Features: Officer's grip; aluminum frame; Commander-length slide; full-length guide rod; button-rifled barrel; skeletonized hammer; trigger with overtravel; frame has black oxide finish; slide is parkerized
MSRP. **$759.00**

Armscor/Rock Island Armory

ARMSCOR/ROCK ISLAND ARMORY TCM ROCK ULTRA CCO

ARMSCOR/ROCK ISLAND ARMORY TCM PREMIUM FS

ARMSCOR/ROCK ISLAND ARMORY TCM STANDARD FS

ARMSCOR/ROCK ISLAND ARMORY TCM STANDARD MS

ARMSCOR/ROCK ISLAND ARMORY XT 22 MAGNUM

ARMSCOR/ROCK ISLAND ARMORY XT MAGNUM PRO

ROCK ULTRA CS

Action: Semiautomatic
Grips: Rubber
Barrel: 3.62 in.
Sights: Dovetail standard front, low-profile, snag-free rear
Weight: 46.4 oz.
Caliber: .45 ACP
Capacity: 7 rounds
Features: Traditional 70-series 1911 design in a compact concealed carry package; snag-free features; checkered rubber grips; all-over parkerized matte finish
MSRP $729.00

TCM PREMIUM FS

Action: Semiautomatic
Grips: G10
Barrel: 5 in.
Sights: Fiber optic front, TRT1 adjustable rear
Weight: 40 oz.
Caliber: .22 TCM
Capacity: 17 rounds
Features: Combat-style hammer; G10 grips; parkerized frame; accessory underrail; skeletonized trigger; slide grooves front and rear
MSRP $949.00

TCM STANDARD FS

Action: Semiautomatic
Grips: Polymer
Barrel: 5 in.
Sights: Fiber optic front, adjustable rear
Weight: 40 oz.
Caliber: .22 TCM
Capacity: 17 rounds
Features: A standard government-sized 1911-style pistol; double-stack magazine; skeletonized hammer and trigger; parkerized finish
MSRP $749.00

TCM STANDARD MS

Action: Semiautomatic
Grips: Polymer
Barrel: 4.5 in.
Sights: Fiber optic front, adjustable rear
Weight: 40 oz.
Caliber: .22 TCM
Capacity: 17 rounds
Features: Similar to the TCM Standard FS, but with a slightly shorter, commander-length barrel; parkerized finish; skeletonized trigger and hammer
MSRP $749.00

XT 22 MAGNUM

Action: Semiautomatic
Grips: Rubber
Barrel: 5 in.
Sights: Fixed
Weight: 2 lb. 3 oz.
Caliber: .22 Mag.
Capacity: 14 rounds
Features: Parkerized frame; single action
MSRP $599.00

XT MAGNUM PRO

Action: Semiautomatic
Grips: G10
Barrel: 5 in.
Sights: None
Weight: 40 oz.
Caliber: .22 WMR
Capacity: 14 rounds
Features: Full-length top rail; bull barrel; parkerized finish
MSRP $749.00

Arsenal, Inc.

ARSENAL, INC. SAM7K

SAM7K

Action: Semiautomatic
Grips: Black polymer
Barrel: 10.5 in.
Sights: Peep rear
Weight: 128 oz.
Caliber: 7.62x39 Warsaw
Capacity: 5 rounds
Features: Milled receiver; short gas system; front sight block; gas block system; chrome-lined hammer-forged barrel; ambidextrous safety lever; scope rail; sling included
MSRP . . . . $1799.99–$1899.99

**AUTO-ORDNANCE
1911 9MM**

**AUTO-ORDNANCE
1911BKO**

**AUTO-ORDNANCE
CUSTOM CASE
HARDENED 1911**

**AUTO-ORDNANCE
IWO JIMA 1911**

**AUTO-ORDNANCE
LIBERTY 1911**

**AUTO-ORDNANCE
REVOLUTION 1911**

**AUTO-ORDNANCE
"SQUADRON"
1911**

1911 9MM

Action: Semiautomatic
Grips: Plastic
Barrel: 5 in.
Sights: Low-profile blade front, notch rear
Weight: 39 oz.
Caliber: 9mm
Capacity: 9 rounds
Features: Faithful GI replica in 9mm; "Model 1911 U.S. Army" on left frame side; brown plastic checkered grips; matte finish
MSRP **$956.00**

1911BKO

Action: Semiautomatic
Grips: Brown checkered plastic, checkered wood grips
Barrel: 5 in.
Sights: Blade front, rear drift adjustable sight
Weight: 39 oz.
Caliber: .45 ACP
Capacity: 7+1 rounds
Features: Single-action 1911 Colt design; WWII parkerized; stainless steel or blued metal finish
MSRP **$899.00**

CUSTOM CASE HARDENED 1911

Action: Semiautomatic
Grips: Wood
Barrel: 5 in.
Sights: Low-profile blade front, notch rear
Weight: 39 oz.

Caliber: .45 ACP
Capacity: 7 rounds
Features: Gorgeous deep color case hardening on all metalwork; wood grips with raised military "U.S." logo
MSRP **$1546.00**

IWO JIMA 1911

Action: Semiautomatic
Grips: Wood
Barrel: 5 in.
Sights: GI
Weight: 36.8 oz.
Caliber: .45 ACP
Capacity: 7 rounds
Features: Honors the 75th anniversary of the Battle of Iwo Jima with grips emblazoned with "Among the men who fought on Iwo Jima, uncommon valor was a common virtue"; engraving by Outlaw Ordnance on both sides of slide and frame; finished in Cerakote OD green with copper highlights
MSRP **$1247.00**

LIBERTY 1911

Action: Semiautomatic
Grips: Goncalo wood
Barrel: 5 in.
Sights: GI
Weight: 36.8 oz.
Caliber: .45 ACP
Capacity: 7 rounds
Features: Left grip panel has "DTOM"—Don't Tread on Me; right grip panel has Liberty Bell in a circle of stars; left slide engraved with

"Don't Tread"; right side engraved with "Liberty Death"; mixed Cerakote finish of brown and black
MSRP **$1476.00**

REVOLUTION 1911

Action: Semiautomatic
Grips: Copper
Barrel: 5 in.
Sights: GI
Weight: 36.8 oz.
Caliber: .45 ACP
Capacity: 7 rounds
Features: Solid copper grips with Liberty Bell design on right, Declaration of Independence on left; engravings of Benjamin Franklin, John Adams, George Washington, Paul Revere, and John Hancock by Outlaw Ordnance across the slide and frame
MSRP **$1338.00**

"SQUADRON" 1911

Action: Semiautomatic
Grips: Wood
Barrel: 5 in.
Sights: Low-profile blade front, notch rear
Weight: 39 oz.
Caliber: .45 ACP
Capacity: 7 rounds
Features: Custom graphics on slide/frame include the "shark mouth" of the P-40 warhawk fighter plane appearing at the muzzle; Army Air Corps insignia; "rivet" pattern; wood grips with raised military "U.S." logo
MSRP **$1259.00**

Beretta USA

92A1

Action: Semiautomatic
Grips: Plastic
Barrel: 4.9 in.
Sights: 3-Dot System
Weight: 34.4 oz.
Caliber: 9mm, .40 S&W
Capacity: 12 or 17 rounds, restricted capacity 10 rounds
Features: Removable front sight; Picatinny rail, internal recoil buffer; captive recoil spring assembly
MSRP . . . . $749.00–$775.00

92FS FUSION

Action: Semiautomatic
Grips: Carbon fiber and walnut
Barrel: 4.9 in.
Sights: Three-dot
Weight: N/A
Caliber: 9mm, 9x21
Capacity: 15 rounds
Features: A very limited edition with just 60 made in 9mm and 30 in 9x21; hand mirror-polished metal treatment; breech bolt, bolt release button, and trigger guard hand mirror-polished and checkered; short-barrel recoil operation; carbon fiber grips with a walnut insert inlaid with special silver plate bearing the PB and Fusion logos
MSRP $8500.00

92FSR 22 SNIPER GRAY

Action: Semiautomatic
Grips: Plastic
Barrel: 4.9 in.
Sights: Dovetailed front and rear
Weight: 26.08 oz.
Caliber: .22 LR
Capacity: 10, 15 rounds
Features: DA/SA .22 LR version of maker's famed 9mm; open slide design; reversible magazine release; ambidextrous decocker/safety; combat trigger guard; 1913 Picatinny rail; Sniper Gray frame finish
MSRP $479.00

92FSR 22 SUPPRESSOR READY KIT

Action: Semiautomatic
Grips: Plastic
Barrel: 4.9 in.
Sights: Suppressor-height front and rear
Weight: 26.08 oz.
Caliber: .22 LR
Capacity: 10, 15 rounds
Features: DA/SA .22 LR version of

maker's famed 9mm; open slide design; reversible magazine release; ambidextrous decocker/safety; combat trigger guard; 1913 Picatinny rail; suppressor-height sights; extended threaded barrel with thread protector and mock suppressor
MSRP $549.00

92G ELITE LTT

Action: Semiautomatic
Grips: G10
Barrel: 4.7 in.
Sights: Red fiber optic front, blacked out notch rear
Weight: 33.3 oz.
Caliber: 9mm
Capacity: 15 rounds
Features: A collaboration with Landon Tactical that features the M9A1 frame; Vertec slide with added front serrations; exclusive radiused trigger guard; beveled mag well; ultra-thin VZ/LTT G10 grips; oversized mag release; no lanyard ring; solid steel guide rod; DA/SA with decocker; ships with three magazines
MSRP $1149.00

92X CENTURION

Action: Semiautomatic
Grips: Synthetic
Barrel: 4.25 in.
Sights: Orange-dot front, black-out notch rear
Weight: 28.5 oz.
Caliber: 9mm
Capacity: 10, 17 rounds
Features: A compact slide pairs with a Vertec full-length grip and a straight backstrap for maximum round count and hand accommodation; decocking safety that can be converted to a decocker only; high-visibility orange front sight against a blacked-out square-notch rear; oversized mag release; Gen 3 barrel locking block
MSRP $699.00

92X COMPACT, COMPACT WITH RAIL

Action: Semiautomatic
Grips: Synthetic
Barrel: 4.25 in.
Sights: Orange-dot front, black-out notch rear
Weight: 27.1 oz.
Caliber: 9mm
Capacity: 10, 13 rounds
Features: Smart double-stack carry choice with a decocking safety that

BERETTA 92A1

BERETTA 92FS FUSION

BERETTA 92FSR_22 SNIPER GRAY

BERETTA 92FSR_22 SUPPRESSOR READY KIT

BERETTA 92G ELITE LTT

BERETTA 92X CENTURION

BERETTA 92X COMPACT, COMPACT WITH RAIL

can be converted to a decocker only; high-visibility orange front sight against a blacked-out square-notch rear; oversized mag release; Gen 3 barrel locking block; Vertec grip frame accommodates a wide variety of hand sizes; front- and backstrap checkering
MSRP $699.00

BERETTA 92X FULL-SIZE

BERETTA 92X PERFORMANCE

BERETTA APX CENTURION

BERETTA 3032 TOMCAT INOX

BERETTA APX COMBAT

BERETTA APX COMPACT

BERETTA APX FDE

92X FULL-SIZE

Action: Semiautomatic
Grips: Synthetic
Barrel: 4.7 in.
Sights: Orange-dot front, black-out notch rear
Weight: 33.3 oz.
Caliber: 9mm
Capacity: 10, 15, 17 rounds
Features: This is a fine choice for a full-size carry, nightstand use, and lots of target practice with features such as a decocking safety that can be converted to a decocker only; high-visibility orange front sight against a blacked-out square-notch rear; oversized mag release; Gen 3 barrel locking block; 3-slot Picatinny accessory rail
MSRP $699.00

92X PERFORMANCE

Action: Semiautomatic
Grips: Synthetic
Barrel: 4.9 in.
Sights: Red fiber optic front, adjustable rear
Weight: 47.6 oz.
Caliber: 9mm, 9x21
Capacity: 15 rounds
Features: Open Brigadier slide that reduces weight and aids barrel cooling; Vertec steel frame with front and rear grip checkering and accessory rail fore of the trigger guard; front and rear slide serrations; oversized magazines with bumper pads; skeletonized hammer; oversized, reversible magazine release; raised frame profile for higher grip position
MSRP $1599.00

3032 TOMCAT INOX

Action: Semiautomatic
Grips: Plastic
Barrel: 2.5 in.
Sights: Fixed, open
Weight: 14.5 oz.
Caliber: .32 ACP, .380 ACP
Capacity: 7+1 round
Features: Double-action; tip-up barrel latch; Inox has stainless steel slide and barrel; titanium alloy frame in black or gray; double- or single-trigger
MSRP $539.00

APX CENTURION

Action: Semiautomatic
Grips: Polymer
Barrel: 3.7 in.
Sights: Drift adjustable three-dot front and rear
Weight: 27.7 oz.
Caliber: 9mm, .40 S&W
Capacity: 10, 13, 15 rounds
Features: A mid-size striker-fire suitable for concealed carry; doublestack magazine; aggressive slide serrations front and rear; 6-pound trigger with audible reset; under rail; standard model available in black or flat dark earth; RDO variant is red-dot-optic ready with slide cuts that take four different mounting plates; Combat is also RDO and has a threaded barrel

Black:	$399.00
Flat dark earth:	$419.00
RDO:	$549.00
Combat:	$579.00

APX COMBAT

Action: Semiautomatic
Grips: Polymer
Barrel: 4.9 in.

Sights: Drift-adjustable front and rear, optics plates
Weight: 33.3 oz.
Caliber: 9mm
Capacity: 10, 17 rounds
Features: Striker-fired DA/SA pistol; threaded barrel; slide cut out to accept four different optics mounting plates for reflex red dot sights from Burris, Trijicon, Leupold, and C-More; interchangeable backstraps
MSRP $579.00

APX COMPACT

Action: Semiautomatic
Grips: Polymer
Barrel: 3.7 in.
Sights: Drift adjustable three-dot front and rear
Weight: 26.4 oz.–27.2 oz.
Caliber: 9mm, .40 S&W
Capacity: 10, 13 rounds
Features: Short-gripped CCW version of the popular APX with flush-fit magazines; under rail; in black or FDE

Black:	$399.00
FDE:	$419.00

APX FDE

Action: Semiautomatic
Grips: Polymer
Barrel: 4.9 in.
Sights: Drift-adjustable
Weight: 33.3 oz.
Caliber: 9mm
Capacity: 10, 15, 17 rounds
Features: Developed for law enforcement and military personnel; easy-to-find controls; under frame accessory rail; three interchangeable backstraps; slide stop is ambidextrous; mag release is reversible
MSRP $419.00

Beretta USA

BERETTA APX RDO

BERETTA APX TARGET

BERETTA BU-9 NANO

BERETTA M9

BERETTA M9A1

BERETTA M9A3 BLACK

BERETTA NANO

BERETTA PICO

APX RDO

Action: Semiautomatic
Grips: Polymer
Barrel: 4.9 in.
Sights: Drift-adjustable front and rear, optics plates
Weight: 33.3 oz.
Caliber: 9mm, .40 S&W
Capacity: 10, 15, 17 rounds
Features: Striker-fired DA/SA pistol; slide cut out to accept four different optics mounting plates for reflex red dot sights from Burris, Trijicon, Leupold, and C-More; interchangeable backstraps
MSRP **$549.00**

APX TARGET

Action: Semiautomatic
Grips: Polymer
Barrel: 4.76 in.
Sights: Fiber optic front, adjustable rear
Weight: 31 oz.
Caliber: 9mm
Capacity: 17 rounds
Features: Great capacity in a striker-fire designed for competition, featuring four mounting plates that accommodate four headlining red-dot reflex sights; interchangeable backstrap set; full-length slide serrations; 5-lb. trigger break
MSRP **$699.00**

BU-9 NANO

Action: Semiautomatic
Grips: Technopolymer
Barrel: 3.07 in.
Sights: 3-dot low profile
Weight: 17.67 oz.
Caliber: 9mm
Capacity: 6+1 rounds
Features: Interchangeable sights; ambidextrous magazine release button; serialized sub-chassis; patent-

pending striker deactivator; technopolymer grip frame; three variations available include black, pink, Flat Dark Earth
MSRP **$450.00**

M9

Action: Semiautomatic
Grips: Plastic
Barrel: 4.9 in.
Sights: Dot-and-Post system
Weight: 33.3 oz.
Caliber: 9mm
Capacity: 15 rounds, restricted capacity 10+1 rounds
Features: Has distinctive military style markings; chrome-lined bore; double-action; automatic firing pin block; ambidextrous manual safety; lightweight forged aluminum alloy frame w/ combat-style trigger guard
MSRP **$649.00**

M9A1

Action: Semiautomatic
Grips: Plastic
Barrel: 4.9 in.
Sights: 3-Dot System
Weight: 33.9 oz.
Caliber: 9mm
Capacity: 15+1 rounds, restricted capacity 10+1 rounds
Features: Picatinny rail; magazine well bevel; sand-resistant magazine
MSRP **$750.00**

M9A3

Action: Semiautomatic
Grips: Polymer
Barrel: 5 in.
Sights: Three-dot night sights
Weight: 33.4 oz.
Caliber: 9mm
Capacity: 10, 17 rounds
Features: An updated classic with

night sights; under rail; textured grips; threaded barrel; decocker; lanyard ring; made in Italy; in black, flat dark earth, flat dark earth frame/black slide combo, black slide/green frame combo, black slide/grey frame combo, green slide/frame with black barrel and grips combo
MSRP . . . . **$1099.00–$1100.00**

NANO

Action: Semiautomatic
Grips: Polymer
Barrel: 3 in.
Sights: Three-dot white
Weight: 19.8 oz.
Caliber: 9mm
Capacity: 8 rounds
Features: Just a smidge bigger than the tiny Pico in order to take the smidge bigger 9mm, the Nano is available with a Robin's Egg Blue frame and matte stainless slide, Sniper Gray frame with matte black slide, Rosa (pink) frame with black slide, and flat dark earth frame with black slide
MSRP **$450.00**

PICO

Action: Semiautomatic
Grips: Technopolymer
Barrel: 2.7 in.
Sights: Front and rear adjustable
Weight: 11.5 oz.
Caliber: .380 ACP
Capacity: 6+1 rounds
Features: Stainless steel sub-chassis engraved with serial number; snag-free slide and frame; barrel can be replaced with a .32 ACP barrel; dovetail quick-change sights; frames available in flat dark earth, light aqua blue, black, or purple
MSRP **$300.00**

BERETTA PX4 COMPACT

BERETTA PX4 STORM COMPACT

BERETTA PX4 COMPACT CARRY

BERETTA PX4 STORM FULL SIZE

BERETTA U22 NEOS

PX4 COMPACT

Action: Semiautomatic
Grips: Polymer
Barrel: 3.2 in.
Sights: Drift-adjustable white three dot
Weight: 27.3 oz.
Caliber: 9mm
Capacity: 15 rounds
Features: A super-concealable pistol with a full palm grip thanks to a double-stack magazine; under rail; front and rear slide serrations; DA/SA with decocker; with gray frame and black slide or in all-over Flat Dark Earth
MSRP **$650.00**

PX4 STORM COMPACT

Action: Semiautomatic
Grips: Plastic
Barrel: 3.2 in.
Sights: 3-Dot System
Weight: 27.3 oz.
Caliber: 9mm, .40 S&W
Capacity: 12 or 15 rounds; full size

magazines 9mm: 17 or 20 rounds, .40 S&W: 14 or 17 rounds; restricted capacity 10 rounds
Features: Ambidextrous side stop lever; integral Picatinny rail; bruiton non-reflective black coating; visible automatic firing pin block
MSRP . . . . **$599.00–$650.00**

PX4 STORM COMPACT CARRY

Action: DA/SA
Grips: Synthetic
Barrel: 3.2 in.
Sights: High-visibility night sights
Weight: 27.3 oz.
Caliber: 9mm
Capacity: 15 rounds
Features: Rotating barrel; grey Cerakote slide; Picatinny rail; competition trigger; double stack magazine; Talon grips; reversible magazine release; lightweight polymer frame; stealth levers decock only
MSRP **$899.00**

PX4 STORM FULL SIZE

Action: Semiautomatic
Grips: Plastic
Barrel: 4 in.
Sights: 3-Dot System
Weight: 27.7 oz.
Caliber: 9mm, .40 S&W, .45 ACP
Capacity: 9, 10, 17 rounds
Features: Picatinny rail; innovative locked-breech with a rotating barrel system; visible automatic firing pin block; ambidextrous safety; reversible magazine release; available in Inox finish; California-compliant model available with and without night sights
MSRP . . . . **$649.00–$749.00**

U22 NEOS

Action: Semiautomatic
Grips: Plastic
Barrel: 4.5 in., 6 in.
Sights: Target
Weight: 31.7–36.2 oz.
Caliber: .22 LR
Capacity: 10+1 rounds
Features: Single-action; removable colored grip inserts; deluxe model features adjustable trigger, replaceable sights; optional 7.5 in. barrel
MSRP **$325.00**

Bersa

BERSA BP9CC WITH THREADED BARREL

BERSA BP CONCEALED CARRY SERIES

BP9CC WITH THREADED BARREL

Action: Semiautomatic
Grips: Polymer
Barrel: 4 in.
Sights: Interchangeable front and rear
Weight: 22 oz.
Caliber: 9mm
Capacity: 8 rounds
Features: An everyday carry gun featuring a threaded barrel; short reset DAO; interchangeable Sig-type front, Glock-type rear sights; matte finish
MSRP **$406.99**

BP CONCEALED CARRY SERIES

Action: Short reset DAO
Grips: Integral to frame
Barrel: 3.3 in.
Sights: Interchangeable front and rear
Weight: 21.5 oz.
Caliber: 9mm, .380 ACP, .40 S&W
Capacity: 6+1 or 8+1 rounds
Features: Bersa polymer concealed carry; high impact polymer frame; Picatinny rail, polygonal rifling, and loaded chamber indicator; ambidextrous magazine release; striker fired; micro-polished bore with sharp, deep rifling; 3-dot sight system; integral locking system; automatic firing pin safety
MSRP . . . . **starting at $311.00**

Bersa

BERSA THUNDER 9 PRO XT

BERSA THUNDER 380

BERSA THUNDER 380 COMBAT PLUS

BERSA THUNDER 380 CONCEALED CARRY

BERSA THUNDER 380 WITH THREADED

BERSA TPR9C WITH THREADED BARREL

BERSA TPR9C DUOTONE, MATTE

THUNDER 9 PRO XT

Action: DA/SA
Grips: Checkered black polymer
Barrel: 4.96 in.
Sights: Fiber optic front sight, adjustable rear
Weight: 33.9 oz.
Caliber: 9mm
Capacity: 10–17 rounds
Features: Dovetailed front fiber optic sight; windage and elevation adjustable rear sights; ambidextrous controls for easy handling; 5-inch competition barrel fitted to slide for maximum precision; Cerakote finish to protect against abrasion, wear, and corrosion
MSRP $835.00

THUNDER 380

Action: Semiautomatic
Grips: Black polymer
Barrel: 3.5 in.
Sights: 3-Dot system
Weight: 20 oz.
Caliber: .380 ACP
Capacity: 7+1 rounds
Features: Combat style trigger guard; extended slide release; micro-polished bore with sharp, deep rifling; integral locking system; available in matte, matte with pink rubber wraparound grips, duotone, or Cerakote nickel
MSRP . . . . $261.99–$406.99

THUNDER 380 COMBAT PLUS

Action: DA/SA
Grips: Olive rubber wrap-around
Barrel: 3.5 in.

Sights: Dovetail front, notched-bar dovetail rear
Weight: 20.5 oz.
Caliber: .380 ACP
Capacity: 8+1, 15+1
Features: Decocker for safer conceal carry; flat-bottom 8 shot magazine; integral locking system for the ultimate in safety; micro-polished bore with sharp, deep rifling for greater accuracy; slim side release for a lower profile; u-shaped combat rear sight for optimum sighting in low-light situations
MSRP $399.00

THUNDER 380 CONCEALED CARRY

Action: Semiautomatic
Grips: Black polymer
Barrel: 3.2 in.
Sights: Blade front and notched-bar dovetailed rear
Weight: 16.4 oz.
Caliber: .380 ACP
Capacity: 8+1 rounds
Features: Extra low profile sights; combat style trigger guard; slim slide release; integral locking system; available with Crimson Trace laser
MSRP $316.00

THUNDER 380 WITH THREADED BARREL, 22 WITH THREADED BARREL

Action: Semiautomatic
Grips: Polymer
Barrel: 4.3 in.
Sights: blade front, notch/bar rear
Weight: 19.4–20.5 oz.
Caliber: .22 LR, .380 ACP
Capacity: 10, 8 rounds

Features: Reminiscent of Walther's small handguns, features include checkered polymer grips; threaded barrel; magazine disconnect; .380 has a dovetail front sight, while the .22 has a low-profile integral blade
MSRP $327.00

TPR9, TPR9C WITH THREADED BARREL

Action: Semiautomatic
Grips: Polymer
Barrel: 5 in., 4.1 in.
Sights: Interchangeable Sig type front and rear
Weight: 31.2 oz., 23.5 oz.
Caliber: 9mm
Capacity: 17, 13 rounds
Features: Intended as a duty gun and perfectly serviceable as a carry or home-defense pistol, these threaded barrel models feature interchangeable Sig-type sights; matte finish; textured grips; alloy frames; steel slides; DA with manual safety; TPR9C is slightly shorter in both barrel and grip length
MSRP $515.00

TPR9C DUOTONE, MATTE

Action: Semiautomatic
Grips: Polymer
Barrel: 3.25 in.
Sights: Interchangeable Sig Sauer-type front and rear
Weight: 23 oz.
Caliber: 9mm
Capacity: 10, 13 rounds
Features: Compact DA/SA for concealed carry; Browning Petter locking action that enhances reliability
MSRP . . . . $349.99–$405.99

Big Horn Armory, Inc.

BIG HORN ARMORY AR500 .500 AUTO MAX PISTOL

AR500 .500 AUTO MAX PISTOL

Action: Semiautomatic
Grips: Synthetic
Barrel: 10 in.
Sights: None
Weight: 8 lb. 1 oz.
Caliber: .500 Auto Max

Capacity: 5, 9 rounds
Features: A big round in a fast-handling pistol package; threaded barrel; M-LOK forearm with brace, Picatinny rail and sling swivels; hard-anodized aluminum action
MSRP $2199.00

Bond Arms

BOND ARMS BACKUP

BOND ARMS BLACKJACK

BOND ARMS, INC. BULLPUP 9

BOND ARMS CENTURY 2000

BOND ARMS MAMA BEAR

BOND ARMS MINI 45

BOND ARMS GIRL MINI

BOND ARMS PATRIOT

BACKUP

Action: Break-top
Grips: Rubber
Barrel: 2.5 in.
Sights: Blade front, fixed rear
Weight: 18.5 oz.
Caliber: .357 Mag., .38 Spl., .40 S&W, .45 ACP, .45 Colt
Capacity: 2 rounds
Features: Interchangable barrels; rebounding hammer; retracting firing pins; crossbolt safety
MSRP $540.00

BLACKJACK

Action: Break-top
Grips: Wood
Barrel: 3.5 in.
Sights: Blade front, fixe rear
Weight: 22 oz.
Caliber: .45 LC/.410-bore
Capacity: 2 rounds
Features: A sleek matte black finish on the metalwork is complemented by the dark wood grips of black ash that wear an inletted ace of spades design
MSRP $689.00

BULLPUP 9

Action: Semiautomatic
Grips: Rosewood
Barrel: 3.35 in.
Sights: Dovetail drift-adjustable non-illuminated three-dot
Weight: 17.5 oz.
Caliber: 9mm Luger

Capacity: 7 rounds
Features: Based on the XR-9 by Boberg Arms; Bond Arms purchased the patents and rights to that gun in 2016, basing its new Bullpup on it
MSRP $1099.00

CENTURY 2000

Action: Break-top
Grips: Custom laminated black ash or rosewood
Barrel: 3.5 in.
Sights: Blade front, fixed rear
Weight: 21 oz.
Caliber: .357 Mag./.38 Spl., .410/.45 LC
Capacity: 2 rounds
Features: Interchangeable barrels; automatic extractor; rebounding hammer; retracting firing pins; crossbolt safety; spring-loaded cammed locking lever; trigger guard; stainless steel with satin polish finish
MSRP $567.00

MAMA BEAR

Action: Break-top
Grips: Pink wood
Barrel: 2.5 in.
Sights: Blade front, fixed rear
Weight: 18.5 oz.
Caliber: .357 Mag, .38 Spl.
Capacity: 2 rounds
Features: Stainless steel double barrel and frame; automatic spent casing extractor; rebounding hammer; retracting ring pins; crossbolt safety; spring-loaded, cammed locking lever; laser-carved American Flag and bald eagle grips
MSRP $541.00

MINI 45, GIRL MINI

Action: Break-top
Grips: Rosewood or pink
Barrel: 2.5 in.
Sights: Blade front, fixed rear
Weight: 18 oz.–19 oz.
Caliber: .45 Colt (Mini 45), .357 Mag. (Girl Mini)
Capacity: 2 rounds
Features: The Bond Mini was developed as a special edition gun that is even easier to conceal and carry, but still packs the same power Bond Arms guns are known for; comes in two models the Mini .45 and the Girl Mini; Girl Mini has slightly smaller barrel and pink grips
MSRP $534.00

PATRIOT

Action: Break-top
Grips: Rosewood
Barrel: 3 in.
Sights: Blade front, fixed rear
Weight: 21.5 oz.
Caliber: .45 Colt, .410
Capacity: 2 rounds
Features: Stainless steel double barrel and frame; automatic spent casing extractor; rebounding hammer; retracting ring pins; crossbolt safety; spring-loaded, cammed locking lever; laser-carved American Flag and bald eagle grips
MSRP $648.00

Bond Arms

BOND ARMS, INC. PT2A (PROTECT THE SECOND AMENDMENT)

BOND ARMS ROUGHNECK

BOND ARMS ROWDY

BOND ARMS SNAKE SLAYER

BOND ARMS SNAKE SLAYER IV

BOND ARMS, INC. TEXAN

BOND ARMS TEXAS DEFENDER

BOND TEXAS RANGER - SPECIAL EDITION

PT2A (PROTECT THE SECOND AMENDMENT)

Action: Break-top
Grips: Rosewood
Barrel: 4.25 in.
Sights: Front blade, fixed rear
Weight: 23.5 oz.
Caliber: .45 LC/.410-bore, .357 Mag.
Capacity: 2 rounds
Features: Custom extended rosewood grips; "The Right of the People to Keep and Bear Arms" is emblazoned on right side of top barrel; "shall not be infringed" on right side of bottom barrel; cross-bolt safety; stainless steel barrels; compatibility with all Bond barrels; automatic extractors; BAD premium leather driving holster
MSRP $887.00

ROUGHNECK

Action: Break-top
Grips: Rubber
Barrel: 2.5 in.
Sights: Integral
Weight: 19 oz.
Caliber: 9mm, .357 Mag., .45 ACP
Capacity: 2 rounds
Features: Designed to work with smooth-lined holsters, this two-shot has a bead-blasted stainless finish with polished barrel flats, trigger, and takedown mechanism
MSRP $269.00

ROWDY

Action: Break-top
Grips: Rubber
Barrel: 3 in.
Sights: Integral
Weight: 20 oz.
Caliber: .410-bore, .45 LC
Capacity: 2 rounds

Features: Similar to the Roughneck, but with a longer barrel and chambering for the .410 shotshell/.45 LC centerfire
MSRP $299.00

SNAKE SLAYER

Action: Break-top
Grips: Extended custom rosewood
Barrel: 3.5 in.
Sights: Blade front, fixed rear
Weight: 22 oz.
Caliber: .357 Mag./.38 Spl., .410/.45 LC
Capacity: 2 rounds
Features: Interchangeable barrels; automatic extractor; rebounding hammer; retracting firing pins; crossbolt safety; spring-loaded cammed locking lever; trigger guard; stainless steel with satin polish finish
MSRP $603.00

SNAKE SLAYER IV

Action: Break-top
Grips: Extended custom rosewood
Barrel: 4.25 in.
Sights: Blade front, fixed rear
Weight: 23.5 oz.
Caliber: .357 Mag./.38 Spl., .410/.45 LC
Capacity: 2 rounds
Features: Automatic extractor; interchangeable barrels; rebounding hammer; retracting firing pins; crossbolt safety; spring-loaded cammed locking lever; trigger guard; stainless steel with satin polish finish
MSRP $648.00

TEXAN

Action: Break-top
Grips: Rosewood

Barrel: 6 in.
Sights: Front ramp
Weight: 23.5 oz.
Caliber: .45 LC/.410-bore
Capacity: 2 rounds
Features: Bond's first six-inch production model; patented rebounding hammer; cross-bolt safety; automatic spent casing extractor; spring-loaded cammed locking lever; compatible with all Bond Arms barrels; rosewood grips are extended and engraved
MSRP $700.00

TEXAS DEFENDER

Action: Break-top
Grips: Custom laminated black ash or rosewood
Barrel: 3 in.
Sights: Blade front and fixed rear
Weight: 20 oz.
Caliber: 45 Colt/.410
Capacity: 2 rounds
Features: Interchangeable barrels; automatic extractor; rebounding hammer; retracting firing pins; crossbolt safety; spring-loaded cammed locking lever; trigger guard; stainless steel with satin polish finish
MSRP $543.00

TEXAS RANGER - SPECIAL EDITION

Action: Break-top
Grips: Texas mesquite
Barrel: 3.5 in.
Sights: Blade front, fixed rear
Weight: 22 oz.
Caliber: .410/.45 LC
Capacity: 2 rounds
Features: Bond Arms has been chosen to represent the prestigious Texas Rangers in their historic 200th Anniversary; gun and knife grips are made from real Texas mesquite wood, the Texas Ranger Stars are handmade by Texas inmates in the Texas Department of Corrections, and it is gold engraved on the barrel; custom glass top display case included
MSRP $1355.00

Bond Arms

BOND ARMS Z SLAYER

Z SLAYER
Action: Break-top
Grips: Black ash
Barrel: 3.5 in.
Sights: Integral
Weight: 22 oz.
Caliber: .410-bore, .45 LC
Capacity: 2 rounds

Features: Zombie-green frame and barrels, the barrels sporting—yikes!—red "blood" splatter; trigger guard, hammer, and break-open mechanism in matte black; special black ash grips have a big "Z" emblazoned on them
MSRP................$697.00

Browning

BROWNING 1911-22 A1 COMPACT

BROWNING 1911-22 A1 FULL SIZE

BROWNING 1911-22 BLACK LABEL MEDALLION

BROWNING 1911-22 GRAY FULL-SIZE, COMPACT

BROWNING 1911-380 BLACK LABEL MEDALLION PRO COMPACT

BROWNING 1911-380 BLACK LABEL MEDALLION PRO WITH RAIL

1911-22 A1 COMPACT
Action: Semiautomatic
Grips: Walnut
Barrel: 3.6 in.
Sights: A1 front, rear
Weight: 14 oz.
Caliber: .22 LR
Capacity: 10 rounds
Features: A flyweight rimfire in a compact frame; machined alloy slide with gray anodized finish; checkered walnut grips; hard case and one magazine included
MSRP................$699.99

1911-22 A1 FULL SIZE
Action: Semiautomatic
Grips: Brown composite
Barrel: 4.25 in.
Sights: Fixed
Weight: 15 oz.
Caliber: 22 LR
Capacity: 10+1 rounds
Features: Alloy frame in matte blued finish; stainless steel barrel block with matte blued finish; blowback action; single-action trigger; detachable magazine; manual thumb safety; grip safety
MSRP................$699.99

1911-22 BLACK LABEL MEDALLION
Action: Semiautomatic
Grips: Rosewood
Barrel: 3.625 in., 4.25 in.
Sights: Combat white dot
Weight: 13 oz., 15 oz.
Caliber: .22LR
Capacity: 10 rounds
Features: Available in full-size or compact 85-percent scale of 1911 package; checkered grips; extended slide release; machined aluminum slide; ambidextrous thumb safety; skeletonized trigger and hammer
MSRP................$749.99

1911-22 GRAY FULL-SIZE, COMPACT
Action: Semiautomatic
Grips: Walnut
Barrel: 4.25 in., 3.625 in.
Sights: A1 front and rear
Weight: 15 oz., 14 oz.
Caliber: .22 LR
Capacity: 10 rounds
Features: Blue alloy frame with gray anodized alloy slide; walnut grips with diamond pattern; comes with one magazine and hard case
MSRP................$679.99

1911-380 BLACK LABEL MEDALLION PRO COMPACT
Action: Semiautomatic
Grips: Laminate
Barrel: 3.625 in. (compact), 4.25 in. (full-size)
Sights: Steel three-dot combat or steel bar-dot combat night sights
Weight: 16 oz. (compact), 18 oz. (full-size)
Caliber: .380 ACP
Capacity: 8 rounds
Features: 85 percent-scale 1911; compact and full-size versions; stainless steel slide and rosewood laminate grips; ambidextrous manual thumb safety; extended slide release beavertail grip safety; two magazines; Commander hammer; target crown
Combat sights...........$899.99
Night sights.............$979.99

1911-380 BLACK LABEL MEDALLION PRO WITH RAIL
Action: Semiautomatic
Grips: Wood
Barrel: 4.25 in., 3.625 in.
Sights: Combat white dot
Weight: 18 oz., 16 oz.
Caliber: .380 ACP
Capacity: 8 rounds
Features: Matte black frame; blackened slide with stainless steel finished flats; rosewood grips with checkering and gold Buck Mark logo; under-barrel Picatinny rail; extended ambidextrous thumb safety; extended slide release; Commander-style hammer; optional night sights; with two magazines and ABS case
MSRP...........$899.99–$979.99

Browning

BROWNING BUCK MARK CONTOUR GRAY URX

BROWNING BUCK MARK FIELD TARGET

BROWNING BUCK MARK MEDALLION ROSEWOOD

BROWNING BUCK MARK PLUS CAMPER UFX SR

BROWNING BUCK MARK PLUS PRACTICAL URX

BROWNING BUCK MARK PLUS STAINLESS UDX

BROWNING BUCK MARK PLUS VISION AMERICAN SUPPRESSOR READY

BUCK MARK CONTOUR GRAY URX

Action: Semiautomatic
Grips: Ultragrip RX
Barrel: 5.5 in.
Sights: Patridge front, adjustable rear
Weight: 36 oz.
Caliber: .22 LR
Capacity: 10 rounds
Features: Contoured steel barrel in matte black; anodized gray full-length top rail; gray anodized frame; URX grips with finger molds; 16-click adjustable Pro Target rear sight; one magazine and pistol rug
MSRP................**$639.99**

BUCK MARK FIELD TARGET, FIELD TARGET SUPPRESSOR READY

Action: Semiautomatic
Grips: Laminate cocobolo
Barrel: 5.5 in.
Sights: Pro Target adjustable
Weight: 38 oz.
Caliber: .22 LR
Capacity: 10 rounds
Features: Suppressor-ready; full-length Picatinny rail on top; barrel profile is heavy bull
Field Target **$659.99**
Suppressor-ready........**$679.99**

BUCK MARK MEDALLION ROSEWOOD

Action: Semiautomatic
Grips: Laminated rosewood
Barrel: 5.5 in.
Sights: TRUGLO/Marble Arms fiber optic front, Pro Target adjustable rear
Weight: 34 oz.
Caliber: .22 LR
Capacity: 11 rounds

Features: A new look for the Buck Mark with blackened, polished-flats slab-sided barrel; adjustable rear sight and fiber optic front; textured grip panels
MSRP.................**$579.99**

BUCK MARK PLUS CAMPER UFX SR

Action: Semiautomatic
Grips: Ultragrip FX
Barrel: 6 in.
Sights: TruGlo/Marble Arms fiber optic front, white outline Pro Target rear
Weight: 34 oz.
Caliber: .22 LR
Capacity: 10 rounds
Features: Suppressor-ready; Browning ambidextrous Ultragrip FX grips; long tapered bull barrel with a matte finish; topside Picatinny rail for optics mounting; pistol rug
MSRP.................**$579.99**

BUCK MARK PLUS PRACTICAL URX

Action: Semiautomatic
Grips: Ultragrip RX ambidextrous
Barrel: 5.5 in.
Sights: Pro-target adjustable rear; Truglo/Marble's fiber-optic front
Weight: 34 oz.
Caliber: .22 LR
Capacity: 10+1 rounds
Features: Tapered bull barrel with matte blued finish; matte gray finish receiver
MSRP.................**$519.99**

BUCK MARK PLUS STAINLESS UDX, ROSEWOOD UDX

Action: Semiautomatic

Grips: Laminate
Barrel: 5.5 in.
Sights: TruGlo fiber optic front; white outline Pro-Target rear
Weight: 34 oz.
Caliber: .22 LR
Capacity: 10 rounds
Features: Wood laminate UDX grips (Utragrip Deluxe); stainless steel frame and slabside barrel with polished flats; SA trigger; Picatinny top rail for optics; grip frame machined with finger grooves that match up to textured wood grips; slab-side barrel has high-polished flats
Stainless................**$679.99**
Rosewood **$639.99**

BUCK MARK PLUS VISION AMERICAN SUPPRESSOR READY

Action: Semiautomatic
Grips: UFX overmolded
Barrel: 5.9 in.
Sights: Fiber optic front, adjustable rear
Weight: 27 oz.
Caliber: .22 LR
Capacity: 10 rounds
Features: Vision barrel of an inner steel tube surrounded by a tensioned aluminum sleeve of anodized blue that has white stars and cutouts to reveal red underneath; anodized blue frame; barrel threaded ½x28 and has a muzzle brake; TruGlo/Marble Arms front sight, Pro Target rear; half-length topside optics rail; pistol rug
MSRP.................**$799.99**

Browning

BROWNING BUCK MARK PLUS VISION BLACK/GOLD SUPPRESSOR READY

BROWNING BUCK MARK PLUS VISION UFX BLACK, BLUE, RED

BUCK MARK PLUS VISION BLACK/GOLD SUPPRESSOR READY
Action: Semiautomatic
Grips: UFX overmolded
Barrel: 5.9 in.
Sights: Fiber optic front, adjustable rear
Weight: 27 oz.
Caliber: .22 LR
Capacity: 10 rounds

Features: Similar to the Americana, but with aggressive diamond cutouts in the outer barrel sleeve that reveal gold underneath; all over matte black finish; pistol rug
MSRP $749.99

BUCK MARK PLUS VISION UFX BLUE
Action: Semiautomatic

Grips: UFX overmolded
Barrel: 5.9 in.
Sights: Fiber optic front, adjustable rear
Weight: 27 oz.
Caliber: .22 LR
Capacity: 10 rounds
Features: Vision barrel; steel inner barrel wrapped in aluminum sleeve with sawtooth cuts; barrel threaded ½x28 with removable muzzle brake; Picatinny optics rail; TruGlo/Marble Arms front sight; 16-click Pro Target rear sight with white outline; pistol rug; matte black frame; sleeve colors in black, red, or blue
MSRP $779.99

B&T (Brügger & Thomet)

B&T (BRÜGGER & THOMET) USWA1

BRÜGGER & THOMET STATION SIX

STATION SIX
Action: Bolt
Grips: Polymer
Barrel: 5.1 in.
Sights: Blade front, notch rear
Weight: 31 oz.
Caliber: 9mm, .45 ACP
Capacity: 5 rounds
Features: An integrally suppressed take on the WWII-era Welrod pistol; rotating bolt action; manually operated bolt to eliminate the sounds associated with semiautomatic actions; suppressor utilizes rubber wipes instead of metal baffles; left-side thumb safety and grip safety; training suppressor available for additional $400
MSRP $2250.00

USWA1
Action: Semiautomatic
Grips: Polymer
Barrel: 4.33 in.
Sights: Aimpoint NANO
Weight: 40.8 oz.
Caliber: 9mm
Capacity: 17, 19, 30 rounds
Features: Swiss-made with unique design; interchangeable grip panels; Aimpoint NANO red dot sight; APL tac light; sling; cleaning kit; hard case; optional stock kit is available with all the attendant NFA paperwork and taxes
MSRP $2350.00

Cabot Guns

CABOT GUNS APOCALYPSE

APOCALYPSE
Action: Semiautomatic
Grips: G10
Barrel: 4.25 in., 5 in.
Sights: Tritium front, ledge rear
Weight: N/A
Caliber: 9mm, .45 ACP
Capacity: 9, 8 rounds
Features: Full-size Government or Commander barrel lengths; slide of Damascus stainless steel in a long tongue pattern, deep etched, VC heritage finish; 13-degree front and rear slide serrations; rhombus cut

frontstrap and mainspring housing checkering; one-piece extended magwell and mainspring housing; scalloped "idiot-proof" slide stop; one-piece full-length guide rod; integral rail; machined in place Perfect Fit ejector; aluminum tristar trigger; trigger in Tri Star, flat serrated, or ICON; optional accessory rail; barrel in either flush cut and crowned or threaded; optional Surefire X300 light
MSRP . . . . starting at $7995.00

Cabot Guns

CABOT GUNS GRAN TORINO SS

CABOT GUNS REBELLION

CABOT GUNS THE AMERICAN JOE COMMANDER

CABOT GUNS THE GENTLEMAN'S CARRY

CABOT GUNS THE ICON

CABOT GUNS THE NATIONAL STANDARD

GRAN TORINO SS

Action: Semiautomatic
Grips: Carbon fiber
Barrel: 5 in.
Sights: Reverse dovetail front, low-mount fixed rear
Weight: N/A
Caliber: 9mm, .45 ACP
Capacity: 8, 9 rounds
Features: Complete stainless steel construction; chatoyant carbon fiber grips with luminescent silver flakes and inlaid Cabot medallion; Racing Vector rear slide serrations; top slide serrations; hand-fit match grade barrel with custom crown; front of guide rod has engraved star; aluminum Cabot Tristar trigger; machined in place ejector; Rhombus-textured front strap and mainspring housing
MSRP . . . . starting at $4895.00

REBELLION

Action: Semiautomatic
Grips: G10, choice of wood
Barrel: 4.25 in.
Sights: Customer choice
Weight: N/A
Caliber: 9mm
Capacity: 9 rounds
Features: Aircraft-grade aluminum frame; speed-cut rails; match-grade bull barrel; front and rear slide serrations; carry cut; lowered ejection port; rhombus-cut checkering on frontstrap and mainspring housing; "idiot-proof" scratch-proof slide stop; standard or extended magwell; two-tone or black finish; trigger in Cabot flat, flat serrated, Cabot Tri Star, or ICON; right-hand or ambidextrous safety
MSRP . . . . starting at $4995.00

THE AMERICAN JOE COMMANDER

Action: Semiautomatic
Grips: Aluminum
Barrel: 4.25 in.
Sights: Cabot reverse dovetail white-dot front, low-mount fixed rear
Weight: 33.5 oz.
Caliber: .45 ACP
Capacity: 8 rounds
Features: The original American Joe now in Commander-length slide; "Tire Tread" USA engraving at front of slide; wing and spiderweb engraving designed by Joe Faris covering the rest of the slide; special flag grips
MSRP . . . . starting at $4895.00

THE GENTLEMAN'S CARRY

Action: Semiautomatic
Grips: Walnut
Barrel: 4.25 in.
Sights: Reverse dovetail tritium front, Warren-style U-notch tritium rear
Weight: N/A
Caliber: .45 ACP, 9mm
Capacity: 8 rounds
Features: Rhombus-cut checkering on the frontstrap and mainspring housing; bobtail cut frame; Carry Cut slide and slide serrations; hand-polished ramp' Cabot's Idiot Scratch-Proof slide star; aluminum trigger skeletonized with a tristar pattern; checkered walnut grips with inlaid Cabot medallion
MSRP . . . . starting at $5295.00

THE ICON

Action: Semiautomatic
Grips: Stainless steel
Barrel: 4.25 in., 5 in.
Sights: Reverse dovetail front, Cabot ACE fixed rear
Weight: N/A

Caliber: .45 ACP, 9mm
Capacity: 8 rounds
Features: Made from U.S. sourced stainless steel; choice of Government-length or Commander-length national match-grade barrels with reverse crowns; 24 lines-per-inch rhombus cut checkering on the mainspring housing and frontstrap; Cabot's beavertail safety grip; barrel bushing; mainspring housing with rhombus cuts; Idiot Scratch Proof takedown lever; full-length guide rod; stainless steel monochrome grips
MSRP . . . . starting at $4995.00

THE NATIONAL STANDARD

Action: Semiautomatic
Grips: G10, choice of wood
Barrel: 4.25 in., 5 in.
Sights: Customer choice
Weight: N/A
Caliber: 9mm, .45 ACP
Capacity: 9, 8 rounds
Features: Hand-polished satin slide flats; steel billet Cabot frame and slide; rhombus cut frontstrap and mainspring housing; machined in place Perfect Fit ejector; aluminum tristar trigger; flats in stainless matte, black diamond-like-carbon vapor deposition finish (with or w/o polished flats); rear sight in Cabot ledge, low-mount adjustable rear, fixed tritium, or low-mount adjustable tritium; front sight in white dot, gold bead, fiber optic, or tritium; magwell in standard or extended; trigger in Cabot Tri Star, flat serrated, or ICON; optional accessory rail; barrel in either flush cut and crowned or threaded; right hand or ambidextrous setup
MSRP . . . . starting at $4795.00

CABOT GUNS VINTAGE CLASSIC

VINTAGE CLASSIC

Action: Semiautomatic
Grips: Walnut
Barrel: 5 in.
Sights: Gold bead Cabot reverse dovetail front, low-mount fixed rear
Weight: N/A
Caliber: .45 ACP
Capacity: 8 rounds
Features: Cabot frame and slide from

416 stainless steel billet; proprietary hardening and vintage "classic" finish; Cabot Trinity Stripes rear slide serrations; beveled magazine well; lowered and flared ejection port; Cabot aluminum TriStar trigger; match-grade hand-fit barrel; rhombus-cut front strap and mainspring housing checkering; sight and grip options
MSRP . . . . starting at $4995.00

Canik USA

CANIK USA TP9 ELITE COMBAT

CANIK USA TP9 ELITE SC

CANIK USA TP9 ELITE SC, SC WITH SHIELD SMS2 OPTIC

CANIK USA TP9SFX

TP9 ELITE COMBAT

Action: Semiautomatic
Grips: Polymer
Barrel: 4.73 in.
Sights: Fiber optic front, drift adjustable rear
Weight: 25.8 oz.
Caliber: 9mm
Capacity: 15, 18 rounds
Features: A sleek-looking striker-fired Canik pistol with a fluted, match-grade threaded barrel; aluminum Speed Funnel magwell; flat-faced aluminum trigger; optics-ready slide with adapter plates; extended mag release; retention holster with slide lock release; changeable backstraps; textured grip; Cerakote slide in flat dark earth (Combat) or black nitride (Combat Executive)
Combat: $849.99

Combat Executive:. $779.99
Combat with Vortex Viper
red-dot: $949.00

TP9 ELITE SC

Action: Semiautomatic
Grips: Polymer
Barrel: 3.6 in.
Sights: Phosphorous white front, black-out rear
Weight: 24.78 oz.
Caliber: 9mm
Capacity: 12, 15 rounds
Features: A nicely designed carry gun with striker-status and loaded chamber indicators; nitride-coated match-grade barrel; reversible magazine release and slide stop; red-dot optic mounting interface; interchangeable backstraps; tungsten Cerakote finish overnitride finish on slide; accessory rail
MSRP $439.99

TP9 ELITE SC WITH SHIELD SMS2 OPTIC

Action: Semiautomatic
Grips: Synthetic
Barrel: 3.6 in.
Sights: Phosphorous white dot front, blackout rear
Weight: 24 oz.

Caliber: 9mm
Capacity: 12, 15 rounds
Features: Two interchangeable backstraps; micro red-dot interface with cowitness feature; reversible magazine release; under-barrel rail; match-grade barrel; tungsten Cerakote finish over a nitride slide; 12-round magazine has finger rest, 15-round magazine is extended; optional SMS Shield red-dot sight factory mounted
MSRP $699.99

TP9SFX

Action: SA
Grips: Plastic
Barrel: 5.2 in.
Sights: Industry-standard dovetail sight cuts & four red dot interface plates; removable red dot over
Weight: 29.92 oz.
Caliber: 9mm Luger
Capacity: 20+1 rounds
Features: Improved single action trigger with 3.5–4 lb. pull; lightening cuts on slide to reduce muzzle rise; reversible ambidextrous cocking lever; adjustable length reversible magazine catch; Picatinny rail; Tungsten grey Cerakote over phosphate
MSRP $549.99

Caracal USA

CARACAL USA
CAR816 A2

CARACAL USA
ENHANCED F

CAR816 A2
Action: Semiautomatic
Grips: Synthetic
Barrel: 11.5 in., 14.5 in., 16 in.
Sights: None
Weight: 6 lb. 15 oz.

Caliber: 5.56 NATO
Capacity: 10, 30 rounds
Features: Capitalizing on the AR pistol trend and featuring a short-stroke gas operated piston system; modified M4 barrel contour; black nitride finish; EDT Sharp Shooter trigger; SBA3 pistol brace; 9-inch key-lock M-LOK handguard; black or Flat Dark Earth
MSRP . . . .**$1849.99–$1929.00**

ENHANCED F
Action: Semiautomatic
Grips: Polymer
Barrel: 4 in.

Sights: Three-dot
Weight: 28 oz.
Caliber: 9mm
Capacity: 10, 18 rounds
Features: Striker-fired polymer frame; integrated trigger safety; firing pin safety; drop safety; rail interface for light and laser mounting; full-length steel slide guide; fully supported chamber; cold-hammer-forged barrel; Quick Sights, 3-dot night sights, and suppressor-height sights available
MSRP **$699.99**
Night Sights/Quick Sights: . .**$773.00**
Suppressor-Height 3-Dot: . .**$799.00**

Charles Daly

CHARLES DALY
1911 FIELD GRADE

CHARLES DALY
PAK-9

1911 FIELD GRADE
Action: Semiautomatic
Grips: Wood
Barrel: 5 in.
Sights: Blade front, notch rear
Weight: 38 oz.
Caliber: .45 ACP
Capacity: 8 rounds
Features: Standard Colt Government fare; matte blue finish; beavertail grip safety; diamond-pattern walnut grips
MSRP **$547.00**

PAK-9
Action: Semiautomatic
Grips: Synthetic

Barrel: 6.3 in.
Sights: Flip-up front, rear
Weight: 96 oz.
Caliber: 9mm
Capacity: 10, 30 rounds
Features: Pistol take on an AK-47 with a slim grip and integrated trigger guard; standard model takes Beretta magazines; interchangeable magazine adaptor upgrade allows for use of Glock magazines and comes with both a 10-round Beretta-style mag and a 30-round Glock-type magazine
Standard **$680.00**
With Glock mag adaptor . . .**$710.00**

Charter Arms

CHARTER ARMS BOOMER

CHARTER ARMS
BULLDOG

BOOMER
Action: DAO revolver
Grips: Rubber
Barrel: 2 in. tapered
Sights: None
Weight: 20 oz.
Caliber: .44 Spl.
Capacity: 5 rounds
Features: Designed specifically for concealed carry; DAO hammer; full rubber combat grips; matte stainless finish; tapered barrel for reduced kick
MSRP **$438.20**

BULLDOG
Action: DA revolver
Grips: Rubber; Crimson Trace lasergrips
Barrel: 2.5 in., 3 in. or 5 in. in target model
Sights: Fixed, adjustable rear on

Target model
Weight: 21 oz.
Caliber: .44 Spl.
Capacity: 5 rounds
Features: A larger concealed carry revolver, with DA/SA exposed hammer; available configurations include: Blue Standard; Tiger; Classic with 3-in. barrel, no underlug, exposed crane, and full wood grips; black Nitride; On Duty semi-concealed hammer in all stainless; Stainless Standard; Stainless DAO with concealed hammer; matte stainless with Crimson Trace laser grips; and Target with ramp front sight and adjustable rear
MSRP . . . .**$425.60–$631.40**

CHARTER ARMS CHIC LADY DAO

CHARTER ARMS OFF DUTY

CHARTER ARMS MAG PUG

CHARTER ARMS ON DUTY

CHARTER ARMS PATHFINDER

CHARTER ARMS PITBULL

CHARTER ARMS PITBULL 9MM BLACKNITRIDE

CHARTER ARMS PITBULL .40 S&W BLACKNITRIDE

CHIC LADY

Action: DA/SA, DAO revolver
Grips: Rubber
Barrel: 2 in.
Sights: Fixed
Weight: 12 oz.
Caliber: .38 Spl.
Capacity: 5 rounds
Features: High-polish stainless-steel pink anodized aluminum frame; frame based on Undercover Lite models; DA/SA exposed hammer version also available with Crimson Trace laser grips
MSRP . . . . $441.00–$684.60

MAG PUG

Action: DA revolver
Grips: Rubber; Crimson Trace lasergrips
Barrel: 2.2 in., 4.2 in.
Sights: Fixed, adjustable rear on Target model
Weight: 23 oz.
Caliber: .357 Mag.
Capacity: 5 rounds
Features: Traditional spurred hammer and full-size grips; optional Crimson Trace grip; stainless steel frame; blued and stainless finish
MSRP . . . . $408.80–$600.60

OFF DUTY

Action: DA revolver
Grips: Crimson Trace lasergrip
Barrel: 2 in.
Sights: Serrated front, rear notch
Weight: 12 oz.
Caliber: .38 Spl. +P
Capacity: 5 rounds
Features: Lightweight, concealed hammer DAO concealed carry revolver of aircraft-grade aluminum and stainless steel; finishes include: black frame/high-polished stainless barrel and cylinder; black frame/matte stainless barrel and cylinder; matte aluminum frame/matte gray barrel and cylinder
MSRP . . . . $420.00–$452.20

ON DUTY

Action: DA revolver
Grips: Rubber; Crimson Trace lasergrips
Barrel: 2 in.
Sights: Fixed
Weight: 12 oz.
Caliber: .357 Mag., .38 Spl. +P
Capacity: 5 rounds
Features: Unique semi-concealed hammer design; constructed of heat-treated aluminum; allows single-action and double-action operations while minimizing the risk of snagging the hammer on clothing; standard or Crimson Trace grip
MSRP $418.60

PATHFINDER

Action: DA revolver
Grips: Rubber; Crimson Trace lasergrips
Barrel: 2 in., 4.2 in.
Sights: Fixed, adjustable rear on Target model
Weight: 12 oz.–24 oz.
Caliber: .22 LR, .22 Mag.
Capacity: 6 rounds
Features: Choice of stainless steel or aluminum frames, has exposed hammer for DA/SA operation; aluminum frame Lite models in .22 Mag only available in brushed silver frame with matte blue barrel and cylinder; pink frame with matte silver cylinder and barrel; lavender frame with matte silver barrel and cylinder; and matte black frame with matte stainless barrel and cylinder; steel frame models are in .22 LR and .22

WMR, with choice of barrel lengths, all in all stainless
MSRP . . . . $378.00–$429.80

PITBULL

Action: DA/SA
Grips: Rubber
Barrel: 2.5 in.
Sights: Fixed
Weight: 22 oz.
Caliber: .40 S&W, 9mm,.45 ACP
Capacity: 5 rounds
Features: Unique design provides a dual coil spring assembly located in the extractor which allows for the insertion and retention of rimless cartridges, so no moon clips are required
MSRP . . . . $506.80–$527.80

PITBULL 9MM BLACKNITRIDE

Action: DA/SA revolver
Grips: Rubber
Barrel: 2.2 in.
Sights: Fixed
Weight: 22 oz.
Caliber: 9mm
Capacity: 5 rounds
Features: Rimless cartridge extractor assembly system; dual coil spring assembly located in the extractor; nitride adds hardness to the finish and reduces friction and wear; scratch-resistant surface; extended life in the rifling and chambers
MSRP $522.00

PITBULL .40 S&W BLACKNITRIDE

Action: DA/SA revolver
Grips: Rubber
Barrel: 2.3 in.
Sights: Fixed
Weight: 20 oz.
Caliber: .40 caliber
Capacity: 5 rounds
Features: Dual coil spring assembly located in the extractor; nitride adds hardness to the finish and reduces friction and wear; scratch-resistant surface; extended life in the rifling and chambers
MSRP $527.80

Charter Arms

CHARTER ARMS PITBULL .45 ACP BLACKNITRIDE

CHARTER ARMS .38 UNDERCOVER

CHARTER ARMS PROFESSIONAL BLACKNITRIDE

CHARTER ARMS UNDERCOVER BLACKNITRIDE

CHARTER ARMS UNDERCOVER LITE

PITBULL .45 ACP BLACKNITRIDE

Action: DA/SA revolver
Grips: Rubber
Barrel: 2.5 in.
Sights: Fixed
Weight: 22 oz.
Caliber: .45 ACP
Capacity: 5 rounds
Features: Rimless cartridge extractor assembly system; dual coil spring assembly located in the extractor; nitride adds hardness to the finish and reduces friction and wear; scratch-resistant surface
MSRP $527.80

PROFESSIONAL BLACKNITRIDE

Action: Revolver
Grips: Walnut
Barrel: 3 in.

Sights: Fiber optic front
Weight: N/A
Caliber: .32 H&R Mag.
Capacity: 7 rounds
Features: This undervalued round finds a home in a carry-ready revolver that has a full underlug; handsome black nitride finish
MSRP $438.00

UNDERCOVER

Action: DA revolver
Grips: Checkered compact rubber or Crimson Trace lasergrips
Barrel: 2 in.
Sights: Fixed
Weight: 16 oz.
Caliber: .38 Spl. +P
Capacity: 5 rounds
Features: Stainless steel frame; blued, stainless, tiger & black, DAO available; compact and lightweight, this revolver is ideal for concealed carry situations; 3-point cylinder lock-up
MSRP . . . . $358.40–$565.60

UNDERCOVER BLACKNITRIDE

Action: DA/SA revolver

Grips: Rubber
Barrel: 2 in.
Sights: Fixed
Weight: 16 oz.
Caliber: .38 Spl.
Capacity: 5 rounds
Features: Compact and lightweight; ideal for concealed carry due to 2 in. barrel and superior safety features; nitride adds hardness to the finish and reduces friction and wear; scratch-resistant surface
MSRP $533.40

UNDERCOVER LITE

Action: DA revolver
Grips: Rubber, compact
Barrel: 2 in.
Sights: Fixed
Weight: 12 oz.
Caliber: .38 Spl. +P
Capacity: 5 rounds
Features: Frame is constructed from aircraft-grade aluminum and steel; traditional spurred hammer; optional DAO (double action trigger); many finishes and special editions available
MSRP . . . . $357.00–$481.38

Chiappa Firearms

CHIAPPA FIREARMS 1873 REVOLVER S.A.A. REGULATOR CENTERFIRE

CHIAPPA FIREARMS CBR-9 BLACK RHINO PISTOL WITH ARM BRACE

CHIAPPA FIREARMS CHARGING RHINO GEN II 60DS

1873 REVOLVER S.A.A. REGULATOR CENTERFIRE

Action: SA revolver
Grips: Black polymer
Barrel: 4.75 in.
Sights: Fixed front
Weight: 32 oz.
Caliber: .45 LC, .38 Spec.
Capacity: 6 rounds
Features: Centerfire cartridge; perfect for competition or plinking
MSRP $443.00

CBR-9 BLACK RHINO PISTOL WITH ARM BRACE

Action: Semiautomatic
Grips: Polymer
Barrel: 9 in.
Sights: Flip-up fiber optic front and rear
Weight: 76.8 oz.
Caliber: 9mm
Capacity: 18 rounds
Features: Designed as a personal defense weapon, but it's also likely a ball on the range with its arm brace
MSRP $2269.00

CHARGING RHINO GEN II 60DS

Action: Revolver
Grips: Laminate
Barrel: 6 in.
Sights: Fiber optic front, adjustable rear
Weight: 32 oz.
Caliber: 9mm
Capacity: 6 rounds
Features: The Gen II is a DAO revolver with gray laminate grips with textured blue side inserts; Cerakote slate finish; comes with 10 moon clips; hammer spring and trigger return springs are separated for individual tuning; top-side and under-barrel rails; California-compliant version available
MSRP $1691.00

CHIAPPA FIREARMS FAS 6007

CHIAPPA FIREARMS RHINO 30 DS HUNTER, 60 DS HUNTER

CHIAPPA FIREARMS RHINO REVOLVER 30DS X SPECIAL EDITION

CHIAPPA FIREARMS RHINO 200DS REVOLVER

CHIAPPA FIREARMS RHINO REVOLVER MATCH MASTER

CHIAPPA FIREARMS RHINO NEBULA

FAS 6007

Action: Semiautomatic
Grips: Wood
Barrel: 5.63 in.
Sights: Two-position front, adjustable rear
Weight: 37.6 oz.
Caliber: .22 LR
Capacity: 5 rounds
Features: Developed in collaboration with Olympic shooters; adjustable palm rest; a rear sight with an adjustable window; adjustable grip; outside access set screws for hammer and hammer weight; modular weights; adjustable trigger; shock buffer
MSRP **$1630.00**

RHINO 30 DS HUNTER, 60 DS HUNTER

Action: Revolver
Grips: Walnut
Barrel: 3 in., 6 in.
Sights: Fiber optic front, adjustable rear
Weight: 28.8 oz.–32 oz.
Caliber: .357 Mag.
Capacity: 6 rounds
Features: Frame and barrel in "Hunter" OD Green Cerakote; barrels have vent ribs; stippled walnut grips with finger grooves; Rhino's distinct flat-sided

cylinder; long-barrel version has accessory rail; includes three moon clips
30 DS Hunter: **$1287.00**
60 DS Hunter: **$1437.00**

RHINO 30DS X SPECIAL EDITION

Action: Revolver
Grips: G10
Barrel: 3 in.
Sights: Fiber optic front, adjustable rear
Weight: 44.8 oz.
Caliber: .357 Mag.
Capacity: 6 rounds
Features: The unique Rhino revolver in a nifty 3-inch barrel with upgraded G10 grips; brushed stainless steel finish
MSRP **$1603.00**

RHINO 200DS

Action: Revolver
Grips: Wood
Barrel: 6 in.
Sights: Front blade; adjustable rear
Weight: 37 oz.
Caliber: .357, .40 S&W, .357 Mag/9mm combo
Capacity: 6 rounds
Features: Rhino barrel is aligned with the bottom most chamber, which lowers the center of gravity and yields a

centerline of the bore more in line with the shooter's arm allowing for the most natural "point ability" while engaging a target; reduces both recoil and muzzle flip which insures subsequent shots are on target faster; frame available in chrome, black, or gold finish
MSRP . . . . **$1127.00–$1316.00**

RHINO MATCH MASTER

Action: Revolver
Grips: Micarta
Barrel: 6 in.
Sights: Aristocrat front, adjustable rear
Weight: 46.6 oz.
Caliber: .38 Spec.
Capacity: 6 rounds
Features: Unique bottom-cylinder barrel alignment; Hogue Micarta grips; Ergal frame; steel barrel and breech shield; cylinder block, cylinder rotation, and hammer block safeties
MSRP **$3116.00**

RHINO NEBULA

Action: Revolver
Grips: Laminate
Barrel: 6 in.
Sights: Fiber optic front and rear
Weight: 33.6 oz.
Caliber: .357 Mag.
Capacity: 6 rounds
Features: The unique bottom chamber/barre alignment that is the Rhino now in a snazzy, mixed-color PVD metal finish and otherworldly blue laminate grips; top and bottom rails, fiber optics front and back with an adjustable rear; three moon clips provided; DA/SA or SA-only option
MSRP . . . . **$1509.00–$1725.00**

Christensen Arms

CHRISTENSEN ARMS CA9MM PISTOL

CA9MM

Action: Semiautomatic
Grips: Synthetic
Barrel: 7.5 in., 10 in.

Sights: None
Weight: 88 oz.
Caliber: 9mm
Capacity: 10, 15, 17 rounds
Features: 7075 forged aluminum upper and lower; nitride finished 416R stainless steel barrel carbon-fiber wrapped, button rifled, and ½x28 threaded; three-prong flash hider;

6.25- or 9.25-in. handguard M-LOK compatible, full aluminum rail, and with two quick detach mounts; SBA3 pistol brace; flared magwell; Gen4 Glock magazine compatible
Black Anodized **$1699.99**
Cerakote **$1749.99**

Cimarron Firearms Co.

CIMARRON 1872 OPEN TOP NAVY

CIMARRON 1911

CIMARRON 1911 WILD BUNCH COMBO

CIMARRON FIREARMS ANGEL EYES

CIMARRON FIREARMS BAD BOY

CIMARRON FIREARMS EL MALO 2

CIMARRON FIREARMS EVIL ROY COMPETITION

CIMARRON FRONTIER

CIMARRON HOLY SMOKER

1872 OPEN TOP NAVY

Action: SA revolver
Grips: Walnut
Barrel: 4.75, 5.5, 7.5 in.
Sights: Fixed, open
Weight: 40 oz.
Caliber: .44 Spl.; .44 Colt, .44 Russian
Capacity: 6 rounds
Features: Forged, color case-hardened frame; Army or Navy grip; charcoal blued, standard blued, or original barrel finish
MSRP..................$598.78

1911

Action: Semiautomatic
Grips: Walnut
Barrel: 5 in.
Sights: Open, fixed
Weight: 39.52 oz.
Caliber: .45 ACP
Capacity: 8+1 rounds
Features: Correct historical markings; diamond checkered walnut grips; nickel, polished blued, and parkerized finish; optional WWI-style lanyard magazine
MSRP...........$608.83–$895.05

1911 WILD BUNCH COMBO

Action: Semiautomatic
Grips: Diamond checkered walnut
Barrel: 5 in.
Sights: Fixed
Weight: 39.52 oz.
Caliber: .45 ACP
Capacity: 8+1 rounds
Features: Correct historical markings; the original 1911 frame with a Type 1 smooth mainspring housing; combo includes the 1911 in polished blue finish and the Tanker shoulder holster, a reproduction of the rig used by William Holden in the movie The Wild Bunch
MSRP..................$1192.07

ANGEL EYES

Action: Revolver
Grips: Wood
Barrel: 8 in.
Sights: Blade front, integral rear
Weight: N/A
Caliber: .45 LC
Capacity: 6 rounds
Features: Part of the Hollywood The Good, the Bad, and the Ugly series, this revolver is named after that movie's Angel Eyes character, played by Lee Van Cleef, and this gun replicates the one that character carried in the movie; 1858 Remington-style, single-action; cold case-hardened barrel with a brass trigger guard and grip frame; smooth wood grip; "Angel Eyes" engraving on the frame
MSRP..................$662.84

BAD BOY

Action: Revolver
Grips: Wood
Barrel: 6 in., 8 in.
Sights: Ramp front, adjustable rear
Weight: N/A
Caliber: .44 Mag., 10mm Auto
Capacity: 6 rounds
Features: Model P pre-war frame single action; octagonal barrel; flat top; adjustable rear sight
MSRP..................$790.28

EL MALO 2

Action: Revolver
Grips: Walnut
Barrel: 3.5, 5.5 in.
Sights: Iron front
Weight: N/A
Caliber: .357 Mag., .45 LC
Capacity: 6 rounds
Features: El Malo is Spanish for "The Bad" and this revolver is based on the 1873 Colt Single Action Army; octagon barrel; case-colored pre-war frame; low and wide competition hammer; one-piece walnut grip; .357 has 5.5-in. barrel, .45 LC has 3.5-in. barrel
.357 Mag................$700.94
.45 LC...................$620.80

EVIL ROY COMPETITION

Action: Revolver
Grips: Walnut
Barrel: 4.75 in., 5.5 in.
Sights: Blade front, integral rear
Weight: 38 oz.–40.1 oz.
Caliber: .357 Mag., .44-40, .45 LC
Capacity: 6 rounds
Features: Competition-ready single-action with a tuned action; square notch rear sight paired with a wide front blade; slim walnut grip; some models available with a low, wide hammer
Blued...................$896.44
Stainless...............$1072.61

FRONTIER

Action: SA
Grips: Walnut
Barrel: 3.5 in., 4.75 in., 5.5 in., 7.5 in.
Sights: Fixed
Weight: 4 lb. 8 oz.
Caliber: .45 Colt
Capacity: N/A
Features: High-polished stainless finish; walnut grips; pre-war frame
MSRP..................$843.81

HOLY SMOKER

Action: SA revolver
Grips: Walnut
Barrel: 4.75 in.
Sights: Open, fixed
Weight: 36 oz.
Caliber: .45 Colt
Capacity: 6 rounds
Features: Revolver made famous in *3:10 to Yuma* film; standard blued finish; case-hardened pre-war frame; gold-plated sterling silver cross inlayed on both sides of one-piece walnut grip
MSRP..................$834.60

Cimarron Firearms Co.

CIMARRON MAN WITH NO NAME

CIMARRON FIREARMS MODEL 3 1ST MODEL AMERICAN

CIMARRON MODEL P JR

CIMARRON FIREARMS PISTOLEER

CIMARRON FIREARMS PLINKERTON

CIMARRON FIREARMS THE BLUE AND THE GRAY SERIES 1851 RICHARDS-MASON

CIMARRON FIREARMS THE BLUE AND THE GRAY SERIES LEECH & RIGDON

CIMARRON THUNDERER

MAN WITH NO NAME

Action: SA revolver
Grips: Walnut
Barrel: 4.75 in., 5.5 in.
Sights: Open, fixed
Weight: 42.56 oz.–44.16 oz.
Caliber: .45 Colt
Capacity: 6 rounds
Features: Model P in .45 Colt; sterling silver snake on both sides of walnut grip
MSRP **$849.81**

MODEL 3 1ST MODEL AMERICAN

Action: Revolver
Grips: Wood
Barrel: 5, 8 in.
Sights: Blade front, integral rear
Weight: 49 oz.
Caliber: .45 LC, .44 Colt, .44 WCF
Capacity: 6 rounds
Features: A break-barrel replica of the original S&W model; single-action; smooth walnut grips; all-over blued finish
MSRP **$1312.58**

MODEL P JR.

Action: SA revolver
Grips: Walnut
Barrel: 3.5 in., 4.75 in., 5.5 in.
Sights: Fixed, open
Weight: 35.2 oz.
Caliber: .38 Spl., .22 LR, .32-20 Win./.32 H&R Dual Cylinder
Capacity: 6 rounds
Features: Fashioned after the 1873 Colt SAA but on a smaller scale; color case-hardened frame
MSRP . . . . **$519.63–$719.74**

PISTOLEER

Action: Revolver
Grips: Wood
Barrel: 4.75 in.
Sights: Blade front, integral rear
Weight: 40 oz.
Caliber: .45 LC, .357 Mag.
Capacity: 6 rounds
Features: Traditionally styled single-action; smooth walnut grips; steel frame; blued frame, cylinder, and barrel; stainless or nickel-plated backstrap and trigger guard; designed by Cimarron founder and CEO Mike Harvey, made by Uberti
MSRP **$574.00**

PLINKERTON

Action: Revolver
Grips: Plastic
Barrel: 4.75 in.
Sights: Blade front, integral rear
Weight: 34 oz.
Caliber: .22 LR/.22 Mag.
Capacity: 6 rounds
Features: Dual-cylinder single-action in all-over matte black finish; black plastic grips are checkered and have gold Cimarron medallion inset; manufactured by Chiappa
MSRP **$218.01**

THE BLUE AND THE GRAY SERIES 1851 RICHARDS-MASON

Action: Cartridge conversion SAO
Grips: Walnut
Barrel: 7.5 in.
Sights: Post front
Weight: 45.2 oz.
Caliber: .38 Spec.
Capacity: 6 rounds
Features: Limited-edition run faithful to the original and featuring a lightly engraved unfluted cylinder; case-hardened frame with brass accents; pure silver CSA flag inlay in one-piece wooden grips
MSRP **$637.73**

THE BLUE AND THE GRAY SERIES LEECH & RIGDON

Action: Cartridge conversion SAO
Grips: Walnut
Barrel: 7.5 in.
Sights: Post front
Weight: 42.8 oz.
Caliber: .36
Capacity: 6 rounds
Features: Limited-edition run faithful to the original and featuring a charcoal blue unfluted cylinder and barrel; case-hardened frame with brass accents; pure silver CSA flag inlay in one-piece wooden grips
MSRP **$740.31**

THUNDERER

Action: SA revolver
Grips: Walnut, ivory, mother of pearl or black hard rubber
Barrel: 3.5 in. w/ ejector, 4.75 in., 5.5 in., 7.5 in.
Sights: Fixed, open
Weight: 38–43.60 oz.
Caliber: .45 LC, .44 Spl., .44 WCF, .357 Mag., .45 LC/.45 ACP Dual Cylinder
Capacity: 6 rounds
Features: Designed in 1990 by Cimarron founder & president "Texas Jack" Harvey; forged, stainless finish
Blued . . . . **$654.77–$669.27**
Stainless **$863.57**
Dual .45 ACP/.45 LC **$778.26**

Cimarron Firearms Co.

CIMARRON THUNDERSTORM

CIMARRON U.S.V. ARTILLERY

CIMARRON WYATT EARP FRONTIER BUNTLINE

THUNDERSTORM

Action: SA revolver
Grips: Walnut
Barrel: 3.5 in., 4.75 in.
Sights: Front, rear
Weight: 35.7 oz.–39.68 oz.
Caliber: .45 Colt, .357 Mag./.38 Spl.
Capacity: 6 rounds
Features: Checkered grips; stainless steel or standard blued finishes; wide front sights and deep rear notch; smooth action and hand-knurled hammer
Blued $920.14
Stainless . . . . $975.00–$1091.71

TUCO

Action: Revolver
Grips: Wood
Barrel: 7.5 in.
Sights: Blade front, integral rear
Weight: N/A
Caliber: .45 LC

Capacity: 6 rounds
Features: Part of the Hollywood The Good, the Bad, and the Ugly series, this revolver is named after that movie's Tuco character, played by Eli Wallach, and this gun replicates the one that character created in the movie from various parts; this is a conversion revolver with a leech and Rigdon-style barrel and loading lever; color case-hardened blue; smooth wood grips; lanyard ring
MSRP $651.69

U.S.V. ARTILLERY

Action: SA revolver
Grips: Walnut
Barrel: 5.5 in.
Sights: Fixed, open
Weight: 40 oz.
Caliber: .45 LC
Capacity: 6 rounds
Features: Old model case-hardened with US Artillery markings; stock is a solid piece of walnut with RAC Cartouche; blued, charcoal blued, or original finish
MSRP . . . . $697.34–$814.91

WYATT EARP FRONTIER BUNTLINE

Action: SA revolver
Grips: Walnut
Barrel: 10 in.
Sights: Open, fixed
Weight: 43.04 oz.
Caliber: .45 LC
Capacity: 6 rounds
Features: Revolver made famous in the film *Tombstone*; one-piece walnut grips with silver inlaid medallion; case-hardened frame with blue barrel and cylinder
MSRP $1005.63

Citadel by Legacy Sports

M-1911

Action: Semiautomatic
Grips: Cocobolo
Barrel: 3.5 in., 5 in.
Sights: Fixed
Weight: 33.6–37.6 oz.
Caliber: 9mm, .45 ACP
Capacity: 7 or 8 rounds
Features: Choice of Government or Officer models with a Series 70 firing system; extended slide stop, skeletonized hammer and trigger, matte blue finish; includes two magazines
MSRP $819.00

M1911 GOVERNMENT AMERICAN FLAG

Action: Semiautomatic
Grips: Wood
Barrel: 5 in.
Sights: Blade front, drift-adjustable rear
Weight: 36.8 oz.–38.8 oz.
Caliber: 9mm, .45 ACP
Capacity: 8, 10 rounds
Features: Citadel's 1911 Government wrapped in eye-catching red-white-and-blue or Grayscale American flag graphics; skeletonized trigger and hammer, extended beavertail grip safety; full-length guide rod; ambidextrous safety
MSRP $1209.00

CITADEL M-1911 PISTOLS

CITADEL M1911 GOVERNMENT AMERICAN FLAG

Colt's Manufacturing Company

COLT COBRA   COLT COMBAT UNIT RAIL GUN   COLT COMPETITION PISTOL   COLT CUSTOM COMPETITION PISTOL

COLT DEFENDER   COLT COMPETITION SS   COLT GOLD CUP   COLT KING COBRA

COBRA

Action: Revolver
Grips: Rubber
Barrel: 2 in.
Sights: Fiber optic front
Weight: 25 oz.
Caliber: .38 Spl.
Capacity: 6 rounds
Features: DA revolver with all-steel contruction; small frame and barrel ideal for concealed carry; Hogue Overmolded grip has been moved rearward to manage recoil on standard model; Classic version has medallion wood grips, brass front bead, and polished cylinder

Cobra:	$699.00
Classic Cobra:	$749.00
Night Cobra:	$899.00
Bright Cobra:	$1299.00
Cobra TT:	$749.00

COMBAT UNIT RAIL GUN

Action: Semiautomatic
Grips: G10
Barrel: 5 in.
Sights: Novak night sight front, Novak Low Mount Carry rear
Weight: 40 oz.
Caliber: 9mm, .45 ACP
Capacity: 8 rounds (.45 ACP), 9 rounds (9mm)
Features: Upgraded duty-ready 1911 with 1913 Picatinny rail; checkered and scalloped gray G10 grips; designed with Special Forces trainers Daryl Holland and Ken Hackathorn

MSRP **$1599.00**

COMPETITION PISTOL

Action: SA
Grips: G10 grips
Barrel: 5 in.
Sights: Fiber optic front, Novak adjustable rear
Weight: 36 oz.
Caliber: .38 Super, .45 ACP, 9mm
Capacity: 8 or 9 rounds
Features: Dual spring recoil system; undercut trigger guard; upswept beavertail grip safety; National Match barrel

Standard:	$899.00
SS 9mm, .45 ACP:	$999.00
SS .38 Super:	$1049.00
Titanium:	$999.00
Competition Plus:	$1199.00

CUSTOM COMPETITION PISTOL

Action: Semiautomatic
Grips: G10
Barrel: 5 in.
Sights: Novak fiber optic front, Bomar-style rear
Weight: N/A
Caliber: .45 ACP
Capacity: 8 rounds
Features: Hand-assembled by Colt's Custom Shop gunsmiths; blended magwell; frontstrap checkering; stainless steel slide and frame; wide slide serrations front and rear

MSRP **$2299.00**

DEFENDER

Action: Semiautomatic
Grips: Rubber finger-grooved
Barrel: 5 in.
Sights: White dot carry front and rear
Weight: 30 oz.
Caliber: .45 ACP, 9mm
Capacity: 7+1 rounds, 8+1 rounds
Features: Beveled magazine well; black skeletonized aluminum trigger; Series 80 firing system; beavertail grip and standard thumb safety; stainless steel slide, Teflon coated receiver; aluminum alloy frame

MSRP **$999.00**

GOLD CUP

Action: Semiautomatic
Grips: Black composite
Barrel: 5 in.
Sights: Dovetail front, adjustable rear
Weight: 39 oz.
Caliber: 9mm, .38 Super, .45 ACP
Capacity: 8+1 rounds
Features: Beveled magazine well; beavertail grip safety; Colt competition blue G10 grips; wide aluminum 3-Hole trigger adjustable for over travel; stainless steel frame finish and material; enhanced hammer. National Match version appears in blue and adds target sights, National Match barrel, wood grips with inset gold Colt medallion

Gold Cup:	$1199.00–$1249.00
Trophy:	$1699.00–$1749.00
National Match:	$1299.00

KING COBRA

Action: Revolver
Grips: Hogue
Barrel: 3 in.
Sights: Brass bead front, groove rear
Weight: 28 oz.
Caliber: .357 Mag.
Capacity: 6 rounds
Features: Colt continues reintroductions of long-discontinued classics with the King Cobra .357 Mag.; a brushed stainless finish; Hogue overmolded grips; user-replaceable front sight; Linear Leaf (LL2) trigger; heavy frame; full lug

MSRP **$899.00**

Colt's Manufacturing Company

COLT LIGHTWEIGHT COMMANDER

COLT PYTHON

COLT SINGLE ACTION ARMY

LIGHTWEIGHT COMMANDER
Action: SA
Grips: G10 grips
Barrel: 4.25 in.
Sights: Novak sights
Weight: 29.4 oz.
Caliber: .45 ACP, 9mm
Capacity: 8 or 9 rounds
Features: Shorter profile and lower weight than a traditional full-size Government model; dual spring recoil system; undercut trigger guard; upswept beavertail grip safety
MSRP $999.00

PYTHON
Action: Revolver
Grips: Walnut
Barrel: 4.25 in., 6 in.
Sights: Orange insert ramp front, adjustable rear
Weight: 46 oz.
Caliber: .357 Mag.
Capacity: 6 rounds
Features: An oldie but a goodie returns to the fold with checkered target-style walnut grips; polished steel finish; redesigned guts have twelve fewer parts than original Python; metal under the rear sight has been made sturdier with 30% more steel
MSRP $1499.00

SINGLE ACTION ARMY
Action: SA revolver
Grips: Black composite eagle
Barrel: 4.75 in., 5.5 in., 7.5 in.
Sights: Fixed
Weight: 46 oz.
Caliber: .357 Mag., .45 Colt
Capacity: 6 rounds
Features: Case-colored frame; transfer bar; second generation style cylinder bushing; blued or nickel finish
MSRP $1799.00

Culper Precision

CULPER PRECISION ATOMIC 6

ATOMIC 6
Action: Semiautomatic
Grips: Polymer
Barrel: 4 in.
Sights: Trijicon night sights
Weight: 16.4 oz.
Caliber: 9mm
Capacity: 15 rounds
Features: CO-cured carbon fiber and steel slide based on the Glock Gen4 foundation; threaded or non-threaded, match-grade, DLC-coated barrel with box fluted target crown; custom SoftShoot recoil management system; installed Zev Pro upper parts kit; set of three grip sizing panels; enhanced trigger guard; Apex trigger
MSRP . . . . $2499.00–$3035.00

CZ-USA (Ceska Zbrojovka)

CZ-USA 75 B

CZ–USA 75 B Ω CONVERTIBLE

CZ-USA 75 COMPACT

75 B
Action: Semiautomatic
Grips: Plastic
Barrel: 4.6 in.
Sights: Fixed, 3-dot system
Weight: 35.2 oz.
Caliber: 9mm
Capacity: 10, 16 rounds
Features: Steel frame; high-capacity double column magazines; hammer forged barrels; ergonomic grip and controls; DA/SA; firing pin block safety; black polycoat finish
MSRP $745.00

75 B Ω CONVERTIBLE
Action: Semiautomatic
Grips: Plastic
Barrel: 4.6 in.
Sights: Fixed
Weight: 35.2 oz.
Caliber: 9mm Luger
Capacity: 10, 16 rounds
Features: Swappable safety/decocker; interlocking trigger design for easy disassembly and reassembly without tools
MSRP $745.00

75 COMPACT
Action: Semiautomatic
Grips: Plastic
Barrel: 3.8 in.
Sights: Fixed, 3-dot system
Weight: 32.48 oz.
Caliber: 9mm Luger
Capacity: 10, 14 rounds
Features: Black polycoat, dual tone, satin nickel frame finishes; manual safety; steel frame; high capacity double column magazines; hammer forged barrels
MSRP $779.00

CZ-USA (Ceska Zbrojovka)

CZ–USA 75 P-01 Ω CONVERTIBLE

CZ-USA 75 SP-01

CZ–USA 75 TACTICAL SPORT ORANGE

CZ-USA 75 TS CZECHMATE

CZ–USA ACCUSHADOW 2

CZ–USA BREN 2 MS

CZ-USA P-01

CZ–USA P-07

CZ–USA P-07 OD GREEN

75 P-01 Ω CONVERTIBLE

Action: Semiautomatic
Grips: Rubber
Barrel: 3.8 in.
Sights: Fixed
Weight: 28 oz.
Caliber: 9mm Luger
Capacity: 10, 14 rounds
Features: Swappable safety/decocker; interlocking trigger design for easy disassembly and reassembly without tools; compact size and reduced weight ideal for discrete carry
MSRP . . . . $779.00–$799.00

75 SP-01

Action: Semiautomatic
Grips: Rubber
Barrel: 4.6 in.
Sights: 3-Dot tritium night
Weight: 38.4 oz.
Caliber: 9mm Luger
Capacity: 10, 18 rounds
Features: Based upon the Shadow Target; decocking lever; safety stop on hammer; firing pin safety; steel frame
MSRP $899.00

75 TACTICAL SPORT ORANGE

Action: Semiautomatic
Grips: Thin aluminum
Barrel: 5.4 in.
Sights: Adjustable
Weight: 48 oz.
Caliber: 9mm Luger; .40 S&W
Capacity: 10, 16, 20 rounds
Features: Ambidextrous manual safety; slimmer trigger guard; improved grip geometry; thumb stop; long slide; full-length dust cover; light pull and short reset
MSRP $1955.00

75 TS CZECHMATE

Action: Semiautomatic
Grips: Aluminum
Barrel: 5.4 in.
Sights: Fixed, C-more red dot
Weight: 48 oz.
Caliber: 9mm
Capacity: 20, 26 rounds
Features: Built upon a modified version of the CZ 75 TS frame; features a single-action trigger mechanism; red-dot sight; includes spare barrel; includes three 20-round magazines and one 26-round magazine; all-steel pistol is finished in black matte
MSRP $3669.00

ACCUSHADOW 2

Action: Semiautomatic
Grips: Polymer
Barrel: 4.89 in.
Sights: Fiber optic front, HAJO rear
Weight: 46.5 oz.
Caliber: 9mm
Capacity: 17 rounds
Features: Steel frame; new quarter-turn bushing; short-reset trigger; hand-fit disconnector; custom hammer; safety is ambidextrous
MSRP $2405.00

BREN 2 MS

Action: Semiautomatic
Grips: Synthetic
Barrel: 8 in., 9 in., 11 in., 14 in.
Sights: Folding adjustable
Weight: 5 lb. 6 oz.–5 lb. 14 oz.
Caliber: 5.56X45mm, 7.62X39mm
Capacity: 30 rounds
Features: Totally redesigned Bren replacing the 805 version. Features include trimmed aluminum receiver; carbon fiber-reinforced lower; forward-positioned swappable charging handle; AR-style bolt catch/release system; swappable barrels; designed for add-on buffer tube installation
MSRP $2085.00

P-01

Action: Semiautomatic
Grips: Rubber
Barrel: 3.8 in.
Sights: Fixed
Weight: 28.8 oz.
Caliber: 9mm Luger
Capacity: 10, 14 rounds
Features: Decocking lever; safety stop on hammer; firing pin safety; black polycoat frame finish; black or pink grips; single- or double-action
MSRP $779.00

P-07

Action: Semiautomatic
Grips: Synthetic
Barrel: 3.8 in.
Sights: Fixed
Weight: 27 oz.
Caliber: 9mm
Capacity: 10, 15 rounds
Features: Ambidextrous safety or decocker; firing pin block
MSRP $585.00

P-07 OD GREEN

Action: Semiautomatic
Grips: Polymer
Barrel: 3.75 in.
Sights: Tritium night sights
Weight: 27.7 oz.
Caliber: 9mm
Capacity: 10, 15 rounds
Features: OD Green polymer frame; tritium nights sights; double-stack magazine
MSRP . . . . $559.00–$619.00

CZ-USA (Ceska Zbrojovka)

CZ-USA P-07 SUPPRESSOR-READY

CZ–USA P-09

CZ-USA P-09 OD GREEN

CZ-USA P-10 C

CZ-USA P-10 S FDE, OD GREEN

CZ–USA SCORPION EVO 3 S1 PISTOL

CZ-USA SHADOW 2 SA

CZ-USA SHADOW 2 BLACK & BLUE

P-07 SUPPRESSOR-READY

Action: Semiautomatic
Grips: Polymer
Barrel: 4.36 in.
Sights: High tritium thee-dot
Weight: 28.7 oz.
Caliber: 9mm
Capacity: 17 rounds
Features: Updated version of the CZ 75 P-07 Duty; interchangeable backstraps; nitrided finish on the slide; frame has been dehorned; interchangeable safety and decocker; muzzle is threaded ½×28 to accept suppressors
MSRP . . . . $559.00–$619.00

P-09

Action: Semiautomatic
Grips: Synthetic
Barrel: 4.53 in. or 5.23 in. (suppressor model)
Sights: Fixed
Weight: 30 oz.
Caliber: 9mm Luger
Capacity: 19 rounds
Features: Ambidextrous safety or decocker; firing pin block
MSRP $609.00

P-09 OD GREEN

Action: Semiautomatic
Grips: Polymer
Barrel: 4.54 in.
Sights: Tritium night sights
Weight: 31 oz.
Caliber: 9mm
Capacity: 10, 19 rounds
Features: OD Green polymer frame; night sights; ambidextrous decocker that can be converted to a manual safety; three backstrap sizes for a custom grip fit
MSRP . . . . $629.00–$659.00

P-10 C

Action: Semiautomatic
Grips: Polymer
Barrel: 4.02 in.
Sights: Metal three-dot
Weight: 26 oz.
Caliber: 9mm
Capacity: 10, 12 rounds
Features: Striker-fired pistol; ergonomically designed with a mild palm swell, deep beavertail, and three interchangeable backstraps; trigger engineered to break at 4–4.5 lb. with a short reset; fiber-reinforced polymer frame with nitride finish
MSRP . . . . $579.00–$605.00

P-10 S FDE, OD GREEN

Action: Semiautomatic
Grips: Polymer
Barrel: 3.5 in.
Sights: Fixed tritium night sights
Weight: 24.4 oz.
Caliber: 9mm
Capacity: 10, 12 rounds
Features: A lightweight striker-fire carry gun with a fiber-reinforced polymer frame; ambidextrous slide release; reversible magazine release; choice of flat dark earth or OD green frames, both with black slides; slide serrations fore and aft
MSRP . . . . $619.00–$649.00

SCORPION EVO 3 S1 PISTOL

Action: Semiautomatic
Grips: Polymer
Barrel: 7.72 in.
Sights: Low-profile fully adjustable aperture and post, 4 rear aperture sizes
Weight: 5 lb.
Caliber: 9mm Luger
Capacity: 10+1 rounds, 20+1 rounds
Features: Scorpion sub-gun, imported as a pistol; blowback-operated; 11-in. Picatinny rail; ambidextrous controls; non-reciprocating charging handle is swappable and reach to the trigger is adjustable; arm brace adapter adds an AR-style pistol buffer tube to the rear of the action; barrel threaded a 18x1 to accept the factory flash hider and also a ½x28 underneath flash hider for easy addition of suppressor or after market muzzle device
MSRP . . . . $1059.00–$1255.00

SHADOW 2 BLACK & BLUE, URBAN GREY

Action: Semiautomatic
Grips: Aluminum
Barrel: 4.89 in.
Sights: Fiber optic front, HAJO rear
Weight: 46.5 oz.
Caliber: 9mm
Capacity: 17 rounds
Features: Higher beavertail; undercut trigger guard; contoured slide; increased weight at the dust cover/rail helps keep muzzle down; steel frame with nitride finish; blue aluminum grips checkered to match front and backstraps; reversible mag release
Black & Blue $1359.00
Urban Grey $1455.00

SHADOW 2 SA

Action: Semiautomatic
Grips: Aluminum
Barrel: 4.89 in.
Sights: Fiber optic front, HAJO rear
Weight: 46.5 oz.
Caliber: 9mm
Capacity: 17 rounds
Features: A SAO target pistol with a steel frame; thin aluminum grips in sky blue; blue trigger; accessory rail; checkered front and backstraps
MSRP $1455.00

Dan Wesson Firearms

DAN WESSON BRUIN

CZ-USA ECP

DAN WESSON GUARDIAN

DAN WESSON KODIAK

DAN WESSON RAZORBACK RZ-10

DAN WESSON SPECIALIST

DAN WESSON TCP

DAN WESSON V-BOB, V-BOB TWO-TONE

BRUIN

Action: Semiautomatic
Grips: Synthetic
Barrel: 6.3 in.
Sights: Adjustable titrium with titrium/fiber optic front
Weight: 42.9 oz.
Caliber: 10mm Auto; .45 ACP
Capacity: 8 or 9 rounds
Features: Long slide for a long sight radius; 6.3 in. barrel allows full-power 10mm loads as much time as possible to use their powder charge; tritium/fiber optic combo front sight to make sure the front glows day or night
MSRP...................**$2235.00**

ECP

Action: Semiautomatic
Grips: G10
Barrel: 4 in.
Sights: Brass front, U-notch rear
Weight: 29 oz.
Caliber: 9mm, .45 ACP
Capacity: 9, 8 rounds
Features: Forged aluminum frame; duty finish; single-action; match-grade bull barrel; bobbed mainspring housing; tri-topped slide with aggressive serrations and top rib to reduce glare
9mm....................**$1705.00**
.45 ACP...............**$1739.00**

GUARDIAN

Action: Semiautomatic
Grips: Wood
Barrel: 4.25 in.
Sights: Fixed
Weight: 29 oz.
Caliber: 9mm Luger, .38 Super, .45 ACP
Capacity: 8 (.45 ACP) or 9 rounds
Features: Ambidextrous thumb safety; grip safety; fixed night sights
MSRP........ **$1586.00–$1649.00**

KODIAK

Action: Semiautomatic

Grips: G10
Barrel: 6.03 in.
Sights: Fiber optic front, adjustable rear
Weight: 47.1 oz.
Caliber: 10mm
Capacity: 8 rounds
Features: Dan Wesson recommits to the 10mm with a long-barreled 1911 design in a choice of tri-tone with a stainless slide, black frame, and bronze controls, or an all Duty black frame/slide with bronze controls; textured tan and black G10 grips; dustcover rail; forged stainless frame
MSRP.........**$2435.00–$2505.00**

RAZORBACK RZ-10

Action: Semiautomatic
Grips: Diamond-checkered cocobolo
Barrel: 5 in.
Sights: Fixed
Weight: 38.4 oz.
Caliber: 10mm
Capacity: 9 rounds
Features: Razorback is back in 2012 in limited quantities; serrated Clark-style target rib; 1911 model; stainless steel frame; manual thumb safety, grip safety
MSRP...................**$1725.00**

SPECIALIST

Action: Semiautomatic
Grips: G10 VZ Operator II grips
Barrel: 5 in.
Sights: Fixed tritium
Weight: 37 oz.
Caliber: 9mm, 10mm, .45 ACP
Capacity: 8+1 or 10 rounds
Features: Full size single-stack pistol; matte stainless steel or black Duty finishes; forged slide and frame; Clark-style serrated rib with tritium dual-colored night sights stacked in a straight eight-type pattern; tactical ledge rear sight with single rear amber dot and green front with white target ring; Picatinny rail; undercut trigger

guard with 25 lpi front strap checkering; ambidextrous thumb safety; two magazines with bumper pads included
MSRP.........**$1825.00–$2225.00**

TCP

Action: Semiautomatic
Grips: G10
Barrel: 4 in.
Sights: Brass blade front, notch rear
Weight: 32 oz.
Caliber: 9mm, .45 ACP
Capacity: 8 rounds
Features: TCP is Tactical Commander Pistol. Features aggressive slide serrations; ramped bull barrel with 30-degree crown; tapered grip profile; under barrel accessory rail; flat K-style trigger; top rib for reduced glare; one-piece magwell; square hammer
MSRP.........**$1809.00–$1845.00**

V-BOB, V-BOB TWO-TONE

Action: Semiautomatic
Grips: G10
Barrel: 4.25 in.
Sights: Fixed night sight front, U-notch rear
Weight: 36.5 oz.
Caliber: .45 ACP
Capacity: 8 rounds
Features: A Commander-sized 1911 with a bobbed mainspring housing; recessed slide stop to better accommodate laser grips; match-grade barrel; ambidextrous safety; tapered grips; inset serrations at rear of slide to reduce glare; front night sight is a a large orange ring; in bead-blasted duty black or stainless or available as a two-tone with a duty black slide and bead-blasted stainless frame
Two-tone..............**$1965.00**
Stainless...............**$1949.00**
Duty Black.............**$2215.00**

Dan Wesson Firearms

DAN WESSON VALOR

VALOR

Action: Semiautomatic
Grips: G10
Barrel: 5 in.
Sights: Fixed night sight front, U-notch rear
Weight: 39.7 oz.
Caliber: .45 ACP
Capacity: 7 rounds

Features: A favorite model in the Dan Wesson lineage returns in 2020 in a choice of stainless bead-blasted or black Duty Coat finishes; inset rear slide serrations; recessed slide stop for use with laser grips; Stan Chen SI magwell; tactical ambidextrous safety; checkered front and backstrap
MSRP . . . . $1965.00–$2295.00

Daniel Defense

DANIEL DEFENSE DDM4 V7P

DANIEL DEFENSE DDM4 PDW

DDM4 PDW

Action: Semiautomatic
Grips: Synthetic
Barrel: 7 in.
Sights: None
Weight: 91.2 oz.
Caliber: .300 BLK
Capacity: 30 rounds
Features: Maxim Defense CQB pistol brace; multiple M-LOK slots; S2W "strength to weight" barrel profile; pistol-length gas system; SLR M-LOK MOD2 plain front handstop
Black $2015.00
Cobalt, FDE $22015.00

DDM4 V7P

Action: Semiautomatic
Grips: Synthetic
Barrel: 10.3 in.
Sights: None
Weight: 87 oz.
Caliber: 5.56 NATO, .300 BL
Capacity: N/A
Features: Chrome-moly vanadium steel barrel; carbine-length gas system; Daniel Defense flash suppressor; SB Tactical SBO pistol brace; MFR 9.0 rail
Black $1870.00
Mil Spec+ $2057.00

Dark Storm Industries

DARK STORM INDUSTRIES DS1 VARIANT 1 PISTOL

DARK STORM INDUSTRIES DS-6 TYPHOON PISTOL

DARK STORM INDUSTRIES DS-15 TYPHOON PISTOL

DS1 VARIANT 1 PISTOL, FIXED MAGAZINE

Action: Semiautomatic
Grips: Synthetic
Barrel: 12.5 in.
Sights: None
Weight: N/A
Caliber: 5.56 NATO
Capacity: 30 rounds
Features: SB Tactical SBA3 stabilizing brace; carbine gas system; DSI competition compensator; optic ready; ambidextrous sling plate, charging handle, and 90-degree safety selector
MSRP . . . . $1595.00–$1695.00

DS-9 TYPHOON PISTOL

Action: Semiautomatic
Grips: Synthetic
Barrel: 7.5 in.
Sights: None
Weight: N/A
Caliber: 9mm
Capacity: 17 rounds
Features: Similar to the DS-15 Typhoon Pistol but available only with the removeable magazine; choice of black or Flat Dark Earth furniture
MSRP . . . . $1395.00–$1495.00

DS-15 TYPHOON PISTOL

Action: Semiautomatic
Grips: Synthetic
Barrel: 7.5 in.
Sights: None
Weight: N/A
Caliber: 5.56 NATO, .300 Blackout
Capacity: 30 rounds
Features: Billet 7075 aluminum lower; forged upper with forward assist; 6-inch M-LOK forearm with ultra-narrow profile; threaded Nitrite barrel; choice of PMAG or fixed mag configurations; choice of black or FDE furniture; steel micro gas block; pistol gas system
MSRP . . . . $1295.00–$1395.00

Davide Pedersoli & C.

DAVIDE PEDERSOLI HOWDAH

HOWDAH
Action: Break-open side-by-side
Grips: Walnut
Barrel: 10 in.
Sights: Dovetail front
Weight: 63.5 oz.
Caliber: .45 LC/.410-bore
Capacity: 2 rounds
Features: Based on Ithaca's 1920 Auto & Burglar pistol; case hardened

action; oil finished walnut stock; manual extractors; automatic safety on hammers; cartridge chamber allows interchangeable use of .45 LC or .410-bore

Standard	$1739.00
Deluxe	$2146.00
Alaskan	$2091.00
Vintage	$2405.00

Del-Ton

LIMA M-LOK PISTOL
Action: Semiautomatic
Grips: Synthetic
Barrel: 7.5 in.
Sights: None
Weight: 4 lb. 13 oz.
Caliber: 5.56x45mm
Capacity: 30 rounds
Features: Forged 7075

aluminum upper and lower hard-coat anodized; round forward assist; heavy-profile threaded barrel; low-profile gas block; 6.5-inch free-floating M-LOK handguard; full-length top rail
MSRP **$660.00**

DEL-TON LIMA M-LOK PISTOL

Devil Dog Arms

DDA 1911
Action: Semiautomatic
Grips: NBD
Barrel: 3.5 in., 4.25 in., 5 in.
Sights: Kensight DFS fixed white dot sights
Weight: N/A
Caliber: 9mm, .45 ACP
Capacity: 10 rounds (9mm), 8 rounds (.45 ACP)
Features: First 1911 offerings from this

maker; available in full-size, Officer, and Commander versions; two caliber choices; black oxide, FDE Cerakote, or Boron nitride finish options; investment cast 4140 steel frames; 4140 billet steel machined slides with a custom flat-top design; button-rifled 416 stainless barrels with match-fit bushing; three-hole aluminum trigger; optional accessory rail; oversized slide serrations
MSRP . . . . **$1149.00–$1449.00**

DEVIL DOG ARMS DDA 1911

Diamondback Firearms

DIAMONDBACK FIREARMS DB9

DIAMONDBACK FIREARMS DBAM29 (AM2)

DB9
Action: Semiautomatic
Grips: Polymer
Barrel: 3.1 in.
Sights: White three-dot
Weight: 13.4 oz.
Caliber: 9mm
Capacity: 6 rounds
Features: Fabulously slim, lightweight, and affordable carry 9mm that features a striker-fire action; a short-reset non-safety trigger; deep front and rear slide serrations; Glock-compatible sights; enhanced grip texturing
MSRP . . . . **$305.00–$322.00**

DBAM29 (AM2)
Action: Semiautomatic
Grips: Polymer
Barrel: 3.5 in.
Sights: White three-dot
Weight: 22 oz.
Caliber: 9mm
Capacity: 17 rounds
Features: Lots of folks think they can improve on a GLOCK, and some even do it successfully, like Diamondback Firearms with its new AM2 that features an all-steel captured recoil system; black nitride slide; safety trigger; creative grip texturing; accessory rail; Glock-compatible sights
Standard . . . . **$415.00–$435.00**
With laser . . . . **$635.00–$643.00**

Diamondback Firearms

DIAMONDBACK FIREARMS DBX57

DBX57
Action: Semiautomatic
Grips: Aluminum
Barrel: 8 in.
Sights: None
Weight: 48 oz.–59.2 oz.
Caliber: 5.7x28mm
Capacity: 20 rounds
Features: Firing the unique 5.7x28mm, this dual gas piston pistol has a locked breech operating system; threaded barrel with DBX muzzle device; rear Picatinny rail for mounting the included side-folding brace; AR-15 mil-spec trigger; top-side full-length Picatinny rail
MSRP $1352.00

DoubleStar Corp.

DOUBLESTAR CORP. ARP7

DOUBLESTAR CORP. PHD 1911

DOUBLESTAR CORP. STAR10-P

ARP7
Action: Semiautomatic
Grips: Synthetic
Barrel: 7.5 in.
Sights: None
Weight: 5 lb. 6 oz.
Caliber: 5.56 NATO, .300 Blackout, 9mm
Capacity: 30 rounds
Features: An AR-style pistol featuring: free-floating barrel with M4 feed ramp; billet winter trigger guard; billet backbone charging handle; Ergo grip; direct gas impingement; Doublestar seven-inch Cloak M-LOK handguard
5.56 NATO $1429.99
.300 BLK $1385.99

PHD 1911
Action: SA
Grips: Magpul MOE 1911 grip panels
Barrel: 5 in.
Sights: XS Express titrium front sight, XS Express rear sight
Weight: 33 oz.
Caliber: .45 ACP
Capacity: 8 rounds
Features: Aggressive rear cocking serrations for a sure grip in the harshest of environments; flat-topped and serrated slide to reduce glare; round butt and Wilson combat high-ride beavertail grip safety
MSRP $1506.99

STAR10-P
Action: Semiautomatic
Grips: Synthetic
Barrel: 12.5 in.
Sights: None
Weight: N/A
Caliber: .308 Win.
Capacity: 20 rounds
Features: A big caliber in a compact handgun package with forged aluminum upper and lower; direct gas impingement action; low-profile gas block; heavy stainless steel barrel; flat trigger group; lots of rail
MSRP $2414.99

DoubleTap Defense LLC

DOUBLETAP
Action: DAO semiautomatic
Grips: Synthetic
Barrel: 3 in.
Sights: Front blade
Weight: 12 oz.–14 oz.
Caliber: .45 ACP, 9mm
Capacity: 2+2 rounds
Features: Titanium frame with a MIL-STD finish that resists corrosion; integral grips house additional two spare rounds; ported barrel reduces muzzle flip and recoil; ambidextrous thumb latch to eject spent rounds; quick-change interchangable barrels; comes with one barrel and you can purchase extra conversion kits; firearm and conversion kit available ported and non-ported
Aluminum: . . . . $499.00–$569.00
Conversion kits: . . . $199.00–$269.00

DOUBLETAP DEFENSE LLC DOUBLETAP

Ed Brown Products

ED BROWN 18 CLASSIC CUSTOM

ED BROWN BO 18 KOBRA CARRY LIGHTWEIGHT

ED BROWN PRODUCTS BO/EB ZEV 19 RMR

ED BROWN EVO KC9 G4, G4 AMBI

ED BROWN SIGNATURE EDITION

ED BROWN PRODUCTS EVO KC9 G4 VTX

EVO KC9 G4 VTX

Action: Semiautomatic
Grips: Wood
Barrel: 4 in.
Sights: Blade front, red-dot rear
Weight: 35 oz.
Caliber: 9mm
Capacity: 9 rounds
Features: The popular EVO line gets an upgrade with a factory-mounted Vortex Venom red-dot sight; Black Gen4 finish; thinned and shortened slide with 7-top custom cuts and front and rear slide serrations; "snakeskin" treatment to forestrap and bobtail housing; bull barrel
MSRP.........$2545.00–$2895.00

18 CLASSIC CUSTOM

Action: Semiautomatic
Grips: Cocobolo wood
Barrel: 5 in.
Sights: Adjustable rear, cross dovetail front
Weight: 40 oz.
Caliber: .45 ACP
Capacity: 7+1 rounds
Features: Single-action; single-stack government model frame; special mirror finished side; two-piece guide rod for smoother cycling and easier disassembly; stainless or blued finish
MSRP........ $3695.00–$3795.00

BO 18 KOBRA CARRY LIGHTWEIGHT

Action: Semiautomatic
Grips: Cocobolo wood
Barrel: 4.25 in.
Sights: Fixed dovetail front night with high visibility white outlines
Weight: 35 oz.
Caliber: 9mm, .45 ACP
Capacity: 7+1 rounds
Features: Stainless Commander bobtail frame with a matte finish holds a seven-round magazine; black fixed rear sight paired with an orange HD XR front sight; skeletonized trigger; checkered walnut grips; "snakeskin" treatment to front strap, mainspring housing, and slide; recessed slide stop and crown among many custom upgrades offered
MSRP........ $3195.00–$3295.00

EB ZEV

Action: Semiautomatic
Grips: G10
Barrel: 4.25 in.
Sights: Tall night sights, Trijicon RMR reflex red dot
Weight: 40 oz.
Caliber: 9mm
Capacity: 8 rounds
Features: The result of a partnership with ZEV Technologies, this Commander-size pistol sports ZEV dimpled barrel; ZEV Orion slide cut package; Alien front strap and mainspring housing; EVO-series HDXR orange front sight; Gen 2 Chen magwell; flush barrel with recessed crown; recessed slide stop
MSRP................. $4195.00

EVO KC9 G4, G4 AMBI

Action: Semiautomatic
Grips: Ed Brown custom
Barrel: 4 in.
Sights: Orange HD XR night sight front, notch rear
Weight: 34 oz.
Caliber: 9mm
Capacity: 9 rounds
Features: EVO is for Evolution, Ed Brown's slimmed and lightened 9mm 1911 featuring Ed's snakeskin treatment to the front strap and his own Bobtail mainspring housing; 7-top custom slide with serrations; bull barrel; flat wire recoil system; two versions, a stainless finish with black textured grips, or a black Gen4 finish with textured brown ombre grips
Standard $2495.00
Ambi $2595.00

SIGNATURE EDITION

Action: Semiautomatic
Grips: Buckeye burl
Barrel: 5 in.
Sights: Adjustable rear, cross dovetail front
Weight: 40 oz.
Caliber: .45 ACP
Capacity: 7+1 rounds
Features: Based on the timeless Classic Custom pistol, with hand relief engraving by our master engraver; single stack government model frame; special mirror finished slide; 50 lpi serrations on back of slide to match serrated adjustable sight; adjustable rear sight buried deep into slide; gold bead front sight
MSRP.................$8195.00

EMF Company, Inc.

EMF 1873 GREAT WESTERN II ALCHIMISTA II

1873 GREAT WESTERN II ALCHIMISTA II, JR., DLX III

Action: SA revolver
Grips: Walnut
Barrel: 3.5 in., 4.75 in., 5.5 in., 7.5 in.
Sights: Fixed
Weight: 33.6 oz.
Caliber: .357 Mag., .44-40, .45 LC
Capacity: 6 rounds
Features: Standard case-hardening; stainless steel; three variations: Alchimista I has checkered walnut 1860 walnut grips, wide setback trigger, case hardened frame; Alchimista III is similar to II but with octagonal barrel; Jr. has a round barrel in the shortest configuration and engraved in Old Silver and Blue
II:.....................$650.00
DLX III: $745.00
Jr.:.....................$775.00

EMF Company, Inc.

EMF 1873 GREAT WESTERN II BUNTLINE

EMF 1873 GREAT WESTERN II CALIFORNIAN

EMF COMPANY, INC. 1873 GREAT WESTERN II DELUXE GRANDE CALIFORNIAN

EMF 1873 GREAT WESTERN II LIBERTY

EMF 1873 GREAT WESTERN II ALL BLUE PALADIN

EMF 1873 GREAT WESTERN II PONY EXPRESS

EMF COMPANY, INC. 1873 GREAT WESTERN II US MARSHAL

1873 GREAT WESTERN II BUNTLINE

Action: Revolver
Grips: Walnut or Ultra Ivory
Barrel: 12 in.
Sights: Fixed
Weight: N/A
Caliber: .45 LC
Capacity: 6 rounds
Features: Deep color case hardened finish; first version was designed by Colt for Ned Buntline
Walnut grips: **$660.00**
Ultra Ivory grips: **$690.00**

1873 GREAT WESTERN II CALIFORNIAN

Action: SA revolver
Grips: Walnut
Barrel: 4.75 in., 5.5 in., 7.5 in.
Sights: Fixed
Weight: 48 oz.
Caliber: .357 Mag., .44-40 Win., .45 LC
Capacity: 6 rounds
Features: Standard case-hardening; steel frame
MSRP **$590.00**

1873 GREAT WESTERN II DELUXE GRANDE CALIFORNIAN

Action: Revolver

Grips: Wood
Barrel: 4.75 in.
Sights: Blade front, integral notch rear
Weight: N/A
Caliber: .357 Mag., .45 LC
Capacity: 6 rounds
Features: Gorgeous single-action with a color-case-hardened frame; grips checkered in a pattern reminiscent of fleur-de-lis; Victorian scroll work and sunburst engraving on high-polished blue barrel and cylinder
MSRP **$690.00**

1873 GREAT WESTERN II LIBERTY

Action: Revolver
Grips: Ultra Ivory
Barrel: 4.75 in., 5.5 in.
Sights: Fixed
Weight: N/A
Caliber: .357 Mag., .45 LC
Capacity: 6 rounds
Features: Manufactured in Italy; all blued barrel, cylinder, and frame; factory laser engraved
MSRP **$675.00**

1873 GREAT WESTERN II PALADIN

Action: Revolver
Grips: Ultra Ivory
Barrel: 7.5 in.
Sights: Fixed
Weight: N/A
Caliber: .45 LC
Capacity: 6 rounds

Features: Single action; all blued barrel, cylinder, and frames as seen in Hollywood westerns
MSRP **$640.00**

1873 GREAT WESTERN II PONY EXPRESS

Action: SA revolver
Grips: Walnut express grips
Barrel: 3.5 in.
Sights: Fixed
Weight: 32 oz.
Caliber: .357 Mag., .45 LC
Capacity: 6 rounds
Features: Designed by Dave Anderson, one of the pioneering gunmakers in Cowboy Action Shooting and intended for mounted shooting competitors; available in an Express (bird's head) grip and turned-down hammer or a standard grip and Bisley hammer, both in bright stainless, or in a case hardened version with Express grip
MSRP . . . . **$705.00–$945.00**

1873 GREAT WESTERN II US MARSHAL

Action: Revolver
Grips: Walnut
Barrel: 4.75 in.
Sights: Blade front, integral notch rear
Weight: N/A
Caliber: .357 Mag., .45 LC
Capacity: 6 rounds
Features: Features a color case-hardened frame; blued barrel and cylinder; brass backstrap and trigger guard; walnut grips have "US Marshal" in its star logo
MSRP **$560.00**

European American Armory (EAA)

EUROPEAN AMERICAN ARMORY GIRSAN MC9 MATCH TV

GIRSAN MC9 MATCH

Action: Semiautomatic
Grips: Polymer
Barrel: 4.63 in.
Sights: Dot front, red-dot optic rear
Weight: 25 oz.
Caliber: 9mm
Capacity: 17 rounds

Features: Sports slide cuts to keep the barrel cool; porting; rear slide serrations; accessory rail; distinctive red magazine well and trigger; interchangeable backstraps; FAR-DOT (Fast Acquisition Red Dot) system
MSRP **$681.00**

European American Armory (EAA)

EUROPEAN AMERICAN ARMORY GIRSAN MC9 STANDARD

EAA GIRSAN MC1911 MATCH

EAA GIRSAN MC1911 MATCH ELITE

EUROPEAN AMERICAN ARMORY GIRSAN MC1911S HUNTER

EUROPEAN AMERICAN ARMORY GIRSAN REGARD MC

EUROPEAN AMERICAN ARMORY BOUNTY HUNTER

GIRSAN MC9 STANDARD

Action: Semiautomatic
Grips: Polymer
Barrel: 4.2 in.
Sights: White dot front, rear
Weight: 22.4 oz.
Caliber: 9mm
Capacity: 17 rounds
Features: No-frills striker-fire with generous capacity; accessory rail; available with EAA's FAR-DOT system; available with threaded barrel
MSRP . . . . $442.00–$754.00

GIRSAN MC1911 MATCH

Action: Semiautomatic
Grips: Laminate
Barrel: 5 in.
Sights: Fully adjustable target
Weight: 40 oz.
Caliber: .45 ACP
Capacity: 8 rounds
Features: A well-rounded full-size 1911 Govt. pistol built by GiRSAN for EAA and featuring an extended beavertail; steel slide and frame; extended ambidextrous safety; long-hole hammer; checkered frame
MSRP . . . . $776.00–$796.00

GIRSAN MC1911 MATCH ELITE

Action: Semiautomatic
Grips: G10
Barrel: 5 in.
Sights: Fully adjustable target
Weight: 40 oz.
Caliber: .45 ACP
Capacity: 8 rounds
Features: Enhanced competition pistol based on the GiRSAN MC1911 Match but with the addition of a competition barrel, mag well and barrel; cone/barrel lock-up; aggressive slide serrations; in a matte hard chrome finish
MSRP $882.00

GIRSAN MC1911S HUNTER

Action: Semiautomatic
Grips: Polymer
Barrel: 6 in.
Sights: White dot front, adjustable rear
Weight: 51.2 oz.
Caliber: 10mm
Capacity: 8 rounds
Features: Another entry into the "return of the 10mm" trend, this one with an appropriately long barrel; weight to take the bite out of the recoil; long-hole hammer; rear slide serrations; target barrel; extended beavertail safety; checkered frame
MSRP . . . . $721.00–$740.00

GIRSAN REGARD MC

Action: Semiautomatic
Grips: Polymer
Barrel: 4.9 in.
Sights: White dot front and rear
Weight: 34.4 oz.
Caliber: 9mm
Capacity: 18 rounds
Features: Modeled after the Beretta 92FS, this one has big capacity; accessory rail; website says this is a single-action, but with a decocker on the slide, we're going with DA/SA; in all black, flat dark earth frame with black grip panels, barrel and touchpoints, or silver frame with black grip panels, barrel and operating controls
MSRP . . . . $468.00–$638.00

WEIHRAUCH BOUNTY HUNTER

Action: SA revolver
Grips: Walnut
Barrel: 4.5 in., 6.75 in., 7.5 in.
Sights: Fixed, open
Weight: 39–41 oz.
Caliber: .357 Mag.,.44 Mag., .22 LR/.22 WMR, 45 LC
Capacity: 6 or 8 rounds
Features: Transfer bar safety; steel or alloy frame; in blued or nickel finishes
MSRP . . . . $383.00–$591.00

Faxon Firearms

FAXON FIREARMS FX-19 HELLFIRE

FAXON FIREARMS FX-19 PATRIOT

FX-19 HELLFIRE

Action: Semiautomatic
Grips: Polymer
Barrel: 4.5 in.
Sights: Suppressor-height night sights
Weight: 18 oz.
Caliber: 9mm

Capacity: 15 rounds
Features: A semi-custom pistol based on the Glock frame--but with a 1911 grip angle--and taking Glock 19 magazines, featuring DLC Diamond-Like-Coating finish; deep slide serrations fore, aft, and top; optics mounting cuts; Overwatch trigger; extended magazine release; suppressor-height night sights; threaded muzzle
MSRP $1189.00

FX-19 PATRIOT

Action: Semiautomatic

Grips: Polymer
Barrel: 4 in.
Sights: Fiber optic front, blacked-out rear
Weight: 18 oz.
Caliber: 9mm
Capacity: 19 rounds
Features: Similar to the Hellfire, but with a fiber optic front/blacked-out rear sight combo and one standard Glock 19 magazine; unthreaded muzzle
MSRP $1049.00

Fightlite Industries

SCR M-LOK
Action: Semiautomatic
Grips: Synthetic
Barrel: 7.25 in.
Sights: None
Weight: 63 oz.
Caliber: 5.56 NATO, .300 Blackout
Capacity: 10 rounds
Features: Short-barreled, grip stock

rifle-caliber carbine pistol; overall length of about 20 inches;barrel of 4150 Vanadium that is gas-ferritic nitrocarbonized and threaded; hardcoat anodized finish on the aluminum receiver; choice of KeyMod or M-LOK handguards
MSRP...................$865.00

FIGHTLITE INDUSTRIES SCR M-LOK

FK BRNO U.S.

7.5 FK FIELD PISTOL

7.5 FK FIELD PISTOL
Action: Semiautomatic
Grips: Aluminum G10
Barrel: 6 in.
Sights: Three-point butterfly
Weight: 44.8 oz.
Caliber: 7.5 FK

Capacity: 16 rounds
Features: Designed for long-distance silhouette with the proprietary 7.5 FK cartridge; proprietary recoil attenuating system; streamlined slide, frame, and grip; G10 grips; dark gray nitride finish; SA
MSRP.....................$7500.00

FN America

FN AMERICA FN 503
FN AMERICA FN 509 COMPACT
FN AMERICA FN-509 COMPACT MRD
FN AMERICA FN 509 COMPACT TACTICAL
FN AMERICA FN 509 LS EDGE

FN-503
Action: Semiautomatic
Grips: Polymer
Barrel: 3.1 in.
Sights: Low-profile drift-adjustable front, rear
Weight: 21 oz.
Caliber: 9mm
Capacity: 6, 8 rounds
Features: A sweet CCW gun; striker-fired; low-profile iron sights; metal trigger; loaded chamber indicator; rear cocking serrations; barrel with recessed target crown; oversized controls; with one 6-round flush-fit magazine and one 8-round extended
MSRP..................$579.00

FN-509 COMPACT
Action: Semiautomatic
Grips: Polymer
Barrel: 3.7 in.
Sights: Low-profile HiViz front, rear
Weight: 25.5 oz.
Caliber: 9mm

Capacity: 10, 12, 15 rounds
Features: Nice mid-size carry option with aggressive texturing on the frontstrap, grip sides, and interchangeable backstraps; external extractor; loaded chamber indicator; ambidextrous controls; accessory rail; flat-faced trigger; compatible with FN 509 24-round magazines; comes with two 10-round magazines or a 12-/15-round duo; MRD is optics ready
MSRP..................$719.00

FN-509 COMPACT MRD
Action: Semiautomatic
Grips: Polymer
Barrel: 3.7 in.
Sights: Combat-style front and rear
Weight: 25.5 oz.
Caliber: 9mm
Capacity: 10, 12, 15 rounds
Features: FN grows its 509 series with a compact model for concealed carry. Features include DAO operation; aggressively textured grip, front and backstrap, and magazine finger rest
MSRP..................$799.00

FN-509 COMPACT TACTICAL
Action: Semiautomatic

Grips: Polymer
Barrel: 4.32 in.
Sights: Trijicon night sights front, rear
Weight: 26.2 oz.
Caliber: 9mm
Capacity: 10, 12, 24 rounds
Features: All the features of the other 509 Compact models, but this one comes with a threaded barrel; suppressor-height Trijicon three-dot green night sights; comes with three 10-round magazines or a 12-/24-round duo; in black or flat dark earth
MSRP..................$1069.00

FN-509 LS EDGE
Action: Semiautomatic
Grips: Polymer
Barrel: 5 in.
Sights: Fiber optic front, MRD blackout notch rear
Weight: 31 oz.
Caliber: 9mm
Capacity: 10, 17 rounds
Features: Long-slide with lightning cuts and rear slide serrations; accessory rail; aggressively textured grip, frontstrap, and interchangeable backstraps; target-crowned hammer-forged barrel; flat-face facet-edge trigger; conical striker reduces trigger weight; low-profile optics mounting system accommodates most name brand red-dot reflex optics; compatible with FN 24-round FN 509 magazines; flared graphite anodized aluminum magwell
MSRP..................$1569.00

FN AMERICA FN-509 MIDSIZE

FN AMERICA FN-509 TACTICAL

FN AMERICA FN FIVE-SEVEN SERIES

FN AMERICA FNX-9

FN AMERICA FNX-45

FN AMERICA FNX-45 TACTICAL

FN-509 MIDSIZE

Action: Semiautomatic
Grips: Polymer
Barrel: 4 in.
Sights: Three-dot luminescent
Weight: 26.5 oz.
Caliber: 9mm
Capacity: 10, 15 rounds
Features: Designed for everyday carry with higher-profile combat-style sights that can make racking in stressed times easier; front and rear slide serrations; striker-fired double-action; loaded chamber indicator; ambidextrous controls; two textured backstraps; under rail
MSRP $719.00

FN-509 TACTICAL

Action: Semiautomatic
Grips: Polymer
Barrel: 4.5 in.
Sights: Three-dot night sights
Weight: 27.9 oz.
Caliber: 9mm
Capacity: 10, 17, 24 rounds
Features: Duty or competition ready with optics mounting plate; suppressor-height night sights, under rail; threaded barrel; interchangeable backstraps; ambidextrous slide stop

and mag release; available in black or Flat Dark Earth
MSRP $1069.00

FN FIVE-SEVEN SERIES

Action: SA semiautomatic
Grips: Plastic
Barrel: 4.8 in.
Sights: Adjustable 3-dot
Weight: 20.8 oz.
Caliber: 5.7x28mm
Capacity: 10 or 20 round magazines
Features: Integrated accessory rail for mounting tactical lights or lasers; reversible magazine button; ambidextrous manual safety levers; hammer-forged, chrome lined barrel; adjustable three-dot target sights available with matte or flat dark earth
MSRP $1319.00

FNX-9

Action: Semiautomatic
Grips: Interchangeable backstraps with lanyard eyelets
Barrel: 4 in.
Sights: 3-Dot system
Weight: 21.9 oz.
Caliber: 9mm, .40 S&W
Capacity: 17 rounds
Features: Ergonomic polymer black frame with low bore axis; checkered

and ribbed grip panels; stainless steel slide and hammer-forged stainless barrel; DA/SA ambidextrous controls
MSRP $739.00

FNX-45

Action: DA/SA Semiautomatic
Grips: Interchangeable backstraps with lanyard eyelets
Barrel: 4.5 in.
Sights: Fixed 3-dot
Weight: 33.2 oz.
Caliber: .45 ACP
Capacity: 15 rounds
Features: Polymer frame with stainless steel barrel; external extractor with loaded chamber indicator; front and rear cocking serrations; Picatinny rail; manual, ambidextrous safety
MSRP $869.00

FNX-45 TACTICAL

Action: DA/SA semiautomatic
Grips: Textured polymer
Barrel: 5.3 in.
Sights: High-profile night sights
Weight: 33.6 oz.
Caliber: .45 ACP
Capacity: 15 rounds
Features: Stainless steel slide; external extractor with loaded chamber indicator; high-profile combat night sights; hammer-forged stainless steel barrel; flat dark earth or black polymer frame; Picatinny rail; fully ambidextrous
MSRP $1379.00

FoldAR

DOUBLE FOLDAR15 GEN3

Action: Semiautomatic
Grips: Polymer
Barrel: 9 in.
Sights: None
Weight: 94.4 oz.–97.6 oz.
Caliber: .223 Wylde, .300 BLK
Capacity: 10, 20 rounds
Features: The folding AR pistol features

a fully adjustable gas block; Dead Foot Arms folding pistol brace; Aero Precision X15 lower; A2 compensator; shortened mil-spec bolt carrier group that's in black nitride; Magpul M-LOK rail; SHUT upper/lower locking hinge; folded length is 10.75 in.
MSRP $2399.00

FOLDAR DOUBLE FOLDAR15 GEN3

Freedom Arms

FREEDOM ARMS MODEL 83 PREMIER GRADE

FREEDOM ARMS MODEL 83 RIMFIRE

FREEDOM ARMS MODEL 97 PREMIER GRADE

MODEL 83 PREMIER GRADE

Action: SA revolver
Grips: Hardwood
Barrel: 4.75 in., 6 in., 7.5 in., 10 in.
Sights: Fixed or adjustable
Weight: 52.5 oz.
Caliber: .500 Wyoming Express, .475 Linebaugh, .454 Casull, .44 Rem. Mag., .41 Rem. Mag., .357 Mag.
Capacity: 5 rounds
Features: Adjustable sight models are drilled and tapped for scope mounts; stainless steel, brush finish and impregnated hardwood grips
MSRP . . . . $2930.00–$3040.00

MODEL 83 RIMFIRE

Action: SA revolver
Grips: Hardwood
Barrel: 10 in.
Sights: Adjustable
Weight: 55.5 oz.
Caliber: .22 LR
Capacity: 5 rounds
Features: Drilled and tapped for scope mounts; stainless steel frame; matte finish; match grade chambers
MSRP $2815.00

MODEL 97 PREMIER GRADE

Action: SA revolver

Grips: Laminated hardwood
Barrel: 4.5 in., 5.5 in., 7.5 in., or 10 in.
Sights: Adjustable or fixed
Weight: 39 oz.
Caliber: .45 Colt, .44 Spl., .41 Rem. Mag., .357 Mag., .327 Fed., .224-32 FA, .22 LR, .17 HMR,
Capacity: 5 or 6 rounds
Features: Impregnated hardwood grips; stainless steel frame; brush stainless finish
MSRP . . . . $2480.00–$2510.00

Glock

GLOCK G19 GEN5 MOS

GLOCK G19X

GLOCK G44

Compact

G19 GEN5 MOS

Action: Semiautomatic
Grips: Polymer
Barrel: 4.02 in.
Sights: Drift adjustable rear, post front
Weight: 23.81 in.
Caliber: 9mm
Capacity: 15, 17, 24, 31, 33 rounds
Features: Fully updated with Gen5 technology, including the Modular Backstrap System, the GLOCK Marksman Barrel, nDLC finish, ambidextrous slide stop, flared mag well and now with the MOS Modular Optics System that allows mounting of multiple electronic red-dot and reflex sights
MSRP $745.00

G19X

Action: Semiautomatic

Grips: Polymer
Barrel: 4 in.
Sights: Fixed
Weight: 31.4 oz.
Caliber: 9mm
Capacity: 17 rounds
Features: GLOCK's first "crossover" pistol; originally developed for military; GLOCK's signature Coyote coloring, including on the factory-colored slide; GLOCK Marksman Barrel; tough nPVD slide coating; ambidextrous slide stop levers; a stock without finger grooves; lanyard loop; Coyote-colored hard case; two 17-round and two 17+2-round magazines unique to the 19X
MSRP $749.00

G38

Action: Semiautomatic
Grips: Polymer
Barrel: 4.01 in.

Sights: Fixed
Weight: 26.83 oz.
Caliber: .45 G.A.P.
Capacity: 8, 10 rounds
Features: Striker-fired, polymer framed pistol with safe action system, trigger safety, hexagonal barrel, DAO action
MSRP $614.00

G44

Action: Semiautomatic
Grips: Polymer
Barrel: 4.02 in.
Sights: White-dot front, white outline notch rear
Weight: 12.63 oz.
Caliber: .22 LR
Capacity: 10 rounds
Features: Glock's first rimfire with a hybrid steel/polymer slide; interchangeable backstraps; supplied with two load-assist magazines
MSRP $430.00

GLOCK G45

GLOCK G43X

GLOCK G48

GLOCK G34 GEN5 MODULAR OPTIC SYSTEM (MOS)

GLOCK G40 GEN4

G45

Action: Semiautomatic
Grips: Polymer
Barrel: 4.02 in.
Sights: Drift adjustable rear, post front
Weight: 30.34 oz.
Caliber: 9mm
Capacity: 17, 19, 24, 31, 33 rounds
Features: A second offering in what GLOCK is calling its Crossover pistols. Intended primarily for duty carry, this one combines the slide of the G19 with a full-size G17 frame and adds a non-reflective black hard surface finish
Standard **$699.00**
MOS **$745.00**

Compact Slimlines

G43X

Action: Semiautomatic
Grips: Polymer
Barrel: 3.41 in.
Sights: Drift adjustable rear, post front
Weight: 18.7 oz.
Caliber: 9mm
Capacity: 10 rounds
Features: The smaller of two new slimline GLOCK pistols for 2019 intended for CCW practitioners. Features a silver mPVD finish on the slide; forward slide serrations; Gen5 GLOCK Marksman Barrel
MSRP **$538.00**

G48

Action: Semiautomatic
Grips: Polymer

Barrel: 4.17 in.
Sights: Drift adjustable rear, post front
Weight: 20.74 oz.
Caliber: 9mm
Capacity: 10 rounds
Features: The larger of two new slimline GLOCK pistols for 2019 intended for CCW practitioners. Features a silver mPVD finish on the slide; forward slide serrations; Gen5 GLOCK Marksman Barrel
Standard **$538.00**
MOS **$582.00**

Competition

G34 GEN5 MODULAR OPTIC SYSTEM (MOS)

Action: Semiautomatic
Grips: Polymer
Barrel: 5.31 in.
Sights: Fixed
Weight: 25.7 oz.
Caliber: 9mm
Capacity: 17 rounds
Features: Glock's Modular Optics System (MOS), which allows the mounting of various red dot and reflex sights without the need to machine the slide for a custom mount; GLOCK's improved nDLC finish; GLOCK Marksman Barrel; improved barrel crown; grip frame without finger grooves
MSRP **$899.00**

G41 GEN4, G41 GEN4 MOS

Action: Semiautomatic
Grips: Polymer

Barrel: 5.31 in.
Sights: Fixed
Weight: 27 oz.
Caliber: .45 ACP
Capacity: 10, 13 rounds
Features: Striker-fired, polymer framed pistol with safe action system, trigger safety, hexagonal barrel, DAO action; Gen4 has modular backstrap design, rough-textured grip, enlarged and reversible magazine release, and is available in Glock's MOS—Modular Optic System—configuration, which simplifies mounting of many modern pistol red dot and reflex sight optics
G41 Gen4 MOS: **$840.00**
G41 Gen4: **$729.00**

Long Slide

G40 GEN4 MOS

Action: Semiautomatic
Grips: Polymer
Barrel: 6.02 in.
Sights: Fixed
Weight: 28.15 oz.
Caliber: 10mm
Capacity: 15 rounds
Features: Striker-fired, polymer framed pistol with safe action system, trigger safety, hexagonal barrel, DAO action; Gen4 has modular backstrap design, rough-textured grip, enlarged and reversible magazine release, and is available in Glock's MOS—Modular Optic System—configuration, which simplifies mounting of many modern pistol red dot and reflex sight optics.
MSRP **$840.00**

Glock

GLOCK G17 GEN5 MOS

GLOCK STANDARD G17

GLOCK G20 GEN4

GLOCK G21 GEN4

GLOCK G26 GEN5

GLOCK G29 GEN4

GLOCK G26

Standard

G17 GEN5 MOS
Action: Semiautomatic
Grips: Polymer
Barrel: 4.49 in
Sights: Drift adjustable rear, post front
Weight: 24.87 oz.
Caliber: 9mm
Capacity: 17, 19, 24, 31, 33 rounds
Features: Fully updated with Gen5 technology, including the Modular Backstrap System, the GLOCK Marksman Barrel, nDLC finish, ambidextrous slide stop, flared mag well and now with the MOS Modular Optics System that allows mounting of multiple electronic red-dot and reflex sights
MSRP. $745.00

G20SF, G20 GEN4
Action: Semiautomatic
Grips: Polymer
Barrel: 4.6 in.
Sights: Fixed
Weight: 30.71 in.
Caliber: 10mm
Capacity: 10, 15 rounds
Features: Striker-fired, polymer framed pistol with safe action system, trigger safety, hexagonal barrel, DAO action; SF designation model has a reduced circumference backstrap. Gen4 has modular backstrap design, rough-textured grip, enlarged and reversible magazine release
G20 Gen4: $687.00
G20SF: $637.00

G21 SF, G21 GEN4
Action: Semiautomatic
Grips: Polymer
Barrel: 4.6 in.
Sights: Fixed
Weight: 29.30 in.
Caliber: .45 ACP

Capacity: 10, 13 rounds
Features: Striker-fired, polymer framed pistol with safe action system, trigger safety, hexagonal barrel, DAO action; SF designation model has a reduced circumference backstrap. Gen4 has modular backstrap design, rough-textured grip, enlarged and reversible magazine release
G21 Gen4: $687.00
G21 SF: $637.00

G31, G31 GEN4
Action: Semiautomatic
Grips: Polymer
Barrel: 4.48 in.
Sights: Fixed
Weight: 26.12 oz.
Caliber: .357 SIG
Capacity: 10, 15 round
Features: Striker-fired, polymer framed pistol with safe action system, trigger safety, hexagonal barrel, DAO action; Gen4 has modular backstrap design, rough-textured grip, enlarged and reversible magazine release
MSRP. $599.00

G37 GEN4
Action: Semiautomatic
Grips: Polymer
Barrel: 4.48 in.
Sights: Fixed
Weight: 28.95 oz.
Caliber: .45 G.A.P.
Capacity: 10 rounds
Features: Striker-fired, polymer framed pistol with safe action system, trigger safety, hexagonal barrel, DAO action; Gen4 has modular backstrap design, rough-textured grip, enlarged and reversible magazine release
MSRP. $614.00

Subcompact

G26 GEN5
Action: Semiautomatic

Grips: Polymer
Barrel: 3.42 in.
Sights: Fixed
Weight: 21.7 oz.
Caliber: 9mm
Capacity: 10 rounds
Features: GLOCK's improved nDLC finish; GLOCK Marksman Barrel; improved barrel crown; grip frame without finger grooves
MSRP. $647.00

G29SF, G29 GEN4
Action: Semiautomatic
Grips: Polymer
Barrel: 3.77 in.
Sights: Fixed
Weight: 26.83 oz.
Caliber: 10mm
Capacity: 10, 15 rounds
Features: Striker-fired, polymer framed pistol with safe action system, trigger safety, hexagonal barrel, DAO action; SF designation model has a reduced circumference backstrap. Gen4 has modular backstrap design, rough-textured grip, enlarged and reversible magazine release
G29 Gen4: $687.00
G29SF: $637.00

G33, G33 GEN4
Action: Semiautomatic
Grips: Polymer
Barrel: 3.42 in.
Sights: Fixed
Weight: 21.89 oz.
Caliber: .357 SIG
Capacity: 9, 13, 15 rounds
Features: Striker-fired, polymer framed pistol with safe action system, trigger safety, hexagonal barrel, DAO action; Gen4 has modular backstrap design, rough-textured grip, enlarged and reversible magazine release
MSRP. $599.00

Glock

GLOCK G33 GEN4

GLOCK G36

GLOCK G42

G39 GEN4

Action: Semiautomatic
Grips: Polymer
Barrel: 3.42 in.
Sights: Fixed
Weight: 24.18 oz.
Caliber: .45 G.A.P.
Capacity: 6, 8, 10 rounds
Features: Striker-fired, polymer framed pistol with safe action system, trigger safety, hexagonal barrel, DAO action
MSRP $614.00

Subcompact Slimline

G36

Action: Semiautomatic
Grips: Polymer
Barrel: 3.77 in.
Sights: Fixed
Weight: 22.42 oz.
Caliber: .45 ACP
Capacity: 6 rounds
Features: Striker-fired, polymer framed pistol with safe action system, trigger safety, hexagonal barrel, DAO action, single-stack magazine
MSRP $637.00

G42

Action: Semiautomatic
Grips: Polymer
Barrel: 3.25 in.
Sights: Fixed
Weight: 13.76 oz.
Caliber: .380 ACP
Capacity: 6 rounds
Features: Striker-fired, polymer framed pistol with safe action system, trigger safety, hexagonal barrel, DAO action, single-stack magazine
MSRP $480.00

Hämmerli

HÄMMERLI MODEL X-ESSE LONG

MODEL X-ESSE

Action: Semiautomatic
Grips: Composite
Barrel: 4.5 in., 5.9 in.
Sights: Adjustable
Weight: 27.9–31 oz.
Caliber: .22 LR
Capacity: 10 rounds
Features: Single-action, two-stage trigger; universal hi-grip
MSRP $1239.00

Heckler & Koch

HECKLER & KOCH HK45

HECKLER & KOCH HK45 COMPACT

HK45

Action: Semiautomatic
Grips: Polymer
Barrel: 4.53 in.
Sights: Fixed
Weight: 31 oz.
Caliber: .45 ACP
Capacity: 10 rounds
Features: DA/SA with control lever; integral Picatinny rail; ambidextrous controls with dual slide releases; modified Browning linkless recoil operating system; polygonal rifling; open square notch rear sight with contrast points; low profile drift adjustable three-dot sights; available in black, RAL8000 green brown, and olive finishes
MSRP . . . . $849.00–$949.00

HK45 COMPACT

Action: Semiautomatic
Grips: Synthetic
Barrel: 3.94 in.
Sights: Adjustable 3-dot
Weight: 28.48 oz.
Caliber: .45 ACP
Capacity: 8 or 10 rounds
Features: Picatinny rail molded into the polymer frame dust cover; slim-line grip profiles with user replaceable grip panels; ambidextrous controls with dual slide releases and enlarged magazine release; uses the proven modified Browning linkless recoil operating system; O-ring barrel; contoured and radiused slide with forward slide (grasping) grooves and anti-glare longitudinal ribs; polymer frame; available in black, RAL8000 green brown, and olive finishes
MSRP . . . . $849.00–$949.00

Heckler & Koch

HECKLER & KOCH HK45 COMPACT TACTICAL

HECKLER & KOCH HK45 TACTICAL

HECKLER & KOCH HK416 .22LR

HECKLER & KOCH MARK 23

HECKLER & KOCH P30

HECKLER & KOCH P30 L

HECKLER & KOCH P30SK

HECKLER & KOCH P2000

HK45 COMPACT TACTICAL

Action: Semiautomatic
Grips: Textured polymer
Barrel: 4.57 in.
Sights: 3-dot
Weight: 29.12 oz.
Caliber: .45 ACP
Capacity: 10 rounds
Features: Proprietary internal mechanical recoil reduction system; O-ring barrel; cold-hammer-forged barrel; available in black, RAL8000 green brown, and olive finishes; supplied with one additional backstrap; night sights optional
MSRP.................**$1029.00**

HK45 TACTICAL

Action: Semiautomatic
Grips: Polymer with finger grooves
Barrel: 5.16 in.
Sights: 3-dot tritium night sights
Weight: 31.7 oz.
Caliber: .45 ACP
Capacity: 10 rounds
Features: Polymer frame; recoil-operated with modified Browning locking system; threaded barrel; Picatinny rail; key-based HK Lock-Out system; nine different trigger firing modes; available in black, RAL8000 green brown, and olive finishes; supplied with one additional backstrap; night sights optional
MSRP.................**$1029.00**

HK416 .22LR

Action: Semiautomatic
Grips: Synthetic
Barrel: 8.5 in.
Sights: Flip-up front, rear
Weight: 72 oz.
Caliber: .22 LR
Capacity: 10, 20, 30 rounds
Features: The looks of the real-deal

HK416 but in a semiauto rimfire; last-round bolt hold-open; pistol grip with storage compartment; RIS rail interface with M-LOK; functional dust cover; aluminum receiver
MSRP.................**$529.00**

MARK 23

Action: Semiautomatic
Grips: Polymer
Barrel: 5.9 in.
Sights: 3-Dot
Weight: 39.4 oz.
Caliber: .45 ACP
Capacity: 12+1 rounds
Features: Threaded O-ring barrel with polygonal bore profile; match grade trigger; one piece machined steel slide; frame mounted decocking lever and separate ambidextrous safety lever; HK recoil reduction system; ambidextrous magazine release lever
MSRP.................**$2639.00**

P30

Action: Semiautomatic
Grips: Polymer
Barrel: 3.86 in.
Sights: Fixed
Weight: 26.08 oz.
Caliber: 9mm, .40 S&W
Capacity: 10, 15 rounds
Features: Corrosion proof fiber-reinforced polymer frame; multiple trigger firing modes; HK recoil reduction system; blued finish; Picatinny rail; ambidextrous magazine release levers and side release
MSRP...........**$839.00–$949.00**

P30 L

Action: Semiautomatic
Grips: Polymer
Barrel: 4.4 in.
Sights: Fixed

Weight: 27.5 oz.
Caliber: 9mm, .40 S&W
Capacity: 10, 13, or 15 rounds
Features: Interchangeable backstraps and side panel grips in small, medium, and large sizes; ambidextrous slide and magazine releases levers; integral Picatinny rail; modular design allows DA trigger or DA/SA system, with a decocking button
MSRP...........**$839.00–$949.00**

P30SK

Action: Semiautomatic
Grips: Rubber
Barrel: 3.27 in.
Sights: Fixed
Weight: 23.99 oz.
Caliber: 9mm
Capacity: 10 rounds
Features: Picatinny rail; interchangeable backstraps and lateral grip panels; available in multiple trigger firing modes including HK's enhanced double action only Law Enforcement Modification (LEM); trigger modes include conventional double action/single action (DA/SA)
MSRP...........**$839.00–$949.00**

P2000, P2000 SK

Action: Semiautomatic
Grips: Polymer
Barrel: 3.26–3.66 in.
Sights: 3-Dot
Weight: 23.8–25.9 oz.
Caliber: 9mm, .40 S&W
Capacity: 9–13 rounds
Features: LEM trigger system; double-action; pre-cock hammer; ambidextrous magazine release and interchangeable grip straps; mounting rail
MSRP...........**$929.00–$1039.00**

SP5

Action: Semiautomatic
Grips: Synthetic
Barrel: 8.86 in.
Sights: Post front, adjustable rear
Weight: 82 oz.
Caliber: 9mm
Capacity: 10, 15, 30 rounds
Features: If you've always yearned for an MP5, this is the next best thing in a super-compact 9mm that has a delayed blowback system; equipped with "bungee" sling
MSRP $3279.00

SP5K PDW

Action: Semiautomatic
Grips: Synthetic
Barrel: 5.83 in.
Sights: Ghost ring front, adjustable rear
Weight: 67.2 oz.
Caliber: 9mm
Capacity: 10, 15, 30 rounds
Features: A semiauto version of the famed MP5K with many of the same features, including a Navy-style threaded tri-lug adaptor; paddle magazine release; fluted chamber; "K" designation indicates shorter barrel and receiver
MSRP $3279.00

USP

Action: Semiautomatic
Grips: Polymer
Barrel: 4.25–4.41 in.
Sights: 3-Dot
Weight: 27.2–31.36 oz.
Caliber: 9mm, .40 S&W, .45 ACP
Capacity: 12, 13, 15 rounds
Features: Browning-type action with a patented recoil reduction system; double and single action modes; available in nine trigger/firing mode configurations; fiber-reinforced polymer frame; blued finish; ambidextrous magazine release trigger
MSRP . . . . $1119.00–$1379.00

USP COMPACT

Action: Semiautomatic
Grips: Polymer
Barrel: 3.58–3.80 in.
Sights: Fixed
Weight: 25.6–28.2 oz.
Caliber: 9mm, .40 S&W, .45 ACP
Capacity: 8, 12, 13 rounds
Features: Corrosion proof fiber-reinforced polymer frame; ambidextrous magazine release lever; grooved target triggers; nine trigger

HECKLER & KOCH SP5

HECKLER & KOCH SP5K PDW

HECKLER & KOCH USP

HECKLER & KOCH USP COMPACT

HECKLER & KOCH USP TACTICAL

HECKLER & KOCH VP40

HECKLER & KOCH VP9SK

HECKLER & KOCH VP9 TACTICAL OR

firing modes
MSRP . . . . $1149.00–$1379.00

USP TACTICAL

Action: Semiautomatic
Grips: Synthetic
Barrel: 4.86 in.
Sights: Adjustable
Weight: 28.16 oz.
Caliber: 9mm, .45 ACP
Capacity: 10 or 15 rounds
Features: High profile target sights; target sights with micrometer adjustment for windage and elevation; one piece machined, nitro-carburized steel slide; nine trigger firing modes; HK recoil reduction system; corrosion resistant "Hostile Environment" blued finish; corrosion proof fiber-reinforced polymer frame; oversized trigger guard for use with gloves; choice of flat and extended floorplate magazines; ambidextrous magazine release lever; extended slide release; extractor doubles as a loaded chamber indicator; patented Lock-Out Safety device
MSRP . . . . $1559.00–$1669.00

VP9, VP40

Action: Semiautomatic
Grips: Rubber
Barrel: 4.09 in.
Sights: Fixed
Weight: 26.56 oz.
Caliber: .40 S&W, 9mm
Capacity: 10, 13, 15 rounds
Features: Ergonomic handgun grip design that includes three changeable

backstraps and six grip side panels; ambidextrous controls; extended Picatinny rail molded into the polymer frame; captive flat recoil spring; supplied with two additional backstraps and two sets of lateral grip plates; night sights optional; specialty versions available with gray, OD Green, or Flat Dark Earth frames; tactical versions add threaded barrels and night sights; now available optics ready
MSRP . . . . $839.00–$999.00

VP9SK

Action: Semiautomatic
Grips: Polymer
Barrel: 3.39 in.
Sights: Drift-adjustable front, rear
Weight: 23.07 oz.
Caliber: 9mm
Capacity: 10, 13, 15 rounds
Features: A light subcompact striker-fire with an adjustable grip; slide and magazine release are ambidextrous; grip is finger-grooved and textured; slide has serrations front and rear; accessory rail; magazines are available flush or with a finger rest extension; available in black, Flat Dark Earth, Gray, or OD Green frames
MSRP . . . . $839.00–$999.00

VP9 TACTICAL OR

Action: Semiautomatic
Grips: Polymer
Barrel: 4.7 in.
Sights: Night sights front, rear
Weight: 26.8 oz.
Caliber: 9mm
Capacity: 10, 17 rounds
Features: Suppressor- and optics-ready; threaded barrel; suppressor-height night sights; optics slide cut with five mounting plates; supplied with three 10- or three 17-round magazines
MSRP $1059.00

Heizer Defense

HEIZER DEFENSE PKO45

PKO45

Action: Semiautomatic
Grips: Stainless steel
Barrel: 2.75 in.
Sights: Low-profile three-dot
Weight: 28 oz.
Caliber: .45 ACP
Capacity: 5, 7 rounds
Features: Uses guide-rod-over-barrel configuration; front strap grip safety; one-groove accessory rail; loaded chamber indicator; available in Ghost Grey, Copperhead, and Tactical Black finishes; company plans to produce the gun in 9mm and .40 S&W
MSRP $949.00

Henry Repeating Arms

HENRY REPEATING ARMS MARE'S LEG

MARE'S LEG

Action: Lever
Stock: Walnut
Barrel: 12.5 in.–12.9 in.
Sights: Open
Weight: 4 lb. 7 oz.–5 lb. 13 oz.
Caliber: .22 LR, .22 WMR, .357 Mag., .44 Mag., .45 Colt
Magazine: 5–10 rounds depending on caliber
Features: Centerfire: American walnut; Marble fully adjustable semi-buckhorn rear with reversible white diamond insert and brass beaded front sights; brasslite receiver, brass buttplate, and blued barrel; .22 S/L/LR: American walnut; fully adjustable rear, with hooded front sight; blued metal barrel and lever
.22 LR $508.00
.22 Mag. $525.00
Centerfire $1133.00

Heritage Manufacturing

HERITAGE MANUFACTURING BARKEEP

HERITAGE MANUFACTURING HONOR BETSY ROSS

HERITAGE MANUFACTURING USA FLAG

BARKEEP

Action: Revolver
Grips: Pearl, wood
Barrel: 2.68 in.
Sights: Blade front, integral notch rear
Weight: 35.5 oz.
Caliber: .22 LR
Capacity: 6 rounds
Features: A snubby .22 single-action that can option a compatible .22 WMR cylinder; multiple grip and metal finishes available
MSRP . . . . $180.15–$208.83

HONOR BETSY ROSS

Action: Revolver
Grips: Wood
Barrel: 4.75, 6.5, 16 in.
Sights: Blade front, integral notch rear
Weight: 30.1 oz., 45.2 oz.
Caliber: .22 LR
Capacity: 6 rounds
Features: A very special revolver with a carbine rifle-length barrel; special grips with the original Betsy Ross flag star configuration
MSRP . . . . $173.36–$210.88

USA FLAG

Action: Revolver
Grips: N/A
Barrel: 4.75 in., 6.5 in.
Sights: Blade front, integral notch rear
Weight: 30.1 oz., 33.4 oz.
Caliber: .22 LR
Capacity: 6 rounds
Features: Several variants in the USA Flag series of all blue-finished revolvers: USA Flag has grips that highlight both the stars and the stripes; Gold USA Flag has same stars and stripes grips, but with a vintage golden look; USA Flag 01 has grips of white stars on a blue background with just a bit of the red stripes at the heel; and USA Flag 02 has a bigger stars and stripes representation in a "wavy" presentation
MSRP . . . . $149.94–$173.33

Hi-Point Firearms

HI-POINT FIREARMS C9

HI-POINT FIREARMS C9 CAMO

HI-POINT FIREARMS MODEL CF-380

HI-POINT FIREARMS MODEL JHP45 ACP

HI-POINT FIREARMS YEET CANNON G1

C9

Action: Semiautomatic
Grips: Polymer
Barrel: 3.5 in.
Sights: Three dot, adjustable rear
Weight: 29 oz.
Caliber: 9mm
Capacity: 8, 10 rounds
Features: A compact CCW pistol rated +P; last round hold-open; black powdercoat finish; high-impact grips with easy-grip finish; magazine disconnect safety; manual thumb safety
MSRP . . . . $199.00–$305.00

C9 CAMO

Action: Semiautomatic
Grips: Polymer
Barrel: 3.5 in.
Sights: Three dot, adjustable rear
Weight: 29 oz.
Caliber: 9mm
Capacity: 8, 10 rounds
Features: Compact CCW pistol rated +P; last round hold-open; black powdercoat finish; high-impact grips with easy-grip finish; magazine disconnect safety; manual thumb safety; available in what looks to be Muddy Girl purple camo, a woodland camo, or a tan/cream digital camo
MSRP $229.00

CF-380

Action: Semiautomatic
Grips: Polymer
Barrel: 3.5 in.
Sights: 3-Dots adjustable
Weight: 29 oz.
Caliber: .380 ACP
Capacity: 8 or 10 rounds
Features: High-impact polymer frame; black powder coat with chrome rail; durable, easy-grip finish; quick on-off thumb safety; free extra rear peep sight; in black with or without hard case or in hydro-dipped pink camo; available with a built-in Laserlyte laser or with an integral compensator
MSRP . . . . $179.00–$289.00

JHP45, JCP40

Action: Semiautomatic
Grips: Polymer
Barrel: 4.5 in.
Sights: 3-Dots adjustable
Weight: 35 oz.
Caliber: .40 S&W, .45 ACP
Capacity: 10 rounds
Features: Polymer frame; quick on-off thumb safety; operations safety sheet; +P rated; free extra rear peep sight; free trigger lock; black finish available as standalone gun or with one of three package choices: with Laserlyte, with hard case, with Galco Kydex holster; camo versions (no packages) available in hydro-dipped Desert Digital, pink, or Woodlands
MSRP . . . . $199.00–$306.00

YEET CANNON G1

Action: Semiautomatic
Grips: Polymer
Barrel: 3.5 in.
Sights: Three dot, adjustable rear
Weight: 29 oz.
Caliber: 9mm
Capacity: 8, 10 rounds
Features: As the story goes, Hi-Point held a contest to name this gun, then threw away the votes to the consternation of just about everyone, and then, under advisement of H&K to listen to their customers, the company did, and voila, the YEET Cannon G1. Yeet means, more or less, to throw forcefully.
MSRP . . . . $210.00–$249.99

Ideal Conceal

IDEAL CONCEAL IC380

IC380

Action: Two-shot
Grips: Synthetic
Barrel: N/A
Sights: Ultra-low-profile front blade, raised groove rear
Weight: N/A
Caliber: .380 ACP
Capacity: 2 rounds
Features: A two-shot pistol that folds to look like a cell-phone; one side unfolds to become the grip and provide access to the trigger
MSRP $600.00

Israel Weapon Industries (IWI)

MASADA

Action: Semiautomatic
Grips: Polymer
Barrel: 4.1 in.
Sights: Combat-style
Weight: 22.9 oz.
Caliber: 9mm
Capacity: 17 rounds
Features: A striker-fired pistol with an interchangeable trigger system; tactile and visible loaded chamber indicator; polygonal rifled barrel; front and rear slide cocking serrations; visible round count magazines; underside accessory rail; ambidextrous control; optional night sights
MSRP $480.00

ISRAEL WEAPON INDUSTRIES (IWI) MASADA

Iver Johnson Arms, Inc.

IVER JOHNSON 1911 A1 CHROME

IVER JOHNSON POCKET ACE

1911A1 CHROME

Action: Semiautomatic
Grips: Black Dymondwood, black synthetic pearl
Barrel: 5 in.
Sights: GI fixed dovetail front and rear
Weight: 38 oz.
Caliber: .38 Super, .45 ACP
Capacity: 8 round
Features: Polished chrome finish; black Dymondwood grips or synthetic black pearl grips; slightly beveled magazine well; slide sports rear gripping serrations
MSRP . . . . $934.00–$1138.00

POCKET ACE

Action: Revolver
Grips: Wood
Barrel: 2 in.
Sights: None
Weight: 7 oz.
Caliber: .22 LR
Capacity: 4 rounds
Features: Four-shot pepperbox; rotating firing pin; sighting grove; wood grips; ambidextrous release lever also functions as a safety
MSRP . . . . N/A

Kahr Arms

KAHR ARMS CM9

KAHR ARMS CM45

CM9

Action: Semiautomatic
Grips: Textured polymer
Barrel: 3 in.
Sights: Adjustable
Weight: 15.9 oz.
Caliber: 9mm
Capacity: 6+1 rounds
Features: Trigger cocking double-action; lock breech; Browning-type recoil lug; passive striker block; no magazine disconnect; drift adjustable, white bar-dot combat sights; available in Armor Black, Kryptek Camo, or matte stainless slide with front night sight
MSRP . . . . $518.00–$565.00

CM45

Action: DAO semiautomatic
Grips: Synthetic
Barrel: 3.24 in.
Sights: Fixed
Weight: 17.3 oz.
Caliber: .45 ACP
Capacity: 5+1 rounds
Features: Trigger cocking DAO; lock breech; "Browning-type" recoil lug; passive striker block; no magazine disconnect; textured grips; drift adjustable white bar-dot combat rear sight; pinned in polymer front sight
MSRP $518.00

Kahr Arms

KAHR ARMS CT45

KAHR ARMS CT380

KAHR ARMS CW9 BURNT BRONZE

KAHR ARMS CW45

KAHR ARMS CW380

KAHR ARMS P9 SERIES

KAHR ARMS P40 SERIES

KAHR ARMS P45 BLACK WITH NIGHT SIGHTS

KAHR ARMS P380

CT45

Action: Semiautomatic
Grips: Synthetic
Barrel: 4.04 in.
Sights: Fixed
Weight: 23.7 oz.
Caliber: .45 ACP
Capacity: 7+1 rounds
Features: Trigger cocking DAO; lock breech; "Browning-type" recoil lug; passive striker block; no magazine disconnect; textured grips; drift adjustable white bar-dot combat rear sight; pinned in polymer front sight; black polymer frame, matte stainless steel slide
MSRP $484.00

CT380

Action: Semiautomatic
Grips: Synthetic
Barrel: 3 in.
Sights: Fixed
Weight: 11.44 oz.
Caliber: .380 ACP
Capacity: 7+1 rounds
Features: Textured polymer grips; trigger cocking DAO; lock breech; Browning-type recoil lug; passive striker block; no magazine disconnect; drift adjustable white bar-dot combat rear sight; pinned in polymer front sight; available
MSRP $447.00

CW9 BURNT BRONZE

Action: Semiautomatic
Grips: Polymer
Barrel: 3.6 in.
Sights: Pinned polymer front dot, drift-adjustable two-dot rear
Weight: 16.8 oz.
Caliber: 9mm
Capacity: 6 rounds
Features: Lightweight and slim; DAO action; Burnt Bronze Cerakote slide finish
MSRP $546.00

CW45

Action: Semiautomatic
Grips: Textured polymer
Barrel: 3.64 in.
Sights: Adjustable
Weight: 21.7 oz.
Caliber: .45 ACP
Capacity: 6+1 rounds
Features: Trigger cocking double-action; lock breech; Browning-type recoil lug; passive striker block; no magazine disconnect; drift adjustable, white bar-dot combat rear sight, pinned in polymer front sight; black frame; matte stainless steel slide
MSRP $502.00

CW380

Action: DAO semiautomatic
Grips: Black polymer
Barrel: 2.58 in.
Sights: Adjustable white bar-dot combat rear, pinned in polymer front
Weight: 10.2 oz.
Caliber: .380 ACP
Capacity: 6+1 rounds
Features: Lock breech; modified Browning type recoil lug; "safe cam" action; conventional rifled barrel; metal-injection-molded slide stop lever; slide lock after last round; available with front night sight
MSRP . . . . $447.00–$494.00

P9 SERIES

Action: Semiautomatic
Grips: Textured polymer
Barrel: 3.6 in.
Sights: Adjustable
Weight: 16.9 oz.
Caliber: 9mm
Capacity: 7+1 rounds
Features: Trigger cocking DAO; lock breech; Browning-type recoil lug; passive striker block; no magazine disconnect
MSRP . . . . $795.00–$996.00

P40 SERIES

Action: Semiautomatic
Grips: Textured polymer
Barrel: 3.6 in.
Sights: Adjustable
Weight: 18.7 oz.
Caliber: .40 S&W
Capacity: 6+1 rounds
Features: Trigger cocking DAO; lock breech; Browning-type recoil lug; passive striker block; no magazine disconnect; black polymer frame; six versions available: with matte stainless slide; with matte stainless slide and night sights
MSRP $795.00

P45 SERIES

Action: Semiautomatic
Grips: Textured polymer
Barrel: 3.54 in.
Sights: Adjustable
Weight: 18.5 oz.
Caliber: .45 ACP
Capacity: 5+1 or 6+1 rounds
Features: Trigger cocking DAO; lock breech; Browning-type recoil lug; passive striker block; no magazine disconnect; black polymer frame
MSRP . . . . $762.00–$795.00

P380 SERIES

Action: Semiautomatic
Grips: Textured polymer
Barrel: 2.5 in.
Sights: Adjustable
Weight: 11.27 oz.
Caliber: .380 ACP
Capacity: 6+1 rounds
Features: Trigger cocking DAO; lock breech; Browning-type recoil lug; passive striker block; no magazine disconnect
MSRP $776.00

Kahr Arms

KAHR ARMS PM9

KAHR ARMS PM40 WITH EXTERNAL SAFETY

KAHR ARMS PM45

KAHR ARMS S9

KAHR ARMS ST9

PM9 SERIES

Action: Semiautomatic
Grips: Textured polymer
Barrel: 3 in.
Sights: Night sights
Weight: 15.9 oz.
Caliber: 9mm
Capacity: 6+1 or 7+1 rounds
Features: Trigger cocking DAO; lock breech; Browning-type recoil lug; passive striker block; no magazine disconnect; California-approved variant
MSRP $795.00

PM40 SERIES

Action: Semiautomatic
Grips: Textured polymer
Barrel: 3 in.
Sights: Night sights
Weight: 17.7 oz.
Caliber: .40 S&W
Capacity: 5+1 or 6+1 rounds
Features: Trigger cocking DAO; lock breech; Browning-type recoil lug; passive striker block; no magazine

disconnect; California-approved variant
MSRP $795.00

PM45 SERIES

Action: Semiautomatic
Grips: Textured polymer
Barrel: 3.24 in.
Sights: Night sights
Weight: 19.3 oz.
Caliber: .45 ACP
Capacity: 6+1 rounds
Features: Trigger cocking DAO; lock breech; Browning-type recoil lug; passive striker block; no magazine disconnect; eight versions available: with matte stainless slide; with matte stainless slide and night sights; with matte stainless or black slide; night sights
MSRP $795.00

S9

Action: Semiautomatic
Grips: Polymer
Barrel: 3.6 in.
Sights: Pinned polymer front dot,

drift-adjustable two-dot rear
Weight: 15.8 oz.
Caliber: 9mm
Capacity: 7 rounds
Features: Intended primarily for concealed carry; stainless slide has grip serrations front and rear; accessory rail in front of the trigger guard; textured frame with ridges on the front and backstraps for improved purchase.; DAO pistol; Browning-type recoil lug; lock breech; passive striker block; no magazine disconnect; includes two magazines with a pinky rest
MSRP $477.00

ST9

Action: Semiautomatic
Grips: Polymer
Barrel: 4 in.
Sights: Pinned polymer front dot, drift-adjustable two-dot rear
Weight: 18.5 oz.
Caliber: 9mm
Capacity: 8 rounds
Features: Intended primarily for concealed carry; stainless slide has grip serrations front and rear; accessory rail in front of the trigger guard; textured frame with ridges on the front and backstraps for improved purchase.; DAO pistol; Browning-type recoil lug; lock breech; passive striker block; no magazine disconnect; includes two magazines with a pinky rest
MSRP $456.00

Kel-Tec

KEL-TEC CP33

CP33

Action: Semiautomatic
Grips: Polymer
Barrel: 5.5 in.
Sights: Adjustable fiber optic
Weight: 24 oz.
Caliber: .22 LR

Capacity: 33 rounds
Features: Loads of target fun with the 33-round double-double-stack magazine; fiber optic adjustable sights; full-length topside rail for optics
MSRP $550.00

KEL-TEC P17

KEL-TEC P-32

KEL-TEC P50

KEL-TEC PMR-30

P17

Action: Semiautomatic
Grips: Polymer
Barrel: 3.93 in.
Sights: Fiber optic front, adjustable rear
Weight: 12.8 oz.
Caliber: .22 LR
Capacity: 16 rounds
Features: A compact striker-fire rimfire with a textured grip; generous magazine capacity; accessory rail; threaded barrel; ambidextrous mag release and safety; three magazines included
MSRP $199.00

P-32

Action: Semiautomatic

Grips: Polymer
Barrel: 2.7 in.
Sights: Fixed
Weight: 6.6 oz.
Caliber: .32 ACP
Capacity: 7+1 rounds
Features: Steel barrel and slide; locked breech mechanism
MSRP $360.00

P50

Action: Semiautomatic
Grips: Synthetic
Barrel: 9.5 in.
Sights: None
Weight: 51.2 oz.
Caliber: 5.7x28mm
Capacity: 50 rounds
Features: The highlight of this gun may be its two—TWO—50-round

magazines; abundant Picatinny rails; quick-detach mounts; under rail; magazine lies on top of the grip/frame
MSRP $1095.00

PMR-30

Action: SA Semiautomatic
Grips: Nylon
Barrel: 4.3 in.
Sights: Picatinny accessory rail under barrel
Weight: 13.6 oz.
Caliber: .22 WMR
Capacity: 30 rounds
Features: Blowback/locked breech system; lightweight but full sized; urethane recoil buffer; disassembles for cleaning with removal of one pin
MSRP $545.00

Kimber

KIMBER AEGIS ELITE CUSTOM, CUSTOM (OI)

KIMBER AEGIS ELITE PRO, PRO (OI)

KIMBER AEGIS ELITE ULTRA

AEGIS ELITE CUSTOM, CUSTOM (OI)

Action: Semiautomatic
Grips: G-10
Barrel: 5 in.
Sights: Venom reflex red dot sight
Weight: 38 oz.
Caliber: .45 ACP, 9mm
Capacity: 8, 9 rounds
Features: Full-size 1911; textured green/black/gray G-10 grips; full-length guide rod; 24 lines-per-inch frontstrap checkering; stainless steel frame in satin silver; matte black Kim Pro II finish on the stainless steel slide; cross-hatched slide serrations front and back; round heel frame; OI

is optics included
MSRP . . . . $1604.00–$1624.00

AEGIS ELITE PRO, PRO (OI)

Action: Semiautomatic
Grips: G-10
Barrel: 4 in.
Sights: Venom reflex red dot sight
Weight: 38 oz.
Caliber: .45 ACP, 9mm
Capacity: 7, 9 rounds
Features: Mid-size 1911; textured green/black/gray G-10 grips; full-length guide rod; 24 lines-per-inch frontstrap checkering; stainless steel frame in satin silver; stainless steel slide in matte black Kim Pro II finish; cross-hatch serrations at the rear of

the slide; round heel frame; OI is optics included
Pro . . . . $1169.00–$1189.00
Pro (OI) . . . . $1604.00–$1624.00

AEGIS ELITE ULTRA

Action: Semiautomatic
Grips: G-10
Barrel: 3 in.
Sights: Green and red fiber optic
Weight: 25 oz.
Caliber: .45 ACP, 9mm
Capacity: 7, 8 rounds
Features: Compact version in the Aegis Elite series; cross-hatch serrations only at the rear of the slide
MSRP . . . . $1169.00–$1189.00

Kimber

KIMBER AMETHYST ULTRA II

KIMBER CAMP GUARD 10

KIMBER CUSTOM II (TWO-TONE)

KIMBER CUSTOM TLE/RL II (TFS)

KIMBER EVO SP (CDP)

KIMBER EVO SP (CS)

KIMBER EVO SP SELECT (BLACK)

KIMBER EVO SP SELECT (STAINLESS)

KIMBER EVO SP (TWO-TONE)

AMETHYST ULTRA II

Action: Semiautomatic
Grips: Micarta thin grips
Barrel: 3 in.
Sights: Fixed titrium night sights
Weight: 25 oz.
Caliber: .45 ACP, 9mm
Capacity: 7 or 8 rounds
Features: Ambidextrous thumb safety; full-length guide rod; amethyst purple PVD coating on small parts and fine engraving; front strap serrations and checkering; purple ball-milled Micarta thin grips
MSRP . . . . $1883.00–$1903.00

CAMP GUARD 10

Action: Semiautomatic
Grips: Rosewood
Barrel: 5 in.
Sights: Tactical wedge
Weight: 38 oz.
Caliber: 10mm
Capacity: 8 rounds
Features: Designed in partnership with Rocky Mountain Elk Foundation for use in the backcountry; stainless steel frame, slide, and barrel; front strap checkering at 30 lines per inch
MSRP $1393.00

CUSTOM II (TWO-TONE)

Action: Semiautomatic
Grips: Smooth/checkered rosewood
Barrel: 5 in.
Sights: Fixed, low profile
Weight: 38 oz.
Caliber: .45 ACP, 9mm
Capacity: 7 or 9 rounds
Features: Brushed polished carbon slide; stainless frame; full-length guide rod; sainless steel match-grade barrel
MSRP . . . . $951.00–$972.00

CUSTOM TLE/RL II (TFS)

Action: Semiautomatic
Grips: G10

Barrel: 5 in.
Sights: Fixed
Weight: 39 oz.
Caliber: .45 ACP, 9mm
Capacity: 7 rounds
Features: Threaded for suppression; Meprolight Tritium 3-dot night sight; Picatinny rail
MSRP . . . . $1318.00–$1332.00

EVO SP (CDP)

Action: Semiautomatic
Grips: G-10
Barrel: 3.16 in.
Sights: Tritium night sights
Weight: 19 oz.
Caliber: 9mm
Capacity: 7 rounds
Features: CDP is Custom Defense Package. Fancier take on the Two-Tone, with the aluminum frame in KimPro Charcoal Gray; FNC Black-finished stainless steel slide; Carry Melt treatment; red/black G10 grips and backstrap with checkering; front strap checkering
MSRP $883.00

EVO SP (CS)

Action: Semiautomatic
Grips: G-10
Barrel: 3.16 in.
Sights: Tritium night sights
Weight: 18 oz.
Caliber: 9mm
Capacity: 7 rounds
Features: CS is the Custom Shop offering in the EVO line of carry guns, with Stiplex-inspired texturing on the slide, front strap, grips and backstrap; KimPro Charcoal Gray finish on the aluminum frame
MSRP $965.00

EVO SP SELECT (BLACK)

Action: Semiautomatic
Grips: Nylon

Barrel: 3.16 in.
Sights: White three-dot
Weight: 19 oz.
Caliber: 9mm
Capacity: 7 rounds
Features: A smartly priced everyday carry gun with interchangeable grip system (side flats and backstrap) in checkered brown nylon; stainless steel slide in FNC black finish; aluminum frame in Kimpro II Black
MSRP $638.00

EVO SP SELECT (STAINLESS)

Action: Semiautomatic
Grips: Nylon
Barrel: 3.16 in.
Sights: White three-dot
Weight: 19 oz.
Caliber: 9mm
Capacity: 7 rounds
Features: Similar to the EVO SP Select (Black) model, but frame in Kimpro II Silver, slide in Kimpro Silver over FNC, and interchangeable checkered nylon grip/backstrap in black
MSRP $638.00

EVO SP (TWO-TONE)

Action: Semiautomatic
Grips: Nylon
Barrel: 3.16 in.
Sights: Tritium night sights
Weight: 19 oz.
Caliber: 9mm
Capacity: 7 rounds
Features: Terrific striker-fired CCW pistol featuring an aluminum frame in KimPro Silver finish; stainless steel slide in FNC Black; diamond checkering on grips; bushing-less match-grade barrel; checkered nylon backstrap; front strap checkering
MSRP $795.00

KIMBER HERO CUSTOM

KIMBER K6S DASA 2"

KIMBER K6S DASA 3"

KIMBER K6S (DASA) 4-IN. COMBAT

KIMBER K6S (DASA) 4-IN. TARGET

KIMBER K6S STAINLESS

KIMBER K6S STAINLESS 3"

KIMBER K6S TEXAS EDITION

KIMBER KHX CUSTOM/RL (OI)

HANDGUNS

HERO CUSTOM

Action: Semiautomatic
Grips: Composite
Barrel: 5 in.
Sights: Green and red fiber optic
Weight: 38 oz.
Caliber: .45 ACP
Capacity: 7 rounds
Features: Full-size 1911; Desert Tan Kim Pro II finish on the frame; matte black Kim Pro II finish on the slide; composite checkered grips in Kryptek Highlander camo; match grade stainless steel barrel and bushing; aluminum three-hole trigger; the American flag is engraved in tan on the slide
MSRP $1066.00

K6S DASA 2"

Action: Revolver
Grips: Walnut
Barrel: 2 in.
Sights: White three-dot
Weight: 23 oz.
Caliber: .357 Mag., .38 Spec.
Capacity: 6 rounds
Features: Compact powerhouse with Kimber's unique cylinder fluting; boot-style walnut grip; DA/SA exposed hammer; overbrushed stainless finish with minimal engraving; serrated backstrap
MSRP $1117.00

K6S DASA 3"

Action: Revolver
Grips: Walnut
Barrel: 3 in.
Sights: White three-dot
Weight: 25.1 oz.
Caliber: .357 Mag.
Capacity: 6 rounds
Features: The extra inch of barrel also gets you enough grip for a three-finger hold; overbrushed stainless finish with minimal engraving; serrated backstrap
MSRP $1117.00

K6S (DASA) 4-IN. COMBAT

Action: Revolver
Grips: Walnut
Barrel: 4 in.
Sights: White three-dot
Weight: 25.5 oz.
Caliber: .357 Mag.
Capacity: 6 rounds
Features: Great for competition or self-defense, this revolver has a non-stacking DA/SA trigger; three-finger-groove round butt combat grips with diamond checkering; flat-sided full underlug; serrated backstrap; brushed stainless finish
MSRP $1131.00

K6S (DASA) 4-IN. TARGET

Action: Revolver
Grips: Walnut
Barrel: 4 in.
Sights: Adjustable combat target
Weight: 25.5 oz.
Caliber: .357 Mag.
Capacity: 6 rounds
Features: A solid full-size target revolver with adjustable sights; brushed stainless finish; diamond-checkered extended walnut grips; non-stacking DA/SA trigger; flat-sided full underlug
MSRP $1131.00

K6S STAINLESS

Action: Revolver
Grips: Rubber
Barrel: 2 in.
Sights: Low-profile removable dovetail sights
Weight: 23 oz.
Caliber: .357 Mag.
Capacity: 6 rounds
Features: Stainless steel barrel; low-profile removable front and rear dovetail sights; smooth no-stack double action trigger; superior ergonomic grip contour; serrated backstrap
MSRP $985.00

K6S STAINLESS 3"

Action: Revolver
Grips: Walnut
Barrel: 3 in.
Sights: White dot
Weight: 25.1 oz.
Caliber: .357 Mag.
Capacity: 6 rounds
Features: Snub-nose small grip revolver; full crane shroud; longer barrel and grip than other K6s models; brushed stainless steel finish; smooth walnut grips
MSRP $1025.00

K6S TEXAS EDITION

Action: Revolver
Grips: G10
Barrel: 2 in.
Sights: White three-dot
Weight: 23 oz.
Caliber: .357 Mag.
Capacity: 6 rounds
Features: A generous six-round cylinder on this special Texas Edition gets paired with smooth satin finish; serrated backstrap; ivory G10 grips with "Texas" and "Come and Take it" emblazoned in gold
MSRP $1543.00

KHX CUSTOM (OI)

Action: Semiautomatic
Grips: G-10
Barrel: 5 in.
Sights: Trijicon RMR red-dot, white-dot co-witness sights
Weight: 38 oz.
Caliber: 9mm, 10mm, .45 ACP
Capacity: 8 rounds
Features: A serious competition or even a home-defense gun, with full-length guide rod; match-grade barrel and bushing; Hogue Magrip G10 panels; aluminum trigger; Trijicon RMR Type 2 red-dot sight with 3.25 MOA dot; co-witness sights; KimPro II Gray finish on frame and slide
MSRP . . . . $2121.00–$2141.00

Kimber

KIMBER KHX CUSTOM, CUSTOM (OR)

KIMBER KHX CUSTOM (OI)

KIMBER KHX PRO, PRO (OR)

KIMBER KHX ULTRA

KIMBER MICRO 9 AMETHYST

KIMBER MICRO 9 BEL AIR

KIMBER MICRO 9 DESERT NIGHT

KIMBER MICRO 9 DESERT TAN (LG)

KIMBER MICRO 9 ECLIPSE

KHX CUSTOM, CUSTOM (OR)

Action: Semiautomatic
Grips: G-10
Barrel: 5 in.
Sights: Fiber optics
Weight: 38 oz.
Caliber: .45 ACP, 9mm
Capacity: 7, 9 rounds
Features: Full-size 1911; "snakeskin" textured Hogue Magrip G-10 grip panels; textured gripping areas on the slide; Stiplex front strap stippling; OR stands for "optics ready"; milled slide
Custom . . . . $1448.00–$1468.00
Custom (OR) . . . $1244.00–$1264.00

KHX CUSTOM/RL (OI)

Action: Semiautomatic
Grips: G-10
Barrel: 5 in.
Sights: Trijicon RMR red-dot, white-dot co-witness sights
Weight: 39 oz.
Caliber: 9mm, 10mm, .45 ACP
Capacity: 8 rounds
Features: Similar to the KHX Custom (OI), but with the addition of an under-barrel accessory rail
MSRP . . . . $2175.00–$2230.00

KHX PRO, PRO (OR)

Action: Semiautomatic
Grips: G-10
Barrel: 4 in.
Sights: Fiber optics
Weight: 38 oz.
Caliber: .45 ACP, 9mm
Capacity: 7, 9 rounds
Features: Hogue Magrip G-10 grip with a built-in red laser; G-10 mainspring housing; OR stands for "optics ready"; milled side
Pro . . . . $1448.00–$1468.00
Pro (OR) (9mm only) $1264.00

KHX ULTRA

Action: Semiautomatic
Grips: G-10
Barrel: 3 in.
Sights: Fiber optics
Weight: 38 oz.
Caliber: .45 ACP, 9mm
Capacity: 7, 8 rounds
Features: G-10 mainspring housing; Hogue Enhanced Magrip G-10 grips with a built-in red laser; slide grip texturing appears only at the rear
MSRP . . . . $1448.00–$1468.00

MICRO 9 AMETHYST

Action: Semiautomatic
Grips: G10
Barrel: 3.15 in.
Sights: Standard night sights
Weight: 15.6 oz.
Caliber: 9mm
Capacity: 7 rounds
Features: Vertical serrations on the black/purple G10 grips, lower backside of the frame, and rear of the slide; aluminum frame in Kimpro II Silver finish; stainless steel slide gets a purple PVD finish on the flats as well as border scroll engraving; ramped barrel
MSRP $1201.00

MICRO 9 BEL AIR

Action: Semiautomatic
Grips: Ivory micarta
Barrel: 3.15 in.
Sights: Three-dot white
Weight: 15.6 oz.
Caliber: 9mm
Capacity: 6 rounds
Features: Kimber's unique Bel Air Blue finish on the aluminum frame; mirror-polished stainless slide; stainless steel barrel; bull-length guide rod; single-action
MSRP $980.00

MICRO 9 DESERT NIGHT (DN)

Action: Semiautomatic
Grips: Rubber
Barrel: 3.15 in.
Sights: TruGlo TFX Pro day/night sights
Weight: 15.6 oz.
Caliber: 9mm
Capacity: 7 rounds
Features: Desert Tan finish on an aluminum frame; Hogue wrap-around grips; matte black steel slide; full-length guide rod; matte black stainless slide; DN designates day/night sights
MSRP $848.00

MICRO 9 DESERT TAN (LG)

Action: Semiautomatic
Grips: Crimson Trace laser grips
Barrel: 3.15 in.
Sights: White-dot
Weight: 15.6 oz.
Caliber: 9mm
Capacity: 6 rounds
Features: Super slim, super lightweight concealed carry pistol; stainless barrel; bull-length guide rod; aluminum frame; single-action
MSRP $876.00

MICRO 9 ECLIPSE

Action: Semiautomatic
Grips: G-10
Barrel: 3.15 in.
Sights: Tritium night sights
Weight: 15.6 oz.
Caliber: 9mm
Capacity: 7 rounds
Features: Charcoal gray finish on an aluminum frame; stainless steel slide with polished flats; checkered gray G-10 grips; round-heel frame; 30 lines-per-inch front strap checkering; full-length guide rod; tritium night sights
MSRP $822.00

KIMBER MICRO 9 ESV (BLACK)

KIMBER MICRO 9 KHX

KIMBER MICRO 9 NIGHTFALL (DN)

KIMBER MICRO 9 SAPPHIRE

KIMBER MICRO 9 STAINLESS (DN)

KIMBER MICRO 9 TRIARI

KIMBER MICRO AMETHYST

KIMBER MICRO DESERT NIGHT

KIMBER MICRO ECLIPSE

MICRO 9 ESV (BLACK)

Action: Semiautomatic
Grips: G-10
Barrel: 3.15 in.
Sights: Night sights
Weight: 15.35 oz.
Caliber: 9mm
Capacity: 7 rounds
Features: Shaving a couple ounces off the EVO line thanks to slide serrations. Two versions: (Black) has gold Titanium Nitride coating, black Altamont G-10 grips, KimPro II Black slide and frame; (Gray) has Rose Copper coated barrel, black Altamont G-10 grips, KimPro II Gray slide and frame
MSRP $918.00

MICRO 9 KHX

Action: Semiautomatic
Grips: G-10
Barrel: 3.15 in.
Sights: Red fiber optic front, green fiber optic rear
Weight: 15.6 oz.
Caliber: 9mm
Capacity: 7 rounds
Features: Outstanding features in the CCW pistol include hexagonal dot "serrations" fore and aft on the slide, that pattern repeated in part on the Hogue G-10 grips and backstrap; KimPro II Gray finish on slide and frame
MSRP $918.00

MICRO 9 NIGHTFALL (DN)

Action: Semiautomatic
Grips: Rubber
Barrel: 3.15 in.
Sights: TruGlo TFX Pro day/night sights

Weight: 15.6 oz.
Caliber: 9mm
Capacity: 7 rounds
Features: Satin silver finish on an aluminum frame; Hogue wrap-around grips; all-over matte black finish
MSRP $848.00

MICRO 9 SAPPHIRE

Action: Semiautomatic
Grips: G10
Barrel: 3.15 in.
Sights: Three-dot tritium night sights
Weight: 15.6 oz.
Caliber: 9mm
Capacity: 6 rounds
Features: Brilliant blue PVD finish on slide; coordinated blue and black G10 grips; slide has scroll engraving enhancements; aluminum frame; stainless steel barrel
MSRP $1201.00

MICRO 9 STAINLESS (DN)

Action: Semiautomatic
Grips: Rubber
Barrel: 3.15 in.
Sights: TruGlo TFX Pro day/night sights
Weight: 15.6 oz.
Caliber: 9mm
Capacity: 7 rounds
Features: Satin silver finish on an aluminum frame; Hogue wrap-around grips; full-length guide rod; satin silver finish on the stainless steel slide; DN designates day/night sights
MSRP $795.00

MICRO 9 TRIARI

Action: Semiautomatic
Grips: Micarta
Barrel: 3.15 in.
Sights: Red fiber optic front, green fiber optic rear
Weight: 15.6 oz.
Caliber: 9mm
Capacity: 7 rounds
Features: Black Linen Micarta grips with a stacked cube pattern;

aluminum frame with Kimpro II Black finish; stainless slide in black oxide finish with stacked-cube serration patterning front and rear; rear sight has cocking ledge; solid aluminum trigger; match-grade barrel
MSRP $876.00

MICRO AMETHYST

Action: Semiautomatic
Grips: G10
Barrel: 2.75 in.
Sights: Three-dot tritium night sights
Weight: 13.4 oz.
Caliber: .380 ACP
Capacity: 6 rounds
Features: Concealed carry gun in vibrant purple PVD finish; engraved scroll accents; aluminum frame; stainless steel barrel; bull-length guide rod; single-action
MSRP $1131.00

MICRO DESERT NIGHT (NS)

Action: Semiautomatic
Grips: G10
Barrel: 2.75 in.
Sights: Night sights
Weight: 13.4 oz.
Caliber: .380 ACP
Capacity: 6 rounds
Features: Concealed carry gun; Desert Tan KimPro finish; black-finished slide; stainless steel slide and barrel; bull-length guide rod
MSRP $706.00

MICRO ECLIPSE

Action: Semiautomatic
Grips: Rosewood
Barrel: 2.75 in.
Sights: Tactical wedge tritium night sights
Weight: 13.4 oz.
Caliber: .380 ACP
Capacity: 9 rounds
Features: Matte black finish on an aluminum frame; satin silver finish on the slide; Carry Melt treatment; thin ball-milled rosewood grips; round-heel frame; 30 lines-per-inch front strap checkering; full-length guide rod; tactical wedge night sights
MSRP $819.00

Kimber

KIMBER MICRO STAINLESS ROSEWOOD (NS)

KIMBER PRO COVERT

KIMBER PRO RAPTOR II

KIMBER RAPIDE (BLACK ICE)

KIMBER ROSE GOLD ULTRA II

KIMBER SAPPHIRE ULTRA II

KIMBER STAINLESS II

KIMBER STAINLESS TARGET (LS)

KIMBER SUPER JÄGARE

MICRO STAINLESS ROSEWOOD (NS)

Action: Semiautomatic
Grips: Rosewood
Barrel: 2.75 in.
Sights: Low-profile three-dot tritium night sights
Weight: 13.4 oz.
Caliber: .380 ACP
Capacity: 6 rounds
Features: Mild recoil; smooth trigger pulls; full-length guide rod; aluminum frame with anodized finish
MSRP **$652.00**

PRO COVERT

Action: Semiautomatic
Grips: Urban Camouflage Crimson Trace laser grips
Barrel: 4 in.
Sights: Tactical wedge tritium night sights
Weight: 28 oz.
Caliber: .45 ACP
Capacity: 7 rounds
Features: Carry Melt treatment; 30 lines per inch checkering on front strap; Charcoal Gray and KimPro II finish; aluminum frame
MSRP **$1604.00**

PRO RAPTOR II

Action: Semiautomatic
Grips: Zebra wood, scale pattern
Barrel: 4 in.
Sights: Tactical wedge 3-dot
Weight: 35 oz.
Caliber: .45 ACP, 9mm
Capacity: 8 rounds
Features: Available in all stainless or all blue; match grade barrel;

ambidextrous thumb safety; full-length guide rod; blue in .45 ACP only, stainless available in both calibers
Blue **$1359.00**
Stainless **$1468.00**

RAPIDE (BLACK ICE)

Action: Semiautomatic
Grips: G10
Barrel: 5 in.
Sights: TruGlo TFX Pro Day/Night
Weight: 38 oz.
Caliber: 9mm, 10mm, .45 ACP
Capacity: 8, 9 rounds
Features: A unique take on cosmetics with aggressively textured Black Rapide G10 grips; stainless steel slide in Kimpro II Silver/Gray with lightning cuts and front and rear cocking serrations; Kimber Stiplex frontstrap stippling; V-cut aluminum trigger
MSRP . . . . **$1645.00–$1665.00**

ROSE GOLD ULTRA II

Action: Semiautomatic
Grips: G10
Barrel: 3 in.
Sights: Tactical wedge
Weight: 25 oz.
Caliber: .45 ACP, 9mm
Capacity: 7 rounds
Features: Personal defense gun; finished in Rose Gold PVD coating; solid aluminum trigger; aluminum round-heel frame; ambidextrous thumb safety; ball-milled front strap
MSRP . . . . **$1883.00–$1903.00**

SAPPHIRE ULTRA II

Action: Semiautomatic
Grips: G-10
Barrel: 3 in.
Sights: Tactical Wedge night sights
Weight: 25 oz.
Caliber: 9mm, .45 ACP
Capacity: 8 rounds
Features: Highly-polished stainless steel slide and small parts are finished with bright blue PVD finish accented with fine engraving; blue/black ball-milled G-10 thin grips and short

trigger; ambidextrous thumb safety; Tactical Wedge night sights
MSRP . . . . **$1883.00–$1903.00**

STAINLESS II

Action: Semiautomatic
Grips: Synthetic
Barrel: 5 in.
Sights: Fixed, low profile
Weight: 38 oz.
Caliber: .45 ACP, 9mm. 10mm
Capacity: 7 or 9 rounds
Features: Aluminum frame with satin silver finish; stainless stell slide; steel match-grade barrel; double-diamond textured grips ; blue in .45 ACP only, stainless available in both calibers
MSRP . . . . **$992.00–$1012.00**

STAINLESS TARGET (LS)

Action: Semiautomatic
Grips: Rosewood
Barrel: 6 in.
Sights: Kimber adjustable
Weight: 42 oz.
Caliber: .45 ACP, 10mm
Capacity: 7, 8 rounds
Features: Full-size 1911 with a longer slide for bull's-eye or other precision competition; slide and frame are finished in a satin silver; LS stands for Long Slide
MSRP . . . . **$1182.00–$1203.00**

SUPER JÄGARE

Action: Semiautomatic
Grips: Micarta
Barrel: 6 in.
Sights: DeltaPoint Pro optic
Weight: 42 oz.
Caliber: 10mm
Capacity: 8 rounds
Features: Designed for close-range big-game and varmint hunting; stainless steel frame and slide; frame has round heel and high cut trigger guard; finished in KimPro and Charcoal Gray; slide has carbon coating and Super Carry pattern on its flat top; Carry Melt treatment; match-grade bushing; solid aluminum trigger
MSRP **$2869.00**

Kimber

KIMBER SUPER MATCH II

KIMBER ULTRA CDP

KIMBER TACTICAL ENTRY II

KIMBER ULTRA CARRY II (TWO-TONE) (LG)

Weight: 25 oz.
Caliber: .45 ACP
Capacity: 7 rounds
Features: Black matte finish; aluminum frame; steel slide; full-length guide rod
MSRP **$1046.00**

SUPER MATCH II

Action: Semiautomatic
Grips: Walnut
Barrel: 5 in.
Sights: Adjustable
Weight: 38 oz.
Caliber: .45 ACP
Capacity: 8 rounds
Features: Ambidextrous thumb safety; full-length guide rod; stainless steel frame with satin silver finish; front strap checkering and checkering under trigger guard
MSRP **$2916.00**

TACTICAL ENTRY II

Action: Semiautomatic

Grips: Laminated double diamond, Kimber logo
Barrel: 5 in.
Sights: Meprolight tritium 3-dot night, fixed
Weight: 40 oz.
Caliber: .45 ACP
Capacity: 7 rounds
Features: Ambidextrous thumb safety; full-length guide rod; stainless steel frame and slide; matte gray Kim Pro II frame finish
MSRP **$1490.00**

ULTRA CARRY II

Action: Semiautomatic
Grips: Black synthetic double diamond
Barrel: 3 in.
Sights: Fixed, low profile

ULTRA CDP

Action: Semiautomatic
Grips: Rosewood double diamond
Barrel: 3 in.
Sights: Meprolight tritium 3-dot night, fixed
Weight: 25 oz.
Caliber: 9mm, .45 ACP
Capacity: 7 rounds
Features: Ambidextrous thumb safety, Carry Melt treatment, aluminum frame with charcoal gray KimPro II finish, stainless slide is flat-topped with satin silver finish
MSRP . . . . **$1325.00–$1359.00**

Kriss USA

KRISS USA SPHINX SDP COMPACT

SPHINX SDP COMPACT

Action: Semiautomatic
Grips: Composite

Barrel: 3.7 in., 4.35 in.
Sights: Fiber optic/tritium front, tritium rear
Weight: 27.5 oz.
Caliber: 9mm
Capacity: 15+1 rounds
Features: Upper frame machined from aeronautic-grade hard-anodized aluminum; integral recoil buffer; Picatinny rail; polymer lower frame;

Defiance fiber optic/tritium day-night green front sight with tritium two-dot red rear sight; internal firing pin safety, drop safety, hammer safety, and integrated slide-position safety; Cerakote finish
Standard: . . . . **$999.00–$1049.00**
Threaded: . . . . . **$1049.00–$1099.00**

Les Baer Custom

LES BAER 1911 BLACK BAER 9MM

1911 BLACK BAER 9MM

Action: Semiautomatic
Grips: Black recon
Barrel: 4.25 in.
Sights: Fixed rear combat night sight, dovetail front night sight
Weight: N/A
Caliber: 9mm

Capacity: 9 rounds
Features: Compact concealed carry; slide fitted to frame; rear serrated slide; speed trigger with crisp 4 lb. pull; tactical extended combat safety; Dupont S coating on complete pistol for maximum corrosion resistance
MSRP **$3223.00**

Les Baer Custom

LES BAER CUSTOM AMERICAN HANDGUNNER SPECIAL EDITION 1911

LES BAER CUSTOM BAER 1911 GUNSITE

LES BAER CUSTOM BAER 1911 KENAI SPECIAL

AMERICAN HANDGUNNER SPECIAL EDITION 1911

Action: Semiautomatic
Grips: VZ
Barrel: 5 in.
Sights: Baer tritium adjustable
Weight: N/A
Caliber: .45 ACP
Capacity: 8 rounds
Features: A tribute to readers of the iconic *American Handgunner* magazine, with the pub's title engraved on the deep blue slide; stainless-finish frame; custom stainless bushing rod; Baer's low-mount Rolo adjustable rear sight and a dovetailed front with tritium inserts; extended ejector; speed trigger set to 4 lbs.; flat serrated mainspring housing; rounded corner Tactical package
MSRP $3144.00

BAER 1911 GUNSITE

Action: Semiautomatic
Grips: Wood
Barrel: 5 in.
Sights: Dovetail tritium front, fixed rear
Weight: N/A
Caliber: .45 ACP
Capacity: 8 rounds

Features: A tribute the legendary Gunsite Academy firearms training center with wood grips bearing the Gunsite logo; serial numbers starting with GAI-; solid match trigger; dehorned; Gunsite logo engraved on slide
MSRP $2439.00

BAER 1911 KENAI SPECIAL

Action: Semiautomatic
Grips: Baer Recon
Barrel: 5 in.
Sights: Fiber optic front, low-mount Baer adjustable with hidden leaf rear
Weight: N/A
Caliber: 10mm
Capacity: 9 rounds
Features: Baer jumps into the new-generation 10mm game with all-steel construction; 4-pound speed trigger; beveled mag well; tuned action; checkered high-cut front strap; flat serrated mainspring housing
MSRP $3925.00

Live Q or Die Q, LLC

LIVE Q OR DIE HONEY BADGER PISTOL

LIVE Q OR DIE MINI FIX

LIVE Q OR DIE SUGAR WEASEL

HONEY BADGER PISTOL

Action: Semiautomatic
Grips: Synthetic
Barrel: 7 in.
Sights: None
Weight: 4 lb. 8 oz.
Caliber: .300 BLK
Capacity: 20 rounds
Features: Clear-coat hard anodized aluminum receiver in tan; free-floating M-LOK handguard; AR-type controls; 5/8x24 threaded tapered muzzle with Cherry Bomb muzzle brake; two-stage match trigger; two-position telescopic brace; adjustable low-profile gas block
MSRP $2999.00

MINI FIX

Action: Bolt
Grips: Synthetic
Barrel: 8 in.
Sights: None
Weight: 4 lb. 7 oz.
Caliber: .300 BLK
Capacity: 20 rounds
Features: Based on the company's rifle

The Fix, the Mini Fix is a bolt-action pistol with a one-piece receiver; stabilizing brace; 45-degree short-throw bolt; full-length topside rail; free-floating Q-sert handguard; 5/8x24 threaded tapered muzzle with Cherry Bomb muzzle brake; two-stage match trigger
MSRP $3299.00

SUGAR WEASEL

Action: Semiautomatic
Grips: Synthetic
Barrel: 7 in.
Sights: None
Weight: 4 lb. 10 oz.
Caliber: .300 BLK
Capacity: 20 rounds
Features: A semiauto AR-type pistol an M16 spec receiver; direct impingement design in a pistol length gas system with adjustable gas block; single-stage trigger; six-position SBA3 pistol stabilizing brace; six-inch M-LOK handguard; 5/8x24 threaded muzzle with Cherry Bomb muzzle brake
MSRP $1999.00

LWRC International

LWRCI SMG-45

SMG-45
Action: Semiautomatic
Grips: Synthetic
Barrel: 8.5 in.
Sights: Magpul MBUS Pro
Weight: 94 oz.
Caliber: .45 ACP
Capacity: 25 rounds
Features: LWRCI dubs this a pistol-caliber "sub-gun" and it features a short recoil/delayed blowback action; LWRCI rail panels at 3, 6, and 9 o'clock; LWRCI Ultra Combat grip; anodized nitride nickel-boron metal surface treatment; chromoly steel barrel; ambidextrous lower controls; LWRCI Advanced Fire Control Group
MSRP **$2995.00**

Magnum Research

MAGNUM RESEARCH .429 DESERT EAGLE MARK XIX

MAGNUM RESEARCH BFR (BIGGEST FINEST REVOLVER)

MAGNUM RESEARCH DESERT EAGLE 1911

MAGNUM RESEARCH DESERT EAGLE 1911 C STAINLESS

MAGNUM RESEARCH DESERT EAGLE 1911 G STAINLESS

MAGNUM RESEARCH DESERT EAGLE 1911 U STAINLESS

MAGNUM RESEARCH DESERT EAGLE BLACK TIGER STRIPE

.429 DESERT EAGLE MARK XIX
Action: Semiautomatic
Grips: Soft rubber
Barrel: 6 in.
Sights: Fixed combat type
Weight: 68.3 oz.
Caliber: .429 DE
Capacity: 7 rounds
Features: A new caliber from Magnum Research in a new gun featuring single-action; integral muzzle brake; Picatinny rails topside and under barrel; polygonal rifling with 1:18 twist; stainless finish
MSRP $2143.00

BFR (BIGGEST FINEST REVOLVER)
Action: SA revolver
Grips: Rubber, optional wood
Barrel: 5 in., 6.5 in., 7.5 in., 10 in.
Sights: Adjustable rear, fixed front
Weight: 57.6–85 oz.
Caliber: Long Cylinder: .30-30 Win., .444 Marlin, .45 LC/.410, .45-70 Govt., .450 Marlin, .44 Mag., .460 S&W Mag., .500 S&W Mag.; Short Cylinder: .22 Hornet, .454 Casull, .480 Ruger/.475 Linebaugh, .50AE, .500 JRH
Capacity: 5 rounds
Features: Both long and short-cylinder models are made of stainless steel; barrels are stress-relieved and cut rifled; rubber grips; Weaver style scope mount
MSRP . . . . $1219.00–$1391.00

DESERT EAGLE 1911 SERIES
Action: SA semiautomatic
Grips: Checkered wood
Barrel: 3 in., 5 in., 4.3 in.
Sights: Fixed
Weight: 36 oz. (5 in. barrel), 32 oz. (4.3 in. barrel), 25.8 oz. (3-in. barrel)
Caliber: .45 ACP
Capacity: 6, 8 rounds
Features: Seven variants comprise this series: C has 4.33-in. barrel, allover stainless or blue finish; G has 5.05-in. barrel, allover stainless or blue finish; U Stainless has a 3-in. barrel, allover stainless or blue finish; GR is in allover blue only, with 5.05-in barrel, and accessory rail
MSRP . . . . $851.00–$1062.00

DESERT EAGLE BLACK TIGER STRIPE
Action: Semiautomatic
Grips: Hard rubber
Barrel: 6 in.
Sights: Fixed combat style
Weight: 70 oz.–71 oz.
Caliber: .50 AE, .44 Mag.
Capacity: 8 rounds
Features: Desert Eagle in unique black tiger stripe finish
MSRP **$2122.00**

Magnum Research

MAGNUM RESEARCH DESERT EAGLE CASE HARDENED

MAGNUM RESEARCH DESERT EAGLE COMBO CALIBER PACKAGE

MAGNUM RESEARCH DESERT EAGLE L5 5-INCH BARREL WITH MUZZLE BRAKE, NY-OKAY

MAGNUM RESEARCH DESERT EAGLE TUNGSTEN

MAGNUM RESEARCH DESERT EAGLE WHITE MATTE DISTRESSED

MAGNUM RESEARCH DESERT EAGLE WITH INTEGRAL MUZZLE BRAKE

DESERT EAGLE CASE HARDENED

Action: Semiautomatic
Grips: Walnut, Hogue
Barrel: 6 in.
Sights: Fixed combat-type
Weight: 72.4 oz.
Caliber: .357 Mag., .44 Mag., .50 AE
Capacity: 7, 8, 9 rounds
Features: Gold trigger; walnut grips with the engraved Desert Eagle logo; includes a pair of Hogue grips
MSRP **$2368.00**

DESERT EAGLE COMBO CALIBER PACKAGE

Action: Semiautomatic
Grips: Polymer
Barrel: 6 in.
Sights: Fixed combat-type
Weight: 69.8 oz.–70.6 oz.
Caliber: .44 Mag./.50 AE
Capacity: 7, 8 rounds
Features: Comes assembled as a .44 Mag. with an 8-round magazine; .50 AE barrel with a .50 AE 7-round magazine included; both barrels have a Weaver-style rail on top
MSRP **$1949.00**

DESERT EAGLE L5 5-INCH BARREL WITH MUZZLE BRAKE, NY-OKAY

Action: SA semiautomatic
Grips: Plastic composite
Barrel: 5 in.
Sights: Fixed combat
Weight: 2 lb. 9 oz.
Caliber: .50 AE, .44 Mag., .357 Mag.
Capacity: 9 rounds
Features: Black aluminum frame; black slide/barrel with integral muzzle brake and full Weaver-style accessory rail
MSRP **$1900.00**

DESERT EAGLE TUNGSTEN

Action: SA semiautomatic
Grips: Plastic composite
Barrel: 6 in.
Sights: Fixed combat
Weight: 4 lb. 6.6 oz.
Caliber: .44 Magnum, .50 A.E.
Capacity: 8 rounds
Features: Tungsten Cerakote finish; high-quality carbon steel barrel; frame and slide with full Weaver-style accessory rail
MSRP **$1891.00**

DESERT EAGLE WHITE MATTE DISTRESSED

Action: Semiautomatic
Grips: Hard rubber
Barrel: 6 in.
Sights: Fixed combat style
Weight: 70 oz.–71 oz.
Caliber: .50 AE, .44 Mag.
Capacity: 8 rounds
Features: Desert Eagle in unique White Matte Distressed finish
MSRP **$1999.00**

DESERT EAGLE WITH INTEGRAL MUZZLE BRAKE

Action: Semiautomatic
Grips: Hard rubber
Barrel: 6 in.
Sights: Fixed combat style
Weight: 71 oz.–74 oz.
Caliber: .50 AE, .44 Mag., .357 Mag.
Capacity: 8 rounds
Features: Three-port integral muzzle brakel; Weaver-style accessory rail; black or stainless finish
MSRP . . . . **$1708.00–$2143.00**

Masterpiece Arms

MASTERPIECE ARMS MPA935DMG

MPA935DMG

Action: Semiautomatic
Grips: Synthetic
Barrel: 5.5 in.
Sights: Adjustable front, rear
Weight: N/A
Caliber: 9mm
Capacity: 17, 33 rounds
Features: Compatible with 17- and 30-round Glock magazines only, this unique pistol sports a barrel threaded ½x28; side cocker; scope mount; lower Picatinny rail; Ergo grip; MPA short handguard; side folding KAK Shockwave 2.0 arm brace; decal grip panels; barrel extension; no tax stamp required with the KAK arm brace; black or multiple Cerakote colors to choose from
MSRP **$791.00**

HANDGUNS

MASTERPIECE ARMS DS9 HYBRID

DS9 HYBRID

Action: Semiautomatic
Grips: Aluminum
Barrel: 5 in.
Sights: Accuracy X Shot base, Kensight
Weight: N/A
Caliber: 9mm
Capacity: 17, 20 rounds
Features: Hand-lapped frame to slide fit; full-length light rail frame; machined aluminum grip; Koenig hammer, sear, and disconnector; custom machined aluminum trigger shoe; FGW slide machining; slide lightning cuts; Wolff springs; MPA magwell; one-piece tool-less guide rod; iron sights or a slide-cut option with customer choice of mounting plates that accommodate a wide variety of reflex red-dot sights; in a hybrid black/stainless; hybrid stainless/blue; hybrid black/blue
MSRP **$2999.00**

Maxim Defense

MAXIM DEFENSE MDX:508

MAXIM DEFENSE PDX

MDX:508

Action: Semiautomatic
Grips: Synthetic
Barrel: 8.5 in.
Sights: None
Weight: N/A
Caliber: 5.56 NATO, .300 BLK, 7.62x39mm
Capacity: 20 rounds
Features: A small-platform AR-type with a full-length top rail; HATEBRAKE muzzle brake; SCW stock or brace; in Arid or black; also available as an SBR
MSRP **$2495.00**

PDX

Action: Semiautomatic
Grips: Aluminum
Barrel: 5.5 in.
Sights: None
Weight: 91 oz.
Caliber: 5.56 NATO, 7.62X29mm NATO
Capacity: N/A
Features: A CQC design featuring Maxim's all-new Heartbrake muzzle "booster"; MD's aluminum SCW stock system with 4-inch length; combo black and Arid tan color finishes; overall length just 18.75 inches
MSRP **$2295.00**

MG Arms

MG ARMS DRAGONFLY

MG ARMS DRAGONSLAYER

MG ARMS WRAITHE

DRAGONFLY

Action: Revolver
Grips: Customer choice
Barrel: 4 in.
Sights: Blade front, adjustable rear
Weight: 21 oz.
Caliber: .32 H&R Mag., .38 Spec. +P, .44 Spec.
Capacity: 6 rounds
Features: MG says this is the world's lightest single-action; colors in PTFE or Cerakote; titanium cylinder; titanium sleeved barrel; customer choice of grips; half-cock loading; limited product of 25 per year
MSRP **$1295.00**

DRAGONSLAYER

Action: Revolver
Grips: Customer choice
Barrel: Customer choice 4.5 in.–10 in.
Sights: Ramp front, adjustable rear
Weight: 36 oz.
Caliber: .45 LC +P, .454 Casull, .475 Linebaugh, .500 Linebaugh
Capacity: 5 rounds
Features: A big-bore for the hunters with multiple custom options including barrel length, metal finish colors, ceramic or Teflon finishes, barrel porting, and grips; limited production to 25 per year
MSRP **$1895.00**

WRAITHE

Action: Semiautomatic
Grips: Custom G10
Barrel: 4.5 in.
Sights: Night or fixed
Weight: 18 oz.–20 oz.
Caliber: .45 ACP, 9mm
Capacity: 8+1, 9+1 rounds
Features: Aluminum alloy bobtail frame; custom grip panels; high ride beavertail safety; two Wilson magazines included, available in olive drab, black or desert tan
MSRP **$2895.00**

Mossberg (O. F. Mossberg & Sons)

MOSSBERG MC2C

MOSSBERG MC2C STAINLESS TWO-TONE

MC2C

Action: Semiautomatic
Grips: Glass-reinforced polymer
Barrel: 3.9 in.
Sights: White three-dot
Weight: 21 oz.
Caliber: 9mm
Capacity: 13, 15 rounds
Features: Just two ounces more than the smaller MC1sc, but double the capacity. Features stainless steel barrel and slide; matte black finish; available with cross-bolt safety
Standard sights $505.00
TruGlog Pro sights $613.00

MC2C STAINLESS TWO-TONE

Action: Semiautomatic
Grips: Glass-reinforced polymer
Barrel: 3.9 in.
Sights: White three-dot
Weight: 21 oz.
Caliber: 9mm
Capacity: 13, 15 rounds
Features: Identical to the all-black base MC2c model, but with a matte stainless slide; available with cross-bolt safety
MSRP $505.00

Nighthawk Custom

NIGHTHAWK CUSTOM AGENT2

NIGHTHAWK CUSTOM AGENT 2 COMMANDER

NIGHTHAWK CUSTOM BOB MARVEL CUSTOM

NIGHTHAWK CUSTOM BORDER SPECIAL

NIGHTHAWK CUSTOM CHAIRMAN

AGENT 2

Action: Semiautomatic
Grips: G10
Barrel: 5 in.
Sights: Fiber optic front, Heinie black ledge rear
Weight: 40.1 oz.
Caliber: 9mm, .45 ACP
Capacity: 8, 10 rounds
Features: Match-grade, crowned, flush-cut barrel; Nighthawk/Agency custom trigger; Ultra Hi-Cut front strap; one-piece magwell/mainspring housing; extended and angled magazine release; Agency slide serrations front and aft; Smoke Cerakote finish; Railscales G10 grip
MSRP $4999.00

AGENT 2 COMMANDER

Action: Semiautomatic
Grips: G10
Barrel: 4.25 in.
Sights: Fiber optic front, Heinie ledge rear
Weight: 38.6 oz.
Caliber: 9mm, .45 ACP
Capacity: 10 rounds
Features: Jointly designed by Nighthawk and Agency Arms, this smart-looking pistol has cuts at the front-strap, mainspring housing, and controls to match the custom Railscales grips; red Nighthawk front sight with serrated Heinie ledge rear; extended, faceted, and angled magazine release; crowned, flush-cut match-grade barrel; smoke Cerakote finish; Agency front and rear slide serrations; light rail
MSRP $4999.00

BOB MARVEL CUSTOM

Action: Semiautomatic
Grips: Custom Mil Tac
Barrel: 4.25 in.
Sights: Novak tritium night sight front, tritium adjustable rear
Weight: 38 oz.
Caliber: 9mm, .45 ACP
Capacity: 8+1 rounds
Features: Incorporates new Nighthawk/Marvel Everlast Recoil System allowing for at least 10,000 rounds before a spring change is necessary and reduced recoil and muzzle flip
MSRP $4899.00

BORDER SPECIAL

Action: Semiautomatic
Grips: Cocobolo
Barrel: 4.25 in.
Sights: Gold bead post front, Heinie Black Slant-Pro rear
Weight: 34.1 oz.
Caliber: .45 ACP, 9mm
Capacity: 8 rounds
Features: Built on concealed carry cut; Commander-sized frame and slide; frame and mainspring housing dehorned for carry; match-grade barrel; ultra high-cut front strap; fluted barrel hood; Elite Midnight Cerakote finish; optional black, two-tone, or all-stainless upgrades available
MSRP $3999.00

CHAIRMAN

Action: Semiautomatic
Grips: G10
Barrel: 6 in.
Sights: Gold bead front, adjustable black rear
Weight: 40.9 oz.
Caliber: 9mm, .45 ACP
Capacity: 10 rounds
Features: Long-slide 9mm featuring Nighthawk's aluminum tri-cavity trigger; Ultra Hi-Cut front strap; match-grade crowned barrel; DLC frame/slide finish with cutouts revealing the gold titanium nitride barrel; heavy angle lightning slide cuts; Railscale G10 grips
MSRP $4599.00

NIGHTHAWK CUSTOM COMPLETE CUSTOM STIPPLE

NIGHTHAWK CUSTOM FIREHAWK

NIGHTHAWK CUSTOM GLOBAL RESPONSE PISTOL

NIGHTHAWK CUSTOM HEINIE LADY HAWK 2.0

NIGHTHAWK CUSTOM KESTREL

NIGHTHAWK CUSTOM/KORTH MONGOOSE .357

NIGHTHAWK CUSTOM KORTH NXA

NIGHTHAWK CUSTOM KORTH NXR

COMPLETE CUSTOM STIPPLE

Action: Semiautomatic
Grips: Cocobolo
Barrel: 5 in.
Sights: Nighthawk tritium front, Heinie 2-Dot Slant-Pro tritium rear
Weight: 38.8 oz.
Caliber: .45 ACP, 9mm
Capacity: 8 rounds
Features: Aggressively stippled on top and rear of slide, front strap, mainspring housing, hammer top, slide stop, mag release, recoil spring plug, thumb safety, and grip safety pad; heavy French border; round butt mainspring housing; beveled frame; front and rear cocking serrations
MSRP $4799.00

FIRE HAWK

Action: Semiautomatic
Grips: Agent 1; G10
Barrel: 5 in.
Sights: Gold bead front, Heinie black slant pro rear
Weight: N/A
Caliber: 9mm, .45 ACP
Capacity: 8, 10 rounds
Features: Government-sized .45 featuring a French border; solid trigger; match-grade barrel; Ultra Hi-Cut front strap; compensator; rear slide serrations only; black finish with Agent 1 grips or stainless with G10 grips
MSRP $4599.00

GLOBAL RESPONSE PISTOL (GRP)

Action: SA Semiautomatic
Grips: Micarta gator grips
Barrel: 5 in.
Sights: Night
Weight: 39 oz.
Caliber: .45 ACP, .30 Super Carry
Capacity: 8 rounds
Features: 1911 design; Lanyard loop integrated into the mainspring housing; forged slide stop axle is cut

flush with the frame; Heinie Slant-Pro Night Sights, Novak Low Mount Night Sights, or Novak Extreme Duty Adjustable Night Sights are standard; Perma Kote finish in black, sniper gray, green, coyote tan, titanium blued, and hard chrome
MSRP $3499.00

HEINIE LADY HAWK 2.0

Action: Semiautomatic
Grips: Obsidian; abalone; zinc
Barrel: 4.25 in.
Sights: Tritium front, Heinie straight edge slant pro rear
Weight: 36 oz.
Caliber: 9mm, .45 ACP
Capacity: 8, 10 rounds
Features: Commander frame; match-grade barrel; scalloped front strap and mainspring housing; beveled frame; Nighthawk tri-cavity aluminum trigger; complete dehorning; DLC frame/slide finish with a rose gold TICN finish on barrel and controls
MSRP $4799.00

KESTREL

Action: Semiautomatic
Grips: Ultra-Thin Alumagrips
Barrel: 4.25 in.
Sights: Heinie Slant pro straight eight night sights
Weight: 34.25 oz.
Caliber: .45 ACP, 9mm
Capacity: 7-10 rounds
Features: Reduced overall frame circumference; magazine well beveled for insertion; hand serrated rear of slide; Heinie Signature scalloped front strap and mainspring housing; tactical checkered extended magazine release; standard black nitride finish with stainless controls and optional stainless steel upgrade
MSRP $4199.00

KORTH MONGOOSE .357

Action: Revolver
Grips: Hogue

Barrel: 3 in., 4 in., 5.25 in., 6 in.
Sights: Gold bead front post, adjustable rear
Weight: 37.6 oz.
Caliber: .357 Mag.
Capacity: 6 rounds
Features: Partnership with German manufacturer Korth; revolver has an AISI 4140 aluminum frame; skeletonized high-speed hammer; easy access cylinder release; optional 9mm cylinder designed for use without moon clips
MSRP $3699.00

KORTH NXR

Action: Revolver
Grips: Walnut
Barrel: 4 in., 6 in.
Sights: Ramp front, adjustable rear
Weight: 55.3 oz.
Caliber: .44 Mag.
Capacity: 6 rounds
Features: A super choice for a hunting tool, this revolver sports an integral Picatinny rail on top for optics and under barrel for weights; ventilated barrel housing; nDLC coating; Turkish walnut grips with finger grooves; 416R hammer-forged barrel; front side has removable side panels for fast change-out
MSRP . . . .$5199.00–$5299.00

KORTH NXS

Action: Revolver
Grips: Walnut
Barrel: 4 in., 6 in.
Sights: Ramp front, adjustable rear
Weight: 50.7 oz.
Caliber: .357 Mag.
Capacity: 8 rounds
Features: Complexly ventilated barrel shroud; wide swing-out cylinder cut for use with moon clips; Jim Wilson walnut grips with finger grooves; nDLC finish on metalwork; dual top-side Picatinny rails; under-barrel rail for lights or weights; optional 9mm cylinder with moon clips cuts
MSRP $5299.00

Nighthawk Custom

NIGHTHAWK CUSTOM NHC CLASSIC

NIGHTHAWK CUSTOM PRESIDENT

NIGHTHAWK CUSTOM T3

NIGHTHAWK CUSTOM T4

NIGHTHAWK CUSTOM THE BULL

NIGHTHAWK CUSTOM THE BULL COMMANDER

NIGHTHAWK CUSTOM THE BULL OFFICER

NHC CLASSIC

Action: Semiautomatic
Grips: Cocobolo
Barrel: 5 in.
Sights: Gold bead front post, Heinie Black Ledge rear
Weight: 36.9 oz.
Caliber: .45 ACP
Capacity: 8 rounds
Features: Custom offering; slide top has been flattened and accented with arrow pattern and French border; curved slide stop; round butt mainspring housing; frame dehorning; ultra high-cut front strap; stainless finish with script engraving at slide rear; threaded barrel available
MSRP $4399.00

PRESIDENT

Action: Semiautomatic
Grips: G10
Barrel: 5 in.
Sights: Gold bead front, Heinie black ledge rear
Weight: 38.2 oz.
Caliber: 9mm, .30 Super Carry
Capacity: 10 rounds
Features: Government frame; Nighthawk tri-cavity trigger; complete dehorning; match-grade crowned barrel; DLC finish with gold titanium nitride barrel; heavy-angle lightning slide cuts; Railscale G10 grips
MSRP $4599.00

T3

Action: SA semiautomatic
Grips: G10 grips
Barrel: 4.25 in.
Sights: Heinie Straight Eight Slant-Pro, night

Weight: 34.6 oz.
Caliber: .45 ACP, 9mm
Capacity: 7 rounds
Features: Frame based on Officer model; extended magazine well; Heinie Slant-Pro Straight Eights Night Sights are standard; mainspring housing and rear of slide are horizontally serrated to match; top of slide serrated to reduce glare; Nighthawk Custom lightweight aluminum trigger that has been blacked-out using Perma Kote; available in black nitride finish
MSRP $3999.00

T4

Action: Semiautomatic
Grips: Slim
Barrel: 3.8 in.
Sights: Fixed
Weight: 34.3 oz.
Caliber: 9mm
Capacity: 9 or 10 rounds
Features: Similar to the T3, but with a shorter 3.8-in. barrel platform; match-grade barrel is crowned and recessed with the slide; slide cuts reduce weight and carry cuts at the front aid in holstering; hinned aluminum grips; complete dehorning; ultra high-cut frontstrap
MSRP $3999.00

THE BULL

Action: Semiautomatic
Grips: Carbon fiber
Barrel: 5 in.
Sights: Nighthawk tritium front, Heinie Ledge Straight Eight tritium rear
Weight: 38.8 oz.

Caliber: .45 ACP, 9mm
Capacity: 8 rounds
Features: Government frame with French border; bow tie plug; match-grade bull barrel; frame dehorning; Elite Smoke Cerakote finish
MSRP $3999.00

THE BULL COMMANDER

Action: Semiautomatic
Grips: Carbon fiber
Barrel: 4.25 in., 5 in.
Sights: Tritium front, Heinie Straight Eight tritium ledge rear
Weight: 36.7 oz.
Caliber: .45 ACP, 9mm
Capacity: 8 rounds
Features: Choice of Government or Commander frames; Nighthawk curved slide stop; coarse rear slide serrations; beveled frame and slide bottom; Nighthawk Bow Tie plug and Bull Nose cut on the front of the slide; French border
MSRP $3999.00

THE BULL OFFICER

Action: Semiautomatic
Grips: Carbon fiber
Barrel: 3.8 in.
Sights: Tritium front, Heinie ledge rear
Weight: 32 oz.
Caliber: 9mm
Capacity: 8 rounds
Features: A single-stack 9mm in an Officer's foundation with a black nitride finish forged frame; bull-nose slide front; bow-tie plug; French border; shortened slide stop; beveled frame; rear slide serrations; completely dehorned
MSRP $3999.00

NIGHTHAWK CUSTOM THUNDER RANCH COMBAT SPECIAL

NIGHTHAWK CUSTOM TRI-CUT CARRY 9MM

NIGHTHAWK CUSTOM TROOPER

NIGHTHAWK CUSTOM TRS COMMANDER

NIGHTHAWK CUSTOM TRS COMP

NIGHTHAWK CUSTOM TURNBULL VIP 1

THUNDER RANCH COMBAT SPECIAL

Action: Semiautomatic
Grips: Linen/Micarta
Barrel: 5 in.
Sights: Gold bead front, Heinie ledge rear
Weight: 41.3 oz.
Caliber: 9mm, .45 ACP
Capacity: 8 rounds
Features: Created by Nighthawk with cooperation from the Thunder Ranch firearm training facility, this special full-size build has front and rear slide serrations; GI numb-style thumb safety; 25 lpi checkering on frontstrap and mainspring housing; lanyard loop; linen/Micarta grips; smoked nitride finish; slide has Thunder Ranch logo
MSRP $3799.00

TRI-CUT CARRY 9MM

Action: Semiautomatic
Grips: Aluminum
Barrel: 4.25 in.
Sights: Nighthawk tritium front, Heinie Ledge Straight Eight tritium rear
Weight: 34.7 oz.
Caliber: 9mm
Capacity: 10 rounds
Features: Commander-sized frame with custom tri-cut angled design; pneumatic stippling; slide ports; flat-faced Nighthawk Custom trigger; angled mag release
MSRP $4999.00

TROOPER

Action: Semiautomatic
Grips: G10
Barrel: 5 in.
Sights: Tritium front, Heinie Straight Eight tritium ledge rear
Weight: 37.1 oz.
Caliber: .45 ACP, 9mm
Capacity: 8 rounds
Features: Government frame; match-grade crowned barrel; Nighthawk tri-cavity trigger; complete dehorning; black nitride finish; Gator Back G10 grips
MSRP $3299.00

TRS COMMANDER

Action: Semiautomatic
Grips: Polymer
Barrel: 4.25 in.
Sights: Tritium front, Heinie ledge rear
Weight: 36.7 oz.
Caliber: 9mm
Capacity: 17 rounds
Features: A double-stack on a Commander build with a match-grade barrel; full-length dust cover; unique dimpling on slide matches pattern on grip; ultra high-cut frontstrap; solid aluminum trigger with flat serrated face; complete dehorning
MSRP $4399.00

TRS COMP

Action: Semiautomatic
Grips: Polymer
Barrel: 5 in.
Sights: Gold bead front, Heinie ledge rear
Weight: 39.6 oz.
Caliber: 9mm
Capacity: 17 rounds
Features: A double-stack Government frame build with precision ported compensator; monolithic slide; full-length dust cover; aluminum trigger with flat serrated face; dimpling pattern at rear of slide matches pattern on the grip; ultra high-cut frontstrap; complete dehorning
MSRP $4999.00

TURNBULL VIP 1

Action: Semiautomatic
Grips: Mastodon ivory
Barrel: 5 in.
Sights: Gold bead front, Heinie solid black Slant-Pro rear
Weight: 37.4 oz.
Caliber: .45 ACP
Capacity: 8 rounds
Features: Very Impressive Pistol is a collaboration between Nighthawk Custom and Doug Turnbull; mastodon ivory grips; custom display case; all-over charcoal blue finish
MSRP $8999.00

Nighthawk Custom

NIGHTHAWK CUSTOM VICE PRESIDENT

NIGHTHAWK CUSTOM VIP

NIGHTHAWK CUSTOM VIP AGENT 2

NIGHTHAWK CUSTOM VIP BLACK

NIGHTHAWK CUSTOM WAR HAWK CCO

NIGHTHAWK CUSTOM WAR HAWK GOVERNMENT

VICE PRESIDENT

Action: Semiautomatic
Grips: G10
Barrel: 5 in.
Sights: Gold bead front, Heinie ledge rear
Weight: 38.2 oz.
Caliber: 9mm
Capacity: 10 rounds
Features: Part of Nighthawk's Boardroom Series, this custom build gets a Commander foundation stainless steel slide with nDLC finish, aggressive rear serrations and muzzle-end windows that show off the gold titanium nitride barrel with crown; custom Ascend scaled G10 grips from Railscales; aluminum Nighthawk tri-cavity trigger; 25 lpi checkering on frontstrap and one-piece mainspring housing; completely dehorned
MSRP $4599.00

VIP

Action: Semiautomatic
Grips: Giraffe bone
Barrel: 5 in.
Sights: Heinie black rear, 14k gold bead front
Weight: 39.78 oz.
Caliber: .45 ACP
Capacity: 8 rounds
Features: Custom vertical front strap and mainspring serrations; 14k plated gold bead front sight and crowned barrel; deep hand engraving featured throughout; antiqued nickel finish; custom cocobolo hardwood presentation case
MSRP $8999.00

VIP AGENT 2

Action: Semiautomatic
Grips: Mammoth ivory

Barrel: 5 in.
Sights: Gold bead front, Heinie ledge rear
Weight: 39.6 oz.
Caliber: .45 ACP
Capacity: 10 rounds
Features: Mammoth ivory G10 grips by Railscales; polished charcoal blue slide; color case-hardened frame; crowned flush-cut match-grade barrel; slide is faceted and has side windows; forged frame with lightened Recon rail; Nighthawk/Agency custom trigger; pistol is a join creation of Nighthawk, Agency Arms, and Turnbull restoration
MSRP $8999.00

VIP BLACK

Action: Semiautomatic
Grips: Girrafe bone
Barrel: 5 in.
Sights: Gold bead front, Heinie black slant pro rear
Weight: N/A
Caliber: .45 ACP
Capacity: 8 rounds
Features: Government frame; 14k solid gold front bead sight; giraffe bone grips; hand serrations at rear of slide and at ejection port match the Heinie sight; hand engraving; comes in custom walnut case
MSRP $8999.00

WAR HAWK CCO

Action: Semitautomatic
Grips: Synthetic
Barrel: 4.25 in.
Sights: Fixed
Weight: 34.7 oz.
Caliber: 9mm
Capacity: 8 rounds

Features: Unique tri-cut slide with bold angles; serrated arrow style slide top; heavy bevel on bottom of slide; hand serrated rear of slide; barrel is crowned and beveled with the bushing; one-piece fully machined 20 LPI checkered mainspring housing/magwell; high-cut front strap; hightweight solid aluminum match grade trigger; thin G10 in hyena brown; Heinie Slant Pro Straight Eight Tritium night sights; Nighthawk Custom/Marvel EVERLAST recoil system; War Hawk logo engraved on slide; stainless steel frame standard; black nitride finish
MSRP $4399.00

WAR HAWK GOVERNMENT

Action: Semitautomatic
Grips: Synthetic
Barrel: 5 in.
Sights: Fixed
Weight: 39.6 oz.
Caliber: 9mm, .45 ACP
Capacity: 8 rounds
Features: Unique multi-faceted slide; serrated arrow style slide top; heavy bevel on bottom of slide; hand serrated rear of slide; barrel is crowned and beveled with the bushing; lightweight aluminum medium solid match trigger; aggressive G10 hyena brown grips; red fiber optic front sights; Tritium dot front sight upgrade available; Jardine Hook rear sight; tactical magazine catch; Nighthawk Custom/Marvel EVERLAST recoil system; War Hawk logo engraved on slide
MSRP $4399.00

NORTH AMERICAN ARMS .32 ACP GUARDIAN

NORTH AMERICAN ARMS .380 ACP GUARDIAN

NORTH AMERICAN ARMS 1860 EARL

NORTH AMERICAN ARMS MINI MASTER SERIES REVOLVER

NORTH AMERICAN ARMS BLACK WIDOW

NORTH AMERICAN ARMS MINI-REVOLVER

NORTH AMERICAN ARMS RANGER II

.32 ACP GUARDIAN

Action: DAO semiautomatic
Grips: Polymer
Barrel: 2.5 in.
Sights: Fixed, open
Weight: 13.5 oz.
Caliber: .32 ACP
Capacity: 6+1 rounds
Features: Stainless steel; double action only
MSRP **$430.00**

.380 ACP GUARDIAN

Action: DAO semiautomatic
Grips: Composite
Barrel: 2.49 in.
Sights: Fixed, open
Weight: 18.72 oz.
Caliber: .380 ACP
Capacity: 6+1 rounds
Features: Stainless steel; double action only
MSRP **$430.00**

1860 EARL

Action: SA revolver
Grips: Rosewood
Barrel: 3 in., 4 in.
Sights: Stainless steel post front sight
Weight: 9.7 oz.
Caliber: .22 Mag.
Capacity: 5 rounds
Features: Replica of 1860s Hogleg, with faux loading lever and pin, octagonal barrel, rosewood grips; available with .22 LR conversion cylinder
Standard **$315.00**
With conversion cylinder. . .**$350.00**

BLACK WIDOW

Action: Revolver
Grips: Rubber
Barrel: 2 in.
Sights: Marble Arms fixed or adjustable
Weight: 8.9 oz.
Caliber: .22 Win. Mag.
Capacity: 5 rounds
Features: A short-barreled .22 Win. Mag. with oversized grips to hang onto; SA only; non-fluted cylinder; vent rib; stainless available with fixed or adjustable sights; PVD black and stainless versions available with .22 LR conversion cylinders
Stainless: . . . . **$305.00–$330.00**
PVD Black:. **$335.00**
PVD Black w/conversion cylinder:. **$370.00**
Stainless w/conversion cylinder:. . . . . . . **$339.00–$365.00**

MINI MASTER SERIES REVOLVER

Action: SA revolver
Grips: Rubber
Barrel: 4 in.
Sights: Fixed or adjustable
Weight: 10.7 oz.
Caliber: .22 LR, .22 Mag.
Capacity: 5 rounds
Features: Conversion cylinder or adjustable sights available
Standard . . . . **$315.00–$345.00**
With conversion cylinder . . . . **$350.00–$385.00**

MINI-REVOLVER

Action: SA revolver
Grips: Laminated rosewood
Barrel: 1.2 in., 1.625 in.
Sights: Fixed, open
Weight: 4 oz.–6.2 oz.
Caliber: .22 Short, .22 LR, .22 Mag.
Capacity: 5 rounds
Features: Features NAA's safety cylinder so mini-revolver can be carried fully loaded; .22 LR available with folding "holster grip." .22 Mag available ported or with folding "holster grip"
.22 Short **$239.00**
.22 LR. **$239.00**
.22 LR with holster grip **$269.00**
.22 Mag.–standard **$249.00**
.22 Mag. with laser. **$375.00**
.22 Mag. with conversion cylinder . . . . **$285.00–$315.00**
.22 Mag. with holster grip. . .**$280.00**
.22 Mag. with ported barrel . . . . **$269.00–$305.00**

RANGER II

Action: Revolver
Grips: Rosewood
Barrel: 1.63, 2.5, 4 in.
Sights: Bead front
Weight: 6.9 oz.
Caliber: .22 Win. Mag.
Capacity: 5 rounds
Features: Tiny break-top revolver has rosewood boot grip; star ejector; fully ribbed barrel; bead-blast stainless finish on barrel and frame, polished finish on cylinder
Standard . . . . **$499.00–$575.00**
With conversion cylinder . . . . **$600.00–$680.00**

North American Arms

NORTH AMERICAN ARMS SIDEWINDER

NORTH AMERICAN ARMS THE PUG

NORTH AMERICAN ARMS THE WASP

SIDEWINDER

Action: Revolver
Grips: Laminated rosewood
Barrel: 1.5, 2.5, 4 in.
Sights: Stainless steel post
Weight: 6.7 oz.
Caliber: .22 Mag.
Capacity: 5 rounds
Features: Features NAA's safety cylinder; stainless steel frame; available .22 LR conversion
Standard . . . . $369.00–$410.00
**With conversion
   cylinder** . . . . $469.00–$535.00

THE PUG

Action: Revolver
Grips: Rubber
Barrel: 1 in.
Sights: XS white dot, tritium
Weight: 6.4 oz.
Caliber: .22 Mag.
Capacity: 5 rounds
Features: Oversized pebble-textured rubber grips enable the handler to keep a firm grip
Standard $345.00
Standard ported. $365.00
Tritium sights $370.00

THE WASP

Action: SA revolver
Grips: Rubber pebble finish
Barrel: 1.125 in., 1.625 in.
Sights: Stainless post
Weight: 5.9 oz.–7.2 oz.
Caliber: .22 Mag.
Capacity: 5 rounds
Features: Stainless steel frame; vent rib barrel; skeleton hammer; .22 LR conversion cylinders available; brushed sides, matte contours, black inlay
Standard $280.00
With conversion cylinder. . .$316.00

Tritium ported $385.00
**Standard with conversion
   cylinder** $380.00
**Tritium with conversion
   cylinder** $399.00

Nosler, Inc.

NOSLER M48 NCH

M48 NCH

Action: Bolt
Grips: Synthetic
Barrel: 15 in.
Sights: None
Weight: N/A
Caliber: .22 Nosler, .24 Nosler, 6mm Creedmoor, 6.5 Creedmoor, 7mm-08

Rem., .308 Win.
Capacity: 1 round
Features: The bolt handgun comes back to life with a one-piece billet aluminum frame; Nosler's Model 58 short-action; Cerakoted metalwork; bedded action; free-floating barrel
MSRP. $2495.00

Patriot Ordnance Factory, Inc.

PATRIOT ORDNANCE FACTORY MINUTEMAN

PATRIOT ORDNANCE FACTORY RENEGADE PLUS

MINUTEMAN

Action: Semiautomatic
Grips: Synthetic
Barrel: 9 in.
Sights: None
Weight: 88 oz.
Caliber: 5.56 NATO, .350 Legend
Capacity: N/A
Features: A direct impingement pistol with a straight, drop-in match-grade trigger; ambidextrous rear QD sling swivel plate; carbine-length gas system; POF three-prong flash-hider; Renegade rail; ambidextrous Strike Eagle charging handle; nitride heat-treated barrel; anti-tilt buffer tube
MSRP . . . . $1518.00–$1650.00

RENEGADE PLUS

Action: Semiautomatic
Grips: Synthetic
Barrel: 10.5 in.
Sights: None
Weight: 5 lb. 13 oz.
Caliber: 5.56 NATO, .300 Blackout
Capacity: 20, 30 rounds
Features: Identical to the company's now discontinued rifle configuration, but in pistol form featuring a nine-inch rail; five-position SB Tactical SBA3 arm brace; M-LOK compatibility; Dictator nine-position gas block; straight gas tube; in black or Burnt Bronze; Ultimate Bolt Carrier Group; match-grade trigger; ambidextrous receiver
MSRP . . . . $1927.00–$2059.00

Polymer80

POLYMER80 P80 PFC9

POLYMER80 P80 PFS9

P80 PFC9

Action: Semiautomatic
Grips: Polymer
Barrel: 4.02 in.
Sights: White dot front, serrated rear
Weight: 21.16 oz.
Caliber: 9mm
Capacity: 10, 15 rounds
Features: The smaller of two guns produced by a company best known for its slides, frames, and 80% kits, this striker-fire pistol takes Glock 17 magazines and features an underside Picatinny rail; front and rear slide serrations; textured grip surface
MSRP $599.00

P80 PFS9

Action: Semiautomatic
Grips: Polymer
Barrel: 4.49 in.
Sights: White dot front, serrated rear
Weight: 24 oz.
Caliber: 9mm
Capacity: 10, 15, 17 rounds
Features: Utilizing Glock 17 mags, this full-size pistol has an improved grip angle; undercut trigger guard; extended beavertail; flared magwell; under rail; serrated slide
MSRP $599.00

Red Arrow Weapons

RED ARROW WEAPONS RAW15 300 BLACKOUT PISTOL

RAW15 300 BLACKOUT PISTOL

Action: Semiautomatic
Grips: Synthetic
Barrel: 10.5 in.

Sights: None
Weight: 88 oz.
Caliber: .300 BLK
Capacity: 30 rounds
Features: This might stretch the definition of pistol, but it's not alone in the crowd of MSR legal pistols; Diamondback barrel that's melonite coated; pistol-length gas system; CMC

3.5-lb. single-stage trigger; forged aluminum lower; forged aluminum A3 upper, flattop and T-marked; Magpul P-Mag magazine; Tailhook Mod 2 brace; A2-style flash hider; ATI pistol buffer tube; 9-in. M-LOK S-rail handguard; in midnight bronze or in all-over black with flash red highlights
MSRP . . . . $1260.00–$1287.00

Rock River Arms

ROCK RIVER ARMS 1911 POLY

ROCK RIVER ARMS LAR-9 7-INCH PISTOL WITH SBA3 ARM BRACE

ROCK RIVER ARMS LAR-15LH LEF-T

1911 POLY

Action: SA semiautomatic
Grips: Polymer
Barrel: 5 in.
Sights: Dovetail front and rear
Weight: 32.6 oz.
Caliber: .45 ACP
Capacity: 7 rounds
Features: Chromoly barrel; polymer frame and mainspring housing; steel frame insert; steel slide; parkerized finish on metal; RRA overmolded grips; aluminum speed trigger; beavertail grip safety; RRA dovetail front and rear sights
MSRP $1100.00

LAR-9 7-INCH PISTOL WITH SBA3 ARM BRACE

Action: Semiautomatic
Grips: Synthetic
Barrel: 7 in.
Sights: None
Weight: 5 lb. 6 oz.
Caliber: 9mm
Capacity: N/A
Features: Tons of 9mm fun in a pistol featuring an extruded aluminum upper; billet aluminum lower with integral winter trigger guard; flared mag well takes Glock magazines; SBA3 five-position arm brace; two-stage trigger; threaded A2 flash hider
MSRP $1080.00

LAR-15LH LEF-T

Action: Semiautomatic
Grips: Synthetic
Barrel: 10.5 in.
Sights: None
Weight: 101 oz.
Caliber: 5.56 NATO
Capacity: 10 rounds
Features: This rifle-round pistol features a threaded A2 flash hider; SB Tactical SBA3 adjustable stabilizing arm brace; Hogue rubber grip; left-side operation/ejection; ambidextrous mag release; left-hand charging handle; forged upper/lower; low-profile gas block
MSRP $1130.00

Rock River Arms

ROCK RIVER ARMS LAR-15 RRAGE 7-INCH PISTOL

ROCK RIVER ARMS LAR-BT9G

ROCK RIVER ARMS LAR-PDS PISTOL

LAR-15 RRAGE 7-INCH PISTOL

Action: Semiautomatic
Grips: Synthetic
Barrel: 7 in.
Sights: None
Weight: 4 lb. 13 oz.
Caliber: 5.56mm NATO/.223 Rem.
Capacity: 20 rounds
Features: Featuring a low-profile gas block; A2 pistol grip; A2 flash hider; single-stage trigger; free-floating aluminum M-LOK-compatible handguard; SBX-K stabilizing arm brace; long A2 flash hider
MSRP **$990.00**

LAR-BT9G

Action: Semiautomatic
Grips: Rubber
Barrel: 4.5 in., 7 in., 10 in.
Sights: None, flip-up front, rear
Weight: 6 lb.
Caliber: 9mm
Capacity: 10, 15, 17, 30 rounds
Features: Glock magazine-compatible, the three guns in this series feature billet aluminum lowers with extruded aluminum uppers; RRA two-stage trigger; free-floating M-LOK handguard; A2 flash hider; Hogue rubber grip; low Pro M-LOK compatible handstop and NPS flip-up sights on 4.5-in. model; flared magwell; integral winter trigger guard; adjustable SB Tactical SBA3 stabilizing arm brace
MSRP . . . . **$1385.00–$1495.00**

LAR-PDS PISTOL

Action: Gas-operated semiautomatic
Grips: Hogue rubber
Barrel: 8 in. chromoly
Sights: Picatinny rail
Weight: 80 oz.
Caliber: 5.56 NATO
Capacity: 30 rounds
Features: Forged lower; Hogue rubber grip; A2 flash hider; two-position regulator; not compatible with suppressors; one version has injection-molded ribbed handguard, second version has an aluminum tri-rail handguard
Ribbed handguard **$1325.00**
Tri-rail handguard **$1385.00**

Ruger (Sturm, Ruger & Co.)

RUGER 22 CHARGER TAKEDOWN

RUGER 22 CHARGER LITE

RUGER AMERICAN PISTOL DUTY

RUGER AR-556 PISTOL FLAG SERIES

22 CHARGER

Action: Semiautomatic
Grips: Synthetic
Barrel: 8, 10 in.
Sights: None
Weight: 52 oz.
Caliber: .22 LR
Capacity: 15 rounds
Features: Cold hammer-forged barrel; threaded barrel; Picatinny rail; A2-style grip; adjustable bipod
Standard . . . . **$379.00–$419.00**
Takedown **$509.00**

22 CHARGER LITE

Action: Semiautomatic
Grips: Polymer
Barrel: 10 in.
Sights: None
Weight: 57 oz.
Caliber: .22 LR
Capacity: 15 rounds
Features: This handy takedown pistol has a new Picatinny brace mount attachment point; A2-style grip; aluminum alloy barrel sleeve; threaded barrel with thread cap and compatible with Silent-SR suppressor
MSRP **$719.00**

AMERICAN PISTOL COMPETITION, DUTY

Action: Semiautomatic
Grips: Ergonomic wrap-around
Barrel: 4.2, 5 in.
Sights: Three-dot; fiber optic front with adjustable rear
Weight: 30 oz.–31.5 oz.
Caliber: 9mm Luger, .45 ACP
Capacity: 10 or 17 rounds
Features: Trigger features a short takeup with positive reset; recoil-reducing barrel cam; low-mass slide; Novak LoMount Carry three-dot sights; modular wrap-around grip system for adjusting palm swell and trigger reach; ambidextrous slide stop and magazine release
MSRP **$669.00**

AR-556 PISTOL FLAG SERIES

Action: Semiautomatic
Grips: Polymer
Barrel: 10.5 in.
Sights: None
Weight: 99.2 oz.
Caliber: 5.56 NATO
Capacity: 30 rounds
Features: Ultra maneuverable, this handy rifle-cartridge pistol features an SB Tactical SBA3 stabilizing brace; free-floating handguard with Magpul M-LOK attachment slots at 3, 6, and 9 o'clock; carbine-length gas system; 1:8 twist rate to stabilize bullets from 35 to 77 grains; Ruger flash suppressor; staked gas key; American flag graphics
MSRP **$1109.00**

Ruger (Sturm, Ruger & Co.)

RUGER AMERICAN PISTOL COMPACT

RUGER BEARCAT

RUGER CUSTOM SHOP SR1911 COMPETITION

RUGER CUSTOM SHOP SUPER GP100 COMPETITION

RUGER EC9S

RUGER GP100

RUGER GP100 .22 LR

RUGER GP100 7-ROUND .357 MAG.

AMERICAN PISTOL COMPACT

Action: Semiautomatic
Grips: Glass-filled nylon
Barrel: 3.55 in.
Sights: Novak low-mount carry three-dot
Weight: 29.2 oz.
Caliber: 9mm
Capacity: 17 rounds
Features: Generous capacity makes this a great carry choice; ergonomic wrap-around grip module; gray Cerakote finish; approved for +P use; grip frame texturing; slide serrations; ambidextrous slide stop and magazine release; mil-spec Picatinny rail; tool-less takedown
MSRP................$669.00

BEARCAT

Action: SA revolver
Grips: Hardwood
Barrel: 4.2 in.
Sights: Blade front, integral notch
Weight: 24 oz.
Caliber: .22 LR
Capacity: 6 rounds
Features: Alloy steel with blued finish or stainless steel frame with satin stainless finish; decorative cylinder; transfer bar mechanism; features one piece frame
Blue/alloy steel..........$799.00
Stainless/stainless steel....$849.00

CUSTOM SHOP SR1911 COMPETITION

Action: Semiautomatic
Grips: G10
Barrel: 5 in.
Sights: Fiber optic front, adjustable target rear
Weight: 40 oz.
Caliber: .45 ACP, 9mm
Capacity: 8 rounds
Features: Hogue Piranha G10 grips on the 9mm, textured G10 grips on the .45; low-profile hammer; match trigger with flat-faced shoe; tuned sear spring; undercut trigger guard; ambidextrous slide stop and mag release; competition barrel with fitted lug, fitted bushing, and target crown; black-nitrided stainless steel frame paired with a stainless finish slide having black nitride-filled serrations
.45 ACP...............$2309.00
9mm.................$2619.00

CUSTOM SHOP SUPER GP100 COMPETITION

Action: Revolver
Grips: Hogue hardwood
Barrel: 5.5 in.
Sights: Fiber optic front, adjustable rear
Weight: 47 oz.
Caliber: .357 Mag., 9mm
Capacity: 8 rounds
Features: Triple-locking cylinder with PVD finish; hand-finished hardwood grips by Hogue; Super Redhawk action; centering boss on trigger; centering shims on hammer; cylinder and extractor cut for moon clip use; .357 in all blue, 9mm with blue cylinder and stainless frame/barrel
MSRP.................$1749.00

EC9S

Action: Semiautomatic
Grips: Glass-filled nylon
Barrel: 3.12 in.
Sights: Integral
Weight: 17.2 oz.
Caliber: 9mm
Capacity: 7 rounds
Features: Striker-fired lightweight has checkered grip; alloy steel barrel; pinky floorplate that can be added to magazine; polymer IWB holster included
MSRP..........$339.00–$379.00

GP100

Action: DA revolver
Grips: Black hogue monogrip
Barrel: 3 in., 4.2 in., 6 in.
Sights: Ramp front, fixed or adjustable rear
Weight: 36 oz.–45 oz.
Caliber: .327 Fed Mag., .357 Mag., .44 Spl.
Capacity: 5, 6, 7 rounds
Features: Satin stainless or blued finish; stainless steel or alloy steel frame; cushioned rubber grip; transfer bar; triple-locking cylinder
MSRP.......... $949.00–$1029.00

GP100 .22 LR

Action: DA revolver
Grips: Cushioned rubber with wood insert
Barrel: 5.5 in.
Sights: Fiber optic front, adjustable rear
Weight: 42 oz
Caliber: .22 LR
Capacity: 10 rounds
Features: Triple-locking cylinder locked into the frame at the front, rear, and bottom; patented grip frame design accommodates a wide variety of custom grips; takedown of integrated subassemblies requires no special tools
MSRP.................$1029.00

GP100 7-ROUND .357 MAG.

Action: DA/SA
Grips: Rubber with hardwood inserts
Barrel: 2.5 in., 4.2 in., 6 in.
Sights: Fiber optic front, adjustable rear
Weight: 36 oz., 40 oz., 43.5 oz.
Caliber: .357 Mag.
Capacity: 7 rounds
Features: Cylinder locks into the frame at the front, rear and bottom, improving alignment and reliability; adjustable sights at the rear with a fiber optic front; three barrel lengths
MSRP.................$1069.00

Ruger (Sturm, Ruger & Co.)

RUGER GP100 MATCH CHAMPION

RUGER LC380

RUGER LCP

RUGER LCP II

RUGER LCP II EXTENDED MAGAZINE

RUGER LCRX

RUGER LCRX 3-INCH .357 MAG.

RUGER LITE RACK LCP II

GP100 MATCH CHAMPION

Action: DA revolver
Grips: Wood
Barrel: 4.2 in.
Sights: Fixed or adjustable
Weight: 38 oz.
Caliber: .357 Mag., 10mm
Capacity: 6 rounds
Features: Hogue stippled hardwood; fiber optic front site; triple-locking cylinder; easy takedown; features a slab-sided, half-lug barrel
MSRP. **$1199.00**

LC380

Action: Semiautomatic
Grips: Black, glass-filled nylon
Barrel: 3.12 in.
Sights: Adjustable 3-dot
Weight: 17.2 oz.
Caliber: .380 ACP
Capacity: 7+1 rounds
Features: Hardened alloy steel slide; checkered grip frame; finger grip extension floorplate; three safeties and loaded chamber indicator; blued finish; California-approved version available
MSRP. **$659.00**

LCP

Action: Semiautomatic
Grips: Glass-filled nylon
Barrel: 2.75 in.
Sights: Integral, Viridian E-Series red laser
Weight: 9.9 oz.
Caliber: .380 ACP
Capacity: 6+1 rounds
Features: Alloy steel barrel and slide; blued finish; fixed/LaserMax CenterFire sights; black, glass-filled nylon grips; standard model is all black and is available with a built-in laser; non-laser model also available with stainless finish or American flag slides
Standard . . . . **$319.00–$359.00**

LCP II

Action: Semiautomatic
Grips: Glass-filled nylon
Barrel: 2.75 in.
Sights: Fixed front and rear
Weight: 10.6 oz.
Caliber: .380 ACP, .22 LR
Capacity: 6 rounds
Features: Updated from the original; improved sights and trigger; last round hold open; larger grip surface
Standard . . . . **$419.00–$469.00**
With laser. . . . . **$519.00–$559.00**

LCP II EXTENDED MAGAZINE

Action: Semiautomatic
Grips: Glass-filled nylon
Barrel: 2.75 in.
Sights: Integral
Weight: 11 oz.
Caliber: .380 ACP
Capacity: 8 rounds
Features: This handy little CCW .380 keeps you in the game with a seven-round extended magazine that also offers a little extra grip purchase. Comes with a pocket holster. Note: Ruger states that 7-round LCP magazines are not compatible with this LCP II firearm.
MSRP. **$419.00**

LCR

Action: DA/SA
Grips: Rubber
Barrel: 1.87 in.
Sights: Adjustable
Weight: 13.5 oz.–17.2 oz.
Caliber: .38 Spl. +P, 22 LR, 22 WMR, .327 Fed. Mag., .357 Mag., 9mm Luger
Capacity: 5–8 rounds
Features: Hogue Tamer monogrip; adjustable black blade rear sight; Ionbond Diamondblack cylinder finish
MSRP. . . . . **$719.00–$829.00**

LCRX

Action: DA/SA revolver
Grips: Rubber
Barrel: 1.87 in.–3 in.
Sights: Fixed
Weight: 13.5 oz.
Caliber: .22 LR, .22 WMR, .38 Spec. +P, .327 Fed. Mag., .357 Mag., 9mm
Capacity: 5 rounds
Features: High-strength stainless steel cylinder features an Ionbond Diamondblack finish; Grip Peg allows a variety of grip styles to be installed; external hammer that allows for single-action mode; also available with Crimson Trace lasergrips
MSRP. . . . . **$719.00–$829.00**

LCRX 3-INCH .357 MAG.

Action: Revolver
Grips: Hogue Tamer Monogrip
Barrel: 3 in.
Sights: Pinned front ramp, adjustable blade rear
Weight: 21.3 oz.
Caliber: .357 Mag.
Capacity: 5 rounds
Features: A little extra barrel and the longer Hogue Tamer grip make handling the .357 Mag. in a carry gun more manageable
MSRP. **$829.00**

LITE RACK LCP II

Action: Semiautomatic
Grips: Glass-filled nylon
Barrel: 2.75 in.
Sights: Integral
Weight: 11.2 oz.
Caliber: .22 LR
Capacity: 10 rounds
Features: A featherweight rimfire with an all-new floorplate assembly that permits ten rounds in the mag while still minimizing the pistol's profile; lightened recoil spring; last shot hold-open; manual push-forward-off safety
MSRP. **$419.00**

Ruger (Sturm, Ruger & Co.)

RUGER MARK IV 22/45 LITE WITH BLACK ANODIZED UPPER AND GOLD THREADED BARREL

RUGER MARK IV 22/45 LITE WITH DIAMOND GRAY ANODIZED FINISH, TARGET LAMINATE GRIPS

RUGER MARK IV 22/45 LITE WITH GOLD ANODIZED UPPER AND BLACK THREADED BARREL

RUGER MARK IV TARGET

RUGER MARK IV TARGET 10-INCH

RUGER MARK IV HUNTER

RUGER MARK IV STANDARD

RUGER MARK IV TACTICAL

RUGER MARK IV TARGET WITH THREADED BULL BARREL

MARK IV 22/45 LITE WITH BLACK ANODIZED UPPER AND GOLD THREADED BARREL

Action: Semiautomatic
Grips: Checkered 1911-style
Barrel: 4.4 in.
Sights: Adjustable rear, fixed front
Weight: 25 oz.
Caliber: .22 LR
Capacity: 10 rounds
Features: A sleek black finish is complemented by the sight here and there of the gold-finished barrel threaded for suppressor; Picatinny topside rail is standard
MSRP. **$699.00**

MARK IV 22/45 LITE WITH DIAMOND GRAY ANODIZED FINISH, TARGET LAMINATE GRIPS

Action: Semiautomatic
Grips: Laminate
Barrel: 4.4 in.
Sights: Adjustable rear, fixed front
Weight: 27 oz.
Caliber: .22 LR
Capacity: 10 rounds
Features: Features include: one-button takedown; polymer frame; laminate grips with target finger grooves; aluminum receiver; ambidextrous safety; drop-free magazine; magazine disconnect; Diamond Gray anodized finish
MSRP. **$759.00**

MARK IV 22/45 LITE WITH GOLD ANODIZED UPPER AND BLACK THREADED BARREL

Action: Semiautomatic
Grips: Checkered 1911-style
Barrel: 4.4 in.
Sights: Adjustable rear, fixed front

Weight: 25 oz.
Caliber: .22 LR
Capacity: 10 rounds
Features: A flashy and fun target pistol with a Gold anodized aluminum receiver; polymer frame with black, checkered 1911-style grips; threaded barrel
MSRP. **$699.00**

MARK IV HUNTER

Action: SA semiautomatic
Grips: Checkered laminate
Barrel 6.88 in.
Sights: Fiber optic front sight, adjustable rear
Weight: 44 oz.
Caliber: .22 LR
Capacity: 10 rounds
Features: Stainless steel frame with satin finish; fluted bull barrel; one-button takedown; drop-free magazine
MSRP. . . . . **$949.00–$1009.00**

MARK IV STANDARD

Action: Semiautomatic
Grips: Synthetic
Barrel: 4.75 in., 6 in.
Sights: Fixed blade front, fixed notch rear
Weight: 28.2–30.1 oz.
Caliber: .22 LR
Capacity: 10 rounds
Features: Tapered barrel; naturally pointing grip angle; ambidextrous safety; bolt stop; drop-free magazines; magazine disconnect; one-button takedown
MSRP. **$539.00**

MARK IV TACTICAL

Action: Semiautomatic
Grips: Synthetic
Barrel: 4.4 in.
Sights: Fixed blade front, adjustable rear
Weight: 34.6 oz.
Caliber: .22 LR
Capacity: 10 rounds
Features: Threaded barrel; Picatinny

rails both top and bottom; drop-free magazines; magazine disconnect
MSRP. **$7090.00**

MARK IV TARGET

Action: Semiautomatic
Grips: Laminate, synthetic
Barrel: 5.5 in.
Sights: Fixed front, adjustable rear
Weight: 35.6 oz.–42.8 oz.
Caliber: .22 LR
Capacity: 10 rounds
Features: Latest version of Ruger's esteemed .22-caliber SA handguns; one-piece CNC-machined frame; ambidextrous manual safety; drop-free mag design; magazine disconnect; one-button takedown; two magazines; blued or stainless steel options
Blued . . . . **$639.00–$709.00**
Stainless. . . . . **$799.00–$829.00**

MARK IV TARGET 10-INCH

Action: Semiautomatic
Grips: Synthetic
Barrel: 10 in.
Sights: Fixed front, adjustable rear
Weight: 46.3 oz.
Caliber: .22 LR
Capacity: 10 rounds
Features: A looooong-barreled one for the bull's-eye circuit with a cold hammer forged barrel; contoured ejection port; one-button takedown; in all-blue or all-stainless finish
Blued **$699.00**
Stainless. **$839.00**

MARK IV TARGET WITH THREADED BULL BARREL

Action: Semiautomatic
Grips: Synthetic
Barrel: 5.5 in.
Sights: Fixed front, adjustable rear
Weight: 42.8 oz.
Caliber: .22 LR
Capacity: 10 rounds
Features: Threaded bull barrel; includes two drop-free magazines
MSRP. **$829.00**

Ruger (Sturm, Ruger & Co.)

RUGER NEW MODEL SUPER BLACKHAWK

RUGER PC CHARGER

RUGER REDHAWK WITH SLEEVE AND SHROUD BARREL

RUGER RUGER-57

RUGER SECURITY-9

RUGER SECURITY-9 COMPACT PRO

RUGER SECURITY-9 COMPACT WITH HOGUE GRIP SLEEVE

RUGER SECURITY-9 COMPACT WITH VIRIDIAN E-SERIES RED LASER

RUGER SECURITY-9 PRO

NEW MODEL SUPER BLACKHAWK

Action: SA revolver
Grips: Hardwood, laminate
Barrel: 4.62 in., 5.5 in., 7.5 in., 10.5 in.
Sights: Ramp front, adjustable rear
Weight: 45–55 oz.
Caliber: .44 Rem. Mag.
Capacity: 6 rounds
Features: Alloy steel or stainless steel frame; blued or satin stainless finish; transfer bar mechanism; western-style grip; Bisley Hunter variation has 7.5-in. barrel, black laminate grips
Standard ...... **$1019.00–$1059.00**
Hunter **$1179.00**
Bisley Hunter **$1179.00**

PC CHARGER

Action: Semiautomatic
Grips: Glass-filled polymer
Barrel: 6.5 in.
Sights: None
Weight: 5 lb. 3 oz.
Caliber: 9mm
Capacity: 17 rounds
Features: A chassis-built pistol that takes standard AR grips; integral aluminum Picatinny rails; flared interchangeable magwells to accommodate Ruger or Glock magazines; integrated rear quick-detach cups; six-position CNC-milled handguard with a handstop and Type III hardcoat anodized aluminum and M-LOK slots at 3, 6, and 9 o'clock; Dead Blow action; reversible magazine release and charging handle; threaded heavy-contour barrel
MSRP **$869.00**

REDHAWK WITH SLEEVE AND SHROUD BARREL

Action: DA/SA
Grips: Hardwood
Barrel: 4.2, 5.5, 7.5 in.
Sights: Color insert front blade, white outline adjustable rear
Weight: 44 oz., 49 oz.

Caliber: .357 Mag., .45 ACP, .44 Mag.
Capacity: 8 rounds
Features: Two cold hammer-forged sleeve and shroud barrel models; satin stainless finish; colored front sight insert is easily replaced
MSRP **$1339.00**

RUGER-5.7

Action: Semiautomatic
Grips: Glass-filled nylon
Barrel: 4.94 in.
Sights: Fiber optic front, adjustable rear
Weight: 24.5 oz.
Caliber: 5.7x28mm
Capacity: 10, 20 rounds
Features: Suitable as a full-size carry or a competition gun, this new Secure Action fire-control pistol features an internal hammer; billet steel slide with front and rear serrations
MSRP **$869.00**

SECURITY-9

Action: Semiautomatic
Grips: Glass-filled nylon
Barrel: 4 in.
Sights: Drift-adjustable front and rear
Weight: 23.7 oz.
Caliber: 9mm
Capacity: 10, 15 rounds
Features: Aluminum chassis; full-length rails; blued alloy steel slide; Ruger's Secure Action found on the LCP II; textured grip frame
Standard **$459.00**
Night sights **$649.00**
With Viridian E-Series red laser **$529.00**
With Hogue grip sleeve **$479.00**

SECURITY-9 COMPACT PRO

Action: Semiautomatic
Grips: Glass-filled nylon
Barrel: 3.42 in.
Sights: Steel tritium
Weight: 21.9 oz.
Caliber: 9mm

Capacity: 10 rounds
Features: Through-hardened alloy steel slide; Secure Action system; textured grip frame
MSRP **$649.00**

SECURITY-9 COMPACT WITH HOGUE GRIP SLEEVE

Action: Semiautomatic
Grips: Glass-filled nylon
Barrel: 3.42 in.
Sights: Drift adjustable
Weight: 22.5 oz.
Caliber: 9mm
Capacity: 10 rounds
Features: A top choice for those who like a very compact handgun for everyday carry, but are frustrated with the lack of hand purchase many offer—the Hogue sleeve grip remedies that problem
MSRP **$479.00**

SECURITY-9 COMPACT WITH VIRIDIAN E-SERIES RED LASER

Action: Semiautomatic
Grips: Glass-filled nylon
Barrel: 3.42 in.
Sights: Drift adjustable
Weight: 22.4 oz.
Caliber: 9mm
Capacity: 10 rounds
Features: Similar to the Compact Pro, but with a factory-installed Viridian E-Series red laser
MSRP **$529.00**

SECURITY-9 PRO

Action: Semiautomatic
Grips: Glass-filled nylon
Barrel: 4 in.
Sights: Steel tritium
Weight: 23.8 oz.
Caliber: 9mm
Capacity: 15 rounds
Features: Slim feel but longer grip; hard-coat anodized aluminum chassis; full-length guide rod rails
MSRP **$649.00**

Ruger (Sturm, Ruger & Co.)

**RUGER SINGLE-SIX
.17 HMR**

RUGER SP101

**RUGER SP101
MATCH
CHAMPION**

**RUGER SR22
RIMFIRE PISTOL**

**RUGER
SR1911**

**RUGER SP101
WITH BLUED
ALLOY STEEL
FINISH**

**RUGER SR1911
LIGHTWEIGHT
COMMANDER-STYLE
9MM**

SINGLE-SIX (NEW MODEL)

Action: SA revolver
Grips: Black checkered hard rubber
Barrel: 6.5, 7.5 in.
Sights: Ramp or front bead, adjustable rear
Weight: 35, 45 oz.
Caliber: .17 HMR
Capacity: 6 rounds
Features: Cold hammer-forged barrel; checkered hard-rubber grips; .17 HMR is in blue; .22 LR is in stainless and has integral scope mount grooves
MSRP $779.00

SP101

Action: DA/SA
Grips: Wood and rubber
Barrel: 2.25 in.–4.2 in.
Sights: Fixed
Weight: 25 oz.–30 oz.
Caliber: .22 LR, .38 Spl +P, .327 Fed. Mag., .357 Mag., 9mm
Capacity: 6 rounds
Features: Features a light-gathering front sight, windage and elevation adjustable rear sight; triple-locking cylinder; easy takedown
MSRP . . . . $719.00–$769.00

SP101 MATCH CHAMPION

Action: DA/SA
Grips: Hardwood
Barrel: 4.2 in.
Sights: Fiber optic front, adjustable rear
Weight: 30 oz.
Caliber: .357 Mag.
Capacity: 5 rounds
Features: Target crown barrel; checkered hardwood grips; full-lug barrel
MSRP $1059.00

SP101 WITH BLUED ALLOY STEEL FINISH

Action: Revolver
Grips: Cushioned rubber, engraved wood
Barrel: 2.25 in.
Sights: Integral rear, black ramp front
Weight: 26 oz.
Caliber: .357 Mag.
Capacity: 5 rounds
Features: A lightweight CCW option in the powerful .357 Mag round; prominent feature is the unexposed backstrap, which improves shooter comfort.
MSRP $889.00

SR22

Action: DA semiautomatic
Grips: Polymer
Barrel: 3.5 in., 4.5 in.
Sights: Adjustable 3-dot
Weight: 17.5 oz.
Caliber: .22 LR
Capacity: 10 rounds
Features: 3-dot sight system has fixed front sight and adjustable rear sight; polymer frame and two interchangeable rubberized grips; underside Picatinny rail; aluminum slide; ambidextrous manual thumb safety/decocking lever; ambidextrous magazine release; Talo Distributor exclusives were offered in purple, black, flat dark earth, red titanium Cerakote, yellow Cerakote, and turquoise Cerakote finishes
Blued . . . . $549.00–$569.00
Stainless. $579.00
Threaded blue $599.00

SR1911

Action: Semiautomatic
Grips: G10, Wood
Barrel: 4.25 in., 5 in.
Sights: Fixed, adjustable
Weight: 29.3 oz.–39 oz.
Caliber: .45 ACP
Capacity: 7+1 rounds, 8+1 rounds
Features: Anodized aluminum frame; stainless steel barrel; standard recoil guide system and flat mainspring housing; rear slide serrations allow for positive grip; now available as a Target model with checkered G10 grips, low-glare stainless finish, and Bomar-style adjustable sights
MSRP $1169.00

SR1911 LIGHTWEIGHT COMMANDER-STYLE

Action: Semiautomatic
Grips: G10
Barrel: 4.25 in.
Sights: Novak drift-adjustable three-dot
Weight: 29.3 oz.
Caliber: .45 ACP, 9mm
Capacity: 9 rounds
Features: Classic 1911 70-series style in Commander-length slide
MSRP $1209.00

Ruger (Sturm, Ruger & Co.)

RUGER SR1911 OFFICER-STYLE

RUGER SR1911 OFFICER-STYLE

RUGER SR1911 TARGET

RUGER SUPER GP100 9MM

RUGER SUPER REDHAWK

RUGER VAQUERO BISLEY

RUGER VAQUERO BLUED

RUGER WRANGLER

SR1911 OFFICER-STYLE

Action: Semiautomatic
Grips: G-10
Barrel: 3.6 in.
Sights: Novak three-dot
Weight: 31 oz.
Caliber: .45 ACP
Capacity: 8 rounds
Features: A sleek carry 1911-style pistol featuring: skeletonized hammer and trigger; round mainspring housing; oversized beavertail grip safety; oversized ejection port; comes with two seven-round magazines; accepts other 1911 magazines, parts and accessories
MSRP $1209.00

SR1911 LIGHTWEIGHT OFFICER-STYLE

Action: Semiautomatic
Grips: G-10
Barrel: 3.6 in.
Sights: Drift-adjustable three-dot **Novak**
Weight: 27.2, 31 oz.
Caliber: 9mm
Capacity: 8 rounds
Features: 9mm is the lightweight version, .45 ACP in the standard; anodized aluminum frame; checkered G10 grips; low-glare stainless finish
MSRP $1209.00

SR1911 TARGET

Action: Semiautomatic
Grips: G10
Barrel: 5 in.
Sights: Bomar-style adjustable
Weight: 39 oz.–40.4 oz.
Caliber: 9mm, 10mm, .45 ACP
Capacity: 8 rounds

Features: Classic 1911 70-series style; oversized ejection port; skeletonized aluminum trigger
MSRP $1229.00

SUPER GP100 9MM

Action: Revolver
Grips: Hardwood
Barrel: 6 in.
Sights: Fiber optic front, adjustable rear
Weight: 45.6 oz.
Caliber: 9mm
Capacity: 8 rounds
Features: Chamfered ejector and chamber mouths ease use of included moon clips; cold hammer-forged, vented shrouded barrel with half-lug; Super Redhawk action; stainless barrel shroud/frame finish; blue cylinder and barrel
MSRP $1809.00

SUPER REDHAWK

Action: DA revolver
Grips: Black Hogue Tamer monogrip
Barrel: 2.5 in., 7.5 in., 9.5 in.
Sights: Ramp front, adjustable rear
Weight: 53 oz.–58 oz.
Caliber: 10mm, .44 Mag., .454 Casull, .480 Ruger
Capacity: 6 rounds
Features: Satin stainless finish; triple-locking cylinder; integral scope system; corrosion-resistant; extended frame; dual chambering; transfer bar; Alaskan model has short 2.5-in. barrel
MSRP . . . . $1429.00–$1459.00

VAQUERO BISLEY

Action: SA revolver
Grips: Simulated ivory
Barrel: 5.5 in.

Sights: Fixed
Weight: 41 oz.–45 oz.
Caliber: .45 Colt, .357 Mag.
Capacity: 6 rounds
Features: Stainless steel frame with high-gloss stainless finish
MSRP $1109.00

VAQUERO BLUED

Action: SA revolver
Grips: Hardwood
Barrel: 4.62 in., 5.5 in.
Sights: Fixed
Weight: 40 oz.–43 oz.
Caliber: .45 Colt, .357 Mag.
Capacity: 6 rounds
Features: Blued finish alloy steel; reverse Indexing Pawl; ejector rod head; transfer bar mechanism; internal lock
MSRP $1019.00

WRANGLER

Action: Revolver
Grips: Synthetic
Barrel: 4.62 in.
Sights: Blade front, integral rear
Weight: 30 oz.
Caliber: .22 LR
Capacity: 6 rounds
Features: A fun plinker or a great tool for low-cost SASS practice, the Ruger Wrangler has an aluminum alloy frame; checkered synthetic grips; Cerakote finish in choice of black, silver, or burnt bronze
MSRP $269.00

SAR USA B6, B6C

SAR USA K2 45

SAR USA K12 SPORT

SAR USA MODEL 2000

SAR USA P8L, P8S

SAR USA SAR9, SAR9 COMPACT

SAR USA SAR9-X PLATINUM

B6, B6C

Action: Semiautomatic
Grips: Polymer
Barrel: 4.5 in., 3.8 in.
Sights: Three dot combat
Weight: 28.2 oz., 25.2 oz.
Caliber: 9mm
Capacity: 17, 13 rounds
Features: A full-size and compact pair of pistols practical for target shooting or self-defense; low-profile combat sights; DA/SA; textured grip frame; blue or stainless slide; frame available in different colors including black and OD green
Full-size **$349.99**
Compact **$299.99**

K2 45, K2 45C

Action: Semiautomatic
Grips: Polymer
Barrel: 4.7 in.
Sights: Three dot with adjustable target rear
Weight: 40.2 oz.
Caliber: .45 ACP
Capacity: 14 rounds
Features: A full-size and compact pair of double-stack .45s, designed as licensed copies of the CZ-75 from what we've read; underside Picatinny rail; forged alloy steel frame; two-position frame safety; DA/SA; in all blue or all stainless finish
Full-size **$649.00**
Compact **$599.00**

K12 SPORT

Action: Semiautomatic
Grips: Polymer
Barrel: 4.7 in.
Sights: Three dot with adjustable target rear
Weight: 46.9 oz.
Caliber: 9mm
Capacity: 17 rounds
Features: Crowned barrel; SA firing system; checkered front- and back-strap; front and rear slide serrations; allover stainless metalwork with grey polymer grips; supplied with two magazines
MSRP **$799.99**

MODEL 2000

Action: Semiautomatic
Grips: Polymer
Barrel: 4.5 in.
Sights: Three dot front, rear
Weight: 35.2 oz.
Caliber: 9mm
Capacity: 17 rounds
Features: Good for target or carry; forged steel frame; DA/SA; low-drag combat sights; crowned barrel; in all blue or all stainless metalwork
MSRP **$569.99**

P8L, P8S

Action: Semiautomatic
Grips: Polymer
Barrel: 4.6 in., 3.8 in.
Sights: Three dot low-profile combat, adjustable rear
Weight: 37.9 oz., 35.8 oz.
Caliber: 9mm
Capacity: 17 rounds

Features: A great one for target competition; ported slide for heat dissipation; crowned and ported barrel; forged alloy steel frame; S model has slightly shorter barrel; metalwork in all black or all stainless
MSRP . . . . **$529.99–$549.99**

SAR9, SAR9 COMPACT

Action: Semiautomatic
Grips: Polymer
Barrel: 4.4 in., 4.0 in.
Sights: Three dot low-profile combat
Weight: 27.1 oz., 26.8 oz.
Caliber: 9mm
Capacity: 17 rounds
Features: A lightweight carry gun with double-stack capacity; striker-fire; polymer frame; low barrel axis; 20-degree grip angle; safety trigger
MSRP **$499.99**

SAR9-X PLATINUM

Action: Semiautomatic
Grips: Polymer
Barrel: 4.4 in.
Sights: Three dot low-profile combat
Weight: 27.5 oz.
Caliber: 9mm
Capacity: 15, 17 rounds
Features: Supplied with one flush-fit 15-round and an extended 17-round magazine, this lightweight CCW/target pistol has a striker-fire mechanism; Picatinny rail; Cerakote gray finish; slide venting to reduce heat build-up; front and rear slide serrations; one source says this comes with the weapon light pictured, but most make no mention of it so we're going without
MSRP **$499.99**

SCCY Firearms

SCCY CPX-2RD

CPX-1RD, CPX-2RD

Action: Semiautomatic

Grips: Polymer
Barrel: 3.1 in.
Sights: Low-profile blade front, Crimson Trace red-dot
Weight: 17.5 oz.
Caliber: 9mm
Capacity: 10 rounds
Features: This CCW striker-fire has a

heat-treated slide in natural stainless or black nitride finish; bar stock barrel; all-steel recoil system; aircraft-grade heat-treated aluminum alloy frame
CPX-1RD **$429.99**
CPX-2RD **$409.99**

SCCY Firearms

SCCY CPX-4RD

SCCY DVG-1

CPX-3RD, CPX-4RD

Action: Semiautomatic
Grips: Polymer
Barrel: 3.1 in.
Sights: Low-profile blade front, Crimson Trace red-dot
Weight: 17.5 oz.
Caliber: 9mm

Capacity: 10 rounds
Features: Similar to the 1RD and 2RD models, this version gets a barrel with Quad-Lock technology that improves repeatable accuracy
CPX-3RD $409.99
CPX-4RD $429.99

DVG-1, DVG-1RD

Action: Semiautomatic

Grips: Polymer
Barrel: 3 in.
Sights: Low-profile front, rear
Weight: 15.5 oz.
Caliber: 9mm
Capacity: 10 rounds
Features: A refinement of SCCY's CPX series; a straight trigger with a 5.5-lb. trigger; black nitride coating; optional Crimson Trace red-dot
DVG-1 . . . . $369.99
DVG-1RD $469.99

Shadow Systems, LLC

SAR USA SAR9, SAR9 COMPACT

SHADOW SYSTEMS DR920 ELITE

SHADOW SYSTEMS MR920 COMBAT

SHADOW SYSTEMS MR920 ELITE, ELITE LONG SLIDE

DR920 COMBAT

Action: Semiautomatic
Grips: Polymer
Barrel: 4.5 in., 5 in.
Sights: Green tritium night sight front, black serrated rear
Weight: 23 oz.
Caliber: 9mm
Capacity: 17 rounds
Features: This full-size striker-fire pistol has a 416R stainless steel barrel; textured polymer frame; front and rear slide serrations; option of a threaded barrel; black or flat dark earth frame choices; interchangeable backstraps; extended beavertail; recoil control ledge on frame; optional magwell; spiral-fluted match barrel gives a unique look
MSRP . . . . Starting at $889.00

DR920 ELITE

Action: Semiautomatic
Grips: Polymer
Barrel: 4.5 in., 5 in.

Sights: Green tritium night sight front, black serrated rear
Weight: 22.5 oz.
Caliber: 9mm
Capacity: 17 rounds
Features: Identical to the Combat full-size version, but with additional slide enhancements that include topside serrations and lightning windows for weight reduction
MSRP . . . . Starting at $989.00

MR920 COMBAT

Action: Semiautomatic
Grips: Polymer
Barrel: 4 in., 4.5 in., 5 in.
Sights: Green tritium night sight front, black serrated rear
Weight: 21.5 oz.
Caliber: 9mm
Capacity: 15 rounds
Features: A compact striker-fire pistol with an aggressively textured frame; aluminum flat-faced trigger; spiral-fluted match-grade barrel available standard or threaded and finished in choice of bronze TiCN or black

nitride; interchangeable backstraps; optional magwell; frame has recoil ledge; extended beavertail for a higher grip
MSRP . . . . Starting at $799.00

MR920 ELITE, ELITE LONG SLIDE

Action: Semiautomatic
Grips: Polymer
Barrel: 4 in., 4.5 in., 5 in.
Sights: Green tritium night sight front, black serrated rear
Weight: 20.9 oz.
Caliber: 9mm
Capacity: 15 rounds
Features: Both models are identical to the Combat version in most features, but the slides feature topside serrations in addition to the side serrations front and rear, and they also boast lightning cuts for weight reduction; long slide version is ½-in. longer at 4.5-in. unthreaded, 5-in. threaded
Elite: . . . . starting at $969.00
Elite Long Slide: . starting at $999.00

SIG SAUER M18 COMMEMORATIVE

SIG SAUER MCX RATTLER CANEBRAKE 5 .5-INCH

SIG SAUER MCX RATTLER PCB

SIG SAUER MPX COPPERHEAD

SIG SAUER MPX K

SIG SAUER P210 TARGET

SIG SAUER P220 NIGHTMARE FULL-SIZE

SIG SAUER P226 EQUINOX FULL-SIZE

M18 COMMEMORATIVE

Action: Semiautomatic
Grips: Polymer
Barrel: 3.9 in.
Sights: SIGLITE front, rear
Weight: 28.1 oz.
Caliber: 9mm
Capacity: 17, 21 rounds
Features: A limited release run of SIG's commemorative take on the official US service pistol; striker-fired; slide cut for optic plate/mounting; ambidextrous safety; grip modules; all-over coyote tan; ships with two 21-round magazine and one 17-round
MSRP **$1563.99**

MCX RATTLER CANEBRAKE 5.5-INCH

Action: Semiautomatic
Grips: PCB
Barrel: 5.5 in.
Sights: None
Weight: 6 lb. 8 oz.
Caliber: .300 Blackout
Capacity: 30 rounds
Features: NFA firearm comes with an inert training device so new owners can head to the range while paperwork clears the feds; suppressor ready; SD handguard; flat, two-stage match trigger; folding PCB brace in Coyote tan; upper and lower in Cerakote E190
MSRP **$2897.00**

MCX RATTLER PCB

Action: Semiautomatic
Grips: N/A
Barrel: 5.5 in.
Sights: None
Weight: 82 oz.
Caliber: .300 BLK, 5.56 NATO
Capacity: 30 rounds

Features: Pistol version of Sig's short-barreled rifle takes standard AR mags; sports PDW upper; three-position telescoping PSB pistol brace; M-LOK handguard is free-floating; action is gas piston
MSRP **$2999.00**

MPX COPPERHEAD

Action: Semiautomatic
Grips: Synthetic
Barrel: 3.5 in.
Sights: None
Weight: 72 oz.
Caliber: 9mm
Capacity: 30 rounds
Features: A barrel of fun in an uber-small package featuring a monolithic upper; barrel with flared flash hider; two-position Pivoting Contour Brace; completely ambidextrous controls; short-stroke gas piston; fully close bolt firing operation; Elite Series Cerakote finish in an eye-catching FDE
MSRP **$1909.99**

MPX K

Action: Semiautomatic
Grips: Synthetic
Barrel: 4.5 in.
Sights: None
Weight: 96 oz.
Caliber: 9mm
Capacity: 30 rounds
Features: Semiauto take on the submachine gun featuring a dual-side selector switch, magazine release, charging handle, and bolt; full-length Picatinny rail; free-floating eight-inch Keymod handguard; three-position telescoping brace; operation from a fully closed bolt
MSRP **$2161.99**

P210 TARGET

Action: Semiautomatic

Grips: Walnut
Barrel: 4.8 in.
Sights: Adjustable
Weight: 36.9 oz.
Caliber: 9mm
Capacity: 8 rounds
Features: Ergonomic walnut grips; frontstrap stippling; sleek controls; target trigger; reversed rail design; single-action-only; the slide is Nitron-coated to reduce wear
MSRP **$1699.00**

P220 NIGHTMARE FULL-SIZE

Action: Semiautomatic
Grips: G10
Barrel: 4.4 in.
Sights: X-RAY3 day/night sights
Weight: 30.4 oz.
Caliber: .45 ACP
Capacity: 8 rounds
Features: From the SIG Custom Works shop the full-size single-stack with a blacked-out frame; contrasting nickel-plated controls; Hogue Classic Contour SL G10 grips; under rail; Negrini case and two magazines
MSRP **$1248.99**

P226 EQUINOX ELITE FULL-SIZE

Action: Semiautomatic
Grips: G10
Barrel: 4.4 in.
Sights: X-RAY3 day/night sights
Weight: 34 oz.
Caliber: 9mm
Capacity: 15 rounds
Features: From SIG Custom Works, this special P226 has an Equinox slide; contrasting nickel-plated controls; Hogue SL G10 grips; SRT trigger; two steel magazines and Custom Works Negrini case
MSRP **$1390/99**

SIG Sauer

SIG SAUER P226 LEGION FULL-SIZE

SIG SAUER P226 MK25

SIG SAUER P229 LEGION RX COMPACT

SIG SAUER P238

SIG SAUER P320 M17

SIG SAUER P320 NITRON COMPACT

P226 LEGION FULL-SIZE

Action: DA/SA
Grips: Checkered G10 grips
Barrel: 4.4 in.
Sights: X-ray blacked-out day/night rear
Weight: 34 oz.
Caliber: 9mm
Capacity: 10, 12, 15 rounds
Features: Legion gray PVD finish; enhanced action with SRT; low-profile slide catch and decocking levers; reduced and contoured beavertail
MSRP $1461.99

P226 MK25 FULL-SIZE

Action: SA/DA semiautomatic
Grips: Polymer
Barrel: 4.4 in.
Sights: SIGLITE night sights
Weight: 34 oz.–35 oz.
Caliber: 9mm
Capacity: 10 or 15 rounds
Features: New designation of the Navy's P226 9mm variant issued to U. S. Navy SEALs; still with phosphated internals; (three) 15 round magazines; classic two-piece polymer grips; anchor engraved on slide; Picatinny rail; actual UID scanable serial number label; packaged with FDE grip band and a certificate of authenticity; available in black Nitron or in Desert Tan Nitron; black version can be had with threaded barrel
MSRP $1187.00

P229

Action: Semiautomatic
Grips: FDE polymer
Barrel: 3.9 in.
Sights: Contrast, Siglite night optional
Weight: 34.4 oz.
Caliber: 9mm, .40 S&W, .357 SIG
Capacity: 9mm: 10, 13 rounds; .357 SIG: 10, 12 rounds, .40 S&W: 10, 12 rounds

Features: Mid-size 9mm double-stack pistol comes in several versions (note that all Legion models have Legion Gray finish): Legion Compact SAO is a single-action-only with accessory rail, P-SAIT trigger, XRAY3 day/night sights, X-Five undercut trigger guard; Legion Compact has X-Ray sights, SIG rail, P-SAIT trigger, black G10 grips, alloy frame, PVD finish, double-/single-action; Legion RXP Compact has all the other features of this line plus a ROMEO1 PRO sight; Legion Compact SAO RXP has same features as Compact SAO, but gets a ROMEO1 PRO sight; Nitron variant has black nitron finish, SIGlite sights, E2 grip
Elite Compact $1086.99
Nitron Compact $959.99
Legion Compact $1299.99
Legion Compact SAO $1319.99
Legion RXP Compact $1749.99

P238

Action: SA semiautomatic
Grips: Fluted polymer, Rosewood Tribal, Pearl, Tribal Engraved Aluminum, Hogue pink rubber
Barrel: 2.7 in.
Sights: Siglite night
Weight: 15.2 oz.
Caliber: .380 ACP (9mm Short)
Capacity: 6 rounds
Features: Ultra compact, single-action-only (miniature 1911 design) .380 carry pistol; available only in a two-tone black frame/grey slide and grip, California compliant version
MSRP $739.00

P320

Action: DAO semiautomatic
Grips: Synthetic
Barrel: 3.6 in.–4.7 in.
Sights: Fixed

Weight: 25 oz.–29.4 oz.
Caliber: .40 S&W, 9mm, .357 SIG, .45 ACP
Capacity: 10–17 rounds
Features: Expansive line of subcompact, compact and full-size modular striker-fired pistols with three-point takedown and interchangeable grip sets. 2020 lineup includes eight full-size (all 9mm), two carry (both 9mm), and seven compact models (four in 9mm, as well as Nitron models in .357 SIG, .40 S&W, and .45 ACP)

XFull-Size	$728.00
X-VTAC	$796.99
Nitron Full-Size	$529.99
RXP Full-Size	$898.99–$989.99
RXP XFull-Size	$1002.99–$1081.99
AXG Pro	$1223.99
AXG Classic	$1218.99–$1238.99
AXG Equinox	$1325.99
AXG Scorpion	$1129.99
XCarry Spectre	$1099.99–$1152.99
XCarry Legion	$1020.99–$1046.99
Nitron Compact	$578.99–$679.00
RXP Compact	$884.99
RXP XCompact	$999.99–$1011.99
XCompact	$607.99–$728.00
XCompact Spectre	$1119.99
XFive Legion	$1073.99
P320Max	$1785.99

P320 M17

Action: Semiautomatic
Grips: Polymer
Barrel: 4.7 in.
Sights: Night sight rear plate, SIGLITE front
Weight: 29.6 oz.
Caliber: 9mm
Capacity: 17 rounds
Features: Recently awarded the MHS--Modular Handgun Contract--from the U.S. Army, this striker-fired mil-spec pistol is now available to the public. Features include optics-ready PVD0-coated slide in Coyote tan; removeable night sight plate; available with or without manual safety; carry-length Coyote grip module
MSRP . . . . $653.99–$768.00

SIG SAUER P320-M18

SIG SAUER P365 SAS

SIG SAUER P365 XL

SIG SAUER P365 XL ROMEOZERO

SIG SAUER P938 BLACKWOOD

SIG SAUER P938 LEGION

SIG SAUER P238 NITRON

SIG SAUER SIGM400 TREAD PISTOL

SIG SAUER SP2022 NITRON FULL-SIZE

P320-M18

Action: Semiautomatic
Grips: Polymer
Barrel: 3.9 in.
Sights: SIGLITE front, rear
Weight: 28.1 oz.
Caliber: 9mm
Capacity: 10, 17 rounds
Features: Optic-ready striker-fired 9mm with a curved trigger; M1913 accessory rail; polymer medium carry grip module; stainless steel frame and slide in PVD-coated Coyote Tan
MSRP $687.99

P365 SAS

Action: Semiautomatic
Grips: Polymer
Barrel: 3.1 in.
Sights: FT Bullseye
Weight: 17.8 oz.
Caliber: 9mm
Capacity: 10 rounds
Features: SAS—SIG Anti-Snag— treatment of rounded edges; ported slide for reduced muzzle flip; flat controls; carbon steel barrel; stainless steel slide with Nitron finish
MSRP $679.99

P365 XL

Action: Semiautomatic
Grips: Polymer
Barrel: 3.7 in.
Sights: XRAY3 day/night sights
Weight: 20.7 oz.

Caliber: 9mm
Capacity: 12 rounds
Features: At home on the range, in the nightstand, or your everyday-carry holster with features like an extended beavertail; 365 Xseries grip module; integrated carry magwell; flat trigger; optics-ready slide that works with SIG's RomeoZero and RMSc optics
MSRP $679.99

P365 XL ROMEOZERO

Action: Semiautomatic
Grips: Polymer
Barrel: 3.7 in.
Sights: XRAY3 front sight, RomeoZero optic
Weight: 20.7 oz.
Caliber: 9mm
Capacity: 10, 12 rounds
Features: Lightweight striker-fired pistol; Xseries straight trigger; carbon steel barrel; stainless steel frame and slide; Nitron finish
MSRP $829.99

P938

Action: SA semiautomatic
Grips: Synthetic or wood
Barrel: 3 in.
Sights: Siglite, FT Bullseye
Weight: 16 oz.
Caliber: 9mm
Capacity: 6+1, 7+1 rounds
Features: 9mm version of the P238 family, with similar aesthetics; single-action-only; ambidextrous safety.
BRX: $699.99
SAS: $779.99

P938 LEGION

Action: Semiautomatic
Grips: Polymer
Barrel: 3 in.

Sights: XRAY3 day/night sights
Weight: 17 oz.
Caliber: 9mm
Capacity: 7 rounds
Features: The smallest of the smallest 9mms in a SAO platform with seven-round magazine; Legion Gray Cerakote finish; front and rear cocking serrations on slide; extended mag well
MSRP $779.99

SIGM400 TREAD PISTOL

Action: Semiautomatic
Grips: Synthetic
Barrel: 11.5 in.
Sights: None
Weight: 96 oz.
Caliber: 5.56 NATO
Capacity: 30 rounds
Features: A direct-impingement AR platform in a pistol configuration with single-stage trigger; FNC carbon steel barrel; M-LOK accessory rail; adjustable stabilizing brace
MSRP $949.99

SP2022

Action: Semiautomatic
Grips: Polymer
Barrel: 3.9 in.
Sights: Siglite
Weight: 29 oz.
Caliber: 9mm, .40 S&W
Capacity: 12, 15 rounds
Features: SIG's original full-size polymer pistol, available in Nitron black; DA/SA; contrast sights; polymer grip; steel magazine
MSRP $679.99

Smith & Wesson

SMITH & WESSON M&P BODYGUARD 38 CRIMSON TRACE LASER

SMITH & WESSON MODEL 10

SMITH & WESSON MODEL 19 CLASSIC

SMITH & WESSON MODEL 27 CLASSICS

SMITH & WESSON MODEL 29 CLASSICS

SMITH & WESSON MODEL 36 CLASSICS

SMITH & WESSON MODEL 57 CLASSICS

SMITH & WESSON MODEL 60

SMITH & WESSON MODEL 60 LADYSMITH

Revolvers

M&P BODYGUARD 38 CRIMSON TRACE LASER

Action: Revolver
Grips: Polymer
Barrel: 1.875 in.
Sights: Black ramp front, groove rear
Weight: 14.4 oz.
Caliber: .38 Spec.
Capacity: 5 rounds
Features: Aluminum alloy frame; gray polymer grips; top-frame mounted red Crimson Trace laser; PVD coated stainless steel cylinder; ambidextrous cylinder release; DA only
MSRP. **$563.00**

MODEL 10

Action: SA/DA revolver
Grips: Wood
Barrel: 4 in.
Sights: Black blade, fixed
Weight: 36 oz.
Caliber: .38 S&W Spl. +P
Capacity: 6 rounds
Features: Carbon steel frame; carbon steel cylinder; blued finish; medium size frame; exposed hammer
MSRP. **$812.00**

MODEL 19 CLASSIC

Action: Revolver
Grips: Wood
Barrel: 4.25 in.
Sights: Red ramp front, adjustable black blade rear
Weight: 37.2 oz.
Caliber: .357 Mag.
Capacity: 6 rounds
Features: A true classic is back in S&W's lineup, featuring a high-

polished blue finish; traditional thumbpiece; half-lug; carbon steel frame and cylinder; checkered custom wood grips with S&W silver medallion
MSRP. **$903.00**

MODEL 27 CLASSICS

Action: SA/DA revolver
Grips: Checkered square butt walnut
Barrel: 4 in., 6.5 in.
Sights: Pinned serrated ramp front; Micro adjustable with cross serrations
Weight: 48.5 oz.
Caliber: .357 Mag., .38 S&W Spl. +P
Capacity: 6 rounds
Features: Carbon steel frame; bright blued finish
MSRP. . . . . **$1093.00–$1131.00**

MODEL 29 CLASSICS

Action: Revolver
Grips: Checkered square butt walnut; 6 in. model features Altamont Service walnut grips
Barrel: 4 in., 6.5 in.
Sights: Red ramp, micro adjustable rear
Weight: 48.5 oz.
Caliber: .44 Mag., .44 S&W Spl.
Capacity: 6 rounds
Features: Carbon steel frame in blue; blued with machine engraving and grips with enhanced carvings also available in 4-inch barrel only
MSRP. . . . . **$1071.00–$1229.00**

MODEL 36 CLASSICS

Action: Revolver
Grips: Wood
Barrel: 1.8 in.
Sights: Integral front, fixed rear
Weight: 19.5 oz.

Caliber: .38 S&W Spl. +P
Capacity: 5 rounds
Features: Small sized frame; exposed hammer; carbon steel frame and cylinder; blued finish; single or double action
MSRP. **$829.00**

MODEL 57 CLASSICS

Action: DA N-frame revolver
Grips: Checkered square-butt walnut
Barrel: 6 in.
Sights: Pinned red ramp front, micro adjustable white outline rear;
Weight: 4.8 oz.
Caliber: .41 Mag.
Capacity: 6 rounds
Features: Bright blued finish; carbon steel frame; classic style thumbpiece; color case wide spur hammer; color case wide serrated target trigger
MSRP. **$1078.00**

MODEL 60

Action: Revolver
Grips: Synthetic, wood
Barrel: 2.125 in., 3 in.
Sights: Black blade front, adjustable rear
Weight: 21.4 oz.–23.2 oz.
Caliber: .357 Mag., .38 S&W Spl. +P
Capacity: 5 rounds
Features: Satin stainless finish; single- or double-action; stainless steel fame and cylinder. Lady Smith has finger-grooved wood grips designed for smaller hands, brushed stainless finish, and is engraved with "Lady Smith" on the frame.
2.125-in. barrel: **$795.00**
3-in. barrel **$826.00**

SMITH & WESSON MODEL 66

SMITH & WESSON MODEL 66 COMBAT MAGNUM

SMITH & WESSON MODEL 69

SMITH & WESSON MODEL 69 COMBAT MAGNUM

SMITH & WESSON MODEL 442 ENGRAVED

SMITH & WESSON PERFORMANCE CENTER MODEL 460XVR 14-IN BARREL WITH BIPOD

SMITH & WESSON MODEL 586

SMITH & WESSON MODEL 617

MODEL 66

Action: DA/SA revolver
Grips: Synthetic
Barrel: 4.25 in.
Sights: Adjustable
Weight: 36.9 oz.–37.4 oz.
Caliber: .38 S&W Spl. +P, .357 Mag.
Capacity: 6 rounds
Features: Full top strap and barrel serration; ball-detent lock-up; two-piece barrel; matte stainless finish
MSRP $914.00

MODEL 66 COMBAT MAGNUM

Action: Revolver
Grips: Synthetic
Barrel: 2.75 in.
Sights: Red ramp front, white outline adjustable rear
Weight: 33.5 oz.
Caliber: .357 Mag., .38 Spl. +P
Capacity: 6 rounds
Features: K-frame revolver; full top strap and barrel serration; ball detent lockup; two-piece barrel; full-length extractor rod
MSRP $914.00

MODEL 69

Action: DA/SA revolver
Grips: Synthetic
Barrel: 4.25 in.
Sights: Adjustable
Weight: 34.4 oz.–37.4 oz.
Caliber: .44 Mag., .44 Spl.
Capacity: 5 rounds
Features: Full top strap and barrel serration; ball-detent lock-up; two-piece barrel
MSRP $914.00

MODEL 69 COMBAT MAGNUM

Action: Revolver
Grips: Synthetic
Barrel: 2.75 in.
Sights: Red ramp front, white outline adjustable rear
Weight: 34.4 oz.–37.4 oz.
Caliber: .44 Mag.
Capacity: 5 rounds
Features: Full top strap and barrel serration; ball detent lockup; two-piece barrel; full-length extractor rod
MSRP $914.00

MODEL 460XVR, PERFORMANCE CENTER 460XVR, PERFORMANCE CENTER HIVIZ 460XVR

Action: SA/DA revolver
Grips: Synthetic
Barrel: 3.5 in., 7 in., 8.38-in., 10.5 in., 12 in., 14 in.
Sights: Vary with model
Weight: 72.02 oz.–79.3 oz.
Caliber: .460 S&W Mag., .45 LC, .454 Casull, .460 S&W Mag.
Capacity: 5 rounds
Features: Highest muzzle velocity revolver in the world, gain-twist rifling; HIVIZ gets muzzle brake, integral scope base, unfluted cylinder, HIVIZ fiber optic front sight and adjustable white outline rear, PC-tuned action, full underlug on 7.5-in. barrel; 14-in. Barrel with Bipod gets bipod, black ramp front sight, adjustable rear sight, muzzle brake, top and bottom accessory/optics rails, chrome hammer, chrome trigger with trigger stop, PC-tuned action (.460 S&W Mag); 12-inch barrel has sling swivels and integrated Picatinny topside rail, removeable Patridge front sight; 10.5-inch barrel has interchangeable fiber optic front sight, adjustable rear sight, muzzle brake, graduated underlug, sling swivels; 3.5-inch barrel has unfluted cylinder, HiViz green fiber optic front and adjustable rear sights; Model 460XVR has 8.38-inch barrel, removeable compensator, gain twist barrel, interchangeable front sight and adjustable rear, full underlug
MSRP . . . . $1638.00–$1839.00

MODEL 586

Action: SA/DA revolver
Grips: Wood
Barrel: 4 in., 6 in.
Sights: Adjustable
Weight: 46.3 oz.
Caliber: .357 Mag., .38 S&W Spl. +P
Capacity: 6 rounds
Features: Carbon steel frame and cylinder with blued finish; adjustable white outline rear sight and red ramp front sight; square-butt design; checkered wood grips
MSRP $911.00

MODEL 617

Action: SA/DA revolver
Grips: Synthetic
Barrel: 4 in., 6 in.
Sights: Partridge front, adjustable rear
Weight: 38.9 oz.–44.1 oz.
Caliber: .22 LR
Capacity: 10 rounds
Features: Stainless steel frame and cylinder with satin stainless finish; medium size frame with exposed hammer
MSRP $893.00

Smith & Wesson

SMITH & WESSON MODEL 629

SMITH & WESSON MODEL 629 DELUXE

SMITH & WESSON MODEL 642 LASERMAX

SMITH & WESSON MODEL 648

SMITH & WESSON MODEL 686 PLUS 3-5-7 MAGNUM SERIES

SMITH & WESSON MODEL 686 PLUS DELUXE

SMITH & WESSON MODEL 686

SMITH & WESSON MODEL GOVERNOR

SMITH & WESSON MODEL S&W 500

MODEL 629, 629 CLASSIC

Action: SA/DA revolver
Grips: Synthetic
Barrel: 3 in., 4.125 in., 5 in., 6 in., 6.5 in.
Sights: Red ramp, adjustable white outline
Weight: 39.6 oz.–50.7 oz.
Caliber: .44 Mag, .44 S&W Spl.
Capacity: 6 rounds
Features: Stainless steel frame and cylinder with satin stainless finish; exposed hammer
MSRP . . . . **$1009.00–$1049.00**

MODEL 629 DELUXE

Action: Revolver
Grips: Wood
Barrel: 3 in., 6.5 in.
Sights: Red ramp front, white outline adjustable rear
Weight: 39.6 oz.–50.7 oz.
Caliber: .44 Mag., .44 S&W Spl.
Capacity: 6 rounds
Features: N-frame revolver; all-stainless construction; textured wood grips
MSRP . . . . **$1039.00–$1067.00**

MODEL 642 LASERMAX

Action: DAO
Grips: Synthetic
Barrel: 1.88 in.
Sights: Fixed front, integral rear
Weight: 15.5 oz.
Caliber: .38 S&W Special +P
Capacity: 5 rounds
Features: No-snag, hammerless design; rapid target acquisition of the LaserMax sighting system; matte silver finish
MSRP **$764.00**

MODEL 648

Action: Revolver
Grips: Synthetic
Barrel: 6 in.
Sights: Partridge front, adjustable rear
Weight: 46.2 oz.
Caliber: .22 Mag.
Capacity: 8 rounds
Features: Double-/single-action in all stainless steel; K-frame; eight-round cylinder; full underlug
MSRP **$812.00**

MODEL 686

Action: Revolver
Grips: Synthetic
Barrel: 4.125, 6 in.
Sights: Varies with model
Weight: 44.8 oz.
Caliber: .357 Mag.
Capacity: 6 rounds
New Features: L-frame six-shot revolver in satin stainless finish; red ramp front sight, adjustable white outline rear, synthetic grips, full underlug
MSRP **$893.00**

MODEL 686 PLUS 3-5-7 MAGNUM SERIES

Action: Revolver
Grips: Wood
Barrel: 3, 5, 7 in.
Sights: Red ramp front, white outline adjustable rear
Weight: 37.4 oz. (3-in. barrel), 37.4 oz. (5-in. barrel)
Caliber: .357 Mag.
Capacity: 7 rounds
Features: Collector's Model 686 L-frame; custom black/silver wood grips bearing "357"; cylinder is unfluted
MSRP **$939.00**

MODEL 686 PLUS DELUXE

Action: Revolver
Grips: Wood
Barrel: 6 in.
Sights: Red ramp front, white outline adjustable rear
Weight: 34.1 oz.–51.2 oz.
Caliber: .357 Mag.
Capacity: 7 rounds
Features: S&W's classic 686 L-frame revolver; all stainless steel
MSRP **$939.00**

MODEL GOVERNOR

Action: SA/DA revolver
Grips: Synthetic, Crimson Trace
Barrel: 2.75 in.
Sights: Tritium front, fixed rear
Weight: 30.3 oz.
Caliber: .45 Colt, .45 ACP, .410
Capacity: 6 rounds
Features: Patented heat-treated scandium frame; PVD coated cylinder; matte silver finish; furnished with two full moon clips and three two-shot moon clips for use with .45 ACP
MSRP . . . . **$865.00–$925.00**

MODEL S&W 500, 500 PERFORMANCE CENTER

Action: SA/DA revolver
Grips: Synthetic
Barrel: 3.5, 7.5, 10.5 in.
Sights: Orange ramp front, adjustable rear; fiber optic front
Weight: 55.6 oz.–79.6 oz.
Caliber: .500 S&W Mag.
Capacity: 5 rounds
Features: Performance Center models have removeable compensator, choice of 7.5 or 10.5-in. barrel (this barrel choice comes with a sling), and orange ramp front sight; standard model has 3.5-in. barrel and has a green fiber-optic front sight
MSRP **$1689.00**
Performance Center: . . . .**$1659.00–$1676.00**

SMITH & WESSON PERFORMANCE CENTER MODEL 19 CARRY COMP

SMITH & WESSON PERFORMANCE CENTER MODEL 327

SMITH & WESSON PERFORMANCE CENTER MODEL 327 TRR8

SMITH & WESSON PERFORMANCE CENTER MODEL 442 CRIMSON TRACE LG 105

SMITH & WESSON PERFORMANCE PERFORMANCE CENTER MODEL 686 PLUS

SMITH & WESSON PERFORMANCE CENTER MODEL 637 ENHANCED ACTION

SMITH & WESSON PERFORMANCE CENTER MODEL 642 ENHANCED ACTION

SMITH & WESSON PERFORMANCE CENTER MODEL 686

PERFORMANCE CENTER MODEL 19 CARRY COMP

Action: Revolver
Grips: Wood/synthetic
Barrel: 2.5, 3 in.
Sights: Tritium ramp front, adjustable black blade rear
Weight: 34.1 oz.
Caliber: .357 Mag.
Capacity: 6 rounds
Features: Features a carbon steel frame and cylinder; stainless steel Power Port vented barrel; tritium front sight; PC-tuned action; custom grips of wood and synthetic materials; trigger overtravel stop
MSRP . . . . $1168.00–$1172.00

PERFORMANCE CENTER MODEL 327

Action: Revolver
Grips: Wood
Barrel: 2 in.
Sights: Orange ramp front sight, integral "U" rear
Weight: 23.1 oz.
Caliber: .357 Mag., .38 S&W Spl. +P
Capacity: 8 rounds
Features: Color case with overtravel stop; color case tear drop with pinned sear; exposed hammer; matte black finish; scandium alloy frame and titanium alloy cylinder; smooth DA with Wolff Mainspring
MSRP $1384.00

PERFORMANCE CENTER MODEL 327 TRR8

Action: SA/DA revolver
Grips: Synthetic
Barrel: 5 in.
Sights: Interchangeable front; adjustable V-notch rear
Weight: 35.3 oz.
Caliber: .357 Mag., .38 S&W Spl. +P
Capacity: 8 rounds
Features: Scandium alloy frame; stainless steel cylinder; matte black; exposed hammer; equipment rails
MSRP $1400.00

PERFORMANCE CENTER MODEL 442 CRIMSON TRACE LG 105

Action: Revolver
Grips: Crimson Trace
Barrel: 1.875 in.
Sights: Ramp front, groove rear, Crimson Trace red laser
Weight: 15 oz.
Caliber: .38 Spec.
Capacity: 5 rounds
Features: Concealed hammer DA only revolver with high-polished parts, including cylinder flutes; carbon steel cylinder in stainless finish; aluminum alloy frame in matte black finish; Crimson Trace LG 105 red laser grips; +P rated; Performance Center tuned action; no internal lock
MSRP $822.00

PERFORMANCE CENTER MODEL 637 ENHANCED ACTION

Action: Revolver
Grips: Wood
Barrel: 1.875 in.
Sights: Integral ramp front
Weight: 15 oz.
Caliber: .38 Spl. +P
Capacity: 5 rounds
Features: J-frame with Performance Center-tuned action; stainless steel barrel; aluminum alloy frame; matte silver finish; custom wood grips
MSRP $605.00

PERFORMANCE CENTER MODEL 642 ENHANCED ACTION

Action: Revolver

Grips: Wood, synthetic
Barrel: 1.875 in.
Sights: Integral ramp front
Weight: 15 oz.
Caliber: .38 Spl. +P
Capacity: 5 rounds
Features: J-frame with Performance Center-tuned action; stainless steel barrel; aluminum alloy frame; matte silver finish; custom wood grips with pinkie extension or black synthetic frame-level grips DAO has concealed hammer
MSRP . . . . $568.00–$605.00

PERFORMANCE CENTER MODEL 686

Action: Revolver
Grips: Wood, synthetic
Barrel: 2.5 in., 4 in.
Sights: Red ramp front, *adjustable rear*
Weight: 34.1 oz.
Caliber: .357 Mag.
Capacity: 7 rounds
Features: Unfluted cylinder; Performance Center-tuned action; custom teardrop hammer; precision crowned barrel; cylinder cut for moon clips; 2.5-in. barrel has custom wood grips with finger grooves, while 4-in. barrel has black synthetic fingergroove grips
MSRP . . . . $1046.00–$1169.00

PERFORMANCE CENTER MODEL 686 PLUS

Action: Revolver
Grips: Synthetic
Barrel: 5 in.
Sights: Interchangeable blade front, adjustable rear
Weight: 38.4 oz.
Caliber: .357 Mag.
Capacity: 7 rounds
Features: Slanted half-underlug; unfluted cylinder; vent rib; Performance Center-tuned action; custom teardrop hammer; speed-release cylinder thumbpiece; includes an orange front blade, which can be subbed out for the user's choice
MSRP $1046.00

Smith & Wesson

SMITH & WESSON
PERFORMANCE CENTER
MODEL 929

PERFORMANCE
CENTER MODEL 986

SMITH & WESSON
PERFORMANCE CENTER
PRO SERIES MODEL 442
MOON CLIP

SMITH & WESSON
PERFORMANCE CENTER
PRO SERIES MODEL 627

SMITH & WESSON
PERFORMANCE CENTER PRO
SERIES MODEL 640

SMITH & WESSON
PERFORMANCE CENTER
PRO SERIES MODEL 986

SMITH & WESSON
M&P9 M2.0
COMPACT FDE
THUMB SAFETY

SMITH & WESSON M&P9 M2.0
COMPACT OR

PERFORMANCE CENTER MODEL 929

Action: DA/SA revolver
Grips: Synthetic
Barrel: 6.5 in.
Sights: Adjustable
Weight: 44.2 oz.
Caliber: 9mm
Capacity: 8 rounds
Features: Removable compensator; titanium cylinder; Jerry Miculek signature; chrome teardrop hammer; chrome trigger with stop
MSRP $1269,00

PERFORMANCE CENTER MODEL 986

Action: Revolver
Grips: Wood
Barrel: 2.5 in.
Sights: Red ramp front, adjustable rear
Weight: 31.7 oz.
Caliber: 9mm
Capacity: 7 rounds
Features: L-frame 9mm with unfluted cylinder; custom barrel with recessed crown; trigger overstop travel; bossed mainspring; Performance Center-tuned action; stainless steel barrel and frame; titanium cylinder; moon clips
MSRP . . . . $1169.00–$1229.00

PERFORMANCE CENTER PRO SERIES MODEL 442 MOON CLIP

Action: DA revolver
Grips: Synthetic
Barrel: 1.87 in.
Sights: Integral front, fixed rear
Weight: 15 oz.
Caliber: .38 S&W Spl. +P
Capacity: 5 rounds
Features: Aluminum alloy frame; stainless steel cylinder; matte black

finish; internal hammer; cylinder cut for moon clips
MSRP $568.00

PERFORMANCE CENTER PRO SERIES MODEL 627

Action: SA/DA revolver
Grips: Synthetic
Barrel: 4 in.
Sights: varies with model
Weight: 37.8 oz.–46.7 oz.
Caliber: .357 Mag.
Capacity: 8 rounds
Features: Performance Center Pro Series with 4-in. barrel has matte silver finish, chamfered charge holes, custom barrel with recessed precision crown, bossed mainspring, Hogue grips, interchangeable front sight, adjustable rear
MSRP $1064.00

PERFORMANCE CENTER PRO SERIES MODEL 640

Action: DA revolver
Grips: Synthetic
Barrel: 2.1 in.
Sights: Black blade front, fixed rear
Weight: 23 oz.
Caliber: .357 Mag.
Capacity: 5 rounds
Features: Stainless steel frame, barrel, and cylinder, front and rear dovetail tritium night sights, concealed hammer, cylinder cut for moon clips, satin stainless finish
MSRP $919.00

PERFORMANCE CENTER PRO SERIES MODEL 986

Action: DA/SA revolver
Grips: Synthetic
Barrel: 5 in.

Sights: Adjustable
Weight: 34.9 oz.
Caliber: 9mm
Capacity: 7 rounds
Features: Titanium, fluted cylinder; precision crowned barrel; cylinder cut for moonclips
MSRP $1229.00

Semiautomatics

M&P9 M2.0 COMPACT FDE THUMB SAFETY

Action: Semiautomatic
Grips: Polymer
Barrel: 4 in.
Sights: White three-dot
Weight: 27 oz.
Caliber: 9mm
Capacity: 10, 15 rounds
Features: Striker-fired pistol with a manual thumb safety; stainless steel barrel finished in Armonite; stainless slide finished in Cerakote flat dark earth; four interchangeable palm swell size inserts; accessory rail
MSRP $598.00

M&P9 M2.0 COMPACT OR

Action: Semiautomatic
Grips: Polymer
Barrel: 4 in.
Sights: Three dot front, rear
Weight: 27 oz.
Caliber: 9mm
Capacity: 15 rounds
Features: This compact in the M&P line gets a slide cut to be optic ready (OR) as well as an underside Picatinny rail; modular grip; front and rear slide "wave" serrations; steel three-dot sights
MSRP $654.00

SMITH & WESSON M&P9 M2.0 COMPACT THREADED BARREL

SMITH & WESSON M&P9 SHIELD M2.0 INTEGRATED CRIMSON TRACE LASER

SMITH & WESSON M&P9 SHIELD EZ WITH CRIMSON TRACE LASERGUARD

SMITH & WESSON M&P22 COMPACT CERAKOTE FLAT DARK EARTH THREADED

SMITH & WESSON M&P 45 SHIELD M2.0 WITH CRIMSON TRACE RED LASER

SMITH & WESSON M&P 380 SHIELD EZ

SMITH & WESSON M&P BODYGUARD 380

SMITH & WESSON M&P BODYGUARD 380 ENGRAVED

M&P9 M2.0 COMPACT THREADED BARREL

Action: Semiautomatic
Grips: Polymer
Barrel: 4.625 in.
Sights: Suppressor-height white-dot front, rear
Weight: 27.4 oz.
Caliber: 9mm
Capacity: 10, 15 rounds
Features: Striker-fired pistol with a threaded stainless steel barrel finished in Armonite; stainless slide finished in Armonite; four interchangeable palm swell size inserts; accessory rail
MSRP $598.00

M&P9 SHIELD M2.0 INTEGRATED CRIMSON TRACE LASER

Action: Semiautomatic
Grips: Polymer
Barrel: 3.1 in.
Sights: Steel three-dot white
Weight: 18.8 oz.
Caliber: 9mm, .40 S&W
Capacity: 7, 8 rounds
Features: Super-compact striker-fired pistol; built-in Crimson Trace Laser in red
MSRP $627.00

M&P9 SHIELD EZ

Action: Semiautomatic
Grips: Polymer
Barrel: 3.675 in.
Sights: White three-dot
Weight: 23.2 oz.–23.8 oz.
Caliber: 9mm
Capacity: 8 rounds
Features: Single-stack striker-fire with a stainless steel slide and barrel with Armornite finish; accessory rail;

no-trigger-pull disassembly; EZ is for an easier to rack slide; grip safety; reversible magazine release
Gun only . . . . $521.00–$695.00
With laser $627.00

M&P22 COMPACT CERAKOTE FLAT DARK EARTH THREADED

Action: Semiautomatic
Grips: Polymer
Barrel: 3.5 in.
Sights: White three-dot
Weight: 15.3 oz.
Caliber: .22 LR
Capacity: 10 rounds
Features: Reduced scale version of full-size M&P pistols; ambidextrous manual safety; reversible magazine release; Picatinny accessory rail; magazine safety; threaded barrel; two magazines
MSRP $449.00

M&P 45 SHIELD M2.0 WITH CRIMSON TRACE RED LASER

Action: Semiautomatic
Grips: Polymer
Barrel: 3.3 in.
Sights: Steel three dot
Weight: 23.1 oz.
Caliber: .45 ACP
Capacity: 6, 7 rounds
Features: A lightweight carry gun in .45 ACP featuring a built-in Crimson Trace laser in red; improved trigger; Armonite finish on metalwork; available with or without manual thumb safety
MSRP $539.00

M&P 380 SHIELD EZ

Action: Semiautomatic
Grips: Polymer
Barrel: 3.675 in.

Sights: Fixed white-dot front, adjustable white-dot rear
Weight: 18.5 o.
Caliber: .380 ACP
Capacity: 8 rounds
Features: An EDC pistol featuring a grip safety; drift adjustable rear sight; under rail; tactile loaded chamber indicator; metalwork including barrel Armonite finished; internal hammer fired; available with or without thumb safety
MSRP $454.00

M&P BODYGUARD 380

Action: DA semiautomatic
Grips: Synthetic
Barrel: 2.75 in.
Sights: Adjustable
Weight: 11.85 oz.
Caliber: .380 ACP
Capacity: 6+1 rounds
Features: Stainless steel drift adjustable sights; ergonomic grip; high-strength polymer frame; external takedown lever and slide stop; manual thumb safety; double action fire control (2nd strike compatibility); available with integral Crimson Trace; and with an engraved stainless slide
Gun only $396.00
With laser $475.00

M&P BODYGUARD 380 ENGRAVED

Action: Semiautomatic
Grips: Polymer
Barrel: 2.75 in.
Sights: Drift adjustable front and rear
Weight: 12 oz.
Caliber: .380 ACP
Capacity: 6 rounds
Features: Ultra-compact carry gun; DAO; custom machine-engraved matte silver slide
MSRP $430.00

Smith & Wesson

SMITH & WESSON
PERFORMANCE
CENTER M&P9 M2.0
PORTED BARREL &
SLIDE

SMITH & WESSON
PERFORMANCE CENTER
M&P9 M2.0 PORTED
BARREL & SLIDE C.O.R.E.
READY

SMITH & WESSON
PERFORMANCE
CENTER M&P9 M2.0
PRO SERIES C.O.R.E.
READY

SMITH & WESSON
PERFORMANCE
CENTER M&P40
M2.0 PORTED
BARREL & SLIDE

SMITH & WESSON
PERFORMANCE
CENTER M&P40
M2.0 PORTED
BARREL & SLIDE
C.O.R.E. READY

SMITH & WESSON
PERFORMANCE CENTER
M&P40 M2.0 PRO SERIES
C.O.R.E. READY

SMITH & WESSON
PERFORMANCE CENTER
M&P SHIELD EZ

PERFORMANCE CENTER M&P9 M2.0 PORTED BARREL & SLIDE

Action: Semiautomatic
Grips: Polymer
Barrel: 4.25 in., 5 in.
Sights: Green fiber optic front, adjustable red fiber optic rear
Weight: 27.7 oz., 29.8 oz.
Caliber: 9mm
Capacity: 10, 17 rounds
Features: Striker-fired pistol with a stainless steel barrel finished in Armonite; stainless slide finished in Armonite; four interchangeable palm swell size inserts; accessory rail; barrel and slide are ported; PC-tuned action; trigger stop
MSRP . . . . $760.00–$781.00

PERFORMANCE CENTER M&P9 M2.0 PORTED BARREL & SLIDE C.O.R.E. READY

Action: Semiautomatic
Grips: Polymer
Barrel: 4.25 in., 5 in.
Sights: White three-dot
Weight: 27.7 oz., 29.8 oz.
Caliber: 9mm
Capacity: 10, 17 rounds
Features: Striker-fired pistol with a stainless steel barrel finished in Armonite; four interchangeable palm swell size inserts; accessory rail; barrel and slide are ported; slide is C.O.R.E. and comes with optics mounting kit; larger slide stop; PC-tuned action; trigger stop
MSRP $774.00

PERFORMANCE CENTER M&P9 M2.0 PRO SERIES C.O.R.E. READY

Action: Semiautomatic

Grips: Polymer
Barrel: 4.25 in., 5 in.
Sights: White three-dot
Weight: 29 oz.
Caliber: 9mm
Capacity: 10, 17 rounds
Features: Striker-fired pistol with a stainless steel barrel finished in Armonite; stainless slide finished in Armonite; four interchangeable palm swell size inserts; accessory rail; slide is C.O.R.E. and comes with optics mounting kit; larger slide stop; PC-tuned action; trigger stop
MSRP . . . . $774.00–$795.00

PERFORMANCE CENTER M&P40 M2.0 PORTED BARREL & SLIDE

Action: Semiautomatic
Grips: Polymer
Barrel: 4.25 in., 5 in.
Sights: Green fiber optic front, adjustable red fiber optic rear
Weight: 28.7 oz., 30.1 oz.
Caliber: .40 S&W
Capacity: 10, 15 rounds
Features: Striker-fired pistol with a stainless steel barrel finished in Armonite; stainless slide finished in Armonite; four interchangeable palm swell size inserts; accessory rail; barrel and slide are ported; slide is C.O.R.E. and includes mounting kit; enlarged slide stop
MSRP . . . . $760.00–$781.00

PERFORMANCE CENTER M&P40 M2.0 PORTED BARREL & SLIDE C.O.R.E. READY

Action: Semiautomatic
Grips: Polymer
Barrel: 4.25 in., 5 in.
Sights: White three-dot
Weight: 28.7 oz., 30.1 oz.

Caliber: .40 S&W
Capacity: 10, 15 rounds
Features: Striker-fired pistol with a stainless steel barrel finished in Armonite; stainless slide finished in Armonite; four interchangeable palm swell size inserts; accessory rail; slide is C.O.R.E. and comes with optics mounting kit; larger slide stop; PC-tuned action; trigger stop
MSRP $774.00

PERFORMANCE CENTER M&P40 M2.0 PRO SERIES C.O.R.E. READY

Action: Semiautomatic
Grips: Polymer
Barrel: 4.25 in., 5 in.
Sights: White three-dot
Weight: 29.4 oz.
Caliber: .40 S&W
Capacity: 10, 15 rounds
Features: Striker-fired pistol with a stainless steel barrel finished in Armonite; stainless slide finished in Armonite; four interchangeable palm swell size inserts; accessory rail; slide is C.O.R.E. and comes with optics mounting kit
MSRP . . . . $760.00–$781.00

PERFORMANCE CENTER M&P SHIELD EZ

Action: Semiautomatic
Grips: Polymer
Barrel: 3.8 in.
Sights: Hi-Viz Litewave tritium/Litepipe
Weight: 23.02 oz.
Caliber: .380 ACP, 9mm
Capacity: 8 rounds
Features: A micro-compact loaded with premium tritium/fiber optic sights; a slide with lightning cuts; ported barrel; Performance Center action; loaded chamber indicator; aluminum grip safety; Picatinny rail; two magazines; choice of manual or no thumb safety; black, silver, or gold accents
.380 ACP $564.00
9mm $643.00

SMITH & WESSON
PERFORMANCE CENTER SW22
VICTORY TARGET MODEL
6-INCH CARBON FIBER BARREL

SMITH & WESSON
PERFORMANCE CENTER
SW22 VICTORY TARGET
MODEL FIBER OPTIC SIGHTS

SMITH & WESSON
SD9, SD40 FLAT DARK
EARTH FRAME FINISH

SMITH & WESSON
SD9, SD40 GRAY
FRAME FINISH

SMITH &
WESSON SD9 VE

SMITH & WESSON
SW22 VICTORY

SMITH &
WESSON SW1911
ENGRAVED

PERFORMANCE CENTER SW22 VICTORY TARGET MODEL 6-INCH CARBON FIBER BARREL

Action: Semiautomatic
Grips: Tandemkross hiveGrip
Barrel: 6 in.
Sights: None
Weight: 33.1 oz.
Caliber: .22 LR
Capacity: 10 rounds
Features: An optics-ready target pistol with carbon fiber barrel; custom muzzle brake; Tandemkross hiveGrip with target thumb rest and texturing; top-side optics rail; flat face trigger; stainless steel frame; extended mag release; adjustable trigger stop; equipped with red-dot sight
MSRP $945.00

PERFORMANCE CENTER SW22 VICTORY TARGET MODEL FIBER OPTIC SIGHTS

Action: Semiautomatic
Grips: Tandemkross hiveGrip
Barrel: 6 in.
Sights: Adjustable fiber optic
Weight: 38.2 oz.
Caliber: .22 LR
Capacity: 10 rounds
Features: One for rimfire match competition, featuring a fluted target barrel; Tandemkross hiveGrip with thumb rest and texturing; flat face trigger; adjustable trigger stop; beveled magazine well; fiber optic

sights with adjustable rear; custom muzzle break; Picatinny rail; stainless steel frame and barrel
MSRP $746.00

SD9, SD40 FLAT DARK EARTH FRAME FINISH

Action: Semiautomatic
Grips: Synthetic
Barrel: 4 in.
Sights: White three-dot
Weight: 22.3 oz.
Caliber: 9mm, .40 S&W
Capacity: 14, 16 rounds
Features: Self-Defense Trigger textured grip; accessory rail; slide serrations front; gray frame with matte black slide
MSRP $406.00

SD9, SD40 GRAY FRAME FINISH

Action: Semiautomatic
Grips: Synthetic
Barrel: 4 in.
Sights: White three-dot
Weight: 22.3 oz.
Caliber: 9mm, .40 S&W
Capacity: 14, 16 rounds
Features: Self-Defense Trigger textured grip; accessory rail; slide serrations front; frame is in Flat Dark Earth
MSRP $406.00

SD9 VE AND SD40 VE

Action: Striker Fired
Grips: Textured polymer
Barrel: 4 in.
Sights: White dot front, fixed 2-dot rear

Weight: 22.7 oz.
Caliber: 9mm, .40 S&W
Capacity: 10+1, 14+1, 16+1 rounds
Features: Lightweight polymer frame; front and rear slide serrations; Self Defense Trigger; ergonomic grip; Picatinny rail; two-tone finish Standard and low capacity
MSRP . . . . $406.00–$455.00

SW22 VICTORY

Action: SA
Grips: Polymer
Barrel: 5.5 in.
Sights: Green fiber optic front, adjustable fiber optic rear
Weight: 36 oz.
Caliber: .22 LR
Capacity: 10+1 rounds
Features: Removable interchangeable match-grade barrel; textured grip panels with finger cuts for easy magazine removal; Kryptek Highlander finish or stainless with threaded barrel
MSRP . . . . $454.00–$487.00

SW1911 ENGRAVED

Action: SA
Grips: Wood laminate E-Series
Barrel: 5 in.
Sights: White dot front, white 2-dot rear
Weight: 39.1 oz.
Caliber: .45 ACP
Capacity: 8+1 rounds
Features: Glass bead finish; machine scroll engraving; engraved, wooden presentation case
MSRP $1279.00

Springfield Armory

SPRINGFIELD ARMORY 1911 EMP

SPRINGFIELD ARMORY 1911 LOADED

SPRINGFIELD ARMORY 1911 RONIN OPERATOR

SPRINGFIELD ARMORY 1911 TRP

SPRINGFIELD ARMORY DEFEND YOUR LEGACY 1911 MIL-SPEC

SPRINGFIELD ARMORY DEFEND YOUR LEGACY XD

SPRINGFIELD ARMORY HELLCAT MICRO-COMPACT OSP

1911 EMP

Action: Semiautomatic
Grips: Thin line cocobolo wood
Barrel: 3 in.
Sights: Low-profile tritium
Weight: 27 oz.
Caliber: 9mm
Capacity: 9 rounds
Features: In 2022, available only in a California-compliant model; Forged stainless steel, satin finish; dual spring recoil system with full length guide rod; match-grade bull barrel with fully supported ramp
MSRP.................$1287.00

1911 LOADED

Action: Semiautomatic
Grips: Synthetic
Barrel: 5 in.
Sights: Fixed combat, 3-dot tritium
Weight: 34–43 oz.
Caliber: .45 ACP, 9mm
Features: Forged steel; integral accessory rail; GI-style recoil system. Six versions include Marine Corps Operator with gray G10 grips, Olive Drab Armory Kote frame and Black Armory Kote slide; Marine Corps Operator with Olive Drab Armory Kote frame, Black Armory Kote slide, and wraparound Pachmayr grips; Operator with all-over Black Armory Kote and black G10 grips; Loaded with Black-T slide, Parkerized frame, and cocobolo grips; Loaded Stainless with stainless frame and slide and cocobolo grips
Marine Corps Operator . . . $1347.00
Loaded black $978.00
Loaded stainless. $1034.00
Loaded Target .45. . . . . $1097.00
Loaded Target 9mm $1097.00

1911 RONIN

Action: Semiautomatic
Grips: Laminate

Barrel: 4.25 in., 5 in.
Sights: Fiber optic front, tactical-rack white dot rear
Weight: 41 oz.
Caliber: 9mm, .45 ACP
Capacity: 8, 9 rounds
Features: A very nice full- or Commander-size pistol for competition or carry, with a duo-tone forged slide and frame; checkered "crossed cannon" laminate grips; hammer-forged barrel; magazines with basepad; grip safety with memory bump; Gen2 speed trigger;
MSRP..................$899.00

1911 TRP

Action: Semiautomatic
Grips: G10 composite
Barrel: 5 in.
Sights: Front tritium 3-dot, fixed low profile combat rear, dovetail
Weight: 42–45 oz.
Caliber: .45 ACP
Capacity: 2–7 rounds
Features: Forged National Match frames, National Match barrels, three-dot low-profile combat tritium sights, two-piece National Match guide rod, G10 grips. Five versions include: Black Armory Kote with gray/black grips; Stainless Steel with black grips; Operator with gray/black grips and rail; Operator Tactical Gray with gray/black grips and rail; Operator Black Armory Kote with black grips and full-length under-rail
Black Armory Kote $1695.00
Stainless steel $1695.00
Operator Full Rail $1780.00

DEFEND YOUR LEGACY 1911 MIL-SPEC

Action: Semiautomatic
Grips: Wood
Barrel: 5 in.
Sights: Three-dot combat
Weight: 39 oz.
Caliber: .45 ACP

Capacity: 7 rounds
Features: Faithful to GI originals with a fully forged frame and slide in Parkerized finish; checkered wood grips; match-grade barrel; GI-style recoil system
Parkerized $709.00
Stainless. $809.00

DEFEND YOUR LEGACY XD

Action: Semiautomatic
Grips: Polymer
Barrel: 3 in.
Sights: Steel three-dot
Weight: 26 oz.
Caliber: 9mm
Capacity: 13 rounds
Features: A subcompact with great capacity; full-length guide rod with dual springs; forged steel slide with Melonite finish; steel barrel with Melonite finish;
MSRP..................$440.00

HELLCAT MICRO-COMPACT

Action: Semiautomatic
Grips: Polymer
Barrel: 3 in.
Sights: Tritium front, tactical-rack U-Dot rear
Weight: 17.9 oz.
Caliber: 9mm
Capacity: 11, 13 rounds
Features: A micro-compact with capacity and features that include a steel, hammer-forged barrel with Melonite finish; Adaptive Grip Texture; full-length guide rod; dual captive recoil springs; billet machined slide with Melonite finish; OSP is an optics-ready version
Standard . . . . $587.00–$630.00
OSP $620.00
OSP with Hex Wasp
 red-dot $820.00
OSP with Shield SMSC
 red-dot $827.00

SPRINGFIELD ARMORY XD-M ELITE PRECISION

SPRINGFIELD ARMORY XD-M ELITE

SPRINGFIELD ARMORY XD-S MOD.2 OSP

XD-M ELITE

Action: Semiautomatic
Grips: Polymer
Barrel: 3.8 in., 4.5 in.
Sights: Fiber optic front, tactical-rack U-Dot rear
Weight: 28 oz., 29 oz.
Caliber: 9mm
Capacity: 20 rounds
Features: Match Enhanced Trigger Assembly; removeable magwell; match-grade chamber; loaded chamber indicator; ambidextrous slide stop; forged steel slide with Melonite finish and front and rear slide serrations; hammer-forged steel barrel with Melonite finish

Standard	$609.00
OSP	$653.00
OSP 4.5-in. barrel threaded	$733.00

XD-M ELITE PRECISION

Action: Semiautomatic
Grips: Polymer
Barrel: 5.25 in.
Sights: Fiber optic front, adjustable target rear
Weight: 30 oz.
Caliber: 9mm
Capacity: 22 rounds
Features: Match Enhanced Trigger Assembly; removeable magwell; match-grade chamber; loaded

chamber indicator; ambidextrous slide stop; forged steel slide with Melonite finish and front and rear slide serrations

MSRP **$674.00**

XD-S MOD.2 OSP

Action: Semiautomatic
Grips: Polymer
Barrel: 3.3 in.
Sights: Three dot low-profile front, rear
Weight: 21.5 oz.–22.5 oz.
Caliber: 9mm, .45 ACP
Capacty: 5, 6, 7, 9 rounds
Features: This small footprint, slim, single-stack has a slide cutout for reflex/micro red-dot optics mounting; comes with one 7-round flush and one 9-round extended magazine; available with factory installed Crimson Trace red-dot sight
Standard .... **$440.00–$465.00**
With Crimson Trace red-dot **$568.00**

Staccato 2011

STACCATO 2011 C2 DPO CARRY, C2 DPO TACTICAL

STACCATO 2011 P, P DPO

STACCATO 2011 STACCATO XC

C2, C2 OPTICS READY

Action: Semiautomatic
Grips: G2
Barrel: 3.9 in.
Sights: Fiber optic front, drift adjustable rear
Weight: 25.7 oz.
Caliber: 9mm
Capacity: 16 rounds
Features: A very svelte, optics-ready double-stack for home-defense, with a Dawson Universal Optic System rear optics mounting plate cutout (plates sold separately); flush-fit 11-degree crown barrel; 3.9 Recoil Master Light recoil system; alloy frame; accessory rail; ambidextrous safety; black diamond-like-carbon finish
C2 ....$1999.00–$2548.99
C2 Optics Ready ....$2299.00–$2848.99

P, P OPTICS READY

Action: Semiautomatic
Grips: G2
Barrel: 4.4 in.
Sights: Fiber optic front, T.A.S.II rear
Weight: 33 oz.
Caliber: 9mm
Capacity: 17, 20 rounds
Features: Actually designed for and utilized by a wide range of law enforcement agencies, you get a full-size frame with a shorter slide; bull barrel; Dawson 4.4 adaptive tool-less recoil system; billet frame with accessory rail; DPO version has Dawson Universal Optic System slide cut for optics mounting plates (plates sold separately); ships with two 17-round and one 20-round mags
P .... **$2099.00–$2799.00**
P Optics Ready .... **$2499.00–$2699.00**

STACCATO XC

Action: Semiautomatic
Grips: Synthetic
Barrel: 5 in.
Sights: Dawson fiber optic front, DUO rear
Weight: N/A
Caliber: 9mm
Capacity: 17, 20 rounds
Features: Gets the DUO (Dawson Universal Optic) Tactical Carry system which works with Leupold Delta Point Pro and Trijicon RMR red-dots with co-witness-height sights; competition bull barrel; Dawson 5.0 Adaptive Tool-less recoil system; 2011 G2 full-length grip with Tactical Advantage magwell
MSRP **$4299.00**

Staccato 2011

STACCATO 2011
STACCATO XL

STACCATO XL

Action: Semiautomatic
Grips: Synthetic
Barrel: 5.4 in.
Sights: Dawson fiber optic front, adjustable STI rear
Weight: N/A
Caliber: 9mm, .40 S&W
Capacity: 15, 16, 18, 20 rounds
Features: The first of the Staccato line to be available in .40 S&W (as well as 9mm); bull barrel; ambidextrous safety; 2.5-lb. trigger; Dawson 5.4 Adaptive Tool-less recoil system; 2011 G2 grip with Tactical Advantage Magwell; billet steel frame; in Diamond Like all black or Tuxedo black frame/chrome slide
MSRP . . . . $3399.00–$3499.00

Standard Manufacturing Co.

STANDARD
MANUFACTURING
CO. S333
THUNDERSTRUCK

STANDARD
MANUFACTURING
CO. SINGLE
ACTION REVOLVER
NICKEL PLATED

STANDARD
MANUFACTURING
CO. SINGLE ACTION
REVOLVER NICKEL
PLATED C-COVERAGE
ENGRAVING

S333 THUNDERSTRUCK

Action: Revolver
Grips: Polymer
Barrel: 1.25 in.
Sights: Ramp front, integral raised groove rear
Weight: N/A
Caliber: .22 Win. Mag.
Capacity: 8 rounds
Features: Interesting double-barrel revolver; each pull of the trigger fires two shots simultaneously; DAO
MSRP $429.00

SINGLE ACTION REVOLVER NICKEL PLATED

Action: Revolver
Grips: Walnut
Barrel: 4.75 in., 5.5 in., 7.5 in.
Sights: Blade front, groove rear
Weight: 40 oz.
Caliber: .45 LC
Capacity: 6 rounds
Features: A solid 4140 steel SA revolver with one- or two-piece figured walnut grips; full nickel-plating with fire-blued screws and pins
MSRP $1995.00

SINGLE ACTION REVOLVER NICKEL PLATED C-COVERAGE ENGRAVING

Action: Revolver
Grips: Walnut
Barrel: 4.75 in., 5.5 in., 7.5 in.
Sights: Blade front, groove rear
Weight: 40 oz.
Caliber: .45 LC
Capacity: 6 rounds
Features: Similar to Standard's full nickel-plated SA, but with 75% scroll engraving on frame, barrel, and cylinder; two-piece grip only
MSRP $3495.00

Steyr Arms

STEYR A2 MF

A2 MF

Action: Semiautomatic
Grips: Polymer
Barrel: 4.5 in.
Sights: Trapezoid
Weight: 27 oz.
Caliber: 9mm
Capacity: 10, 17 rounds
Features: MF stands for Modular Frame, which features interchangeable, textured backstraps and grips; trigger, drop, indirect firing pin safeties and manual lock; 5-pound trigger; under rail
MSRP $685.00

Stoeger Industries

STOEGER STR-9

STR-9

Action: Semiautomatic
Grips: Polymer
Barrel: 4.17 in.
Sights: Three-dot; tritium
Weight: 24 oz.
Caliber: 9mm
Capacity: 15 rounds
Features: Striker-fire pistol; double-stack magazine; aggressive slide serrations fore and aft; backstrap and grip texturing; fingergrooves; under rail. Three configurations: 1 magazine/1 backstrap; 3 magazines/3 backstraps; 3 magazines/3 backstraps with tritium sights
MSRP . . . . $329.00–$399.00

410 • Shooter's Bible 114th Edition

www.skyhorsepublishing.com

Stoeger Industries

STOEGER INDUSTRIES STR-9S COMBAT

STOEGER INDUSTRIES STR-9 OPTIC READY

STOEGER INDUSTRIES STR-9C COMPACT

STR-9 OPTIC READY

Action: Semiautomatic
Grips: Polymer
Barrel: 4.17 oz.
Sights: Three dot front, rear
Weight: 26 oz.
Caliber: 9mm
Capacity: 10, 15 rounds
Features: Optics-ready, double-stack pistol; four optics mounting plates included; choice of 10- or 15-round magazine
MSRP **$399.00**

STR-9C COMPACT

Action: Semiautomatic
Grips: Polymer
Barrel: 3.8 in.
Sights: Tritium
Weight: 24 oz.
Caliber: 9mm
Capacity: 10, 13 rounds
Features: A smartly priced option for CCW or target practice; 10- or 13-round magazine option; striker-fired; slide serrations
MSRP **$399.00**

STR-9S COMBAT

Action: Semiautomatic
Grips: Polymer
Barrel: 4.67 in.
Sights: Three dot front, adjustable rear
Weight: 28.8 oz.
Caliber: 9mm
Capacity: 10, 20 rounds
Features: Combat striker-fired model; threaded barrel; slide cut for mounting optics and four mounting plates; three interchangeable backstraps; in nitride hardened black with three 20-round magazines; optic not included
MSRP **$599.00**

Taurus International Manufacturing, Inc.

TAURUS 44

TAURUS 82

TAURUS .380 AUTO REVOLVER

TAURUS 605

TAURUS 692

TAURUS 856

TAURUS 608

Revolvers

44

Action: Revolver
Grips: Soft rubber
Barrel: 4 in., 6.5 in., 8.4 in.
Sights: Fixed
Weight: 45–57 oz.
Caliber: .44 Mag.
Capacity: 6 rounds
Features: Transfer bar; ported barrel; matte stainless steel finish; double and single-action
4.5-, 6-in.barrel: **$727.03**
8.4-in barrel: **745.27**

82

Action: Revolver
Grips: Rubber
Barrel: 4 in.
Sights: Fixed
Weight: 36.5 oz.
Caliber: .38 Spl. +P
Capacity: 6 rounds
Features: Transfer bar; steel construction with blued finish; single/double-action trigger
MSRP **$474.48**

.380 AUTO REVOLVER

Action: Revolver
Grips: Rubber
Barrel: 1.75 in.
Sights: Adjustable rear
Weight: 15.5 oz.
Caliber: .380 ACP
Capacity: 5 rounds
Features: Double-action trigger; fully enclosed hammer; blued or matte stainless finish; bobbed hammer
Blue **$536.97**
Stainless. **$576.70**

605

Action: Revolver
Grips: Rubber
Barrel: 2 in.
Sights: Fixed
Weight: 24 oz.
Caliber: .357 Mag
Capacity: 5 rounds
Features: Transfer bar safety; steel construction with blued or stainless finish; single-double action trigger
MSRP . . . .**$388.57–$540.68**

608

Action: Revolver
Grips: Rubber
Barrel: 4 in., 6.5 in.
Sights: Fixed front, adjustable rear

Weight: 44 oz.–51 oz.
Caliber: .357 Mag
Capacity: 8 rounds
Features: Matte stainless steel finish; transfer bar; large frame; steel frame; Taurus security system; porting
MSRP **$852.75**

692

Action: Revolver
Grips: Rubber
Barrel: 3 in., 6.5 in.
Sights: Fixed front, adjustable rear
Weight: 35.27 oz., 45.85 oz.
Caliber: .357 Mag., 9mm
Capacity: 7 rounds
Features: User can swap out .38 Special/.357 Mag. cylinder for one in 9mm; unfluted cylinder and porting; 6.5-in. barrel has a vent rib; matte blue or matte stainless finish
Blue . . . .**$639.45–$717.75**
Stainless. . . . .**$691.95–$776.78**

856

Action: Revolver
Grips: Rubber
Barrel: 2 in.
Sights: Serrated ramp front, notch rear
Weight: 16 oz., 22 oz.
Caliber: .38 Spec.
Capacity: 6 rounds
Features: Snub-nosed .38; ribbed rubber grips; matte blue, matte stainless, matte natural anodized and black oxide finishes; UL model is Ultralight 16 oz.; both versions +P rated
MSRP . . . .**$376.05–$550.53**

Taurus International Manufacturing, Inc.

TAURUS DEFENDER 856, DEFENDER 856 ULTRA-LITE

TAURUS JUDGE

TAURUS RAGING HUNTER

TAURUS RAGING BULL 444

TAURUS TRACKER 17

TAURUS RAGING JUDGE 513

TAURUS TRACKER 44

TAURUS TRACKER 627

TAURUS TRACKER 992

HANDGUNS

DEFENDER 856, DEFENDER 856 ULTRA-LITE

Action: Revolver
Grips: Laminate, rubber
Barrel: 3 in.
Sights: Orange outline night sight front
Weight: 16 oz.–35 oz.
Caliber: .38 Spec.
Capacity: 6 rounds
Features: +P rated. Several configurations include: tungsten Cerakote finish with brown Altamont wood grips; matte stainless finish with Hogue rubber grips; matte stainless frame/barrel and matte black cylinder finishes with gray/black VZ laminate grips; hard-anodized black finish Hogue rubber grips; Ultra-Lite models in the matte stainless or hard anodized matte black
MSRP . . . . **$446.12–$466.28**

JUDGE

Action: Revolver
Grips: Taurus rubber grips
Barrel: 3 in.
Sights: Red fiber optic, fixed
Weight: 29–36.8 oz.
Caliber: .45 Colt/.410
Capacity: 5 rounds
Features: Firing pin block, transfer bar safety; compact frame; matte stainless steel finish; steel construction
MSRP . . . . **$501.53–$615.37**

RAGING BULL 444

Action: Revolver
Grips: Rubber w/cushioned insert
Barrel: 6.5 in., 8.38 in.
Sights: Partridge front, adjustable rear
Weight: 53 oz.–63 oz.
Caliber: .44 Mag.
Capacity: 6 rounds
Features: Steel construction with

blued or stainless steel finish; transfer bar; dual lockup cylinder; porting; Taurus security system
MSRP **$944.50**

RAGING HUNTER

Action: Revolver
Grips: Rubber
Barrel: 5.12 in., 6.75 in., 8.375 in.
Sights: Fixed front, adjustable rear
Weight: 55 oz.
Caliber: .357 Mag., .44 Mag., .454 Casull, .460 S&W Mag.
Capacity: 6 rounds
Features: Optics rail; a steel sleeved barrel in an aluminum housing, porting, and cushioned grip inserts in all-over matte black or a two-tone with a stainless frame
Blue . . . .**$1021.73–$1065.00**
Stainless. $1032.13–1081.67

RAGING JUDGE 513

Action: Revolver
Grips: Rubber with soft cushion insert
Barrel: 3 in., 6.5 in.
Sights: Fiber optic front, fixed rear
Weight: 60.6 oz.–73 oz.
Caliber: .410/.45 Colt, .454 Casull
Capacity: 6 rounds
Features: Stainless steel finish; "Raging Bull" backstrap for added cushioning
MSRP **$1167.75**

TRACKER 17

Action: Revolver
Grips: Rubber with ribs
Barrel: 6.5 in.
Sights: Fixed front, adjustable rear
Weight: 47 oz.
Caliber: .17 HMR
Capacity: 7 rounds
Features: Matte stainless steel or blued finish; transfer bar; steel frame; porting

Blue **$595.60**
Stainless **$654.23**

TRACKER 44

Action: Revolver
Grips: Rubber with ribs
Barrel: 4 in.
Sights: Fixed front, adjustable rear
Weight: 35 oz.
Caliber: .44 Mag.
Capacity: 5 rounds
Features: Matte stainless steel or blued finish; transfer bar; steel frame; barrel porting; vent rib
Blue **$635.93**
Stainless **$654.17**

TRACKER 627

Action: Revolver
Grips: Rubber with ribs
Barrel: 4, 6.5 in.
Sights: Fixed front, adjustable rear
Weight: 35–40 oz.
Caliber: .357 Mag.
Capacity: 6 rounds
Features: Matte stainless steel medium frame revolver; barrel porting; 6.5-inch barrel has topside vent rib
MSRP **$588.30**

TRACKER 992

Action: Revolver
Grips: Taurus Ribber
Barrel: 4 in., 6.5 in.
Sights: Adjustable
Weight: 55 oz.
Caliber: .22 LR
Capacity: 9 rounds
Features: The versatile Tracker 992 easily transforms from .22 LR to .22 Magnum in seconds with its breakthrough removable cylinder; perfect for plinking, target practice, or varmint hunting
Blue: **$639.45**
Stainless: **$776.68**

Taurus International Manufacturing, Inc.

TAURUS 22 POLY

TAURUS 92

TAURUS 1911 COMMANDER

TAURUS 1911 OFFICER

TAURUS G2C

TAURUS G2S

TAURUS G3

TAURUS G3C

TAURUS SPECTRUM

Semiautomatics

22 POLY

Action: Semiautomatic
Grips: Polymer
Barrel: 2.3 in.
Sights: Fixed
Weight: 11.3 oz.
Caliber: .22 LR
Capacity: 8+1
Features: Polymer/blued steel construction; blue or stainless slide and barrel; tip-up barrel
Blue $280.62
Stainless. $297.62

92

Action: Semiautomatic
Grips: Checkered rubber
Barrel: 5 in.
Sights: Fixed-1 dot front, fixed-2 dots rear
Weight: 34 oz.
Caliber: 9mm
Capacity: 10+1 or 17+1 rounds
Features: Blued finish; steel/alloy construction; firing pin block, hammer decocker, manual safety
MSRP. $598.70

1911 COMMANDER

Action: Semiautomatic
Grips: Synthetic
Barrel: 4.2 in.
Sights: Novak drift adjustable front and rear
Weight: 38 oz.
Caliber: .45 ACP
Capacity: 8 rounds
Features: Numerous finishes and grip combinations; Novak drift-adjustable sights; grip safety; manual safety
MSRP. . . . . $626.27–$715.00

1911 OFFICER

Action: Semiautomatic

Grips: Synthetic
Barrel: 3.5 in.
Sights: Novak drift adjustable front and rear
Weight: 34.5 oz.
Caliber: .45 ACP
Capacity: 6 rounds
Features: Standard matte black finish or Cerakote finishes in tungsten, desert sand, and MS green; shortest model in the 1911 line
MSRP. . . . . $639.45–$739.20

G2C

Action: Semiautomatic
Grips: Polymer
Barrel: 3.2 oz.
Sights: Blade front, adjustable rear
Weight: 22 oz.
Caliber: 9mm, .40 S&W
Capacity: 12, 10 rounds
Features: A double-stack striker-fire good for CCW, target practice, or competition
MSRP. . . . . $299.97–$316.63

G2S

Action: Semiautomatic
Grips: Polymer
Barrel: 3.2 in.
Sights: Blade front, adjustable rear
Weight: 20 oz.
Caliber: 9mm, .40 S&W
Capacity: 7, 6 rounds
Features: A single-stack striker-fire for home-defense and target practice; various frame and slide color options available
MSRP. . . . . $278.57–$295.58

G3

Action: Semiautomatic
Grips: Polymer
Barrel: 4 in.
Sights: White three-dot
Weight: 25 oz.

Caliber: 9mm
Capacity: 10, 15, 17 rounds
Features: A single-action striker-fire with a safety trigger; a carbons steel slide in matte black or a stainless steel slide in matte stainless; full-size frame
Standard $357.00
Tenifer . . . . $339.65–$357.00
Optics Ready Tenifer $449.65

G3C

Action: Semiautomatic
Grips: Polymer
Barrel: 3.2 in.
Sights: Fixed front, drift adjustable rear
Weight: 22 oz.
Caliber: 9mm
Capacity: 10, 12 rounds
Features: A small, lightweight, and affordable double-stack carry option with a striker-fire action; stainless steel barrel; Tennifer finish in black; accessory rail; three magazines included in choice of 10- or 12-round
Stainless. $357.00
Tenifer $339.65
Optics Ready Tenifer $449.65

SPECTRUM

Action: Semiautomatic
Grips: Soft-touch overmold
Barrel: 2.8 in.
Sights: Integral low-profile front and rear
Weight: 10 oz.
Caliber: .380 ACP
Capacity: 6 rounds
Features: Ultralight striker-fired micro-pistol; soft-touch overmold grip; slide serrations; soft-edged frame; reversible magazine release; customizable color options
MSRP. $224.24

Taylor's & Co. Firearms

TAURUS TH9

TAURUS TX22

TAURUS TX-22 COMPETITION

TAYLOR'S & CO. FIREARMS 1860 ARMY LONG CYLINDER

TAYLOR'S & CO. 1873 CATTLEMAN PHOTO ENGRAVED

TAYLOR'S & CO. 1873 GUNFIGHTER

TAYLOR'S & CO. 1873 TAYLOR GAMBLER

TAYLOR'S & CO. FIREARMS GUNFIGHTER DEFENDER

TH9

Action: Semiautomatic
Grips: Synthetic
Barrel: 3.54 in., 4.27 in.
Sights: Novak drift adjustable front and rear
Weight: 28.2 oz., 25 oz.
Caliber: 9mm
Capacity: 13, 19 rounds
Features: Lightweight polymer frame DA/SA; dual trigger safety system; ambidextrous controls; underbarrel Picatinny rail; interchangeable backstrap
MSRP . . . . $376.95–$381.67

TX22

Action: Semiautomatic
Grips: Polymer
Barrel: 4.1 in.
Sights: Blade front, notch rear
Weight: 17.3 oz.
Caliber: .22 LR
Capacity: 10 rounds
Features: A .22 pistol to fill the hands; striker-fire action; Taurus' Pittman Trigger System
MSRP $348.43

TX22 COMPETITION

Action: Semiautomatic
Grips: Polymer
Barrel: 5.25 in.
Sights: White dot front, fully adjustable rear
Weight: 23 oz.
Caliber: .22 LR
Capacity: 10, 16 rounds
Features: A very lightweight rimfire designed for more serious target shooting, with a striker-fire action; threaded barrel; aggressive serrations on the aluminum slide; full-size polymer frame; four optics mounting plates; with three magazines
MSRP . . . . $533.33–$589.32

1860 ARMY LONG CYLINDER CONVERSION

Action: Revolver
Grips: Walnut
Barrel: 8 in.
Sights: Blade front, integral rear
Weight: 41.6 oz.
Caliber: .45 LC
Capacity: 6 rounds
Features: Originally a cap-n-ball blackpowder design, this one takes modern .45 LC rounds; forged steel frame; longer Army-sized walnut grips; case-hardened frame; blued cylinder, backstrap, barrel, and loading lever; brass trigger guard
MSRP $643.48

1873 CATTLEMAN PHOTO ENGRAVED

Action: Revolver
Grips: Walnut
Barrel: 4.75 in., 5.5 in., 7.5 in.
Sights: Fixed
Weight: 2 lb. 4 oz.–3 lb. 6 oz.
Caliber: .357 Mag., .45 LC
Capacity: 6 rounds
Features: Coin finish with charcoal blued screws; laser-engraved and hand chased; forged frame
MSRP . . . . $1014.81–$1167.73

1873 GUNFIGHTER

Action: Revolver
Grips: Walnut
Barrel: 5.5 in.

Sights: Fixed
Weight: 2 lb. 5 oz.
Caliber: .357 Mag., .45 Colt
Capacity: 6 rounds
Features: Special Army-sized grip; steel trigger guard and backstrap; choice of full nickel finish or blue barrel/cylinder with case-hardened frame; forged frame
Blue . . . . $625.12–$777.68
Nickel. . . . . $747.10–$899.66
**Blued checkered
 grips** . . . . $661.50–$814.06

1873 TAYLOR GAMBLER

Action: Revolver
Grips: Walnut
Barrel: 4.75 in., 5.5 in.
Sights: Fixed
Weight: 2 lb. 5 oz.
Caliber: .357 Mag., .45 Colt
Capacity: 6 rounds
Features: Checkered walnut grip; blued color case-hardened frame
MSRP . . . . $625.04–$804.60

GUNFIGHTER DEFENDER

Action: Revolver
Grips: Walnut
Barrel: 4.75 in., 5.5 in.
Sights: Blade front, integral rear
Weight: 39.2 oz., 40 oz.
Caliber: .357 Mag., .45 LC
Capacity: 6 rounds
Features: This single-action wears extra-long smooth walnut grips; forged steel frame; a low, flat hammer-spur makes this a good choice for competition
MSRP . . . . $695.15–$847.71

Taylor's & Co. Firearms

TAYLOR'S & CO. RUNNIN' IRON

TAYLOR'S & CO. SMOKE WAGON

RUNNIN' IRON
Action: Revolver
Grips: Checkered walnut

Barrel: 3.5 in., 4.75 in.
Sights: Wider fixed, open
Weight: 39 oz.
Caliber: .45 Colt, .357 Mag.
Capacity: 6 rounds
Features: Designed for the sport of mounted shooting; stainless or blued with low, wide hammer spur; checkered, one-piece gunfighter style grips in walnut or black polymer; wide trigger and extra clearance at front and rear of cylinder
MSRP . . . . $698.73–$844.98

SMOKE WAGON
Action: SA revolver

Grips: Checkered wood
Barrel: 3.5 in., 4.75 in., 5.5 in.
Sights: Open rear sight groove, wide angle front sight blade
Weight: 40 oz.
Caliber: .357 Mag., .45 Colt, .44-40 Win.
Capacity: 6 rounds
Features: Low profile hammer; custom tuning, custom hammer and base pin springs; jig-cut positive angles on trigger and sears; wire bolt and trigger springs
MSRP . . . . $657.93–$818.90

TNW Firearms

AERO SURVIVAL PISTOL
Action: Semiautomatic
Grips: Synthetic
Barrel: 8 in.
Sights: none
Weight: 48oz.
Caliber: 9mm, 10mm, .40 S&W, .45 ACP, .460 Rowland, .357 SIG
Capacity: Varies with magazine
Features: Reduced SBR version of TNW's Aero Survival Rifle; compact, lightweight, and easily disassembled; takes Glock-style magazines; available in OD green, dark earth, hard-anodized black, or Aero grey; some restricted state versions available
MSRP $799.00

TNW FIREARMS AERO SURVIVAL PISTOL

Traditions Firearms

TRADITIONS FIREARMS FRONTIER

TRADITIONS FIREARMS RAWHIDE

FRONTIER SERIES
Action: Revolver
Grips: Simulated ivory or walnut
Barrel: 3.5 in., 4.75 in., 5.5 in., 7.5 in.
Sights: Front blade
Weight: N/A
Caliber: .357 Mag., .44 Mag., .45 Colt, .44-40 Win.
Capacity: 6 rounds
Features: 1873 single action revolvers; deep bluing and nickel frames and barrel or color case hardened frame; transfer bar safety system provides the highest lever of safety offered in an 1873 single action
MSRP . . . . $605.00–$740.00

RAWHIDE SERIES
Action: Revolver
Grips: Walnut
Barrel: 4.75 in., 5.5 in., 7.5 in.
Sights: Front blade

Weight: N/A
Caliber: .45 Colt, .357 Mag., .22 LR, and .22 LR/.22 Mag.
Capacity: 6 rounds
Features: Quality single action shooter features at an affordable price; matte black finish that provides excellent corrosion resistance; transfer bar system provides the highest level of safety offered in an 1873 single action
MSRP . . . . $237.00–$474.00

Trailblazer Firearms

HANDGUNS

TRAILBLAZER FIREARMS LIFECARD .22LR

LIFECARD .22LR
Action: Single-shot

Grips: Aluminum
Barrel: 3 in.
Sights: None
Weight: 7 oz.
Caliber: .22LR
Capacity: 1 round
Features: Half-inch thick; barrel, bolt, and trigger are 4140 pre-hardened steel; handle is aluminum billet; folds to size of a stack of credit cards; full-size handle when unfolded; firearm will not fire when closed
MSRP . . . . $299.00–$359.00

TROY

TROY INDUSTRIES A4 PISTOL

A4 PISTOL WITH SBA3 BRACE
Action: Semiautomatic
Grips: Synthetic

Barrel: 10.5 in.
Sights: Flip-up front, rear
Weight: 67.2 oz.
Caliber: 5.56 NATO
Capacity: 30 rounds
Features: Gas-operated MSR pistol with features by the maker that include a standard trigger; SOCC92 BattleRail forend; control group; M4 front and rear folding BattleSight; 30-round BattleMag; Medieval muzzle brake; SBA3 pistol brace
MSRP $1200.00

Uberti

UBERTI 1851 NAVY CONVERSION

UBERTI 1851 NAVY CONVERSION WILD BILL

UBERTI 1860 ARMY CONVERSION

UBERTI 1871–1872 OPEN-TOP CONVERSION

UBERTI 1873 SA CATTLEMAN

UBERTI 1873 .22 LR

1851 NAVY CONVERSION
Action: Revolver
Grips: Walnut
Barrel: 4.75 in., 5.5 in., 7.5 in.
Sights: Fixed, open
Weight: 42 oz.
Caliber: .38 Spl.
Capacity: 6 rounds
Features: Case-hardened frame octagonal barrel; brass backstrap and trigger guard; conversion revolver frames are retro-fitted with loading gates to accommodate metallic cartridges like the originals
MSRP $679.00

1851 NAVY CONVERSION WILD BILL
Action: Revolver
Grips: Simulated ivory
Barrel: 7.5 in.
Sights: Bead front, groove rear
Weight: 43 oz.
Caliber: .38 Special
Capacity: 6 rounds
Features: Based on the 1851 Navy with an unfluted barrel sporting light engraving; classic grip of simulated ivory; front bead; color case hardened frame; cylinder and barre in blue
MSRP $899.00

1860 ARMY CONVERSION
Action: Revolver
Grips: Walnut
Barrel: 4.75 in., 5.5 in., 8 in.
Sights: Fixed, open
Weight: 42 oz.
Caliber: .38 Spl., .45 Colt
Capacity: 6 rounds
Features: Case-hardened frame; round barrel; steel backstrap and trigger guard; conversion revolver frames are retro-fitted with loading gates to accommodate metallic cartridges like the originals
MSRP $699.00

1871–1872 OPEN-TOP CONVERSION
Action: Revolver
Grips: Walnut
Barrel: 4.75 in., 5.5 in., 7.5 in.
Sights: Fixed, open
Weight: 42 oz.
Caliber: .38 Spl., .45 Colt
Capacity: 6 rounds
Features: 1872 model has steel backstrap and trigger guard; 1871 model has brass backstrap and trigger guard; case-hardened frame; round barrel; blued conversion revolver frames are retro-fitted with loading gates to accommodate metallic cartridges
1871 Navy $629.00
1872 Army $649.00

1873 CATTLEMAN
Action: Revolver
Grips: Walnut
Barrel: 4.75 in., 5.5 in., 7.5 in.
Sights: Fixed, open
Weight: 37 oz.
Caliber: .45 Colt
Capacity: 6 rounds
Features: Case-hardened frame; brass or steel backstrap and trigger guard; blued, nickel or stainless steel finish; fluted cylinder
Charcoal blue . . . . . $779.00–$829.00
Nickel $799.00
Stainless . . . . $849.00–$879.00

1873 CATTLEMAN .22 LR
Action: Revolver
Grips: Walnut
Barrel: 4.75 in., 5.5 in., 7.5 in.
Sights: Fixed, open
Weight: 36.8 oz.
Caliber: .22 LR
Capacity: 12 rounds
Features: Ideal for cowboy-action shooting practice; case-hardened frame; blued finish
MSRP $679.00

UBERTI 1873 CATTLEMAN BONNEY

UBERTI 1873 CATTLEMAN CALLAHAN

UBERTI 1873 CATTLEMAN CHISHOLM

UBERTI 1873 CATTLEMAN DESPERADO

UBERTI FIREARMS 1873 CATTLEMAN NEW MODEL DALTON

UBERTI FIREARMS 1873 SINGLE ACTION CATTLEMAN NEW MODEL DOC

UBERTI FIREARMS 1873 SINGLE ACTION CATTLEMAN NEW MODEL JESSE

UBERTI FIREARMS 1873 CATTLEMAN TEDDY

UBERTI FIREARMS 1875 NO. 3 2ND MODEL TOP-BREAK HARDIN

1873 CATTLEMAN BONNEY

Action: Revolver
Grips: Simulated bison horn
Barrel: 5.5 in.
Sights: Blade front, groove rear
Weight: 37 oz.
Caliber: .45 LC
Capacity: 6 rounds
Features: Part of Uberti's 1873 Cattleman Series; SA; bird's head grip of simulated bison; color case hardened frame; blued barrel and cylinder
MSRP $899.00

1873 CATTLEMAN CALLAHAN

Action: Revolver
Grips: Walnut, black or mother-of-pearl synthetic
Barrel: 4.75 in., 6 in., 7.5 in.
Sights: Fixed
Weight: 42 oz.
Caliber: .44 Mag.
Capacity: 6 rounds
Features: Blued, stainless, case-hardened or Old West finish; target model has angled front target sight and adjustable notched rear blade
MSRP $729.00

1873 CATTLEMAN CHISHOLM

Action: Revolver
Grips: Checkered walnut
Barrel: 4.75 in., 5.5 in.
Sights: Fixed, open
Weight: 37 oz.
Caliber: .45 Colt
Capacity: 6 rounds
Features: Complete matte finished steel; fluted barrel
MSRP $699.00

1873 CATTLEMAN DESPERADO

Action: Revolver
Grips: Bison horn style
Barrel: 4.75 in., 5.5 in.
Sights: Fixed, open
Weight: 37 oz.
Caliber: .45 Colt
Capacity: 6 rounds
Features: Full nickel-plated steel; fluted barrel
MSRP $1029.00

1873 CATTLEMAN NEW MODEL DALTON

Action: Revolver
Grips: Pearl-style
Barrel: 5.5 in.
Sights: Blade front, notch rear
Weight: 36.8 oz.
Caliber: .357 Mag., .45 Colt
Capacity: 6 rounds
Features: Embellished with nearly full-coverage engraving; case-colored frame; polished blue barrel, hammer, trigger guard; based in the revolver owned by Bob Dalton of the famous Dalton gang
MSRP $1249.00

1873 SINGLE ACTION CATTLEMAN NEW MODEL DOC

Action: Revolver
Grips: Bison horn
Barrel: 5.5 in.
Sights: Metal blade front, receiver notch rear
Weight: 36.8 oz.
Caliber: .45 Colt
Capacity: 6 rounds
Features: Based on gambler and gunslinger Doc Holliday's revolver; short-barreled, nimble single-action 1873; all-over nickel-plating and pearl-style grips in a bird's-head design
MSRP $1029.00

1873 CATTLEMAN NEW MODEL JESSE

Action: Revolver
Grips: Pearl-style
Barrel: 4.75 in.
Sights: Metal blade front, receiver notch rear
Weight: 35.2 oz.
Caliber: .45 Colt
Capacity: 6 rounds
Features: Based on Jesse James' 1873 Colt; fluted cylinder; all-over polished blue finish; dark bison-horn grips
MSRP $899.00

1873 CATTLEMAN NEW MODEL TEDDY

Action: Revolver
Grips: Simulated ivory
Barrel: 5.5 in.
Sights: Blade front, integral rear
Weight: 36.8 oz.
Caliber: .45 LC
Capacity: 6 rounds
Features: Sporting full laser engraving mimicking that of Roosevelt's Colt, this revolver is in full nickel-plated steel; fluted cylinder
MSRP $1399.00

1875 NO. 3 2ND MODEL TOP-BREAK HARDIN

Action: Revolver
Grips: Simulated buffalo horn
Barrel: 7 in.
Sights: Blade front, integral rear
Weight: 41.6 oz.
Caliber: .45 LC
Capacity: 6 rounds
Features: This top-break revolver comes with a case-hardened frame and blue barrel/cylinder for an eye-catching combination; fluted cylinder
MSRP $1699.00

Uberti

UBERTI 1875 FRONTIER

UBERTI FIREARMS 1875 SINGLE ACTION ARMY OUTLAW FRANK

UBERTI BIRD'S HEAD

UBERTI FIREARMS EL PATRON GRIZZLY PAW

UBERTI FIREARMS SHORT STROKE CMS PRO

UBERTI STALLION

UBERTI TOP BREAK REVOLVER

1875 OUTLAW & FRONTIER

Action: Revolver
Grips: Walnut
Barrel: 5.5 in. (Frontier), 7.5 in.
Sights: Fixed, open
Weight: 40–45 oz.
Caliber: .45 Colt
Capacity: 6 rounds
Features: Case-hardened or full nickel plated steel frame; steel backstrap and trigger guard; fluted cylinder
Outlaw case-hardened frame: $699.00
Outlaw full nickel-plating:. . .$829.00
Frontier case-hardened frame: $699.00

1875 SINGLE ACTION ARMY OUTLAW FRANK

Action: Revolver
Grips: Ivory-style
Barrel: 7.5 in.
Sights: Metal blade front, receiver notch rear
Weight: 44.8 oz.
Caliber: .357 Mag., .45 Colt
Capacity: 6 rounds
Features: Replica of the 1875 Remington carried by outlaw Jesse James' brother Frank James; all-over nickel-plating; ivory-style grips; lanyard ring
MSRP. $1099.00

BIRD'S HEAD

Action: Revolver
Grips: Walnut
Barrel: 3.5 in., 4 in., 4.75 in., 5.5 in.
Sights: Fixed, open
Weight: 35 oz.
Caliber: .38 Spl., .45 Colt, .357 Mag.
Capacity: 6 rounds
Features: Case-hardened frame; steel backstrap and trigger guard; blued finish; bird head shape grip; Bird's Head Stallion Old West Defense is chambered in .38 Spl., has full matte finish, 3.5-in. barrel
Standard $679.00
Stallion Old West Defense . . . $679.00

BISLEY

Action: Revolver
Grips: Bisley target style walnut
Barrel: 4.75 in., 5.5 in., 7.5 in.
Sights: Fixed, open
Weight: 40 oz.
Caliber: .45 Colt, .357 Mag.
Capacity: 6 rounds
Features: Case-hardened frame; steel backstrap and trigger guard; blued finish; fluted cylinder
MSRP. $699.00

EL PATRON GRIZZLY PAW

Action: Revolver
Grips: Walnut
Barrel: 4.75 in., 5.5 in.
Sights: EasyView sights
Weight: 36.8 oz.
Caliber: .357 Mag., .45 Colt
Capacity: 6 rounds
Features: Made for those with larger hands ("grizzly paws"); checkered walnut 1860 Army grips; blued barrel and cylinder; blued, case-hardened frame; cylinder has numbered chambers
MSRP. $779.00

SHORT STROKE CMS PRO

Action: Revolver
Grips: Walnut
Barrel: 3.5 in.
Sights: Blade front, notch rear
Weight: N/A
Caliber: .357 Mag., .45 Colt
Capacity: 6 rounds
Features: Designed specifically for cowboy action competition; short-stroke hammer that Uberti says has 20% less travel than other single-action revolvers; custom mainspring housing; checkered grip
MSRP. . . . . $879.00–$1029.00

STALLION

Action: Revolver
Grips: Walnut
Barrel: 4.75 in., 5.5 in., 6.5 in.
Sights: Fixed, open
Weight: 32 oz.
Caliber: .22 LR, .22 LR/Mag.
Capacity: 6 or 10 round
Features: Case-hardened frame; brass or steel backstrap and trigger guard; blued finish; fluted cylinder
.22 LR $549.00
.22 Mag. $649.00
10-shot .22 LR. $599.00

TOP BREAK REVOLVERS

Action: Revolver
Grips: Walnut or pearl-style
Barrel: 3.5 in., 5 in., 7 in.
Sights: Fixed, open
Weight: 40 oz.
Caliber: .45 Colt, .38 Spl., .44-40 Win.
Capacity: 6 rounds
Features: Full nickel plated steel or blued steel frame and blackstrap; case-hardened trigger guard
No. 3 Russian. $1349.00
1875 No. 3 blued $1349.00
1875 No. 3 nickel-plated. . . $1829.00

Ultimate Arms, LLC

ULTIMATE ARMS MAGNA T5 COMMANDER TAC

MAGNA T5 COMMANDER MATCH, COMMANDER TAC

Action: Semiautomatic
Grips: Carbon fiber
Barrel: 4.25 in.
Sights: Blade front, drift-adjustable
rear
Weight: 23 oz.
Caliber: .45 ACP
Capacity: 8 rounds
Features: Commander-length slide/barrel; full-size grip
MSRP. $1999.00

Ultimate Arms, LLC

ULTIMATE ARMS MAGNA T5 GOVERNMENT

MAGNA T5 GOVERNMENT MATCH, GOVERNMENT TAC

Action: Semiautomatic
Grips: Carbon fiber
Barrel: 5 in.
Sights: Fiber optic front, adjustable rear
Weight: 28 oz.
Caliber: .45 ACP
Capacity: 8 rounds
Features: A magnesium frame from forged billet makes this a strong and light full-size 1911 featuring a competition trigger; front and rear slide serrations; match-grade barrel
MSRP **$1999.00**

Volquartsen Firearms

VOLQUARTSEN FIREARMS BLACK MAMBA

VOLQUARTSEN FIREARMS SCORPION .22 LR

VOLQUARTSEN FIREARMS SCORPION .22 WMR

VOLQUARTSEN FIREARMS MAMBA-TF

VOLQUARTSEN FIREARMS MAMBA-X

VOLQUARTSEN FIREARMS MINI-MAMBA

BLACK MAMBA

Action: Semiautomatic
Grips: Polymer
Barrel: 4.5 in., 6 in.
Sights: Front ramp blade, adjustable rear
Weight: N/A
Caliber: .22 LR
Capacity: 10 rounds
Features: A combination of Volquartsen's Scorpion target pistol and the takedown functionality of a Ruger 2245 frame; stainless steel threaded barrel with removeable compensator; Tandemkross hiveGrip; Volquartsen accurizing kit, DLC-coated competition bolt, magazine release, and magazine pads; choice of black, OD Green, or Flat Dark Earth upper; top and under rails; Hi-Viz fiber optic front sight available on some versions
MSRP . . . . **$1409.00–$1800.00**

MAMBA-TF

Action: Semiautomatic
Grips: Polymer
Barrel: 4.5 in., 6 in.
Sights: Fiber optic front, target rear
Weight: 35 oz.
Caliber: .22 LR
Capacity: 10 rounds
Features: Push-button takedown for simple disassembly; Volquartsen LLV Competition upper; stainless steel barrel; laser-hardened stainless steel breech; integral top and underside Picatinny rails; aluminum frame retrofitted with Volquartsen Accurizing Kit; textured grip with pronounced finger grooves; metal in black, Arctic,

or Battleworn finishes
MSRP . . . . **$1504.00–$1868.00**

MAMBA-X

Action: Semiautomatic
Grips: Polymer
Barrel: 4.5 in.
Sights: None
Weight: 28 oz.
Caliber: .22 LR
Capacity: 10 rounds
Features: Volquartsen takes a cue from the centerfire crowd, with its LLV Competition Upper configured with a slide cut for red-dot sight mounting; DLC-coated competition bolt; single-port compensator; ½x28 threaded barrel; black anodized aluminum frame with Volquartsen Accurizing Kit; Hogue grips; compatible with a wide range of name-brand red-dots
MSRP **$1409.00**

MINI-MAMBA

Action: Semiautomatic
Grips: Rubber
Barrel: 3 in.
Sights: Fiber optic front, adjustable rear
Weight: 25 oz.
Caliber: .22 LR
Capacity: 10 rounds
Features: This is Volquartsen's smallest Mamba package and it features a black anodized aluminum Ruger Mk IV 22/45 frame; Hogue grips; barrel threaded ½x28; DLC-coated competition bolt; LLV Competition upper; integral topside Picatinny rail
MSRP **$1437.00**

SCORPION .22 LR

Action: Semiautomatic
Grips: Hogue
Barrel: 4.5 in., 6 in.
Sights: Front ramp fiber optic, adjustable target rear
Weight: 32 oz.
Caliber: .22 LR
Capacity: 10 rounds
Features: A 1911-angled frame with Hogue finger-groove grips; competition bolt; compensator; under and top rails; eye-catching finishes ranging from a full-coverage American flag to Battleworn grey and numerous grip options; some models available compensated; target or fiber optic sights
MSRP . . . . **$1410.00–$1854.00**

SCORPION .22 WMR

Action: Semiautomatic
Grips: G10
Barrel: 6 in.
Sights: Front ramp fiber optic, adjustable tritium rear
Weight: 67 oz.
Caliber: .22 WMR
Capacity: 9 rounds
Features: A dedicated small-game and varmint pistol with compensator; VZ Grips G10 panels in Predator Green; black nitride finish; under rail and topside rail; optional no sight version with black stainless finish; optional target sight version with black VZ Grip panels and black nitride finish
MSRP . . . . **$1934.00–$2463.00**

WALTHER CCP (CONCEALED CARRY PISTOL)

WALTHER CCP M2 .380

WALTHER CREED

WALTHER P22

WALTHER P99AS

WALTHER P99AS COMPACT

WALTHER PKK/S

WALTHER PPK/S .22

WALTHER PPQ M2 .45 ACP

CCP (CONCEALED CARRY PISTOL)
Action: Semiautomatic
Grips: Synthetic
Barrel: 3.54 in.
Sights: Adjustable
Weight: 22.33 oz.
Caliber: 9mm
Capacity: 8+1 rounds
Features: Available in black or stainless steel; interchangeable front sight with white dot; adjustable rear sight; reversible magazine release
MSRP. . . . . **starting at $419.00**

CCP M2 .380
Action: Semiautomatic
Grips: Polymer
Barrel: 3.54 in.
Sights: White three-dot
Weight: 19.4 oz.
Caliber: .380 ACP
Capacity: 8 rounds
Features: External safety; slide serrations front and rear; aggressive grip texture; reversible mag release; in a stainless slide, black slide, or a black slide with a built-in Viridian laser
MSRP. **$499.99**

CREED
Action: Semiautomatic
Grips: None
Barrel: 4 in.
Sights: Three-dot, low profile
Weight: 26.6 oz.
Caliber: 9mm
Capacity: 16, 10 rounds
Features: Economically priced, polymer frame; DAO pre-set trigger pistol; firing pin and drop safeties; ambidextrous magazine release button; 1913 Picatinny rail
MSRP. **$429.99**

P22
Action: DA/SA semiautomatic
Grips: Polymer
Barrel: 3.42 in., 5 in.
Sights: 3-dot adjustable low-profile
Weight: 17 oz., 22 oz.
Caliber: .22 LR
Capacity: 10 rounds
Features: Threaded barrel, interchangeable with target barrel; loaded chamber indicator; external slide stop; 3 safeties; two magazine styles; available with integrated laser-set; available in black, nickel, and military finish; now available with laser, Target models with 5-in. barrels available in black, Flat Dark Earth, or nickel
MSRP. . . . . **$309.00–$449.00**

P99AS
Action: DA semiautomatic
Grips: Black polymer frame and grips
Barrel: 4 in. stainless steel with Tenifer finish
Sights: Front and rear tritium night
Weight: 24 oz.–25.6 oz.
Caliber: 9mm, .40 S&W
Capacity: 15 (9mm) or 12 (.40 S&W) rounds
Features: The first pistol with a firing pin block combines advantages of a traditional DA pull with SA trigger and a decocking button safety integrated into slide, allowing users the ability to decock the striker, preventing inadvertent firing in both DA and SA
MSRP. . . . . **$505.00–$699.00**

P99AS COMPACT
Action: Striker-fired semiautomatic
Grips: Polymer
Barrel: 3.5 in.
Sights: 3-dot adjustable low-profile
Weight: 20.8 oz.–22.4 oz.
Caliber: 9mm, .40 S&W
Capacity: 10 (9mm) or 8 (.40 S&W) rounds
Features: Flat-bottom magazine buttplate, finger rest magazine buttplate; molded with a Weaver-style rail; interchangeable backstraps; hammerless striker system and integral safety devices come standard
MSRP. . . . . **$469.00–$545.00**

PPK AND PPK/S
Action: DA/SA semiautomatic
Grips: Polymer
Barrel: 3.3 in.
Sights: Fixed, open
Weight: 22.4 oz. (PPK), 24 oz. (PPK/S)
Caliber: .380 ACP
Capacity: 6 (PPK) or 7 (PPK/S) rounds
Features: Firing pin safety; manual safety with decocking function; double- and single-action trigger; extended beaver tail; nickel plated or blued finish
MSRP. **$849,00**

PPK/S .22
Action: DA/SA semiautomatic
Grips: Polymer
Barrel: 3.3 in.
Sights: Fixed, open
Weight: 24 oz.
Caliber: .22 LR
Capacity: 10 rounds
Features: Manual safety; top strap waved to reduce glare; internal slide stop; iconic PPK/S frame; beaver tail extension; nickel plated or black finish
MSRP. **$421.99**

PPQ M2 .45 ACP
Action: Striker-fired semiautomatic
Grips: Ergonomic polymer
Barrel: 4.25 in.
Sights: Three dot polymer
Weight: 28 oz.
Caliber: .45 ACP
Capacity: 12 rounds
Features: Custom Picatinny accessory rail; quick-defense trigger; ergonomic, non-slip, cross-directional grip surface; three safeties; Tenifer coating on slide and barrel; front and rear slide serrations; ambidextrous slide stop
MSRP. **$722.99**

Walther Arms

WALTHER PPQ M2

WALTHER PPQ SC

WALTHER PPS M2

WALTHER Q4 STEEL FRAME OR

WALTHER Q4 TAC

WALTHER Q5 MATCH

PPQ M2 9MM

Action: Striker-fired semiautomatic
Grips: Polymer
Barrel: 4 in., 4.1 in., 4.6 in., 5 in.
Sights: 3-dot adjustable low-profile
Weight: 24 oz. (9mm), 25.6 oz. (.40 S&W)
Caliber: 9mm
Capacity: 15 (9mm), 15/17 (9mm Navy SD) or 11 (.40 S&W) rounds
Features: Quick defense trigger; three safeties; Tenifer coated slide and barrel with matte finish
MSRP $549.99

PPQ SC

Action: Semiautomatic
Grips: Synthetic
Barrel: 3.5 in.
Sights: Three-dot, windage-adjustable rear
Weight: 21.2 oz.
Caliber: 9mm
Capacity: 10, 15 rounds
Features: Sub-Compact is easy to conceal; unique grip texturing; wide trigger guard with serrations on the front for extra purchase; accessory rail; low-profile snag-resistant sights; interchangeable backstraps; ambidextrous slide release; slide has a Tenifer coating
MSRP $435.00

PPS M2

Action: Striker-fired semiautomatic
Grips: Ergonomic polymer
Barrel: 3.18 in.
Sights: Three dot metal
Weight: 21.1 oz.
Caliber: 9mm
Capacity: 6, 7, 8 rounds
Features: Front and rear slide serrations; smooth, light trigger; ergonomic, non-slip, cross-directional grip surface; cocking indicator; chamber viewport; slide stop; magazine release conveniently placed for thumb operation; three magazine options; LE (Law Enforcement) variation comes equipped with phosphoric sights and three magazines
MSRP . . . . $429.99–$599.99

Q4 STEEL FRAME

Action: Semiautomatic
Grips: Polymer
Barrel: 4 in.
Sights: LPA with adjustable rear
Weight: 39.7 oz.
Caliber: 9mm
Capacity: 15 rounds
Features: Double-stack, steel-frame, striker-fire pistol that has an ergonomic wrap-around grip; extended beavertail; optics-ready slide; Picatinny accessory rail
MSRP $1349.00

Q4 TAC

Action: Semiautomatic
Grips: Synthetic
Barrel: 4.6 in.
Sights: Fiber optic front sight, adjustable target rear
Weight: 26 oz.
Caliber: 9mm
Capacity: 15, 17 rounds
Features: Ambidextrous slide stop and mag release; texturing on the grip; wide trigger guard with serrations for additional purchase; ergonomic and finger-grooved grip; magazine with finger rest; interchangeable backstraps for a custom fit; threaded barrel for suppressor add-ons; slide has been milled to be optics ready
MSRP $749.00

Q5 MATCH

Action: Semiautomatic
Grips: Synthetic
Barrel: 5 in.
Sights: Fiber optic front sight, adjustable target rear
Weight: 27.9 oz.
Caliber: 9mm
Capacity: 15 rounds
Features: Optics-ready slide; Picatinny rail; Walther ergonomic grip; ported slide; blue Quick Defense trigger; front and rear slide serrations; ambidextrous slide stop
MSRP $979.99

Wilson Combat

WILSON COMBAT ACP, ACP COMMANDER, ACP COMPACT

ACP, ACP COMMANDER, ACP COMPACT

Action: Semiautomatic
Grips: G10
Barrel: 4 in., 4.25 in., 5 in.
Sights: Fiber optic front, battlesight rear
Weight: 36.9 oz.–41.6 oz.
Caliber: 9mm, .45 ACP
Capacity: 8, 10 rounds

Features: With a full-size carbon steel frame, this pistol gets a Bullet Proof tactical thumb safety and high-grip beavertail safety; G10 Eagle Claw grip panels ; carbon steel slide with Eagle Claw rear serrations
.45 ACP . . . . starting at $2595.00
9mm . . . . starting at $2695.00

Wilson Combat

WILSON COMBAT AR9 PISTOL

WILSON COMBAT CQB ELITE COMBAT

WILSON COMBAT CQB ELITE COMMANDER

WILSON COMBAT CQB ELITE PROFESSIONAL

WILSON COMBAT EDC X9

WILSON COMBAT EDC X9L

WILSON COMBAT EXPERIOR 5-IN. DOUBLE STACK

AR9 PISTOL

Action: Semiautomatic
Grips: Synthetic
Barrel: 8 in., 11.3 in.
Sights: None
Weight: 86 oz.–96 oz.
Caliber: 9mm
Capacity: 10, 15, 17 rounds
Features: A pistol-caliber MSR pistol with billet aluminum lower and flat-top upper; Q-Comp flash hider on threaded muzzle; Bravo Company Mfg. pistol grip; Shockwave forearm support; Wilson's TTU M2 trigger; Armor-Tuff and hard-anodized finishes; M-LOK rail
MSRP . . . . starting at $2095.00

CQB ELITE COMPACT

Action: Semiautomatic
Grips: G10
Barrel: 4 in.
Sights: Fiber optic front, battlesight rear
Weight: 36.8 oz.
Caliber: .45 ACP, 9mm
Capacity: 7, 8 rounds
Features: With a carbon steel compact frame and slide; tactical thumb safety, high-ride beavertail safety, round-butt magazine well, and magazine release; starburst G10 grips
.45 ACP . . . . . . starting at $3565.00
9mm. . . . . starting at $3665.00

CQB ELITE COMMANDER

Action: Semiautomatic
Grips: G10
Barrel: 4.25 in.
Sights: Fiber optic front, battlesight rear
Weight: 38.3 oz.
Caliber: 9mm, .45 ACP
Capacity: 7, 8 rounds

Features: Similar to the CQB Compact, but with Wilson's Professional carbon steel frame and 4.25-in. match-grade barrel and bushing
.45 ACP . . . . . starting at $3565.00
9mm. . . . . starting at $3665.00

CQB ELITE PROFESSIONAL

Action: Semiautomatic
Grips: G10
Barrel: 4 in.
Sights: Fiber optic front, battlesight rear
Weight: 44 oz.
Caliber: 9mm, .45 ACP
Capacity: 7, 8 rounds
Features: A combo of the Compact and the Commander, with Wilson's Professional-size frame and Compact 4-in. match-grade cone barrel
.45 ACP . . . . . . starting at $3565.00
9mmstarting at $3665.00

EDC X9

Action: Semiautomatic
Grips: G10
Barrel: 4 in.
Sights: Fiber optic front, battlesight rear
Weight: 29.9 oz.
Caliber: 9mm
Capacity: 15, 18 rounds
Features: Double-stack aluminum X frame; Bullet Proof concealment hammer, thumb safety, and magazine release; tri-top slide with external extractor; X-TAC treatment to front- and backstrap; reliability-enhanced cone barrel with a reverse flush-cut crown; fluted chamber and barrel
MSRP . . . . starting at $2995.00

EDC X9L

Action: Semiautomatic
Grips: G10
Barrel: 5 in.
Sights: Fiber optic front, battlesight rear
Weight: 32.4 oz.
Caliber: 9mm
Capacity: 15, 18 rounds
Features: Double-stack aluminum X frame; Bullet Proof concealment hammer, thumb safety, and magazine release; tri-top slide with external extractor; X-TAC treatment to front- and backstrap; reliability enhanced barrel and bushing with a reverse flush-cut crown; fluted chamber
MSRP . . . . starting at $3095.00

EXPERIOR 5-IN. DOUBLE STACK, COMMANDER DOUBLE-STACK, COMPACT DOUBLE-STACK

Action: Semiautomatic
Grips: G10
Barrel: 4 in., 4.25 in., 5 in.
Sights: Fiber optic front, battlesight rear
Weight: 30.5 oz.–41 oz.
Caliber: 9mm
Capacity: 15, 18 rounds
Features: A compact aluminum frame with a longer slide and features like frontstrap and mainspring housing with TRAK pattern texturing; aluminum mag well; Bullet Proof magazine release, concealment hammer safety, and tactical thumb safety; stainless steel slide
5-in. . . . . starting at $3235.00
Commander. . . starting at $2185.00
Compact . . . . . starting at $3095.00

WILSON COMBAT EXPERIOR 6-IN. LONGSLIDE

WILSON COMBAT EXPERIOR FULL-SIZE

WILSON COMBAT EXPERIOR PROFESSIONAL

WILSON COMBAT TACTICAL CARRY COMMANDER

WILSON COMBAT VICKERS ELITE

WILSON COMBAT X-TAC ELITE COMMANDER

WILSON COMBAT X-TAC PROFESSIONAL

EXPERIOR 6-IN. LONGSLIDE

Action: Semiautomatic
Grips: G10
Barrel: 6 in.
Sights: Fiber optic front, battlesight rear
Weight: 44.1 oz.
Caliber: 9mm, .45 ACP
Capacity: 8, 10 rounds
Features: Full-size carbon steel frame with WAVE rails; frontstrap, mainspring housing and G10 grips have TRAK pattern texturing; Bullet Proof round-butt mag well, magazine release; concealment beavertail grip safety, and tactical thumb safety
.45 ACP . . . . . . starting at $3890.00
9mm. . . . . starting at $3990.00

EXPERIOR FULL-SIZE, COMMANDER, COMMANDER COMPACT, COMPACT, SUB-COMPACT

Action: Semiautomatic
Grips: G10
Barrel: 4 in., 4.25 in., 5 in.
Sights: Fiber optic front, battlesight rear
Weight: 36.4 oz.–40.2 oz.
Caliber: 9mm, .45 ACP
Capacity: 8, 10 rounds
Features: Carbon steel frame with WAVE rails; frontstrap, mainspring housing and G10 grips have TRAK pattern texturing; Bullet Proof round-butt mag well, magazine release; concealment beavertail grip safety, and tactical thumb safety
.45 ACP . . . . . . starting at $3890.00
9mm. . . . . starting at $3990.00

EXPERIOR PROFESSIONAL

Action: Semiautomatic
Grips: G10
Barrel: 4 in.
Sights: Fiber optic front, battlesight rear
Weight: 38.2 oz.
Caliber: 9mm, .45 ACP
Capacity: 8, 10 rounds
Features: Professional-size carbon steel frame with WAVE rails; frontstrap, mainspring housing and G10 grips have TRAK pattern texturing; Bullet Proof round-butt mag well, magazine release; concealment beavertail grip safety, and tactical thumb safety; carbon steel slide
.45 ACP . . . . . . starting at $3890.00
9mm. . . . . starting at $3990.00

TACTICAL CARRY COMMANDER

Action: Semiautomatic
Grips: G10
Barrel: 4.25 in.
Sights: Fiber optic front, battlesight rear
Weight: 37.8 oz.
Caliber: 9mm, .45 ACP
Capacity: 8, 10 rounds
Features: Wilson's Professional-size carbon steel frame with a match-grade barrel and bushing with a reverse flush-cut crown; fluted chamber; Bullet Proof concealment beavertail grip safety, tactical thumb safety, and magazine release; countersunk slide stop
.45 ACP . . . . . . starting at $3890.00
9mm. . . . . starting at $3990.00

VICKERS ELITE

Action: Semiautomatic
Grips: G10
Barrel: 5 in.
Sights: Battlesight with gold bead front

Weight: 41.6 oz.
Caliber: 9mm, .45 ACP
Capacity: 8, 9 rounds
Features: A full-size competition gun designed with Larry Vickers, featuring a carbon steel frame; high-cut and checkered front strap; Bullet Proof mag well, mag release and thumb safety; carbon steel slide with heavy underside machine chamfering and serrations fore and aft; match-grade barrel with flush cut reverse crown; countersunk slide stop
.45 ACP . . . . . . starting at $3990.00
9mm. . . . . starting at $4090.00

X-TAC ELITE COMMANDER

Action: Semiautomatic
Grips: G10
Barrel: 4.5 in.
Sights: Fiber optic front, battlesight rear
Weight: 44.3 oz.
Caliber: 9mm, .45 ACP
Capacity: 8, 10 rounds
Features: Wilson's Professional-size carbon steel frame with a slightly longer match-grade barrel with a reverse flush-cut crown; Bullet Proof high-ride beavertail grip safety, tactical thumb safety, and magazine release
.45 ACP . . . . . . starting at $3790.00
9mm. . . . . starting at $3890.00

X-TAC PROFESSIONAL

Action: Semiautomatic
Grips: G10
Barrel: 4.25 in.
Sights: Fiber optic front, battlesight rear
Weight: 38 oz.
Caliber: 9mm, .45 ACP
Capacity: 8, 10 rounds
Features: Wilson's Professional-size carbon steel frame; Bullet Proof high-ride beavertail grip safety, tactical thumb safety, and magazine release
.45 ACP . . . . starting at $2960.00
9mm. . . . . starting at $3060.00

Wilson Combat

WILSON COMBAT X-TAC SUPERGRADE

WILSON COMBAT X-TAC SUPERGRADE COMMANDER

X-TAC SUPERGRADE
Action: Semiautomatic
Grips: G10
Barrel: 5 in.
Sights: Fiber optic front, battlesight rear
Weight: 46 oz.
Caliber: 9mm, .45 ACP
Capacity: 8, 10 rounds
Features: The Supergrade has a full-size carbon steel frame with a round butt; Bullet Proof magazine release, tactical thumb safety, and high-ride beavertail grip safety; X-TAC frontstrap and mainspring housing treatment, rear slide cocking serrations
.45 ACP . . . . . . starting at $4995.00
9mm. . . . . starting at $5055.00

X-TAC SUPERGRADE COMMANDER, COMPACT, PROFESSIONAL
Action: Semiautomatic
Grips: G10
Barrel: 4 in., 4.25 in.
Sights: Fiber optic front, battlesight rear
Weight: 38.4 oz.–43.3 oz.
Caliber: 9mm, .45 ACP
Capacity: 7, 8, 10 rounds
Features: Similar to the full-size Supergrade, but with a Professional-size frame in the Commander/Professional; Compact has Officer's size frame
.45 ACP . . . . . . starting at $4995.00
9mm. . . . . starting at $5055.00

ZEV Technologies

ZEV TECHNOLOGIES OZ9 COMBAT

ZEV TECHNOLOGIES OZ9C HYPERCOMP

ZEV TECHNOLOGIES OZ9 ELITE STANDARD, OZ9C ELITE COMPACT

ZEV TECHNOLOGIES OZ9C ELITE X GRIP

OZ9 COMBAT
Action: Semiautomatic
Grips: Polymer
Barrel: 4.5 in.
Sights: Fiber optic front, battle sight rear
Weight: 28 oz.
Caliber: 9mm
Capacity: 17 rounds
Features: Double-stack high-end striker fire with ZEV's windowless Citadel slide; PRO match barrel; PRO curved-face trigger; optic-ready slide cut; steeper grip angle for straighter pointing; full-length solid steel frame; accessory rail; slide has serrations front and rear and is serrated across the top to reduce glare
MSRP. $1499.00

OZ9 ELITE STANDARD, OZ9C ELITE COMPACT
Action: Semiautomatic
Grips: Polymer

Barrel: 4.49 in., 4 in.
Sights: Fiber optic front, battle sight rear
Weight: 28 oz., 26.25 oz.
Caliber: 9mm
Capacity: 15 rounds
Features: Similar to other OZ9 models, this one has a top slide cutout behind the front sight; optics mounting plate cutout; threaded barrel; underside rail; in all black, black frame/slide with bronze barrel, or flat dark earth frame/slide with black barrel
MSRP. . . . . $1815.00–$2235.00

OZ9C ELITE X GRIP
Action: Semiautomatic
Grips: Polymer
Barrel: 4 in.
Sights: Fiber optic front, battle sight rear
Weight: 27 oz.
Caliber: 9mm
Capacity: 17 rounds
Features: A hybrid OZ9, with the

slide of the OZ9c compact model and the longer grip of the standard OZ9; optics ready; PRO magwell
MSRP. . . . . $1763.00–$2235.00

ZEV TECHNOLOGIES OZ9C HYPERCOMP
Action: Semiautomatic
Grips: Polymer
Barrel: 4 in.
Sights: Three dot front, rear
Weight: 28 oz.
Caliber: 9mm
Capacity: 15 rounds
Features: Ready for trophy winning with a bronze Cerakote barrel ported across the top instead of the sides; slide serrations fore and aft; underside rail; textured grip; wide magwell; optics ready; fully integrated locking block on full-length steel frame; PRO flat-faced trigger
MSRP. $1815.00

BLACK POWDER

Cimarron Firearms

**CIMARRON FIREARMS
1851 NAVY**

**CIMARRON
FIREARMS CO.
WALKER'S WALKER**

1851 NAVY LONDON
Action: Revolver
Stock: Wood
Barrel: 7.5 in.
Sights: Front blade, groove
Weight: 2 lb. 11 oz.
Caliber: .36, .44
Features: Reproduction of the 1851 cap-and-ball revolver originally known as the Percussion Peacemaker; frame is in a case-hardened finish; walnut grips are smooth; barrel is octagonal
MSRP $426.12

WALKER'S WALKER
Action: Revolver
Stock: Walnut
Barrel: 9 in.
Sights: Low blade front
Weight: 72 oz.
Caliber: .44
Features: A beefy revolver with a long barrel in limited edition and featuring a brass trigger guard; steel backstrap; one-piece grips; Cimarron's own original finish with military markings; ships in a glass and walnut presentation case
MSRP $794.97

Cooper Firearms of Montana

**COOPER FIREARMS OF
MONTANA MUZZLELOADER**

MUZZLELOADER
Action: Bolt/inline
Stock: Wood
Barrel: N/A
Sights: None
Weight: N/A
Caliber: .45, .50
Features: Synthetic and wood stock versions; left-hand available; fluted barrel; sealed and removeable plug; 209 shotgun primer ignition; adjustable single-stage trigger; synthetic stock available in Excalibur or Open Country Long-Range stocks; wood stock available in Classic, Custom Classic, Schnabel, and Jackson Game styles, and upgraded wood is available
Synthetic . . . . . . $2795.00–$3045.00
Wood . . . . $4125.00–$4375.00

CVA (Connecticut Valley Arms)

**CVA ACCURA
X-TREME LR-X**

**CVA ACCURA
X-TREME MR-X**

CVA OPTIMA V2

ACCURA X-TREME LR-X
Action: Break-action
Stock: Synthetic
Barrel: 30 in.
Sights: None
Weight: 7 lb. 4 oz.
Bore/Caliber: .45, .50
Features: This is considered a long-range muzzleloader, featuring a QRBP quick-release breech plug; DuraSight rail; Quake Claw sling; fluted premium Bergara threaded barrel; stock in Veil Wildland with flat dark earth Cerakote metalwork or Realtree Hillside camo stock with Patriot Brown Cerakote metalwork; .50-cal available with Williams rear peep and fiber optic front sights
MSRP . . . . $675.00–$710.00

ACCURA X-TREME MR-X
Action: Break-action
Stock: Synthetic
Barrel: 26 in.
Sights: None
Weight: 7 lb. 1 oz.
Bore/Caliber: .45, .50
Features: Similar to the LR-X, but with a more manageable barrel length, featuring a QRBP quick-release breech plug; DuraSight rail; Quake Claw sling; fluted premium Bergara threaded barrel; stock in Veil Alpine or Realtree Rockslide camo, both with Sniper Grey Cerakote metalwork; .50-cal available with Williams rear peep and fiber optic front sights
MSRP . . . . $595.00–$705.00

OPTIMA V2
Action: Break-action
Stock: Realtree Xtra Green or black
Barrel: 26 in.
Sights: Fiber optic sights or mount
Weight: 6 lb. 10 oz.
Bore/Caliber: .50
Features: Modeled on Accura V2; stainless steel barrel; quick release breech plug; ambidextrous stock, thumbhole stock option; includes DuraSight Dead-On scope mount and ramrod
MSRP . . . . $325.00–$370.00

CVA (Connecticut Valley Arms)

CVA OPTIMA V2 LR

CVA OPTIMA V2 NORTHWEST

CVA ARMS PARAMOUNT

CVA PARAMOUNT PRO

CVA PARAMOUNT HTR

CVA PARAMOUNT PRO COLORADO

CVA WOLF

OPTIMA V2 LR
Action: Break-action
Stock: Synthetic
Barrel: 26 in.
Sights: None
Weight: 6 lb. 10 oz.
Caliber: .50
Features: Breech lever trigger-guard actuation; Optima's trigger and internal parts; finger-removable Quick-Release breech plug; PalmSaver ramrod; reversible hammer spur; DuraSight Dead-On scope mount; stainless steel barrel or Nitride treated; Realtree Xtra Green stock
MSRP . . . . **$400.00–$585.00**

OPTIMA V2 NORTHWEST
Action: Break-action
Stock: Synthetic
Barrel: 26 in.
Sights: Fiber optics
Weight: 6 lb. 10 oz.
Bore/Caliber: .50
Features: Meets open-breech/ignition requirements of Idaho, Oregon, and Washington; quick release breech plug; stainless steel hardware and Realtree Xtra Green standard stock
MSRP **$350.00**

PARAMOUNT
Action: Bolt

Stock: Synthetic
Barrel: 26 in.
Sights: None
Weight: N/A
Caliber: .45
Features: Billed as the world's first long-range muzzleloader capable of killing shots 300 yards and beyond. Features include free-floating Bergara barrel; CVA VariFlame breech plus; aluminum chassis; takes new PowerBelt ELR bullets spedifically designed for this muzzleloader
MSRP **$1190.00**

PARAMOUNT HTR
Action: Bolt
Stock: Synthetic
Barrel: 26 in.
Sights: None
Weight: 9 Lb. 9.6 oz.
Bore/Caliber: .40, .45
Features: Internal aluminum chassis and adjustable cheek riser; free-floating barrel threaded for CVA muzzle brake; designed to use .40-cal. 225-gr. PowerBelt ELR or .45-cal. 285-gr. PowerBelt ELR projectiles and magnum loads of Blackhorn 209
MSRP **$1240.00**

PARAMOUNT PRO
Action: Bolt
Stock: Fiberglass
Barrel: 26 in.
Sights: None
Weight: 8 lb. 12 oz.
Caliber: .45

Features: Free-floating barrel of nitride-treated stainless steel; Grayboe stock; TriggerTech trigger; self-deploying ramrod; VariFlame breech plug; Quake CLAW flush cup sling; Cerakote finish in bronze
MSRP **$1905.00**

PARAMOUNT PRO COLORADO
Action: Bolt
Stock: Fiberglass
Barrel: 26 in.
Sights: Peep
Weight: 8 lb. 12 oz.
Caliber: .50
Features: Identical to the Paramount Pro, but with the addition of Williams peep sights
MSRP **$1905.00**

WOLF
Action: Break-action in-line
Stock: Synthetic
Barrel: 24 in.
Sights: DuraSight fiber optic; includes 3–9x32mm KonusShot scope
Weight: 6 lb. 4 oz.
Bore/Caliber: .50
Features: Bullet-guiding muzzle; new tool-free QR breech plug system; ambidextrous compact or standard stock in black or camo; reversible hammer spur; blued or stainless barrel
MSRP . . . . **$205.00–$390.95**

Davide Pedersoli & C.

DAVIDE PEDERSOLI 1763 LEGER (1766) CHARLEVILLE

1763 LEGER (1766) CHARLEVILLE
Action: Dropping block
Stock: Walnut
Barrel: 44.7 in.

Sights: Open
Weight: 10 lb. 2 oz.
Caliber: .69
Magazine: None
Features: Creedmoor sight; tunnel front sight; replica of French infantry musket
MSRP **$1441.00**

Davide Pedersoli & C.

DAVIDE PEDERSOLI 1805 HARPER'S FERRY PERCUSSION PISTOL

DAVIDE PEDERSOLI 1850 UNDERHAMMER COOK PISTOL

DAVIDE PEDERSOLI 1854 LORENZ INFANTRY RIFLE TYPE II

DAVIDE PEDERSOLI 1860 VOLUNTEER

DAVIDE PEDERSOLI BAKER CAVALRY SHOTGUN

DAVIDE PEDERSOLI BOUTET 1ER EMPIRE

DAVIDE PEDERSOLI CONTINENTAL TARGET PISTOL CAPTION

DAVIDE PEDERSOLI COOK & BROTHER ARTILLERY CARBINE

DAVIDE PEDERSOLI DERRINGER PHILADELPHIA

DAVIDE PEDERSOLI COOK & BROTHER RIFLE

1805 HARPER'S FERRY PERCUSSION PISTOL

Action: Percussion cap
Stock: American walnut
Barrel: 10.06 in.
Sights: Bead front
Weight: 2 lb. 10.6 oz.
Bore/Caliber: .54
Features: Brass furniture; smooth bore; chromed and satin finished barrel; old silver case hardened lock
MSRP **$810.00**

1850 UNDERHAMMER COOK PISTOL

Action: Percussion
Stock: Walnut
Barrel: 7.8 in.
Sights: Blade front, notch rear
Weight: 2 lb. 2 oz.
Bore/Caliber: .36
Features: A target shooting pistol that will be coveted by MLAIC competitors; front sight adjustable for windage, rear sight adjustable for elevation; walnut grip in a rather inverted teardrop design; match-grade barrel
MSRP **$1118.00**

1854 LORENZ INFANTRY RIFLE TYPE II

Action: Percussion
Stock: Walnut
Barrel: 37 in.
Sights: N/A
Weight: 9 lb.
Caliber: .54
Features: Conceived by the Austrian Lieutenant Joseph Lorenz; official production started in 1854, replacing the Augustin rifle among Austrian troops; used in Italy during the second Independence War, as well as in the Balkans; then largely exported to America, equipping both the Union and the Confederate armies,

becoming one of the most used rifles during the American Civil War
MSRP **$1941.00**

1860 VOLUNTEER

Action: Percussion
Stock: Walnut
Barrel: 33 in.
Sights: Tunnel front, Creedmoor rear
Weight: 8 lb. 13 oz.
Caliber: .451
Features: The British N.R.A., for the first time, organized a national event held at Wimbledon in 1860, inspiring Pedersoli's Volunteer Rifle; broach rifled with an optimal twist for target shooting at 100-150 meters; oil-finished, hand-checkered stock
MSRP **$2122.00**

BAKER CAVALRY SHOTGUN

Action: Percussion
Stock: Walnut
Barrel: 11.25 in.
Sights: None
Weight: 5 lb. 12 oz.
Bore/Caliber: 20 Ga.
Features: Single trigger back action, side-by-side shotgun; reproduces a gun made by London gunsmith Ezekiel Baker in 1850; case-hardened
MSRP **$1491.00**

BOUTET 1ER EMPIRE

Action: Flintlock
Stock: Hardwood
Barrel: 10 in.
Sights: Fixed
Weight: 2 lb. 14 oz.
Bore/Caliber: .45
Features: Napoleon wrote with flattering appreciation about the style and prestige of the Boutet guns, which Pedersoli now proudly introduces with fine checkering on sides; metal buttplate; ramrod has horn tip; single set trigger; on lock two lines are engraved with MANUF RE/a Versailles.
MSRP **$1590.00**

CONTINENTAL TARGET PISTOL

Action: Percussion, flintlock
Stock: Walnut
Barrel: 11 in.
Sights: Front, windage adjustable rear
Weight: 2 lb. 3 oz.
Caliber: .45, .44
Features: Reproduction of target pistol of Central European style; set trigger; octagonal barrel; chrome finished
Percussion **$707.00**
Flintlock **$806.00**

COOK & BROTHER ARTILLERY CARBINE

Action: Caplock
Stock: Walnut
Barrel: 24 in.
Sights: None
Weight: 6 lb. 10 oz.
Bore/Caliber: .58
Features: Inspired by English model guns; brass garnitures; blued barrel; case-hardened lock
MSRP **$1372.00**

COOK & BROTHER RIFLE

Action: Muzzleloading
Stock: Walnut
Barrel: 33 in.
Chokes: IC, M, F
Sights: Fixed
Weight: 8 lb. 10 oz.
Bore/Gauge: .58
Features: Brass garnitures; brown colour barrel
MSRP **$1471.00**

DERRINGER PHILADELPHIA

Action: Percussion
Stock: Walnut
Barrel: 3.06 in.
Sights: None
Weight: 8.6 oz.
Bore/Caliber: .45
Features: Originally manufactured by John Henry Derringer; brass furniture; case-hardened lock; original markings on the Action: Derringer/Philadelphia
MSRP **$666.00**

Davide Pedersoli & C.

DAVIDE PEDERSOLI ENFIELD 3 BAND P1853 WHITWORTH WITH HEXAGONAL RIFLING

DAVIDE PEDERSOLI GIBBS SHOTGUN

DAVIDE PEDERSOLI KODIAK EXPRESS MK VI

DAVIDE PEDERSOLI MAMELOUK

DAVIDE PEDERSOLI ENFIELD 3 BAND P1853 RIFLE MUSKET

DAVIDE PEDERSOLI HAWKEN HUNTER RIFLE

DAVIDE PEDERSOLI LA BOHEMIENNE SIDE-BY-SIDE SHOTGUN

DAVIDE PEDERSOLI GIBBS SHORT RANGE RIFLE

DAVIDE PEDERSOLI HOWDAH HUNTER PISTOL

DAVIDE PEDERSOLI LE PAGE TARGET FLINTLOCK PISTOL

ENFIELD 3 BAND P1853 RIFLE MUSKET

Action: Percussion
Stock: Walnut
Barrel: 39 in.
Sights: Adjustable rear
Weight: 8 lb. 13 oz.
Bore/Caliber: .577
Features: Ladder rear sight with a slider assembled on a base with steps; steel barrel bands; brass furniture; ramrod tip is shaped with characteristic jag slot
MSRP $1471.00

ENFIELD 3 BAND P1853 WHITWORTH WITH HEXAGONAL RIFLING

Action: Percussion cap
Stock: American walnut
Barrel: 36 in.
Sights: Creedmoor sight, tunnel front
Weight: 9 lb. 7.4 oz.
Bore/Caliber: .451
Features: Hammer-forged browned finish hexagonal barrel; lock parts with light colour case hardened finish
MSRP $2326.00

GIBBS SHORT RANGE RIFLE

Action: Percussion
Stock: Walnut
Barrel: 32 in.
Sights: Tunnel front, Creedmoor rear
Weight: 10 lb. 9.6 oz.
Caliber: .45
Features: Modeled on the original Gibbs; equipped with a barrel made for target shooting at 100-150 meters
MSRP $2342.00

GIBBS SHOTGUN

Action: Percussion
Stock: Walnut
Barrel: 32.3 in.
Sights: None
Weight: 8 lb. 9 oz.

Bore/Caliber: 12 Ga.
Features: Octagonal to round barrel; case-hardened color-finished lock; grip and forend caps with ebony inserts; pistol grip stock
Standard $1877.00
Deluxe $4024.00

HAWKEN HUNTER RIFLE

Action: Percussion, flintlock
Stock: Wood
Barrel: 28.4 in.
Chokes: IC, M, F
Sights: Adjustable rear, fixed front
Weight: 8 lb. 10 oz.
Bore/Gauge: .50, .54
Features: American walnut stock features a microcell thick butt plate; double set triggers
Percussion $941.00
Percussion left-hand $971.00
Flintlock. $1012.00
Flintlock left-hand $1042.00

HOWDAH HUNTER PISTOL

Action: Caplock
Stock: Walnut
Barrel: 11.25 in.
Sights: None
Weight: 5 lb. 1 oz.
Bore/Caliber: .45 LC, .45/.410, .50, .58
Features: Engraved locks with wild animal scenes; case-hardened color finish; checkered walnut pistol grip with steel butt cap
Shotgun $1072.00
.50-caliber $1182.00
.58-caliber $1202.00
20-ga./.50-caliber
  combo $1182.00

KODIAK EXPRESS MK VI

Action: Percussion
Stock: Hardwood
Barrel: 24.25 in.
Sights: Creedmore
Weight: 10 lb. 2 oz.

Bore/Caliber: .50, .54, .58
Features: A very manageable gun, perfectly balanced; particularly suitable for wild boar hunting; practical rubber buttplate; half pistol grip stock; equipped with ghost sights
MSRP $1688.00

LA BOHEMIENNE SIDE-BY-SIDE SHOTGUN

Action: Hinged breech
Stock: Checkered walnut
Barrel: 28 in.
Chokes: cyl/mod choke tubes
Weight: 7 lb.
Bore/Caliber: 12 Ga.
Features: Rust brown finish barrel; interchangeable chokes; color case-hardened frame; hand-engraved locks
MSRP $2475.00

LE PAGE TARGET PISTOL

Action: Flintlock, percussion
Stock: Walnut
Barrel: 10.5 in.
Sights: Adjustable
Weight: 2 lb. 10 oz.
Bore/Caliber: .31, .36, .44 (percussion); .44, .45 (flintlock)
Features: Smoothbore .45 available; adjustable single-set trigger; brightly polished lock with a roller frizzen spring
Percussion $1181.00
Flintlock. $1553.00

MAMELOUK

Action: Flintlock
Stock: Hardwood
Barrel: 7.6 in.
Sights: Fixed
Weight: 1 lb. 10 oz.
Bore/Caliber: N/A
Features: Like all the firearms equipping Napoleon's Imperial Guards, the Mameluke pistols were made at the Manufacture of Versailles under the technical management of Nicolas-Noël Boutet; the trigger guard, buttcap, screw washers of the lock, and ramrod tip are brass
MSRP $838.00

Davide Pedersoli & C.

MANG IN GRAZ MATCH

Action: Percussion
Stock: Walnut
Barrel: 11.4 in.
Sights: Fixed
Weight: 2 lb. 10 oz.
Bore/Caliber: .38, .44
Features: Fluted grip; octagonal, rifled barrel in brown rust finish; adjustable single set trigger; breech plug shows a typical mask of the period; barrel and tang enriched with gold inlays
MSRP $2127.00

MISSISSIPPI US MODEL 1841

Action: Percussion
Stock: Walnut
Barrel: 33 in.
Sights: Open rear
Weight: 9 lb. 8 oz.
Bore/Caliber: .54, .58
Features: Considered the best-looking ordnance rifle of its period; brass furniture; browned barrel; notched rear sight; case-hardened lock; ramrod with brass tip
MSRP $1509.00

MORTIMER TARGET RIFLE

Action: Flintlock
Stock: English-style European walnut
Barrel: 36.4 in.
Sights: Target
Weight: 10 lb. 2 oz.
Bore/Caliber: .54
Features: Case-colored lock; stock has cheekpiece and hand checkering; 7-groove barrel
MSRP $2273.00

PLAINS SHOTGUN "THE FAST BACK ACTION"

Action: Caplock
Stock: Walnut
Barrel: 27.5 in., 28.5 in.
Sights: None
Weight: 7 lb. 5 oz.–7 lb. 8 oz.
Bore/Caliber: 12, 20 Ga.
Features: Single trigger; side-by-side shotgun; fast second shot, thanks to back action lock reducing minor residues of black powder in lock parts
MSRP $1532.00

RICHMOND 1862, TYPE III

Action: Percussion
Stock: Walnut
Barrel: 39.75 in.
Sights: None
Weight: 9 lb. 14 oz.

DAVIDE PEDERSOLI MANG IN GRAZ MATCH

DAVIDE PEDERSOLI MISSISSIPPI US MODEL 1841

DAVIDE PEDERSOLI MORTIMER TARGET RIFLE

DAVIDE PEDERSOLI PLAINS SHOTGUN "THE FAST BACK VACTION"

DAVIDE PEDERSOLI RICHMOND 1862, TYPE III

DAVIDE PEDERSOLI SIDE-BY-SIDE SHOTGUN CLASSIC STANDARD, DELUXE

DAVIDE PEDERSOLI SPRINGFIELD MODEL 1861 US

DAVIDE PEDERSOLI SWISS MATCH STANDARD FLINTLOCK

DAVIDE PEDERSOLI TATHAM & EGG PISTOL

Bore/Caliber: .58
Features: Manufactured based on the U.S. 1855 Model with the Maynard tape ignition system; except for the lock's profile, the brass buttplate, and the stock nose cap, the gun's appearance resembles the U.S. Model 1861
MSRP $1404.00

SIDE-BY-SIDE SHOTGUN CLASSIC, CLASSIC EXTRA DELUXE

Action: Percussion
Stock: Walnut
Barrel: 28.5 in.
Sights: Brass bead
Weight: 7 lb.
Caliber: 20 ga., 12 ga.
Features: Standard has a walnut stock, case-hardened receiver, and blued barrels; deluxe has wood, scroll-engraved receiver in a coin finish and rust-brown barrels
Classic . . . . $1314.00–$1416.00
Extra Deluxe $5719.00

SPRINGFIELD MODEL 1861 US

Action: Caplock
Stock: Walnut
Barrel: 40 in.
Sights: None
Weight: 9 lb. 14 oz.
Bore/Caliber: .58

Features: More efficient than earlier smooth bored muskets used by both sides in the American Civil War; satin finish barrel; stock with three bands; coin-colored finish on the steel furniture
MSRP $1441.00

SWISS MATCH STANDARD FLINTLOCK

Action: Flintlock
Stock: Walnut
Barrel: 30.8 in.
Sights: Adjustable
Weight: 16 lb. 5 oz.
Bore/Caliber: .40
Features: Octagonal conical profile barrel with rust brown finish; lock is case-hardened; steel ramrod; double-set trigger; steel hook buttplate
MSRP $3925.00

TATHAM & EGG PISTOL

Action: Flintlock
Stock: Walnut
Barrel: 10.06 in.
Sights: Adjustable rear
Weight: 2 lb. 6.7 oz.
Bore/Caliber: .45 (smooth), .42
Features: Ergonomic grip; set trigger; PMG-quality trigger; case-hardened metal parts
MSRP $1617.00

Davide Pedersoli & C.

DAVIDE PEDERSOLI TRADITIONAL HAWKEN TARGET RIFLE

DAVIDE PEDERSOLI ZOUAVE US MODEL 1863

TRADITIONAL HAWKEN TARGET RIFLE

Action: Percussion, flintlock
Stock: Wood
Barrel: 28.4 in.
Chokes: IC, M, F
Sights: Adjustable rear, fixed front
Weight: 8 lb. 10 oz.
Bore/Gauge: .50, .54
Features: Double set trigger; adjust-able buckhorn rear sight; American walnut stock is enriched with a brass patch box; left-handed version available

Percussion	$869.00
Percussion left-hand	$915.00
Flintlock	$936.00
Flintlock left-hand	$964.00

ZOUAVE US MODEL 1863

Action: Percussion
Stock: Hardwood
Barrel: 33 in.
Sights: Front, rear
Weight: 9 lb. 4 oz.
Bore/Caliber: .58
Features: Intended for the U.S. Artillery Department and never distributed to any Civil War army division; features brass furnitures; ramrod with a tulip tip; three-leaf rear sight; two sling swivels; the lock shows the Eagle stamp and the U.S. letters in front of the hammer
MSRP $1471.00

Dixie Gun Works

DIXIE GUN WORKS PEDERSOLI SCREW BARREL PISTOL

DIXIE GUN WORKS SHARPS NEW MODEL 1859 MILITARY CARBINE

DIXIE GUN WORKS SPANISH MUSKET

PEDERSOLI SCREW BARREL PISTOL

Action: Traditional caplock
Stock: European walnut
Barrel: 3 in.
Sights: None
Weight: 12 oz.
Bore/Caliber: .44
Features: Color case-hardened lock; single folding trigger; combination nipple/barrel wrench included
MSRP $345.00

SHARPS NEW MODEL 1859 MILITARY CARBINE

Action: Dropping block
Stock: Walnut
Barrel: 22 in.
Sights: Adjustable open
Weight: 8 lb.
Bore/Caliber: .54
Features: Steel furniture; color case-hardened; single trigger; single barrel band; saddle bar with ring
MSRP $2150.00

SPANISH MUSKET

Action: Flintlock muzzleloading
Stock: Full, European walnut 56 in.
Barrel: 44.75 in.
Sights: Steel stud front
Weight: 10 lb.
Bore/Caliber: .68 round ball
Features: Brass buttplate, trigger guard, and barrel bands; bright steel sideplates; steel ramrod
MSRP $1450.00

EMF Company, Inc.

EMF 1860 ARMY REVOLVER

EMF 1863 REMINGTON POCKET STEEL

1860 ARMY REVOLVER

Action: Caplock revolver
Stock: Walnut
Barrel: 8 in.
Sights: Fixed
Weight: 41.6 oz.
Bore/Caliber: .44
Features: Case-hardened frame; blued barrel
Brass: $265.00

Case-hardened:	$285.00
Steel:	$310.00
Old Silver:	$335.00
Deluxe Engraved Old Silver:	$605.00
London:	$300.00
Old West frame	$330.00
Snub-nosed case-hardened:	$335.00

1863 REMINGTON POCKET STEEL

Action: Caplock revolver
Stock: Walnut
Barrel: 3.5 in.
Sights: Fixed
Weight: 21 oz.
Bore/Caliber: .36
Features: Steel frame, blued barrel
MSRP $405.00

Gunwerks

GUNWERKS MUZZLELOADER RIFLE SYSTEM .45-CAL.

MAGNUS MUZZLELOADER RIFLE SYSTEM

Action: Bolt
Stock: Carbon fiber
Barrel: 26 in.
Sights: Revic EXO open sights
Weight: N/A
Bore/Caliber: .45
Features: Truly a custom build; an example build: carbon fiber stock in carbon black; factory-mounted Kahles K318i Max scope; Gunwerks Picatinny scope rings; Low Pro two-piece 20 MOA scope bases; underside Picatinny rail; adjustable recoil pad; TT Primary adjustable trigger; GLR action; G8-profile barrel in a graphite finish and with a directional muzzle brake
MSRP . . . . **starting at $11,234.00**

Lyman

LYMAN DEERSTALKER FLINTLOCK

LYMAN GREAT PLAINS FLINTLOCK

LYMAN PLAINS PISTOL

LYMAN TRADE RIFLE

DEERSTALKER RIFLE

Action: Traditional cap or flint
Stock: Walnut
Barrel: 24 in.
Sights: Fiber optic front and rear
Weight: 10 lb. 6 oz.
Bore/Caliber: .50, .54
Features: Quiet single trigger; metal blackened to avoid glare; black rubber recoil pad; left-hand available
MSRP . . . . **$625.00–$725.00**

GREAT PLAINS RIFLE

Action: Traditional cap or flint
Stock: Walnut
Barrel: 32 in.
Sights: Adjustable open
Weight: 11 lb. 10 oz.
Bore/Caliber: .50, .54
Features: Double-set triggers; Hawken style percussion "snail" with clean-out screw; separate ramrod entry thimble and nose cap; left-hand available
MSRP . . . . **$995.00–$1275.00**

PLAINS PISTOL

Action: Percussion, flintlock
Stock: Walnut
Barrel: 6 in.
Sights: Fixed
Weight: 3 lb. 2 oz.
Bore/Caliber: .50, .54
Features: Blackened iron furniture; polished brass trigger guard and ramrod tips; hooked patent breech takes down quickly for easy cleaning
MSRP **$465.00**

TRADE RIFLE

Action: Percussion caplock, flintlock
Stock: Walnut
Barrel: 28 in.
Sights: Adjustable open
Weight: 10 lb. 13 oz.
Bore/Caliber: .50, .54
Features: Brass furniture; originally developed for the early Indian fur trade
Percussion **$625.00**
Flintlock **$689.95**

Shiloh Rifle

SHILOH SHARPS 1863 MILITARY CARBINE

SHILOH SHARPS 1863 SPORTING RIFLE

1863 MILITARY CARBINE

Action: Percussion
Stock: Wood
Barrel: 22 in.
Sights: Iron block front sight, Lawrence ladder rear
Weight: 7 lb. 8 oz.
Bore/Caliber: .45, .50, .54
Features: This round barrel model has a forearm barrel band; single trigger; lever catch; color case-hardened finish; numerous upgrades including pack harden and various levels of antique metal finishes, patchbox, ebony pistol grip, saddle bar and ring, upgraded wood and finishes, brass escutcheons, and custom bedding, various sling swivels, and checkering upgrades
MSRP . . . . **starting at $2057.00**

1863 SPORTING RIFLE

Action: Percussion
Stock: Wood
Barrel: 26 in., 28 in., 30 in., 32 in., 34 in.
Sights: Blade front, buckhorn rear
Weight: N/A
Bore/Caliber: .45, .50, .54
Features: One for blackpowder cartridge metallic silhouette; optional color case-hardened finish; numerous upgrades including pack harden and various levels of antique metal finishes, patchbox, ebony pistol grip, barrel finish, upgraded wood and finishes, brass escutcheons, custom bedding, various sling swivels, forearm designs, rear barrel sights, vernier tang sights, drilling and tapping, and checkering upgrades
MSRP . . . . **starting at $2057.00**

SHILOH RIFLE 1874 CREEDMOOR TARGET RIFLE

SHILOH RIFLE 1874 QUIGLEY

SHILOH RIFLE 1877 #1 SHILOH ENGLISH RIFLE

1874 CREEDMOOR TARGET RIFLE

Action: Lever-action falling block
Stock: Walnut
Barrel: 32 in.
Sights: V aiming rear; blade front
Weight: 9 lb.
Bore/Caliber: All popular black powder cartridges from .38-55 to .50-90
Features: Pistol grip; single trigger; AA finish on American black walnut; polished barrel; octagon barrel; pewter tip
MSRP................$3312.00

1874 QUIGLEY

Action: Falling block
Stock: Walnut
Barrel: 34 in.
Sights: Semi buckhorn rear, midrange vernier tang, #111 globe aperture front
Weight: 12 lb. 8 oz.
Bore/Caliber: .45-70 Govt. or .45-110
Features: Military buttstock; patchbox; heavy octagonal barrel; pewter tip; Hartford collars; double set triggers; antique or standard color finish; gold inlay initials in gold oval
MSRP................$3689.00

1877 #1 SHILOH ENGLISH RIFLE

Action: Breechloading
Stock: Wood
Barrel: 26 in.–34 in.
Sights: Adjustable
Weight: N/A
Bore/Caliber: .38-55, .40-50BN, .40-50ST, .40-65, .40-70ST, .40-70BN, .40-90BN, .45-70, .45-90, .45-100
Features: Standard pistol grip; standard forearm; standard color cased; full or semi buckhorn rear sight; blade front sight; single trigger
MSRP................$2300.00

Taylor's & Co. Firearms

TAYLOR'S & CO. 1842 SMOOTHBORE MUSKET

TAYLOR'S & CO. 1847 WALKER

TAYLOR'S & CO. 1848 DRAGOONS

TAYLOR'S & CO. THE ACE

TAYLOR'S & CO. LE MAT CAVALRY

1842 SMOOTHBORE MUSKET

Action: Percussion
Stock: Walnut
Barrel: 42 in.
Sights: Military style
Weight: 9 lb. 12 oz.
Bore/Caliber: .69
Features: The Springfield replica has all the features of the original, including a one-piece, oil-finished walnut stock; original-style barrel bands; and completely interchangeable parts; the percussion lock has a V-style mainspring; features the lock with stamping noting 1842 and Springfield; NSSA approved, with certificate of authenticity and a brass medallion featuring the model and serial number
MSRP................$1394.10

1847 WALKER

Action: Caplock revolver
Stock: Walnut
Barrel: 9 in.

LE MAT CAVALRY

Sights: Fixed
Weight: 4 lb. 12 oz.
Bore/Caliber: .44
Features: Blued finish; round barrel
Antique finish..........$642.64
Case-hardened/blue.......$507.70
Charcoal blue...........$607.88

1848 DRAGOONS

Action: Caplock revolver
Stock: Walnut
Barrel: 7.5 in.
Sights: Fixed
Weight: 4 lb.–4 lb. 14 oz.
Bore/Caliber: .44
Features: First used by the U.S. Army's Mounted Rifles 1st Cavalry in 1833 and they went on to see considerable use during the 1850 and during the Civil War; blued finish; six-round capacity; available in 1st, 2nd, and 3rd models, as well as the Whitney variation
1st, 2nd, 3rd............$499.52
Whitneyville............$507.70

1858 THE ACE

Action: Caplock
Stock: PVC
Barrel: 3 in.
Sights: Blade front, integral notch rear
Weight: 2 lb. 7oz.
Bore/Caliber: .44/.45 LC
Features: An 1858 snubby for the caplock crowd that can also use a conversion cylinder in .45 LC; octagon barrel; brass trigger guard
MSRP...........$393.09–$431.09

LE MAT CAVALRY

Action: Caplock revolver
Stock: Walnut
Barrel: 8 in.
Sights: Fixed
Weight: 5 lb.
Bore/Caliber: .44 or 20 Ga.
Features: Blued steel finish; nine-shot .44 caliber revolver with a 20 Ga. single-shot barrel was a favorite among Confederate cavalry troops; case-hardened hammer and trigger; lanyard ring; trigger guard with spur
MSRP................$1383.53

Thompson/Center Arms

THOMPSON/CENTER ARMS IMPACT!SB

IMPACT!SB
Action: Break-open
Stock: Synthetic
Barrel: 26 inv.
Sights: Fiber optic front, adjustable rear
Weight: 6 lb. 15 oz.
Caliber: .50
Features: Featuring a hand-removeable triple lead thread breech plug; Power Rod aluminum ramrod; single-0shot sliding hood design; adjustable stock with spacers. Five finish/stock options: blued/black; Silver Weather Shield/Realtree Edge; Silver Weather Shield/black; blued/Mossy Oak Bottomland; Silver Weather Shield/ Mossy Oak Break-Up Country
MSRP . . . . $269.00–$332.00

Traditions Firearms

TRADITIONS FIREARMS 1851 NAVY REVOLVER

TRADITIONS FIREARMS 1858 ARMY REVOLVER

TRADITIONS FIREARMS 1860 ARMY REVOLVER

TRADITIONS FIREARMS BUCKSTALKER XT

TRADITIONS FIREARMS BUCKSTALKER XT NORTHWEST MAGNUM

TRADITIONS FIREARMS DEERHUNTER RIFLE

TRADITIONS FIREARMS HAWKEN WOODSMAN RIFLE

1851 NAVY REVOLVER
Action: Caplock revolver
Stock: Walnut
Barrel: 7.5 in.
Sights: Fixed
Weight: 2 lb. 8 oz.
Bore/Caliber: .44, .36
Features: Octagonal barrel and lever-style loader; brass, antiqued, or old silver frame and guard
MSRP . . . . $287.00–$323.00

1858 ARMY REVOLVER
Action: Caplock
Stock: Walnut
Barrel: 8 in.
Sights: Fixed
Weight: 2 lb. 12 oz.
Bore/Caliber: .44
Features: Octagonal barrel and lever style loader; brass frame and guard; top strap and post sights
MSRP $329.00

1860 ARMY REVOLVER
Action: Caplock
Stock: Simulated ivory, walnut
Barrel: 8 in.
Sights: Fixed
Weight: 2 lb. 12 oz.
Bore/Caliber: .44
Features: Blued barrel and cylinder; choice of brass or case-hardened steel frames
Brass $337.00
Steel $370.00

BUCKSTALKER XT
Action: Hinged breach
Stock: Synthetic
Barrel: 24 in.
Sights: None
Weight: 6 lb. 6 oz.
Bore/Caliber: .50
Features: This upgrades the current Buckstalker line with a premium-grade chromoly steel barrel; Elite XT trigger system; rebounding hammer; Accelerator breech plug; Speed Load system; accuracy to the 200-yard mark; various packages include: Vista camo stock with silver Cerakote barrel, with or without 3–9x40 scope and with or without case; black stock with silver Cerakote barrel, with or without 3-9x40 scope and with or without case; black stock with blued barrel, scope, and with or without case; Youth model in all black
MSRP . . . . $338.00–$429.00

BUCKSTALKER XT NORTHWEST MAGNUM
Action: Hinged breech
Stock: Synthetic
Barrel: 24 in.
Sights: Fiber optic front, adjustable rear
Weight: 6 lb. 6 oz.
Bore/Caliber: .50
Features: Similar to the Buckstalker XT, but designed specifically for hunters in Idaho and Oregon who need an open breech, open sights, and musket ignition
MSRP $305.00

DEERHUNTER RIFLE
Action: Traditional cap or flint
Stock: Synthetic or hardwood
Barrel: 24 in.
Sights: Lite Optic adjustable
Weight: 6 lb.
Bore/Caliber: .50
Features: Octagonal performance barrels; blued or nickel barrel finish; percussion models are drilled and tapped to accept scope mounts; non-slip recoil pad; stock comes in black synthetic or hardwood
Hardwood . . . . $368.00–$431.00
Synthetic . . . . $290.00–$378.00

HAWKEN WOODSMAN RIFLE
Action: Traditional cap or flint
Stock: Hardwood
Barrel: 28 in.
Sights: Adjustable rear hunting
Weight: 7 lb. 13 oz.
Bore/Caliber: .50
Features: Hooked breech for easy barrel removal; double-set triggers in an oversized glove-fitting trigger guard; inletted solid brass patch box; left-hand model available; octagonal blued barrel
Flintlock $575.00
Percussion $529.00

TRADITIONS FIREARMS KENTUCKY PISTOL

TRADITIONS FIREARMS KENTUCKY RIFLE DELUXE

TRADITIONS FIREARMS NITROFIRE

TRADITIONS FIREARMS PENNSYLVANIA RIFLE

TRADITIONS FIREARMS PURSUIT XT

TRADITIONS FIREARMS PURSUIT XT NORTHWEST MAGNUM, PURSUIT XT LDR NORTHWEST MAGNUM

TRADITIONS FIREARMS TRAPPER PISTOL

TRADITIONS FIREARMS VORTEK STRIKERFIRE

TRADITIONS FIREARMS VORTEK STRIKERFIRE LDR

KENTUCKY PISTOL

Action: Traditional caplock
Stock: Hardwood
Barrel: 10 in.
Sights: Fixed
Weight: 2 lb. 8 oz.
Bore/Caliber: .50
Features: Brass furniture; case-colored sidelock and brass ramrod thimble
MSRP $279.00

KENTUCKY RIFLE DELUXE

Action: Flintlock
Stock: Walnut
Barrel: 33.5 in.
Sights: Blade front, notch rear
Weight: N/A
Caliber: .50
Features: A handsome traditional flintlock with case-hardened flintlock; wooden ramrod; double-set triggers; 1:66 twist; brass furniture
MSRP . . . . $475.00–$578.00

NITROFIRE

Action: Break-open
Stock: Synthetic
Barrel: 26 in.
Sights: None
Weight: N/A
Caliber: .50
Features: First muzzleloader to utilize Federal's Firestick propellant charge, which is breech loaded; projectiles load from muzzle; Elite XT trigger system with rebounding hammer, captive half-cock; Cerakote finish on metalwork; stocks in black and in camo by Mossy Oak, Realtree, and Go Wild; VAPR Twist barrel with 1:24 rifling added in 2022
MSRP . . . . $549.00–$699.00

PENNSYLVANIA RIFLE

Action: Percussion caplock, flintlock
Stock: Walnut
Barrel: 20 in.
Sights: Adjustable primitive style rear
Weight: 8 lb. 8 oz.
Bore/Caliber: .50

Features: Brass stock inlay ornamentation and toe plate; cheekpiece; solid brass patch box
Flintlock $912.00
Percussion $879.00

PURSUIT XT

Action: Hinged breech
Stock: Synthetic
Barrel: 26 in.
Sights: None
Weight: 5 lb. 12 oz.
Bore/Caliber: .50
Features: An upgrade to the current Pursuit G4 Ultralight series; VAPR Twist barrel; Elite XT trigger; chromoly barrel; 209 primer ignition; 200-plus yard accuracy; numerous stock and metal finish combinations, including Cerakote metalwork, wood stocks, and full-coverage camo, available with and without 3–9x40 factory mounted scope and with or without cases
MSRP . . . . $362.00–$591.00

PURSUIT XT NORTHWEST MAGNUM, LDR NORTHWEST MAGNUM

Action: Hinged breech
Stock: Synthetic
Barrel: 26 in., 30 in.
Sights: Fiber optic front, adjustable rear
Weight: 5 lb. 12 oz.
Bore/Caliber: .50
Features: Similar to the Pursuit XT, but designed specifically for hunters in Idaho and Oregon who need an open breech, open sights, and musket ignition; available in black or Realtree Edge stocks with gray Cerakote metalwork; LDR has a 30-in. barrel and comes with a black stock and grey Cerakote metalwork
Northwest Magnum $390.00
LDR Northwest Magnum . . .$438.00

TRAPPER PISTOL

Action: Traditional cap or flint
Stock: Hardwood
Barrel: 9.75 in.
Sights: Primitive-style adjustable rear
Weight: 2 lb. 14 oz.

Bore/Caliber: .50
Features: Octagonal blued barrel; double set triggers
Flintlock $416.00
Percussion $365.00

VORTEK STRIKERFIRE

Action: Strikerfire
Stock: Soft Touch synthetic
Barrel: 28 in.
Sights: Fiber optic
Weight: N/A
Bore/Caliber: .50
Features: This rifle takes in-line muzzleloaders to the next level by taking away the external hammer and using an internal StrikerFire System; to cock the gun, simply slide the striker button forward until it locks and fire; the recessed de-cocking buttons allows for quick and quiet de-cocking of the firearm and the gun is also equipped with an automatic de-cocking mechanism—when the gun is opened, it is automatically de-cocked; also includes: two-stage trigger; CeraKote finish; Realtree Xtra, black, Mossy Oak Break-Up Country; most options available with 3-9x40mm Traditions Duplex scopes; VAPR Twist barrel with 1:24 rifling added in 2022
MSRP . . . . $428.00–$543.00

VORTEK STRIKERFIRE LDR

Action: Strikerfire
Stock: Synthetic
Barrel: 30 in.
Sights: None
Weight: 6 lb. 8 oz.
Bore/Caliber: .50
Features: Made for long-distance muzzleloader shooting, out to 300 yards; TAC2 two-stage competition-type trigger; 3–9x40 scope; nitride finish on metalwork; Hogue over-molded grip panels; recoil-reducing buttstock and buttpad; chromoly tapered and fluted barrel; recessed decocking button; stock in Realtree Edge; available with or without case and scope; VAPR Twist barrel with 1:24 rifling added in 2022
MSRP . . . . $438.00–$543.00

BLACK POWDER

Uberti

UBERTI 1847 WALKER

UBERTI 1848 DRAGOON

UBERTI 1849 POCKET REVOLVER

UBERTI 1851 NAVY REVOLVER

UBERTI 1858 NEW ARMY REVOLVER

UBERTI 1860 ARMY REVOLVER

UBERTI 1861 NAVY REVOLVER

UBERTI 1862 POCKET NAVY REVOLVER

UBERTI 1862 POLICE REVOLVER

1847 WALKER

Action: Caplock revolver
Stock: Walnut
Barrel: 9 in.
Sights: Fixed, open
Weight: 4 lb. 8 oz.
Bore/Caliber: .44
Features: Case-hardened frame, steel backstrap, brass trigger guard; blued finish
MSRP $479.00

1848 DRAGOON

Action: Caplock revolver
Stock: Walnut
Barrel: 7.5 in.
Sights: Fixed, open
Weight: 4 lb. 2 oz.
Bore/Caliber: .44
Features: Case-hardened frame; steel or brass backstrap and trigger guard; engraved
MSRP $479.00

1849 POCKET REVOLVER

Action: Caplock revolver
Stock: Walnut
Barrel: 4 in.
Sights: Fixed, open
Weight: 1 lb. 8 oz.
Bore/Caliber: .31
Features: Case-hardened frame; brass backstrap and trigger guard; blued octagonal barrel; engraved
MSRP . . . .$379.00–$399.00

1851 NAVY REVOLVER

Action: Caplock revolver
Stock: Walnut
Barrel: 7.5 in.
Sights: Fixed, open
Weight: 2 lb. 10 oz.
Bore/Caliber: .36
Features: Color case-hardened frame; oval or squareback trigger guard; brass or steel backstrap and trigger guard; octagonal barrel (Leech-Rigdon model has round barrel)
MSRP . . . .$349.00–$399.00

1858 NEW ARMY REVOLVER

Action: Caplock revolver
Stock: Walnut

Barrel: 8 in.
Sights: Fixed, open
Weight: 2 lb. 11 oz.
Bore/Caliber: .44
Features: Blued or stainless steel frame and backstrap; brass trigger guard; octagonal barrel
Blue $429.00
Stainless $529.00

1860 ARMY REVOLVER

Action: Caplock revolver
Stock: Walnut
Barrel: 7.5 in.
Sights: Fixed, open
Weight: 2 lb. 10 oz.
Bore/Caliber: .44
Features: Case-hardened frame, steel backstrap, brass trigger guard; blued, round barrel
MSRP . . . .$379.00–$399.00

1861 NAVY REVOLVER

Action: Caplock revolver
Stock: Walnut
Barrel: 7.5 in.
Sights: Fixed, open
Weight: 2 lb. 10 oz.
Bore/Caliber: .36
Features: Case-hardened frame, steel or brass backstrap and trigger guard
MSRP $399.00

1862 POCKET NAVY REVOLVER

Action: Caplock revolver
Stock: Walnut

Barrel: 5.5 in., 6.5 in.
Sights: Fixed, open
Weight: 1 lb. 11 oz.
Bore/Caliber: .36
Features: Case-hardened frame; brass backstrap and trigger guard; octagonal, blued barrel
MSRP $429.00

1862 POLICE REVOLVER

Action: Caplock revolver
Stock: Walnut
Barrel: 5.5 in., 6.5 in.
Sights: Fixed, open
Weight: 1 lb. 10 oz.
Bore/Caliber: .36
Features: Case-hardened frame; brass backstrap and trigger guard; fluted round barrel
MSRP $429.00

BLACK POWDER

SCOPES
Accufire Technology

ACCUFIRE TECHNOLOGY NOCTIS V1

ACCUFIRE TECHNOLOGY INCENDIS THERMAL

ACCUFIRE TECHNOLOGY NOCTIS TR1

ACCUFIRE TECHNOLOGY PROSPECTIS ATRO-8

ACCUFIRE TECHNOLOGY PROSPECTIS ATRO-20

ACCUFIRE TECHNOLOGY PROSPECTIS EVRO-6

ACCUFIRE TECHNOLOGY PROSPECTIS EVRO-12

NOCTIS V1
Available in: 1–6X
Features: Compact day/night vision unit with loads of features, including HD-quality night vision; savable presets; ballistic calculations; fifty downloadable reticles; HD video recording in all light levels; built-in Wi-Fi
MSRP $699.00

INCENDIS THERMAL
Available in: 1–4X30mm
Weight: 14.8 oz.
Length: 5.9 in.
Main Dia.: N/A
Exit Pupil: 20–15mm
Field of View: N/A
Eye Relief: N/A
Features: A thermal imaging scope with

1X, 2X, and 4X magnification; heat display in white hot, black hot, red accent, and green hot; focus-adjustable objective lens; can be used as a standalone scope, a handheld unit, and as a forward mounted aid
MSRP $2999.00

NOCTIS TR1
Available in: 1–16x60mm
Weight: 36.4 oz.
Length: 14.7 in.
Obj. Dia.: 60mm
Main Dia.: N/A
Exit Pupil: N/A
Field of View: 31.2m@100m
Eye Relief: 2.4 in.
Features: A night vision scope in a traditional presentation; can be used with quick-detach and return-to-zero mounts; on-board ballistics calcuator; Wi-Fi streaming and gallery sends to Android and iOS devices; Accufire Smart Range Finder; HD recording and streaming; color correction technology; rechargeable lithium batteries; built-in microphone; multi-band coatings; multiple reticles and color schemes
MSRP $999.00

PROSPECTIS ATRO-8
Available in: 1–8x24mm
Weight: 19.4 oz.
Length: 10.31 in.
Main Dia.: 30mm
Exit Pupil: N/A
Field of View: 105–14.3 ft.@100 yd.
Eye Relief: 3.21–3.3 in.
Features: Accufire CQB-Comp illuminated reticle in the first focal plane; locking turrets
MSRP $939.00

PROSPECTIS ATRO-20
Available in: 2.5–29x50mm
Weight: 27.51 oz.
Length: 14.56 in.
Main Dia.: 34mm
Exit Pupil: N/A
Field of View: 40–6.2 ft.@100 yd.
Eye Relief: 3.22 in.
Features: Illuminated Tango-20 reticle in the first focal plane that appears as a simple crosshair at the lowest magnification; fast-mag lever; ZRT locking turrets
MSRP $1199.00

PROSPECTIS EVRO-6
Available in: 1–6x24mm
Weight: 15.34 oz.
Length: 10.31 in.
Main Dia.: 30mm
Exit Pupil: N/A
Field of View: 112–19 ft.@100 yd.
Eye Relief: 3.85–5.35 in.
Features: Second focal plane illuminated reticle with 12 adjustment points; locking turrets; .5-MRAD clicks
MSRP $649.00

PROSPECTIS EVRO-12
Available in: 3–12x50mm
Weight: 23.98 oz.
Length: 13.97 in.
Main Dia.: 30mm
Exit Pupil: N/A
Field of View: 30.53–8.13 ft.@100 yd.
Eye Relief: 2.83–3.54 in.
Features: Uncomplicated, non-illuminated mil-spec reticle in the first focal plane that offers precise shot placement; green glass coatings; fast-mag lever; locking turrets; intended for hunting applications
MSRP $479.00

Armament Technology Inc.

ARMAMENT TECHNOLOGY ELCAN SPECTERDR 1X/4X DUAL ROLE OPTIC

ELCAN SPECTERDR 1X/4X DUAL ROLE OPTIC
Available in: 1X/4X
Weight: 23.2 oz.
Length: 6.02 in.
Obj. Dia.: N/A
Main Dia.: N/A
Exit Pupil: 8mm
Field of View: 48.8–11.4m@100m
Eye Relief: 2.75 in.

Features: Throw lever changes the optic from a 4X magnified sight to a 1X CQB sight—this is not a zoom and eye relief is identical between the two; choice of setup between 5.56 and 7.62 ballistic reticles, user-selected illumination for both crosshairs and the red dot; mounts on a Picatinny rail
MSRP . . . . $2079.00–$2499.00

OPTICS

ARMAMENT TECHNOLOGY ELCAN SPECTERDR 1.5X/6X

ARMAMENT TECHNOLOGY ELCAN SPECTERTR 1X/3X/9X

TANGENT THETA LONG-RANGE HUNTER

TANGENT THETA PROFESSIONAL

ATHLON ARES ETR UHD

ATHLON CRONUS BTR GEN2 UHD

ATHLON HELOS BTR GEN2

ATHLON MIDAS TSP1

ELCAN SPECTERDR 1.5X/6X

Available in: 1.5X/6X
Weight: 24.86 oz.
Length: 7.2 in.
Obj. Dia.: N/A
Main Dia.: N/A
Exit Pupil: 7mm
Field of View: 28.7–7m@100m
Eye Relief: 2.75 in.
Features: Similar to the 1X/4X SpecterDR, but with larger magnification on both the low and high end; not a zoom, but two separate magnification levels accessed by the throw of a lever; choice of illuminated reticles calibrated for 5.56 or 7.62 NATO
MSRP . . . . $2503.00–$2998.00

ELCAN SPECTERTR 1X/3X/9X

Available in: 1X/3X/9X
Weight: 29.98 oz.
Length: 10.43 in.
Obj. Dia.: N/A
Main Dia.: N/A
Exit Pupil: 11.7mm
Field of View: 28.7m@100m
Eye Relief: 3 in.
Features: One more step up from the 1X/4X SpecterDR with three throw-lever magnification levels; 1X can provide both-eyes-open shooting; five illumination levels each for both the reticle and the red dot; Picatinny rail mounting; reticles available for either 5.56 or 7.62 NATO
MSRP $2049.00

TANGENT THETA LONG-RANGE HUNTER

Available in: 3-15x50mm
Weight: 26.98 oz.
Length: 13.7 oz.
Obj. Dia.: 50mm
Main Dia.: 30mm

Field of View: 7.3–1.6 degrees
Features: A premium riflescope for the hunter, with a first focal plane illuminated LRH MRAD reticle
MSRP $3974.00

TANGENT THETA PROFESSIONAL

Available in: 5–25X
Weight: 40.57 oz.
Length: 16.73 in.
Main Dia.: 34mm
Exit Pupil: 11–2.3mm
Field of View: 7.6–1.6m @ 100m
Twilight Factor: 16.73–37.42
Eye Relief: 3.54 in.
Features: Water- and shockproof; adjustable parallax; illuminated reticle; 3–15x50 also available
5–25X . . . . $5092.00–$6980.00
3–15X $4550.00

ARES ETR UHD

Available in: 1–10x24mm, 3–18x50mm, 4.5–30x56mm
Weight: 26.9 oz., 31.4 oz., 36.5 oz.
Length: 10 in., 14.2 in., 15.3 in.
Main Dia.: 34mm
Exit Pupil: N/A
Field of View: 117.3–11.7 ft.@100 yd., 39.2–6.65 ft.@100 yd., 24.5–3.75 ft.@100 yd.
Eye Relief: 3.7 in., 3.74 in., 3.9 in.
Features: These are first focal plane scopes with high-precision erector systems; extra-low dispersion glass; precision zero-stop turrets; locking windage turret; illuminated reticles in ATMR2 MOA, ATMR3 MIL, APLR2 MOA, APLR5 MOA, APRS1 MIL, and APRS6 MIL
MSRP . . . . $1212.49–$1562.49

CRONUS BTR GEN2 UHD

Available in: 1–6x24mm, 4.5–29x56mm
Weight: 18.8 oz., 35.8 oz.
Length: 10.6 in., 14.4 in.
Obj. Dia.: 24mm, 56mm
Main Dia.: 34mm
Exit Pupil: 11.4–4mm, 8.8–1.9mm
Field of View: 106.9–17.7 ft.@100 yd., 24.8–3.83 ft.@100 yd.
Eye Relief: 3.6–4 in., 3.6–3.8 in.
Features: Extra-low dispersion glass; internal stainless steel-component turrets produce sharp, loud, and tactile clicks; true zero stop; reticles for both models are illuminated; XPL-coated exterior lenses
1–6X $1374.00
4.5–29X $1999.99

HELOS BTR GEN2

Available in: 1–10x28mm, 2–12x42mm, 4–20x50mm, 6–24x56mm
Weight: 18.3 oz.–34.5 oz.
Length: 10.3 in., 11.8 in., 13.3 in., 14.3 in.
Main Dia.: 30mm, 34mm
Exit Pupil: N/A
Field of View: 110–10 ft.@100 yd., 55.7–9.6 ft.@100 yd., 27.9–5.6 ft.@100 yd., 19.9–5.12 ft.@100 yd.
Eye Relief: 3.2 in., 3.6 in., 3.6 in., 3.7 in.
Features: Lenses with XPL external coatings; locking turrets; precision zero stop; heat-treated one-piece tube construction; all reticles are illuminated
MSRP . . . . $624.99–$787.49

MIDAS TSP1

Available in: 1X21mm
Weight: 6.25 oz.
Length: 2.7 in.
Main Dia.: N/A
Exit Pupil: N/A
Field of View: 66 ft.@100 yd.
Eye Relief: 3.2 in.
Features: Prism red-dot optic; can be used even when the batteries are dead and the etched-glass reticle unilluminated; when the TSP1 reticle is illuminated choice of red or green; Picatinny rail mount
MSRP $387.49

OPTICS

Armament Technology Incorporated

ATHLON MIDAS TSP3

ATHLON MIDAS TSP4

MIDAS TSP3
Available in: 3X
Weight: 16 oz.
Length: 5.1 in.
Obj. Dia.: 28mm

Main Dia.: N/A
Exit Pupil: N/A
Field of View: 32.5 ft.@100 yd.
Eye Relief: 3.2 in.
Features: Prism optic of 3X with a TSP3 etched-glass reticle illuminated in selectable red or green; reticle is usable without illumination being activated
MSRP....................$349.99

MIDAS TSP4
Available in: 3.9X
Weight: 16.8 oz.

Length: 5.7 in.
Obj. Dia.: 30mm
Main Dia.: N/A
Exit Pupil: N/A
Field of View: 24.9 ft.@100 yd.
Eye Relief: 3.1 in.
Features: Prism optic with a fixed 3.9X; etched-glass TSP4 reticle in selectable red or green illumination; Smart Power Management System
MSRP....................$362.49

ATN Corp.

ATN THOR 4 SERIES

ATN CORP. X-SIGHT 4K INT

ATN X-SIGHT 4K PRO

ATN CORP. X-SIGHT LTV

THOR 4 SERIES
Available in: 1.25–5x, 2–8x, 4.5–18x, 7–28x, 1-10x, 1.5–15x, 2.5–25x, 4–40x
Weight: 31 oz.–37 oz.
Length: 13.1–14.8 in.
Main Dia.: 30mm
Eye Relief: 3.5 in.
Features: Thermal vision Smart HD scopes; Gen4 sensor that will display in black hot, white hot, or color modes; can record and stream video; Smart rangefinder; ballistic calculator that displays target profile and environmental conditions; 3D gyroscope; 3D accelerometer; recoil-activated video; e-barometer; microphone; SD card; HD display
MSRP......... $1999.00–$4799.00

X-SIGHT 4K INT
Available in: 3–14x, 5–20x
Weight: 33 oz.
Length: 13.8 in.
Main Dia.: 30mm

Field of View: 460 ft.@1000 yd.
Eye Relief: 90mm
Features: A smart HD day/night riflescope with built-in SD card recording capabilities in 1080P full HD, streaming at 720p; spin to zoom wheel; one-shot zero capabilities; smart rangefinder; recoil-activated recording; 1280x720 HD micro display; 3D gyroscope and accelerometer
3–14X:................$1199.00
5–20X:................$1299.00

X-SIGHT 4K PRO
Available in: 3–14x, 5–20x
Weight: 33.6 oz.
Length: 13.8 in.
Main Dia.: 30mm
Eye Relief: 3.5 in.
Features: Smart scope with day and night capabilities; video records in 1080 Full HD; built-in rangefinder that lets you zero in one shot; ballistic calculator; recoil-activated and streaming video capabilities; a built-

in compass; Smooth Zoom
3–14x:.................$699.00
5–20x:.................$799.00

X-SIGHT LTV
Available in: 3–9X, 5–15X
Weight: 26.2 oz.–27.5 oz.
Length: 12.2 in., 13 in.
Obj. Dia.: N/A
Main Dia.: 30mm
Exit Pupil: N/A
Field of View: N/A
Eye Relief: 90mm
Features: A day/night scope with a One Shot Zero reticle; recoil-resistant hardened aluminum alloy construction; ATN Obsidian LT Core for ultra low-power consumption (10+ hours continuous use); 720P HD video recording; HD night vision mode; multiple reticle patterns to choose from
3–9X:..................$599.00
5–15X:.................$679.00

Barska

BARSKA AR6 1–6X24MM

AR6 1–6X24MM
Available in: 1–6X24mm
Weight: 17.6 oz.
Length: 11 in.
Main Dia.: 30mm
Exit Pupil: 4–11mm
Field of View: 75.78–12.79 ft @ 100 yds

Twilight Factor: 4.9–12
Eye Relief: 3.7 in.
Features: Water- and fogproof; red or green illuminated reticle; dual cantilever ring scope mount, flip-up scope caps
MSRP...................$311.99

Barska

LEVEL HD, LEVEL HD FFP

Available in: 1–4x24mm, 1–6x24mm
Weight: 16 oz.
Length: 10 in., 10.5 in.
Main Dia.: 30mm
Exit Pupil: 5.88–2.29mm, 8–3.5mm
Field of View: 25–7.6 ft.@100 yd., 18.8 ft.–5.7 ft.@100 yd.
Eye Relief: 4.76–3.94 in., 3.9–3.5 in.
Features: Close and mid-range shooting applications will find favor with the scope featuring an illuminated HRS Quick Shot .223 BDC reticle; fully multi-coated optics; reticle can be red or green and adjusted for brightness; lockable turrets; 1–6X has first focal plane glass-etched reticle
SFP.....................$298.99
FFP....................$518.99

BARSKA LEVEL HD, LEVEL HD FFP

Brownells

BROWNELLS RETRO CARRY HANDLE SCOPE

RETRO CARRY HANDLE SCOPE

Available in: 4X21mm
Weight: 13.3 oz.
Length: 6.1 in.
Main Dia.: 1 in.
Eye Relief: 3.11 in.
Features: Brownells says they found the original company that manufactured this sight during the 1970s and had them build this new version with a fixed focal plane
MSRP......................$299.99

Burris

BURRIS 2–7X SCOUT SCOPE

BURRIS DROPTINE RIFLESCOPE 4.5–14X42MM

BURRIS ELIMINATOR IV LASER

BURRIS FULLFIELD E1 3–9X40MM ILLUMINATED

2–7X SCOUT SCOPE

Available in: 2–7X32mm
Weight: 13 oz.
Length: 9.7 in.
Main Dia.: 1 in.
Exit Pupil: 16–4.6mm
Field of View: 21–7 ft @ 100 yds
Twilight Factor: 8–15
Eye Relief: 11–21 in.
Features: Ballistic Plex reticle; fully multi-coated; variable power; low mounting capabilities; black matte finish; Scout also available in a fixed-power 2.75x20mm
X20:.....................$299.00
X32:.....................$479.00

DROPTINE RIFLESCOPE 4.5–14X42MM

Available in: 4.5–14X42mm
Weight: 18 oz.
Length: 13 in.
Main Dia.: 1 in.
Exit Pupil: 9–3mm
Field of View: 22–7.5 ft @ 100 yds
Twilight Factor: 13.75–24.25
Eye Relief: 3.1 in.–3.8 in.
Features: Nitrogen filled; multi-coated lenses; Ballistic Plex reticle or G2B Mil-Dot reticle; adjustable parallax; 3–9x50 also available
4.5–14X:................$189.00
3–9X:.......... $143.00–$155.00

ELIMINATOR IV LASERSCOPE

Available in: 4-16x50mm
Weight: 28.8 oz.
Length: 13.5 in.
Exit Pupil: 16–4.2mm
Field of View: 33–9 ft.@100 yd.
Eye Relief: 3.5–4 in.
Features: Enhanced ballistic software with an onboard calculator and blue-tooth laser activation; internal digital inclinometer; smart-dope card; built-in laser rangefinder; X96 rear focal plane reticle with five illumination settings; 50 MOA windage/elevation adjustment
MSRP.................$2039.00

FULLFIELD E1 3–9X40MM ILLUMINATED

Available in: 3–9X40mm
Weight: 12 oz.
Length: 11.4 in.
Main Dia.: 1 in.
Exit Pupil: 17–5mm
Field of View: 45–13 ft @ 100 yds
Twilight Factor: 10.95–18.97
Eye Relief: 3.1–4.1 in.
Features: A series of cascading dots to the left and right of the reticle help compensate for crosswinds. The dots represent a 10 mph crosswind (+/-1.5-in. at 400 yds) for most hunting cartridges. For a 5 mph crosswind, halve the distance between dot and reticle. For 20 mph crosswind, simply double the distance. Also available in 4.5–14x42 and 6.5–20x50
3–9X: $227.00
4.5–14X:.................$263.00
6.5–20X:................$347.00

OPTICS

Burris

BURRIS FULLFIELD IV

BURRIS MSR RIFLESCOPE 4.5–14X42MM

BURRIS RT-6

BURRIS RT-15, RT-25 LONG-RANGE

BURRIS SIGNATURE HD

BURRIS T.M.P.R. 3, T.M.P.R. 5

FULLFIELD IV

Available in: 2.5–10x42mm, 3–12x42mm, 3–12x56mm, 4–16x50mm, 6–24x50mm
Weight: 16.8 oz.–18.4 oz.
Length: 11.6 in., 12 in.
Main Dia.: 1 in., 30mm
Exit Pupil: 10.1–4.6mm, 11–4mm, 13.7–5.4mm, 1.8–3.4mm, 9.4–2.7mm
Field of View: 46–11 ft.@100 yd., 38–9 ft.@100 yd., 40–1 ft.@100 yd., 26–6.5 ft.@100 yd., 2–5.1 ft.@100 yd.
Eye Relief: 3.5–3.8 in., 3.5–3.9 in., 3.3–3.5 in.
Features: Fourth generation of economical rear focal plane Fullfields; nitrogen-field tubes, waterproof, shockproof, and fogproof; easy turn turret knobs, and multicoated lenses.
2.5–1X: . . . . $203.00–$239.00
3–12X42mm: . . . . . . $263.00–$335.00
3–12X56mm: $359.00
4–16X: . . . . $383.00–$455.00
6–24X: . . . . $479.00–$539.00

MSR RIFLESCOPE 4.5–14X42MM

Available in: 4.5–14X42mm
Weight: 18 oz.
Length: 13 in.
Main Dia.: 1 in.
Exit Pupil: 9–3mm
Field of View: 22–7.5 ft @ 100 yds
Twilight Factor: 13.75–24.25
Eye Relief: 3.1–3.8 in.
Features: Shock-, water-, and fogproof; nitrogen filled; multi-coated lenses; Ballistic Plex reticle; adjustable parallax; 3–9x40 also available
4.5–14X: $335.00
3–9X: $239.00

RT-6

Weight: 17.4 oz.
Length: 10.3 in.

Power: 1–6x24mm
Obj. Diameter: 24mm
Exit Pupil: 11.5 mm–5.2mm
Eye Relief: 3.3–4 in.
Field of View: 18.5–106 in.
Features: Intended for 3-gun competition; illuminated reticle; integrated adjustable throw lever; eleven brightness levels; tube is 30mm; ballistic AR mil reticle with trajectory compensation to 600 yards
MSRP $419.00

RT-15, RT-25 LONG-RANGE

Available in: 3–5X50mm, 5–25X56mm
Weight: 23.2 oz., 24.8 oz.
Length: 13.2 in., 14.3 in.
Main Dia.: 30mm
Exit Pupil: 8–3.3mm, 8–2.2mm=
Field of View: 37.5–7.5 ft.@100 yd., 22.5–4.5 ft.@100 yd.
Eye Relief: 3.5–3.8 in., 3.3–3.6 in.
Features: First focal plane scopes for distance shooting, adjustable throw lever, zero-stop click turrets, side parallax adjustment, SCR2 Mil reticle
3–15X: $719.00
5–25X: $839.00

SIGNATURE HD

Available in: 2–10x40mm, 3–15x44mm, 5–25x50mm
Weight: 17.6 oz.–24 oz.
Length: 11.7 in.–14.3 in.
Main Dia.: 1 in., 30mm
Exit Pupil: 8–3.5mm, 8–3.3mm, 8–2.2mm
Field of View: 54–10.8 ft.@100 yd., 37.5–7.5 ft.@100 yd., 22.5–4.5 ft.@100 yd.
Eye Relief: 3.5–3.8 in., 3.3–3.6 in.
Features: Second focal plane scopes with multi-coated glass, push-pull locking turrets

---

2–10X: $431.00
3–15X: . . . . $575.00–$599.00
5–25X: . . . . $719.00–$875.00

THERMAL RIFLESCOPE

Available in: 1.7–6.8x35mm, 2.9–9.2x50mm
Weight: N/A
Length: N/A
Obj. Dia.: 35mm, 50mm
Main Dia.: N/A
Exit Pupil: N/A
Field of View: N/A
Eye Relief: N/A
Features: Thermal scope for rifle work with 10 reticle options; 7 color pallette settings; stadiametric ranging; adjustable brightness and contrast; hot track feature; one-hand operation; 400x300 resolution; manual focus
MSRP . . . . $3899.00–$4199.00

T.M.P.R. 3, T.M.P.R. 5

Available in: 3X32mm, 5X32mm
Weight: 18.2 oz.
Length: 5.6 in.
Field of View: 40 ft.
Eye Relief: 2.2 in.
Features: Modular combo optics package for law enforcement, self-defense, and action sports use; prism optic in 3x or 5x; Ballistic AR reticle; Burris' FastFire M3 red dot sight; Burris T.M.P.R. red laser; components may be purchased individually; ballistic reticle is illuminated digitally at seven levels with a choice of red, blue, or green viewing options; prism is night-vision compatible with three settings and three color choices; CR123 battery; quick-detach mounting base
3x: . . . . $839.00–$1259.00
5x: . . . . $899.00–$1319.00

OPTICS

BURRIS VERACITY 2–10X42MM

BURRIS XTR III TACTICAL

VERACITY 2–10X42MM

Available in: 2–10X42mm
Weight: 22.7 oz.
Length: 13.5 in.
Main Dia.: 30mm
Exit Pupil: 21–4.2mm
Field of View: 52–10.5 ft @ 100 yds
Twilight Factor: 9.17–20.49
Eye Relief: 3.5 in.–4.25 in.
Features: Ballistic E1 FFP MOA reticle with PTC technology; E1 Hunter knobs; parallax adjustment; 3–15x50, 4–20x50, and 5–25x50 also available

2–10X: $719.00
3–15X: $875.00
4–20X: $959.00
5–25X: $1079.00

XTR III TACTICAL

Available in: 3.3–18x50mm, 5.5–30x56mm
Weight: 29.8 oz., 32 oz.
Length: 13.3 in., 15.4 in.
Main Dia.: 34mm
Exit Pupil: 8.6–2.7mm, 8.6–1.8 in.
Field of View: 37.7–6.8 ft.@100 yd., 23–4.2 ft.@100 yd.
Eye Relief: 3.25–4 in.
Features: Premium first focal plane scopes with big fields of view, big adjustment range, "Dragon Scale" knurling at adjustment points, and optional Race dial with a writable surface

3.3–18X. . . . . $1929.00–$1999.00
5.5–30X standard . . .$2159.00–$2219.00

Bushnell

BUSHNELL AR OPTICS 1–4X24MM

BUSHNELL AR OPTICS 1–6X24

BUSHNELL AR OPTICS 3–12X40MM

BUSHNELL AR OPTICS 4.5–18X40MM

BUSHNELL BANNER 2

AR OPTICS 1–4X24MM

Available in: 1–4X 24mm
Weight: 17.3 oz.
Length: 3.6 in.
Main Dia.: 30mm
Exit Pupil: 13–6mm
Field of View: 110–36 ft @ 100 yds
Twilight Factor: 4.9–9.8
Eye Relief: 3.6 in.
Features: Designed for tactical applications; first focal plane reticles in Drop-Zone 223, and illuminated BTR-1; fully multi-coated glass; anti-reflective coating on all air-to-glass surfaces; 120 MOA elevation, 140 MOA windage adjustment ranges
MSRP . . . . $149.99–$324.99

AR OPTICS 1–6X24MM

Available in: 1–6x24mm
Weight: 16.5 oz.
Length: 10.2 in.
Main Dia.: 30mm
Exit Pupil: N/A
Field of View: 100–16 ft.@100 yd.
Eye Relief: 3.6 in.
Features: Illuminated BTR-1 reticle in the second focal plane; throw-down power lever for quick changes; capped turrets; IPX7 waterproof construction
MSRP $279.99

AR OPTICS 3–12X40MM

Available in: 3–12X40mm
Weight: 21.3 oz.
Length: 12 in.
Main Dia.: 1 in.
Exit Pupil: 13.7–3.7mm
Field of View: 33–11 ft @ 100 yds
Twilight Factor: 11–21.9
Eye Relief: 3.7 in.
Features: Target turrets; side parallax FOCUS; Drop Zone 223 reticle in the second focal plane; fully multicoated optics; 50 MOA elevation, 85 MOA windage adjustment range; Rainguard
MSRP $179.99

AR OPTICS 4.5–18X40MM

Available in: 4.5–18X40mm
Weight: 21.5 oz.
Length: 12.4 in.
Main Dia.: 1 in.
Exit Pupil: 8.6–2.3mm
Field of View: 22–7.3 ft @ 100 yds
Twilight Factor: 13.4–26.8
Eye Relief: 3.7 in.
Features: Target turrets; side parallax FOCUS; fully multi-coated optics; Drop-Zone second focal plane reticles available calibrated for 6.5 Creedmoor, .224 Valkyrie, .308 Win., and .223; 50 MOA elevation, 80 MOA windage adjustment range; Rainguard; multi-turret option also available with Windhold reticle and five different caliber turrets
MSRP . . . .$179.99–$279.99

BANNER 2

Available in: 3–9x40mm, 4–12x40mm, 3–9x50mm, 6–18x50mm
Weight: 16.5 oz.–21.6 oz.
Length: 12.3 in., 13.4 in., 13.5 in., 13 in.
Main Dia.: 1 in.
Exit Pupil: N/A
Field of View: 37–12.2 ft.@100 yd., 27–9 ft.@100 yd., 33.6–10.4 ft.@100 yd., 17.3–6 ft.@100 yd.
Eye Relief: 3.5 in., 3.3 in., 3.5 in., 3.9 in.
Features: Second focal plane DOA QBR reticle; capped, non-locking turrets with 60 MOA windage/elevation adjustment; multicoated and ultra wideband coatings; EXO Barrier; IPX7 waterproofing; adjustable objective; aluminum body
MSRP . . . . $89.99–$139.99

OPTICS

Bushnell

BUSHNELL ENGAGE

BUSHNELL LEGEND 3–9X40, 6–18X50, 4–12X40

BUSHNELL MATCH PRO

BUSHNELL NITRO

BUSHNELL PRIME

ENGAGE
Available in: 2–7x36mm, 3–9x40mm, 3–9x50mm, 4–12x40mm, 6–18x50mm, 2.5–10x44mm, 3–12x42mm, 4–16x44mm, 6–24x50mm
Weight: 11.4–23.7 oz.
Length: 12.8–14.3 in.
Main Dia.: 1 in., 30mm
Exit Pupil: varies
Field of View: varies
Eye Relief: 3.5–4 in.
Features: New Deploy MOA reticle that is compatible with a range of calibers; locking turrets; toolless zero reset; EXO lens barrier; some models have side focus
MSRP . . . . $189.99–$467.99

LEGEND 3–9X40, 6–18X50, 4–12X40
Available in: 3–9x40mm, 6–18x50mm, 4–12x40mm
Weight: 14.8 oz., 18.4 oz., 17.3 oz.
Length: 15.1 in., 12 in., 14.4 in.
Main Dia.: 1 in.
Exit Pupil: N/A
Field of View: N/A
Eye Relief: 3.5 in., 3.9 in., 3.9 in.
Features: Rainguard HD coating; choice of DOA QBR second focal plane reticle or illuminated Multi-X reticle second focal plane; aluminum body
MSRP . . . . $129.99–$224.95

MATCH PRO
Available in: 6–24x50mm
Weight: 29.8 oz.
Length: 14.01 in.
Obj. Dia.: 50mm
Main Dia.: 30mm
Field of View: 18–4 ft.@100 yd.
Eye Relief: 3.74 in.
Features: A heavyweight for today's distant target games, this first focal plane scope has choice of non-illuminated or illuminated Deploy Mil etched glass reticle; 65 MOA of elevation/windage adjustment
MSRP . . . . $449.99–$499.99

NITRO
Available in: 2.5–10x44mm, 3–12x44mm
Weight: 23.9 oz., 24.2 oz.
Length: 13.4 in., 13.7 in.
Main Dia.: 30mm
Field of View: 37–9 ft.@100 yd. (2.5–10X), 34.8–8.6 ft.@100yd. (3–12X)
Eye Relief: 3.6 in.
Features: Designed for hunters working at close to middle ranges. Second focal plane copes have a matte gray or black finish; variety of Multi-Plex and Deploy reticles; capped target turrets; Ultra-Wide Band Coating; EXO Barrier Protection; IPX7 waterproofing
2.5–10X: $349.99
3–12X: $399.99

PRIME
Available in: 1–4x32mm, 3–9x40mm, 3–12x40mm, 4-12x40mm, 6–18x50mm
Weight: 13.4 oz., 16.6 oz., 17 oz., 18.6 oz., 19 oz.
Length: 10.4 in., 12.8 in., 12 in., 12.8 in., 15 in.
Main Dia.: 1 in.
Field of View: 105–26 ft.@100 yd. (1–4X), 31–11 ft.@100 yd. (3–9X), 29–7.5 ft,@100 yd. (3–12X), 26–9 ft.@100 yd. (4–12X), 18–6 ft.@100 yd. (6–18X)
Eye Relief: 3.9 in. (1–4X), 3.3 in. (3–9X), 3.7 in. (3.5–10X), 3.5 in. (3–12X), 3.3 in. (4–12X), 3.5 n. (6–18X)
Features: Lightweight and compact second focal plane package in a power range for every target or hunting application. Features include multi-coated optics; EXO Barrier Protection; IPX7 waterproofing; Ultra Wide Band coatings; Multi-X reticle; 3–12X is a multi-turret design with six turrets calibrated for popular calibers, including two for muzzleloader loads
MSRP . . . . $139.99–$299.99

Cabela's

CABELA'S RIMFIRE RIFLESCOPE 3–9X40MM

CABELA'S LEVER ACTION 3–9X40MM

LEVER ACTION 3–9X40MM
Available in: 3–9X40mm
Weight: 14.64 oz.
Length: 13 in.
Main Dia.: 1 in.
Exit Pupil: 13.33–4.44mm
Field of View: 30.55–9.6 ft @ 100 yds
Twilight Factor: 10.95–18.97
Eye Relief: 5.5 in.
Features: Ballistic glass reticles specifically engineered for use with a particular Hornady LEVERevolution round; tube is machined aluminum and lenses are multi-coated; windage and elevation are adjustable in ¼ MOA clicks; in .45-70 Govt., .44 Mag., and .30-30 Win. reticles
MSRP $99.99

RIMFIRE RIFLESCOPE 3–9X40MM
Available in: 3–9X40mm
Weight: 13.4 oz.
Length: 12 in.
Main Dia.: 1 in.
Exit Pupil: 13.33–4.44mm
Field of View: 37.7–12.4 ft @ 100 yds
Twilight Factor: 10.95–18.97
Eye Relief: 4 in.
Features: For hunting, target shooting, or plinking with a rimfire rifle; parallax-free at 50 yards; multi-coated glass optics; extended eye relief and an expanded exit pupil; low-profile windage and elevation turrets; Duplex reticle; also available in 2-7x32, 4X
MSRP $99.99

OPTICS

Carl Zeiss Sports Optics

CARL ZEISS SPORTS OPTICS CONQUEST V4

CARL ZEISS SPORTS OPTICS VICTORY V8

CONQUEST V4
Available in: 1–4x24mm, 3–12x56mm, 4–16x44mm, 6–24x50mm
Weight: 16.6 oz. (1–4x), 21.5 oz. (3–12x), 22.6 oz. (4–16x), 24.4 oz. (6–24x)
Length: 10.08 in. (1–4x), 14.5 in. (3–12x), 14 in. (4–16), 14.5 in. (6–24x)
Main Dia.: 30mm
Exit Pupil: 11.9–24mm (1–4x), 9.2–4.7mm (3–12x), 8.5–2.8mm (4–16x), 7.5–2.1mm (6–24x)
Field of View: 114–28.5 ft.@100 yd. (1–4x), 38–9.5 ft.@100 yd. (3–12x), 28.5–7.1 ft.@100 yd. (4–16x), 19–4.8 ft.@100 yd. (6–24x)
Twilight Factor: 3.5–9.8 (1–4x), 9.1–25.9 (3–12x), 11.5–26.5 (4–16x), 16.4–34.6 (6–24x)
Eye Relief: 3.5 in.
Features: Multiple reticles available, all second focal plane: 1–4x #60 illuminated center dot, ZQAR (on external turret option), 3–12x Z-Plex, Plex illuminated, 4–16x Z-Plex, ZMOA-2, 6–24x ZBR-1, ZMOA-1
MSRP . . . . $699.99–$1299.99

VICTORY V8
Available in: 1–8x30mm, 1.8–14x50mm, 2.8–20x56mm, 4.8–35x60mm
Weight: 21 oz.–34 oz.
Length: 12 in.–15.75 in.
Main Dia.: 36mm
Exit Pupil: 9.9–3.9mm, 10.3–3.7mm, 9.8–2.8mm, 9.9–1.4mm
Field of View: 110–15 ft @ 100 yds, 63–8.5 ft @ 100 yds, 42–5.7 ft @ 100 yds, 24–3.3 ft @ 100 yds
Twilight Factor: 3.1–15.5; 5.1–26; 7.9–33; 13.6–45.8
Eye Relief: 3.75 in.
Features: Largest zoom range; interaction of 92 percent transmission; fluoride lens elements and SCHOTT HT glass ensures outstanding image quality and target resolution; large exit pupils and extremely large fields of view ensure fast target acquisition, an excellent overview of the hunting situation, no shadowing, and an immediate round image; compact design; generous adjustment range of 100 clicks enables you to stay on target at distances up to 600 yds; a fiber optic thinner than a human hair provides the finest illuminated dot in the world, resulting in 0.1188 in. subtension at 100 yds
MSRP . . . . $2999.99–$4444.43

C-More Systems

C-MORE SYSTEMS C3 1–6X24MM COMPETITION

C3 1–6X24MM COMPETITION
Available in: 1–6x24mm
Weight: 22 oz.
Length: 10.5 in.
Main Dia.: 30mm
Exit Pupil: 12–4.1mm
Field of View: 108.3–19.8 ft @ 100 yds
Eye Relief: 4.25 in.
Features: Lockable windage and elevation turrets; TJ1I competition ballistic reticle with 1.5 in. illuminated red dot; 11 entensity settings; nitrogen filled; waterproof, fogproof, and shockproof; quick-zoom power adjustment ring; coated optics
MSRP $1999.99

Crimson Trace Corp.

CRIMSON TRACE BRUSHLINE PRO

BRUSHLINE PRO
Available in: 2–7x32mm, 2.5–10x42mm, 3–9x40mm, 3–9x50mm, 3–12x42mm, 4–16x42mm, 4–16x50mm, 6–24x50mm
Weight: N/A
Length: N/A
Main Dia.: 1 in., 30mm
Exit Pupil: N/A
Field of View: N/A
Eye Relief: N/A
Features: Designed for hunters, line has 24 models with second focal plane reticles (Plex, BDC, BDC Legend, BDC Rimfire, BDC Predator, BDC Muzzleloader); nitrogen purged; waterproof; lifetime guarantee

MSRP . . . . $224.99–$779.99

Crimson Trace Corp.

CRIMSON TRACE HARDLINE PRO

HARDLINE PRO
Available in: 1–6x24mm, 2–7x32mm, 3–9x40mm, 3–12x42mm, 4–12x40mm, 4–12x42mm, 4–16x50mm, 5–20x50mm, 6–24x50mm
Weight: N/A
Length: N/A
Main Dia.: 30mm
Exit Pupil: N/A
Field of View: N/A
Eye Relief: N/A

Features: 23 variations in this new line, most with second focal plane reticles (MOA ILL, MIL ILL, BDC Comp, MR1-MOA, MR1-MIL, BDC Long-Range, BDC Carbine, BDC Blackout, Mildot) and a couple in the first focal plane (illuminated MOA ILL and MIL ILL); intended for target and tactical shooters; fully multicoated; nitrogen purged; lifetime warranty
MSRP . . . . $624.99–$1099.99

EoTech

EOTECH VUDU SERIES

VUDU SERIES
Available in: 1–6x24mm, 1–8x24mm, 2.5–10x44mm, 3.5–18x50mm, 8–32x50mm, 5-25x50mm
Weight: 19.75 oz.–33.23 oz.

Length: 10.63 in.–14.84 in.
Obj. Dia.: 24mm–50mm
Main Dia.: 30mm, 34mm
Exit Pupil: 11.4–4mm, 11.4–4.4mm, 10–2.4mm
Field of View: 105.8–17.7 ft @ 100 yds, 44–11 ft @100 yds, 30–6 ft @100 yds
Eye Relief: 3.15–4 in., 3.43–3.94 in., 3.39–3.94 in.
Features: Allows for fast target engagement at low power; at higher power provides the resolution and

accuracy required to tackle longer shots; extremely clear XC High-Density glass; foversized and precision-machined turrets; EZ Chek zero stop feature; side-mounted parallax adjustment; 1–6X, 2.5-10X, 3.5–18X and 5–25X have first focal plane reticles, second focal plane reticles in the 8–32X and a second 3.5–18X model
FFP . . . . $1399.00–$2099.00
SFP . . . . $1399.00–$1799.00

GPO

GPO GPOTAC

GPO PASSION 3X

GPO PASSION 4X

GPOTAC
Available in: 1–6x24mm, 1–8x24mm, 2.5– 20x50mm, 4.5–27X50mm
Length: 10.6 in.–14.8 in.
Exit Pupil: Varies with model/magnification
Eye Relief: 3.54–4.33 in.

Field of View: Varies with model/magnification
Features: 1–8x, 2.5–10X, and 4.5–27 models have a 34mm tube, 1–6x has a 30mm. Features of both include, iControl illumination with a custom Mil-Spec Horseshoe reticle, Double HD objective lenses, and oversized target turrets. These are first focal plane scopes; also now available in a 2.5–20x50 and a 4.5– 27x50, both with illuminated reticles.
MSRP . . . . $1452.62–$1999.99

PASSION 3X
Available in: 3–9X42mm, 4–12X42mm, 6–18X50mm
Weight: 13.8 oz.–18.2 oz.
Length: 11.7 in.–13.2in.
Exit Pupil: Varies with model/magnification
Eye Relief: 3.54–3.74 in.
Field of View: Varies with model/magnification
Features: Entry-level scopes; 1-in. tubes; generous eye relief; fast focus ocular lenses; proprietary lens coatings;

metal turret caps; clicks are ¼-MOA; with or without illuminated reticles
MSRP . . . . $421.04–$736.83

PASSION 4X
Available in: 3–12X56mm, 6–24X50mm
Weight: 22.6 oz.–23.3 oz.
Length: 13.4 in. (3–12x56mm), 15.5 in. (6–24x50mm)
Exit Pupil: 19–4.7mm
Eye Relief: 3.54 in.
Field of View: 37–14 ft @ 100 yds
Features: Entry-level scopes; 30mm tubes; generous eye relief; fast focus ocular lenses; proprietary lens coatings; metal turret caps; clicks are .36-in. in the 3-12x model, ¼-MOA in the 6-24x model; 3-12x models come with standard or illuminated G4 reticle; 6-24X has Plex reticle; parallax free at 100m for 3-12x; 6-24mm has side-adjustment parallax correction
3–12X $736.83
6–24X $1210.52

OPTICS

GPO SPECTRA 4X

GPO SPECTRA 5X

GPO SPECTRA 6X

GPO SPECTRA 8X

SPECTRA 4X

Available in: 2.5–10x44mm, 4–16x50mm
Weight: 21.9 oz.–24 oz.
Length: 13.3 in., 14.7 in.
Main Dia.: 30mm
Exit Pupil: N/A
Field of View: 49.3 ft.@100 yd., 32.8 ft.@100 yd.
Eye Relief: 3.75mm
Features: Traditional G4 plex reticle; PASSIONtrac reset turrets; GPOBright lens coatings; DoubleHD objective lens technology; 2.5-10X available in standard or illuminated reticle, 4–12X with G4 illuminated or G4-Drop illuminated ballistic reticle; .1 MRAD turret clicks
MSRP . . . . $610.52–$821.04

SPECTRA 5X

Available in: 3–15x56mm
Weight: 29.3 oz.
Length: 14.6 in.
Main Dia.: 30mm
Exit Pupil: N/A
Field of View: 34.7 ft.@100 yd.
Eye Relief: 3.75mm
Features: iControl illuminated G4 reticle; PASSIONtrac reset turrets; GPObright lens coatings; DoubleHD objective lens technology; removable magnification throw lever
MSRP $1052.62

SPECTRA 6X

Available in: 1–6x24mm, 1.5–9x32mm, 1.5–9x44mm, 2–12x44mm, 2–12x50mm, 3–18x56mm
Weight: 16.9 oz.–29.3 oz.
Length: 11.4 in.–14.6 in.
Main Dia.: 30mm
Exit Pupil: N/A

Field of View: 128–22 ft.@100 yd., 86–14 ft.@100 yd., 86–14 ft.@100 yd., 65–11 ft.@100 yd., 65–11 ft.@100 yd., 34–6 ft.@100 yd.
Eye Relief: 4mm, 3.75mm
Features: Illuminated G4-Drop reticle; PASSIONtrac reset turrets; GPObright lens coatings; DoubleHD objective lens technology; .1 MRAD clicks
MSRP . . . . $842.09–$1157.88

SPECTRA 8X

Available in: 1–8x24mm, 2–16x44mm, 2.5–20x50mm
Weight: 17.8 oz.–25.3 oz.
Length: 10.1 in.–14.8 in.
Main Dia.: 30mm
Exit Pupil: N/A
Field of View: 123–15 ft.@100 yd., 59–8 ft.@100 yd., 48–6 ft.@100 yd.
Eye Relief: 3.5mm
Features: G4 illuminated reticles, and the 2–16X is also available in an illuminated BR reticle; PASSIONtrac reset turrets; GPObright lens coatings; DoubleHD objective lens technology; .1 MRAD
MSRP . . . . $1263.15–$1452.62

Hawke Sport Optics, LLC

HAWKE SPORT OPTICS .350 LEGEND

HAWKE SPORT OPTICS FRONTIER 30

HAWKE SPORT OPTICS FRONTIER 30 SF

.350 LEGEND

Available in: 2.5–10x50mm, 3–12x56mm
Weight: 21.6 oz., 22.4 oz.
Length: 13.1 in., 13.7 in.
Main Dia.: 30mm
Exit Pupil: 20–5mm, 18–5mm
Field of View: 49.8–12.5 ft.@100 yd., 41.5–1.4 ft.@100 yd.
Eye Relief: 4 in.

Features: Designed specifically to partner with the .350 Legend straight-wall cartridge, with precise holdover points; illuminated 35 Legend reticle in the second focal plane
2.5–10X $529.00
3–12X $549.00

FRONTIER 30

Available in: 1–6x24mm
Weight: 19.7 oz.
Length: 10.4 in.
Main Dia.: 30mm
Exit Pupil: 24–4mm
Field of View: 108–17.6 ft.@100 yd.
Eye Relief: 4 in.
Features: Designed for tactical applications with a wide field of view; generous eye relief; second focal plane; 21 layers fully multicoated; illuminated etched glass Tactical Dot (6X), L4A Dot or Circle Dot reticle with six brightness levels
MSRP . . . . $749.00–$769.00

FRONTIER 30 SF

Available in: 2.5–15x50mm, 4–24x50mm, 5–30x56mm
Weight: 23.4 oz., 24.5 oz.
Length: 13.7 in., 13.9 in.
Main Dia.: 30mm
Exit Pupil: 20–3mm (2.5–15X), *10–2mm (5–30X), 12.5–2.1mm (4–24X)*
Field of View: 42–6.9 ft.@100 yd. (2.5–15X), 22.8–3.9 ft.@100 yd. (5–30X), 28.2–4.8 ft.@1000 yd. (4–24X)
Eye Relief: 4 in.
Features: Super tool for hunters especially those shooting magnum calibers, thanks to the 4-inch eye relief; big objective; side focus parallax adjustment; second focal plane; illuminated glass etched LR Dot or Mil Pro reticles
MSRP . . . . $899.00–$949.00

Hawke Sport Optics, LLC

HAWKE SPORT OPTICS
FRONTIER 30 SF FFP

HAWKE SPORT OPTICS
SIDEWINDER 30 FFP

HAWKE
SPORT OPTICS
SIDEWINDER 30 SF

HAWKE SPORT OPTICS
VANTAGE

HAWKE SPORT OPTICS
VANTAGE 30 WA FFP

HAWKE SPORT OPTICS
VANTAGE 30 WA IR

FRONTIER 30 SF FFP

Available in: 3–15x50mm,
5–25x56mm, 4–20X50mm
Weight: 26.3 oz., 28.8 oz., 22.2 oz.
Length: 13.2 in.
Main Dia.: 30mm
Exit Pupil: 16.7–3.3mm (3–15X),
11.2–2.3mm (5–25X), 12.5–2.5mm
(4–20X)
Field of View: 36.7–7.3 ft.@100 yd.
(3–15X), 21.7–4.3 ft.@100 yd.
(5–25X), 28.5–5.7 ft.@100 yd. (4–20X)
Eye Relief: 4 in.
Features: A mid-size hunter's tool in
the underutilized 5X category; 1/10
MRAD locking turrets; first focal Plane
illuminated etched glass Mil Pro reti-
cle with six brightness settings
MSRP . . . .$1049.00–$1149.00

SIDEWINDER 30 FFP

Available in: 4–16x50mm,
6–24x56mm
Weight: 25.6 oz., 27.3 oz.
Length: 13.3 in., 14.3 in.
Obj. Dia.: 50mm, 56mm
Main Dia.: 30mm
Exit Pupil: N/A
Field of View: 31.8–8.1ft.@100 yd.,
21.3–5.4 ft.@100 yd.
Eye Relief: 4 in.
Features: Dual LED reticle
illumination; mono-tube chassis;
distortion-free low-dispersion crown
glass; fully multicoated lenses (18
layers, ion-assisted); fast-focus eyebell
with locking ring; side focus with
removable index-matched side wheel;
zoom magnification throw lever;
exposed locking turrets with witness
window
MSRP . . . . $899.00–$929.00

SIDEWINDER 30 SF

Available in: 4.5–14x44mm, 6.5–
20x44mm, 4–16x50mm,
6–24x56mm, 8–32x56mm
Weight: 24 oz.–27.3 oz.
Length: 13.3 in.–15.5 in.
Main Dia.: 30mm
Exit Pupil: N/A
Field of View: 28.2–9ft.@100 yd.,
19.5–6.3 ft.@100 yd., 31.8–8.1
ft.@100 yd., 21.3–5.4 ft.@100 yd.,
15.9–3.9ft.@100 yd.
Eye Relief: 4 in.
Features: Second focal plane scopes;
dual LED reticle illumination; mono-
tube chassis; distortion-free low-
dispersion crown glass; fully
multicoated lenses (18 layers, ion-
assisted); fast-focus eyebell with
locking ring; side focus with
removable index-matched side wheel;
zoom magnification throw lever;
exposed locking turrets with witness
window
MSRP . . . . $679.00–$749.00

VANTAGE

Available in: 4x32mm, 2–7x32mm,
3–9x4mm, 3–9x50, 4–12x40mm,
4–12X50mm
Weight: 11.1 oz.–20.3 oz.
Length: 11.5 in.–13.8 in.
Main Dia.: 1 in.
Exit Pupil: 8mm, 16–5mm, 13–4mm,
17–6mm, 10–3mm
Field of View: 28.5 ft.@100 yd., 46.6–
14.1 ft.@100 yd., 39–12.7 ft.@100

yd., 33.6–11 ft.@100 yd., 26.2–8.7
ft.@100 yd.
Eye Relief: 3.5 in.
Features: A truly economical line of
second focal plane all-purpose scopes
that include adjustable objective
options; glass-etched 30/30 Duplex or
Mil-Dot reticles; 1/4-MOA turrets

4X	**$99.00–$109.00**
2–7X	**$119.00–$129.00**
3–9X40	**$139.00–$149.00**
3–9X50	**$149.00–$159.00**
4–12X40	**$159.00–$169.00**
4–12X50	**$169.00**

VANTAGE 30 WA FFP

Available in: 4–16x50mm,
6–24x50mm
Weight: 26.3 oz., 26.6 oz.
Length: 13.7 in., 14.9 in.
Main Dia.: 30mm
Exit Pupil: 12.5–3.1mm, 8.3–2.1mm
Field of View: 21–5.2 ft.@100 yd.
Eye Relief: 3.5 in.
Features: The only first focal plane
models in the Vantage line, these two
scopes have illuminated green/red ret-
icles with five brightness settings;
side-focus control; 1/10 MRAD lock-
ing turrets

4–16X	**$519.00**
6–24X	**$549.00**

VANTAGE 30 WA IR

Available in: 1–4x24mm, 1.5–
6x44mm, 2.5–10x50mm, 3–9x42mm,
3–12x56mm
Weight: 14.9 oz.–23.6 oz.
Length: 11.1 in.–13.4 in.
Main Dia.: 30mm
Exit Pupil: 24–6mm, 29.3–7.3mm,
20–5mm, 14–4.7mm, 18–5mm
Field of View: 126–31.5 ft.@100 yd.,
80.4–19.8 ft.@100 yd., 50.4–12.6
ft.@100 yd., 42.2–13.1 ft.@100 yd.,
42.8–1.7 ft.@100 yd.
Eye Relief: 3.5 in.
Features: Moving to a 30mm tube,
this wide-angle series has illuminated
glass-etched reticles with five brightness settings and in red and green; 1/2-
MOA clicks
MSRP . . . . $279.00–$349.00

OPTICS

Hawke Sport Optics, LLC

HAWKE SPORT OPTICS
VANTAGE 30 WA SF IR

HAWKE SPORT
OPTICS VANTAGE IR

HAWKE SPORT OPTICS
VANTAGE SF

VANTAGE 30 WA SF IR

Available in: 4–16x50mm, 6–24x50mm
Weight: 26.1 oz., 26.3 oz.
Length: 13.7 in., 15.4 in.
Main Dia.: 30mm
Exit Pupil: 12.5–3.1mm, 8.3–2.1mm
Field of View: 28.8–7.8 ft.@100 yd., 20.7–5.4 ft.@100 yd.
Eye Relief: 3.5 in.
Features: All the features of the 30 WA IR, but with side-focus design; ¼-MOA clicks
4–16X $439.00
6–24X $459.00

VANTAGE IR

Available in: 2–7x32mm, 3–9x40mm, 3–9x50mm, 4–12x40mm, 4–12x50mm, 4–16x50mm, 6–24x50mm
Weight: 15.9 oz.,–22 oz.
Length: 11.5 in.–15.6 in.
Main Dia.: 1 in.
Exit Pupil: 16–5mm, 13–4mm, 17–6mm, 10–3.3mm, 13–4mm, 13–3mm, 8–2mm
Field of View: 46.6–14.1 ft.@100 yd., 39–12 ft.@100 yd., 33.6–11 ft.@100 yd., 26.2–8.7 ft.@100 yd., 26.2–8.7 ft.@100 yd.; 23.6–6.2 ft.@100 yd., 15.1–4.2 ft.@100 yd.
Eye Relief: 3.5 in.
Features: Illuminated reticles with five brightness settings; fast-focus eyeball; glass-etched reticle in green and red; some models have adjustable objective
MSRP . . . . $179.00–$299.00

VANTAGE SF

Available in: 3–12x44mm, 4–16x44mm, 6–24x44mm
Weight: 17.3 oz.–18.7 oz.
Length: 13.3 in.–14.7 in.
Main Dia.: 1 in.
Exit Pupil: 15–4mm, 11–3mm, 7–2mm
Field of View: 30.6–77 ft.@100 yd., 22.9–5.8 ft.@100 yd., 15.3–3.8 ft.@100 yd.
Eye Relief: 3.5 in.
Features: Budget-friendly side-focus models; ¼-MOA clicks; fully multi-coated optics; 100 MOA elevation/windage; knurled posi-grip power selector; second focal plane ½ Mil Dot reticle
3–12X $289.00
4–16X $309.00
6–24X $329.00

Hi-Lux Precision Optics

HI-LUX
CMR4 1–4X24MM

HI-LUX PRECISION
OPTICS LEATHERWOOD
ART M1000 PRO

HI-LUX
LEATHERWOOD
ART M1200

HI-LUX M40
TACTICAL HUNTER
3-9X40MM

CLOSE TO MEDIUM RANGE (CMR4) 1–4X24MM

Available in: 1–4X24mm
Weight: 16.5 oz.
Length: 10.2 in.
Main Dia.: 30mm
Exit Pupil: 11.1–6mm
Field of View: 94.8–26.2 ft @ 100 yds
Twilight Factor: 4.89–9.79
Eye Relief: 3 in.
Features: Zero-locking turrets; large external target-style windage and elevation adjustment knobs; power-ring extended lever handle for power change; CMR ranging reticle for determining range and also BDC hold over value good for .223, .308, and other calibers; red illuminated reticle
MSRP $395.00

M40 TACTICAL HUNTER 3-9X40MM

Available in: 3–9X40mm
Weight: 16.2 in.
Length: 12.5 in.
Main Dia.: 1 in.
Exit Pupil: 13.3–4.4mm
Field of View: 37.7–12.6 ft @ 100 yds
Twilight Factor: 10.95–18.97
Eye Relief: 3.25 in.
Features: This is a dual focal plane reticle scope, with a glass-etched ranging reticle in the first focal plane and a .223/5.56 BDC reticle in the second
MSRP $249.00

LEATHERWOOD ART M1000 PRO

Available in: 2–10x42mm

Weight: 32 oz.
Length: 12 in.
Main Dia.: 30mm
Eye Relief: 3.5 in.
Features: 50th anniversary of Jim Leatherwood's Automatic Ranging Trajectory (ART) scope; distance to target can be accomplished by framing targets of known size within the HR1 reticle or dialing the cam to a known distance, either way eliminating holdover guesswork
MSRP $515.00

LEATHERWOOD ART M1200

Available in: 6–24X50mm
Weight: 29 oz.
Length: 15.5 in.
Main Dia.: 30mm
Exit Pupil: 8.5–2mm
Field of View: 12–4 ft @ 100 yds
Twilight Factor: 17.32–34.64
Eye Relief: 3.25 in.
Features: Auto-ranging trajectory; multi-coated lenses; second focal plane; nitrogen gas filled; waterproof; ZRO-LOK system
MSRP $585.00

OPTICS

Hi-Lux Precision Optics

HI-LUX TOBY BRIDGES HIGH PERFORMANCE MUZZLELOADER

HI-LUX WM. MALCOLM 2.5X M73G4

HI-LUX WM. MALCOLM 6X LONG TELESCOPIC

HI-LUX WM. MALCOM 8X USMC SNIPER SCOPE

TOBY BRIDGES HIGH PERFORMANCE MUZZLELOADER 3–9X40MM

Available in: 3–9X40mm
Weight: 15.8 oz.
Length: 12.5 in.
Main Dia.: 1 in.
Exit Pupil: 13.3–4.4mm
Field of View: 39–13 ft @ 100 yds
Twilight Factor: 10.9–19
Eye Relief: 3.25 in.
Features: The TB/ML scope is designed for in-line ignition muzzle-loaders and saboted bullets. It offers multiple reticles for shooting at ranges out to 250 yards.
MSRP **$129.00**

WM. MALCOLM 2.5X M73G4

Available in: 2.5X16mm
Weight: 11.8 in.
Length: 8.3 oz.
Main Dia.: ¾ in.
Exit Pupil: 4mm
Field of View: 24.9 ft @ 100 yds
Twilight Factor: 6.33
Eye Relief: 3.54 in.
Features: Built to bring the vintage sniper rifle competition shooter a top quality scope that surpasses the quality of the WWII originals used on the M1903A4 sniper rifles; modern erector tube and quality multi-coated

lenses for superior light transmission; offers a minimum total of 60 MOA with either windage or elevation when those adjustments are at center
MSRP **$385.00**

WM. MALCOLM 6X LONG TELESCOPIC

Available in: 6X16mm
Weight: 32.5 oz.
Length: 30.5 in.
Main Dia.: .75 in.
Exit Pupil: 5.8mm
Field of View: 10 ft @ 100 yds
Twilight Factor: 9.79
Eye Relief: 4 in.
Features: A modern copy of the Model 1855 W. Malcolm riflescopes; early-style mounts for scoping original and replica 19th century breechloading rifles (Sharps, rolling block, high wall, etc.) or late period long-range percussion muzzleloading bullet rifles; ¾-in. (steel) scope tube; interchangeable front extension tubes to mount on rifles with barrels of 30 to 34 inches; also in 3x17-in. and 6x18-in. short Malcolms
MSRP **$475.00**

WM. MALCOLM 6X TWO-TONE SHORT RIFLE TELESCOPE

Available in: 6X17mm
Weight: 18 oz.

HI-LUX PRECISION OPTICS WM. MALCOLM 6X TWO-TONE SHORT RIFLE TELESCOPE

Length: 18 in.
Main Dia.: .75 in.
Exit Pupil: N/A
Field of View: 12 ft.@100 yd.
Eye Relief: 4 in.
Features: Gloss black and brass scope for a deserving vintage gun; clickless micrometer adjustment rear mount; fine cross reticle; sliding lock ring mitigates the impact of recoil to the scope and needs to be "reset to battery" after each shot

MSRP **$475.00**

WM. MALCOLM 8X USMC SNIPER SCOPE

Available in: 8X31mm
Weight: 25.4 oz.
Length: 22.1 in.
Main Dia.: .75 in.
Exit Pupil: 4.2mm
Field of View: 11 ft @ 100 yds
Twilight Factor: 15.75
Eye Relief: 3.15 in.
Features: Fully multi-coated lens; fine cross reticle; elevation and wind adjustment ¼ MOA per click at the mounts
MSRP **$575.00**

Kahles

KAHLES K16I

KAHLES K318I

K16I

Available in: 1–6X24mm
Weight: 16.9 oz.

Length: 10.9 in.
Obj. Dia.: 24mm
Main Dia.: 30mm
Exit Pupil: 9.65–3.81mm
Field of View: 127–20.1 ft @ 100 yds
Twilight Factor: 4.9–12
Eye Relief: 3.74 in.
Features: Rear focal plane; illuminated; integrated magnification throw lever allows for instant magnification changes even in the most adverse environmental conditions
MSRP **$2049.00**

K318I

Available in: 3.5–18x50mm
Weight: 33.2 oz.
Length: 12.3 in.
Main Dia.: 34mm
Field of View: 27.8–5.5 ft.@100 yd.
Eye Relief: 3.6 in.
Features: A solid scope for mid-range work with an illuminated reticle in the first focal plane; TWIST GUARD windage protection; reticle choices of MSR/Ki, SKMR3, and MOAK
MSRP **$3349.00**

OPTICS

KAHLES K525I

KAHLES K521I DLR

KAHLES K624I

KAHLES K1050

K525I

Available in: 5–25x56mm
Weight: 34.2 oz.
Length: 14.8 in.
Main Dia.: 34mm
Exit Pupil: 9.5–2.3mm
Field of View: 21.7–4.4 ft.@100 yd.
Eye Relief: 3.74 in.
Features: A big scope for big calibers going big distances featuring an elevation turret with integrated parallax wheel; illuminated first focal plane reticle in reticle choice of SKMR3, SKMR, MOAK, Mil4+, or MSR2/Ki; TWIST GUARD windage system prevents accidental dial movement
MSRP . . . . $3449.00–$4099.00

K525I DLR

Available in: 5–25x56mm
Weight: 35 oz.
Length: 14.8 in.
Main Dia.: 34mm
Exit Pupil: 9.5–2.3mm
Field of View: 7.7–1.6m@100m
Eye Relief: 3.7 in.
Features: Dynamic Long Range; extra-long throw lever; parallax spinner; illuminated SKMR4 reticle in the first focal plane; turrets with extra-large lettering and 100 clicks per rotation; optional left or right Twist Guard windage
MSRP $3549.00

K624I

Available in: 6–24X56mm
Weight: 33.5 oz.
Length: 15.9 in.
Main Dia.: 34mm
Exit Pupil: 9.3–2.3mm
Field of View: 20–5.1 ft @ 100 yds
Twilight Factor: 18.33–36.66
Eye Relief: 3.54 in.
Features: Front focal plane; illuminated; adjustable parallax; specifically engineered for long range precision
MSRP . . . . $2499.00–$2999.00

K1050

Available in: 10–50X56mm
Weight: 31.4 oz.
Length: 16.9 in.
Main Dia.: 30mm
Exit Pupil: 15.1–5mm
Field of View: 9.5–2 ft @ 100 yds
Twilight Factor: 23.66–52.92
Eye Relief: 3.75 in.
Features: Rear focal plane; adjustable parallax; ultra-precise 1/8 MOA adjustments constructed of hardened steel
MSRP . . . . $2999.00–$3149.00

Konus

KONUS EMPIRE　　**KONUS EVENT**　　**KONUS GLORY**　　**KONUS KONUSFIRE**

EMPIRE

Available in: 3–18x50mm, 5–30x56mm
Weight: 26.8 oz., 34 oz.
Length: 14.68 in., 14.96 in.
Main Dia.: 30mm
Exit Pupil: 8–3mm, 13–2mm
Field of View: 35–6.1 ft.@100 yd., 20.9–3 ft.@100 yd.
Eye Relief: 4 in.
Features: Lockable, zero-reset turrets, dual-color illuminated reticle; locking fast-focus eyepiece; ¼-MOA clicks; level bubble; side knob has both parallax and illumination controls
MSRP . . . . $654.99–$799.99

EVENT

Available in: 1–10x24mm
Weight: 19.2 oz.
Length: 10.45 in.
Main Dia.: 30mm
Exit Pupil: 24–2.4mm
Field of View: 121.2–11.5 ft.@100 yd.
Eye Relief: 3.5–3.7 in.
Features: Removable zoom lever; lockable tactical turrets with zero reset; ½-MOA clicks; two-color illuminated reticle in a circle/dot configuration in the second focal plane; fully multi-coated lenses; fast-focus eyepiece
MSRP $654.49

GLORY

Available in: 3–24x56mm
Weight: 25.69 oz.
Length: 15 in.
Main Dia.: 30mm
Exit Pupil: 7.8–2.3mm
Field of View: 37.6–4.8 ft.@100 yd.
Eye Relief: 3.27–3.77 in.
Features: Constant long eye relief across the magnification spectrum; zero-reset locking turrets; removable zoom lever; redesigned erector system takes heavy recoil; side parallax wheel; illuminated reticle
MSRP $866.99

KONUSFIRE

Available in: 3–9x32mm
Weight: 12.6 oz.
Length: 12 in.
Main Dia.: 1 in.
Exit Pupil: 10.6–3.5mm
Field of View: 36.7–13.1 ft.@100 yd.
Eye Relief: 2.9 in.
Features: Scope for rimfire use with ¼-MOA clicks; coated optics; 30/30 reticle; .22 dovetail mounting rings included
MSRP . . . . $54.99–$79.99

OPTICS

Konus

**KONUS KONUSHOT
4X32MM**

**KONUS KONUSPRO
M-30 4.5–16X40MM**

**KONUS KONUSPRO
PLUS 3–12X50MM**

KONUSHOT
Available in: 3–9X32mm,
3–12X40mm
Weight: 12.6 oz., 11.2 oz., 13.7 oz.
Length: 12.2 in., 12.2 in., 13.3 in.
Main Dia.: 1 in.
Exit Pupil: 8mm, 10.7–3.9mm, 13.3–3.3mm
Field of View: 25.5 ft @ 100 yds,
33.54–11.56 ft @ 100 yds, 27.4–6.9 ft
@ 100 yds
Twilight Factor: 11.31, 9.8–16.97,
10.95–21.91
Eye Relief: 3.4 in., 3 in., 3 in.
Features: Shock-, water-, and fog-proof; nitrogen filled
3–9X: **$109.99**
3–12X: **$99.99**

KONUSPRO EL-30
Available in: 4–16x44mm
Weight: 23.39 oz.
Length: 13.1 in.
Obj. Dia.: 44mm

Main Dia.: 30mm
Exit Pupil: 11–2.7mm
Field of View: 22.6–9.5 ft.@100 yd.
Eye Relief: 3.3–3 in.
Features: Utilizing LCD technology,
the EL-30 features 10 interchangeable
reticles; 1/10-Mil adjustments; locking
tactical turrets
MSRP **$574.99**

KONUSPRO M-30
Available in: 1–4X24mm, 12.5–50X56mm, 6.5–25X44mm, 8.5–32X52mm
Weight: 17.6 oz., 21.1 oz., 28.9 oz.,
31.7 oz., 30.6 oz., 32.3 oz.
Length: 11.6 in., 12.8 in., 16.4 in.,
17.6 in., 18.4 in.
Main Dia.: 30mm
Exit Pupil: 12–6mm, 6.8–1.8mm, 6.1–1.6mm, 4.4–1.15mm
Field of View: 100–25 ft @ 100 yds,
17–4.5 ft @100 yds, 13–3.3 ft @ 100
yds, 9.7–2.5 ft@100 yds

Features: Engraved reticle in second
focal plane; illuminated reticle;
adjustable parallax
MSRP . . . . **$233.49–$518.99**

KONUSPRO PLUS
Available in: 6–24X50mm
Weight: 25.7 oz.
Length: 16.4 in.
Main Dia.: 1 in.
Exit Pupil: 8.3–2.1mm
Field of View: 16.2–4.45 ft @100 yds
Eye Relief: 3.4 in.
Features: engraved reticle in second
focal plane; shock-, water-, and fog-proof; nitrogen filled; illuminated
reticle
MSRP **$269.99**

Leapers, Inc.

**LEAPERS, INC. UTG
1 BUGBUSTER**

**LEAPERS, INC. UTG
CLASSIC**

UTG 1 BUGBUSTER
Available in: 3–9x32mm, 3–12x32mm
Weight: 12 oz., 12.7 oz.
Length: 7.8, 8 in.

Main Dia.: 1 in.
Exit Pupil: 10.6–3.6 in., 10.6–2.7mm,
Field of View: 36.6–21.5 ft.@100 yd.,
31–10 ft.@100 yd.
Eye Relief: 4.3–3.3 in.
Features: Compact scope with True
Strength Platform; mil-dot range-estimating reticle; resettable target turrets;
2-inch sunshade; flip-up lens caps
MSRP . . . .**$149.97–$179.97**

UTG CLASSIC
Available in: 3–12x44mm

Weight: 19.2 oz.
Length: 12.8 in.
Main Dia.: 30mm
Exit Pupil: 14.7–3.7mm
Field of View: 34–8.5 ft.@100 yd.
Eye Relief: 3.3–3 in.
Features: A utilitarian riflescope with
the wire Mil-Dot reticle in the second
focal plane; zero resetting target turrets; side parallax adjustment; 1/4-MOA clicks
MSRP **$114.97**

Leica Camera AG

LEICA AMPLUS 6

AMPLUS 6
Available in: 1–6x24mm, 2.5–15x50mm, 2.5–15x56mm

Weight: 16.9 oz., 24.7 oz., 28.7 oz.
Length: 10.7 in., 14.9 in.
Main Dia.: 30mm
Exit Pupil: 12.2–4.2mm, 11.6–3.4mm,
11.6–3.7mm
Field of View: 38–6.3m@100m,
15–2.8m@100m, 14.8–2.5m@100m
Eye Relief: 3.5 in.

Features: Leica says the 6X zoom is
ideal when shots at running game are
a probability; wide field of view and
exit pupil; extra-fine illuminated dot
L4-a reticle in the secondfocal plane;
BDC option
MSRP . . . . **$1299.00–$1599.00**

Leica Camera AG

LEICA PRS 5–30X56I

PRS 5–30X56I
Available in: 5–30x56mm
Weight: 36.3 oz.

Length: 14.37 in.
Main Dia.: 34mm
Exit Pupil: 9–2mm
Field of View: 8.2–1.3m@100m
Eye Relief: 3.5 in.
Features: Leica dives into the long-range game with a first focal plane 6X; huge elevation adjustment of 320/180 cm, 32/18 Mil (100m); illuminated dot/scale reticle; sunshade and throw lever included
MSRP................**$2699.00**

Leupold & Stevens

LEUPOLD MARK FX-3 6X42MM

LEUPOLD MARK 6 3–18X44MM

LEUPOLD MARK 5HD 3.6–18X44MM

LEUPOLD MARK 8 1.1–8X24MM CQBSS

LEUPOLD MARK 5HD 5–25X56MM

LEUPOLD MARK 6 1–6X20MM

FX-3 6X42MM
Available in: 6X
Weight: 15 oz.
Length: 12.2 in.
Main Dia.: 1 in.
Exit Pupil: 7mm
Field of View: 17.3 ft @ 100 yds
Twilight Factor: 15.87
Eye Relief: 4.4 in.
Features: Fixed-power riflescope; Twilight Light Management System; rear focal plane Wide Duplex reticle; ¼-MOA clicks
MSRP..................**$449.99**

MARK 5HD 3.6–18X44MM
Available in: 3.6–18x44mm
Weight: 26 oz.
Length: 12.6 in.
Main Dia.: 35mm
Exit Pupil: 2.4mm
Field of View: 28.4–5.8 ft.@100 yd.
Eye Relief: 3.54–3.82 in.
Features: Lighter than comparable scopes; 1/10-MIL click adjustments; side-focus parallax adjustment; choice of Horus H59, front focal Tremor 3, TMR illuminated, or TMR reticles; three full rotations of elevation adjustment; quick-throw lever
MSRP........ **$1899.99–$2699.99**

MARK 5HD 5–25X56MM
Available in: 5–25x56mm

Weight: 30 oz.
Length: 15.67 in.
Main Dia.: 35mm
Exit Pupil: 2.2mm
Field of View: 20.5–4.2 ft.@100 yd.
Eye Relief: 3.58–3.82 in.
Features: Reticle choices include front focal TMR, first focal plane CCH, H-59, front focal Tremor 3, TMR illuminated, front focal Tremor 3 illuminated, and front focal TMR
MSRP........ **$2099.99–$2899.99**

MARK 6 1–6X20MM
Available in: 1–6X20mm
Weight: 17 oz.
Length: 10.3 in.
Main Dia.: 1.34 in.
Exit Pupil: 10.2–3.3mm
Field of View: 103.2–17.4 ft @ 100 yds
Twilight Factor: 4.5–11
Eye Relief: 3.7 in.
Features: Scratch-resistant lenses; Twilight Max HD Light Management System; dial illumination control; side-focus; M5C2 elevation control dial; 1/10 Mil click adjustments; first focal plane reticles available in CMR-W 7.62, CMR-W 5.56, or TMR-D reticles, all illuminated
MSRP..................**$2199.99**

MARK 6 3–18X44MM
Available in: 3–18X44mm
Weight: 23.6 oz.

Length: 11.9 in.
Main Dia.: 1.34 in.
Exit Pupil: 10.3–2.4mm
Field of View: 36.8–6.3 ft @ 100 yds
Twilight Factor: 11.5–28.1
Eye Relief: 3.8–3.9 in.
Features: Scratch-resistant lenses; Twilight Max HD Light Management System; dial illumination control; side-focus; M5C2 elevation control dial; 1/10 Mil click adjustments; first focal plane reticles available in TMR (Mk), Tremor 2, and Tremor 3 configurations, all either illuminated and non-illuminated, as well as a non-illuminated H-59 reticle
MSRP........ **$2199.99–$4399.99**

MARK 8 1.1–8X24MM CQBSS
Available in: 1.1–8X24mm
Weight: 23.2 oz.
Length: 11.75 in.
Eye Relief: 3.3–3.7 in.
Field of View: 14.7–92 ft @ 100 yds
Features: Scratch-resistant lenses; Twilight Max HD Light Management System; dial illumination control; easy grip power selector; M5B1 windage/elevation control; bullet drop compensation; 1/10 Mil click adjustments; first focal plane reticles available in H-27D, M-TMR, Mil-Dot, and CMR-W 7.62 designs, all illuminated
MSRP........ **$2999.99–$3799.99**

OPTICS

Leupold & Stevens

LEUPOLD MARK 8 3.5–25X56MM

LEUPOLD & STEVENS VX-3HD

LEUPOLD & STEVENS VX-4.5HD SERVICE RIFLE 1–4.5X24MM

LEUPOLD VX-6HD

LEUPOLD VX-FREEDOM

LEUPOLD VX-FREEDOM MUZZLELOADER ULTIMATESLAM

LEUPOLD VX-FREEDOM RIMFIRE

MARK 8 3.5–25X56MM
Available in: 3.5–25X56mm
Weight: 37 oz.
Length: 16 in.
Eye Relief: 3.3–3.7 in.
Field of View: 4.4–32.5 ft @ 100 yds
Features: Scratch-resistant lenses; Twilight Max HD Light Management System; dial illumination control; easy grip power selector; M5B2 windage/elevation control; bullet drop compensation; 1/10 Mil click adjustments; first focal plane reticles available in Tremor 2, Tremor 3, and TMR (Mk), all illuminated, plus the non-illuminated Horus H-59
MSRP . . . . $2999.99–$4699.99

VX-3HD
Available in: 1.5–5x20mm, 2.5–8x36mm, 3.5–10x40mm, 3.5–10x50mm, 4.5–14x40mm, 4.5–14x50mm
Weight: 9.7 oz.–16.9 oz.
Length: N/A
Main Dia.: 1 in., 30mm
Exit Pupil: N/A
Field of View: 19.9–7.4 ft.@100 yd., 37.5–13.7 ft.@100 yd., 29–11 ft.@100 yd., 29.7–11 ft.@100 yd., 19.9–7.4 ft.@100 yd., 20.5–7.6 ft.@100 yd.
Eye Relief: 3.6–4.4 in.
Features: CDS ZeroLock dial; Guard-Ion lens coating; Elite Optical System; removable throw lever; scratch-resistant lenses; second focal plane CDS-ZL Duplex reticle available in all models, CDS-ZL Boone & Crockett available in 4.5–14x40, and CDS-ZL Wind-Plex available in 4.5–14x40 Side Focus
MSRP . . . . $499.99–$799.99

VX-4.5HD SERVICE RIFLE 1–4.5X24MM
Available in: 1–4.5x24mm
Weight: 13.4 oz.
Length: 10.76 in.
Main Dia.: 30mm
Field of View: 123.2–26.2 ft.@100 yd.
Eye Relief: 3.82–3.7 in.
Features: As the name implies, this is one for Service Rifle matches and features true 1X magnification; Bull-Ring Post Reticle in the second focal plane and available with FireDot illumination; Guard-Ion lens coating
Standard reticle: $1399.99
Firedot reticle: $1499.99

VX-6HD
Available in: 1–6X24mm, 2–12X42mm, 3–18X44mm, 3–18X50mm, 4–24X52mm
Weight: 13.4 oz.–23.4 oz.
Length: 11.2 in.–14.6 in.
Eye Relief: Varies with model
Field of View: Varies with model
Features: Twilight Max Light Management System; CDS-ZL2 dial locks; electronic level; fast-change magnification throw lever; flip-up lens covers; Zero Lock windage adjusment; reversible throw lever for quick-change magnification; Guard Ion lens coating; push-button illumination with power-off motion sensing technology; second generation argon/krypton waterproofing; 2–12X and 3–18X available in Sitka Subalpine camo
MSRP . . . . $1499.99–$2299.99

VX-FREEDOM
Available in: 3–9x40mm, 2–7x33mm, 1.5–4x20mm, 1.5–4x28mm, 3-9x50mm, 4–12x40mm, 4–12x50mm, 3–9x40, 3–9x33mm, 6–18x40mm
Weight: 9.6 oz.–17 oz.
Length: 9.3 in.–14.61 in.
Main Dia.: 1 in.
Exit Pupil: Varies with model
Field of View: Varies with model
Eye Relief: Varies with model
Features: Twilight Light Management System; aluminum tubes; scratch-resistant lenses; ¼-MOA finger clicks; rear focal plane reticles. Multiple features and variations across the line, including Leupold's CDS (Custom Dial System), Fire Dot illumination technology, a wide range of reticle choices, a Scout model in 1.5–4x28mm, a 3–9x33mm with an EFR (Extended Focal Ring), a 3–9x40mm calibrated for the .450 Bushmaster and another for the .350 Legend
MSRP . . . . $299.99–$499.99

VX-FREEDOM MUZZLELOADER ULTIMATESLAM
Available in: 3–9x40mm
Weight: 12.2 oz.
Length: 12.39 in.
Main Dia.: 1 in.
Field of View: 33.7–13.6 ft.@100 yd.
Eye Relief: 4.17
Features: Designed for muzzleloader pressures; houses an Ultimateslam reticle
MSRP $299.99

VX-FREEDOM RIMFIRE
Available in: 2–7x33mm, 3–9x40mm
Weight: 11.1 oz. (2–7x), 12.2 oz. (3–9x)
Length: 11.04 in. (2–7x), 12.39 in (3–9x)
Main Dia.: 1 in.
Exit Pupil: 5mm (2–7x), 4.7mm (3–9x)
Field of View: 43.8–17.8 ft.@100 yd. (2–7x), 33.7–13.6 ft.@100 yd. (3–9x)
Eye Relief: 4.17–3.7 in. (2–7x), 4.17–3.66 in. (3–9x)
Features: Rimfire MOA reticle; Twilight Light Management System; scratch-resistant lenses
MSRP $299.99

Lucid Optics, LLC

LUCID OPTICS L5 4-16X44MM RIFLE SCOPE

LUCID OPTICS L5 6-24X50 RIFLE SCOPE

LUCID OPTICS L7 1–6X24MM

LUCID OPTICS MLX RIFLE SCOPE

L5 4-16X44MM RIFLE SCOPE

Available in: 4–16X44mm
Weight: 18 oz.
Length: 13.25 in.
Main Dia.: 34mm
Exit Pupil: 11–3mm
Field of View: 25.5–8.5 ft @ 100 yds
Twilight Factor: 13.27–8
Eye Relief: 4.25 in.–3.25 in.
Features: Shock-, water-, and fog-proof; adjustable parallax; etched-glass reticle
MSRP $679.99

L5 6-24X50 RIFLE SCOPE

Available in: 6–24X50mm
Weight: 24.5 oz.
Length: 15.5 in.
Main Dia.: 30mm

Exit Pupil: 8.3–2mm
Field of View: 16.5–4.3 ft @ 100 yds
Twilight Factor: 17.32–34.64
Eye Relief: 4.25–3.25 in.
Features: Sniper-style rifle scope with the new L5 reticle; multi-coated lenses; ⅛ MOA turret click value; water-, fog-, and shockproof; matte black finish; available in STRELOK
MSRP $689.99

L7 1–6X24MM

Available in: 1–6x24mm
Weight: 20.40 oz.
Length: 10.75 in.
Main Dia.: 30mm
Exit Pupil: 15–4mm
Field of View: 56–20 ft @ 100 yds
Eye Relief: 3.75–4 in.
Features: Edge-to-edge sharp, crisp

image resolution through the entire magnification range; Lucid blue reticle illumination; windage and elevation turrets offer 60MOA either side of optical center; selectable magnification lever for fast changes to the zoom function
MSRP $659.99

MLX RIFLE SCOPE

Available in: 4.5–18X44mm
Weight: 26 oz.
Length: 13.89 in.
Exit Pupil: 2.4–11mm
Eye Relief: 3.1–3.6 in.
Field of View: 8.5–25 ft @ 100 yds
Features: First focal plane scope; one-piece 6063 aluminum 30mm tube; Mil-based reticle; side parallax adjustment; 1/10 Mil tactile and audible click adjustments
MSRP $879.99

March Scopes/Deon Optical Design Corp.

MARCH SCOPES 5–42X56 MARCH FX WIDE ANGLE

MARCH SCOPES MARCH 1.5–15X42MM SFF

MARCH SCOPES 4-40X52 GENESIS HIGH MASTER WIDE ANGLE FFP

GENESIS HIGH MASTER WIDE ANGLE FFP 4–40X52MM

Available in: 4-40x52mm
Weight: 45.2 oz.
Length: 13 in.
Main Dia.: 34mm
Features: Designed for ultra long-

range applications (up to three miles); 10X zoom ratio; 86 MRAD elevation with .05-MRAD clicks; side focus 20m to infinity; tactical windage dial; Genesis body system tube adjusts on a horizontal/vertical pivot via a gimbled system with return springs keeping the guts tight against the turrets
MSRP $5225.00

MARCH 1.5–15X42MM SFF

Available in: 1.5–15x42mm
Weight: 22 oz.
Length: 10.6 in.
Main Dia.: 30mm
Exit Pupil: 8.7–2.8mm
Field of View: 23.4–2.3m@100m
Eye Relief: 2.9–3.8 in.

Features: 10X zoom with a generous light-gathering objective; choice of MTR-3, MTR-4, or MTR-5 illuminated reticles in the second focal plane; ¼-MOA clicks; zero-reset turrets; fast-focus eyepiece; waterproof to 4 meters; designed for NRA's mid-range tactical rifle competitions
MSRP . . . . $2451.00–$2498.50

MARCH-F 1–10X24MM SHORTY FFP

Available in: 1–10x24mm
Weight: 17.8 oz.
Length: 8.4 in.
Main Dia.: 30mm
Exit Pupil: 8.6–2.4mm
Field of View: 34–3.4m@100m
Eye Relief: 2.8–4 in.
Features: .1-Mil clicks; six illumination levels; capped tactical turrets; dual-reticle--both first and second focal plane reticles put together to produce the visible pattern; fast-focus eyepiece
MSRP $2992.50

March Scopes/Deon Optical Design Corp.

MARCH SCOPES MARCH-F 1–10X24MM SHORTY FFP

MARCH SCOPES MARCH-FX 4.5–28X52MM FFP WIDE ANGLE

MARCH-FX 4.5–28X52MM FFP WIDE ANGLE

Available in: 4.5–28x52mm
Weight: 28.7 oz.–29.8 oz.
Length: 12.5 in.
Main Dia.: 34mm
Exit Pupil: 1.9mm
Field of View: 9.7–1.56m@100m
Eye Relief: 3.5–2.7 in.
Features: Super ED lenses with Anti-Temperature Drift lets the lens system naturally adapt to temperature change and maintain focus for the user; 25° wide-angle ocular; illuminated first focal plane reticles include FML-TR1 and FML-3 with six illumination levels; non-illuminated first focal plane reticles include FML-PDK and FML-LDK; throw lever; middle focus wheel; .1-Mil clicks

MSRP . . . . $3125.50–$3410.50

MARCH-FX WIDE ANGLE 5–42X56MM

Available in: 5–42x56mm
Weight: 33.5 oz.
Length: 14.1 in.
Main Dia.: 34mm
Features: A premium competition model with a 26-degree wide-angle ocular lens with a fast-focus diopter; temperature tolerant anti-drift objective; turret-locking system with zero-set elevation; side focus; six illumination settings

MSRP $3900.00

Meopta USA

MEOPTA MEOSTAR R1 RD

MEOPTA MEOSTAR R2 1–6X24MM

MEOPTA USA OPTIKA6 FFP

MEOPTA USA OPTIKA6 SFP

MEOSTAR R1 SERIES

Available in: 1–4X22MM, 1.5–6X42MM, 3–10X50MM, 3–12X56MM, 4–12X40MM, 4–16X44MM, 7X
Weight: 18.87 oz., 20.6 oz., 15.87 oz., 21.87 oz., 18.27 oz., 24.16 oz.
Length: 12.09 in., 13.54 in., 13.03 in., 14.37 in., 12.91 in., 15.16 in.
Main Dia.: 30mm, 25.4mm
Exit Pupil: 13.5–5.5mm, 14.8–7mm, 16.7–5mm, 14.8–4.6mm, 10–3.3mm, 11–2.8mm, 8mm
Field of View: 117.78–28.22 ft @ 100 yds, 73.49–22.31 ft @ 100 yds, 43.64–13.12 ft @ 100 yds, 36–11.15 ft @ 100 yds, 33.14–11.15 ft @ 100 yds, 16–4.46 ft @ 100 yds, 17.4 ft @ 100 yds
Twilight Factor: 4.69–9.38, 7.94–15.88, 12.25–22.36, 12.96–25.92, 12.65–21.91, 13.27–26.53, 19.8
Eye Relief: 3.31–3.47 in., 3.23–3.74 in., 3.15–3.23 in., 3.03–3.27 in., 3.58–3.15 in., 3.94–3.15 in., 3.3 in.
Features: Features MeoTrak II™ posi-click turret adjustments, nitrogen-purged tube, ion-assisted MeoBright and MeoShield lens coatings, MeoQuick fast focus; second focal plane models some with illuminated reticles

MSRP . . . . $1299.99–$1399.99

MEOSTAR R2 SERIES

Available in: 1–6X24mm, 1.7–10X42mm, 2–12X50mm, 2.5–15X56mm, 8X56mm
Weight: 17.64 oz., 20.32 oz., 21.02 oz., 22.93 oz.
Length: 11.69 in. 3.31–3.47 in., 3.23–3.74 in., 3.15–3.23 in., 3.03–3.27 in., 3.58–3.15 in., 3.94–3.15 in.
Main Dia.: 30mm
Exit Pupil: varies with model
Field of View: varies with model
Twilight Factor: varies with model
Eye Relief: 3.54 in.
Features: Water- and fogproof; MeoLux ion-assisted multi-coatings for 99.8 percent light transmission; MeoQuick fast focus adsjutment; MeoClick tactile turret adjustments; MeoTrack windage and elevation controls; second focal plane illuminated reticles in 4C, 4K, BDC-2, and BDC-3 configurations

MSRP . . . . $1599.99–$2199.99

OPTIKA6 FFP

Available in: 1–6x24mm, 3–18x50mm, 3–18x56mm, 4.5–27x50mm, 5–30x56mm
Weight: 20.4 oz.–36.7 oz.
Length: 10.07 in.–15.44 in.
Main Dia.: 30mm, 34mm
Exit Pupil: 10–4mm, 9.5–2.8mm, 9.5–3.1mm, 9.5–1.9mm
Field of View: 109.5–18.9 ft.@100 yd., 33.6–5.7 ft.@100 yd., 33.3–5.7 ft.@100 yd., 21.9–3.6 ft.@100 yd., 24.6–3.6 ft.@100 yd.
Eye Relief: 3.94 in.
Features: First focal plane; parallax correction on all but 1–6X

MSRP $1099.99

OPTIKA6 SFP

Available in: 1–6x24mm, 2.5–14x44mm, 3–18x50mm, 3–18x56mm, 4.5–27x50mm
Weight: 20.4 oz.–31.1 oz.
Length: 10.07 in.–14.21 in.
Main Dia.: 30mm
Exit Pupil: 10–4mm, 11–2.9mm, 9.5–2.8mm, 9.5–3.1mm, 9.5–1.9mm
Field of View: 109.5–19.9 ft.@100 yd., 39.9–6.9 ft.@100 yd., 33.6–5.7 ft.@100 yd., 33.3–5.7 ft.@100 yd., 21.9–3.6 ft.@100 yd.
Eye Relief: 3.94 in.
Features: Similar to the FFP line, but all with 30mm tubes and second focal plane design

MSRP . . . .$599.99–$799.99

OPTICS

Minox

**MINOX
5–25X56MM LR**

LONG-RANGE 5–25X56MM

Available in: 5–25x56mm
Weight: N/A
Length: 16.6 in.
Main Dia.: 34mm
Exit Pupil: 10.6–2.3mm
Field of View: 7.2–1.6m@100m

Eye Relief: 3.5 in.
Features: This is a big scope for long-range applications (thus the LR in the model name); M* multicoating; first focal plane LR illuminated reticle with 11 settings; IPX7 waterproof
MSRP $1896.94

Nightforce Optics, Inc.

**NIGHTFORCE OPTICS ATACR
7–35X56 F2**

**NIGHTFORCE OPTICS
ATACR (ADVANCED
TACTICAL RIFLESCOPE)
1-8X24 F1**

**NIGHTFORCE OPTICS
NXS 5.5–22X50MM**

**NIGHTFORCE OPTICS
ATACR F1 SERIES**

**NIGHTFORCE OPTICS
PRECISION BENCHREST
8–32X56MM**

ATACR F1 SERIES

Available in: 1–8X24mm, 4–16X42mm, 4–16X50mm, 4–20X50mm, 5–25X56mm, 7–35X56mm
Weight: 21, 30, 38 oz.
Length: 10.6, 12.6 in., 15.37 in.
Main Dia.: 30, 34mm
Exit Pupil: 11.2–3.9mm, 10.3–2.7mm, 8.3–2.3mm,
6–1.6mm
Field of View: 96.1–13.1 ft.@100 yds, 26.9–6.9 ft @ 100 yds, 18.7–4.92 ft @ 100 yds, 14.97–3.44 ft
@ 100 yards
Eye Relief: 3.74 in., 3.35–3.54 in., 3.26–3.58 in.
Features: Front focal plane; multicoated lenses; eyepiece features enhanced engraving, an integrated Power Throw Lever (PTL) and an XtremeSpeed thread for making a fast diopter adjustment; adjustments are standard with the patented Nightforce Hi-Speed ZeroStop, and available in .1 Mrad (12 Mils per revolution) or .25 MOA (30 MOA per revolution) Increments. Available reticles as follows: 1–8X first focal plane FC-DM; 4-16X and 5-25X Horus H59 illuminated, Horus Tremor3 illuminated, Mil-C, Mil-R, Mil-XT, MOAR; 7–35X Horus Tremor3 illuminated, Mil-C, Mil-R, MOAR
1–8X: $2800.00
4-16X: . . . . $2400.00–$2750.00
5-25X: . . . . $2700.00–$3350.00
7-35X: . . . . $3600.00–$3850.00

ATACR 7–35X56 F2

Available in: 7–35x56mm
Weight: 39.3 oz.
Length: 16 in.
Main Dia.: 34mm
Exit Pupil: 6mm (7X), 1.6mm (35X)
Field of View: 97–3.44 ft.@100 yd.
Eye Relief: 3.5 in.
Features: ED glass; 100 MOA total click travel; side parallax adjustment 11 yards to infinity; two-piece locking eyepiece adaptor; power-throw lever; Zero-Stop elevation adjustment; three 30 MOA or 12 MRAD rotation built-in quick-dial options; choice of MOAR-T or MIL-C reticles; second focal plane optics
MSRP $3100.00

NX8 1-8X24 F1

Available in: 1-8x24mm
Weight: 17 oz.
Length: 8.75 in.
Main Dia.: 30mm
Exit Pupil: 7.9mm@1x–3.0mm@8x
Field of View: 106 ft.@100 yd.–13.2 ft. @100 yd.
Eye Relief: 3.75 in.
Features: Illuminated daytime reticle with multiple brightness levels; Power Throw Lever that permits fast magnification changes; first focal plane reticle
MSRP $2326.00

NXS 5.5–22X50MM

Available in: 5.5–22X50mm
Weight: 31 oz.

Length: 15.1 in.
Main Dia.: 30mm
Exit Pupil: 9.1–2.3mm
Field of View: 17.5–4.7 ft @ 100 yds
Twilight Factor: 16.58–33.16
Eye Relief: 3.8 in.
Features: Originally developed for the U.S. military's extreme long range shooting and hard target interdiction; 100 MOA of elevation travel make it ideal for use on the .50 BMG, allowing accurate shots to 2000 yards and beyond; slim profile, easily adaptable to a wide range of mounting systems
MSRP . . . . $1800.00–$2028.00

NXS 5.5–22X56MM

Available in: 5.5–22X56mm
Weight: 32 oz.
Length: 15.2 in.
Main Dia.: 30mm
Exit Pupil: 10.2–2.5mm
Field of View: 17.5–4.7 ft @ 100 yds
Twilight Factor: 17.54–35.09
Eye Relief: 3.9 in. *Fe*atures: Advanced field tactical riflescope for long-range applications; maximum clarity and resolution across the entire magnification range, exceptional low-light performance; available with ZeroStop technology and 1/8 and . MOA or .1 Mil-Radian adjustments; available with MOAR, MOAR-T, MIL-R, or MIL-DOT reticles
MSRP . . . . $1800.00–$2090.00

OPTICS

Nightforce Optics, Inc.

NIGHTFORCE OPTICS NXS 8–32X56MM

NIGHTFORCE OPTICS NXS 5.5–22X56MM

NIGHTFORCE OPTICS SHOOTER HUNTER VARMINTER (SHV) 4–14X56MM

NXS 8–32X56MM

Available in: 8–32X56mm
Weight: 34 oz.
Length: 15.9 in.
Main Dia.: 30mm
Exit Pupil: 7–1.8mm
Field of View: 12.1–3.1 ft @ 100 yds
Twilight Factor: 21.16–42.33
Eye Relief: 3.8 in.
Features: For long-range hunting, competition, and target shooting; choice of five different reticles for the shooter's chosen application; offered with .125 MOA, .250 MOA or .1 Mil-Radian Hi-Speed adjustments; equipped with ZeroStop; second focal plane reticles available in MOAR, MOAR-T, NP-2DD, MIL-R, or MIL-DOT, all with analog illumination
MSRP . . . . $1900.00–$2190.00

PRECISION BENCHREST 8–32X56MM, 12-42X56MM

Available in: 8–32X56mm, 12–42X56mm

Weight: 36 oz.
Length: 16.6 in.
Main Dia.: 30mm
Exit Pupil: 5.6–1.7mm, 4–1.4mm
Field of View: 9.4–3.1 ft @ 100 yds, 6.7–2.3 ft. @ 100 yds
Twilight Factor: 21.16–42.33
Eye Relief: 2.9 in.
Features: Superior resolution; adjustable objective; parallax adjustment from 25 yards to infinity; target adjustments calibrated in 1/8 click) MOA values, and can be re-indexed to zero after sighting in; eyepiece allows for fast reticle focusing; second plane reticles in a choice of NP-R2 or NP-2DD configurations with analog illumination
8-32X: $1326.00
12-42X: $1473.00

SHOOTER HUNTER VARMINTER (SHV) SERIES

Available in: 3–10X42mm, 4–14X56mm, 5–20X56mm

Weight: 20.8 oz., 26.9 oz., 29.1 oz.
Length: 11.6 in., 14.8 in., 15.2 in.
Main Dia.: 30mm
Exit Pupil: 10.7–4.4mm, 12–3.6mm, 8.7–2.5mm
Field of View: 34.9–11 ft @ 100 yds, 24.9–7.3 ft @ 100 yds, 17.9–5 ft @ 100 yds
Twilight Factor: 11.22–20.49, 14.97–28, 16.73–33.47
Eye Relief: 3.5 in., 3.15–3.54 in., 3.15–3.54 in.
Features: European-style fast-focus eyepiece, side parallax adjustment, capped .25-MOA adjustments, and multiple reticle choices, including illuminated options, at a consumer-friendly price point.
3–10X: $985.00
4–14x56mm: . . . . . $995.00–$1290.00
5–20X: . . . . $1195.00–$1345.00

Nikko Stirling

NIKKO STIRLING DIAMOND FFP

NIKKO STIRLING DIAMOND LONG RANGE

DIAMOND FFP

Available in: 4–16X44mm, 6–24X50mm
Weight: 24.2 oz.–24 oz.
Length: 13 in.–14.2 in.
Eye Relief: 3.9 in., 3.5 in.
Field of View: Varies with model
Features: First focal plane (FFP) optics allow for range-finding shot corrections via reticle; 30mm main body

tube; glass-etched illuminated skeleton HMD or PRR reticles; fully multi-coated lenses; parallax turret houses illumination
MSRP . . . . starting at $379.00

DIAMOND LONG RANGE

Available in: 4–16X50mm, 6–24x50mm, 10-40x56m
Weight: 16.5 oz.

Length: 14.2 in.
Power: 4–16X, 6–24X, 10-40X
Main Dia.: 30mm
Field of View: 32.1–8 ft @ 100 yds, 21.4–5.4 ft @ 100 yds, 10.5–2.6 ft.@100 yds
Eye Relief: 4.5 in.
Features: Fully multi-coated lens; Zerostop turrets; dual-color red/green illumination settings; 4–16X features LR HMD reticle, 6–24X houses LR Hold Fast reticle
MSRP . . . . starting at $229.00

Primary Arms

PRIMARY ARMS SLX 1–8X24MM FFP

SLX 1–8X24MM FFP

Available in: 1–8x24mm
Weight: 17.9 oz.

Main Dia.: 30mm
Exit Pupil: 9–3mm
Field of View: 105–4.3 ft.@100 yd.
Eye Relief: 3.3–3.2 in.
Features: A first focal plane compact 8X with illuminated ACSS Raptor 5.56

reticle; capped, low-profile, finger-adjustable turrets; moveable and replaceable magnification ring fin; fully multi-coated lenses; 1/4-MOA clicks
MSRP $479.99

Primary Arms

**PRIMARY ARMS SLX
2.5 COMPACT PRISM**

**PRIMARY ARMS SLX
4–16X44MM**

SLX 2.5 COMPACT PRISM

Available in: 2.5x32mm
Weight: 14.9 oz.
Main Dia.: 30mm
Exit Pupil: 10.16mm
Field of View: 37.5 ft.@100 yd.
Eye Relief: 2.7 in.
Features: A workhorse CQB scope with an illuminated ACSS CQB-M1 reticle that has BDC ranging to 600 yards with .223/.308 applications; prism construction; Type II hardcoat anodized finish; ½-MOA clicks; optional Picatinny rail for red-dot piggybacking
MSRP. $249.99

SLX 4–14X44MM

Available in: SLX 4–14X44mm
Weight: 25.4 oz.
Length: 14.3 in.
Main Dia.: 30mm
Exit Pupil: 11.2–3.3mm
Field of View: 27.2–7.85 ft.@100 yd.
Eye Relief: 3.22–3.14 in.
Features: HUD-308, RGRID, ARC-2-MOA, and Apollo illuminated reticles to choose from; first focal plane; side-adjustable parallax; fast-focus eyepiece
MSRP. . . . . $279.99–$299.99

PULSAR (Yukon Advanced Optics Worldwide)

**PULSAR
DIGISIGHT
ULTRA LRF
N450, N455**

**PULSAR THERMION
XM30**

**PULSAR TRAIL 2
LRF XP50, XQ50**

DIGISIGHT ULTRA LRF N450, N455

Available in: 4.5–18X
Weight: 38.8 oz.
Length: 14.56 in.
Obj. Dia.: N/A
Main Dia.: N/A
Exit Pupil: N/A
Field of View: N/A
Eye Relief: 1.96 in.

Features: Thermal imaging riflescope with 10 reticle shapes and 6 color choices; scalable ballistic reticles; zoom zeroing; 5 shooting profiles and 50 distance savings; can utilize the Stream Vision app for iOS and Android; extreme operating conditions from -25ºC to +50ºC; side incline and elevation angle sensor; long-range 850nm infrared illuminator wavelength for improved nighttime sensitivity on N450 model with a detection range of 550m; N455 has 940nm invisible infrared illumination wavelength with 500m detection; picture-in-picture; IPX7 waterproof; wide-angle eyepiece; Weaver rail mount; integrated video recorder
MSRP. $1500.00

THERMION XM30

Available in: 3.5–14x25mm
Weight: 26.5 oz.
Length: 15.2 in.
Main Dia.: N/A
Exit Pupil: N/A
Field of View: 45.9 ft.@100 yd.
Eye Relief: 2 in.
Features: Thermal imaging riflescope with 320x420 resolution; 1,400-yd. detection range; 8X digital zoom; picture-in-picture zoom; built-in recording with sound; one-shot

zeroing with freeze function; 13 reticles; choice of identification modes; choice of viewing modes, including color; five hours of battery life; holds five rifle profiles and 50 zero points; stadiametric rangefinder

MSRP. $2299.97

TRAIL 2 LRF XP50, XQ50

Available in: 2–16X, 3.5–14X
Weight: 28.21 oz.
Length: 13.6 in.
Obj. Dia.: N/A
Main Dia.: N/A
Exit Pupil: N/A
Field of View: N/A
Eye Relief: 1.96 in.
Features: A thermal imaging riflescope with a wide-angle six-lens eyepiece; AMOLED display; photo and video recorder with 16GB internal memory; 1,800m detection range; eight reticles customizable for color and scalable ballistic style; .03-second instant startup; recoil-rated up to .375 H&H/12-ga./9.3X64; stores five zeroing profiles; picture in picture display; Wi-Fi Stream Vision connectivity with iOS and Android smart devices; IPX7 waterproof; integrated laser rangefinder
XP50:. $5999.97
XQ50:. $4229.97

OPTICS

Riton Optics

RITON OPTICS CONQUER SERIES

RITON OPTICS TACTIX SERIES

RITON OPTICS PATRIOPTIC

RITON OPTICS PRIMAL SERIES

CONQUER SERIES
Available in: 3–15x44mm, 3–18x50mm, 3–24x50mm, 3–24x56mm, 4–32x56mm, 5–25x50mm, 6–24x50mm
Weight: 24 oz.–37 oz.
Length: 12.62 in.–15.37 in.
Main Dia.: 30mm, 34mm
Exit Pupil: 14.7–2.9mm, 7.5–2.9mm, 6.6–2.2mm, 7–1.6mm, 10.2–2.2mm, 8.2–2.1mm
Field of View: 38.3–7.6 ft.@100 yd., 35–6.2 ft.@100 yd., 35–6.4 ft.@100 yd., 27–3.4 ft.@100 yd., 22.5–4.5 ft.@100 yd., 16.8–4.4 ft.@100 yd.
Eye Relief: 3.7 in., 3.4 in., 3.5 in., 3.5 in., 3.7 in., 3.9 in.
Features: This series of scopes vary in features, but all have removable throw levers, HD glass, fast focus eyepieces
MSRP . . . . $389.00–$2299.99

PATRIOPTIC
Available in: 1–8x28mm
Weight: 25 oz.
Length: 10.9 in.
Main Dia.: 34mm
Exit Pupil: 7.5–2.9mm
Field of View: 105.8–13.1 ft@100 yd.
Eye Relief: 3.5 in.
Features: An impressive field of view is complemented by zero-reset capped turrets; 175 MOA of adjustment; fully multi-coated, full wide-band and waterproof coatings; removable throw lever; first focal plane illuminated CM1 reticle in daylight green; fast-focus eyepiece
MSRP $1776.00

PRIMAL SERIES
Available in: 1–8x28mm, 3–9x40mm, 3–15x 44, 3–18x44, 4–16x44mm
Weight: 22 oz.–27 oz.
Length: 10.75 in.–13.37 in.
Power: 1–8X, 3–9X, 3–15X, 3–18X, 4–16X

Obj. Dia.: 28mm, 40mm, 44mm
Main Dia.: 1 in., 30mm, 34mm
Exit Pupil: 7.5–2.9mm, 10.6–3.5mm, 14.7–2.9mm, 8.2–2.8mm, 11–2.8mm
Field of View: 105.8–13.1 ft.@100 yd., 41–13 ft.@100 yd., 38.3–7.6 ft.@100 yd., 35–6.2 ft.@100 yd., 24.1–6.3 ft.@100 yd.
Eye Relief: 3.4 in., 3.9 in.
Features: The scopes in this series vary widely in features
MSRP . . . . $249.99–$1299.99

TACTIX SERIES
Available in: 1–6x24mm, 1–8x24mm, 1–8x28mm
Weight: 19.3 oz.–25 oz.
Length: 10.25 in.–10.9 in.
Main Dia.: 30mm
Exit Pupil: 8.5–4mm, 7.5–3mm, 7.5–2.9mm
Field of View: 111.2–18.33 ft.@100 yd., 105.8–13.1 ft.@100 yd.
Eye Relief: 3.5 in.
Features: Features in this series vary
MSRP . . . . $599.99–$1299.99

Schmidt & Bender

SCHMIDT & BENDER EXOS

SCHMIDT & BENDER PM II HIGH POWER

SCHMIDT & BENDER PM II ULTRA BRIGHT

EXOS
Available in: 3–21x50mm
Weight: 32.6 oz.
Length: 13.4 in.
Main Dia.: 34mm
Exit Pupil: 11.4–2.5mm
Field of View: 13–1.9m@100m
Eye Relief: 3.5 in.
Features: Features an illuminated second focal plane D7 reticle with 11 settings and auto shutoff; locking elevation turret; Minimum Deviation System
MSRP . . . . $3299.99–$3999.99

PM II HIGH POWER
Available in: 5–45x56mm
Weight: 39.03 oz.
Length: 17 in.
Main Dia.: 34mm
Exit Pupil: 8.8–1.2mm
Field of View: 7.8–.9m@100m
Twilight Factor: 16.7–50.2
Eye Relief: 3.54 in.
Features: Developed via a U.S. SOCOM request for a scope to cover extreme distances; reticles available include TReMoR2, H58, MSR, Police, P3L, H2CMR, H37, P4L, Klein, and P4LF
MSRP . . . . $5499.99–$6599.00

PM II ULTRA BRIGHT
Available in: 3–12x54mm, 4–16x56mm
Weight: 32.52 oz. (3–12x), 33.79 oz. (4–16x)
Length: 13.8 in. (3–12x), 15.2 in. (4–16x)
Main Dia.: 34mm
Exit Pupil: 12–4.5mm (3–12x), 12–3.5mm (4–16x)
Field of View: 12.5–3.1m@100m (3–12x), 9.4–2.3m@100m (4–16x)
Twilight Factor: 12.7–25.5 (3–12x), 15–29.9 (4–16x)
Eye Relief: 3.54 in.
Features: More than 96 percent light transmission; "reverse" design is rounder and sports flattened turrets; reticle choices include TReMoR3, P3L, and P4LF; other reticles can be installed at request
MSRP . . . . $3799.99–$4899.99

Schmidt & Bender

SCHMIDT & BENDER POLAR T96

POLAR T96
Available in: 3–12x54mm, 4–16x56mm, 2.5–10x50mm

Weight: 23.92–28.57 oz.
Length: 13 in., 14 in.
Main Dia.: 34mm
Exit Pupil: 12–4.5mm (3-12x), 12–3.5mm (4–16x), 12–5mm (2.5–10x)
Field of View: 12.5–3.1m@100m, 9.4–3m@100m, 15–3.75m
Eye Relief: 3.54 in.

Features: Model is named based on its 96 percent light transmission; dusk-proof reticles; choice of reticle in the first or second focal plane; reticle choices include L7, L4, D7, and D4
MSRP . . . . **$2599.99–$3699.99**

Sightmark (Sellmark Corporation)

SIGHTMARK CORE HX 3–9X40 VHR

SIGHTMARK WRAITHE 4K MAX 3–24X50MM

SIGHTMARK WRAITHE HD 2–16X28MM

CORE HX 3–9X40 VHR
Available in: 3–9x40mm
Weight: 14.2 oz.
Length: 12.26 in.
Main Dia.: 1 in.
Exit Pupil: 13.3–4.4mm
Field of View: 11.8–4.07m@100m

Eye Relief: 4–3.7mm
Features: VHR stands for Venison Hunter Riflescope; rangefinding BDC reticle in the second focal plane; resettable capped turrets; hard anodized finish; 70 MOA of adjustment; also available with a .350 Legend 150-gr. BDC reticle or .450 Bushmaster 250-gr. BDC reticle
MSRP **$159.99**

WRAITHE 4K MAX 3–24X50MM
Available in: 3–24x50mm
Weight: 34.6 oz.
Length: 12 in.
Main Dia.: N/A
Exit Pupil: N/A
Field of View: 31.5 ft.@100 yd.
Eye Relief: 2.7 in.
Features: Ultra high-definition digital riflescope with a 4000x3000 CMOS sensor that picks up objects out to 300 yards at night; detachable 850nm infrared illuminator has a run time of 90 minutes on max; UHD 4K video

recording with audio; 10 reticle options in nine colors; IPX5 water-resistant rating; rechargeable battery with eight-hour life
MSRP **$999.99**

WRAITHE HD 2–16X28MM
Available in: 2–16x28mm
Weight: 33.3 oz.
Length: 10 in.
Main Dia.: N/A
Exit Pupil: N/A
Field of View: 42 ft.@100 yd.
Eye Relief: 2.4 in.
Features: A night/day digital riflescope with an 850nm infrared illuminator; detection of objects out to 200 yards at night; black-and-white, green, or night and day color modes; aluminum body; 1080p HD video recording; 10 reticle options in nine colors; five firearm profile saves; IP55 water-resistant rating; 20ºF–122ºF operating range; includes fixed Picatinny mount and additional Weaver rail
MSRP **$599.99**

Sightron

SIGHTRON S-TAC 3–16X42FFP

SIGHTRON S-TAC FFP 4–20X50MM ZERRO STOP

S-TAC 3–16X42MM FFP ZERO STOP
Available in: 3–16x42mm
Weight: 24.8 oz.
Length: 13.3 in.
Main Dia.: 30mm
Exit Pupil: N/A

Field of View: 29.2–6.1 ft.@100 yd.
Eye Relief: 4.1–3.6 in.
Features: Fast-focus eyepiece; resettable zero-stop turrets in ExacTrack .1 MRAD or MOA adjustment; pop-up zoom ring lever; Zact-7 Revcoat multicoating; illuminated MOA-5 or Mil-Hash-2 reticle in the first focal plane
MSRP **$659.99**

S-TAC FFP 4–20X50MM ZERRO STOP
Available in: 4–20x50mm

Weight: 25.6 oz.
Length: 15 in.
Main Dia.: 30mm
Field of View: 22.2–4.36 ft.@100 yd.
Eye Relief: 3.9–3.7 in.
Features: A nice entry for long-range work, with ample eye relief and magnification; tactical resettable turret knobs; side focus; illuminated Mil-Hash 4 reticle in the first focal plane; fast-focus eyepiece; zoom ring lever
MSRP **$789.99**

OPTICS

SIG Sauer

SIG SAUER SIERRA3BDX

SIG SAUER TANGO4

SIG SAUER SIERRA6 BDX

SIG SAUER WHISKEY3

SIERRA3BDX

Available in: 2.5x8x32mm, 3–18x44mm, 3.5–10x42mm, 4.5–14x44mm, 4.5–14x50mm, 6.5–20x52mm
Main Dia.: 30mm
Exit Pupil: varies with model
Field of View: varies with model
Features: A rangefinder and scope all in one via SIG's BDX-R1 reticle—BDX stands for Ballistic Data Exchange—which includes an illuminated auto-holdover dot when the scope is paired with Sig's BDX-capable KILO rangefinders; SpectralCoat lenses; anti-cant digital LevelPlex technology; second focal plane
MSRP . . . . $506.99–$878.99

SIERRA6BDX

Available in: 3–18x44mm, 2–12x40mm, 5–30x56mm
Weight: 23.8 oz., 30.04 oz.
Main Dia.: 34mm, 30mm
Exit Pupil: 8.2–2.4mm, 8.4–3.3mm, 8.1–1.9mm

Field of View: 34.9–8 ft.@100 yd., 52.5–8.7 ft.@100 yd., 21–3.5 ft.@100 yd.
Eye Relief: 3.9 in., 3.7 in.
Features: A second focal plane rifle-scope with adjustments in ¼-MOA; eight daytime/two night vision settings; IPX7 waterproofing; Argon-gas purged; 60 MOA total windage/elevation adjustment
MSRP . . . . $1013.99–$1588.99

TANGO4

Available in: 1–4x24mm, 6–24x50mm
Weight: 20.1 oz.–26.9 oz.
Length: 10 in.–15.6 in.
Main Dia.: 30mm
Exit Pupil: 15.4–6.1mm, 8–2.1mm
Field of View: 98–24 ft @ 100 yds, 16.8–4.2 ft @ 100 yds
Eye Relief: 3.3 in.
Features: Low dispersion glass provides industry-leading optical clarity for any situation; offered in first focal plane with multiple, illuminated reticle options; MOTAC (Motion

Activated Illumination) powers up when it senses motion and powers down when it does not; provides for optimum operational safety and enhanced battery life; dependable waterproof (IPX-7 rated for complete immersion up to 1 meter) and fog-proof performance; LockDown Zero System features a resettable zero, zero-stop, and auto-locks down at zero
MSRP . . . . $549.99–$878.99

WHISKEY3

Available in: 2–7x32mm, 3–9x50mm, 4–12x40mm, 4–12x50mm
Weight: 14.8 oz.–18.8 oz.
Length: 11.2 in.–14 in.
Main Dia.: 25.4mm
Exit Pupil: 15–4.5mm, 15–4.8mm, 15.1–5.6mm, 10–3.3mm
Field of View: 45.4–13.1 ft @ 100 yds, 33.9–11.3 ft @ 100 yds, 23.6–7.9 ft @ 100 yds
Eye Relief: 3.5 in.
Features: 3X optical zoom offered in second focal plane (SFP) with multiple reticle options; low dispersion glass provides industry-leading optical clarity for any situation; European-style eyepiece for a smooth, fast, and precise reticle adjustment; dependable waterproof (IPX-7 rated for complete immersion up to 1 meter) and fogproof performance
MSRP . . . . $109.99–$312.99

Simmons

SIMMONS .22 MAG 3–9X32MM

SIMMONS PROTARGET RIFLESCOPES

.22 MAG 3–9X32MM

Available in: 3–9X32mm
Weight: 10 oz.
Length: 12 in.
Main Dia.: 1 in.
Exit Pupil: 10.7–3.6mm
Field of View: 31.4–10.5 ft @ 100 yds
Twilight Factor: 9.8–17
Eye Relief: 3.75 in.
Features: One piece tube construction; fully coated optics; waterproof; fogproof; shockproof; Truplex reticle; RF Rings with available Adjustable Objective; matte or silver finish
MSRP $82.45

PROTARGET RIFLESCOPES

Available in: 2.5–10x40mm, 4–16x40mm, 6–24x44
Weight: 20–20.4 oz.
Main Dia.: 1 in.
Field of View: 31–10.5 ft.@100 yd. (2.5–10x), 33-8.6 ft.@100 yd. (4–16x), 17–4.5 ft.@100 yd. (6–24x)
Eye Relief: 3.9 in.
Features: Three dedicated rimfire scopes with TruPlex reticles and side parallax adjustment; 3–9x and 6–24x have turrets calibrated for .22 LR; 3–12x's turrets are calibrated for .17 HMR; 3–12x and 6–24x have side focus adjustment; multi-coated glass; matte finish; supplied with rings
MSRP . . . . $179.95–$224.95

OPTICS

Simmons

SIMMONS OPTICS PROTARGET RIMFIRE

SIMMONS WHITETAIL CLASSIC

PROTARGET RIMFIRE
Available in: 4x32, 2–7x32mm, 3–9x40mm
Weight: 8.8 oz.–11.2 oz.
Main Dia.: 1 in.
Exit Pupil: 8mm, 13.5–4.4mm, 13–4.2mm
Field of View: 26 ft.@100 yd., 49–15 ft.@100 yd., 32–11 ft.@100 yd.
Eye Relief: 3.5 in.
Features: Designed specifically for rimfire accuracy, this series of scopes feature a Truplex reticle; 35 MOA windage/elevation with ¼-MOA clicks; capped exposed turrets
MSRP . . . . $42.95–$64.99

WHITETAIL CLASSIC
Available in: 1–4x20mm, 2–7x32mm, 3–9x40mm, 4–12x40mm, 6–24x50mm
Weight: 13.29–19.4 oz.
Length: 9.76–15.98 in.
Main Dia.: 1 in.
Exit Pupil: varies
Field of View: varies
Eye Relief: varies
Features: Five utilitarian zoom magnifications; second focal plane optics with 1-in. tubes; Black Granite finish and red highlights; waterproof, fogproof, and shockproof
MSRP . . . . $61.99–$155.99

Steiner

STEINER M7XI, M7XI IFS

STEINER T5XI SERIES

M7XI, M7XI IFS
Available in: 2.9X20–50mm
Weight: 40.6 oz.
Length: 13.8 in.
Main Dia.: 34mm
Field of View: 12–1.7m@100m
Eye Relief: 3.23–3.43 in.
Features: A compact tactical scope with low-profile turrets; Intelligent Firing Solution; built-in ballistic calculator and sensor suite; Bluetooth connectivity; customizable display; first focal plane reticle; side-focus parallax adjustment
M7Xi: . . . . $4219.99–$4944.99
M7Xi IFS $6829.99

T5XI
Available in: 1–5X24mm
Weight: 19.4 oz.
Length: 11.3 in.
Main Dia.: 30mm
Field of View: 108–21 ft.@100 yd.
Eye Relief: 3.5–4 in.
Features: A compact scope with 5X zoom for action shooting sports; low-profile turrets; 3TR 3-Gun reticle calibrated for 5.56 or 7.62 NATO; one-piece 30mm tube; tapered all-metal magnification ring; locking diopter; throw lever; sun shade included
MSRP . . . . 1804.99–$1977.99

Swarovski Optik

SWAROVSKI OPTIK X5(I) 3.5–18X50MM

SWAROVSKI OPTIK X5(I) 5–25X56 P 1/4 MOA

X5(I) 3.5–18X50MM
Available in: 3.5–18X50mm
Weight: 28.6 oz.–32.1 oz.
Length: 14.4 in.–14.8 in.
Main Dia.: 30mm
Exit Pupil: 9.5–2.8mm
Field of View: 30–6.3 ft @ 100 yds
Twilight Factor: 11–30
Eye Relief: 3.7 in.
Features: The X5(i) from SWAROVSKI OPTIK redefines accuracy; new spring retention system and turrets are part of the total package promoting accuracy and offering across the entire adjustment range an accurate impact point adjustment of ¼ MOA in terms of both elevation and windage even in the most extreme situations; use the SUBZERO function to go below the sight-in distance
MSRP . . . . $3110.00–$3221.00

X5(I) 5–25X56 P 1/4 MOA
Available in: 5–25X56mm
Weight: 32.1 oz.
Length: 14.8 in.
Exit Pupil: 2.3–9.5mm
Field of View: 4.5–21 ft @ 100 yds
Features: High-luminosity rifle scope with 25x magnification; three reticle options; 30mm tube; 10 illumination brightness settings
MSRP $3477.00

Swarovski Optik

SWAROVSKI OPTIK Z3 3–10X42MM

SWAROVSKI OPTIK Z5(I) 5–25X52MM

SWAROVSKI OPTIK Z6I 5–30X50MM P

SWAROVSKI OPTIK Z8I

Z3 3–10X42MM
Available in: 3–10X42mm
Weight: 12.7 oz.
Length: 12.6 in.
Main Dia.: 1 in.
Exit Pupil: 12.6–4.2mm
Field of View: 33–11.7 ft @ 100 yds
Twilight Factor: 11.22–20.49
Eye Relief: 3.5 in.
Features: Z3 riflescopes have a 3x zoom factor and are the lightest riflescopes in the Swarovski Optik line; perfect fit for many of today's lightweight rifles; reticles for the Z3 include the 4A, Plex, BRX, and BRX Heavy; also available in 3–10x40mm and 4–12x50mm
MSRP $854.00

Z5(I) 5–25X52MM
Available in: 5–25X52mm
Weight: 17.5 oz.
Length: 14.6 in.
Main Dia.: 1 in.
Exit Pupil: 9.6–2.1mm
Field of View: 21.9–4.5 ft @ 100 yds
Twilight Factor: 16.12–36.05
Eye Relief: 3.75 in.
Features: The Z5 Riflescope line features a 5x zoom factor; a third parallax-adjustment turret; and long eye relief; with reticles available in #4, Plex, Fine in the 5–25x, and BRX/BRH; also available with the ballistic turrets; also in 3.5–18x44mm, 2.4–12x50mm
5–25X . . . . **$1943.00–$1999.00**
2.4–12X . . . . . . **$1654.00–$1766.00**
3.5–18X . . . . . . **$1810.00–$1888.00**

Z6I 5–30X50MM P
Available in: 5–30X50mm
Weight: 22.6 oz.
Length: 15.67 in.
Main Dia.: 30mm
Exit Pupil: 9.5–1.7mm
Field of View: 23.7–3.9 ft @ 100 yds
Twilight Factor: 14.1–38.7
Eye Relief: 3.74 in.

Features: New 2nd Generation scopes feature slimmer design that enables a clearer view of the controls and of the hunting situation; parallax turret also features a lock-in position at the 100 yds mark; more prominent ribbing on the magnification ring; 4A-I, 4W-I reticles available
MSRP . . . . **$2543.00–$2666.00**

Z8I
Available in: 1–8X24mm, 1.7–13.3X42mm, 2–16X50mm, 2.3–18X56mm
Weight: 18.2 oz.–25.6 oz.
Length: 14 in.–14.3 in.
Exit Pupil: Varies with model
Field of View: Varies with model
Features: Illuminated 8x zoom in a 30mm tube; Flexchange, a switchable reticle; multiple reticles to choose from
MSRP . . . . **$3032.00–$4110.00**

Tasco

TASCO RIMFIRE

TASCO SPORTSMAN

RIMFIRE
Available in: 4x32mm, 3–9x40mm
Weight: 4 oz.–11.6 oz.
Length: 11 in.–12.2 in.
Power: 4X, 3–9X
Main Dia.: .75 in., 1 in.
Exit Pupil: 8mm, 14–4.4mm
Field of View: 26 ft.@100 yd., 32–11 ft.@100 yd.
Eye Relief: 2.5–3.6 in.
Features: Very budget-friendly line of rimfire rifle scopes in a variety of fixed and variable powers to fit any job at hand
MSRP . . . . **$42.99–$56.99**

SPORTSMAN
Available in: 3–9x40mm, 3–9x50mm, 4–12x40mm
Weight: 14.9 oz.–17.2 oz.
Power: 3–9X, 4–12X
Length: 13 in.–13.5 in.
Main Dia.: 1 in.
Exit Pupil: 100–4.6mm, 10.5–5.5mm
Field of View: 39–12.7 ft.@100 yd., 33-10 ft.@100 yd., 27–9 ft.@100 yd.
Eye Relief: 3.5 in.
Features: Economical line of scopes for centerfire rifles, with 1-in. main tubes; 30/30 reticle in the second focal plane
MSRP . . . . **$59.99–$69.99**

Tract Optics

TRACT OPTICS 22FIRE

22FIRE
Available in: 3–9X40mm, 4–12X40mm
Weight: 15.2 oz., 16 oz.
Length: 12.2 in. (3–9x40mm), 13.9 in. (4–12x40mm)
Exit Pupil: Varies with model
Eye Relief: 3.5 in.
Field of View: Varies with model

Features: 22Rifle line designed specifically to maximize accuracy with .22-caliber rifles; Impact BDC or T-Plex reticle; BDC designed for longer-distance work, while T-Plex is suitable for target practice and small-game hunting
MSRP $224.00

Tract Optics

TRACT OPTICS RESPONSE

TRACT OPTICS TORIC SERIES

TRACT OPTICS TORIC UHD 30MM

RESPONSE

Available in: 4–16X42mm
Weight: 19.6 oz.
Length: 13.1 in.
Exit Pupil: 10.5–2.6mm
Eye Relief: 3.5 in.
Field of View: 22–2.5 ft @ 100 yds

Features: Response line consists of three scopes; intended for use with ARs/MSRs in the .223 reticles and the AR10 platform with the .308 reticle; exposed tactical type turrets; glassetched reticles with windage correction
MSRP $474.00

TORIC

Available in: 2–10x42mm, 3–15x42mm, 3–15x50mm
Weight: 18.6 oz.–22.3 oz.
Length: 13.2 in.–13.9 in.
Power: 2–10X, 3–15X, 3–15X
Obj. Dia.: 42mm–50mm
Main Dia.: 1 in.
Exit Pupil: 10.7–4.2mm, 10–2.8mm, 10–3.3mm
Field of View: 49–9.9 ft @ 100 yds, 34–6.9 ft @ 100 yds, 34.3–6.8 ft @ 100 yds
Eye Relief: 4 in.
Features: Schott HT glass; glass etched BDC and T-Plex reticle (w/ windage correction in the BDC)
2–10X $694.00
3–15X $794.00

TORIC UHD 30MM

Available in: 2.5–15X44mm
Weight: 27.2 oz.
Length: 13.8 in.
Main Dia.: 30mm
Field of View: 41.7–7.1 ft.@100 yd.
Eye Relief: 3.9–4 in.
Features: Available in choice of second (illuminated BDC) or first focal plane (non-illuminated MOA) reticles; capped windage and elevation turrets; ¼-MOA clicks; side focus parallax adjustment; Argon gas purged; magnification ring has rear-facing numbers; fully multi-coated high-definition ED lens and Schott high-transmission glass; FFP has locking turret with zero stop
FFP $1094.00
SFP $1194.00

Trijicon

TRIJICON ACCUPOINT 4–16X50MM

TRIJICON CREDO

TRIJICON ACOG WITH .300 BLK RETICLE 3X30MM

TRIJICON CREDO HX

ACCUPOINT 4–16X50MM

Available in: 4–16x50mm
Weight: 24.2 oz.
Length: 13.9 in.
Main Dia.: 30mm
Exit Pupil: 9.3–3.1mm
Field of View: 25.8–6.4 ft.@100 yd.
Eye Relief: 3.6–3.7 in.
Features: Fiber optic and tritium illuminated reticle; operates without a battery; illumination automatically adjusts to lighting conditions; aircraft-quality aluminum body; available with a standard Duplex crosshair in green, an MOA-Dot crosshair in green, a Mil-Dot crosshair in green, or a BAC triangle post in red, green, or yellow
MSRP . . . . $1399.00–$1499.00

ACOG WITH .300 BLK RETICLE 3X30MM

Available in: 3X30mm
Weight: 11.64 oz.
Length: 6.1 in.
Exit Pupil: 10mm
Field of View: 19.3 ft @ 100 yds
Twilight Factor: 9.5
Eye Relief: 1.9 in.
Features: TA60 Mount; designed for law enforcement and military applications; .300 BLK Ballistic Reticle for subsonic and supersonic rounds; bullet drop compensator; Bindon Aiming Concept (BAC), fiber optics & tritium illuminated); available with amber, green, or red crosshair reticle
**MSRP . . . .
$1407.00**

ASCENT

Available in: 1–4x24mm, 3–12x40mm
Weight: 15.9 oz., 17.8 oz.
Length: varies with model
Main Dia.: 30mm
Exit Pupil: varies with model
Field of View: varies with model
Eye Relief: varies with model
Features: Tested to military standards, the two scopes in this line have anti-scratch glass, wide fields of view, knurled adjustment points, easy-focus eyepieces, and BDC Target Hold reticle in the second focal plane
1-4X: $650.00
3–12X: $699.00

CREDO

Available in: 1–4x24mm, 1–6x24mm, 1–8x28mm, 2–10x36mm, 2.5–10x56mm, 2.5–15x42mm, 2.5–15x56mm, 3–9x40mm, 4–16X50mm
Weight: varies with model
Length: varies with model
Main Dia.: 1 in., 30mm, 34mm
Exit Pupil: varies with model
Field of View: varies with model
Eye Relief: varies with model
Features: Designed for both-eyes-open shooting, the Credo line has a wide range of variable powers to choose from
MSRP . . . . $799.00–$1799.00

OPTICS

Trijicon

TRIJICON ASCENT

TRIJICON HURON

TRIJICON TENMILE

TRIJICON TENMILE HX

TRIJICON VCOG 1–6X24MM RIFLESCOPE

CREDO HX

Available in: 1–4x24mm, 1–6x24mm, 1–8x28mm, 2.5–10x56mm, 2.5–15x42mm, 2.5–15x56mm, 4–16x50
Weight: varies with model
Length: varies with model
Main Dia.: 30mm, 34mm
Exit Pupil: varies with model
Field of View: varies with model
Eye Relief: varies with model
Features: Similar to the Credo line, the HX designates reticles and power ranges for hunters
MSRP . . . . $999.00–$1799.00

HURON

Available in: 1–4x24mm, 2.5–10x40mm, 3–9x40mm, 3–12x40mm
Weight: varies with model
Length: varies with model
Main Dia.: 1 in., 30mm
Exit Pupil: varies with model
Field of View: varies with model
Eye Relief: varies with model
Features: Second focal plane reticle scopes designed for whitetail deer

hunters, with aircraft-grade aluminum bodies, fast-focus eyepieces, BDC Hunter Holds reticle, ¼-MOA click adjustments, and wide fields of view
MSRP . . . . $650.00–$699.00

TENMILE

Available in: 3–18x44mm, 4–24x50mm, 4.5–30x56mm, 5–25x50mm, 5–50x56, 6–24x56mm
Weight: varies with model
Length: varies with model
Main Dia.: 30mm, 34mm
Exit Pupil: varies with model
Field of View: varies with model
Eye Relief: varies with model
Features: Big tubes, big objectives, and big power ranges help those in the long-range game go the distance, and scopes include repositionable magnification knob, sunshade, battery, and Tenebraex flip lens caps
MSRP . . . . $1399.00–$2700.00

TENMILE HX

Available in: 3–18x44mm, 3–18x50mm, 5–25x50mm,

6–24x50mm
Weight: varies with model
Length: varies with model
Main Dia.: 30mm
Exit Pupil: varies with model
Field of View: varies with model
Eye Relief: varies with model
Features: Similar to the Tenmile series for target games, the HX here indicates powers and reticles suitable for hunting applications at distance
MSRP . . . . $1399.00–$2199.00

VCOG 1–6X24MM

Available in: 1–6X24mm
Weight: 23.2 oz.
Length: 10.05 in.
Exit Pupil: 10.4–3.8mm
Field of View: 95–15.9 ft @ 100 yds
Twilight Factor: 12
Eye Relief: 4 in.
Features: Designed and built in the U.S.; Mil Spec, hard-coat finish; 90 MOA of windage and elevation adjustment; fully multi-coated lenses; waterproof; seven different reticle choices, between centered crosshair and horseshoe/dot reticle; red illuminated reticle; six brightness settings; matte finish
MSRP . . . . $2800.00–$3050.00

Truglo

TRUGLO BUCKLINE

TRUGLO EMINUS

TRUGLO NEXUS

BUCKLINE

Available in: 3–9x32mm, 3–9x32mm, 3–9x40mm, 3–9x50mm, 4x32mm
Main Dia.: .375 in., 1 in.
Features: Super economical scope series has a rubber-coated speed-focus eyepiece; BDC dot or Duplex reticles; fully coated lenses; water-resistant and fogproof; Weaver-style or 3/8-in. rings supplied
MSRP . . . . $29.99–$39.99

EMINUS

Available in: 3–9x42mm, 4–16x44mm, 6–24x50mm
Power: 3-9X, 4–16X, 6–24X

Main Dia.: 30mm
Features: A full-size scope for MSRs with side-focus wheel; illuminated TacPlex reticle; multi-coated lenses; hardcoat anodized matte black finish; leaf-spring turret control; ¼-MOA clicks; locking target turrets; supplied with APTUS-M1 mount
MSRP . . . . $248.99–$390.99

NEXUS

Available in: 3–9x42mm, 4–12x44mm
Features: Rubber-coated speed-focus eyepiece; non-illuminated BDC MOA-based or Duplex reticle
MSRP . . . . $131.99–$152.99

TRUGLO OMNIA

TRUGLO TRU-BRITE 30

OMNIA

Available in: 1–4x24mm, 1–6x24mm, 1–8x24mm
Main Dia.: 30mm
Features: A tactical sight with illuminated A.P.T.R. reticle; multi-coated lenses; hardcoat anodized matte black finish; leaf-spring turret control; ½-MOA clicks; locking target turrets
MSRP . . . . **$248.99–$414.99**

TRU-BRITE 30

Available in: 1–4x24mm

Weight: 13.4 oz.–15.1 oz.
Length: 9.88 in.
Main Dia.: 30mm
Field of View: 93.6–23.03 @ 100 yds
Eye Relief: 3.75 in.
Features: Includes two pre-calibrated BDC turrets in calibers .223 (55 grain) and .308 (168 grain) to engage targets up to 800 yards away; ½ MOA windage/elevation adjustments
MSRP **$119.99**

U.S. Optics

U.S. OPTICS FOUNDATION SERIES

U.S. OPTICS TS SERIES

FOUNDATION SERIES

Available in: 1.8–10x42mm, 10x42mm, 3.2–17x50mm, 5–25x52mm
Weight: 25.7 oz.–33.4 oz.
Length: 12.98 in.–17.93 in.
Main Dia.: 34mm
Exit Pupil: 3.2mm, 3mm
Field of View: 36–11 ft.@100 yd., 11.3 ft.@100 yd., 25.25–8 ft.@100 yd., 25.25–8 ft.@100 yd.
Eye Relief: 3.2 in.
Features: A U.S.-made line of premium optics that include aircraft-grade aluminum bodies, low-profile ER3K elevation knobs, capped US#1 windage knob, integrated and adjustable parallax, 180-degree magnification throw, choice of hard coat black anodized finish or a variety of Cerakote colors, reticles available in red, blue, or green illumination

1.8–10X	**starting at $2499.00**
10X42	**starting at $1999.00**
3.2–17X	**starting at $2899.00**
5–25X	**starting at $3449.00**

TS SERIES

Available in: 1–6x24mm, 1–8x24mm, 3–12x44mm, 2.5–20x50mm, 5–25X50mm
Weight: 17.9 oz.–28.7 oz.
Length: 10.75 in., 10.5 in., 9.6 in., 14.64 in., 14.17 in.
Main Dia.: 30mm
Exit Pupil: 4mm, 3mm, 3mm, 2.5mm, 2mm
Field of View: N/A
Eye Relief: 2 in.
Features: First or second focal plane illuminated and non-illuminated reticles

1–6X	**starting at $695.00**
1–8X	**starting at $795.00**
3–12X	**starting at $595.00**
2.5–20X	**starting at $1495.00**
5–25X	**starting at $995.00**

Vortex Optics

VORTEX CROSSFIRE II 3–12X56 AO

VORTEX CROSSFIRE II SCOUT

CROSSFIRE II 3–12X56 AO

Available in: 3–12X56mm
Weight: 21.1 oz.
Length: 14.3 in.
Main Dia.: 30mm
Field of View: 36.7–9.2 ft @ 100 yds
Twilight Factor: 12.96–25.92
Eye Relief: 3.5 in.

Features: Second focal plane V-Brite illuminated reticle; capped reset turrets; adjustable objective; hard anodized finish
MSRP **$369.99**

CROSSFIRE II SCOUT

Available in: 2–7x32mm

Weight: 12 oz.
Length: 10.5 in.
Main Dia.: 25.4mm
Field of View: 18.3–5.2 ft @ 100 yds
Eye Relief: 9.45 in.
Features: Fully multi-coated; second focal plane reticle; single-piece tube; capped reset turrets
MSRP **$199.99**

Vortex Optics

VORTEX DIAMONDBACK TACTICAL

VORTEX GOLDEN EAGLE HD

VORTEX RAZOR HD AMG

VORTEX RAZOR HD GEN II SERIES 4.5–27X56MM

VORTEX RAZOR HD GEN II-E

VORTEX OPTICS RAZOR HD GEN III

VORTEX OPTICS SPITFIRE HD GEN II 3X, 5X

VORTEX STRIKE EAGLE

DIAMONDBACK TACTICAL

Available in: 4–12X40mm, 4–16X44mm, 6–24X50mm
Weight: 16.2 oz., 23.1 oz., 24.6 oz.
Length: 12.5 in.
Eye Relief: 3.8 in., 3.9 in.
Field of View: 7.9–23.6 ft @ 100 yds (4–12x), 26.9–6.7 ft @ 100 yds, 18–4.5 ft @ 100 yds
Features: 3–9X and 4–12X have second focal plane reticle (VMR-1); 4–16X and 6–24X have first focal plane reticle (glass-etched EBR-2C MOA); XD lens elements; XR full multi-coatings; fast focus eyepiece; fiber optic turret rotation indicator
4–12X: $349.99
4–16X: $449.99
6–24X: $499.99

GOLDEN EAGLE HD

Available in: 15–60x52mm
Weight: 29.7 oz.
Length: 16.1 in.
Main Dia.: 30mm
Field of View: 6.3–1.7 ft @ 100 yds
Eye Relief: 3.9 in.
Features: Apochromatic objective lens system uses index-matched lenses to correct color across the entire visual spectrum; extra-fine resolution turret
MSRP $2499.99

RAZOR HD AMG

Available in: 6–24x50mm
Weight: 28.8 oz.
Length: 15.2 in.
Main Dia.: 30mm
Field of View: 20.4–5.1 ft @ 100 yds
Eye Relief: 3.6 in.
Features: ALO proprietary automated laser optical alignment process; apochromatic objective lens system uses

index-matched lenses to correct color across the entire visual spectrum; optically indexed lenses; high-density, extra-low dispersion glass; first focal plane reticle; illuminated reticle; side focus adjustment
MSRP $3699.99

RAZOR HD GEN II 4.5–27X56MM

Available in: 4.5–27X56mm
Weight: 48.5 oz.
Length: 14.4 in
Main Dia.: 34mm
Field of View: 25.3–4.4 ft @ 100 yds
Twilight Factor: 15.87–38.88
Eye Relief: 3.7 in.
Features: Front focal plane; shock-, water-, and fogproof; adjustable parallax; illuminated reticle; glass-etched reticle
MSRP $3599.99

RAZOR HD GEN II-E

Available in: 1–6x24mm
Weight: 21.5 oz.
Length: 10.1 in.
Main Dia.: 30mm
Field of View: 115.2–20.5 ft.@100 yd.
Eye Relief: 4 in.
Features: Optically indexed lens for clarity; XR Plus fully multi-coated lenses; HD lens elements; second focal plane reticle; illuminated center dot with intensity lock; Armor-Tek finish for reduced external wear; reticles include VRM-2 MOA, VRM-2 MRAD, and JM-1 BDC
MSRP $1999.99

RAZOR HD GEN III

Available in: 1-10x24mm
Weight: 21.5 oz.
Length: 10.1 in.

Main Dia.: 34mm
Field of View: 116–11.7 ft.@100 yd.
Eye Relief: 3.6 in.
Features: When everyone in the CQB scope game goes 8X, Vortex steps up the game with a first focal plane 10X
MSRP $3599.99

SPITFIRE HD GEN II 3X, 5X

Available in: 3X21mm, 5X25mm
Weight: 9 oz., 10.3 oz.
Length: 3 in., 3.6 in.
Main Dia.: N/A
Exit Pupil: N/A
Field of View: 37.9 ft.@100 yd., 23.3 ft.@100 yd.
Eye Relief: 2.6 in., 2.7 in.
Features: Small magnified optic intended for use with most 5.56 cartridges thanks to the illuminated AR-BDC4 reticle that includes holdovers to 600 yards; 12 brightness settings include two night vision settings; includes multi-height mounting system
3X: $549.99
5X: $649.99

STRIKE EAGLE

Available in: 1–6x24mm, 1–8x24mm
Weight: 17.6 oz., 16.5 oz.
Length: 10.5 in., 10 in.
Main Dia.: 30mm
Field of View: 116.5–19.2 ft @ 100 yds, 116,6–14.4 ft @ 100 yds
Eye Relief: 3.5 in., 4.1 in.
Features: Second focal plane; glass-etched, illuminated reticles in a light-weight package and with fast-focus eyepieces; reticle is the EBR-4
1–6X $499.99
1–8X . . . . $599.99–$799.99

OPTICS

VORTEX HS LR RFP SERIES 4–16X44MM

VORTEX VIPER HST SERIES 6–24X50MM

VORTEX VIPER PST GEN II

VIPER HUNTING SHOOTING LONG RANGE (HS LR) 4–16X50MM

Available in: 4–16X50mm
Weight: 19.8 oz.
Length: 13.7 in.
Main Dia.: 30mm
Field of View: 27.4–7.4 ft @ 100 yds
Twilight Factor: 13.27–26.53
Eye Relief: 4 in.

Features: Rear focal plane; shock-, water-, and fogproof; adjustable parallax; 4–16X features Dead-Hold BDC reticle; also available in a 6–24X50mm with a first focal plane XLR reticle
4–16X: $899.99
6–24X: $1249.99

VIPER HUNTING SHOOTING TACTICAL (HST) 6–24X50MM

Available in: 6–24X50mm
Weight: 22.6 oz.
Length: 15.5 in.
Main Dia.: 30mm
Field of View: 17.8–5.1 ft @ 100 yds
Twilight Factor: 17.32–34.64
Eye Relief: 4 in.
Features: Choice of VMR-1 MRAD or MOA reticles in the second focal plane; shock-, water-, and fogproof; adjustable parallax; 4–16x44 also available
4–16X: $849.99
6–24X: $949.99

VIPER PST GEN II

Available in: 1–6X24mm, 2–10X32mm, 3–15X44mm, 5–25X50mm
Weight: 22.7 oz.–31.2 oz.
Length: 10.9 in.–16 in.
Eye Relief: 3.4–3.8 in.
Field of View: Varies with model
Features: Extra-low dispersion (XD) glass; multiple anti-reflection coatings on all air-to-glass surfaces; glass-etched, illuminated reticles; Reticle and focal plane options available are: 1–6x VMR-2 MRAD or MOA second focal plane; 2–10x EBR-4 MRAD or MOA first focal plane; 3–15x EBR-4 MOA second focal plane or EBR-2C MRAD or MOA first focal plane; 5–25x EBR-4 MOA second focal plane or EBR-2C MRAD or MOA first focal plane.
1–6x: $899.99
2–10x: $1149.99
3–15x: $1199.99
5–25x: $1299.99

SIGHTS

AIMPOINT 9000SC

AIMPOINT ACRO P-1

AIMPOINT COMPM5B

AIMPOINT MICRO H-2

9000SC

Type: Red-dot
Weight: 7.4 oz.
Length: 6.3 in.
Obj. Dia.: 38mm

Features: Ideal for short length action rifles, semi-automatic firearms, and magnum handguns; ACET technology for longer battery life; available in 2 or 4 MOA dot sizes; two-ring configuration for mounting; waterproof; matte finish
MSRP $523.00

ACRO P-1

Type: Red-dot/reflex red-dot
Weight: 2.1 oz.
Length: 1.9 in.
Power: 1X
Obj. Dia.: N/A
Field of View: Unlimited
Eye Relief: Unlimited
Features: Reflex collimator sight with a 3.5 MOA red dot; lithium CR1225 battery; four night vision and six daylight settings; optimized for pistol use
MSRP .... $667.00–$699.93

COMPM5B

Type: Red-dot/reflex red-dot
Weight: 9 oz.
Length: 3.3 in.
Power: 1X
Obj. Dia.: N/A

Aimpoint

Field of View: N/A
Eye Relief: Unlimited
Features: Reflex dot for MSR-use with a 2 MOA red-dot; AAA battery; four night vision and six daylight illumination settings; 39mm spacer and LRP Lever Release Picatinny mount; flip-up lens covers; hard anodized non-reflective finish
MSRP .... $938.00–$1123.00

MICRO H-2 AND T-2

Type: Red-dot
Weight: 4.6 oz.–4.8 oz.
Length: 2.7 in.–3.16 in.
Power: 1X
Features: Advanced optical lenses for even better light transmission; can be used on shotguns, rifles, handguns or archery tackle; transparent front and rear flip-up lens covers are included; reinforced protection of the turrets for even greater ruggedness; 12 daylight settings; available in 2 MOA dot size; can be "piggybacked" on larger magnifying optics using an adapter.
H-2 .... $829.00–$1236.00
T-2 .... $886.00–$1031.00

OPTICS

Aimpoint

AIMPOINT PRO

PRO
Type: Red-dot
Weight: 7.8 oz.
Length: 5.1 in.
Power: 1X
Features: Parallax free optic; 2 MOA dot for accurate target engagement at all distances; four night vision settings and six daylight settings; modular QRP2 mount includes removable spacer that indexes the sight at optimal height for co-witness, with the standard iron sights on AR15/M16/M4 carbine style weapons
MSRP . . . . $495.00–$619.00

Armament Technology, Inc.

ARMAMENT TECHNOLOGY XOPTEK

XOPTEK
Type: Red-dot/reflex red-dot
Weight: 1.3 oz.
Length: 1.8 in.
Power: 1X
Obj. Dia.: N/A
Field of View: N/A
Eye Relief: N/A
Features: With a 4 MOA red-dot, this super-micro reflex 60 MOA of adjustment; five illumination settings; Picatinny rail mount or Elcan SpecterDR mount; choice of 4 or 6 MOA with either mount option
MSRP $399.00

Athlon Optics

ATHLON MIDAS LE   **ATHLON MIDAS TSR1**   **ATHLON MIDAS TSR2**   **ATHLON MIDAS TSR3**

MIDAS LE GEN II
Type: Red-dot/reflex red-dot
Weight: 2.8 oz.
Length: 3.55 in.
Power: 1X
Obj. Dia.: 28x36mm
Field of View: N/A
Eye Relief: N/A
Features: Intended for close-range engagements; LE reticle of an illuminated circle and dot
MSRP $374.99

MIDAS TSR1
Type: Red-dot/reflex red-dot
Weight: 2.8 oz.
Length: 1.88 in.
Power: 1X
Obj. Dia.: 24x17mm
Field of View: N/A
Eye Relief: Unlimited
Features: 3 MOA dot; can be used on guns with slide cuts and mounting plates by removing the Picatinny rail mount
MSRP $312.49

MIDAS TSR2
Type: Red-dot/reflex red-dot
Weight: 6.7 oz.
Length: 2.8 in.
Power: 1X
Obj. Dia.: 20mm
Field of View: N/A
Eye Relief: Unlimited
Features: 2 MOA red dot in a more conventional tubed body; fully multicoated glass; Smart Power Management System sends the unit to sleep after five minutes of no activity
MSRP $237.49

MIDAS TSR3
Type: Red-dot/reflex red-dot
Weight: 10.6 oz.
Length: 3.7 in.
Power: 1X
Obj. Dia.: 36mm
Field of View: N/A
Eye Relief: Unlimited
Features: A good choice for PPC competition or game and predator hunting, with a 2 MOA red dot that has 10 daylight settings and three night vision settings; motion activation sensor
MSRP $279.99

Barska

BARSKA 1X20 HQ RED DOT

1X20 HQ RED DOT
Type: Red-dot
Weight: 7 oz.
Length: 2.95 in.
Power: 1X20mm
Obj. Dia.: 20mm
Exit Pupil: 18mm
Field of View: 36 ft.@100 yd.
Eye Relief: Unlimited
Features: Red-dot auto adjusts for external lighting conditions via a light sensor; integrated QD mount
MSRP $117.99

OPTICS

BARSKA 1X30 HQ RED DOT

BARSKA 1X30 ION REFLEX SIGHT

BARSKA 1X40 ION REFLEX SIGHT

1X30 HQ RED DOT
Type: Red-dot
Weight: 10.8 oz.
Length: 4.13 in.
Power: 1X30mm

Obj. Dia.: 30mm
Exit Pupil: 26mm
Field of View: 57 ft.@100 yd.
Eye Relief: Unlimited
Features: Similar to the 1X20 version, including auto-adjusting brightness; 1 MOA adjustments
MSRP. $129.99

1X30 ION REFLEX SIGHT
Type: Reflex sight
Weight: 3.9 oz.
Length: 2.37 in.
Power: 1X30mm
Obj. Dia.: 30mm
Exit Pupil: 26–20mm
Field of View: Unlimited
Eye Relief: Unlimited

Features: A compact, affordable reflex with choice of four reticle patterns; Picatinny rail mount
MSRP. $104.99

1X40 ION REFLEX SIGHT
Type: Reflex sight
Weight: 6.2 oz.
Length: 3.6 in.
Power: 1X40mm
Obj. Dia.: 40mm
Exit Pupil: 28–44mm
Field of View: Unlimited
Eye Relief: Unlimited
Features: A slightly bigger reflex with choice of four reticles; quick release Picatinny/Weaver-type mount
MSRP. $90.99

Blaser

BLASER RD20

RD20
Type: Red-dot/reflex red-dot

Weight: 6.8 oz.
Length: 3.85 in.
Power: 1X
Obj. Dia.: 36mm
Field of View: N/A
Eye Relief: Unlimited

Features: Developed for Blaser's own rifles, this red-dot optic has scratch-resistant lenses; Intelligent Illumination Control with 30 settings; power-saving mode; Blaser saddle mount; 2 MOA dot
MSRP. $1365.00

British Small Arms Co. (BSA)

BSA TACTICAL WEAPON ILLUMINATED SIGHT

TACTICAL WEAPON ILLUMINATED SIGHT
Type: Red-dot
Weight: 22 oz.
Length: 8.75 in.
Power: 1X
Field of View: 3.7–19.3 ft @ 100 yds
Eye Relief: 2 in.

Features: Fully multicoated optics; easy one-piece mounting; 5/8-inch Weaver-style rail; illuminated red dot; rubber eye guard; output power: 5mW; wave length: 650 nm; attachable 140 lumen LED flashlight
With flashlight: $119.90

Browning

BROWNING BUCK MARK REFLEX SIGHT

BUCK MARK REFLEX SIGHT
Type: Red-dot reflex sight
Power: 1X
Field of View: 47 ft @ 100 yds
Eye Relief: Unlimited
Features: The Buck Mark has an aluminum housing, four red reticle patterns, a seven-position brightness rheostat powered by a lithium battery, and mounts on a standard Weaver-styled base
MSRP. $83.99

Burris

AR-536
Type: Red-dot
Weight: 18.75 oz.
Length: 5.75 in.
Power: 5X
Obj. Dia.: 36mm
Field of View: 20 ft @ 100 yds

BURRIS AR-536

Eye Relief: 2.5–3.5 in.
Features: Ballistic/CQTM lighted reticle; 600 yard range; multi-coated lenses; adjustable diopter; three Picatinny rail mounting points; black matte finish; max adj. 60 MOA; one-year warranty
MSRP. $419.00

Burris

BURRIS FASTFIRE 3

BURRIS FASTFIRE 4

BURRIS FASTFIRE RD

BURRIS RT-1

BURRIS RT-3

FASTFIRE 3

Type: Reflex sight
Weight: 0.9 oz.
Power: 1X
Features: 3 or 8 MOA dot; power button with three levels of brightness; low battery warning indicator and see-through protective cap; ideally suited for use on pistols and AR-15s where fast target acquisition is desired, the FastFire red-dot sight will also match up well with carbines, lever guns, and shotguns; available Picatinny mount
MSRP $299.00

FASTFIRE 4

Type: Reflex sight
Weight: 1.6 oz.
Length: 1.9 in.
Field of View: Infinite
Features: Change between a 3 MOA red dot, 11 MOA red dot, or either in a red circle; removeable weather shield; impact-resistant housing
MSRP $419.00

FASTFIRE RD

Type: Red-dot
Weight: 6.4 oz.
Length: 2.8 in.
Obj. Dia.: 35.5mm
Field of View: Infinite
Features: Features a 2 MOA red dot; alloy housing; 90 MOA elevation/windage; 1 MOA click value; runs off a AAA battery
MSRP $299.00

RT-1

Type: Red-dot
Weight: 4.8 oz.
Length: 2.75 in.

Power: 1X
Obj. Dia.: 25mm
Field of View: Infinite
Features: True 1X magnification; 2 MOA red-dot; 45 MOA elevation/windage; ½-MOA clicks; CR2032 battery; comes with high and low base mounts
MSRP $359.00

RT-3

Type: Red-dot
Weight: 8.8 oz.
Length: 3.5 in.
Power: 3X
Obj. Dia.: 33.8mm
Field of View: Infinite
Features: True 3X magnification; 50 MOA elevation/windage; CR2032 battery; Ballistic 3X red dot reticle; integrated Picatinny rail mount
MSRP $455.00

Bushnell Outdoor Products

BUSHNELL AR OPTICS ADVANCE

BUSHNELL AR OPTICS TRS-26

BUSHNELL AR OPTICS FIRST STRIKE 2.0

AR OPTICS ADVANCE

Type: Reflex sight
Power: 1X
Features: 5-MOA dot; compact design compatible with a large selection of semiautomatic pistols
MSRP $159.99

AR OPTICS FIRST STRIKE 2.0

Type: Red dot
Weight: 2.1 oz.
Length: 2.4 in.

Power: 1X
Exit Pupil: 22 mm
Field of View: Unlimited
Eye Relief: Unlimited
Features: Five brightness settings; side battery compartment that requires no tools to access
MSRP $189.99

AR OPTICS TRS-26

Type: Red dot
Weight: 13.2 oz.
Power: 1x
Obj. Dia.: 26mm
Field of View: Unlimited
Eye Relief: Unlimited
Features: Compact red dot replacing an older version; brighter, five-setting dot; enhanced battery life; push-button controls
MSRP $149.99

BUSHNELL RXS-100

BUSHNELL RXS-250

RXS-100

Type: Red-dot/reflex red-dot
Weight: 1.3 oz.
Length: 1.8 in.
Power: 1X
Obj. Dia.: N/A
Field of View: N/A
Eye Relief: Unlimited
Features: Ultralight micro reflex with a 4 MOA dot and eight brightness settings; side battery door; CR2032 battery; Weaver-style low-rise mount included; can be used on pistols, MSRs, and shotguns
MSRP $99.99

RXS-250

Type: Red-dot/reflex red-dot
Weight: 1.4 oz.
Length: 1.8 oz.
Power: 1X
Obj. Dia.: N/A
Field of View: N/A
Eye Relief: Unlimited
Features: 4 MOA red-dot reflex has 10 brightness settings; CR2032 battery; 12-hour auto-shutoff with no button pressed; IPX7 water resistant; Weaver-style mount included and will mount to a Deltapoint Pro standard plate; 1 MOA clicks; chamfered hood edges help prevent snags
MSRP $249.99

C-More Systems

C-MORE SYSTEMS RTSB-V5

RTSB-V5

Type: Reflex sight
Field of View: Infinite
Features: V5-hardened electronics; motion-sensing system with auto-off; 1 MOA click adjustments; removeable battery tray eliminates need to rezero; choice of 3, 6, 8, or 10 MOA red dot
MSRP $389.00

Crimson Trace Corp.

CRIMSON TRACE CMR-201 RAIL MASTER

CRIMSON TRACE CMR-204 RAIL MASTER PRO

CRIMSON TRACE CMR-205 RAIL MASTER PRO

CRIMSON TRACE CMR-206 RAIL MASTER PRO

CRIMSON TRACE CMR-207G RAIL MASTER PRO

CRIMSON TRACE CMR-301 RAIL MASTER PRO

CMR-201 RAIL MASTER

Type: Laser/light
Features: Made for Picatinny or Weaver rail-equipped pistol, rifles, and shotguns; ambidextrous "tap" on/off controls; 5mW red laser; five-minute auto shutoff
MSRP $189.99

CMR-204 RAIL MASTER PRO

Type: Laser/light
Features: Made for Picatinny or Weaver rail-equipped pistol, rifles, and shotguns; ambidextrous "tap" on/off controls; combination green laser with 100 Lumen white light; four modes include laser/light constant on, laser constant on, light constant on, and laser w/light dazzler
MSRP $433.99

CMR-205 RAIL MASTER PRO

Type: Laser/light
Features: Similar to the CMR-204, but with a red laser
MSRP $333.99

CMR-206 RAIL MASTER PRO

Type: Laser/light
Features: Made for Picatinny or Weaver rail-equipped pistol, rifles, and shotguns; ambidextrous "tap" on/off controls; 5mW green laser with momentary, strobe, and constant-on functionality; five-minute auto shutoff
MSRP $206.99

CMR-207G RAIL MASTER PRO

Type: Laser/light
Features: For any Picatinny/Weaver rail-equipped firearm, this is a combo laser and a 400 Lumen tactical light; choice of red or green laser
MSRP $284.99

CMR-301 RAIL MASTER PRO

Type: Laser/light
Features: A two-for-one package for just about any MSR/AR-type rifle, with a green laser paired with 1,000-lumen tactical light; needs M1913 Picatinny rail or similar rail at least 2 ¾-in. to mount
MSRP $314.99

OPTICS

Crimson Trace Corp.

CRIMSON TRACE CTS-1250

CRIMSON TRACE CTS-1550

CRIMSON TRACE RAD MAX, RAD MAX PRO

CRIMSON TRACE RAD PRO

CRIMSON TRACE RAD MICRO

CRIMSON TRACE RAD MICRO PRO

CTS-1250

Type: Red-dot/reflex red-dot
Weight: 1 oz.
Length: 1.8 in.
Power: 1X
Obj. Dia.: N/A
Field of View: N/A
Eye Relief: Unlimited
Features: With a bigger 3.25 MOA red dot; seven daylight and three night settings; 1 MOA clicks; fully multi-coated lens; industry standard mounting interface for pistols
MSRP....................$259.99

CTS-1550

Type: Red-dot/reflex red-dot
Weight: N/A
Length: N/A
Power: 1X
Obj. Dia.: N/A
Field of View: N/A
Eye Relief: Unlimited
Features: 3 MOA red dot; underside battery compartment allows for co-witnessing iron sights; industry-standard mounting interface; ambient light sensor automatically adjusts dot brightness; coated lenses; designed for compact and subcompact pistols
MSRP...................$179.99

RAD MAX, RAD MAX PRO

Type: Red-dot/reflex red-dot
Weight: 0.5 oz.
Length: N/A
Power: 1X
Obj. Dia.: N/A
Field of View: N/A
Eye Relief: Unlimited
Features: 3.25 MOA red dot; utilizes Picatinny rail mount; 10 brightness levels
RAD Max...............$399.99
RAD Max Pro...........$$449.99

RAD MICRO

Type: Red-dot/reflex red-dot
Weight: N/A
Length: N/A
Power: 1X
Obj. Dia.: N/A
Field of View: N/A
Eye Relief: Unlimited
Features: Rapid Aiming Dot; super-compact reflex sight with 3 MOA red dot; aerograde aluminum construction; ambient light sensor; high efficiency LED battery; bottom positioned battery access
Red....................$224.99
Green..................$249.99

RAD MICRO PRO

Type: Red-dot/reflex red-dot
Weight: 0.3 oz.
Length: N/A
Power: 1X
Obj. Dia.: N/A
Field of View: N/A
Eye Relief: Unlimited
Features: 3 MOA red dot
Red....................$274.99
Green..................$299.99

RAD PRO

Type: Red-dot/reflex red-dot
Weight: N/A
Length: N/A
Power: 1X
Obj. Dia.: N/A
Field of View: N/A
Eye Relief: Unlimited
Features: Top-accessible battery compartment; CR1632 battery; shake-to-wake function; sleep function; large operating buttons for brightness; includes low-mount Picatinny; snag-free design
Red....................$299.99
Green..................$324.99

Davide Pedersoli & C.

DAVIDE PEDERSOLI ENGLISH REAR SIGHT–428

DAVIDE FIBER OPTIC FRONT AND REAR SIGHT–409

150 UNIVERSAL CREEDMOOR SIGHT, MIDDLE AND LONG RANGE, MODELS USA 465 AND 430

Features: Tang sight with elevation and windage adjustment in the eye piece; for long-distance target shooting both with muzzle-loading and breech-loading rifles; 2.1875–2.3125-in. between two mounting holes; 2- and 3-in. elevation adjustments
USA 430 Long Range:......$236.00
USA 465 Middle Range:....$234.00

ENGLISH REAR SIGHT, MODEL USA 428

Features: Rear sight with convex base, with two adjustable and folding leaves

Flat base................$142.00
Convex base.............$142.00

FIBER OPTIC FRONT AND REAR SIGHT, MODEL USA 409

Features: Front sight and rear sight set for muzzleloading rifles (Model 410 for breechloaders); front sight with dovetail base; rear sight with base for octagonal barrel
From:.................$140.00

474 • Shooter's Bible 114th Edition

Davide Pedersoli & C.

DAVIDE PEDERSOLI FOLDING FRONT SIGHT

DAVIDE PEDERSOLI UNIVERSAL CREEDMOOR SIGHT–430

DAVIDE PEDERSOLI "SOULE TYPE" MIDDLE RANGE SET-170

DAVIDE PEDERSOLI SPIRIT LEVEL TUNNEL SIGHT ADJUSTABLE–425

DAVIDE PEDERSOLI GHOST CREEDMOOR SIGHT-USA 422

FOLDING FRONT SIGHT

Features: Globe sight for long-range when raised, or fold down for built-in blade for close range; ball/detent locking mechanism; 3/8-in. dovetail base; ½-in. high

From:. $104.00

GHOST CREEDMOOR SIGHT-USA 422

Features: A tang sight inspired by some models in use in the 1800s, economic, functional, and useful for hunting; adjustable in elevation and

windage; can fit several gun types; small eye piece ring enables a quick, instinctive aim at the target; when quickly shouldering the rifle, the open ring provides a clear sight picture with low light condition; distance between the two mounting holes is 1¾-in.

From:. $86.00

"SOULE TYPE" MIDDLE RANGE SET, MODEL USA 170

Features: Wooden-box set including Soule XL Middle Range Sight; tunnel front sight with a micrometric screw for windage adjustment, spirit level, and fifteen interchangeable inserts; professional "Hadley Style" eyepiece with eight varying diameter viewing

holes, depending on available light, on a rotating disk which can be selected without disassembling or loosening the eyepiece, and a rubber ring on the eyepiece; six interchangeable glass bubbles (spirit level) with different colors for varying light conditions; 3-in. elevation adjustment

From:. $634.00

SPIRIT LEVEL TUNNEL SIGHT ADJUSTABLE WITH 12 INSERTS SET, MODEL USA 425

Features: Spirit level tunnel sight with micrometer adjustment for windage, equipped with twelve interchangeable inserts; also available in 15 and 18 insert sets

From:. $232.00

EOTech

EOTECH HOLOGRAPHIC HYBRID SIGHT

EOTECH HWS 300 BLACKOUT

EOTECH HWS 518

HOLOGRAPHIC HYBRID SIGHT (HHS)

Type: Holographic sight
Power: 3X
Eye Relief: 2.2 in.
Features: The HHS kits combine the

speed of the EXPS holographic weapon sight and the extended range versatility by adding a magnifier; available in four configurations: HHS I houses the EXPS3 red-dot and pairs with a G33 magnifier; HHS II houses the EXPS2 red-dot paired with a G33 magnifier; HHS Green is a green-dot EXPS2 with a switch-to-side-mount and a 3X magnifier; HHS V houses an EXPS3-4 red-dot with a bigger G45 magnifier and is night-vision compatible

HHS I. $1179.00
HHS II $1169.00
HHS Green $1279.00
HHS V $1389.00

HWS 300 BLACKOUT

Type: Red-dot/reflex sight
Weight: 9 oz.
Length: 3.8 in.
Power: 1X
Field of View: 90 ft @ 100 yds
Eye Relief: Unlimited
Features: Designed with tactical shooters in mind, this optic offers a

two-dot ballistic drop reticle that allows the shooter to zero either subsonic or supersonic rounds in the same reticle pattern; offered in the XPS2 platform, it is the shortest and lightest HWS sight available; its size and weight make it convenient for hunters, military and law enforcement officers to carry; the single compact lithium 123 battery configuration opens up more space on the rail for rear iron sights or magnifiers

MSRP. $619.00

HWS 518

Type: Red-dot/reflex red-dot
Weight: 11.5 oz.
Length: 5.6 in.
Power: 1X
Obj. Dia.: N/A
Field of View: N/A
Eye Relief: Unlimited
Features: Uses two AA batteries; one- or two-dot 68 MOA reticle models available, both in red
MSRP. $619.00

OPTICS

EOTech

EOTECH HWS 552

EOTECH HWS 558

EOTECH HWS EXPS2

EOTECH HWS XPS2

EOTECH HWS XPS3

HWS 552

Type: Red-dot/reflex red-dot
Weight: 11.5 oz.
Length: 5.6 in.
Power: 1X
Obj. Dia.: N/A
Field of View: N/A
Eye Relief: Unlimited
Features: EoTech calls this an "operator grade" sight, and it's night-vision compatible; uses two AA batteries; 20 daylight settings with 10 additional settings for Gen1-Gen3 night vision devices; utilizes the 68 MOA 1-dot reticle in red
MSRP $645.00

HWS 558

Type: Red-dot/reflex red-dot
Weight: 13.8 oz.
Length: 5.6 in.
Power: 1X
Obj. Dia.: N/A
Field of View: N/A
Eye Relief: Unlimited
Features: A night-vision compatible holographic sight with a quick-release locking mount; compatible with Gen1-Gen3 night vision devices; 20 daylight settings and 10 nighttime; uses 2 AA batteries

MSRP $719.00

HWS EXPS2

Type: Red-dot/reflex red-dot
Weight: 11.2 oz.
Length: 3.8 in.
Power: 1X
Obj. Dia.: N/A
Field of View: N/A
Eye Relief: Unlimited
Features: Allows for cowitnessing of iron sights; locking, quick-detach lever; side buttons allow addition of magnifier; two-dot 68 MOA reticle has a center dot for 50- and 200-yard use, a second dot below that for 500-yard use, and the bottom post for 7 yards, while the 68 MOA reticle design with a 1 MOA dot is useful at 7, 50, and 200 yards, both designed for use with a 62-gr. .223 round at 2,900 fps; both reticles are red, have 20 brightness settings
Red $659.00
Green. $769.00

HWS XPS2

Type: Red-dot/reflex red-dot
Weight: 9 oz.

Length: 3.8 in.
Power: 1X
Obj. Dia.: N/A
Field of View: N/A
Eye Relief: Unlimited
Features: 68 MOA reticle design, with a 1 MOA dot useful at 7, 50, and 200 yards with a 62-gr. .223 round at 2,900 fps; CR123 battery; 20 daylight settings; .5 MOA adjustments
Red $609.00
Green. $725.00
Thin Blue Line $609.00

HWS XPS3

Type: Red-dot/reflex red-dot
Weight: 9 oz.
Length: 3.8 in.
Power: 1X
Obj. Dia.: N/A
Field of View: N/A
Eye Relief: Unlimited
Features: Night-vision compatible holographic sight; works with Gen1-Gen3 night vision devices; CR123 battery; 20 daylight settings and 10 nighttime; offered in one- or two-dot 68 MOA reticle in red
MSRP $719.00

Firefield

FIREFIELD IMPACT MINI

FIREFIELD IMPACT XL, XLT

IMPACT MINI

Type: Red-dot/reflex red-dot
Weight: 1 oz.
Length: 1.9 in.
Power: 1X
Obj. Dia.: 16x21mm
Field of View: N/A
Eye Relief: Unlimited
Features: Very small reflex red-dot mounts to Weaver or Picatinny rail; generous 120 MOA windage/elevation adjustment; aluminum housing; AR Red lens coating; CR1632 battery; 5 MOA dot
MSRP . . . . $57.47–$69.97

IMPACT XL, XLT

Type: Red dot
Weight: 5.6, 7.8 oz.
Length: 3.6 in.
Power: 1x
Eye Relief: Unlimited
Battery Life: 25–250 hours (XL); 40–250 hours (XLT)
Features: Multiple reticle options; AR-red coated lenses; parallax correction; ample windage; elevation adjustments; neoprene cover; adjustment tools; XLT has a quick-detach mount, digital controls, and a protective hood
XL. $68.97
XLT $91.97

FIREFIELD SPEEDSTRIKE

SPEEDSTRIKE
Type: Laser
Weight: 6.3 oz.
Length: 4.25 in.
Battery Life: 80 hours (red); 25 hours (green)
Laser Power Output: Less than 5 mw
Laser Wavelength: 632 nm
Features: Available in green; modular mount; windage and elevation adjustments can be made without tools; pressure-pad activated
MSRP $91.97

Hawke Sport Optics, LLC

HAWKE SPORT OPTICS ENDURANCE

HAWKE SPORT OPTICS MICRO REFLEX

HAWKE SPORT OPTICS REFLEX WIDE VIEW

ENDURANCE REFLEX SIGHT
Type: Red-dot/reflex red-dot
Weight: 6.5 oz., 8.5 oz.
Length: 2.8 in., 3.5 in.
Power: 1X
Obj. Dia.: 25mm, 30mm
Field of View: N/A
Eye Relief: Unlimited
Features: "Old-school" style tubular red-dot optics; 25-layer multicoated glass; 3 MOA dot in red with eight brightness settings; high quick-release and low Weaver mounts; standby mode after five minutes of no movement; in 1X25 and 1X30
MSRP . . . . $209.00–$229.00

MICRO REFLEX
Type: Red-dot/reflex red-dot
Weight: 2.5 oz.
Length: 1.9 in.
Power: 1X
Obj. Dia.: N/A
Field of View: N/A
Eye Relief: Unlimited
Features: Reflex red-dot sight available in 3 MOA dot; 1 MOA clicks; Weaver rail mount; standby mode after five minutes of no movement; 25 layers of multicoating
MSRP $159.00

REFLEX WIDE VIEW
Type: Red-dot/reflex red-dot
Weight: 3 oz.
Length: 2.3 in.
Power: 1X
Obj. Dia.: N/A
Field of View: N/A
Eye Relief: Unlimited
Features: 25-layer multicoated glass; 3 MOA dot in red with eight brightness settings; Weaver mounts; standby mode after five minutes of no movement
MSRP . . . . $179.00–$189.00

Hi-Lux Precision Optics

HI-LUX PRECISION OPTICS MAX TAC DOT (MTD-30)

HI-LUX PRECISION OPTICS MM-2

HI-LUX PRECISION OPTICS TD-3

MAX TAC DOT (MTD-30)
Type: Red-dot/reflex red-dot
Weight: 8.9 oz.
Length: 3.9 in.
Power: 1X
Obj. Dia.: 30mm
Field of View: N/A
Eye Relief: Unlimited
Features: A slim and super-rugged tubular red dot; 4 MOA red dot; fully multi-coated lenses; Picatinny mount is machined into the housing
MSRP $120.00

MM-2
Type: Red-dot/reflex red-dot
Weight: 3.8 oz.
Length: 2.5 in.
Power: 1X
Obj. Dia.: 20mm
Field of View: N/A
Eye Relief: Unlimited
Features: Collimator reflex red-dot sight that comes with a low mount; glass coatings reduce glare; co-witness lower 1/3 or AR riser is included; 2 MOA dot
MSRP $229.00

TD-3
Type: Red-dot/reflex red-dot
Weight: 2 oz.
Length: 1.78 in.
Power: 1X
Obj. Dia.: 28x19mm
Field of View: N/A
Eye Relief: Unlimited
Features: Reflex sight intended for mounting on optics-ready slide cuts; 1 MOA clicks; lowest two brightness settings are night-vision compatible
MSRP $169.00

HE407C-GR X2
Type: Red-dot/reflex red-dot
Weight: 1.5 oz.
Length: 1.78 in.
Power: 1X
Obj. Dia.: .63x.91 in.
Field of View: N/A
Eye Relief: Unlimited
Features: Same as the HS407C X2, but with a green 2 MOA dot
MSRP $299.99

OPTICS

HIVIZ

HIVIZ LIGHTWAVE

HIVIZ LIGHTWAVE H3

HIVIZ LIGHTWAVE H3 EXPRESS

HIVIZ LITEWAVE H3 COMPSIGHT

LIGHTWAVE

Features: The wave design of the front sight housing produces a sharper, brighter sight; available in green, red, or white front with a two-dot adjustable green rear for a variety of rifles; as a single front for shotguns; and as a Lighwave front/rear pair for a variety of handguns

Shotgun $55.00
Handgun . . . . $34.95–$55.95

LIGHTWAVE H3

Features: Combines tritium with a fiber optic pipe for a brighter sight; all-steel construction; green front with choice of green or orange two-dot rear

Shotgun $55.00
Handgun . . . . $55.00–$135.00

LIGHTWAVE H3 EXPRESS

Features: HiViz brings the competition to XS Sights, with a big front tritium/pip "dot" gathering light via the "wave" housing, sitting over a single fiber optic vertical line in the rear sight; green front with choice of orange or green rear

MSRP $135.00

LITEWAVE H3 COMPSIGHT

Features: For shotgunners, this sight combines tritium with HIVIZ's LightPipe technology; all-steel construction; green pipe

MSRP $55.00

Holosun

HOLOSUN HE407C-GR X2

HOLOSUN HE507C-GR X2, HS507C X2

HOLOSUN HE508T-GR X2, HE508T-RD X2

HOLOSUN HE509T-RD

HOLOSUN HE512C-GD, HS512C

HE407C-GR X2

Type: Red-dot/reflex red-dot
Weight: 1.5 oz.
Length: 1.78 in.
Power: 1X
Obj. Dia.: .63x.91 in.
Field of View: N/A
Eye Relief: Unlimited
Features: Same as the HS407C X2, but with a green 2 MOA dot
MSRP $299.99

HE507C-GR X2, HS507C X2

Type: Red-dot/reflex red-dot
Weight: 1.5 oz.
Length: 1.78 in.

Power: 1X
Obj. Dia.: .63x.91 in.
Field of View: N/A
Eye Relief: Unlimited
Features: Open reflex with a lock mode that prevents the activation buttons from changing settings if accidentally depressed; Solar Failsafe design; Shake Awake function; Multi-reticle system of a 32 MOA circle with a 2 MOA dot that can be used together or separately; Super LED display; model with GR in the name is green, the other is red

Red: $364.69
Green: $399.00

HE508T-GR X2, HE508T-RD X2

Type: Red-dot/reflex red-dot
Weight: 2 oz.
Length: 1.78 in.
Power: 1X
Obj. Dia.: .63x.91 in.
Field of View: N/A
Eye Relief: Unlimited
Features: Reflex with titanium housing instead of aluminum; Solar Failsafe function; Shake Awake function, Super Led 2 MOA dot in a 32 MOA circle in choice of green or red, and the Multiple Reticle System allows the user to use circle and dot together or separately

Red: $435.28
Green: $470.58

HE509T-RD

Type: Red-dot/reflex red-dot
Weight: 1.72 oz.
Length: 1.6 in.
Power: 1X
Obj. Dia.: .63x.91 in.
Field of View: N/A
Eye Relief: Unlimited
Features: Enclosed reflex sight with titanium housing; Solar Failsafe feature; Shake Awake feature; Super LED Multiple Reticle System with a 32 MOA circle and 2 MOA dot, all in red, that can be used together or individually
MSRP $505.87

HE512C-GD, HS512C

Type: Red-dot/reflex red-dot
Weight: 8.1 oz.
Length: 3.35 in.
Power: 1X
Obj. Dia.: .91x1.26 in.
Field of View: N/A
Eye Relief: Unlimited
Features: Intended for carbine and rifle applications; enclosed reflex sight; Holosun's Gold Super LED display; Shake Awake function; Solar Failsafe function; Multiple reticle system with a 65 MOA circle and a 2 MOA dot, choice of gold or red, that can be used together or each element separately; Gold model number ends in "GD"

Red: $423.52
Gold: $458.81

OPTICS

Holosun

HOLOSUN
HE512T-RD,
HE512T-GR

HOLOSUN
HS407C X2,
HS407CO
X2

HOLOSUN
HS407K X2

HOLOSUN
HS507K X2

HE512T-RD, HE512T-GR
Type: Red-dot/reflex red-dot
Weight: 9.1 oz.
Length: 3.35 in.
Power: 1X
Obj. Dia.: .91x1.26 in.
Field of View: N/A
Eye Relief: Unlimited
Features: Enclosed reflex has a titanium housing; Solar Failsafe function; Shake Awake function; Super LED display; Multiple Reticle System with a 65 MOA circle and a 2 MOA dot, available in choice of red or green; that can be used together or each element separately; multilayer reflective glass; RD model is red, GR model is green
Red:. $588.22
Green: $623.52

HS407C X2, HS407CO X2
Type: Red-dot/reflex red-dot
Weight: 1.5 oz.

Length: 1.78 in.
Power: 1X
Obj. Dia.: .63x.91 in.
Field of View: N/A
Eye Relief: Unlimited
Features: A reflex sight with multilayer glass coatings; shake-awake feature; Solar Failsafe; red 2 MOA dot; 10 daylight settings and two nighttime; 1 MOA clicks; CO X2 model has a an 8 MOA open circle red dot
HS407C X2: $282.34
HS407CO X2: $317.64

HS407K X2
Type: Red-dot/reflex red-dot
Weight: 1 oz.
Length: 1.6 in.
Power: 1X
Obj. Dia.: .58x.77 in.
Field of View: N/A
Eye Relief: Unlimited

Features: 6 MOA red dot; Shake Awake; Super LED; multilayer reflective glass; 10 daylight and two nighttime brightness settings
MSRP. $258.81

HS507K X2
Type: Red-dot/reflex red-dot
Weight: 1 oz.
Length: 1.6 in.
Power: 1X
Obj. Dia.: .58x.77 in.
Field of View: N/A
Eye Relief: Unlimited
Features: Super small reflex with Shake Awake function; multi-reticle system has red 32 MOA circle with a 2 MOA dot, both in red only, that can be used together or each element separately
MSRP. $341.16

Kahles

KAHLES
HELIA RD

HELIA RD
Type: Reflex sight
Weight: 1.4 oz.
Length: 2.16 in.
Power: 1X
Obj. Dia.: 26X22mm

Features: Anti-reflection lens coating for clear view; 2 MOA red-dot with four illumination settings; includes Picatinny rail mount
MSRP. $369.00

Konus

KONUS SIGHTPRO
ATOMIC 2.0

KONUS SIGHTPRO
ATOMIC QR

KONUS SIGHTPRO
FISSION 2.0

SIGHTPRO ATOMIC 2.0
Type: Red-dot
Weight: 3.8 oz.
Length: 2.4 in.
Power: 1X
Field of View: 76 ft @ 100 yds
Features: Illuminated reticle dots; fits both Picatinny and Weaver rails
MSRP $124.99

SIGHTPRO ATOMIC QR
Type: Red-dot
Weight: 6.5 oz.
Length: 2.5 in.
Power: 1X

Features: Illuminated reticle dots; fits both Picatinny and Weaver rails
MSRP. $89.00

SIGHTPRO FISSION 2.0
Type: Red-dot/reflex sight
Weight: 1.76 oz.
Length: 1.7 in.
Power: 1X
Field of View: 115 ft @ 100 yds
Features: Illuminated reticle dots; fits both Picatinny and Weaver rails
MSRP. $179.99

Lasermax

LASERMAX GRIPSENSE LIGHT AND LASERS

LASERMAX LIGHTNING LASER WITH GRIPSENSE

GRIPSENSE LIGHT AND LASERS

Type: Laser
Weight: 1.5 oz.
Battery Life: At least 4 hours
Laser Power Output: Less than 5 mw
Laser Wavelength: 510–535 nm
Red . . . . **$113.99–$241.67**
Green. . . . . **$197.92–$241.67**

LIGHTNING LASER WITH GRIPSENSE

Type: Laser
Weight: .5 oz.
Features: Dual-activation via the GripSense technology that does not alter grip, or via push-button; steady or pulse beam; Rail Vise mounting technology; fits Picatinny or Weaver-type rails; red or green beam
Red **$165.10**
Green. **$220.51**

Leapers, Inc.

LEAPERS UTG ITA RED/GREEN CLOSE QUARTERS BATTLE (CQB) T-DOT SIGHT

LEAPERS UTG OP3 SL, SLS

LEAPERS, INC. UTG PRO FLIP-UP SIGHTS, PICATINNY

UTG OP3 SL, SLS

Type: Red-dot/reflex red-dot
Weight: 1.81 oz.
Length: 1.89 in.
Power: 1X
Obj. Dia.: N/A
Field of View: N/A
Eye Relief: Unlimited
Features: An IPSX7 waterproof-rated reflex red-dot with an aluminum housing; 1 MOA clicks; removable low-profile Picatinny base; can co-witness with suppressor-height iron sights; side-loading battery compartment; 4 MOA dot with eight brightness settings; compatible with most optics-ready pistols; SLS model has additional Surrounding Light Sensor that can automatically brighten/dampen dot intensity
SL. **$164.97**
SLS. **$174.97**

UTG ITA RED/GREEN CLOSE QUARTERS BATTLE (CQB) T-DOT SIGHT

Type: Red-dot
Weight: 13.1 oz.
Length: 6.1 in.
Power: 1X
Field of View: 85 ft @ 100 yds
Eye Relief: Unlimited
Features: Completely sealed; shock-proof, fogproof, and rainproof; 4 MOA red/green single dot reticle or quick-to-acquire red/green T-dot reticle; premium zero lockable and zero resettable target turrets; TactEdge angled integral sunshade reduces glare off the lens while maintaining superb light transmission clarity
MSRP. **$99.97**

UTG PRO FLIP-UP SIGHTS, PICATINNY

Features: Aircraft-grade aluminum construction with reinforced steel components; matte black anodized finish; fits most Picatinny rails; locks upon flipping up, push-button spring lowers sights; front sight is standard elevation for AR-15 A2 front sight post
Front:. **$42.97**
Rear: **$42.97**

Leica Camera AG

LEICA CAMERA AG TEMPUS ASPH

TEMPUS ASPH

Type: Reflex sight
Weight: 1.41 oz.
Power: 1X
Obj. Dia.: 21X25mm

Features: Utilizes an aspheric lens for a more exacting red-dot image; aluminum housing; choice of 2 or 3.5 MOA dot
MSRP. **$639.00**

Leupold & Stevens

LEUPOLD & STEVENS DELTAPOINT MICRO

DELTAPOINT MICRO

Type: Red-dot/reflex red-dot
Weight: 1.1 oz.
Length: N/A
Power: 1X
Obj. Dia.: N/A
Field of View: N/A
Eye Relief: Unlimited

Features: A very low-profile and concealable red-dot that's the same height as most factory iron sights; fully enclosed design; 3 MOA dot; CR1632 battery; eight illumination settings with night vision-compatible illumination; currently available for Glock and S&W M&P pistols
MSRP. **$399.99**

OPTICS

Leupold & Stevens

LEUPOLD DELTAPOINT PRO

LEUPOLD
& STEVENS
DELTAPOINT PRO
6 MOA

LEUPOLD
& STEVENS
VX-FREEDOM RDS

DELTAPOINT PRO
Type: Red-dot/reflex sight
Weight: 1.95 oz.
Length: 1.82 in.
Power: 1X
Eye Relief: Unlimited
Features: Water- and fogproof;
DiamondCoat; removable, adjustable
rear sight; tool-less, spring actuated
battery compartment; illuminated
reticle available
MSRP . . . . $449.99–$549.99

DELTAPOINT PRO 6 MOA
Type: Red-dot/reflex red-dot
Weight: 2 oz.
Length: N/A
Power: 1X
Obj. Dia.: N/A
Field of View: N/A
Eye Relief: Unlimited
Features: Designed for competitors
and personal-defense, the large 6
MOA red dot is appropriate for close-

quarters engagements; motion sensor
technology; in black or flat dark earth;
daylight bright illumination with eight
settings
MSRP $449.99

FREEDOM RDS
Type: Red-dot
Weight: 6.9 oz.
Length: 5.5 in.
Power: 1X
Features: 1MOA dot reticle; one ver-
sion has ¼ MOA click adjustments, a
second has exposed BDC elevation
turrets designed for use with the .223
Rem. 55-grain load; built-in Motion
Sensor Technology saves battery life
Optic only: $279.99
With mount: $299.99
With mount/BDC reticle: . . . $399.99

Lucid Optics, LLC

LUCID
OPTICS HDX

LUCID OPTICS
LITL MO

LUCID OPTICS M7

HDX
Type: Red-dot
Weight: 11 oz.
Length: 4.35 in.
Field of View: Infinite
Features: Roughly have the weight of
the original HD7, the HDx has a 3
MOA base; is shockproof up to .458
SOCOM; auto-brightness control
MSRP $355.99

LITL MO
Type: Reflex sight
Weight: 1 oz.
Obj. Dia.: 28X19mm
Field of View: Infinite
Features: Just one ounce! This micro
reflex sight has a 3MOA red dot; ½-

MOA adjustments; shockproof up to
.458 SOCOM use
MSRP $369.99

M7
Type: Red-dot
Weight: 4.4 oz.
Length: 2.6 in.
Power: 1X
Obj. Dia.: 25mm
Field of View: Infinite
Features: A very small red dot optic
with an M5 reticle that sports a 4
MOA red dot within a 32 MOA
circle; Picatinny rail adaptor included;
11 brightness settings; modular
mounting system
MSRP $299.99

OPTICS

Meopta USA

MEOPTA MEOMAG3
MAGNIFIER

MEOMAG3 MAGNIFIER
Type: Magnifier
Weight: 7.48 oz.
Length: 4.65 in.
Power: 3x
Obj. Dia.: 20mm
Exit Pupil: 5.4 mm
Field of View: 7 degrees
Eye Relief: 60mm

Features: Works with both Meopta
and other red dot sights on the market; works as a monocular; waterproof, shockproof, and fogproof;
Meopta's Fast Opening Lens Covers;
optional accessories include fixed,
quick-release and hinge mounts, tactical carry pouch, and a hard case
MSRP $999.99

Minox

MINOX RV1

RV1
Type: Red-dot
Weight: 3.38 oz.
Length: 2.51 in.
Power: 1X
Field of View: Infinite
Features: A very small and lightweight red-dot with a 2 MOA dot; 100 MOA elevation/windage in 1 MOA clicks; three night, six daylight, and extra-bright daylight settings; IPX7 waterproofing
MSRP $283.67

Newcon Optik

NEWCON OPTIK NC 4X32

NEWCON OPTIK NC 6X50

NEWCON OPTIK NC BURD

NC 4X32
Type: Red-dot/reflex red-dot
Weight: 16.47 oz.
Length: 5.39 in.
Power: 4X
Obj. Dia.: 32mm
Field of View: N/A
Eye Relief: 2.83 in.
Features: Holographic sight with illuminated reticle in user-selectable red or green; Picatinny mount and topside rail; night vision/thermal compatible
MSRP $565.00

NC 6X50
Type: Red-dot/reflex red-dot
Weight: 20.56 oz.
Length: 6.61 in.
Power: 6X
Obj. Dia.: 50mm
Field of View: N/A
Eye Relief: 2.83 in.
Features: Holographic sight with illuminated BDC rangefinding reticle in user-selectable red or green; Designed to take heavy recoil; Picatinny mount and topside rail
MSRP $767.00

NC BURD
Type: Red-dot/reflex red-dot
Weight: 2.2 oz.
Length: 1.8 in.
Power: 1X
Obj. Dia.: N/A
Field of View: N/A
Eye Relief: Unlimited
Features: Intended as back-up red-dot for CQB engagements; can be used on rifles, shotguns, and optics-ready pistols; side-loading battery compartment; integrates with Newcon's NC 4X32 and 6X50 optics; infrared compatible; adjustable LED; Picatinny mount
MSRP $337.00

Night Fision

NIGHT FISION ACCUR8

NIGHT FISION COSTA

NIGHT FISION OPTICS READY STEALTH

NIGHT FISION PERFECT DOT

NIGHT FISION SUPPRESSOR HEIGHT

ACCUR8
Features: Night sights with a black circle rear and front circle in choice of blue, orange, red, white, or yellow; for Glock, CZ-USA, S&W
MSRP $110.00

COSTA
Features: Serrated matte black rear, circle night sight front in choice of orange, white, or yellow; for Glock
MSRP $110.00

OPTICS READY STEALTH
Features: Works in conjunction with slide-mounted reflex sights; front ring in orange, yellow, or black dots; rear square-notch sight in serrated matte black or serrated matte black with two black dots; for Glock, CZ-USA, SIG Sauer
MSRP . . . . $99.00–$119.00

PERFECT DOT
Features: Night sights with choice of square-notch rear, u-notch rear, front sight only, and suppressor height; front ring available in white, orange, red, yellow, and blue; rear available in white or black dot; available for Canik, H&K, Springfield Armory, Novak 1911
MSRP . . . . $48.00–$121.75

SUPPRESSOR HEIGHT
Features: Flat matte black rear with a night sight circle front in white, yellow, orange, red, or blue, and orange and yellow are also available with Night Fision's Dome Glow glowing ring; for Glock, Canik, SIG Sauer, S&W
MSRP . . . . $48.00–$129.00

OPTICS

Primary Arms

PRIMARY ARMS SLX ADVANCED PUSH-BUTTON MICRO RED DOT GENII

PRIMARY ARMS SLX MD-25

SLX ADVANCED PUSH-BUTTON MICRO RED DOT GENII

Type: Red-dot/reflex red-dot
Weight: 3.8 oz.
Length: N/A
Power: 1X
Obj. Dia.: N/A
Field of View: N/A
Eye Relief: Unlimited
Features: Redesigned body has low-profile shield adjustment turrets; night-vision compatible; true daylight bright settings; 12 illumination settings; ½ MOA clicks; 2 MOA red dot
MSRP $149.99

SLX MD-25

Type: Red-dot/reflex red-dot
Weight: 6.5 oz.
Length: N/A
Power: 1X
Obj. Dia.: N/A
Field of View: N/A
Eye Relief: Unlimited
Features: Super-compact tubular-designed red-dot with 12 brightness settings; night-vision compatible; aluminum housing; 2 MOA dot; ½ MOA clicks
MSRP $169.99

Riton Optics

RITON OPTICS X1 TACTIX ARD

RITON OPTICS X1 TACTIX RRD

RITON OPTICS X3 TACTIX MPRD

RITON OPTICS X3 TACTIX PRD

X1 TACTIX ARD

Type: Red-dot
Weight: 3.5 oz.
Length: 2.48 in.
Power: 1X
Obj. Dia.: 23mm
Field of View: Infinite

Features: In Riton's (X1) price level, this optic sports 120 MOA elevation/windage with 1-MOA clicks; parallax fixed at 50 yd., six brightness settings
MSRP $229.99

X1 TACTIX RRD

Type: Red-dot
Weight: 9.5 oz.
Length: 3.76 in.
Power: 1X
Obj. Dia.: 29mm
Main Dia.: 30mm
Field of View: Infinite
Features: A more substantial red-dot in Riton's budget-friendly (X1) family, this optic has a 30mm tube; 2 MOA dot with six brightness levels; 120 MOA elevation/windage with 1-MOA clicks; 40,000 hours battery life
MSRP $229.99

X3 TACTIX MPRD

Type: Red-dot/reflex red-dot
Weight: 0.6 oz.
Length: 1.6 in.

Power: 1X
Obj. Dia.: N/A
Field of View: N/A
Eye Relief: Unlimited
Features: 10 levels of illumination, night-vision compatible on levels 1 and 2; water/fog/shock proof; CR2032 battery; 3 MOA red dot; 1 MOA clicks; optics ready footprint is S&W Shield RMSc-type
MSRP $299.99

X3 TACTIX PRD

Type: Reflex red-dot
Weight: 1.12 oz.
Length: 1.8 in.
Power: 1X
Field of View: Infinite
Features: A micro reflex in Riton's (X3) price level family that features a 3 MOA red dot with six levels of illumination; 45 MOA total adjustment in 1 MOA increments
MSRP $299.99

Shield Sights

SHIELD SIGHTS RMSC

SHIELD SIGHTS RMSW

RMSC

Type: Reflex red dot
Weight: .57 oz.

Length: 17 in.
Power: 1x
Features: Reflex Mini Sight Compact; designed specifically for use on sub-compact pistols; with a 4 MOA or 8 MOA dot
MSRP $450.00

RMSW

Type: Reflex sight

Power: 1X
Field of View: Unlimited
Eye Relief: Unlimited
Features: Model stands for Reflex Mini Sight Waterproof; gasket sealed and watertight to 20 meters for up to thirty minutes; hard-coated S1O2 polymer lens; 4 MOA or 8 MOA dot
MSRP $650.00

OPTICS

Shield Sights

SHIELD SIGHTS SMS2

SMS2
Type: Reflex sight
Power: 1X
Field of View: Unlimited
Eye Relief: Unlimited

Features: Updated "2.0" version of the original Shield Mini Sight (SMS); available with 1 MOA, 4 MOA, 8 MOA, or 65/1 MOA ring/dot
MSRP **$350.00**

Sightmark (Sellmark Corporation)

SIGHTMARK ULTRA SHOT A-SPEC

SIGHTMARK ULTRA SHOT R-SPEC

SIGHTMARK ULTRA SHOT M-SPEC FMS

SIGHTMARK MINI SHOT A-SPEC M1 GREEN, RED

SIGHTMARK ELEMENT MINI SOLAR RED-DOT

MINI SHOT A-SPEC M1 GREEN, RED
Type: Red-dot/reflex red-dot
Weight: 2.3 oz.
Length: 1.85 in.
Power: 1X
Obj. Dia.: 22x17mm
Field of View: N/A
Eye Relief: Unlimited
Features: Green or red 2 MOA illuminated dot; aluminum alloy housing; parallax free; 10 brightness levels; 110 MOA adjustment
MSRP **$119.99**

MTS MINI SOLAR RED DOT
Type: Red-dot/reflex red-dot
Weight: 5.5 oz.
Length: 2.96 in.
Power: 1X
Obj. Dia.: 22mm
Field of View: N/A
Eye Relief: Unlimited
Features: Solar power or CR2032 battery; recoil rated to .338 Win. Mag.; AR Red lens coating; IP67 waterproof rating; 120 MOA

elevation, 160 windage adjustable; 1 MOA click; adjustable mounting height; Eclipse light management system; 3 MOA dot; hinged battery door
MSRP **$239.99**

ULTRA SHOT A-SPEC
Type: Reflex sight
Weight: 10.8 oz.
Length: 4.33 in.
Power: 1X
Obj. Dia.: 33X24mm
Field of View: Unlimited
Eye Relief: Unlimited
Features: The A stands for Advanced. Features include: scratch-resistant wide-angle lens; aluminum hood and shield; 120 MOA windage and elevation adjustments in 1 MOA clicks; recoil-rated up to .338-caliber; one-hour shutoff; battery life of 2000 hours
MSRP **$179.99**

ULTRA SHOT M-SPEC FMS, M-SPEC LQD
Type: Reflex sight
Weight: 9.6 oz.

Length: 4.01 in.
Power: 1X
Obj. Dia.: 33X24mm
Field of View: Unlimited
Eye Relief: Unlimited
Features: Useful across law enforcement, hunting, and target competition disciplines, this rugged reflex sight's feature includes: waterproof to 40 feet; ability to handle recoil up to .50 BMG; 12-hour auto off with five minute motion activation shutoff/on; 65 MOA dot; 120 MOA of windage and elevation adjustment in 1 MOA clicks; 2000 hours of battery life; integrated sunshade; quick-detach option with the LQD version
FMS: **$239.99**
LQD: **$299.99**

ULTRA SHOT R-SPEC
Type: Reflex sight
Weight: 10.7 oz.
Length: 4.33 in.
Power: 1X
Obj. Dia.: 33X24mm
Field of View: Unlimited
Eye Relief: Unlimited
Features: The R stands for Range. Features include: 10 brightness settings; 120 MOA of windage and elevation adjustment with 1 MOA clicks; choice of four each red or green reticles; one-hour auto shutoff
MSRP **$155.99**

SIG Sauer

SIG SAUER BRAVO3

BRAVO3
Type: Red-dot
Weight: 22 oz.
Length: 6.45 in.
Power: 3X
Obj. Dia.: 24mm
Exit Pupil: 8mm
Field of View: 10 degrees

Features: A 3X red dot in SIG's battlesight family with choice of .300 BLK or .223/5.56 NATO Horseshoe dot; 120 MOA windage/elevation with ½-MOA clicks; motion-activated illumination with eight daytime and three night vision settings
MSRP **$422.99**

SIG Sauer

SIG SAUER BRAVO5

SIG SAUER ECHO3

SIG SAUER JULIET4 MAGNIFIER

SIG SAUER LIMA365

SIG SAUER ROMEO-MSR

SIG SAUER ROMEO ZERO

SIG SAUER ROMEO1

SIG SAUER ROMEO1PRO

SIG SAUER ROMEO3MAX

SIG SAUER ROMEO3XL

BRAVO5
Type: Red-dot
Weight: 23 oz.
Length: 6.45 in.
Power: 5X
Obj. Dia.: 30mm
Exit Pupil: 6.4mm
Field of View: 6 degrees
Features: Similar to the BRAVO3, including the same reticle choices, but in a 5X magnification
MSRP $481.99

ECHO3
Type: Reflex sight
Weight: 14.3 oz.
Length: 4.3 in.
Power: 1–6X, 2–12X
Obj. Dia.: 23mm
Features: A thermal imaging reflex sight with multiple reticles including active and custom fixed reticles; 11 color palettes; six brightness settings; 150 MOA elevation/windage travel
1–6X **$2746.99**
2–12X **$3295.99**

JULIET4 MAGNIFIER
Type: Magnifier
Weight: 12.5 oz.
Length: 4.2 in.
Power: 4X
Obj. Dia.: 24mm
Exit Pupil: 6mm
Field of View: 6.25 degrees
Eye Relief: 65mm
Features: Included spacers allow height adjustment; stand-alone or with red dot sight; aircraft grade CNC aluminum housing; quick release mount with recoil lugs; IPX-8 waterproofing of 20 meters per 1 hour; protectors for front thread-in lens and rear flip back lens
MSRP . . . . $422.99–$447.99

LIMA365
Type: Laser
Features: Designed specifically for SIG's P365 compact handgun, the rail-mounted laser is available in either red or green
MSRP . . . . $177.99–$245.99

ROMEO-MSR
Type: Reflex sight
Weight: 4.9 oz.
Length: 3.1 in.
Power: 1X
Obj. Dia.: 20mm
Features: Houses a green 2MOA dot; IPX7 waterproofing; ten day, two night vision illumination settings; 100 MOA total windage/elevation travel
MSRP $109.99

ROMEO ZERO
Type: Reflex sight
Weight: 0.4 oz.
Length: 1.6 in.
Power: 1X
Obj. Dia.: 24mm
Features: Choice of 3 or 6 MOA dot in red; eight daytime illumination settings; 20,000-hour runtime
MSRP $168.99

ROMEO1
Type: Red-dot/reflex sight
Weight: 0.8 oz.
Length: 1.8 in.
Power: 1X
Eye Relief: Unlimited
Features: Also available with a universal mount with rear sight dovetail adapters for the most popular handguns on the market; also available with either an M1913 Picatinny or KeyMod Rail interface for use with today's MSR platforms; molded glass aspheric lens with high performance coatings for superior light transmittance and zero distortion; manual illumination controls that remember your last used settings; MOTAC (Motion Activated Illumination) powers up when it senses motion and powers down when it does not; top-loading CR1632 battery, allowing for quick battery replacement without having to remove the sight from the firearm; extremely strong and lightweight aircraft grade CNC magnesium housing waterproof (IPX-7 rated for complete immersion up to 1 meter)
MSRP $354.99

ROMEO1PRO
Type: Reflex sight
Weight: 1 oz.
Length: 1.8 in.
Power: 1X
Obj. Dia.: 30mm
Features: Choice of 3 or 6 MOA dot; 10 daytime and two night vision illumination settings; 100 MOA total elevation/windage travel
Black $439.99
Flat dark earth $464.99

ROMEO3MAX
Type: Reflex sight
Weight: 1.5 oz.
Length: 2.1 in.
Power: 1X
Obj. Dia.: 30mm
Features: Choice of 3 or 6 MOA dot; 10 daytime and two night vision illumination settings
MSRP $675.99

ROMEO3XL
Type: Reflex sight
Weight: 1.5 oz.
Length: 2.1 in.
Power: 1X
Obj. Dia.: 35mm
Features: Choice of 3 or 6 MOA dot; 10 daytime and two night vision illumination settings
MSRP $675.99

OPTICS

SIG Sauer

SIG SAUER ROMEO4H

SIG SAUER ROMEO4S

SIG SAUER ROMEO4T

SIG SAUER ROMEO5

SIG SAUER ROMEO7

SIG SAUER ROMEO8H

SIG SAUER ROMEO8T

ROMEO4H
Type: Red-dot
Weight: 3.4 oz.
Power: 1X
Obj. Diameter: 20mm
Features: Designed for a AR-platform pistols, MSRs, and shotguns; four reticle options; side-loading battery has 50,000+ hours of life
MSRP . . . . $371.99–$422.99

ROMEO4S
Type: Red-dot
Weight: 3.4 oz.
Power: 1X
Obj. Diameter: 20mm
Features: Solar powered red-dot runs in excess of 100,000+ with solar and battery usage; designed for AR-platform pistols, MSRs, and shotguns; lens caps and quick-release mount; four reticle choices
MSRP $481.99

ROMEO4T
Type: Red-dot
Weight: 3.2 oz.
Power: 1X
Obj. Diameter: 20mm
Features: Solar powered red dot runs in excess of 100,000+ with solar and battery usage; designed for

AR-platform pistols, MSRs, and shotguns; lens caps and quick-release mount; four reticle choices; tactical version designed for harsh environments
MSRP . . . . $583.99–$609.99

ROMEO5
Type: Red dot
Weight: 6 oz.
Length: 2.47 in.
Power: 1X
Obj. Dia.: 20mm
Eye Relief: Infinite
Features: Mounts on any platform; 2 MOA dot; motion-activated illumination; 10 brightness settings; front-mounting AAA battery or side-loading CR2032 battery; waterproof and fogproof; Picatinny low mount and co-witness 1.41-inch riser mount included; torx tool; battery; lens cloth; lens covers; reticles include 2 MOA dot with 65 MOA circle, 2 MOA red dot, 2 MOA green dot with triangle holds
MSRP . . . . $139.99–$168.99

ROMEO7
Type: Red-dot
Weight: 12.5 oz.
Length: 4.75 in.
Power: 1X
Eye Relief: Unlimited
Features: Low dispersion glass lens design with high-performance coatings for excellent light transmittance and zero distortion; 2 MOA dot is

optimal for close quarters battle to mid-range target engagement; MOTAC (Motion Activated Illumination) powers up when it senses motion and powers down when it does not; 62,500 hours of continuous battery life in medium illumination setting; ready to mount with a standard QD mount provided, but can be customized with vertical spacers to fit a variety of systems
MSRP $219.99

ROMEO8H
Type: Red-dot
Power: 1X
Obj. Dia.: 38mm
Eye Relief: Unlimited
Features: Similar to the 8T, but with a 2 MOA red ballistic circle dot
MSRP $608.99

ROMEO8T
Type: Red-dot
Power: 1X
Obj. Dia.: 38mm
Eye Relief: Unlimited
Features: Intended for use on MSR rifle platforms and on shotguns; 2 MOA/65 MOA circle reticle; MOTAC motion activated illumination power up/down; LED illumination for daytime use; four integrated user-selectable reticles; lens covers; ½ hex bolt mount; 100,000 hours battery life; waterproof and fog-proof
MSRP . . . . $726.99–$752.99

Steiner

STEINER DRS 1X

DRS 1X
Type: Reflex sight
Weight: 10.4 oz.
Length: 3.88 in.
Power: 1X

Features: Choice of three reticle options; seven illumination settings; 50 MOA windage and elevation adjustment
MSRP $789.99

OPTICS

STEINER MICRO REFLEX SIGHT (MRS)

STEINER T536

STEINER TOR FUSION

STEINER TOR MINI

MICRO REFLEX SIGHT (MRS)

Type: Red-dot/reflex
Weight: 2.5 oz.
Power: 1X
Eye Relief: Unlimited
Features: Picatinny mount; waterproof; holographic sight; adjustable for windage and elevation; illuminated
MSRP $619.99

T332, T432, T536

Type: Red-dot
Weight: 15.9 oz., 16.6 oz., 17.8 oz.
Length: 4.8 in., 5 in., 5.7 in.
Power: 3X, 4X, 5X
Obj. Dia.: 32mm
Field of View: 10.5m@100m

Eye Relief: 2.56 in.
Features: Intended mostly for AR-platform use, these T-dot red-dot sights are shockproof, fogproof, and waterproof and have 50 MOA elevation/windage travel
T332 . . . .$749.99
T432 . . . .$821.99
T536 . . . .$937.99

TOR FUSION

Type: Laser
Features: A rail-mounted combo white light and aiming laser; laser available in red or green; left and right activation buttons; mil-spec engineering; anodized aluminum housing; dustproof; splash-proof;

windage and elevation adjustment screws; auto-mode that senses motion like draw from a holster and automatically turns on the laser; boost mode forces unit to maximum output
MSRP $436.99

TOR MINI

Type: Laser
Features: Similar to the Micro, but intended for rail mounting forward of the trigger guard. Red and green lasers available; low, medium, high, and high pulse modes plus setting memory; auto-on senses movement such as retrieval from a nightstand safe and automatically activates laser; ambidextrous use
MSRP $389.99

Trijicon

TRIJICON GLOCK SUPPRESSOR BRIGHT & TOUGH NIGHT SIGHTS

TRIJICON FIBER SIGHTS

TRIJICON HD XR NIGHT SIGHTS

TRIJICON MACHINE GUN REFLEX SIGHT (MGRS)

TRIJICON DI NIGHT SIGHTS

BRIGHT & TOUGH SUPPRESSOR NIGHT SIGHTS

Features: Three-dot iron sights; shock-resistant design; increase night-fire accuracy by as much as 5x; available for a wide variety of Glock, FNH, H&K, SIG Sauer, Smith & Wesson, and Springfield Armory handguns
MSRP $145.00

DI NIGHT SIGHTS

Features: Uses both tritium and fiber optics with an interchangeable fiber optic pipe; tritium lamp is capped

with a sapphire jewel; serrated notch/two-dot rear; available for Glock, SIG Sauer, S&W, and Springfield Armory pistols
MSRP $150.00

FIBER SIGHTS

Features: Front post is .110-inch wide with a .060-inch-diameter fiber; rear sight is blacked out with a .125-inch square notch, is steeply hooked for one-handed slide manipulation as needed, and has rounded edges to reduce snagging; red front installed, red and green replacements included
MSRP $105.00

HD XR NIGHT SIGHTS

Features: Thin front sight post pro-

vides a larger field of view; available for Beretta, FNH, GLOCK, H&K, Sig Sauer, Smith & Wesson, and Springfield Armory handguns; front sight choice of yellow or orange outline
Front sight only: $99.00
Front and rear: $175.00

MACHINE GUN REFLEX SIGHT (MGRS)

Type: Red-dot/reflex sight
Weight: 66.9 oz.
Length: 8.78 in.
Power: 1x
Features: Created to withstand the constant, violent battering of machine guns; large objective lens with a 3-inch-by-2-inch viewing area; 35 MOA segmented circle reticle; centered 3 MOA dot for precise aiming at close combat to extended ranges; powered by a single CR123A battery that lasts 1000 hours of continuous operation
MSRP $4499.00

Trijicon

TRIJICON MINIATURE RIFLE OPTIC (MRO)

TRIJICON MINIATURE RIFLE OPTIC (MRO) PATROL

TRIJICON MRO HD

TRIJICON RMRCC RED-DOT

MINIATURE RIFLE OPTIC (MRO)

Type: Red-dot
Weight: 4.1 oz.
Length: 2.6 in.
Power: 1X
Eye Relief: Unlimited
Features: Large viewing area; adjustable brightness settings; ambidextrous brightness control; easy-to-set adjusters; aircraft-grade aluminum housing; surface-flush adjusters; waterproof to 30 meters; single lithium battery

Green dot:. . . . . . . $613.00–$749.00
Red dot:. . . . . $579.00–$639.00

MINIATURE RIFLE OPTIC (MRO) PATROL

Type: Red dot
Weight: 5.1 oz.
Length: 4.1 in.
Power: 1X
Obj. Dia.: 25mm
Eye Relief: Infinite
Features: Lens covers; Kill Flash feature that eliminates glare; quick-release mount in full height or co-witness configurations; 70 MOAs of adjustment are in 0.5-MOA increments; runs for five years of continuous use on its 2032 battery; available without mount

Red dot . . . . $579.00–$639.00
Green dot . . . . $613.00–$739.00

MRO HD

Type: Red-dot/reflex red-dot
Weight: 4.6 oz.
Length: 2.9 in.
Power: 1X
Obj. Dia.: N/A
Field of View: N/A
Eye Relief: Unlimited
Features: Miniature Rifle Optic; can be used on rifles, carbines, and shotguns; both-eyes-open application; ambidextrous brightness controls; advanced lens coatings; fully sealed and waterproof; sub-flush adjusters; 70 MOA of adjustment; 16 illumination settings on the 68 MOA reticle with 2 MOA red dot; available as a standalone optic/no mount, with low mount, with full co-witness mount, with lower 1/3 co-witness mount, and as a combo unit with a full co-witness mount with a 3X magnifier and quick-release side mount

MSRP . . . . $919.00–$1428.00

RMRCC

Type: Red-dot/reflex red-dot
Weight: 1 oz.
Length: 1.8 in.
Power: 1X
Obj. Dia.: N/A
Field of View: N/A
Eye Relief: Unlimited
Features: 3.25 or 6.5 MOA red dot; eight illumination settings include two for night vision; forged aluminum housing; lock-in and lock-out modes; CR2032 battery; multi-coated lenses; waterproof to 20m/66 ft.; snag-free design

MSRP $699.00

Truglo

TRUGLO FIBER OPTIC PRO

TRUGLO SIGHT LINE HANDGUN LASER

TRUGLO TRITON 30MM TRI-COLOR TACTICAL TG8230GB

TRUGLO TRUTEC MICRO

TRUGLO TFX

FIBER OPTIC PRO

Features: Patented light reflector design; blacked-out rear with serrated anti-glare face
MSRP $76.99

SIGHT LINE HANDGUN LASER

Type: Laser
Features: Red or green laser created for pistol Picatinny/Weaver, Glock and other rail mounts; pulse and constant beam modes; adjustable recoil lug
MSRP . . . . $86.99–$161.99

TRITON 30MM TRI-COLOR TACTICAL RED DOT

Weight: 6.4 oz.
Length: 5.2 in.
Power: 1X
Obj. Dia.: 30mm
Features: Weaver style mount; multi-coated lenses; tri-color illuminated reticle; Model #TG8230B has 5 MOA single dot; Model #TG8230GB has 3 MOA center dot and surrounding aiming ring

Picatinny mount: $98.99
Cantilever mount: $141.99

TRUTEC MICRO

Type: Reflex sight
Power: 1X
Obj. Dia.: 23X17mm
Eye Relief: Unlimited
Features: Ten brightness settings; compatible with most pistol optics mounting plates/platforms; shock-, water-, and fog-resistant; includes ABS hardshell cover; aluminum body
MSRP $218.99

TFX

Features: Day/night sights with a combination of tritium and fiber optic pipe; white contrasting ring around front sight dot; for a wide range of handguns
MSRP . . . . $76.99–$153.99

OPTICS

Vortex Optics

VORTEX CROSSFIRE

VORTEX SPARC AR

VORTEX OPTICS SPARC SOLAR

VORTEX SPITFIRE AR PRISM

VORTEX STRIKEFIRE II

VORTEX VENOM

VORTEX VIPER

CROSSFIRE

Type: Red dot
Weight: 5.2 oz.
Length: 2.5 in.
Power: 1X
Eye Relief: Infinite

Features: Daylight-bright 2 MOA dot; 100 MOA of elevation and windage adjustment; parallax-free viewing
MSRP $219.99

SPARC AR

Weight: 7.5 oz.
Length: 2.9 in.
Power: 1X
Eye Relief: Unlimited
Features: Fully multi-coated; bright red dot highly visible in daylight; ten variable illumination settings; waterproof, fogproof, and shockproof; hard anodized finish; twelve-hour auto-shutdown feature
MSRP $274.99

SPARC SOLAR

Type: Red-dot/reflex red-dot
Weight: 5.9 oz.
Length: 2.6 in.
Power: 1X
Obj. Dia.: N/A
Field of View: N/A
Eye Relief: Unlimited
Features: Red-dot sight with a 2 MOA dot; parallax free; 1 MOA clicks; power source auto-switches from sun to battery depending on amount of sun; CR2032 battery; includes low mount and lower 1/3 co-witness mounts
MSRP $399.99

SPITFIRE AR PRISM

Type: Red-dot
Weight: 11.2 oz.
Length: 4.3 in.
Power: 1X, 3X

Field of View: 29 ft @ 100 yds
Eye Relief: 3.8 in.
Features: Fully multi-coated; prism-based design; twelve variable illumination settings; waterpoof and shockproof; hard anodized finish; red or green reticle option
MSRP $349.99

STRIKEFIRE II

Type: Red-dot
Weight: 7.2 oz.
Length: 5.6 in.
Power: 1X
Features: Shock-, water-, and fogproof; illuminated red dot; red/green dot cantilever and low mount models available
MSRP $274.99

VENOM

Type: Red-dot/reflex sight
Weight: 1.1 oz.
Length: 1.9 in.
Power: 1X
Eye Relief: Unlimited
Features: Bright red dot; Picatinny mount; choice of 3 or 6 MOA dots; machined aluminum housing
MSRP $349.99

VIPER

Type: Red-dot/reflex sight
Weight: 1.37 oz.
Length: 1.8 in.
Power: 1X
Eye Relief: Unlimited
Features: Bright red dot; Picatinny mount; 6 MOA dot
MSRP $349.99

Williams Gun Sight Company

WILLIAMS GUN SIGHT COMPANY AR-15 FOLDING TACTICAL SIGHT

AR-15 FOLDING TACTICAL SIGHT

Features: CNC high-grade machined aluminum construction; upright lock; fit any Picatinny-style rail; windage and elevation adjustments
MSRP $139.95

XS Sights

XS SIGHTS DXT

DXT

Features: Defensive Express Tritium available in Big Dot or Standard Dot versions for the CZ P10C, Kimber Micro 9 and 380, and BerettaPico
MSRP . . . . $137.00–$212.00

XS Sights

XS SIGHTS DXT2 BIG DOT NIGHT SIGHTS   **XS SIGHTS DXW**

XS SIGHTS F8 NIGHT SIGHTS   **XS SIGHTS XT12**

DXT2 BIG DOT NIGHT SIGHTS

Features: Available in orange or yellow, the sight design naturally allows the shooter to focus on the front sight; dot absorbs light and glows when conditions aren't dark enough to sustain the visible glow of tritium; available for a wide variety of handgun models and with yellow or orange front sights

MSRP . . . . $39.00–$155.00

DXW

Features: Defensive Express White Rear available in Big Dot or Standard Dot versions for the CZ P10C, Kimber Micro 9 and 380, and Beretta Pico

MSRP . . . . $104.00–$175.99

F8 NIGHT SIGHTS

Weight: 2.4 oz.
Features: Presents a figure 8 top-to-bottom alignment of front and rear sight; orange ring of the sight absorbs ambient light to glow in low light conditions; wide notch rear allows more light around the front sight for quicker acquisition and also reduces glare in daylight; available for a variety of GLOCK, Sig Sauer, Smith & Wesson, Springfield, and FNH pistols

MSRP . . . . $71.00–$104.00

XT12

Features: Pistol sight designed to be secondary or backup sights for use during CQB engagements and also useful for 3-gun competition; front sight is orange ember glow; taller bases than in previous generations; fully ambidextrous for left-/right-hand shooting on top rail installations

MSRP . . . . $59.99–$155.00

RANGEFINDERS
ATN Corp.

ATN LASERBALLISTICS 1000, 1500

LASERBALLISTICS 1000, 1500

Weight: 5.4 oz.
Length: 4.17 in.
Power: 6X
Features: Pairs with ATN's Smart HD Bluetooth scopes; gives the distance to your target in five seconds, then moves the reticle of those scopes accordingly via the mobile app for a shot in under 15 seconds; range is from 5–1000 yds (Model 1000) and 5–1500 yds (Model 1500); waterproof

1000: $279.00
1500: $349.00

Bushnell Outdoor Products

BUSHNELL BONE COLLECTOR 850 LRF REALTREE EDGE

BUSHNELL NITRO 1800

BUSHNELL PRIME 1300/1700

BONE COLLECTOR 850 LRF REALTREE EDGE

Weight: 6.34 oz.
Length: 4.3 in.
Power: 6X24mm
Obj. Dia.: 24mm
Field of View: N/A
Eye Relief: N/A
Features: Range up to 850 yards or meters; 3-volt CR2 battery; ARC mode; IPX4 water resistance; all-glass optical system; fast-ranging scan mode; includes leather lanyard and battery

MSRP $139.99

NITRO 1800

Weight: 5.7 oz.
Length: 4.19 in.
Power: 6X
Obj. Dia.: 24mm
Features: With a stellar 2,000 yards reflective range (trees 1,200 yards, deer 800 yards), this is top choice for long-range target shooters more than hunters

MSRP $349.99

PRIME 1300, 1700

Weight: 5.9 oz.
Length: 4.27 in.
Power: 6X
Obj. Dia.: 24mm
Features: Running off a 3-volt CR2 battery; regular, bow, and rifle ARC modes; bull's-eye and brush scanning modes; IPX4 waterproofing; Rainguard glass coating; EXO Barrier

Prime 1300: $173.99
Prime 1700: $203.99

OPTICS

Hawke Sport Optics, LLC

HAWKE SPORT OPTICS VANTAGE

VANTAGE 400, 600, 900
Weight: 6 oz.
Length: 3.8 in.

Power: 6X
Obj. Dia.: 21mm
Field of View: 420 ft.@1000 yd.
Eye Relief: 0.7 in.
Features: BK7 prism; fully multi-coated lenses; standard, horizontal distance, angle, rain, and hunt modes; auto shut-off, water- and fog-proofed; ranging distances are 400, 600, and 900 meters relative to the same model numbers
400: $219.00
600: $239.00
900: $259.00

Kahles

KAHLES HELIA RF-M

HELIA RF-M
Weight: 7.5 oz.
Length: 4 in.
Power: 7X
Obj. Dia.: 25mm
Exit Pupil: 3.6mm
Field of View: 6.7 degrees
Eye Relief: 15mm
Features: A generous 7X rangefinder with an ergonomic housing; targeting to 2,000m; Enhanced Angle Compensation function; scan mode
MSRP. $549.00

Leica Camera AG

LEICA CAMERA AG RANGEMASTER CRF 2400-R

LEICA CAMERA AG RANGEMASTER CRF 2800 COM

RANGEMASTER CRF 2400-R
Type: Rangefinder
Weight: 6.5 oz.
Length: 4.5 in.
Power: 7X
Obj. Dia.: 24mm
Exit Pupil: 3.4mm
Field of View: 347 ft.@1,000 yd.
Eye Relief: 15mm
Features: Updated LED display adjusts to ambient light for better viewing; decimal results to 200 yards; equivalent horizontal range to 1200 yards
MSRP. $550.00

RANGEMASTER CRF 2800 COM
Weight: 6.7 oz.
Power: 7X
Obj. Dia.: 24mm
Exit Pupil: 3.4mm
Field of View: 115m @1,000 yd.
Eye Relief: 15mm
Features: Leica's ABC ballistic system; measurements to 2800 yards; works in combination with Leica's hunting app to relay information via Bluetooth to calculate holdover and distance corrections for given environmental conditions
MSRP. $749.00

Leupold & Stevens

RX-1600I TBR/W

LEUPOLD & STEVENS RX-1400I TBR/W

RX-1400I TBR/W
Weight: 5.1 oz.
Length: 4 in.
Power: 5X21mm
Obj. Dia.: 21mm
Field of View: 368 ft.@1000 yd.
Eye Relief: 18.3 mm
Features: True Ballistic Range/Wind (TBR/W) for firearm use; bow mode; line of sight; last target mode; TOLED display; max ranging capability 1400 yds.
MSRP. $199.99

RX-2800 TBR/W
Weight: 7.3 oz.
Length: 4.3 in.
Power: 7X
Field of View: 318 ft.@1000 yd.
Eye Relief: 16 mm
Features: Powered by Alpha IQ; OLED display; scan mode; trophy scale analysis; True Ballistic Range with Wind
MSRP. $599.99

OPTICS

Leupold & Stevens

LEUPOLD
RX-2800 TBR/W

RX-1600I TBR/W

Weight: 7.8 oz.
Length: 3.8 in.
Power: 6X
Exit Pupil: 3.6mm
Field of View: 315 ft.@1000 yd.
Eye Relief: 17mm
Features: Fully multi-coated glass;

Leupold's DNA technology; scan mode; choice of three reticles; line-of-sight distance; trophy scale technology; built-in inclinometer; True Ballistic Range with Wind; fold-down rubber eye cup; OLED display
MSRP $399.99

Newcon Optik

NEWCON
OPTIK LRM 2K

NEWCON OPTIK
LRM 1800S

NEWCON
OPTIK LRM
2200SI

NEWCON
OPTIK LRM
3500M

LRM 2K

Weight: 5.8 oz.
Length: 4.17 in.
Power: 7X
Obj. Dia.: 24mm
Field of View: 7.5 degrees
Eye Relief: 16mm
Features: Very lightweight rangefinder capable of reading targets to 2,000 meters (about 1.24 miles); built-in inclinometer; bluetooth compatible and works with NC Cronus App; speed detection; yards/meters display; TOLED display; in green/black
MSRP $674.00

LRM 1800S

Weight: 15.69 oz.
Length: 5 in.
Power: 7X
Obj. Dia.: 25mm
Field of View: 8 degrees
Eye Relief: 15mm
Features: Built-in speed detector; last 10 reading recall; target quality indicator; reticle pattern selection; meters/yards readings; scan mode
MSRP $488.78

LRM 2200SI

Weight: 15.69 oz.
Length: 5 in.
Power: 7X
Obj. Dia.: 25mm
Eye Relief: 15mm
Features: A compact monocular rangefinder capable of reading targets to 2,200 meters (about 1.36 miles); built-in inclinometer; bluetooth compatible and works with NC Cronus App; first/last target logic
MSRP $969.99

LRM 3500M

Weight: 16 oz.
Length: 4.6 in.
Power: 6.5X
Obj. Dia.: 30mm
Field of View: 7 degrees
Eye Relief: 20mm
Features: A full-featured rangefinder goes the distance to 5 km; etched reticle in mils; last ten readings recall; first/last target logic; declination correction; digital compass; user and target GPS coordinates; bluetooth capability/Android compatible; Kestrel ballistic calculator
MSRP . . . . $6858.00–$7512.00

Vortex Optics

VORTEX OPTICS
RAZOR HD 4000

RAZOR HD 4000

Weight: 9.9 oz.
Length: 4.49 in.
Power: 7X
Obj. Dia.: 25mm
Field of View: 341.25 ft.@1000 yd.
Eye Relief: .62 in.

Features: Reflective range of up to 2,400 yards; ELR mode to 4,000 yards; scan mode; line of sight mode; anti-reflective coatings on all air to surface glass; rubber armor; magnesium chassis; angle compensated ranging
MSRP $729.99

OPTICS

MUZZLELOADING BULLETS

BULLETS

AMMUNITION

Aguila Ammunition

AGUILA 5.56X45MM

AGUILA MINISHELL

5MM REMINGTON SJHP
Features: The unusual 5mm necked rimfire round in a semi-jacketed hollowpoint; 2200 fps velocity
Available in: 5mm Remington (30 gr.)
Box 50: **$46.99**

5.56X45MM
Features: Bulk packs of 300 rounds with full metal jacket boattails
Available in: 5.56x45mm (55 gr.)

Box 300. . . . .**$355.99**
Box 1200. . . . . **$941.99**

MINISHELL
Description: SAAMI-approved in 2019, this 12 ga. 1.75-in. shotshell offers less recoil than traditional 2.75-in. shotshells
Available in: 12 ga. No. 7 ½ 5/8-oz. load, 12 ga. No. 4 Buck 5/8-oz. load, 12 ga. 7/8-oz. slug
Box of 20: . . . .**$19.49–$28.99**

Alexander Arms

ALEXANDER ARMS .50 BEOWULF

.50 BEOWULF
Features: Several configurations available, including 200-gr. frangible Inceptor ARX; 350-gr. Hornady XTP jacketed hollowpoint; 350-gr. plated round-shoulder; 400-gr. Hawk jacketed flat-point; 300-gr. Hornady FTX
Box 20: . . . .**$38.99–$55.99**

6.5 GRENDEL
Features: A long-range favorite available in 123-gr. Lapua Scenar hollowpoint; 120-gr. Nosler Ballistic Tip; 129-gr. Hornady SST
Box 20: . . . .**$38.99–$40.99**

Allegiance Ammunition

ALLEGIANCE POWERSTRIKE

HOGSTRIKE
Description: A frangible round with a thick solid core that penetrates tough game hides and fragments into soft fluid tissue and creates devastating wound channels
Available in: .308 Win. (150 gr.), 5.56 NATO (80 gr., 100 gr.)
Box 20: . . . .**$39.19–$49.02**

ONESTRIKE
Features: A frangible offering intended for use where metal enclosures or crowds are a concern; HET High Energy Transfer frangible core; fragments on light barriers
Available in: 5.56 NATO (55 gr., 80 gr.), 9mm (90 gr.)
Box 20: . . . .**$29.95–$39.95**

POWERSTRIKE
Description: Jacketed frangible self-defense ammo
Available in: 9mm (95 gr., 115 gr.)
Box of 20: . . . .**$29.79–$29.95**

RANGESTRIKE
Features: A frangible round for target practice; USA made to NATO spec; same point of impact as the company's tactical line
Available in: 9mm (65 gr., 115 gr., 124 gr.)
Box 50: . . . .**$13.72–$45.50**

SILENTSTRIKE
Features: A subsonic, frangible round made of compressed tungsten powder and with a high-density core that will penetrate even thick clothing; fragmentation of core occurs both horizontally and vertically upon hitting fluid-filled tissue
Available in: 5.56 NATO (80 gr., 95 gr. [non-frangible], 100 gr. [hybrid/subsonic], 110 gr.), .300 BLK (150 gr.), .308 Win. (150 gr.); 9mm (140 gr.)
Box 20: . . . .**$29.95–$49.02**

Apex Ammunition

APEX TURKEY NINJA TSS

PREDATOR TSS
Description: A full lineup of 12-ga. shotshells loaded with Tungsten Super Shot for predator hunting
Available in: 12 ga. (3 in., 3½ in.)
Box of 5: . . . .**$45.99–$68.99**

TURKEY NINJA TSS
Description: You don't have to guess that this stuff is for serious turkey hunters with a unique No. 8.5 shot size
Available in: 12 ga. (3 in., 3½ in.), 20 ga. (3 in.), 28 ga. (2¾ in.), .410 (3 in.)
Box of 5: **$41.99–68.99**

UPLAND BIRD TSS
Description: Utilizes Tungsten Super Shot
Available in: 12 ga. (2¾ in.), 20 ga. (2¾ in.); shot sizes #7.5, #8, #9 in both gauges
Box 10: . . . .**$49.99–$65.99**

AMMUNITION

Apex Ammunition

APEX WATERFOWL S3 STEEL

WATERFOWL S3 STEEL

Description: A premium all-steel load for waterfowlers
Available in: 12 ga. (2¾ in.), 20 ga.

(2¾ in.); #BB, #4, and #2 in 12-ga.; #4 and #2 in 20-ga.
Box 25: **$24.99**

WATERFOWL TSS

Description: Utilizes Apex's own Tungsten Super Shot
Available in: 12 ga. (2 ¾ in.), 20 ga. (2 ¾ in.); #7.5, #8, #9 in both gauges
Box 10: . . . .**$49.99–$65.99**

WATERFOWL TSS/S3 STEEL BLEND

Description: Shell holds a combination Tungsten Super Shot with S3 steel shot
Available in: 12 ga. (2¾ in., #BB, #4, or #2); 20 ga. (2¾ in., #4)
Box 25: . . . .**$45.99–$46.99**

Barnes Bullets

BARNES PRECISION MATCH

BARNES BULLETS VOR-TX EXPANDER SHOTSHELL

PRECISION MATCH

Description: Engineered for precision at extreme distances, with very low standard deviations; Loaded with Barnes match-grade OTM (Open Tip Match) boattail
Available in: 5.56 NATO, .308 Win., .300 Win. Mag., .338 Lapua Mag., 6.5 Creedmoor, 6mm Creedmoor, .260 Rem., .300 BLK, 6.5 Grendel , 6.5 PRC
Box 20: . . . .**$34.99–$135.99**

TAC-XPD

Description: Loaded with Barnes TAC-XP bullets, the all-copper construction and very large, deep hollow-point cavity expand, penetrate, and perform consistently and optimally for personal and home defense
Available in: .357 Mag., .380 ACP, 9mm, 9mm +P, .45 ACP +P, .40 S&W
Box 20: . . . .**$24.99–$31.99**

VOR-TX

Description: Provides maximum tissue and bone destruction, pass-through penetration, and devastating energy transfer; multiple grooves in the bullet's shank reduce pressure and improve accuracy; bullets open instantly on contact causing the nose to peel back into four sharp-edged copper petals
Available in: *Rifle:* .223 Rem., .22-250 Rem., 5.56 NATO, .243 Win., .25-06 Rem., 6.5 Grendel, 6.5 Creedmoor, .260 Rem., .270 Win., .270 WSM, 7mm-08 Rem., 7mm Rem. Mag., .30-30 Win., .308 Win., .30-06 Spfd., .300 BLK, .300 WSM, .300 Win. Mag., .300 RUM, .300 Wby. Mag., .338 Win. Mag., .338 Lapua Mag., .35 Whelen, .45-70

Gov't., 9.3X62mm, 7X64 Brenneke, .450 Bushmaster
Rifle LR: 6mm Creedmoor, 6.5 Creedmoor, .270 Win., 7mm Rem. Mag., 7mm RUM, .30-06 Spfd., .300 Win. Mag., .300 RUM, .338 RUM, .375 RUM
Hunting Handgun: .357 Mag., 10mm, .41 Rem. Mag., .44 Mag., .45 Colt, .454 Casull
Safari: .375 H&H Mag., .416 Rem. Mag., .416 Rigby, .458 Win. Mag., .458 Lott, .470 Nitro Express, .500 Nitro Express
Euro: 7x64 Brenneke, .308 Win., .30-06 Spfd., 8x57 JS, 9.3x62mm
Rifle . . . .**$34.99–$150.99**
Rifle LR . . . .**$47.99–$88.99**
Safari . . . .**$97.99–$220.99**
Handgun . . . .**$23.99–$51.99**

VOR-TX EXPANDER SHOTSHELL

Description: Rifle-like precision for slug shotguns; blue polymer-tipped all-copper body; flat trajectory
Available in: 12 ga. (3 in., 2¾ in.), 20 ga. (3 in., 2¾ in.)
Box of 5: . . . .**$18.99–$20.99**

Berger Bullets

BERGER EXTREME OUTER LIMITS ELITE HUNTER

EXTREME OUTER LIMITS ELITE HUNTER

Description: Long-nosed bullet that has a hybrid ogive that minimizes wind drift; J4 Precision jacket promotes rapid expansion after just two

to three inches of penetration
Available in: 6.5 Creedmoor (156 gr.)
Box of 20.0: **$64.99**

AMMUNITION

Black Hills Ammunition

BLACK HILLS FACTORY NEW RIFLE

Rifle Ammunition

BLACK HILLS GOLD

Description: Bullets by Barnes; lead-free non-toxic rounds; high-performance hunting ammunition
Available in: .22–250 Rem., .243 Win., .25-06 Rem., .260 Rem., .270 Win., 7mm Rem. Mag., .300 Win. Mag., .308 Win., .30-06 Spfd., .338 Lapua; 6.5 Creedmoor
Box 20: . . . . **$49.99–$79.99**

FACTORY NEW RIFLE

Description: Bullets by manufacturers such as Hornady, Barnes, and Nosler; high-performance hunting ammunition; certain calibers available in Molycoat

Available in: .223 Rem., .308 Win. Match, .300 Win. Mag., .338 Lapua, .338 Norma Mag. , .300 Whisper, 5.56 NATO
Box 50: . . . . **$39.99–$129.99**

Handgun Ammunition
COWBOY ACTION

Description: Designed to meet the needs of cowboy-action pistol shooters with its new virgin brass and premium-quality hard-cast bullets; velocities are moderate to provide low recoil and excellent accuracy
Available in: .32 H&R, .32-20 Win., .38 LC, .38 Spl., .38-40 Win., .44-40 Win., .44 Russian, .44 Spl., .44 Colt, .45 Schofield, .45 Colt, .38-55 Win., .357 Mag.
Box 50: . . . . **$43.99–$59.99**

FACTORY NEW HANDGUN

Description: Used by the U.S. Military in all four branches for its reliability
Available in: .32 H&R Mag., .380

ACP, 9mm Luger, .38 Spl., .357 Mag., .40 S&W, .44 Mag., .45 ACP
Box of 20 . . . . **$19.99–$35.99**
Box of 50 . . . . **$51.99–$94.99**

HONEYBADGER

Description: A unique fluted projectile—not a hollowpoint—designed for self-defense purposes; a .45-70 load is likely suitable for ranch and varmint/predator work
Available in: .38 Spec. +P (100 gr.), .380 ACP (60 gr.), .44 Mag. (160 gr.), .44 Spec. (125 gr.), .45 ACP (235 gr.), .45-70 Gov't. (325 gr.), 9mm (100 gr.), .357 Mag. (127 gr.)
Box 20: . . . . **$31.99–$94.99**

MK 262 MOD 1-C, MIL PACK

Description: The result of a 1999 request from the US Navy to develop a 5.56 NATO precision round; no lot ships if it doesn't shoot sub-2-in. groups; 2750 fps, 1293 ft.-lbs.
Available in: 5.56 NATO (77 gr.)
Box of 460: **$759.00**

Boss Shotshells

BOSS SHOTSHELLS TOM

TOM

Description: Dedicated copper-plated tungsten loads for a range of shotgun gauges/bores for the turkey hunter
Available in: 12 ga. (3 in., 2¾ in.), 20 ga. (3 in., 2¾ in.), 28-ga. (2¾ in), .410-bore (3-in.)
Box 5: . . . . **$40.00–$60.00**

UNMUZZLED

Description: A line of copper-plated Bismuth shells without the historically high cost; a variety of 3-inch and 2 ¾-inch 12 ga. and 20 ga. loads, 2 ¾-inch 16 and 28 ga., and 3-in. .410 bore loadings
Available in: 10 ga., 12 ga., 16 ga., 20 ga., 28 ga., .410 bore
Box 25: . . . . **$31.00–$60.00**

Brenneke USA

ATS

Description: ATS stands for Anti-Terror Slug; super-hard slug; can be used with any shotgun barrel type; patented rear slides into the slug point after impact; 1680 fps, 2639 ft.-lbs.
Available in: 12-ga. (2 ¾ in., 424 gr.)
Box of 5: **$13.99**

BLACK MAGIC MAGNUM

Description: The Black Magic Magnum and Black Magic Short Magnum are two of the most powerful cartridges available on the market,

offering tremendous knockdown power up to 100/60 yds; clean speed coating reduces lead fouling inside the barrel by almost 100 percent
Available in: 12 Ga. (3 in.)
Box 5: **$18.49**

BRENNEKE 28

Description: The moderate recoil makes the 28 Ga. a perfect slug for young hunters who will be introduced to slug shooting; 28 Ga. is a multi-talent: small game, home defense, and all around shooting

Available in: 28 Ga. (2¾ in.)
Box 5: **$13.99**

CLASSIC MAGNUM

Description: Invented by Wilhelm Brenneke in 1898, the classic is the ancestor of all modern shotgun slugs; this state-of-the-art slug provides long-range stopping power, consistently flat trajectories, and a patented B.E.T. wad column
Available in: 12 Ga. (2¾ in.), 16 Ga. (2¾ in.)
Box 5: **$12.99**

Brenneke USA

BRENNEKE CLOSE ENCOUNTER

BRENNEKE ATS

BRENNEKE TOPAS

CLOSE ENCOUNTER

Description: The .410 Close Encounter is the perfect choice if you are a fan of 2½-in. .410/.45 revolvers. They are powerful without having bad recoil, and they have an incredible frontal area and the legendary Brenneke penetration
Available in: .410 (2½ in.)
Box 5: $10.15

HEAVY FIELD SHORT MAGNUM GREEN LIGHTNING

Description: The original "Emerald" slug with patented B.E.T wad and famous stopping power; for all barrel types; range up to 100 yds.
Available in: 12 Ga., 20 Ga. (2¾ in.)
MSRP $13.99

K.O. SLUG

Description: The KO is an improved Foster-type slug with excellent penetration; range up to 60 yds; for all barrel types

Available in: 12 Ga. (2¾ in.), 20 Ga. (2¾ in.)
MSRP . . . .$8.99–$9.99

MAGNUM CRUSH

Description: Delivers a force of more than 3.800 ft/lbs, weighs a full 1½ oz. / 666 gr. and the flat trajectory is ideal for bigger game; special coating to reduce lead fouling and broad ribs for optimum groove engagement
Available in: 12 Ga. (3 in.)
Box 5: $13.41

TOPAS

Description: New sabot design with cup deploys a sub-caliber slug; barrel-friendly; 2/3-oz. slug at 1673 fps, 1919 ft-lbs.
Available in: 12-ga. (2 ¾ in.)
Box of 5: $5.83

Browning Ammunition

BROWNING BPT PERFORMANCE TARGET

BPR PERFORMANCE RIMFIRE

Description: BPR provides reliability and performance in 22 long rifle ammunition that you can expect from The Best There Is in rimfire ammunition.
Available in: .22 LR
Box of 1000 . . . .$99.99

BPT PERFORMANCE TARGET

Description: BPT Performance Target is a premium training product that can be used to hone your handgun skills. It is a matched training counterpart to BXP Personal Defense.
Available in: .223 Rem., .38 Spec., .380 ACP, .40 S&W, .45 ACP, 9mm
Box of 50 handgun . . . $41.99–$65.99
Box of 20 .223 Rem. $14.99

BPT TARGET LOAD

Description: BPT Performance Target utilizes premium, hard shot to help deliver tight patterns and maximum target breaking energy. The smooth hull allows for a sleek profile and smooth ejection.
Available in: 2¾-inch 12- (No. 7½, 8), 20- (No. 7½), 16- (No. 8) and 28-gauge (No. 7½); 2½-inch .410-boren (No. 7½)
Box of 25: . . . .$11.99–$24.99

BXC BIG GAME

Description: BXC Controlled Expansion Terminal Tip is designed specifically for use on big game like elk, moose, mule deer, and bear. The Terminal Tip and bonded bullet design allow for deep penetration through thick, tough hide and bone. The brass tip, heavy bullet weight, and boat-tail are integral components to delivering precision accuracy, maximum downrange velocity, and long-range, on-target performance.
Available in: .270 Win., .30-06 Spfd., .300 Win. Mag., .300 WSM, .308 Win., 7mm Rem. Mag., 6.5 Creedmoor, .270 WSM, .28 Nosler
Box of 20: . . . .$56.99–$88.99

BXD UPLAND

Description: BXD Upland Extra Distance launches premium-plated shot at high velocities to achieve premium in-the-field performance. Nickel-plated shot helps keep shot round resulting in high velocity retention and energy transfer as well as tighter downrange patterns.
Available in: 12 ga. (2¾ in.), 20 ga. (2¾ in.), 16 ga. (2¾ in.)
Box of 25: . . . .$20.99–$24.99

BXD WATERFOWL

Description: BXD Waterfowl Extra Distance is launched at high velocities utilizing an optimized long-range wad and plated round steel shot. Combining round steel with a cutting edge wad design results in a lethal combination of energy retention, penetration, and pattern density that is critical in achieving long-range performance. No. 2, 4, and BB shot sizes available in 12-gauge, No. 2 shot only for 20-gauge.
Available in: 12 (3 in., 3.5 in.), 20 (3 in.)
Box of 25: . . . .$23.99–$25.99

BXR DEER

Description: BXR Rapid Expansion Matrix Tip is designed specifically for use on whitetail, blacktail, mule deer, and antelope. The proprietary matrix tip design allows for high downrange velocity and energy retention while also initiating rapid positive expansion. The jacket and tip combination yields precision accuracy and rapid energy transfer, and generates massive knockdown power.
Available in: .243 Win., .270 Win., .270 WSM, .30-06 Spfd., .30-30 Win., .300 Win. Mag., .300 WSM, .308 Win. 6.5 Creedmoor, 7mm Rem. Mag., 7mm-08
Box of 20: . . . .$34.99–$51.99

Browning Ammunition

BROWNING BXV PREDATOR & VARMINT

BROWNING WICKED BLEND

BXS DEER

Description: Solid copper expansion sabot slug designed to increase accuracy, penetration, and energy transfer
Available in: 12-ga. sabot slug, 00 Buckshot, or rifled slug, 20-ga. sabot slug, all in 5-count boxes; 20-count boxes of rifle cartridges in .270 Win., .30-06 Spfd., .300 Win. Mag., .300 WSM, .308 Win., 6.5 Creedmoor, 7mm Rem. Mag.
Sabot slugs: $18.99
Buckshot: $10.99
Rifled slug: $5.99
Rifle cartridges: . . . . .$52.99–$62.99

BXV PREDATOR & VARMINT

Description: Polymer tip improves BC and results in flatter trajectory and higher downrange velocity
Available in: .223 Win., .243 Win., .22 Hornet, .22-250
Box of 20: . . . .$31.99–$42.99

LONG RANGE PRO HUNTER

Description: Designed for long-range hunting with a Sierra Tipped GameKing bullet
Available in: 6.5 Creedmoor, .270 Win., .300 Win. Mag., .308 Win., .300 WSM, .30-06 Spfd.
Box of 20: . . . .$57.90–$62.50

WICKED BLEND

Description: Holds Browning's Wicked Wad with rear stabilizing pellets that provide a straighter shot and decrease shot slinging; slotted sidewalls improve choke responsiveness; stacked payloads of 12 ga. In BB/No. 1, No.2/No. 4 Bismuth, 20-ga. in No. 2/No. 4 Bismuth
Available in: 12 ga. (3 ½ in., 3 in.), 20 ga. (3 in.)
Box of 25: . . . .$29.99–$39.99

TSS TUNGSTEN TURKEY

Description: Super-dense loads for gobbler season; shot sizes BB, 6, 5, and 4 across magnum 12- and 20 ga. and .410-bore loads; duplex loads are also to be made available in smaller shot size combos
Available in: 12 ga. (3½ in., 3 in.), 20 ga. (3 in.), .410-bore (3 in.)
Box 10: . . . .$35.99–$47.99

X-POINT DEFENSE

Description: BXP Personal Defense is designed for superior personal defense performance in reliability, expansion, and penetration. The X-Point is designed to shield the hollow point through intermediate barriers.
Available in: .380 ACP, 9mm. .40 S&W, 10mm Auto, .45 ACP
Box of 20: . . . .$23.99–$29.99

Buffalo Bore Ammunition

BUFFALO BORE .32 WINCHESTER SPECIAL

.32 WINCHESTER SPECIAL

Description: Available in a 170-gr. jacketed flat-nose and a 200-gr. hard-cast gas-checked
Available in: .32 Win. Spec.
Box of 20: $50.22

CCI Ammunition

.22 WIN. MAG. MAXI MAG

Description: A favorite of varmint shooters; 40 gr. TMJ flat nose at 1875 fps, or 40 gr. jacketed HP at 1875 fps; both loads give over 1400 fps from a 6-in. revolver; clean-burning propellants keep actions cleaner; sure-fire CCI priming; reusable plastic box with dispenser lid
Available in: .22 Win. Mag.
Box of 50 . . . .$17.99–$20.99
Box of 125 . . . .$44.99

A17 VARMINT TIP

Description: Optimized for feeding and function in the Savage Arms A17 semiautomatic rifle and can be fired through bolt-action .17 HMR firearms; 100 fps faster than other .17 HMR loads of the same weight; Varmint Tip bullet provides rapid expansion; CCI-made and primed case
Available in: .17 HMR
Box 50: $19.99
Box of 200 . . . .$$77.99

A22 MAGNUM GAMEPOINT

Description: GamePoint bullet; designed around Savage's semiautomatic A22 Magnum rifle
Available in: .22 WMR (35 gr.)
Box of 200 . . . .$85.99

BIG 4

Description: Centerfire handgun shotshells with larger No. 4 pellets for extended range and penetration
Available in: .38 Spl., .44 Spl., .45 Colt, 9mm
Box 10: . . . .$20.99–$26.99

BLAZER .22 LR BULK PACK

Description: A 525-count box of lead roundnose for hours of plinking fun
Available in: .22 LR (38 gr.)
Box of 425 . . . .$39.99
Box of 525 . . . .$47.99
Box of 1500. . . . .$141.99

BLAZER 9MM

Description: Designed for high-volume training; Speer TMJ bullet in reloadable brass case, non-reloadable aluminum case, or non-reloadable case with Clean Fire primer
Available in: 9mm (124 gr., 147 gr.)
Aluminum case/50 . . . .$19.99
Aluminum case/100 . . . .$32.99
Brass case/50 . . . .$23.99
Brass case/250 . . . .$108.99
Brass case/500 . . . .$219.99
Cleanfire/50 . . . .$26.99–$33.99

AMMUNITION

CCI BLAZER 10MM

CCI MAXI-MAG POUR PACK

CCI MAXI-MAG MEATEATER

CCI CLEAN-22 REALTREE

CCI GREEN TAG

BLAZER 10MM

Description: Full-power, full metal jacket 10mm loads in reloadable brass cases or non-reloadable aluminum cases
Available in: 10mm (180 gr.)
Brass case/50 . . . .$31.99
Aluminum case/50 . . . .$30.99

CLEAN-22

Description: A coated polymer bullet leaves no residue behind while reducing traditional copper and lead fouling, even in suppressors; sub-sonic and high-velocity loads; will cycle in semiautomatics
Available in: .22 LR (40 gr.)
Box 100: $12.99

CLEAN-22 PINK

Description: Bullets wear a pink polymer coating that reduces copper and lead fouling; a portion of the sales go to fight breast cancer; lead roundnose
Available in: .22 LR (40 gr.)
Box of 400: $49.99

CLEAN-22 REALTREE

Description: Special Realtree bottle holds 400 rounds of its Clean-22 wearing a green, tan, and black polymer bullet coating that reduces copper fouling
Available in: .22 LR
Box of 400: $49.99

CLEAN-22 SUPPRESSOR POUR PACK

Description: Uses polymer bullet coating to reduce barrel and suppressor fouling; reliable functioning in semiautomatic firearms; 1,000 fps
Available in: .22 LR (45 gr.)
Box of 200: $35.99

COPPER-22 MEATEATER

Description: One of three loads developed in partnership with hunting personality Steven Rinella; official rimfire ammunition of Rinella's MeatEater brand
Available in: .22 LR (21 gr.)
Box of 50: $13.99

GREEN TAG

Description: Our first and still most-popular match rimfire product; tight manufacturing and accuracy specs mean you get the consistency and accuracy that the unforgiving field of competition demands; the rimfire match ammo leaves the muzzle sub-sonic which means no buffeting in the transonic zone; clean-burning propellants keep actions cleaner. Sure-fire CCI priming; reusable plastic box with dispenser lid
Available in: .22 LR (40 gr. lead round nose)
Box of 100: $28.99

HMR TNT

Description: A 17-gr. Speer TNT hollow point answers requests from varmint hunters and gives explosive performance over the .17's effective range; clean-burning propellants keep actions cleaner; sure-fire CCI priming; reusable plastic box with dispenser lid
Available in: .17 HMR 17-gr. TNT hollow point or 16-gr. lead-free green TNT solid hollow point
TNT/50 . . . .$19.99
TNT Green/50 . . . .$21.99

MAXI-MAG MEATEATER

Description: One of three loads developed in partnership with hunting personality Steven Rinella; official rimfire ammunition of Rinella's MeatEater brand
Available in: .22 WMR (40 gr.)
Box of 200: $73.99

MAXI-MAG POUR PACK

Description: "Milk"-carton bulk packs of 125
Available in: .22 WMR (40 gr.)
Box of 125: $52.99

MINI-MAG

Description: CCI's first rimfire product and still the most popular; Mini-Mag. hollow points are high-velocity products and offer excellent all-around performance for small game and varmints; clean-burning propellants keep actions cleaner; sure-fire CCI priming; reusable plastic box with dispenser lid
Available in: .22 LR (40 gr. gilded round nose or 36 gr. gilded lead hollow point)
Box 100: $11.99

MINI-MAG MEATEATER

Description: One of three loads developed in partnership with hunting personality Steven Rinella; official rimfire ammunition of Rinella's MeatEater brand
Available in: .22 LR (36 gr.)
Box of 300: $36.99

MINI-MAG SEGMENTED HOLLOW POINT

Description: New bullet design splits into three equal parts upon impact
Available in: .22 LR (40 gr.)
Box 100: $11.99

PISTOL MATCH

Description: Designed expressly for high-end semiautomatic match pistols; singe-die tooling and great care in assembly lets you wring the last bit of accuracy from your precision pistol; clean-burning propellants keep actions cleaner; sure-fire CCI priming; reusable plastic box with dispenser lid
Available in: .22 LR (40 gr. lead round nose bullet)
Box 50: $14.99

QUIET-22

Description: Ideal for bolt-action and single shot .22 LR rifles (and perfectly safe in semiautomatics), this new reduced report cartridge generates ¼ the perceived noise level of standard velocity .22 LR
Available in: .22 LR
Box 50: $5.99

QUIET-22 SEMI-AUTO

Description: Reduced report in a round that reliably cycles semiautomatics; noise reduced with or without suppressors; low velocity
Available in: .22 LR (45 gr., 735 fps)
Box of: 50
MSRP $5.99

SELECT .22 LR

Description: The .22 Long Rifle Select is built for semiautomatic competition; reliable operation, accuracy, and consistency make Select an ideal choice for competition shooters
Available in: .22 LR
Box of 100: $23.99

CCI Ammunition

CCI VNT .17 MACH 2, .22 WMR

STANGERS .22 LR

Description: Named for the drawl of YouTube personality 22plinkster, this is CCI Stinger ammo in special edition packaging; varmint load at 1,640 fps

Available in: .22 LR (32 gr.)

Box of 100:. $19.99

SUPPRESSOR 22 LONG RIFLE

Description: Subsonic velocity of 970 fps minimizes sound signature through suppressed firearms; HP bullet; consistent function in semiautomatic firearms; clean-burning powders

Available in: .22 LR

Box 50:. $8.99

VNT

Description: Special Speer VNT bullet design for varmint hunters favoring these speedy specialty rimfire rounds; polymer tip and thin jacket; nickel-plated cases

Available in: .17 Mach 2 (17 gr.), .22 WMR (30 gr.)

.17 Mach 2/50. . . . .$11.99
.17 HMR/50 . . . .$19.99
.17 HMR/125. . . . .$51.99
.17 HMR/250. . . . .$101.99
.22 WMR/125 . . . .$52.99
.22 WMR/250 . . . .$106.99

Cor-Bon

COR-BON MPR

CORBON HUNTER

Rifle

DPX, T-DPX RIFLE

Description: This is an optimum load for Law Enforcement; lead-free projectile; reduced recoil due to lighter weight projectile; deep penetration on soft tissue 12–17-in.

Available in: .223 Rem., .243 Win., .270 Win., .30-06 Spfd., .30-30 Win., .300 BLK, .300 Win. Mag., .308 Win., .338 Lapua, .338 RUM, .338 Win. Mag., .340 Wby. Mag., .444 Marlin, .458 SOCOM, 6.5-284 Norma, 7.62X39

Box 20:. . . . . $39.99–$129.99

MULTI-PURPOSE RIFLE (MPR)

Description: Features a gilding metal jacket with a specially formulated lead core and a green acetal resin tip, which reduces drag, producing extremely high ballistic coefficient, and also creates more reliable feeding in magazine fed firearms; provides rapid, explosive expansion without excessive penetration; aerodynamic resin tip offers extreme accuracy at long-range precision competition and also improves feeding in magazine fed rifles; reliably expands for humane kills on varmints and deer-size game, giving just the right amount of penetration

Available in: .223 Rem., .22-250 Rem., 30-06 Spfd., .300 BLK, 300 Win. Mag., .308 Win.

Box 20:. . . . . $39.99–$47.99

Handgun
DPX HANDGUN

Description: DPX is a solid copper hollowpoint bullet that combines the best of the lightweight high-speed JHPs and the heavyweight, deep-penetrating JHPs; the copper bullet construction allows it to conquer hard barriers like auto glass and steel

Available in: 10mm, .32 ACP, .357 Mag., .357 SIG, .375 JDJ, .38 Spec. +P, .38 Super +P, .380 ACP, .40 S&W, .400 CORBON, .44 Mag. .44 Spl., .45 ACP, .45 ACP +P, .45 Colt +P, .454 Casull, .460 S&W, .500 S&W, 9mm, 9mm +P

Box 20:. . . . . $29.99–$84.99

GLASER SAFETY SLUG

Description: Originally designed for use by Sky Marshals on airplanes, today the slug is recommended for anyone concerned with over-penetration; copper jacket; filled with a compressed load of #12 or #6 lead shot, then capped with a round polymer ball that enhances feeding and reloading. Silver line is designed for more penetration than the blue line and is a preferred choice in colder climates where thick, heavy clothing would be prevalent

Available in: Silver line: 10mm, .44 Mag. Pow'RBall: 38 Spec. +P, .357 Mag., .38 Super +P, .380 ACP, 9mm +P, 9mm

Silver box of 20 . . . . . $39.99–$44.99
Blue box of 20 . . . .$39.99
Pw'RBall box of 20 . . . $31.99–$34.99

HUNTER

Description: Bone-breaking loads for the handgun hunter; expanding bullet varieties include Swift A-frame, Swift Scirocco II, Bonded Core Jacketed Soft Point, jacketed soft point, and jacketed hollowpoint; non-expanding bullets include Round Nose Penetrator, hard cast, and full metal jacket

Available in: .45 Colt +P, .454 Casull, .460 Rowland, .460 S&W Mag., .500 S&W Mag.

Box 20:. . . . . $35.99–$84.99

D Dupleks USA

DUPO 28

Description: An expanding slug of non-toxic steel and polyethylene construction; works in smoothbore and rifled barrels; 1,460 fps with 2,050 ft.-lb. of muzzle energy

Available in: 12 ga. (2¾ in.)

Box of 5: $10.00

D DUPLEKS MONOLIT 28

HEXOLIT 32

Description: Expanding slug with polymer bearing bands that prevent slug contact with the barrel, so safe for use in both rifled and smoothbore barrels; one-piece wad column; six-

piece fragmentation after hit; eco-friendly for use in areas that prohibit lead projectiles
Available in: 12 ga. (2¾ in.)
Box 5:. **$12.99**

KAVIAR SLUG

Description: Home-defense frangible hollowpoint slug made of a combination of pellets and polyethylene; reduced recoil; also suitable for use on steel targets; designed for smoothbore, suitable for rifled bores
Available in: 12 ga. (2¾ in.)
Box 5:. **$15.99**

MONOLIT 28

Description: A deep-penetrating slug of solid non-toxic steel/polyethylene construction; can be used in both smoothbores and rifled barrels; flat ogive; 1,460 fps/2,070 ft-lb. muzzle energy
Available in: 12 ga. (2¾ in.)
Box of 5: **$6.95**

MONOLIT 32

Description: A solid steel hunting slug suitable for both rifled and smooth bores; obstacle penetrating; one-piece wad; flat fore-front; self-stabilizing
Available in: 12 ga. (2¾ in.)
Box 5:. **$9.99**

Eley

ELEY ACTION

ELEY .38 SUPER COMP

ELEY ACTION PLUS

ACTION .22 LR

Description: A subsonic round with reduced recoil; 1060 fps; designed specifically for use in semiautomatics, especially those high-end guns for competition; boxes of 50 and 500
Available in: .22 LR (42 gr.)
Box of 50 . . . .**$12.95**

.38 SUPER COMP

Description: A major power-factor round for IPSC/USPSA and 3-Gun competitors; rimless case; copper-

jacketed bullet
Available in: .38 Super (124 gr.)
Box of 50:. **$25.99**

ACTION PLUS .22 LR

Description: A supersonic round traveling at 1150 fps; designed for high-end semiautomatic competition rifles; boxes of 50 and 500
Available in: .22 LR (46 gr.)
Box of 500:. **$41.99**

Environ-Metal/Hevi-Shot

ENVIRON-METAL/ HEVI-SHOT HEVI-BISMUTH UPLAND

ENVIRON-METAL/HEVI-SHOT HEVI-METAL LONGER RANGE

HEVI-BISMUTH UPLAND

Description: Bismuth loads in 12- and 20-ga., No. 5 only
Available in: 12 ga. (2¾ in.), 20 ga. (2¾ in.)
Box of 25:. **$73.99**

HEVI-BISMUTH WATERFOWL

Description: Bismuth loads for the waterfowler
Available in: 10 ga. (3½ in.), 12 ga. (3½ in., 3 in., 2¾ in.), 16 ga. (2¾ in.),

20 ga. (3 in.), 28 ga. (2¾ in., 3 in.)
Box of 25:. . . . . **$58.99–$104.99**

HEVI-HAMMER

Description: A unique duplex load of steel shot under Bismuth shot and with a layer of flax seed under the crimp
Available in: 12 ga. (3 in.), 20 ga. (3 in.)
Box of 25:. . . . . **$31.99–$41.99**

HEVI-METAL LONGER RANGE

Description: Improved bismuth pellets are 16 percent denser than previous Hevi-Shot Heavier Than Steel shot
Available in: 10 ga. (3½ in.), 12 ga. (3½ in., 3 in., 2¾ in.), 20 ga. (3 in.)
Box of 25:. . . . . **$42.99–$71.99**

HEVI-METAL TURKEY

Features: A layered load that com-

bines premium steel shot with HEVI-Shot pellets; timeless testing of various shot load methods found layering to provide the most pellets on target and the best knockdown performance
Available in: 12 Ga. (3 in., 3½ in.), 20 Ga. (3 in.)
Box 5:. . . . .**$21.99–$25.49**

HEVI-SHOT DEAD COYOTE!

Description: With these HEVI-Shot T-shot loads, you can be deadly at ranges you never thought possible with a 12 gauge; the 3-in. load pounds out 50 perfectly round pellets at 1,350 fps. 10 percent heavier than lead, 54 percent denser than steel; every 50 rounds includes a dry-storage box.
Available in: 12 Ga. (3 in., 3½ in.)
3-in/10 . . . .**$100.79**
3.5-in/10 . . . .**$102.59**

HEVI-SHOT MAGNUM BLEND

Features: Put more lethal pellets in your pattern with a combination of No. 5, 6, and 7 HEVI-13 shot, and boost your lethal range by 14 to 17 percent; buffered and moly-coated pellets produce a denser pattern than conventional shot; HEVI-13 delivers 40 percent more knockdown energy and up to 40 percent longer range than lead shells
Available in: 10 Ga. (3½-in.), 12 Ga. (3 in., 3½ in.) 20 Ga. (3 in.)
Box 5: . . . . **$36.49–$63.99**

Federal Ammunition

FEDERAL AMERICAN EAGLE MSR AMMO CANS

FEDERAL BYOB

FEDERAL HAMMERDOWN

Rifle Ammunition

AMERICAN EAGLE BUCKETS

Description: Practice ammo in bulk and reasonably priced for hours of fun on the range
Available in: .223 Rem. (55 gr.)
Box of 300 . . . . **$265.99**
Box of 1000 . . . . **$829.99-861.99**

AMERICAN EAGLE FULL METAL JACKET BOATTAIL

Description: Accurate, non-expanding bullets; flat shooting trajectory, leaves small exit holes in game, and put clean holes in paper; smooth, reliable feeding into semiautomatics
Available in: .300 BLK, .223 Rem., 5.56 NATO, .308 Win., .20-06 Spfd.
Box 20 . . . . **$19.99–$38.99**

AMERICAN EAGLE MSR AMMO CANS

Description: If .223/5.56 NATO is your game, this is how to stock up your ammo supply; all are full metal jacket boattails; comes in heavy-duty metal can
Available in: .223 Rem. (55 gr.), 5.56 NATO (55 gr.). 5.56 NATO (62 gr.)
Box 420: . . . . **$391.99–$389.99**

BYOB

Description: Bulk rimfire in "Bring Your Own Bucket" packs
Available in: .17 HMR (17 gr. jacketed hollowpoint), .22 LR (36 gr. copper-plated hollowpoint), .22 WMR (50 gr. jacketed hollowpoint)
.17 HMR/250 . . . . **$77.99**
.22 LR/450 . . . . **$45.99**
.22 LR/825 . . . . **$69.99**
.22 LR/1375 . . . . **$117.99**
.22 WMR/250 . . . . **$72.99**

FUSION RIFLE

Description: This specialized deer bullet electrochemically joins pure copper to an extreme pressure-formed core to ensure optimum performance. The result is high terminal energy on impact that radiates lethal shock throughout the target. This energy is optimized through mass weight retention, a top secretive tip-skiving process and superior bullet integrity.
Available in: .223 Rem., .22-250 Rem., .224 Valkyrie, .243 Win., .25-06 Rem., 6.5 Grendel, 6.5x55 Swedish Mauser, .260 Rem., 6.8 SPC, .270 Win., .270 WSM, 7mm-08, .280 Rem., 7mm Rem. Mag., 7mm WSM, 7.62x39 Soviet, .30-30 Win. 6.5 Creedmoor, .308 Win., .30-06 Spfd., .300 Win. Mag., .300 WSM, .338 Federal, .338 Win. Mag., .35 Whelen, .375 H&H Mag.,.45-70 Govt., .450 Bushmaster, .350 Legend, 6.8 SPC, 6.5 PRC
Box 20: . . . . **$32.99–$79.99**

GOLD MEDAL BERGER HYBRID

Description: Rounds feature a Berger bullet with a high BC to provide flat trajectories, less wind drift, and surgical long-range accuracy; Gold Medal match primers; Federal brass; specially formulated propellants
Available in: 6mm Creedmoor, 6.5 Creedmoor, .300 Win. Mag., .300 Norma Mag.
Box 20: . . . . **$48.99–$143.99**

GOLD MEDAL SIERRA MATCHKING BOATTAIL HOLLOWPOINT

Description: Long ranges are its specialty; excellent choice for everything from varmints to big game animals; tapered, boattail design provides extremely flat trajectories; higher downrange velocity for more energy at the point of impact; reduced wind drift
Available in: .223 Rem., .224 Valiyrie, 6mm Creedmoor, 6.5 Creedmoor, .260 Rem., .308 Win., 7.62x51 NATO, .30-06 Spfd., .300 Win. Mag., .338 Lapua Mag.
Box 20: . . . . **$35.99–$149.99**

HAMMERDOWN

Description: Designed for lever-action rifles; bullets optimized for terminal performance; nickel-plated cases
Available in: .357 Mag. (170 gr.), .327 Fed. (127 gr.), .44 Mag. (270 gr.), .45 Colt (250 gr.), .30-30 Win. (150 gr.), .45-70 Govt. (300 gr.)
Handgun/20 . . . . **$25.99–$39.99**
Rifle/20 . . . . **$36.99–$65.99**

HUNTER MATCH .22 LONG RIFLE

Features: High-velocity long-range round; hollowpoint designed for optimum expansion at 100 yards; nickel-plated case
Available in: .22 LR
Box 50: **$7.99**

NON-TYPICAL

Description: New line designed for deer hunting; soft-point bullet with a concentric jacket
Available in: .243 Win., 6.5 Creedmoor, .270 Win., .30-30 Win., .308 Win., .30-06 Spfd., .300 Win. Mag., 7mm Rem. Mag. .450 Bushmaster, .350 Legend, 7mm-08 Rem.
Box 20: . . . . **$28.99–$57.99**

POWER-SHOK COPPER

Description: Copper-alloy construction; hollow-point design expands consistently; accurate, reliable performance; large wound channels and efficient energy transfer to the target; lead-free; California-legal; federal brass and primers
Available in: .243 Win, .270 Win., .308 Win., .30-06 Spfd., .300 Blackout, .300 Win. Mag., .300 WSM
Box 20: . . . . **$35.99–$60.99**

FEDERAL PREMIUM CENTERFIRE SWIFT SCIROCCO II

FEDERAL PREMIUM TERMINAL ASCENT

FEDERAL SWIFT SCIROCCO II

FEDERAL PUNCH .22 LR

PREMIUM CENTERFIRE BARNES TSX

Description: One of Federal's most popular hunting designs resurrected. Deep hollowpoint, monolithic bullet design has more than 99% weight retention
Available in: .223 Rem., .224 Valkyrie, .243 Win., .25-06 Rem., 6.5 Creedmoor, .270 Win., .270 WSM, 7mm-08 Rem., .308 Win., .30-30 Win., .30-06 Spfd., 7mm Rem. Mag., .300 WSM, .300 Win. Mag.
Box 20:. . . . .$40.99–$71.99

PREMIUM CENTERFIRE BERGER HYBRID HUNTER

Description: Features a low-drag bullet profile with a hybrid tangent/secant ogive design. Very high BC; Gold Medal primers; nickel-plated brass
Available in: 6.5 Creedmoor, .270 Win., .270 WSM, 7mm Rem. Mag., .280 Ackley Improved, .30-06 Spfd., .300 Win., .300 WSM
Box 20:. . . . .$49.99–$68.99

PREMIUM CENTERFIRE NOSLER PARTITION

Description: Bullet features a partitioned lead core and shank that allows the front half to mushroom while the rear core remains intact for deep penetration and stopping power
Available in: .223 Rem., .22-250 Rem., 6mm Rem., .243 Win., .25-06 Rem., .270 Win., .270 WSM, .280 Rem., 7mm Rem. Mag., .30-30 Win., .308 Win. .30-06 Spfd., .300 Win. Mag., .300 WSM, .338 Win. Mag., .338 RUM, .375 H&H
Box 20:. . . . .$39.99–$104.99

PREMIUM CENTERFIRE SIERRA GAMEKING BOATTAIL SOFTPOINT

Description: Proven performer on small game and thin-skinned medium game; aerodynamic tip for a flat trajectory; exposed soft point expands rapidly for hard hits, even as velocity slows at longer ranges
Available in: .243 Win., .25-06 Rem., .260 Rem., .270 Win., 7-30 Waters, 7mm Rem. Mag., .308 Win., .30-06 Spfd.
Box 20:. . . . .$40.99–$55.99

PREMIUM CENTERFIRE SWIFT SCIROCCO II

Description: Advanced streamlined bullet design with a high B.C.; improved secant ogive; tapered copper jacket bonded to a lead core; polymer tip for low-velocity expansion
Available in: .243 Win. (90 gr.) 6.5 Creedmoor (130 gr.), .270 Win. (130 gr.), .270 WSM (130 gr.), 7mm Rem. Mag. (150 gr.), .308 Win. (165 gr.), .30-06 Spfd. (165 gr.), .300 Win. Mag. (180 gr.), .300 WSM (180 gr.)
Box of 20:. . . . .$56.99–$76.99

PREMIUM CENTERFIRE TERMINAL ASCENT

Description: Long sleek bullets have high B.C. and Federal's AccuChannel groove technology that reduces drag and improves accuracy; Slipstream polymer tip; copper shank; bonded lead core
Available in: 6.5 Creedmoor (130 gr.), 6.5 PRC (130 gr.), .270 Win. (136 gr.), .270 WSM (136 gr.), .280 Ackley Improved (155 gr.), 7mm Rem. Mag. (155 gr.), .308 Win. (175 gr.), .30-06 Spfd. (175 gr.), .300 Win. Mag. (200 gr.), .300 WSM (200 gr.), .28 Nosler
Box of 20:. . . . . $57.99–$104.99

PREMIUM CENTERFIRE TROPHY BONDED TIP

Description: Built on the Trophy Bonded Bear Claw platform to provide deep penetration and high weight retention; sleek profile, with tapered heel and translucent polymer tip; nickel-plated; available as component
Available in: .223 Rem., .270 Win., .270 WSM, .270 Wby. Mag., 7mm-08 Rem., .280 Rem., 7mm Rem. Mag., 7mm WSM, 7mm Wby. Mag., 7mm STW, .308 Win., .30-06 Spfd., .300 H&H Mag., .300 Wby. Mag., .300 Win. Mag., .300 RUM, .300 WSM, .338 Federal, .338 Win. Mag.
Box 20:. . . . .$27.99–$115.99

PREMIUM SAFARI TROPHY BONDED BEAR CLAW

Description: Ideal for medium to large dangerous game; jacket and core are 100 percent fusion-bonded for reliable bullet expansion from 25 yds to extreme ranges; bullet retains 95 percent of its weight for deep penetration; hard solid copper base tapering to a soft, copper nose section for controlled expansion
Available in: .375 H&H Mag., .45-70 Gov't.
.45-70 Gov't./20 . . . . $95.99
.375 H&H/20 . . . .$128.99

PREMIUM SAFARI TROPHY BONDED SLEDGEHAMMER SOLID

Description: Use it on the largest, most dangerous game in the world; Jack Carter design maximizes stopping power; bonded bronze solid with a flat nose that minimizes deflection off bone and muscle for a deep straight wound channel
Available in: .375 H&H Mag., .416 Rigby, .416 Rem. Mag., .458 Win. Mag., .458 Lott, .470 NE
Box 20:. . . . . $147.99–$304.99

PREMIUM CENTERFIRE TROPHY COPPER MEATEATER

Description: The "official ammunition" of Steve Rinella's MeatEater brand; tipped bullet cavity; grooved bullet shank; boattail, polymer tip
Available in: .223 Rem., .243 Win., .25-06 Rem., 6.5 Creedmoor, .270 Win., .270 WSM, 7mm-08 Rem., .280 Rem., 7mm Rem. Mag., 7mm WSM, .30-30 Win., .308 Win., .30-06 Spfd., .300 Win. Mag., .300 WSM, .338 Federal, .338 Win. Mag., .338 Lapua Mag., 6.5 PRC
Box 20:. . . . .$37.99–$112.99

PREMIUM SAFARI WOODLEIGH HYDRO SOLID

Description: Provides safari hunters superb accuracy, consistent performance, and tremendous impact; special heavy jackets provide excellent weight retention, up to 100 percent for solids
Available in: 9.3x62 Mauser, 9.3x74 R, .370 Sako Mag., .375 H&H Mag., .416 Rigby, .416 Rem. Mag., .458 Win. Mag., 458 Lott, .470 NE, .500 NE
Box 20:. . . . . $151.99–$342.99

Federal Ammunition

FEDERAL MILITARY GRADE BALL

FEDERAL PRACTICE & DEFEND PACKS

FEDERAL SWIFT A-FRAME .327 FEDERAL, 10MM

FEDERAL PUNCH

PUNCH .22 LR

Description: Intended for self-defense with a max velocity of 1,070 fps from a 2-in. barreled handgun, 1650 fps from a 24-in. barreled rifle; nickel-plated case; lead-core bullet
Available in: .22 LR (29 gr.)
Box of 50: **$9.99**

PREMIUM SWIFT SCIROCCO II

Description: Bullet has a proprietary polymer tip; advanced secant ogive; bonded tapered copper jacket
Available in: .243 Win., 6.5 Creedmoor, .270 Win., .270 WSM, 7mm Rem. Mag., .308 Win., .30-06 Spfd., .300 Win. Mag., .300 WSM
Box of 20: . . . . **$56.99–$76.99**

SYNTECH PCC

Description: Created specifically for better functionality in pistol-caliber carbine rifles, especially those used in competition; Total Synthetic Jacket reduces heat and fouling
Available in: 9mm (130 gr.)
Box of 50: **$28.99**

VARMINT & PREDATOR

Description: A line of coyote and prairie dog ammo priced for high-volume shooters; V-Max bullets; Federal brass and primer
Available in: .204 Ruger, .22 Hornet, .222 Rem., .223 Rem., .224 Valkyrie, .22-250 Rem., .220 Swift, .243 Win., .25-06 Rem., 6.5 Creedmoor, .308 Win.
Box 20 . . . . **$26.99–$38.99**

V-SHOK SPEER TNT GREEN HOLLOWPOINT

Description: Brings non-tox technology to the Federal Premium V-Shok varmint hunting line; a totally lead-free bullet that couples explosive expansion with match-grade accuracy
Available in: .223 Rem., .22-250 Rem., .17 HMR, .22 WMR
Box 20 . . . . **$34.99**
Box 50 (.22 WMR/.17 HMR) . . . . **$19.99–$20/99**

Handgun Ammunition

AMERICAN EAGLE FULL METAL JACKET

Description: Good choice for range practice and reducing lead fouling in the barrel; jacket extends from the nose to the base, preventing bullet expansion and barrel leading; primarily as military ammunition for recreational shooting
Available in: 5.7X28, .25 ACP, .32 ACP, .327 Federal, .380 ACP, 9mm Luger, .357 SIG, .38 Spl., .40 S&W, 10mm, .45 ACP
Box 50: . . . . **$28.99–$44.99**

AMERICAN EAGLE LEAD ROUND NOSE

Description: Great training round for practicing at the range; 100 percent lead with no jacket; excellent accuracy and very economical
Available in: .38 Spl.
Box 50: **$36.99**

FUSION

Description: Bullet weights and velocities have been developed to be lethal on whitetails, without pounding the shooter
Available in: .357 Mag., 10mm Auto .44 Rem. Mag., .454 Casull, .460 S&W, .500 S&W, 50 Action Express
Box 20: . . . . **$29.99–$59.99**

MILITARY GRADE BALL

Description: High-grade full-metal-jacket practice ammo that has a staked primer; mouth and primer sealed; NATO spec brass; assembled to NATO requirements
Available in: 9mm (124 gr.)
Box of 50: **$29.99**

PERSONAL DEFENSE HST

Description: Provides near 100 percent weight retention through most barriers; consistent expansion, optimum penetration, and superior terminal performance, it's specially designed hollow point won't plug while passing through a variety of barriers
Available in: .45 ACP
Box 20: **$40.99**

PERSONAL DEFENSE HYDRA-SHOK DEEP

Features: New version of Hydra-Shok, intended for better results when fired through barriers; 50-percent deeper penetration than original Hydra-Shok
Available in: 9mm
Box 20: **$34.99**

PERSONAL DEFENSE REVOLVER

Description: Economical personal defense round for revolvers; quick, positive expansion
Available in: .32 H&R Mag., .357 Mag.
.32 H&R/20 . . . . **$30.99**
.357 Mag./20 . . . . **$34.99**

PRACTICE & DEFEND PACKS

Description: Boxes of ballistically paired Syntech Training Match rounds (50 count) and HST self-defense loads (50 count)
Available in: 9mm (124 gr., 147 gr.), .40 S&W (180 gr.), .45 ACP (230 gr.)
Box of 100: . . . . **$80.99–$97.99**

PREMIUM SWIFT A-FRAME

Description: Intended mostly for hunting applications; excellet expansion; nickel-plated cases
Available in: .327 Fed. Mag., .357 Mag., 10mm Auto, .41 Rem. Mag., .44 Rem. Mag., .454 Casull, .460 S&W, .500 S&W
Box of 20 . . . . **$60.99–$98.99**

PUNCH

Description: These personal defense loads get a Punch jacketed hollow-point bullet with a skived jacket and soft lead core; nickel-plated brass cases; sealed primer
Available in: .380 ACP (85 gr.), .38 Spec. +P (120 gr.), 9mm (124 gr.), .40 S&W (165 gr.), .45 ACP (230 gr.), 10mm Auto (200-gr.)
Box of 20: . . . . **$21.99–$35.99**

SOLID CORE

Description: Touted as hunting rounds, these are heavy-hitting bone-crushing rounds; Syntech jacket reduces fouling; super-hard lead core
Available in: 9mm +P (147 gr.), .357 Mag. (180 gr.), .40 S&W (200 gr.), 10mm Auto (200 gr.), .45 ACP +P (240 gr.), .44 Mag. (300 gr.)
Box of 20: . . . . **$36.99–$42.99**

FEDERAL SYNTECH BULK BUCKET

FEDERAL BISMUTH MEATEATER

SYNTECH ACTION PISTOL

Description: Designed for action shooting competitors; flat-nosed bullets help with steel target knockdown while reducing bullet fracturing and splash back; Federal's TSJ–Total Synthetic Jacket–reduces bore fouling; clean powders; Federal's lead-free Catalyst primer
Available in: 9mm (150 gr.), .40 S&W (205 gr.), .45 ACP (.220 gr.)
Box 50: . . . . **$28.99–$34.99**

SYNTECH BULK BUCKET

Description: Save money and practice more with these handgun rounds in bulk; lead-free Catalyst primer; Syntech projectiles with TSJ polymer jackets
Available in: 9mm (124 gr.), .40 S&W (165 gr.), .45 ACP (230 gr.)
9mm/250. . . . .**$117.99**
9mm/500. . . . .**$257.99**
.40 S&W/350. . . . .**$232.99**
.45 ACP/300. . . . .**$225.99**

SYNTECH DEFENSE

Description: Hollowpoint design separates into three segments for additional trauma, while the core continues penetration; Catalyst lead-free primer; polymer jacket reduces fouling
Available in: 9mm (138 gr.), .40 S&W (175 gr.), .45 ACP (205 gr.)
Box 20 . . . .**$24.99–$26.99**
Box 50 . . . .**$44.99–$58.99**

SYNTECH PCC

Description: A 9mmm load specifically developed for reliable functionality in pistol-caliber carbines; minimizes splashback so a great choice for competitors; synthetic jacket reduces fouling; lead-free Catalyst primer
Available in: 9mm (130 gr.)
Box 50: **$28.99**

SYNTECH RANGE

Description: Polymer-encapsulated bullet eliminates metal contact with the bore; Catalyst lead-free primer; no copper jacket means improved safety when used on steel targets; reduced recoil
Available in: 9mm, .40 S&W, .45 ACP, 10mm Auto
9mm/50 . . . .**$28.99**
.40 S&W/50. . . . .**$34.99**
.45 ACP/50 . . . .**$37.99**
10mm Auto. **$46.99**

SYNTECH TRAINING MATCH

Description: Provides the same velocities, trajectories, and point of impact's as Federal's Personal Defense HST and Tactical HST loadings, but with a Catalyst lead-free primer and synthetic bullet jacket that reduces fouling; purple bullet color makes use as a training round easily identifiable
Available in: 9mm (124 gr., 147 gr.), .40 S&W (180 gr.), .45 ACP (230 gr.)
9mm/50 . . . .**$26.99–$28.99**
.40 S&W/50. . . . .**$34.99**
.45 ACP/50 . . . .**$37.99**

Shotgun Ammunition

3RD DEGREE WITH HEAVYWEIGHT TSS MEATEATER

Description: The "official" turkey ammunition of Steve Rinella's MeatEater brand; three-stage payload of 20% No. 6 Flitestopper, 40% copper-plated No. 5, and 40% Heavyweight TSS shot; Flitecontrol Flex wad; portion of the proceeds go to benefit the National Wild Turkey Federation
Available in: 12 ga. (3½ in., 3 in.)
Box of 5: . . . .**$30.99–$35.99**

BISMUTH MEATEATER

Description: A return to bismuth non-toxic shot makes this the "official" waterfowl/upland load for Steven Rinella's MeatEater brand; Flitecontrol Fex wad; lead-free Catalyst primer
Available in: 12 ga. (3 in., 2¾ in.), 20 ga. (3 in.)
Box of 25: . . . .**$66.99–$76.99**

BLACK CLOUD FS STEEL

Available in: 10-gauge 3½-inch No. 2, BB; 12-gauge 3½-inch No. 3, 2, 1, BB, BBB; 12-gauge 3-inch No. 4, 3, 2, 1, BB, BBB; 12-gauge 2¾-inch No. 4, 3, 2, BB; 20-gauge 3-inch No. 4, 3, 2, 1
Box 25: . . . .**$25.99–$47.99**

BLACK CLOUD TSS

Description: A new and improved duplex Black Cloud with Heavyweight Tungsten Super Shot pellets (60%) and Flitestopper Steel (40%) backed by Flitecontrol Flex wad; Catalyst lead-free primer
Available in: 12-gauge 3-in. 1¼-ounce load in No. 7 TSS/BB FS Steel or No. 9 TSS/No. 3 FS Steel; 20-gauge 2¾-inch 1 1/8-ounce load in No. 9 TSS/No. 3 FS Steel
Box 10: . . . .**$45.99–$50.99**

GOLD MEDAL GRAND PAPER

Available in: 12 Ga. (2¾ in.) only, in 11/8-oz. loads of 7.5 or 8, or 1-oz. load of 8
Box of 25: **$18.99**

GOLD MEDAL GRAND PLASTIC

Available in: 12-gauge 2¾-inch No. 9, 8, 7½; general target shooting and dedicated competition loads available in a variety of velocities and payloads
Box of 25: . . . .**$13.99–$14.99**

GRAND SLAM

Description: FLITECONTROL FLEX wad; load of copper-plated lead shot; 20 ga. is available in No. 5 only; 12 ga. is available in 4, 5, and 6; 10 ga. is available in 4 and 5
Available in: 10 ga. (3.5 in.), 12 ga. (2.75 in., 3 in., 3.5 in.), 20 ga. (3 in.)
Box 5: . . . .**$17.99–$29.99**

HEAVYWEIGHT TSS

Description: Four duplex loads of HEAVYWEIGHT TSS (Tungsten Super Shot) and a single-size fine-shot TSS load provide superior pellet counts-- more than double the pellet count of a No. 5 load in the same weight
Available in: 12-ga. 3.5-in. #7/9 2½-oz., #9 or #7 2 ¼-oz., 12-ga. 3-in. #7/9 2-oz., #9 or #7 1¾-oz., 20-ga. 3-in. #8/10 or #7/9 1 5/8-oz., 20-ga. 3-in. #9 or #7 1 ½-oz., .410-bore 3-in. #9 13/16-oz.
Box 5: . . . .**$42.99–$92.99**

HI-BIRD

Description: Two-piece wad features SoftCell technology to decrease perceived recoil and produce more consistent long-range patterns; dense long-range patterns and increased down-range energy
Available in: 12-gauge 2¾-inch No. 8, 7, 6, 5, 4
Box 25: . . . .**$14.99–$18.99**

AMMUNITION

Federal Ammunition

FEDERAL PERSONAL DEFENSE SHOTSHELLS FORCE X2

FEDERAL SPEED-SHOK SNOW GOOSE

PERSONAL DEFENSE SHOTSHELLS

Description: Just as the name implies, buckshot loads for personal-/home-defense use; one of two 12-gauge loads keep shot column tight with Flitecontrol wad; .410 is suitable for revolver use

Available in: .410-bore (3-inch #4 Buck, #000 Buck; 2½-inch No. 4 shot, #000 Buck); 12-gauge (2¾-inch #00 Buck with Flitecontrol or #4 Buck without); 20-gauge (2¾-inch #4 Buck)

.410-bore/20 . . . . **$24.99–$28.00**
12-ga./10 . . . . **$27.99**
12-ga. with Flitecontrol wad/5$11.99

PERSONAL DEFENSE SHOTSHELLS FORCE X2

Description: Defensive loads of FX2 buckshot designed to split in two upon impact, doubling the number of wound channels; nine-pellet load

Available in: 12 ga. (2¾ in.)
Box of 10: **$27.99**

PRAIRIE STORM FS STEEL

Available in: Boxes of 25 in 12-ga. 2 ¾-in. #3, 4, 5, and 6; 12-ga. 3-in. #3, 4, 5, and 6; 16-ga. 2 ¾-in. #4, 5, and 6; 20-ga. 3-in. #3, 4, 5, and 6; 28-ga. 2 ¾-in. #6

12-ga. 2 3/4-in. . . . . . . **$29.99–$30.99**
12-ga. 3-in. . . . . **$31.99–$35.99**
16-ga. **$42.99**
20-ga. . . . . **$30.99–$33.99**
28-ga. **$40.99**

SHORTY

Description: Just 1¾-inches long, perfect for use in short-chambered older guns and offers performance similar to 2 ¾-inch shells

Available in: 12 ga.; Shot size: #4 Buck, rifled slug, 8

Box 10: . . . . **$7.99–$10.99**

SPEED-SHOK SNOW GOOSE

Description: Just for snow goose hunters and their long, big limit seasons with two moderately priced steel loads

Available in: 12-ga. 3-in; No. 2 or BB

Box 25: **$19.99**

SPEED-SHOK WATERFOWL

Available in: Box of 25 in 10 ga. (3½ in., No. T, BBB, BB, 2); 12 ga. (3½ in., No. T, BBB, BB, 1, 2, 3, 4); 12 ga. (3 in., No. T, BBB, BB, 1, 2, 3, 4, 6); 12 ga. (2¾ in., No. BB, 2, 3, 4, 6); 16 ga. (2¾ in., No. BB, 2, 4); 20 ga. (3 in., No. 1, 2, 3, 4); 20 ga. (2¾ in., No. 4, 6, 7); 28 ga. (2¾ in., No. 6); .410-bore (3-in. No. 6)

10-ga. **$41.99**
12-ga. 3.5-in. **$28.99**
12-ga. 3-in. **$19.99**
12-ga. 2 3/4-in. **$18.99**
16-ga. . . . . **$32.99–$34.99**
20-ga. 3-in. **$21.99**
20-ga. 2 3/4-in. **$16.99**
28-ga. **$25.99**
.410-bore **$25.99**

TOP GUN, TOP GUN SUBSONIC

Available in: 12- or 20-gauge 2.75-inch in No. 7., 8, 9; multiple loadings available, including a subsonic load in 12-gauge in No. 7.

Top Gun/25 . . . . **$9.99–$18.99**
Subsonic/5 . . . . **$13.99**

TOP GUN STEEL

Available in: 12 Ga., 20 Ga. (2¾ in.); Shot size: 7

Box 25: **$12.99**

UPLAND STEEL

Description: Quail, woodcock, pheasant and other upland game on lands with traditional ammo restrictions are now easier to add to the dinner table with these high-velocity steel loads

Available in: 12 ga. (2¾ in. 11/8-ounce No. 6, 7.5); 20 ga. (2¾ in. ¾-ounce No. 5, 7.5)

12-ga./25 . . . . **$14.99–$28.99**
20-ga./25 . . . . **$14.99**
28-ga. **$28.99**
.410-bore **$24.99**

Shotgun Slugs

TROPHY COPPER SABOT SLUG

Description: A copper slug that incorporates some of the most advanced technology in the industry; better accuracy, less drop, manageable recoil (similar to a .30-06 Spfd.) and consistent penetration and expansion; unique two-part sabot design achieves accuracy through a clean launch and improved projectile support

Available in: 12 Ga., 20 Ga. (2¾ in., 3 in.)

12-ga./5 . . . . **$18.99–$20.99**
20-ga./5 . . . . **$18.99–$21.99**

TRUBALL RIFLED SLUG

Available in: 12, 20 Ga. (2¾ in., 3 in.)
12-ga./5 . . . . **$6.99–$7.99**
12-ga./5 . . . . **$5.99–$7.99**

Rifle Ammunition

RANGE DYNAMICS RIFLE

Description: Training and target loads for rifle shooters, most calibers sold in bulk

Available in: 4.6X30 HK, .223 Rem., 5.56 NATO, .300 BLK, .308 Win., .30-06 Spfd.

Box of 20 . . . . **$21.99–$36.95**

Handgun Ammunition

COWBOY ACTION

Description: Loaded with brass reloadable cases, noncorrosive primers, smokeless powders, and lead bullets coated with lube to reduce leading in the barrel; velocity is on par with what you would expect from

Fiocchi USA

period-correct ammo while keeping the recoil to a minimum for timed Cowboy Action competition and to reduce wear and tear on older guns

Available in: .45 Colt, .44 Spec., .357 Mag., .38 Spec., .38 S&W Short, .32 S&W Long, .45-70 Gov't., .44 S&W Russian, .44-40 Win.

Box 50: . . . . **$28.95–$59.99**

Fiocchi USA

FIOCCHI RANGE DYNAMICS HANDGUN

RANGE DYNAMICS HANDGUN
Description: Training and target load sold in bulk; reloadable brass cases
Available in: .25 ACP, .32 ACP, .32

RIFLE AMMUNITION
Features: A range of bullets for training and all types of hunting situations worldwide; GECO offers five different bullet types to cover every hunting situation; GECO PLUS for shooting big game, GECO EXPRESS for the long distance shot, GECO SOFTPOINT as the real all-rounder, GECO SWISS MATCH for .223 competitors, and GECO ZERO, a lead-free line for hunters; made in Germany, which means outstanding accuracy and reliable bullet performance
Available calibers: .223 Rem., .243 Win., .270 WSM, .270 Win., .280 Rem., .30-06 Spfd., .300 Win. Mag., .308 Win., 6.5x55 Swedish Mauser, 7mm Rem. Mag., 7x57, 7x57R, 7x64,

7x65R, 8x57 IRS, 8x57 IS, 9.3x62, 9.3x74R
MSRP . . . .$9.99–$29.99

RIMFIRE AMMUNITION
Description: Target shooters can always depend on the cartridges perfect functioning, consistent performance and good precision.; reliable rimfire ammunition to guarantee required standards of accuracy at a favorable price
Available in: .22 LR Rifle, .22 LR Semi-Auto
Box 500: . . . .$14.99–$39.99

PISTOL AMMUNITION
Description: GECO offers 18 loads with cartridges in nine different cali-

S&W Long, .380 ACP, 9mm, .357 SIG, .38 Spec., .357 Mag., .40 S&W, 10mm Auto, .45 ACP, .45 Colt
Box of 50 . . . .$21.99–$61.99

GECO

GECO RIMFIRE AMMUNITION

bers; these cover all relevant fields of application like precision shooting, dynamic sport disciplines, hunting, protection, and self-defense.
Available in: .38 Super, .40 S&W, .45ACP, 6.35 Browning, 7.65 Browning (.32 ACP), 9mm Browning Court (.380 ACP), 9mm, 9mm Makarov, 9x21., .357 Mag., .38 Spl. .357 SIG
Box 50: . . . .$8.49–$30.82

Grasso Holdings/GH Ammunition

GRASSO HOLDINGS/GH AMMUNITION TULAMMO

MAXXTECH
Features: Economical brass-cased ammunition for range practice; Boxer primed, full metal jacket except for the lead .22 LR rimfire
Available in: .380 ACP, 9mm, .40 S&W, .45 ACP, .22 LR, .223 Rem.
Box of: 50/100 (pistol), 20/50 (rifle), 250 (.22 LR)
MSRP . . . . .N/A

TULAMMO
Features: Russian-made steel-cased ammo designed to be range-friendly by minimizing spark risks with a non-steel, brass-jacketed projectile; legal in all 50 states; Berdan primers
Available in: .223 Rem., .30 Carbine, .308 Win., 5.45x39mm, 7.62x39, 7.62x54R
20 rounds . . . .$8.29–$20.00

Hornady Manufacturing

Rifle Ammunition

AMERICAN GUNNER RIFLE
Description: The American Gunner line of ammunition is a collection of tried-and-true, versatile loads that are popular with shooters for their target

shooting, hunting, or self-defense needs. Made in the USA with premium components, American Gunner ammunition combines generations of ballistics know-how with modern technology. Hornady introduces new rifle calibers to complement the handgun offerings currently available. These rifle options are loaded with

match grade hollow point bullets for a broad range of use including self-defense, target shooting, and varmint/small game hunting.
Available in: .223 Rem., 6.5 Creedmoor, .300 BLK, .308 Win., 7.652x39
Box 50: . . . .$64.99–$108/99

Hornady Manufacturing

HORNADY SUPERFORMANCE MATCH

HORNADY OUTFITTER

AMERICAN WHITETAIL

Description: Loaded with Hornady InterLock Bullets, optimized loads specifically for deer hunting, and select propellants for greater consistency
Available in: 6.5 Creedmoor, .243 Win., .25-06 Rem., .270 Win., 7mm-08 Rem., 7mm Rem. Mag, 30-30 Win., .308 Win., 30-06 Spfd., .300 Win. Mag, .300 WSM
Box 20: . . . .**$37.99–$54.99**

BLACK

Description: Designed to function across a wide variety of platforms including direct impingement, gas piston, suppressed, unsuppressed, inertia, bolt, pump, supersonic, subsonic, rifle, mid-length, carbine, or pistol; seven bullet types; 00 buckshot comes in a box of 10
Available in: 5.45x39, .223 Rem., 5.56 NATO, 6.5 Grendel, .224 Valkyrie, 6mm ARC, 6mm Creedmoor, 6.8mm SPC, .300 BLK, 7.62x39, .308 Win., .450 Bushmaster
Box 20: . . . .**$28.99–$48.99**

CRITICAL DEFENSE RIFLE

Description: Corrosion-resistant nickel-plated cases; Critical Defense offers improved expansion with limited penetration in self-defense rifles
Available in: .223 Rem., .30 Carbine, .308 Win.
Box 20: . . . .**$39.99–$44.99**

CUSTOM

Description: Depending on caliber, Custom ammo is loaded with Hornady SST, InterBond, InterLock, or V-MAX bullets
Available in: .22 Hornet, .218 Bee, .223 Rem., .243 Win., .250 Savage, 6.5 Grendel, .264 Win. Mag., 6.8 SPC, .275 Rigby, .308 Win., .300 BLK, .30-40 Krag, .300 H&H Mag., .303 British, .350 Legend, .358 Win., .405 Win., .450 Bushmaster
Box 20: . . . .**$33.99–$107.99**

CUSTOM LITE

Description: CustomLite ammunition is recommended for children, women, and anyone new to the game; offer minimum recoil and a reduced muzzle blast; often paired with SST and RN bullets
Available in: .243 Win, 7mm-08 Rem., .308 Win., .30-06 Spfd.
From: **$55.99**

DANGEROUS GAME

Description: These bullets are among the largest offered by Hornady and feature the DGS (Dangerous Game Solid) and the DGX (Dangerous Game eXpanding); made with hard lead/antimony alloy cone and surrounded by a copper-clad steel jacket; straighter penetration comes from a flat meplat that creates more energy than traditional round bullets
Available in: 9.3x62 Mauser, 9.3x74R, .376 Steyr., .375 H&H, .375 H&H Superformance, .375 Ruger, .375 Ruger Superformance, .450/.400 Nitro Express, .416 Ruger, .416 Rem. Mag., .416 Rigby, .404 Jeffery, .450 Nitro Express 3.25-in., .450 Rigby, .458 Win. Mag. Superformance, .458 Win. Mag., .458 Lott, .470 Nitro Express 3.25-in., .500 Nitro Express
Box 20: . . . .**$83.99–$243.99**

FRONTIER

Description: Frontier is American made; military grade; brass cases; wide variety of bullet weights and profiles
Available in: .223 Rem., 5.56 NATO, .300 BLK, 6.5 Grendel
Box 20: . . . .**$12.99–$34.99**

LEVEREVOLUTION

Description: LEVERevolution bullets travel at a speed of 250 fps and have a faster muzzle velocity than most other conventional lever gun loads; are unbelievably accurate and offer incomparable terminal performance; available in FTX and MonoFlex
Available in: .25-35 Win., 7-30 Waters, .30-30 Win., .307 Win., .308 Marlin Express, .32 Win. Spec., .338 Marlin Express, .348 Win., .35 Rem., .444 Marlin, .45-70 Govt., .450 Marlin
Box 20: . . . .**$34.99–$77.99**

MATCH

Description: Match bullets feature a boattail hollow point design that provides both accuracy and speed; these bullets' jackets feature near-zero wall thickness, which leads to uniformity throughout the jacket; case weight and internal capacity are also consistent throughout Match ammunition
Available in: .223 Rem., .224 Valkyrie, .260 Rem., 6mm ARC, 6mm Creedmoor, 6.5 Creedmoor, 6.5 PRC, .308 Win., .300 Win. Mag., .300 PRC, .338 Lapua Mag., .50 BMG (box 10)
Box 20: . . . .**$39.99–$186.99**

OUTFITTER

Description: Dedicated hunting line of rifle cartridges featuring: corrosion-resistant, waterproof nickel-plated cases; copper-alloy expanding CX bullets have 95% weight retention
Available in: .243 Win., .257 Wby. Mag., 6.5 Creedmoor, 6.5mm PRC, .270 Win., .270 WSM, 7mm WSM, 7mm Rem. Mag., .308 Win., .30-06 Spfd., .300 WSM, .300 Win. Mag., .300 Wby. .300 PRC, Mag., .300 RUM, .338 Win. Mag., .375 H&H Mag., .375 Ruger
Box 20: . . . .**$54.90–$109.99**

PRECISION HUNTER

Description: Best-in-class BCs, match-accurate hunting loads, topped with ELD-X Heat Shield Tip bullets
Available in: .243 Win., 6mm ARC, 6mm Creedmoor, .25-06 Rem., .257 Wby. Mag., 6.5 Creedmoor, 6.5 PRC, .270 Win., .270 WSM, 7mm-08 Rem., .280 Rem., .280 Ackley Improved, 7mm WSM, 7mm Rem. Mag., .28 Nosler, 7mm STW, .308 Win., .30-06 Spfd., .300 Rem. SAUM, .300 Ruger Compact Mag., .300 Win. Mag., .300 WSM, .300 Wby. Mag., .300 PRC, .300 RUM. .30-378 Wby. Mag., .338 Lapua Mag., 6mm ARC
Box 20: . . . .**$51.99–$188.99**

SUBSONIC

Description: Subsonic .300 Blackout wears a 190-gr. Sub-X (Subsonic eXpanding) bullet; lead core; gilded metal jacket; Flex Tip insert; muzzle velocity is 1,050 fps; muzzle energy is 465 ft-lbs.
Available in: .300 BLK, .30-30 Win., .450 Bushmaster, .45-70 Gov't. (1895 Marlin), .350 Legend
Box 20: . . . .**$39.99–$62.99**

SUPERFORMANCE

Description: Superformance bullets are 100–200 fps faster than any other traditional type of bullet on the market today. In addition to their speed, they also offer minimal recoil, muzzle blast, temperature sensativity, and inaccuracies; these bullets are versatile and can be paired with all types of firearms, including semiautomatics, lever guns, and pump actions

Available in: .223 Rem., 5.56 NATO, .243 Win., 6mm Rem., 6mm Creedmoor, .25-06 Rem., .257 Roberts +P, .260 Rem., , 6.5 Creedmoor, 6.5x55 Swedish, .270 Win., 7mm-08 Rem., 7mm Rem. Mag., .300 Savage, .308 Win., .30 TC, .30-06 Spfd., .300 Ruger Compact Mag., .300 Win. Mag., .300 WSM, .338 Ruger Compact Mag., .338 Win. Mag., .35 Whelen, .444 Marlin

Box 20: . . . .$36.99–$79.99

SUPERFORMANCE MATCH

Description: Achieves muzzle velocity 100 to 200 fps faster than conventional .308 Win. loads; AMAX or Hornady Boattail Hollowpoint Match bullets featuring AMP (Advanced Manufacturing Process) jackets

Available in: .223 Rem., 5.56 NATO, .308 Win.

Box 20: . . . .$38.99–$59.99

Handgun Ammunition

AMERICAN GUNNER HANDGUN

Description: XTP (eXtreme Terminal Performance) bullets are exceptionally accurate and deliver excellent versatility and superior ballistic performance; propellants are matched to each load to ensure optimal pressure, velocity, volume and consistency from lot to lot; high quality primers and Hornady cases combine to deliver consistent shooting in the field

Available in: .380 ACP, .40 S&W, .45 ACP, 9mm, 9mm +P, .38 Spl., .357 Mag.

Box 25: . . . .$24.99–$34.99

COWBOY

Description: These swaged bullets flatten instead of fragment when they reach their targets; diamond knurling ensures that the entire surface of the bullet is well-lubed

Available in: .44-40 Win., .45 Colt

Box 20: . . . .$19.99–$24.33

CRITICAL DEFENSE HANDGUN

Description: Critical Defense bullets are custom-designed for individual loads, and their shiny silver nickel plating prevents bullet corrosion; Critical Defense ammunition is cannelured and crimped to avoid bullet setback, and clean burning and stable propellants reduce recoil

Available in: .25 ACP, .32 ACP, .32 NAA, 32 H&R Mag., .327 Fed. Mag., .380 ACP, 9mm, 9mm Lite, 9X18 Makarov, .38 Spec., .38 Spec. Lite, .38 Spec. +P, .357 Mag., .40 S&W, .44 Spec., .45 ACP, .45 Colt

Box 25: . . . .$29.99–$39.99

CRITICAL DUTY

Description: Features FlexLock Bullets, crimped and nickel-plated cases, interlocking bands, and a core made of high-antimony lead; these bullets are among the top choices of law enforcement and military professionals and highly reliable

Available in: .357 Mag., .40 S&W, .45 ACP +P, .357 SIG, 9mm, 9mm Luger +P, 10mm Auto

Box 25: . . . .$32.99–$37.99

HANDGUN HUNTER

Description: A top-end choice for those pursing game with a handgun; MonoFlex projectiles contain a copper alloy; deep cavity has elastomer material that compresses upon impact before pushing out for rapid and wide expansion

Available in: 9mm +P (115 gr.), .357 Mag. (130 gr.), .40 S&W (135 gr.), 10mm Auto (135 gr.), .44 Mag. (200 gr.), .454 Casull (200 gr.), .460 S&W Mag. (200 gr.)

Box of 20, 25: . . . .$41.99–$58.99

Shotgun Ammunition

AMERICAN GUNNER SHOTGUN

Description: Reduced recoil rifled

HORNADY HEAVY MAGNUM COYOTE

HORNADY AMERICAN GUNNER SHOTGUN

slugs or 00 buckshot; rifled slug is 1 oz., 00 buck holds eight high-antimony swaged pellets

Available in: 12 ga.

Box 5: . . . .$14.99–$19.99

AMERICAN WHITETAIL RIFLED SLUG

Description: Rifled slug for smooth-bore barrels; 12 gauge 1-ounce rifled, foster style slug or 325-grain InterLock slug; hollow point, tough lead-alloy core; 1,600 feet per second

Available in: 12 Ga.

Box 5: . . . .$14.99–$19.99

CUSTOM LITE SHOTGUN SLUGS

Description: Delivers 25 percent less recoil than standard loads; for rifled barrels only; FTX bullet improves ballistic coefficient and aids in expansion; lower recoil and muzzle blast while maintaining accuracy and effectiveness out to 150 yds; innovative sabot design enhances accuracy

Available in: 12 Ga., 20 Ga. (2¾ in.)

Box 5: $24.99

HEAVY MAGNUM COYOTE

Description: Loaded with 1 ½ oz. of nickel plated lead shot in either a BB or 00 buckshot for close range predators; features Hornady Versatite wad for more impact on target; 1,300 fps

Available in: 12 Ga. (3 in., 00 buckshot or BB)

Box 10: $24.99

SST SLUGS

Description: Sharp points at the end of these slugs allow for faster and more accurate shooting; able to reach your target from an impressive 200 yards away; each shot delivers more than 1200 ft.-lbs. of energy

Available in: 12, 20 Ga. (2¾ in)

Box 5: . . . .$18.99–$21.99

Rimfire Ammunition

VARMINT EXPRESS RIMFIRE .17 HMR

Description: The 17 HMR is one of the most accurate rimfire bullets ever made; polymer tip fragments rapidly and dramatically on impact, and its flat trajectory adds to its accuracy and consistency

Available in: .17 HMR

Box 50: $24.99

Hornady Manufacturing

VARMINT EXPRESS RIMFIRE .17 MACH 2

Description: These V-MAX bullets are known for their rapid fragmentation and consistent accuracy; these bullets are made in America and hand inspected; paired with Varmint Express products, ignition is fast and easy
Available in: .17 Mach2
Box 50:. $15.99

VARMINT EXPRESS RIMFIRE .17 WSM

Description: 20 grain V-Max bullet that provides tack-driving accuracy; muzzle velocity of 3,000 feet per second; fills the gap between the rimfire 17 HMR and centerfire 17 Hornet
Available in: .17 WSM (20 gr.)
Box 50:. $22.99

VARMINT EXPRESS RIMFIRE .22 WMR

Description: The .22 WMR guarantees accurate shooting from more than 125 feet; has a muzzle velocity of 2,200 fps and is one of the most requested products Hornady offers; available in 25, 30, and 45 gr.
Available in: .22 WMR
Box 50:. $22.99

Inceptor Ammunition

INCEPTOR SPORT & CARRY COMBO

PREFERRED DEFENSE ARX

Description: Non-expanding projectile of a copper/polymer matrix for special critical defense use; 1780 fps, 633 ft.-lb.
Available in: 9mm, 9mm +P, .40

S&W, 10mm Auto, .45 ACP, .38 Spec., .357 Mag.
Box 20:. . . . . starting at $24.99

SPORT & CARRY COMBO

Description: They say to train with ammo ballistically equal to your carry ammo, and you can do that without breaking the bank with this combo pack that boasts 100 rounds of Inceptor's RNP roundnose practice ammo with 25 rounds of its hollowpoint ARX Preferred Defense rounds
Available in: .380 ACP, 9mm +P, .40 S&W, .45 ACP, .38 Spec.

Box 120:. . . . . starting at $55.99

SPORT UTILITY-HANDGUN

Description: Lead-free injection-molded copper-polymer projectiles loaded to tight specifications in high-quality brass cases; RNP (Round Nose Precision) profile in handgun cartridges or with the SRR (Short-Range Rifle) in rifle cartridges
Available in: .380 ACP, 9mm, 9mm +P, .38 Spec., .40 S&W, .45 ACP
Box 50:. . . . . starting at $17.99

Jarrett Rifles

JARRETT TROPHY AMMUNITION

TROPHY AMMUNITION

Description: Jarrett's high-performance cartridges are in ten round boxes; cases are from Norma with Jarrett's headstamp

Available in: .243 Win., .270 Win., 7mm Rem. Mag., .30-06 Spfd., .300 WM, .300 Jarrett, .375 H&H, .416 Rem. Mag.
MSRP. . . . . $29.12–$82.81

Kent Cartridge

KENT CARTRIDGE BISMUTH UPLAND

BISMUTH UPLAND

Description: Bismuth-based shot is 24 percent denser than steel; safe to use in any choke; doesn't harm barrels; loaded to optimal velocities for max ballistic performance
Available in: 12- and 20-gauge 3- and 2 ¾-inch in No. 5 and 6; 16-gauge 2¾-inch in No. 5 only
Box of: 25
MSRP. . . . . $29.12–$82.81

BISMUTH WATERFOWL

Description: Bismuth-based shot is 24 percent denser than steel; safe to use in any choke; doesn't harm barrels; loaded to optimal velocities for max ballistic performance
Available in: 12-gauge 3½- and 3-inch in No. 3, 4; 12-gauge 2¾-inch in No. 4; 20-gauge 3-inch in No. 3, 4
Box 25:. . . . . $33.99–$45.99

ELITE LOW-RECOIL/TRAINING

Description: The new Elite Low-Recoil/Training load from Kent comes two ways: a 12-ga. 2.5-in. shell with a 0.75-oz. load, and a 12-ga. 2.75-in. shell with a 0.75-oz. load; loaded

with No. 8 to muzzle velocity of 1,200 fps; Kent's Diamond Shot ensures solid break
Available in: 12 ga.
Box 25 . . . .$11.99

ELITE PRO TARGET

Description: Loaded with Diamond Shot; all 2.75 in. Shot sizes: 7.5, 8, 8.5
Available in: 12, 20 ga.
Case 250:. $119.99

ELITE STEEL TARGET

Description: Two 12-ga. 2.75-in. loads: a 1-oz. load at 1,290 fps and a 0.75-oz. load at 1,215 fps, both in No. 7
Available in: 12 ga.
Case 250. . . . .$119.00

FASTEEL 2.0
Description: Zinc-plated shots; nickel-plated case heads; high-performance wad ensures consistent patterns in the coldest conditions; 12 ga. 3½-, 3-, 2¾-inch in a range of BB to No. 6; 20 ga. 3-inch in Nos. 2, 3, and 4
Available in: 12 ga., 20 ga.
Box 25 . . . . **$15.99–$17.99**

STEEL DOVE
Description: Two 12-ga. 2.75-in. loads: a 1-oz. and a 1.125-oz.; One 20-ga. 2.75-in. 0.875-oz. load; Shot size: 6
Available in: 12, 20 ga.
Case 250 . . . . **$92.90–$98.00**

Kent Cartridge

Kynoch Ammunition

KYNOCH RIFLE AMMUNITION

Description: Kynoch hunting ammunition is now standardized on Woodleigh soft nosed and solid bullets, recognized world wide as the most reliable big game bullets currently manufactured;

Kynamco offers virtually the whole range of classic British Nitro Express from its purpose-built factory
Available in: .300 Flanged, .303 British, .318 Westley Richards, 9.5X57 Mannlicher, .333 Jeffery Flanged. .350 Rigby, .400/.360 Westley Richards, .375 Flanged 2½-inch, .375 Flanged, .400 Purdey, .405 Winchester, .450/400 3- and 3½-inch, .416 Rigby, .404 Jeffery, .425 Westley Richards, .450 NE, .450 No. 2 NE, .450 Rigby, .577/.450 Martini Henry, .500/.450 NE, .500/.465 NE, .470 NE, .475 No. 2 Eley, .475 No. 2 Jeffery, .476 Westley Richards, .505 Gibbs, .500 Jeffery, .500 NE, .577 NE, .600 NE, .700 NE; currently available in the U.S. from M.W. Reynolds (mwreynolds.com) in Denver, Colorado.
MSRP . . . contact mwreynolds.com

Lapua

LAPUA NATURALIS (3RD GENERATION)

CENTERFIRE SPORT
Description: Lapua's extremely accurate target shooting cartridges are loaded with the best target bullets—Scenar, FMJBT, D46 and Lock Base; numerous world championships, Olympic championships, and other top competition gold medals, as well as many official world records in different disciplines, are shot with the Lapua cartridges
Available in: .222 Rem., .223 Rem., .243 Win., 6mm BR Norma, 6.5 Creedmoor, 6.5x47 Lapua, 6.5x55 Swedish, 7.62x39, .308 Win., .30-06 Spfd., 7.62x53R, .338 Lapua Mag.
Box 50: . . . . **$39.99–$54.99**

NATURALIS 3RD GENERATION
Description: Bullet mushrooming begins immediately on impact; bullet expands symmetrically and without shattering; gives a maximal shock effect to the hunted game; top premium copper bullet; 3rd Generation has updated bullet design with a monolithic pure copper body that can produce weight retention up to 100 percent; new boattail design eases reloading and improves ballistics; controlled expansion is procured via a polymer valve tip
Available in: .222 Rem., .243 Win., 6.5 Creedmoor, 6.5x47 Lapua, 6.5x55 Swedish Mauser, 7x64, 7x65R, ,308 Win., .30-06 Spfd., 8x57 JS, 8x57 JRS, 338 Lapua, 9.3X62
MSRP . . . . **Starting at $69.99**

Magnum Research

.429 DE MAGNUM
Description: Designed specifically for Magnum Research's 429 DE Mark XIX pistol; Starline brass; more energy and velocity than a .44 Mag.
Available in: .429 DE (240 gr.) soft-point, (210 gr.) hollowpoint
Box 20: **$42.00**

MAGNUM RESEARCH .429 DE MAGNUM

Magtech Ammunition

SPORT SHOOTING HANDGUN
Description: The 100 percent solid copper hollow-point projectile features a six-petal hollow-point specifically designed to deliver tight groups, superior expansion, virtually 100 percent weight retention, and increased penetration over jacketed lead-core bullets
Available in: .25 ACP, .32 ACP, .32 S&W, .32 S&W Long, .380 ACP, 9mm, 9mm +P, 9X19 NATO, 9X21mm, .38 S&W, .38 Spec., .38 Spec. +P, .38 Super, .357 Mag., .40 S&W, 10mm Auto, .44040 Win., .44 Spec., .44 Mag., .45 G.A.P., .45 ACP, .454 Casull, .500 S&W
Box of 20, 50: . . . . . . **$20.99–$119.99**

MAGTECH AMMUNITION

Nexus Ammunition

NEXUS AMMUNITION SUBSONIC

HUNTING GRADE

Description: Uses same proprietary loading methods as Nexus' Match line; lead projectiles
Available in: .223 Rem. (79-gr.), .300 BLK (125-gr.)
Box 20: . . . .$35.99–$56.99

MATCH GRADE

Description: Proprietary loading process; competition-ready
Available in: .260 Rem., .223 Rem., .338 Lapua, .300 Win. Mag., .300 Norma, .308 Win., 6.5x47 Lapua, 6.5 Creedmoor
Box of 20: . . . . $39.99–$75.99

POWDER CORE

Description: Heavy-metal powder core technology replaces solid lead in the projectile; improved spin stability;

higher B.C.; improved shot-to-shot consistency
Available in: .223 Rem. (79-gr.)
Box of 20: $35.99

SUBSONIC

Description: Subsonic ammo to pair with your favorite suppressor
Available in: .300 BLK (220-gr.), .308 Win. (175-, 220-gr.
Box 20: . . . .$39.99–$59.99

Norma Ammunition

NORMA RANGE & TRAINING FRANGIBLE

NORMA SAFEGUARD

BONDSTRIKE

Description: Long-range hunting application; polymer tip match-style boattail projectiles with proprietary bonding produce extreme wound channels; initial offerings all in 180 gr.
Available in: .308 Win., .30-06 Spfd., .300 Win. Mag., .300 WSM, .300 RUM
Box 20: . . . . $69.99–$105.99

HEXAGON

Description: Match-grade line of

competition ammunition for handguns; consistent velocities; unique bullet has stabilizing grooves
Available in: .357 Mag. (180 gr.), 9mm (124 gr.), .45 ACP (200 gr.)
Box of 50: . . . . $19.99–$29.99

MHP

Description: High-expansion self-defense round with an all copper monolithic hollowpoint
Available in: 9mm, .380 ACP
Box of: 20
MSRP . . . .$22.79–$23.74

RANGE & TRAINING

Description: Full metal jacket ball ammo for the practice range
Available in: .32 ACP (73 gr.), .380 ACP (95 gr.), 9mm (115 gr.), 9mm Makarov (95 gr.), .38 Spec. (158

gr.).357 Mag. (158 gr.), .40 S&W (180 gr.)
Box of 50: . . . . $20.99–$34.99

RANGE & TRAINING FRANGIBLE

Description: An affordable line of frangible training ammunition; non-lead; great for use with steel targets
Available in: .40 S&W (122 gr.), .45 ACP (147 gr.)
Box of 50: . . . . $24.99–$39.49

SAFEGUARD

Description: A jacketed hollowpoint designed for self-defense use
Available in: 9mm (115 gr., 124 gr.), .38 Spec. (158 gr.), .357 Mag. (158 gr.), .45 ACP (230 gr.)
Box of 50: . . . . $39.99–$48.99

Nosler

NOSLER BALLISTIC TIP

Rifle Ammunition
BALLISTIC TIP

Description: Dedicated whitetail round with a bullet that has a fully tapered jacket, lead alloy core, heavy

jacketed base to improve mushrooming, and polymer tip
Available in: 6.5 Creedmoor, 6.5 Grendel, 6.5 PRC, 6mm Creedmoor, 7.62X39mm, 7mm Rem. Mag., 7mm-08 Rem., .25-06, .30-06 Spfd., .30-30 Win., .243 Win., .260 Rem., .270 Win., .280 AI; .280 Rem., .300 BLK, .300 Win. Mag., .308 Win.
Box of 20: . . . . $45.99–$77.77

MATCH GRADE

Description: Match Grade Ammunition consists of Nosler's precisely-designed Custom Competition bullet along with NoslerCustom Brass; each piece of

brass is checked for correct length, neck-sized, chamfered, trued and flash holes are checked for proper alignment; powder charges are meticulously weighed and finished rounds are visually inspected and polished
Available in: .223 Rem., 5.56X45 .22 Nosler, 6mm Creedmoor, 6.5 Creedmoor, 6.5 Grendel, .260 Rem., 6.5-284 Norma, .26 Nosler, .28 Nosler, 6.8 SPC, .30 Nosler, .300 BLK, .308 Win., .300 Win. Mag., .33 Nosler, .338 Lapua Mag., .33 Nosler
Box 20: . . . .$39.95–$144.95

Nosler

NOSLER TROPHY GRADE LONG-RANGE

TROPHY GRADE SAFARI

Description: Loaded with either the Partition or Nosler Solid and designed for the same point of impact with either bullet, Safari Ammunition provides the ultimate versatility for any dangerous game situation
Available in: .500 Jeffery, 505 Gibbs, 9.3x62 Mauser, .375 Flanged, .375 H&H, .404 Jeffery, .416 Rem. Mag., .416 Rigby, .450 Rigby, .458 Lott, .458 Win. Mag., .470 NE, .500 NE, .500/.416 NE
Box 20:. . . . . $159.49–$224.95

TROPHY GRADE

Description: Manufactured to Nosler's strictest quality standards, Trophy Grade Ammunition uses Nosler Custom Brass and Nosler Bullets to attain optimum performance, no matter where your hunting trip takes you. Whether you want your ammunition loaded with AccuBond, Partition Ballistic Tip or, E-Tip, NoslerCustom Trophy Grade Ammunition will have the right load for the right game.
Available in: .223 Rem., .22 Nosler, 6mm Creedmoor, .243 Win., .25-06 Rem., .257 Roberts, .257 Wby. Mag., 6.5 Creedmoor, 6.5x55 Swedish, .260

Rem., 6.5-284 Norma, .264 Win. Mag., .26 Nosler, .27 Nosler, .270 Win., .270 WSM, 7mm-08, 7x57 Mauser, .280 Rem., .28 Nosler, 7mm SAUM, .280 Ackley Improved, 7mm Rem. Mag., 7mm STW, 7mm RUM, .308 Win., .30–06 Spfd., .300 SAUM, .300 H&H, .300 WSM, .300 Win. Mag., .300 Wby. Mag., .30 Nosler, .30-378 Wby. Mag., .300 RUM, .325 WSM, .338 Win. Mag., .340 Wby. Mag., .338 RUM, .338 Lapua, .33 Nosler, .35 Whelen, 9.3X62, .375 H&H, .416 Rem. Mag.
Box 20:. . . . . $58.95–$165.49

TROPHY GRADE LONG-RANGE

Description: More fuel for the fires stoking the long-range trend, these loaded with Nosler's Accubond Long-Range high B.C. bonded-core bullet; long ogive; boattail
Available in: 6.5–284 Norma (129 gr.), 6.5 Creedmoor (129 gr., 142 gr.), 6.5 Grendel (129 gr.), .26 Nosler (142 gr.), .260 Rem. (129 gr.), 6.5 PRC (142 gr.), .27 Nosler (165 gr.), .270 Wby. Mag. (150 gr.), .270 Win. (150 gr.), .270 WSM (150 gr.), .28 Nosler (175 gr.), .280 Ackley Improved (150 gr.), 7mm Rem. Mag. (168 gr.), 7mm RUM (175 gr.), 7mm STW (175 gr.), .308 Win. 1(68 gr.), .30-06 Spfd. (168 gr.), .30 Nosler (210 gr.), .300 RUM (210 gr.), .300 Win. Mag. (190 gr.), .300 WSM (190 gr.), .300 Wby. Mag.

(210 gr.), .30-378 Wby. Mag. (210 gr.), .33 Nosler (265 gr.), 7mm-08 Rem. (150 gr.)
Box of 20:. . . . . $59.95–$153.49

VARMAGEDDON

Description: Featuring a highly accurate polymer tip or hollow point combined with flat base design, Varmageddon products were created for the high-volume varmint shooter who requires the utmost precision; loaded with Nosler Custom Brass, Varmageddon ammunition provides the highest levels of performance for any varmint hunter
Available in: .17 Rem. Fireball, .17 Rem., .204 Ruger, .22 Hornet, .221 Rem. Fireball, .222 Rem., .223 Rem., .22 Nosler, .22-250 Rem., 6mm Creedmoor, .243 Win., 6.5 Grendel, .300 BLK, .308 Win.
Box 20:. . . . . $35.95–$88.49

Handgun Ammunition

DEFENSE HANDGUN

Description: Bonded 'Performance' bullets for higher weight retention and maximum barrier penetration; either jacketed hollow point or polymer tipped configuration
Available in: 9mm +P, .40 S&W, .45 ACP +P
Box 20:. . . . . $35.49–$44.49

NovX

NOVX RNP CROSSTRAINER, RNP +P CROSS TRAINER

ENGAGEMENT EXTREME, ENGAGMENT EXTREME +P

Description: Lead free; projectiles are a copper-polymer creation; cases are stainless steel; fluted bullet design; 65-gr. 9mm at 1,672 fps/358 ft-lbs standard pressure (1,710 fps/422 ft-lbs in the +P.)
Available in: 9mm, 9mm +P
Box 20:. $31.99

CROSSTRAINER/ COMPETITION

Description: Roundnose design; 65-gr. at 1,600 fps, 347 ft-lbs standard pressure
Available in 9mm
Box 26:. . . . . $23.99–$24.99

PMC Ammunition

PMC BRONZE LINE - HANDGUN

Rifle Ammunition

BRONZE LINE - RIFLE

Description: For shooters and hunters who appreciate affordable quality ammunition, the PMC Bronze Line

offers reliable performance for every shooting application; Full Metal Jacket (FMJ) bullet types
Available in: .223 Rem., .308 Win., 7.62x39, .50 BMG
Box 20:. . . . . $10.99–$41.99

PMC Ammunition

PMC ERANGE

X-TAC
Description: PMC's exacting adherence to precise specifications of military and law enforcement organizations assures that X-TAC ammunition will perform perfectly in that fraction of a second when a serious threat arises and your life is on the line
Available in: 5.56, 7.62x51
Box 20:................$14.89

X-TAC MATCH
Description: X-TAC ammo performance comined with Sierra Bullets' ballistics
Available in: .223 Rem., .308 Win., .50
.223/20 ....$29.99
.308/20 ....$27.99
.50/10 ....$99.99

Handgun Ammunition

BRONZE LINE - HANDGUN
Description: The same quality and dependability built into our Starfire ammunition is incorporated throughout our extensive line of PMC training ammunition and standard hollow point or soft point ammunition.
Available in: .25 ACP, .32 ACP, .380 ACP, .38 Spl., .38 Super +P, 9mm Luger, .357 Mag., 10mm ACP, .40 S&W, .44 S&W Spl., .44 Rem. Mag., .45 ACP
From:............$19.89–$34.89

ERANGE
Description: PMC's eRange environmentally friendly ammunition utilizes a reduced hazard primer that is the first of this type in the industry, an encapsulated metal jacket (EMJ) bullet which completely encloses the surface of the bullet core with precision made copper alloy, and powder with clean-burning characteristics and smooth fire for increased barrel life
Available in: .380 ACP, .38 Spl., .38 Spl. +P, .357 Mag., 9mm Luger, .40 S&W, .44 Rem., .45 ACP
From:.................... **N/A**

SFX
Description: A personal-defense load with "hyper-expanding" hollowpoint. Replaces the old Starfire line and meets current law enforcement ammo protocols
Available in: 9mm (124 gr.)
Box 20:................ $16.99

Polyfrang, LLC

POLYFRANG HANDGUN
Description: US-made lead-free and frangible cartridges for 9mm or .40 S&W; reduces splashback on steel targets; safe for use with suppressors
Available in: 9mm (90 gr.), .40 S&W (115 gr.)
Box 50:.................. **N/A**

POLYFRANG RIFLE
Description: US-made lead-free and frangible cartridges; reduces splashback on steel targets; safe for use with suppressors; .223 comes 50 rounds to the box
Available in: .223 Rem/5.56 NATO. (45 gr.)
Box 20:.................. **N/A**

POLYFRANG RIFLE

Remington Ammunition

REMINGTON HYPERSONIC BONDED

Rifle Ammunition
CORE-LOKT
Description: The bonded bullet retains up to 95 percent of its original weight with maximum penetration and energy transfer; features a progressively tapered jacket design, the Core-Lokt Ultra Bonded bullet initiates and controls expansion nearly 2x
Available in: .223 Rem., 6mm Rem., 6mm Creedmoor, .243 Win., .25-06 Rem., 6.5x55 Swedish Mauser, 6.5 Creedmoor, .260 Rem., .270 Win., .270 WSM. 7mm-08 Rem., .280 Rem., 7mm Rem. Mag., .30 Carbine, .30-30 Win., .300 Savage, .308 Win., .30-06 Spfd., .300 Win. Mag., .300 WSM, .300 Wby. Mag., .300 RUM, .303 British, .32 Win. Spec., .338 Win. Mag., .338 RUM, .35 Rem., .35 Whelen, .45-70 Gov't., .450 Bushmaster, .250 Savage, .25-20 Win., .257 Roberts, .264 Win. Mag., .300 RSAUM, .30-40 Krag, .308 Marlin Express, .30 Rem. AR, .444 Marlin, 7.62x39, 7mm RSAUM, 7mm RUM, 7x57 Mauser, 7x64 Brenneke
Box 20:.......... $28.99–$121.99

HYPERSONIC BONDED
Description: Super-flat trajectories via a Core-Lokt Ultra Bonded projectile; souped up velocities; pointed soft point profile
Available in: .223 Rem., .243 Win., .270 Win., .30-06 Spfd., .300 Win. Mag., .308 Win.
Box 20:............$38.99–$56.99

PREMIER MATCH
Description: Loaded with match-grade bullets, this ammunition employs special loading practices to ensure world-class performance and accuracy with every shot
Available in: .223 Rem., 6.8 SPC, .300 BLK, .308 Win.,. 6.5 Creedmoor, .260 Rem., 6mm Creedmoor
Box 20:............$33.99–$51.99

AMMUNITION

REMINGTON SUBSONIC RIFLE

PREMIER SCIROCCO BONDED

Description: A hunting round with a polymer-tipped boattail whose core is bonded to the jacket; deep penetration and high weight retention
Available in: .243 Win., .270 Win., 7mm Rem. Mag., 7mm RUM, .30-06 Spfd., .300 WSM, .300 Win. Mag., .300 RUM, 6.5 Creedmoor, .308 Win.
Box 20:. . . . . $64.99–$100.99

SUBSONIC RIFLE

Description: A round resulting from the partnership of AAC and Remington; designed to work ideally with silencer-equipped firearms; special heel design reduces lead residue and fouling
Available in: .300 BLK
Box 20:. $32.99

Handgun Ammunition

SUBSONIC HANDGUN

Description: A round resulting from the partnership of AAC and Remington; designed to work ideally with silencer-equipped firearms; special heel design reduces lead residue and fouling
Available in: 9mm, .45 ACP
Box 50:. . . . . $23.99–$35.99

Rimfire Ammunition

PREMIER MAGNUM RIMFIRE

Description: Repackaged and repriced in 2019; .17 HMR in AccuTip; .22 Win. Mag. In Accutip, jacketed hollowpoint, or pointed softpoint
Available in: .17 HMR, .22 Win. Mag.
Box 50:. . . . . $18.99–$20.99

Shotgun Ammunition

AMERICAN CLAY AND FIELD

Description: Nothing that flies stands a chance against these dual-purpose rounds. Expect the densest, most consistent patterns possible, no matter the day's pursuit. Featuring a premium STS primer, reloadable hull, our patented Power Piston wad, and high-hardness lead shot, they deliver flawless performance and consistent patterning, whether your target is winged or clay.
Available in: 12, 20, 28, .410
Box 25:. . . . . $13.99–$16.99

GUN CLUB TARGET

Description: Loaded with Gun Club Grade Shot, Premier STS Primers, and Power Piston One-Piece Wads, these high-quality shells receive the same care in loading as top-of-the-line Premier STS and Nitro .27 shells
Available in: 12, 20 Ga. (2¾ in.); Shot sizes: 7.5, 8, 9
Box 25:. $10.99

EXPRESS EXTRA LONG RANGE

Description: Suitable for everything from quail to farm predators
Available in: 12, 16, 20, 28 Ga. (2¾ in.), .410 (2½ in., 3 in.); Shot sizes: 2, 4, 5, 6, 7.5
From:. . . . . $18.99–$30.99

HEAVY DOVE

Description: A sure bet for all kinds of upland game, ShurShot loads have earned the reputation as one of the best-balanced, best-pattering upland field loads available; shells combine an ideal balance of powder charge and shot payload to deliver effective velocities and near-perfect patterns with mild recoil for high-volume upland hunting situations
Available in: 12, 20 Ga. (2¾ in.); Shot sizes: 6, 7.5, 8
From:. . . . . $12.99–$13.99

HYPERSONIC STEEL

Description: With unprecedented velocity and the highest downrange pattern energies ever achieved, Remington HyperSonic Steel takes lethality to new heights and lengths
Available in: 10 Ga. (3½ in.), 12 Ga. (3 in., 3½ in.), 20 Ga. (3 in.); Shot sizes: BB, BBB, 1, 2, 3, 4
From:. . . . . $34.99–$45.99

NITRO PHEASANT

Description: Uses Remington's own Copper-Lokt copper-plated lead shot with high antimony content; hard shot stays rounder for truer flight, tighter patterns, and greater penetration; available in both high-velocity and magnum loadings
Available in: 12, 20 Ga. (2¾ in., 3 in.); Shot sizes: 4, 5, 6
From:. . . . . $30.99–$33.99

NITRO-STEEL HIGH-VELOCITY

Description: Greater hull capacity means heavier charges and larger pellets, which makes these loads ideal for large waterfowl; delivers denser patterns for greater lethality and is zinc plated to prevent corrosion
Available in: 10 Ga. (3½ in.), 12 Ga. (2¾ in., 3 in., 3½ in.), 16 Ga. (2¾ in.), 20 Ga. (3 in.); Shot sizes: T, BBB, BB, 1, 2, 3, 4
From:. . . . . $29.99–$43.99

NITRO TURKEY

Description: These loads contain Nitro Mag. extra-hard lead shot that is as hard and round as copper-plated shot; will pattern as well as other copper-plated, buffered loads without the higher cost
Available in: 12 Ga. (2¾ in., 3 in., 3½ in.), 20 Ga. (3 in.); Shot sizes: 4, 5, 6
Box 5, 10:. . . . . $11.99–$17.99

PHEASANT

Description: For the broadest selection in game-specific Upland shotshells, Remington Upland Loads are the perfect choice with high-velocity and long-range performance for any pheasant hunting situation; standard high-base payloads feature Power Piston one-piece wads
Available in: 12, 16, 20 Ga. (2¾ in.); Shot sizes: 4, 5, 6, 7.5
From:. . . . . $18.99–$28.99

PREMIER STS

Description: STS Target Loads have taken shot-to-shot consistency to a new performance level, setting the standard at all major skeet, trap, and sporting clays shooting across the country, while providing handloaders with unmatched reloading ease and hull longevity; available in most gauges, Premier STS shells are the most reliable, consistent, and reloadable shells you can shoot
Available in: 12, 20, 28 Ga. (2¾ in.), .410 (2½ in.); Shot sizes: 7.5, 8, 8.5, 9
From:. . . . . $14.99–$19.99

Remington Ammunition

REMINGTON ULTIMATE DEFENSE SHOTSHELL .410-BORE

SPORTSMAN HI-SPEED STEEL

Description: Sportsman Hi-Speed Steel's sealed primer, high-quality steel shot, and consistent muzzle velocities combine to provide reliability in adverse weather, while delivering exceptional pattern density and retained energy; a high-speed steel load that is ideal for short-range high-volume shooting during early duck seasons or over decoys
Available in: 10 Ga. (3½ in.), 12 Ga. (2¾ in., 3 in., 3½ in.), 20 Ga. (2¾ in.); Shot sizes: BB, 1, 2, 3, 4, 6, 7
From: . . . .$16.99–$43.99

Shotgun Slugs & Buckshot

EXPRESS, EXPRESS MAGNUM BUCKSHOT

Description: A combination of heavy cushioning behind the shot column and a granulated polymer buffering helps maintain pellet roundness for tight, even patterns
Available in: 12 (2¾ in., 3 in., 3½ in.), 20 Ga. (2¾ in.); Shot sizes: 000, 00, 0, 1, 3, 4
Box 5: . . . .$8.99–$12.99

PREMIER ACCUTIP BONDED SABOT

Description: Guided by our new Power Port Tip, the AccuTip Bonded Sabot Slug delivers a degree of accuracy and terminal performance unmatched by any other we tested; yields over 95 percent weight retention thanks to its spiral nose cuts, bonded construction, and high-strength cartridge brass jacket; designed for fully-rifled barrels only
Available in: 12, 20 Ga. (2¾ in., 3 in.)
Box 5: . . . .$21.99–$24.99

SLUGGER HIGH VELOCITY

Description: This is the first high-velocity Foster-style lead slug which exits the barrel at 1800 fps, 13 percent faster than standard 1-oz. slugs; the ⅞ oz. Slugger High Velocity delivers 200 ft.-lbs. more energy at 50 yards with flatter trajectory on deer than standard 1-oz. slugs; designed for the avid deer hunter using smooth bore guns
Available in: 12 Ga. (2¾ in., 3 in.), 20 Ga. (2¾ in.)
Box 5: . . . .$7.99–$10.99

SLUGGER RIFLED

Description: Remington redesigned their 12-gauge Slugger Rifled Slug for a 25 percent improvement in accuracy; at 1760 fps muzzle velocity, the 3-in. 12-gauge Magnum slug shoot 25 percent flatter than regular 12 gauge slugs
Available in: 12 Ga. (2¾ in., 3 in.), 16 Ga. (2¾ in.), 20 Ga. (2¾ in.), .410 (2½ in.)
Box 5: . . . .$5.99–$10.99

ULTIMATE DEFENSE BUCKSHOT

Description: Dense patterns and big knock-down power; short-range patterns through smoothbores are tight; .410-bore loads house four lead 000 buckshot pellets
Available in: 12 ga 3 in., 2 ¾ in., 20 ga. 3 in., .410-bore 2 ½ in., 3 in. 12 ga. in 00 or No. 4 Buck; 20 ga. in No. 3 Buck; .410-bore in 000 Buck
12-ga./5 . . . .$7.99–$9.99
20-ga./5 . . . . $7.99
.410-bore/10 . . . .$24.99

Rio Ammunition

RIO TARGET LOAD LOW RECOIL

ROYAL ECO BLUESTEEL

Description: Features an environmentally friendly water-soluble wad
Available in: 12 ga. (3 in.); No. BB, 2, 3, 4, 5, and 6
Box 25 . . . . $9.99

ROYAL PHEASANT

Description: A new line of copper-plated upland loads; designed for stopping power and patterns
Available in: 12, 20, 28 ga.
Case 250: $160.00

ROYAL TURKEY BUFFERED MAGNUM

Description: Offered in 12-ga. 3-in. with a Max Dram Equivalent and 1.75 oz. of shot, or a 3.5-in. Max Dram 2-oz. load in your choice of 4, 5, or 6 shot
Available in: 12 ga.
Box 10: $13.49

SPREADER

Description: Velocity of 1,350 fps; 25 percent higher dispersion than other spreader wads
Box 10: $3.41

TARGET LOAD LOW RECOIL

Description: A sound choice for new shooters; 12 ga. 2¾-inch 1-ounce, 2½ DE, 1,135 fps, Nos. 7, 7.5, 8, and 9
Available in: 28 ga., 12 ga.
Case 250: $69.99

VINTAGE 1896 PAPER

Description: Rio's line of five loads uses single-based powders for minimal fouling; unique dust-stopping membrane on primers; Kraft paper hulls; premium lead shot. Five 12 ga. 2¾-inch loadings: Paper Light 1 1/8 oz., 2¾ DE, No. 7.5, 8; Paper 1 1/8 oz., 3 DE, No. 7.5, 8, 9; Paper HC 1 1/8 oz., 3¼ DE, No. 7.5, 8; Paper Light 1 oz., 2¾ DE, No. 7.5, 8, 9; and Sporting 1-ounce, 3 DE, No. 7.5, 8
Box 10 . . . . $7.99

VINTAGE 1896 PAPER HELICE

Description: Designed specifically for the challenging game of Helice; three 12 ga. 1-ounce 2 ¾-inch loads, one at 3 DE and 1,250 fps, one at Max DE and 1,300 fps, and a third at Max DE in a high-velocity 1,350 fps, all in Nos. 7.5 and 8
Available in: 12 ga.
Case 250 . . . .$140.99

Rio Ammunition

WING & TARGET LITE, HIGH VELOCITY

Description: A soft-shooting load

SIERRA OUTDOOR MASTER

SIERRA PRAIRIE ENEMY

GAMECHANGER

Description: A line of centerfire rifle ammo for big-game hunters, these rounds sporting Sierra's Tipped GameKing projectile

offered in a Lite version with a 12 ga. 2¾-inch 1-ounce load at 1,150 fps and a High Velocity with the same

Available in: .223 Rem., 6mm Creedmoor, .243 Win., 6.5 Creedmoor, .270 Win., 7mm Rem. Mag., .300 BLK., .308 Win., .30-06 Spfd., .300 Win. Mag.
Box of 20: . . . . $44.99–$79.99

OUTDOOR MASTER

Description: A full line of handgun cartridges with a Power Jacket topped with a Sports Master jacketed hollow-point; skives in the jacket control expansion; brass casings can be

payload at 1,350 fps; Nos. 7.5, 8
Available in: 12 ga.
Case 250: $79.99

Sierra Bullets

reloaded
Available in: .380 Auto (115 gr.), 9mm (115 gr., 124 gr.), .40 S&W (180 gr.), .45 ACP (185 gr.)
Box of 20: . . . . $21.99–$26.99

PRAIRIE ENEMY

Description: A varmint getter loaded with Sierra's BlitzKing bullet
Available in: .22-250 Rem., .223 Rem., .204 Ruger, .243 Win., .224 Valkyrie, 6.5 Creedmoor
Box of 20: . . . . $37.99–$49.99

SIG Sauer

SIG SAUER ELITE COPPER HUNTING

SIG SAUER SBR SOLID COPPER BLACK CASE

Rifle Ammunition
ELITE BALL RIFLE

Description: Intended for training purposes with a full metal jacket projectile. Available in: 55-grain .223 Rem. with a muzzle velocity of 3,240 fps and 1,282 ft.-lb. of energy; 150-grain .308 Win. with a muzzle velocity of 2,900 fps and 2802 ft-lb. of energy
Available in: .223 Rem., .300 BLK, .308 Win., .277 Fury
Box 20: . . . . $15.95–$33.95

ELITE COPPER HUNTING

Description: A precision cartridge for hunters
Available in: .30-06 (150 gr.), .308 Win. (150 gr.), .300 Win. Mag. (165 gr.), .300 BLK (120 gr.)
Box of 20: . . . . $42.95–$62.95

ELITE HUNTER TIPPED

Description: Long-range hunting application; deep penetration and impressive expansion thanks to concentric blackened jacket; improved B.C. with translucent yellow tip
Available in: .243 Win., .260 Rem., .270 Win., .30-06 Spfd., .308 Win., .300 Win. Mag., 6.5 Creedmoor, 6mm Creedmoor
Box of 20: . . . . $32.95–$59.95

ELITE MATCH GRADE OTM (OPEN TIP MATCH)

Description: Engineered to match the ballistics of SIG's V-Crown defensive ammo line as a more affordable match-grade loading
Available in: 6.5 Creedmoor, .30-06
Available in: 6mm Creedmoor, .30-06 Spfd., .300 Win. Mag., 6.5 Creedmoor, .223 Rem., .308 Win., .300 BLK
Box 20: . . . . $30.95–$57/95

SBR SOLID COPPER BLACK CASE

Description: A supersonic duty round for short barreled rifles, wearing a distinctive black oxide case; solid copper projectile; 1897 fps, 959 ft.-lbs. of energy out of a 6.75-in. barrel
Available in: .300 BLK (120 gr.)
Box of 20: $37.95

VARMINT & PREDATOR

Description: Single-based extruded powders; smoke gray-tipped projectiles designed for expansion; match-grade accuracy; flat trajectories
Available in: .223 Rem. (40 gr.), .22-250 Rem. (40 gr.), .243 Win. (55 gr.)
MSRP . . . .$27.95–$38.95

Handgun Ammunition

365 ELITE FMJ
Description: Training ammo designed specifically for short-barreled handguns; offers reduced recoil; 1050 fps; 282 ft.-lb. energy
Available in: 9mm (115 gr.)
Box 50: . . . .$22.95–$23.95

365 ELITE V-CROWN
Description: Carry ammo designed specifically for short-barreled handguns; offers reduced recoil; 1050 fps; 282 ft.-lb. energy
Available in: 9mm (115 gr.)
Box 20: . . . .$23.95–$24.95

ELITE BALL M17
Description: Military-grade ammunition for 9mm handguns and carbine rifles capable of handling +P pressures. Muzzle velocity 1198 fps; muzzle energy 395 ft.-lb. Designed for training
Available in: 9mm +P
Box 50: $23.95

AMMUNITION

Ammunition • 517

SIG SAUER 365 ELITE V-CROWN

SIG SAUER MATCH ELITE COMPETITION

ELITE V-CROWN M17

Description: Military-grade ammunition for 9mm handguns and carbine rifles capable of handling +P pressures. Muzzle velocity 1198 fps; muzzle energy 395 ft.-lb. Designed with a

stacked hollowpoint for maximum weight retention and expansion
Available in: 9mm +P
Box 20: **$24.95**

MATCH ELITE V-CROWN COMPETITION

Description: Designed for competitive handgun practitioners, specifically those shooting minor power factors; low recoil; coated nickel cases; velocities range from 860 to 900 fps
Available in: 9mm (115 gr., 147 gr.)
Box 50: **$53.95**

MATCH ELITE COMPETITION

Description: Designed with input from Max Michel and Lena Miculek, jacketed hollowpoint with reduced charge weight to lower recoil; 880 fps, 254 ft.-lbs.
Available in: 9mm (147 gr.)
Box of 50: **$53.95**

Speer

SPEER GOLD DOT G2

GOLD DOT G2

Description: Personal-defense rounds in standard bullet weights featuring an exclusive new shallow-dish nose design filled with an elastomer that, upon impact, is forced into several fis-

sures internal to the bullet, forcing expansion
Available in: 9mm (147 gr.), .40 S&W (180 gr.), .45 ACP +P (230 gr.)
Box of 20: . . . .**$36.99–$41.99**

Steinel Ammunition

STEINEL AMMUNITION .500 AUTO MAX

RIFLE AMMUNITION

Description: A comprehensive line of custom premium rifle ammunition for some of the world's more unusual calibers; new Starline brass; Hodgdon powders
Available in: 12.7x42 (with a Hornady XTP or FP-XTP for use in Beowulf uppers); match-grade .223 Rem. softpoints; .30-30 with a Lehigh Defense Controlled Chaos hollowpoint); .308

Win. with a boattail hollowpoint; .357 Maximum with a Lehigh Defense Xtreme Penetrator bullet or a flat-nose soft-point for single-shot use; .44 Magnum ultimate solid copper hollowpoint Ultimate Deer or a hardcast, wide meplat WLNC Heavy Hitter bullet; .45 LC with a hardcast bullet and loaded only for modern lever rifles, T/C Contenders, and Ruger's Blackhawk, Super Blackhawk, Bisley, and Redhawk actions; .45-70 Gov't Goldilocks load intended for 100-yard shots on deer and loaded with a Hornady JHP; .45-70 Gov't High-Power load for other applications, a brass monolithic design for target work, and a light-recoil JHP for use in Trapdoor Springfields; .450 Bushmaster with an XTP Mag, FTX

flex-tip or solid copper expanding hollowpoint Maker topping; .458 SOCOM in JHP, solid copper expanding hollowpoint Maker, FTX flex-tip, or brass monolithic bullets; .458 Win. in solid brass or dangerous game solids; .500 Auto Max for Big Horn Armory's AR500 in Lehigh Match Warhead brass, XTP Mag jacketed hollowpoint, or wide flatnose hardcast; 6.5X50 Arisaka in a softpoint; 6.5X52 Carcano in a roundnose or softpoint; 7.7X58 Japanese Arisaka in a softpoint or in an accurized full metal jacketed boattail; and just to throw in something normal, a full metal jacket .30-06 Spfd. for M1 Garand use
Box 20: . . . .**$19.99–$57.99**

TB Ammunition, LLC

GPM QUADRA-SHOCK

Description: An economical lead-free alternative in a variety of rifle and pistol calibers; non-frangible bullets
Available in: .223 Rem., .243 Win.,

.270 Win., .30-06 Spfd., .30-30 Win., .300 AAC, .308 Win., .380 ACP, .40 S&W, .357 SIG, .45 ACP, 9mm
Box of: 20, 50
Rifle calibers: . . . . . . **$15.99–$39.99**
Handgun calibers: . . . **$26.99–$32.99**

TB AMMUNITION, LLC GPM QUADRA-SHOCK

WEATHERBY MAGNUM

Features: Weatherby Magnum cartridges are loaded with a variety of popular bullet types for a wide range of shooting purposes

Available in: .224, .240, .257, 6.5-300, 6.5 RPM, .270, .30-378, .300, 7mm, .338-378, .340, .375, .378, .416, .460
MSRP. . . . . $69.00–$179.00

Weatherby

WEATHERBY 6.5-300 WEATHERBY MAGNUM

Winchester Ammunition

WINCHESTER AMMUNITION DEER SEASON COPPER IMPACT XP

WINCHESTER AMMUNITION DEFENDER RIFLE

WINCHESTER AMMUNITION EXPEDITION LONG RANGE

WINCHESTER M-22 SUBSONIC

Rifle Ammunition

17 WINCHESTER SUPER MAGNUM

Description: A .27 caliber shellcase necked down to a .17 caliber bullet; surpasses the downrange velocity, energy, trajectory and wind bucking characteristics of both the .17 HMR and .22 WMR; available in Varmint HE, Varmint HV, and VarmintX lines.
Available in: .17 WSM
Box 50: $24.99

BALLISTIC SILVERTIP

Description: Solid-based boattail design delivers excellent long-range accuracy; the ballistic plastic polycarbonate Silvertip bullet initiates rapid fragmentation; in medium to larger calibers, special jacket contours extend range and reduce cross-wind drift; harder lead core ensures expansion
Available in: 6.5 Creedmoor, 6.8 Western,.22-250 Rem., .223 Rem., .223 WSSM, .243 Win., .243 WSSM, .25-06 Rem., .25 WSSM, .270 Win., .270 WSM, .280 Rem., .300 Win. Mag., .30–06 Spfd., .300 WSM, .30–30 Win., .308 Win., 7mm Rem. Mag., 7mm-08 Rem., 7mm WSM, .45-70 Gov't.
Box 20: . . . . $38.99–$43.99

DEER SEASON COPPER IMPACT XP

Description: Wears a huge polymer tip, Winchester's Extreme Point, over a copper-solid boattail bullet for extreme weight retention and big wound channels
Available in: .270 WSM (130 gr.), .300 WSM (150 gr.), .350 Legend (150 gr.), 6.5 Creedmoor (125 gr.), .243 Win. (85 gr.), .30-06 Spfd. (150 gr.), .308 Win. (150 gr.)
Box of 20: . . . . $36.99–$66.99

DEER SEASON XP

Description: Large diameter polymer tip accelerates bullet expansion; built specifically for deer hunting; alloyed leather core; contoured jacket
Available in: .223 Rem., .243 Win., 25-06 Win., .270 Win., .270 WSM, .30-06 Spfd., .30-30 Win., .300 BLK, .300 Win. Mag., .350 Legend, 7.62X39, .450 Bushmaster, 6.5 Creedmoor, 7mm Rem. Mag., 7mm-08 Rem., 6.8 Spl.
Box 20: . . . . $28.99–$49.99

DEFENDER RIFLE

Description: A protected holllowpoint with Split Core technology and a tapered copper alloy jacket provides quick shock, deep penetration, and 1.5X expansion
Available in: .350 Legend (160 gr.), 5.56 NATO
Box of 20: $45.99

EXPEDITION BIG GAME

Description: Polymer tip; bonded alloyed lead core; jacket technology; Lubalox (black oxide) coating; controlled expansion
Available in: .270 Win., .270 WSM, .30-06 Spfd., .300 Win. Mag., .300 WSM, .325 WSM, .338 Win. Mag., .338 Lapua Mag., 7mm Rem. Mag.
Box 20: . . . . $53.99–$135.99

EXPEDITION LONG RANGE

Description: Boattail bullets wear a polymer tip, have extended ogive, a bonded alloy core, and a jacket designed for maximum expansion at both close and long ranges
Available in: .308 Win. (168 gr.), 6.5 PRC (142 gr.), 6.8 Western (165 gr.), .270 Win. (150 gr.), .300 Win. Mag. (190 gr.), .300 WSM (190 gr.), .30-06 Spfd. (190 gr.), 6.5 Creedmoor (142 gr.), 7mm Rem. Mag. (168 gr.)
Box of 20: . . . . $53.99–$74.99

M-22 SUBSONIC

Description: Specifically designed to reliably function semiautomatic rifles and pistols at subsonic velocities. Subsonic velocities offer low noise in both suppressed and non-supressed firearms. Bullet is a black copper-plated roundnose.
Available in: .22 LR (45 gr.)
Box 100. . . . .$15.80

MATCH

Description: Combining proven Winchester technology with proven bullets, the hollow point boat tail design provides the precision match shooters demand; sleek bullet profile, large boattail and small hollow point maximizes long-range accuracy
Available in: .223 Rem., 5.56 NATO, 6.5 Creedmoor, .308 Win., .338 Lapua, 6.5 PRC, 6.8 Western
Box 20: . . . . $35.99–$63.99

PDX1 DEFENDER

Description: Given the recent popularity of modern sporting rifles (MSR) among shooters and hunters, Winchester has designed a product using Split Core Technology (SCT) for personal defense; SCT technology, using a quick expansion front lead core and a deep driving bonded rear lead core, creates the ultimate .223 Rem. Home Defense load
Available in: .223 Rem., .308 Win., 7.62x39
Box 20: . . . . $44.99–$62.99

Winchester Ammunition

WINCHESTER AMMUNITION ACTIVE DUTY

POWER MAX BONDED
Description: Featuring a contoured jacked bonded to a lead core; protected hollowpoint
Available in: .350 Legend (160 gr.), .223 Rem. (64 gr.), .243 Win. (100 gr.), .270 Win. (150 gr.), .270 WSM (130 gr.), .300 Win. Mag. (150 gr., 180 gr.), .300 WSM (150 gr.)
Box of 20: . . . . **$29.99–$91.99**

SUPER SUPPRESSED
Description: Optimized for suppressed rifles and specialty handguns with a fully encapsulated bullet backed by a brass disc that reduces fouling; reduced noise with subsonic speeds
Available in: .350 Legend (265 gr.), .300 BLK (200 gr.), .308 Win. (168 gr.)
Box 20: . . . . **$22.99–$35.99**

SUPER-X HOLLOW POINT
Available in: .204 Ruger, .218 Bee, .22 Hornet, .30-30 Win., .45-70 Gov't.
MSRP . . . . **$19.99–$129.99**

SUPER-X HOLLOW SOFT POINT
Available in: .30 Carbine, .44 Rem. Mag.
Box 50: . . . . **$34.99–$69.99**

SUPER-X LEAD
Available in: .32-20 Win.
Box of 50: **$72.99**

SUPER-X POSITIVE EXPANDING POINT
Available in: .25-06 Rem., .25 WSSM
Box 20: . . . . **$54.99–$55.99**

SUPER-X POWER-POINT
Available in: .22-250 Rem., .223 Rem., .223 WSSM, .243 Win., .243 WSSM, .25-35 Win., .257 Roberts +P, .264 Win. Mag., .270 Win., .270 WSM, .284 Win., .300 Savage, .30-06 Spfd., .300 WSM, .30–30 Win., .303 British, .30-40 Krag, .307 Win., .308 Win., .300 Win. Mag., .325 WSM, .32 Win. Spl., .338 Win. Mag., .348 Win.

Mag., .356 Win., 35 Rem., .375 Win., .38-40 Win., .38-55 Win., .44-40 Win., 6.5x55 Swede, 6mm Rem., 7.62x39mm, 7x57 Mauser, 7mm Rem. Mag., 7mm-08 Rem., 8x57 Mauser, .350 Legend, .450 Bushmaster
Box 20: . . . . **$20.99–$105.99**

USA READY
Description: Intended for competition and training; offered in a variety of common rifle and pistol cartridges; match grade primers; flat-nose or open-tip bullets depending on caliber
Available in: .223 Rem. (62 gr.), .300 BLK (125 gr.), .308 Win. (168 gr.), 6.5 Creedmoor (125 gr.), .45 ACP (230 gr.), .40 S&W (165 gr.), 9mm (115 gr.), 6.8 SPC (115 gr.)
Rifle, box 20: . . . . **$19.99–$27.99**
Handgun, box 50: . . . **$23.99–$38.99**

VARMINT X
Description: Polymer tip, alloy jacket, lead core, and rapid fragmentation
Available in: .17 Hornet, .22 Hornet, .204 Ruger; .22-250 Rem.; .223 Rem.; .243 Win.
Box 20: . . . . **$22.99–$56.99**

VARMINT X LEAD FREE
Description: Features zinc core technology used in Winchester's Super Clean pistol ammo
Available in: .22-250 Rem., .223 Rem., .243 Rem.
Box 20: . . . . **$26.99–$37.99**

WWII VICTORY SERIES
Description: Intended to be a collector's item; standard FMJ ball; in special cartons and wood boxes
Available in: .30-06 Spfd., .30 Carbine
Box 20: **$38.99**

Handgun Ammunition

ACTIVE DUTY
Description: Winchester says this round was "selected to serve as the ammunition supplier for the U.S. Army Modular Handgun System;" loaded to M1152 military specifications; flat-nose full metal jacket; military-grade primer
Available in: 9mm (115 gr.)
Box of 100: **$47.99**

DEFENDER HANDGUN
Description: The Winchester Supreme Elite Bonded PDX1, which was cho-

sen by the FBI as their primary service round, is engineered to maximize terminal ballistics, as defined by the demanding FBI test protocol, which simulates real-world threats
Available in: .357 Mag., .357 SIG, .380 ACP, .38 Spl., +P, .40 S&W, .45 Colt, .45 ACP, 9mm Luger +P, 9mm, 10mm Auto
Box of 20: . . . . **$26.99–$43.99**

DUAL BOND
Description: Dual Bond offers a large hollow point cavity, which provides consistent upsets at a variety of ranges and impact velocities; the heavy outer jacket is mechanically bonded to the inner bullet; inner bullet utilizes a proprietary bonding process for a combination of knockdown power, solid penetration, and significant tissue damage
Available in: .44 Rem. Mag., .454 Cassull, .460 S&W Mag., .500 S&W Mag.
Box 20: . . . . **$48.99–$123.99**

PLATINUM TIP HOLLOW POINT
Description: Patented notched reserve taper bullet jacket, plated heavy wall jacket, and two-part hollow point cavity for uniform bullet expansion, massive energy depot
Available in: .41 Rem. Mag., .44 Rem. Mag., .454 Casull, .500 S&W
Box 20: . . . . **$64.99–$124.99**

SUPER SUPPRESSED
Description: Optimized for suppressed handguns and PCCs with a fully encapsulated bullet backed by a brass disc that reduces fouling
Available in: 9mm (147 gr.), .45 ACP (230 gr.)
Box 50: . . . . **$22.99–$38.99**

SUPER-X BLANK-BLACK POWDER
Available in: .32 S&W
Box 50: **$38.99**

SUPER-X BLANK-SMOKELESS
Available in: .38 Spl.
Box 50: **$78.49**

SUPER-X EXPANDING POINT
Available in: .25 ACP
Box 50: **$81.99**

Winchester Ammunition

SUPER-X JACKETED HOLLOW POINT

Available in: .357 Mag., .38 Spl. +P, .454 Casull, .45 Win. Mag., .460 S&W Mag., .500 S&W Mag.

Box 20 . . . . **$66.99–$107.99**

SUPER-X JACKETED SOFT POINT

Available in: .357 Mag.

Box 50: **$102.99**

SUPER-X LEAD ROUND NOSE

Available in: .32 Short Colt, .32 S&W Long, .32 S&W, .38 Spl., .38 S&W, .44 S&W Spl., .45 Colt

Box of 50: . . . . **$28.99–$67.99**

SUPER-X LEAD SEMI-WAD CUTTER

Available in: .38 Spl.

Box 50: **$49.99**

SUPER-X LEAD SEMI-WAD CUTTER HP

Available in: .38 Spl. +P

Box 50: **$66.99**

SUPER-X LEAD SEMI-WADCUTTER SUPER MATCH

Available in: .38 Spl.

Box 50: **$43.99**

SUPER-X SILVERTIP HOLLOW POINT

Available in: 10mm Auto, .32 ACP, .357 Mag., .380 ACP, .38 Super Auto +P, .38 Spl. +P, .38 Spl., .40 S&W, .41 Rem. Mag., .44 Rem. Mag., .44 S&W Spl., .45 ACP, .45 Colt, .45 GAP, 9x23 Win., 9mm Luger

Box 20, 50: . . . . **$17.49–$44.99**

USA FULL METAL JACKET (USA WHITE BOX)

Available in: .25 ACP, .32 ACP, .357 SIG, .38 Spec., .38 Super +P, .380 ACP, .40 S&W, .45 ACP, .45 G.A.P., 7.62X39 Tokarev, 9mm, 9mm Makarov, 9mm NATO, 10MM

From: . . . . **$30.99–$69.99**

W TRAIN & DEFEND

Description:: A straightforward solution for new shooters interested in training to become more proficient with their personal defense ammunition; ballistically-matched ammunition pairs range-ready TRAIN (T) rounds with threat-stopping, technologically-driven DEFEND (D) rounds, each designed for less felt recoil

Available in: .38 Spl., .380 ACP, .40 S&W, 9mm, .45 ACP

.45 ACP, .40 S&W, 9mm/20 . . . . **$16.99–$24.00**

.38 Spec., .380 ACP/50 . . . . **$24.95–$27.87**

WIN1911

Description: Provides a choice of personal defense or training ammunition that has been matched for ballistic performance and engineered for the same feel and function; high-accuracy, ballistically matched full metal jacket and jacketed hollow point offerings make this an ideal ammunition choice

Available in: .45 ACP

Box 50: **$66.99**

WWII VICTORY SERIES

Description: Intended to be a collector's item;standard ball; period-correct loading for a muzzle velocity of 850 fps; special headstamp; packed in specialty carton and in wood boxes

Available in: .45 ACP (230 gr.)

Box 50: **$40.00**

Rimfire Ammunition

SUPER SUPPRESSED

Description: Designed for suppressed .22 LR rifles and handguns, featuring a black copperplated bullet with a roundnose profile; reduced muzzle flash; subsonic performance in both handguns and rifles

Available in: .22 LR (45 gr.)

Box 100: **$15.99**

SUPER-X #12 SHOT

Available in: .22 LR

Box 50: **$16.99**

SUPER-X FULL METAL JACKET

Available in: .22 Win. Mag.

Box 50: **$17.99**

SUPER-X JACKETED HOLLOW POINT

Available in: .17 HMR, .22 Win. Mag.

Box 50: **$17.99**

SUPER-X LEAD ROUND NOSE

Available in: .22 LR, .22 Long, .22 Short

.22 Short/50 . . . . **$6.99**

.22 LR/100 . . . . **$12.99**

WINCHESTER WWII VICTORY SERIES (RIFLE)

WINCHESTER AMMUNITION WILDCAT

SUPER-X LEAD ROUND NOSE, STANDARD VELOCITY

Available in: .22 LR

Box of 50: **$9.99**

SUPER-X POWER-POINT PLATED LEAD HOLLOW POINT

Available in: .22 LR

Box 50: **$14.99**

VARMINT HIGH ENERGY

Available in: .22 LR, .22 Win. Mag., .17 WSM

Box of 50: **$24.99**

VARMINT HIGH VELOCITY

Available in: .22 Win. Mag., .17 HMR, .17 WSM

Box of 50: **$22.99**

WILDCAT

Description: A valued-priced round for target shooting and small game; available in a 500-count box with a Dynapoint bullet or a 50-count box with a lead round nose

Available in: .22 LR (40 gr.)

Box 50 . . . . **$5.99**

Box 5000 . . . . **$574.99**

Shotgun Ammunition

AA DIAMOND GRADE

Description: A top-end round for the competitive clay crowd; super-hard copper-plated shot

Available in: 12 ga. (2¾ in.)

Box of 25: . . . . **$13.99–$15.99**

AA STEEL

Description: Steel shot; high-strength hull; AA wads

Available in: 12 (2¾ in.); Shot sizes: 7.5, 8

Box of 25: **$21.09**

Winchester Ammunition

WINCHESTER AMMUNITION ROOSTER XR

WINCHESTER AMMUNITION DEFENDER SHOTGUN

WINCHESTER AMMUNITION DOUBLE X DIAMOND GRADE

AA TARGET LOADS

Description: The hunter's choice for a wide variety of game bird applications, available in an exceptionally broad selection of loadings, from 12-gauge to .410 bore, with shot size options ranging from BBs all the way down to 9s—suitable for everything from quail to farm predators
Available in: 12, 20, 28 Ga. (2¾ in.), .410 (2½ in.); Shot sizes: 7.5, 8, 8.5, 9
Box 25:. . . . .$14.99–$16.99

AA TRAACKER

Description: Stay centered in the pattern all the way to the target; Shot-trap core design captures a portion of the shot to stabilize the wad; unique dove-tail petals allows the wad to spin-stabilize and track in the center of the pattern; available in bright orange for low light conditions and in black for bright light conditions
Available in: 12 Ga. (2¾ in.), 20 Ga. (2 ¾ in.)
Box 25:. $11.34

BLIND SIDE MAGNUM PHEASANT

Description: High Packing density for increased powder charge with hinged wad results in 1675 fps; high velocity HEX Shot allows reduced leads and increased pellet energy; diamond cut wad design provides choke responsiveness for increased kill zone; Drylok Super Steel System keeps your powder dry
Available in: 12 (2¾ in., 3 in.)
Box: $23.99

BLIND SIDE WATERFOWL

Description: High Packing density for increased powder charge with hinged wad results in 1675 fps; high velocity HEX Shot allows reduced leads and increased pellet energy; diamond cut wad design provides choke responsiveness for increased kill zone; Drylok Super Steel System keeps your powder dry
Available in: 12 (2¾ in., 3 in., 3½ in.), 20 (3 in.)
Box: . . . . $28.99–$32.99

DEFENDER SHOTGUN

Description: Intended to deliver massive shock with plated 00 buckshot backed by a 1-oz. rifled slug; grex buffering improves patterns; 12- and 20-ga. in this line also available with a segmenting slug;
Available in: 12 ga., 20 ga.
Box of 10, 20: . . . . $21.99–$24.99

DOUBLE X DIAMOND GRADE

Description: Designed specifically for turkey hunting with a ¾-oz. payload of 8% antimony copper-plated pellets; 1100 fps
Available in: .410 bore
Box of 10:. $16.99

LONG BEARD XR

Description: Features Shot-Lok technology; offers the tightest patterns and longest shot capability of any traditional turkey load with twice the pellets in a 10-in. circle out to 60 yds
Available in: 12 Ga. (3 in., 3½ in.), 20 Ga. (3 in.)
Box 10:. . . . . $23.99–$26.99

ROOSTER LOK'D & LETHAL XR

Description: Protects shot during in-bore acceleration; shot launches from barrel near perfectly round for extremely tight long-range patterns; greater penetration over standard lead loads beyond 50 yards; devastating terminal on-target performances
Available in: 12 (2¾ in., 3 in.)
Box 15: . . . .$31.99–$35.99

SUPER PHEASANT

Available in: 12 Ga. (2¾ in., 3 in.), 20 Ga. (3 in.); Shot sizes: 4, 5, 6
Box 25:. . . . .$25.99–$30.99

SUPER TARGET

Available in: 12, 20 Ga. (2¾ in.); Shot sizes: 7, 7.5, 8, 9
Box 25:. . . . .$9.99–$11.99

SUPER-X TRIALS AND BLANKS

Available in: 10 Ga. (2⅞ in.), 12 Ga. (2¾ in.)
Box 25:. . . . .$51.99–$68.99

SUPER-X TURKEY LOADS

Available in: 12 Ga. (2¾ in., 3 in.); Shot sizes: 4, 5, 6
Box 10: . . . .$14.99–$15.99

SUPER-X XPERT HI-VELOCITY STEEL

Available in: 12 Ga. (2. in., 3 in., 3½ in.), 20 Ga. (3 in.); Shot sizes: BB, 1, 2, 3, 4
Box 25:. . . . .$16.99–$19.99

VARMINT-X

Description: Shot-Lok technology; 50 percent more pellets in a 10 in. circle at 40 yds; greater penetration over standard lead loads beyond 40 yds; devastating terminal on-target performance
Available in: 12 Ga. (3 in.); Shot size: BB
Box 10:. $34.09

XPERT SNOW GOOSE

Description: Continuing the trend of ammo designed for specific species, XPERT Snow Goose uses features from Winchester's XPERT Steel and Blind Side lines, with XPERT Steel Shot and the Diamond Cut Wad; 12 ga. 3-inch BB, No. 1, No 2 1,475 fps; 12 ga. 3 ½-inch BB, No. 1. No. 2 1550 fps
Available in: 12 ga.
Box 25:. $19.99

XTENDED RANGE BISMUTH

Description: A fresh non-lead alternative with the hard hits bismuth provides; patented Shot-Lok wad protects the shot from deformation during barrel travel; 12 ga. 3-inch 1 5/8-ounce No. 5 at 1200 fps is primarily a turkey load, but suitable for a variety of ducks as well
Available in: 12 ga.
Box 10:. $38.99

Winchester Ammunition

WINCHESTER AMMUNITION PDX1 DEFENDER SEGMENTING SLUG

Shotgun Ammunition– Slugs & Buckshot

DEER SEASON COPPER IMPACT XP

Description: Species-dedicated round for whitetail hunters featuring a wide polymer tip with a hollow nose; solid copper construction; streamlined, boattail profile
Available in: .243 Win. (85 gr.), .270 Win. (130 gr.), .300 Win. Mag. (150 gr.), .30-06 Spfd. (150 gr.), .308 Win. (150 gr.)
Box 20: **$17.99**

DEER SEASON SHOTGUN SLUG

Description: A new species-dedicated shotgun slug for whitetail hunters; 1 1/8-ounce rifled slug; 1600 fps muzzle velocity; rear-stabilized wad
Available in: 12 ga.
Box 5: **$7.99**

PDX1 12 SLUG AND BUCK

Description: The 12-gauge PDX1 Defender ammunition features a distinctive black hull, black oxide high-base head and three pellets of Grex buffered 00 plated buckshot nested on top of a 1 oz. rifled slug; an ideal, tight patterning personal defense load; slug/buckshot combination provides optimum performance at short and long ranges while compensating for aim error
Available in: 12 Ga. (2¾ in.)
Box 10: **$23.99**

PDX1 DEFENDER SEGMENTING SLUG

Description: The uniquely designed slug segments into three pieces when fired into FBI protocol barriers such as bare, light cloth, and heavy cloth covered ballistic gelatin; the round is designed to compensate for aim error over traditional slugs.
Available in: 12 Ga. (2¾ in.), 20 Ga. (2¾ in.)
Box 10: **$23.99**

SUPER-X BUCKSHOT

Available in: 12 Ga. (2¾ in., 3 in., 3½ in.), 20 Ga. (2¾ in.), .410 (2½ in., 3 in.); Shot sizes: 4, 3, 1, 00, 000.
Box 5: . . . . **$7.99–$19.99**

MUZZLELOADING BULLETS

Barnes Bullets

BARNES BULLETS SPIT-FIRE TMZ

EXPANDER MZ

Description: 100 percent copper with a large, hollow cavity; six copper petals with double-diameter expansion; full weight retention
Available in: .45 (195 gr.), .50 (250, 300 gr.), .54 (275, 325 gr.)
Box 15: . . . . **$21.99–$36.99**

SPIT-FIRE TMZ

Description: 100 percent copper boattail design with streamlined polymer tip for faster expansion; expands at 1050 fps.; remains intact at extreme velocities; redesigned sabot loads faster while retaining tight gas seal
Available in: .50 (250, 290 gr.)
Box 15 . . . . **$22.99–$23.99**
Box 24 . . . . **$34.99–$35.99**

Harvester Muzzleloading (J-Ron, Inc.)

HARVESTER SCORPION PT GOLD

CRUSHED RIB SABOT

Description: 50 percent less loading friction; consistent ignition and superb accuracy
Available in: .45 (.400); .50 (.400, .429–.430, .451–.452)
Box 50: **$9.99**

SABER TOOTH BELTED

Description: Copper-clad belted bullets in Harvester Crush Rib Sabot
Available in: .50 (250, 270, 300, 350 gr.)
MSRP **$15.99**

SCORPION FUNNEL POINT MAG

Description: Electroplated copper plating does not separate from lead core; loaded in Harvester Crush Rib Sabots
Available in: .50 (240, 260, 300 gr.); .54 (240, 260, 300 gr.)
MSRP . . . . **$9.99–$13.99**

SCORPION PT GOLD

Description: Scorpion PT Gold Ballistic Tip Bullets are electroplated with copper plating that does not separate from lead core; offers greater accuracy at longer ranges than a hollow point; 3 percent antimony makes the bullet harder than pure lead
Available in: .45 (240, 260, 300 gr.); .50 ((240, 260, 300 gr.)
MSRP . . . . **$15.99–$25.99**

AMMUNITION

Hodgdon Powder Co.

TRIPLE SEVEN FIRESTAR PELLETS

Description: Star-shaped pellet designed for .50-caliber muzzleloaders utilizing 209 primers for ignition; long grooves provide more surface for ignition compared to traditional pellets

Available in: .50-caliber

Box 60:.....................**$29.99**

HODGDON POWDER TRIPLE SEVEN FIRESTAR PELLETS

Hornady Manufacturing

HORNADY MONOFLEX ML

GREAT PLAINS - PA CONICAL

Description: Delivers greater accuracy and more knock-down power; PA bullets are prelubed with special knurled grooves on the bearing surface to hold the lubricant on the bullet—no need for a patch or sabot

Available: in .50-caliber 240-grain

Box of 50: **$15.99**

MONOFLEX ML

Description: Constructed with the Hornady Flex Tip and retaining 95 percent of its original weight, it's available in both a High Speed/Low Drag sabot and Lock-N-Load Speed Sabot

Available in: .50 cal. sabot with .45 cal. (250 gr.) bullet

Box of 20:................**$35.99**

Knight Rifles

BLOODLINE BULLETS

Description: Individually machined, double knurled bullets for increased visual blood trails

Available in: .45 (185, 200 gr.); .50 (220, 250, 275, 300, 350 gr.); .52 (220, 275, 300, 350 gr.); .54 (325 gr.)

Box 20:............**$20.99–$33.99**

RED HOT BULLETS

Description: Saboted Barnes solid copper bullet with superior expansion

Available in: .45 (175, 195 gr.); .50 (250, 300, 350 gr.); .52 (275, 350, 375 gr.)

MSRP........... **$19.99–$35.99**

KNIGHT RIFLES BLOODLINE BULLETS

PowerBelt Bullets

POWERBELT COPPER

AEROLITE

Description: Designed specifically for use with standard 100-grain loads; AeroLite's shape is noticeably longer and more aerodynamic than other PowerBelts of similar weight; longer length is made possible by the massive hollow point cavity that is filled by an oversized polycarbonate point

Available in: .45 (250 gr.), .50 (250, 300 gr.)

MSRP....................**$28.00**

AEROTIP ELR

Description: Designed specifically for the CVA Paramount long-range bolt-action muzzleloader; 280-grain; .452 BC; best used in 1:22 twist

Type: ELR

Available in: .45

Box 15:...................**$34.00**

COPPER

Description: Thin copper plating reduces bore friction while allowing for optimal bullet expansion; available in four tip designs: Hollow Point, AeroTip, Flat Point, and Steel Tip

Available in: .45 (195, 225, 275 gr.); .50 (223, 245, 295, 348, 405, 444 gr.); .54 (295, 348 gr.)

MSRP.............**$14.00–$28.95**

PLATINUM

Description: Proprietary hard plating and aggressive bullet taper design for improved ballistic coefficient; large-size fluted gas check produces higher and more consistent pressures

Available in: .45 (223, 300 gr.); .50 (270, 300, 338 gr.)

MSRP.............**$15.00–$28.00**

PURE LEAD

Description: Pure lead, available in four different grain weights in Hollow Point and 444 in Flat Point

Available in: .50 (295, 348 gr.); .54 (345, 405 gr.)

Box 15:............**$11.00–$28.00**

Swift Bullet Company

SWIFT A-FRAME MUZZLELOADING BULLETS

A-FRAME MUZZLELOADING BULLETS
Description: Muzzleloader and heavy revolver A-Frame bullets are one in the same; initiate expansion at 950 feet per second, expand to .65x their original caliber, and maintain 97% of their weight; virtually indestructible at velocities in excess of 3000 feet per second
Available in: .50 (240, 300 gr.); .54 (265, 325 gr.)
Box of 10:. **$19.25**

Thompson/Center Arms

MAXI-BALL
Description: An exceptionally accurate bullet and the preferred bullet for penetration needed for large game like elk; lubricating grooves (maxi wide grooves)
Available in: .50 (275, 350 gr.)
Box 20:. . . . .**$24.00–$29.99**

SHOCK WAVE SABOTS
Description: Polymer tip spire point bullet with sabot; incorporates harder lead core with walls interlocked with the jacket for maximum weight retention and expansion; available with spire point or bonded bullets
Available in: Bonded Core in Super Glide Sabots .50 (250 gr.); Controlled Expansion in Super Glide Sabot .50 (250, 300 gr.); Bonded Core in Mag Express Sabots .50 (250, 300 gr.); Controlled Expansion in Mag Express Sabots .50 (200, 250, 300 gr.) and .45 (200 gr.)
MSRP. . . . . **$19.99–$24.99**

SUPER 45 XR SABOTS
Description: Centerfire weight performance without the recoil, Super 45 XR sabots have a flatter trajectory, provide deep penetration, and nearly 2 times the expansion of its original diameter.
Available in: .45 (155 gr.)
Box 30:. **$19.99**

THOMPSON/CENTER SHOCK WAVE SABOTS

Umarex

UUMAREX ARX

UMAREX/INCEPTOR ARX
Description: Designed in conjunction with PolyCase Ammunition Development Lab; SpeedBand sabot available calibers include .357, .40, and .45, while a .45-caliber option has Umarex's base-style SpeedBelt; acceptable for use in large-bore airguns, including Umarex's Hammer .50-caliber
Available in: .50
Box of 15:. **$24.99**

BULLETS

Due to extreme demand and limited supplies, pricing on components has varied too widely during 2021 to include MSRP here. Anticipating that prices will eventually settle down in 2022, we expect the 114th edition to include component MSRP. Purchasers of components should do their research across manufacturer, distributor, and retailer websites to assess availability and best pricing.

Barnes Bullets

Barnes continues to develop leading-edge products with a wide range of workability and functionality using an incredibly broad range of purpose-built components and ammunition. Barnes's most popular hunting bullets, the all-copper TSX line, also comes with a streamlined polymer tip. The Barnes Buster line can be used for both rifles and handguns.

Rifle Bullets

BANDED SOLIDS

Caliber & Description	9.3MM RN	9.3MM RN	416 RN	416 RN	404 JEFF RN	470 NITRO RN	505 GIBBS RN	500 NITRO FN	500 JEFF RN	50 BMG BORE RIDER	50 BMG BORE RIDER	577 NITRO FN	600 NITRO FN
Diameter, Inches	.366	.366	.416	.416	.422	.474	.504	.509	.510	.510	.510	.583	.618
Weight, Grains	250	286	350	.400	.400	.500	525	570	535	750	800	750	900
Density	.267	.305	.289	.33	.321	.318	.295	.314	.294	.412	.439	.315	.337
Ballistic Coefficient	.214	.247	.217	.261	.261	.243	.267	.243	.238	1.070	1.095	.257	.380
Catalog Number	30466	30467	30520	30526	30536	30649	30685	30690	30694	30703	30707	30713	30714

From: N/A

> **LEGEND**
> **Type of Bullet**
> BT – Boattail
> FB – Flat Base
> FN – Flat Nose
> RN – Round Nose
> S – Spitzer
> SP – Soft Point
> SS – Semi-Spitzer

BARNES BUSTER

Caliber & Description	44 MAG. FN FB	454 CASULL FN FB	45/70 FN FB	500 S&W FN FB
Diameter, Inches	.429	.451	.458	.500
Weight, Grains	300	325	400	400
Density	.233	.228	.272	.229
Ballistic Coefficient	.241	.206	.242	.220
Catalog Number	30545	30572	30644	30672

Box 50: N/A

Barnes Bullets

BARNES ORIGINAL

Caliber & Description	30-30 WIN FNSP	348 WIN FN SP	348 WIN FN SP	375 WIN FN SP	38/55 FN SP	38/55 FN SP	45/70 SSSP	45/70 FN SP	45/70 SSSP	45/70 FN SP	50/110 WIN FN SP	50/110 WIN FN SP
Diameter, Inches	.308	.348	.348	.375	.375	.377	.458	.458	.458	.458	.510	.510
Weight, Grains	190	220	250	255	255	255	300	300	400	400	300	450
Jckt.	-	.032	.032	.032	.032	.032	.032	.032	.032	.032	.032	.032
Density	.286	.260	.295	.259	.259	.256	.204	.204	.272	.272	.165	.247
Ballistic Coefficient	.296	.301	.327	.290	.290	.290	.291	.227	.389	.302	.183	.274
Catalog Number	30360	30437	30438	30496	30497	30498	30611	30612	30613	30614	30682	30683

From: N/A

LRX BULLETS

Caliber & Description	22 BT	6MM BT	6.5MM BT	270 BT	7MM BT	7MM BT	7MM BT	30 BT	30 BT	30 BT	30 BT	338 BT	338 LAPUA BT	338 LAPUA BT	375 BT
Diameter, Inches	.224	.243	.264	.277	.284	.284	.284	.308	.308	.308	.308	.338	.338	.338	.375
Weight, Grains	77	95	127	129	139	145	168	175	190	200	212	250	265	280	270
Density	.216	230	.257	.240	.246	.257	.257	.264	.286	.301	.319	.313	.331	.350	.274
Ballistic Coefficient	.404	.436	.468	.463	.470	.486	.550	.508	.540	.546	.705	.602	.575	.667	.449
Catalog Number	30881	30862	30228	30262	30295	30282	30284	30318	30377	30374	30376	31150	30434	30432	30483

Box 50: N/A

MATCH BURNER BULLETS

Caliber & Description	22 FB	22 BT	22 BT	6MM FB	6MM BT	6MM BT	6.5MM BT	6.5MM BT	6.5MM BT	7MM BT	30 PALMA FB	30 BT
Diameter, Inches	.224	.224	.224	.243	.243	.243	.264	.264	.264	.284	.308	.308
Weight, Grains	52	69	85	68	105	112	120	140	145	171	155	175
Density	.148	.196	.242	.165	.254	.271	.246	.287	.297	.303	.233	.264
Ballistic Coefficient	.224	.339	.410	.267	.511	.624	.460	.586	.703	.645	.467	.521
Catalog Number	30160	30162	30164	30205	31120	31122	30234	31144	30102	30285	30381	30385

Box 100: N/A

LEGEND

Type of Bullet

BT – Boattail
FB – Flat Base
FN – Flat Nose
RN – Round Nose
S – Spitzer
SP – Soft Point
SS – Semi-Spitzer

AMMUNITION

Barnes Bullets

M/LE Reduced Ricochet, Limited Penetration (RRLP) Bullets

Caliber & Description	223/5.56 FB	6.8MM FB	30 FB	7.62X39 FB
Diameter, Inches	.224	.277	.308	.310
Weight, Grains	55	85	150	108
Density	.157	.158	.226	.161
Ballistic Coefficient	.225	.229	.357	.243
Catalog Number	30161	30252	30313	30390

From: N/A

M/LE TAC-TX Bullets

Caliber & Description	6.5mm BT	6.5mm BT	6.5mm BT	6.8mm BT	300 BLK	300 BLK	30 FB	30 BT	338 BT	338 BT	458 SOCOM BT
Diameter, Inches	.264	.264	.264	.277	.308	.308	.308	.308	.338	.338	.458
Weight, Grains	100	115	120	95	110	120	110	168	225	265	300
Density	.205	.236	.246	.177	.166	.181	.166	.253	.281	.331	.204
Ballistic Coefficient	.359	.387	.443	.292	.289	.358	.295	.470	.514	.575	.236
Catalog Number	30236	31142	30237	30253	30321	30320	30358	30359	30420	30419	30640

From: N/A

Multi-Purpose Green (MPG) Bullets

Caliber & Description	223 FB	6.8MM FB	30 FB	7.62X39 FB
Diameter, Inches	.224	.277	.308	.310
Weight, Grains	55	85	150	108
Density	.157	.158	.226	.161
Ballistic Coefficient	.225	.229	.357	.243
Catalog Number	30161	30249	30331	30388

From: N/A

TSX Bullets

Caliber & Description	22 FB	22 FB	22 FB	22 FB	22 BT	22 BT	224 VALKYRIE BT	6MM BT	25 BT	25 FB	6.5MM BT	6.5MM FB	6.5MM BT	6.8MM FB	6.8MM BT	270 BT	270 BT
Diameter, Inches	.224	.224	.224	.224	.224	.224	.224	.243	.257	.257	.264	.264	.264	.277	.277	.277	.277
Weight, Grains	45	50	53	55	62	70	78	85	100	115	120	130	120	85	110	130	140
Density	.128	.142	.151	.157	.177	.199	.222	.206	.216	.249	.246	.266	.266	.158	.205	.242	.261
Ballistic Coefficient	.188	.197	.204	.209	.287	.314	.383	.333	.336	.335	.381	.365	.411	.246	.323	.374	.404
Catalog Number	30176	30174	30180	30182	30190	30193	30204	30212	30222	30224	30244	30246	31140	30254	30260	30264	30266

AMMUNITION

Caliber & Description	270 FB	7MM BT	7MM BT	7MM BT	7MM FB	7MM FB	30 FN FB	30 FB	30 BT	30 BT	30 BT	30 BT	30 BT	30 FB	7.62X39 BT
Diameter, Inches	.277	.284	.284	.284	.284	.284	.308	.308	.308	.308	.308	.308	.308	.308	.310
Weight, Grains	150	120	140	150	160	175	150	110	130	150	165	168	180	200	123
Density	.279	.213	.248	.266	.283	.310	.226	.166	.196	.226	.248	.253	.271	.301	.183
Ballistic Coefficient	.386	.349	.394	.408	.392	.417	.184	.264	.340	.369	.398	.404	.453	.423	.275
Catalog Number	30269	30287	30289	30293	30291	30294	30334	30341	30345	30347	30349	30351	30353	30356	30391

Caliber & Description	303/7.65MM FB	8MM BT	8MM BT	338 BT	338 BT	338 FB	338 FB	338 LAPUA BT	35 FB	35 FB	9.3MM FB	9.3MM FB	375 FB	375 FB	375 FB
Diameter, Inches	.311	.323	.323	.338	.338	.338	.338	.338	.358	.358	.366	.366	.375	.375	.375
Weight, Grains	150	180	200	185	210	225	250	285	200	225	250	286	235	270	300
Density	.222	.246	.274	.231	.263	.281	.313	.356	.223	.251	.267	.305	.239	.274	.305
Ballistic Coefficient	.322	.381	.421	.352	.404	.386	.425	.585	.284	.359	.361	.411	.270	.326	.357
Catalog Number	30393	30396	30398	30408	30410	30412	30415	30417	30455	30457	30469	30473	30486	30489	30491

Caliber & Description	375 FB	405 WIN FB	416 FB	416 FB	416 FB	404 JEFFERY FB	450 FB	458 FB	458 FB	458 FB	458 FB	45/70 FN	45/70 FN	470 NITRO FB
Diameter, Inches	.375	.411	.416	.416	.416	.422	.451	.458	.458	.458	.458	.458	.458	.474
Weight, Grains	350	300	300	350	400	400	275	300	350	450	500	250	300	500
Density	.356	.254	.248	.289	.330	.321	.193	.204	.238	.306	.341	.170	.204	.318
Ballistic Coefficient	.425	.281	.298	.345	.392	.378	.215	.234	.278	.369	.412	.136	.163	.363
Catalog Number	30494	30516	30527	30529	30532	30537	30628	30615	30617	30619	30622	30629	30630	30647

Caliber & Description	505 GIBBS FB	500 NITRO FB	50 BMG BT	577 NITRO FB
Diameter, Inches	.505	.509	.510	.583
Weight, Grains	525	570	647	750
Density	.294	.314	.355	.315
Ballistic Coefficient	.320	.369	.572	.402
Catalog Number	30688	30692	30700	30712

From: N/A

VARMIN-A-TOR

Caliber & Description	20 FB	22 FB	22 FB	6mm FB	6mm FB
Diameter, Inches	.204	.224	.224	.243	.243
Weight, Grains	32	40	50	58	72
Density	.110	.114	.142	.140	.174
Ballistic Coefficient	.159	.153	.192	.173	.208
Catalog Number	30092	30168	30178	30207	30210

From: N/A

VARMINT GRENADE

Caliber & Description	20 FB	22 HORNET FB	22 FB	223 FB	6MM FB
Diameter, Inches	.204	.224	.224	.224	.243
Weight, Grains	26	30	36	50	62
Density	.089	.085	.102	.142	.150
Ballistic Coefficient	.131	.101	.149	.183	.199
Catalog Number	30090	30170	30171	30198	30214

Box 100: N/A

AMMUNITION

Barnes Bullets

Handgun Bullets

M/LE TAC-XP PISTOL BULLETS

Caliber & Description	380 ACP	9MM	9MM	.357 SIG	38 SPL.	357 MAG.	10MM/40 S&W	10MM/40 S&W	10MM/40 S&W	44 SPL.	45 ACP/45 GAP	45 ACP
Diameter, Inches	.355	.355	.355	.355	.355	.357	.400	.400	.400	.429	.451	.451
Weight, Grains	80	95	115	125	110	125	125.	140	155	200	160	185
Density	.091	.108	.130	.142	.123	.140	.112	.125	.138	.155	.112	.130
Ballistic Coefficient	.107	.120	.167	.159	.156	.160	.113	.128	.189	.138	.133	.167
Catalog Number	30440	30444	30442	30446	30449	30451	30500	30502	30504	30539	30550	30552

Box 40: N/A

XPB PISTOL BULLETS

Caliber & Description	357 Mag.	41 Mag.	44 Mag.	44 Mag.	45 Colt	45 Colt	454 Casull	460 S&W	460 S&W	480 Ruger	500 S&W XPB	500 S&W XPB	500 S&W XPB
Diameter, Inches	.357	.410	.429	.429	.451	.451	.451	.451	.451	.475	.500	.500	.500
Weight, Grains	140	180	200	225	200	225	250	200	275	275	275	325	375
Density	.157	.153	.155	.175	.140	.158	.176	.140	.193	.174	.157	.186	.214
Ballistic Coefficient	.150	.126	.138	.166	-	.146	.141	.160	.215	.155	.141	.228	.261
Catalog Number	30453	30512	30541	30543	30556	30558	30562	30554	30548	30659	30663	30665	30667

Box 20: N/A

Berger Bullets

Famous for their superior performance in benchrest matches, Berger bullets also include hunting designs. From .17 to .30, all Bergers feature fourteen jackets with a wall concentricity tolerance of .0003. Lead cores are 99.9 percent pure and swaged in dies to within .0001 of a round. Berger's line includes several profiles: Match, Low Drag, Very Low Drag, Length Tolerant, and Maximum-Expansion, besides standard flat-base and boattail.

HUNTING

Caliber & Description	6mm VLD	6mm VLD	6mm	6mm VLD	6mm VLD	25 VLD"	6.5mm VLD	6.5mm VLD	270 VLD	270 Classic	270 VLD	270 VLD	7mm VLD	270 EOL	7mm VLD	7mm Classic	7mm VLD	7mm EOL	30 VLD	30 VLD	30 Classic	30 VLD	30 VLD	30 Classic	30 VLD	30 VLD	338 Elite	338 Elite
Diameter, Inches	.243	.243	.243	.243	.243	.257	.264	.264	.277	.277	.277	.277	.284	.277	.284	.284	.284	.284	.308	.308	.308	.308	.308	.308	.308	.308	.338	.338
Weight, Grains	87	95	95	105	115	115	130	140	130	130	140	150	140	170	168	168	180	195	155	168	168	175	185	185	190	210	250	300
Density	.210	.230	-	.254	.278	.249	.266	.287	.241	-	.260	.279	.248	-	.298	-	.319	.345	.233	.253	-	.264	.279	-	.286	.316	-	-
Ballistic Coefficient	.412	.480	.427	.532	.545	.466	.552	.612	.452	.497	.487	.531	.510	.662	.617	.604	.659	.754	.439	.473	.496	.498	.549	.547	.570	.631	.682	.818
Catalog Number	24524	24527	24570	24528	24530	25513	26503	26504	27501	27570	27502	27503	28503	27575	28501	28570	28502	28550	30508	30510	30570	30512	30513	30571	30514	30515	33554	33556

Box 100: N/A

AMMUNITION

Berger Bullets

TARGET

Caliber & Description	22 FBHP	22 FBHP	22 VLD	22 BTHP	22 VLD	22 VLD	22 VLD	22 LRBTHP	22 VLD	6mm FBHP	6mm BR	6mm BTHP	6mm FBHP	6mm FBHP	6mm BTHP	6mm VLD
Diameter, Inches	.224	.224	.224	.224	.224	.224	.224	.224	.224	.243	.243	.243	.243	.243	.243	.243
Weight, Grains	52	55	70	73	75	80	80.5	82	90	62		65	65	68	90	95
Density	.148	.157	.199	.208	.214	.228	.229	.233	.256	.150	-	.157	.157	.165	.218	.230
Ballistic Coefficient	.242	.262	.371	.343	.423	.445	.436	.444	.551	.253	.277	.270	.265	.280	.411	.480
Catalog Number	22408	22410	22418	22420	22421	22422	22427	22424	22423	24404	24407	24408	24409	24411	24425	24427

Caliber & Description	6mm BTHP	6mm VLD	6mm Hybrid	6mm BTHP	6mm VLD	6.5mm BTHP	6.5mm VLD	6.5mm VLD	6.5mm LRBTHP	6.5mm Hybrid	7mm VLD	7mm VLD	7mm Hybrid
Diameter, Inches	.243	.243	.243	.243	.243	.264	.264	.264	.264	.264	.284	.284	.284
Weight, Grains	105	105	105	108	115	120	130	140	140	140	168	180	180
Density	.254	.254	.254	.261	.278	.245	.266	.287	.287	.287	.298	.319	.319
Ballistic Coefficient	.493	.495	.547	.551	.545	.453	.552	.612	.592	.618	.617	.659	.674
Catalog Number	24428	24429	24433	24431	24430	26402	26403	26401	26409	26414	28401	28405	28407

Caliber & Description	30 FBHP	30 FBHP	30 VLD	30 Hybrid	30 LRBTHP	30 VLD	30 Hybrid	30 LRBTHP	30 VLD	30 Juggernaut	30 VLD	30 Hybrid
Diameter, Inches	.308	.308	.308	.308	.308	.308	.308	.308	.308	.308	.308	.308
Weight, Grains	115	150	155	155	155.5	168	168	175	175	185	185	185
Density	.183	.226	.233	.233	.234	.253	.253	.264	.264	.279	.279	.279
Ballistic Coefficient	.296	.398	.439	.483	.464	.473	.519	.515	.498	.560	.549	.569
Catalog Number	30421	30407	30408	30426	30416	30410	30425	30420	30412	30418	30413	30424

Caliber & Description	30 Hybrid	30 LRBTHP	30 VLD	30 Hybrid	30 Hybrid
Diameter, Inches	.308	.308	.308	.308	.308
Weight, Grains	200	210	210	215	230
Density	.301	.316	.316	-	-
Ballistic Coefficient	.624	.626	.631	.696	.743
Catalog Number	30427	30419	30415	30429	30430

Box 100: N/A

LEGEND
Type of Bullet

BT – Boattail
FB – Flat Base

HP – Hollow Point
LD – Low Drag
LR – Long Range
VLD – Very Low Drag

AMMUNITION

Berger Bullets

VARMINT

Caliber & Description	17 FBHP	20 FBHP	20 BTHP	20 LRBTHP	22 FBHP	22 FBHP	22 FBHP	22 FBHP	22 FBHP	6mm LDHP	6mm FBHP	6mm LDHP
Diameter, Inches	.172	.204	.204	.204	.224	.224	.224	.224	.224	.243	.243	.243
Weight, Grains	25	35	40	55	40	52	55	60	64	69	80	88
Density	.121	.120	.137	.188	.114	.148	.157	.171	.182	.167	.194	.213
Ballistic Coefficient	.150	.176	.225	.381	.155	.197	.210	.278	.294	.291	.306	.391
Catalog Number	17308	20303	20304	20306	22303	22309	22311	22312	22316	24313	24321	24323

Box 100: N/A

Hornady Bullets

Hornady's product line includes over 300 bullets, ranging from .17 caliber all the way up to the .50 caliber A-MAX bullet for the .50 BMG. Hornady is always working to originate the next technological innovation. From prairie dogs to dangerous game, they have the perfect bullet to meet every hunting and shooting need.

Rifle Bullets

ELD MATCH

Caliber & Description	6.5mm	7mm	30	338
Diameter, Inches	.264	.284	.308	.338
Weight, Grains	140	162	208	285
Density	.287	.287	.313	.356
Ballistic Coefficient	.305	.329	.335	.394
Catalog Number	26331	28403	30731	33381

MSRP N/A

ELD-X

Caliber & Description	30	30	30	30	6.5mm	7mm	7mm
Diameter, Inches	.308	.308	.308	.308	.264	.284	.284
Weight, Grains	178	200	212	220	143	162	175
Density	.268	.301	.319	.331	.293	.287	.310
Ballistic Coefficient	.271	.315	.336	.325	.315	.315	.340
Catalog Number	3074	3076	3077	3078	2635	2840	2841

MSRP N/A

FMJ BULLETS

Caliber & Description	22 FMJ-BT	30 FMJ	30 FMJ-BT	303 FMJ-BT	7.62 FMJ
Diameter, Inches	.224	.308	.308	.3105	.310
Weight, Grains	55	110	150	174	123
Density	.157	.166	.226	.255	.183
Ballistic Coefficient	.243	.178	.398	.470	.266
Catalog Number	2267	3017	3037	3131	3478

MSRP N/A

AMMUNITION

InterBond

Caliber & Description	6mm BT	25 BT	6.5mm BT	270 BT	270 BT	7mm BT	7mm BT	30 BT	30 BT	30 BT	338 BT	416 RN
Diameter, Inches	.243	.257	.264	.277	.277	.284	.284	.308	.308	.308	.338	.416
Weight, Grains	85	110	129	130	150	139	154	150	165	180	225	400
Density	.206	.238	.264	.242	.279	.246	.525	.226	.248	.271	.281	.330
Ballistic Coefficient	.395	.390	.485	.460	.525	.486	.273	.415	.447	.480	.515	.311
Catalog Number	24539	25419	26209	27309	27409	28209	28309	30309	30459	30709	33209	41659

MSRP N/A

InterLock

Caliber & Description	22 SP	6mm BT SP	25 SP	25 BTSP	25 RN	25 HP	6.5mm SP	6.5mm SP	6.5mm RN	6.5mm Carcano RN	270 SP	270 BTSP	270 SP	7mm BTSP	7mm SP	7mm SP	7mm BTSP	7mm RN	7mm SP
Diameter, Inches	.227	.243	.257	.257	.257	.257	.264	.264	.264	.268	.277	.277	.277	.284	.284	.284	.284	.284	.284
Weight, Grains	70	100	100	117	117	120	129	140	160	160	130	140	150	139	139	154	162	175	175
Density	.194	.242	.216	.253	.253	.260	.264	.287	.328	.321	.242	.261	.279	.246	.246	.273	.287	.310	.310
Ballistic Coefficient	.296	.405	.357	.391	.243	.394	.445	.465	.283	.275	.409	.486	.462	.453	.392	.433	.514	.285	.462
Catalog Number	2280	2453	2540	2552	2550	2560	2620	2630	2640	2645	2730	2735	2740	2825	2820	2830	2845	2855	2850

Caliber & Description	30 BTSP	30 RN	30 SP	30 BTSP	30 SP	30 FP	30 BTSP	30 RN	30 SP	30 BTSP	30 RN	7.62 SP	303 SP	303 RN	32 FP	8mm SP
Diameter, Inches	.308	.308	.308	.308	.308	.308	.308	.308	.308	.308	.308	.310	.312	.312	.321	.323
Weight, Grains	150	150	150	165	165	170	180	180	180	190	220	123	150	174	170	150
Density	.226	.226	.226	.248	.248	.256	.271	.271	.271	.286	.331	.183	.220	.255	.236	.205
Ballistic Coefficient	.349	.186	.338	.435	.387	.189	.452	.241	.425	.491	.300	.252	.361	.262	.249	.290
Catalog Number	3033	3035	3031	3045	3040	3060	3072	3075	3070	3085	3090	3140	3120	3130	3210	3232

Hornady Bullets

Caliber & Description	8mm RN	8mm SP	338 SP RP	338 SP RP	338 RN	338 SP RP	348 FP	35 RN	35 SP RP	35 SP RP	9.3 SP RP	375 FP	375 SP RP	375 SP RP
Diameter, Inches	.323	.323	.338	.338	.338	.338	.348	.358	.358	.358	.366	.375	.375	.375
Weight, Grains	170	195	200	225	250	250	200	200	200	250	286	220	225	270
Density	.233	.267	.250	.281	.313	.313	.236	.223	.223	.279	.305	.223	.229	.229
Ballistic Coefficient	.217	.410	.361	.397	.291	.431	.246	.195	.282	.375	.410	.217	.320	.380
Catalog Number	3235	3236	3310	3320	3330	3335	3410	3515	3510	3520	3560	3705	3706	3711

LEGEND
Type of Bullet
- BT – Boat Tail
- CT – Combat Target
- FMJ – Full Metal Jacket
- FP – Flat Point
- HB – Hollow Base
- L – Lead
- RN – Round Nose
- SP – Spire Point
- SX – Super Explosive
- SWC – Semi-Wadcutter
- WC – Wadcutter

Caliber & Description	405 FP	405 SP	416 RN	44 FP	45 HP	45 FP	45 RN	45 RN
Diameter, Inches	.411	.411	.416	.430	.458	.458	.458	.458
Weight, Grains	300	300	400	265	300	350	350	500
Density	.251	.251	.330	.205	.204	.238	.238	.341
Ballistic Coefficient	.215	.250	.311	.186	.197	.195	.189	.287
Catalog Number	41050	41051	4165	4300	4500	4503	4502	4504

LEGEND
Type of Bullet
- BT – Boat Tail
- CT – Combat Target
- FMJ – Full Metal Jacket
- FP – Flat Point
- HB – Hollow Base
- L – Lead
- RN – Round Nose
- SP – Spire Point
- SX – Super Explosive
- SWC – Semi-Wadcutter
- WC – Wadcutter

MSRP N/A

MATCH A-MAX

Caliber & Description	6.5mm	22	22	22	6mm	6.5mm	6.5mm	6.5mm	7mm	30	30	30 MOLY	30	30	338 BT	50
Diameter, Inches	.264	.224	.224	.224	.243	.264	.264	.264	.284	.308	.308	.308	.308	.308	.338	.510
Weight, Grains	100	52	75	80	105	120	123	140	162	155	168	168	178	208	285	750
Density	.246	.148	.214	.228	.254	.246	.252	.287	.287	.233	.253	.253	.268	.313	.356	.412
Ballistic Coefficient	.390	.247	.435	.453	.500	.465	.510	.585	.625	.435	.475	.475	.495	.325	.720	1.050
Catalog Number	26101	22492	22792	22832	24562	26172	26171	26332	28402	30312	30502	30504	30712	30732	3338	5165

MSRP N/A

SST

Caliber & Description	6mm	25	6.5mm	6.5mm	6.5mm	270	270	270	270	7mm SST	7mm SST	7mm SST	30	30	30	30
Diameter, Inches	.243	.257	.264	.264	.264	.277	.277	.277	.277	.284	.284	.284	.308	.308	.308	.308
Weight, Grains	95	117	123	129	140	120	130	140	150	139	154	162	125	150	150	165
Density	.230	.253	.252	.264	.287	.223	.242	.261	.279	.246	.273	.287	.185	.226	.226	.248
Ballistic Coefficient	.355	.390	.510	.485	.520	.400	.460	.495	.525	.486	.525	.550	.305	.415	.370	.447
Catalog Number	24532	25522	26173	26202	26302	2716	27302	27352	27402	28202	28302	28452	3019	30302	30303	30452

AMMUNITION

Hornady Bullets

Caliber & Description	30	7.62	338	338	8mm BT
Diameter, Inches	.308	.310	.338	.338	
Weight, Grains	180	123	200	225	170
Density	.271	.183	.250	.281	.233
Ballistic Coefficient	.480	.260	.455	.515	.455
Catalog Number	30702	3142	33102	33202	3233

MSRP N/A

TRADITIONAL VARMINT

Caliber & Description	17 HP	20 SP	22 JET	22 Hornet	22 Hornet	22 HP BEE	22 SP	22 SP SX	22 SP	22 SP	22 SP SX	22 HP	22 SP	6mm HP
Diameter, Inches	.172	.204	.222	.223	.224	.224	.224	.224	.224	.224	.224	.224	.224	.243
Weight, Grains	25	45	40	45	45	45	50	50	55	55	55	60	60	75
Density	.121	.155	.116	.129	.128	.128	.142	.142	.157	.157	.157	.171	.171	.181
Ballistic Coefficient	.187	.245	.104	.202	.202	.108	.214	.214	.235	.235	.235	.271	.264	.294
Catalog Number	1710	22008	2210	2220	2230	2229	2245	2240	2265	2266	2260	2275	2270	2420

Caliber & Description	6mm BTHP	6mm SP	25 FP	25 HP	25 SP	270 SP	270 HP	270 BTHP	7mm HP	30 Short Jacket	30 SP	30 RN	30 SP
Diameter, Inches	.243	.243	.257	.257	.257	.277	.277	.277	.284	.308	.308	.308	.308
Weight, Grains	87	87	60	75	87	100	110	110	120	100	110	110	130
Density	.210	.210	.130	.162	.188	.186	.205	.205	.213	.151	.166	.166	.196
Ballistic Coefficient	.376	.327	.101	.257	.322	.307	.352	.360	.334	.152	.256	.150	.295
Catalog Number	2442	2440	2510	2520	2530	2710	2720	27200	2815	3005	3010	3015	3020

MSRP N/A

AMMUNITION

Hornady Bullets

V-Max

Caliber & Description	17	17	20	20	22	22	22	22 MOLY	22	22	22	22 MOLY	22	6mm
Diameter, Inches	.172	.172	.204	.204	.224	.224	.224	.224	.224	.224	.224	.224	.224	.243
Weight, Grains	20	25	32	40	35	40	50	50	53	55	55	55	60	58
Density	.097	.121	.110	.137	.100	.114	.142	.142	.151	.157	.157	.157	.171	.140
Ballistic Coefficient	.185	.230	.210	.275	.109	.200	.242	.242	.290	.255	.255	.255	.265	.250
Catalog Number	21710	17105	22004	22006	22252	22241	22261	22613	22265	22272	22271	22713	22281	22411

Caliber & Description	6mm	6mm	6mm	25	6.5mm	270	7mm	30
Diameter, Inches	.243	.243	.243	.257	.264	.277	.284	.308
Weight, Grains	65	75	87	75	95	110	120	110
Density	.157	.181	.210	.162	.195	.205	.213	.166
Ballistic Coefficient	.280	.330	.400	.290	.365	.370	.365	.290
Catalog Number	22415	22420	22440	22520	22601	22721	22810	23010

LEGEND
Type of Bullet
BT – Boat Tail
CT – Combat Target
FMJ – Full Metal Jacket
FP – Flat Point
HB – Hollow Base
L – Lead
RN – Round Nose
SP – Spire Point
SX – Super Explosive
SWC – Semi-Wadcutter
WC – Wadcutter

MSRP N/A

Handgun Bullets

FMJ BULLETS

Caliber & Description	9mm FMJ-RN	9mm FMJ-RN	10mm FMJ-FP	45 SWC	45 FMJ-RN	9mm FMJ	9mm FMJ-RN	10mm FMJ-FP	45 FMJ-CT
Diameter, Inches	.355	.355	.400	.451	.451	.355	.355	.400	.451
Weight, Grains	115	124	180	185	230	100	147	200	200
Density	.130	.141	N/A	.130	.162	.141	.167	.179	.140
Ballistic Coefficient	.140	.145	N/A	.068	.184	.158	.212	.182	.115
Catalog Number	35557	355771	400471	45137	45177	35527B	35597B	40077B	45157B

MSRP N/A

FRONTIER LEAD BULLETS

Caliber & Description	32 HBWC	32 SWC	38	38 HBWC	38 LRN	38 SWC	38 SWC HP	44 Cowboy	44 Cowboy
Diameter, Inches	.314	.314	.358	.358	.358	.358	.358	.427	.430
Weight, Grains	90	90	140	148	158	158	158	205	180
Density	.130	.130	.157	.165	.176	.176	.176	.161	.139
Ballistic Coefficient	.040	.096	.127	.047	.159	.135	.139	.123	.114
Catalog Number	10028	10008	10078	10208	10508	10408	10428	11208	11058

FRONTIER/ LEAD BULLETS (CONT.)

Caliber & Description	44 SWC	44 SWC HP	45 L-C/T	45 SWC	45 LRN	45 FP Cowboy
Diameter, Inches	.430	.430	.452	.452	.452	.454
Weight, Grains	240	240	200	200	230	255
Density	.185	.185	.140	.140	.162	.177
Ballistic Coefficient	.182	.204	.081	.070	.207	.117
Catalog Number	11108	11118	12208	12108	12308	12458

MSRP N/A

HAP BULLETS

Caliber & Description	9mm	9mm	10mm	45	45	10mm	45
Diameter, Inches	.356	.356	.400	.451	.451	.400	.451
Weight, Grains	115	125	180	185	230	200	200
Density	.130	.141	.161	.130	.162	.179	.140
Ballistic Coefficient	.129	.158	.164	.139	.188	.199	151
Catalog Number	355281	355721	400421	451051	451611	40061B	45159B

MSRP N/A

LEGEND
Type of Bullet
BT – Boat Tail
CT – Combat Target
FMJ – Full Metal Jacket
FP – Flat Point
HB – Hollow Base
L – Lead
RN – Round Nose
SP – Spire Point
SX – Super Explosive
SWC – Semi-Wadcutter
WC – Wadcutter

XTP BULLETS

Caliber & Description	30 RN	30 HP	32 HP	32 HP	32 HP	9mm HP	9mm HP	38 HP	9mm HP	38 FP	9mm HP	38 HP	38 HP	38 FP	38 HP	38 HP	9x18mm HP	10mm HP	10mm HP
Diameter, Inches	.308	.309	.312	.312	.312	.355	.355	.357	.355	.357	.355	.357	.357	.357	.357	.357	.365	.400	.400
Weight, Grains	86	90	60	85	100	90	115	110	124	125	147	125	140	158	158	180	95	155	180
Density	.130	.136	.088	.125	.147	.102	.130	.123	.141	.140	.167	.140	.157	.177	.177	.202	.102	.138	.161
Ballistic Coefficient	.105	.115	.090	.145	.170	.099	.129	.131	.165	.148	.212	.151	.169	.199	.206	.230	.127	.137	.164
Catalog Number	3100	31000	32010	32050	32070	35500	35540	35700	35571	35730	35580	35710	35740	35780	35750	35771	36500	40000	40040

Caliber & Description	10mm HP	41 HP	44 HP	44 HP	44 HP	44 HP	45 HP	45 HP	45 HP	45	45 HP	45 HP	45	475 MAG	50	500 MAG	500 FP
Diameter, Inches	.400	.410	.430	.430	.430	.300	.451	.451	.451	.452	.452	.452	.452	.475	.500	.500	.500
Weight, Grains	200	210	180	200	240	300	185	200	230	240	250	300	300	325	300	350	500
Density	.179	.178	.139	.155	.185	.232	.130	.140	.162	.168	.175	.210	.210	.206	.171	.192	.275
Ballistic Coefficient	.199	.182	.138	.170	.205	.245	.139	.151	.188	.160	.146	.180	.200	.150	.120	.145	.185
Catalog Number	40060	41000	44050	44100	44200	44280	45100	45140	45160	45220	45200	45230	45235	47500	50101	50100	50105

MSRP N/A

AMMUNITION

Lapua

Rifle Bullets

Lapua precision bullets are made from the best raw materials and meet the toughest precision specifications. Each bullet is subject to visual inspection and tested with advanced measurement devices.

D46

Manufactured to the strictest tolerances for concentricity, uniformity of shape, and weight; 7.62mm (.308) available
Box 100:..**N/A**

D166

Superbly accurate FMJBT bullet for 7.62mm (.311) cartridges
Box 100:..**N/A**

FMJ

Ten rounds loaded with Lapua's .30 S374 8.0/123gr FMJ bullet from 100m can easily achieve groupings less than; 30mm .224, 6.5mm, 7.62mm (.308, .311) available
Box 100:..**N/A**

LOCK BASE

A distinctive Full Metal Jacket Boat Tail bullet that has many applications from sport shooting to battlefield; streamlined ballistic shape combined with patented base design; 7.62mm and .338 available
Box 100:..**N/A**

MEGA

Soft point bullet with a protective copper jacket bullet at its best in the field and typically more than duplicates on impact; mechanical bonding locks the lead alloy in place; 6.5mm, 7.62mm, and 9.3mm available
Box 100:..**N/A**

LAPUA NATURALIS THIRD GENERATION

Market leaders in terminal ballistic performance, and they can be used in hunting areas where lead-core bullets are prohibited. 5.69 (50 gr.), 6mm (90 gr.), 6.5mm (140 gr.), 7mm (155 gr.), 8mm (180 gr.), 9.3mm (250 gr.), .338 (231 gr.) available.
Box 50:..**N/A**

SCENAR

Scenar Hollow Point Boat Tail bullets have the IBS World Record in 600 yard Heavy Gun 5-shot group (.404") and hold the official world ISSF record of 600 out of 600 possible; also available in Coated Silver Jacket version; .244, 6mm, 6.5mm, 7.62mm, and .338 available
Box 100:..**N/A**

SCENAR-L

A refinement in all manufacturing steps that has resulted in closer weight tolerances, tighter jacket wall concentricity standards, and greater uniformity in every dimension, including the gilding metal cup, lead wire and jacket forming, ending up to core-jacket assembly, boat tail pressing, and tipping ; 6mm, 6.5mm, 7mm, and 7.62mm (.308) available
Box 100:..**N/A**

LAPUA D46   LAPUA D166

LAPUA FMJ S   LAPUA HP

LAPUA LOCK BASE   LAPUA MEGA

LAPUA SCENAR

LAPUA NATURALIS
THIRD GENERATION

LAPUA SCENAR-L

AMMUNITION

Nosler Bullets

Rifle Bullets

ACCUBOND

Caliber & Description	6mm S	25 SWT	6.5mm SWT	6.5mm	270 SWT	270 SWT	7mm SWT	7mm SWT	30 SWT	30 SWT	30 S	30 SWT	30 SWT
Diameter, inches	.243	.257	.264	.264	.277	.277	.277	.277	.284	.284	.308	.308	.308
Weight, Grains	90	110	130	140	100	110	130	140	140	160	125	150	165
Density	.218	.238	.266	.287	.186	.205	.242	.261	.248	.283	.188	.226	.248
Ballistic Coefficient	.376	.418	.488	.509	.323	.370	.435	.496	.485	.531	.366	.435	.475
Catalog Number	56357	53742	56902	57873	57845	54382	54987	54765	59992	54932	52165	56719	55602

Caliber & Description	30 S	30 S	8mm S	338 S	338 S	338 S	338 S	338 S	35 Whelen S	35 Whelen S	9.3mm S	375 S	375 S
Diameter, inches	.308	.308	.323	.338	.338	.338	.338	.338	.358	.358	.366	.375	.375
Weight, Grains	180	200	200	180	200	225	250	300	200	225	250	260	300
Density	.271	.301	.274	.225	.250	.281	.313	.375	.223	.251	.267	.264	.305
Ballistic Coefficient	.507	.588	.450	.372	.414	.550	.575	.720	.365	.421	.494	.473	.485
Catalog Number	54825	54618	54374	57625	56382	54357	57287	54851	54425	50712	59756	54413	53662

Box 50, 100: N/A

BALLISTIC TIP HUNTING

Caliber & Description	6mm S	6mm S	25 S	25 S	6.5mm S	6.5mm S	6.5mm S	270 S	270 S	270 S	7mm S	7mm S
Diameter, inches	.243	.243	.257	.257	.264	.264	.264	.277	.277	.277	.284	.284
Weight, Grains	90	95	100	115	100	120	140	130	140	150	120	140
Density	.218	.230	.216	.249	.205	.246	.287	.242	.261	.279	.213	.248
Ballistic Coefficient	.365	.379	.393	.453	.350	.458	.509	.433	.456	.496	.417	.485
Catalog Number	24090	24095	25100	25115	26100	26120	26140	27130	27140	27150	28120	28140

Caliber & Description	7mm S	30 S	30 S	30 S	30 S	30 S	8mm S
Diameter, inches	.284	.308	.308	.308	.308	.308	.323
Weight, Grains	150	125	150	165	168	180	180
Density	.266	.188	.226	.248	.253	.271	.247
Ballistic Coefficient	.493	.366	.435	.475	.490	.507	.394
Catalog Number	28150	30125	30150	30165	30168	30180	32180

Box 50: N/A

LEGEND

Type of Bullet		Type of Tip	
BT	– Boat Tail	PT	– Purple Tip
HP	– Hollow Point	BT	– Blue Tip
J	– Jacketed	BrT	– Brown Tip
PP	– Protected Point	BuT	– Buckskin Tip
RN	– Round Nose	GT	– Green Tip
S	– Spitzer	GuT	– Gunmetal Tip
SS	– Semi Spitzer	MT	– Maroon Tip
W	– Whelen	OT	– Olive Tip
		RT	– Red Tip
		SLT	– Soft Lead Tip
		YT	– Yellow Tip

AMMUNITION

Nosler Bullets

BALLISTIC TIP VARMINT

Caliber & Description	204 S	204 S	22 S	22 S	22 S	22 S	6mm S	6mm S	6mm S	25 S
Diameter, Inches	.204	.204	.224	.224	.224	.224	.243	.243	.243	.257
Weight, Grains	32	40	40	50	55	60	55	70	80	85
Density	.110	.137	.114	.142	.157	.171	.133	.169	.194	.184
Ballistic Coefficient	.206	.239	.221	.238	.27	.270	.276	.310	.329	.329
Catalog Number	35216	52111	39510	39522	39526	34992	24055	39532	24080	43004

Box 100: N/A

CT BALLISTIC SILVERTIP HUNTING

Caliber & Description	6mm S	25 S	270 S	270 S	7mm S	7mm S	30 S	30 RN	30 S	30 S	8mm S	45-70 RN	338 S
Diameter, Inches	.243	.257	.277	.277	.284	.284	.308	.308	.308	.308	.323	.458	.338
Weight, Grains	95	115	130	150	140	150	150	150	168	180	180	300	200
Density	.230	.249	.242	.279	.248	.266	.226	.226	.253	.271	.247	.204	.250
Ballistic Coefficient	.379	.453	.433	.496	.485	.493	.435	.232	.490	.507	.394	.191	.414
Catalog Number	51040	51050	51075	51100	51105	51110	51150	51165	51160	51170	51693	51834	51200

Box 50: N/A

CUSTOM COMPETITION

Caliber & Description	22 HPBT	22 HPBT	22 HPBT	22 HPBT	6mm HPBT	6mm HPBT	6.5mm HPBT	6.5mm HPBT	6.8mm HPBT	7mm HPBT	30 HPBT	30 HPBT	30 HPBT	30 HPBT	30 HPBT	45 JHP
Diameter, Inches	.224	.224	.224	.224	.243	.243	.264	.264	.277	.284	.308	.308	.308	.308	.308	.451
Weight, Grains	52	69	77	80	105	107	123	140	115	168	140	155	168	175	190	185
Density	.148	.196	.219	.228	.254	.259	.252	.287	.214	.298	.211	.233	.253	.264	.286	.130
Ballistic Coefficient	.220	.305	.340	.415	.517	.525	.510	.529	.375	.520	.396	.450	.462	.505	.530	.142
Catalog Number	53294	17101	22421	25116	53614	49742	53415	26725	45357	53418	53152	53155	53164	53952	53412	44847

Box 100, 250: N/A

E-TIP

Caliber & Description	6mm S	25 S	6.8mm S	270 S	7mm S	7mm S	30 S	30 S	30 S	8mm S	338 S	6.5MM S
Diameter, Inches	.243	.257	.277	.277	.284	.284	.308	.308	.308	.323	.338	264
Weight, Grains	90	100	85	130	140	150	150	168	180	180	200	120
Density	.218	.216	.158	.242	.248	.266	.226	.253	.271	.246	.250	.246
Ballistic Coefficient	.403	.409	.273	.459	.489	.498	.469	.503	.523	.427	.425	.497
Catalog Number	59165	59456	59543	59298	59955	59426	59378	59415	59180	59265	59186	59765

Box 50: N/A

AMMUNITION

PARTITION

Caliber & Description	22 S	6mm S	6mm S	6mm S	25 S	25 S	25 S	6.5mm S	6.5mm S	6.5mm S	270 S	270 S	270 S	270 SS
Diameter, Inches	.224	.243	.243	.243	.257	.257	.257	.264	.264	.264	.277	.277	.277	.277
Weight, Grains	60	85	95	100	100	115	120	100	125	140	130	140	150	160
Density	.171	.206	.230	.242	.216	.249	.260	.205	.256	.287	.242	.261	.279	.298
Ballistic Coefficient	.228	.315	.365	.384	.377	.389	.391	.326	.4479	.490	.416	.432	.465	.434
Catalog Number	16316	16314	16315	35642	16317	16318	35643	16319	16320	16321	16322	35200	.16323	16324

Caliber & Description	7mm S	7mm S	7mm S	7mm S	30 S	30 S	30 RN	30 PP	30 S	30 S	30 SS	8mm S	338 S	338 S
Diameter, Inches	.284	.284	.284	.284	.308	.308	.308	.308	.308	.308	.308	.323	.338	.338
Weight, Grains	140	150	160	175	150	165	170	180	180	200	220	200	210	225
Density	.248	.266	.283	.310	.226	.248	.256	.271	.271	.301	.331	.274	.263	.281
Ballistic Coefficient	.434	.456	.475	.519	.387	.410	.252	.361	.474	.481	.351	.426	.400	.454
Catalog Number	16325	16326	16327	35645	16329	16330	16333	25396	16331	35626	16332	35277	16337	16336

Caliber & Description	338 S	35 S	35 S	9.3mm S	375 S	375 S	416 S	458 PP
Diameter, Inches	.338	.358	.358	.366	.375	.375	.416	.458
Weight, Grains	250	225	250	286	260	300	400	500
Density	.313	.251	.279	.307	.264	.305	.330	.389
Ballistic Coefficient	.473	.430	.446	.482	.314	.398	.390	.341
Catalog Number	35644	44800	44801	44750	44850	44845	45200	44745

Box 25, 50: N/A

LEGEND

Type of Bullet		Type of Tip	
BT	– Boat Tail	PT	– Purple Tip
HP	– Hollow Point	BT	– Blue Tip
J	– Jacketed	BrT	– Brown Tip
PP	– Protected Point	BuT	– Buckskin Tip
RN	– Round Nose	GT	– Green Tip
S	– Spitzer	GuT	– Gunmetal Tip
SS	– Semi Spitzer	MT	– Maroon Tip
W	– Whelen	OT	– Olive Tip
		RT	– Red Tip
		SLT	– Soft Lead Tip
		YT	– Yellow Tip

SOLID

Caliber & Description	9.3mm Solid	375 Solid	375 Solid	416 Solid	458 Solid	470 NE Solid
Diameter, Inches	.366	.375	.375	.416	.458	.474
Weight, Grains	286	260	300	400	500	500
Density	.305	.264	.305	.330	.341	.318
Ballistic Coefficient	.350	.254	.300	.289	.246	.237
Catalog Number	29825	29755	28451	23654	27452	28455

MSRP N/A

LEGEND

Type of Bullet			
BT	– Boattail	J	– Jacketed
FMJ	– Full Metal Jacket	PP	– Protected Point
		RN	– Round Nose
		S	– Spitzer

AMMUNITION

Nosler Bullets

VARMAGEDDON

Caliber& Description	17 FBHP	17 FB Tipped	20 FBHP	20 FB Tipped	22 FB Tipped	22 FBHP	22 FB Tipped	22 FBHP	22 FB Tipped	22 FBHP	6mm FBHP	6mm FB Tipped	6mm FB Tipped	30 FB Tipped
Diameter, Inches	.172	.172	.204	.204	.224	.224	.224	.224	.224	.224	.243	.243	.243	.308
Weight, Grains	20	20	32	32	35	40	40	55	55	62	55	55	70	110
Density	.097	.097	.110	.110	.100	.114	.114	.157	.157	.176	.133	.133	.169	.166
Ballistic Coefficient	.119	.183	.131	.204	.120	.158	.211	.210	.218	.251	.192	.252	.334	.293
Catalog Number	17205	17210	17215	17220	36763	17225	17230	17235	17240	35631	17245	17250	26123	34057

Box 100, 250: N/A

Handgun Bullets

SPORTING PISTOL

Caliber & Description	9mm JHP	9mm JHP	10mm JHP	10mm JHP	10mm JHP	10mm JHP	45 JHP	45 FMJ
Diameter, Inches	.355	.355	.400	.400	.400	.400	.451	.451
Weight, Grains	115	124	135	150	180	200	230	230
Density	.109	.141	.093	.106	.161	.179	.1625	.162
Ballistic Coefficient	.130	.118	.121	.134	.147	.163	.175	.183
Catalog Number	44848	43123	44852	44860	44885	44952	44922	44964

LEGEND
Type of Bullet
BT – Boattail
FB – Flat Base
FN – Flat Nose
RN – Round Nose
S – Spitzer
SP – Soft Point
SS – Semi-Spitzer

Box 250: N/A

SPORTING REVOLVER

Caliber & Description	38 JHP	41 JHP	44 JHP	44 JHP	44 JHP	44 JHP	45 Colt JHP
Diameter, Inches	.357	.410	.429	.429	.429	.429	.451
Weight, Grains	158	210	200	240	240	300	250
Density	.182	.170	.151	.173	.177	.206	.177
Ballistic Coefficient	.177	.178	155	.186	.186	.233	.176
Catalog Number	44841	43012	44846	44842	44868	42069	43013

Sierra Bullets

Box 100, 250: N/A

Rifle Bullets

BLITZKING

Caliber & Description	20	20	224	224	224	6mm	6mm	257	257
Diameter, Inches	.204	.204	.224	.224	.224	.243	.243	.257	.257
Weight, Grains	32	39	40	50	55	55	70	70	90
Density	.110	.134	.114	.142	.157	.133	.169	.151	.195
Ballistic Coefficient	.221	.287	.196	.248	.185	.225	.299	.260	.388
Catalog Number	1032	1039	1440	1450	1455	1502	1507	1605	1616

From: N/A

GameKing

Caliber & Description	22 FMJBT	22 SBT	22 HPBT	22 SBT	6mm HPBT	6mm FMJBT	6mm SBT	25 HPBT	25 SBT	25 SBT	25 HPBT	6.5mm HPBT
Diameter, Inches	.224	.224	.224	.224	.243	.243	.243	.257	.257	.257	.257	.264
Weight, Grains	55	55	55	65	85	90	100	90	100	117	120	130
Density	.157	.257	.157	.185	.206	.218	.242	.195	.216	.253	.260	.266
Ballistic Coefficient	.272	.250	.185	.303	.282	.387	.430	.250	.355	.410	.350	.355
Catalog Number	1355	1365	1390	1395	1530	1535	1560	1615	1625	1630	1650	1728

Caliber & Description	6.5mm SBT	270 SBT	270 HPBT	270 SBT	270 SBT	7mm HPBT	7mm SBT	7mm SBT	7mm SBT	7mm HPBT	7mm SBT	30 FMJBT
Diameter, Inches	.264	.277	.277	.277	.277	.284	.274	.284	.284	.284	.284	.308
Weight, Grains	140	130	140	140	150	140	140	150	160	160	175	150
Density	.287	.242	.261	.261	.279	.248	.248	.266	.283	.283	.310	.226
Ballistic Coefficient	.495	.436	.337	.457	.483	.375	.416	.436	.455	.384	.533	.408
Catalog Number	1730	1820	1835	1845	1840	1912	1905	1913	1920	1925	1940	2115

Caliber & Description	30 SBT	30 HPBT	30 SBT	30 SBT	30 SBT	8mm SBT	338 SBT	338 SBT	35 SBT	375 SBT	375 SBT
Diameter, Inches	.308	.308	.308	.308	.308	.323	.338	.338	.358	.375	.375
Weight, Grains	150	165	165	180	200	220	215	250	225	250	300
Density	.226	.248	.248	.271	.301	.301	.269	.313	.251	.254	.305
Ballistic Coefficient	.380	.363	.404	.501	.560	.521	.485	.565	.370	.353	.475
Catalog Number	2125	2140	2145	2160	2165	2420	2610	2600	2850	2950	3000

From: N/A

MatchKing

Caliber & Description	22 HPBT	22 HP	22 HPBT	22 HPBT	22 HPBT	22 HPBT	6mm HPBT	6mm HPBT	6mm HPBT	25 HPBT	6.5mm HPBT	6.5mm HPBT	6.5mm HPBT	6.5mm HPBT
Diameter, Inches	.224	.224	.224	.224	.224	.224	.243	.243	.243	.257	.264	.264	.264	.264
Weight, Grains	52	53	69	77	80	90	70	107	95	100	107	120	123	140
Density	.148	.151	.196	.219	.228	.256	.169	.259	.230	.216	.219	.246	.252	.287
Ballistic Coefficient	.225	.224	.301	.372	.420	.504	.259	.527	.480	.394	.430	.421	.510	.535
Catalog Number	1410	1400	1380	9377T	9390T	9290T	1505	1570	1537	1628	1715	1725	1727	1740

Sierra Bullets

MatchKing (cont.)

Caliber & Description	6.5mm HPBT	270 HPBT	270 HPBT	7mm HPBT	7mm HPBT	7mm HPBT	7mm HPBT	7mm HPBT	7mm HPBT	30 HP	30 HPBT	30 HPBT	30 HPBT	30 HPBT	30 HPBT	30 HPBT
Diameter, Inches	.264	.277	.277	.284	.284	.284	.284	.284	.284	.308	.308	.308	.308	.308	.308	.308
Weight, Grains	142	115	135	130	150	168	175	180	183	125	135	150	155	168	175	180
Density	.291	.214	.251	.230	.266	.298	.310	.319	.324	.188	.203	.226	.233	.253	.264	.271
Ballistic Coefficient	.595	.318	.488	.395	.429	.488	.608	.660	.707	.349	.390	.417	.450	.462	.505	.475
Catalog Number	1742	1815	1833	1903	1915	1930	1975	1980	1983	2121	2123	2190	2155	2200	2275	2220

Caliber & Description	30 HPBT	30 HPBT	30 HPBT	30 HPBT	30 HPBT	303 HPBT	8mm HPBT	338 HPBT	338 HPBT	375 HPBT
Diameter, Inches	.308	.308	.308	.308	.308	.311	.323	.338	.338	.375
Weight, Grains	190	200	210	220	240	174	200	250	300	350
Density	.286	.301	.316	.331	.361	.257	.274	.313	.375	.355
Ballistic Coefficient	.533	.565	.645	.629	.711	.499	.520	.587	.768	.805
Catalog Number	2210	2230	9240T	2240	9245T	2315	2415	2650	9300T	9350T

LEGEND

BT – Boattail
FMJ – Full Metal Jacket
FN – Flat Nose
HC – Hollow Cavity
HP – Hollow Point
J – Jacketed
RN – Round Nose
S – Spitzer
SMP – Semi-Pointed
SP – Soft Point

From: N/A

Pro-Hunter

Caliber & Description	6mm S	25 S	25 S	6.5mm S	270 S	270 S	7mm S	7mm S	30 HP/FN	30 FN	30 FN
Diameter, Inches	.243	.257	.257	.264	.277	.277	.284	.284	.308	.308	.308
Weight, Grains	100	100	117	120	110	130	120	140	125	150	170
Density	.242	.216	.253	.246	.205	.242	.213	.248	.188	.226	.256
Ballistic Coefficient	.373	.330	.388	.356	.318	.370	.328	.377	.119	.185	.205
Catalog Number	1540	1620	1640	1720	1810	1830	1900	1910	2020	2000	2010

Caliber & Description	30 RN	30 FMJ	30 S	30 S	30 RN	30 S	30 RN	30 RN
Diameter, Inches	.308	.308	.308	.308	.308	.308	.308	.308
Weight, Grains	110	110	125	150	150	180	180	220
Density	.166	.166	.188	.226	.226	.271	.271	.331
Ballistic Coefficient	.144	.144	.279	.336	.200	.407	.240	.310
Catalog Number	2100	2105	2120	2130	2135	2150	2170	2180

Sierra Bullets

PRO-HUNTER (CONT.)

Caliber & Description	303 S	303 S	303 S	8mm S	8mm S	338 S	35 RN	375 FN	45-70 HP/FN
Diameter, Inches	.311	.311	.311	.323	.323	.338	.358	.375	.458
Weight, Grains	125	150	180	150	175	225	200	200	300
Density	.185	.222	.266	.205	.240	.281	.223	.203	.204
Ballistic Coefficient	.274	.344	.411	.336	.381	.462	.148	.195	.120
Catalog Number	2305	2300	2310	2400	2410	2620	2800	2900	8900

VARMINTER

Caliber & Description	22 Hornet	22 Hornet	22 Hornet	22 Hornet	22 HP
Diameter, Inches	.223	.223	.224	.224	.224
Weight, Grains	40	45	40	45	40
Density	.115	.129	.114	.128	.114
Ballistic Coefficient	.117	.132	.116	.131	.155
Catalog Number	1100	1110	1200	1210	1385

From: N/A

Caliber & Description	22 S	22 S	22 S	22 Blitz	22 Blitz	22 SMP	22 S	22 HP	22 SMP	6mm HP	6mm HP	6mm SBT Blitz	6mm S	25 HP	25 S	6.5mm HP	6.5mm HP	270 HP	7mm HP	30 HP
Diameter, Inches	.224	.224	.224	.224	.224	.224	.224	.224	.224	.243	.243	.243	.243	.257	.257	.264	.264	.277	.284	.308
Weight, Grains	45	50	50	50	55	55	55	60	63	60	75	80	85	75	87	85	100	90	100	110
Density	.128	.142	.142	.142	.157	.157	.157	.171	.179	.145	.181	.194	.206	.162	.188	.174	.205	.168	.177	.166
Ballistic Coefficient	.210	.192	.222	.222	.237	.204	.237	.246	.231	.182	.217	.319	.315	.189	.293	.225	.259	.195	.209	.177
Catalog Number	1310	1320	1330	1340	1345	1350	1360	1375	1370	1500	1510	1515	1520	1600	1610	1700	1710	1800	1895	2110

From: N/A

TIPPED MATCHKING

Caliber & Description	224	224	243	264	284	308	308	308	308
Diameter, Inches	.224	.224	.243	.264	.284	.308	.308	.308	.308
Weight, Grains	69	77	95	130	160	125	155	168	175
Density	.196	.219	.243	.264	.284	.188	.233	.253	.264
Ballistic Coefficient	.375	.420	.500	.518	.600	.343	.519	.535	.545
Catalog Number	7169	7177	7295	7430	7660	7725	7755	7768	7775

From: N/A

Handgun Bullets

SPORTS MASTER

Caliber & Description	30 RN	32 JHC	9mm JHP	9mm JHP	9mm JHP	38 JHP Blitz	38 JHP	38 JSP	38 JHP	38 JHC	38 JSP	10mm JHP	10mm JHP
Diameter, Inches	.308	.312	.355	.355	.355	.357	.357	.357	.357	.357	.357	.400	.400
Weight, Grains	85	90	90	115	125	110	125	125	140	158	158	135	150
Density	.128	.132	.102	.130	.142	.123	.140	.140	.157	.177	.177	.121	.134
Ballistic Coefficient	.102	.125	.095	.107	.124	.120	.133	.133	.0776	.100	.100	.105	.120
Catalog Number	8005	8030	8100	8110	8125	8300	8320	8310	8325	8360	8340	8425	8430

Sierra Bullets

Handgun Bullets

Caliber & Description	10mm JHP	10mm JHP	41 JHC	41 JHC	44 JHC	44 JHC	44 JHC	44 JSP	45 JHP	45 JHP	45 JHC	45 JSP	50 JHP	50 JSP
Diameter, Inches	.400	.400	.410	.410	.4295	.4295	.4295	.4295	.4515	.4515	.4515	.4515	.500	.500
Weight, Grains	165	180	170	210	180	210	240	300	185	230	240	300	350	400
Density	.147	.161	.144	.178	.139	.163	.186	.232	.130	.161	.168	.210	.200	.229
Ballistic Coefficient	.130	.140	.123	.165	.130	.160	.185	.230	.100	.145	.150	.192	.155	.185
Catalog Number	8445	8460	8500	8520	8600	8620	8610	8630	8800	8805	8820	8830	5350	5400

From: N/A

V-Crown

Caliber & Description	9mm JHP	9mm JHP	9mm JHP	10mm JHP	45 JHP
Diameter, Inches	.355	.355	.355	.400	.4515
Weight, Grains	90	124	125	165	200
Density	.109	.160	.168	.147	.143
Ballistic Coefficient	.094	.120	.122	.132	.118
Catalog Number	9990	9924	9925	9465	9820

Box 100: N/A

Speer Bullets

Rifle Bullets

BOAT TAIL BULLETS

Caliber & Description	22 Match* HP	6mm SSP	6mm SSP	25 SHP	25 SSP	270 SSP	270 SSP	7mm SSP
Diameter, Inches	.224	.243	.243	.257	.257	.277	.277	.284
Weight, Grains	52	85	100	100	120	130	150	130
Density	.148	.206	.242	.216	.260	.242	.279	.230
Ballistic Coefficient	.253	.380	.446	.393	.480	.412	.489	.424
Catalog Number	1036	1213	1220	1408	1410	1458	1604	1624

*Match bullets are not recommended for use on game animals.

Caliber & Description	7mm SSP	7mm Match* HP	7mm SSP	30 SSP	30 SSP	30 Match* HP	30 SSP	338 SSP	375 SSP
Diameter, Inches	.284	.284	.284	.308	.308	.308	.308	.338	.375
Weight, Grains	145	145	160	150	165	168	180	225	270
Density	.257	.257	.284	.226	.248	.253	.271	.281	.274
Ballistic Coefficient	.472	.468	.519	.417	.520	.534	.545	.497	.478
Catalog Number	1628	1631	1634	2022	2034	2040	2052	2406	2472

*Match bullets are not recommended for use on game animals.

From: N/A

AMMUNITION

Speer Bullets

GRAND SLAM

Caliber & Description	6mm SP	25 HCSP	270 HCSP	270 HCSP	7mm HCSP	7mm HCSP	7mm HCSP	30 HCSP	30 HCSP	30 HCSP	338 HCSP	375 HCSP
Diameter, Inches	.243	.257	.277	.277	.284	.284	.284	.308	.308	.308	.338	.375
Weight, Grains	100	120	130	150	145	160	175	150	165	180	250	285
Density	.242	.260	.242	.279	.257	.283	.310	.226	.248	.271	.313	.290
Ballistic Coefficient	.327	.356	.332	.378	.353	.389	.436	.295	.354	.374	.436	.354
Catalog Number	1222	1415	1465	1608	1632	1638	1643	2026	2038	2063	2408	2473

From: N/A

HOT-COR BULLETS*

Caliber & Description	6mm SSP	25 SPFN	25 SSP	25 SSP	25 SSP	6.5mm SSP	6.5mm SSP	270 SSP	270 SSP	7mm SSP	7mm SPFN	7mm SSP
Diameter, Inches	.243	.257	.257	.257	.257	.264	.264	.277	.277	.284	.284	.284
Weight, Grains	90	75	87	100	120	120	140	130	150	130	130	145
Density	.218	.162	.188	.216	.260	.246	.287	.242	.279	.230	.230	.257
Ballistic Coefficient	.365	.135	.300	.334	.405	.392	.498	.383	.455	.394	.257	.416
Catalog Number	1217	1237	1241	1405	1411	1435	1441	1459	1605	1623	1625	1629

* Not recommended for lever-action rifles.

Caliber & Description	7mm SSP	30 Spire SP	30 FNSP	30 SPFN	30 RNSP	30 SSP	30 Mag-Tip	30 SSP	30 SSP	30 SPRN	30 SSP	30 SSP	7.62x39 SSP
Diameter, Inches	.284	.308	.308	.308	.308	.308	.308	.308	.308	.308	.308	.308	.310
Weight, Grains	160	110	130	150	150	150	150	165	170	180	180	200	123
Density	.283	.166	.196	.226	.226	.226	.226	.248	.256	.271	.271	.301	.183
Ballistic Coefficient	.504	.245	.213	.255	.235	.377	.301	.444	.298	.304	.441	.478	.283
Catalog Number	1635	1855	2007	2011	2017	2023	2025	2035	2041	2047	2053	2211	2213

* Not recommended for lever-action rifles.

Caliber & Description	303 SSP	303 RNSP	32 FNSP	8mm SSP	8mm SSSP	8mm SSP	338 SSP	35 FNSP	35 FNSP	35 SSP	9.3mm SSSP	375 SSSP	416 Mag-Tip	45 FNSP
Diameter, Inches	.311	.311	.321	.323	.323	.323	.338	.358	.358	.358	.366	.375	.416	.458
Weight, Grains	150	180	170	150	170	200	200	180	220	250	270	235	350	350
Density	.222	.266	.236	.205	.233	.274	.250	.201	.245	.279	.288	.239	.289	.238
Ballistic Coefficient	.351	.299	.283	.343	.311	.440	.426	.236	.286	.422	.361	.301	.332	.218
Catalog Number	2217	2223	2259	2277	2283	2285	2405	2435	2439	2453	2459	2471	2477	2478

From: N/A

Speer Bullets

JACKETED HP BULLETS

Caliber & Description	22 Hornet	45
Diameter, Inches	.224	.458
Weight, Grains	33	300
Density	.094	.204
Ballistic Coefficient	.080	.206
Catalog Number	1014	2482

From: N/A

SPECIAL PURPOSE BULLETS*

Caliber & Description	30 SPRN	30 HP	45 SPFN
Diameter, Inches	.308	.308	.458
Weight, Grains	100	110	400
Density	.151	.166	.272
Ballistic Coefficient	.144	.128	.259
Catalog Number	1805	1835	2479

From: N/A

TNT BULLETS

Caliber & Description	204 HP	22 HP	22 HP	6mm HP	25 HP	6.5mm HP	270 HP	7mm HP	30 HP
Diameter, Inches	.204	.224	.224	.243	.247	.264	.277	.284	.308
Weight, Grains	39	50	55	70	87	90	90	110	125
Density	.134	.142	.157	.169	.188	.184	.168	.195	.188
Ballistic Coefficient	.202	.228	.233	.279	.337	.281	.303	.384	.341
Catalog Number	1015	1030	1032	1206	1246	1445	1446	1616	1986

From: N/A

Handgun Bullets

GOLD DOT BULLETS

Caliber & Description	25 HP	32 Auto HP	327 Fed. Mag. HP	327 Fed. Mag. HP	380 Auto HP	9mm HP	9mm HP	9mm HP	357 SIG HP	38 Spl. HPSB	38 HPSB	357 Mag. HP	40/10mm HP
Diameter, Inches	.251	.312	.312	.312	.355	.355	.355	.355	.355	.357	.357	.357	.400
Weight, Grains	35	60	100	115	90	115	124	147	125	110	135	125	155
Density	.079	.088	.147	.168	.102	.130	.141	.167	.142	.123	.151	.177	.138
Ballistic Coefficient	.091	.118	.137	.180	.101	.125	.134	.164	.141	.117	.141	.140	.123
Catalog Number	3985	3986	3990	3988	3992	3994	3998	4002	4360	4009	4014	4012	4400

Caliber & Description	40/10mm HP	40/10mm HP	40/10mm HPSB	44 Spl. HP	44 Mag. HP	45 Auto HP	45 Auto HP	45 Auto HP	45 HPSB
Diameter, Inches	.400	.400	.400	.429	.429	.451	.451	.451	.451
Weight, Grains	165	180	180	.200	210	185	200	230	230
Density	.147	.161	.161	.155	.163	.130	.140	.162	.162
Ballistic Coefficient	.138	.143	.148	.145	.154	.109	.138	.143	.148
Catalog Number	4397	4406	4401	4427	4428	4470	4478	4483	4482

From: N/A

AMMUNITION

Speer Bullets

JACKETED BULLETS

Caliber & Description	9mm Luger FN JSP	38 Spl./357 Mag. JHP	38 Spl./357 Mag. JSP	38 Spl./357 Mag. JHP	38 Spl./357 Mag. JHP	38 Spl./357 Mag. JHP	38 Spl./357 Mag. JSP
Diameter, Inches	.355	.357	.357	.357	.357	.357	.357
Weight, Grains	124	110	125	125	140	158	158
Density	.141	.123	.140	.140	.157	.177	.177
Ballistic Coefficient	.115	.113	.129	.129	.145	.163	.164
Catalog Number	3997	4007	4011	4013	4203	4211	4217

Caliber & Description	44 Mag. JSP	44 Mag. JSP	45 Colt/460 S&W JHP	45 Colt/460 S&W JSP	50 Action Express JHP
Diameter, Inches	.429	.429	.451	.451	.186
Weight, Grains	240	300	260	300	325
Density	.186	.233	.183	.211	.186
Ballistic Coefficient	.169	.213	.183	.199	.169
Catalog Number	4454	4463	4481	4485	4495

From: N/A

LEGEND

FN	– Flat Nose	S	– Spitzer
HB	– Hollow Base	SP	– Soft Point
HC	– Hot-Cor	SS	– Semi-Spitzer
HP	– Hollow Point	SWC	– Semi-Wadcutter
J	– Jacketed	WC	– Wadcutter
RN	– Round Nose		

LEAD HANDGUN BULLETS

Caliber & Description	32 S&W HBWC	9mm Luger RN	38 HBWC	38 SWC	38 SWC HP	38 RN	44 SWC	45 Auto SWC	45 Auto RN	45 Colt SWC
Diameter, Inches	.314	.356	.358	.358	.358	.358	.430	.452	.452	.452
Weight, grains	98	125	148	158	158	158	240	200	230	250
Density	.142	.141	.165	.176	.176	.176	.185	.140	.161	.175
Ballistic Coefficient	.044	.155	.050	.123	.121	.170	.151	.078	.160	.117
Bulk Part No.	4600	4602	4618	4624	4628	4648	4661	4678	4691	4684
Bulk Count	1000	500	500	500	500	500	500	500	500	500

From: N/A

AMMUNITION

Swift Bullet Company

Rifle Bullets

The Scirocco II rifle bullet starts with a tough, pointed polymer tip that reduces air resistance, prevents tip deformation, and blends into the radius of its secant ogive nose section.

The Scirocco II has a bonded core construction with a pure lead core encased in a tapered, progressively thickening jacket of pure copper. The Swift A-Frame bullet with its midsec-tion wall of copper is less aerodynamic than the Scirocco, but it produces a broad mushroom while carrying almost all its weight through muscle and bone.

A-FRAME

Caliber & Description	25 SS	25 SS	6.5mm SS	6.5mm SS	270 SS	270 SS	270 SS	7mm SS	7mm SS	7mm SS	30-30 FN	30 SS	30-30 FN	30 SS	30 SS	8mm SS	8mm SS
Diameter, Inches	.257	.257	.264	.264	.277	.277	.277	.284	.284	.284	.308	.308	.308	.308	.308	.323	.323
Weight, Grains	100	120	120	140	130	140	150	140	160	175	150	165	170	180	200	200	200
Density	.216	.260	.246	.287	.242	.261	.279	.248	.283	.310	.226	.248	.256	.271	.301	.274	.301
Ballistic Coefficient	.318	.382	.344	.401	.323	.414	.444	.335	.450	.493	.220	.367	.266	.400	.444	.357	.393

Caliber & Description	338 SS	338 SS	338 SS	348 FN	35 SS	35 SS	35 SS	9.3mm SS	9.3mm SS	9.3mm SS	375 SS	375 SS	375 SS	400 SS	400 SS
Diameter, Inches	.338	.338	.338	.348	.358	.358	.358	.366	.366	.366	.375	.375	.375	.410	.410
Weight, Grains	225	250	275	200	225	250	280	250	286	300	250	270	300	350	400
Density	.281	.313	.344	.236	.251	.279	.312	.267	.305	.320	.254	.274	.305	.297	.339
Ballistic Coefficient	.384	.427	.469	.245	.312	.347	.388	.285	.385	.342	.271	.349	.325	.321	.367

AMMUNITION

Swift Bullet Company

Caliber & Description	416 SS	416 SS	404 SS	45-70 FN	458 FN	458 SS	458 SS	470 RN	505 RN	505 RN	50 FN	500 RN	500 RN
Diameter, Inches	.416	.416	.423	.457	.458	.458	.458	.475	.505	.505	.509	.509	.509
Weight, Grains	350	400	400	350	400	450	500	500	535	570	450	535	570
Density	.289	.330	.319	.238	.272	.307	.341	.329	.300	.319	.247	.294	.313
Ballistic Coefficient	.321	.367	.375	.172	.258	.325	.361	.364	.285	.306	.180	.285	.306

MSRP N/A

SCIROCCO

Caliber & Description	224 BTS	224 BTS	6mm BTS	25 BTS	6.5mm BTS	270 BTS	7mm BTS	30 BTS	30 BTS	30 BTS	338 BTS
Diameter, Inches	.224	.224	.243	.257	.264	.277	.284	.308	.308	.308	.338
Weight, Grains	62	75	90	100	130	130	150	150	165	180	210
Density	.177	.214	.218	.216	.266	.242	.266	.226	.248	.271	.263
Ballistic Coefficient	.307	.419	.419	.429	.571	.450	.515	.430	.470	.520	.507

MSRP N/A

> **LEGEND**
> **BT** – Boattail
> **FN** – Flat Nose
> **HP** – Hollow Point
> **RN** – Round Nose
> **S** – Spitzer
> **SS** – Semi-Spitzer

Handgun Bullets

A-FRAME HUNTING REVOLVER BULLETS

Caliber & Description	357 HP	357 HP	41 HP	44 HP	44 HP	44 HP	45 HP	45 HP	45 HP	50 HP
Diameter, Inches	.357	.357	.410	.430	.430	.430	.452	.452	.452	.499
Weight, Grains	158	180	210	240	280	300	265	300	325	325
Density	.177	.202	.178	.185	.216	.232	.185	.210	.227	.186
Ballistic Coefficient	.183	.189	.159	.119	.139	.147	.129	.153	.171	.135

MSRP N/A

> **LEGEND**
> **BT** – Boattail
> **FN** – Flat Nose
> **HP** – Hollow Point
> **RN** – Round Nose
> **S** – Spitzer
> **SS** – Semi-Spitzer

Woodleigh Bullets

HYDROSTATICALLY STABILIZED

Hydrostatic stabilization is a method of producing pierced hollow bars to very precise concentricity to produce a bullet that resists deflection and achieves deep straight-line penetration. It's non-toxic and environmentally sensitive. It can be used in most nitro double and magazine rifles.

10–20 per box: N/A

Caliber	Diameter	"Weight, Grains"	Catalog Number
7mm	.284	140	H7mm
308	.308	150	H308A
308	.308	180	H308
303	.312	215	H303
8mm	.323	170	H8mm
338	.338	185	H338A
338	.338	225	H338
358	.358	225	H358
9.3	.366	232	H9.3A
9,3	.366	286	H9.3
375 Win.	.375	235	H375A
375	.375	300	H375
450/400 3"	.410	400	H450/400

Caliber	Diameter	"Weight, Grains"	Catalog Number
416	.416	400	H416
404 Jeffery	.422	400	H404
450	.458	325	H450BPE
45/70	.458	400	H45/70
458	.458	450	H458A
458	.458	480	H458
465	.468	480	H465
470	.474	500	H470
500	.510	570	H500
50 Alaskan	.510	400	H50 Alaskan
505	.505	525	H505
577	.585	750	H577

98% & 95% RETAINED WEIGHT 300 WIN MAG 180GR PP

458 X 500GN SN RECOVERED FROM BUFFALO

270 WIN 150GN PP 86% RETAINED WEIGHT

94% RETAINED WEIGHT 300 WIN MAG 180GR PP

500/465 RECOVERED FROM BUFFALO

TRADITIONAL BULLETS

Fashioned from gilding-metal-clad steel 2mm thick, jackets on FMJ bullets are heavy at the nose for extra impact resistance. The jacket then tapers toward the base to assist rifling engraving. Woodleigh Weldcore Soft Nose bullets are made from 90/100 gilding metal (90 percent copper; 10 percent zinc) 1.6 mm thick.
50 per box: N/A

Caliber Diameter	Type	Weight, Grains	SD	BC	Catalog Number
6.5mm .264	PP SN	140	.287	.444	80
	PP SN	160	.328	.509	80A
	RN SN	160	.328	.285	80B
270 Win .277	PP SN	130	.242	.409	72
	PP SN	150	.279	.463	73
	PP SN	180	.334	.513	73A
7mm .284	PP SN	140	.248	.436	74
	PP SN	160	.283	.486	75
	PP SN	175	.310	.510	76
275 H&H .287	PP SN	160	.277	.474	77
	PP SN	175	.304	.509	78
308 .308	PP SN	130	.189	.302	65I
	PP SN	150	.226	.310	65F
	PP SN	165	.248	.320	65A
	PP SN	180	.271	.376	65B
	RN SN	220	.331	.367	65C
	FMJ	220	.331	.359	65
30-30 .308	FN SN	150	.226	.246	65H
30-06 .308	PP SN	240	.361	.401	65G
300 Win. Mag. .308	PP SN	180	.271	.435	65D
	PP SN	200	.301	.450	65E
303 British .312	PP SN	174	.255	.362	68A
	RN SN	215	.316	.359	68
303/ 7.62x39mm .312	PP SN	130	.180	.295	68B
8mm .323	RN SN	196	.268	.315	64B
	RN SN	220	.301	.355	64C
	RN SN	250	.343	.403	64D
325 Win. (8mm) .323	PP SN	200	.274	.406	64F
	PP SN	220	.301	.448	64G
8x57 .318	RN SN	200	.283	.331	64E
318 WR .330	RN SN	250	.328	.420	63
	FMJ	250	.328	.364	64
333 Jeffery .333	RN SN	250	.322	.335	60
	RN SN	300	.386	.418	61
	FMJ	300	.386	.418	62
338 Fed .338	PP SN	180	.226	.361	56C
	PP SN	200	.251	.401	56D
33 Win. .338	FN SN	200	.246	.234	56E
338 Mag .338	PP SN	225	.281	.425	56A
	RN SN	250	.313	.332	56
	PP SN	250	.313	.431	56B
	FMJ	250	.313	.326	57
	RN SN	300	.375	.416	58
	FMJ	300	.375	.414	59
348 Win. .348	FN SN	250	.295	.281	348
358 .358	RN SN	225	.251	.263	51
	PP SN	225	.251	.372	51A
	FMJ	225	.251	.263	52
	RN SN	250	.279	.300	53
	PP SN	250	.279	.400	53A
	PP SN	275	.307	.450	53B
	RN SN	310	.346	.458	54
	FMJ	310	.346	.458	55
9.3 .366	RN SN	250	.267	.281	47A
	PP SN	250	.267	.381	47C
	RN SN	286	.305	.321	47
	PP SN	286	.305	.396	47B
	FMJ	286	.305	.305	48
	RN SN	320	.341	.359	49
	PP SN	320	.341	.457	49A
	FMJ	320	.341	.341	50
375 Mag. .375	PP SN	235	.239	.310	42A
	RN SN	270	.274	.250	42
	PP SN	270	.274	.370	43A
	RN SN	300	.305	.277	44HD
	RN SN	300	.305	.277	44
	PP SN	300	.305	.380	45A
	FMJ	300	.305	.275	46
	RN SN	350	.356	.321	46B
	RN SN	350	.356	.323	46BHD
	PP SN	350	.356	.400	46C
	FMJ	350	.356	.307	46D
400 Purdey .405	RN SN	230	.200	.181	81
450/400 Nitro .408	RN SN	400	.344	.307	40A
450/400 Nitro .411	RN SN	400	.338	.307	40
450/400 Ruger .410	RN SN	400	.338	.307	40B
450/400 Ruger .408	FMJ	400	.344	.300	41A
.410 Ruger	FMJ	400	.338	.300	41
405 Win. .412	RN SN	300	.252	.194	71
416 Rigby .416	PP SN	340	.281	.330	39
	RN SN	410	.338	.307	37A
	FMJ	410	.338	.300	38
	RN SN	450	.371	.338	37B
	FMJ	450	.371	.330	38B"
416 Rem. .416	RN SN	400	.330	.305	37C
	FMJ	400	.330	.300	38C
	RN SN	450	.371	.338	37N
	FMJ	450	.371	.330	38N
404 Jeffery .422	RN SN	350	.281	.293	35
	RN SN	400	.321	.335	33A
	FMJ	400	.321	.330	34
	RN SN	450	.361	.360	33B
	FMJ	450	.361	.355	34B
10.75x68mm .423	RN SN	347	.277	.290	36
	FMJ	347	.277	.288	36A
444 Marlin .430	FN SN	280	.216	.186	444

Woodleigh Bullets

Caliber Diameter	Type	Weight, Grains	SD	BC	Catalog Number
425 WR .435	RN SN	410	.310	.222	31
	FMJ	410	.310	.221	32
11.2 Schuler .440	RN SN	401	.296	.325	67
458 Mag. .458	PP SN	400	.272	.340	30
	RN SN	480	.327	.328	24A
	FMJ	480	.327	.325	25A
	RN SN	500	.341	.310	26
	PP SN	500	.341	.378	26A
	FMJ	500	.341	.310	28
	RN SN	550	.375	.340	27
	FMJ	550	.375	.326	29
450 BPE .458	RN SN	350	.238	.250	30A
45/70 .458	FN SN	405	.276	.204	30B
	FN SN	300	.205	.196	30C
450 Nitro .458	RN SN	480	.327	.328	24
	FMJ	480	.327	.325	25
465 Nitro .468	RN SN	480	.313	.334	22
	FMJ	480	.313	.330	23
470 Nitro .474	RN SN	500	.318	.374	20
	FMJ	500	.318	.370	21
476 WR .476	RN SN	520	.328	.385	18
	FMJ	520	.328	.380	19
475 No. 2 .483	RN SN	480	.294	.309	15
	FMJ	480	.294	.300	16
475 No. 2 Jeffery .488	RN SN	500	.300	.315	13
	FMJ	500	.300	.300	14

Caliber Diameter	Type	Weight, Grains	SD	BC	Catalog Number
500 S&W MAG .500	FN SN	400	.229	.182	83
505 Gibbs .505	RN SN	525	.294	.345	11
	FMJ	525	.294	.340	12
	PP SN	600	.336	.360	11A
	FMJ	600	.336	.360	12A
500 Jeffery .510	RN SN	535	.294	.350	9
	PP SN	535	.294	.310	9A
	FMJ	535	.294	.340	10
	PP SN	600	.330	.350	10B
	FMJ	600	.330	.355	10A
500 BP .510	RN SN	440	.242	.255	8
50 Alaskan & 50/110 Win. .510	FN SN	500	.275	.219	82
500 Nitro .510	RN SN	450	.247	.257	06A
	RN SN	570	.313	.368	6
	FMJ	570	.313	.350	7
577 BP Express .585	RN SN	650	.271	.292	5
577 Nitro .585	RN SN	650	.271	.292	3A
	RN SN	750	.313	.346	3
577 Nitro .584	FMJ	650	.272	.292	4A
	FMJ	750	.314	.351	4
600 Nitro .620	RN SN	900	.334	.371	1
	FMJ	900	.334	.334	2
700 Nitro .700	RN SN	1000	.292	.340	A
	FMJ	1000	.292	.340	B

AMMUNITION

Centerfire Rifle Ballistics
Comprehensive Ballistics Tables for Currently Manufactured Sporting Rifle Cartridges

No more collecting catalogs and peering at microscopic print to find out what ammunition is offered for a cartridge, and how it performs relative to other factory loads! *Shooter's Bible* has assembled the data for you, in easy-to-read tables, by cartridge.

Data is taken from manufacturers' charts; your chronograph readings may vary. Listings are not intended as recommendations. For example, the data for the .44 Magnum at 400 yards shows its effective range is much shorter. The lack of data for a 285-grain .375 H&H bullet beyond 300 yards does not mean the bullet has no authority farther out. Besides ammunition, the rifle, sights, conditions and shooter ability all must be considered when contemplating a long shot. Accuracy and bullet energy both matter when big game is in the offing.

Barrel length affects velocity, and at various rates depending on the load. As a rule, figure 50 fps per inch of barrel, plus or minus, if your barrel is longer or shorter than 22 inches.

Bullets are given by make, weight (in grains) and type. Most type abbreviations are self-explanatory: BT=Boat-Tail, FMJ=Full Metal Jacket, HP=Hollow Point, SP=Soft Point—except in Hornady listings, where SP is the firm's Spire Point. TNT and TXP are trademarked designations of Speer and Norma. XLC identifies a coated Barnes X bullet. HE indicates a Federal High Energy load, similar to the Hornady LM (Light Magnum) and HM (Heavy Magnum) cartridges.

Arc (trajectory) is based on a zero range published by the manufacturer, from 100 to 300 yards. If a zero does not fall in a yardage column, it lies halfway between—at 150 yards, for example, if the bullet's strike is "+" at 100 yards and "-" at 200.

.17 HORNET TO .222 REMINGTON

CARTRIDGE BULLET	RANGE, YARDS:	0	100	200	300	400
.17 HORNET						
Hornady 15.5 NXT SPF		0	100	200	300	400
	velocity, fps	3860	2924	2159	1531	1108
	energy, ft-lb	513	294	160	81	42
	arc, inches	-1.5	+1.4	0	-9.1	-33.7
Hornady 20 V-MAX		0	100	200	300	400
	velocity, fps	3650	3077	2574	2122	1721
	energy, ft-lb	592	420	294	200	132
	arc, inches	-1.5	+1.1	0	-6.4	-20.7
.17 REMINGTON						
Rem. 20 AccuTip BT	velocity, fps	4250	3594	3028	2529	2081
	energy, ft-lb	802	574	407	284	192
	arc, inches		+1.3	+1.3	-2.5	-11.8
Rem. 20 Fireball	velocity, fps	4000	3380	2840	2360	1930
	energy, ft-lb	710	507	358	247	165
	arc, inches		+1.6	+1.5	-2.8	-13.5
Rem. 25 HP Power-Lokt	velocity, fps	4040	3284	2644	2086	1606
	energy, ft-lb	906	599	388	242	143
	arc, inches		+1.8	0	-3.3	-16.6
.204 RUGER						
Federal 32 Nosler Ballistic Tip	velocity, fps	4030	3465	2968	2523	2119
	arc, inches		+0.7	0	-4.7	-14.9
Federal 40 Ballistic Tip	velocity, fps	3650	3200	2790	2420	2080
	energy, ft-lb	1185	910	695	520	385
	arc, inches		+1.0	0	-5.4	-16.9
Hornady 32 V-Max	velocity, fps	4225	3632	3114	2652	2234
	energy, ft-lb	1268	937	689	500	355
	arc, inches		+0.6	0	-4.2	-13.4
Hornady 40 V-Max	velocity, fps	3900	3451	3046	2677	2335
	energy, ft-lb	1351	1058	824	636	485
	arc, inches		+0.7	0	-4.5	-13.9
Rem. 32 AccuTip	velocity, fps	4225	3632	3114	2652	2234
	Energy, ft-lb	1268	937	689	500	355
	Arc, inches		+0.6	0	-4.1	-13.1
Rem. 40 AccuTip	velocity, fps	3900	3451	3046	2677	2336
	energy, ft-lb	1351	1058	824	636	485
	arc, inches		+0.7	0	-4.3	-13.2
Win. 32 Ballistic Silver Tip	velocity, fps	4050	3482	2984	2537	2132
	energy, ft-lb	1165	862	632	457	323
	arc, inches		+0.7	0	-4.6	-14.7
Win. 34 HP	velocity, fps	4025	3339	2751	2232	1775
	energy, ft-lb	1223	842	571	376	238
	arc, inches		+0.8	0	-5.5	-18.1

CARTRIDGE BULLET	RANGE, YARDS:	0	100	200	300	400
.218 BEE						
Win. 46 Hollow Point	velocity, fps	2760	2102	1550	1155	961
	energy, ft-lb	778	451	245	136	94
	arc, inches		0	-7.2	-29.4	
.22 HORNET						
Federal 30 Speer TNT	velocity, fps	3150	2150	1390	990	830
	energy, ft-lb	660	310	130	65	45
	arc, inches		+3.3	0	-22.8	-78.7
Federal 45 JSP	velocity, fps	2690	2100	1590	1210	1000
	energy, ft-lb	725	440	255	145	100
	arc, inches		+3.3	0	-17.6	-59.5
Hornady 35 V-Max	velocity, fps	3100	2278	1601	1135	929
	energy, ft-lb	747	403	199	100	67
	arc, inches		+2.8	0	-16.9	-60.4
Rem. 35 AccuTip	velocity, fps	3100	2271	1591	1127	924
	energy, ft-lb	747	401	197	99	66
	arc, inches		+1.5	-3.5	-22.3	-68.4
Rem. 45 Pointed Soft Point	velocity, fps	2690	2042	1502	1128	948
	energy, ft-lb	723	417	225	127	90
	arc, inches		0	-7.1	-30.0	
Rem. 45 Hollow Point	velocity, fps	2690	2042	1502	1128	948
	energy, ft-lb	723	417	225	127	90
	arc, inches		0	-7.1	-30.0	
Win. 34 Jacketed HP	velocity, fps	3050	2132	1415	1017	852
	energy, ft-lb	700	343	151	78	55.
	arc, inches		0	-6.6	-29.9	
Win. 45 Soft Point	velocity, fps	2690	2042	1502	1128	948.
	energy, ft-lb	723	417	225	127	90
	arc, inches		0	-7.7	-31.3	
Win. 46 Hollow Point	velocity, fps	2690	2042	1502	1128	948.
	energy, ft-lb	739	426	230	130	92
	arc, inches		0	-7.7	-31.3	
.221 REMINGTON FIREBALL						
Rem. 50 AccuTip BT	velocity, fps	2995	2605	2247	1918	1622
	energy, ft-lb	996	753	560	408	292
	arc, inches		+1.8	0	-8.8	-27.1
.222 REMINGTON						
Federal 40 Ballistic Tip	velocity, fps	3450	2990	2570	2190	1840
	energy, ft-lb	1055	790	585	425	300
	arc, inches		+1.2	0	-6.5	-20.4

CARTRIDGE BULLET	RANGE, YARDS:	0	100	200	300	400
Federal 43 Speer TNT	velocity, fps:	3400	2750	2180	1680	1290
	energy, ft-lb:	1105	720	450	270	160
	arc, inches:		+1.6	0	-9.2	-31.4
Federal 50 Hi-Shok	velocity, fps:	3140	2600	2120	1700	1350
	energy, ft-lb:	1095	750	500	320	200
	arc, inches:		+1.9	0	-9.7	-31.6
Federal 55 FMJ boat-tail	velocity, fps:	3020	2740	2480	2230	1990
	energy, ft-lb:	1115	915	750	610	484
	arc, inches:		+1.6	0	-7.3	-21.5
Hornady 40 V-Max	velocity, fps:	3600	3117	2673	2269	1911
	energy, ft-lb:	1151	863	634	457	324
	arc, inches:		+1.1	0	-6.1	-18.9
Hornady 50 V-Max	velocity, fps:	3140	2729	2352	2008	1710
	energy, ft-lb:	1094	827	614	448	325
	arc, inches:		+1.7	0	-7.9	-24.4
Norma 50 Soft Point	velocity, fps:	3199	2667	2193	1771	
	energy, ft-lb:	1136	790	534	348	
	arc, inches:		+1.7	0	-9.1	
Norma 50 FMJ	velocity, fps:	2789	2326	1910	1547	
	energy, ft-lb:	864	601	405	266	
	arc, inches:		+2.5	0	-12.2	
Norma 62 Soft Point	velocity, fps:	2887	2457	2067	1716	
	energy, ft-lb:	1148	831	588	405	
	arc, inches:		+2.1	0	-10.4	
PMC 50 Pointed Soft Point	velocity, fps:	3044	2727	2354	2012	1651
	energy, ft-lb:	1131	908	677	494	333
	arc, inches:		+1.6	0	-7.9	-24.5
PMC 55 Pointed Soft Point	velocity, fps:	2950	2594	2266	1966	1693
	energy, ft-lb:	1063	822	627	472	350
	arc, inches:		+1.9	0	-8.7	-26.3
Rem. 50 Pointed Soft Point	velocity, fps:	3140	2602	2123	1700	1350
	energy, ft-lb:	1094	752	500	321	202
	arc, inches:		+1.9	0	-9.7	-31.7
Rem. 50 HP Power-Lokt	velocity, fps:	3140	2635	2182	1777	1432
	energy, ft-lb:	1094	771	529	351	228
	arc, inches:		+1.8	0	-9.2	-29.6
Rem. 50 AccuTip BT	velocity, fps:	3140	2744	2380	2045	1740
	energy, ft-lb:	1094	836	629	464	336
	arc, inches:		+1.6	0	-7.8	-23.9
Win. 40 Ballistic Silvertip	velocity, fps:	3370	2915	2503	2127	1786
	energy, ft-lb:	1009	755	556	402	283
	arc, inches:		+1.3	0	-6.9	-21.5
Win. 50 Pointed Soft Point	velocity, fps:	3140	2602	2123	1700	1350
	energy, ft-lb:	1094	752	500	321	202
	arc, inches:		+2.2	0	-10.0	-32.3

.222 REMINGTON MAGNUM

CARTRIDGE BULLET	RANGE, YARDS:	0	100	200	300	400
Nosler 40 BT	velocity, fps:	3600	3140	2726	2347	2000
	energy, ft-lb:	1150	876	660	489	355
	arc, inches:	-1.5	+1.0	0	-5.7	-17.8
Nosler 50 BT	velocity, fps:	3340	2917	2533	2179	1855
	energy, ft-lb:	1238	945	712	527	382
	arc, inches:	-1.5	+1.3	0	-6.8	-20.9

.223 REMINGTON

CARTRIDGE BULLET	RANGE, YARDS:	0	100	200	300	400
Black Hills 36 Varmint Grenade	velocity, fps:	w3750				
	energy, ft-lb:	1124				
	arc, inches:					
Black Hills 40 Nosler B. Tip	velocity, fps:	3600				
	energy, ft-lb:	1150				
	arc, inches:					
Black Hills 50 V-Max	velocity, fps:	3300				
	energy, ft-lb:	1209				
	arc, inches:					
Black Hills 52 Match HP	velocity, fps:	3300				
	energy, ft-lb:	1237				
	arc, inches:					
Black Hills 55 Softpoint	velocity, fps:	3250				
	energy, ft-lb:	1270				
	arc, inches:					

CARTRIDGE BULLET	RANGE, YARDS:	0	100	200	300	400
Black Hills 55 TSX	velocity, fps:	3200				
	energy, ft-lb:	1250				
	arc, inches:					
Black Hills 60 SP or V-Max	velocity, fps:	3150				
	energy, ft-lb:	1322				
	arc, inches:					
Black Hills 60 Partition	velocity, fps:	3150				
	energy, ft-lb:	1322				
	arc, inches:					
Black Hills 62 TSX	velocity, fps:	3100				
	energy, ft-lb:	1323				
	arc, inches:					
Black Hills 68 Heavy Match	velocity, fps:	2850				
	energy, ft-lb:	1227				
	arc, inches:					
Black Hills 69 OTM	velocity, fps:	2875				
	energy, ft-lb:	1266				
	arc, inches:					
Black Hills 69 Sierra MK	velocity, fps:	2850				
	energy, ft-lb:	1245				
	arc, inches:					
Black Hills 73 Berger BTHP	velocity, fps:	2750				
	energy, ft-lb:	1226				
	arc, inches:					
Black Hills 75 Heavy Match	velocity, fps:	2750				
	energy, ft-lb:	1259				
	arc, inches:					
Black Hills 77 Sierra MKing	velocity, fps:	2750				
	energy, ft-lb:	1293				
	arc, inches:					
Black Hills 77 Tipped MatchKing	velocity, fps:	2750				
	energy, ft-lb:	1293				
	arc, inches:					
Federal 40 Ballistic Tip	velocity, fps:	3700	3210	2770	2370	2010
	energy, ft-lb:	1215	915	680	500	360
	arc, inches:		+0.9	0	-5.5	-17.3
Federal 43 Speer TNT	velocity, fps:	3600	2920	2330	1810	1390
	energy, ft-lb:	1235	810	515	315	185
	arc, inches:		+1.3	0	-7.9	-27.1
Federal 50 Jacketed HP	velocity, fps:	3400	2910	2460	2060	1700
	energy, ft-lb:	1285	940	675	470	320
	arc, inches:		+1.3	0	-7.1	-22.7
Federal 50 Speer TNT HP	velocity, fps:	3300	2860	2450	2080	1750
	energy, ft-lb:	1210	905	670	480	340
	arc, inches:		+1.4	0	-7.3	-22.6
Federal 52 Sierra MatchKing BTHP	velocity, fps:	3300	2860	2460	2090	1760
	energy, ft-lb:	1255	945	700	505	360
	arc, inches:		+1.4	0	-7.2	-22.4
Federal 55 Hi-Shok	velocity, fps:	3240	2750	2300	1910	1550
	energy, ft-lb:	1280	920	650	445	295
	arc, inches:		+1.6	0	-8.2	-26.1
Federal 55 FMJ boat-tail	velocity, fps:	3240	2950	2670	2410	2170
	energy, ft-lb:	1280	1060	875	710	575
	arc, inches:		+1.3	0	-6.1	-18.3
Federal 55 Sierra GameKing BTHP	velocity, fps:	3240	2770	2340	1950	1610
	energy, ft-lb:	1280	935	670	465	315
	arc, inches:		+1.5	0	-8.0	-25.3
Federal 55 Trophy Bonded	velocity, fps:	3100	2630	2210	1830	1500
	energy, ft-lb:	1175	845	595	410	275
	arc, inches:		+1.8	0	-8.9	-28.7
Federal 55 Nosler Bal. Tip	velocity, fps:	3240	2870	2530	2220	1920
	energy, ft-lb:	1280	1005	780	600	450
	arc, inches:		+1.4	0	-6.8	-20.8
Federal 55 Sierra BlitzKing	velocity, fps:	3240	2870	2520	2200	1910
	energy, ft-lb:	1280	1005	775	590	445
	arc, inches:		+-1.4	0	-6.9	-20.9

Centerfire Rifle Ballistics

.223 REMINGTON TO 5.6X52 R

CARTRIDGE BULLET	RANGE, YARDS:	0	100	200	300	400
Federal 60 Partition	velocity, fps:	3160	2740	2350	2000	1680
	energy, ft-lb:	1330	1000	735	530	375
	arc, inches:		+1.6	0	-7.9	-24.8
Federal 62 FMJ	velocity, fps:	3020	2650	2310	2000	1710
	energy, ft-lb:	1225	970	735	550	405
	arc, inches:		+1.7	0	-8.4	-25.5
Federal 64 Hi-Shok SP	velocity, fps:	3090	2690	2325	1990	1680
	energy, ft-lb:	1360	1030	770	560	400
	arc, inches:		+1.7	0	-8.2	-25.2
Federal 69 Sierra MatchKing BTHP	velocity, fps:	3000	2720	2460	2210	1980
	energy, ft-lb:	1380	1135	925	750	600
	arc, inches:		+1.6	0	-7.4	-21.9
Hornady 40 V-Max	velocity, fps:	3800	3305	2845	2424	2044
	energy, ft-lb:	1282	970	719	522	371
	arc, inches:		+0.8	0	-5.3	-16.6
Hornady 53 Hollow Point	velocity, fps:	3330	2882	2477	2106	1710
	energy, ft-lb:	1305	978	722	522	369
	arc, inches:		+1.7	0	-7.4	-22.7
Hornady 55 V-Max	velocity, fps:	3240	2859	2507	2181	1891
	energy, ft-lb:	1282	998	767	581	437
	arc, inches:		+1.4	0	-7.1	-21.4
Hornady 75 BTHP Superformance Match	velocity, fps:	2930	2695	2471	2259	2057
	energy, ft-lb:	1430	1209	1017	850	705
	arc, inches:		+1.7	0	-7.4	-21.6
Hornady 55 TAP-FPD	velocity, fps:	3240	2854	2500	2172	1871
	energy, ft-lb:	1282	995	763	576	427
	arc, inches:		+1.4	0	-7.0	-21.4
Hornady 55 Urban Tactical	velocity, fps:	2970	2626	2307	2011	1739
	energy, ft-lb:	1077	842	650	494	369
	arc, inches:		+1.5	0	-8.1	-24.9
Hornady 60 Soft Point	velocity, fps:	3150	2782	2442	2127	1837
	energy, ft-lb:	1322	1031	795	603	450
	arc, inches:		+1.6	0	-7.5	-22.5
Hornady 60 TAP-FPD	velocity, fps:	3115	2754	2420	2110	1824
	energy, ft-lb:	1293	1010	780	593	443
	arc, inches:		+1.6	0	-7.5	-22.9
Hornady 60 Urban Tactical	velocity, fps:	2950	2619	2312	2025	1762
	energy, ft-lb:	1160	914	712	546	413
	arc, inches:		+1.6	0	-8.1	-24.7
Hornady 75 BTHP Match	velocity, fps:	2790	2554	2330	2119	1926
	energy, ft-lb:	1296	1086	904	747	617
	arc, inches:		+2.4	0	-8.8	-25.1
Hornacy 75 TAP-FPD	velocity, fps:	2790	2582	2383	2193	2012
	energy, ft-lb:	1296	1110	946	801	674
	arc, inches:		+1.9	0	-8.0	-23.2
Hornady 75 BTHP Tactical	velocity, fps:	2630	2409	2199	2000	1814
	energy, ft-lb:	1152	966	805	666	548
	arc, inches:		+2.0	0	-9.2	-25.9
PMC 40 non-toxic	velocity, fps:	3500	2606	1871	1315	
	energy, ft-lb:	1088	603	311	154	
	arc, inches:		+2.6	0	-12.8	
PMC 50 Sierra BlitzKing	velocity, fps:	3300	2874	2484	2130	1809
	energy, ft-lb:	1209	917	685	504	363
	arc, inches:		+1.4	0	-7.1	-21.8
PMC 52 Sierra HPBT Match	velocity, fps:	3200	2808	2447	2117	1817
	energy, ft-lb:	1182	910	691	517	381
	arc, inches:		+1.5	0	-7.3	-22.5
PMC 53 Barnes XLC	velocity, fps:	3200	2815	2461	2136	1840
	energy, ft-lb:	1205	933	713	537	398
	arc, inches:		+1.5	0	-7.2	-22.2
PMC 55 HP boat-tail	velocity, fps:	3240	2717	2250	1832	1473
	energy, ft-lb:	1282	901	618	410	265
	arc, inches:		+1.6	0	-8.6	-27.7
PMC 55 FMJ boat-tail	velocity, fps:	3195	2882	2525	2169	1843
	energy, ft-lb:	1246	1014	779	574	415
	arc, inches:		+1.4	0	-6.8	-21.1
PMC 55 Pointed Soft Point	velocity, fps:	3112	2767	2421	2100	1806
	energy, ft-lb:	1182	935	715	539	398
	arc, inches:		+1.5	0	-7.5	-22.9

CARTRIDGE BULLET	RANGE, YARDS:	0	100	200	300	400
PMC 64 Pointed Soft Point	velocity, fps:	2775	2511	2261	2026	1806
	energy, ft-lb:	1094	896	726	583	464
	arc, inches:		+2.0	0	-8.8	-26.1
PMC 69 Sierra BTHP Match	velocity, fps:	2900	2591	2304	2038	1791
	energy, ft-lb:	1288	1029	813	636	492
	arc, inches:		+1.9	0	-8.4	-25.3
Rem. 50 AccuTip BT	velocity, fps:	3300	2889	2514	2168	1851
	energy, ft-lb:	1209	927	701	522	380
	arc, inches:		+1.4	0	-6.9	-21.2
Rem. 55 Pointed Soft Point	velocity, fps:	3240	2747	2304	1905	1554
	energy, ft-lb:	1282	921	648	443	295
	arc, inches:		+1.6	0	-8.2	-26.2
Rem. 55 HP Power-Lokt	velocity, fps:	3240	2773	2352	1969	1627
	energy, ft-lb:	1282	939	675	473	323
	arc, inches:		+1.5	0	-7.9	-24.8
Rem. 55 AccuTip BT	velocity, fps:	3240	2854	2500	2172	1871
	energy, ft-lb:	1282	995	763	576	427
	arc, inches:		+1.5	0	-7.1	-21.7
Rem. 55 Metal Case	velocity, fps:	3240	2759	2326	1933	1587
	energy, ft-lb:	1282	929	660	456	307
	arc, inches:		+1.6	0	-8.1	-25.5
Remington 62 Core-Lokt Ultra Bonded	velocity, fps:	3100	2695	2324	1983	1676
	energy, ft-lb:	1323	1000	743	541	386
	arc, inches:		+1.7				
Rem. 62 HP Match	velocity, fps:	3025	2572	2162	1792	1471
	energy, ft-lb:	1260	911	643	442	298
	arc, inches:		+1.9	0	-9.4	-29.9
Rem. 69 BTHP Match	velocity, fps:	3000	2720	2457	2209	1975
	energy, ft-lb:	1379	1133	925	747	598
	arc, inches:		+1.6	0	-7.4	-21.9
Win. 40 Ballistic Silvertip	velocity, fps:	3700	3166	2693	2265	1879.
	energy, ft-lb:	1216	891	644	456	314
	arc, inches:		+1.0	0	-5.8	-18.4
Win. 45 JHP	velocity, fps:	3600				
	energy, ft-lb:	1295				
	arc, inches:					
Win. 50 Ballistic Silvertip	velocity, fps:	3410	2982	2593	2235	1907.
	energy, ft-lb:	1291	987	746	555	404
	arc, inches:		+1.2	0	-6.4	-19.8
Win. 53 Hollow Point	velocity, fps:	3330	2882	2477	2106	1770
	energy, ft-lb:	1305	978	722	522	369
	arc, inches:		+1.7	0	-7.4	-22.7
Win. 55 Pointed Soft Point	velocity, fps:	3240	2747	2304	1905	1554.
	energy, ft-lb:	1282	921	648	443	295
	arc, inches:		+1.9	0	-8.5	-26.7
Win. 55 Super Clean NT	velocity, fps:	3150	2520	1970	1505	1165
	energy, ft-lb:	1212	776	474	277	166
	arc, inches:		+2.8	0	-11.9	-38.9
Win. 55 FMJ	velocity, fps:	3240	2854			
	energy, ft-lb:	1282	995			
	arc, inches:					
Win. 55 Ballistic Silvertip	velocity, fps:	3240	2871	2531	2215	1923
	energy, ft-lb:	1282	1006	782	599	451
	arc, inches:		+1.4	0	-6.8	-20.8
Win. 64 Power-Point	velocity, fps:	3020	2656	2320	2009	1724
	energy, ft-lb:	1296	1003	765	574	423
	arc, inches:		+1.7	0	-8.2	-25.1
Win. 64 Power-Point Plus	velocity, fps:	3090	2684	2312	1971	1664
	energy, ft-lb:	1357	1024	760	552	393
	arc, inches:		+1.7	0	-8.2	-25.4
Winchester 69 BTHP Match	velocity, fps:	3060	2740	2442	2163	1902
	energy, ft-lb:	1434	1150	913	716	554
	arc, inches:		+1.6	0	-7.4	-22.4

5.6x52 R

CARTRIDGE BULLET	RANGE, YARDS:	0	100	200	300	400
Norma 71 Soft Point	velocity, fps:	2789	2446	2128	1835	
	energy, ft-lb:	1227	944	714	531	
	arc, inches:		+2.1	0	-9.9	

CARTRIDGE BULLET	RANGE, YARDS:	0	100	200	300	400
.22 PPC						
A-Square 52 Berger	velocity, fps:	3300	2952	2629	2329	2049
	energy, ft-lb:	1257	1006	798	626	485
	arc, inches:		+1.3	0	-6.3	-19.1
.225 WINCHESTER						
Win. 55 Pointed Soft Point	velocity, fps:	3570	3066	2616	2208	1838.
	energy, ft-lb:	1556	1148	836	595	412
	arc, inches:		+2.4	+2.0	-3.5	-16.3
.224 WEATHERBY MAGNUM						
Wby. 55 Pointed Expanding	velocity, fps:	3650	3192	2780	2403	2056
	energy, ft-lb:	1627	1244	944	705	516
	arc, inches:		+2.8	+3.7	0	-9.8
.22-250 REMINGTON						
Black Hills 50 Nos. Bal. Tip	velocity, fps:	3700				
	energy, ft-lb:	1520				
	arc, inches:					
Black Hills 60 Nos. Partition	velocity, fps:	3550				
	energy, ft-lb:	1679				
	arc, inches:					
Federal 40 Nos. Bal. Tip	velocity, fps:	4150	3610	3130	2700	2300
	energy, ft-lb:	1530	1155	870	645	470
	arc, inches:		+0.6	0	-4.2	-13.2
Federal 40 Sierra Varminter	velocity, fps:	4000	3320	2720	2200	1740
	energy, ft-lb:	1420	980	660	430	265
	arc, inches:		+0.8	0	-5.6	-18.4
Federal 43 Speer TNT	velocity, fps:	4000	3250	2650	2070	1590
	energy, ft-lb:	1530	1010	655	405	240
	arc, inches:		+0.9	0	-6.1	-20.8
Federal 55 Hi-Shok	velocity, fps:	3680	3140	2660	2220	1830
	energy, ft-lb:	1655	1200	860	605	410
	arc, inches:		+1.0	0	-6.0	-19.1
Federal 55 Sierra BlitzKing	velocity, fps:	3680	3270	2890	2540	2220
	energy, ft-lb:	1655	1300	1020	790	605
	arc, inches:		+0.9	0	-5.1	-15.6
Federal 55 Sierra GameKing BTHP	velocity, fps:	3680	3280	2920	2590	2280
	energy, ft-lb:	1655	1315	1040	815	630
	arc, inches:		+0.9	0	-5.0	-15.1
Federal 55 Trophy Bonded	velocity, fps:	3600	3080	2610	2190	1810.
	energy, ft-lb:	1585	1155	835	590	400.
	arc, inches:		+1.1	0	-6.2	-19.8
Hornady 35 NTX Superformance Varmint	velocity, fps:	4450	3736	3128	2598	2125
	energy, ft-lb:	1539	1085	761	524	351
	arc, inches:		+0.5	0	-4.1	-13.4
Hornady 40 V-Max	velocity, fps:	4150	3631	3147	2699	2293
	energy, ft-lb:	1529	1171	879	647	467
	arc, inches:		+0.5	0	-4.2	-13.3
Hornady 50 V-Max	velocity, fps:	3800	3349	2925	2535	2178
	energy, ft-lb:	1603	1245	950	713	527
	arc, inches:		+0.8	0	-5.0	-15.6
Hornady 50 V-Max Superformance Varmint	velocity, fps:	4000	3517	3086	2696	2337
	energy, ft-lb:	1776	1373	1057	807	606
	arc, inches:		+0.7	0	-4.3	-13.5
Hornady 53 Hollow Point	velocity, fps:	3680	3185	2743	2341	1974.
	energy, ft-lb:	1594	1194	886	645	459
	arc, inches:		+1.0	0	-5.7	-17.8
Hornady 55 V-Max	velocity, fps:	3680	3265	2876	2517	2183
	energy, ft-lb:	1654	1302	1010	772	582
	arc, inches:		+0.9	0	-5.3	-16.1
Hornady 60 Soft Point	velocity, fps:	3600	3195	2826	2485	2169
	energy, ft-lb:	1727	1360	1064	823	627
	arc, inches:		+1.0	0	-5.4	-16.3

CARTRIDGE BULLET	RANGE, YARDS:	0	100	200	300	400
Norma 53 Soft Point	velocity, fps:	3707	3234	2809	1716	
	energy, ft-lb:	1618	1231	928	690	
	arc, inches:		+0.9	0	-5.3	
PMC 50 Sierra BlitzKing	velocity, fps:	3725	3264	2641	2455	2103
	energy, ft-lb:	1540	1183	896	669	491
	arc, inches:		+0.9	0	-5.2	-16.2
PMC 50 Barnes XLC	velocity, fps:	3725	3280	2871	2495	2152
	energy, ft-lb:	1540	1195	915	691	514.
	arc, inches:		+0.9	0	-5.1	-15.9.
PMC 55 HP boat-tail	velocity, fps:	3680	3104	2596	2141	1737
	energy, ft-lb:	1654	1176	823	560	368
	arc, inches:		+1.1	0	-6.3	-20.2
PMC 55 Pointed Soft Point	velocity, fps:	3586	3203	2852	2505	2178
	energy, ft-lb:	1570	1253	993	766	579
	arc, inches:		+1.0	0	-5.2	-16.0
Rem. 50 AccuTip BT (also in EtronX)	velocity, fps:	3725	3272	2864	2491	2147
	energy, ft-lb:	1540	1188	910	689	512
	arc, inches:		+1.7	+1.6	-2.8	-12.8
Rem. 55 Pointed Soft Point	velocity, fps:	3680	3137	2656	2222	1832
	energy, ft-lb:	1654	1201	861	603	410
	arc, inches:		+1.9	+1.8	-3.3	-15.5
Rem. 55 HP Power-Lokt	velocity, fps:	3680	3209	2785	2400	2046.
	energy, ft-lb:	1654	1257	947	703	511
	arc, inches:		+1.8	+1.7	-3.0	-13.7
Rem. 60 Nosler Partition (also in EtronX)	velocity, fps:	3500	3045	2634	2258	1914
	energy, ft-lb:	1632	1235	924	679	488
	arc, inches:		+2.1	+1.9	-3.4	-15.5
Win. 40 Ballistic Silvertip	velocity, fps:	4150	3591	3099	2658	2257
	energy, ft-lb:	1530	1146	853	628	453
	arc, inches:		+0.6	0	-4.2	-13.4
Win. 50 Ballistic Silvertip	velocity, fps:	3810	3341	2919	2536	2182
	energy, ft-lb:	1611	1239	946	714	529.
	arc, inches:		+0.8	0	-4.9	-15.2
Win. 55 Pointed Soft Point	velocity, fps:	3680	3137	2656	2222	1832
	energy, ft-lb:	1654	1201	861	603	410
	arc, inches:		+2.3	+1.9	-3.4	-15.9
Win. 55 Ballistic Silvertip	velocity, fps:	3680	3272	2900	2558	2240
	energy, ft-lb:	1654	1307	1027	799	613
	arc, inches:		+0.9	0	-5.0	-15.4
Win. 64 Power-Point	velocity, fps:	3500	3086	2708	2360	2038
	energy, ft-lb:	1741	1353	1042	791	590
	arc, inches:		+1.1	0	-5.9	-18.0
.220 SWIFT						
Federal 52 Sierra MatchKing BTHP	velocity, fps:	3830	3370	2960	2600	2230
	energy, ft-lb:	1690	1310	1010	770	575
	arc, inches:		+0.8	0	-4.8	-14.9
Federal 55 Sierra BlitzKing	velocity, fps:	3800	3370	2990	2630	2310.
	energy, ft-lb:	1765	1390	1090	850	650
	arc, inches:		+0.8	0	-4.7	-14.4
Federal 55 Trophy Bonded	velocity, fps:	3700	3170	2690	2270	1880
	energy, ft-lb:	1670	1225	885	625	430
	arc, inches:		+1.0	0	-5.8	-18.5
Hornady 40 V-Max	velocity, fps:	4200	3678	3190	2739	2329
	energy, ft-lb:	1566	1201	904	666	482
	arc, inches:		+0.5	0	-4.0	-12.9
Hornady 50 V-Max	velocity, fps:	3850	3396	2970	2576	2215.
	energy, ft-lb:	1645	1280	979	736	545
	arc, inches:		+0.7	0	-4.8	-15.1
Hornady 50 SP	velocity, fps:	3850	3327	2862	2442	2060.
	energy, ft-lb:	1645	1228	909	662	471
	arc, inches:		+0.8	0	-5.1	-16.1
Hornady 55 V-Max	velocity, fps:	3680	3265	2876	2517	2183
	energy, ft-lb:	1654	1302	1010	772	582
	arc, inches:		+0.9	0	-5.3	-16.1
Hornady 60 Hollow Point	velocity, fps:	3600	3199	2824	2475	2156
	energy, ft-lb:	1727	1364	1063	816	619
	arc, inches:		+1.0	0	-5.4	-16.3
Norma 50 Soft Point	velocity, fps:	4019	3380	2826	2335	
	energy, ft-lb:	1794	1268	887	605	
	arc, inches:		+0.7	0	-5.1	

Centerfire Rifle Ballistics

.220 SWIFT TO .243 WINCHESTER

CARTRIDGE BULLET	RANGE, YARDS:	0	100	200	300	400
Rem. 50 Pointed Soft Point	velocity, fps:	3780	3158	2617	2135	1710
	energy, ft-lb:	1586	1107	760	506	325
	arc, inches:		+0.3	-1.4	-8.2	
Rem. 50 V-Max boat-tail	velocity, fps:	3780	3321	2908	2532	2185
(also in EtronX)	energy, ft-lb:	1586	1224	939	711	530
	arc, inches:		+0.8	0	-5.0	-15.4
Win. 40 Ballistic Silvertip	velocity, fps:	4050	3518	3048	2624	2238.
	energy, ft-lb:	1457	1099	825	611	445
	arc, inches:		+0.7	0	-4.4	-13.9
Win. 50 Pointed Soft Point	velocity, fps:	3870	3310	2816	2373	1972
	energy, ft-lb:	1663	1226	881	625	432
	arc, inches:		+0.8	0	-5.2	-16.7

.223 WSSM

CARTRIDGE BULLET	RANGE, YARDS:	0	100	200	300	400
Win. 55 Ballistic Silvertip	velocity, fps:	3850	3438	3064	2721	2402
	energy, ft-lb:	1810	1444	1147	904	704
	arc, inches:		+0.7	0	-4.4	-13.6
Win. 55 Pointed Softpoint	velocity, fps:	3850	3367	2934	2541	2181
	energy, ft-lb:	1810	1384	1051	789	581
	arc, inches:		+0.8	0	-4.9	-15.1
Win. 64 Power-Point	velocity, fps:	3600	3144	2732	2356	2011
	energy, ft-lb:	1841	1404	1061	789	574
	arc, inches:		+1.0	0	-5.7	-17.7

6MM PPC

CARTRIDGE BULLET	RANGE, YARDS:	0	100	200	300	400
A-Square 68 Berger	velocity, fps:	3100	2751	2428	2128	1850
	energy, ft-lb:	1451	1143	890	684	516
	arc, inches:		+1.5	0	-7.5	-22.6

6x70 R

CARTRIDGE BULLET	RANGE, YARDS:	0	100	200	300	400
Norma 95 Nosler Bal. Tip	velocity, fps:	2461	2231	2013	1809	
	energy, ft-lb:	1211	995	810	654	
	arc, inches:		+2.7	0	-11.3	

.243 WINCHESTER

CARTRIDGE BULLET	RANGE, YARDS:	0	100	200	300	400
Black Hills 55 Nosler B. Tip	velocity, fps:	3800				
	energy, ft-lb:	1763				
	arc, inches:					
Black Hills 95 Nosler B. Tip	velocity, fps:	2950				
	energy, ft-lb:	1836				
	arc, inches:					
Federal 70 Nosler Bal. Tip	velocity, fps:	3400	3070	2760	2470	2200
	energy, ft-lb:	1795	1465	1185	950	755.
	arc, inches:		+1.1	0	-5.7	-17.1
Federal 70 Speer TNT HP	velocity, fps:	3400	3040	2700	2390	2100
	energy, ft-lb:	1795	1435	1135	890	685
	arc, inches:		+1.1	0	-5.9	-18.0
Federal 80 Sierra Pro-Hunter	velocity, fps:	3350	2960	2590	2260	1950
	energy, ft-lb:	1995	1550	1195	905	675
	arc, inches:		+1.3	0	-6.4	-19.7
Federal 85 Sierra GameKing BTHP	velocity, fps:	3320	3070	2830	2600	2380
	energy, ft-lb:	2080	1770	1510	1280	1070
	arc, inches:		+1.1	0	-5.5	-16.1
Federal 85 Trophy Copper	velocity, fps:	3200	2950	2710	2480	2270
	energy, ft-lb:	1935	1640	1385	1160	970
	arc, inches:		+1.3	0	-6.0	-17.6
Federal 90 Trophy Bonded	velocity, fps:	3100	2850	2610	2380	2160.
	energy, ft-lb:	1920	1620	1360	1130	935
	arc, inches:		+1.4	0	-6.1	-19.2
Federal 100 Hi-Shok	velocity, fps:	2960	2700	2450	2220	1990
	energy, ft-lb:	1945	1615	1330	1090	880
	arc, inches:		+1.6	0	-7.5	-22.0
Federal 100 Sierra GameKing BTSP	velocity, fps:	2960	2760	2570	2380	2210
	energy, ft-lb:	1950	1690	1460	1260	1080
	arc, inches:		+1.5	0	-6.8	-19.8
Federal 100 Nosler Partition	velocity, fps:	2960	2730	2510	2300	2100
	energy, ft-lb:	1945	1650	1395	1170	975.
	arc, inches:		+1.6	0	-7.1	-20.9
Hornady 58 V-Max Superformance Varmint	velocity, fps:	3925	3465	3052	2676	2330
	energy, ft-lb:	1984	1546	1200	922	699
	arc, inches:		+0.7	0	-4.4	-13.8
Hornady 75 Hollow Point	velocity, fps:	3400	2970	2578	2219	1890
	energy, ft-lb:	1926	1469	1107	820	595

CARTRIDGE BULLET	RANGE, YARDS:	0	100	200	300	400
	arc, inches:		+1.2	0	-6.5	-20.3
Hornady 80 GMX Superformance	velocity, fps:	3425	3081	2763	2468	2190
	energy, ft-lb:	2084	1686	1357	1082	852
	arc, inches:		+1.1	0	-5.7	-17.1
Hornady 87 SST Custom Lite	velocity, fps:	2800	2574	2359	2155	1961
	energy, ft-lb:	1514	1280	1075	897	743
	arc, inches:		+1.9	0	-8.1	-23.8
Hornady 95 SST Superformance	velocity, fps:	3185	2908	2649	2404	2172
	energy, ft-lb:	2140	1784	1480	1219	995
	arc, inches:		+1.3	0	-6.3	-18.6
Hornady 100 BTSP	velocity, fps:	2960	2728	2508	2299	2099
	energy, ft-lb:	1945	1653	1397	1174	979
	arc, inches:		+1.6	0	-7.2	-21.0
Hornady 100 BTSP LM	velocity, fps:	3100	2839	2592	2358	2138
	energy, ft-lb:	2133	1790	1491	1235	1014
	arc, inches:		+1.5	0	-6.8	-19.8
Norma 80 FMJ	velocity, fps:	3117	2750	2412	2098	
	energy, ft-lb:	1726	1344	1034	782	
	arc, inches:		+1.5	0	-7.5	
Norma 100 FMJ	velocity, fps:	3018	2747	2493	2252	
	energy, ft-lb:	2023	1677	1380	1126	
	arc, inches:		+1.5	0	-7.1	
Norma 100 Soft Point	velocity, fps:	3018	2748	2493	2252	
	energy, ft-lb:	2023	1677	1380	1126	
	arc, inches:		+1.5	0	-7.1	
Norma 100 Oryx	velocity, fps:	3018	2653	2316	2004	
	energy, ft-lb:	2023	1563	1191	892	
	arc, inches:		+1.7	0	-8.3	
PMC 80 Pointed Soft Point	velocity, fps:	2940	2684	2444	2215	1999
	energy, ft-lb:	1535	1280	1060	871	709
	arc, inches:		+1.7	0	-7.5	-22.1
PMC 85 Barnes XLC	velocity, fps:	3250	3022	2805	2598	2401
	energy, ft-lb:	1993	1724	1485	1274	1088
	arc, inches:		+1.6	0	-5.6	16.3
PMC 85 HP boat-tail	velocity, fps:	3275	2922	2596	2292	2009
	energy, ft-lb:	2024	1611	1272	991	761
	arc, inches:		+1.3	0	-6.5	-19.7
PMC 100 Pointed Soft Point	velocity, fps:	2743	2507	2283	2070	1869
	energy, ft-lb:	1670	1395	1157	951	776
	arc, inches:		+2.0	0	-8.7	-25.5
PMC 100 SP boat-tail	velocity, fps:	2960	2742	2534	2335	2144
	energy, ft-lb:	1945	1669	1425	1210	1021
	arc, inches:		+1.6	0	-7.0	-20.5
Rem. 75 AccuTip BT	velocity, fps:	3375	3065	2775	2504	2248
	energy, ft-lb:	1897	1564	1282	1044	842
	arc, inches:		+2.0	+1.8	-3.0	-13.3
Remington 80 Copper Solid Tipped	velocity, fps:	3350	3011	2696	2403	2128
	energy, ft-lb:	1993	1610	1291	1025	894
	arc, inches:		+1.2	0	-6.1	-18.1
Rem. 80 Pointed Soft Point	velocity, fps:	3350	2955	2593	2259	1951
	energy, ft-lb:	1993	1551	1194	906	676
	arc, inches:		+2.2	+2.0	-3.5	-15.8
Rem. 80 HP Power-Lokt	velocity, fps:	3350	2955	2593	2259	1951
	energy, ft-lb:	1993	1551	1194	906	676
	arc, inches:		+2.2	+2.0	-3.5	-15.8
Rem. 90 Nosler Bal. Tip (also in EtronX) or Scirocco	velocity, fps:	3120	2871	2635	2411	2199
	energy, ft-lb:	1946	1647	1388	1162	966
	arc, inches:		+1.4	0	-6.4	-18.8
Rem. 95 AccuTip	velocity, fps:	3120	2847	2590	2347	2118
	energy, ft-lb:	2053	1710	1415	1162	946
	arc, inches:		+1.5	0	-6.6	-19.5
Rem. 100 PSP Core-Lokt (also in EtronX)	velocity, fps:	2960	2697	2449	2215	1993
	energy, ft-lb:	1945	1615	1332	1089	882
	arc, inches:		+1.6	0	-7.5	-22.1
Rem. 100 PSP boat-tail	velocity, fps:	2960	2720	2492	2275	2069
	energy, ft-lb:	1945	1642	1378	1149	950
	arc, inches:		+2.8	+2.3	-3.8	-16.6
Speer 100 Grand Slam	velocity, fps:	2950	2684	2434	2197	
	energy, ft-lb:	1932	1600	1315	1072	
	arc, inches:		+1.7	0	-7.6	-22.4

CARTRIDGE BULLET	RANGE, YARDS:	0	100	200	300	400
Win. 55 Ballistic Silvertip	velocity, fps:	4025	3597	3209	2853	2525
	energy, ft-lb:	1978	1579	1257	994	779
	arc, inches:		+0.6	0	-4.0	-12.2
Win. 80 Pointed Soft Point	velocity, fps:	3350	2955	2593	2259	1951.
	energy, ft-lb:	1993	1551	1194	906	676
	arc, inches:		+2.6	+2.1	-3.6	-16.2
Win. 95 Ballistic Silvertip	velocity, fps:	3100	2854	2626	2410	2203
	energy, ft-lb:	2021	1719	1455	1225	1024
	arc, inches:		+1.4	0	-6.4	-18.9
Win. 95 Supreme Elite XP3	velocity, fps:	3100	2864	2641	2428	2225
	energy, ft-lb:	2027	1730	1471	1243	1044
	a rc, inches:		+1.4	0	-6.4	-18.7
Win. 100 Power-Point	velocity, fps:	2960	2697	2449	2215	1993
	energy, ft-lb:	1945	1615	1332	1089	882
	arc, inches:		+1.9	0	-7.8	-22.6.
Win. 100 Power-Point Plus	velocity, fps:	3090	2818	2562	2321	2092
	energy, ft-lb:	2121	1764	1458	1196	972
	arc, inches:		+1.4	0	-6.7	-20.0

6MM REMINGTON

CARTRIDGE BULLET	RANGE, YARDS:	0	100	200	300	400
Federal 80 Sierra Pro-Hunter	velocity, fps:	3470	3060	2690	2350	2040
	energy, ft-lb:	2140	1665	1290	980	735
	arc, inches:		+1.1	0	-5.9	-18.2
Federal 100 Hi-Shok	velocity, fps:	3100	2830	2570	2330	2100
	energy, ft-lb:	2135	1775	1470	1205	985
	arc, inches:		+1.4	0	-6.7	-19.8
Federal 100 Nos. Partition	velocity, fps:	3100	2860	2640	2420	2220
	energy, ft-lb:	2135	1820	1545	1300	1090
	arc, inches:		+1.4	0	-6.3	-18.7
Hornady 95 SST Superformance	velocity, fps:	3235	2955	2693	2445	2211
	energy, ft-lb:	2207	1842	1530	1261	1031
	arc, inches:		+1.3	0	-6.1	-18.0
Hornady 100 SP boat-tail	velocity, fps:	3100	2861	2634	2419	2231
	energy, ft-lb:	2134	1818	1541	1300	1088
	arc, inches:		+1.3	0	-6.5	-18.9
Hornady 100 SPBT LM	velocity, fps:	3250	2997	2756	2528	2311
	energy, ft-lb:	2345	1995	1687	1418	1186
	arc, inches:		+1.6	0	-6.3	-18.2
Rem. 75 V-Max boat-tail	velocity, fps:	3400	3088	2797	2524	2267
	energy, ft-lb:	1925	1587	1303	1061	856
	arc, inches:		+1.9	+1.7	-3.0	-13.1
Rem. 100 PSP Core-Lokt	velocity, fps:	3100	2829	2573	2332	2104.
	energy, ft-lb:	2133	1777	1470	1207	983
	arc, inches:		+1.4	0	-6.7	-19.8
Rem. 100 PSP boat-tail	velocity, fps:	3100	2852	2617	2394	2183.
	energy, ft-lb:	2134	1806	1521	1273	1058
	arc, inches:		+1.4	0	-6.5	-19.1
Win. 100 Power-Point	velocity, fps:	3100	2829	2573	2332	2104
	energy, ft-lb:	2133	1777	1470	1207	983
	arc, inches:		+1.7	0	-7.0	-20.4

.243 WSSM

CARTRIDGE BULLET	RANGE, YARDS:	0	100	200	300	400
Win. 55 Ballistic Silvertip	velocity, fps:	4060	3628	3237	2880	2550
	energy, ft-lb:	2013	1607	1280	1013	794
	arc, inches:		+0.6	0	-3.9	-12.0
Win. 95 Ballistic Silvertip	velocity, fps:	3250	3000	2763	2538	2325
	energy, ft-lb:	2258	1898	1610	1359	1140
	arc, inches:		+1.2	0	5.7	16.9
Win. 95 Supreme Elite XP3	velocity, fps	3150	2912	2686	2471	2266
	energy, ft-lb	2093	1788	1521	1287	1083
	arc, inches		+1.3	0	-6.1	-18.0
Win. 100 Power Point	velocity, fps:	3110	2838	2583	2341	2112
	energy, ft-lb:	2147	1789	1481	1217	991
	arc, inches:		+1.4	0	-6.6	-19.7

CARTRIDGE BULLET	RANGE, YARDS:	0	100	200	300	400

.240 WEATHERBY MAGNUM

CARTRIDGE BULLET		0	100	200	300	400
Wby. 87 Pointed Expanding	velocity, fps:	3523	3199	2898	2617	2352
	energy, ft-lb:	2397	1977	1622	1323	1069
	arc, inches:		+2.7	+3.4	0	-8.4
Wby. 90 Barnes-X	velocity, fps:	3500	3222	2962	2717	2484
	energy, ft-lb:	2448	2075	1753	1475	1233
	arc, inches:		+2.6	+3.3	0	-8.0
Wby. 95 Nosler Bal. Tip	velocity, fps:	3420	3146	2888	2645	2414
	energy, ft-lb:	2467	2087	1759	1475	1229
	arc, inches:		+2.7	+3.5	0	-8.4
Wby. 100 Pointed Expanding	velocity, fps:	3406	3134	2878	2637	2408
	energy, ft-lb:	2576	2180	1839	1544	1287
	arc, inches:		+2.8	+3.5	0	-8.4
Wby. 100 Partition	velocity, fps:	3406	3136	2882	2642	2415
	energy, ft-lb:	2576	2183	1844	1550	1294
	arc, inches:		+2.8	+3.5	0	-8.4

.25-20 WINCHESTER

CARTRIDGE BULLET		0	100	200	300	400
Rem. 86 Soft Point	velocity, fps:	1460	1194	1030	931	858
	energy, ft-lb:	407	272	203	165	141
	arc, inches:		0	-22.9	-78.9	-173.0
Win. 86 Soft Point	velocity, fps:	1460	1194	1030	931	858.
	energy, ft-lb:	407	272	203	165	141
	arc, inches:		0	-23.5	-79.6	-175.9

.25-35 WINCHESTER

CARTRIDGE BULLET		0	100	200	300	400
Win. 117 Soft Point	velocity, fps:	2230	1866	1545	1282	1097
	energy, ft-lb:	1292	904	620	427	313
	arc, inches:		+2.1	-5.1	-27.0	-70.1

.250 SAVAGE

CARTRIDGE BULLET		0	100	200	300	400
Rem. 100 Pointed SP	velocity, fps:	2820	2504	2210	1936	1684.
	energy, ft-lb:	1765	1392	1084	832	630
	arc, inches:		+2.0	0	-9.2	-27.7
Win. 100 Silvertip	velocity, fps:	2820	2467	2140	1839	1569
	energy, ft-lb:	1765	1351	1017	751	547
	arc, inches:		+2.4	0	-10.1	-30.5

.257 ROBERTS

CARTRIDGE BULLET		0	100	200	300	400
Federal 120 Nosler Partition	velocity, fps:	2780	2560	2360	2160	1970
	energy, ft-lb:	2060	1750	1480	1240	1030
	arc, inches:		+1.9	0	-8.2	-24.0
Hornady 117 SP boat-tail	velocity, fps:	2780	2550	2331	2122	1925
	energy, ft-lb:	2007	1689	1411	1170	963
	arc, inches:		+1.9	0	-8.3	-24.4
Hornady 117 SP boat-tail LM	velocity, fps:	2940	2694	2460	2240	2031
	energy, ft-lb:	2245	1885	1572	1303	1071
	arc, inches:		+1.7	0	-7.6	-21.8
Hornady 117 SST Superformance	velocity, fps:	2946	2707	2480	2265	2060
	energy, ft-lb:	2255	1903	1598	1332	1102
	arc, inches:		+1.6	0	-7.3	-21.4
Rem. 117 SP Core-Lokt	velocity, fps:	2650	2291	1961	1663	1404
	energy, ft-lb:	1824	1363	999	718	512
	arc, inches:		+2.6	0	-11.7	-36.1
Win. 117 Power-Point	velocity, fps:	2780	2411	2071	1761	1488
	energy, ft-lb:	2009	1511	1115	806	576.
	arc, inches:		+2.6	0	-10.8	-33.0

.25-06 REMINGTON

CARTRIDGE BULLET		0	100	200	300	400
Black Hills 100 Nos. Bal. Tip	velocity, fps:	3200				
	energy, ft-lb:	2273				
	arc, inches:					
Black Hills 100 Barnes XLC	velocity, fps:	3200.				
	energy, ft-lb:	2273				
	arc, inches:					
Black Hills 115 Barnes X	velocity, fps:	2975				
	energy, ft-lb:	2259				
	arc, inches:					

Centerfire Rifle Ballistics

.25-06 REMINGTON TO 6.5X55 SWEDISH

CARTRIDGE BULLET	RANGE, YARDS:	0	100	200	300	400
Federal 90 Sierra Varminter	velocity, fps:	3440	3040	2680	2340	2030
	energy, ft-lb:	2365	1850	1435	1100	825
	arc, inches:		+1.1	0	-6.0	-18.3
Federal 100 Barnes XLC	velocity, fps:	3210	2970	2750	2540	2330
	energy, ft-lb:	2290	1965	1680	1430	1205
	arc, inches:		+1.2	0	-5.8	-17.0
Federal 100 Nosler Bal. Tip	velocity, fps:	3210	2960	2720	2490	2280
	energy, ft-lb:	2290	1940	1640	1380	1150.
	arc, inches:		+1.2	0	-6.0	-17.5
Federal 100 Trophy Copper	velocity, fps:	3210	2970	2740	2520	2310
	energy, ft-lb:	2290	1955	1665	1410	1185
	arc, inches:		+1.2	0	-5.9	-17.2
Federal 115 Nosler Partition	velocity, fps:	2990	2750	2520	2300	2100
	energy, ft-lb:	2285	1930	1620	1350	1120
	arc, inches:		+1.6	0	-7.0	-20.8
Federal 115 Trophy Bonded	velocity, fps:	2990	2740	2500	2270	2050
	energy, ft-lb:	2285	1910	1590	1310	1075
	arc, inches:		+1.6	0	-7.2	-21.1
Federal 117 Sierra Pro Hunt.	velocity, fps:	2990	2730	2480	2250	2030
	energy, ft-lb:	2320	1985	1645	1350	1100
	arc, inches:		+1.6	0	-7.2	-21.4
Federal 117 Sierra GameKing BTSP	velocity, fps:	2990	2770	2570	2370	2190
	energy, ft-lb:	2320	2000	1715	1465	1240
	arc, inches:		+1.5	0	-6.8	-19.9
Hornady 90 GMX Superformance	velocity, fps:	3350	3001	2679	2378	2098
	energy, ft-lb:	2243	1799	1434	1130	879
	arc, inches:		+1.2	0	-6.0	-18.3
Hornady 117 SP boat-tail	velocity, fps:	2990	2749	2520	2302	2096
	energy, ft-lb:	2322	1962	1649	1377	1141
	arc, inches:		+1.6	0	-7.0	-20.7
Hornady 117 SP boat-tail LM	velocity, fps:	3110	2855	2613	2384	2168
	energy, ft-lb:	2512	2117	1774	1476	1220
	arc, inches:		+1.8	0	-7.1	-20.3
Hornady 117 SST Superformance	velocity, fps:	3110	2862	2627	2405	2193
	energy, ft-lb:	2513	2127	1793	1502	1249
	arc, inches:		+1.4	0	-6.4	-18.9
PMC 100 SPBT	velocity, fps:	3200	2925	2650	2395	2145
	energy, ft-lb:	2273	1895	1561	1268	1019
	arc, inches:		+1.3	0	-6.3	-18.6
PMC 117 PSP	velocity, fps:	2950	2706	2472	2253	2047
	energy, ft-lb:	2261	1900	1588	1319	1088
	arc, inches:		+1.6	0	-7.3	-21.5
Rem. 100 PSP Core-Lokt	velocity, fps:	3230	2893	2580	2287	2014
	energy, ft-lb:	2316	1858	1478	1161	901
	arc, inches:		+1.3	0	-6.6	-19.8
Rem. 115 Core-Lokt Ultra	velocity, fps:	3000	2751	2516	2293	2081
	energy, ft-lb:	2298	1933	1616	1342	1106
	arc, inches:		+1.6	0	-7.1	-20.7
Rem. 120 PSP Core-Lokt	velocity, fps:	2990	2730	2484	2252	2032
	energy, ft-lb:	2382	1985	1644	1351	1100
	arc, inches:		+1.6	0	-7.2	-21.4
Speer 120 Grand Slam	velocity, fps:	3130	2835	2558	2298	
	energy, ft-lb:	2610	2141	1743	1407	
	arc, inches:		+1.4	0	-6.8	-20.1
Win. 85 Ballistic Silvertip	velocity, fps	3470	3156	2863	2589	2331
	energy, ft-lb:	2273	1880	1548	1266	1026
	arc, inches:		+1.0	0	-5.2	-15.7
Win. 90 Pos. Exp. Point	velocity, fps:	3440	3043	2680	2344	2034
	energy, ft-lb:	2364	1850	1435	1098	827
	arc, inches:		+2.4	+2.0	-3.4	-15.0
Win. 110 AccuBond CT	velocity, fps:	3100	2870	2651	2442	2243
	energy, ft-lb:	2347	2011	1716	1456	1228
	arc, inches:		+1.4	0	-6.3	-18.5
Win. 115 Ballistic Silvertip	velocity, fps:	3060	2825	2603	2390	2188
	energy, ft-lb:	2391	2038	1729	1459	1223
	arc, inches:		+1.4	0	-6.6	-19.2
Win. 120 Pos. Pt. Exp.	velocity, fps:	2990	2717	2459	2216	1987
	energy, ft-lb:	2382	1967	1612	1309	1053
	arc, inches:		+1.6	0	-7.4	-21.8

.25 WINCHESTER SUPER SHORT MAGNUM

CARTRIDGE BULLET	RANGE, YARDS:	0	100	200	300	400
Win. 85 Ballistic Silvertip	velocity, fps:	3470	3156	2863	2589	2331
	energy, ft-lb:	2273	1880	1548	1266	1026
	arc, inches:		+1.0	0	-5.2	-15.7
Win. 110 AccuBond CT	velocity, fps:	3100	2870	2651	2442	2243.
	energy, ft-lb:	2347	2011	1716	1456	1228
	arc, inches:		+1.4	0	-6.3	-18.5
Win. 115 Ballistic Silvertip	velocity, fps:	3060	2844	2639	2442	2254
	energy, ft-lb:	2392	2066	1778	1523	1298
	arc, inches:		+1.4	0	-6.4	-18.6
Win. 120 Pos. Pt. Exp.	velocity, fps:	2990	2717	2459	2216	1987
	energy, ft-lb:	2383	1967	1612	1309	1053
	arc, inches:		+1.6	0	-7.4	-21.8

.257 WEATHERBY MAGNUM

CARTRIDGE BULLET	RANGE, YARDS:	0	100	200	300	400
Federal 115 Nosler Partition	velocity, fps:	3150	2900	2660	2440	2220
	energy, ft-lb:	2535	2145	1810	1515	1260
	arc, inches:		+1.3	0	-6.2	-18.4
Federal 115 Trophy Bonded	velocity, fps:	3150	2890	2640	2400	2180
	energy, ft-lb:	2535	2125	1775	1470	1210
	arc, inches:		+1.4	0	-6.3	-18.8
Wby. 87 Pointed Expanding	velocity, fps:	3825	3472	3147	2845	2563
	energy, ft-lb:	2826	2328	1913	1563	1269
	arc, inches:		+2.1	+2.8	0	-7.1
Wby. 100 Pointed Expanding	velocity, fps:	3602	3298	3016	2750	2500
	energy, ft-lb:	2881	2416	2019	1680	1388
	arc, inches:		+2.4	+3.1	0	-7.7
Wby. 115 Nosler Bal. Tip	velocity, fps:	3400	3170	2952	2745	2547
	energy, ft-lb:	2952	2566	2226	1924	1656.
	arc, inches:		+3.0	+3.5	0	-7.9
Wby. 115 Barnes X	velocity, fps:	3400	3158	2929	2711	2504
	energy, ft-lb:	2952	2546	2190	1877	1601
	arc, inches:		+2.7	+3.4	0	-8.1
Wby. 117 RN Expanding	velocity, fps:	3402	2984	2595	2240	1921
	energy, ft-lb:	3007	2320	1742	1302	956
	arc, inches:		+3.4	+4.31	0	-11.1
Wby. 120 Nosler Partition	velocity, fps:	3305	3046	2801	2570	2350
	energy, ft-lb:	2910	2472	2091	1760	1471
	arc, inches:		+3.0	+3.7	0	-8.9

6.53 (.257) SCRAMJET

CARTRIDGE BULLET	RANGE, YARDS:	0	100	200	300	400
Lazzeroni 85 Nosler Bal. Tip	velocity, fps:	3960	3652	3365	3096	2844
	energy, ft-lb:	2961	2517	2137	1810	1526
	arc, inches:		+1.7	+2.4	0	-6.0
Lazzeroni 100 Nosler Part.	velocity, fps:	3740	3465	3208	2965	2735
	energy, ft-lb:	3106	2667	2285	1953	1661.
	arc, inches:		+2.1	+2.7	0	-6.7

6.5x50 JAPANESE

CARTRIDGE BULLET	RANGE, YARDS:	0	100	200	300	400
Norma 156 Alaska	velocity, fps:	2067	1832	1615	1423	
	energy, ft-lb:	1480	1162	904	701	
	arc, inches:		+4.4	0	-17.8	

6.5x52 CARCANO

CARTRIDGE BULLET	RANGE, YARDS:	0	100	200	300	400
Norma 156 Alaska	velocity, fps:	2428	2169	1926	1702	
	energy, ft-lb:	2043	1630	1286	1004	
	arc, inches:		+2.9	0	-12.3	

6.5x55 SWEDISH

CARTRIDGE BULLET	RANGE, YARDS:	0	100	200	300	400
Federal 140 Hi-Shok	velocity, fps:	2600	2400	2220	2040	1860
	energy, ft-lb:	2100	1795	1525	1285	1080
	arc, inches:		+2.3	0	-9.4	-27.2

CARTRIDGE BULLET	RANGE, YARDS:	0	100	200	300	400
Federal 140 Trophy Bonded	velocity, fps:	2550	2350	2160	1980	1810
	energy, ft-lb:	2020	1720	1450	1220	1015
	arc, inches:		+2.4	0	-9.8	-28.4
Federal 140 Sierra MatchKg. BTHP	velocity, fps:	2630	2460	2300	2140	2000
	energy, ft-lb:	2140	1880	1640	1430	1235
	arc, inches:		+16.4	+28.8	+33.9	+31.8
Hornady 129 SP LM	velocity, fps:	2770	2561	2361	2171	1994
	energy, ft-lb:	2197	1878	1597	1350	1138
	arc, inches:		+2.0	0	-8.2	-23.2
Hornady 140 SP Interlock	velocity, fps:	2525	2341	2165	1996	1836
	energy, ft-lb:	1982	1704	1457	1239	1048
	arc, inches:		+2.4	0	-9.9	-28.5
Hornady140 SP LM	velocity, fps:	2740	2541	2351	2169	1999
	energy, ft-lb:	2333	2006	1717	1463	1242
	arc, inches:		+2.4	0	-8.7	-24.0
Norma 120 Nosler Bal. Tip	velocity, fps:	2822	2609	2407	2213	
	energy, ft-lb:	2123	1815	1544	1305	
	arc, inches:		+1.8	0	-7.8	
Norma 139 Vulkan	velocity, fps:	2854	2569	2302	2051	
	energy, ft-lb:	2515	2038	1636	1298	
	arc, inches:		+1.8	0	-8.4	
Norma 140 Nosler Partition	velocity, fps:	2789	2592	2403	2223	
	energy, ft-lb:	2419	2089	1796	1536	
	arc, inches:		+1.8	0	-7.8	
Norma 156 TXP Swift A-Fr.	velocity, fps:	2526	2276	2040	1818	
	energy, ft-lb:	2196	1782	1432	1138	
	arc, inches:		+2.6	0	-10.9	
Norma 156 Alaska	velocity, fps:	2559	2245	1953	1687	
	energy, ft-lb:	2269	1746	1322	986	
	arc, inches:		+2.7	0	-11.9	
Norma 156 Vulkan	velocity, fps:	2644	2395	2159	1937	
	energy, ft-lb:	2422	1987	1616	1301	
	arc, inches:		+2.2	0	-9.7	
Norma 156 Oryx	velocity, fps:	2559	2308	2070	1848	
	energy, ft-lb:	2269	1845	1485	1183	
	arc, inches:		+2.5	0	-10.6	
PMC 139 Pointed Soft Point	velocity, fps:	2850	2560	2290	2030	1790
	energy, ft-lb:	2515	2025	1615	1270	985
	arc, inches:		+2.2	0	-8.9	-26.3
PMC 140 HP boat-tail	velocity, fps:	2560	2398	2243	2093	1949
	energy, ft-lb:	2037	1788	1563	1361	1181
	arc, inches:		+2.3	0	-9.2	-26.4
PMC 140 SP boat-tail	velocity, fps:	2560	2386	2218	2057	1903
	energy, ft-lb:	2037	1769	1529	1315	1126
	arc, inches:		+2.3	0	-9.4	-27.1
PMC 144 FMJ	velocity, fps:	2650	2370	2110	1870	1650
	energy, ft-lb:	2425	1950	1550	1215	945
	arc, inches:		+2.7	0	-10.5	-30.9
Rem. 140 PSP Core-Lokt	velocity, fps:	2550	2353	2164	1984	1814
	energy, ft-lb:	2021	1720	1456	1224	1023
	arc, inches:		+2.4	0	-9.8	-27.0
Speer 140 Grand Slam	velocity, fps:	2550	2318	2099	1892	
	energy, ft-lb:	2021	1670	1369	1112	
	arc, inches:		+2.5	0	-10.4	-30.6
Win. 140 Soft Point	velocity, fps:	2550	2359	2176	2002	1836
	energy, ft-lb:	2022	1731	1473	1246	1048.
	arc, inches:		+2.4	0	-9.7	-28.1

6.5 GRENDEL

CARTRIDGE BULLET	RANGE, YARDS:	0	100	200	300	400
Hornady 123 A-MAX	velocity, fps:	2590	2420	2256	2099	1948
	energy, ft-lb:	1832	1599	1390	1203	1037
	arc, inches:	-2.4	+1.8	0	-8.6	-25.1
Hornady 123 SST	velocity, fps:	2620	2449	2284	2126	1974

CARTRIDGE BULLET	RANGE, YARDS:	0	100	200	300	400
	energy, ft-lb:	1875	1638	1425	1234	1064
	arc, inches:	-2.4	+1.7	0	-8.4	-24.5

6.5 CREEDMOOR

CARTRIDGE BULLET	RANGE, YARDS:	0	100	200	300	400
Hornady 120 GMX	velocity, fps:	3050	2850	2659	2476	2300
	energy, ft-lb:	2479	2164	1884	1634	1410
	arc, inches:	-1.5	+1.4	0	-6.3	-18.3
Hornady 129 SST	velocity, fps:	2950	2756	2571	2394	2223
	energy, ft-lb:	2493	2176	1894	1641	1415
	arc, inches:	-1.5	+1.5	0	-6.8	-19.7
Hornady 140 A-MAX	velocity, fps:	2710	2557	2410	2267	2129
	energy, ft-lb:	2283	2033	1805	1598	1410
	arc, inches:	-1.5	+1.9	0	-7.9	-22.6
Nosler 140 BT	velocity, fps:	2550	2380	2217	2060	1910
	energy, ft-lb:	2021	1761	1527	1319	1134
	arc, inches:	-1.5	+2.3	0	-9.4	-27.0

.260 REMINGTON

CARTRIDGE BULLET	RANGE, YARDS:	0	100	200	300	400
Federal 140 Sierra GameKing BTSP	velocity, fps:	2750	2570	2390	2220	2060
	energy, ft-lb:	2350	2045	1775	1535	1315
	arc, inches:		+1.9	0	-8.0	-23.1
Federal 140 Trophy Bonded	velocity, fps:	2750	2540	2340	2150	1970
	energy, ft-lb:	2350	2010	1705	1440	1210
	arc, inches:		+1.9	0	-8.4	-24.1
Rem. 120 Nosler Bal. Tip	velocity, fps:	2890	2688	2494	2309	2131
	energy, ft-lb:	2226	1924	1657	1420	1210
	arc, inches:		+1.7	0	-7.3	-21.1
Rem. 120 AccuTip	velocity, fps:	2890	2697	2512	2334	2163
	energy, ft-lb:	2392	2083	1807	1560	1340
	arc, inches:		+1.6	0	-7.2	-20.7
Rem. 125 Nosler Partition	velocity, fps:	2875	2669	2473	2285	2105.
	energy, ft-lb:	2294	1977	1697	1449	1230
	arc, inches:	+1.71	0	-7.4	-21.4	
Rem. 140 PSP Core-Lokt (and C-L Ultra)	velocity, fps:	2750	2544	2347	2158	1979
	energy, ft-lb:	2351	2011	1712	1448	1217
	arc, inches:		+1.9	0	-8.3	-24.0
Speer 140 Grand Slam	velocity, fps:	2750	2518	2297	2087	
	energy, ft-lb:	2351	1970	1640	1354	
	arc, inches:		+2.3	0	-8.9	-25.8

6.5-284

CARTRIDGE BULLET	RANGE, YARDS:	0	100	200	300	400
Norma 120 Nosler Bal. Tip	velocity, fps:	3117	2890	2674	2469	
	energy, ft-lb:	2589	2226	1906	1624	
	arc, inches:		+1.3	0	-6.2	
Norma 140 Nosler Part.	velocity, fps:	2953	2750	2557	2371	
	energy, ft-lb:	2712	2352	2032	1748	
	arc, inches:		+1.5	0	-6.8	

6.5-284 NORMA

CARTRIDGE BULLET	RANGE, YARDS:	0	100	200	300	400
Nosler 120 Ballistic Tip	velocity, fps:	3000	2792	2594	2404	2223
	energy, ft-lb:	2398	2077	1793	1540	1316
	arc, inches:	-1.5	+1.4	0	-6.6	-17.1
Nosler 125 PT	velocity, fps:	3000	2788	2585	2392	2207
	energy, ft-lb:	2497	2157	1855	1588	1352
	arc, inches:	-1.5	+1.5	0	-6.7	-19.5
Nosler 130 AccuBond	velocity, fps:	2900	2709	2526	2351	2182
	energy, ft-lb:	2427	2118	1842	1595	1374
	arc, inches:	-1.5	+1.5	0	-6.9	-18.4

6.5 REMINGTON MAGNUM

CARTRIDGE BULLET	RANGE, YARDS:	0	100	200	300	400
Nosler 125 PT	velocity, fps:	3025	2811	2608	2414	2228
	energy, ft-lb:	2539	2194	1888	1617	1377
	arc, inches:	-1.5	+1.5	0	-6.6	-19.1

Centerfire Rifle Ballistics

6.5 REMINGTON MAGNUM TO .270 WINCHESTER

CARTRIDGE BULLET	RANGE, YARDS:	0	100	200	300	400
Rem. 120 Core-Lokt PSP	velocity, fps:	3210	2905	2621	2353	2102
	energy, ft-lb:	2745	2248	1830	1475	1177
	arc, inches:		+2.7	+2.1	-3.5	-15.5

.264 WINCHESTER MAGNUM

CARTRIDGE BULLET	RANGE, YARDS:	0	100	200	300	400
Nosler 100 Ballistic Tip	velocity, fps:	3400	3105	2829	2569	2324
	energy, ft-lb:	2567	2141	1777	1465	1199
	arc, inches:	-1.5	+1.0	0	-5.5	-16.1
Nosler 130 AccuBond	velocity, fps:	3100	2900	2709	2527	2351
	energy, ft-lb:	2774	2428	2119	1843	1595
	arc, inches:	-1.5	+1.2	0	-6.0	-17.5
Rem. 140 PSP Core-Lokt	velocity, fps:	3030	2782	2548	2326	2114
	energy, ft-lb:	2854	2406	2018	1682	1389
	arc, inches:		+1.5	0	-6.9	-20.2
Win. 140 Power-Point	velocity, fps:	3030	2782	2548	2326	2114.
	energy, ft-lb:	2854	2406	2018	1682	1389
	arc, inches:		+1.8	0	-7.2	-20.8

6.8MM REMINGTON SPC

CARTRIDGE BULLET	RANGE, YARDS:	0	100	200	300	400
Hornady 110 BTHP (16-in. barrel)	velocity, fps:	2570	2332	2107	1895	1697
	energy, ft-lb:	1613	1328	1084	877	703
	arc, inches:	-2.4	+2.0	0	-9.9	-29.5
Hornady 120 SST (16-in. barrel)	velocity, fps:	2460	2250	2051	1863	1687
	energy, ft-lb:	1612	1349	1121	925	758
	arc, inches:	-2.4	+2.3	0	-10.5	-31.1
Rem. 115 Open Tip Match (and HPBT Match)	velocity, fps:	2800	2535	2285	2049	1828
	energy, ft-lb:	2002	1641	1333	1072	853
	arc, inches:		+2.0	0	-8.8	-26.2
Rem. 115 Metal Case	velocity, fps:	2800	2523	2262	2017	1789
	energy, ft-lb:	2002	1625	1307	1039	817
	arc, inches:		+2.0	0	-8.8	-26.2
Rem. 115 Sierra HPBT (2005; all vel. @ 2775)	velocity, fps:	2775	2511	2263	2028	1809
	energy, ft-lb:	1966	1610	1307	1050	835
	arc, inches:		+2.0	0	-8.8	-26.2.
Rem. 115 CL Ultra	velocity, fps:	2775	2472	2190	1926	1683
	energy, ft-lb:	1966	1561	1224	947	723
	arc, inches:		+2.1	0	-9.4	-28.2

.270 WINCHESTER

CARTRIDGE BULLET	RANGE, YARDS:	0	100	200	300	400
Black Hills 130 Nos. Bal. T.	velocity, fps:	2950				
	energy, ft-lb:	2512				
	arc, inches:					
Black Hills 130 Barnes XLC	velocity, ft-lb:	2950				
	energy, ft-lb:	2512				
	arc, inches:					
Federal 130 Barnes XLC And Triple Shock	velocity, fps:	3060	2840	2620	2420	2220
	energy, ft-lb:	2705	2320	1985	1690	1425
	arc, inches:		+1.4	0	-6.4	-18.9
Federal 130 Hi-Shok	velocity, fps:	3060	2800	2560	2330	2110
	energy, ft-lb:	2700	2265	1890	1565	1285
	arc, inches:		+1.5	0	-6.8	-20.0
Federal 130 Nosler Bal. Tip	velocity, fps:	3060	2840	2630	2430	2230
	energy, ft-lb:	2700	2325	1990	1700	1440
	arc, inches:		+1.4	0	-6.5	-18.8
Federal 130 Nos. Partition And Solid Base	velocity, fps:	3060	2830	2610	2400	2200
	energy, ft-lb:	2705	2310	1965	1665	1400
	arc, inches:		+1.4	0	-6.5	-19.1
Federal 130 Sierra GameKing	velocity, fps:	3060	2830	2620	2410	2220
	energy, ft-lb:	2700	2320	1980	1680	1420
	arc, inches:		+1.4	0	-6.5	-19.0
Federal 130 Sierra Pro-Hunt.	velocity, fps:	3060	2830	2600	2390	2190
	energy, ft-lb:	2705	2305	1960	1655	1390
	arc, inches:	+1.4	0	-6.4	-19.0	
Federal 130 Trophy Bonded	velocity, fps:	3060	2810	2570	2340	2130
	energy, ft-lb:	2705	2275	1905	1585	1310
	arc, inches:		+1.5	0	-6.7	-19.8
Federal 130 Trophy Bonded Tip	velocity, fps:	3060	2840	2630	2430	2240
	energy, ft-lb:	2705	2330	2000	1710	1455
	arc, inches:		+1.4	0	-6.4	-18.7
Federal 140 Trophy Bonded	velocity, fps:	2940	2700	2480	2260	2060
	energy, ft-lb:	2685	2270	1905	1590	1315
	arc, inches:		+1.6	0	-7.3	-21.5

CARTRIDGE BULLET	RANGE, YARDS:	0	100	200	300	400
Federal 140 Trophy Bonded Tip	velocity, fps:	2950	2740	2550	2360	2180
	energy, ft-lb:	2705	2340	2015	1730	1475
	arc, inches:		+1.6	0	-6.9	-20.1
Federal 140 Tr. Bonded HE	velocity, fps:	3100	2860	2620	2400	2200.
	energy, ft-lb:	2990	2535	2140	1795	1500
	arc, inches:		+1.4	0	-6.4	-18.9
Federal 140 Nos. AccuBond	velocity, fps:	2950	2760	2580	2400	2230.
	energy, ft-lb:	2705	2365	2060	1790	1545
	arc, inches:		+1.5	0	-6.7	-19.6
Federal 150 Hi-Shok RN	velocity, fps:	2850	2500	2180	1890	1620
	energy, ft-lb:	2705	2085	1585	1185	870
	arc, inches:		+2.0	0	-9.4	-28.6
Federal 150 Sierra GameKing	velocity, fps:	2850	2660	2480	2300	2130
	energy, ft-lb:	2705	2355	2040	1760	1510
	arc, inches:		+1.7	0	-7.4	-21.4
Federal 150 Sierra GameKing HE	velocity, fps:	3000	2800	2620	2430	2260
	energy, ft-lb:	2995	2615	2275	1975	1700
	arc, inches:		+1.5	0	-6.5	-18.9
Federal 150 Nosler Partition	velocity, fps:	2850	2590	2340	2100	1880.
	energy, ft-lb:	2705	2225	1815	1470	1175
	arc, inches:		+1.9	0	-8.3	-24.4
Hornady 120 SST Custom Lite	velocity, fps:	2675	2288	1935	1619	1351
	energy, ft-lb:	1907	1395	998	699	486
	arc, inches:		+2.6	0	-12.0	-37.4
Hornady 130 GMX Superformance	velocity, fps:	3190	2975	2770	2575	2387
	energy, ft-lb:	2937	2554	2215	1913	1645
	arc, inches:		+1.2	0	-5.7	-16.8
Hornady 130 SST (or Interbond)	velocity, fps:	3060	2845	2639	2442	2254
	energy, ft-lb:	2700	2335	2009	1721	1467
	arc, inches:		+1.4	0	-6.6	-19.1
Hornady 130 SST LM (or Interbond)	velocity, fps:	3215	2998	2790	2590	2400
	energy, ft-lb:	2983	2594	2246	1936	1662
	arc, inches:		+1.2	0	-5.8	-17.0
Hornady 130 SST Superformance	velocity, fps:	3200	2984	2779	2583	2396
	energy, ft-lb:	2956	2570	2229	1926	1656
	arc, inches:		+1.2	0	-5.7	-16.7
Hornady 140 SP boat-tail	velocity, fps:	2940	2747	2562	2385	2214
	energy, ft-lb:	2688	2346	2041	1769	1524
	arc, inches:		+1.6	0	-7.0	-20.2
Hornady 140 SP boat-tail LM	velocity, fps:	3100	2894	2697	2508	2327.
	energy, ft-lb:	2987	2604	2261	1955	1684
	arc, inches:		+1.4	0	6.3	-18.3
Hornady 140 SST Superformance	velocity, fps:	3090	2894	2707	2568	2355
	energy, ft-lb:	2968	2604	2278	1986	1724
	arc, inches:		+1.3	0	-6.1	-17.6
Hornady 150 SP	velocity, fps:	2800	2684	2478	2284	2100
	energy, ft-lb:	2802	2400	2046	1737	1469
	arc, inches:		+1.7	0	-7.4	-21.6
Norma 130 SP	velocity, fps:	3140	2862	2601	2354	
	energy, ft-lb:	2847	2365	1953	1600	
	arc, inches:		+1.3	0	-6.5	
Norma 130 FMJ	velocity, fps:	2887	2634	2395	2169	
	energy, ft-lb:					
	arc, inches:		+1.8	0	-7.8	
Norma 150 SP	velocity, fps:	2799	2555	2323	2104	
	energy, ft-lb:	2610	2175	1798	1475	
	arc, inches:		+1.9	0	-8.3	
Norma 150 Oryx	velocity, fps:	2854	2608	2376	2155	
	energy, ft-lb:	2714	2267	1880	1547	
	arc, inches:		+1.8	0	-8.0	
PMC 130 Barnes X	velocity, fps:	2910	2717	2533	2356	2186
	energy, ft-lb:	2444	2131	1852	1602	1379
	arc, inches:		+1.6	0	-7.1	-20.4
PMC 130 SP boat-tail	velocity, fps:	3050	2830	2620	2421	2229
	energy, ft-lb:	2685	2312	1982	1691	1435
	arc, inches:		+1.5	0	-6.5	-19.0
PMC 130 Pointed Soft Point	velocity, fps:	2950	2691	2447	2217	2001
	energy, ft-lb:	2512	2090	1728	1419	1156
	arc, inches:		+1.6	0	-7.5	-22.1
PMC 150 Barnes X	velocity, fps:	2700	2541	2387	2238	2095
	energy, ft-lb:	2428	2150	1897	1668	1461
	arc, inches:		+2.0	0	-8.1	-23.1

CARTRIDGE BULLET	RANGE, YARDS:	0	100	200	300	400
PMC 150 SP boat-tail	velocity, fps:	2850	2660	2477	2302	2134
	energy, ft-lb:	2705	2355	2043	1765	1516.
	arc, inches:		+1.7	0	-7.4	-21.4
PMC 150 Pointed Soft Point	velocity, fps:	2750	2530	2321	2123	1936
	energy, ft-lb:	2519	2131	1794	1501	1248
	arc, inches:		+2.0	0	-8.4	-24.6
Rem. 100 Pointed Soft Point	velocity, fps:	3320	2924	2561	2225	1916
	energy, ft-lb:	2448	1898	1456	1099	815
	arc, inches:		+2.3	+2.0	-3.6	-16.2
Rem. 115 PSP Core-Lokt mr	velocity, fps:	2710	2412	2133	1873	1636
	energy, ft-lb:	1875	1485	1161	896	683
	arc, inches:		+1.0	-2.7	-14.2	-35.6
Rem. 130 PSP Core-Lokt	velocity, fps:	3060	2776	2510	2259	2022
	energy, ft-lb:	2702	2225	1818	1472	1180
	arc, inches:		+1.5	0	-7.0	-20.9
Rem. 130 Bronze Point	velocity, fps:	3060	2802	2559	2329	2110
	energy, ft-lb:	2702	2267	1890	1565	1285
	arc, inches:		+1.5	0	-6.8	-20.0
Rem. 130 Swift Scirocco	velocity, fps:	3060	2838	2677	2425	2232
	energy, ft-lb:	2702	2325	1991	1697	1438
	arc, inches:		+1.4	0	-6.5	-18.8
Rem. 130 AccuTip BT	velocity, fps:	3060	2845	2639	2442	2254
	energy, ft-lb:	2702	2336	2009	1721	1467
	arc, inches:		+1.4	0	-6.4	-18.6
Rem. 140 Swift A-Frame	velocity, fps:	2925	2652	2394	2152	1923
	energy, ft-lb:	2659	2186	1782	1439	1150
	arc, inches:		+1.7	0	-7.8	-23.2
Rem. 140 PSP boat-tail	velocity, fps:	2960	2749	2548	2355	2171
	energy, ft-lb:	2723	2349	2018	1724	1465
	arc, inches:		+1.6	0	-6.9	-20.1
Rem. 140 Nosler Bal. Tip	velocity, fps:	2960	2754	2557	2366	2187
	energy, ft-lb:	2724	2358	2032	1743	1487
	arc, inches:		+1.6	0	-6.9	-20.0
Rem. 140 PSP C-L Ultra	velocity, fps:	2925	2667	2424	2193	1975
	energy, ft-lb:	2659	2211	1826	1495	1212
	arc, inches:		+1.7	0	-7.6	-22.5
Rem. 150 SP Core-Lokt	velocity, fps:	2850	2504	2183	1886	1618
	energy, ft-lb:	2705	2087	1587	1185	872
	arc, inches:		+2.0	0	-9.4	-28.6
Rem. 150 Nosler Partition	velocity, fps:	2850	2652	2463	2282	2108
	energy, ft-lb:	2705	2343	2021	1734	1480
	arc, inches:		+1.7	0	-7.5	-21.6
Speer 130 Grand Slam	velocity, fps:	3050	2774	2514	2269	
	energy, ft-lb:	2685	2221	1824	1485	
	arc, inches:		+1.5	0	-7.0	-20.9
Speer 150 Grand Slam	velocity, fps:	2830	2594	2369	2156	
	energy, ft-lb:	2667	2240	1869	1548	
	arc, inches:		+1.8	0	-8.1	-23.6
Win. 130 Power-Point	velocity, fps:	3060	2802	2559	2329	2110
	energy, ft-lb:	2702	2267	1890	1565	1285.
	arc, inches:		+1.8	0	-7.1	-20.6
Win. 130 Power-Point Plus	velocity, fps:	3150	2881	2628	2388	2161
	energy, ft-lb:	2865	2396	1993	1646	1348
	arc, inches:		+1.3	0	-6.4	-18.9
Win. 130 Silvertip	velocity, fps:	3060	2776	2510	2259	2022.
	energy, ft-lb:	2702	2225	1818	1472	1180
	arc, inches:		+1.8	0	-7.4	-21.6
Win. 130 Ballistic Silvertip	velocity, fps:	3050	2828	2618	2416	2224
	energy, ft-lb:	2685	2309	1978	1685	1428
	arc, inches:		+1.4	0	-6.5	-18.9
Win. 140 AccuBond	velocity, fps:	2950	2751	2560	2378	2203
	energy, ft-lb:	2705	2352	2038	1757	1508
	arc, inches:		+1.6	0	-6.9	-19.9

CARTRIDGE BULLET	RANGE, YARDS:	0	100	200	300	400
Win. 140 Fail Safe	velocity, fps:	2920	2671	2435	2211	1999
	energy, ft-lb:	2651	2218	1843	1519	1242
	arc, inches:		+1.7	0	-7.6	-22.3
Win. 150 Power-Point	velocity, fps:	2850	2585	2336	2100	1879
	energy, ft-lb:	2705	2226	1817	1468	1175
	arc, inches:		+2.2	0	-8.6	-25.0
Win. 150 Power-Point Plus	velocity, fps:	2950	2679	2425	2184	1957
	energy, ft-lb:	2900	2391	1959	1589	1276
	arc, inches:		+1.7	0	-7.6	-22.6
Win. 150 Partition Gold	velocity, fps:	2930	2693	2468	2254	2051
	energy, ft-lb:	2860	2416	2030	1693	1402
	arc, inches:		+1.7	0	-7.4	-21.6
Win. 150 Supreme Elite XP3	velocity, fps:	2950	2763	2583	2411	2245
	energy, ft-lb:	2898	2542	2223	1936	1679
	arc, inches:		+1.5	0	-6.9	-15.5

.270 WINCHESTER SHORT MAGNUM

CARTRIDGE BULLET	RANGE, YARDS:	0	100	200	300	400
Black Hills 140 AccuBond	velocity, fps:	3100				
	energy, ft-lb:	2987				
	arc, inches:					
Federal 130 Nos. Bal. Tip	velocity, fps:	3300	3070	2840	2630	2430
	energy, ft-lb:	3145	2710	2335	2000	1705
	arc, inches:		+1.1	0	-5.4	-15.8
Federal 130 Nos. Partition And Nos. Solid Base And Barnes TS	velocity, fps:	3280	3040	2810	2590	2380
	energy, ft-lb:	3105	2665	2275	1935	1635
	arc, inches:		+1.1	0	-5.6	-16.3
Federal 130 Trophy Copper	velocity, fps:	3280	3060	2850	2650	2460
	energy, ft-lb:	3105	2700	2345	2025	1745
	arc, inches:		+1.1	0	-5.4	-15.8
Federal 140 Nos. AccuBond	velocity, fps:	3200	3000	2810	2630	2450
	energy, ft-lb:	3185	2795	2455	2145	1865
	arc, inches:		+1.2	0	-5.6	-16.2
Federal 140 Trophy Bonded	velocity, fps:	3130	2870	2640	2410	2200
	energy, ft-lb:	3035	2570	2160	1810	1500
	arc, inches:		+1.4	0	-6.3	18.7
Federal 140 Trophy Bonded Tip	velocity, fps:	3200	2980	2770	2580	2390
	energy, ft-lb:	3185	2765	2390	2060	1770
	arc, inches:		+1.2	0	-5.8	-16.7
Federal 150 Nos. Partition	velocity, fps:	3160	2950	2750	2550	2370
	energy, ft-lb:	3325	2895	2515	2175	1870
	arc, inches:		+1.3	0	-5.9	-17.0
Norma 130 FMJ	velocity, fps:	3150	2882	2630	2391	
	energy, ft-lb:					
	arc, inches:		+1.5	0	-6.4	
Norma 130 Ballistic ST	velocity, fps:	3281	3047	2825	2614	
	energy, ft-lb:	3108	2681	2305	1973	
	arc, inches:		+1.1	0	-5.5	
Norma 140 Barnes X TS	velocity, fps:	3150	2952	2762	2580	
	energy, ft-lb:	3085	2709	2372	2070	
	arc, inches:		+1.3	0	-5.8	
Norma 150 Nosler Bal. Tip	velocity, fps:	3280	3046	2824	2613	
	energy, ft-lb:	3106	2679	2303	1972	
	arc, inches:		+1.1	0	-5.4	
Norma 150 Oryx	velocity, fps:	3117	2856	2611	2378	
	energy, ft-lb:	3237	2718	2271	1884	
	arc, inches:		+1.4	0	-6.5	
Win. 130 Bal. Silvertip	velocity, fps:	3275	3041	2820	2609	2408
	energy, ft-lb:	3096	2669	2295	1964	1673
	arc, inches:		+1.1	0	-5.5	-16.1
Win. 140 AccuBond	velocity, fps:	3200	2989	2789	2597	2413
	energy, ft-lb:	3184	2779	2418	2097	1810
	arc, inches:		+1.2	0	-5.7	-16.5
Win. 140 Fail Safe	velocity, fps:	3125	2865	2619	2386	2165
	energy, ft-lb:	3035	2550	2132	1769	1457
	arc, inches:		+1.4	0	-6.5	-19.0
Win. 150 Ballistic Silvertip	velocity, fps:	3120	2923	2734	2554	2380.
	energy, ft-lb:	3242	2845	2490	2172	1886.
	arc, inches:		+1.3	0	-5.9	-17.2

Centerfire Rifle Ballistics

.270 WINCHESTER SHORT MAGNUM TO 7MM-08 REMINGTON

CARTRIDGE BULLET	RANGE, YARDS:	0	100	200	300	400
Win. 150 Power Point	velocity, fps:	3150	2867	2601	2350	2113
	energy, ft-lb:	3304	2737	2252	1839	1487
	arc, inches:		+1.4	0	-6.5	-19.4
Win. 150 Supreme Elite XP3	velocity, fps:	3120	2926	2740	2561	2389
	energy, ft-lb:	3242	2850	2499	2184	1901
	arc, inches:		+1.3	0	-5.9	-17.1

.270 WEATHERBY MAGNUM

CARTRIDGE BULLET	RANGE, YARDS:	0	100	200	300	400
Federal 130 Nosler Partition	velocity, fps:	3200	2960	2740	2520	2320
	energy, ft-lb:	2955	2530	2160	1835	1550·
	arc, inches:		+1.2	0	-5.9	-17.3
Federal 130 Sierra GameKing BTSP	velocity, fps:	3200	2980	2780	2580	2400
	energy, ft-lb:	2955	2570	2230	1925	1655
	arc, inches:		+1.2	0	-5.7	-16.6
Federal 140 Trophy Bonded	velocity, fps:	3100	2840	2600	2370	2150.
	energy, ft-lb:	2990	2510	2100	1745	1440
	arc, inches:		+1.4	0	-6.6	-19.3
Federal 130 Trophy Bonded Tip	velocity, fps:	3200	2970	2760	2560	2360
	energy, ft-lb:	2955	2555	2200	1885	1610
	arc, inches:		+1.2	0	-5.9	-16.9
Wby. 100 Pointed Expanding	velocity, fps:	3760	3396	3061	2751	2462
	energy, ft-lb:	3139	2560	2081	1681	1346
	arc, inches:		+2.3	+3.0	0	-7.6
Wby. 130 Pointed Expanding	velocity, fps:	3375	3123	2885	2659	2444
	energy, ft-lb:	3288	2815	2402	2041	1724
	arc, inches:		+2.8	+3.5	0	-8.4
Wby. 130 Nosler Partition	velocity, fps:	3375	3127	2892	2670	2458.
	energy, ft-lb:	3288	2822	2415	2058	1744
	arc, inches:		+2.8	+3.5	0	-8.3
Wby. 140 Nosler Bal. Tip	velocity, fps:	3300	3077	2865	2663	2470.
	energy, ft-lb:	3385	2943	2551	2204	1896
	arc, inches:		+2.9	+3.6	0	-8.4
Wby. 140 Barnes X	velocity, fps:	3250	3032	2825	2628	2438
	energy, ft-lb:	3283	2858	2481	2146	1848
	arc, inches:		+3.0	+3.7	0	-8.7
Wby. 150 Pointed Expanding	velocity, fps:	3245	3028	2821	2623	2434
	energy, ft-lb:	3507	3053	2650	2292	1973
	arc, inches:		+3.0	+3.7	0	-8.7
Wby. 150 Nosler Partition	velocity, fps:	3245	3029	2823	2627	2439.
	energy, ft-lb:	3507	3055	2655	2298	1981
	arc, inches:		+3.0	+3.7	0	-8.

7-30 WATERS

CARTRIDGE BULLET	RANGE, YARDS:	0	100	200	300	400
Federal 120 Sierra GameKing BTSP	velocity, fps:	2700	2300	1930	1600	1330.
	energy, ft-lb:	1940	1405	990	685	470
	arc, inches:		+2.6	0	-12.0	-37.6

7MM MAUSER (7x57)

CARTRIDGE BULLET	RANGE, YARDS:	0	100	200	300	400
Federal 140 Sierra Pro-Hunt.	velocity, fps:	2660	2450	2260	2070	1890.
	energy, ft-lb:	2200	1865	1585	1330	1110
	arc, inches:		+2.1	0	-9.0	-26.1
Federal 140 Nosler Partition	velocity, fps:	2660	2450	2260	2070	1890.
	energy, ft-lb:	2200	1865	1585	1330	1110
	arc, inches:		+2.1	0	-9.0	-26.1
Federal 175 Hi-Shok RN	velocity, fps:	2440	2140	1860	1600	1380
	energy, ft-lb:	2315	1775	1340	1000	740
	arc, inches:		+3.1	0	-13.3	-40.1
Hornady 139 SP boat-tail	velocity, fps:	2700	2504	2316	2137	1965
	energy, ft-lb:	2251	1936	1656	1410	1192
	arc, inches:		+2.0	0	-8.5	-24.9
Hornady 139 SP Interlock	velocity, fps:	2680	2455	2241	2038	1846
	energy, ft-lb:	2216	1860	1550	1282	1052
	arc, inches:		+2.1	0	-9.1	-26.6
Hornady 139 SP boat-tail LM	velocity, fps:	2830	2620	2450	2250	2070
	energy, ft-lb:	2475	2135	1835	1565	1330
	arc, inches:		+1.8	0	-7.6	-22.1
Hornady 139 SP LM	velocity, fps:	2950	2736	2532	2337	2152.
	energy, ft-lb:	2686	2310	1978	1686	1429
	arc, inches:		+2.0	0	-7.6	-21.5

CARTRIDGE BULLET	RANGE, YARDS:	0	100	200	300	400
Hornady 139 SST Superformance	velocity, fps:	2760	2575	2397	2227	2063
	energy, ft-lb:	2351	2046	1774	1530	1314
	arc, inches:		+1.9	0	-7.9	-22.9
Norma 150 Soft Point	velocity, fps:	2690	2479	2278	2087	
	energy, ft-lb:	2411	2048	1729	1450	
	arc, inches:		+2.0	0	-8.8	
PMC 140 Pointed Soft Point	velocity, fps:	2660	2450	2260	2070	1890
	energy, ft-lb:	2200	1865	1585	1330	1110.
	arc, inches:		+2.4	0	-9.6	-27.3
PMC 175 Soft Point	velocity, fps:	2440	2140	1860	1600	1380
	energy, ft-lb:	2315	1775	1340	1000	740
	arc, inches:		+1.5	-3.6	-18.6	-46.8
Rem. 140 PSP Core-Lokt	velocity, fps:	2660	2435	2221	2018	1827
	energy, ft-lb:	2199	1843	1533	1266	1037
	arc, inches:		+2.2	0	-9.2	-27.4
Win. 145 Power-Point	velocity, fps:	2660	2413	2180	1959	1754
	energy, ft-lb:	2279	1875	1530	1236	990
	arc, inches:		+1.1	-2.8	-14.1	-34.4

7x57 R

CARTRIDGE BULLET	RANGE, YARDS:	0	100	200	300	400
Norma 150 FMJ	velocity, fps:	2690	2489	2296	2112	
	energy, ft-lb:	2411	2063	1756	1486	
	arc, inches:		+2.0	0	-8.6	
Norma 154 Soft Point	velocity, fps:	2625	2417	2219	2030	
	energy, ft-lb:	2357	1999	1684	1410	
	arc, inches:		+2.2	0	-9.3	
Norma 156 Oryx	velocity, fps:	2608	2346	2099	1867	
	energy, ft-lb:	2357	1906	1526	1208	
	arc, inches:		+2.4	0	-10.3	

7MM-08 REMINGTON

CARTRIDGE BULLET	RANGE, YARDS:	0	100	200	300	400
Black Hills 140 AccuBond	velocity, fps:	2700				
	energy, ft-lb:					
	arc, inches:					
Federal 140 Nosler Partition	velocity, fps:	2800	2590	2390	2200	2020
	energy, ft-lb:	2435	2085	1775	1500	1265
	arc, inches:		+1.8	0	-8.0	-23.1
Federal 140 Nosler Bal. Tip And AccuBond	velocity, fps:	2800	2610	2430	2260	2100
	energy, ft-lb:	2440	2135	1840	1590	1360.
	arc, inches:		+1.8	0	-7.7	-22.3
Federal 140 Tr. Bonded HE	velocity, fps:	2950	2660	2390	2140	1900
	energy, ft-lb:	2705	2205	1780	1420	1120
	arc, inches:		+1.7	0	-7.9	-23.2
Federal 140 Trophy Copper	velocity, fps:	2800	2610	2440	2260	2100
	energy, ft-lb:	2435	2125	1845	1595	1370
	arc, inches:		+1.8	0	-7.7	-22.2
Federal 150 Sierra Pro-Hunt.	velocity, fps:	2650	2440	2230	2040	1860
	energy, ft-lb:	2340	1980	1660	1390	1150
	arc, inches:		+2.2	0	-9.2	-26.7
Hornady 120 SST Custom Lite	velocity, fps:	2675	2435	2207	1992	1790
	energy, ft-lb:	1907	1579	1298	1057	854
	arc, inches:		+2.2	0	-9.4	-27.5
Hornady 139 SP boat-tail LM	velocity, fps:	3000	2790	2590	2399	2216
	energy, ft-lb:	2777	2403	2071	1776	1515
	arc, inches:		+1.5	0	-6.7	-19.4
Norma 140 Ballistic ST	velocity, fps:	2822	2633	2452	2278	
	energy, ft-lb:	2476	2156	1870	1614	
	arc, inches:		+1.8	0	-7.6	
PMC 139 PSP	velocity, fps:	2850	2610	2384	2170	1969
	energy, ft-lb:	2507	2103	1754	1454	1197
	arc, inches:		+1.8	0	-7.9	-23.3
Rem. 120 Hollow Point	velocity, fps:	3000	2725	2467	2223	1992
	energy, ft-lb:	2398	1979	1621	1316	1058
	arc, inches:		+1.6	0	-7.3	-21.7
Rem. 140 PSP Core-Lokt	velocity, fps:	2860	2625	2402	2189	1988
	energy, ft-lb:	2542	2142	1793	1490	1228
	arc, inches:		+1.8	0	-7.8	-22.9
Rem. 140 PSP boat-tail	velocity, fps:	2860	2656	2460	2273	2094
	energy, ft-lb:	2542	2192	1881	1606	1363
	arc, inches:		+1.7	0	-7.5	-21.7

CARTRIDGE BULLET	RANGE, YARDS:	0	100	200	300	400
Rem. 140 AccuTip BT	velocity, fps	2860	2670	2488	2313	2145
	energy, ft-lb	2543	2217	1925	1663	1431
	arc, inches:		+1.7	0	-7.3	-21.2
Rem. 140 Nosler Partition	velocity, fps	2860	2648	2446	2253	2068
	energy, ft-lb	2542	2180	1860	1577	1330
	arc, inches:		+1.7	0	-7.6	-22.0
Speer 145 Grand Slam	velocity, fps	2845	2567	2305	2059	
	energy, ft-lb	2606	2121	1711	1365	
	arc, inches:		+1.9	0	-8.4	-25.5
Win. 140 Power-Point	velocity, fps	2800	2523	2268	2027	1802.
	energy, ft-lb	2429	1980	1599	1277	1010
	arc, inches:		+2.0	0	-8.8	-26.0
Win. 140 Power-Point Plus	velocity, fps	2875	2597	2336	2090	1859
	energy, ft-lb	2570	1997	1697	1358	1075
	arc, inches:		+2.0	0	-8.8	26.0
Win. 140 Fail Safe	velocity, fps	2760	2506	2271	2048	1839
	energy, ft-lb	2360	1953	1603	1304	1051
	arc, inches:		+2.0	0	-8.8	-25.9
Win. 140 Ballistic Silvertip	velocity, fps	2770	2572	2382	2200	2026
	energy, ft-lb	2386	2056	1764	1504	1276
	arc, inches:		+1.9	0	-8.0	-23.8

7x64 BRENNEKE

CARTRIDGE BULLET	RANGE, YARDS:	0	100	200	300	400
Federal 160 Nosler Partition	velocity, fps	2650	2480	2310	2150	2000
	energy, ft-lb	2495	2180	1895	1640	1415
	arc, inches:		+2.1	0	-8.7	-24.9
Norma 140 AccuBond	velocity, fps	2953	2759	2572	2394	
	energy, ft-lb	2712	2366	2058	1782	
	arc, inches:		+1.5	0	-6.8	
Norma 154 Soft Point	velocity, fps	2821	2605	2399	2203	
	energy, ft-lb	2722	2321	1969	1660	
	arc, inches:		+1.8	0	-7.8	
Norma 156 Oryx	velocity, fps	2789	2516	2259	2017	
	energy, ft-lb	2695	2193	1768	1410	
	arc, inches:		+2.0	0	-8.8	
Norma 170 Vulkan	velocity, fps	2756	2501	2259	2031	
	energy, ft-lb	2868	2361	1927	1558	
	arc, inches:		+2.0	0	-8.8	
Norma 170 Oryx	velocity, fps	2756	2481	2222	1979	
	energy, ft-lb	2868	2324	1864	1478	
	arc, inches:		+2.1	0	-9.2	
Norma 170 Plastic Point	velocity, fps	2756	2519	2294	2081	
	energy, ft-lb	2868	2396	1987	1635	
	arc, inches:		+2.0	0	-8.6	
PMC 170 Pointed Soft Point	velocity, fps	2625	2401	2189	1989	1801
	energy, ft lb	2601	2175	1808	1493	1224
	arc, inches:		+2.3	0	-9.6	-27.9
Rem. 175 PSP Core-Lokt	velocity, fps	2650	2445	2248	2061	1883
	energy, ft-lb	2728	2322	1964	1650	1378
	arc, inches:		+2.2	0	-9.1	-26.4
Speer 160 Grand Slam	velocity, fps	2600	2376	2164	1962	
	energy, ft-lb	2401	2006	1663	1368	
	arc, inches:		+2.3	0	-9.8	-28.6
Speer 175 Grand Slam	velocity, fps	2650	2461	2280	2106	
	energy, ft-lb	2728	2353	2019	1723	
	arc, inches:		+2.4	0	-9.2	-26.2

7x65 R

CARTRIDGE BULLET	RANGE, YARDS:	0	100	200	300	400
Norma 150 FMJ	velocity, fps	2756	2552	2357	2170	
	energy, ft-lb	2530	2169	1850	1569	
	arc, inches:		+1.9	0	-8.2	
Norma 156 Oryx	velocity, fps	2723	2454	2200	1962	
	energy, ft-lb	2569	2086	1678	1334	
	arc, inches:		+2.1	0	-9.3	

CARTRIDGE BULLET	RANGE, YARDS:	0	100	200	300	400
Norma 170 Plastic Point	velocity, fps	2625	2390	2167	1956	
	energy, ft-lb	2602	2157	1773	1445	
	arc, inches:		+2.3	0	-9.7	
Norma 170 Vulkan	velocity, fps	2657	2392	2143	1909	
	energy, ft-lb	2666	2161	1734	1377	
	arc, inches:		+2.3	0	-9.9	
Norma 170 Oryx	velocity, fps	2657	2378	2115	1871	
	energy, ft-lb	2666	2135	1690	1321	
	arc, inches:		+2.3	0	-10.1	

.284 WINCHESTER

CARTRIDGE BULLET	RANGE, YARDS:	0	100	200	300	400
Win. 150 Power-Point	velocity, fps	2860	2595	2344	2108	1886
	energy, ft-lb	2724	2243	1830	1480	1185
	arc, inches:		+2.1	0	-8.5	-24.8

.280 REMINGTON

CARTRIDGE BULLET	RANGE, YARDS:	0	100	200	300	400
Federal 140 Sierra Pro-Hunt.	velocity, fps	2990	2740	2500	2270	2060
	energy, ft-lb	2770	2325	1940	1605	1320
	arc, inches:		+1.6	0	-7.0	-20.8
Federal 140 Trophy Bonded	velocity, fps	2990	2630	2310	2040	1730
	energy, ft-lb	2770	2155	1655	1250	925
	arc, inches:		+1.6	0	-8.4	-25.4
Federal 140 Trophy Bonded Tip	velocity, fps	2950	2730	2520	2330	2140
	energy, ft-lb	2705	2320	1980	1680	1420
	arc, inches:		+1.6	0	-7.0	-20.6
Federal 140 Tr. Bonded HE	velocity, fps	3150	2850	2570	2300	2050
	energy, ft-lb	3085	2520	2050	1650	1310
	arc, inches:		+1.4	0	-6.7	-20.0
Federal 140 Nos. AccuBond And Bal. Tip And Solid Base	velocity, fps	3000	2800	2620	2440	2260
	energy, ft-lb	2800	2445	2130	1845	1590
	arc, inches:		+1.5	0	-6.5	-18.9
Federal 150 Hi-Shok	velocity, fps	2890	2670	2460	2260	2060
	energy, ft-lb	2780	2370	2015	1695	1420
	arc, inches:		+1.7	0	-7.5	-21.8
Federal 150 Nosler Partition	velocity, fps	2890	2690	2490	2310	2130
	energy, ft-lb	2780	2405	2070	1770	1510.
	arc, inches:		+1.7	0	-7.2	-21.1
Federal 150 Nos. AccuBond	velocity, fps	2800	2630	2460	2300	2150
	energy, ft-lb	2785	2455	2155	1885	1645
	arc, inches:		+1.8	0	-7.5	-21.5
Federal 160 Trophy Bonded	velocity, fps	2800	2570	2350	2140	1940
	energy, ft-lb	2785	2345	1960	1625	1340
	arc, inches:		+1.9	0	-8.3	-24.0
Hornady 139 SPBT LMmoly	velocity, fps	3110	2888	2675	2473	2280.
	energy, ft-lb	2985	2573	2209	1887	1604
	arc, inches:		+1.4	0	-6.5	-18.6
Hornady 139 SST Superformance	velocity, fps	3090	2891	2700	2518	2343
	energy, ft-lb	2947	2579	2250	1957	1694
	arc, inches:		+1.3	0	-6.1	-17.7
Norma 156 Oryx	velocity, fps	2789	2516	2259	2017	
	energy, ft-lb	2695	2193	1768	1410	
	arc, inches:		+2.0	0	-8.8	
Norma 170 Plastic Point	velocity, fps	2707	2468	2241	2026	
	energy, ft-lb	2767	2299	1896	1550	
	arc, inches:		+2.1	0	-9.1	
Norma 170 Vulkan	velocity, fps	2592	2346	2113	1894	
	energy, ft-lb	2537	2078	1686	1354	
	arc, inches:		+2.4	0	-10.2	
Norma 170 Oryx	velocity, fps	2690	2416	2159	1918	
	energy, ft-lb	2732	2204	1760	1389	
	arc, inches:		+2.2	0	-9.7	
Rem. 140 PSP Core-Lokt	velocity, fps	3000	2758	2528	2309	2102
	energy, ft-lb	2797	2363	1986	1657	1373
	arc, inches:		+1.5	0	-7.0	-20.5
Rem. 140 PSP boat-tail	velocity, fps	2860	2656	2460	2273	2094
	energy, ft-lb	2542	2192	1881	1606	1363
	arc, inches:		+1.7	0	-7.5	-21.7
Rem. 140 Nosler Bal. Tip	velocity, fps	3000	2804	2616	2436	2263
	energy, ft-lb	2799	2445	2128	1848	1593
	arc, inches:		+1.5	0	-6.8	-19.0

Centerfire Rifle Ballistics

.280 REMINGTON TO 7MM REMINGTON MAGNUM

CARTRIDGE BULLET	RANGE, YARDS:	0	100	200	300	400
Rem. 140 AccuTip	velocity, fps:	3000	2804	2617	2437	2265
	energy, ft-lb:	2797	2444	2129	1846	1594
	arc, inches:		+1.5	0	-6.8	-19.0
Rem. 150 PSP Core-Lokt	velocity, fps:	2890	2624	2373	2135	1912
	energy, ft-lb:	2781	2293	1875	1518	1217
	arc, inches:		+1.8	0	-8.0	-23.6
Rem. 165 SP Core-Lokt	velocity, fps:	2820	2510	2220	1950	1701
	energy, ft-lb:	2913	2308	1805	1393	1060.
	arc, inches:		+2.0	0	-9.1	-27.4
Speer 145 Grand Slam	velocity, fps:	2900	2619	2354	2105	
	energy, ft-lb:	2707	2207	1784	1426	
	arc, inches:		+2.1	0	-8.4	-24.7
Speer 160 Grand Slam	velocity, fps:	2890	2652	2425	2210	
	energy, ft-lb:	2967	2497	2089	1735	
	arc, inches:		+1.7	0	-7.7	-22.4
Win. 140 Fail Safe	velocity, fps:	3050	2756	2480	2221	1977
	energy, ft-lb:	2893	2362	1913	1533	1216
	arc, inches:		+1.5	0	-7.2	-21.5
Win. 140 Ballistic Silvertip	velocity, fps:	3040	2842	2653	2471	2297
	energy, ft-lb:	2872	2511	2187	1898	1640
	arc, inches:		+1.4	0	-6.3	-18.4

.280 ACKLEY IMPROVED

CARTRIDGE BULLET	RANGE, YARDS:	0	100	200	300	400
Nosler 140 AccuBond	velocity, fps:	3150	2947	2753	2567	2389
	energy, ft-lb:	3084	2700	2355	2048	1774
	arc, inches:	-1.5	+1.1	0	-5.0	-16.8
Nosler 150 ABLR	velocity, fps:	2930	2775	2626	2482	2342
	energy, ft-lb:	2858	2565	2297	2052	1827
	arc, inches:	-1.5	+1.5	0	-6.6	-18.7
Nosler 160 Partition	velocity, fps:	2950	2752	2562	2380	2206
	energy, ft-lb:	3091	2690	2332	2013	1729
	arc, inches:	-1.5	+1.5	0	-6.7	-19.4

7MM REMINGTON MAGNUM

CARTRIDGE BULLET	RANGE, YARDS:	0	100	200	300	400
A-Square 175 Monolithic Solid	velocity, fps:	2860	2557	2273	2008	1771
	energy, ft-lb:	3178	2540	2008	1567	1219
	arc, inches:		+1.92	0	-8.7	-25.9
Black Hills 140 Nos. Bal. Tip	velocity, fps:	3150				
	energy, ft-lb:	3084				
	arc, inches:					
Black Hills 140 Barnes XLC	velocity, fps:	3150				
	energy, ft-lb:	3084				
	arc, inches:					
Black Hills 140 Nos. Partition	velocity, fps:	3150				
	energy, ft-lb:	3084				
	arc, inches:					
Federal 140 Nosler Bal. Tip And AccuBond	velocity, fps:	3110	2910	2720	2530	2360.
	energy, ft-lb:	3005	2630	2295	1995	1725
	arc, inches:		+1.3	0	-6.0	-17.4
Federal 140 Nosler Partition	velocity, fps:	3150	2930	2710	2510	2320
	energy, ft-lb:	3085	2660	2290	1960	1670
	arc, inches:		+1.3	0	-6.0	-17.5
Federal 140 Trophy Bonded	velocity, fps:	3150	2910	2680	2460	2250.
	energy, ft-lb:	3085	2630	2230	1880	1575
	arc, inches:		+1.3	0	-6.1	-18.1
Federal 140 Trophy Copper	velocity, fps:	3150	2950	2760	2570	2400
	energy, ft-lb:	3085	2705	2360	2055	1785
	arc, inches:		+1.3	0	-5.9	-16.9
Federal 150 Hi-Shok	velocity, fps:	3110	2830	2570	2320	2090
	energy, ft-lb:	3220	2670	2200	1790	1450
	arc, inches:		+1.4	0	-6.7	-19.9
Federal 150 Nosler Bal. Tip	velocity, fps:	3110	2910	2720	2540	2370
	energy, ft-lb:	3220	2825	2470	2150	1865
	arc, inches:		+1.3	0	-6.0	-17.4
Federal 150 Nos. Solid Base	velocity, fps:	3100	2890	2690	2500	2310
	energy, ft-lb:	3200	2780	2405	2075	1775
	arc, inches:		+1.3	0	-6.2	-17.8
Federal 150 Sierra GameKing BTSP	velocity, fps:	3110	2920	2750	2580	2410
	energy, ft-lb:	3220	2850	2510	2210	1930
	arc, inches:		+1.3 0	-5.9	-17.0	

CARTRIDGE BULLET	RANGE, YARDS:	0	100	200	300	400
Federal 150 Trophy Copper	velocity, fps:	3025	2830	2650	2470	2300
	energy, ft-lb:	3045	2675	2335	2035	1765
	arc, inches:		+1.4	0	-6.4	-18.4
Federal 160 Barnes XLC	velocity, fps:	2940	2760	2580	2410	2240
	energy, ft-lb:	3070	2695	2360	2060	1785
	arc, inches:		+1.5	0	-6.8	-19.6
Federal 160 Sierra Pro-Hunt.	velocity, fps:	2940	2730	2520	2320	2140
	energy, ft-lb:	3070	2640	2260	1920	1620
	arc, inches:		+1.6	0	-7.1	-20.6
Federal 160 Nosler Partition	velocity, fps:	2950	2770	2590	2420	2250.
	energy, ft-lb:	3090	2715	2375	2075	1800
	arc, inches:		+1.5	0	-6.7	-19.4
Federal 160 Nos. AccuBond	velocity, fps:	2950	2770	2600	2440	2280.
	energy, ft-lb:	3090	2730	2405	2110	1845
	arc, inches:		+1.5	0	-6.6	-19.1
Federal 160 Trophy Bonded	velocity, fps:	2940	2660	2390	2140	1900
	energy, ft-lb:	3070	2505	2025	1620	1280.
	arc, inches:		+1.7	0	-7.9	-23.3
Federal 165 Sierra GameKing BTSP	velocity, fps:	2950	2800	2650	2510	2370.
	energy, ft-lb:	3190	2865	2570	2300	2050
	arc, inches:		+1.5	0	-6.4	-18.4
Federal 175 Hi-Shok	velocity, fps:	2860	2650	2440	2240	2060
	energy, ft-lb:	3180	2720	2310	1960	1640
	arc, inches:		+1.7	0	-7.6	-22.1
Federal 175 Trophy Bonded	velocity, fps:	2860	2600	2350	2120	1900
	energy, ft-lb:	3180	2625	2150	1745	1400
	arc, inches:		+1.8	0	-8.2	-24.0
Hornady 139 SPBT	velocity, fps:	3150	2933	2727	2530	2341
	energy, ft-lb:	3063	2656	2296	1976	1692
	arc, inches:		+1.2	0	-6.1	-17.7
Hornady 139 SPBT HMmoly	velocity, fps:	3250	3041	2822	2613	2413
	energy, ft-lb:	3300	2854	2458	2106	1797
	arc, inches:		+1.1 0	-5.7	-16.6	
Hornady 139 SST (or Interbond)	velocity, fps:	3150	2948	2754	2569	2391
	energy, ft-lb:	3062	2681	2341	2037	1764
	arc, inches:		+1.1	0	-5.7	-16.7
Hornady 139 SST Custom Lite	velocity, fps:	2800	2613	2434	2262	2097
	energy, ft-lb:	2420	2108	1829	1579	1357
	arc, inches:		+1.8	0	-7.7	-22.2
Hornady 139 SST LM (or Interbond)	velocity, fps:	3250	3044	2847	2657	2475
	energy, ft-lb:	3259	2860	2501	2178	1890
	arc, inches:		+1.1	0	-5.5	-16.2
Hornady 139 SPBT HMmoly	velocity, fps:	3250	3041	2822	2613	2413
	energy, ft-lb:	3300	2854	2458	2106	1797.
	arc, inches:		+1.1	0	-5.7	-16.6
Hornady 154 Soft Point	velocity, fps:	3035	2814	2604	2404	2212
	energy, ft-lb:	3151	2708	2319	1977	1674
	arc, inches:		+1.3	0	-6.7	-19.3
Hornady 154 SST (or Interbond)	velocity, fps:	3035	2850	2672	2501	2337
	energy, ft-lb:	3149	2777	2441	2139	1867
	arc, inches:		+1.4	0	-6.5	-18.7
Hornady 162 SP boat-tail	velocity, fps:	2940	2757	2582	2413	2251
	energy, ft-lb:	3110	2735	2399	2095	1823
	arc, inches:		+1.6	0	-6.7	-19.7
Hornady 162 SST Superformance	velocity, fps:	3030	2856	2689	2527	2372
	energy, ft-lb:	3302	2933	2600	2298	2023
	arc, inches:		+1.4	0	-6.2	-17.8
Hornady 175 SP	velocity, fps:	2860	2650	2440	2240	2060.
	energy, ft-lb:	3180	2720	2310	1960	1640
	arc, inches:		+2.0	0	-7.9	-22.7
Norma 140 Nosler Bal. Tip	velocity, fps:	3150	2936	2732	2537	
	energy, ft-lb:	3085	2680	2320	2001	
	arc, inches:		+1.2	0	-5.9	
Norma 140 Barnes X TS	velocity, fps:	3117	2912	2716	2529	
	energy, ft-lb:	3021	2637	2294	1988	
	arch, inches:		+1.3	0	-6.0	
Norma 150 Scirocco	velocity, fps:	3117	2934	2758	2589	
	energy, ft-lb:	3237	2869	2535	2234	
	arc, inches:		+1.2	0	-5.8	
Norma 156 Oryx	velocity, fps:	2953	2670	2404	2153	
	energy, ft-lb:	3021	2470	2002	1607	
	arc, inches:		+1.7	0	-7.7	

7MM REMINGTON MAGNUM TO 7MM WINCHESTER SHORT MAGNUM

CARTRIDGE BULLET	RANGE, YARDS:	0	100	200	300	400
Norma 170 Vulkan	velocity, fps:	3018	2747	2493	2252	
	energy, ft-lb:	3439	2850	2346	1914	
	arc, inches:		+1.5	0	-2.8	
Norma 170 Oryx	velocity, fps:	2887	2601	2333	2080	
	energy, ft-lb:	3147	2555	2055	1634	
	arc, inches:		+1.8	0	-8.2	
Norma 170 Plastic Point	velocity, fps:	3018	2762	2519	2290	
	energy, ft-lb:	3439	2880	2394	1980	
	arc, inches:		+1.5	0	-7.0	
PMC 140 Barnes X	velocity, fps:	3000	2808	2624	2448	2279
	energy, ft-lb:	2797	2451	2141	1863	1614
	arc, inches:		+1.5	0	-6.6	18.9
PMC 140 Pointed Soft Point	velocity, fps:	3099	2878	2668	2469	2279
	energy, ft-lb:	2984	2574	2212	1895	1614
	arc, inches:		+1.4	0	-6.2	-18.1
PMC 140 SP boat-tail	velocity, fps:	3125	2891	2669	2457	2255
	energy, ft-lb:	3035	2597	2213	1877	1580
	arc, inches:		+1.4	0	-6.3	-18.4
PMC 160 Barnes X	velocity, fps:	2800	2639	2484	2334	2189
	energy, ft-lb:	2785	2474	2192	1935	1703
	arc, inches:		+1.8	0	-7.4	-21.2
PMC 160 Pointed Soft Point	velocity, fps:	2914	2748	2586	2428	2276
	energy, ft-lb:	3016	2682	2375	2095	1840
	arc, inches:		+1.6	0	-6.7	-19.4
PMC 160 SP boat-tail	velocity, fps:	2900	2696	2501	2314	2135
	energy, ft-lb:	2987	2582	2222	1903	1620
	arc, inches:		+1.7	0	-7.2	-21.0
PMC 175 Pointed Soft Point	velocity, fps:	2860	2645	2442	2244	2957
	energy, ft-lb:	3178	2718	2313	1956	1644
	arc, inches:		+2.0	0	-7.9	-22.7
Remington 140 Copper Solid Tipped	velocity, fps:	3175	2964	2762	2570	2385
	energy, ft-lb:	3133	2730	2372	2053	1768
	arc, inches:		+1.4	0	-6.0	-17.6
Rem. 140 PSP Core-Lokt mr	velocity, fps:	2710	2482	2265	2059	1865
	energy, ft-lb:	2283	1915	1595	1318	1081
	arc, inches:		+1.0	-2.5	-12.8	-31.3
Rem. 140 PSP Core-Lokt	velocity, fps:	3175	2923	2684	2458	2243
	energy, ft-lb:	3133	2655	2240	1878	1564
	arc, inches:		+2.2	+1.9	-3.2	-14.2
Rem. 140 PSP boat-tail	velocity, fps:	3175	2956	2747	2547	2356
	energy, ft-lb:	3133	2715	2345	2017	1726
	arc, inches:		+2.2	+1.6	-3.1	-13.4
Rem. 150 AccuTip	velocity, fps:	3110	2926	2749	2579	2415
	energy, ft-lb:	3221	2850	2516	2215	1943
	arc, inches:		+1.3	0	-5.9	-17.0
Rem. 150 PSP Core-Lokt	velocity, fps:	3110	2830	2568	2320	2085
	energy, ft-lb:	3221	2667	2196	1792	1448
	arc, inches:		+1.3	0	-6.6	-20.2
Rem. 150 Nosler Bal. Tip	velocity, fps:	3110	2912	2723	2542	2367
	energy, ft-lb:	3222	2825	2470	2152	1867
	arc, inches:		+1.2	0	-5.9	-17.3
Rem. 150 Swift Scirocco	velocity, fps:	3110	2927	2751	2582	2419
	energy, ft-lb:	3221	2852	2520	2220	1948
	arc, inches:		+1.3	0	-5.9	-17.0
Rem. 160 Swift A-Frame	velocity, fps:	2900	2659	2430	2212	2006
	energy, ft-lb:	2987	2511	2097	1739	1430
	arc, inches:		+1.7	0	-7.6	-22.4
Rem. 160 Nosler Partition	velocity, fps:	2950	2752	2563	2381	2207
	energy, ft-lb:	3091	2690	2333	2014	1730
	arc, inches:		+0.6	-1.9	-9.6	-23.6
Rem. 175 PSP Core-Lokt	velocity, fps:	2860	2645	2440	2244	2057
	energy, ft-lb:	3178	2718	2313	1956	1644
	arc, inches:		+1.7	0	-7.6	-22.1
Speer 145 Grand Slam	velocity, fps:	3140	2843	2565	2304	
	energy, ft-lb:	3174	2602	2118	1708	
	arc, inches:		+1.4	0	-6.7	
Speer 175 Grand Slam	velocity, fps:	2850	2653	2463	2282	
	energy, ft-lb:	3156	2734	2358	2023	
	arc, inches:		+1.7	0	-7.5	-21.7
Win. 140 Fail Safe	velocity, fps:	3150	2861	2589	2333	2092
	energy, ft-lb:	3085	2544	2085	1693	1361
	arc, inches:		+1.4	0	-6.6	-19.5
Win. 140 Ballistic Silvertip	velocity, fps:	3100	2889	2687	2494	2310
	energy, ft-lb:	2988	2595	2245	1934	1659.
	arc, inches:		+1.3	0	-6.2	-17.9
Win. 140 AccuBond CT	velocity, fps:	3180	2965	2760	2565	2377
	energy, ft-lb:	3143	2733	2368	2044	1756
	arc, inches:		+1.2	0	-5.8	-16.9
Win. 150 Power-Point	velocity, fps:	3090	2812	2551	2304	2071
	energy, ft-lb:	3181	2634	2167	1768	1429
	arc, inches:		+1.5	0	-6.8	-20.2
Win. 150 Power-Point Plus	velocity, fps:	3130	2849	2586	2337	2102
	energy, ft-lb:	3264	2705	2227	1819	1472
	arc, inches:		+1.4	0	-6.6	-19.6
Win. 150 Ballistic Silvertip	velocity, fps:	3100	2903	2714	2533	2359
	energy, ft-lb:	3200	2806	2453	2136	1853
	arc, inches:		+1.3	0	-6.0	-17.5
Win. 160 AccuBond	velocity, fps:	2950	2766	2590	2420	2257
	energy, ft-lb:	3091	2718	2382	2080	1809
	arc, inches:		+1.5	0	-6.7	-19.4
Win. 160 Partition Gold	velocity, fps:	2950	2743	2546	2357	2176
	energy, ft-lb:	3093	2674	2303	1974	1682
	arc, inches:		+1.6	0	-6.9	-20.1
Win. 160 Fail Safe	velocity, fps:	2920	2678	2449	2331	2025
	energy, ft-lb:	3030	2549	2131	1769	1457
	arc, inches:		+1.7	0	-7.5	-22.0
Win. 175 Power-Point	velocity, fps:	2860	2645	2440	2244	2057
	energy, ft-lb:	3178	2718	2313	1956	1644
	arc, inches:		+2.0	0	-7.9	-22.7

7MM REMINGTON SHORT ULTRA MAGNUM

CARTRIDGE BULLET	RANGE, YARDS:	0	100	200	300	400
Rem. 140 PSP C-L Ultra	velocity, fps:	3175	2934	2707	2490	2283
	energy, ft-lb:	3133	2676	2277	1927	1620.
	arc, inches:		+1.3	0	-6.0	-17.7
Rem. 150 PSP Core-Lokt	velocity, fps:	3110	2828	2563	2313	2077
	energy, ft-lb:	3221	2663	2188	1782	1437
	arc, inches:		+2.5	+2.1	-3.6	-15.8
Rem. 160 Partition	velocity, fps:	2960	2762	2572	2390	2215
	energy, ft-lb:	3112	2709	2350	2029	1744
	arc, inches:		+2.6	+2.2	-3.6	-15.4
Rem. 160 PSP C-L Ultra	velocity, fps:	2960	2733	2518	2313	2117
	energy, ft-lb:	3112	2654	2252	1900	1592
	arc, inches:		+2.7	+2.2	-3.7	-16.2

7MM WINCHESTER SHORT MAGNUM

CARTRIDGE BULLET	RANGE, YARDS:	0	100	200	300	400
Federal 140 Nos. AccuBond	velocity, fps:	3250	3040	2840	2660	2470
	energy, ft-lb:	3285	2875	2515	2190	1900
	arc, inches:		+1.1	0	-5.5	-15.8
Federal 140 Nos. Bal. Tip	velocity, fps:	3310	3100	2900	2700	2520
	energy, ft-lb:	3405	2985	2610	2270	1975
	arc, inches:		+1.1	0	-5.2	15.2
Federal 150 Nos. Solid Base	velocity, fps:	3230	3010	2800	2600	2410
	energy, ft-lb:	3475	3015	2615	2255	1935
	arc, inches:		+1.3	0	-5.6	-16.3
Federal 150 Trophy Copper	velocity, fps:	3140	2940	2750	2570	2400
	energy, ft-lb:	3285	2885	2525	2205	1915
	arc, inches:		+1.3	0	-5.9	-16.9
Federal 160 Nos. AccuBond	velocity, fps:	3120	2940	2760	2590	2430
	energy, ft-lb:	3460	3065	2710	2390	2095
	arc, inches:		+1.3	0	-5.9	-16.8
Federal 160 Nos. Partition	velocity, fps:	3160	2950	2750	2560	2380.
	energy, ft-lb:	3545	3095	2690	2335	2015.
	arc, inches:		+1.2	0	-5.9	-16.9

Centerfire Rifle Ballistics

7MM WINCHESTER SHORT MAGNUM TO 7MM REMINGTON ULTRA MAGNUM

CARTRIDGE BULLET	RANGE, YARDS:	0	100	200	300	400
Federal 160 Barnes TS	velocity, fps:	2990	2780	2590	2400	2220
	energy, ft-lb:	3175	2755	2380	2045	1750
	arc, inches:		+1.5	0	-6.6	-19.4
Federal 160 Trophy Bonded	velocity, fps:	3120	2880	2650	2440	2230
	energy, ft-lb:	3460	2945	2500	2105	1765
	arc, inches:		+1.4	0	-6.3	-18.5
Federal 160 Trophy Bonded Tip	velocity, fps:	3000	2820	2640	2470	2310
	energy, ft-lb:	3195	2820	2480	2170	1895
	arc, inches:		+1.5	0	-6.4	-18.5
Win. 140 Bal. Silvertip	velocity, fps:	3225	3008	2801	2603	2414
	energy, ft-lb:	3233	2812	2438	2106	1812
	arc, inches:		+1.2	0	-5.6	-16.4
Win. 140 AccuBond CT	velocity, fps:	3225	3008	2801	2604	2415
	energy, ft-lb:	3233	2812	2439	2107	1812
	arc, inches:		+1.2	0	-5.6	-16.4
Win. 150 Power Point	velocity, fps:	3200	2915	2648	2396	2157
	energy, ft-lb:	3410	2830	2335	1911	1550
	arc, inches:		+1.3	0	-6.3	-18.6
Win. 160 AccuBond	velocity, fps:	3050	2862	2682	2509	2342
	energy, ft-lb:	3306	2911	2556	2237	1950
	arc, inches:		1.4	0	-6.2	-17.9
Win. 160 Fail Safe	velocity, fps:	2990	2744	2512	2291	2081
	energy, ft-lb:	3176	2675	2241	1864	1538
	arc, inches:		+1.6	0	-7.1	-20.8

7MM WEATHERBY MAGNUM

CARTRIDGE BULLET	RANGE, YARDS:	0	100	200	300	400
Federal 160 Nosler Partition	velocity, fps:	3050	2850	2650	2470	2290
	energy, ft-lb:	3305	2880	2505	2165	1865
	arc, inches:		+1.4	0	-6.3	-18.4
Federal 160 Sierra GameKing BTSP	velocity, fps:	3050	2880	2710	2560	2400
	energy, ft-lb:	3305	2945	2615	2320	2050
	arc, inches:		+1.4	0	-6.1	-17.4
Federal 160 Trophy Bonded	velocity, fps:	3050	2730	2420	2140	1880.
	energy, ft-lb:	3305	2640	2085	1630	1255
	arc, inches:		+1.6	0	-7.6	-22.7
Federal 160 Trophy Bonded Tip	velocity, fps:	3100	2910	2730	2560	2390
	energy, ft-lb:	3415	3015	2655	2330	2035
	arc, inches:		+1.3	0	-6.0	-17.2
Hornady 139 GMX Superformance	velocity, fps:	3300	3091	2891	2701	2519
	energy, ft-lb:	3361	2948	2580	2252	1958
	arc, inches:		+1.1	0	-5.2	-15.2
Hornady 154 Soft Point	velocity, fps:	3200	2971	2753	2546	2348.
	energy, ft-lb:	3501	3017	2592	2216	1885
	arc, inches:		+1.2	0	-5.8	-17.0
Hornady 154 SST (or Interbond)	velocity, fps:	3200	3009	2825	2648	2478
	energy, ft-lb:	3501	3096	2729	2398	2100
	arc, inches:		+1.2	0	-5.7	-16.5
Hornady 175 Soft Point	velocity, fps:	2910	2709	2516	2331	2154
	energy, ft-lb:	3290	2850	2459	2111	1803
	arc, inches:		+1.6	0	-7.1	-20.6
Wby. 139 Pointed Expanding	velocity, fps:	3340	3079	2834	2601	2380.
	energy, ft-lb:	3443	2926	2478	2088	1748
	arc, inches:		+2.9	+3.6	0	-8.7
Wby. 140 Nosler Partition	velocity, fps:	3303	3069	2847	2636	2434
	energy, ft-lb:	3391	2927	2519	2159	1841
	arc, inches:		+2.9	+3.6	0	-8.5
Wby. 150 Nosler Bal. Tip	velocity, fps:	3300	3093	2896	2708	2527
	energy, ft-lb:	3627	3187	2793	2442	2127
	arc, inches:		+2.8	+3.5	0	-8.2
Wby. 150 Barnes X	veloctiy, fps:	3100	2901	2710	2527	2352
	energy, ft-lb:	3200	2802	2446	2127	1842
	arc, inches:		+3.3	+4.0	0	-9.4
Wby. 154 Pointed Expanding	velocity, fps:	3260	3028	2807	2597	2397
	energy, ft-lb:	3634	3134	2694	2307	1964
	arc, inches:		+3.0	+3.7	0	-8.8
Wby. 160 Nosler Partition	velocity, fps:	3200	2991	2791	2600	2417
	energy, ft-lb:	3638	3177	2767	2401	2075.
	arc, inches:		+3.1	+3.8	0	-8.9
Wby. 175 Pointed Expanding	velocity, fps:	3070	2861	2662	2471	2288
	energy, ft-lb:	3662	3181	2753	2373	2034
	arc, inches:		+3.5	+4.2	0	-9.9

7MM DAKOTA

CARTRIDGE BULLET	RANGE, YARDS:	0	100	200	300	400
Dakota 140 Barnes X	velocity, fps:	3500	3253	3019	2798	2587
	energy, ft-lb:	3807	3288	2833	2433	2081
	arc, inches:		+2.0	+2.1	-1.5	-9.6
Dakota 160 Barnes X	velocity, fps:	3200	3001	2811	2630	2455
	energy, ft-lb:	3637	3200	2808	2456	2140
	arc, inches:		+2.1	+1.9	-2.8	-12.5

7MM STW

CARTRIDGE BULLET	RANGE, YARDS:	0	100	200	300	400
A-Square 140 Nos. Bal. Tip	velocity, fps:	3450	3254	3067	2888	2715
	energy, ft-lb:	3700	3291	2924	2592	2292
	arc, inches:		+2.2	+3.0	0	-7.3
A-Square 160 Nosler Part.	velocity, fps:	3250	3071	2900	2735	2576.
	energy, ft-lb:	3752	3351	2987	2657	2357
	arc, inches:		+2.8	+3.5	0	-8.2
A-Square 160 SP boat-tail	velocity, fps:	3250	3087	2930	2778	2631
	energy, ft-lb:	3752	3385	3049	2741	2460
	arc, inches:		+2.8	+3.4	0	-8.0
Federal 140 Trophy Bonded	velocity, fps:	3330	3080	2850	2630	2420
	energy, ft-lb:	3435	2950	2520	2145	1815
	arc, inches:		+1.1	0	-5.4	-15.8
Federal 150 Trophy Bonded	velocity, fps:	3250	3010	2770	2560	2350.
	energy, ft-lb:	3520	3010	2565	2175	1830
	arc, inches:		+1.2	0	-5.7	-16.7
Federal 160 Sierra GameKing BTSP	velocity, fps:	3200	3020	2850	2670	2530.
	energy, ft-lb:	3640	3245	2890	2570	2275
	arc, inches:		+1.1	0	-5.5	-15.7
Federal 160 Trophy Bonded Tip	velocity, fps:	3100	2910	2730	2560	2390
	energy, ft-lb:	3415	3015	2655	2330	2035
	arc, inches:		+1.3	0	-6.0	-17.2
Nosler 175 ABLR	velocity, fps:	2900	2760	2625	2493	2366
	energy, ft-lb:	3267	2960	2677	2416	2175
	arc, inches:	-1.5	+1.5	0	-6.6	-18.8
Rem. 140 PSP Core-Lokt	velocity, fps:	3325	3064	2818	2585	2364
	energy, ft-lb:	3436	2918	2468	2077	1737
	arc, inches:		+2.0	+1.7	-2.9	-12.8
Rem. 140 Swift A-Frame	velocity, fps:	3325	3020	2735	2467	2215
	energy, ft-lb:	3436	2834	2324	1892	1525
	arc, inches:		+2.1	+1.8	-3.1	-13.8
Speer 145 Grand Slam	velocity, fps:	3300	2992	2075	2435	
	energy, ft-lb:	3506	2882	2355	1909	
	arc, inches:		+1.2	0	-6.0	-17.8
Win. 140 Ballistic Silvertip	velocity, fps:	3320	3100	2890	2690	2499
	energy, ft-lb:	3427	2982	2597	2250	1941
	arc, inches:		+1.1	0	-5.2	-15.2
Win. 150 Power-Point	velocity, fps:	3250	2957	2683	2424	2181
	energy, ft-lb:	3519	2913	2398	1958	1584
	arc, inches:		+1.2	0	-6.1	-18.1
Win. 160 Fail Safe	velocity, fps:	3150	2894	2652	2422	2204
	energy, ft-lb:	3526	2976	2499	2085	1727
	arc, inches:		+1.3	0	-6.3	-18.5

7MM REMINGTON ULTRA MAGNUM

CARTRIDGE BULLET	RANGE, YARDS:	0	100	200	300	400
Nosler 175 ABLR	velocity, fps:	3040	2896	2756	2621	2490
	energy, ft-lb:	3590	3258	2952	2669	2409
	arc, inches:	-1.5	+1.3	0	-5.9	-16.9
Rem. 140 PSP Core-Lokt	velocity, fps:	3425	3158	2907	2669	2444
	energy, ft-lb:	3646	3099	2626	2214	1856
	arc, inches:		+1.8	+1.6	-2.7	-11.9
Rem. 140 Nosler Partition	velocity, fps:	3425	3184	2956	2740	2534
	energy, ft-lb:	3646	3151	2715	2333	1995
	arc, inches:		+1.7	+1.6	-2.6	-11.4
Rem. 160 Nosler Partition	velocity, fps:	3200	2991	2791	2600	2417
	energy, ft-lb:	3637	3177	2767	2401	2075
	arc, inches:		+2.1	+1.8	-3.0	-12.9

BALLISTICS

7.21 (.284) FIREHAWK

CARTRIDGE BULLET	RANGE, YARDS:	0	100	200	300	400
Lazzeroni 140 Nosler Part.	velocity, fps:	3580	3349	3130	2923	2724
	energy, ft-lb:	3985	3488	3048	2656	2308
	arc, inches:		+2.2	+2.9	0	-7.0
Lazzeroni 160 Swift A-Fr.	velocity, fps:	3385	3167	2961	2763	2574
	energy, ft-lb:	4072	3565	3115	2713	2354
	arc, inches:		+2.6	+3.3	0	-7.8

7.5x55 SWISS

CARTRIDGE BULLET	RANGE, YARDS:	0	100	200	300	400
Norma 180 Soft Point	velocity, fps:	2651	2432	2223	2025	
	energy, ft-lb:	2810	2364	1976	1639	
	arc, inches:		+2.2	0	-9.3	
Norma 180 Oryx	velocity, fps:	2493	2222	1968	1734	
	energy, ft-lb:	2485	1974	1549	1201	
	arc, inches:		+2.7	0	-11.8	

7.62x39 RUSSIAN

CARTRIDGE BULLET	RANGE, YARDS:	0	100	200	300	400
Federal 123 Hi-Shok	velocity, fps:	2300	2030	1780	1550	1350
	energy, ft-lb:	1445	1125	860	655	500.
	arc, inches:	0	-7.0	-25.1		
Federal 124 FMJ	velocity, fps:	2300	2030	1780	1560	1360
	energy, ft-lb:	1455	1135	875	670	510
	arc, inches:		+3.5	0	-14.6	-43.5
PMC 123 FMJ	velocity, fps:	2350	2072	1817	1583	1368
	energy, ft-lb:	1495	1162	894	678	507
	arc, inches:	0	-5.0	-26.4	-67.8	
PMC 125 Pointed Soft Point	velocity, fps:	2320	2046	1794	1563	1350
	energy, ft-lb:	1493	1161	893	678	505.
	arc, inches:	0	-5.2	-27.5	-70.6	
Rem. 125 Pointed Soft Point	velocity, fps:	2365	2062	1783	1533	1320
	energy, ft-lb:	1552	1180	882	652	483
	arc, inches:	0	-6.7	-24.5		
Win. 123 Soft Point	velocity, fps:	2365	2033	1731	1465	1248
	energy, ft-lb:	1527	1129	818	586	425
	arc, inches:		+3.8	0	-15.4	-46.3

.30 CARBINE

CARTRIDGE BULLET	RANGE, YARDS:	0	100	200	300	400
Federal 110 Hi-Shok RN	velocity, fps:	1990	1570	1240	1040	920
	energy, ft-lb:	965	600	375	260	210
	arc, inches:	0	-12.8	-46.9		
Federal 110 FMJ	velocity, fps:	1990	1570	1240	1040	920
	energy, ft-lb:	965	600	375	260	210
	arc, inches:	0	-12.8	-46.9		
Hornady 110 FTX	velocity, fps:	2000	1601	1279	1067	
(20-inch barrel)	energy, ft-lb:	977	626	399	278	
	arc, inches:	0	-12.9	-47.2		
Magtech 110 FMC	velocity, fps:	1990	1654			
	energy, ft-lb:	965	668			
	arc, inches:	0				
PMC 110 FMJ	(and RNSP)velocity, fps:	1927	1548	1248		
	energy, ft-lb:	906	585	380		
	arc, inches:	0	-14.2			
Rem. 110 Soft Point	velocity, fps:	1990	1567	1236	1035	923
	energy, ft-lb:	967	600	373	262	208
	arc, inches:	0	-12.9	-48.6		
Win. 110 Hollow Soft Point	velocity, fps:	1990	1567	1236	1035	923
	energy, ft-lb:	967	600	373	262	208
	arc, inches:	0	-13.5	-49.9		

.30 T/C HORNADAY

CARTRIDGE BULLET	RANGE, YARDS:	0	100	200	300	400
Hornady 150	velocity, fps	3000	2772	2555	2348	
	energy, ft-lb	2997	2558	2176	1836	
	arc, inches	-1.5	+1.5	0	-6.9	

CARTRIDGE BULLET	RANGE, YARDS:	0	100	200	300	400
Hornady 165	velocity, fps	2850	2644	2447	2258	
	energy, ft-lb	2975	2560	2193	1868	
	arc, inches	-1.5	+1.7	0	-7.6	

.30-30 WINCHESTER

CARTRIDGE BULLET	RANGE, YARDS:	0	100	200	300	400
Federal 125 Hi-Shok HP	velocity, fps:	2570	2090	1660	1320	1080
	energy, ft-lb:	1830	1210	770	480	320
	arc, inches:		+3.3	0	-16.0	-50.9
Federal 150 Hi-Shok FN	velocity, fps:	2390	2020	1680	1400	1180
	energy, ft-lb:	1900	1355	945	650	460
	arc, inches:		+3.6	0	-15.9	-49.1
Federal 170 Hi-Shok RN	velocity, fps:	2200	1900	1620	1380	1190
	energy, ft-lb:	1830	1355	990	720	535
	arc, inches:		+4.1	0	-17.4	-52.4
Federal 170 Sierra Pro-Hunt.	velocity, fps:	2200	1820	1500	1240	1060
	energy, ft-lb:	1830	1255	845	575	425
	arc, inches:		+4.5	0	-20.0	-63.5
Federal 170 Nosler Partition	velocity, fps:	2200	1900	1620	1380	1190
	energy, ft-lb:	1830	1355	990	720	535
	arc, inches:		+4.1	0	-17.4	-52.4
Hornady 150 Round Nose	velocity, fps:	2390	1973	1605	1303	1095
	energy, ft-lb:	1902	1296	858	565	399
	arc, inches:	0	-8.2	-30.0		
Hornady 160 Evolution	velocity, fps:	2400	2150	1916	1699	
	energy, ft-lb:	2046	1643	1304	1025	
	arc, inches:		+3.0	0.2	-12.1	
Hornady 170 Flat Point	velocity, fps:	2200	1895	1619	1381	1191
	energy, ft-lb:	1827	1355	989	720	535
	arc, inches:	0	-8.9	-31.1		
Norma 150 Soft Point	velocity, fps:	2329	2008	1716	1459	
	energy, ft-lb:	1807	1344	981	709	
	arc, inches:		+3.6	0	-15.5	
PMC 150 Starfire HP	velocity, fps:	2100	1769	1478		
	energy, ft-lb:	1469	1042	728		
	arc, inches:	0	-10.8			
PMC 150 Flat Nose	velocity, fps:	2300	1943	1627		
	energy, ft-lb:	1762	1257	881		
	arc, inches:	0	-7.8			
PMC 170 Flat Nose	velocity, fps:	2150	1840	1566		
	energy, ft-lb:	1745	1277	926		
	arc, inches:	0	-8.9			
Rem. 55 PSP (sabot)	velocity, fps:	3400	2693	2085	1570	1187
"Accelerator"	energy, ft-lb:	1412	886	521	301	172
	arc, inches:		+1.7	0	-9.9	-34.3
Rem. 150 SP Core-Lokt	velocity, fps:	2390	1973	1605	1303	1095
	energy, ft-lb:	1902	1296	858	565	399
	arc, inches:	0	-7.6	-28.8		
Rem. 170 SP Core-Lokt	velocity, fps:	2200	1895	1619	1381	1191
	energy, ft-lb:	1827	1355	989	720	535
	arc, inches:	0	-8.3	-29.9		
Rem. 170 HP Core-Lokt	velocity, fps:	2200	1895	1619	1381	1191.
	energy, ft-lb:	1827	1355	989	720	535
	arc, inches:	0	-8.3	-29.9		
Speer 150 Flat Nose	velocity, fps:	2370	2067	1788	1538	
	energy, ft-lb:	1870	1423	1065	788	
	arc, inches:		+3.3	0	-14.4	-43.7
Win. 150 Hollow Point	velocity, fps:	2390	2018	1684	1398	1177
	energy, ft-lb:	1902	1356	944	651	461
	arc, inches:	0	-7.7	-27.9		
Win. 150 Power-Point	velocity, fps:	2390	2018	1684	1398	1177
	energy, ft-lb:	1902	1356	944	651	461
	arc, inches:	0	-7.7	-27.9		
Win. 150 Silvertip	velocity,fps:	2390	2018	1684	1398	1177
	energy, ft-lb:	1902	1356	944	651	461
	arc, inches:	0	-7.7	-27.9		

Centerfire Rifle Ballistics

.30-30 WINCHESTER TO .308 WINCHESTER

CARTRIDGE BULLET	RANGE, YARDS:	0	100	200	300	400
Win. 150 Power-Point Plus	velocity, fps:	2480	2095	1747	1446	1209
	energy, ft-lb:	2049	1462	1017	697	487
	arc, inches:		0	-6.5	-24.5	
Win. 170 Power-Point	velocity, fps:	2200	1895	1619	1381	1191
	energy, ft-lb:	1827	1355	989	720	535.
	arc, inches:		0	-8.9	-31.1	
Win. 170 Silvertip	velocity, fps:	2200	1895	1619	1381	1191
	energy, ft-lb:	1827	1355	989	720	535
	arc, inches:		0	-8.9	-31.1	

.300 SAVAGE

CARTRIDGE BULLET	RANGE, YARDS:	0	100	200	300	400
Federal 150 Hi-Shok	velocity, fps:	2630	2350	2100	1850	1630
	energy, ft-lb:	2305	1845	1460	1145	885
	arc, inches:		+2.4	0	-10.4	-30.9
Federal 180 Hi-Shok	velocity, fps:	2350	2140	1940	1750	1570
	energy, ft-lb:	2205	1825	1495	1215	985
	arc, inches:		+3.1	0	-12.4	-36.1
Hornady 150 SST	velocity, fps:	2740	2499	2272	2056	1852
	energy, ft-lb:	2500	2081	1718	1407	1143
	arc, inches:		+2.1	0	-8.8	-25.8
Rem. 150 PSP Core-Lokt	velocity, fps:	2630	2354	2095	1853	1631
	energy, ft-lb:	2303	1845	1462	1143	806.
	arc, inches:		+2.4	0	-10.4	-30.9
Rem. 180 SP Core-Lokt	velocity, fps:	2350	2025	1728	1467	1252
	energy, ft-lb:	2207	1639	1193	860	626
	arc, inches:		0	-7.1	-25.9	
Win. 150 Power-Point	velocity, fps:	2630	2311	2015	1743	1500
	energy, ft-lb:	2303	1779	1352	1012	749
	arc, inches:		+2.8	0	-11.5	-34.4

.307 WINCHESTER

CARTRIDGE BULLET	RANGE, YARDS:	0	100	200	300	400
Win. 180 Power-Point	velocity, fps:	2510	2179	1874	1599	1362
	energy, ft-lb:	2519	1898	1404	1022	742
	arc, inches:		+1.5	-3.6	-18.6	-47.1

.30-40 KRAG

CARTRIDGE BULLET	RANGE, YARDS:	0	100	200	300	400
Rem. 180 PSP Core-Lokt	velocity, fps:	2430	2213	2007	1813	1632.
	energy, ft-lb:	2360	1957	1610	1314	1064
	arc, inches, s:		0	-5.6	-18.6	
Win. 180 Power-Point	velocity, fps:	2430	2099	1795	1525	1298
	energy, ft-lb:	2360	1761	1288	929	673
	arc, inches, s:		0	-7.1	-25.0	

7.62x54R RUSSIAN

CARTRIDGE BULLET	RANGE, YARDS:	0	100	200	300	400
Norma 150 Soft Point	velocity, fps:	2953	2622	2314	2028	
	energy, ft-lb:	2905	2291	1784	1370	
	arc, inches:		+1.8	0	-8.3	
Norma 180 Alaska	velocity, fps:	2575	2362	2159	1967	
	energy, ft-lb:	2651	2231	1864	1546	
	arc, inches:		+2.9	0	-12.9	
Winchester 180 FMJ	velocity, fps:	2580	2401	2230	2066	1909
	energy, ft-lb:	2658	2304	1987	1706	1457
	arc, inches:	-1.5	+2.6	0	-9.6	-27.3
Winchester 180 SP	velocity, fps:	2625	2302	2003	1729	1485
	energy, ft-lb:	2751	2117	1603	1195	882
	arc, inches:	-1.5	+2.9	0	-11.6	-34.9

.308 MARLIN EXPRESS

CARTRIDGE BULLET	RANGE, YARDS:	0	100	200	300	400
Hornady 160	velocity, fps	2660	2438	2226	2026	1836
	energy, ft-lb	2513	2111	1761	1457	1197
	arc, inches	-1.5	+3.0	+1.7	-6.7	-23.5
Hornady 140 MonoFlex	velocity, fps:	2800	2532	2279	2040	1818

CARTRIDGE BULLET	RANGE, YARDS:	0	100	200	300	400
	energy, ft-lb:	2437	1992	1614	1294	1027
	arc, inches:	-1.5	+2.0	0	-8.7	-25.8

.308 WINCHESTER

CARTRIDGE BULLET	RANGE, YARDS:	0	100	200	300	400
Black Hills 150 Nosler B. Tip	velocity, fps:	2800				
	energy, ft-lb:	2611				
	arc, inches:					
Black Hills 165 Nosler B. Tip (and SP)	velocity, fps:	2650				
	energy, ft-lb:	2573				
	arc, inches:					
Black Hills 168 Barnes X (and Match)	velocity, fps:	2650				
	energy, ft-lb:	2620				
	arc, inches:					
Black Hills 175 Match	velocity, fps:	2600				
	energy, ft-lb:	2657				
	arc, inches:					
Black Hills 180 AccuBond	velocity, fps:	2600				
	energy, ft-lb:	2701				
	arc, inches:					
Federal 150 Barnes XLC	velocity, fps:	2820	2610	2400	2210	2030
	energy, ft-lb:	2650	2265	1925	1630	1370
	arc, inches:		+1.8 0	-7.8	-22.9	
Federal 150 FMJ Boat-Tail	velocity, fps:	2820	2620	2430	2250	2070
	energy, ft-lb:	2650	2285	1965	1680	1430
	arc, inches:		+1.8 0	-7.7	-22.4	
Federal 150 Hi-Shok	velocity, fps:	2820	2530	2260	2010	1770
	energy, ft-lb:	2650	2140	1705	1345	1050
	arc, inches:		+2.0	0	-8.8	-26.3
Federal 150 Nosler Bal. Tip.	velocity, fps:	2820	2610	2410	2220	2040
	energy, ft-lb:	2650	2270	1935	1640	1380
	arc, inches:		+1.8	0	-7.8	-22.7
Federal 150 Trophy Copper	velocity, fps:	2820	2630	2440	2260	2090
	energy, ft-lb:	2650	2295	1980	1700	1455
	arc, inches:		+1.8	0	-7.6	-22.2
Federal 155 Sierra MatchKg. BTHP	velocity, fps:	2950	2740	2540	2350	2170
	energy, ft-lb:	2995	2585	2225	1905	1620
	arc, inches:		+1.9	0	-8.9	-22.6
Federal 165 Sierra GameKing BTSP	velocity, fps:	2700	2520	2330	2160	1990
	energy, ft-lb:	2670	2310	1990	1700	1450
	arc, inches:		+2.0	0	-8.4	-24.3
Federal 165 Trophy Bonded	velocity, fps:	2700	2440	2200	1970	1760
	energy, ft-lb:	2670	2185	1775	1425	1135
	arc, inches:		+2.2	0	-9.4	-27.7
Federal 165 Tr. Bonded HE	velocity, fps:	2870	2600	2350	2120	1890
	energy, ft-lb:	3020	2485	2030	1640	1310
	arc, inches:		+1.8	0	-8.2	-24.0
Federal 168 Sierra MatchKg. BTHP	velocity, fps:	2600	2410	2230	2060	1890
	energy, ft-lb:	2520	2170	1855	1580	1340.
	arc, inches:		+2.1	0	+8.9	+25.9
Federal 180 Hi-Shok	velocity, fps:	2620	2390	2180	1970	1780
	energy, ft-lb:	2745	2290	1895	1555	1270
	arc, inches:		+2.3	0	-9.7	-28.3
Federal 180 Nosler Partition	velocity, fps:	2620	2430	2240	2060	1890
	energy, ft-lb:	2745	2355	2005	1700	1430.
	arc, inches:		+2.2	0	-9.2	-26.5
Federal 180 Nosler Part. HE	velocity, fps:	2740	2550	2370	2200	2030
	energy, ft-lb:	3000	2600	2245	1925	1645
	arc, inches:		+1.9	0	-8.2	-23.5
Federal 180 Sierra Pro-Hunt.	velocity, fps:	2620	2410	2200	2010	1820
	energy, ft-lb:	2745	2315	1940	1610	1330
	arc, inches:		+2.3	0	-9.3	-27.1
Federal 180 Trophy Bonded Tip	velocity, fps:	2620	2450	2280	2120	1960
	energy, ft-lb:	2745	2390	2070	1790	1535
	arc, inches:		+2.2	0	-8.9	-25.5
Hornady 110 TAP-FPD	velocity, fps:	3165	2830	2519	2228	1957
	energy, ft-lb:	2446	1956	1649	1212	935
	arc, inches:		+1.4	0	-6.9	-20.9
Hornady 110 Urban Tactical	velocity, fps:	3170	2825	2504	2206	1937
	energy, ft-lb:	2454	1950	1532	1189	916
	arc, inches:		+1.5	0	-7.2	-21.2

BALLISTICS

BALLISTICS

CARTRIDGE BULLET	RANGE, YARDS:	0	100	200	300	400
Hornady 125 SST Custom Lite	velocity, fps:	2675	2389	2121	1871	1642
	energy, ft-lb:	1986	1584	1248	971	748
	arc, inches:		+2.3	0	-10.1	-30.1
Hornady 150 SP boat-tail	velocity, fps:	2820	2560	2315	2084	1866
	energy, ft-lb:	2648	2183	1785	1447	1160
	arc, inches:		+2.0	0	-8.5	-25.2
Hornady 150 SP LM	velocity, fps:	2980	2703	2442	2195	1964
	energy, ft-lb:	2959	2433	1986	1606	1285
	arc, inches:	+1.6 0	-7.5	-22.2		
Hornady 150 SST (or Interbond)	velocity, fps:	2820	2593	2378	2174	1984
	energy, ft-lb:	2648	2240	1884	1574	1311
	arc, inches:		+1.9	0	-8.1	-22.9
Hornady 150 SST LM (or Interbond)	velocity, fps:	3000	2765	2541	2328	2127
	energy, ft-lb:	2997	2545	2150	1805	1506
	arc, inches:		+1.5	0	-7.1	-20.6
Hornady 155 A-Max	velocity, fps:	2815	2610	2415	2229	2051
	energy, ft-lb:	2727	2345	2007	1709	1448
	arc, inches:		+1.9	0	-7.9	-22.6
Hornady 155 TAP-FPD	velocity, fps:	2785	2577	2379	2189	2008
	energy, ft-lb:	2669	2285	1947	1649	1387
	arc, inches:		+1.9	0	-8.0	-23.3
Hornady 165 GMX Superformance	velocity, fps:	2750	2550	2358	2174	1999
	energy, ft-lb:	2771	2381	2037	1732	1464
	arc, inches:		+1.9	0	-8.2	-23.8
Hornady 165 SP boat-tail	velocity, fps:	2700	2496	2301	2115	1937
	energy, ft-lb:	2670	2283	1940	1639	1375
	arc, inches:		+2.0	0	-8.7	-25.2
Hornady 165 SPBT LM	velocity, fps:	2870	2658	2456	2283	2078
	energy, ft-lb:	3019	2589	2211	1877	1583
	arc, inches:		+1.7	0	-7.5	-21.8
Hornady 165 SST LM (or Interbond)	velocity, fps:	2880	2672	2474	2284	2103
	energy, ft-lb:	3038	2616	2242	1911	1620
	arc, inches:		+1.6	0	-7.3	-21.2
Hornady 168 BTHP Match	velocity, fps:	2700	2524	2354	2191	2035.
	energy, ft-lb:	2720	2377	2068	1791	1545
	arc, inches:		+2.0	0	-8.4	-23.9
Hornady 168 BTHP Match LM	velocity, fps:	2640	2630	2429	2238	2056
	energy, ft-lb:	3008	2579	2201	1868	1577
	arc, inches:		+1.8	0	-7.8	-22.4
Hornady 168 A-Max Match	velocity fps:	2620	2446	2280	2120	1972
	energy, ft-lb:	2560	2232	1939	1677	1450
	arc, inches:		+2.6	0	-9.2	-25.6
Hornady 168 A-Max	velocity, fps:	2700	2491	2292	2102	1921
	energy, ft-lb:	2719	2315	1959	1648	1377
	arc, inches:		+2.4	0	-9.0	-25.9
Hornady 168 TAP-FPD	velocity, fps:	2700	2513	2333	2161	1996
	energy, ft-lb:	2719	2355	2030	1742	1486
	arc, inches:		+2.0	0	-8.4	-24.3
Hornady 178 BTHP Match	velocity, fps:	2600	2436	2278	2125	1979
	energy, ft-lb:	2672	2345	2050	1785	1548
	arc, inches:		+2.2	0	-8.9	-25.5
Hornady 180 A-Max Match	velocity, fps:	2550	2397	2249	2106	1974
	energy, ft-lb:	2598	2295	2021	1773	1557
	arc, inches:		+2.7	0	-9.5	-26.2
Norma 150 Nosler Bal. Tip	velocity, fps:	2822	2588	2365	2154	
	energy, ft-lb:	2653	2231	1864	1545	
	arc, inches:		+1.6	0	-7.1	
Norma 150 Soft Point	velocity, fps:	2861	2537	2235	1954	
	energy, ft-lb:	2727	2144	1664	1272	
	arc, inches:		+2.0	0	-9.0	
Norma 165 TXP Swift A-Fr.	velocity, fps:	2700	2459	2231	2015	
	energy, ft-lb:	2672	2216	1824	1488	
	arc, inches:		+2.1	0	-9.1	

CARTRIDGE BULLET	RANGE, YARDS:	0	100	200	300	400
Norma 180 Plastic Point	velocity, fps:	2612	2365	2131	1911	
	energy, ft-lb:	2728	2235	1815	1460	
	arc, inches:		+2.4	0	-10.1	
Norma 180 Nosler Partition	velocity, fps:	2612	2414	2225	2044	
	energy, ft-lb:	2728	2330	1979	1670	
	arc, inches:		+2.2	0	-9.3	
Norma 180 Alaska	velocity, fps:	2612	2269	1953	1667	
	energy, ft-lb:	2728	2059	1526	1111	
	arc, inches:		+2.7	0	-11.9	
Norma 180 Vulkan	velocity, fps:	2612	2325	2056	1806	
	energy, ft-lb:	2728	2161	1690	1304	
	arc, inches:		+2.5	0	-10.8	
Norma 180 Oryx	velocity, fps:	2612	2305	2019	1755	
	energy, ft-lb:	2728	2124	1629	1232	
	arc, inches:		+2.5	0	-11.1	
Norma 200 Vulkan	velocity, fps:	2461	2215	1983	1767	
	energy, ft-lb:	2690	2179	1747	1387	
	arc, inches:		+2.8	0	-11.7	
PMC 147 FMJ boat-tail	velocity, fps:	2751	2473	2257	2052	1859
	energy, ft-lb:	2428	2037	1697	1403	1150
	arc, inches:		+2.3	0	-9.3	-27.3
PMC 150 Barnes X	velocity, fps:	2700	2504	2316	2135	1964
	energy, ft-lb:	2428	2087	1786	1518	1284
	arc, inches:		+2.0	0	-8.6	-24.7
PMC 150 Pointed Soft Point	velocity, fps:	2750	2478	2224	1987	1766
	energy, ft-lb:	2519	2045	1647	1315	1039
	arc, inches:		+2.1	0	-9.2	-27.1
PMC 150 SP boat-tail	velocity, fps:	2820	2581	2354	2139	1935
	energy, ft-lb:	2648	2218	1846	1523	1247.
	arc, inches:		+1.9	0	-8.2	-24.0
PMC 168 Barnes X	velocity, fps:	2600	2425	2256	2095	1940
	energy, ft-lb:	2476	2154	1865	1608	1379
	arc, inches:		+2.2	0	-9.0	-26.0
PMC 168 HP boat-tail	velocity, fps:	2650	2460	2278	2103	1936
	energy, ft-lb:	2619	2257	1935	1649	1399
	arc, inches:		+2.1	0	-8.8	-25.6
PMC 168 Pointed Soft Point	velocity, fps:	2559	2354	2160	1976	1803
	energy, ft-lb:	2443	2067	1740	1457	1212
	arc, inches:		+2.4	0	-9.9	-28.7
PMC 168 Pointed Soft Point	velocity, fps:	2600	2404	2216	2037	1866
	energy, ft-lb:	2476	2064	1709	1403	1142
	arc, inches:		+2.3	0	-9.8	-28.7
PMC 180 Pointed Soft Point	velocity, fps:	2550	2335	2132	1940	1760
	energy, ft-lb:	2599	2179	1816	1504	1238.
	arc, inches:		+2.5	0	-10.1	-29.5
PMC 180 SP boat-tail	velocity, fps:	2620	2446	2278	2117	1962
	energy, ft-lb:	2743	2391	2074	1790	1538
	arc, inches:		+2.2	0	-8.9	-25.4
Rem. 125 PSP C-L MR	velocity, fps:	2660	2348	2057	1788	1546
	energy, ft-lb:	1964	1529	1174	887	663
	arc, inches:		+1.1	-2.7	-14.3	-35.8
Rem. 150 PSP Core-Lokt	velocity, fps:	2820	2533	2263	2009	1774
	energy, ft-lb:	2648	2137	1705	1344	1048
	arc, inches:		+2.0	0	-8.8	-26.2
Rem. 150 PSP C-L Ultra	velocity, fps:	2620	2404	2198	2002	1818
	energy, ft-lb:	2743	2309	1930	1601	1320
	arc, inches:		+2.3	0	-9.5	-26.4
Rem. 150 Swift Scirocco	velocity, fps:	2820	2611	2410	2219	2037
	energy, ft-lb:	2648	2269	1935	1640	1381
	arc, inches:		+1.8	0	-7.8	-22.7
Rem. 165 AccuTip	velocity, fps:	2700	2501	2311	2129	1958.
	energy, ft-lb:	2670	2292	1957	1861	1401.
	arc, inches:		+2.0	0	-8.6	-24.8
Rem. 165 PSP boat-tail	velocity, fps:	2700	2497	2303	2117	1941.
	energy, ft-lb:	2670	2284	1942	1642	1379
	arc, inches:		+2.0	0	-8.6	-25.0
Rem. 165 Nosler Bal. Tip	velocity, fps:	2700	2613	2333	2161	1996
	energy, ft-lb:	2672	2314	1995	1711	1460
	arc, inches:		+2.0	0	-8.4	-24.3

Centerfire Rifle Ballistics

.308 WINCHESTER TO .30-06 SPRINGFIELD

CARTRIDGE BULLET	RANGE, YARDS:	0	100	200	300	400
Rem. 165 Swift Scirocco	velocity, fps:	2700	2513	2233	2161	1996
	energy, fps:	2670	2313	1994	1711	1459
	arc, inches:		+2.0	0	-8.4	-24.3
Rem. 168 HPBT Match	velocity, fps:	2680	2493	2314	2143	1979
	energy, ft-lb:	2678	2318	1998	1713	1460
	arc, inches:		+2.1	0	-8.6	-24.7
Rem. 180 SP Core-Lokt	velocity, fps:	2620	2274	1955	1666	1414
	energy, ft-lb:	2743	2066	1527	1109	799
	arc, inches:		+2.6	0	-11.8	-36.3
Rem. 180 PSP Core-Lokt	velocity, fps:	2620	2393	2178	1974	1782
	energy, ft-lb:	2743	2288	1896	1557	1269
	arc, inches:		+2.3	0	-9.7	-28.3
Rem. 180 Nosler Partition	velocity, fps:	2620	2436	2259	2089	1927.
	energy, ft-lb:	2743	2371	2039	1774	1485
	arc, inches:		+2.2	0	-9.0	-26.0
Speer 150 Grand Slam	velocity, fps:	2900	2599	2317	2053	
	energy, ft-lb:	2800	2249	1788	1404	
	arc, inches:		+2.1	0	-8.6	-24.8
Speer 165 Grand Slam	velocity, fps:	2700	2475	2261	2057	
	energy, ft-lb:	2670	2243	1872	1550	
	arc, inches:		+2.1	0	-8.9	-25.9
Speer 180 Grand Slam	velocity, fps:	2620	2420	2229	2046	
	energy, ft-lb:	2743	2340	1985	1674	
	arc, inches:		+2.2	0	-9.2	-26.6
Win. 150 Power-Point	velocity, fps:	2820	2488	2179	1893	1633
	energy, ft-lb:	2648	2061	1581	1193	888
	arc, inches:		+2.4	0	-9.8	-29.3
Win. 150 Power-Point Plus	velocity, fps:	2900	2558	2241	1946	1678
	energy, ft-lb:	2802	2180	1672	1262	938
	arc, inches:		+1.9	0	-8.9	-27.0
Win. 150 Partition Gold	velocity, fps:	2900	2645	2405	2177	1962
	energy, ft-lb:	2802	2332	1927	1579	1282.
	arc, inches:		+1.7	0	-7.8	-22.9
Win. 150 Ballistic Silvertip	velocity, fps:	2810	2601	2401	2211	2028
	energy, ft-lb:	2629	2253	1920	1627	1370.
	arc, inches:		+1.8	0	-7.8	-22.8
Win. 150 Fail Safe	velocity, fps:	2820	2533	2263	2010	1775
	energy, ft-lb:	2649	2137	1706	1346	1049
	arc, inches:		+2.0	0	-8.8	-26.2
Win. 150 Supreme Elite XP3	velocity, fps:	2825	2616	2417	2226	2044
	energy, ft-lb:	2658	2279	1945	1650	1392
	arc, inches:		+1.8	0	-7.8	-22.6
Win. 168 Ballistic Silvertip	velocity, fps:	2670	2484	2306	2134	1971
	energy, ft-lb:	2659	2301	1983	1699	1449
	arc, inches:		+2.1	0	-8.6	-24.8
Win. 168 HP boat-tail Match	velocity, fps:	2680	2485	2297	2118	1948
	energy, ft-lb:	2680	2303	1970	1674	1415
	arc, inches:		+2.1	0	-8.7	-25.1
Win. 180 Power-Point	velocity, fps:	2620	2274	1955	1666	1414
	energy, ft-lb:	2743	2066	1527	1109	799
	arc, inches:		+2.9	0	-12.1	-36.9
Win. 180 Silvertip	velocity, fps:	2620	2393	2178	1974	1782
	energy, ft-lb:	2743	2288	1896	1557	1269
	arc, inches:		+2.6	0	-9.9	-28.9

.30-06 SPRINGFIELD

CARTRIDGE BULLET	RANGE, YARDS:	0	100	200	300	400
A-Square 180 M & D-T	velocity, fps:	2700	2365	2054	1769	1524
	energy, ft-lb:	2913	2235	1687	1251	928
	arc, inches:		+2.4	0	-10.6	-32.4
A-Square 220 Monolythic Solid	velocity, fps:	2380	2108	1854	1623	1424
	energy, ft-lb:	2767	2171	1679	1287	990
	arc, inches:		+3.1	0	-13.6	-39.9
Black Hills 150 Nosler B. Tip	velocity, fps:	2900				
	energy, ft-lb:	2770				
	arc, inches:					
Black Hills 165 Nosler B. Tip	velocity, fps:	2750				
	energy, ft-lb:	2770				
	arc, inches:					
Black Hills 168 Hor. Match	velocity, fps:	2700				
	energy, ft-lb:	2718				
	arc, inches:					
Black Hills 180 Barnes X	velocity, fps:	2650				
	energy, ft-lb:	2806				
	arc, inches:					
Black Hills 180 AccuBond	velocity, ft-lb:	2700				
	energy, ft-lb:					
	arc, inches:					
Federal 125 Sierra Pro-Hunt.	velocity, fps:	3140	2780	2450	2140	1850
	energy, ft-lb:	2735	2145	1660	1270	955
	arc, inches:		+1.5	0	-7.3	-22.3
Federal 150 Hi-Shok	velocity, fps:	2910	2620	2340	2080	1840
	energy, ft-lb:	2820	2280	1825	1445	1130
	arc, inches:		+1.8	0	-8.2	-24.4
Federal 150 Sierra Pro-Hunt.	velocity, fps:	2910	2640	2380	2130	1900
	energy, ft-lb:	2820	2315	1880	1515	1205
	arc, inches:		+1.7	0	-7.9	-23.3
Federal 150 Sierra GameKing BTSP	velocity, fps:	2910	2690	2480	2270	2070
	energy, ft-lb:	2820	2420	2040	1710	1430
	arc, inches:		+1.7	0	-7.4	-21.5
Federal 150 Nosler Bal. Tip	velocity, fps:	2910	2700	2490	2300	2110
	energy, ft-lb:	2820	2420	2070	1760	1485
	arc, inches:		+1.6	0	-7.3	-21.1
Federal 150 FMJ boat-tail	velocity, fps:	2910	2710	2510	2320	2150
	energy, ft-lb:	2820	2440	2100	1800	1535
	arc, inches:		+1.6	0	-7.1	-20.8
Federal 165 Sierra Pro-Hunt.	velocity, fps:	2800	2560	2340	2130	1920
	energy, ft-lb:	2875	2410	2005	1655	1360
	arc, inches:		+1.9	0	-8.3	-24.3
Federal 165 Sierra GameKing BTSP	velocity, fps:	2800	2610	2420	2240	2070.
	energy, ft-lb:	2870	2490	2150	1840	1580
	arc, inches:		+1.8	0	-7.8	-22.4
Federal 165 Sierra GameKing HE	velocity, fps:	3140	2900	2670	2450	2240.
	energy, ft-lb:	3610	3075	2610	2200	1845
	arc, inches:		+1.5	0	-6.9	-20.4
Federal 165 Nosler Bal. Tip	velocity, fps:	2800	2610	2430	2250	2080
	energy, ft-lb:	2870	2495	2155	1855	1585
	arc, inches:		+1.8	0	-7.7	-22.3
Federal 165 Trophy Bonded	velocity, fps:	2800	2540	2290	2050	1830.
	energy, ft-lb:	2870	2360	1915	1545	1230
	arc, inches:		+2.0	0	-8.7	-25.4
Federal 165 Tr. Bonded HE	velocity, fps:	3140	2860	2590	2340	2100
	energy, ft-lb:	3610	2990	2460	2010	1625.
	arc, inches:		+1.6	0	-7.4	-21.9
Federal 165 Trophy Copper	velocity, fps:	2800	2620	2450	2280	2120
	energy, ft-lb:	2870	2515	2190	1900	1645
	arc, inches:		+1.8	0	-7.6	-22.0
Federal 168 Sierra MatchKg. BTHP	velocity, fps:	2700	2510	2320	2150	1980
	energy, ft-lb:	2720	2350	2010	1720	1460
	arc, inches:		+16.2	+28.4	+34.1	+32.3
Federal 180 Barnes XLC	velocity, fps:	2700	2530	2360	2200	2040
	energy, ft-lb:	2915	2550	2220	1930	1670
	arc, inches:	+2.0	0	-8.3	-23.8	
Federal 180 Hi-Shok	velocity, fps:	2700	2470	2250	2040	1850
	energy, ft-lb:	2915	2435	2025	1665	1360
	arc, inches:		+2.1	0	-9.0	-26.4
Federal 180 Sierra Pro-Hunt. RN	velocity, fps:	2700	2350	2020	1730	1470
	energy, ft-lb:	2915	2200	1630	1190	860
	arc, inches:		+2.4	0	-11.0	-33.6
Federal 180 Nosler Partition	velocity, fps:	2700	2500	2320	2140	1970
	energy, ft-lb:	2915	2510	2150	1830	1550
	arc, inches:		+2.0	0	-8.6	-24.6

CARTRIDGE BULLET	RANGE, YARDS:	0	100	200	300	400
Federal 180 Nosler Part. HE	velocity, fps:	2880	2690	2500	2320	2150
	energy, ft-lb:	3315	2880	2495	2150	1845
	arc, inches:		+1.7	0	-7.2	-21.0
Federal 180 Sierra GameKing BTSP	velocity, fps:	2700	2540	2380	2220	2080
	energy, ft-lb:	2915	2570	2260	1975	1720
	arc, inches:		+1.9	0	-8.1	-23.1
Federal 180 Barnes XLC	velocity, fps:	2700	2530	2360	2200	2040.
	energy, ft-lb:	2915	2550	2220	1930	1670
	arc, inches:		+2.0	0	-8.3	-23.8
Federal 180 Sierra Pro-Hunt.	velocity, fps:	2700	2350	2020	1730	1470
	RN energy, ft-lb:	2915	2200	1630	1190	860
	arc, inches:		+2.4	0	-11.0	-33.6
Federal 180 Trophy Bonded	velocity, fps:	2700	2460	2220	2000	1800
	energy, ft-lb:	2915	2410	1975	1605	1290
	arc, inches:		+2.2	0	-9.2	-27.0
Federal 180 Tr. Bonded HE	velocity, fps:	2880	2630	2380	2160	1940
	energy, ft-lb:	3315	2755	2270	1855	1505
	arc, inches:		+1.8	0	-8.0	-23.3
Federal 180 Trophy Bonded Tip	velocity, fps:	2700	2520	2350	2190	2030
	energy, ft-lb:	2915	2540	2219	1910	1645
	arc, inches:		+2.0	0	-8.4	-23.9
Federal 200 Trophy Bonded	velocity, fps:	2540	2320	2120	1920	1740
	energy, ft-lb:	2865	2395	1990	1640	1345
	arc, inches:		+2.5	0	-10.1	-29.9
Federal 220 Sierra Pro-Hunt. RN	velocity, fps:	2410	2130	1870	1630	1420
	energy, ft-lb:	2835	2215	1705	1300	985
	arc, inches:		+3.1	0	-13.1	-39.3
Hornady 125 SST Custom Lite	velocity, fps:	2700	2412	2143	1891	1660
	energy, ft-lb:	2023	1615	1274	993	765
	arc, inches:		+2.3	0	-9.9	-29.5
Hornady 150 GMX Superformance	velocity, fps:	3080	2848	2628	2418	2218
	energy, ft-lb:	3159	2701	2300	1948	1639
	arc, inches:		+1.4	0	-6.4	-18.8
Hornady 150 SP	velocity, fps:	2910	2617	2342	2083	1843
	energy, ft-lb:	2820	2281	1827	1445	1131
	arc, inches:		+2.1	0	-8.5	-25.0
Hornady 150 SP LM	velocity, fps:	3100	2815	2548	2295	2058
	energy, ft-lb:	3200	2639	2161	1755	1410
	arc, inches:		+1.4	0	-6.8	-20.3
Hornady 150 SP boat-tail	velocity, fps:	2910	2683	2467	2262	2066.
	energy, ft-lb:	2820	2397	2027	1706	1421
	arc, inches:		+2.0	0	-7.7	-22.2
Hornady 150 SST (or Interbond)	velocity, fps:	2910	2802	2599	2405	2219
	energy, ft-lb:	3330	2876	2474	2118	1803
	arc, inches:		+1.5	0	-6.6	-19.3
Hornady 150 SST LM	velocity, fps:	3100	2860	2631	2414	2208
	energy, ft-lb:	3200	2724	2306	1941	1624
	arc, inches:		+1.4	0	-6.6	-19.2
Hornady 165 GMX Superformance	velocity, fps:	2940	2731	2532	2341	2158
	energy, ft-lb:	3167	2732	3248	2007	1706
	arc, inches:		+1.5	0	-7.0	-20.4
Hornady 165 SP boat-tail	velocity, fps:	2800	2591	2392	2202	2020
	energy, ft-lb:	2873	2460	2097	1777	1495
	arc, inches:		+1.8	0	-8.0	-23.3
Hornady 165 SPBT LM	velocity, fps:	3015	2790	2575	2370	2176
	energy, ft-lb:	3330	2850	2428	2058	1734
	arc, inches:		+1.6	0	-7.0	-20.1
Hornady 165 SST (or Interbond)	velocity, fps:	2800	2598	2405	2221	2046
	energy, ft-lb:	2872	2473	2119	1808	1534
	arc, inches:		+1.9	0	-8.0	-22.8
Hornady 165 SST LM	velocity, fps:	3015	2802	2599	2405	2219
	energy, ft-lb:	3330	2878	2474	2118	1803.
	arc, inches:		+1.5	0	-6.5	-19.3
Hornady 168 A-Max Garand Match	velocity, fps:	2710	2523	2343	2171	2006
	energy, ft-lb:	2739	2374	2048	1758	1501
	arc, inches:		+2.3	0	-8.6	-24.6
Hornady 168 HPBT Match	velocity, fps:	2790	2620	2447	2280	2120.
	energy, ft-lb:	2925	2561	2234	1940	1677.
	arc, inches:		+1.7	0	-7.7	-22.2
Hornady 180 SP	velocity, fps:	2700	2469	2258	2042	1846
	energy, ft-lb:	2913	2436	2023	1666	1362
	arc, inches:		+2.4	0	-9.3	-27.0
Hornady 180 SPBT LM	velocity, fps:	2880	2676	2480	2293	2114
	energy, ft-lb:	3316	2862	2459	2102	1786
	arc, inches:		+1.7	0	-7.3	-21.3

CARTRIDGE BULLET	RANGE, YARDS:	0	100	200	300	400
Norma 150 Nosler Bal. Tip	velocity, fps:	2936	2713	2502	2300	
	energy, ft-lb:	2872	2453	2085	1762	
	arc, inches:		+1.6	0	-7.1	
Norma 150 Soft Point	velocity, fps:	2972	2640	2331	2043	
	energy, ft-lb:	2943	2321	1810	1390	
	arc, inches:		+1.8	0	-8.2	
Norma 180 Alaska	velocity, fps:	2700	2351	2028	1734	
	energy, ft-lb:	2914	2209	1645	1202	
	arc, inches:		+2.4	0	-11.0	
Norma 180 Nosler Partition	velocity, fps:	2700	2494	2297	2108	
	energy, ft-lb:	2914	2486	2108	1777	
	arc, inches:		+2.1	0	-8.7	
Norma 180 Plastic Point	velocity, fps:	2700	2455	2222	2003	
	energy, ft-lb:	2914	2409	1974	1603	
	arc, inches:		+2.1	0	-9.2	
Norma 180 Vulkan	velocity, fps:	2700	2416	2150	1901	
	energy, ft-lb:	2914	2334	1848	1445	
	arc, inches:		+2.2	0	-9.8	
Norma 180 Oryx	velocity, fps:	2700	2387	2095	1825	
	energy, ft-lb:	2914	2278	1755	1332	
	arc, inches:		+2.3	0	-10.2	
Norma 180 TXP Swift A-Fr.	velocity, fps:	2700	2479	2268	2067	
	energy, ft-lb:	2914	2456	2056	1708	
	arc, inches:		+2.0	0	-8.8	
Norma 180 AccuBond	velocity, fps:	2674	2499	2331	2169	
	energy, ft-lb:	2859	2497	2172	1881	
	arc, inches:		+2.0	0	-8.5	
Norma 200 Vulkan	velocity, fps:	2641	2385	2143	1916	
	energy, ft-lb:	3098	2527	2040	1631	
	arc, inches:		+2.3	0	-9.9	
Norma 200 Oryx	velocity, fps:	2625	2362	2115	1883	
	energy, ft-lb:	3061	2479	1987	1575	
	arc, inches:		+2.3	0	-10.1	
PMC 150 X-Bullet	velocity, fps:	2750	2552	2361	2179	2005
	energy, ft-lb:	2518	2168	1857	1582	1339
	arc, inches:		+2.0	0	-8.2	-23.7
PMC 150 Pointed Soft Point	velocity, fps:	2773	2542	2322	2113	1916
	energy, ft-lb:	2560	2152	1796	1487	1222.
	arc, inches:		+1.9	0	-8.4	-24.6
PMC 150 SP boat-tail	velocity, fps:	2900	2657	2427	2208	2000
	energy, ft-lb:	2801	2351	1961	1623	1332
	arc, inches:		+1.7	0	-7.7	-22.5
PMC 150 FMJ	velocity, fps:	2773	2542	2322	2113	1916
	energy, ft-lb:	2560	2152	1796	1487	1222
	arc, inches:		+1.9	0	-8.4	-24.6
PMC 168 Barnes X	velocity, fps:	2750	2569	2395	2228	2067
	energy, ft-lb:	2770	2418	2101	1818	1565
	arc, inches:		+1.9	0	-8.0	-23.0
PMC 180 Barnes X	velocity, fps:	2650	2487	2331	2179	2034
	energy, ft-lb:	2806	2472	2171	1898	1652
	arc, inches:		+2.1	0	-8.5	-24.3
PMC 180 Pointed Soft Point	velocity, fps:	2650	2430	2221	2024	1839
	energy, ft-lb:	2807	2359	1972	1638	1351
	arc, inches:		+2.2	0	-9.3	-27.0
PMC 180 SP boat-tail	velocity, fps:	2700	2523	2352	2188	2030
	energy, ft-lb:	2913	2543	2210	1913	1646
	arc, inches:		+2.0	0	-8.3	-23.9
PMC 180 HPBT Match	velocity, fps:	2800	2622	2456	2302	2158
	energy, ft-lb:	3133	2747	2411	2118	1861
	arc, inches:		+1.8	0	-7.6	-21.7
Rem. 55 PSP (sabot) "Accelerator"	velocity, fps:	4080	3484	2964	2499	2080
	energy, ft-lb:	2033	1482	1073	763	528.
	arc, inches:		+1.4	+1.4	-2.6	-12.2
Rem. 125 PSP C-L MR	velocity, fps:	2660	2335	2034	1757	1509
	energy, ft-lb:	1964	1513	1148	856	632
	arc, inches:		+1.1	-3.0	-15.5	-37.4
Rem. 125 Pointed Soft Point	velocity, fps:	3140	2780	2447	2138	1853
	energy, ft-lb:	2736	2145	1662	1269	953.
	arc, inches:		+1.5	0	-7.4	-22.4
Rem. 150 AccuTip	velocity, fps:	2910	2686	2473	2270	2077
	energy, ft-lb:	2820	2403	2037	1716	1436
	arc, inches:		+1.8	0	-7.4	-21.5

Centerfire Rifle Ballistics

.30-06 SPRINGFIELD TO .300 BLACKOUT

CARTRIDGE BULLET	RANGE, YARDS:	0	100	200	300	400
Rem. 150 PSP Core-Lokt	velocity, fps:	2910	2617	2342	2083	1843
	energy, ft-lb:	2820	2281	1827	1445	1131
	arc, inches:		+1.8	0	-8.2	-24.4
Rem. 150 Bronze Point	velocity, fps:	2910	2656	2416	2189	1974
	energy, ft-lb:	2820	2349	1944	1596	1298
	arc, inches:		+1.7	0	-7.7	-22.7
Rem. 150 Nosler Bal. Tip	velocity, fps:	2910	2696	2492	2298	2112.
	energy, ft-lb:	2821	2422	2070	1769	1485
	arc, inches:		+1.6	0	-7.3	-21.1
Rem. 150 Swift Scirocco	velocity, fps:	2910	2696	2492	2298	2111
	energy, ft-lb:	2820	2421	2069	1758	1485
	arc, inches:		+1.6	0	-7.3	-21.1
Rem. 165 AccuTip	velocity, fps:	2800	2597	2403	2217	2039
	energy, ft-lb:	2872	2470	2115	1800	1523
	arc, inches:		+1.8	0	-7.9	-22.8
Rem. 165 PSP Core-Lokt	velocity, fps:	2800	2534	2283	2047	1825.
	energy, ft-lb:	2872	2352	1909	1534	1220
	arc, inches:		+2.0	0	-8.7	-25.9
Rem. 165 PSP boat-tail	velocity, fps:	2800	2592	2394	2204	2023
	energy, ft-lb:	2872	2462	2100	1780	1500
	arc, inches:		+1.8	0	-7.9	-23.0
Rem. 165 Nosler Bal. Tip	velocity, fps:	2800	2609	2426	2249	2080.
	energy, ft-lb:	2873	2494	2155	1854	1588
	arc, inches:		+1.8	0	-7.7	-22.3
Rem. 168 PSP C-L Ultra	velocity, fps:	2800	2546	2306	2079	1866
	energy, ft-lb:	2924	2418	1984	1613	1299
	arc, inches:		+1.9	0	-8.5	-25.1
Rem. 180 SP Core-Lokt	velocity, fps:	2700	2348	2023	1727	1466
	energy, ft-lb:	2913	2203	1635	1192	859
	arc, inches:		+2.4	0	-11.0	-33.8
Rem. 180 PSP Core-Lokt	velocity, fps:	2700	2469	2250	2042	1846
	energy, ft-lb:	2913	2436	2023	1666	1362
	arc, inches:		+2.1	0	-9.0	-26.3
Rem. 180 PSP C-L Ultra	velocity, fps:	2700	2480	2270	2070	1882
	energy, ft-lb:	2913	2457	2059	1713	1415
	arc, inches:		+2.1	0	-8.9	-25.8
Rem. 180 Bronze Point	velocity, fps:	2700	2485	2280	2084	1899.
	energy, ft-lb:	2913	2468	2077	1736	1441
	arc, inches:		+2.1	0	-8.8	-25.5
Rem. 180 Swift A-Frame	velocity, fps:	2700	2465	2243	2032	1833
	energy, ft-lb:	2913	2429	2010	1650	1343
	arc, inches:		+2.1	0	-9.1	-26.6
Rem. 180 Nosler Partition	velocity, fps:	2700	2512	2332	2160	1995
	energy, ft-lb:	2913	2522	2174	1864	1590
	arc, inches:		+2.0	0	-8.4	-24.3
Rem. 220 SP Core-Lokt	velocity, fps:	2410	2130	1870	1632	1422
	energy, ft-lb:	2837	2216	1708	1301	988
	arc, inches, s:		0	-6.2	-22.4	
Speer 150 Grand Slam	velocity, fps:	2975	2669	2383	2114	
	energy, ft-lb:	2947	2372	1891	1489	
	arc, inches:		+2.0	0	-8.1	-24.1
Speer 165 Grand Slam	velocity, fps:	2790	2560	2342	2134	
	energy, ft-lb:	2851	2401	2009	1669	
	arc, inches:		+1.9	0	-8.3	-24.1
Speer 180 Grand Slam	velocity, fps:	2690	2487	2293	2108	
	energy, ft-lb:	2892	2472	2101	1775	
	arc, inches:		+2.1	0	-8.8	-25.1
Win. 125 Pointed Soft Point	velocity, fps:	3140	2780	2447	2138	1853
	energy, ft-lb:	2736	2145	1662	1269	953
	arc, inches:		+1.8	0	-7.7	-23.0
Win. 150 Power-Point	velocity, fps:	2920	2580	2265	1972	1704
	energy, ft-lb:	2839	2217	1708	1295	967
	arc, inches:		+2.2	0	-9.0	-27.0
Win. 150 Power-Point Plus	velocity, fps:	3050	2685	2352	2043	1760
	energy, ft-lb:	3089	2402	1843	1391	1032
	arc, inches:		+1.7	0	-8.0	-24.3
Win. 150 Silvertip	velocity, fps:	2910	2617	2342	2083	1843
	energy, ft-lb:	2820	2281	1827	1445	1131
	arc, inches:		+2.1	0	-8.5	-25.0

CARTRIDGE BULLET	RANGE, YARDS:	0	100	200	300	400
Win. 150 Partition Gold	velocity, fps:	2960	2705	2464	2235	2019
	energy, ft-lb:	2919	2437	2022	1664	1358.
	arc, inches:		+1.6	0	-7.4	-21.7
Win. 150 Ballistic Silvertip	velocity, fps:	2900	2687	2483	2289	2103
	energy, ft-lb:	2801	2404	2054	1745	1473
	arc, inches:		+1.7	0	-7.3	-21.2
Win. 150 Fail Safe	velocity, fps:	2920	2625	2349	2089	1848
	energy, ft-lb:	2841	2296	1838	1455	1137
	arc, inches:		+1.8	0	-8.1	-24.3
Win. 165 Pointed Soft Point	velocity, fps:	2800	2573	2357	2151	1956
	energy, ft-lb:	2873	2426	2036	1696	1402
	arc, inches:		+2.2	0	-8.4	-24.4
Win. 165 Fail Safe	velocity, fps:	2800	2540	2295	2063	1846
	energy, ft-lb:	2873	2365	1930	1560	1249
	arc, inches:		+2.0	0	-8.6	-25.3
Win. 168 Ballistic Silvertip	velocity, fps:	2790	2599	2416	2240	2072
	energy, ft-lb:	2903	2520	2177	1872	1601
	arc, inches:		+1.8	0	-7.8	-22.5
Win. 180 Ballistic Silvertip	velocity, fps:	2750	2572	2402	2237	2080
	energy, ft-lb:	3022	2644	2305	2001	1728
	arc, inches:		+1.9	0	-7.9	-22.8
Win. 180 Power-Point	velocity, fps:	2700	2348	2023	1727	1466
	energy, ft-lb:	2913	2203	1635	1192	859
	arc, inches:		+2.7	0	-11.3	-34.4
Win. 180 Power-Point Plus	velocity, fps:	2770	2563	2366	2177	1997
	energy, ft-lb:	3068	2627	2237	1894	1594
	arc, inches:		+1.9	0	-8.1	-23.6
Win. 180 Silvertip	velocity, fps:	2700	2469	2250	2042	1846
	energy, ft-lb:	2913	2436	2023	1666	1362
	arc, inches:		+2.4	0	-9.3	-27.0
Win. 180 AccuBond	velocity, fps:	2750	2573	2403	2239	2082
	energy, ft-lb:	3022	2646	2308	2004	1732
	arc, inches:		+1.9	0	-7.9	-22.8
Win. 180 Partition Gold	velocity, fps:	2790	2581	2382	2192	2010
	energy, ft-lb:	3112	2664	2269	1920	1615
	arc, inches:		+1.9	0	-8.0	-23.2
Win. 180 Fail Safe	velocity, fps:	2700	2486	2283	2089	1904
	energy, ft-lb:	2914	2472	2083	1744	1450
	arc, inches:		+2.1	0	-8.7	-25.5
Win. 150 Supreme Elite XP3	velocity, fps:	2925	2712	2508	2313	2127
	energy, ft-lb:	2849	2448	2095	1782	1507
	arc, inches:		+1.6	0	-7.2	-20.8
Win. 180 Supreme Elite XP3	velocity, fps:	2750	2579	2414	2256	2103
	energy, ft-lb:	3022	2658	2330	2034	1768
	arc, inches:		+1.9	0	-7.8	-22.5

.300 BLK (.300 WHISPER)

CARTRIDGE BULLET	RANGE, YARDS:	0	100	200	300	400
Barnes 110 Tac/TX	velocity, fps:	2350	1810	1369		
	energy, ft-lb:	1349	800	458		
	arc, inches:	-1.5	-6.7	-55.5		
Black Hills 125 OTM	velocity, fps:	2200				
	energy, ft-lb:	1343				
	arc, inches					
Black Hills 220 OTM	velocity, fps:	1000				
	energy, ft-lb:	488				
	arc, inches					
Hornady 110 V-Max (16-inch barrel)	velocity, fps:	2375	2094	1834	1597	1389
	energy, ft-lb:	1378	1071	821	623	471
	arc, inches:		+3.20	0	-13.7	-41.0
Hornady 110 V-MAX	velocity, fps:	2375	2094	1834	1597	
	energy, ft-lb:	1378	1071	821	623	
	arc, inches:	-1.5	+3.2	0	-13.7	
Hornady 208 A-MAX	velocity, fps:	1020	987	959		
	energy, ft-lb:	480	450	424		
	arc, inches:	-1.5	0	-34.1		

.300 H&H MAGNUM TO .300 WINCHESTER MAGNUM

.300 H&H MAGNUM

CARTRIDGE BULLET	RANGE, YARDS:	0	100	200	300	400
Federal 180 Barnes TSX	velocity, fps:	2880	2680	2480	2290	2120
	energy, ft-lb:	3315	2860	2460	2105	1790
	arc, inches:	-1.5	+1.7	0	-7.3	-21.3
Federal 180 Nosler Partition	velocity, fps:	2880	2620	2380	2150	1930
	energy, ft-lb:	3315	2750	2260	1840	1480
	arc, inches:		+1.8 0		-8.0	-23.4
Federal 180 Trophy Bonded Tip	velocity, fps:	2880	2700	2520	2350	2180
	energy, ft-lb:	3315	2900	2530	2200	1900
	arc, inches:		+1.6	0	-7.1	-20.6
Handload, 165 Sierra HP	velocity, fps:	3000	2784	2579	2382	2195
	energy, ft-lb:	3297	2840	2436	2079	1764
	arc, inches:	-1.5	+1.5	0	-6.7	-19.5
Handload, 190 Hornady	velocity, fps:	2800	2615	2437	2266	2102
	energy, ft-lb:	3307	2884	2505	2166	1864
	arc, inches:	-1.5	+1.8	0	-7.7	-22.1
Hornady 180 InterBond	velocity, fps:	2870	2678	2493	2316	2146
	energy, ft-lb:	3292	2865	2484	2144	1841
	arc, inches:	-1.5	+1.	0	-7.3	-21.0
Win. 180 Fail Safe	velocity, fps:	2880	2628	2390	2165	1952
	energy, ft-lb:	3316	2762	2284	1873	1523
	arc, inches:		+1.8 0		-7.9	-23.2

.308 NORMA MAGNUM

CARTRIDGE BULLET	RANGE, YARDS:	0	100	200	300	400
Norma 180 TXP Swift A-Fr.	velocity, fps:	2953	2704	2469	2245	
	energy, ft-lb:	3486	2924	2437	2016	
	arc, inches:		+1.6	0	-7.3	
Norma 180 Oryx	velocity, fps:	2953	2630	2330	2049	
	energy, ft-lb:	3486	2766	2170	1679	
	arc, inches:		+1.8	0	-8.2	
Norma 200 Vulkan	velocity, fps:	2903	2624	2361	2114	
	energy, ft-lb:	3744	3058	2476	1985	
	arc, inches:	0	+1.8	0	-8.0	
Nosler 180 AB	velocity, fps:	2975	2787	2608	2435	2269
	energy, ft-lb:	3536	3105	2718	2371	2058
	arc, inches:	-1.5	+1.5	0	-6.6	-19.1

.300 WINCHESTER MAGNUM

CARTRIDGE BULLET	RANGE, YARDS:	0	100	200	300	400
A-Square 180 Dead Tough	velocity, fps:	3120	2756	2420	2108	1820
	energy, ft-lb:	3890	3035	2340	1776	1324
	arc, inches:		+1.6	0	-7.6	-22.9
Black Hills 180 Nos. Bal. Tip	velocity, fps:	3100				
	energy, ft-lb:	3498				
	arc, inches:					
Black Hills 180 Barnes X	velocity, fps:	2950				
	energy, ft-lb:	3498				
	arc, inches:					
Black Hills 180 AccuBond	velocity, fps:	3000				
	energy, ft-lb:	3597				
	arc, inches:					
Black Hills 190 Match	velocity, fps:	2950				
	energy, ft-lb:	3672				
	arc, inches:					
Federal 150 Sierra Pro Hunt.	velocity, fps:	3280	3030	2800	2570	2360.
	energy, ft-lb:	3570	3055	2600	2205	1860
	arc, inches:		+1.1	0	-5.6	-16.4
Federal 150 Trophy Bonded	velocity, fps:	3280	2980	2700	2430	2190
	energy, ft-lb:	3570	2450	2420	1970	1590
	arc, inches:		+1.2	0	-6.0	-17.9
Federal 165 Trophy Copper	velocity, fps:	3050	2860	2680	2500	2330
	energy, ft-lb:	3410	2995	2620	2290	1990
	arc, inches:		+1.4	0	-6.3	-18.0
Federal 180 Sierra Pro Hunt.	velocity, fps:	2960	2750	2540	2340	2160
	energy, ft-lb:	3500	3010	2580	2195	1860
	arc, inches:		+1.6	0	-7.0	-20.3

CARTRIDGE BULLET	RANGE, YARDS:	0	100	200	300	400
Federal 180 Barnes XLC	velocity, fps:	2960	2780	2600	2430	2260
	energy, ft-lb:	3500	3080	2700	2355	2050
	arc, inches:		+1.5	0	-6.6	-19.2
Federal 180 Trophy Bonded	velocity, fps:	2960	2700	2460	2220	2000
	energy, ft-lb:	3500	2915	2410	1975	1605
	arc, inches:		+1.6	0	-7.4	-21.9
Federal 180 Tr. Bonded HE	velocity, fps:	3100	2830	2580	2340	2110
	energy, ft-lb:	3840	3205	2660	2190	1790
	arc, inches:		+1.4	0	-6.6	-19.7
Federal 180 Nosler Partition	velocity, fps:	2960	2700	2450	2210	1990
	energy, ft-lb:	3500	2905	2395	1955	1585
	arc, inches:		+1.6	0	-7.5	-22.1
Federal 190 Sierra MatchKg. BTHP	velocity, fps:	2900	2730	2560	2400	2240
	energy, ft-lb:	3550	3135	2760	2420	2115
	arc, inches:		+12.9	+22.5	+26.9	+25.1
Federal 200 Sierra GameKing BTSP	velocity, fps:	2830	2680	2530	2380	2240
	energy, ft-lb:	3560	3180	2830	2520	2230
	arc, inches:		+1.7	0	-7.1	-20.4
Federal 200 Nosler Part. HE	velocity, fps:	2930	2740	2550	2370	2200
	energy, ft-lb:	3810	3325	2885	2495	2145
	arc, inches:		+1.6	0	-6.9	-20.1
Federal 200 Trophy Bonded	velocity, fps:	2800	2570	2350	2150	1950
	energy, ft-lb:	3480	2935	2460	2050	1690
	arc, inches:		+1.9	0	-8.2	-23.9
Hornady 150 SP boat-tail	velocity, fps:	3275	2988	2718	2464	2224
	energy, ft-lb:	3573	2974	2461	2023	1648
	arc, inches:		+1.2	0	-6.0	-17.8
Hornady 150 SST (and Interbond)	velocity, fps:	3275	3027	2791	2565	2352
	energy, ft-lb:	3572	3052	2593	2192	1842
	arc, inches:		+1.2	0	-5.8	-17.0
Hornady 150 SST Custom Lite	velocity, fps:	2800	2582	2375	2177	1988
	energy, ft-lb:	2611	2220	1878	1578	1316
	arc, inches:		+1.9	0	-8.0	-23.5
Hornady 165 SP boat-tail	velocity, fps:	3100	2877	2665·	2462	2269.
	energy, ft-lb:	3522	3033	2603	2221	1887
	arc, inches:		+1.3	0	-6.5	-18.5
Hornady 165 SST	velocity, fps:	3100	2885	2680	2483	2296
	energy, ft-lb:	3520	3049	2630	2259	1930
	arc, inches:		+1.4	0	-6.4	-18.6
Hornady 180 SP boat-tail	velocity, fps:	2960	2745	2540	2344	2157
	energy, ft-lb:	3501	3011	2578	2196	1859
	arc, inches:		+1.9	0	-7.3	-20.9
Hornady 180 SST	velocity, fps:	2960	2764	2575	2395	2222
	energy, ft-lb:	3501	3052	2650	2292	1974
	arc, inches:		+1.6	0	-7.0	-20.1.
Hornady 180 SPBT HM	velocity, fps:	3100	2879	2668	2467	2275
	energy, ft-lb:	3840	3313	2845	2431	2068
	arc, inches:		+1.4	0	-6.4	-18.7
Hornady 190 BTHP Match	velocity, fps:	2930	2760	2596	2438	2286
	energy, ft-lb:	3717	3297	2918	2574	2262
	arc, inches:		+1.5	0	-6.7	-19.3
Hornady 190 SP boat-tail	velocity, fps:	2900	2711	2529	2355	2187
	energy, ft-lb:	3549	3101	2699	2340	2018
	arc, inches:		+1.6	0	-7.1	-20.4
Norma 150 Nosler Bal. Tip	velocity, fps:	3250	3014	2791	2578	
	energy, ft-lb:	3519	3027	2595	2215	
	arc, inches:		+1.1	0	-5.6	
Norma 150 Barnes TS	velocity, fps:	3215	2982	2761	2550	
	energy, ft-lb:	3444	2962	2539	2167	
	arc, inches:		+1.2	0	-5.8	
Norma 165 Scirocco	velocity, fps:	3117	2921	2734	2554	
	energy, ft-lb:	3561	3127	2738	2390	
	arc, inches:		+1.2	0	-5.9	
Norma 180 Soft Point	velocity, fps:	3018	2780	2555	2341	
	energy, ft-lb:	3641	3091	2610	2190	
	arc, inches:		+1.5	0	-7.0	
Norma 180 Plastic Point	velocity, fps:	3018	2755	2506	2271	
	energy, ft-lb:	3641	3034	2512	2062	
	arc, inches:		+1.6	0	-7.1	
Norma 180 TXP Swift A-Fr.	velocity, fps:	2920	2688	2467	2256	
	energy, ft-lb:	3409	2888	2432	2035	
	arc, inches:		+1.7	0	-7.4	

Centerfire Rifle Ballistics

.300 WINCHESTER MAGNUM TO .300 REMINGTON SHORT ULTRA MAGNUM

BALLISTICS

CARTRIDGE BULLET	RANGE, YARDS:	0	100	200	300	400
Norma 180 AccuBond	velocity, fps:	2953	2767	2588	2417	
	energy, ft-lb:	3486	3061	2678	2335	
	arc, inches:		+1.5	0	-6.7	
Norma 180 Oryx	velocity, fps:	2920	2600	2301	2023	
	energy, ft-lb:	3409	2702	2117	1636	
	arc, inches:		+1.8	0	-8.4	
Norma 200 Vulkan	velocity, fps:	2887	2609	2347	2100	
	energy, ft-lb:	3702	3023	2447	1960	
	arc, inches:		+1.8	0	-8.2	
Norma 200 Oryx	velocity, fps:	2789	2510	2248	2002	
	energy, ft-lb:	3455	2799	2245	1780	
	arc, inches:		+2.0	0	-8.9	
PMC 150 Barnes X	velocity, fps:	3135	2918	2712	2515	2327
	energy, ft-lb:	3273	2836	2449	2107	1803
	arc, inches:		+1.3	0	-6.1	-17.7
PMC 150 Pointed Soft Point	velocity, fps:	3150	2902	2665	2438	2222
	energy, ft-lb:	3304	2804	2364	1979	1644.
	arc, inches:		+1.3	0	-6.2	-18.3
PMC 150 SP boat-tail	velocity, fps:	3250	2987	2739	2504	2281
	energy, ft-lb:	3517	2970	2498	2088	1733
	arc, inches:		+1.2	0	-6.0	-17.4
PMC 180 Barnes X	velocity, fps:	2910	2738	2572	2412	2258
	energy, ft-lb:	3384	2995	2644	2325	2037
	arc, inches:		+1.6	0	-6.9	-19.8
PMC 180 Pointed Soft Point	velocity, fps:	2853	2643	2446	2258	2077
	energy, ft-lb:	3252	2792	2391	2037	1724
	arc, inches:		+1.7	0	-7.5	-21.9
PMC 180 SP boat-tail	velocity, fps:	2900	2714	2536	2365	2200
	energy, ft-lb:	3361	2944	2571	2235	1935
	arc, inches:		+1.6	0	-7.1	-20.3
PMC 180 HPBT Match	velocity, fps:	2950	2755	2568	2390	2219
	energy, ft-lb:	3478	3033	2636	2283	1968
	arc, inches:		+1.5	0	-6.8	-19.7
Rem. 150 PSP Core-Lokt	velocity, fps:	3290	2951	2636	2342	2068
	energy, ft-lb:	3605	2900	2314	1827	1859
	arc, inches:		+1.6	0	-7.0	-20.2
Rem. 150 PSP C-L MR	velocity, fps:	2650	2373	2113	1870	1646
	energy, ft-lb:	2339	1875	1486	1164	902
	arc, inches:		+1.0	-2.7	-14.3	-35.8
Rem. 150 PSP C-L Ultra	velocity, fps:	3290	2967	2666	2384	2120
	energy, ft-lb:	3065	2931	2366	1893	1496
	arc, inches:		+1.2	0	-6.1	-18.4
Rem. 180 AccuTip	velocity, fps:	2960	2764	2577	2397	2224
	energy, ft-lb:	3501	3053	2653	2295	1976
	arc, inches:		+1.5	0	-6.8	-19.6
Rem. 180 PSP Core-Lokt	velocity, fps:	2960	2745	2540	2344	2157
	energy, ft-lb:	3501	3011	2578	2196	1424
	arc, inches:		+2.2	+1.9	-3.4	-15.0
Rem. 180 PSP C-L Ultra	velocity, fps:	2960	2727	2505	2294	2093
	energy, ft-lb:	3501	2971	2508	2103	1751
	arc, inches:		+2.7	+2.2	-3.8	-16.4
Rem. 180 Nosler Partition	velocity, fps:	2960	2725	2503	2291	2089
	energy, ft-lb:	3501	2968	2503	2087	1744
	arc, inches:		+1.6	0	-7.2	-20.9
Rem. 180 Nosler Bal. Tip	velocity, fps:	2960	2774	2595	2424	2259.
	energy, ft-lb:	3501	3075	2692	2348	2039
	arc, inches:		+1.5	0	-6.7	-19.3
Rem. 180 Swift Scirocco	velocity, fps:	2960	2774	2595	2424	2259
	energy, ft-lb:	3501	3075	2692	2348	2039
	arc, inches:		+1.5	0	-6.7	-19.3
Rem. 190 PSP boat-tail	velocity, fps:	2885	2691	2506	2327	2156
	energy, ft-lb:	3511	3055	2648	2285	1961
	arc, inches:		+1.6	0	-7.2	-20.8

CARTRIDGE BULLET	RANGE, YARDS:	0	100	200	300	400
Rem. 190 HPBT Match	velocity, fps:	2900	2725	2557	2395	2239
	energy, ft-lb:	3547	3133	2758	2420	2115
	arc, inches:		+1.6	0	-6.9	-19.9
Rem. 200 Swift A-Frame	velocity, fps:	2825	2595	2376	2167	1970
	energy, ft-lb:	3544	2989	2506	2086	1722
	arc, inches:		+1.8	0	-8.0	-23.5
Speer 180 Grand Slam	velocity, fps:	2950	2735	2530	2334	
	energy, ft-lb:	3478	2989	2558	2176	
	arc, inches:		+1.6	0	-7.0	-20.5
Speer 200 Grand Slam	velocity, fps:	2800	2597	2404	2218	
	energy, ft-lb:	3481	2996	2565	2185	
	arc, inches:		+1.8	0	-7.9	-22.9
Win. 150 Power-Point	velocity, fps:	3290	2951	2636	2342	2068.
	energy, ft-lb:	3605	2900	2314	1827	1424
	arc, inches:		+2.6	+2.1	-3.5	-15.4
Win. 150 Fail Safe	velocity, fps:	3260	2943	2647	2370	2110
	energy, ft-lb:	3539	2884	2334	1871	1483
	arc, inches:		+1.3	0	-6.2	-18.7
Win. 165 Fail Safe	velocity, fps:	3120	2807	2515	2242	1985
	energy, ft-lb:	3567	2888	2319	1842	1445
	arc, inches:		+1.5	0	-7.0	-20.0
Win. 180 Power-Point	velocity, fps:	2960	2745	2540	2344	2157
	energy, ft-lb:	3501	3011	2578	2196	1859
	arc, inches:		+1.9	0	-7.3	-20.9
Win. 180 Power-Point Plus	velocity, fps:	3070	2846	2633	2430	2236
	energy, ft-lb:	3768	3239	2772	2361	1999
	arc, inches:		+1.4	0	-6.4	-18.7
Win. 180 Ballistic Silvertip	velocity, fps:	2950	2764	2586	2415	2250
	energy, ft-lb:	3478	3054	2673	2331	2023
	arc, inches:		+1.5	0	-6.7	-19.4
Win. 180 AccuBond	velocity, fps:	2950	2765	2588	2417	2253
	energy, ft-lb:	3478	3055	2676	2334	2028
	arc, inches:		+1.5	0	-6.7	-19.4
Win. 180 Fail Safe	velocity, fps:	2960	2732	2514	2307	2110
	energy, ft-lb:	3503	2983	2528	2129	1780
	arc, inches:		+1.6	0	-7.1	-20.7
Win. 180 Partition Gold	velocity, fps:	3070	2859	2657	2464	2280
	energy, ft-lb:	3768	3267	2823	2428	2078
	arc, inches:		+1.4	0	-6.3	-18.3
Win. 150 Supreme Elite XP3	velocity, fps:	3260	3030	2811	2603	2404
	energy, ft-lb:	3539	3057	2632	2256	1925
	arc, inches:		+1.1	0	-5.6	-16.2
Win. 180 Supreme Elite XP3	velocity, fps:	3000	2819	2646	2479	2318
	energy, ft-lb:	3597	3176	2797	2455	2147
	arc, inches:		+1.4	0	-6.4	-18.5

.300 REMINGTON SHORT ULTRA MAGNUM

CARTRIDGE BULLET	RANGE, YARDS:	0	100	200	300	400
Rem. 150 PSP C-L Ultra	velocity, fps:	3200	2901	2672	2359	2112
	energy, ft-lb:	3410	2803	2290	1854	1485
	arc, inches:		+1.3	0	-6.4	-19.l
Rem. 165 PSP Core-Lokt	velocity, fps:	3075	2792	2527	2276	2040
	energy, ft-lb:	3464	2856	2339	1828	1525
	arc, inches:		+1.5	0	-7.0	-20.7
Rem. 180 Partition	velocity, fps:	2960	2761	2571	2389	2214
	energy, ft-lb:	3501	3047	2642	2280	1959
	arc, inches:		+1.5	0	-6.8	-19.7
Rem. 180 PSP C-L Ultra	velocity, fps:	2960	2727	2506	2295	2094
	energy, ft-lb:	3501	2972	2509	2105	1753
	arc, inches:		+1.6	0	-7.1	-20.9
Rem. 190 HPBT Match	velocity, fps:	2900	2725	2557	2395	2239
	energy, ft-lb:	3547	3133	2758	2420	2115
	arc, inches:		+1.6	0	-6.9	-19.9

.300 WINCHESTER SHORT MAGNUM TO .300 WEATHERBY MAGNUM

.300 WINCHESTER SHORT MAGNUM

CARTRIDGE BULLET	RANGE, YARDS:	0	100	200	300	400
Black Hills 175 Sierra MKing	velocity, fps:	2950				
	energy, ft-lb:	3381				
	arc, inches:					
Black Hills 180 AccuBond	velocity, fps:	2950				
	energy, ft-lb:	3478				
	arc, inches:					
Federal 150 Nosler Bal. Tip	velocity, fps:	3200	2970	2755	2545	2345
	energy, ft-lb:	3410	2940	2520	2155	1830.
	arc, inches:		+1.2	0	-5.8	-17.0
Federal 160 Trophy Bonded Tip	velocity, fps:	3130	2910	2710	2510	2320
	energy, ft-lb:	3590	3110	2680	2305	1970
	arc, inches:		+1.3	0	-6.0	-17.6
Federal 165 Nos. Partition	velocity, fps:	3130	2890	2670	2450	2250
	energy, ft-lb:	3590	3065	2605	2205	1855.
	arc, inches:		+1.3	0	-6.2	-18.2
Federal 165 Nos. Solid Base	velocity, fps:	3130	2900	2690	2490	2290
	energy, ft-lb:	3590	3090	2650	2265	1920
	arc, inches:		+1.3	0	-6.1	-17.8
Federal 180 Barnes TS And Nos. Solid Base	velocity, fps:	2980	2780	2580	2400	2220
	energy, ft-lbs:	3550	3085	2670	2300	1970
	arc, inches:		+1.5	0	-6.7	-19.5
Federal 180 Grand Slam	velocity, fps:	2970	2740	2530	2320	2130
	energy, ft-lb:	3525	3010	2555	2155	1810
	arc, inches:		+1.5	0	-7.0	-20.5
Federal 180 Trophy Bonded	velocity, fps:	2970	2730	2500	2280	2080
	energy, ft-lb:	3525	2975	2500	2085	1725
	arc, inches:		+1.5	0	-7.2	-21.0
Federal 180 Nosler Partition	velocity, fps:	2975	2750	2535	2290	2126
	energy, ft-lb:	3540	3025	2570	2175	1825
	arc, inches:		+1.5	0	-7.0	-20.3
Federal 180 Nos. AccuBond	velocity, fps:	2960	2780	2610	2440	2280
	energy, ft-lb:	3500	3090	2715	2380	2075
	arc, inches:		+1.5	0	-6.6	-19.0
Federal 180 Hi-Shok SP	velocity, fps:	2970	2520	2115	1750	1430
	energy, ft-lb:	3525	2540	1785	1220	820
	arc, inches:		+2.2	0	-9.9	-31.4
Norma 150 FMJ	velocity, fps:	2953	2731	2519	2318	
	energy, ft-lb:					
	arc, inches:		+1.6	0	-7.1	
Norma 150 Barnes X TS	velocity, fps:	3215	2982	2761	2550	
	energy, ft-lb:	3444	2962	2539	2167	
	arc, inches:		+1.2	0	-5.7	
Norma 180 Nosler Bal. Tip	velocity, fps:	3215	2985	2767	2560	
	energy, ft-lb:	3437	2963	2547	2179	
	arc, inches:		+1.2	0	-5.7	
Norma 180 Oryx	velocity, fps:	2936	2542	2180	1849	
	energy, ft-lb:	3446	2583	1900	1368	
	arc, inches:		+1.9	0	-8.9	
Win. 150 Power-Point	velocity, fps:	3270	2903	2565	2250	1958
	energy, ft-lb:	3561	2807	2190	1686	1277
	arc, inches:		+1.3	0	-6.6	-20.2
Win. 150 Ballistic Silvertip	velocity, fps:	3300	3061	2834	2619	2414
	energy, ft-lb:	3628	3121	2676	2285	1941
	arc, inches:		+1.1	0	-5.4	-15.9
Win. 165 Fail Safe	velocity, fps:	3125	2846	2584	2336	2102
	energy, ft-lb:	3577	2967	2446	1999	1619
	arc, inches:		+1.4	0	-6.6	-19.6
Win. 180 Ballistic Silvertip	velocity, fps:	3010	2822	2641	2468	2301.
	energy, ft-lb:	3621	3182	2788	2434	2116
	arc, inches:		+1.4	0	-6.4	-18.6
Win. 180 AccuBond	velocity, fps:	3010	2822	2643	2470	2304
	energy, ft-lb:	3622	3185	2792	2439	2121
	arc, inches:		+1.4	0	-6.4	-18.5
Win. 180 Fail Safe	velocity, fps:	2970	2741	2524	2317	2120
	energy, ft-lb:	3526	3005	2547	2147	1797
	arc, inches:		+1.6	0	-7.0	-20.5
Win. 180 Power Point	velocity, fps:	2970	2755	2549	2353	2166
	energy, ft-lb:	3526	3034	2598	2214	1875
	arc, inches:		+1.5	0	-6.9	-20.1
Win. 150 Supreme Elite XP3	velocity, fps:	3300	3068	2847	2637	2437
	energy, ft-lb:	3626	3134	2699	2316	1978
	arc, inches:		+1.1	0	-5.4	-15.8
Win. 180 Supreme Elite XP3	velocity, fps:	3010	2829	2655	2488	2326
	energy, ft-lb:	3621	3198	2817	2473	2162
	arc, inches:		+1.4	0	-6.4	-18.3

.300 RUGER COMPACT MAGNUM

CARTRIDGE BULLET	RANGE, YARDS:	0	100	200	300	400
Hornady 150 SST	velocity, fps:	3310	3065	2833	2613	2404
	energy, ft-lb:	3648	3128	2673	2274	1924
	arc, inches:	-1.5	+1.1	0	-5.4	-16.0
Hornady 165 GMX	velocity, fps:	3130	2911	2703	2504	2314
	energy, ft-lb:	3589	3105	2677	2297	1963
	arc, inches:	-1.5	+1.3	0	-6.1	-17.7
Hornady 180 SST	velocity, fps:	3040	2840	2649	2466	2290
	energy, ft-lb:	3693	3223	2804	2430	2096
	arc, inches:	-1.5	+1.4	0	-6.4	-18.5

.300 WEATHERBY MAGNUM

CARTRIDGE BULLET	RANGE, YARDS:	0	100	200	300	400
A-Square 180 Dead Tough	velocity, fps:	3180	2811	2471	2155	1863.
	energy, ft-lb:	4041	3158	2440	1856	1387
	arc, inches:		+1.5	0	-7.2	-21.8
A-Square 220 Monolythic Solid	velocity, fps:	2700	2407	2133	1877	1653
	energy, ft-lb:	3561	2830	2223	1721	1334
	arc, inches:		+2.3	0	-9.8	-29.7
Federal 180 Nosler Partition	velocity, fps:	3190	2980	2780	2590	2400
	energy, ft-lb:	4055	3540	3080	2670	2305
	arc, inches:		+1.2	0	-5.7	-16.7
Federal 180 Nosler Part. HE	velocity, fps:	3330	3110	2810	2710	2520
	energy, ft-lb:	4430	3875	3375	2935	2540
	arc, inches:		+1.0	0	-5.2	-15.1
Federal 180 Sierra GameKing BTSP	velocity, fps:	3190	3010	2830	2660	2490
	energy, ft-lb:	4065	3610	3195	2820	2480
	arc, inches:		+1.2	0	-5.6	-16.0
Federal 180 Trophy Bonded	velocity, fps:	3190	2950	2720	2500	2290
	energy, ft-lb:	4065	3475	2955	2500	2105
	arc, inches:		+1.3	0	-5.9	-17.5
Federal 180 Tr. Bonded HE	velocity, fps:	3330	3080	2850	2750	2410
	energy, ft-lb:	4430	3795	3235	2750	2320
	arc, inches:		+1.1	0	-5.4	-15.8
Federal 180 Trophy Copper	velocity, fps:	3100	2910	2740	2560	2400
	energy, ft-lb:	3840	3395	2990	2625	2300
	arc, inches:		+1.3	0	-6.0	-17.1
Federal 200 Trophy Bonded	velocity, fps:	2900	2670	2440	2230	2030
	energy, ft-lb:	3735	3150	2645	2200	1820
	arc, inches:		+1.7	0	-7.6	-22.2
Hornady 150 SST (or Interbond)	velocity, fps:	3375	3123	2882	2652	2434
	energy, ft-lb:	3793	3248	2766	2343	1973
	arc, inches:		+1.0	0	-5.4	-15.8
Hornady 165 GMX Superformance	velocity, fps:	3140	2921	2713	2515	2325
	energy, ft-lb:	3612	3126	2697	2317	1980
	arc, inches:		+1.3	0	-6.0	-17.5
Hornady 180 SP	velocity, fps:	3120	2891	2673	2466	2268.
	energy, ft-lb:	3890	3340	2856	2430	2055
	arc, inches:		+1.3	0	-6.2	-18.1
Hornady 180 SST	velocity, fps:	3120	2911	2711	2519	2335
	energy, ft-lb:	3890	3386	2936	2535	2180
	arc, inches:		+1.3	0	-6.2	-18.1
Rem. 180 PSP Core-Lokt	velocity, fps:	3120	2866	2627	2400	2184
	energy, ft-lb:	3890	3284	2758	2301	1905
	arc, inches:		+2.4	+2.0	-3.4	-14.9

Centerfire Rifle Ballistics

.300 WEATHERBY MAGNUM TO .303 BRITISH

CARTRIDGE BULLET	RANGE, YARDS:	0	100	200	300	400
Rem. 190 PSP boat-tail	velocity, fps:	3030	2830	2638	2455	2279
	energy, ft-lb:	3873	3378	2936	2542	2190.
	arc, inches:		+1.4	0	-6.4	-18.6
Rem. 200 Swift A-Frame	velocity, fps:	2925	2690	2467	2254	2052
	energy, ft-lb:	3799	3213	2701	2256	1870
	arc, inches:		+2.8	+2.3	-3.9	-17.0
Speer 180 Grand Slam	velocity, fps:	3185	2948	2722	2508	
	energy, ft-lb:	4054	3472	2962	2514	
	arc, inches:		+1.3	0	-5.9	-17.4
Wby. 150 Pointed Expanding	velocity, fps:	3540	3225	2932	2657	2399
	energy, ft-lb:	4173	3462	2862	2351	1916
	arc, inches:		+2.6	+3.3	0	-8.2
Wby. 150 Nosler Partition	velocity, fps:	3540	3263	3004	2759	2528
	energy, ft-lb:	4173	3547	3005	2536	2128
	arc, inches:		+2.5	+3.2	0	-7.7
Wby. 165 Pointed Expanding	velocity, fps:	3390	3123	2872	2634	2409
	energy, ft-lb:	4210	3573	3021	2542	2126
	arc, inches:		+2.8	+3.5	0	-8.5
Wby. 165 Nosler Bal. Tip	velocity, fps:	3350	3133	2927	2730	2542
	energy, ft-lb:	4111	3596	3138	2730	2367
	arc, inches:		+2.7	+3.4	0	-8.1
Wby. 180 Pointed Expanding	velocity, fps:	3240	3004	2781	2569	2366
	energy, ft-lb:	4195	3607	3091	2637	2237
	arc, inches:		+3.1	+3.8	0	-9.0
Wby. 180 Barnes X	velocity, fps:	3190	2995	2809	2631	2459
	energy, ft-lb:	4067	3586	3154	2766	2417
	arc, inches:		+3.1	+3.8	0	-8.7
Wby. 180 Bal. Tip	velocity, fps:	3250	3051	2806	2676	2503
	energy, ft-lb:	4223	3721	3271	2867	2504
	arc, inches:		+2.8	+3.6	0	-8.4
Wby. 180 Nosler Partition	velocity, fps:	3240	3028	2826	2634	2449
	energy, ft-lb:	4195	3665	3193	2772	2396
	arc, inches:		+3.0	+3.7	0	-8.6
Wby. 200 Nosler Partition	velocity, fps:	3060	2860	2668	2485	2308
	energy, ft-lb:	4158	3631	3161	2741	2366
	arc, inches:		+3.5	+4.2	0	-9.8
Wby. 220 RN Expanding	velocity, fps:	2845	2543	2260	1996	1751.
	energy, ft-lb:	3954	3158	2495	1946	1497
	arc, inches:		+4.9	+5.9	0	-14.6

.300 DAKOTA

CARTRIDGE BULLET	RANGE, YARDS:	0	100	200	300	400
Dakota 165 Barnes X	velocity, fps:	3200	2979	2769	2569	2377
	energy, ft-lb:	3751	3251	2809	2417	2070
	arc, inches:		+2.1	+1.8	-3.0	-13.2
Dakota 200 Barnes X	velocity, fps:	3000	2824	2656	2493	2336
	energy, ft-lb:	3996	3542	3131	2760	2423
	arc, inches:		+2.2	+1.5	-4.0	-15.2

.300 PEGASUS

CARTRIDGE BULLET	RANGE, YARDS:	0	100	200	300	400
A-Square 180 SP boat-tail	velocity, fps:	3500	3319	3145	2978	2817
	energy, ft-lb:	4896	4401	3953	3544	3172
	arc, inches:		+2.3	+2.9	0	-6.8
A-Square 180 Nosler Part.	velocity, fps:	3500	3295	3100	2913	2734
	energy, ft-lb:	4896	4339	3840	3392	2988
	arc, inches:		+2.3	+3.0	0	-7.1
A-Square 180 Dead Tough	velocity, fps:	3500	3103	2740	2405	2095
	energy, ft-lb:	4896	3848	3001	2312	1753
	arc, inches:		+1.1	0	-5.7	-17.5

.300 REMINGTON ULTRA MAGNUM

CARTRIDGE BULLET	RANGE, YARDS:	0	100	200	300	400
Federal 180 Trophy Bonded	velocity, fps:	3250	3000	2770	2550	2340
	energy, ft-lb:	4220	3605	3065	2590	2180
	arc, inches:		+1.2	0	-5.7	-16.8
Federal 180 Trophy Copper	velocity, fps:	3150	2960	2780	2610	2440
	energy, ft-lb:	3965	3505	3090	2715	2380
	arc, inches:		+1.2	0	-5.8	-16.6

CARTRIDGE BULLET	RANGE, YARDS:	0	100	200	300	400
Federal 200 Partition	velocity, fps:	3070	2870	2680	2490	2320
	energy, ft-lb:	4185	3655	3180	2760	2380
	arc, inches:		+1.4	0	-6.2	-18.0
Rem. 150 Swift Scirocco	velocity, fps:	3450	3208	2980	2762	2556
	energy, ft-lb:	3964	3427	2956	2541	2175
	arc, inches:		+1.7	+1.5	-2.6	-11.2
Remington 165 Copper Solid	velocity, fps:	3250	3035	2821	2617	2422
	energy, ft-lb:	3893	3373	2916	2602	2390
	arc, inches:		+1.4	0	-5.8	-16.7
Rem. 180 Nosler Partition	velocity, fps:	3250	3037	2834	2640	2454
	energy, ft-lb:	4221	3686	3201	2786	2407
	arc, inches:		+2.4	+1.8	-3.0	-12.7
Rem. 180 Swift Scirocco	velocity, fps:	3250	3048	2856	2672	2495
	energy, ft-lb:	4221	3714	3260	2853	2487
	arc, inches:		+2.0	+1.7	-2.8	-12.3
Rem. 180 PSP Core-Lokt	velocity, fps:	3250	2988	2742	2508	2287
	energy, ft-lb:	3517	2974	2503	2095	1741
	arc, inches:		+2.1	+1.8	-3.1	-13.6
Rem. 200 Nosler Partition	velocity, fps:	3025	2826	2636	2454	2279
	energy, ft-lb:	4063	3547	3086	2673	2308
	arc, inches:		+2.4	+2.0	-3.4	-14.6

.30-378 WEATHERBY MAGNUM

CARTRIDGE BULLET	RANGE, YARDS:	0	100	200	300	400
Nosler 210 ABLR	velocity, fps:	3040	2907	2778	2653	2531
	energy, ft-lb:	4308	3940	3599	3282	2987
	arc, inches:	-1.5	+1.3	0	-5.8	-16.6
Wby. 165 Nosler Bal. Tip	velocity, fps:	3500	3275	3062	2859	2665
	energy, ft-lb:	4488	3930	3435	2995	2603
	arc, inches:		+2.4	+3.0	0	-7.4
Wby. 180 Nosler Bal. Tip	velocity, fps:	3420	3213	3015	2826	2645
	energy, ft-lb:	4676	4126	3634	3193	2797
	arc, inches:		+2.5	+3.1	0	-7.5
Wby. 180 Barnes X	velocity, fps:	3450	3243	3046	2858	2678.
	energy, ft-lb:	4757	4204	3709	3264	2865
	arc, inches:		+2.4	+3.1	0	-7.4
Wby. 200 Nosler Partition	velocity, fps:	3160	2955	2759	2572	2392.
	energy, ft-lb:	4434	3877	3381	2938	2541
	arc, inches:		+3.2	+3.9	0	-9.1

7.82 (.308) WARBIRD

CARTRIDGE BULLET	RANGE, YARDS:	0	100	200	300	400
Lazzeroni 150 Nosler Part.	velocity, fps:	3680	3432	3197	2975	2764
	energy, ft-lb:	4512	3923	3406	2949	2546.
	arc, inches:		+2.1	+2.7	0	-6.6
Lazzeroni 180 Nosler Part.	velocity, fps:	3425	3220	3026	2839	2661
	energy, ft-lb:	4689	4147	3661	3224	2831
	arc, inches:		+2.5	+3.2	0	-7.5
Lazzeroni 200 Swift A-Fr.	velocity, fps:	3290	3105	2928	2758	2594.
	energy, ft-lb:	4808	4283	3808	3378	2988
	arc, inches:		+2.7	+3.4	0	-7.9

7.65x53 ARGENTINE

CARTRIDGE BULLET	RANGE, YARDS:	0	100	200	300	400
Norma 174 Soft Point	velocity, fps:	2493	2173	1878	1611	
	energy, ft-lb:	2402	1825	1363	1003	
	arc, inches:		+2.0	0	-9.5	
Norma 180 Soft Point	velocity, fps:	2592	2386	2189	2002	
	energy, ft-lb:	2686	2276	1916	1602	
	arc, inches:		+2.3	0	-9.6	

.303 BRITISH

CARTRIDGE BULLET	RANGE, YARDS:	0	100	200	300	400
Federal 150 Hi-Shok	velocity, fps:	2690	2440	2210	1980	1780
	energy, ft-lb:	2400	1980	1620	1310	1055
	arc, inches:		+2.2	0	-9.4	-27.6
Federal 180 Sierra Pro-Hunt.	velocity, fps:	2460	2230	2020	1820	1630
	energy, ft-lb:	2420	1995	1625	1315	1060
	arc, inches:		+2.8	0	-11.3	-33.2
Federal 180 Tr. Bonded HE	velocity, fps:	2590	2350	2120	1900	1700
	energy, ft-lb:	2680	2205	1795	1445	1160
	arc, inches:		+2.4	0	-10.0	-30.0
Hornady 150 Soft Point	velocity, fps:	2685	2441	2210	1992	1787
	energy, ft-lb:	2401	1984	1627	1321	1064
	arc, inches:		+2.2	0	-9.3	-27.4

CARTRIDGE BULLET	RANGE, YARDS:	0	100	200	300	400
Hornady 150 SP LM	velocity, fps:	2830	2570	2325	2094	1884.
	energy, ft-lb:	2667	2199	1800	1461	1185
	arc, inches:		+2.0	0	-8.4	-24.6
Hornady 174 BTHP	velocity, fps:	2430	2252	2082	1919	1765
	energy, ft-lb:	2281	1959	1674	1423	1204
	arc, inches:		+2.7	0	-10.7	-30.9
Norma 150 Soft Point	velocity, fps:	2723	2438	2170	1920	
	energy, ft-lb:	2470	1980	1569	1228	
	arc, inches:		+2.2	0	-9.6	
PMC 174 FMJ (and HPBT)	velocity, fps:	2400	2216	2042	1876	1720
	energy, ft-lb:	2225	1898	1611	1360	1143
	arc, inches:		+2.8	0	-11.2	-32.2
PMC 180 SP boat-tail	velocity, fps:	2450	2276	2110	1951	1799
	energy, ft-lb:	2399	2071	1779	1521	1294
	arc, inches:		+2.6	0	-10.4	-30.1
Rem. 180 SP Core-Lokt	velocity, fps:	2460	2124	1817	1542	1311
	energy, ft-lb:	2418	1803	1319	950	687
	arc, inches, s:		0	-5.8	-23.3	
Win. 180 Power-Point	velocity, fps:	2460	2233	2018	1816	1629
	energy, ft-lb:	2418	1993	1627	1318	1060
	arc, inches, s:		0	-6.1	-20.8	

7.7x58 JAPANESE ARISAKA

CARTRIDGE BULLET	RANGE, YARDS:	0	100	200	300	400
Norma 174 Soft Point	velocity, fps:	2493	2173	1878	1611	
	energy, ft-lb:	2402	1825	1363	1003	
	arc, inches:		+2.0	0	-9.5	
Norma 180 Soft Point	velocity, fps:	2493	2291	2099	1916	
	energy, ft-lb:	2485	2099	1761	1468	
	arc, inches:		+2.6	0	-10.5	

.32-20 WINCHESTER

CARTRIDGE BULLET	RANGE, YARDS:	0	100	200	300	400
Rem. 100 Lead	velocity, fps:	1210	1021	913	834	769
	energy, ft-lb:	325	231	185	154	131
	arc, inches:		0	-31.6	-104.7	
Win. 100 Lead	velocity, fps:	1210	1021	913	834	769
	energy, ft-lb:	325	231	185	154	131
	arc, inches:		0	-32.3	-106.3	

.32 WINCHESTER SPECIAL

CARTRIDGE BULLET	RANGE, YARDS:	0	100	200	300	400
Federal 170 Hi-Shok	velocity, fps:	2250	1920	1630	1370	1180
	energy, ft-lb:	1910	1395	1000	710	520
	arc, inches:		0	-8.0	-29.2	
Hornady 165 FTX	velocity, fps:	2410	2145	1897	1669	
	energy, ft-lb:	2128	1685	1318	1020	
	arc, inches:	-1.5	+3.0	0	-12.8	
Rem. 170 SP Core-Lokt	velocity, fps:	2250	1921	1626	1372	1175
	energy, ft-lb:	1911	1393	998	710	521
	arc, inches:		0	-8.0	-29.3	
Win. 170 Power-Point	velocity, fps:	2250	1870	1537	1267	1082
	energy, ft-lb:	1911	1320	892	606	442
	arc, inches:		0	-9.2	-33.2	

8MM MAUSER (8x57)

CARTRIDGE BULLET	RANGE, YARDS:	0	100	200	300	400
Federal 170 Hi-Shok	velocity, fps:	2360	1970	1620	1330	1120
	energy, ft-lb:	2100	1465	995	670	475
	arc, inches:		0	-7.6	-28.5	
Hornady 195 SP	velocity, fps:	2550	2343	2146	1959	1782
	energy, ft-lb:	2815	2377	1994	1861	1375
	arc, inches:		+2.3	0	-9.9	-28.8.
Hornady 195 SP (2005)	velocity, fps:	2475	2269	2074	1888	1714
	energy, ft-lb:	2652	2230	1861	1543	1271
	arc, inches:		+2.6	0	-10.7	-31.3
Norma 123 FMJ	velocity, fps:	2559	2121	1729	1398	
	energy, ft-lb:	1789	1228	817	534	
	arc, inches:		+3.2	0	-15.0	

CARTRIDGE BULLET	RANGE, YARDS:	0	100	200	300	400
Norma 196 Oryx	velocity, fps:	2395	2146	1912	1695	
	energy, ft-lb:	2497	2004	1591	1251	
	arc, inches:		+3	0	-12.6	
Norma 196 Vulkan	velocity, fps:	2395	2156	1930	1720	
	energy, ft-lb:	2497	2023	1622	1289	
	arc, inches:		3.0	0	-12.3	
Norma 196 Alaska	velocity, fps:	2395	2112	1850	1611	
	energy, ft-lb:	2714	2190	1754	1399	
	arc, inches:		0	-6.3	-22.9	
Norma 196 Soft Point (JS)	velocity, fps:	2526	2244	1981	1737	
	energy, ft-lb:	2778	2192	1708	1314	
	arc, inches:		+2.7	0	-11.6	
Norma 196 Alaska (JS)	velocity, fps:	2526	2248	1988	1747	
	energy, ft-lb:	2778	2200	1720	1328	
	arc, inches:		+2.7	0	-11.5	
Norma 196 Vulkan (JS)	velocity, fps:	2526	2276	2041	1821	
	energy, ft-lb:	2778	2256	1813	1443	
	arc, inches:		+2.6	0	-11.0	
Norma 196 Oryx (JS)	velocity, fps:	2526	2269	2027	1802	
	energy, ft-lb:	2778	2241	1789	1413	
	arc, inches:		+2.6	0	-11.1	
PMC 170 Pointed Soft Point	velocity, fps:	2360	1969	1622	1333	1123
	energy, ft-lb:	2102	1463	993	671	476
	arc, inches:		+1.8	-4.5	-24.3	-63.8
Rem. 170 SP Core-Lokt	velocity, fps:	2360	1969	1622	1333	1123
	energy, ft-lb:	2102	1463	993	671	476
	arc, inches:		+1.8	-4.5	-24.3	-63.8.
Win. 170 Power-Point	velocity, fps:	2360	1969	1622	1333	1123
	energy, ft-lb:	2102	1463	993	671	476
	arc, inches:		+1.8	-4.5	-24.3	-63.8

.325 WSM

CARTRIDGE BULLET	RANGE, YARDS:	0	100	200	300	400
Win. 180 Ballistic ST	velocity, fps:	3060	2841	2632	2432	2242
	energy, ft-lb:	3743	3226	2769	2365	2009
	arc, inches:		+1.4	0	-6.4	-18.7
Win. 200 AccuBond CT	velocity, fps:	2950	2753	2565	2384	2210
	energy, ft-lb:	3866	3367	2922	2524	2170
	arc, inches:		+1.5	0	-6.8	-19.8
Win. 220 Power-Point	velocity, fps:	2840	2605	2382	2169	1968
	energy, ft-lb:	3941	3316	2772	2300	1893
	arc, inches:		+1.8	0	-8.0	-23.3

8MM REMINGTON MAGNUM

CARTRIDGE BULLET	RANGE, YARDS:	0	100	200	300	400
A-Square 220 Monolythic Solid	velocity, fps:	2800	2501	2221	1959	1718
	energy, ft-lb:	3829	3055	2409	1875	1442
	arc, inches:		+2.1	0	-9.1	-27.6
Nosler 180 BT	velocity, fps:	3200	2923	2662	2416	2183
	energy, ft-lb:	4092	3414	2832	2333	1905
	arc, inches:	-1.5	+1.3	0	-6.2	-18.4
Rem. 200 Swift A-Frame	velocity, fps:	2900	2623	2361	2115	1885
	energy, ft-lb:	3734	3054	2476	1987	1577
	arc, inches:		+1.8	0	-8.0	-23.9

.338 FEDERAL

CARTRIDGE BULLET	RANGE, YARDS:	0	100	200	300	400
Federal 180 AccuBond	velocity, fps:	2830	2590	2350	2130	1930
	energy, ft-lb:	3200	2670	2215	1820	1480
	arc, inches:	-1.5	+1.8	0	-8.2	-23.9
Federal 185 Barnes TSX	velocity, fps:	2750	2500	2260	2030	1820
	energy, ft-lb:	3105	2560	2090	1695	1355
	arc, inches:	-1.5	+2.0	0	-8.9	-26.2
Federal 200 Tr. Bonded T	velocity, fps:	2630	2430	2240	2060	1890
	energy, ft-lb:	3070	2625	2230	1885	1580
	arc, inches:	-1.5	+2.2	0	-9.2	-26.3
Federal 210 Partition	velocity, fps:	2630	2410	2200	2010	1820
	energy, ft-lb:	3225	2710	2265	1880	1545
	arc, inches:	-1.5	+2.3	0	-9.4	-27.3

Centerfire Rifle Ballistics

.338 MARLIN EXPRESS TO .340 WEATHERBY MAGNUM

CARTRIDGE BULLET	RANGE, YARDS:	0	100	200	300	400
.338 MARLIN EXPRESS						
Hornady 200 FTX	velocity, fps:	2565	2365	2174	1992	`1820
	energy, ft-lb:	2922	2484	2099	1762	1471
	arc, inches:	-1.5	+3.0	+1.2	-7.9	-25.9
.338-06						
A-Square 200 Nos. Bal. Tip	velocity, fps:	2750	2553	2364	2184	2011
	energy, ft-lb:	3358	2894	2482	2118	1796
	arc, inches:		+1.9	0	-8.2	-23.6
A-Square 250 SP boat-tail	velocity, fps:	2500	2374	2252	2134	2019
	energy, ft-lb:	3496	3129	2816	2528	2263
	arc, inches:		+2.4	0	-9.3	-26.0
A-Square 250 Dead Tough	velocity, fps:	2500	2222	1963	1724	1507
	energy, ft-lb:	3496	2742	2139	1649	1261
	arc, inches:		+2.8	0	-11.9	-35.5
Nosler 180 AB	velocity, fps:	2950	2698	2460	2234	2020
	energy, ft-lb:	3477	2909	2418	1994	1631
	arc, inches:	-1.5	+1.6	0	-7.4	-21.8
Nosler 225 AB	velocity, fps:	2600	2441	2287	2139	1997
	energy, ft-lb:	3376	2976	2614	2286	1992
	arc, inches:	-1.5	+2.2	0	-8.8	-25.3
Wby. 210 Nosler Part.	velocity, fps:	2750	2526	2312	2109	1916
	energy, ft-lb:	3527	2975	2403	2074	1712
	arc, inches:		+4.8	+5.7	0	-13.5
.338 RUGER COMPACT MAGNUM						
Hornady 185 GMX	velocity, fps:	2980	2755	2542	2338	2143
	energy, ft-lb:	3647	3118	2653	2242	1887
	arc, inches:	-1.5	+1.5	0	-6.9	-20.3
Hornady 200 SST	velocity, fps:	2950	2744	2547	2358	2177
	energy, ft-lb:	3846	3342	2879	2468	2104
	arc, inches:	-1.5	+1.6	0	-6.9	-20.1
Hornady 225 SST	velocity, fps:	2750	2575	2407	2245	2089
	energy, ft-lb:	3778	3313	2894	2518	2180
	arc, inches:	-1.5	+1.9	· 0	-7.9	-22.7
.338 WINCHESTER MAGNUM						
A-Square 250 SP boat-tail	velocity, fps:	2700	2568	2439	2314	2193
	energy, ft-lb:	4046	3659	3302	2972	2669
	arc, inches:		+4.4	+5.2	0	-11.7
A-Square 250 Triad	velocity, fps:	2700	2407	2133	1877	1653
	energy, ft-lb:	4046	3216	2526	1956	1516
	arc, inches:		+2.3	0	-9.8	-29.8
Federal 200 Trophy Bonded Tip	velocity, fps:	2930	2720	2520	2320	2140
	energy, ft-lb:	3810	3280	2810	2395	2025
	arc, inches:		+1.6	0	-7.1	-20.7
Federal 210 Nosler Partition	velocity, fps:	2830	2600	2390	2180	1980
	energy, ft-lb:	3735	3160	2655	2215	1835
	arc, inches:		+1.8	0	-8.0 ·	-23.3
Federal 225 Sierra Pro-Hunt.	velocity, fps:	2780	2570	2360	2170	1980
	energy, ft-lb:	3860	3290	2780	2340	1960
	arc, inches:		+1.9	0	-8.2	-23.7
Federal 225 Trophy Bonded	velocity, fps:	2800	2560	2330	2110	1900
	energy, ft-lb:	3915	3265	2700	2220	1800
	arc, inches:		+1.9	0	-8.4	-24.5
Federal 225 Tr. Bonded HE	velocity, fps:	2940	2690	2450	2230	2010
	energy, ft-lb:	4320	3610	3000	2475	2025
	arc, inches:		+1.7	0	-7.5	-22.0
Federal 225 Barnes XLC	velocity, fps:	2800	2610	2430	2260	2090
	energy, ft-lb:	3915	3405	2950	2545	2190
	arc, inches:		+1.8	0	-7.7	-22.2
Federal 250 Nosler Partition	velocity, fps:	2660	2470	2300	2120	1960
	energy, ft-lb:	3925	3395	2925	2505	2130.
	arc, inches:		+2.1	0	-8.8	-25.1

CARTRIDGE BULLET	RANGE, YARDS:	0	100	200	300	400
Federal 250 Nosler Part HE	velocity, fps:	2800	2610	2420	2250	2080
	energy, ft-lb:	4350	3775	3260	2805	2395
	arc, inches:	+1.8	0	-7.8	-22.5	
Hornady 185 GMX Superformance	velocity, fps:	3080	2851	2633	2426	2228
	energy, ft-lb:	3897	3338	2848	2417	2038
	arc, inches:	+1.4	0	-6.4	-18.8	
Hornady 200 SST Superformance	velocity, fps:	3030	2820	2620	2429	2246
	energy, ft-lb:	4077	3532	3049	2621	2240
	arc, inches:	+1.4	0	-6.5	-18.9	
Hornady 225 Soft Point HM	velocity, fps:	2920	2678	2449	2232	2027
	energy, ft-lb:	4259	3583	2996	2489	2053
	arc, inches:	+1.8	0	-7.6	-22.0	
Norma 225 TXP Swift A-Fr.	velocity, fps:	2740	2507	2286	2075	
	energy, ft-lb:	3752	3141	2611	2153	
	arc, inches:	+2.0	0	-8.7		
Norma 230 Oryx	velocity, fps:	2756	2514	2284	2066	
	energy, ft-lb:	3880	3228	2665	2181	
	arc, inches:	+2.0	0	-8.7		
Norma 250 Nosler Partition	velocity, fps:	2657	2470	2290	2118	
	energy, ft-lb:	3920	3387	2912	2490	
	arc, inches:	+2.1	0	-8.7		
PMC 225 Barnes X	velocity, fps:	2780	2619	2464	2313	2168
	energy, ft-lb:	3860	3426	3032	2673	2348.
	arc, inches:	+1.8	0	-7.6	-21.6	
Rem. 200 Nosler Bal. Tip	velocity, fps:	2950	2724	2509	2303	2108
	energy, ft-lb:	3866	3295	2795	2357	1973
	arc, inches:	+1.6	0	-7.1	-20.8	
Rem. 210 Nosler Partition	velocity, fps:	2830	2602	2385	2179	1983
	energy, ft-lb:	3734	3157	2653	2214	1834
	arc, inches:	+1.8	0	-7.9	-23.2	
Rem. 225 PSP Core-Lokt	velocity, fps:	2780	2572	2374	2184	2003
	energy, ft-lb:	3860	3305	2815	2383	2004
	arc, inches:	+1.9	0	-8.1	-23.4	
Rem. 225 PSP C-L Ultra	velocity, fps:	2780	2582	2392	2210	2036
	energy, ft-lb:	3860	3329	2858	2440	2071
	arc, inches:	+1.9	0	-7.9	-23.0	
Rem. 225 Swift A-Frame	velocity, fps:	2785	2517	2266	2029	1808
	energy, ft-lb:	3871	3165	2565	2057	1633
	arc, inches:	+2.0	0	-8.8	-25.2	
Rem. 250 PSP Core-Lokt	velocity, fps:	2660	2456	2261	2075	1898
	energy, ft-lb:	3927	3348	2837	2389	1999
	arc, inches:	+2.1	0	-8.9	-26.0	
Speer 250 Grand Slam	velocity, fps:	2645	2442	2247	2062	
	energy, ft-lb:	3883	3309	2803	2360	
	arc, inches:	+2.2	0	-9.1	-26.2	
Win. 200 Power-Point	velocity, fps:	2960	2658	2375	2110	1862
	energy, ft-lb:	3890	3137	2505	1977	1539
	arc, inches:	+2.0	0	-8.2	-24.3	
Win. 200 Ballistic Silvertip	velocity, fps:	2950	2724	2509	2303	2108
	energy, ft-lb:	3864	3294	2794	2355	1972
	arc, inches:	+1.6	0	-7.1	-20.8	
Win. 225 AccuBond	velocity, fps:	2800	2634	2474	2319	2170
	energy, ft-lb:	3918	3467	3058	2688	2353
	arc, inches:	+1.8	0	-7.4	-21.3	
Win. 230 Fail Safe	velocity, fps:	2780	2573	2375	2186	2005
	energy, ft-lb:	3948	3382	2881	2441	2054
	arc, inches:	+1.9	0	-8.1	-23.4	
Win. 250 Partition Gold	velocity, fps:	2650	2467	2291	2122	1960
	energy, ft-lb:	3899	3378	2914	2520	2134
	arc, inches:	+2.1	0	-8.7	-25.2	
.340 WEATHERBY MAGNUM						
A-Square 250 SP boat-tail	velocity, fps:	2820	2684	2552	2424	2299
	energy, ft-lb:	4414	3999	3615	3261	2935
	arc, inches:	+4.0	+4.6	0	-10.6	
A-Square 250 Triad	velocity, fps:	2820	2520	2238	1976	1741
	energy, ft-lb:	4414	3524	2781	2166	1683
	arc, inches:	+2.0	0	-9.0	-26.8	
Federal 225 Trophy Bonded	velocity, fps:	3100	2840	2600	2370	2150
	energy, ft-lb:	4800	4035	3375	2800	2310
	arc, inches:	+1.4	0	-6.5	-19.4	

CARTRIDGE BULLET	RANGE, YARDS:	0	100	200	300	400
Wby. 200 Pointed Expanding	velocity, fps:	3221	2946	2688	2444	2213
	energy, ft-lb:	4607	3854	3208	2652	2174
	arc, inches:		+3.3	+4.0	0	-9.9
Wby. 200 Nosler Bal. Tip	velocity, fps:	3221	2980	2753	2536	2329
	energy, ft-lb:	4607	3944	3364	2856	2409
	arc, inches:		+3.1	+3.9	0	-9.2
Wby. 210 Nosler Partition	velocity, fps:	3211	2963	2728	2505	2293
	energy, ft-lb:	4807	4093	3470	2927	2452
	arc, inches:		+3.2	+3.9	0	-9.5
Wby. 225 Pointed Expanding	velocity, fps:	3066	2824	2595	2377	2170
	energy, ft-lb:	4696	3984	3364	2822	2352
	arc, inches:		+3.6	+4.4	0	-10.7
Wby. 225 Barnes X	velocity, fps:	3001	2804	2615	2434	2260
	energy, ft-lb:	4499	3927	3416	2959	2551
	arc, inches:		+3.6	+4.3	0	-10.3
Wby. 250 Pointed Expanding	velocity, fps:	2963	2745	2537	2338	2149
	energy, ft-lb:	4873	4182	3572	3035	2563
	arc, inches:		+3.9	+4.6	0	-11.1
Wby. 250 Nosler Partition	velocity, fps:	2941	2743	2553	2371	2197
	energy, ft-lb:	4801	4176	3618	3120	2678
	arc, inches:		+3.9	+4.6	0	-10.9

.330 DAKOTA

CARTRIDGE BULLET	RANGE, YARDS:	0	100	200	300	400
Dakota 200 Barnes X	velocity, fps:	3200	2971	2754	2548	2350
	energy, ft-lb:	4547	3920	3369	2882	2452
	arc, inches:		+2.1	+1.8	-3.1	-13.4
Dakota 250 Barnes X	velocity, fps:	2900	2719	2545	2378	2217
	energy, ft-lb:	4668	4103	3595	3138	2727
	arc, inches:		+2.3	+1.3	-5.0	-17.5

.338 REMINGTON ULTRA MAGNUM

CARTRIDGE BULLET	RANGE, YARDS:	0	100	200	300	400
Federal 210 Nosler Partition	velocity, fps:	3025	2800	2585	2385	2190
	energy, ft-lb:	4270	3655	3120	2645	2230
	arc, inches:		+1.5	0	-6.7	-19.5
Federal 250 Trophy Bonded	velocity, fps:	2860	2630	2420	2210	2020
	energy, ft-lb:	4540	3850	3245	2715	2260.
	arc, inches:		+0.8	0	-7.7	-22.6
Rem. 250 Swift A-Frame	velocity, fps:	2860	2645	2440	2244	2057
	energy, ft-lb:	4540	3882	3303	2794	2347
	arc, inches:		+1.7	0	-7.6	-22.1
Rem. 250 PSP Core-Lokt	velocity, fps:	2860	2647	2443	2249	2064
	energy, ft-lb:	4540	3888	3314	2807	2363
	arc, inches:		+1.7	0	-7.6	-22.0

.338 NORMA MAGNUM

CARTRIDGE BULLET	RANGE, YARDS:	0	100	200	300	400
Black Hills 300 MatchKing	velocity, fps:	2725				
	energy, ft-lb:	4946				
	arc, inches					

.338 LAPUA

CARTRIDGE BULLET	RANGE, YARDS:	0	100	200	300	400
Black Hills 250 Sierra MKing	velocity, fps:	2950				
	energy, ft-lb:	4831				
	arc, inches:					
Black Hills 300 Sierra MKing	velocity, fps:	2800				
	energy, ft-lb:	5223				
	arc, inches:					
Hornady 250 BTHP Match	velocity, fps:	2900	2761	2626	2495	2368
	energy, ft-lb:	4668	4230	3827	3455	3112
	arc, inches:		+1.5	0	-6.6	-18.8
Hornady 285 BTHP	velocity, fps:	2745	2616	2491	2369	2251
	energy, ft-lb:	4768	4331	3926	3552	3206
	arc, inches:	-1.5	+1.8	0	-7.4	-21.0

CARTRIDGE BULLET	RANGE, YARDS:	0	100	200	300	600
Lapua 250 Scenar	velocity, fps:	2970	2823	2680	2539	2141
	energy, ft-lb:	4896	4424	3985	3579	2545
	arc, inches:	-1.5	+3.0	+4.0	0	-47.0
Lapua 300 Scenar	velocity, fps:	2723	2600	2482	2367	2042
	energy, ft-lb:	4938	4504	4102	3731	2778
	arc, inches:	-1.5	+4.0	+5.0	0	-54.0

CARTRIDGE BULLET	RANGE, YARDS:	0	100	200	300	400
Nosler 225 AB	velocity, fps:	3000	2826	2659	2498	2342
	energy, ft-lb:	4495	3990	3532	3117	2741
	arc, inches:	-1.5	+1.4	0	-6.3	-18.3

.338-378 WEATHERBY MAGNUM

CARTRIDGE BULLET	RANGE, YARDS:	0	100	200	300	400
Wby. 200 Nosler Bal. Tip	velocity, fps:	3350	3102	2868	2646	2434
	energy, ft-lb:	4983	4273	3652	3109	2631
	arc, inches:	0	+2.8	+3.5	0	-8.4
Wby. 225 Barnes X	velocity, fps:	3180	2974	2778	2591	2410.
	energy, ft-lb:	5052	4420	3856	3353	2902
	arc, inches:	0	+3.1	+3.8	0	-8.9
Wby. 250 Nosler Partition	velocity, fps:	3060	2856	2662	2475	2297
	energy, ft-lb:	5197	4528	3933	3401	2927
	arc, inches:	0	+3.5	+4.2	0	-9.8

8.59 (.338) TITAN

CARTRIDGE BULLET	RANGE, YARDS:	0	100	200	300	400
Lazzeroni 200 Nos. Bal. Tip	velocity, fps:	3430	3211	3002	2803	2613
	energy, ft-lb:	5226	4579	4004	3491	3033
	arc, inches:		+2.5	+3.2	0	-7.6
Lazzeroni 225 Nos. Partition	velocity, fps:	3235	3031	2836	2650	2471
	energy, ft-lb:	5229	4591	4021	3510	3052
	arc, inches:		+3.0	+3.6	0	-8.6
Lazzeroni 250 Swift A-Fr.	velocity, fps:	3100	2908	2725	2549	2379
	energy, ft-lb:	5336	4697	4123	3607	3143
	arc, inches:		+3.3	+4.0	0	-9.3

.338 A-SQUARE

CARTRIDGE BULLET	RANGE, YARDS:	0	100	200	300	400
A-Square 200 Nos. Bal. Tip	velocity, fps:	3500	3266	3045	2835	2634
	energy, ft-lb:	5440	4737	4117	3568	3081
	arc, inches:		+2.4	+3.1	0	-7.5
A-Square 250 SP boat-tail	velocity, fps:	3120	2974	2834	2697	2565.
	energy, ft-lb:	5403	4911	4457	4038	3652
	arc, inches:		+3.1	+3.7	0	-8.5
A-Square 250 Triad	velocity, fps:	3120	2799	2500	2220	1958
	energy, ft-lb:	5403	4348	3469	2736	2128
	arc, inches:		+1.5	0	-7.1	-20.4.

.338 EXCALIBER

CARTRIDGE BULLET	RANGE, YARDS:	0	100	200	300	400
A-Square 200 Nos. Bal. Tip	velocity, fps:	3600	3361	3134	2920	2715
	energy, ft-lb:	5755	5015	4363	3785	3274
	arc, inches:		+2.2	+2.9	0	-6.7
A-Square 250 SP boat-tail	velocity, fps:	3250	3101	2958	2684	2553
	energy, ft-lb:	5863	5339	4855	4410	3998
	arc, inches:		+2.7	+3.4	0	-7.8
A-Square 250 Triad	velocity, fps:	3250	2922	2618	2333	2066
	energy, ft-lb:	5863	4740	3804	3021	2370
	arc, inches:		+1.3	0	-6.4	-19.2

.348 WINCHESTER

CARTRIDGE BULLET	RANGE, YARDS:	0	100	200	300	400
Win. 200 Silvertip	velocity, fps:	2520	2215	1931	1672	1443.
	energy, ft-lb:	2820	2178	1656	1241	925
	arc, inches:		0	-6.2	-21.9	

.357 MAGNUM

CARTRIDGE BULLET	RANGE, YARDS:	0	100	200	300	400
Federal 180 Hi-Shok HP Hollow Point	velocity, fps:	1550	1160	980	860	770
	energy, ft-lb:	960	535	385	295	235
	arc, inches:		0	-22.8	-77.9	-173.8
Win. 158 Jacketed SP	velocity, fps:	1830	1427	1138	980	883
	energy, ft-lb:	1175	715	454	337	274
	arc, inches:		0	-16.2	-57.0	-128.3

.35 REMINGTON

CARTRIDGE BULLET	RANGE, YARDS:	0	100	200	300	400
Federal 200 Hi-Shok	velocity, fps:	2080	1700	1380	1140	1000
	energy, ft-lb:	1920	1280	840	575	445
	arc, inches:		0	-10.7	-39.3	

Centerfire Rifle Ballistics

.35 REMINGTON TO 9.3X74 R

BALLISTICS

CARTRIDGE BULLET	RANGE, YARDS:	0	100	200	300	400
Hornady 200 Evolution	velocity, fps:	2225	1963	1721	1503	
	energy, ft-lb:	2198	1711	1315	1003	
	arc, inches:		+3.0	-1.3	-17.5	
Rem. 150 PSP Core-Lokt	velocity, fps:	2300	1874	1506	1218	1039
	energy, ft-lb:	1762	1169	755	494	359
	arc, inches:		0	-8.6	-32.6	
Rem. 200 SP Core-Lokt	velocity, fps:	2080	1698	1376	1140	1001
	energy, ft-lb:	1921	1280	841	577	445
	arc, inches:		0	-10.7	-40.1	
Win. 200 Power-Point	velocity, fps:	2020	1646	1335	1114	985
	energy, ft-lb:	1812	1203	791	551	431
	arc, inches:		0	-12.1	-43.9	

.356 WINCHESTER

CARTRIDGE BULLET	RANGE, YARDS:	0	100	200	300	400
Win. 200 Power-Point	velocity, fps:	2460	2114	1797	1517	1284
	energy, ft-lb:	2688	1985	1434	1022	732
	arc, inches:		+1.6	-3.8	-20.1	-51.2

.358 WINCHESTER

CARTRIDGE BULLET	RANGE, YARDS:	0	100	200	300	400
Hornady 200 SP	velocity, fps:	2475	2180	1906	1655	1434
	energy, ft-lb:	2720	2110	1612	1217	913
	arc, inches:	-1.5	+2.9	0	-12.6	-37.9
Win. 200 Silvertip	velocity, fps:	2490	2171	1876	1610	1379
	energy, ft-lb:	2753	2093	1563	1151	844
	arc, inches:		+1.5	-3.6	-18.6	-47.2

.35 WHELEN

CARTRIDGE BULLET	RANGE, YARDS:	0	100	200	300	400
Federal 225 Trophy Bonded	velocity, fps:	2600	2400	2200	2020	1840
	energy, ft-lb:	3375	2865	2520	2030	1690.
	arc, inches:		+2.3	0	-9.4	-27.3
Hornady 200 SP	velocity, fps:	2910	2585	2283	2001	1742
	energy, ft-lb:	3760	2968	2314	1778	1347
	arc, inches:	-1.5	+1.9	0	-8.6	-25.9
Rem. 200 Pointed Soft Point	velocity, fps:	2675	2378	2100	1842	1606
	energy, ft-lb:	3177	2510	1958	1506	1145
	arc, inches:		+2.3	0	-10.3	-30.8
Rem. 250 Pointed Soft Point	velocity, fps:	2400	2197	2005	1823	1652
	energy, ft-lb:	3197	2680	2230	1844	1515
	arc, inches:		+1.3	-3.2	-16.6	-40.0

.350 REMINGTON MAGNUM

CARTRIDGE BULLET	RANGE, YARDS:	0	100	200	300	400
Nosler 225 PT	velocity, fps:	2550	2349	2158	1976	1804
	energy, ft-lb:	3248	2758	2327	1951	1626
	arc, inches:	-1.5	+2.4	0	-9.9	-28.7

.358 NORMA MAGNUM

CARTRIDGE BULLET	RANGE, YARDS:	0	100	200	300	400
A-Square 275 Triad	velocity, fps:	2700	2394	2108	1842	1653
	energy, ft-lb:	4451	3498	2713	2072	1668
	arc, inches:		+2.3	0	-10.1	-29.8
Norma 250 TXP Swift A-Fr.	velocity, fps:	2723	2467	2225	1996	
	energy, ft-lb:	4117	3379	2748	2213	
	arc, inches:		+2.1	0	-9.1	
Norma 250 Woodleigh	velocity, fps:	2799	2442	2112	1810	
	energy, ft-lb:	4350	3312	2478	1819	
	arc, inches:		+2.2	0	-10.0	
Norma 250 Oryx	velocity, fps:	2756	2493	2245	2011	
	energy, ft-lb:	4217	3451	2798	2245	
	arc, inches:		+2.1	0	-9.0	

.358 STA

CARTRIDGE BULLET	RANGE, YARDS:	0	100	200	300	400
A-Square 275 Triad	velocity, fps:	2850	2562	2292	2039	1764
	energy, ft-lb:	4959	4009	3208	2539	1899.
	arc, inches:		+1.9	0	-8.6	-26.1

9.3x57

CARTRIDGE BULLET	RANGE, YARDS:	0	100	200	300	400
Norma 232 Vulkan	velocity, fps:	2329	2031	1757	1512	
	energy, ft-lb:	2795	2126	1591	1178	
	arc, inches:		+3.5	0	-14.9	
Norma 232 Oryx	velocity, fps:	2362	2058	1778	1528	
	energy, ft-lb:	2875	2182	1630	1203	
	arc, inches:		+3.4	0	-14.5	
Norma 285 Oryx	velocity, fps:	2067	1859	1666	1490	
	energy, ft-lb:	2704	2188	1756	1404	
	arc, inches:		+4.3	0	-16.8	
Norma 286 Alaska	velocity, fps:	2067	1857	1662	1484	
	energy, ft-lb:	2714	2190	1754	1399	
	arc, inches:		+4.3	0	-17.0	

9.3x62

CARTRIDGE BULLET	RANGE, YARDS:	0	100	200	300	400
Federal 286 Swift A-Frame	velocity, fps:	2360	2150	1950	1760	1580
	energy, ft-lb:	3535	2930	2405	1960	1590
	arc, inches:		+2.9	0	-11.6	-31.0
Federal 286 TSX	velocity, fps:	2360	2160	1970	1790	
	energy, ft-lb:	3535	2965	2465	2035	
	arc, inches:	-1.5	+3.0	0	-12.0	
Federal 286 Woodleigh Hydro	velocity, fps:	2360	2050	1760	1510	
	energy, ft-lb:	3535	2665	1975	1445	
	arc, inches::	-1.5	+3.4	0	-14.7	
Hornady 286 SP-HP	velocity, fps:	2350	2155	1961	1778	
	energy, ft-lb:	3537	2949	2442	2008	
	arc, inches:	-1.5	+3.0	0	-12.1	
Norma 232 Oryx	velocity, fps:	2625	2294	1988	1708	
	energy, ft-lb:	3535	2700	2028	1497	
	arc, inches:	-1.5	+2.5	0	-11.4	
Norma 250 A-Frame	velocity, fps:	2625	2322	2039	1778	
	energy, ft-lb:	3826	2993	2309	1755	
	arc, inches:	-1.5	+2.5	0	-10.9	
Norma 286 Plastic Point	velocity, fps:	2362	2141	1931	1736	
	energy, ft-lb:	3544	2911	2370	1914	
	arc, inches:	-1.5	+3.1	0	-12.4	
Nosler 250 AccuBond	velocity, fps:	2550	2376	2208	2048	1894
	energy, ft-lb:	3609	3133	2707	2328	1992
	arc, inches:	-1.5	+2.3	0	-9.5	-27.2
Nosler 286 Partition	velocity, fps:	2350	2179	2015	1859	1711
	energy, ft-lb:	3506	3014	2578	2194	1859
	arc, inches:	-1.5	+2.9	0	-11.5	-33.1

9.3x64

CARTRIDGE BULLET	RANGE, YARDS:	0	100	200	300	400
A-Square 286 Triad	velocity, fps:	2700	2391	2103	1835	1602
	energy, ft-lb:	4629	3630	2808	2139	1631
	arc, inches:		+2.3	0	-10.1	-30.8

.370 SAKO

CARTRIDGE BULLET	RANGE, YARDS:	0	100	200	300	400
Federal 286 TSX	velocity, fps:	2550	2370	2190	2020	1860
	energy, ft-lb:	4130	3555	3045	2595	2195
	arc, inches:	-1.5	+2.4	0	-9.6	-27.5

370 SAKO MAGNUM

CARTRIDGE BULLET	RANGE, YARDS:	0	100	200	300	400
Federal 286 Swift A-Frame	velocity, fps:	2550	2330	2120	1920	1730
	energy, ft-lb:	4130	3440	2845	2330	1900
	arc, inches:		+2.5	0	-10.1	-30.0
Federal 286 TSX	velocity, fps:	2550	2370	2190	2020	1860
	energy, ft-lb:	4130	3555	3045	2595	2195
	arc, inches:		+2.4	0	-9.5	-27.5
Federal 286 Woodleigh Hydro Solid	velocity, fps:	2550	2230	1920	1650	1410
	energy, ft-lb:	4130	3145	2350	1730	1265
	arc, inches:		+2.8	0	-12.4	-37.5

9.3x74 R

CARTRIDGE BULLET	RANGE, YARDS:	0	100	200	300	400
A-Square 286 Triad	velocity, fps:	2360	2089	1844	1623	
	energy, ft-lb:	3538	2771	2157	1670	
	arc, inches:		+3.6	0	-14.0	
Federal 286 Swift A-Frame	velocity, fps:	2360	2150	1950	1760	1580
	energy, ft-lb:	3535	2930	2405	1960	1590
	arc, inches:		+2.9	0	-11.6	-31.0
Federal 286 TSX	velocity, fps:	2360	2160	1970	1790	1630
	energy, ft-lb:	3535	2965	2465	2035	1675
	arc, inches:		+2.9	0	-11.1	-29.9
Federal 286 Woodleigh Hydro Solid	velocity, fps:	2360	2050	1760	1510	1300
	energy, ft-lb:	3535	2665	1975	1445	1065
	arc, inches:		+3.4	0	-14.7	-45.0
Hornady 286	velocity, fps	2360	2136	1924	1727	1545
	energy, ft-lb	3536	2896	2351	1893	1516
	arc, inches	-1.5	0	-6.1	-21.7	-49.0
Norma 232 Vulkan	velocity, fps:	2625	2327	2049	1792	
	energy, ft-lb:	3551	2791	2164	1655	
	arc, inches:		+2.5	0	-10.8	
Norma 232 Oryx	velocity, fps:	2526	2191	1883	1605	
	energy, ft-lb:	3274	2463	1819	1322	
	arc, inches:		+2.9	0	-12.8	

CARTRIDGE BULLET	RANGE, YARDS:	0	100	200	300	400
Norma 285 Oryx	velocity, fps:	2362	2114	1881	1667	
	energy, ft-lb:	3532	2829	2241	1758	
	arc, inches:		+3.1	0	-13.0	
Norma 286 Alaska	velocity, fps:	2362	2135	1920	1720	
	energy, ft-lb:	3544	2894	2342	1879	
	arc, inches:		+3.1	0	-12.5	
Norma 286 Plastic Point	velocity, fps:	2362	2135	1920	1720	
	energy, ft-lb:	3544	2894	2342	1879	
	arc, inches:		+3.1	0	-12.5	

.375 WINCHESTER

CARTRIDGE BULLET	RANGE, YARDS:	0	100	200	300	400
Win. 200 Power-Point	velocity, fps:	2200	1841	1526	1268	1089
	energy, ft-lb:	2150	1506	1034	714	
	arc, inches:			0	-9.5	-33.8

.375 FLANGED

CARTRIDGE BULLET	RANGE, YARDS:	0	100	200	300	400
Nosler 300 PT	velocity, fps:	2400	2191	1993	1806	1632
	energy, ft-lb:	3836	3198	2646	2173	1775
	arc, inches:	-1.5	+2.9	0	-11.7	-34.0

.375 H&H MAGNUM

CARTRIDGE BULLET	RANGE, YARDS:	0	100	200	300	400
A-Square 300 SP boat-tail	velocity, fps:	2550	2415	2284	2157	2034
	energy, ft-lb:	4331	3884	3474	3098	2755
	arc, inches:		+5.2	+6.0	0	-13.3
A-Square 300 Triad	velocity, fps:	2550	2251	1973	1717	1496
	energy, ft-lb:	4331	3375	2592	1964	1491
	arc, inches:		+2.7	0	-11.7	-35.1
Federal 250 Trophy Bonded	velocity, fps:	2670	2360	2080	1820	1580
	energy, ft-lb:	3955	3100	2400	1830	1380
	arc, inches:		+2.4	0	-10.4	-31.7
Federal 270 Hi-Shok	velocity, fps:	2690	2420	2170	1920	1700
	energy, ft-lb:	4340	3510	2810	2220	1740
	arc, inches:		+2.4	0	-10.9	-33.3
Federal 300 Hi-Shok	velocity, fps:	2530	2270	2020	1790	1580
	energy, ft-lb:	4265	3425	2720	2135	1665
	arc, inches:		+2.6	0	-11.2	-33.3
Federal 300 Nosler Partition	velocity, fps:	2530	2320	2120	1930	1750
	energy, ft-lb:	4265	3585	2995	2475	2040
	arc, inches:		+2.5	0	-10.3	-29.9
Federal 300 Trophy Bonded	velocity, fps:	2530	2280	2040	1810	1610
	energy, ft-lb:	4265	3450	2765	2190	1725
	arc, inches:		+2.6	0	-10.9	-32.8
Federal 300 Tr. Bonded HE	velocity, fps:	2700	2440	2190	1960	1740
	energy, ft-lb:	4855	3960	3195	2550	2020
	arc, inches:		+2.2	0	-9.4	-28.0
Federal 300 Trophy Bonded Sledgehammer Solid	velocity, fps:	2530	2160	1820	1520	1280.
	energy, ft-lb:	4265	3105	2210	1550	1090
	arc, inches, s:		0	-6.0	-22.7	-54.6
Federal 300 TSX	velocity, fps:	2470	2240	2010	1800	1610
	energy, ft-lb:	4065	3325	2700	2170	1735
	arc, inches:		+2.7	0	-11.3	-33.6
Federal 300 Woodleigh Hydro Solid	velocity, fps:	2500	2180	1880	1610	1380
	energy, ft-lb:	4165	3160	2355	1735	1270
	arc, inches:		+2.9	0	-20.1	-46.3
Hornady 250 GMX Superformance	velocity, fps:	2890	2675	2471	2275	2088
	energy, ft-lb:	4636	3973	3388	2873	2421
	arc, inches:		+1.7	0	-7.4	-21.5
Hornady 270 SP HM	velocity, fps:	2870	2620	2385	2162	1957
	energy, ft-lb:	4937	4116	3408	2802	2296
	arc, inches:		+2.2	0	-8.4	-23.9
Hornady 300 FMJ RN HM	velocity, fps:	2705	2376	2072	1804	1560
	energy, ft-lb:	4873	3760	2861	2167	1621
	arc, inches:		+2.7	0	-10.8	-32.1
Norma 300 Soft Point	velocity, fps:	2549	2211	1900	1619	
	energy, ft-lb:	4329	3258	2406	1747	
	arc, inches:		+2.8	0	-12.6	
Norma 300 TXP Swift A-Fr.	velocity, fps:	2559	2296	2049	1818	
	energy, ft-lb:	4363	3513	2798	2203	
	arc, inches:		+2.6	0	-10.9	

CARTRIDGE BULLET	RANGE, YARDS:	0	100	200	300	400
Norma 300 Oryx	velocity, fps:	2559	2292	2041	1807	
	energy, ft-lb:	4363	3500	2775	2176	
	arc, inches:		+2.6	0	-11.0	
Norma 300 Barnes Solid	velocity, fps:	2493	2061	1677	1356	
	energy, ft-lb:	4141	2829	1873	1234	
	arc, inches:		+3.4	0	-16.0	
PMC 270 PSP	velocity, fps:					
	energy, ft-lb:					
	arc, inches:					
PMC 270 Barnes X	velocity, fps:	2690	2528	2372	2221	2076
	energy, ft-lb:	4337	3831	3371	2957	2582
	arc, inches:		+2.0	0	-8.2	-23.4
PMC 300 Barnes X	velocity, fps:	2530	2389	2252	2120	1993
	energy, ft-lb:	4263	3801	3378	2994	2644
	arc, inches:		+2.3	0	-9.2	-26.1
Rem. 270 Soft Point	velocity, fps:	2690	2420	2166	1928	1707
	energy, ft-lb:	4337	3510	2812	2228	1747
	arc, inches:		+2.2	0	-9.7	-28.7
Rem. 300 Swift A-Frame	velocity, fps:	2530	2245	1979	1733	1512
	energy, ft-lb:	4262	3357	2608	2001	1523
	arc, inches:		+2.7	0	-11.7	-35.0
Speer 285 Grand Slam	velocity, fps:	2610	2365	2134	1916	
	energy, ft-lb:	4310	3540	2883	2323	
	arc, inches:		+2.4	0	-9.9	
Speer 300 African GS Tungsten Solid	velocity, fps:	2609	2277	1970	1690	
	energy, ft-lb:	4534	3453	2585	1903	
	arc, inches:		+2.6	0	-11.7	-35.6
Win. 270 Fail Safe	velocity, fps:	2670	2447	2234	2033	1842
	energy, ft-lb:	4275	3590	2994	2478	2035
	arc, inches:		+2.2	0	-9.1	-28.7
Win. 300 Fail Safe	velocity, fps:	2530	2336	2151	1974	1806
	energy, ft-lb:	4265	3636	3082	2596	2173
	arc, inches:		+2.4	0	-10.0	-26.9

.375 DAKOTA

CARTRIDGE BULLET	RANGE, YARDS:	0	100	200	300	400
Dakota 270 Barnes X	velocity, fps:	2800	2617	2441	2272	2109
	energy, ft-lb:	4699	4104	3571	3093	2666
	arc, inches:		+2.3	+1.0	-6.1	-19.9
Dakota 300 Barnes X	velocity, fps:	2600	2316	2051	1804	1579
	energy, ft-lb:	4502	3573	2800	2167	1661
	arc, inches:		+2.4	-0.1	-11.0	-32.7

.375 RUGER

CARTRIDGE BULLET	RANGE, YARDS:	0	100	200	300	400
Hornady 250 GMX Superformance	velocity, fps:	2890	2675	2471	2275	2088
	energy, ft-lb:	4636	3973	3388	2873	2421
	arc, inches:		+1.7	0	-7.4	-21.5
Hornady 270 SP	velocity, fps:	2840	2600	2372	2156	1951
	energy, ft-lb:	4835	4052	3373	2786	2283
	arc, inches:	-1.5	+1.8	0	-8.0	-23.6
Hornady 300 Solid	velocity, fps	2660	2344	2050	1780	1536
	energy, ft-lb	4713	3660	2800	2110	1572
	arc, inches	-1.5	+2.4	0	-10.8	-32.6
Nosler 260 AB	velocity, fps:	2900	2703	2514	2333	2160
	energy, ft-lb:	4854	4217	3649	3143	2693
	arc, inches:	-1.5	+1.6	0	-7.1	-20.7

.375 WEATHERBY MAGNUM

CARTRIDGE BULLET	RANGE, YARDS:	0	100	200	300	400
A-Square 300 SP boat-tail	velocity, fps:	2700	2560	2425	2293	2166
	energy, ft-lb:	4856	4366	3916	3503	3125
	arc, inches:		+4.5	+5.2	0	-11.9
A-Square 300 Triad	velocity, fps:	2700	2391	2103	1835	1602
	energy, ft-lb:	4856	3808	2946	2243	1710
	arc, inches:		+2.3	0	-10.1	-30.8
Wby. 300 Nosler Part.	velocity, fps:	2800	2572	2366	2140	1963
	energy, ft-lb:	5224	4408	3696	3076	2541
	arc, inches:		+1.9	0	-8.2	-23.9

Centerfire Rifle Ballistics

.375 JRS TO .416 REMINGTON MAGNUM

CARTRIDGE BULLET	RANGE, YARDS:	0	100	200	300	400
.375 JRS						
A-Square 300 SP boat-tail	velocity, fps:	2700	2560	2425	2293	2166.
	energy, ft-lb:	4856	4366	3916	3503	3125
	arc, inches:		+4.5	+5.2	0	-11.9
A-Square 300 Triad	velocity, fps:	2700	2391	2103	1835	1602
	energy, ft-lb:	4856	3808	2946	2243	1710
	arc, inches:		+2.3	0	-10.1	-30.8
.375 REMINGTON ULTRA MAGNUM						
Nosler 260 AB	velocity, fps:	2950	2750	2560	2377	2202
	energy, ft-lb:	5023	4367	3783	3262	2799
	arc, inches:	-1.5	+1.6	0	-6.9	-19.9
Nosler 300 PT	velocity, fps:	2750	2524	2309	2105	1912
	energy, ft-lb:	5036	4244	3553	2953	2435
	arc, inches:	-1.5	+2.0	0	-8.5	-24.9
Rem. 270 Soft Point	velocity, fps:	2900	2558	2241	1947	1678
	energy, fps:	5041	3922	3010	2272	1689
	arc, inches:		+1.9	0	-9.2	-27.8
Rem. 300 Swift A-Frame	velocity, fps:	2760	2505	2263	2035	1822
	energy, fps:	5073	4178	3412	2759	2210
	arc, inches:		+2.0	0	-8.8	-26.1
.375 A-SQUARE						
A-Square 300 SP boat-tail	velocity, fps:	2920	2773	2631	2494	2360
	energy, ft-lb:	5679	5123	4611	4142	3710
	arc, inches:		+3.7	+4.4	0	-9.8
A-Square 300 Triad	velocity, fps:	2920	2596	2294	2012	1762
	energy, ft-lb:	5679	4488	3505	2698	2068
	arc, inches:		+1.8	0	-8.5	-25.5
.376 STEYR						
Hornady 225 SP	velocity, fps:	2600	2331	2078	1842	1625
	energy, ft-lb:	3377	2714	2157	1694	1319
	arc, inches:		+2.5	0	-10.6	-31.4
Hornady 270 SP	velocity, fps:	2600	2372	2156	1951	1759
	energy, ft-lb:	4052	3373	2787	2283	1855
	arc, inches:		+2.3	0	-9.9	-28.9
.378 WEATHERBY MAGNUM						
A-Square 300 SP boat-tail	velocity, fps:	2900	2754	2612	2475	2342
	energy, ft-lb:	5602	5051	4546	4081	3655
	arc, inches:		+3.8	+4.4	0	-10.0
A-Square 300 Triad	velocity, fps:	2900	2577	2276	1997	1747
	energy, ft-lb:	5602	4424	3452	2656	2034
	arc, inches:		+1.9	0	-8.7	-25.9
Wby. 270 Pointed Expanding	velocity, fps:	3180	2921	2677	2445	2225
	energy, ft-lb:	6062	5115	4295	3583	2968
	arc, inches:		+1.3	0	-6.1	-18.1
Wby. 270 Barnes X	velocity, fps:	3150	2954	2767	2587	2415
	energy, ft-lb:	5948	5232	4589	4013	3495
	arc, inches:		+1.2	0	-5.8	-16.7
Wby. 300 RN Expanding	velocity, fps:	2925	2558	2220	1908	1627.
	energy, ft-lb:	5699	4360	3283	2424	1764
	arc, inches:		+1.9	0	-9.0	-27.8
Wby. 300 FMJ	velocity, fps:	2925	2591	2280	1991	1725
	energy, ft-lb:	5699	4470	3461	2640	1983
	arc, inches:		+1.8	0	-8.6	-26.1
.38-40 WINCHESTER						
Win. 180 Soft Point	velocity, fps:	1160	999	901	827	
	energy, ft-lb:	538	399	324	273	
	arc, inches:			0	-23.4	-75.2

CARTRIDGE BULLET	RANGE, YARDS:	0	100	200	300	400
.38-55 WINCHESTER						
Black Hills 255 FN Lead	velocity, fps:	1250				
	energy, ft-lb:	925				
	arc, inches:					
Win. 255 Soft Point	velocity, fps:	1320	1190	1091	1018	
	energy, ft-lb:	987	802	674	587	
	arc, inches:			0	-33.9	-110.6
.41 MAGNUM						
Win. 240 Platinum Tip	velocity, fps:	1830	1488	1220	1048	
	energy, ft-lb:	1784	1180	792	585	
	arc, inches:			0	-15.0	-53.4
.450/.400 NITRO EXPRESS						
A-Square 400 Triad	velocity, fps:	2150	1910	1690	1490	
	energy, ft-lb:	4105	3241	2537	1972	
	arc, inches:		+4.4	0	-16.5	
Hornady 400 DGS, DGX	velocity, fps:	2050	1820	1609	1420	
	energy, ft-lb:	3732	2940	2298	1791	
	arc, inches:	-0.9	0	-9.7	-32.8	
.404 JEFFERY						
A-Square 400 Triad	velocity, fps:	2150	1901	1674	1468	1299
	energy, ft-lb:	4105	3211	2489	1915	1499
	arc, inches:		+4.1	0	-16.4	-49.1
Hornady 400 DGS, DGX	velocity, fps:	2300	2046	1809	1592	
	energy, ft-lb:	4698	3717	2906	2251	
	arc, inches:	-1.5	0	-6.9	-24.4	
Norma 450 Woodleigh SP	velocity, fps:	2150	2048	1949	1853	1760
	energy, ft-lb:	4620	4191	3795	3430	3096
	arc, inches:	-1.5	+.2	0	-2.5	-7.6
.405 WINCHESTER						
Hornady 300 Flatpoint	velocity, fps:	2200	1851	1545	1296	
	energy, ft-lb:	3224	2282	1589	1119	
	arc, inches:		0	-8.7	-31.9	
Hornady 300 SP Interlock	velocity, fps:	2200	1890	1610	1370	
	energy, ft-lb:	3224	2379	1727	1250	
	arc, inches:		0	-8.3	-30.2	
.416 TAYLOR						
A-Square 400 Triad	velocity, fps:	2350	2093	1853	1634	1443
	energy, ft-lb:	4905	3892	3049	2371	1849
	arc, inches:		+3.2	0	-13.6	-39.8
.416 HOFFMAN						
A-Square 400 Triad	velocity, fps:	2380	2122	1879	1658	1464
	energy, ft-lb:	5031	3998	3136	2440	1903
	arc, inches:		+3.1	0	-13.1	-38.7
.416 REMINGTON MAGNUM						
A-Square 400 Triad	velocity, fps:	2380	2122	1879	1658	1464
	energy, ft-lb:	5031	3998	3136	2440	1903
	arc, inches:		+3.1	0	-13.2	-38.7
Federal 400 Trophy Bonded Sledgehammer Solid	velocity, fps:	2400	2150	1920	1700	1500
	energy, ft-lb:	5115	4110	3260	2565	2005
	arc, inches:		0	-6.0	-21.6	-49.2
Federal 400 Trophy Bonded	velocity, fps:	2400	2180	1970	1770	1590
	energy, ft-lb:	5115	4215	3440	2785	2245
	arc, inches:		0	-5.8	-20.6	-46.9
Rem. 400 Swift A-Frame	velocity, fps:	2400	2175	1962	1763	1579
	energy, ft-lb:	5115	4201	3419	2760	2214
	arc, inches:		0	-5.9	-20.8	

CARTRIDGE BULLET	RANGE, YARDS:	0	100	200	300	400

.416 RIGBY

CARTRIDGE BULLET		0	100	200	300	400
A-Square 400 Triad	velocity, fps:	2400	2140	1897	1673	1478
	energy, ft-lb:	5115	4069	3194	2487	1940
	arc, inches:		+3.0	0	-12.9	-38.0
Federal 400 Trophy Bonded	velocity, fps:	2370	2150	1940	1750	1570
	energy, ft-lb:	4990	4110	3350	2715	2190
	arc, inches:		0	-6.0	-21.3	-48.1
Federal 400 Trophy Bonded Sledgehammer Solid	velocity, fps:	2370	2120	1890	1660	1460
	energy, ft-lb:	4990	3975	3130	2440	1895
	arc, inches:		0	-6.3	-22.5	-51.5
Federal 410 Woodleigh Weldcore	velocity, fps:	2370	2110	1870	1640	1440
	energy, ft-lb:	5115	4050	3165	2455	1895
	arc, inches:		0	-7.4	-24.8	-55.0
Federal 410 Solid	velocity, fps:	2370	2110	2870	1640	1440
	energy, ft-lb:	5115	4050	3165	2455	1895
	arc, inches:		0	-7.4	-24.8	-55.0
Hornady 400 DGX, DGS	velocity, fps:	2415	2156	1915	1691	
	energy, ft-lb:	5180	4130	3256	2540	
	arc, inches:	-1.5	0	-6.0	-21.6	
Norma 400 TXP Swift A-Fr.	velocity, fps:	2350	2127	1917	1721	
	energy, ft-lb:	4906	4021	3266	2632	
	arc, inches:		+3.1	0	-12.5	
Norma 400 Barnes Solid	velocity, fps:	2297	1930	1604	1330	
	energy, ft-lb:	4687	3310	2284	1571	
	arc, inches:		+3.9	0	-17.7	

.416 RUGER

CARTRIDGE BULLET		0	100	200	300	400
Hornady 400 DGS, DGX	velocity, fps:	2400	2151	1917	1700	
	energy, ft-lb:	5116	4109	3264	2568	
	arc, inches:	-1.5	0	-6.0	-21.6	

.500/416 NITRO EXPRESS

CARTRIDGE BULLET	RANGE, YARDS:	0	50	100	150	200
Norma 450 Woodleigh SP	velocity, fps:	2100	1991	1886	1785	1688
	energy, ft-lb:	4408	3963	3556	3185	2849
	arc, inches:	-1.5	+.3	0	-2.7	-8.2

.416 DAKOTA

CARTRIDGE BULLET	RANGE, YARDS:	0	100	200	300	400
Dakota 400 Barnes X	velocity, fps:	2450	2294	2143	1998	1859
	energy, ft-lb:	5330	4671	4077	3544	3068
	arc, inches:		+2.5	-0.2	-10.5	-29.4

.416 WEATHERBY

CARTRIDGE BULLET		0	100	200	300	400
A-Square 400 Triad	velocity, fps:	2600	2328	2073	1834	1624
	energy, ft-lb:	6004	4813	3816	2986	2343
	arc, inches:		+2.5	0	-10.5	-31.6
Wby. 350 Barnes X	velocity, fps:	2850	2673	2503	2340	2182
	energy, ft-lb:	6312	5553	4870	4253	3700
	arc, inches:		+1.7	0	-7.2	-20.9
Wby. 400 Swift A-Fr.	velocity, fps:	2650	2426	2213	2011	1820
	energy, ft-lb:	6237	5227	4350	3592	2941
	arc, inches:		+2.2	0	-9.3	-27.1
Wby. 400 RN Expanding	velocity, fps:	2700	2417	2152	1903	1676
	energy, ft-lb:	6474	5189	4113	3216	2493
	arc, inches:		+2.3	0	-9.7	-29.3
Wby. 400 Monolithic Solid	velocity, fps:	2700	2411	2140	1887	1656
	energy, ft-lb:	6474	5162	4068	3161	2435
	arc, inches:		+2.3	0	-9.8	-29.7

10.57 (.416) METEOR

CARTRIDGE BULLET		0	100	200	300	400
Lazzeroni 400 Swift A-Fr.	velocity, fps:	2730	2532	2342	2161	1987
	energy, ft-lb:	6621	5695	4874	4147	3508
	arc, inches:		+1.9	0	-8.3	-24.0

.425 EXPRESS

CARTRIDGE BULLET		0	100	200	300	400
A-Square 400 Triad	velocity, fps:	2400	2136	1888	1662	1465
	energy, ft-lb:	5115	4052	3167	2454	1906
	arc, inches:		+3.0	0	-13.1	-38.3

.44-40 WINCHESTER

CARTRIDGE BULLET		0	100	200	300	400
Rem. 200 Soft Point	velocity, fps:	1190	1006	900	822	756
	energy, ft-lb:	629	449	360	300	254
	arc, inches:		0	-33.1	-108.7	-235.2
Win. 200 Soft Point	velocity, fps:	1190	1006	900	822	756
	energy, ft-lb:	629	449	360	300	254
	arc, inches:		0	-33.3	-109.5	-237.4

.44 REMINGTON MAGNUM

CARTRIDGE BULLET		0	100	200	300	400
Federal 240 Hi-Shok HP	velocity, fps:	1760	1380	1090	950	860
	energy, ft-lb:	1650	1015	640	485	395
	arc, inches:		0	-17.4	-60.7	-136.0
Rem. 210 Semi-Jacketed HP	velocity, fps:	1920	1477	1155	982	880
	energy, ft-lb:	1719	1017	622	450	361
	arc, inches:		0	-14.7	-55.5	-131.3
Rem. 240 Soft Point	velocity, fps:	1760	1380	1114	970	878
	energy, ft-lb:	1650	1015	661	501	411
	arc, inches:		0	-17.0	-61.4	-143.0
Rem. 240 Semi-Jacketed Hollow Point	velocity, fps:	1760	1380	1114	970	878
	energy, ft-lb:	1650	1015	661	501	411
	arc, inches:		0	-17.0	-61.4	-143.0
Rem. 275 JHP Core-Lokt	velocity, fps:	1580	1293	1093	976	896
	energy, ft-lb:	1524	1020	730	582	490
	arc, inches:		0	-19.4	-67.5	-210.8
Win. 210 Silvertip HP	velocity, fps:	1580	1198	993	879	795
	energy, ft-lb:	1164	670	460	361	295
	arc, inches:		0	-22.4	-76.1	-168.0
Win. 240 Hollow Soft Point	velocity, fps:	1760	1362	1094	953	861
	energy, ft-lb:	1650	988	638	484	395
	arc, inches:		0	-18.1	-65.1	-150.3
Win. 250 Platinum Tip	velocity, fps:	1830	1475	1201	1032	931
	energy, ft-lb:	1859	1208	801	591	481
	arc, inches:		0	-15.3	-54.7	-126.6.

.444 MARLIN

CARTRIDGE BULLET		0	100	200	300	400
Rem. 240 Soft Point	velocity, fps:	2350	1815	1377	1087	941
	energy, ft-lb:	2942	1755	1010	630	472
	arc, inches:		+2.2	-5.4	-31.4	-86.7
Hornady 265 Evolution	velocity, fps:	2325	1971	1652	1380	
	energy, ft-lb:	3180	2285	1606	1120	
	arc, inches:		+3.0	-1.4	-18.6	
Hornady 265 FP LM	velocity, fps:	2335	1913	1551	1266	
	energy, ft-lb:	3208	2153	1415	943	
	arc, inches:		+2.0	-4.9	-26.5	
Hornady 265 InterLock FP	velocity, fps:	2400	1974	1601	1295	
	energy, ft-lb:	3389	2294	1508	987	
	arc, inches:		+3.8	0	-17.5	
Rem. 240 Soft Point	velocity, fps:	2350	1815	1377	1087	941
	energy, ft-lb:	2942	1755	1010	630	472
	arc, inches:		+2.2	-5.4	-31.4	-86.7

.45-70 GOVERNMENT

CARTRIDGE BULLET		0	100	200	300	400
Black Hills 405 FPL	velocity, fps:	1250				
	energy, ft-lb:					
	arc, inches:					
Federal 300 Sierra Pro-Hunt. HP FN	velocity, fps:	1880	1650	1430	1240	1110
	energy, ft-lb:	2355	1815	1355	1015	810
	arc, inches:		0	-11.5	-39.7	-89.1
PMC 350 FNSP	velocity, fps:					
	energy, ft-lb:					
	arc, inches:					
Rem. 300 Jacketed HP	velocity, fps:	1810	1497	1244	1073	969
	energy, ft-lb:	2182	1492	1031	767	625
	arc, inches:		0	-13.8	-50.1	-115.7

Centerfire Rifle Ballistics

.45-70 GOVERNMENT TO .460 WEATHERBY MAGNUM

CARTRIDGE BULLET	RANGE, YARDS:	0	100	200	300	400
Rem. 405 Soft Point	velocity, fps:	1330	1168	1055	977	918
	energy, ft-lb:	1590	1227	1001	858	758
	arc, inches:		0	-24.0	-78.6	-169.4
Win. 300 Jacketed HP	velocity, fps:	1880	1650	1425	1235	1105
	energy, ft-lb:	2355	1815	1355	1015	810
	arc, inches:		0	-12.8	-44.3	-95.5
Win. 300 Partition Gold	velocity, fps:	1880	1558	1292	1103	988
	energy, ft-lb:	2355	1616	1112	811	651
	arc, inches:		0	-12.9	-46.0	-104.9.

.450 BUSHMASTER

CARTRIDGE BULLET	RANGE, YARDS:	0	100	200	300	400
Hornady 250 SST-ML	velocity, fps:	2200	1840	1524	1268	
	energy, ft-lb	2686	1879	1289	893	
	arc, inches	-2.0	+2.5	-3.5	-24.5	

.450 MARLIN

CARTRIDGE BULLET	RANGE, YARDS:	0	100	200	300	400
Hornady 325 FTX	velocity, fps:	2225	1887	1585	1331	
	energy, ft-lb:	3572	2569	1813	1278	
	arc, inches:	-1.5	+3.0	-2.2	-21.3	
Hornady 350 FP	velocity, fps:	2100	1720	1397	1156	
	energy, ft-lb:	3427	2298	1516	1039	
	arc, inches:		0	-10.4	-38.9	

.450 NITRO EXPRESS (3¼")

CARTRIDGE BULLET	RANGE, YARDS:	0	100	200	300	400
A-Square 465 Triad	velocity, fps:	2190	1970	1765	1577	
	energy, ft-lb:	4952	4009	3216	2567	
	arc, inches:		+4.3	0	-15.4	
Hornady 480 DGS, DGX	velocity, fps:	2150	1881	1635	1418	
	energy, ft-lb:	4927	3769	2850	2144	
	arc, inches:	-1.5	0	-8.4	-29.9	

.450 #2

CARTRIDGE BULLET	RANGE, YARDS:	0	100	200	300	400
A-Square 465 Triad	velocity, fps:	2190	1970	1765	1577	
	energy, ft-lb:	4952	4009	3216	2567	
	arc, inches:		+4.3	0	-15.4	

.458 WINCHESTER MAGNUM

CARTRIDGE BULLET	RANGE, YARDS:	0	100	200	300	400
A-Square 465 Triad	velocity, fps:	2220	1999	1791	1601	1433
	energy, ft-lb:	5088	4127	3312	2646	2121
	arc, inches:		+3.6	0	-14.7	-42.5
Federal 350 Soft Point	velocity, fps:	2470	1990	1570	1250	1060
	energy, ft-lb:	4740	3065	1915	1205	870
	arc, inches:		-7.5	-29.1	-71.1	
Federal 400 Trophy Bonded	velocity, fps:	2380	2170	1960	1770	1590
	energy, ft-lb:	5030	4165	3415	2785	2255
	arc, inches:		0	-5.9	-20.9	-47.1
Federal 500 Solid	velocity, fps:	2090	1870	1670	1480	1320
	energy, ft-lb:	4850	3880	3085	2440	1945
	arc, inches:		0	-8.5	-29.5	-66.2
Federal 500 Trophy Bonded	velocity, fps:	2090	1870	1660	1480	1310
	energy, ft-lb:	4850	3870	3065	2420	1915
	arc, inches:		0	-8.5	-29.7	-66.8
Federal 500 Trophy Bonded Sledgehammer Solid	velocity, fps:	2090	1860	1650	1460	1300
	energy, ft-lb:	4850	3845	3025	2365	1865
	arc, inches:		0	-8.6	-30.0	-67.8
Federal 510 Soft Point	velocity, fps:	2090	1820	1570	1360	1190
	energy, ft-lb:	4945	3730	2790	2080	1605
	arc, inches:		0	-9.1	-32.3	-73.9
Hornady 500 FMJ-RN HM	velocity, fps:	2260	1984	1735	1512	
	energy, ft-lb:	5670	4368	3341	2538	
	arc, inches:		0	-7.4	-26.4	
Norma 500 TXP Swift A-Fr.	velocity, fps:	2116	1903	1705	1524	
	energy, ft-lb:	4972	4023	3228	2578	
	arc, inches:		+4.1	0	-16.1	

CARTRIDGE BULLET	RANGE, YARDS:	0	100	200	300	400
Norma 500 Barnes Solid	velocity, fps:	2067	1750	1472	1245	
	energy, ft-lb:	4745	3401	2405	1721	
	arc, inches:		+4.9	0	-21.2	
Rem. 450 Swift A-Frame PSP	velocity, fps:	2150	1901	1671	1465	1289
	energy, ft-lb:	4618	3609	2789	2144	1659
	arc, inches:		0	-8.2	-28.9	
Speer 500 African GS Tungsten Solid	velocity, fps:	2120	1845	1596	1379	
	energy, ft-lb:	4989	3780	2828	2111	
	arc, inches:		0	-8.8	-31.3	
Speer African Grand Slam	velocity, fps:	2120	1853	1609	1396	
	energy, ft-lb:	4989	3810	2875	2163	
	arc, inches:		0	-8.7	-30.8	
Win. 510 Soft Point	velocity, fps:	2040	1770	1527	1319	1157
	energy, ft-lb:	4712	3547	2640	1970	1516
	arc, inches:		0	-10.3	-35.6	

.458 LOTT

CARTRIDGE BULLET	RANGE, YARDS:	0	100	200	300	400
A-Square 465 Triad	velocity, fps:	2380	2150	1932	1730	1551
	energy, ft-lb:	5848	4773	3855	3091	2485
	arc, inches:		+3.0	0	-12.5	-36.4
Federal 500 TSX	velocity, fps:	2280	2090	1900	1730	1560
	energy, ft-lb:	5770	4825	4000	3305	2715
	arc, inches:	0	-6.4	-22.7	-50.7	
Hornady 500 RNSP or solid	velocity, fps:	2300	2022	1776	1551	
	energy, ft-lb:	5872	4537	3502	2671	
	arc, inches:		+3.4	0	-14.3	
Hornady 500 InterBond	velocity, fps:	2300	2028	1777	1549	
	energy, ft-lb:	5872	4535	3453	2604	
	arc, inches:		0	-7.0	-25.1	

CARTRIDGE BULLET	RANGE, YARDS:	0	50	100	150	200
Norma 500 Woodleigh SP	velocity, fps:	2100	1982	1868	1758	1654
	energy, ft-lb:	4897	4361	3874	3434	3039
	arc, inches:	-1.5	+.3	0	-2.8	-8.4

.450 ACKLEY

CARTRIDGE BULLET	RANGE, YARDS:	0	100	200	300	400
A-Square 465 Triad	velocity, fps:	2400	2169	1950	1747	1567
	energy, ft-lb:	5947	4857	3927	3150	2534
	arc, inches:		+2.9	0	-12.2	-35.8

.450 RIGBY

CARTRIDGE BULLET	RANGE, YARDS:	0	50	100	150	200
Norma 550 Woodleigh SP	velocity, fps:	2100	1992	1887	1787	1690
	energy, ft-lb:	5387	4847	4352	3900	3491
	arc, inches:	-1.5	+.3	0	-2.7	-8.2

.460 SHORT A-SQUARE

CARTRIDGE BULLET	RANGE, YARDS:	0	100	200	300	400
A-Square 500 Triad	velocity, fps:	2420	2198	1987	1789	1613
	energy, ft-lb:	6501	5362	4385	3553	2890
	arc, inches:		+2.9	0	-11.6	-34.2

.450 DAKOTA

Dakota 500 Barnes Solid	velocity, fps:	2450	2235	2030	1838	1658
	energy, ft-lb:	6663	5544	4576	3748	3051
	arc, inches:		+2.5	-0.6	-12.0	-33.8

.460 WEATHERBY MAGNUM

A-Square 500 Triad	velocity, fps:	2580	2349	2131	1923	1737
	energy, ft-lb:	7389	6126	5040	4107	3351
	arc, inches:		+2.4	0	-10.0	-29.4
Wby. 450 Barnes X	velocity, fps:	2700	2518	2343	2175	2013
	energy, ft-lb:	7284	6333	5482	4725	4050
	arc, inches:		+2.0	0	-8.4	-24.1

BALLISTICS

CARTRIDGE BULLET	RANGE, YARDS:	0	100	200	300	400
Wby. 500 RN Expanding	velocity, fps:	2600	2301	2022	1764	1533.
	energy, ft-lb:	7504	5877	4539	3456	2608
	arc, inches:		+2.6	0	-11.1	-33.5
Wby. 500 FMJ	velocity, fps:	2600	2309	2037	1784	1557
	energy, ft-lb:	7504	5917	4605	3534	2690
	arc, inches:		+2.5	0	-10.9	-33.0

.500/.465

CARTRIDGE BULLET	RANGE, YARDS:	0	100	200	300	400
A-Square 480 Triad	velocity, fps:	2150	1928	1722	1533	
	energy, ft-lb:	4926	3960	3160	2505	
	arc, inches:		+4.3	0	-16.0	

.470 NITRO EXPRESS

CARTRIDGE BULLET	RANGE, YARDS:	0	100	200	300	400
A-Square 500 Triad	velocity, fps:	2150	1912	1693	1494	
	energy, ft-lb:	5132	4058	3182	2478	
	arc, inches:		+4.4	0	-16.5	
Federal 500 Trophy Bond (and Sledgehammer solid)	velocity, fps:	2150	1890	1660	1450	
	energy, ft-lb:	5130	3975	3045	2320	
	arc, inches:	-1.5	0	-9.4	-29.3	
Hornady 500 DGX, DGS	velocity, fps:	2150	1885	1643	1429	
	energy, ft-lb:	5132	3946	2998	2267	
	arc, inches:	-1.5	0	-8.9	-30.9	

CARTRIDGE BULLET	RANGE, YARDS:	0	50	100	150	200
Norma 500 Woodleigh (soft and solid)	velocity, fps:	2100	2002	1906	1814	1725
	energy, ft-lb:	4897	4449	4035	3654	3304
	arc, inches:	-1.5	+.3	0	-2.7	-8.0

.470 CAPSTICK

CARTRIDGE BULLET	RANGE, YARDS:	0	100	200	300	400
A-Square 500 Triad	velocity, fps:	2400	2172	1958	1761	1553
	energy, ft-lb:	6394	5236	4255	3445	2678
	arc, inches:		+2.9	0	-11.9	-36.1

.475 #2

A-Square 480 Triad	velocity, fps:	2200	1964	1744	1544	
	energy, ft-lb:	5158	4109	3240	2539	
	arc, inches:		+4.1	0	-15.6	

.475 #2 JEFFERY

A-Square 500 Triad	velocity, fps:	2200	1966	1748	1550	
	energy, ft-lb:	5373	4291	3392	2666	
	arc, inches:		+4.1	0	-15.6	

.495 A-SQUARE

A-Square 570 Triad	velocity, fps:	2350	2117	1896	1693	1513
	energy, ft-lb:	6989	5671	4552	3629	2899
	arc, inches:		+3.1	0	-13.0	-37.8

.50 BMG

Hornady 750 A-Max	velocity, fps:	2815	2727	2641	2557	2474
	energy, ft-lb:	13,196	12,386	11,619	10,889	10,196
	arc, inches:		+1.4	0	-6.4	-18.2

.500 NITRO EXPRESS (3")

A-Square 570 Triad	velocity, fps:	2150	1928	1722	1533	
	energy, ft-lb:	5850	4703	3752	2975	
	arc, inches:		+4.3	0	-16.1	

CARTRIDGE BULLET	RANGE, YARDS:	0	100	200	300	400
Federal 570 TSX	velocity, fps:	2100	1890	1700	1520	1370
	energy, ft-lb:	5580	4530	3655	2935	2355
	arc, inches:	0	-8.4	-28.7	-64.2	
Hornady 570 DGX, DGS	velocity, fps:	2150	1881	1635	1419	
	energy, ft-lb:	5850	4477	3384	2547	
	arc, inches:	-.9	0	-9.0	-31.1	

CARTRIDGE BULLET	RANGE, YARDS:	0	50	100	150	200
Norma 570 Woodleigh SP	velocity, fps:	2100	2000	1903	1809	1719
	energy, ft-lb:	5583	5064	4585	4145	3742
	arc, inches:	-1.5	+.3	0	-2.7	-8.0
50 BMG Hornady 750 A-MAX	velocity, fps:	2815	2727	2641	2557	2474
	energy, ft-lb:	13196	12386	11619	10889	10196
	arc, inches:	-1.8	+1.4	0	-6.4	-18.2

.500 JEFFERY

CARTRIDGE BULLET	RANGE, YARDS:	0	50	100	150	200
Norma 570 Woodleigh SP	velocity, fps:	2200	2097	1997	1901	1807
	energy, ft-lb:	6127	5568	5050	4573	4134
	arc, inches:	-1.5	+.2	0	-2.4	-7.1

.500 A-SQUARE

CARTRIDGE BULLET	RANGE, YARDS:	0	100	200	300	400
A-Square 600 Triad	velocity, fps:	2470	2235	2013	1804	1620
	energy, ft-lb:	8127	6654	5397	4336	3495
	arc, inches:		+2.7	0	-11.3	-33.5

.505 GIBBS

A-Square 525 Triad	velocity, fps:	2300	2063	1840	1637	
	energy, ft-lb:	6166	4962	3948	3122	
	arc, inches:		+3.6	0	-14.2	

CARTRIDGE BULLET	RANGE, YARDS:	0	50	100	150	200
Norma 600 Woodleigh SP	velocity, fps:	2100	1998	1899	1803	1711
	energy, ft-lb:	5877	5319	4805	4334	3904
	arc, inches:	-1.5	+.3	0	-2.7	-8.1

.577 NITRO EXPRESS

CARTRIDGE BULLET	RANGE, YARDS:	0	100	200	300	400
A-Square 750 Triad	velocity, fps:	2050	1811	1595	1401	
	energy, ft-lb:	6998	5463	4234	3267	
	arc, inches:		+4.9	0	-18.5	

.577 TYRANNOSAUR

A-Square 750 Triad	velocity, fps:	2460	2197	1950	1723	1516
	energy, ft-lb:	10077	8039	6335	4941	3825
	arc, inches:		+2.8	0	-12.1	-36.0

.600 NITRO EXPRESS

A-Square 900 Triad	velocity, fps:	1950	1680	1452	1336	
	energy, ft-lb:	7596	5634	4212	3564	
	arc, inches:		+5.6	0	-20.7	

.700 NITRO EXPRESS

A-Square 1000 Monolithic Solid	velocity, fps:	1900	1669	1461	1288	
	energy, ft-lb:	8015	6188	4740	3685	
	arc, inches:		+5.8	0	-22.2	

Long Range Rifle

6.6 CREEDMOOR TO .338 LAPUA

CARTRIDGE BULLET	RANGE, YARDS:	0	400	600	800	1000
6.6 CREEDMOOR						
Nosler 140 HPBT	velocity, fps:	2550	2229	1932	1662	1426
	energy, ft-lb:	2021	1544	1160	859	632
	arc, inches:	-1.5	0	-26.7	-90.9	-205.9
.264 WINCHESTER MAGNUM						
Nosler 130 AccuBond	velocity, fps:	3100	2709	2350	2019	1718
	energy, ft-lb:	2773	2118	1594	1176	852
	arc, inches:	-1.5	0	-17.6	-60.6	-137.9
6.5-284 NORMA						
Nosler 129 AccuBond	velocity, fps:	2965	2633	2324	2036	1771
Long Range	energy, ft-lb:	2517	1985	1547	1188	899
	arc, inches:	-1.5	0	-18.7	-63.2	-141.6
.270 WSM						
Nosler 150 AccuBond	velocity, fps:	2960	2661	2381	2118	1873
Long Range	energy, ft-lb:	2917	2358	1888	1495	1169
	arc, inches:	-1.5	0	-18.2	-61.1	-135.1
7MM REMINGTON MAGNUM						
Nosler 168 AccuBond	velocity, fps:	2880	2598	2333	2084	1851
Long Range	energy, ft-lb:	3093	2518	2030	1620	1278
	arc, inches:	-1.5	0	-19.2	-64.0	-141.0
7MM STW						
Nosler 175 AccuBond	velocity, fps:	2900	2625	2366	2122	1893
Long Range	energy, ft-lb:	3267	2677	2175	1750	1393
	arc, inches:	-1.5	0	-18.8	-62.4	-137.1
7MM REMINGTON ULTRA MAG						
Nosler 175 AccuBond	velocity, fps:	3040	2756	2490	2239	2002
Long Range	energy, ft-lb:	3590	2952	2409	1948	1558
	arc, inches:	-1.5	0	-16.9	-56.2	-123.5
.308 WINCHESTER						
Barnes 175 OTM	velocity, fps:	2650	2318	2011	1730	1480	1272
	energy, ft-lb:	2730	2089	1571	1163	852	629
	arc, inches:	-1.5	0	-24.6	-83.8	-189.9	-360.0
.300 WSM						
Nosler 190 AccuBond	velocity, fps:	2875	2588	2319	2066	1830
Long Range	energy, ft-lb:	3486	2826	2269	1801	1413
	arc, inches:	-1.5	0	-19.3	-64.7	-142.7

CARTRIDGE BULLET	RANGE, YARDS:	0	400	600	800	1000
.300 WINCHESTER MAGNUM						
Barnes 220 OTM	velocity, fps:	2700	2420	2158	1912	1685	1481
	energy, ft-lb:	3562	2862	2275	1786	1387	1072
	arc, inches:	-1.5	0	-22.4	-74.7	-165.4	-305.3
Nosler 190 AccuBond	velocity, fps:	2870	2583	2314	2062	1826
Long Range	energy, ft-lb:	3474	2816	2260	1794	1407
	arc, inches:	-1.5	0	-19.4	-64.9	-143.3
.300 WEATHERBY MAGNUM						
Nosler 210 AccuBond	velocity, fps:	2825	2575	2339	2115	1905
Long Range	energy, ft-lb:	3720	3092	2551	2087	1691
	arc, inches:	-1.5	0	-19.5	-64.6	-140.8
.300 REMINGTON ULTRA MAG						
Nosler 210 AccuBond	velocity, fps:	2920	2665	2424	2196	1980
Long Range	energy, ft-lb:	3975	3311	2740	2248	1828
	arc, inches:	-1.5	0	-18.1	-60.0	-130.8
.30-378 WEATHERBY MAGNUM						
Nosler 210 AccuBond	velocity, fps:	3040	2778	2531	2297	2076
Long Range	energy, ft-lb:	4308	3599	2987	2461	2009
	arc, inches:	-1.5	0	-16.6	-54.9	-119.7
.338 REMINGTON ULTRA MAG						
Nosler 300 AccuBond	velocity, fps:	2600	2359	2131	1916	1716
	energy, ft-lb:	4502	3707	3026	2447	1963
	arc, inches:	-1.5	0	-23.6	-77.9	-170.2
.338 LAPUA						
Barnes 300 OTM	velocity, fps:	2600	2375	2161	1958	1767	1591
	energy, ft-lb:	4504	3757	3110	2554	2081	1687
	arc, inches:	-1.5	0	-23.2	-76.4	-165.9	-300.1
Nosler 300 AccuBond	velocity, fps:	2650	2406	2176	1959	1755
	energy, ft-lb:	4677	3857	3154	2555	2053
	arc, inches:	-1.5	0	-22.6	-74.7	-163.1

Rimfire cartridges have had a longer run than any centerfire you can name. Horace Smith and Daniel Wesson came up with the first successful .22 rimfires in the United States in 1857. Thirty years later the .22 Long Rifle arrived, courtesy of the J. Stevens Arms & Tool Company. It used 5 grains of black powder to drive a 40-grain bullet, shortly making the transition to smokeless in a case crimped on a heeled bullet. Remington produced the first modern high-speed load in 1930. Current .22 ammo includes myriad Long Rifle listings. The Long (essentially a Short bullet in a Long Rifle case), like the CB and WRF cartridges, is going the way of the dodo. The shot load of #12 "dust" has faded too, though it has dispatched many snakes, and was once hailed as just the ticket for barn mice and rats when you didn't want to perforate the boards. New rimfires have joined the versatile Long Rifle. The .22 WMR (Winchester Magnum Rimfire) came in 1959. More than four decades passed before Hornady necked down the WMR case to form the .17 HMR. A sibling on the CCI Stinger variation of the .22 LR appeared in 2004. Hornady dubbed it the .17 Mach 2. The newest .17, Winchester's Super Mag, arrived in 2013. The .17s and the .22 WMR feature jacketed hollowpoint and polymer-tipped bullets, just like centerfires.

This list is incomplete. For convenience (and given space constraints), it omits duplicate loads—those by the same manufacturer but under different labels). Units: velocity in feet per second, energy in foot-pounds, drop in inches.

.22 TO .17 HORNADY MAGNUM RIMFIRE

CARTRIDGE BULLET	LOAD	MUZZLE VEL./ENERGY	100-YD. VEL./ENERGY
.22			
CCI .22 CB Short	29-gr. RN	710/32	607/24
CCI .22 CB Long	29-gr. RN	710/32	607/24
CCI .22 Short	27-gr. HP	1105/73	868/45
CCI .22 Short	29-gr. RN	1080/75	857/47
CCI .22 Short	29-gr. Target RN	830/44	704/32
CCI .22 Long	29-gr. RN	1215/95	908/53
CCI .22 LR	21-gr. Short Range Green HP	1650/127	912/38
CCI .22 LR	31 gr. #12 birdshot	1000	
CCI .22 LR	32-gr. Stinger HP	1640/191	1066/81
CCI .22 LR	36-gr. HP	1260/127	1003/80
CCI .22 LR	40-gr. Tactical RN	1200/128	964/82
CCI .22 LR	40-gr. Mini-Mag RN	1235/135	998/88
CCI .22 LR	40-gr. Sub-sonic HP	1050/98	897/72
CCI .22 LR	40-gr. Velocitor HP	1435/183	1084/104
CCI .22 LR	40-gr. Small Game Bullet LFN	1235/135	992/87
CCI .22 LR	40-gr. Quiet-22 HP	710/45	640/36
CCI .22 LR	40-gr. Select RN	1200/128	964/82
CCI .22 LR	40-gr. Green Tag RN	1070/102	908/73
CCI .22 LR	45-gr. HP Suppressor	970/95	892/75
Federal .22 LR	25 gr. #12 birdshot		
Federal .22 LR	31-gr. Game-Shok HP	1430/140	1050/75
Federal .22 LR	36-gr. Champion HP	1260/125	1000/80
Federal .22 LR	38-gr. Game-Shok HP	1260/135	1010/85
Federal .22 LR	38-gr. Amer. Eagle HP	1260/135	1010/85
Federal .22 LR	40-gr. Prem. Gold Medal	1200/130	990/85
Federal .22 LR	40-gr. Game-Shok HP	1240/135	1010/90
Federal .22 LR	40-gr. Champion	1240/135	1010/90
Federal .22 LR	45-gr. Amer. Eagle Suppressed	1050/105	910/75
Lapua .22 LR	40-gr. Polar Biathlon	1106/109	914/74
Remington .22 Short	29-gr. RN	1095/77	903/52
Remington .22 LR	33-gr. CBee Low Noise HP	740/40	638/30
Remington .22 LR	33-gr. Yellow Jacket T. C.	1500/165	1075/85

CARTRIDGE BULLET	LOAD	MUZZLE VEL./ENERGY	100-YD. VEL./ENERGY
Remington .22 LR	36-gr. Viper Truncated Cone	1410/159	1056/89
Remington .22 LR	36-gr. Cyclone HP	1280/131	1010/82
Remington .22 LR	38-gr. Sub-sonic HP	1050/93	901/69
Remington .22 LR	40-gr. Target	1150/117	976/85
Remington .22 LR	40-gr. Thunderbolt	1255/140	1017/92
Remington .22 LR	40-gr. Competition RN	1085/105	941/79
Winchester .22 Short	29-gr. RN	1095/77	903/52
Winchester .22 Long	29-gr. RN	770/38	681/30
Winchester .22 LR	31-gr. #12 birdshot	1000	
Winchester .22 LR	26-gr. Varmint LF HP	1650/157	1023/60
Winchester .22 LR	32-gr. Xpediter HP	1640/191	1078/83
Winchester .22 LR	29-gr. Super-X sub-sonic	770/38	681/30
Winchester .22 LR	36-gr. HP	1280/131	975/76
Winchester .22 LR	37-gr. Super-X HP	1280/135	1015/85
Winchester .22 LR	37-gr. Super Speed HP	1330/154	1038/88
Winchester .22 LR	37-gr. Varmint HE HP	1435/169	1080/96
Winchester .22 LR	40-gr. Super-X low-report	1065/101	922/76
Winchester .22 LR	40-gr. DynaPoint	1150/117	976/85
Winchester .22 LR	40-gr. M22 LRN Black	1255/140	1017/92
Winchester .22 LR	40-gr. Power-Point HP	1280/145	1001/89
Winchester .22 LR	40-gr. Super-X	1300/150	1038/96
Winchester .22 LR	40-gr. Hyper Speed HP	1435/183	1070/102

.17 HORNADY MAGNUM RIMFIRE

CARTRIDGE BULLET	LOAD	MUZZLE VEL./ENERGY	100-YD. VEL./ENERGY
CCI .17 HMR	16-gr. TNT Green HP	2500/222	1642/96
CCI .17 HMR	17-gr. TNT JHP	2550/245	1757116
CCI .17 HMR	17-gr. Poly-Tip V-Max	2550/245	1915/138
CCI .17 HMR	20-gr. FMJ	2375/250	1776/140
CCI .17 HMR	20-gr. JSP	2375/250	1754/137
Federal .17 HMR	17-gr. Prem. V-Shok TNT JHP	2530/240	1800/125
Federal .17 HMR	17-gr. Prem. Hornady V-Max	2530/240	1880/135
Hornady .17 Mach 2	15.5-gr. NTX Lead-Free	2050/149	1450/75
Hornady .17 Mach 2	17-gr. V-Max	2100/166	1530/88

Rimfire Ballistics

.17 HORNADY MAGNUM RIMFIRE TO .22 WINCHESTER RIMFIRE

CARTRIDGE BULLET	LOAD	MUZZLE VEL./ENERGY	100-YD. VEL./ENERGY
Hornady .17 HMR	15.5-gr. NTX Lead-Free	2525/236	1829/119
Hornady .17 HMR	17-gr. V-Max	2550/245	1901/136
Hornady .17 HMR	20-gr. XTP	2375/250	1776/140
Remington.17 HMR	17-gr. AccuTip-V	2550/245	1901/136
Winchester .17 HMR	15.5-gr. Varmint LF NTX	2550/224	1901/124
Winchester .17 HMR	17-gr. Poly Tip V-Max	2550/245	1915/138
Winchester .17 HMR	20-gr. Super-X JHP	2375/250	1776/140

.22 WINCHESTER MAGNUM RIMFIRE

CARTRIDGE BULLET	LOAD	MUZZLE VEL./ENERGY	100-YD. VEL./ENERGY
CCI .22 WMR	30 Maxi Mag HP + V	2200/322	1375/126
CCI .22 WMR	30 Poly-Tip V-Max	2200/322	1571/164
CCI .22 WMR	30 TNT JHP	2200/322	1405/131
CCI .22 WMR	30 TNT Green HP	2050/280	1317/116
CCI .22 WMR	40 Maxi Mag HP	1875/312	1319/155
CCI .22 WMR	40 Maxi Mag TMJ	1875/312	1366/166
CCI .22 WMR	40 GamePoint JSP	1875/312	1385/170
CCI .22 WMR	52 #12 birdshot	1000	
Federal .22 WMR	30-gr. Speer TNT HP	2200/320	1420/135
Federal .22 WMR	40-gr. FMJ	1880/315	1310/155
Hornady .22 WMR	30-gr. V-Max	2200/322	1421/134
Remington .22 WMR	33-gr. AccuTip-V	2000/293	1495/164

CARTRIDGE BULLET	LOAD	MUZZLE VEL./ENERGY	100-YD. VEL./ENERGY
Remington .22 WMR	40-gr. JHP	1910/324	1350/162
Remington .22 WMR	40-gr. PSP	1910/324	1340/159
Winchester .22 WMR	28-gr. Varmint LF JHP	2200/301	1394/121
Winchester .22 WMR	30-gr. Varmint HV V-Max	2250/337	1490/148
Winchester .22 WMR	30-gr. Varmint HV JHP	2250/337	1450/140
Winchester .22 WMR	34-gr. Varmint HE JHP	2120/339	1437/156
Winchester .22 WMR	40-gr. Super-X JHP (and FMJ)	1910/324	1326/156
Winchester .22 WMR	45-gr. USA DynaPoint	1550/240	1147/131

.17 WINCHESTER SUPER MAG.

CARTRIDGE BULLET	LOAD	MUZZLE VEL./ENERGY	100-YD. VEL./ENERGY
Winchester .17 Super Mag	20-gr. Varmint HV	3000/400	2504/278
Winchester .17 Super Mag	25-gr. Polymer Tip	2600/375	2230/276

.22 WINCHESTER RIMFIRE

CARTRIDGE BULLET	LOAD	MUZZLE VEL./ENERGY	100-YD. VEL./ENERGY
CCI .22 WRF	45 JHP	1300/169	1013/103
Winchester .22 WRF	45 FN	1300/169	1023/105

Centerfire Handgun Ballistics

Data shown here is taken from manufacturers' charts; your chronograph readings may vary. Barrel lengths for pistol data vary, and depend in part on which pistols are typically chambered in a given cartridge. Velocity variations due to barrel length depend on the baseline bullet speed and the load. Velocity for the .30 Carbine, normally a rifle cartridge, was determined in a pistol barrel.

Listings are current as of February the year *Shooter's Bible* appears (not the cover year). Listings are not intended as recommendations. For example, the data for the .25 Auto gives velocity and energy readings to 100 yards. Few handgunners would call the little .25 a 100-yard cartridge.

Abbreviations: Bullets are designated by loading company, weight (in grains) and type, with these abbreviations for shape and construction: BJHP= brass-jacketed hollowpoint; FN=Flat Nose; FMC=Full Metal Case; FMJ=Full Metal Jacket; HP=Hollowpoint; L=Lead; LF=Lead-Free; +P=a more powerful load than traditionally manufactured for that round; RN=Round Nose; SFHP=Starfire (PMC) Hollowpoint; SP=Softpoint; SWC=Semi Wadcutter; TMJ=Total Metal Jacket; WC=Wadcutter; CEPP, SXT and XTP are trademarked designations of Lapua, Winchester and Hornady, respectively.

.25 AUTO TO .32 S&W LONG

CARTRIDGE BULLET	RANGE, YARDS:	0	25	50	75	100
.25 AUTO						
Federal 50 FMJ	velocity, fps:	760	750	730	720	700
	energy, ft-lb:	65	60	60	55	55
Hornady 35 JHP/XTP	velocity, fps:	900		813		742
	energy, ft-lb:	63		51		43
Magtech 50 FMC	velocity, fps:	760		707		659
	energy, ft-lb:	64		56		48
PMC 50 FMJ	velocity, fps:	754	730	707	685	663
	energy, ft-lb:	62				
Rem. 50 Metal Case	velocity, fps:	760		707		659
	energy, ft-lb:	64		56		48
Speer 35 Gold Dot	velocity, fps:	900		816		747
	energy, ft-lb:	63		52		43
Speer 50 TMJ (and Blazer)	velocity, fps:	760		717		677
	energy, ft-lb:	64		57		51
Win. 45 Expanding Point	velocity, fps:	815		729		655
	energy, ft-lb	66		53		42
Win. 50 FMJ	velocity, fps:	760		707		
	energy, ft-lb	64		56		
.30 LUGER						
Win. 93 FMJ	velocity, fps:	1220		1110		1040
	energy, ft-lb:	305		255		225
7.62x25 TOKAREV						
PMC 93 FMJ	velocity and energy figures not available					
.30 CARBINE						
Win. 110 Hollow SP	velocity, fps:	1790		1601		1430
	energy, ft-lb	783		626		500
.32 AUTO						
Federal 65 Hydra-Shok JHP	velocity, fps:	950	920	890	860	830
	energy, ft-lb:	130	120	115	105	100
Federal 71 FMJ	velocity, fps:	910	880	860	830	810
	energy, ft-lb:	130	120	115	110	105
Hornady 60 JHP/XTP	velocity, fps:	1000		917		849
	energy, ft-lb:	133		112		96
Hornady 71 FMJ-RN	velocity, fps:	900		845		797
	energy, ft-lb:	128		112		100
Magtech 71 FMC	velocity, fps:	905		855		810
	energy, ft-lb:	129		115		103
Magtech 71 JHP	velocity, fps:	905		855		810
	energy, ft-lb:	129		115		103

CARTRIDGE BULLET	RANGE, YARDS:	0	25	50	75	100
PMC 60 JHP	velocity, fps:	980	849	820	791	763
	energy, ft-lb:	117				
PMC 70 SFHP	velocity, fps:	velocity and energy figures not available				
PMC 71 FMJ	velocity, fps:	870	841	814	791	763
	energy, ft-lb:	119				
Rem. 71 Metal Case	velocity, fps:	905		855		810
	energy, ft-lb:	129		115		97
Speer 60 Gold Dot	velocity, fps:	960		868		796
	energy, ft-lb:	123		100		84
Speer 71 TMJ (and Blazer)	velocity, fps:	900		855		810
	energy, ft-lb:	129		115		97
Win. 60 Silvertip HP	velocity, fps:	970		895		835
	energy, ft-lb	125		107		93
Win. 71 FMJ	velocity, fps:	905		855		
	energy, ft-lb	129		115		
.32 S&W						
Rem. 88 LRN	velocity, fps:	680		645		610
	energy, ft-lb:	90		81		73
Win. 85 LRN	velocity, fps:	680		645		610
	energy, ft-lb:	90		81		73
.32 S&W LONG						
Federal 98 LWC	velocity, fps:	780	700	630	560	500
	energy, ft-lb:	130	105	85	70	55
Federal 98 LRN	velocity, fps:	710	690	670	650	640
	energy, ft-lb:	115	105	100	95	90
Lapua 83 LWC	velocity, fps:	240		189*		149*
	energy, ft-lb:	154		95*		59*
Lapua 98 LWC	velocity, fps:	240		202*		171*
	energy, ft-lb:	183		130*		93*
Magtech 98 LRN	velocity, fps:	705		670		635
	energy, ft-lb:	108		98		88
Magtech 98 LWC	velocity, fps:	682		579		491
	energy, ft-lb:	102		73		52
Norma 98 LWC	velocity, fps:	787	759	732		683
	energy, ft-lb:	136	126	118		102
PMC 98 LRN	velocity, fps:	789	770	751	733	716
	energy, ft-lb:	135				
PMC 100 LWC	velocity, fps:	683	652	623	595	569
	energy, ft-lb:	102				
Rem. 98 LRN	velocity, fps:	705		670		635
	energy, ft-lb:	115		98		88

Centerfire Handgun Ballistics

.32 S&W LONG TO 9MM LUGER

CARTRIDGE BULLET	RANGE, YARDS:	0	25	50	75	100
Win. 98 LRN	velocity, fps:	705		670		635
	energy, ft-lb:	115		98		88
.32 SHORT COLT						
Win. 80 LRN	velocity, fps:	745		665		590
	energy, ft-lb	100		79		62
.32-20						
Black Hills 115 FPL	velocity, fps:	800				
	energy, ft-lb:					
.32 H&R MAG						
Black Hills 85 JHP	velocity, fps	1100				
	energy, ft-lb	228				
Black Hills 90 FPL	velocity, fps	750				
	energy, ft-lb					
Black Hills 115 FPL	velocity, fps	800				
	energy, ft-lb					
Federal 85 Hi-Shok JHP	velocity, fps:	1100	1050	1020	970	930
	energy, ft-lb:	230	210	195	175	165
Federal 95 LSWC	velocity, fps:	1030	1000	940	930	900
	energy, ft-lb:	225	210	195	185	170
Hornady 80 FTX		0		50 yds.		100.
	velocity, fps:	1150		1039		963
	energy, ft-lb:	235		192		165
.38 SPECIAL LITE, 4"BBL						
Hornady 90 FTX	velocity, fps:	1200		1037		938
	energy, ft-lb:	288		215		176
9MM MAKAROV						
Federal 90 Hi-Shok JHP	velocity, fps:	990	950	910	880	850
	energy, ft-lb:	195	180	165	155	145
Federal 90 FMJ	velocity, fps:	990	960	920	900	870
	energy, ft-lb:	205	190	180	170	160
Hornady 95 JHP/XTP	velocity, fps:	1000		930		874
	energy, ft-lb:	211		182		161
PMC 100 FMJ-TC	velocity, fps:	velocity and energy figures not available				
Speer 95 TMJ Blazer	velocity, fps:	1000		928		872
	energy, ft-lb:	211		182		161
9x21 IMI						
PMC 123 FMJ	velocity, fps:	1150	1093	1046	1007	973
	energy, ft-lb:	364				
9MM LUGER						
Black Hills 115 JHP	velocity, fps:	1150				
	energy, ft-lb:	336				
Black Hills 115 FMJ	velocity, fps:	1150				
	energy, ft-lb:	336				
Black Hills 115 JHP +P	velocity, fps:	1300				
	energy, ft-lb:	431				
Black Hills 115 EXP JHP	velocity, fps:	1250				
	energy, ft-lb:	400				
Black Hills 124 JHP +P	velocity, fps:	1250				
	energy, ft-lb:	430				
Black Hills 124 JHP	velocity, fps:	1150				
	energy, ft-lb:	363				
Black Hills 124 FMJ	velocity, fps:	1150				
	energy, ft-lb:	363				
Black Hills 147 JHP subsonic	velocity, fps:	975				
	energy, ft-lb:	309				
Black Hills 147 FMJ subsonic	velocity, fps:	975				
	energy, ft-lb:	309				
Federal 105 EFMJ	velocity, fps:	1225	1160	1105	1060	1025
	energy, ft-lb:	350	315	285	265	245

CARTRIDGE BULLET	RANGE, YARDS:	0	25	50	75	100
Federal 115 Hi-Shok JHP	velocity, fps:	1160	1100	1060	1020	990
	energy, ft-lb:	345	310	285	270	250
Federal 115 FMJ	velocity, fps:	1160	1100	1060	1020	990
	energy, ft-lb:	345	310	285	270	250
Federal 124 FMJ	velocity, fps:	1120	1070	1030	990	960
	energy, ft-lb:	345	315	290	270	255
Federal 124 Hydra-Shok JHP	velocity, fps:	1120	1070	1030	990	960
	energy, ft-lb:	345	315	290	270	255
Federal 124 TMJ TMF Primer	velocity, fps:	1120	1070	1030	990	960
	energy, ft-lb:	345	315	290	270	255
Federal 124 Truncated FMJ Match	velocity, fps:	1120	1070	1030	990	960
	energy, ft-lb:	345	315	290	270	255
Federal 124 Nyclad HP	velocity, fps:	1120	1070	1030	990	960
	energy, ft-lb:	345	315	290	270	255
Federal 124 FMJ +P	velocity, fps:	1120	1070	1030	990	960
	energy, ft-lb:	345	315	290	270	255
Federal 135 Hydra-Shok JHP	velocity, fps:	1050	1030	1010	980	970
	energy, ft-lb:	330	315	300	290	280
Federal 147 Hydra-Shok JHP	velocity, fps:	1000	960	920	890	860
	energy, ft-lb:	325	300	275	260	240
Federal 147 Hi-Shok JHP	velocity, fps:	980	950	930	900	880
	energy, ft-lb:	310	295	285	265	255
Federal 147 FMJ FN	velocity, fps:	960	930	910	890	870
	energy, ft-lb:	295	280	270	260	250
Federal 147 TMJ TMF Primer	velocity, fps:	960	940	910	890	870
	energy, ft-lb:	300	285	270	260	245
Hornady 115 JHP/XTP	velocity, fps:	1155		1047		971
	energy, ft-lb:	341		280		241
Hornady 124 JHP/XTP	velocity, fps:	1110		1030		971
	energy, ft-lb:	339		292		259
Hornady 124 TAP-FPD	velocity, fps:	1100		1028		967
	energy, ft-lb:	339		291		257
Hornady 147 JHP/XTP	velocity, fps:	975		935		899
	energy, ft-lb:	310		285		264
Hornady 147 TAP-FPD	velocity, fps:	975		935		899
	energy, ft-lb:	310		285		264
Lapua 116 FMJ	velocity, fps:	365		319*		290*
	energy, ft-lb:	500		381*		315*
Lapua 120 FMJ CEPP Super	velocity, fps:	360		316*		288*
	energy, ft-lb:	505		390*		324*
Lapua 120 FMJ CEPP Extra	velocity, fps:	360		316*		288*
	energy, ft-lb:	505		390*		324*
Lapua 123 HP Megashock	velocity, fps:	355		311*		284*
	energy, ft-lb:	504		388*		322*
Lapua 123 FMJ	velocity, fps:	320		292*		272*
	energy, ft-lb:	410		342*		295*
Lapua 123 FMJ Combat	velocity, fps:	355		315*		289*
	energy, ft-lb:	504		397*		333*
Magtech 115 JHP +P	velocity, fps:	1246		1137		1056
	energy, ft-lb:	397		330		285
Magtech 115 FMC	velocity, fps:	1135		1027		961
	energy, ft-lb:	330		270		235
Magtech 115 JHP	velocity, fps:	1155		1047		971
	energy, ft-lb:	340		280		240
Magtech 124 FMC	velocity, fps:	1109		1030		971
	energy, ft-lb:	339		292		259
Norma 84 Lead Free Frangible (Geco brand)	velocity, fps:	1411				
	energy, ft-lb:	371				
Norma 124 FMJ (Geco brand)	velocity, fps:	1120				
	energy, fps:	341				
Norma 123 FMJ	velocity, fps:	1099	1032	980		899
	energy, ft-lb:	331	292	263		221
Norma 123 FMJ	velocity, fps:	1280	1170	1086		972
	energy, ft-lb:	449	375	323		259

Centerfire Handgun Ballistics

9MM LUGER TO .380 AUTO

CARTRIDGE BULLET	RANGE, YARDS:	0	25	50	75	100
PMC 75 Non-Toxic Frangible	velocity, fps:	1350	1240	1154	1088	1035
	energy, ft-lb:	303				
PMC 95 SFHP	velocity, fps:	1250	1239	1228	1217	1207
	energy, ft-lb:	330				
PMC 115 FMJ	velocity, fps:	1157	1100	1053	1013	979
	energy, ft-lb:	344				
PMC 115 JHP	velocity, fps:	1167	1098	1044	999	961
	energy, ft-lb:	350				
PMC 124 SFHP	velocity, fps:	1090	1043	1003	969	939
	energy, ft-lb:	327				
PMC 124 FMJ	velocity, fps:	1110	1059	1017	980	949
	energy, ft-lb:	339				
PMC 124 LRN	velocity, fps:	1050	1006	969	937	908
	energy, ft-lb:	304				
PMC 147 FMJ	velocity, fps:	980	965	941	919	900
	enerby, ft-lb:	310				
PMC 147 SFHP	velocity, fps:	velocity and energy figures not available				
Rem. 101 Lead Free Frangible	velocity, fps:	1220		1092		1004
	energy, ft-lb:	334		267		226
Rem. 115 FN Enclosed Base	velocity, fps:	1135		1041		973
	energy, ft-lb:	329		277		242
Rem. 115 Metal Case	velocity, fps:	1135		1041		973
	energy, ft-lb:	329		277		242
Rem. 115 JHP	velocity, fps:	1155		1047		971
	energy, ft-lb:	341		280		241
Rem. 115 JHP +P	velocity, fps:	1250		1113		1019
	energy, ft-lb:	399		316		265
Rem. 124 JHP	velocity, fps:	1120		1028		960
	energy, ft-lb:	346		291		254
Rem. 124 FNEB	velocity, fps:	1100		1030		971
	energy, ft-lb:	339		292		252
Rem. 124 BJHP	velocity, fps:	1125		1031		963
	energy, ft-lb:	349		293		255
Rem. 124 BJHP +P	velocity, fps:	1180		1089		1021
	energy, ft-lb:	384		327		287
Rem. 124 Metal Case	velocity, fps:	1110		1030		971
	energy, ft-lb:	339		292		259
Rem. 147 JHP subsonic	velocity, fps:	990		941		900
	energy, ft-lb:	320		289		264
Rem. 147 BJHP	velocity, fps:	990		941		900
	energy, ft-lb:	320		289		264
Speer 90 Frangible	velocity, fps:	1350		1132		1001
	energy, ft-lb:	364		256		200
Speer 115 JHP Blazer	velocity, fps:	1145		1024		943
	energy, ft-lb:	335		268		227
Speer 115 FMJ Blazer	velocity, fps:	1145		1047		971
	energy, ft-lb:	341		280		241
Speer 115 FMJ	velocity, fps:	1200		1060		970
	energy, ft-lb:	368		287		240
Speer 115 Gold Dot HP	velocity, fps:	1200		1047		971
	energy, ft-lb:	341		280		241
Speer 124 FMJ Blazer	velocity, fps:	1090		989		917
	energy, ft-lb:	327		269		231
Speer 124 FMJ	velocity, fps:	1090		987		913
	energy, ft-lb:	327		268		230
Speer 124 TMJ-CF (and Blazer)	velocity, fps:	1090		989		917
	energy, ft-lb:	327		269		231
Speer 124 Gold Dot HP	velocity, fps:	1150		1030		948
	energy, ft-lb:	367		292		247
Speer 124 Gold Dot HP+P	velocity, ft-lb:	1220		1085		996
	energy, ft-lb:	410		324		273
Speer 147 TMJ Blazer	velocity, fps:	950		912		879
	energy, ft-lb:	295		272		252

CARTRIDGE BULLET	RANGE, YARDS:	0	25	50	75	100
Speer 147 TMJ	velocity, fps:	985		943		906
	energy, ft-lb:	317		290		268
Speer 147 TMJ-CF (and Blazer)	velocity, fps:	985		960		924
	energy, ft-lb:	326		300		279
Speer 147 Gold Dot	velocity, fps:	985		960		924
	energy, ft-lb:	326		300		279
Win. 105 Jacketed FP	velocity, fps:	1200		1074		989
	energy, ft-lb:	336		269		228
Win. 115 Silvertip HP	velocity, fps:	1225		1095		1007
	energy, ft-lb:	383		306		259
Win. 115 Jacketed HP	velocity, fps:	1225		1095		
	energy, ft-lb:	383		306		
Win. 115 FMJ	velocity, fps:	1190		1071		
	energy, ft-lb:	362		293		
Win. 115 EB WinClean	velocity, fps:	1190		1088		
	energy, ft-lb:	362		302		
Win. 124 FMJ	velocity, fps:	1140		1050		
	energy, ft-lb:	358		303		
Win. 124 EB WinClean	velocity, fps:	1130		1049		
	energy, ft-lb:	352		303		
Win. 147 FMJ FN	velocity, fps:	990		945		
	energy, ft-lb:	320		292		
Win. 147 SXT	velocity, fps:	990		947		909
	energy, ft-lb:	320		293		270
Win. 147 Silvertip HP	velocity, fps:	1010		962		921
	energy, ft-lb:	333		302		277
Win. 147 JHP	velocity, fps:	990		945		
	energy, ft-lb:	320		291		
Win. 147 EB WinClean	velocity, fps:	990		945		
	energy, ft-lb:	320		291		

9 X 23 WINCHESTER

CARTRIDGE BULLET	RANGE, YARDS:	0	25	50	75	100
Win. 124 Jacketed FP	velocity, fps:	1460		1308		
	energy, ft-lb:	587		471		
Win. 125 Silvertip HP	velocity, fps:	1450		1249		1103
	energy, ft-lb:	583		433		338

.38 S&W

CARTRIDGE BULLET	RANGE, YARDS:	0	25	50	75	100
Rem. 146 LRN	velocity, fps:	685		650		620
	energy, ft-lb:	150		135		125
Win. 145 LRN	velocity, fps:	685		650		620
	energy, ft-lb:	150		135		125

.38 SHORT COLT

CARTRIDGE BULLET	RANGE, YARDS:	0	25	50	75	100
Rem. 125 LRN	velocity, fps:	730		685		645
	energy, ft-lb:	150		130		115

.38 LONG COLT

CARTRIDGE BULLET	RANGE, YARDS:	0	25	50	75	100
Black Hills 158 RNL	velocity, fps:	650				
	energy, ft-lb:					

.380 AUTO

CARTRIDGE BULLET	RANGE, YARDS:	0	25	50	75	100
Black Hills 90 JHP	velocity, fps:	1000				
	energy, ft-lb:	200				
Black Hills 95 FMJ	velocity, fps:	950				
	energy, ft-lb:	190				
Federal 90 Hi-Shok JHP	velocity, fps:	1000	940	890	840	800
	energy, ft-lb:	200	175	160	140	130
Federal 90 Hydra-Shok JHP	velocity, fps:	1000	940	890	840	800
	energy, ft-lb:	200	175	160	140	130
Federal 95 FMJ	velocity, fps:	960	910	870	830	790
	energy, ft-lb:	190	175	160	145	130
Hornady 90 JHP/XTP	velocity, fps:	1000		902		823
	energy, ft-lb:	200		163		135

Centerfire Handgun Ballistics

.380 AUTO TO .38 SPECIAL

CARTRIDGE BULLET	RANGE, YARDS:	0	25	50	75	100
Magtech 85 JHP + P	velocity, fps:	1082		999		936
	energy, ft-lb:	221		188		166
Magtech 95 FMC	velocity, fps:	951		861		781
	energy, ft-lb:	190		156		128
Magtech 95 JHP	velocity, fps:	951		861		781
	energy, ft-lb:	190		156		128
PMC 77 NT/FR	velocity, fps:	1200	1095	1012	932	874
	energy, ft-lb:	223				
PMC 90 FMJ	velocity, fps:	910	872	838	807	778
	energy, ft-lb:	165				
PMC 90 JHP	velocity, fps:	917	878	844	812	782
	energy, ft-lb:	168				
PMC 95 SFHP	velocity, fps:	925	884	847	813	783
	energy, ft-lb:	180				
Rem. 88 JHP	velocity, fps:	990		920		868
	energy, ft-lb:	191		165		146
Rem. 95 FNEB	velocity, fps:	955		865		785
	energy, ft-lb:	190		160		130
Rem. 95 Metal Case	velocity, fps:	955		865		785
	energy, ft-lb:	190		160		130
Rem. 102 BJHP	velocity, fps:	940		901		866
	energy, ft-lb:	200		184		170
Speer 88 JHP Blazer	velocity, fps:	950		920		870
	energy, ft-lb:	195		164		148
Speer 90 Gold Dot	velocity, fps:	990		907		842
	energy, ft-lb:	196		164		142
Speer 95 TMJ Blazer	velocity, fps:	945		865		785
	energy, ft-lb:	190		160		130
Speer 95 TMJ	velocity, fps:	950		877		817
	energy, ft-lb:	180		154		133
Win. 85 Silvertip HP	velocity, fps:	1000		921		860
	energy, ft-lb:	189		160		140
Win. 95 SXT	velocity, fps:	955		889		835
	energy, ft-lb:	192		167		147
Win. 95 FMJ	velocity, fps:	955		865		
	energy, ft-lb:	190		160		
Win. 95 EB WinClean	velocity, fps:	955		881		
	energy, ft-lb:	192		164		

.38 SPECIAL

CARTRIDGE BULLET	RANGE, YARDS:	0	25	50	75	100
Black Hills 125 JHP +P	velocity, fps:	1050				
	energy, ft-lb:	306				
Black Hills 148 HBWC	velocity, fps:	700				
	energy, ft-lb:					
Black Hills 158 SWC	velocity, fps:	850				
	energy, ft-lb:					
Black Hills 158 CNL	velocity, fps:	800				
	energy, ft-lb:					
Federal 110 Hydra-Shok JHP	velocity, fps:	1000	970	930	910	880
	energy, ft-lb:	245	225	215	200	190
Federal 110 Hi-Shok JHP +P	velocity, fps:	1000	960	930	900	870
	energy, ft-lb:	240	225	210	195	185
Federal 125 Nyclad HP	velocity, fps:	830	780	730	690	650
	energy, ft-lb:	190	170	150	130	115
Federal 125 Hi-Shok JSP +P	velocity, fps:	950	920	900	880	860
	energy, ft-lb:	250	235	225	215	205
Federal 125 Hi-Shok JHP +P	velocity, fps:	950	920	900	880	860
	energy, ft-lb:	250	235	225	215	205
Federal 125 Nyclad HP +P	velocity, fps:	950	920	900	880	860
	energy, ft-lb:	250	235	225	215	205
Federal 129 Hydra-Shok JHP+P	velocity, fps:	950	930	910	890	870
	energy, ft-lb:	255	245	235	225	215
Federal 130 FMJ	velocity, fps:	950	920	890	870	840
	energy, ft-lb:	260	245	230	215	205

CARTRIDGE BULLET	RANGE, YARDS:	0	25	50	75	100
Federal 148 LWC Match	velocity, fps:	710	670	630	600	560
	energy, ft-lb:	165	150	130	115	105
Federal 158 LRN	velocity, fps:	760	740	720	710	690
	energy, ft-lb:	200	190	185	175	170
Federal 158 LSWC	velocity, fps:	760	740	720	710	690
	energy, ft-lb:	200	190	185	175	170
Federal 158 Nyclad RN	velocity, fps:	760	740	720	710	690
	energy, ft-lb:	200	190	185	175	170
Federal 158 SWC HP +P	velocity, fps:	890	870	860	840	820
	energy, ft-lb:	280	265	260	245	235
Federal 158 LSWC +P	velocity, fps:	890	870	860	840	820
	energy, ft-lb:	270	265	260	245	235
Federal 158 Nyclad SWC-HP+P	velocity, fps:	890	870	860	840	820
	energy, ft-lb:	270	265	260	245	235
Hornady 125 JHP/XTP	velocity, fps:	900		856		817
	energy, ft-lb:	225		203		185
Hornady 140 JHP/XTP	velocity, fps:	825		790		757
	energy, ft-lb:	212		194		178
Hornady 140 Cowboy	velocity, fps:	800		767		735
	energy, ft-lb:	199		183		168
Hornady 148 HBWC	velocity, fps:	800		697		610
	energy, ft-lb:	210		160		122
Hornady 158 JHP/XPT	velocity, fps:	800		765		731
	energy, ft-lb:	225		205		188
Lapua 123 HP Megashock	velocity, fps:	355		311*		284*
	energy, ft-lb:	504		388*		322*
Lapua 148 LWC	velocity, fps:	230		203*		181*
	energy, ft-lb:	254		199*		157*
Lapua 150 SJFN	velocity, fps:	325		301*		283*
	energy, ft-lb:	512		439*		388*
Lapua 158 FMJLF	velocity, fps:	255		243*		232*
	energy, ft-lb:	332		301*		275*
Lapua 158 LRN	velocity, fps:	255		243*		232*
	energy, ft-lb:	332		301*		275*
Magtech 125 JHP +P	velocity, fps:	1017		971		931
	energy, ft-lb:	287		262		241
Magtech 148 LWC	velocity, fps:	710		634		566
	energy, ft-lb:	166		132		105
Magtech 158 LRN	velocity, fps:	755		728		693
	energy, ft-lb:	200		183		168
Magtech 158 LFN	velocity, fps:	800		776		753
	energy, ft-lb:	225		211		199
Magtech 158 SJHP	velocity, fps:	807		779		753
	energy, ft-lb:	230		213		199
Magtech 158 LSWC	velocity, fps:	755		721		689
	energy, ft-lb:	200		182		167
Magtech 158 FMC-Flat	velocity, fps:	807		779		753
	energy, ft-lb:	230		213		199
PMC 85 Non-Toxic Frangible	velocity, fps:	1275	1181	1109	1052	1006
	energy, ft-lb:	307				
PMC 110 SFHP +P	velocity, fps:	velocity and energy figures not available				
PMC 125 SFHP +P	velocity, fps:	950	918	889	863	838
	energy, ft-lb:	251				
PMC 125 JHP +P	velocity, fps:	974	938	906	878	851
	energy, ft-lb:	266				
PMC 132 FMJ	velocity, fps:	841	820	799	780	761
	energy, ft-lb:	206				
PMC 148 LWC	velocity, fps:	728	694	662	631	602
	energy, ft-lb:	175				
PMC 158 LRN	velocity, fps:	820	801	783	765	749
	energy, ft-lb:	235				
PMC 158 JSP	velocity, fps:	835	816	797	779	762
	energy, ft-lb:	245				

CARTRIDGE BULLET	RANGE, YARDS:	0	25	50	75	100
PMC 158 LFP	velocity, fps:	800		761		725
	energy, ft-lb:	225		203		185
Rem. 101 Lead Free Frangible	velocity, fps:	950		896		850
	energy, ft-lb:	202		180		162
Rem. 110 SJHP	velocity, fps:	950		890		840
	energy, ft-lb:	220		194		172
Rem. 110 SJHP +P	velocity, fps:	995		926		871
	energy, ft-lb:	242		210		185
Rem. 125 SJHP +P	velocity, ft-lb:	945		898		858
	energy, ft-lb:	248		224		204
Rem. 125 BJHP	velocity, fps:	975		929		885
	energy, ft-lb:	264		238		218
Rem. 125 FNEB	velocity, fps:	850		822		796
	energy, ft-lb:	201		188		176
Rem. 125 FNEB +P	velocity, fps:	975		935		899
	energy, ft-lb:	264		242		224
Rem. 130 Metal Case	velocity, fps:	950		913		879
	energy, ft-lb:	261		240		223
Rem. 148 LWC Match	velocity, fps:	710		634		566
	energy, ft-lb:	166		132		105
Rem. 158 LRN	velocity, fps:	755		723		692
	energy, ft-lb:	200		183		168
Rem. 158 SWC +P	velocity, fps:	890		855		823
	energy, ft-lb:	278		257		238
Rem. 158 SWC	velocity, fps:	755		723		692
	energy, ft-lb:	200		183		168
Rem. 158 LHP +P	velocity, fps:	890		855		823
	energy, ft-lb:	278		257		238
Speer 125 JHP +P Blazer	velocity, fps:	945		898		858
	energy, ft-lb:	248		224		204
Speer 125 Gold Dot +P	velocity, fps:	945		898		858
	energy, ft-lb:	248		224		204
Speer 158 TMJ +P (and Blazer)	velocity, fps:	900		852		818
	energy, ft-lb:	278		255		235
Speer 158 LRN Blazer	velocity, fps:	755		723		692
	energy, ft-lb:	200		183		168
Speer 158 Trail Blazer LFN	velocity, fps:	800		761		725
	energy, ft-lb:	225		203		184
Speer 158 TMJ-CF +P (and Blazer)	velocity, fps:	900		852		818
	energy, ft-lb:	278		255		235
Win. 110 Silvertip HP	velocity, fps:	945		894		850
	energy, ft-lb:	218		195		176
Win. 110 Jacketed FP	velocity, fps:	975		906		849
	energy, ft-lb:	232		201		176
Win. 125 Jacketed HP	velocity, fps:	945		898		
	energy, ft-lb:	248		224		
Win. 125 Jacketed HP +P	velocity, fps:	945		898		858
	energy, ft-lb:	248		224		204
Win. 125 Jacketed FP	velocity, fps:	850		804		
	energy, ft-lb:	201		179		
Win. 125 Silvertip HP + P	velocity, fps:	945		898		858
	energy, ft-lb:	248		224		204
Win. 125 JFP WinClean	velocity, fps:	775		742		
	energy, ft-lb:	167		153		
Win. 130 FMJ	velocity, fps:	800		765		
	energy, ft-lb:	185		169		
Win. 130 SXT +P	velocity, fps:	925		887		852
	energy, ft-lb:	247		227		210
Win. 148 LWC Super Match	velocity, fps:	710		634		566
	energy, ft-lb:	166		132		105
Win. 150 Lead	velocity, fps:	845		812		
	energy, ft-lb:	238		219		
Win. 158 Lead	velocity, fps:	800		761		725
	energy, ft-lb:	225		203		185

CARTRIDGE BULLET	RANGE, YARDS:	0	25	50	75	100
Win. 158 LRN	velocity, fps:	755		723		693
	energy, ft-lb:	200		183		168
Win. 158 LSWC	velocity, fps:	755		721		689
	energy, ft-lb:	200		182		167
Win. 158 LSWC HP +P	velocity, fps:	890		855		823
	energy, ft-lb:	278		257		238

.38-40

CARTRIDGE BULLET	RANGE, YARDS:	0	25	50	75	100
Black Hills 180 FPL	velocity, fps:	800				
	energy, ft-lb:					

.38 Super

CARTRIDGE BULLET	RANGE, YARDS:	0	25	50	75	100
Federal 130 FMJ +P	velocity, fps:	1200	1140	1100	1050	1020
	energy, ft-lb:	415	380	350	320	300
PMC 115 JHP	velocity, fps:	1116	1052	1001	959	923
	energy, ft-lb:	318				
PMC 130 FMJ	velocity, fps:	1092	1038	994	957	924
	energy, ft-lb:	348				
Rem. 130 Metal Case	velocity, fps:	1215		1099		1017
	energy, ft-lb:	426		348		298
Win. 125 Silvertip HP +P	velocity, fps:	1240		1130		1050
	energy, ft-lb:	427		354		306
Win. 130 FMJ +P	velocity, fps:	1215		1099		
	energy, ft-lb:	426		348		

.357 Sig

CARTRIDGE BULLET	RANGE, YARDS:	0	25	50	75	100
Federal 125 FMJ	velocity, fps:	1350	1270	1190	1130	1080
	energy, ft-lb:	510	445	395	355	325
Federal 125 JHP	velocity, fps:	1350	1270	1190	1130	1080
	energy, ft-lb:	510	445	395	355	325
Federal 150 JHP	velocity, fps:	1130	1080	1030	1000	970
	energy, ft-lb:	420	385	355	330	310
Hornady 124 JHP/XTP	velocity, fps:	1350		1208		1108
	energy, ft-lb:	502		405		338
Hornady 147 JHP/XTP	velocity, fps:	1225		1138		1072
	energy, ft-lb:	490		422		375
PMC 85 Non-Toxic Frangible	velocity, fps:	1480	1356	1245	1158	1092
	energy, ft-lb:	413				
PMC 124 SFHP	velocity, fps:	1350	1263	1190	1132	1083
	energy, ft-lb:	502				
PMC 124 FMJ/FP	velocity, fps:	1350	1242	1158	1093	1040
	energy, ft-lb:	512				
Rem. 104 Lead Free Frangible	velocity, fps:	1400		1223		1094
	energy, ft-lb:	453		345		276
Rem. 125 Metal Case	velocity, fps:	1350		1146		1018
	energy, ft-lb:	506		422		359
Rem. 125 JHP	velocity, fps:	1350		1157		1032
	energy, ft-lb:	506		372		296
Speer 125 TMJ (and Blazer)	velocity, fps:	1350		1177		1057
	energy, ft-lb:	502		381		307
Speer 125 TMJ-CF	velocity, fps:	1350		1177		1057
	energy, ft-lb:	502		381		307
Speer 125 Gold Dot	velocity, fps:	1375		1203		1079
	energy, ft-lb:	525		402		323
Win. 105 JFP	velocity, fps:	1370		1179		1050
	energy, ft-lb	438		324		257
Win. 125 FMJ FN	velocity, fps:	1350		1185		
	energy, ft-lb:	506		390		

.357 Magnum

CARTRIDGE BULLET	RANGE, YARDS:	0	25	50	75	100
Black Hills 125 JHP	velocity, fps:	1500				
	energy, ft-lb:	625				
Black Hills 158 CNL	velocity, fps:	800				
	energy, ft-lb:					
Black Hills 158 SWC	velocity, fps:	1050				
	energy, ft-lb:					

Centerfire Handgun Ballistics

.357 MAGNUM TO .40 S&W

CARTRIDGE BULLET	RANGE, YARDS:	0	25	50	75	100
Black Hills 158 JHP	velocity, fps:	1250				
	energy, ft-lb:					
Federal 110 Hi-Shok JHP	velocity, fps:	1300	1180	1090	1040	990
	energy, ft-lb:	410	340	290	260	235
Federal 125 Hi-Shok JHP	velocity, fps:	1450	1350	1240	1160	1100
	energy, ft-lb:	580	495	430	370	335
Federal 130 Hydra-Shok JHP	velocity, fps:	1300	1210	1130	1070	1020
	energy, ft-lb:	490	420	370	330	300
Federal 158 Hi-Shok JSP	velocity, fps:	1240	1160	1100	1060	1020
	energy, ft-lb:	535	475	430	395	365
Federal 158 JSP	velocity, fps:	1240	1160	1100	1060	1020
	energy, ft-lb:	535	475	430	395	365
Federal 158 LSWC	velocity, fps:	1240	1160	1100	1060	1020
	energy, ft-lb:	535	475	430	395	365
Federal 158 Hi-Shok JHP	velocity, fps:	1240	1160	1100	1060	1020
	energy, ft-lb:	535	475	430	395	365
Federal 158 Hydra-Shok JHP	velocity, fps:	1240	1160	1100	1060	1020
	energy, ft-lb:	535	475	430	395	365
Federal 180 Hi-Shok JHP	velocity, fps:	1090	1030	980	930	890
	energy, ft-lb:	475	425	385	350	320
Federal 180 Castcore	velocity, fps:	1250	1200	1160	1120	1080
	energy, ft-lb:	625	575	535	495	465
Hornady 125 JHP/XTP	velocity, fps:	1500		1314		1166
	energy, ft-lb:	624		479		377
Hornady 125 JFP/XTP	velocity, fps:	1500		1311		1161
	energy, ft-lb:	624		477		374
Hornady 140 Cowboy	velocity, fps:	800		767		735
	energy, ft-lb:	199		183		168
Hornady 140 JHP/XTP	velocity, fps:	1400		1249		1130
	energy, ft-lb:	609		485		397
Hornady 158 JHP/XTP	velocity, fps:	1250		1150		1073
	energy, ft-lb:	548		464		404
Hornady 158 JFP/XTP	velocity, fps:	1250		1147		1068
	energy, ft-lb:	548		461		400
Lapua 150 FMJ CEPP Super	velocity, fps:	370		527*		303*
	energy, ft-lb:	664		527*		445*
Lapua 150 SJFN	velocity, fps:	385		342*		313*
	energy, ft-lb:	719		569*		476*
Lapua 158 SJHP	velocity, fps:	470		408*		359*
	energy, ft-lb:	1127		850*		657*
Magtech 158 SJSP	velocity, fps:	1235		1104		1015
	energy, ft-lb:	535		428		361
Magtech 158 SJHP	velocity, fps:	1235		1104		1015
	energy, ft-lb:	535		428		361
PMC 85 Non-Toxic Frangible	velocity, fps:	1325	1219	1139	1076	1025
	energy, ft-lb:	331				
PMC 125 JHP	velocity, fps:	1194	1117	1057	1008	967
	energy, ft-lb:	399				
PMC 150 JHP	velocity, fps:	1234	1156	1093	1042	1000
	energy, ft-lb:	512				
PMC 150 SFHP	velocity, fps:	1205	1129	1069	1020	980
	energy, ft-lb:	484				
PMC 158 JSP	velocity, fps:	1194	1122	1063	1016	977
	energy, ft-lb:	504				
PMC 158 LFP	velocity, fps:	800		761		725
	energy, ft-lb:	225		203		185
Rem. 110 SJHP	velocity, fps:	1295		1094		975
	energy, ft-lb:	410		292		232
Rem. 125 SJHP	velocity, fps:	1450		1240		1090
	energy, ft-lb:	583		427		330
Rem. 125 BJHP	velocity, fps:	1220		1095		1009
	energy, ft-lb:	413		333		283
Rem. 125 FNEB	velocity, fps:	1450		1240		1090
	energy, ft-lb:	583		427		330

CARTRIDGE BULLET	RANGE, YARDS:	0	25	50	75	100
Rem. 158 SJHP	velocity, fps:	1235		1104		1015
	energy, ft-lb:	535		428		361
Rem. 158 SP	velocity, fps:	1235		1104		1015
	energy, ft-lb:	535		428		361
Rem. 158 SWC	velocity, fps:	1235		1104		1015
	energy, ft-lb:	535		428		361
Rem. 165 JHP Core-Lokt	velocity, fps:	1290		1189		1108
	energy, ft-lb:	610		518		450
Rem. 180 SJHP	velocity, fps:	1145		1053		985
	energy, ft-lb:	542		443		388
Speer 125 Gold Dot	velocity, fps:	1450		1240		1090
	energy, ft-lb:	583		427		330
Speer 158 JHP Blazer	velocity, fps:	1150		1104		1015
	energy, ft-lb:	535		428		361
Speer 158 Gold Dot	velocity, fps:	1235		1104		1015
	energy, ft-lb:	535		428		361
Speer 170 Gold Dot SP	velocity, fps:	1180		1089		1019
	energy, ft-lb:	525		447		392
Win. 110 JFP	velocity, fps:	1275		1105		998
	energy, ft-lb:	397		298		243
Win. 110 JHP	velocity, fps:	1295		1095		
	energy, ft-lb:	410		292		
Win. 125 JFP WinClean	velocity, fps:	1370		1183		
	energy, ft-lb:	521		389		
Win. 145 Silvertip HP	velocity, fps:	1290		1155		1060
	energy, ft-lb:	535		428		361
Win. 158 JHP	velocity, fps:	1235		1104		1015
	energy, ft-lb:	535		428		361
Win. 158 JSP	velocity, fps:	1235		1104		1015
	energy, ft-lb:	535		428		361
Win. 180 Partition Gold	velocity, fps:	1180		1088		1020
	energy, ft-lb:	557		473		416

.40 S&W

CARTRIDGE BULLET	RANGE, YARDS:	0	25	50	75	100
Black Hills 155 JHP	velocity, fps:	1150				
	energy, ft-lb:	450				
Black Hills 165 EXP JHP	velocity, fps:	1150 (2005: 1100)				
	energy, ft-lb:	483				
Black Hills 180 JHP	velocity, fps:	1000				
	energy, ft-lb:	400				
Black Hills 180 JHP	velocity, fps:	1000				
	energy, ft-lb:	400				
Federal 135 Hydra-Shok JHP	velocity, fps:	1190	1050	970	900	850
	energy, ft-lb:	420	330	280	245	215
Federal 155 FMJ Ball	velocity, fps:	1140	1080	1030	990	960
	energy, ft-lb:	445	400	365	335	315
Federal 155 Hi-Shok JHP	velocity, fps:	1140	1080	1030	990	950
	energy, ft-lb:	445	400	365	335	315
Federal 155 Hydra-Shok JHP	velocity, fps:	1140	1080	1030	990	950
	energy, ft-lb:	445	400	365	335	315
Federal 165 EFMJ	velocity, fps:	1190	1060	970	905	850
	energy, ft-lb:	520	410	345	300	265
Federal 165 FMJ	velocity, fps:	1050	1020	990	960	935
	energy, ft-lb:	405	380	355	335	320
Federal 165 FMJ Ball	velocity, fps:	980	950	920	900	880
	energy, ft-lb:	350	330	310	295	280
Federal 165 Hydra-Shok JHP	velocity, fps:	980	950	930	910	890
	energy, ft-lb:	350	330	315	300	290
Federal 180 High Antim. Lead	velocity, fps:	990	960	930	910	890
	energy, ft-lb:	390	365	345	330	315
Federal 180 TMJ TMF Primer	velocity, fps:	990	960	940	910	890
	energy, ft-lb:	390	370	350	330	315
Federal 180 FMJ Ball	velocity, fps:	990	960	940	910	890
	energy, ft-lb:	390	370	350	330	315

.40 S&W

CARTRIDGE BULLET	RANGE, YARDS:	0	25	50	75	100
Federal 180 Hi-Shok JHP	velocity, fps:	990	960	930	910	890
	energy, ft-lb:	390	365	345	330	315
Federal 180 Hydra-Shok JHP	velocity, fps:	990	960	930	910	890
	energy, ft-lb:	390	365	345	330	315
Hornady 155 JHP/XTP	velocity, fps:	1180		1061		980
	energy, ft-lb:	479		387		331
Hornady 155 TAP-FPD	velocity, fps:	1180		1061		980
	energy, ft-lb:	470		387		331
Hornady 180 JHP/XTP	velocity, fps:	950		903		862
	energy, ft-lb:	361		326		297
Hornady 180 TAP-FPD	velocity, fps:	950		903		862
	energy, ft-lb:	361		326		297
Magtech 155 JHP	velocity, fps:	1025		1118		1052
	energy, ft-lb:	500		430		381
Magtech 180 JHP	velocity, fps:	990		933		886
	energy, ft-lb:	390		348		314
Magtech 180 FMC	velocity, fps:	990		933		886
	energy, ft-lb:	390		348		314
PMC 115 Non-Toxic Frangible	velocity, fps:	1350	1240	1154	1088	1035
	energy, ft-lb:	465				
PMC 155 SFHP	velocity, fps:	1160	1092	1039	994	957
	energy, ft-lb:	463				
PMC 165 JHP	velocity, fps:	1040	1002	970	941	915
	energy, ft-lb:	396				
PMC 165 FMJ	velocity, fps:	1010	977	948	922	899
	energy, ft-lb:	374				
PMC 180 FMJ/FP	velocity, fps:	985	957	931	908	885
	energy, ft-lb:	388				
PMC 180 SFHP	velocity, fps:	985	958	933	910	889
	energy, ft-lb:	388				
Rem. 141 Lead Free Frangible	velocity, fps:	1135		1056		996
	energy, ft-lb:	403		349		311
Rem. 155 JHP	velocity, fps:	1205		1095		1017
	energy, ft-lb:	499		413		356
Rem. 165 BJHP	velocity, fps:	1150		1040		964
	energy, ft-lb:	485		396		340
Rem. 180 JHP	velocity, fps:	1015		960		914
	energy, ft-lb:	412		368		334
Rem. 180 FN Enclosed Base	velocity, fps:	985		936		893
	energy, ft-lb:	388		350		319
Rem. 180 Metal Case	velocity, fps:	985		936		893
	energy, ft-lb:	388		350		319
Rem. 180 BJHP	velocity, fps:	1015		960		914
	energy, ft-lb:	412		368		334
Speer 105 Frangible	velocity, fps:	1380		1128		985
	energy, ft-lb:	444		297		226
Speer 155 TMJ Blazer	velocity, fps:	1175		1047		963
	energy, ft-lb:	475		377		319
Speer 155 TMJ	velocity, fps:	1200		1065		976
	energy, ft-lb:	496		390		328
Speer 155 Gold Dot	velocity, fps:	1200		1063		974
	energy, ft-lb:	496		389		326
Speer 165 TMJ Blazer	velocity, fps:	1100		1006		938
	energy, ft-lb:	443		371		321
Speer 165 TMJ	velocity, fps:	1150		1040		964
	energy, ft-lb:	484		396		340
Speer 165 Gold Dot	velocity, fps:	1150		1043		966
	energy, ft-lb:	485		399		342
Speer 180 HP Blazer	velocity, fps:	985		951		909
	energy, ft-lb:	400		361		330
Speer 180 FMJ Blazer	velocity, fps:	1000		937		886
	energy, ft-lb:	400		351		313
Speer 180 FMJ	velocity, fps:	1000		951		909
	energy, ft-lb:	400		361		330

CARTRIDGE BULLET	RANGE, YARDS:	0	25	50	75	100
Speer 180 TMJ-CF (and Blazer)	velocity, fps:	1000		951		909
	energy, ft-lb:	400		361		330
Speer 180 Gold Dot	velocity, fps:	1025		957		902
	energy, ft-lb:	420		366		325
Win. 140 JFP	velocity, fps:	1155		1039		960
	energy, ft-lb:	415		336		286
Win. 155 Silvertip HP	velocity, fps:	1205		1096		1018
	energy, ft-lb:	500		414		357
Win. 165 SXT	velocity, fps:	1130		1041		977
	energy, ft-lb:	468		397		349
Win. 165 FMJ FN	velocity, fps:	1060		1001		
	energy, ft-lb:	412		367		
Win. 165 EB WinClean	velocity, fps:	1130		1054		
	energy, ft-lb:	468		407		
Win. 180 JHP	velocity, fps:	1010		954		
	energy, ft-lb:	408		364		
Win. 180 FMJ	velocity, fps:	990		936		
	energy, ft-lb:	390		350		
Win. 180 SXT	velocity, fps:	1010		954		909
	energy, ft-lb:	408		364		330
Win. 180 EB WinClean	velocity, fps:	990		943		
	energy, ft-lb:	392		356		

10 MM AUTO

CARTRIDGE BULLET	RANGE, YARDS:	0	25	50	75	100
Federal 155 Hi-Shok JHP	velocity, fps:	1330	1230	1140	1080	1030
	energy, ft-lb:	605	515	450	400	360
Federal 180 Hi-Shok JHP	velocity, fps:	1030	1000	970	950	920
	energy, ft-lb:	425	400	375	355	340
Federal 180 Hydra-Shok JHP	velocity, fps:	1030	1000	970	950	920
	energy, ft-lb:	425	400	375	355	340
Federal 180 High Antim. Lead	velocity, fps:	1030	1000	970	950	920
	energy, ft-lb:	425	400	375	355	340
Federal 180 FMJ	velocity, fps:	1060	1025	990	965	940
	energy, ft-lb:	400	370	350	330	310
Hornady 155 JHP/XTP	velocity, fps:	1265		1119		1020
	energy, ft-lb:	551		431		358
Hornady 180 JHP/XTP	velocity, fps:	1180		1077		1004
	energy, ft-lb:	556		464		403
Hornady 200 JHP/XTP	velocity, fps:	1050		994		948
	energy, ft-lb:	490		439		399
PMC 115 Non-Toxic Frangible	velocity, fps:	1350	1240	1154	1088	1035
	energy, ft-lb:	465				
PMC 170 JHP	velocity, fps:	1200	1117	1052	1000	958
	energy, ft-lb:	543				
PMC 180 SFHP	velocity, fps:	950	926	903	882	862
	energy, ft-lb:	361				
PMC 200 TC-FMJ	velocity, fps:	1050	1008	972	941	912
	energy, ft-lb:	490				
Rem. 180 Metal Case	velocity, fps:	1150		1063		998
	energy, ft-lb:	529		452		398
Speer 200 TMJ Blazer	velocity, fps:	1050		966		952
	energy, ft-lb:	490		440		402
Win. 175 Silvertip HP	velocity, fps:	1290		1141		1037
	energy, ft-lb:	649		506		418

.41 REMINGTON MAGNUM

CARTRIDGE BULLET	RANGE, YARDS:	0	25	50	75	100
Federal 210 Hi-Shok JHP	velocity, fps:	1300	1210	1130	1070	1030
	energy, ft-lb:	790	680	595	540	495
PMC 210 TCSP	velocity, fps:	1290	1201	1128	1069	1021
	energy, ft-lb:	774				
PMC 210 JHP	velocity, fps:	1289	1200	1127	1068	1020
	energy, ft-lb:	774				
Rem. 210 SP	velocity, fps:	1300		1162		1062
	energy, ft-lb:	788		630		526

Centerfire Handgun Ballistics

.41 REMINGTON MAGNUM TO .45 AUTOMATIC (ACP)

CARTRIDGE BULLET	RANGE, YARDS:	0	25	50	75	100
Win. 175 Silvertip HP	velocity, fps:	1250		1120		1029
	energy, ft-lb:	607		488		412
Win. 240 Platinum Tip	velocity, ft-lb:	1250		1151		1075
	energy, ft-lb:	833		706		616

.44 COLT

CARTRIDGE BULLET	RANGE, YARDS:	0	25	50	75	100
Black Hills 230 FPL	velocity, fps:	730				
	energy, ft-lb:					

.44 RUSSIAN

CARTRIDGE BULLET	RANGE, YARDS:	0	25	50	75	100
Black Hills 210 FPL	velocity, fps:	650				
	energy, ft-lb:					

.44 SPECIAL

CARTRIDGE BULLET	RANGE, YARDS:	0	25	50	75	100
Black Hills 210 FPL	velocity, fps:	700				
	energy, ft-lb:					
Federal 200 SWC HP	velocity, fps:	900	860	830	800	770
	energy, ft-lb:	360	330	305	285	260
Federal 250 CastCore	velocity, fps:	1250	1200	1150	1110	1080
	energy, ft-lb:	865	795	735	685	645
Hornady 180 JHP/XTP	velocity, fps:	1000		935		882
	energy, ft-lb:	400		350		311
Magtech 240 LFN	velocity, fps:	750		722		696
	energy, ft-lb:	300		278		258
PMC 180 JHP	velocity, fps:	980	938	902	869	839
	energy, ft-lb:	383				
PMC 240 SWC-CP	velocity, fps:	764	744	724	706	687
	energy, ft-lb:	311				
PMC 240 LFP	velocity, fps:	750		719		690
	energy, ft-lb:	300		275		253
Rem. 246 LRN	velocity, fps:	755		725		695
	energy, ft-lb:	310		285		265
Speer 200 HP Blazer	velocity, fps:	875		825		780
	energy, ft-lb:	340		302		270
Speer 200 Trail Blazer LFN	velocity, fps:	750		714		680
	energy, ft-lb:	250		226		205
Speer 200 Gold Dot	velocity, fps:	875		825		780
	energy, ft-lb:	340		302		270
Win. 200 Silvertip HP	velocity, fps:	900		860		822
	energy, ft-lb:	360		328		300
Win. 240 Lead	velocity, fps:	750		719		690
	energy, ft-lb	300		275		253
Win. 246 LRN	velocity, fps:	755		725		695
	energy, ft-lb:	310		285		265

.44 REMINGTON MAGNUM

CARTRIDGE BULLET	RANGE, YARDS:	0	25	50	75	100
Black Hills 240 JHP	velocity, fps:	1260				
	energy, ft-lb:	848				
Black Hills 300 JHP	velocity, fps:	1150				
	energy, ft-lb:	879				
Federal 180 Hi-Shok JHP	velocity, fps:	1610	1480	1370	1270	1180
	energy, ft-lb:	1035	875	750	640	555
Federal 240 Hi-Shok JHP	velocity, fps:	1180	1130	1080	1050	1010
	energy, ft-lb:	740	675	625	580	550
Federal 240 Hydra-Shok JHP	velocity, fps:	1180	1130	1080	1050	1010
	energy, ft-lb:	740	675	625	580	550
Federal 240 JHP	velocity, fps:	1180	1130	1080	1050	1010
	energy, ft-lb:	740	675	625	580	550
Federal 300 CastCore	velocity, fps:	1250	1200	1160	1120	1080
	energy, ft-lb:	1040	960	885	825	775
Hornady 180 JHP/XTP	velocity, fps:	1550		1340		1173
	energy, ft-lb:	960		717		550
Hornady 200 JHP/XTP	velocity, fps:	1500		1284		1128
	energy, ft-lb:	999		732		565
Hornady 240 JHP/XTP	velocity, fps:	1350		1188		1078
	energy, ft-lb:	971		753		619
Hornady 300 JHP/XTP	velocity, fps:	1150		1084		1031
	energy, ft-lb:	881		782		708
Magtech 240 SJSP	velocity, fps:	1180		1081		1010
	energy, ft-lb:	741		632		623
PMC 180 JHP	velocity, fps:	1392	1263	1157	1076	1015
	energy, ft-lb:	772				
PMC 240 JHP	velocity, fps:	1301	1218	1147	1088	1041
	energy, ft-lb:	900				
PMC 240 TC-SP	velocity, fps:	1300	1216	1144	1086	1038
	energy, ft-lb:	900				
PMC 240 SFHP	velocity, fps:	1300	1212	1138	1079	1030
	energy, ft-lb:	900				
PMC 240 LSWC-GCK	velocity, fps:	1225	1143	1077	1025	982
	energy, ft-lb:	806				
Rem. 180 JSP	velocity, fps:	1610		1365		1175
	energy, ft-lb:	1036		745		551
Rem. 210 Gold Dot HP	velocity, fps:	1450		1276		1140
	energy, ft-lb:	980		759		606
Rem. 240 SP	velocity, fps:	1180		1081		1010
	energy, ft-lb:	721		623		543
Rem. 240 SJHP	velocity, fps:	1180		1081		1010
	energy, ft-lb:	721		623		543
Rem. 275 JHP Core-Lokt	velocity, fps:	1235		1142		1070
	energy, ft-lb:	931		797		699
Speer 240 JHP Blazer	velocity, fps:	1200		1092		1015
	energy, ft-lb:	767		636		549
Speer 240 Gold Dot HP	velocity, fps:	1400		1255		1139
	energy, ft-lb:	1044		839		691
Speer 270 Gold Dot SP	velocity, fps:	1250		1142		1060
	energy, ft-lb:	937		781		674
Win. 210 Silvertip HP	velocity, fps:	1250		1106		1010
	energy, ft-lb:	729		570		475
Win. 240 Hollow SP	velocity, fps:	1180		1081		1010
	energy, ft-lb:	741		623		543
Win. 240 JSP	velocity, fps:	1180		1081		
	energy, ft-lb:	741		623		
Win. 250 Partition Gold	velocity, fps:	1230		1132		1057
	energy, ft-lb:	840		711		620
Win. 250 Platinum Tip	velocity, fps:	1250		1148		1070
	energy, ft-lb:	867		732		635

.44-40

CARTRIDGE BULLET	RANGE, YARDS:	0	25	50	75	100
Black Hills 200 RNFP	velocity, fps:	800				
	energy, ft-lb:					
Hornady 205 Cowboy	velocity, fps:	725		697		670
	energy, ft-lb:	239		221		204
Magtech 225 LFN	velocity, fps:	725		703		681
	energy, ft-lb:	281		247		232
PMC 225 LFP	velocity, fps:	725		723		695
	energy, ft-lb:	281		261		242
Win. 225 Lead	velocity, fps:	750		723		695
	energy, ft-lb:	281		261		242

.45 AUTOMATIC (ACP)

CARTRIDGE BULLET	RANGE, YARDS:	0	25	50	75	100
Black Hills 185 JHP	velocity, fps:	1000				
	energy, ft-lb:	411				
Black Hills 200 Match SWC	velocity, fps:	875				
	energy, ft-lb:	340				
Black Hills 230 FMJ	velocity, fps:	850				
	energy, ft-lb:	368				

Centerfire Handgun Ballistics

CARTRIDGE BULLET	RANGE, YARDS:	0	25	50	75	100
Black Hills 230 JHP	velocity, fps:	850				
	energy, ft-lb:	368				
Black Hills 230 JHP +P	velocity, fps:	950				
	energy, ft-lb:	460				
Federal 165 Hydra-Shok JHP	velocity, fps:	1060	1020	980	950	920
	energy, ft-lb:	410	375	350	330	310
Federal 165 EFMJ	velocity, fps:	1090	1045	1005	975	942
	energy, ft-lb:	435	400	370	345	325
Federal 185 Hi-Shok JHP	velocity, fps:	950	920	900	880	860
	energy, ft-lb:	370	350	335	315	300
Federal 185 FMJ-SWC Match	velocity, fps:	780	730	700	660	620
	energy, ft-lb:	245	220	200	175	160
Federal 200 Exp. FMJ	velocity, fps:	1030	1000	970	940	920
	energy, ft-lb:	470	440	415	395	375
Federal 230 FMJ	velocity, fps:	850	830	810	790	770
	energy, ft-lb:	370	350	335	320	305
Federal 230 FMJ Match	velocity, fps:	855	835	815	795	775
	energy, ft-lb:	375	355	340	325	305
Federal 230 Hi-Shok JHP	velocity, fps:	850	830	810	790	770
	energy, ft-lb:	370	350	335	320	300
Federal 230 Hydra-Shok JHP	velocity, fps:	850	830	810	790	770
	energy, ft-lb:	370	350	335	320	305
Federal 230 FMJ	velocity, fps:	850	830	810	790	770
	energy, ft-lb:	370	350	335	320	305
Federal 230 TMJ TMF Primer	velocity, fps:	850	830	810	790	770
	energy, ft-lb:	370	350	335	315	305
Hornady 185 JHP/XTP	velocity, fps:	950		880		819
	energy, ft-lb:	371		318		276
Hornady 200 JHP/XTP	velocity, fps:	900		855		815
	energy, ft-lb:	358		325		295
Hornady 200 HP/XTP +P	velocity, fps:	1055		982		925
	energy, ft-lb:	494		428		380
Hornady 200 TAP-FPD	velocity, fps:	1055		982		926
	energy, ft-lbs:	494		428		380
Hornady 230 FMJ/RN	velocity, fps:	850		809		771
	energy, ft-lb:	369		334		304
Hornady 230 FMJ/FP	velocity, fps:	850		809		771
	energy, ft-lb:	369		334		304
Hornady 230 HP/XTP +P	velocity, fps:	950		904		865
	energy, ft-lb:	462		418		382
Hornady 230 TAP-FPD	velocity, fps:	950		908		872
	energy, ft-lb:	461		421		388
Magtech 185 JHP +P	velocity, fps:	1148		1066		1055
	energy, ft-lb:	540		467		415
Magtech 200 LSWC	velocity, fps:	950		910		874
	energy, ft-lb:	401		368		339
Magtech 230 FMC	veloctiy, fps:	837		800		767
	energy, ft-lb:	356		326		300
Magtech 230 FMC-SWC	velocity, fps:	780		720		660
	energy, ft-lb:	310		265		222
PMC 145 Non-Toxic Frangible	velocity, fps:	1100	1045	999	961	928
	energy, ft-lb:	390				
PMC 185 JHP	velocity, fps:	903	870	839	811	785
	energy, ft-lb:	339				
PMC 200 FMJ-SWC	velocity, fps:	850	818	788	761	734
	energy, ft-lb:	321				
PMC 230 SFHP	velocity, fps:	850	830	811	792	775
	energy, ft-lb:	369				
PMC 230 FMJ	velocity, fps:	830	809	789	769	749
	energy, ft-lb:	352				
Rem. 175 Lead Free Frangible	velocity, fps:	1020		923		851
	energy, ft-lb:	404		331		281

CARTRIDGE BULLET	RANGE, YARDS:	0	25	50	75	100
Rem. 185 JHP	velocity, fps:	1000		939		889
	energy, ft-lb:	411		362		324
Rem. 185 BJHP	velocity, fps:	1015		951		899
	energy, ft-lb:	423		372		332
Rem. 185 BJHP +P	velocity, fps:	1140		1042		971
	energy, ft-lb:	534		446		388
Rem. 185 MC	velocity, fps:	1015		955		907
	energy, ft-lb:	423		375		338
Rem. 230 FN Enclosed Base	velocity, fps:	835		800		767
	energy, ft-lb:	356		326		300
Rem. 230 Metal Case	velocity, fps:	835		800		767
	energy, ft-lb:	356		326		300
Rem. 230 JHP	velocity, fps:	835		800		767
	energy, ft-lb:	356		326		300
Rem. 230 BJHP	velocity, fps:	875		833		795
	energy, ft-lb:	391		355		323
Speer 140 Frangible	velocity, fps:	1200		1029		928
	energy, ft-lb:	448		329		268
Speer 185 Gold Dot	velocity, fps:	1050		956		886
	energy, ft-lb:	453		375		322
Speer 185 TMJ/FN	velocity, fps:	1000		909		839
	energy, ft-lb:	411		339		289
Speer 200 JHP Blazer	velocity, fps:	975		917		860
	energy, ft-lb:	421		372		328
Speer 200 Gold Dot +P	velocity, fps:	1080		994		930
	energy, ft-lb:	518		439		384
Speer 200 TMJ/FN	velocity, fps:	975		897		834
	energy, ft-lb:	422		357		309
Speer 230 FMJ (and Blazer)	velocity, fps:	845		804		775
	energy, ft-lb:	363		329		304
Speer 230 TMJ-CF (and Blazer)	velocity, fps:	845		804		775
	energy, ft-lb:	363		329		304
Speer 230 Gold Dot	velocity, fps:	890		845		805
	energy, ft-lb:	405		365		331
Win. 170 JFP	velocity, fps:	1050		982		928
	energy, ft-lb:	416		364		325
Win. 185 Silvertip HP	velocity, fps:	1000		938		888
	energy, ft-lb:	411		362		324
Win. 185 FMJ FN	velocity, fps:	910		861		
	energy, ft-lb:	340		304		
Win. 185 EB WinClean	velocity, fps:	910		835		
	energy, ft-lb:	340		286		
Win. 230 JHP	velocity, fps:	880		842		
	energy, ft-lb:	396		363		
Win. 230 FMJ	velocity, fps:	835		800		
	energy, ft-lb:	356		326		
Win. 230 SXT	velocity, fps:	880		846		816
	energy, ft-lb:	396		366		340
Win. 230 JHP subsonic	velocity, fps:	880		842		808
	energy, ft-lb:	396		363		334
Win. 230 EB WinClean	velocity, fps:	835		802		
	energy, ft-lb:	356		329		

.45 GAP

CARTRIDGE BULLET	RANGE, YARDS:	0	25	50	75	100
Federal 185 Hydra-Shok JHP And Federal TMJ	velocity, fps:	1090	1020	970	920	890
	energy, ft-lb:	490	430	385	350	320
Federal 230 Hydra-Shok And Federal FMJ	velocity, fps:	880	870	850	840	820
	energy, ft-lb:	395	380	3760	355	345
Win. 185 STHP	velocity, fps:	1000		938		887
	energy, ft-lb:	411		361		323
Win. 230 JHP	velocity, fps:	880		842		
	energy, ft-lb:	396		363		

Centerfire Handgun Ballistics

.45 GAP TO .500 SMITH & WESSON

CARTRIDGE BULLET	RANGE, YARDS:	0	25	50	75	100
Win. 230 EB WinClean	velocity, fps:	875		840		
	energy, ft-lb:	391		360		
Win. 230 FMJ	velocity, fps:	850		814		
	energy, ft-lb:	369		338		
.45 WINCHESTER MAGNUM						
Win. 260 Partition Gold	velocity, fps:	1200		1105		1033
	energy, ft-lb:	832		705		616
Win. 260 JHP	velocity, fps:	1200		1099		1026
	energy, ft-lb:	831		698		607
.45 SCHOFIELD						
Black Hills 180 FNL	velocity, fps:	730				
	energy, ft-lb:					
Black Hills 230 RNFP	velocity, fps:	730				
	energy, ft-lb:					
.45 COLT						
Black Hills 250 RNFP	velocity, fps:	725				
	energy, ft-lb:					
Federal 225 SWC HP	velocity, fps:	900	880	860	840	820
	energy, ft-lb:	405	385	370	355	340
Hornady 255 Cowboy	velocity, fps:	725		692		660
	energy, ft-lb:	298		271		247
Magtech 250 LFN	velocity, fps:	750		726		702
	energy, ft-lb:	312		293		274
PMC 250 LFP	velocity, fps:	800		767		736
	energy, ft-lb:	355		331		309
PMC 300 +P+	velocity, fps:	1250	1192	1144	1102	1066
	energy, ft-lb:	1041				
Rem. 225 SWC	velocity, fps:	960		890		832
	energy, ft-lb:	460		395		346
Rem. 250 RLN	velocity, fps:	860		820		780
	energy, ft-lb:	410		375		340
Speer 200 FMJ Blazer	velocity, fps:	1000		938		889
	energy, ft-lb:	444		391		351
Speer 230 Trail Blazer LFN	velocity, fps:	750		716		684
	energy, ft-lb:	287		262		239
Speer 250 Gold Dot	velocity, fps:	900		860		823
	energy, ft-lb:	450		410		376
Win. 225 Silvertip HP	velocity, fps:	920		877		839
	energy, ft-lb:	423		384		352
Win. 255 LRN	velocity, fps:	860		820		780
	energy, ft-lb:	420		380		345
Win. 250 Lead	velocity, fps:	750		720		692
	energy, ft-lb:	312		288		266
.454 CASULL						
Federal 300 Trophy Bonded	velocity, fps:	1630	1540	1450	1380	1300
	energy, ft-lb:	1760	1570	1405	1260	1130
Federal 360 CastCore	velocity, fps:	1500	1435	1370	1310	1255
	energy, ft-lb:	1800	1640	1500	1310	1260
Hornady 240 XTP-MAG	velocity, fps:	1900		1679		1483
	energy, ft-lb:	1923		1502		1172
Hornady 300 XTP-MAG	velocity, fps:	1650		1478		1328
	energy, ft-lb:	1813		1455		1175
Magtech 260 SJSP	velocity, fps:	1800		1577		1383
	energy, ft-lb:	1871		1437		1104
Rem. 300 Core-Lokt Ultra	velocity, fps:	1625		1472		1335
	energy, ft-lb:	1759		1442		1187

CARTRIDGE BULLET	RANGE, YARDS:	0	25	50	75	100
Speer 300 Gold Dot HP	velocity, fps:	1625		1477		1343
	energy, ft-lb:	1758		1452		1201
Win. 250 JHP	velocity, fps:	1300		1151		1047
	energy, ft-lb:	938		735		608
Win. 260 Partition Gold	velocity, fps:	1800		1605		1427
	energy, ft-lb:	1871		1485		1176
Win. 260 Platinum Tip	velocity, fps:	1800		1596		1414
	eneryg, ft-lb:	1870		1470		1154
Win. 300 JFP	velocity, fps:	1625		1451		1308
	energy, ft-lb:	1759		1413		1141
.460 SMITH & WESSON						
Federal 275 Expander	velocity, fps:	1800		1640		1500
	energy, ft-lb:	1980		1650		1370
Federal 300 A-Frame	velocity, fps:	1750		1510		1300
	energy, ft-lb:	2040		1510		1125
Hornady 200 SST	velocity, fps:	2250		2003		1772
	energy, ft-lb:	2248		1395		1081
Win. 260 Supreme Part. Gold	velocity, fps	2000		1788		1592
	energy, ft-lb	2309		1845		2012
.475 LINEBAUGH						
Hornady 400 XTP-MAG	velocity, fps:	1300		1179		1093
	energy, ft-lb:	1501		1235		1060
.480 RUGER						
Federal 275 Expander	velocity, fps:	1350		1190		1080
	energy, ft-lb:	1115		870		710
Hornady 325 XTP-MAG	velocity, fps:	1350		1191		1076
	energy, ft-lb:	1315		1023		835
Hornady 400 XTP-MAG	velocity, fps:	1100		1027		971
	energy, ft-lb:	1075		937		838
Speer 275 Gold Dot HP	velocity, fps:	1450		1284		1152
	energy, ft-lb:	1284		1007		810
Speer 325 SP	velocity, fps:	1350		1224		1124
	energy, ft-lb:	1315		1082		912
.50 ACTION EXPRESS						
Hornady 300 XTP/HP	velocity, fps:	1475		1251		1092
	energy, ft-lb:	1449		1043		795
Speer 300 Gold Dot HP	velocity, fps:	1550		1361		1207
	energy, ft-lb:	1600		1234		970
Speer 325 UCHP	velocity, fps:	1400		1232		1106
	energy, ft-lb:	1414		1095		883
.500 SMITH & WESSON						
Federal 275 Expander	velocity, fps:	1660		1440		1250
	energy, ft-lb:	1680		1255		950
Federal 325 A-Frame	velocity, fps:	1800		1560		1350
	energy, ft-lb:	2340		1755		1315
Hornady 350 XTP Mag	velocity, fps:	1900		1656		1439
	energy, ft-lb:	2805		2131		1610
Hornady 500 FP-XTP	velocity, fps:	1425		1281		1164
	energy, ft-lb:	2254		1823		1505
Win. 350 Super-X	velocity, fps	1400		1231		1106
	energy, ft-lb	1523		1178		951
Win. 400 Platinum Tip	velocity, fps:	1800		1647		1505
	energy, ft-lb:	2877		2409		2012

GUNFINDER INDEX

Gunfinder Index

Gunfinder Index